Microsoft® Office 2000/ Visual Basic® Programmer's Guide

David Shank
Mark Roberts
Tamra Myers

Microsoft® Press

PUBLISHED BY
Microsoft Press
A Division of Microsoft Corporation
One Microsoft Way
Redmond, Washington 98052-6399

Library of Congress Cataloging-in-Publication Data
Shank, David, 1954-
Microsoft Office 2000/Visual Basic Programmer's Guide / David Shank, Mark Roberts, Tamra Myers.
p. cm.
Includes index.
ISBN 1-57231-952-6
1. Microsoft Office. 2. Microsoft Visual BASIC. 3. Microsoft Visual Basic for applications. 4. Business--Computer programs.
I. Roberts, Mark, 1957 April 10- II. Myers, Tamra, 1969- .
III. Title.
HF5548.4.M525S46 1999
005.369--dc21 98-44826
CIP

Printed and bound in the United States of America.

2 3 4 5 6 7 8 9 WCWC 4 3 2 1 0 9

Distributed in Canada by Penguin Books Canada Limited.

A CIP catalogue record for this book is available from the British Library.

Microsoft Press books are available through booksellers and distributors worldwide. For further information about international editions, contact your local Microsoft Corporation office or contact Microsoft Press International directly at fax (425) 936-7329. Visit our Web site at mspress.microsoft.com.

Acquisitions Editor: Ben Ryan
Project Editor: Devon Musgrave

Contents

Part 4 Securing Office Solutions 737

Foreword

Congratulations! If you're reading this foreword, you're either using, or considering using, Microsoft® Office 2000 as a part of a custom solution. Either way, the book you hold in your hands is the best available resource for learning how to exploit the programmability features of Office 2000.

Over 2.6 million developers currently use Office as a part of the custom solutions they build. Why are so many developers building solutions with Office? For starters, Office can now be found on over 40 million end users' desktops. Developers have also long recognized that Office exposes hundreds of reusable objects that can be programmatically automated and integrated in order to create custom solutions. Furthermore, developers know that they can save time and effort by taking advantage of the prebuilt objects, functionality, and services provided by the Office applications.

With the Office 2000 release, Microsoft has worked hard to simplify the process of customizing and automating Office. By exposing all of the Office applications' functionality through Component Object Model (COM)-compliant objects and integrating Visual Basic for Applications (VBA) throughout Office, we have made it easier than ever to develop solutions with Office. Having a consistent development language and environment greatly simplifies the developer's efforts in building solutions and working with the objects and services Office exposes. However, the major challenge of developing solutions generally revolves around knowing which objects to instantiate, which properties to set, and the appropriate and available methods to call. With over 600 programmable objects exposed to the developer, Office provides incredible flexibility, but there needs to be some way of identifying the appropriate objects, knowing the most efficient way to access them, and the syntax required for developing solutions with them. That's where this book comes in.

The *Microsoft Office 2000/Visual Basic Programmer's Guide* is intended specifically to help VBA developers take advantage of the applications and components in the Office suite. This book was designed from the ground up to be a comprehensive and accurate guide to building custom solutions that profit from the powerful technologies available in Office. The authors assume you know the basics of VBA and understand something about what it means to work with Office objects, object models, and components. There is no fluff or filler here. This is not a user's guide. This is a "roll up your sleeves and get productive quickly" resource that will help you build your custom Office solutions. The *Microsoft Office 2000/Visual Basic Programmer's Guide* was written by a team of experienced and talented writers and developers who have worked closely with the Office 2000 team throughout the entire development cycle. That experience and knowledge has been included here in the form of insights, tips, tricks, and sample code that will make you immediately productive.

If you have already worked with Office 2000, you know that it contains much that is new and exciting for developers. With VBA now in every application, direct access to SQL Server databases from Microsoft Access, support for ActiveX® Data Objects (ADO), and tight integration with the Web, Office 2000 gives you more ways of customizing Office to meet specific customer needs, and this guide will show you how to take advantage of these new features and technologies in your custom solutions.

So whether you've been developing solutions with Office for years or are just now starting, by opening this book you've taken the most important first step in capitalizing on everything that Office 2000 has to offer developers. The *Microsoft Office 2000/Visual Basic Programmer's Guide* is truly the "developer's owner's manual" to Office 2000.

Neil Charney
Lead Product Manager, Microsoft Developer Tools
Microsoft Corporation
December 1998

Acknowledgements

Writing a book like the *Microsoft Office 2000/Visual Basic Programmer's Guide* was a huge undertaking that required the exceptional effort of many people. But before we acknowledge the efforts of the individuals who made this book a reality, we'd like to thank the people we wrote this book for: Office developers.

We would like to acknowledge those whose energy and creativity never cease to amaze us with what they can do with Office applications, tools, and technologies and for what they demand from Microsoft in terms of changes, improvements, bug fixes, and answers to all those really hard questions. And not just those who call themselves Office developers, but those who work with Office day after day, making it do incredible things not because they can, or because it is cool, or because they can write an article about it, but because they need to get a job done. This book is for you.

The *Microsoft Office 2000/Visual Basic Programmer's Guide* was a team effort and while the authors often get all the credit, the real work is done by lots of people who don't always get the thanks they deserve. We want to thank them now.

First and foremost, we'd like to thank Dana Schmeller. Although her official title was "Editor," she was really so much more than that. She combined the words of three authors and made them speak as one, she caught our errors, she relentlessly kept us to our schedule, she oversaw editing, and copyediting, and production, and art, and all aspects of this project. And although her name does not appear on the cover, this book is as much hers as it is ours.

We'd like give special thanks to: Robin Lyle for contributing her extensive experience, taking care of production and an amazing list of details, helping with scheduling, and working closely with Microsoft Press® to make sure everyone was working from the same page; to Karen Downing for jumping in with editing help during those long, dark, days when it seemed like this project would last forever; to Kristin Lynn Bergsma for her creativity (all the art in this book is hers) and her attention to detail with the appendix; to Olwen Moery for catching all those mistakes nobody else could see; to Diana Rain for her great work indexing this book so that readers will actually be able to find the answers to their questions; and to Erin O'Rourke for her lightning speed in formatting chapters and resolving layout challenges. We'd also like to thank the folks at Microsoft Press who worked with us to create a unique resource for the Office developer, with special thanks to Ben Ryan and Devon Musgrave for the work they did to bring this book to you.

We also want to thank our reviewers, who took the time to carefully read what we wrote and make corrections, additions, suggestions, and improvements to our original words and examples. And we'd like to specially thank Theresa Venhuis, Michael Kaplan, Keith Fink, Howie Dickerman, Peter Hussey, Alyssa Henry, and Joe Robison for going above and beyond the call of duty when reviewing and improving our original work and answering our many, many questions. Your depth and breadth of knowledge is truly amazing.

We'd like to give special thanks to the program managers, developers, and testers on the Microsoft Office 2000, Microsoft Visual Basic®, Microsoft Data Access Components, Visual Data, Microsoft SQL Server™, and Microsoft Internet Explorer teams. You have created a great product and given us lots of cool things to write about.

The authors are grateful to have had the help of so many talented people in creating the book you hold in your hands and the product it describes. To the extent that there are any errors remaining in this book, they are our responsibility alone.

And finally, we'd like to thank our families and loved ones for their gracious support and patience during the long hours it took to produce this book. We cannot give back the lost weekends and evenings, but we can gratefully acknowledge your contributions to this book.

David Shank, Mark Roberts, and Tamra Myers

Preface

The *Microsoft Office 2000/Visual Basic Programmer's Guide* describes how to use the applications and components in Microsoft Office 2000 to build custom solutions. This guide is the definitive resource for developers who are creating custom solutions based on Office applications. From the overall design of your solution to the nitty-gritty details of implementing it, this book tells you what you need to know to get things done quickly and productively.

If you are familiar with one of the Office applications, you can build on that knowledge to work with other applications in the suite. If you know how to work with Visual Basic for Applications (VBA), you'll learn how to build on that knowledge in order to create code modules you can reuse in any application. If you've designed database solutions, you can build on that knowledge in order to create data-driven Web pages that your users can interact with through a Web browser.

Even if you're an expert programmer in one or more of the Office applications, figuring out where to get started when you are building a solution can be a daunting task. The applications and components that make up Microsoft Office expose hundreds of programmable objects that you can manipulate through VBA code. Each of those objects exposes a number of properties and methods that you can use to specify how the object behaves. The prospect of dealing with all these objects can be challenging, but the *Microsoft Office 2000/Visual Basic Programmer's Guide* will show you where to get started.

Office developers have asked for a resource like the *Microsoft Office 2000/Visual Basic Programmer's Guide* for a long time. That time has finally arrived. This guide teaches you how to capitalize on your existing knowledge in order to take full advantage of new and existing features alike. This book is about mastering new and existing technologies, and learning strategies and skills that you can apply to all of your Office programming tasks.

Not only is the information presented here something you can use immediately, but also each chapter includes dozens of code samples to help illustrate the discussions. In addition to the code samples shown in the chapters, the companion CD-ROM contains hundreds of VBA and Microsoft Visual Basic Scripting Edition (VBScript) procedures that you can use right now in your own solutions. The companion CD-ROM also includes white papers that provide in-depth discussions of various technologies and programming issues not covered in the book. Lastly, the "Object Model Diagrams" appendix includes complete object models for every Office application and component. In short, the *Microsoft Office 2000/Visual Basic Programmer's Guide* contains just about everything you need to know to start building custom solutions with Office.

Contents

Who This Guide Is For

This guide is for developers who are creating custom solutions based on Office 2000 applications. These developers form a large and diverse group. We use the term "developer" to include someone doing something as simple as creating a basic VBA procedure as well as someone working on a complex vertical-market solution. What Office developers have in common is that they all use the programmability features of Office technologies.

The *Microsoft Office 2000/Visual Basic Programmer's Guide* is for people looking for answers to Office-based development questions. This book can be used as a reference to answer those hard questions that come up time and again, or this book can be used as a learning tool, which when read from cover to cover, teaches important concepts in application development and design, code maintainability and reusability, and application security and distribution.

But this book is not for everyone. To cover such a wealth of material in a useful manner, we had to make certain assumptions about your level of knowledge. If you are not familiar with the concepts mentioned in the "What You Should Already Know" section later in this preface, this is not the book for you. Your time (and money) will be better spent with one of the many fine introductory resources available for the beginning VBA developer, such as the Mastering Office 2000 Development CD-ROM, or any of the other introductory references mentioned in the "Other Resources" section later in this preface. Then, when you have mastered the fundamentals, you can come back to the *Microsoft Office 2000/Visual Basic Programmer's Guide* to take full advantage of the programmability features in Office 2000.

What This Guide Covers

This guide teaches developers how to work with the applications and components in the Microsoft Office 2000 suite (Microsoft Access, Microsoft Excel, Microsoft FrontPage®, Microsoft PowerPoint®, Microsoft Outlook®, and Microsoft Word). All the VBA code samples throughout this guide are compatible with this version of Office. All the VBScript examples are compatible with Microsoft Internet Explorer 5, which ships as part of Office 2000. As needed, notes describe differences between the Office 2000 applications and earlier versions.

What You Should Already Know

The goal of this guide is to enhance your existing knowledge of the Office applications. We assume you're comfortable with the VBA language and that you understand data types, variable scoping, and how to use the Visual Basic Editor. The VBA code samples are written in VBA version 6.0, which is supported by Microsoft Visual Basic version 6.0, all the Microsoft Office 2000 applications, and other VBA 6.0 host applications. Most of the HTML scripting examples are written in VBScript; a few are written in Microsoft JScript®.

To understand the Web-related technologies in Office 2000, we assume that you have a basic knowledge of HTML and a basic understanding of how scripting works in Web pages. In addition, we assume you know about HTML intrinsic controls as well as how to use ActiveX controls on a Web page.

Many Office-based solutions are designed to manipulate data in one form or another. We assume that you are familiar with the concepts of relational databases and queries and know something of Structured Query Language (SQL) and programmatic data access. A large part of the data access discussion deals with ActiveX Data Objects (ADO). Although we do not assume you are already familiar with ADO, we do assume you have some knowledge of how to work with data programmatically by using Data Access Objects (DAO), Remote Data Objects (RDO), or Open Database Connectivity (ODBC).

Other Resources

Following are descriptions of the various resources you can use to get additional information about programming with VBA in Office.

Microsoft Office Help

Microsoft Office provides an extensive Help system for the VBA language, the objects that Office supports, and the properties and methods of those objects.

You can access Visual Basic Reference Help in any module in the Visual Basic Editor in any of the following three ways:

- Position the insertion point anywhere in an object name, property name, method name, event name, function name, or other keyword you've typed, and then press F1 to get context-sensitive Help for that keyword.
- Click **Microsoft Visual Basic Help** on the **Help** menu in the Visual Basic Editor. You can then ask the Office Assistant a question, click **Search**, and click the topic you want to read in the **What would you like to do?** balloon. (If you do not have the Office Assistant turned on, you will see the Help window instead.)
- Click **Object Browser** on the **View** menu, and then either press F1 or click the **Help** button (the question-mark button above the **Members of** box) for information about the selected object, method, property, event, or function.

After you've displayed a Help topic, you can click the **Show** button in the Help window to display the navigation pane, which contains three tabs: **Contents**, **Answer Wizard**, and **Index**. You can then either look up a specific topic or language keyword by using the **Contents** or **Index** tab or ask a question by using the **Answer Wizard** tab.

Note If you turn off the Office Assistant, Help will behave slightly differently. When you click **Microsoft Visual Basic Help** on the **Help** menu, the Help window will appear with the navigation pane already visible. To turn off the Assistant, right-click the Assistant and then click **Options** on the shortcut menu (or click the **Options** button in the Assistant balloon) and then clear the **Use the Office Assistant** check box on the **Options** tab. (Clicking **Hide the Office Assistant** on the application's **Help** menu doesn't turn off the Assistant.) To turn the Office Assistant back on, click **Show the Office Assistant** on the **Help** menu in the application.

Microsoft Office also provides Help for the VBScript and JScript scripting languages, HTML, and the Dynamic HTML (DHTML) object model. These Help files (Vbscrip5.chm, Jscript5.chm, and Htmlref.chm) are available in the C:\Program Files\Microsoft Visual Studio\Common\IDE\IDE98\MSE\1033 subfolder.

Note The path to these Help files reflects the language ID folder (1033) for U.S. English language support in Office. The language ID folder below C:\Program Files\Microsoft Visual Studio\Common\IDE\IDE98\MSE\ differs for each language.

Microsoft Developer Network (MSDN) Online Web Site

You can get useful and comprehensive information about developing solutions with Microsoft tools and technologies on the MSDN Online Web site at http://msdn.microsoft.com/developer/default.htm.

Microsoft Office Developer Forum Web Site

The latest information focused on developing custom applications for Office is available on the Microsoft Office Developer Forum Web site at http://www.microsoft.com/officedev/.

Microsoft Press

In addition to the *Microsoft Office 2000/Visual Basic Programmer's Guide*, Microsoft Press offers a number of books to help you understand VBA programming. For a listing of the current titles available from Microsoft Press, visit the Microsoft Press Online Web site at http://mspress.microsoft.com/.

In addition to books, Microsoft Press offers training and learning resources to help developers get the most out of Microsoft technology. The Microsoft Press Online Web site offers instant access to all Microsoft Press tools as well as news, chats with technical experts, and other information to help you become more productive quickly.

Mastering Office 2000 Development

Mastering Office 2000 Development is a CD-ROM product available from Microsoft. You can use this self-paced training tool to become proficient with VBA, the Office 2000 object models, and more. More than 40 hours of labs, demos, sample code, and articles—plus valuable tips and techniques—get you up to speed fast, and the powerful Boolean search engine and comprehensive index make it easy to find just the information you need when you need it. Narrated demonstrations, animations, and interactive lab exercises walk you through complex concepts and help you design your own Office 2000-based applications.

A Note About "Where to Go from Here"

At the end of each chapter in the *Microsoft Office 2000/Visual Basic Programmer's Guide,* there is a "Where to Go from Here" section, which provides a list of resources that contain more information about the topics covered in that chapter. Along with pointers to files on the companion CD-ROM and various Web sites, the "Where to Go from Here" sections include references to many other books. For each book, we have referenced the most current version available at the time this guide was written, but because many of these books are updated when a new version of Microsoft Office is released, you may want to check for a newer version. Our intention in all cases is to reference the most up-to-date version of each book cited.

How to Use This Guide

The *Microsoft Office 2000/Visual Basic Programmer's Guide* is divided into four parts encompassing eighteen chapters, with one appendix. Although it is not necessary to read the book front to back, information presented in later chapters builds on material in previous chapters. Feel free to skip to specific chapters, but note that this preface and Chapter 1, "Understanding Office Solution Development," provide a foundation for later chapters.

The following section outlines each of the chapters.

Part 1 Planning Office Solutions

The chapters in this section present an overall view of designing your custom solution, deciding which Office technologies best suit the needs of your solution, and planning for the distribution of your solution once you are ready to put it in the hands of your users.

Chapter 1 Understanding Office Solution Development

This chapter gives an overview of using Office 2000 technologies to develop custom solutions. The discussion provides a roadmap for understanding different aspects of solution development and how these concepts come together in the material presented in this book. When you are finished with this chapter, you'll have a better understanding of how to approach custom solution development and how to use this book to find the information you need.

Chapter 2 Designing and Deploying Office Solutions

Regardless of how simple or complicated your solution is, the development process always begins with fundamental design considerations and ends with choices about how to deliver your solution to users. These can be some of the most important choices you make while developing your custom solution, and this chapter explains what you need to consider in order to design your solution efficiently and effectively.

Part 2 Developing Office Solutions

The chapters in this section form the heart of the book, providing detailed information about creating custom Office solutions.

Chapter 3 Writing Solid Code

This chapter focuses on fundamental coding guidelines, techniques, and suggestions you can employ in your code. Once these fundamentals become second nature to you, you'll discover that your code is easier to understand, debug, modify, and share with other developers. The techniques discussed in this chapter apply whether you are writing VBA code in a VBA project or script behind an HTML page or Active Server page (ASP).

Chapter 4 Understanding Office Objects and Object Models

All Office applications that support VBA and VBScript can use Automation (formerly OLE Automation) code to work with the objects exposed by other Office applications, as well as many other applications and services that expose object models. The key to understanding Automation is to understand objects and object models: what they are, how they work, and how they work together. This chapter and Chapter 5, "Working with Office Applications," provide a solid foundation on which to build your understanding of Office solution development.

Chapter 5 Working with Office Applications

Most Office developers are familiar with at least one Office application. This chapter teaches you how to build on what you know about one Office application in order to master the other Office applications. There are literally hundreds of exposed objects you can work with programmatically, and this chapter leads you through the object models of the Office suite to teach you what you need to build solutions with any of the Office applications.

Chapter 6 Working with Shared Office Components

Microsoft Office includes a set of shared components available in all Office applications. You can use these shared components to search for files, control the Office Assistant, manipulate command bars, read and write document properties, read and write script, and hook add-ins to your Office solution. Because these components are shared among all Office applications, it is easy to write code that uses these components and that will run without modification from within any Office application or custom Office solution.

Chapter 7 Getting the Most Out of Visual Basic for Applications

As you develop applications, you'll find yourself repeatedly performing a number of operations—parsing a file path, for example, or returning all the files in a directory. Rather than rewriting these routines every time you need them, you can begin building an arsenal of procedures that solve common problems. This chapter gives you a head start by providing functions that perform some often-needed operations on strings, numbers, dates and times, files, and arrays. It also explains the key aspects of each procedure and covers fundamental VBA programming issues so that you can continue to expand your code arsenal yourself.

Chapter 8 Error Handling and Debugging

All code contains errors of one kind or another. How you deal with errors may be the most important part of a well-designed application. There are two categories of errors: those you can prevent, known as development errors, and those you can't prevent but can trap, known as run-time errors. You eliminate development errors by "debugging" your code. There are a wide variety of tools included in the Visual Basic Editor and the Microsoft Script Editor that can help you debug VBA code and script. You handle run-time errors by writing error handlers and by writing procedures that can validate program or environmental conditions as appropriate.

Chapter 9 Custom Classes and Objects

Once you understand how to work with the objects exposed by the Office applications and components, you are ready to dive into creating your own reusable objects and organizing those objects into custom object models. Building on the concepts of code maintainability and reusability introduced in earlier chapters, this discussion provides a clear understanding of this powerful technology.

Chapter 10 The Windows API and Other Dynamic-Link Libraries

Understanding how to work directly with the Microsoft Windows® application programming interface (API) is an essential skill for any advanced Office developer. Although you can build sophisticated solutions without using the Windows API, knowing how and when to take advantage of this resource can extend the power and flexibility of your code. This chapter covers the basics of using functions in dynamic-link libraries (DLLs) and presents solutions to common problems by using the Windows API.

Chapter 11 Add-ins, Templates, Wizards, and Libraries

Creating a custom Office solution consists of enhancing and extending powerful applications that you and your users already have on your desktops. An *add-in* extends an application by adding functionality that isn't in the core product itself. This chapter explains how to create Component Object Model (COM) add-ins, which are based on a new technology available to Office 2000 that allows you to build add-ins that work in one or more of the Office applications. This chapter also discusses how to create application-specific add-ins, templates, and specialized forms of add-ins, such as wizards and code libraries.

Chapter 12 Using Web Technologies

Office 2000 contains more Web-related technologies than any previous version of Office. This chapter explains how you can use your existing VBA knowledge to write script in Office documents that will run when the documents are viewed in a Web browser. In addition, this chapter discusses the basics of DHTML and explains how to use cascading style sheets in your HTML documents. This chapter also discusses the new Microsoft Office Web Components, which are powerful ActiveX controls that let you transform Office documents into interactive Web pages. Finally, the chapter includes a discussion of how to programmatically work with Microsoft Office Server Extensions.

Chapter 13 Adding Help to Your Custom Solution

Adding Help to your Microsoft Office solution can reduce the amount of time required to train and support users of your solution. By using the tools provided with Microsoft HTML Help Workshop or your favorite HTML editor, you can author topics for a Help system by using the same tools and technologies you use to create Web pages—including hyperlinks, ActiveX controls, scripting, and DHTML support. You can then compile your topics into a single file and display them by using the same viewer that is used to display Help in Office 2000.

Part 3 Working with Data in Office Solutions

Most Office solutions manage data in one form or another. Whether you are using Microsoft Access to build database applications or one of the other Office applications to work with data stored in a data source, this section tells you what you need to know to access and manipulate data in a variety of situations.

Chapter 14 Working with the Data Access Components of an Office Solution

Office 2000 includes ADO as a powerful new programmatic interface to data no matter where the data resides or what form the data takes. This chapter discusses what you need to know about ADO to make your Office solutions work better and faster with data in any form. If you have developed custom solutions in earlier versions of Office, you are already familiar with DAO. Through side-by-side comparisons of comparable data access techniques and strategies, this chapter teaches ADO by building on what you already know about DAO.

Chapter 15 Retrieving and Analyzing Data

Once you have mastered the techniques for retrieving data, you'll want to know how to display and manipulate that data. This chapter illustrates different ways to present and analyze data. The concepts in this chapter build on the introductory discussions begun in Chapter 1, "Understanding Office Solution Development," about choosing and using the right Office application to meet the requirements of your custom solution.

Chapter 16 Multiuser Database Applications

Building solutions that tap the capabilities of a multiuser database application can be difficult and intimidating. This chapter helps you understand the various types of multiuser database applications and determine which type is best suited to your Office solution.

Part 4 Securing Office Solutions

Security issues take on increasing significance as computer networks expand to include the World Wide Web. In addition, as a developer, you need to know how to protect your investment in the intellectual property that is your custom solution. The chapters in this section discuss what you need to know about securing your custom Office solution, protecting your code, and taking full advantage of the new security-related features of Office 2000.

Chapter 17 Securing Office Documents and Visual Basic for Applications Code

If your solution contains or provides access to sensitive information, such as legal documents or payroll records, you may need to control access to this information. If you are retaining the ownership of the VBA code you develop, you also need to prevent unauthorized access to your solution's code. Furthermore, with the advent of macro viruses, you need to assure users and administrators that they can trust the macros (VBA code) contained in any Office documents that are part of your solution.

This chapter discusses how to address these access security and virus security issues for Word, Excel, and PowerPoint through various means, including the use of digital signatures. It also discusses how to secure VBA code, which applies to Access and FrontPage as well.

Chapter 18 Securing Access Databases

Access provides a sophisticated security environment for controlling access to object definitions and data. This chapter discusses the Access security model and how to implement it successfully, and provides complete code samples for programmatically creating and maintaining security settings. This chapter also discusses how to password-protect a database, how to secure VBA code in an Access database by saving the database as an .mde file, and how to set up security when accessing databases through data access pages.

Appendix Object Model Diagrams

This appendix contains object model diagrams for every Office application and shared Office component. Also included here are object models related to programming the Visual Basic Editor and object models for the data access technologies you are likely to use in a custom Office solution. Internet Explorer and related Web technology object models are also provided.

Typographic Conventions

This guide provides comprehensive examples for many of the topics discussed. The following typographic conventions are used in this guide.

Example of convention	Description
Sub, **If**, **ChDir**, **Print**, **Time$**, **RecordsAffected**, **Recordset, srcElement**	Words in bold, generally with the initial letter capitalized, indicate language-specific keywords with special meaning to VBA or VBScript. Objects, methods, statements, functions, and properties appear in bold, generally with the initial letter capitalized. Concatenated names may contain other capital letters.
expr, path	In syntax, italics indicate placeholders for information you supply. In text, italic letters are used for defined terms, usually the first time they occur in the guide. Italics are also used occasionally for emphasis.
ReadOnly, ***FileName***	In text and syntax, the use of bold and italic together indicates named arguments.

Example of convention	Description
[*expressionlist*]	In syntax, items in square brackets are optional.
{**While** | **Until**}	In syntax, braces and a vertical bar indicate a choice between two or more items. You must choose one of the items unless all of the items are enclosed in square brackets.
`Dim rstCust As ADODB.Recordset`	A monospace font indicates code.
`Set olNewItem = _` `ol.CreateItem(olMailItem)`	The line-continuation character (_) is used to break long lines of code.

`Sub StockSale()`
`.`
`.`
`.`
`End Sub`
	A column of three periods indicates that part of an example has been intentionally omitted.

Code Samples and Programming Style

This guide contains numerous code samples that you can use to experiment with the concepts covered. Unless otherwise noted, the code is compatible with VBA 6.0 as it is implemented in Microsoft Visual Basic 6.0, Microsoft Access 2000, Microsoft Excel 2000, Microsoft FrontPage 2000, Microsoft Outlook 2000, Microsoft PowerPoint 2000, Microsoft Word 2000, and other applications that host VBA 6.0. Additional code samples are written in VBScript, JScript, HTML, and DHTML.

This guide uses the following conventions in VBA sample code:

- Keywords appear with an initial letter capitalized; concatenated words may contain other capital letters. Variables appear in mixed case, constants in uppercase.

```
Dim objDatabase As Object
   Const PROP_NOT_FOUND_ERROR = 3270

   Set objDatabase = CurrentDb
```

- In full procedures, all variables are declared locally or are listed with an initialization procedure that declares public variables. All code has been tested with the VBA **Option Explicit** statement to ensure that there are no undeclared variables.
- An apostrophe (') introduces a comment:

```
' This is a comment.
Dim intNew As Integer  ' This is also a comment.
```

- Control-flow blocks and statements in **Sub**, **Function**, and **Property** procedures are indented:

  ```
  Sub MyCode ()
     Dim intX As Integer
     Dim intP As Integer
     Dim intQ As Integer

     If intX > 0 Then
        intP = intQ
     End If
  End Sub
  ```

- Naming conventions are used to make it easier to identify objects and variables in the code samples. For more information about the naming conventions used in this book, see Chapter 3, "Writing Solid Code."

This guide also uses the following conventions in HTML script samples:

- VBScript is case insensitive; therefore, capitalization of keywords, intrinsic functions, language elements, and variable names is not required.
- The HTML and DHTML naming conventions use a lowercase or lowercase and uppercase concatenated style for object, variable, method, event, function, and property names. For example, the name of the **document** object is lowercase, whereas the name of the **srcElement** property is a concatenated lowercase and uppercase combination.
- Most script examples are written in VBScript. Some examples are written in JScript. Note that JScript is case sensitive.

  Note JScript is the Microsoft implementation of the ECMA-262 language specification.

Using the Companion CD-ROM

Inside the back cover of this guide you can find the companion CD-ROM for the *Microsoft Office 2000/Visual Basic Programmer's Guide*. The companion CD-ROM contains online versions of all the code samples in this guide, white papers that provide additional information about Microsoft Office programming topics, and several sample applications.

Code Samples

This guide contains hundreds of code samples that show how to work with the programming features of Microsoft Office. To help you learn about these features and incorporate them into your applications, the companion CD-ROM contains electronic versions of the code samples used in the book. In addition, the samples subfolder for each chapter contains dozens of code samples that expand on the concepts and ideas presented in the book. Wherever possible, these code samples were written not only so you can learn from studying how they work, but also so that you can use them "as-is" in your custom solutions.

The code samples for the chapters are stored in the Samples subfolder on the companion CD-ROM. The files for each chapter are stored in the subfolder corresponding to the chapter number; for example, the files for Chapter 3 are stored in the Samples\CH03 subfolder. In some cases, the samples for a particular chapter are used in other chapters as well.

▶ To use the code samples

The code samples are designed to be executed from your hard disk. To make sure the samples work properly, you should use the setup program on the companion CD-ROM to transfer the code samples to your machine.

1. Insert the companion CD-ROM in your CD-ROM drive.
2. Double-click Setup.exe in the root folder of the companion CD-ROM.
3. The setup program creates an OPG folder in the root directory of your C drive, and then copies the directory structure of the companion CD-ROM to the C:\OPG folder.

   Important If you do not accept the default drive and path, you will need to modify some of the sample code to point to the drive and path where you installed the files.

   Because files stored on a CD-ROM must have their read-only file attribute set, the setup program also clears the read-only file attribute after copying the files.

Notes

- Some of the examples use data in Northwind.mdb, a sample database that ships with Access 2000. In addition, some of the samples use the Solutions9.mdb sample file, which links to some of the tables in Northwind.mdb. If you have not installed the Northwind sample database, you must do so to take full advantage of the examples in this book.
- If you have Microsoft Office 2000 Developer, you can use the Code Librarian add-in to view and copy many of the reusable procedures included in this book and in the accompanying sample files. To use the Code Librarian, first make sure that you've installed the Microsoft VBA Developer Add-ins from the Office 2000 Developer Tools CD-ROM. In the Visual Basic Editor, load the Code Librarian from the Add-In Manager (**Add-Ins** menu). From the Code Librarian, load the Codelib.mdb database, which by default is located in the C:\Program Files\Microsoft Office\ODETools\V9 folder.
- In Word 2000, security is set by default to High, which means that the code will not run when you open the Word sample files. To use these files, you must change the security setting by pointing to **Macro** on the **Tools** menu, clicking **Security**, and then clicking either **Medium** or **Low** on the **Security Level** tab.
- To run the scripting examples that use scriptlets, your browser's security settings must be set to Medium or Low.

For information about specific file names or additional requirements for the code samples in each chapter, see the discussion regarding a particular sample file in the text of each chapter.

White Papers

A number of white papers pertaining to the Office 2000 applications and the technologies they use are included in the Appendixes folder on the companion CD-ROM. For a list of the white papers and their contents, see WhitePapers.txt in the Appendixes folder.

Sample Applications

Several sample applications are included in the Sample Applications folder on the companion CD-ROM. Complete documentation for these applications is contained in ReadmeSamples.txt in the Sample Applications folder.

Part One

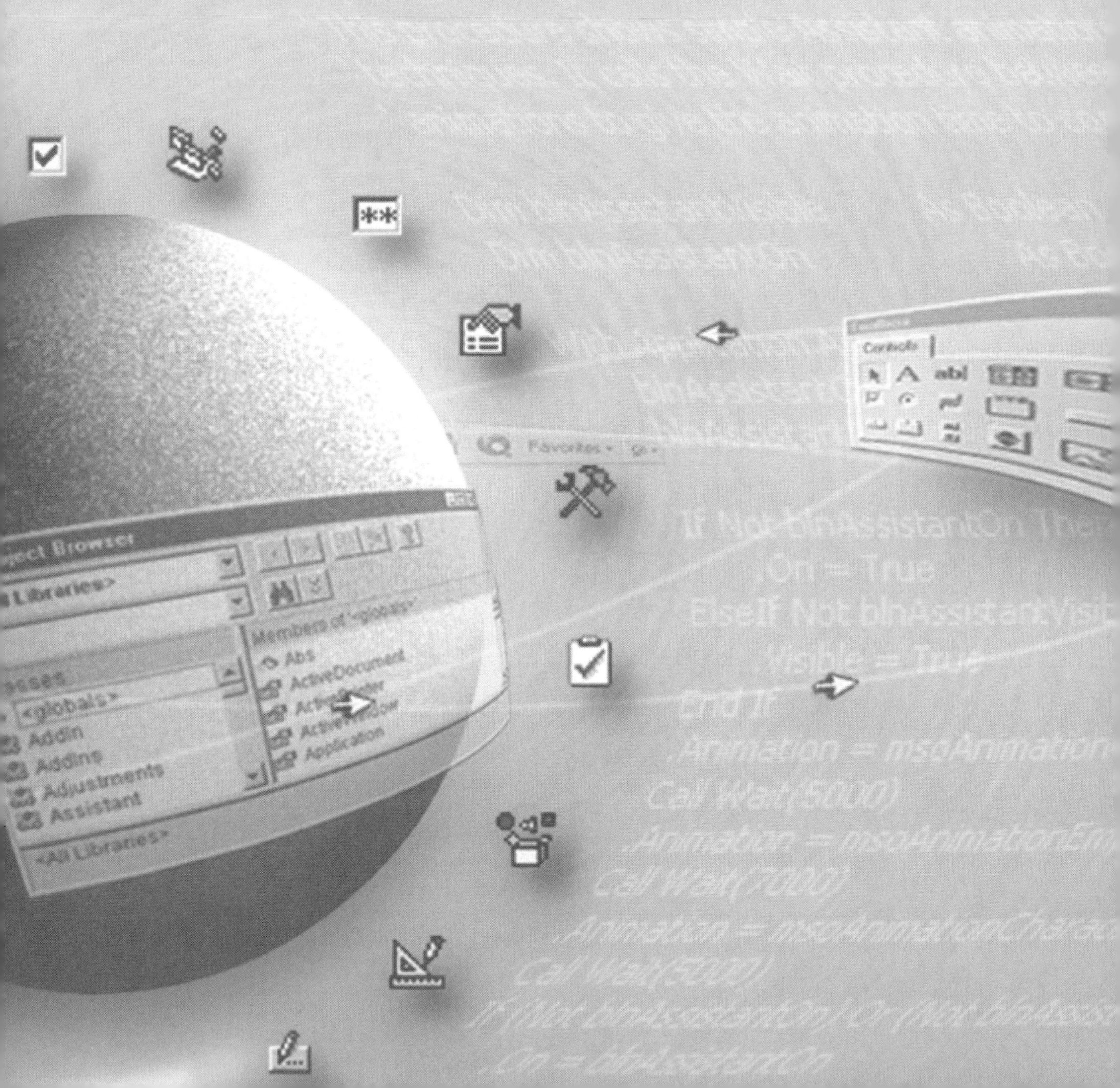

Controls
abl
Favorites
Abs
ActiveDocument
Application
<globals>
Addin
AddIns
Adjustments
Assistant
<All Libraries>
.On = True
End If
Call Wait(5000)
Call Wait(7000)

Planning Office Solutions

What's the first important step in building a solution based on Microsoft Office 2000? As with anything else, planning and design are the keys to successful solution development. Spending a little time on solution design before you begin writing code can make your job more fun. And in the long run, your customers will be happier with the results.

The first chapter in this book, "Understanding Office Solution Development," is just an appetizer. It introduces some of the cool new features you'll find in the Office 2000 suite of applications, such as the new Component Object Model (COM) add-in architecture, the Web-publishing tools that make it easier to create rich, interactive documents that can be shared over the Internet or an intranet, the enhanced security features for protecting your solutions, and the advent of universal data access with ActiveX Data Objects (ADO). This chapter also discusses some of the benefits of building an Office-based solution, such as faster development time and lower support and training costs.

The second chapter, "Designing and Deploying Office Solutions," offers suggestions for the development process. It begins at the beginning, with tips on identifying the customer's needs and modeling the customer's business process before you start coding. This chapter outlines considerations for designing common types of solutions, such as which applications to use, where to store data, how to analyze and present data, how to design an effective user interface, how to design code for reusability, and what kinds of measures you may need to take in order to secure your solution. It also suggests ways to deploy different types of Office-based solutions.

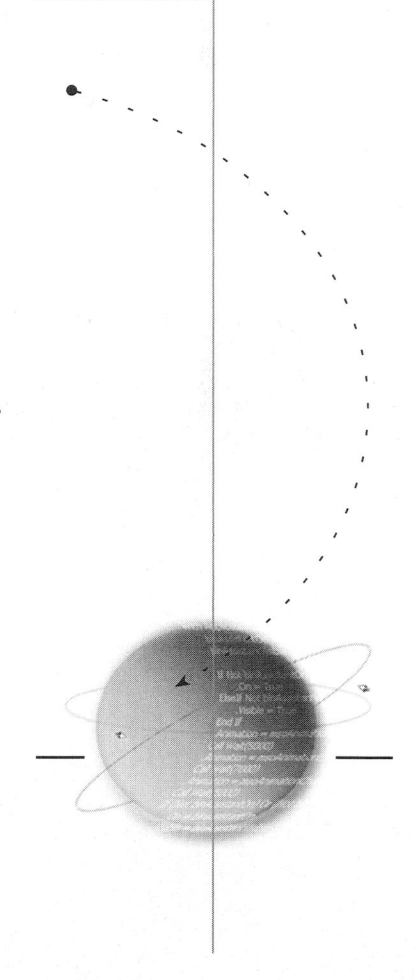

Before you dive into the rest of this book, take some time to look over these first two chapters, so that ideas about planning and design are in the back of your mind as you move forward. Then you can get on to the real fun—designing and building an Office solution that takes full advantage of the exciting technologies at your fingertips.

CHAPTER 1

Understanding Office Solution Development

Developers have been able to build custom solutions based on the applications in Microsoft Office for a long time. Each new version of Office brings new tools and technologies that make it easier to develop and deliver custom Office-based solutions. As companies have standardized on the Office suite of applications, users have become more and more familiar with these applications, and developers have learned to take advantage of the Office tools and technologies to create customized and integrated solutions on top of the Office suite of applications. These are solutions designed to improve users' ability to gather, analyze, customize, publish, and share information.

Microsoft Office 2000 includes powerful new technologies and improved programming models that are designed specifically to aid the developer in building custom Office solutions. The Office applications and components make it easier to connect to and work with corporate data and to move information from the Office applications to the Web.

This book was designed to help you understand the problems associated with custom solution development and give you the information you need to solve problems ranging from the simple to the complex. This chapter provides an overview of Office solution development. It is designed to give you a better understanding of what is new in Microsoft Office 2000 and how to use this book to find the information you need.

Contents

Developing Office Solutions

Office solution development is typically the process of customizing an Office application to perform some function or service. Developing an Office solution can range from writing a simple Visual Basic for Applications (VBA) procedure to creating a sophisticated financial analysis and reporting application. An *Office developer* is anyone who uses the programmability features of Office to make an application do something better, faster, or more efficiently than it could be done before. An *Office solution* is an application that uses an Office application or component as part of its overall architecture.

Every custom solution is, in some sense, an answer to a particular problem or need. Once you understand the problem, the success of your solution will depend on your ability to deliver a response that uses appropriate tools tailored to the experience level of the people who will be using your solution.

The Benefits of Office Programmability

There are currently more than 2.5 million Office developers creating custom solutions that use the applications or components in Microsoft Office. The term "Office developer" includes developers who work exclusively in one or more of the Office applications. It also includes developers working in any language that can access the objects exposed by Office applications. For more than ten years, Microsoft has been making improvements to the Office suite that enable developers to quickly and easily build and deploy custom desktop solutions. These improvements are the reason why Office applications continue to play such an important role in custom solution development:

- **Users and businesses already use the Microsoft Office suite of applications.** Most users already have Office on their desktop. The most recent surveys indicate that more than 40 million people regularly use Office to get their work done. Building solutions based on the Office platform enables developers to target this large base of users. Also, even if you are not developing within the Office development environment, it is still a good idea to take advantage of the objects exposed by Office applications so that your custom applications can leverage existing, proven, and tested Office functionality.

- **Office supports programmable objects and an integrated development environment.** Each Office application exposes its functionality through programmable objects, and each also supports the ability to integrate with other applications by using Automation (formerly OLE Automation). The applications all share the same programming language (Visual Basic for Applications) and integrated development environment (the Visual Basic Editor). Solutions created with VBA run in the same memory space as the host application and therefore execute faster. The programmable objects and powerful development tools in Office let developers build solutions that tightly integrate applications and seamlessly share data and information. In addition, distribution of Office-based solutions is simplified because VBA code and ActiveX controls are part of the application document or project.
- **Faster development cycles mean more affordable solutions.** The use of a single language and development environment also makes solution development faster. What you learn while programming one application applies when working with another application. VBA code written for one application can often be reused in a solution that works with a different application. Developers' skills become more valuable because they can work across many applications. Reducing the number of development environments or languages that developers need to learn means that the time and cost of creating custom solutions is reduced. Reliance on existing components eliminates the need to develop or test large portions of the application. This lets developers quickly build robust solutions that previously might have been cost-prohibitive.
- **Users become part of the solution.** Because solutions are created and run in an environment familiar to the user, support costs are kept to an absolute minimum. Building a solution based on Office technologies lets you define the solution in a context your users are already familiar with. This enables greater user participation in the solution-design process and can dramatically reduce training and support costs. It takes less time and effort to customize applications your users already own than to build new applications from scratch. The more familiar users are with the application, the easier it is going to be for them to understand and use your solution.

Office 2000 Programmability Enhancements

The Office programming model has always been a key factor in the expansion of Office as a solution-development platform. The current version of Office continues the long tradition of giving developers the tools they need to take full advantage of the technologies available in Office applications. The following sections discuss the new programmability features in this version of Office and where these new features are covered in this book.

New Add-in Architecture

Every Office application supports a new add-in architecture that allows developers to create a single add-in that can run in any application. This new add-in model is open to VBA developers and, because it is based on the Component Object Model (COM), it is also available to developers who are using Microsoft Visual Basic versions 5.0 and 6.0, Microsoft Visual C++®, Microsoft Visual J++™, or any language that can create COM components. This wide support for COM add-ins means that developers can now use multiple development environments to create custom solutions in Microsoft Office. The only requirement to connect a COM add-in to an Office application is for the add-in to implement the IDExtensibility2 interface. COM add-ins can be loaded when the host application starts, or on demand. Support has been added to allow the **OnAction** property of a custom command bar button to load a COM add-in. For a complete discussion of how to create, register, load, and work with COM add-ins, see Chapter 11, "Add-ins, Templates, Wizards, and Libraries."

Programming Features

Each of the Office applications has been expanded to expose new objects, methods, and properties. To see complete object model diagrams for all the Office applications, as well as for components used by Office applications, see the "Object Model Diagrams" appendix. For more information about how to work with objects, see Chapter 4, "Understanding Office Objects and Object Models." For additional information about working with the objects exposed by each Office application, see Chapter 5, "Working with Office Applications."

Expanded Event Model

The Office event model has been greatly expanded. Microsoft Word and Microsoft PowerPoint both expose more than two dozen new events, primarily associated with window and document objects. In addition, all Office applications now expose three command bar events:

- The **CommandBarButton** object has a Click event, which occurs when a user clicks a custom command bar button.
- The **CommandBarComboBox** object has a Change event, which occurs when the user makes a selection from a custom combo box on a command bar.
- The **CommandBars** collection object has an Update event, which occurs whenever there is a change to any command bar or command bar control. In addition, the Update event occurs whenever there is any change to any part of the host application, for example, when the insertion point moves between characters in a Word document.

For more information about command bar events, see Chapter 6, "Working with Shared Office Components."

New Language Elements

Several new functions are available to make it easier to format data or parse and manipulate strings. The following VBA functions can be used to format data: **FormatCurrency**, **FormatDateTime**, **FormatNumber**, and **FormatPercent**. You can use the **Split**, **Join**, and **Filter** functions to parse strings. The **Split** function parses a string into an array of substrings. The **Join** function is the opposite of the **Split** function: It creates a string from an array of substrings. Finally, the **Filter** function filters an array and returns an array containing the elements that match the specified criteria. You can also manipulate strings by using the new **Replace** and **InStrRev** functions. The **Round** function rounds a number to a specified number of decimal places. In this version of VBA, you can now write functions that return arrays and you can assign one array to another. For more information about using the new language elements, see Chapter 7, "Getting the Most Out of Visual Basic for Applications."

New Objects

Also new to VBA in Office are the **FileSystemObject** and **Dictionary** objects. The **Dictionary** object is analogous to a VBA collection, except that it can hold objects of different data types. The **FileSystemObject** object lets you work with the drives, directories, and files on your computer as if they were objects and collections of objects with methods and properties you can use to return information about your file system. For more information about using these new objects, see Chapter 7, "Getting the Most Out of Visual Basic for Applications."

The new objects and language elements make it even easier to work with objects exposed by Office applications and the shared Office components. But don't forget that VBA also gives you the ability to create your own objects. Also new to VBA in Office 2000 is the ability to add custom events to objects you create. In addition, you now have the ability to extend your custom objects by implementing interfaces. You can find a complete discussion of how to create and work with custom VBA objects in Chapter 9, "Custom Classes and Objects."

Office Document Virus Protection

Nearly everyone is familiar with the problem of macro viruses, which can range from the merely annoying to the truly destructive. In previous versions of Office, a document that contains VBA code will, depending on application-level settings, display a warning message before opening. It is up to users to choose whether to run the suspect VBA code when they open a document. But developers need to be able to assure users and administrators that they can trust the VBA code in a custom solution.

Microsoft Excel, Microsoft Outlook, Word, and PowerPoint now enable anti-virus software to scan documents as they are being opened to detect the presence of actual viruses, not just regular VBA code. In addition, these Office applications now support Microsoft Authenticode™ technology, which allows developers to digitally "sign" the VBA projects in their solutions by using a digital certificate. Users or network administrators can specify that a certificate is a trusted source, and Office applications then automatically enable the opening of documents containing VBA code from trusted sources. For a complete discussion of the security features in Office applications, including security for Microsoft Access databases and Microsoft FrontPage-based webs, see Chapter 17, "Securing Office Documents and Visual Basic for Applications Code," and Chapter 18, "Securing Access Databases."

Easier Access to Data

The fundamental purpose of most custom Office solutions is to turn data into usable information. This can involve working with data from a wide range of sources. The Microsoft ActiveX Database Objects (ADO) library is a new tool that developers can use to work with data. ADO is the new high-level programming interface to Microsoft's newest and most powerful data access technology, called OLE DB. It provides access to a broader variety of data sources than Microsoft Data Access Objects (DAO), although DAO is still supported and is, in some cases, the preferred way to access data programmatically. For a complete discussion of ADO and information that shows the DAO programmer how to transition to ADO, see Chapter 14, "Working with the Data Access Components of an Office Solution."

Getting at the data you need for your custom solutions is just the start of the story. Knowing how to work with data to turn it into usable information is one of the hallmarks of a successful Office developer. The Office applications now provide so many ways to retrieve data and work with data that deciding which one is the best to use can be a daunting task. There are new data access technologies and new ways to work with data once you get it into an Office application. For a discussion of what you need to know to acquire and work with data in your Office solution, see Chapter 15, "Retrieving and Analyzing Data."

Microsoft Office provides a broad array of tools and technologies for creating multiuser database solutions, and Access provides powerful new tools and features for working with Microsoft SQL Server. For information about creating multiuser database solutions by using different database architectures, see Chapter 16, "Multiuser Database Applications."

Integrating Office with the Web

For the first time, Microsoft Office 2000 seamlessly integrates Office desktop productivity with the ability to share information across an intranet or the Internet. Microsoft Office now contains a set of Web-publishing tools that enable users to manage information instead of documents. In addition, HTML is now a standard Office file format. Developers who need to enable Web-based information sharing and collaboration can use the new Web technologies in Office 2000. Chapter 12, "Using Web Technologies," gives you detailed information about HTML, Dynamic HTML (DHTML), scripting, the Microsoft Script Editor, Microsoft Office Web Components, and Microsoft Office Server Extensions.

Microsoft Script Editor

Office developers are accustomed to using Visual Basic Editor to add VBA code to their Office documents. Now that Office documents support HTML and can be viewed in a Web browser, developers need some way to programmatically work with the objects and script that make up an Office document designed to be displayed on the Web. Access, Excel, FrontPage, PowerPoint, and Word now support the Microsoft Script Editor. The Script Editor is a powerful new integrated development environment designed to let developers easily work with Office documents as Web pages. The Script Editor allows you to work with HTML in a document, add script, add ActiveX and HTML intrinsic controls, and view the results as if the document were displayed in the browser.

For Office developers who have not worked with Web pages extensively, this book provides an overview of what you need to know about how to work with the Script Editor. In addition, it covers scripting in Office documents, an overview of the DHTML object model, and manipulating objects using script. There is also an introduction to cascading style sheets (.css files), scriptlets, and behaviors—in short, a discussion crafted specifically to help Office developers understand the new Internet tools and technologies in Office 2000.

Office Web Components and Office Server Extensions

The new support for HTML as a native file format means Office documents are "Web-ready" by default. Publishing an Office document to the Web is now as easy as saving a file to your computer's hard disk (or saving an Office document to an HTTP server). But publishing a document is only half the challenge. There are new ActiveX controls, called the Microsoft Office Web Components. The Office Web Components are a collection of controls designed to let you publish fully interactive spreadsheets, charts, PivotTable® reports, and databases to the Web. By using the Office Web Components on a Web page, you can sort, filter, add or change data, expand and collapse views, work with PivotTable reports, and display your data in a chart. In addition, the Office Web Components are fully programmable, which lets developers create rich, interactive content for Web-based solutions.

The Microsoft Office Server Extensions library allows developers to programmatically work with the objects that enable online threaded discussions. This feature lets you create custom solutions that use the browser to incorporate online discussions with any Office document or Web page.

Data Access Pages

Microsoft Access has a new Web-related object called a *data access page*. Data access pages are HTML documents that use the features of DHTML and provide a new way for users to interact with data on the Web. You create data access pages by using Access and display them either in Access or in Microsoft Internet Explorer 5. Data access pages allow users to use a Web browser to work with data in an interactive manner and in a way that has never been possible before. You can use them to view, edit, or delete records, and you can use them to sort and filter records as well as group records according to criteria you specify. In addition, while a page is displayed, the user can manipulate what records are displayed and how they are displayed. Although you design these pages in Access, you save them to disk as separate .htm files. The pages can contain data from an Access database (.mdb file) or Access project (.adp file). For more information about working with data access pages, see Chapter 5, "Working with Office Applications."

HTML and Script

You can also use VBA to work with the HTML and script in an Office document. Through the shared Office component library, Excel, PowerPoint, and Word support two new objects—**Scripts** and **HTMLProject**—that expose the properties and methods of the script blocks in a document as well as the properties and methods of the HTML code in the document. For more information about using VBA to work with these objects, see Chapter 6, "Working with Shared Office Components."

You can use VBA in Access to work with the script and HTML code in a data access page. Each data access page has a **Document** property that returns the DHTML **document** object. The **document** object is the gateway to all other objects in a Web page. You can see code examples that use the **Document** property to return the **document** object in Chapter 5, "Working with Office Applications." You can see code examples that work with the **document** object in Chapter 12, "Using Web Technologies."

Creating Help Files

If you have used the Help system in any Office 2000 application, you have already seen the new Office Help system based on compiled HTML files. Now you can create Help files for your custom applications that have all the power and flexibility that you have seen in Web pages—including scripting, DHTML, and ActiveX controls. HTML Help lets you do the following:

- Author your Help files by using the same tools you use to create Web pages.
- Integrate Help topics and context-sensitive Help into your solution's custom dialog boxes, error messages, and forms.
- Use VBA to work directly with the HtmlHelp application programming interface (API).
- Under certain circumstances, use the Answer Wizard Software Development Kit (SDK) to integrate your Help topics with those supplied by an Office application.
- Use the HTML Help ActiveX control to display your custom Help files from within any Web page by using the HTML Help Viewer.

For more information about using HTML Help, see Chapter 13, "Adding Help to Your Custom Solution."

Pulling It All Together

The programmability features of Microsoft Office have always provided developers with powerful tools they can use to modify and integrate Office applications into custom solutions that extend the functionality of Office. With the new tools and technologies in Office 2000, you have more power than ever before to take advantage of the Office platform and extend Office functionality from the desktop to the Web.

All of these features give you many options for developing the right strategy for designing, building, and deploying your custom solution (see Chapter 2, "Designing and Deploying Office Solutions," for more details about designing your custom solutions). Every possible direction has both benefits and limitations. It will be *your* strengths and abilities, the needs of *your* users, and the power of *your* development environment that will determine how you deliver your services to customers.

The *Microsoft Office 2000/Visual Basic Programmer's Guide* is designed to help you get where you need to go now. But there is much more here if you want to take advantage of it. This book not only answers specific questions, it provides code samples that illustrate how to use all Office technologies. In addition, it tells you how to design and build procedures, modules, objects, and solutions in a way that makes them robust, easy to maintain and update, and easy to reuse in other solutions you may build.

Where to Go from Here

For additional information about the subjects discussed in this chapter, see the following resources.

Planning Your Solution

Chapter 2, "Designing and Deploying Office Solutions"

Creating Reusable, Maintainable Code

Chapter 3, "Writing Solid Code"

Chapter 8, "Error Handling and Debugging"

Working with VBA

Chapter 6, "Working with Shared Office Components"

Chapter 7, "Getting the Most Out of Visual Basic for Applications"

Chapter 9, "Custom Classes and Objects"

Chapter 10, "The Windows API and Other Dynamic-Link Libraries"

Chapter 11, "Add-ins, Templates, Wizards, and Libraries"

Working with Data

Chapter 14, "Working with the Data Access Components of an Office Solution"

Chapter 15, "Retrieving and Analyzing Data"

Working with Access Project (.Adp) Files

Chapter 16, "Multiuser Database Applications"

Creating HTML Help Files

Chapter 13, "Adding Help to Your Custom Solution"

Working with Data Access Pages

Chapter 5, "Working with Office Applications"

Chapter 12, "Using Web Technologies"

Creating Multiuser Database Applications

Chapter 16, "Multiuser Database Applications"

Using Microsoft Office Web Components

Chapter 12, "Using Web Technologies"

Chapter 15, "Retrieving and Analyzing Data"

Securing Office Documents and Locking VBA Projects

Chapter 17, "Securing Office Documents and Visual Basic for Applications Code"

Securing Access Databases

Chapter 18, "Securing Access Databases"

CHAPTER 2

Designing and Deploying Office Solutions

Chances are good that you're reading this book because you need to develop a Microsoft Office-based solution for your company. If your company is like most companies, it needs to be done yesterday, and you're already wondering how you're going to get it done on time. However, we're also willing to wager that despite the stress of building a bullet-proof application in record time, you also secretly (or maybe not so secretly) think that writing code in Visual Basic for Applications (VBA) is a lot of fun. And we agree. For many people, coding is more fun than designing and planning a solution, and it's tempting to jump right in and begin coding before you've fully thought through the problems that you're facing. The goal of this chapter is to persuade you to go through that sometimes difficult design process in order to begin coding with a clear goal in mind. Spending a few hours up front on design can mean the difference between delivering the solution that your customer needs a few months down the road, or backtracking to try to convert your many hours of coding work into the solution that you wish you had designed in the first place.

Contents

Beginning the Design Process

The very first thing that you need to do when you begin designing a solution is to identify your customers. Who will be using the solution? It may be just one person, or a small workgroup within your company, or an entire department. Or perhaps you're a consultant building custom solutions for other companies. Or maybe you're building Office based solutions to package and sell through a retail outfit or over the Internet. Whoever your customers are, you should have a thorough understanding of their business processes and their needs before you begin building your solution.

What Do Your Customers Want?

The first step in the design process is to get a clear idea of what your customers want. This can take some time and patience, especially if your customers aren't technical people by nature.

Have your customers tell you in their own words what they want, and ask lots of questions to clarify your customers' goals for yourself. It's a good idea to rephrase your customers' requests and repeat them back to make sure that you're communicating on the same plane. For example, if your customers say that they want to be able to create reports from a set of data, you need to know: Who will be using the reports? Can they be read-only, or do users need to be able to manipulate the data in the report to present it in new ways? Should the reports be available over a corporate intranet, or will they be printed, or will they be e-mailed? The answers to these kinds of questions will begin to eliminate certain design possibilities and shift your focus to others.

You may have to ask the same question several times in several different ways. It may be helpful to diagram or demonstrate multiple possibilities to your customers and ask them to choose the one that best fits what they have in mind. Keep in mind that your customers probably find the planning and design process difficult, and would rather that you just went away and came back with what they want. Simplifying choices for your customers, while keeping their goals in mind, may make the process easier for everyone.

What Do Your Customers Need?

What your customers want and what your customers need aren't always the same thing. Customers may say that they want a particular type of solution because that's what they're familiar with, or because they've seen the technology and think it's cool. As the developer, part of your job is to figure out what solution will best fit your customers' needs, and present persuasive evidence to your customers. That said, keep in mind that in the end, the solution your customers want takes priority over the solution that you want to build. If you can't understand why your customers want a particular solution, it may be that you simply don't understand their needs well enough.

To figure out what your customers need, look at your customers' existing solutions, if there are any, and their business process. For example, if your customers want to create a database to track accounting information that to date has been managed on paper, review the paper system carefully so that you can model the solution on the existing system. Of course, in the process of modeling the existing system, you may find ways to enhance the system within the solution and make your customers' business process more efficient.

Next, find out who will be using the application, and how they will use it. Interview as many people as you can who have used the existing system, or who will use your solution once it has been created. If you're dealing with only one person to create an application that will be used by several people, it's possible that you're getting only a narrow perspective on what the solution needs to do.

Who will use the solution and how they will use it can make a big difference in your design. For example, a database in which multiple users may be entering data simultaneously across a network requires a different design than a database that's managed by one or two people who enter data and then generate reports for other users. The first solution may require record-locking management, full-fledged security, and a means of distributing the front end across a corporate network. The second solution can probably get by with no locking management, minimal security, and a common network share for those using it.

A detailed understanding of your customers' data and business process is crucial to creating a well-designed solution. Spend some time analyzing their data and asking questions about it. Again, it's quite possible that the current solution does not store the data in the most efficient manner. Rather than duplicating this inefficiency, you'll want to improve it if possible—with your customers' agreement, of course!

At the Drawing Table

When you've gathered as much information as you can from your customers, sit down with pencil and paper and sketch out the initial design for the solution—the technologies to be used, the user interface, the organization of the code. Doing this not only gives you a basis to begin working, it's also likely to bring up all kinds of new questions that you need to ask your customers. Nailing down as many issues as you can before you start coding will save you time in the long run.

If your solution is complex, you may want to write a *specification* for it. A specification is a document that outlines your goals in creating the solution, discusses the details of the solution's implementation, and notes unresolved technical and design issues. It's a valuable document, both for you and for your customers, that helps you agree on how the solution will work before you begin creating it. It also provides you and any other programmers working on the project with a road map for the development process.

Of course, you may not be able to foresee every aspect of your solution's design ahead of time. As you develop the solution, you'll most likely learn new ways to do things, encounter unplanned obstacles, and refine your understanding of your customers' needs. The key is to create a flexible design, so that making a change doesn't send you all the way back to the beginning. For example, creating custom objects is a good way to build in flexibility. If you need to modify an object, you need to do so only once, within that object's class module. Using constants in your code is another way to make your code more organized and easier to modify.

If you suspect there may be a more efficient way to do something, indulge your intuition before you dive into the code. There's no point in re-creating the wheel if someone's already built the component that you need.

Building a Prototype

For most Office 2000 solutions, you don't need to build a full-fledged prototype—the solution that you're building can act as the prototype that you show to your customers. When you begin building the solution, however, it's useful to approach it as though it were a prototype, so that you can quickly demonstrate to your customers how the solution is going to work.

Map out a general user interface, but don't spend hours laying out controls and adding graphics if the user interface may need to be altered. Also forego work on the fine details of navigation through the solution, unless that's a critical part for your customers to see.

Build the core part of the application first. For example, if you're building a wizard, focus on the code that generates the basic result, rather than adding in the various options that users will be able to select to fine-tune the outcome. This way you can determine whether you're on the right track for creating the solution that your customers need. Also, once you've tackled the hard problems, you'll have more insight into the way that the final solution will work and a better understanding of your customers' business process.

Use sample data to test your initial design. Don't use live data or your customers' only copy of the data if your solution may modify it. Create a local copy of the data that you can isolate until you've thoroughly tested the solution.

Which Technologies Should You Use?

The first critical design decisions that you need to make are what type of solution you want to create and which application or technologies to use as the basis for your solution. Solutions you create with Office 2000 are likely to fall into one of the following broad categories: data-management applications; document templates; add-ins; and Web applications, either with or without a data-management component.

Each of the Office 2000 applications is better suited to some solutions than to others, and deciding which to use requires some familiarity with the strengths and weaknesses of all of them. One of the goals of this book is to help you become familiar with applications and technologies that you may not have known much about before so that you can use the right tools for the solution. The following sections, as well as later chapters, aim to help you navigate through the possibilities in order to choose the best technologies for your solution.

Where Should You Store Data?

Many solutions involve storing and managing data at some level. Microsoft's new OLE DB technology makes it easier to access data in any format. If you need to work with existing data, you can access it directly through OLE DB or through Open Database Connectivity (ODBC). If you are creating a solution to store new data, or if your customer wants to move existing data into the new solution, you are free to choose the data-storage strategy that makes the most sense for your solution.

Building a Solution to Store New Data

Where should you store your data if you have the freedom to design your data storage from scratch? Although there are many options, if you're building an Office-based solution, you're most likely going to store data in a Microsoft Excel workbook, in a Microsoft Access database (.mdb), or on a database server, such as Microsoft SQL Server.

Should You Store Data in Excel or in a Relational Database?

Many people are well-versed with VBA programming in Excel, but are intimidated by relational databases like Access and SQL Server, which require an understanding of relational database design concepts. Some developers end up using Excel to build data-management solutions that would be better off as relational databases.

Excel is best for storing small amounts of data on which you need to perform calculations, or that you want to present in a grid format. It's also good for storing disparate types of information—numeric, text, and graphical data, such as charts, that doesn't easily conform to a particular structure.

For larger data sets, Excel may not be the ideal application for storing the data, but it's a superior tool for analyzing and presenting data that's stored in another format. You can import data into Excel from any OLE DB or ODBC data source, and use Excel's calculation and analysis tools to analyze the data however you choose. For more information about using Excel for data analysis, see Chapter 15, "Retrieving and Analyzing Data."

Here are a few questions to ask yourself when trying to decide whether to use a relational database rather than Excel to store data:

- Does your data duplicate items that could be stored in one place? For example, are you typing a customer's address repeatedly each time you take an order for that customer? If so, you would be better off storing your data in a relational database, where you can enter customer information in a single table and create relationships with other tables that use that data.
- Do you need to be able to expand the system with more data or more users in the future? If so, it's likely that your solution will become extremely complicated as you add data. Again, you would be better off storing your data in a relational database and using queries to get to the data that you need. A relational database is a better choice for scalability.
- Do you need to store or archive old data? Access is better suited to this task than Excel. On the other hand, if you regularly replace data without archiving it, Excel may be sufficient for your needs. For example, if your application pulls daily stock quotes from a Web page but doesn't need to track stock histories, Excel is ideal.
- Does your solution need to be multiuser? If more than one person may need to access the data at the same time, you can take advantage of the built-in multiuser features in Access. Only one person at a time can open an Excel workbook file, so data entry in Excel is limited to one person at a time.
- Do you need to be able to control and validate data entry? Access is generally better suited for this than Excel. Access provides controls with built-in data binding with which you can easily impose validation rules. You can create bound controls and perform data validation on a UserForm in Excel, but it's more work.

If you decide to store your data in a relational database, you have several options. If you're building either a single-user solution or a multiuser solution for a small workgroup, you can store the data in an Access database (.mdb) or in a Microsoft Database Engine (MSDE) database. Either of these options is available to you if you own Microsoft Office 2000 Professional or Microsoft Office 2000 Premium.

An MSDE database uses a database engine that's similar to the one found in SQL Server, but an MSDE database can't support as many users; best performance is achieved with five or fewer users. The advantage to using MSDE is that you can use it to create a SQL Server database from Access without actually having SQL Server on your computer. It's a good tool for prototyping and designing an enterprise solution that you'll eventually migrate to SQL Server, because you can run an MSDE database under SQL Server without modification. A database server such as SQL Server can support hundreds to thousands of simultaneous users. A properly optimized Access database (.mdb) can support up to 255 simultaneous users, although best performance is achieved with 25-50 users. An Access database is best for small workgroup-based solutions.

For more information about which type of relational database you should use to store the data for your solution, see Chapter 14, "Working with the Data Access Components of an Office Solution," and Chapter 16, "Multiuser Database Applications."

Designing a Relational Database

If you decide to store the data for your solution in an Access database (.mdb), SQL Server database, or other relational database, designing the database structure is likely to be the most challenging part of building the solution. In order to understand how the tables in the database should be structured and how they should relate to one another, you need to understand the data—perfectly. Although it's fairly easy to modify the data model while you're developing the solution, it's much more difficult once your customers are using the solution. So it's important to put as much effort as necessary into the process of designing the data model before you begin writing code. Developing a solution based on a well-designed data model is much more rewarding than working with one that's poorly designed.

There are entire books devoted to designing effective relational data models. If you're new to relational database design, check out the references listed in the "Where to Go from Here" section of this chapter for more information.

Thinking About Data Entry and User Input

If your solution requires that users enter data, another key part of your design process is determining how your solution should get data from users and validate it. The extent to which your solution needs to control user input is another factor in choosing which application to use as the basis for your solution.

If you decide to store the data in a relational database such as an Access or SQL Server database, it's a good idea to separate the solution into two parts: a back-end database and a front-end data-entry component. The back-end database contains the tables, where all of the data is stored, while the front end displays the data and manages data entry. By designing the solution this way, you can store the data in a central location on a network server and distribute a copy of the front-end file or files to each user. You can build the front-end data-entry component in any Office 2000 application or in Microsoft Visual Basic.

Using Access to Create a Data-Entry Component

An Access database makes a good front-end data-entry component for data stored in a relational database. If your back-end database is an Access .mdb file, you can create another .mdb file to function as the front end, and link it to the tables in the back-end database. In the front-end component, create the queries, forms, reports, data access pages, macros, and modules that you need to build the solution and manipulate and display the data.

If your back-end database is a SQL Server database, you can create an Access project file (.adp) to function as the front-end data-entry component. In an Access project, you can create forms, reports, data access pages, macros, and modules, just as you can in an .mdb file; you can also create SQL-specific objects like views, stored procedures, and database diagrams. By using an Access project, you can display the data in a SQL Server database, and you can also create a database or modify the database structure.

Creating either an Access database or an Access project file is the best approach if your solution requires that users enter lots of data, and if you need to control the way that data is stored. The design of your database itself enforces certain rules on the way that users can enter data. For example, a user cannot violate a table's primary key by adding a duplicate record. In addition, you can establish custom validation rules in Access that prevent users from entering invalid data.

For more information about creating an Access-based solution or a client/server solution, see Chapter 5, "Working with Office Applications," Chapter 14, "Working with the Data Access Components of an Office Solution," and Chapter 16, "Multiuser Database Applications."

Validating User Input from Excel, Word, and PowerPoint-Based Solutions

Excel, Microsoft Word, and Microsoft PowerPoint are good for displaying data that's stored in a relational database, but they don't provide much flexibility for entering data into the database. However, if your data is stored in Excel, Word, or PowerPoint, and your solution requires that you control and validate the data that users enter or other user input, you may still need to perform data validation. Here are some ways to control and validate user input from these applications:

- Use the **InputBox** function to prompt users to input small amounts of information. Verify within code that users entered data and that it's the type of data you're expecting. For example, you can use the **IsNumeric** and **IsDate** functions to determine whether users entered a number or a date. For more information about performing data validation in VBA code, see Chapter 7, "Getting the Most Out of Visual Basic for Applications."
- Create a custom dialog box that prompts users to enter data or select options. Using this approach provides more flexibility than using the **InputBox** function does. By using a combo box, for example, you can force users to choose an existing value from a list, thus preventing errors that might occur if users typed the value in themselves.
- Disable controls on the form until users have entered the data that you're expecting. For example, within the Change event procedure for a text box control, you can check whether the value of the text box is a zero-length string (" "). If it is, you can disable the command buttons on the form so that users cannot proceed without entering text or canceling, as shown in the following procedure:

```
' The Len function returns zero if there is no data in the text box,
' and a nonzero value if there is, so using the CBool function
' converts the numeric value to True (nonzero) or False (zero).
Private Sub txtGetData_Change()
   cmdOK.Enabled =  CBool(Len(txtGetData.Value))
End If
```

- Create a wizard that walks users through an operation, prompting them at each step to supply the necessary data. Again, you can prevent users from proceeding by disabling the command buttons that the wizard uses for navigation. For more information about creating wizards, see Chapter 11, "Add-ins, Templates, Wizards, and Libraries."

You can also use these strategies for controlling and validating data input through script in a Web page.

Retrieving, Analyzing, and Presenting Data

Once you've designed the data-storage and data-entry components of your solution, you should begin thinking about how to present and summarize the data in a format that makes sense to users. Although generally not as difficult as database design, determining which data users want to see and building reports to display the data in a usable format can be a more challenging task than it initially seems.

Here are some questions to ask yourself as you design the reporting component of a solution:

- Does the report need to be dynamically linked to the data source, or can it be a static report? If the report needs to display the most up-to-date data, it should be dynamically linked to the data source. On the other hand, if the data is not updated frequently, or if the report needs to be re-created regularly because the structure of the underlying data source changes, you can create a static report.
- Do users need to interact with the data in the report, or can the report be read-only? If users need to perform calculations on the data or manipulate the data to display it in novel ways, you probably want to create the report in Excel or use the Microsoft Office Web Components to create it in a Web page. For information about working with the Office Web Components, see Chapter 12, "Using Web Technologies."
- Do users need to be able to view the report from a Web page, or from within one of the Office applications?
- Does the report need to be nicely formatted?

The following table describes some common types of reports that you can create with Office 2000 applications and their advantages. There are other ways to create reports in addition to those described here. For more information about working with reports, see Chapter 15, "Retrieving and Analyzing Data."

Type of report	Application or technology	Advantages
Static (not dynamically linked to data)	Access report snapshot	You can create a report snapshot by exporting an Access report to a snapshot file (.snp). A report snapshot retains the formatting of the report from which it is created. It can be viewed in the Snapshot Viewer application or embedded in a Web page by using the Snapshot Viewer control (Snapview.ocx). It can also be e-mailed as a stand-alone file to someone who does not have Access. To view a snapshot file, a user must have the Snapshot Viewer, which is included with Access. Users that don't have Access can download it free of charge from the Microsoft Office Developer Forum Web site at http://www.microsoft.com/officedev/index/snapshot.htm.
	Access object saved as HTML	Saving an Access table, query, form, or report as HTML creates a static, unformatted HTML table in a Web page.
Dynamic (linked to data)	Access report	The data in the report is refreshed each time you close and reopen it. An Access report can be nicely formatted, so it may be a good choice for printed reports.

Type of report	Application or technology	Advantages
	Excel query table	A query table is a table in Excel that's dynamically linked to an Excel range or an external data source. You can filter a query table and use it as the data source for a chart, PivotTable report, or PivotChart™ report.
	Excel PivotTable report or PivotChart report	A PivotTable report can be dynamically linked to an Excel range or to an external data source. You can use a PivotTable report to view a single set of data in a variety of configurations. To display the data graphically, you can also create a PivotChart report that's dynamically linked to a PivotTable report. In addition, you can save a PivotTable report or PivotChart report to a Web page to create a dynamic report on a Web page.

Building Add-ins, Wizards, and Templates

The preceding sections emphasize design considerations for solutions that store and display data, which companies commonly need. Other common solutions are those that may not involve data storage, but that help users do their jobs more efficiently. Add-ins, wizards, and templates fall into that category.

There are two types of add-ins that you can create for Office 2000 applications: Component Object Model (COM) add-ins and application-specific add-ins. COM add-ins take advantage of COM technology and can be designed to work in multiple Office 2000 applications and in the Visual Basic Editor. For example, you could create a COM add-in that displays a set of images to be inserted into a Word document, an Excel worksheet, or a PowerPoint presentation. You can build COM add-ins in Microsoft Visual Basic 5.0 or 6.0, or with Microsoft Office 2000 Developer.

Application-specific add-ins, on the other hand, function only in the application in which they were created. For example, you could create an Excel add-in to perform calculations that you need to run repeatedly on different sets of data. Both types of add-ins can be integrated into the users' environment so that they become part of the application.

A wizard is a special type of add-in, and you can create a wizard as either a COM add-in or an application-specific add-in. A wizard walks a user through a process, one step at a time. The Mail Merge Helper in Word is a good example of a wizard that walks a user through a complicated process. Creating a wizard is a good way both to control how users enter information into a document and to speed up the process of formatting the document correctly.

A template forms the basis for a new document, and can contain text, graphics, predefined styles, macros, and code. Templates make it easier for users to create common documents in a standardized format. For example, you could create a Word template displaying your company's logo and address, so that all correspondence from your company has the same look.

For more information about these kinds of solutions, see Chapter 11, "Add-ins, Templates, Wizards, and Libraries."

Thinking About User Interface Design

Another important aspect of solution design is the design of an effective user interface. A good user interface should be attractive, neatly laid out, and well organized. It should also be easy to use and understand. The best solutions are those that users can work with fairly intuitively, without extensive training or documentation.

Any way in which users interact with your solution is part of the user interface. Here are some suggestions for designing an effective user interface:

- Strive for consistency in the way that the solution looks and in the way that users work with it. Be consistent with colors, fonts, and formatting. The solution should be visually appealing but not overwhelming.
- Make it easy for users to navigate through the solution. For example, when the solution starts, you may want to display a switchboard form that provides users with a set of choices.
- Make the solution equally accessible through the mouse or the keyboard. Set the tab order for controls on a form or Web page so that users can move from one control to the next predictably. Take into account users that may have problems seeing the screen or using the mouse or keyboard.
- Whenever possible, provide clear visual clues so that users can figure out what's happening. For example, it's a good idea to change the mouse pointer to an hourglass during lengthy operations so that users do not think that the solution has stopped working.
- Validate data that users enter so that you can immediately prompt users to correct themselves if they've entered the wrong type of data.
- When you create custom toolbars and menus, make sure that they are displayed when the solution is available, and hidden when it is not.
- Implement thorough error handling, and anticipate as many different types of errors as you can. Provide error messages that are clear and succinct.

There are several good resources available that discuss user interface design; see "Where to Go from Here" for more information.

Designing Code for Reusability

Once you've mapped out the overall design for your solution, spend some time thinking about how to structure your code within the solution. There's always more than one way to write the code, and with a little additional effort, you can maximize the reusability of your code. The work you do now to make your code reusable can save you and other developers time in the future, when you can reuse code rather than rewrite it. If you write code with the intention of reusing it in other scenarios, your code may also be easier to maintain because you'll tend to write smaller, more compact procedures that are simpler to modify.

- Whenever practical, write procedures that are atomic—that is, each procedure performs one task. Procedures written in this manner are easier to reuse.
- Adopt a set of coding standards and stick to them. Chapter 3, "Writing Solid Code," makes suggestions for standardizing your coding practices.
- Document your procedures and modules well by adding comments, so that you and other developers can easily figure out later what your code is doing.
- Group similar procedures or procedures that are called together in a module. Not only does this help you to organize your code functionally, but it can also enhance your solution's performance. By default, VBA compiles code on demand, meaning that when you run a procedure, VBA compiles that module and the modules containing any procedures that that procedure calls. Compiling fewer modules results in improved performance. (To further improve performance, be sure to save your code in a compiled state.)
- Develop a library of procedures that you can reuse. Use a code library tool to store procedures and code snippets so that they are immediately available when you need them. Office 2000 Developer includes such a tool, the Code Librarian, which is an add-in for the Visual Basic Editor.
- Create custom objects by encapsulating related code in class modules. You can add properties, methods, and events to custom objects, and organize them into custom hierarchical object models. Once you've built and tested a custom object, you can treat it as a "black box"—you and other programmers can use the object without thinking about the code that it contains. When you do need to maintain the code, you only need to modify it once, within the class module.

- Develop interfaces to extend custom objects. An interface provides a basic set of properties, methods, and events to any custom object that implements the interface. By using an interface, you can create sets of closely related, yet distinct, objects that share common code.
- If you have Visual Basic, you can create Automation (formerly OLE Automation) servers, which are .dll or .exe files that contain custom objects. The advantage to packaging custom objects in separate .dll or .exe files is that you can call them from any VBA project, just as you would call any Automation server, without having to include the code for the object in your project. For more information, see the documentation for Visual Basic 5.0 and Visual Basic 6.0.

For more information about effective code design, see Chapter 3, "Writing Solid Code," Chapter 7, "Getting the Most Out of Visual Basic for Applications," Chapter 9, "Creating Classes and Objects," and Chapter 10, "The Windows API and Other Dynamic-Link Libraries."

Security Considerations

While security may not be the most exciting topic, the fact is that security is taking on an ever-greater importance for programmers as computers become increasingly connected through corporate networks and the Internet. Be sure to discuss the security needs for your solution with your customers.

There are two aspects of security with which you need to concern yourself as an Office solution developer. The first is protecting your intellectual property by securing your code. The second is protecting your solution from viruses and unwelcome users.

To secure your intellectual property, you have the following options:

- You can password-protect the VBA project. For information about locking your VBA project, see Chapter 17, "Securing Office Documents and Visual Basic for Applications Code."
- If your solution involves creating an add-in, you can build a COM add-in, which is compiled into a .dll file. The code contained in the .dll file can't be viewed, so you can distribute the file without worrying about others stealing your code.
- If you're building a solution in Access, you can create an .mde file from the database and distribute that file. Saving your database as an .mde file removes all editable source code and prevents users from viewing or modifying the design of forms, reports, data access pages, or modules. Your VBA code will continue to run, but it cannot be viewed or edited. If your solution is an Access project (.adp) rather than an Access database, you can create an .ade file, which is similar to an .mde file.

Note Although saving a database as an .mde or .ade file prevents users from modifying a data access page from within Access, if they have access to the HTML file, they can still modify the HTML file in another HTML editor. To prevent users from modifying a data access page, you should save the HTML file to a network share and specify read-only permissions for users who need to view the data access page but should not be able to modify it. For more information about using file-system access control to protect access to documents, see Chapter 17, "Securing Office Documents and Visual Basic for Applications Code."

To protect your solution from viruses and from undesired users, you have the following options:

- You can install a VBA virus scanner. For more information about available virus scanners, see the "Where to Go from Here" section at the end of this chapter.
- You can define trusted sources for code. A trusted source is an individual or company that has been certified by a certification authority. You can then set the security level for each Office 2000 application to High to run code only from trusted sources, to Medium to permit users to choose whether to run potentially unsafe code, or to Low to run all code, whether trusted or not.
- You can use Microsoft Jet security to secure a Microsoft Jet database (.mdb). Microsoft Jet allows you to implement user-level security for each object in a database.

For more information about securing your solution, see Chapter 17, "Securing Office Documents and Visual Basic for Applications Code" and Chapter 18, "Securing Access Databases."

Testing Your Solution

Testing your code is a fundamental part of building an Office solution. Thorough testing will save you lots of headaches later on.

In general, you probably find that you test codc as you go, to make sure that each part of the solution works as expected before you move on to the next part. It's also a good idea to test the solution thoroughly once you're done building it, to find things that you missed and to try new or unexpected scenarios. If you have access to other computers, test your solution there to make sure that it behaves as expected on different system configurations.

Once you've tested the solution yourself, get someone else to test it as well. Ideally, you would recruit another developer or a professional tester, but if that's not an option, have your customers begin testing the application.

Before you deploy your solution to all users, choose a subset of users to act as beta testers. Have them keep track of all the bugs they encounter—how they caused the bug, what they expected the solution to do, and what it actually did. You can log run-time errors from within the solution, either in a text file on the users' computers, or to a centrally located database.

Finally, when you're designing your solution, prepare for the worst, and hope for the best! Consider how you will deal with a serious bug should one be discovered after you've fully deployed your solution. If your solution includes a file that may need to be modified for a bug fix—say an .mdb file that is the front end for a database solution—you have little choice but to distribute a new version of that file to all users in order to fix the bug. If your solution is Web-based, however, you may be able to fix the bug in the Web page on the Web server; the next time a user accesses that Web page, the user will see the new version containing the bug fix.

Providing Support for Your Solution

Once your solution is in the hands of users, it's likely that you'll have to provide some level of support for it—answering questions, aiding installation, fixing bugs, and generally helping users to use the solution to get their jobs done. You may be able to avoid some support issues by providing a Help file for the solution. For information about creating Help files, see Chapter 13, "Adding Help to Your Custom Solution."

Deploying Your Solution

When it's time to deploy your Office solution to users, you have lots of alternatives, ranging from copying a file to a common share on a network server to building a full-fledged setup program. How you choose to deploy the solution depends largely on what type of solution you've created.

The following sections outline different ways to deploy various types of Office 2000 solutions.

Building a Setup Program with the Package and Deployment Wizard

If you have Microsoft Office 2000 Developer or Visual Basic 6.0, you can use the Package and Deployment Wizard to create a setup program for your solution. You can build a setup program that's stored in a folder on a network server or published to a Web server. For more information about this wizard, see the documentation for the Package and Deployment Wizard in Office 2000 Developer.

Note If your solution is a template or application-specific add-in, creating a setup program with the Package and Deployment Wizard may not be your best option because the wizard doesn't provide a way to install the template or add-in to the special folders reserved for these on the user's machine. For more information, see the following section, "Deploying Templates and Application-Specific Add-ins."

When you create a setup script with the Package and Deployment Wizard, you can specify where the solution should be installed on users' computers by choosing from a list of installation locations. The following table lists the installation locations from which you can select and provides an example of a path to which the solution might then be installed on a typical user's computer.

Installation location	Example
$(AppPath)	C:\Program Files*ApplicationName*
$(ProgramFiles)	C:\Program Files*ApplicationName*
$(CommonFiles)	C:\Program Files\Common Files
$(CommonFilesSys)	C:\Program Files\Common Files\System
$(WinPath)	C:\Windows
$(WinSysPath)	C:\Windows\System
$(OfficeAddInPath)	C:\Program Files\Microsoft Office\Office

Note When you build a setup program with the Package and Deployment Wizard, a new folder will be created under the user's C:\Program Files folder. By default, the folder is given the name you've provided for the solution. This folder is added even if you are not installing the solution itself to the Program Files folder, and is used to store information for uninstalling the solution.

Deploying Templates and Application-Specific Add-ins

The Package and Deployment Wizard is a good tool for building setup programs for many Office 2000 solutions. However, Office 2000 templates and application-specific add-ins (versus COM add-ins) are exceptions, because they should be installed to special folders on users' machines. The Package and Deployment Wizard does not provide any way to install to these special folders.

On a computer running Microsoft Windows 95 or Windows 98 without user profiles enabled, Office 2000 templates and add-ins should be installed to the following folders, respectively:

C:\Windows\Application Data\Microsoft\Templates
C:\Windows\Application Data\Microsoft\Addins

On a computer running Windows 95 or Windows 98 with user profiles enabled or Microsoft Windows NT® Workstation or Windows NT Server, Office 2000 templates and add-ins should be installed to these folders:

C:*WindowsFolder*\Profiles*UserName*\Application Data\Microsoft\Templates
C:*WindowsFolder*\Profiles*UserName*\Application Data\Microsoft\Addins

Although it's not absolutely necessary to install a template or add-in to one of these foldcrs, there are some advantages to doing so:

- If a Word, Excel, or PowerPoint custom template is stored on users' computers, it must be installed to the Templates folder in order for it to appear in the **New** dialog box (**File** menu). For more information, see "Deploying a Custom Template" later in this chapter.
- Because the Templates and AddIns folders are the default folders for templates and add-ins, installing them there makes it easier for users to locate a template or add-in. For example, Excel add-ins (.xla files) that are installed in the AddIns folder automatically appear in the list of available add-ins in the **Add-ins** dialog box (**Tools** menu), so that users do not have to browse to find the correct file.
- The Templates and AddIns folders are trusted folders, meaning that an add-in or template in one of these folders does not have to be digitally signed by a trusted source in order to run code when security is set to High. These folders are trusted by default, but it's possible to override this setting by clearing the **Trust all installed add-ins and templates** check box on the **Trusted Sources** tab of the **Security** dialog box. To open the **Security** dialog box in the Office 2000 applications, point to **Macro** on the **Tools** menu, and then click **Security**. For more information about using digital signatures, see Chapter 17, "Securing Office Documents and Visual Basic for Applications Code."

Note If you change the default folder for templates and add-ins, the new folder that you specify will be trusted.

There are simple ways to deploy templates and add-ins to the Templates and AddIns folders. You can use one of these strategies, or you can create your own simple custom installation program. The following sections discuss both options.

Understanding User Profiles

In Windows 95 and Windows 98, you have the option of enabling the user profiles feature. A *user profile* is an account maintained by the operating system that keeps track of a particular user's files and system configuration. When you log on to a computer as a user who has a user profile, Windows checks the data it has stored for that user profile, and loads with those settings in place. Additionally, it maintains a folder for files created under that user profile, the C:\Windows\Profiles*UserName* folder.

In Windows NT Workstation and Windows NT Server, user profiles are automatically turned on all the time. Whenever a new user logs in, a user profile is created for that user under the C:\Winnt\Profiles*UserName* folder.

Under either operating system, the system can be secured so that each user has access only to the files, applications, and system configuration defined for his or her user profile. For example, files that are installed by a user who has administrative privileges may not be available to another user who does not share those privileges.

For more information about working with user profiles, see the *Microsoft Office 2000 Resource Kit* (Microsoft Press, 1999).

Deploying a Custom Template

When you create a new document in Word, Excel, or PowerPoint, the **New** dialog box (**File** menu) displays a list of templates that you can choose from to create a new document. The dialog box can display three types of templates: built-in templates that are included with Office 2000; user-created templates, which are stored on users' computers; and workgroup templates, which are stored on a network share. Only templates from certain folders are displayed, however, so if you create a new template, you must save it to the correct location in order for it to be displayed in the dialog box. The following table indicates where the dialog box looks for each type of template.

Type of template	Default location	Notes
Built-in	C:\Program Files \Microsoft Office\Templates *LanguageID*	The language ID is a number indicating the product language. For U.S. English, this is 1033. User-created templates saved here will not appear in the **New** dialog box.
User-created	C:\Windows\Application Data \Microsoft\Templates -or- C:\Windows\Profiles*UserName* \Application Data\Microsoft \Templates	You can change this location in Word or Excel in the **Options** dialog box (**Tools** menu). In order to appear in the **New** dialog box, user-created templates must be stored in the location that's specified in the **Options** dialog box.
Workgroup	Not specified	You can specify a location for workgroup templates in the **Options** dialog box in Word, or from VBA code in Excel or Word. When you set this option, templates in the specified location appear in the **New** dialog box.

As you can see, you have two options for installing a custom template: You can install it locally on users' machines, or you can copy it to a shared folder on a network server.

Installing a Custom Template Locally

To install a custom template locally onto users' machines, you have a couple of options:

- You can e-mail the template to users or instruct users to copy it from a network share, with instructions for where to copy the template to on the users' computers.
- You can create a custom installation program to copy the template to the correct folder. For more information, see "Deploying Application-Specific Add-ins" later in this chapter.

Deploying a Workgroup Template to a Network Share

If you need to deploy a custom template to multiple users, a good way to do it is to copy the template to a shared folder on a network server, so that it is available to everyone who has access to the share.

Once you've copied the template to the shared folder, you need to make sure that every user has specified this path for workgroup templates. Word and Excel both provide an option to specify a path for workgroup templates. You or users can set this option to point to the shared folder for each user's application.

There are several ways to set the workgroup templates option:

- You can instruct each user to set it themselves.
- You can write code to set the option and run the code on all users' computers.
- For custom Word templates, if the Normal.dot file is under administrative control, you can set the option there. In this scenario, the Normal.dot file is probably read-only, so users cannot modify the setting. For more information about administrative control of Office 2000, see the *Microsoft Office 2000 Resource Kit* (Microsoft Press, 1999).

In Word, you can modify the workgroup templates option through VBA code by setting the **DefaultFilePath** property of the **Options** object, passing in the **wdWorkgroupTemplatesPath** constant for the *path* argument, as shown in the following code fragment:

```
Options.DefaultFilePath(wdWorkgroupTemplatesPath) = "\\Server\Share\WorkgroupTemplates"
```

In Excel, you can modify the workgroup templates option through VBA code by setting the **NetworkTemplatesPath** property of the **Application** object:

```
Application.NetworkTemplatesPath = "\\Server\Share\WorkgroupTemplates"
```

For example, if you have Visual Basic, you can write a simple program that launches Word or Excel through Automation to set this option, and then compile the program into an .exe file and distribute it to all of your users through e-mail. When the users run the program, it will set the workgroup templates option correctly for them.

Storing a workgroup template on a common network share is a good idea from a maintenance standpoint, because you can modify the template without having to redistribute the template to every user. However, if you need to deploy the template to users who do not have access to a common network share, you can build a custom installation program to deploy a template. See the following section for more information.

Deploying Application-Specific Add-ins

The AddIns folder under C:\Windows\Application Data\Microsoft or C:\Windows\Profiles*UserName*\Application Data\Microsoft is the default folder for Word, Excel, PowerPoint, and Access application-specific add-ins. The simplest way to deploy an application-specific add-in, of course, is to e-mail the add-in to users or to post it on a network share with instructions for copying it to the correct folder. There is nothing wrong with this approach; however, you can't guarantee that users will copy the add-in correctly, especially if the add-in has any dependent files that may need to be installed to a different folder. If you need more control over the installation process, you can create a custom setup program to install the solution correctly.

Building such a setup program is relatively simple. Although you can build a setup program from any VBA host application, Microsoft Visual Basic is optimal because you can create an executable (.exe) file.

The trickiest part of building a custom setup program is determining the path to the Templates and AddIns folders on users' computers. To determine the location of the Templates and AddIns folders, you need to call three Windows application programming interface (API) functions. These functions are **SHGetSpecialFolderLocation**, **SHGetPathFromIDList**, and **SHGetMalloc**. For more information about working with the Windows API, see Chapter 10, "The Windows API and Other Dynamic-Link Libraries."

A template project for a custom setup program built in Visual Basic 6.0 is available in the Samples\CH02\CustomInstaller subfolder on the companion CD-ROM. The instructions for using the template project to build a custom setup program are in the modInit module. If you don't have Visual Basic 6.0, you can still view and copy the code in the project's modules by opening them with Notepad.

Deploying COM Add-ins

If you've built a COM add-in using Visual Basic 6.0 or Office 2000 Developer, you can create an installation program for it by using the Package and Deployment Wizard included in either Visual Basic 6.0 or Office 2000 Developer. The two wizards are very similar. The installation program needs to deploy the COM add-in dynamic-link library (DLL) as well as any files on which it is dependent, such as type libraries that may not be on users' computers.

A COM add-in DLL created with the add-in designer in Visual Basic 6.0 or Office 2000 Developer is a self-registering DLL, meaning that it will register itself properly when the setup program runs. Once the DLL has registered itself, the COM add-in will appear in the list of available COM add-ins in the **COM Add-ins** dialog box. Therefore, it doesn't matter where you install the DLL, but for the sake of consistency you may want to choose one folder for installing all COM add-ins, such as the AddIns folder under C:\Windows\Application Data\Microsoft or C:\Windows\Profiles*UserName*\Application Data\Microsoft.

If you create a COM add-in with Visual Basic 5.0, the COM add-in DLL is not a self-registering DLL, and you must register it on installation. If you don't have the Package and Deployment Wizard available to you, the easiest approach is to write a simple custom installation program to copy the DLL to users' machines and register it. You can use the Visual Basic 6.0 template project included in the Samples\CH02\CustomInstaller subfolder on the companion CD-ROM to create a setup program to register a COM add-in built in Visual Basic 5.0. If you don't have Visual Basic 6.0, import the modules in the template project into a Visual Basic 5.0 project.

A more complicated option is to use the Visual Basic 5.0 Setup Toolkit to modify the Setup1.vbp project, add code to register the DLL, and recompile the Setup1.exe file. For more information about how to do this, see the documentation for Visual Basic 5.0.

For more information about COM add-ins, see Chapter 11, "Add-ins, Templates, Wizards, and Libraries."

Deploying Access Solutions

In a typical multiuser or client/server database solution, the data is stored in a database on a network server, and the front-end application for entering and viewing data is deployed to each client workstation. If you build an Access database (.mdb) as the front-end application, you can deploy the database to users who don't have Access on their workstations by distributing it together with the run-time version of Access. The run-time version of Access is a version of Access for which certain features have been disabled, including the ability to create and modify databases.

The run-time version of Access is available in Microsoft Office 2000 Developer. When you purchase Office 2000 Developer, you are licensed to distribute the run-time version of Access to as many workstations as you need to.

To distribute your database with the run-time version of Access, use the Package and Deployment Wizard add-in that's included in Office 2000 Developer to create an installation program for your solution. On the **Included Files** page of the wizard, select the **Include Access Runtime** check box to include the run-time version of Access in your installation program.

Note You can distribute only Access databases (.mdb files) with the run-time version of Access. The run-time version of Access does not support Access projects (.adp files).

For more information about distributing the run-time version of Access, see the documentation for Office 2000 Developer.

Deploying Outlook and FrontPage Solutions

Outlook and FrontPage differ from the other Office applications in the way that they store VBA code. Whereas each Excel, Word, Access, or PowerPoint file that you create contains its own VBA project, which is saved with that file, Outlook and FrontPage each provide only a single VBA project where all VBA code is stored. This VBA project is saved as a separate file. For Outlook, this file is named VbaProject.OTM; for FrontPage, it is named Microsoft FrontPage.fpm.

To deploy an Outlook or FrontPage solution, you can develop the solution locally and then distribute the VbaProject.OTM or Microsoft FrontPage.fpm file to users to replace their own file. However, each time you or another developer distributes a solution in this manner, you'll be replacing the user's existing VBAProject.OTM or FrontPage.fpm file, which may very well break existing solutions. A better strategy for building an Outlook or FrontPage solution is to create a COM add-in. The COM add-in runs independently of the VBA project and of other COM add-ins, so your solution won't affect the user's other solutions.

A Note About the Windows Installer

Office 2000 uses the new Microsoft Windows installer, which manages the process of installing Office on the user's computer. The Windows installer is an operating system component that is installed on your machine when you first begin the Office 2000 installation process. In future versions of Windows, the Windows installer will be a fundamental part of the operating system.

In previous versions of Microsoft Office, a product or feature can either be installed on the user's computer, or not installed. If your solution created with a previous version of Office uses a product or feature that may not be installed on a particular user's computer, you need to include error handling in your code for cases where the product or feature is unavailable.

In Office 2000, a feature can be installed, not installed, or *advertised*. An advertised feature is one that's installed the first time the user tries to use it. When you run the Office 2000 installation program and select the **Install on First Use** setting for a particular feature, the Windows installer installs the appropriate shortcuts and icons and registers the feature in the Windows registry, but doesn't actually install the feature itself.

When you're creating an Office 2000 solution, you may want to take into account the fact that certain features may be advertised on the user's computer. To specify that the Windows installer should install a given feature when you refer to it from code, you can use the **FeatureInstall** property of the **Application** object. This property is available in all Office 2000 applications.

By default, the **FeatureInstall** property is set to **msoFeatureInstallNone**. With this setting, the Windows installer will not install on the user's computer any advertised feature used by your code. The other settings for the **FeatureInstall** property instruct the Windows installer to install advertised features as your code requires them. The **msoFeatureInstallOnDemandWithUI** setting gives the user the option to cancel the installation either before it begins or after it has begun, and the **msoFeatureInstallOnDemand** setting gives the user the option to cancel the installation after it has begun.

For example, the Office Assistant is a feature that may be advertised. If you want to use the Office Assistant in your solution, you can set the **FeatureInstall** property to instruct the Windows installer to install the Assistant if it's advertised, as shown in the following procedure:

```
Private Sub cmdOK_Click()
   ' Turns the Assistant on or off, depending on the user's choice
   ' and on the installation state for the Assistant.

   Const ASST_NOT_AVAILABLE As Long = -2147467259

   If optDisplayAsst.Value = True Then
      ' If Assistant is already installed, or not
      ' installed, setting the FeatureInstall property
      ' has no effect. The FeatureInstall property affects
      ' only advertised features.
      Application.FeatureInstall = msoFeatureInstallOnDemandWithUI

      ' Turn on Assistant. If Assistant is not installed,
      ' or if user cancels installation, error will occur here.
      On Error Resume Next
      Assistant.On = True
      ' Handle the error. Note that the same error is returned
      ' whether the Assistant was not installed or the user
      ' cancelled the installation.
      If Err.Number <> 0 Then
         If Err.Number = ASST_NOT_AVAILABLE Then
            MsgBox "Sorry, the Assistant is not currently available."
            GoTo Event_End
         End If
      End If
      Assistant.Visible = True
   Else
      ' Turn Assistant off if it's on.
      Assistant.On = False
   End If

Event_End:
   Unload Me
   Exit Sub
End Sub
```

This procedure appears in the module for the frmDisplayAsst UserForm in the DisplayAssistant.doc sample file, which is available in the Samples\CH02 subfolder on the companion CD-ROM.

For more information about managing the Windows installer from within Office solutions, see Installer.doc in the Appendixes folder on the companion CD-ROM.

Where to Go from Here

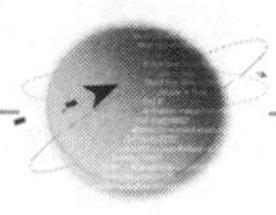

For additional information about the subjects discussed in this chapter, see the following resources. If a file name is listed, that file is located in the Appendixes folder on the companion CD-ROM, unless otherwise noted.

User Interface Design

Cooper, Alan. *About Face: The Essentials of User Interface Design*. Foster City, CA: Programmers Press, a division of IDG Books Worldwide, Inc., 1995.

The Windows Interface Guidelines for Software Design. Redmond, WA: Microsoft Press, 1995.

The Windows Interface Guidelines for Software Design Web site (http://www.microsoft.com/win32dev/uiguide/default.htm)

Virus Protection

Microsoft Excel Web site, virus search add-ins article (http://www.microsoft.com/excel/productinfo/vbavirus/add_in.htm)

Microsoft Excel Web site, virus information article (http://www.microsoft.com/excel/productinfo/vbavirus/emvolc.htm)

Installation and Configuration Issues

Microsoft Office 2000 Resource Kit Web site (http://www.microsoft.com/office/ork/)

Microsoft Office 2000 Resource Kit. Redmond, WA: Microsoft Press, 1999.

Microsoft TechNet Total Cost of Ownership Web site (http://www.microsoft.com/tco/)

Windows installer white paper (Installer.doc)

Database Design and Data Access

Hernandez, Michael. *Database Design for Mere Mortals*. Reading, MA: Addison-Wesley Developers Press, 1997.

Getz, Ken, Paul Litwin, and Mike Gilbert. *Access 2000 Developer's Handbook, Volume 1: Desktop Edition*. Alameda, CA: Sybex, 1999.

Litwin, Paul, Ken Getz, and Mike Gilbert. *Access 2000 Developer's Handbook, Volume 2: Enterprise Edition*. Alameda, CA: Sybex, 1999.

Microsoft Jet Database Engine Programmer's Guide, Third Edition. Redmond, WA: Microsoft Press, 1999.

Microsoft Universal Data Access Web site (http://www.microsoft.com/data/)

Effective Code Design

Getz, Ken, and Mike Gilbert. *Visual Basic Language Developer's Handbook*. Alameda, CA: Sybex, 1999.

Appleman, Dan. *Dan Appleman's Visual Basic 5.0 Programmer's Guide to the Win32® API*. Indianapolis, IN: Macmillan Computer Publishing, 1998.

Code Samples

The code samples shown in this chapter, along with additional examples demonstrating similar techniques, can be copied from the files in the Samples\CH02 subfolder on the companion CD-ROM.

Part Two

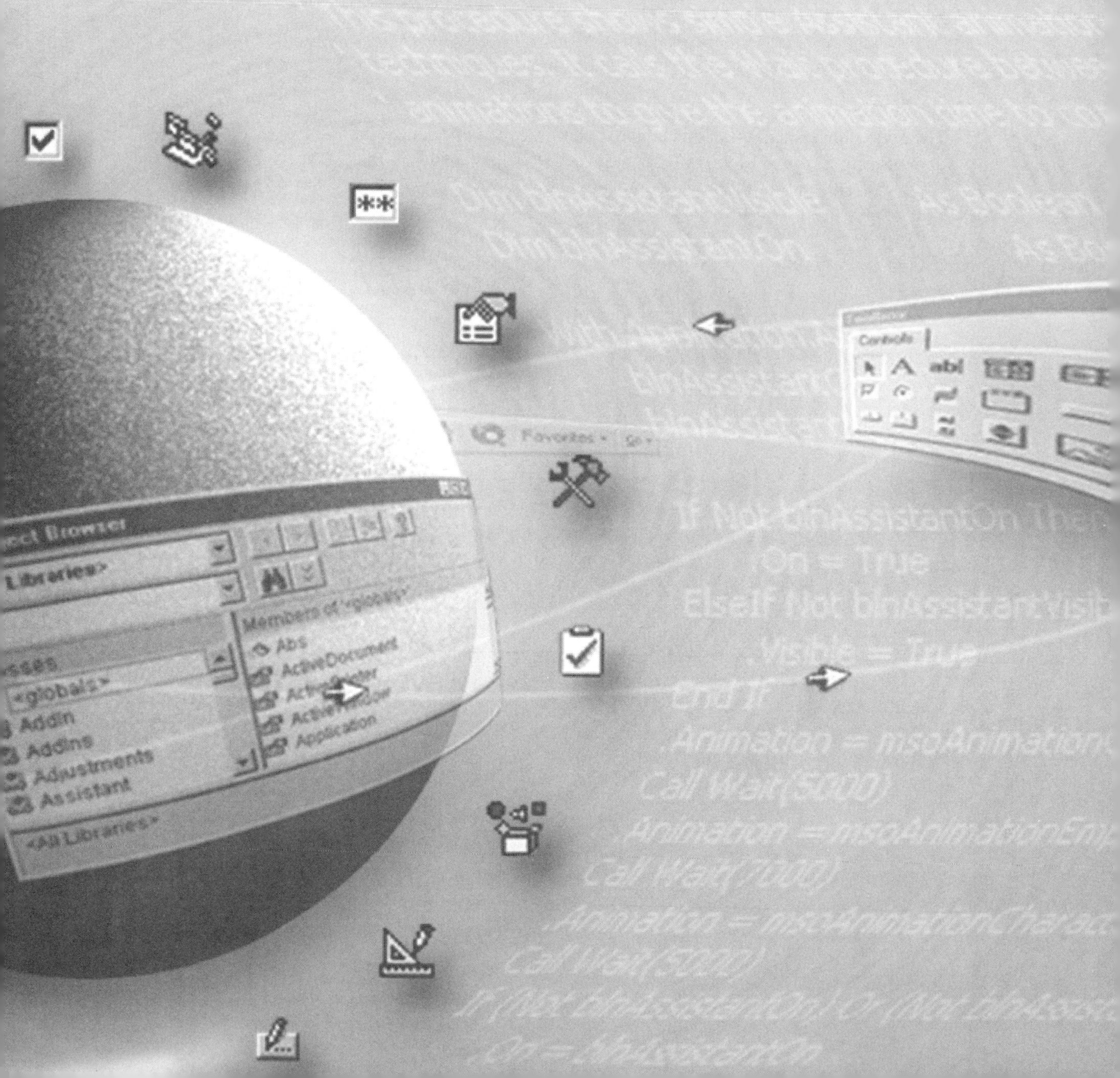
Controls
Favorites
Abs
ActiveDocument
Application
<globals>
AddIn
AddIns
Adjustments
Assistant
<All Libraries>
On = True
Call Wait(5000)

Developing Office Solutions

So what do you need to know in order to build a solution based on Microsoft Office 2000? For starters, it helps to adopt good coding standards and stick to them. This is the subject of Chapter 3, "Writing Solid Code." Chapter 3 addresses necessary evils such as naming conventions and code structure that, in the end, make your code more efficient, more reusable, easier to maintain, and better documented.

Chapter 4, "Understanding Office Objects and Object Models," is an in-depth look at the heart of Office solution-building, the object model. This chapter covers all the ins and outs of working with an application's objects, not only from within that application itself, but also from other applications through Automation (formerly OLE Automation).

From Chapter 5, "Working with Office Applications," you can learn the ropes of writing code with Microsoft Access, Microsoft Excel, Microsoft FrontPage, Microsoft Outlook, Microsoft PowerPoint, and Microsoft Word objects. Chapter 5 provides lots of valuable information and reusable code for working with each Office application's object model.

Chapter 6, "Working with Shared Office Components," is devoted to the objects in the Microsoft Office object model, which all of the Office 2000 applications share. The Office object model provides command bars, file-searching capabilities, the Office Assistant, and objects for working with HTML documents and script.

You can hone your programming skills with Chapter 7, "Getting the Most Out of Visual Basic for Applications." This chapter provides useful procedures for working with strings, numbers, dates, and arrays.

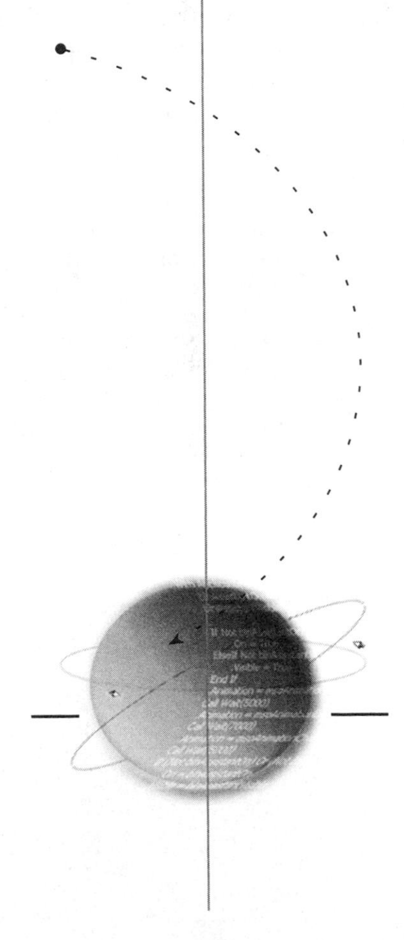

Writing bulletproof code is the subject of Chapter 8, "Error Handling and Debugging." This chapter covers the tools of the trade, the debugging features for Visual Basic for Applications (VBA) code and for script. It also discusses techniques for constructing effective error handlers.

Chapter 9, "Custom Classes and Objects," delves into the intricacies of creating custom objects and object models by using class modules. This chapter demonstrates how to build custom objects with their own properties, methods, and events, and how to leverage your existing code by implementing interfaces.

In Chapter 10, "The Windows API and Other Dynamic-Link Libraries," you can learn the basics of calling functions in DLLs from VBA. This chapter includes examples of calls to Windows API functions that may be useful to VBA developers.

Chapter 11, "Add-ins, Templates, Wizards, and Libraries," walks you through the process of creating a COM add-in for Office applications or for the Visual Basic Editor. It also discusses how to create application-specific add-ins, wizards, and code libraries.

The new Web technologies integrated into Office 2000 are the topic of Chapter 12, "Using Web Technologies." This chapter covers the basics of dynamic HTML, cascading style sheets, and scripting. It also explores the Microsoft Office Web Components, new controls that make it easy to publish interactive data to the Web.

If your solution is complex, you may want to provide a custom Help file for your users. Chapter 13, "Adding Help to Your Custom Solution," gives you the information you need to create your own Help system based on HTML Help.

CHAPTER 3

Writing Solid Code

"Writing solid code" means writing Visual Basic for Applications (VBA) code or script that performs as expected and is reusable, easy to understand, and easy to maintain. Many developers focus all their time and effort on just getting code to work. If you have ever struggled to understand code, whether written by you or someone else, or rewritten the same procedure to work in different solutions, then you understand part of the problem.

Other chapters in this book focus on how to develop solutions that perform as expected. This chapter focuses on fundamental coding guidelines and techniques that should be used when developing Microsoft Office solutions. Once these fundamentals become second nature to you, you will discover that your code is easier to understand, debug, modify, and share with others. The techniques discussed in this chapter apply whether you are writing VBA code or script behind an HTML page or Active Server page (ASP).

One of the most important considerations for an effective Office solution is how well it is designed. If your solution has a user interface, you should be aware of consistency and ease-of-use issues every time you create a dialog box or add a custom toolbar. You need to be just as aware of the design and structure of the code you write. The way you design your code, from how you name variables to when you use class modules, can make a big difference in the maintainability and usability of your code.

There is an old adage that says "There is never time to do it right but there is always time to do it over." When it comes to designing and building Office solutions, there should always be time to do it right. It's a lot easier than trying to do it over.

Contents

Using a Naming Convention

Naming conventions are discussed here in terms of broad outlines only. The purpose of this discussion is to suggest an approach that will help you develop a consistent naming convention.

There are many formal naming conventions and each has its adherents and detractors. You can adopt one of the existing conventions or create one of your own. The important point is that you adopt some convention that would be self-evident to another Office developer and that you apply it consistently.

At a minimum, a useful naming convention will identify and distinguish variable type (object variable, control variable, and data type), variable scope, constants, and procedures, and it should be simple to understand and use. For an example of a naming convention you can adopt or that you can use as the basis for your own convention, see MCS Naming Conventions.doc in the Appendixes folder on the companion CD-ROM.

Naming Variables and Constants

Naming conventions typically use a lowercase prefix or suffix to specify the variable's type and scope. The variable itself should have a meaningful name that describes what it is or what it does. Multiple-word names are concatenated, the first letter of each word is capitalized, and the underscore character is not used. If you used a variable-name template, it would be in the form *prefixNoun* or *prefixNounVerb*.

Constant names should also be descriptive names in the *NOUN* or *NOUN_VERB* format. Constant names are uppercase and use an underscore character to separate words. Although there is nothing technically wrong with adding characters to constant names to specify data type and scope, it is typically not done. A constant is really the same thing as a variable in the sense that both are symbolic representations of data. The difference is that variables can change and constants remain, well, constant.

Both variable and constant names can contain up to 255 characters; however, names that exceed about 25 to 30 characters can become unwieldy. Besides, 25 or 30 characters should be plenty of room to provide descriptive names that clearly convey the purpose of the variable or constant.

Variable Names

As mentioned earlier, variable names use the mixed-case form (*Noun* or *NounVerb*), specifying what the variable is and what it does. This is the descriptive portion of the variable name where the first letter of each word is in uppercase and the rest is in lowercase.

Variable names also have a two- or three-character prefix used to specify the variable's data type. For example, the following statements declare variables with a prefix that specifies the variable's data type:

```
Dim strRecipientName       As String
Dim intItemsProcessed      As Integer
Dim blnContinueProcessing  As Boolean
```

The two-character prefix is typically used to specify an Office **Application** object type. For example:

```
Dim xlApp          As Excel.Application
Dim olNameSpace    As Outlook.NameSpace
Dim wdNewDoc       As Word.Document
```

Use the "obj" prefix when declaring a generic, or late-bound, object variable. Use this prefix even when you are creating a late-bound object variable that represents an Office application. For example:

```
Dim objXLApp       As Object
Dim objWDDocument As Object
Dim objOLMailItem As Object
```

Note Many developers who have worked with the BASIC language for years have developed the habit of specifying data types by using a single-character suffix; for example:

```
Dim FName$
Dim i%
Dim Value&
```

Although BASIC still supports these data-type suffixes, their use is no longer recommended.

Global and module-level variables use an additional single-character prefix to specify their scope. The scope of a variable defines its lifetime and visibility. Global and module-level variables have a permanent lifetime. That is, the memory allocated to the variable remains allocated as long as the application is running. Variables declared within a procedure (except when they are declared by using the **Static** keyword) are visible only within the procedure where they are declared and have a lifetime that lasts only so long as the code within the procedure is executing.

Global variables have a lowercase "g" prefix and are declared in the Declarations section of a module by using the **Public** statement. They are visible to all procedures in all modules in an application. For example, `Public gstrPathToDataSource As String` would be a global variable that contains a string that is the path to the data source used in the application.

A Note on Global Variables

Variables should always be defined using the smallest scope possible. Use global variables only when there is no other way to share the data they contain. Global variables can make your code hard to understand and difficult to maintain. If you find you are using more than a few carefully chosen global variables, you probably need to redesign your code to eliminate them.

Module-level variables have a lowercase "m" prefix and are declared in the Declarations section of a module by using the **Dim** or **Private** statement. They are visible to any procedure within the module in which they are declared. For example, `Dim mrstCustomerRecords As ADODB.Recordset` would be a module-level object variable for customer records. In class modules, module-level variables that are declared with the **Private** statement have a "p_" prefix. Public module-level variables in class modules appear as properties of the class and should not have any prefix to indicate their data type or scope. For more information about naming variables in class modules, see Chapter 9, "Custom Classes and Objects."

Procedure-level variables are created within a procedure by using the **Dim** statement. For example, `Dim intCurrentMailItem As Integer` would be a procedure-level variable used as a loop counter. Procedure-level variables can also be declared by using the **Static** keyword. Static variables retain their value even after the procedure in which they are declared has finished running. Static procedure-level variables have a lowercase "s" prefix. For example, `Static scurTotalSales As Currency` would create a procedure-level static variable used to keep an accumulating total in a procedure that calculates current sales.

User-defined type variables are declared in the Declarations section of a module by using an all uppercase type name with "_TYPE" appended to the type name. You could declare a user-defined type in the following manner:

```
Type EMPLOYEEINFO_TYPE
   strFullName As String
   lngEmployeeID As Long
   datStartDate As Date
   strDepartmentCode As String * 4
   curSalary As Currency
End Type
```

You would declare a module-level variable of type EMPLOYEEINFO_TYPE by using a "udt" prefix. For example, `Dim mudtEmployeeRecord As EMPLOYEEINFO_TYPE`.

Array variables have a lowercase "a" prefix and, unless the variable is a variant, are followed by a pair of parentheses. Array variables are declared by using the **Dim** statement; for example, `Dim alngNum()` is an array variable of type **Long**. An array is a variable that can contain multiple values. Arrays are useful when you need to store a number of values of the same type, but you don't want to create individual variables to store them all. For more information about working with array variables, see Chapter 7, "Getting the Most Out of Visual Basic for Applications."

Here are some examples of variable names that use the general naming guidelines described earlier.

Variable	Data type	Scope
strCompanyName	**String**	Procedure
rstCurrentOrders	**Object**	Procedure
intCurrentRecordCount	**Integer**	Procedure
wdWordApplication	**Object**	Procedure
varClipboardData	**Variant**	Procedure
curAmountPastDue	**Currency**	Procedure
blnProcessNextRecord	**Boolean**	Procedure
molOutlookMailItem	**Object**	Module
mcolCurrentUsers	**Object**	Module
gcnnDBConnection	**Object**	Global
gstrLogonID	**String**	Global
gastrContactNames()	**String** (array)	Global

Constant Names

Constants use multiple-word descriptive names in all uppercase letters with an underscore character between each word. Constants are declared by using the **Const** statement along with the name of the constant, its data type, and its value. For example, the following constant could be declared in the Declarations section of a module to provide the path to the data source used by an application:

```
Public Const DATABASE_PATH As String = "C:\Solutions\Source\AppData.mdb"
```

Note By using the **Public** keyword to declare the constant, it can be used by any procedure in any module in the application. If the **Public** keyword is not used, the constant has a module-level scope, meaning that it is available only to procedures within the module in which it was declared. If the constant is declared within a procedure, it is available only to the code in the procedure and only so long as the code in the procedure is executing.

Here are some examples of constant names that use the general naming guidelines described earlier:

ACCESS_CONNECTSTRING
API_MAX_STRINGBUFFER
SQL_STRING

Note If you create public enumerated constants in a class module, you can use a different naming convention to distinguish them from other constants. For more information about naming enumerated constants in class modules, see Chapter 9, "Custom Classes and Objects."

In addition to constants you declare yourself, Visual Basic for Applications (VBA), Microsoft Visual Basic Scripting Edition (VBScript), and each of the Office applications contain built-in, or intrinsic, constants whose values are predefined. Intrinsic constants should always be used in place of the values they represent. Just like user-defined constants, the advantage to using intrinsic constants is that they make your code more understandable. For example, compare the following two code samples, where one sample uses intrinsic constants and the other does not. See if you agree that intrinsic constants can make a big difference in how easy the code is to understand.

```
If MsgBox("Proceed Now?", 48 + 512 + 3 + 16384, "Continue?") = 7 Then
   DoCmd.OpenForm "Customers", 0, , , 1, 3
End If

If MsgBox("Proceed Now?", vbExclamation + vbDefaultButton3 + _
      vbYesNoCancel + vbMsgBoxHelpButton, "Continue?") = vbNo Then
   DoCmd.OpenForm "Customers", acNormal, , , acFormEdit, acDialog
End If
```

For a complete listing of intrinsic constants available through VBA and each of the Office applications, open the Object Browser, select the appropriate type library from the **Projects/Library** box, type the appropriate constant prefix in the **Search Text** box, and then click **Search** on the **Object Browser** toolbar.

Application/type library	Constant prefix
Access	ac
Excel	xl
FrontPage	fp
Office	mso
OfficeBinder	bind
Outlook	ol
PowerPoint	pp
Word	wd
VBA	vb

For a complete listing of intrinsic constants available through VBScript, see the VBScript Language Reference in the C:\Program Files\Microsoft Visual Studio\Common\IDE\IDE98\MSE\1033\Vbscrip5.chm file.

Note The path to the Vbscrip5.chm Help file reflects the language ID folder (1033) for U.S. English language support in Office. The language ID folder below C:\Program Files\Microsoft Visual Studio\Common\IDE\IDE98\MSE differs for each language.

A Word About Writing Solid Script

Scripting languages are "loosely typed" and as a consequence, all variables used in script have a **Variant** data type. In addition, script is written directly into the HTML code behind a Web page and there are no modules used to contain code as there are in VBA and other strongly typed languages. Finally, scripting languages do not require that you expressly declare variables before you use them.

Given these unique characteristics, does it still make sense to talk about a naming convention in the context of writing script? Absolutely!

The naming conventions and other coding guidelines discussed in this chapter apply just as well to script in an HTML page as they do to VBA code in an Office application. The benefits associated with writing reusable, understandable, and maintainable code can be realized whether you are writing script or VBA code. In fact, there is probably more work to be done persuading script developers to pay attention to issues of code reuse and maintainability. There are just as many benefits to writing solid script as there are to writing solid code.

Even though script is written directly into the HTML code of a Web page, questions of visibility and lifetime are still important. Variables and constants declared within a procedure are local to that procedure and have a lifetime that lasts only so long as the script within the procedure is executing.

Variables and constants declared in script outside a procedure are visible to any script contained in the current HTML page. These variables have the equivalent of the module-level scope described earlier. Variables and constants declared in VBScript by using the **Public** keyword are visible to all script in the current HTML page and to all script in all other currently loaded pages. For example, if you had an HTML page that contained multiple frames designated by a <FRAMESET> tag pair, a variable or constant declared with the **Public** keyword would be visible to all pages loaded within all the frames specified by the <FRAMESET> tag.

In addition, although all script variables have a **Variant** data type, it is important to remember that the **Variant** data type encompasses many different data types and can coerce a variable to the most appropriate data type in a particular context. Although you cannot declare a variable as a specific data type, you should name your variables as if you could. Naming script variables as if they were strongly typed will not prevent you from assigning an integer value to the `strCompanyName` variable, but it will force you to think about how the variable is used and the data subtype it will contain. You declare VBScript variables by using the **Dim** statement and Microsoft JScript variables by using the **var** statement.

Note Unlike VBScript, JScript is a case-sensitive language; if you name a variable `strCompanyName` but refer to it as `STRCompanyName`, you will encounter errors.

Using the Option Explicit Statement

Neither VBScript nor VBA requires you to declare variables before using them. The default behavior in both languages is to allow you to create variables by simply using a variable name in an assignment statement.

However, every experienced developer knows that the failure to use the **Option Explicit** statement to force explicit variable declaration is a coding blunder of the highest order. Using undeclared variables can introduce subtle, hard-to-find bugs into your code that are easily avoided by using this one, simple technique.

To force VBA to insert the **Option Explicit** statement in every module you create, open the Visual Basic Editor, click **Options** on the **Tools** menu, and then click **Require Variable Declaration** on the **Editor** tab.

To force variables to be declared in VBScript, type **Option Explicit** immediately after the first <SCRIPT> tag in your HTML document.

Naming Objects and Controls

Objects and controls, and variables that represent objects and controls, should be named with a prefix that identifies the item and a mixed-case name that clearly identifies what the item's purpose is. In this context, the term *objects* refers to object variables that represent items such as documents, workbooks, forms, reports, recordsets, the application itself, and other items exposed through an Office application's type library. In HTML, the term *objects* refers to HTML intrinsic forms and controls, ActiveX controls, Microsoft Scripting Components (scriptlets), and other objects designated by using the <OBJECT> tag.

When you create a new module or form or add a control to a document, form, or report, the Visual Basic Editor creates a default name for the object, such as Module1, Form3, or TextBox5. You should never use these default names in your code. Develop the habit of specifying a meaningful name for an object as soon as you add it to your project. That way you won't have to revise your code to rename objects later. The name should include a prefix that specifies what the object is and a name that identifies its purpose. For example, you could use modDataAccessCode, frmCustomers, and txtLastName to represent a module, a form, and a text box control. A three-character prefix is preferred, but the important point is that the prefix should be adequate to clearly specify the control type.

Note When you are designing custom object models, you should use object names without prefixes, and instead use names that indicate the purpose of the objects in the model. Custom objects are designed to be used by other developers and are exposed through the Object Browser; therefore, prefixes don't make sense in this context. For more information about creating and using custom objects, see Chapter 9, "Custom Classes and Objects."

When you create HTML objects and controls, you must specify a name by using the object's ID parameter. If you use a tool to add controls to an HTML page, the tool will often insert a default name for an object or control just as the Visual Basic Editor does. For example, if you add a Microsoft Forms 2.0 CommandButton control to an HTML page by using the Microsoft ActiveX Control Pad, the control's ID parameter is given the name CommandButton1 by default. These objects and controls should always be renamed according to the guidelines discussed in this section.

HTML element names (tags) should be entered in all capital letters. Although HTML is case-insensitive, using this convention will help create a visual distinction between HTML elements and other items on the page. You might think of this technique as being equivalent to VBA keywords being highlighted in the Visual Basic Editor.

For example, if you examine the HTML code in the following example (ScriptNaming.htm in the Samples\CH03 subfolder on the companion CD-ROM), the use of uppercase HTML element names clearly distinguishes them from the other items on the page:

```
<HTML>
<HEAD>

<TITLE>
   Office Programmer's Guide, Chapter 3: Formatting HTML Elements
</TITLE>

<STYLE>
   .CenterThisRed {position:absolute; left:40%; top:220; font:bold; color:red}
   .BoldAndBlue {font:bold; color:blue}
</STYLE>

<SCRIPT LANGUAGE="VBSCRIPT">
<!--
   Option Explicit
   Dim strMessage
```

```
    Sub ShowAMessage(strMessage)
       ' Display strMessage in a message box.
       If Len(strMessage) = 0 Then
          strMessage = "You need to enter some text in the " _
             & "'Enter Text Here' text box before you can " _
             & "see it displayed here!"
       End If
       MsgBox strMessage
    End Sub

    Sub cmdMessage_OnClick()
       ShowAMessage(frmSampleForm.txtMessage.Value)
       frmSampleForm.txtMessage.Value = ""
    End Sub
-->
</SCRIPT>

<BODY>
   <CENTER>
   <H1>Enter HTML Elements Using
   <BR>
   <SPAN CLASS = "BoldAndBlue">
   ALL CAPS
   </SPAN>
   </H1>
   </CENTER>

   <HR>

   <DIV ID="ItemsList" CLASS="CenterThisRed">
      <OL>
         <LI>Item One</LI>
         <LI>Item Two</LI>
         <LI>Item Three</LI>
         <LI>Item Four</LI>
      </OL>
   </DIV>

   <CENTER>
   <FORM NAME="frmSampleForm">
      <DIV ID="divTextBoxLabel"
         STYLE="font:bold;
                color:green">
         Enter Text Here:
      </DIV>

      <INPUT TYPE="Text" NAME="txtMessage" SIZE=50>
      <BR>
      <INPUT TYPE="Button" NAME="cmdMessage" VALUE="Display Text">
   </FORM>
   </CENTER>
</BODY>
</HTML>
```

Naming Functions and Subroutines

A well-written procedure performs a single specific task and is named to identify the task performed. If you find it difficult to give a specific name to a procedure because it is performing more than one task, consider breaking the procedure down into multiple procedures so that each discrete piece of functionality can be clearly identified.

When naming a procedure, you should use the *NounVerb* or *VerbNoun* style to create a name that clearly identifies what the procedure does. It is not necessary to use a prefix or suffix to specify the data type of the return value. Keep in mind that when you store related procedures in the same module, the **Procedures** box in the Code window will display those procedures alphabetically. If you stored all your data access code in a module named modDataAccessCode, you could use the *NounVerb* naming style so that related procedures are listed together. For example, the CustomerAdd, CustomerDelete, and CustomerUpdate procedures would all be displayed together in the **Procedures** box.

When you are creating procedures that use arguments, use argument names that adhere to your variable-naming convention. For example, the following procedure uses arguments consisting of three strings, an integer, and a Boolean value:

```
Function RemoveString(ByVal strSource As String, _
                      strStart As String, _
                      strEnd As String, _
                      Optional intEndCount As Integer = 0, _
                      Optional blnReturnChunk As Boolean = False) As String
    .
    .
    .
End Function
```

The RemoveString procedure is available in the modAdditionalSamples module in FormattingExamples.doc in the Samples\CH03 subfolder on the companion CD-ROM.

When you are calling a built-in or custom method or procedure that accepts optional arguments, always use named arguments instead of positional arguments. Named arguments make your code easier to understand, debug, and maintain. A named argument is an argument name followed by a colon and an equal sign (:=), followed by the argument value. When you use named arguments, you don't have to include placeholders for optional arguments not passed to the procedure. The first line in the following example shows how to call a custom procedure using positional arguments. The second line shows how to call the same procedure using named arguments.

```
strModifiedString = RemoveString(strOriginalString, strStartHere, _
   strEndHere, , True)

strModifiedString = RemoveString(strSource:=strOriginalString, _
   strStart:=strStartHere, strEnd:=strEndHere, blnReturnChunk:=True)
```

The next example shows how to use named arguments to call the **Open** method of the Word **Documents** collection. The **Open** method accepts up to 10 arguments, but only the **FileName** argument is required.

```
Application.Documents.Open ReadOnly:=True, FileName:="AUTOSHAPE.DOC", _
   Format:=wdOpenFormatAuto
```

If an argument uses a value that represents a built-in enumerated constant, declare the argument's data type by using the enumerated constant name. For example, if you have an argument that is used to specify one of the seven Outlook item types, declare the argument `As Outlook.OlItemType` rather than `As Integer`. Using this technique means you don't have to validate the argument that is passed to the procedure because by definition the argument value can contain only an existing Outlook item type. For example:

```
Function CreateNewItemB(intItemType As Outlook.OlItemType, _
                        Optional strName As String = "")
   Dim olApp      As New Outlook.Application
   Dim olNewItem  As Object

   Select Case intItemType
      Case olMailItem
         Set olNewItem = olApp.CreateItem(olMailItem)
      Case olAppointmentItem
         Set olNewItem = olApp.CreateItem(olAppointmentItem)
      Case olContactItem
         Set olNewItem = olApp.CreateItem(olContactItem)
      Case olTaskItem
         Set olNewItem = olApp.CreateItem(olTaskItem)
      Case olNoteItem
         Set olNewItem = olApp.CreateItem(olNoteItem)
      Case Else
   End Select
   .
   .
   .
End Function
```

The CreateNewItemB procedure is available in the modAdditionalSamples module in FormattingExamples.doc in the Samples\CH03 subfolder on the companion CD-ROM.

Structuring and Formatting Your Code

How you use structured coding conventions directly affects how easy your code is to understand and maintain. General principles of applying a structure to your code have effects at the application level, the module level, and the procedure level. The corresponding use of formatting—line breaks, white space, and indentation—helps reveal the logic and structure of each procedure.

Structuring Your Code

At the application level, your code is contained in one or more standard modules or class modules and in modules behind forms, reports, or documents. You apply structure to your code at this level by organizing your code logically within these components in your application. Within any module, the procedures should have some relation to each other. For example, you could keep all data access code in a single module. Form, report, or document modules should contain only code that applies directly to the form, report, or document or to controls it contains. At the procedure level, applying a structure to the code means breaking up large procedures into smaller ones and using line breaks, white space, and indentation to organize and illustrate the logical structure of the code. Any general-purpose procedures called by code in these objects should be contained in a separate module. You should also add comments at the module level to provide information on the nature and purpose of the procedures contained in the module.

You should use these principles whether you are writing VBA code or script in an HTML page. You can think of an HTML page as being similar to a VBA application for the purposes of structuring your script. You can think of blocks of script within <SCRIPT> tags as being similar to VBA procedures contained in a module. The script and procedures used between <SCRIPT> tags should be related to other script within the same set of tags. Any general-purpose procedures called from the script in an HTML page should grouped together within their own pair of <SCRIPT> tags or kept in a scriptlet. For more information about creating and using scriptlets, see Chapter 12, "Using Web Technologies."

Formatting Code

Some inexperienced developers feel that although formatting code may make it look "pretty," it is not really worth the time. However, properly formatting code has nothing to do with appearance and everything to do with how easy your code is to understand and maintain. The basic techniques used to format code are line breaks, white space, and indentation. In addition to making the code easier to read, these formatting techniques help document the code by showing the logic and flow of a procedure and by grouping logically related sections of code.

For examples of VBA and VBScript code that use the formatting techniques discussed in this section, see the code samples in the Samples\CH03 subfolder on the companion CD-ROM.

Formatting VBScript vs. VBA Code

Even developers of the most poorly written VBA code usually make some attempt at naming things consistently and adding comments and perhaps some white space where appropriate. But something very different is happening on the Web. It seems that there is no attempt to use naming conventions or formatting techniques to make script easier to understand and maintain; in fact, just the opposite seems to be happening. Perhaps it is the forgiving nature of an HTML page as a scripting environment. Perhaps it is because script in an HTML page is easily viewed by others, and the easier it is to understand, the easier it is for someone to "borrow." If this is a concern of yours, see Chapter 12, "Using Web Technologies," for information about protecting your script.

Line Breaks

In VBA and VBScript code, you break a line by using the line-continuation character, an underscore (_) preceded by a space. You use line breaks to make sure that your code does not extend beyond the right edge of the Code window (usually about 60 characters).

For example, line breaks have been used in the following code so that the entire string can be viewed in the Code window without having to scroll to the right:

```
Dim strMessage As String
strMessage = "Fourscore and seven years ago our fathers " _
   & "brought forth, on this continent, a new nation, " _
   & "conceived in liberty, and dedicated to the " _
   & "proposition that all men are created equal."
MsgBox strMessage
```

Note how an additional tab character is inserted for all lines following the initial line break. This is to create a visual cue that the indented text remains a part of the portion of the string that comes before the line break.

If the line following the continued line is indented as much as the continued line would be, add one more tab to the continued line to distinguish it from the next line. For example:

```
If ActiveSheet.ChartObjects(1).Chart.ChartTitle = _
      ActiveSheet.Range("a2").Value Then
   MsgBox "They are equal."
End If
```

Be careful when you are using line-continuation characters in strings. If you must divide the string into two or more strings, place the line-continuation character between the strings, and then concatenate them using the ampersand (&). It is important to preserve all spaces in the string when it is concatenated. For example:

```
Sub LongString()
   ' This will form a correct SQL string.
   strSQL = "SELECT LastName, FirstName FROM Employees WHERE " _
      & "(BirthDate > #1-1-60#);"

   ' This one will be missing the space between WHERE and (BirthDate).
   strSQL = "SELECT LastName, FirstName FROM Employees WHERE" _
      & "(BirthDate > #1-1-60#);"
End Sub
```

Use the ampersand for all concatenation operations; never use the plus sign (+).

In HTML code you create a line break simply by entering a carriage return. The browser will ignore these line breaks when it renders the page. For example, text in this HTML page will break only where the <BR> element appears:

```
<BODY>
   <CENTER>
   <H2>Office Programmer's Guide
   <BR>Chapter 3
   <BR>HTML Sample Page: Line Breaks</H2>
   <HR>
   <H3>To see an example, click Source
   on the View menu.</H3>
   <BR>
   <BR>
   </CENTER>

   Fourscore and seven
   years ago our fathers
   brought forth, on this
   continent, a new nation,
   conceived in liberty, and
   dedicated to the proposition
   that all men are created equal.

</BODY>
```

You can also use line breaks to format a procedure's argument list. For an example of this technique, see the RemoveString procedure in the previous section.

White Space

Use blank lines to separate logically related blocks of code and to separate introductory (header) comments from the first variable declaration and the last declared variable from the code itself. Precede all comments with a blank line. For examples of procedures that use white space to highlight logically related sections of code and to separate comments from any preceding code, see the code samples in the Samples\CH03 subfolder on the companion CD-ROM.

Indentation

You indent code and comments within a procedure by using a two- to four-space tab stop. (The Visual Basic Editor uses a four-space tab stop by default.) Like white space, indents are used to organize code logically and make it visually appealing. The benefits from this simple technique are substantial. To see VBA and VBScript examples that do not use the general formatting techniques discussed here, take a look at the VBA examples in the modBadCodeFormatting module in FormattingExamples.doc and the script example in ScriptBadFormatting.htm in the Samples\CH03 subfolder on the companion CD-ROM. To see examples that do use the formatting techniques recommended here, see the rest of the sample code in this book.

The following list contains some general guidelines regarding where, when, and how to correctly use indentation to make your code more readable and maintainable:

- Indent all code and comments within a procedure at least one tab stop. The only code lines that are not indented are the beginning and ending of the procedure and line labels used in connection with your error handler.
- If you use line breaks to format a procedure's argument list, use tabs to indent the arguments and their data-type declarations so that they are aligned with the first argument in the list.
- Indent declared variables one tab stop. Declare only one variable on a line. Indent each variable's data-type specifier so that the variable data types are aligned.
- Indent control structures at least one tab stop. If one control structure is embedded within another, indent the embedded structure one tab stop. Indent code within a control structure one additional tab stop.
- If you use a line-continuation character to break a line of code, indent the new line one extra tab stop. This creates a visual cue that the two (or more) lines belong together. If the line following the continued line is indented as much as the continued line would be, add one more tab to the continued line to distinguish it from the next line.
- Indent comments to the same level as the code the comment refers to.

Take a look at how these general techniques are applied in the following procedure:

```
Function GetFileList(strDirPath As String, _
                     Optional strFileSpec As String = "*.*", _
                     Optional strDelim As String = ",") As String

   ' This procedure returns a delimited list of files from the
   ' strDirPath directory that match the strFileSpec argument.
   ' The default delimiter character is a comma. By default, the
   ' procedure returns all files ("*.*") from the designated
   ' directory.

   Dim strFileList    As String   ' Used to collect the file list.
   Dim strFileNames   As String   ' The full path and criteria to search for.
   Dim strTemp        As String   ' Temporarily holds the matching file name.

   ' Make sure that strDirPath ends in a "\" character.
   If Right$(strDirPath, 1) <> "\" Then
      strDirPath = strDirPath & "\"
   End If

   ' This will be our file search criteria.
   strFileNames = strDirPath & strFileSpec

   ' Create a list of matching files delimited by the
   ' strDelim character.
   strTemp = Dir$(strFileNames)
   Do While Len(strTemp) <> 0
      strFileList = strFileList & strTemp & strDelim
      strTemp = Dir$()
   Loop

   If Len(strFileList) > 1 Then
      ' If there are matching files, remove the delimiter
      ' character from the end of the list.
      GetFileList = Left(strFileList, Len(strFileList) - 1)
   Else
      GetFileList = ""
   End If
End Function
```

The GetFileList procedure is available in the modAdditionalSamples module in FormattingExamples.doc in the Samples\CH03 subfolder on the companion CD-ROM.

Using Comments Effectively

If you follow the guidelines discussed so far in this chapter, you are using a naming convention that identifies objects, variables, constants, and procedures, and you are using a prefix to indicate each variable's data type and scope. In addition, you are using white space, line breaks, and indentation to make your code easy to read and to create a visual representation of the code's logic. In other words, you have taken full advantage of all of the benefits that use of a consistent naming convention and structured code will yield. To a large degree, you should now be able to tell how your code is working just by looking at it.

The purpose of adding comments to code is to provide a plain English description of what your code is doing. Comments should provide information that is not otherwise available from reading the code itself. Good comments are written at a higher level of abstraction than the code itself. Comments that simply restate what is already obvious add nothing to the code and should be avoided. In addition, exactly how the code works may change as it gets updated or revised. If your comments speak to how the code works, instead of to what it does, you have created an additional code-maintenance problem because comments that describe how code works need to be revised whenever you change the code. Failing to maintain these comments along with the code creates a risk that the comments will no longer describe the code. Beginning developers often write "how" comments that merely restate what is already obvious from the code itself; for example:

```
' Make sure the length of strSource is not zero and it contains
' a ".txt" extension.
If Len(strSource) > 0 And InStr(strFileName, ".txt") > 0 Then
   ' If strSource does not contain a ":" or a "\" then
   ' return False.
   If InStr(strFileName, ":") = 0 Or InStr(strFileName, "\") = 0 Then
      SaveStringAsTextFile = False
   Else
      ' Get the next available file number.
      intFileNumber = FreeFile
      ' Open the file in Append mode.
      Open strFileName For Append As intFileNumber
      ' Write data to the file on disk.
      Print #intFileNumber, strSource;
      ' Close the file.
      Close intFileNumber
   End If
Else
   ' Return False.
   SaveStringAsTextFile = False
End If
```

As you can see, these comments add nothing that isn't already evident from the code itself. Now take a look at the full version of this procedure that lets the code speak for itself and uses comments that describe only what the code is doing:

```
Function SaveStringAsTextFile(strSource As String, _
                              strFileName As String) As Boolean

   ' Save the string in strSource to the file supplied
   ' in strFileName. If the operation succeeds, return True;
   ' otherwise, return False. If the file described by
   ' strFileName already exists, append strSource to any
   ' existing text in the file.

   Dim intFileNumber As Integer

   On Error GoTo SaveString_Err

   ' Assume that the operation will succeed.
   SaveStringAsTextFile = True

   If Len(strSource) > 0 And InStr(strFileName, ".txt") > 0 Then
      If InStr(strFileName, ":") = 0 Or InStr(strFileName, "\") = 0 Then
         ' Invalid file path submitted.
         SaveStringAsTextFile = False
      Else
         ' Save file to disk.
         intFileNumber = FreeFile
         Open strFileName For Append As intFileNumber
         Print #intFileNumber, strSource;
         Close intFileNumber
      End If
   Else
      SaveStringAsTextFile = False
   End If

SaveString_End:
   Exit Function
SaveString_Err:
   MsgBox Err.Description, vbCritical & vbOKOnly, _
       "Error Number " & Err.Number & " Occurred"
   Resume SaveString_End
End Function
```

The SaveStringAsTextFile procedure is available in the modAdditionalSamples module in FormattingExamples.doc in the Samples\CH03 subfolder on the companion CD-ROM.

At a minimum, you should add comments at the module level to describe the group of related procedures in the module. Add comments at the procedure level to describe the purpose of the procedure itself. For example, the following module-level comments document the public and private procedures (called "methods" in a class module), the properties and their data types, and information about how to use the class as an object:

```
' This class provides services related to creating and sending
' Outlook MailItem objects. It also includes wrappers to handle
' attaching files to a mail message.
'
'  Public Methods:
'     MailAddRecipient(strName As String, Optional fType As Boolean)
'        strName: Name of recipient to add to message.
'        fType:   Outlook MailItem Type property setting.
'     SendMail(Optional blnShowMailFirst As Boolean)
'        blnShowMailFirst: Whether to show the Outlook mail message
'                          before sending it. Set to True programmatically
'                          if unable to resolve recipient addresses.
'
'  Private Methods:
'     InitializeOutlook()
'     CreateMail()
'
'  Public Properties:
'     MailSubject:      (Write only, String)
'     MailMessage:      (Write only, String)
'     MailAttachments:  (Write only, String)
'
'  Usage:From any standard module, declare an object variable of type
'        clsMailMessage. Use that object variable to access the methods
'        and properties of this class.
```

Where needed, add comments to describe the functionality of a particular line or block of code. These comments should be used sparingly and should be used to document any unusual aspects of the code. A blank line should precede all comments and they should be aligned with the code they apply to. Insert comments before the line or block of code they apply to, not on the same line as the code itself.

In certain circumstances you will also use comments to document the arguments passed to a procedure, whether those arguments should be within a certain range of values, whether global variables are changed within the procedure, and the procedure's return values. It is not unusual to include comments that document a procedure's revision history, the names of other procedures that call the current procedure, the author of a procedure (or a revision), or a sample syntax line showing how the procedure is called.

You should make it your practice to write comments at the same time that (or earlier than) you write your code. Some developers write the comments for all of their procedures before they write a single line of code. It can be very effective to design procedures using only comments to describe what the code will do. This is a way to sketch out a framework for a procedure, or several related procedures, without getting bogged down in the details of writing the code itself. Later, when you write the code to implement the framework, your original high-level descriptions can be effective comments. Whatever technique you use, always enter or revise your comments as soon as you write the code. Never "save it for later," because there will often never be time to do it later, or if there is, you will not understand the code as well when you come back to it at some other time.

You add comments to an HTML page by wrapping them in comment tags. The HTML element for a comment is the <!-- and --> tag pair. At a minimum, add comments to document the HTML where necessary. Use an introductory (header) comment to document each subroutine and function in the HTML page. How you add comments to script in an HTML page depends on the scripting language you are using. In VBScript, comments are indicated by an apostrophe (') character. In JScript, you use either //, which indicates that the rest of the line is a comment, or /* *comment text* */, which indicates that all of the *comment text* is a comment, no matter how many lines it spans.

Comments serve an additional purpose when they are used in script in an HTML file. Browsers will ignore any unrecognized HTML tag. However, if the script tags are ignored, the browser will attempt to render the script itself as plain text. This is rarely the behavior you want. The correct way to format script so that older browsers will ignore both the script tags and the script itself is to wrap your script (but not the script tags) in the <!-- and --> comment tags. If you are using VBScript, you will need to use the apostrophe character to add comments to script that is nested within the <!-- and --> comment tags. The following example uses both forms of comment tags:

```
<SCRIPT LANGUAGE="VBSCRIPT">
<!--
   Option Explicit

   Sub UpdateMessage()
      ' This procedure calls code in a scriptlet to get
      ' values for the current day, month, and year, and then
      ' uses the innerHTML property of a <DIV> tag to dynamically
      ' display those values on the page.

      .
      .
      .
-->
</SCRIPT>
```

The preceding code fragment is available in ScriptGoodFormatting.htm in the Samples\CH03 subfolder on the companion CD-ROM.

For more information about writing script in HTML pages, see Chapter 12, "Using Web Technologies."

Designing Code to Be Used Again

Previous sections focused on techniques you can use to write code that is easy to understand and maintain. This section covers techniques you can use to transform that code into reusable components.

A discussion of the principles behind creating high-quality procedures is beyond the scope of this chapter. Complete coverage of this topic is available in *Code Complete* by Steve McConnell (Microsoft Press, 1993).

This section is designed to get you started writing code that can be used in different situations.

What Is Reusable Code?

Reusable code is code that can be used, without modification, to perform a specific "service" regardless of what application uses the code.

There are everyday objects that perform a specific service in different circumstances all around you. Think of a calendar. It gives you the ability to look up days and dates. You can use it to determine that this year your birthday falls on a Tuesday, or that Thanksgiving is on the 25th, or that there are two extra days to file tax returns because April 15th is on a Saturday. Similarly, you can use your address book to create a Christmas card mailing list or find the phone number for your Aunt Sally. When you are building software, "objects" are created in code, and reusable objects that perform specific services in different circumstances are called *components*.

When you use Microsoft Office to build custom solutions, you write code that leverages the power of Office components. Using an Office component means that you not only don't have to write the code yourself, but you are using a component that has been tested and found reliable in different conditions. The day has long passed when any knowledgeable developer would consider writing a custom program to check spelling. Instead, you'd call the spelling checker provided with Word. Similarly, nobody would develop custom code to calculate depreciation or determine principal and interest payments on a long-term loan. Instead, you would call VBA's built-in financial functions or use the Excel **Application** object to handle complex calculations for you.

Just as you can build custom solutions based on components supplied as part of Microsoft Office, you can also build them by using reusable components that you have created yourself. You can think of reusable code from the perspective of the code that will call it to perform its service. It is a "black box" that accepts a known input value and returns a known output value. What happens inside the box (how the procedure actually works) is irrelevant to the code that calls it.

Once you get into the habit of writing reusable procedures, you will often find that you have solutions where groups of related procedures work together to perform a single service or a group of related services. For example, you may have a group of procedures that provides data access services, or another group that consists of string-handling routines. This is an opportunity to group related procedures in their own module (or in a class module that exposes methods and properties to gain access to the procedures). You can then add the module to any solution that needs the services it provides.

Writing Reusable Code

There are many ways to write code that performs some valuable service. Options range from recording a macro that can replay a sequence of keystrokes and menu selections to creating a class module that provides a wrapper around complicated Windows application programming interface (API) functions. In the first example, you have application-specific code that provides a solution, but is not reusable. In the second example, you have created a reusable component that can perform its service from within any solution.

It is not difficult to write reusable code. If there are two ways to code something and one of them will result in a reusable procedure, create the reusable code. It is really a matter of how you approach the problem. If you understand how to create and use class modules, then you already know a great deal about how to approach writing reusable code. For more information about using class modules in Microsoft Office, see Chapter 9, “Custom Classes and Objects.”

The first consideration when you are writing reusable code is to follow all the guidelines suggested in the previous sections of this chapter. In other words, write code that uses a consistent naming convention, is formatted properly, and contains useful comments.

Examine your existing code to make sure that your procedures have a single, specific purpose. Can you describe your procedures in a short, plain sentence? For example, “This procedure accepts an SQL string as an argument and returns a **Recordset** object containing the records described by the string.” If you are unable to simply and clearly describe a procedure, it probably does too many things. Break down complicated procedures into smaller ones that do one thing each. Procedures should contain only code that clearly belongs together.

When you write new procedures, design them to perform a single operation.

Avoid making specific reference to named application objects. For example, the following code makes a specific reference to a combo box control and a text box control on an Access form:

```
strEmployeeName = Forms!frmEmployees!cboEmployeeName
strSQL = "SELECT * FROM Employees WHERE LastName = '" & _
   Mid(strEmployeeName, InStr(strEmployeeName, " ") + 1) & "'"
Set rstAddresses = dbs.OpenRecordset(strSQL)
Forms!frmEmployees!txtHireDate = rstAddresses!HireDate
```

It would not be possible to reuse this code without substantially revising it. The procedure could be rewritten as a function that accepts a table name, a field name, and the record-selection criteria and returns the matching data. This procedure could be used in any solution that needed to retrieve a value from a field in a table:

```
Function GetDataFromField(strTableName As String, _
                          strFieldName As String, _
                          strCriteria As String) As Variant

   ' Returns a value from the field specified by strFieldName
   ' in the table specified by strTableName according to the
   ' criteria specified by strCriteria.

   Dim rstFieldData   As New ADODB.Recordset
   Dim strSQL         As String

   On Error Resume Next

   strSQL = "SELECT " & strFieldName & " FROM " & _
      strTableName & " WHERE " & strCriteria
    rstFieldData.Open strSQL, DATA_CONNECTSTRING & DATA_PATH
   If Err = 0 Then
      GetDataFromField = rstFieldData(strFieldName)
   Else
      GetDataFromField = ""
   End If
End Function
```

The GetDataFromField procedure is available in the modGetAddressCode module in FormattingExamples.doc in the Samples\CH03 subfolder on the companion CD-ROM.

In the previous code sample, you'll notice that two constants were used in place of the database connection string and database path in the ActiveX Data Object (ADO) **Recordset** object's **Open** method. This sample highlights another important consideration when you are writing reusable code: Never hard-code values used in your code. If a string or number is used repeatedly, define a module-level constant and use the constant in your code. If you need to use a string or number in more than one module, declare the constant by using the **Public** keyword. If you have a string or number that is local to a procedure, consider rewriting the procedure to pass the value as an argument or by using a local constant.

Always try to minimize the number of arguments in a procedure and pass in only what is actually needed by the procedure. In addition, make sure that your procedures use all the arguments passed to them.

Group related procedures and the constants they use together in the same module, and where appropriate, consider grouping related procedures together in a class module with a clearly defined interface.

Keep procedures in standard modules and not in modules behind forms or documents. The code in form modules should only be that code that is tied directly to the form itself and the code required for calling general procedures stored in standard modules.

Clearly distinguish between persisting data and communicating it between procedures. Communicate between procedures by passing data as arguments to the procedures. Persist data by writing it to disk or to the Windows registry. Don't use a procedure to write to a global variable so that some other procedure can read data from that global variable. Don't communicate with another procedure by passing data out of the application; for example, using one procedure to write data to a disk file, .ini file, or the registry so that some other procedure can read that data.

The same considerations that go into writing reusable code also apply to writing reusable script. The easiest way to reuse script is to group related procedures together in a scriptlet and then link the scriptlet to the HTML page in which you want to use the script. To see an example of an HTML page that links to reusable code in a scriptlet, copy ScriptGoodFormatting.htm and Scriptlet.htm from the Samples\CH03 subfolder on the companion CD-ROM and open ScriptGoodFormatting.htm in your Web browser. To view the scriptlet code, open Scriptlet.htm in Windows Notepad. For more information about scriptlets, see Chapter 12, "Using Web Technologies."

Where to Go from Here

For additional information about the subjects discussed in this chapter, see the following resources. If a file name is listed, that file is located in the Appendixes folder on the companion CD-ROM, unless otherwise noted.

Naming Conventions

Microsoft Consulting Services Naming Conventions (MCS Naming Conventions.doc)

Microsoft Knowledge Base article: "*Built-in Constants in Visual Basic for Applications*," Q112671 (http://support.microsoft.com/support)

VBScript Intrinsic Constants (Visual Basic Scripting Help located at C:\Program Files\Microsoft Visual Studio\Common\IDE\IDE98\MSE\1033\Vbscrip5.chm)

Writing Reusable Code

McConnell, Steve. *Code Complete*. Redmond, WA: Microsoft Press, 1993.

Using Scriptlets in HTML Files

Chapter 12, "Using Web Technologies"

Scriptlet Technology Web site (http://msdn.microsoft.com/developer/sdk/inetsdk/help/scriptlets/scrlt.htm)

Isaacs, Scott. *Inside Dynamic HTML.* Redmond, WA: Microsoft Press, 1997.

Code Samples

The code samples shown in this chapter, along with additional examples demonstrating similar techniques, can be copied from the files in the Samples\CH03 subfolder on the companion CD-ROM.

CHAPTER 4

Understanding Office Objects and Object Models

Each Microsoft Office application contains a powerful set of tools designed to help you accomplish a related set of tasks. For example, Microsoft Access provides powerful data-management and query capabilities, Microsoft Excel provides mathematical, analytical, and reporting tools, Microsoft Outlook provides tools for sending and receiving e-mail, for scheduling, and for contact and task management, and Microsoft Word lets you create and manage documents, track versions of documents among different users, and create forms and templates. As powerful as these and the other Office applications are on their own, you can also integrate the features from two or more Office applications into a single solution to amplify and focus users' productivity.

The key technology that makes individual Office applications programmable and also makes creating an integrated Office solution possible is the Component Object Model (COM) technology known as *Automation* (formerly called *OLE Automation*). Automation allows a developer to use Visual Basic for Applications (VBA) code to create and control software objects exposed by any application, dynamic-link library (DLL), or ActiveX control that supports the appropriate programmatic interfaces. VBA and Automation allow you to program individual Office applications, for example, to create procedures to automatically create and format documents in Word itself, as well as to run other applications from within a host application. For example, you can run a hidden instance of Excel from within Access to perform mathematical and analytical operations on your Access data. The key to understanding Automation is to understand objects and object models: what they are, how they work, and how they work together. This chapter and Chapter 5, "Working with Office Applications," provide a solid foundation on which to build your understanding of developing custom Office solutions.

To fully master the use of Automation in your Office solutions, you must have detailed working knowledge of the applications you are integrating. It is not the purpose of this chapter, indeed of this book, to teach you all you need to know about any specific Office application. That is the kind of knowledge and experience that can only be gained with further application-specific training and hands-on experience.

Contents

Developing Integrated Office Solutions

The ability to develop an integrated Office solution heavily depends on two technologies:

- The Component Object Model (COM) software architecture
- Visual Basic for Applications (VBA)

The COM software architecture allows software developers to build their applications and services from individual software components, collectively referred to as *COM components* or simply *components*. COM components consist of the physical, compiled files that contain *classes*, which are code modules that define programmable objects. There are two types of COM components: *in-process components* and *out-of-process components*. In-process components are either DLLs or ActiveX controls (.ocx files) and can run only within the process of another application. Out-of-process components are .exe files and run as free-standing applications. A COM component can serve either or both of the following roles in application development:

- Sharing its objects with other applications. This role is called being an *Automation server.*
- Using other components' objects. This role is called being an *Automation client*. In earlier documentation, this role is called being an *Automation controller.*

The Windows operating system and Office suite of applications are examples of products that have been developed by using the COM software architecture. Just because software is developed by using COM doesn't necessarily mean that it can be programmed by using VBA. However, if an application or service supports the COM technology known as Automation, it can expose interfaces to the features of its components as objects that can be programmed from VBA, as well as many other programming languages. To support Automation, an application or service must provide either or both of two methods of exposing its custom interfaces:

- By providing the IDispatch interface. In this way, the application or service can be queried for further information about its custom interfaces. Applications and services that support the IDispatch interface provide information about their custom interfaces at run time by using a method called late binding.
- By allowing direct access at design time to the member functions in its virtual function table, or vtable, that implement its interfaces. Applications and services that support direct access to custom interfaces support what is called vtable binding or early binding.

An application can be said to support Automation if it supports either one, but not necessarily both, of these methods. Most contemporary applications and services provide support for both methods and are referred to as supporting dual interfaces.

For more information about the differences between late binding and early binding, see "Declaring Object Variables" later in this chapter.

To support early binding, an application or service must also supply a *type library* (also known as an *object library*). A type library is a file or part of a file that describes the type of one or more objects. Type libraries do not store objects; they store type information. By accessing a type library, a programming environment can determine the characteristics of an object, such as the interfaces supported by the object and the names and addresses of the members of each interface. With this information, the programming language can be used to work with the exposed interfaces.

In the VBA programming environment, you can establish a connection to a type library, which is called *establishing a reference* to a type library. Once you establish a reference to a type library, you can view information about the objects made available through the type library by using the Object Browser. Establishing a reference to a type library also allows VBA to perform error-checking at compile time to ensure that code written against the type library is free from errors due to improper declarations or from passing values of the wrong type. Additionally, referencing a type library allows you to take advantage of VBA features that simplify writing code, such as automatic listing of the properties and methods of objects exposed by the type library. Further, referencing a type library makes your code run faster because information about the objects you are programming is available to VBA at design time; this information can be used to optimize your code when it is compiled. For more information about referencing type libraries and using the Object Browser, see "Declaring Object Variables" later in this chapter.

The VBA programming environment can be incorporated into applications that support Automation to make them programmable. The suite of Microsoft Office applications, as well as a rapidly growing number of applications such as AutoCAD and Visio, incorporate the VBA programming environment and are written to support both kinds of Automation interfaces. Additionally, many other software components, such as ActiveX controls and DLLs, expose their functionality to VBA programmers through Automation interfaces.

Using the objects, properties, and methods exposed through Automation interfaces, you can use VBA code running in modules associated with the currently open document, template, database, Microsoft FrontPage-based web, or add-in to automate that application. VBA and Automation make it possible to record simple macros to automate keystrokes and mouse actions (in applications that support macro recording), and also to create sophisticated integrated solutions, such as document management, accounting, and database applications.

To produce even more powerful integrated applications, you can use VBA code running in one application to create and work with objects from another installed application or component. For example, if you are developing a solution in Access and you want to use mathematical or other functions available only in Excel, you can use VBA to create an instance of Excel and use its features from code running in Access.

You can think of Automation as a nervous system that makes programmatic communication and feedback between applications and components possible, and as "glue" that lets you integrate features from Office applications and other software components into a custom solution.

VBA's support for Automation provides Office developers with incredible flexibility and power. By taking advantage of Automation, you can use the features exposed through the object models of the entire Office suite of applications (as well as any third-party applications and components that support Automation interfaces) as a set of business-application building blocks. By taking advantage of the prebuilt components exposed through Automation, you don't need to develop your own custom components and procedures every time you want to get something done. In addition to shortening the development time for your solution, using pre-built components also means that you can take advantage of the thousands of hours of design, development, and testing that went into producing them.

By using VBA and objects exposed through Automation, you can select the best set of features to use to perform the tasks you want to accomplish, you can provide the data users need to accomplish their jobs, and you can manage workflow to provide an effective and productive solution.

Understanding Objects and Collections

This section provides an overview of the fundamental concepts behind how Office applications expose their functionality to the VBA language through a hierarchical system of objects and collections of objects called an *object model*. Once you understand how to reference objects in an application's object model, you can use the objects and features available to build your solution.

What Are Objects and Object Models?

An application fundamentally consists of two things: content and functionality. Content refers to the information within an application, that is, the documents, worksheets, tables, or slides and the information they contain. Content also refers to information about the attributes of individual elements in that application, such as the size of a window, the color of a graphic, or the font size of a word. Functionality refers to all the ways you can work with the content in the application, for example, opening, closing, adding, deleting, sending, copying, pasting, editing, or formatting the content in the application.

The content and functionality that make up an application are represented to the Visual Basic language as discrete units called *objects*. For the most part, the set of objects exposed by an application to Visual Basic corresponds to all the objects that you can work with by using the application's user interface. You should already be familiar with many of these objects, such as Access databases, tables, queries, forms, and reports; Excel workbooks, worksheets, and cell ranges; Word documents, sections, paragraphs, sentences, and words; Microsoft Outlook messages, appointments, and contacts; Microsoft PowerPoint presentations and slides; and FrontPage-based webs and pages.

In some cases, actions you can perform with the application's user interface aren't exposed as objects in VBA. For example, there are no objects for digitally signing a VBA project. On the other hand, many objects provide more specific control than is available through the user interface. For example, by using the **Assistant** object you can programmatically perform specific animations of the Office Assistant that aren't exposed directly through the user interface. Also, some objects provide control over lower-level functions of the application that have no user interface. For example, the **Err** object allows you to trap errors so that you can anticipate situations that would otherwise cause your program to stop working, or leave users confused about the correct action to take.

The objects exposed by an application are arranged relative to each other in hierarchical relationships. The top-level object in an Office application is the **Application** object, which represents the application itself. The **Application** object contains other objects that you have access to only when the **Application** object exists (that is, when an instance of the application itself is running). For example, the Excel **Application** object contains **Workbook** objects, and the Word **Application** object contains **Document** objects. Because the **Document** object depends on the existence of the Word **Application** object for its own existence, the **Document** object is said to be the *child* of the **Application** object; conversely, the **Application** object is said to be the *parent* of the **Document** object.

Many child objects have children of their own. For example, the Excel **Workbook** object contains, or is parent to, the **Worksheets** object. The **Worksheets** object is a special kind of object called a *collection* that represents a set of objects—in this case, all the worksheets in the workbook, which in turn are represented as individual **Worksheet** objects within that collection. A parent object can have multiple children; for instance, the Word **Window** object has as children the **Document**, **Panes**, **Selection**, and **View** objects. Additionally, identically named child objects may belong to more than one parent object; for instance, in Word, both the **Application** object and the **Document** object have a **Windows** collection as a child object. However, even though the child objects have the same name, typically their functionality is determined by the parent object; for example, the **Windows** collection for the **Application** object contains all the current document windows in the application, whereas the **Windows** collection for the **Document** object contains only the windows that display the specified document.

Figure 4.1 The Windows Collection Portion of the Word Object Model

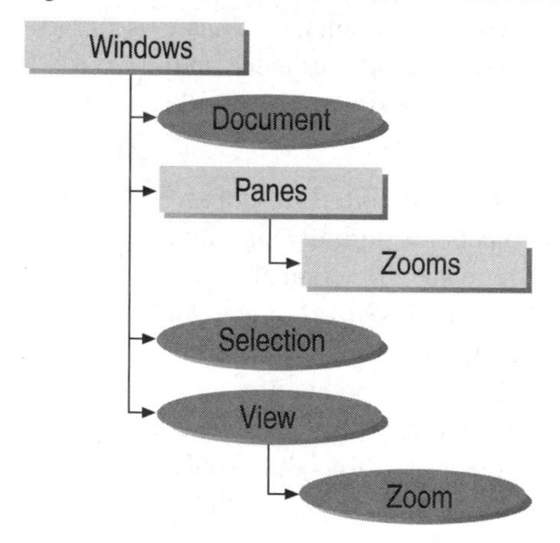

To view graphical representations of the object models for Office applications and shared components, see the "Object Model Diagrams" appendix or see the topics "Microsoft Office Objects," "Microsoft Access Objects," "Microsoft Excel Objects," "Microsoft FrontPage Objects," "Microsoft Outlook Objects," "Microsoft Word Objects," or "Microsoft PowerPoint Objects," in the Visual Basic Reference Help for that application. You can also view the object models for all Office applications as well as other applications that support VBA and Automation, such as AutoCAD and Visio, at the VBA Objects Web site at http://www.inquiry.com/objects/.

In addition to containing child objects, each object in the hierarchy contains content and functionality that apply both to the object itself and to all its child objects. The higher an object is in a hierarchy of nested objects (that is, the more child objects an object has), the wider the scope of its content and functionality. For example, in Excel, the **Application** object contains the size of the application window and the ability to quit the application; the **Workbook** object contains the file name and format of the workbook and the ability to save the workbook; the **Worksheets** collection contains **Worksheet** object names and the ability to add and delete worksheets.

You often don't get to the actual contents of a file, such as the values on an Excel worksheet or the text in a Word document, until you've navigated through several levels in the object hierarchy. This is because the scope of this specific content belongs to a particular functionality of the application. For example, the value in a cell on a worksheet applies only to that cell, not to all cells on the worksheet, so you can't store the value directly in a **Worksheet** object.

To work with the content and functionality exposed by an object, you use *properties* and *methods* of that object. You use properties to determine or change some characteristic of an object, such as its color, dimensions, or state. For example, you can set the **Visible** property of an Excel **Worksheet** object to specify whether a worksheet is visible to the user. You use methods to perform a particular action on an object. For example, you use the **PrintOut** method of the Word **Document** object to print the document. For more information about using properties and methods, see "Using Properties and Methods" later in this chapter.

Some objects also respond to *events*. An event is an action that is typically performed by a user such as clicking a mouse, pressing a key, changing data, or opening a document or form, but can also be performed by program code, or by the system itself. You can write code, called an *event procedure*, that will run whenever an event occurs. For example, you can write code in a form's Open event to size or position the form whenever it is opened. For more information about working with events, see "Working with Events" later in this chapter.

In summary, the representation of content and functionality in an application is divided among the objects in the application's object model. Together, the objects in the object model's hierarchy represent all the content and functionality in the application that is exposed to Visual Basic. Separately, the objects provide access to very specific areas of content and functionality. To determine or set a characteristic of an object, you read or set one of the object's properties. To perform an action on or with an object, you use one of the object's methods. Additionally, some objects provide events that are typically triggered by a user's action, so that you can write code that will run in response to that action.

Working with the Outlook Object Model

Outlook's programming model differs somewhat from the other Office applications. You can work with Outlook's object model in three ways:

- You can write VBA code that runs from a local project file or a COM add-in that is associated with the local installation of Outlook.
- You can use the native scripting environment available within the Outlook forms that are used to display items such as messages and appointments.
- You can use Automation to work with Outlook from other Office applications and applications that support VBA.

To write VBA code that runs from a local project file (VBAProject.OTM), open Outlook, point to **Macro** on the **Tools** menu, and then click **Visual Basic Editor**. In Outlook, the Visual Basic Editor allows you to write code that can be run from this installation of Outlook only. For example, by adding code to the ThisOutlookSession module, you can write code against the following **Application** object events: ItemSend, NewMail, OptionsPagesAdd, Quit, Reminder, and Startup. Just as with other Office applications, you can insert code modules, class modules, and UserForms to further customize your solution, and you can run procedures from menu items or toolbar buttons.

To distribute a solution created by using a local Outlook VBA project, you can export your modules and objects to files and then import them on other machines where Outlook is installed. However, a much better way to distribute your solution is to compile and install your solution as a COM add-in by using the COM add-in designer available in Microsoft Office 2000 Developer or in Microsoft Visual Basic 6.0. For more information about creating COM add-ins, see Chapter 11, "Add-ins, Templates, Wizards, and Libraries." For more information about using VBA within Outlook, see "Working with Microsoft Outlook Objects" in Chapter 5, "Working with Office Applications."

To write script that runs within Outlook items, you use the Outlook Script Editor. Outlook forms (that is, all items you can open in Outlook, such as messages, appointments, and contacts) support scripting in Microsoft Visual Basic Scripting Edition (VBScript) by using the Outlook Script Editor. Because VBScript is a subset of VBA, there are limitations to what you can do; for example, VBScript supports only one data type, the **Variant** data type, and a number of VBA keywords and features aren't supported. For more information about scripting, see Chapter 12, "Using Web Technologies." To access the Outlook Script Editor, you must be in form design mode.

Working with the Outlook Object Model (*continued*)

▶ **To open the Outlook Script Editor**

1. Open the Outlook item you want to base your form on.
2. On the **Tools** menu, point to **Forms**, and then click **Design This Form**. To start from an existing custom form, point to **Forms** on the **Tools** menu, click **Design a Form**, and then select a form.
3. Make any changes you want to the design of the form.
4. On the **Form** menu, click **View Code**.

When working with scripting in Outlook forms, you will most typically be writing event procedures. For example, you may want to write an event procedure for your form's Open event to initialize the form to display a particular tab page and enter default values in certain fields. To add an event handler stub to the Outlook Script Editor, click **Event Handler** on the **Script** menu, select the event you want to work with, and then click **Add**. For more information about the Outlook object model, click **Microsoft Outlook Object Library Help** on the **Help** menu in the Outlook Script Editor.

To work with Outlook from another application, you can use Automation code with either early binding or late binding. To use early binding, establish a reference to the Microsoft Outlook 9.0 object library and then declare and initialize an object variable that references the Outlook **Application** object. For example:

```
Dim olApp As Outlook.Application
Set olApp = New Outlook.Application
```

Similarly, you can use the **CreateObject** function with an object variable declared as type **Object** to initialize a late-bound object variable. For example:

```
Dim olApp As Object
Set olApp = CreateObject("Outlook.Application")
```

Either way, you can then use this object variable to work with the other objects, properties, methods, and events of the Outlook object model.

For more information about using Automation code with Outlook, see "Creating an Object Variable to Automate Another Office Application" later in this chapter, and "Working with Microsoft Outlook Objects" in Chapter 5, "Working with Office Applications."

Working with Objects

To work with the objects exposed by an object model, you must first declare an object variable and set a reference to the object you want to work with. Once you've established a reference to an object, you can work with its properties, methods, or events.

Returning a Reference to an Object

Before you can do anything with an object, you must return a reference to it. To do this, you must build an expression that gains access to one object in the object model and then use properties or methods to move up or down the object hierarchy until you get to the object you want to work with. The properties and methods you use to return the object you start from and to move from one object to another are called *object accessors* or just *accessors*. Accessors typically have the same name as the object they are used to access; for example, the Word **Documents** property is used to access the **Documents** collection. Accessors are typically properties, but in some object models accessors are methods.

The Application Object

A common place to gain access to the object model is the top-level object. In all Office applications and in most applications that support VBA, the top-level object is the **Application** object. However, some applications and components may have a different top-level object. For example, when you are programming the Visual Basic Editor (by using a reference to the Microsoft Visual Basic for Applications Extensibility 5.3 library), the top-level object is the **VBE** object.

You use the **Application** property to return a reference to the **Application** object. The following code fragment returns a reference to the **Application** object and then sets properties to display scroll bars, ScreenTips, and the status bar:

```
Dim wdApp As Application
Set wdApp = Application
With wdApp
   .DisplayScrollBars = True
   .DisplayScreenTips = True
   .DisplayStatusBar = True
End With
```

If you have established references to more than one type library that contains an **Application** object, the **Application** property will always return the **Application** object for the host application. In addition, for any other object that has the same name in two or more referenced type libraries, the accessor property or method will return the object from the first type library referenced in the **Available References** list of the **References** dialog box (**Tools** menu).

For example, the ActiveX Data Objects (ADO) and Data Access Objects (DAO) type libraries both have **Recordset** objects. If you have a reference to the ADO type library followed by the DAO type library, a declaration like the following will always return the ADO **Recordset** object:

```
Dim rstNew As Recordset
```

While you may be able to adjust the priority of references in the **References** dialog box to correct this, a better solution, which eliminates any ambiguity and prevents errors, is to declare an object variable by using the fully qualified *class name*, also called the *programmatic identifier* or *ProgID*, of the object. To do this, combine the name of the application or component that contains the object (as it appears in the Object Browser's **Project/Library** box) with the name of the object separated by a period.

For example, to declare an object variable that will be used to work with the Word **Application** object from another application, you must declare the object variable like this:

```
Dim wdApp As Word.Application
```

Similarly, if you have both the ADO and the DAO type libraries referenced in your project, you should declare object variables to work with **Recordset** objects like this:

```
Dim rstADO As ADODB.Recordset
Dim rstDAO As DAO.Recordset
```

Note You can view the ProgIDs of all installed applications and components on a computer by running the Registry Editor and looking under the \HKEY_CLASSES_ROOT\CLSID subkey.

For more information about using the **References** dialog box, see "Setting References and Working with Object Variables" later in this chapter. For more information about using the Object Browser, see "Using the Object Browser" later in this chapter.

Navigating the Object Hierarchy

To get to an object from the top-level object, you must step through all the objects above it in the hierarchy by using accessors to return one object from another. Many objects, such as workbooks, worksheets, documents, presentations, and slides, are members of *collections*. A collection is an object that contains a set of related objects. You can work with the objects in a collection as a single group rather than as separate entities. Because collections are always one level higher than individual objects in the hierarchy, you usually have to access a collection before you can access an object in that collection. The accessor that returns a collection object usually has the same name as the collection object itself.

For example, the **Documents** property of the Word **Application** object returns the **Documents** collection object, which represents all open documents. The following expression returns a reference to the Word **Documents** collection object:

```
Application.Documents
```

You reference an item in a collection by using either a number that refers to its position in the collection or by using its name. For example, if a document named Report.doc is the first open document in the **Documents** collection, you can reference it in either of the following ways:

```
Application.Documents(1)
```

–or–

```
Application.Documents("Report.doc")
```

To get to an object further down the object hierarchy, simply add additional accessors and objects to your expression until you get to the object you want to work with. For example, the following expression returns a reference to the second paragraph in the **Paragraphs** collection of the first open document:

```
Application.Documents(1).Paragraphs(2)
```

For more information about referencing and working with objects in collections, see "Working with Collections" later in this chapter.

Shortcut Accessors

There are shortcut accessors you can use to gain direct access to objects in the model without having to navigate from the **Application** object. These shortcuts include accessors, such as the **Documents**, **Workbooks**, **Items**, and **Presentations** properties, that you can use by themselves to return a reference to the document collection for the corresponding application. For example, in Word, you can use either of the following statements to open MyDoc.doc:

```
Application.Documents.Open Filename:="c:\docs\mydoc.doc"
```

–or–

```
Documents.Open Filename:="c:\docs\mydoc.doc"
```

There are other shortcut accessors, such as the **ActiveWindow**, **ActiveDocument**, **ActiveWorksheet**, or **ActiveCell** properties that return a direct reference to an active part of an application. The following statement closes the active Word document. Note that the **Application** object and the **Documents** collection object are not explicitly referenced.

```
ActiveDocument.Close
```

Tip When **<globals>** is selected in the **Classes** list in the Object Browser, you can use any accessor that appears in the **Members of** list as a shortcut; that is, you don't have to return the object that the property or method applies to before you use the property or method, because VBA can determine that information from the context in which your code is running.

Referencing the Document or Workbook in Which Code Is Running

When you are using the **ActiveDocument** and **ActiveWorkbook** accessor properties, it is important to remember that the reference returned is to the document or workbook that is currently in use (the topmost window of all open documents or workbooks). In many circumstances, you can reference an active object *implicitly*, that is, without including the entire hierarchy above the object you're referring to. For example, you can create a reference to the active workbook's **Worksheets** collection without preceding the collection with `ActiveWorkbook.` or an explicit reference to the workbook's name or number in the **Workbooks** collection:

```
Worksheets("MySheet")
```

However, using implicit references or references to the **ActiveDocument** or **ActiveWorkbook** accessor properties can create problems if you are developing a global template or add-in and need to make sure your code refers to the add-in or global template itself. Word and Excel provide two special accessor properties that return a reference to the document or workbook in which the VBA code is running: **ThisDocument** and **ThisWorkbook**. Use the **ThisDocument** or **ThisWorkbook** property whenever you need to make sure that your code refers to the document or workbook that contains the code that is running.

For example, both of the following **Set** statements reference the worksheet named Addin Definition. The first makes an explicit reference to the active workbook by using the **ActiveWorkbook** property. The second makes an implicit reference; because it doesn't explicitly refer to a specific workbook, the reference is assumed to be to the active workbook. In either case, the reference made in the **Set** statement will be to the worksheet in whatever workbook happens to be active when the code runs.

```
Set rngMenuDef = ActiveWorkbook.Worksheets("Addin Definition"). _
   Range("MenuDefinition")

Set rngMenuDef = Worksheets("Addin Definition").Range("MenuDefinition")
```

References like these will work correctly while you are developing an add-in or template if you have no other documents or workbooks open while you are testing your code, or if the add-in or template is in the active window when the code is running. However, once your add-in or template is in use, these type of references can cause errors. To make sure that you are referencing the workbook in which code is running, use the **ThisWorkbook** property as shown in the following **Set** statement:

```
Set rngMenuDef = ThisWorkbook.Worksheets("Addin Definition"). _
   Range("MenuDefinition")
```

The Parent Property

To access an object higher up in the object hierarchy from the current object, you can often use the **Parent** property of the object. Using an object's **Parent** property allows you to reference the object that contains the object. For example, if you write a function to work with a control on a form (the function takes an argument of type **Control**), you can use the control's **Parent** property to reference the form that contains the control.

Note that the **Parent** property doesn't always return the object immediately above the current object in the hierarchy, it may return a higher object, especially if the object immediately above the current object is a collection. For example, the **Parent** property of a Word **Document** object returns the **Application** object, not the **Documents** collection. You can use the **TypeName** function to find out what kind of object the **Parent** property of an object refers to. For example, in Word, the following statement displays the type of object that the **Parent** property of the **Document** object refers to:

```
MsgBox TypeName(Documents("Document1").Parent)
```

Tip You can use the **TypeName** function to determine the type of object returned by any expression, not just expressions that use the **Parent** property. The **TypeName** function can also be used to determine the kind of data type returned by an expression, such as **Byte**, **Integer**, or **Long**.

Accessing an Embedded OLE Object's Application

To navigate from an embedded OLE object to the **Application** object of the program it was created with, you can often use the **Application** property of the object. For example, in PowerPoint, the following expression returns a reference to the **Application** object for the application used to create the embedded OLE object in the third shape on the first slide of the active presentation:

```
ActivePresentation.Slides(1).Shapes(3).Object.Application
```

Working with Collections

Although collections and the objects they contain, such as the **Workbooks** collection and the **Workbook** object, are distinct objects each with their own properties and methods, they're grouped as one unit in most object model graphics to reduce complexity. To return a single member of a collection, you usually use the **Item** property or method and pass the name or index number of the member as the *index* argument. For example, in Excel, the following expression returns a reference to an open workbook by passing its name "Sales.xls" to the **Item** property and then invokes the **Close** method to close it:

```
Workbooks.Item("Sales.xls").Close
```

The **Item** property or method is the default for most collections, so you can usually omit it from your expression. For example, in Excel, the following two expressions are equivalent:

```
Workbooks.Item("Sales.xls")
```

–or–

```
Workbooks("Sales.xls")
```

To reference items in a collection by using an index number, simply pass the number of the item to the **Item** property or method of the collection. For example, if Sales.xls is the second workbook in the **Workbooks** collection, the following expression will return a reference to it:

```
Workbooks(2)
```

Note Most collections used in Office applications (except Access) are *one-based*, that is, the index number of the first item in the collection is 1. However, the collections in Access and some components, such as ADO and DAO, are *zero-based*, that is, the index number of the first item is 0. For more information, refer to the Visual Basic Reference Help topic for the collection you want to work with.

Adding Objects to a Collection

You can also create new objects and add them to a collection, usually by using the **Add** method of that collection. The following code fragment creates a new document by using the Professional Memo.dot template and assigns it to the object variable docNew:

```
Const TEMPLATE_PATH  As String = "c:\program files\microsoft office\templates\1033\"
Dim docNew           As Word.Document

Set docNew = Documents.Add(Template:=TEMPLATE_PATH & "memos\professional memo.dot")
```

Note The template path in this example shows the language ID folder (1033) for templates installed by Microsoft Office for U.S. English language support. The language ID folder below C:\Program Files\Microsoft Office\Templates differs for each language. Templates you create yourself should be stored in the C:\Windows\Application Data\Microsoft\Templates folder or in a user profile-specific location. For more information about template deployment, see Chapter 2, "Designing and Deploying Office Solutions."

Working with Objects in a Collection

You can find out how many objects there are in a collection by using the **Count** property. The following Excel example displays a message box with the number of workbooks that are open:

```
MsgBox Workbooks.Count & " workbooks are open."
```

You can perform an operation on all the objects in a collection, or you can set or test a value for all the objects in a collection. To do this, you use a **For Each...Next** structure, or a **For...Next** structure in conjunction with the **Count** property to loop through all the objects in the collection.

Whenever possible, you should use a **For Each...Next** loop when you need to work with all the items in a collection. A **For Each...Next** loop generally performs faster and doesn't require you to use or test a loop counter, which can introduce errors. The following Excel example contains a **For Each...Next** structure that loops through the **Worksheets** collection of a workbook and appends " - By Automation" to the name of each worksheet:

```
Sub CreateExcelObjects()
   Dim xlApp          As Excel.Application
   Dim wkbNewBook     As Excel.Workbook
   Dim wksSheet       As Excel.Worksheet
   Dim strBookName    As String

   ' Create new hidden instance of Excel.
   Set xlApp = New Excel.Application
   ' Add new workbook to Workbooks collection.
   Set wkbNewBook = xlApp.Workbooks.Add
   ' Specify path to save workbook.
   strBookName = "c:\my documents\xlautomation.xls"
   ' Loop through each worksheet and append " - By Automation" to the
   ' name of each sheet. Close and save workbook to specified path.
   With wkbNewBook
      For Each wksSheet In .Worksheets
         wksSheet.Name = wksSheet.Name & " - By Automation"
      Next wksSheet
      .Close SaveChanges:=True, FileName:=strBookName
   End With

   Set wkbNewBook = Nothing
   Set xlApp = Nothing
End Sub
```

The CreateExcelObjects procedure is available in the modSetObjVariable module in Automating&IDE.doc in the Samples\CH04 subfolder on the companion CD-ROM.

Under some circumstances, you must use a **For...Next** loop to work with items in a collection. For example, if you try to use a **For Each...Next** loop to delete all the objects in a collection, only every other object in the collection will be deleted. This is because after deleting the first item, all items in the collection are reindexed so that what was the second item is now the first. When the **Next** statement runs at the end of the first execution of the loop, the pointer is advanced one, skipping that item for the next iteration of the loop. For this reason, to delete all items in a collection, you must use a **For...Next** loop that starts from the end of the collection and works backwards.

The following Binder example uses a **For...Next** structure to loop through the entire **Sections** collection of a binder starting from the end, deleting each section:

```
Sub DeleteDocsFromBinder()
   Dim bindApp          As OfficeBinder.Binder
   Dim intSectionCount  As Integer

   Const ERR_FILE_EXISTS As Long = 6546

   On Error GoTo DeleteDocsFromBinder_Err

   ' Create new hidden instance of Binder.
   Set bindApp = New OfficeBinder.Binder

   With bindApp
      ' Make Binder visible and open binder created with
      ' AddDocsToBinder procedure.
      .Visible = True
      .Open ("C:\My Documents\NewDocs.obd")

      ' Loop through each section and delete it.
      For intSectionCount = .Sections.Count To 1 Step -1
         .Sections(intSectionCount).Delete
      Next
      .Save
      .Close
   End With

DeleteDocsFromBinder_End:
   Set bindApp = Nothing
   Exit Sub

DeleteDocsFromBinder_Err:
   Select Case Err.Number
      Case ERR_FILE_EXISTS
         MsgBox "File already exists."
      Case Else
         MsgBox "Error: " & Error.Number & " " & Error.Description
      Resume DeleteDocsFromBinder_End
   End Select
End Sub
```

The DeleteDocsFromBinder procedure is available in the modSetObjVariable module in Automating&IDE.doc in the Samples\CH04 subfolder on the companion CD-ROM.

Another situation that requires you to use a **For...Next** loop to work with items in a collection is if you need to work with only a certain number of items, say the first ten, or every tenth item.

Using Properties and Methods

To work with the content and functionality exposed by an object, you use *properties* and *methods* of that object. The following Excel example uses the **Value** property of the **Range** object to set the contents of cell B3 on the Sales worksheet in the Current.xls workbook to 3:

```
Workbooks("Current.xls").Worksheets("Sales").Range("B3").Value = 3
```

The following example uses the **Bold** property of the **Font** object to apply bold formatting to cell B3 on the Sales worksheet:

```
Workbooks("Current.xls").Worksheets("Sales").Range("B3").Font.Bold = True
```

The following Word example uses the **Close** method of the **Document** object to close the file named Draft3.doc:

```
Documents("Draft3.doc").Close
```

In general, you use properties to set or read the content, which can include the text or value contained in an object, or other attributes of the object, and you use methods to work with an application's (or VBA's) built-in functionality to perform operations on the content. Be aware, however, that this distinction doesn't always hold true; there are a number of properties and methods in every object model that are exceptions to this rule.

Creating Your Own Objects and Object Models

You can create your own objects and object models by creating and using class modules. For example, you may need to work with complex sets of data that need to be managed in a consistent and reliable way. By creating your own objects, properties, and methods to work with this data in a class module, you can create an object model to make working with your data simpler and less error-prone. Similarly, you can create class modules to create wrapper functions around Windows application programming interface (API) calls or even complex parts of existing object models to make them easier to use.

For detailed information about how to work with class modules, see Chapter 9, "Custom Classes and Objects."

Working with Events

An event is an action that is typically performed by a user, such as clicking a mouse button, pressing a key, changing data, or opening a document or form, but the action can also be performed by program code, or by the system itself. You can write event procedure code to respond to such actions at either of two levels:

- **Document-level or sub-document-level events** These events occur for open documents and in some cases, for objects within them. For example, the Word **Document** object can respond to the Open, New, and Close events; the Excel **Workbook** object can respond to 20 events such as the Open, BeforeClose, and BeforeSave events; and the Excel **Worksheet** object can respond to 8 events, such as the Activate and Calculate events. PowerPoint supports only application-level events.
- **Application-level events** These events occur at the level of the application itself, for example, when a new Word document, Excel workbook, or PowerPoint presentation is created, for which the corresponding events are the NewDocument, NewWorkbook, and NewPresentation events.

Access provides a different model that responds to events on **Form** and **Report** objects, and most of the controls on them, such as **ListBox** and **TextBox** objects. UserForms, which can be used from Excel, Word, and PowerPoint, provide a similar event model to Access forms.

The Outlook **Application** object provides 6 events that can be used from the ThisOutlookSession module or a COM add-in running from an installation of the Outlook application: ItemSend, NewMail, OptionsPagesAdd, Quit, Reminder, and Startup. To create code that responds to a user's actions in the Outlook user interface, you can use the **WithEvents** keyword to declare object variables that can respond to Outlook **Explorer**, **Inspector**, and **MAPIFolder** object events. All Outlook item objects, except the **NoteItem** object, can respond to up to 11 events, such as the Open, Read, and Reply events.

The FrontPage **Application** object provides 10 events that allow your solution to respond to the creation and editing of pages and FrontPage-based webs: OnPageNew, OnPageOpen, OnBeforePageSave, OnAfterPageSave, and OnPageClose, and OnWebNew, OnWebOpen, OnBeforeWebPublish, OnAfterWebPublish, and OnWebClose.

In addition to the events supported by each Office application, the **CommandBarButton** object, **CommandBarComboBox** object, and **CommandBars** collection support events. For information about working with command bar events, see Chapter 6, "Working with Shared Office Components."

Responding to Document-Level Events

To create event procedures for events in Excel workbooks and Word documents, you need to work with the ThisWorkbook or ThisDocument modules. For example, to write an event procedure that will run when a Word document is opened, open the document and then open the Visual Basic Editor. In the Project Explorer, double-click **ThisDocument** to open the ThisDocument module. In the **Object** box in the Code window, click **Document**, and then click **Open** in the **Procedure** box. The Visual Basic Editor will create an event procedure template for the document's Open event. You can then enter any code you want to run whenever the document is opened. For example, the following event procedure sets certain features of the active window and view of a Word document when it is opened:

```
Private Sub Document_Open()
' Set Window and View properties to display document with document map
' in page layout view.
   With ActiveWindow
      .DisplayVerticalScrollBar = True
      .DisplayRulers = False
      .DisplayScreenTips = True
      .DocumentMap = True
      .DocumentMapPercentWidth = 25
      With .View
         .Type = wdPageView
         .WrapToWindow = True
         .EnlargeFontsLessThan = 11
         .ShowAll = False
         .ShowPicturePlaceHolders = False
         .ShowFieldCodes = False
         .ShowBookmarks = False
      End With
   End With
End Sub
```

The Document_Open procedure is available in the ThisDocument module in OpenEvent.doc in the Samples\CH04 subfolder on the companion CD-ROM.

If you want to prevent code written in a document's Open event from running when the document is opened programmatically from another application, you can check the **Application** object's **UserControl** property to determine if the application was opened by a user. To see an example of how to do this, see "Working with Documents That Contain Startup Code" later in this chapter.

Responding to Application-Level Events

In Office 97, Excel was the only Office application that provided a rich set of application-level events. Microsoft Office 2000 now includes a comparable set of events for Word and PowerPoint with similar names across each application. For example, where Excel provides NewWorkbook and WorkbookOpen events, Word provides NewDocument and DocumentOpen events, and PowerPoint provides NewPresentation and PresentationOpen events. Providing consistent event handling and similar names across Word, Excel, and PowerPoint makes it easier to create a COM add-in that works across these applications. FrontPage doesn't supply as extensive a set of application-level events as the other Office applications, but FrontPage events also have similar names; for example, OnPageNew, OnWebNew, OnPageOpen, and OnWebOpen.

The NewDocument, NewWorkbook, NewPresentation, and OnPageNew events are useful for tasks such as automatically formatting new documents and inserting content such as the date, time, author, or latest company logo off the intranet. Similarly, the OnWebNew event can be used to automatically apply themes or to add pages and content to new FrontPage-based webs. The DocumentOpen, WorkbookOpen, PresentationOpen, and OnPageOpen events can be used to retrieve information from the document and update command bar customizations. The DocumentClose, DocumentSave, and DocumentPrint events in Word (and comparable events in Excel and PowerPoint) can be used to ensure that document properties, such as the author or subject, are entered in the document before the document can be closed, saved, or printed. Similarly, the FrontPage OnBeforePageSave, OnBeforeWebPublish, OnPageClose, and OnWebClose events can be used to check page properties or to check the sizes of image files on the page, and to verify hyperlinks before publishing a FrontPage-based web.

To write event procedures for the **Application** object, you must create a new class module and declare an object variable as type **Application** by using the **WithEvents** keyword. For example, you could create a class module named XLEvents and add the following declaration to create a private Excel **Application** object variable to respond to events:

```
Private WithEvents xlApp As Excel.Application
```

Once you have done this, you can click **xlApp** in the **Object** box of the class module's Code window, and then click any of the events in the **Procedure** box to write event procedures to respond to Excel **Application** object events. However, because you can't use the **New** keyword to create an instance of the **Application** object variable when you are declaring it by using the **WithEvents** keyword, you'll need to write a **Set** statement to do so in the class module's Initialize event like this:

```
Private Sub Class_Initialize
   Set xlApp = Excel.Application
End Sub
```

This process is called creating an *event sink*. To activate the event sink, you declare in another module a public (or private) object variable for your event sink class, and then run a procedure that will create an instance of your class before the events you want to handle occur. For example:

```
Public evtEvents As XLEvents

Public Sub InitXLEvents()
   Set evtEvents = New XLEvents
End Sub
```

Creating an event sink in a class module provides a way for you to create an independent object that will respond to application-level events. The VBA project that contains the class module and procedure used to initialize your event sink must be running before any of the events you want to trap occur. Because application-level events are triggered by events that occur while the application itself is being used to open and work with documents, you will most typically implement an event sink in an add-in to trap an application's application-level events, or in Automation code running from another application.

For detailed information about how to create an event sink for application-level events, see Chapter 9, "Custom Classes and Objects."

Using the Object Browser

The Object Browser is available in all Microsoft products that contain the VBA programming environment. The Object Browser allows you to view all objects, methods, properties, events, and constants of all COM components whose type libraries are referenced by the application you are working with. By default, each Office application references a set of type libraries. For example, Word references by default the Visual Basic for Applications, Microsoft Word 9.0, OLE Automation, and Microsoft Office 9.0 type libraries. To manually reference any additional type libraries available on your system, click **References** on the **Tools** menu in the Visual Basic Editor. For more information about setting references, see "Setting References and Working with Object Variables" later in this chapter.

To display the Object Browser, open the Visual Basic Editor, and then click **Object Browser** on the **View** menu. Figure 4.2 shows the Object Browser.

Figure 4.2 The Object Browser

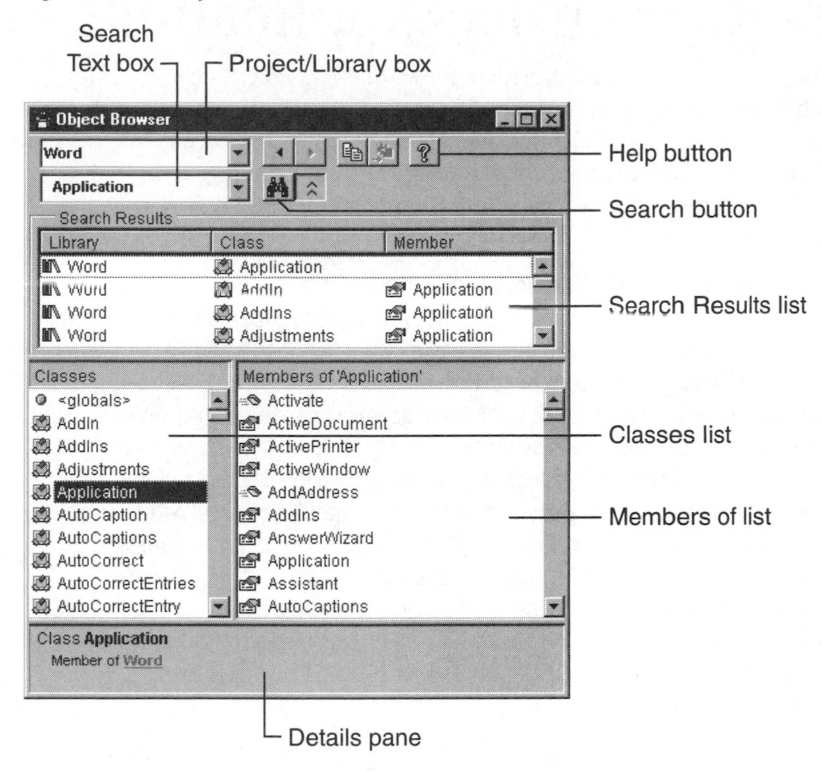

The **Project/Library** box shows all the available referenced type libraries. These libraries allow you to use early binding with the corresponding applications.

The **Search Text** box shows any keywords you have searched for by using the drop-down list. You can also type a word in this box, and then click the **Search** button to search the available libraries for that word. The **Search Results** list displays any classes, properties, methods, events, or constants that contain the word you searched for.

The **Classes** list displays all objects and collections in the library, and the **Members of** list displays all methods, properties, events, and constants associated with the selected object in the **Classes** list. The bottom pane of the dialog box (the **Details** pane) displays other information about the currently selected item, such as what kind of object it is, its data type, what arguments it may take, and what library or collection it is a member of.

If a Help file has been associated with the objects in the type library, you can display a Help topic by clicking the item in either the **Classes** or **Members of** list, and then pressing F1 or clicking the **Help** button in the upper-right corner of the dialog box.

Automating Other Office Applications

This section covers the basic steps required to prepare for automating an Office application from another application. This is often referred to as running code from a host application to automate another application. Although automating one Office application from another is generally accomplished in the same way, there are some important differences regarding how you work with each application; those differences are discussed in this section.

Note When VBA code references an object that is not installed, the Windows installer technology will attempt to install the required feature. In all Office applications except Outlook and FrontPage, you can use the **FeatureInstall** property to control what happens when an uninstalled object is referenced. When this property is set to the default (**msoFeatureInstallOnDemand**), any attempt to use an uninstalled object causes the Windows installer to try to install the requested feature. In some circumstances, this may take some time, and the user may believe that the machine has stopped responding to additional commands. To address this, you can set the **FeatureInstall** property to **msoFeatureInstallOnDemandWithUI** to display a progress meter so that users can see that something is happening as the feature is being installed. If you want to trap the error that is returned and display your own dialog box to the user or take some other custom action, you can set the **FeatureInstall** property to **msoFeatureInstallNone**. For more information and details about application-specific behavior, see Chapter 2, "Designing and Deploying Office Solutions," or search the Office application's Help index for "FeatureInstall property."

Setting References and Working with Object Variables

The first step in automating one Office application from another is referencing the application you want to automate. This reference lets your application "see" the objects exposed by the other application. In most cases, this means setting a reference to the application's type library by using the **References** dialog box.

The References Dialog Box

Before you work with objects exposed by an Office application, you should set a reference to that application by using the **References** dialog box. To open the **References** dialog box, click **References** on the **Tools** menu in the Visual Basic Editor. Figure 4.3 shows the **References** dialog box.

Figure 4.3 The References Dialog Box

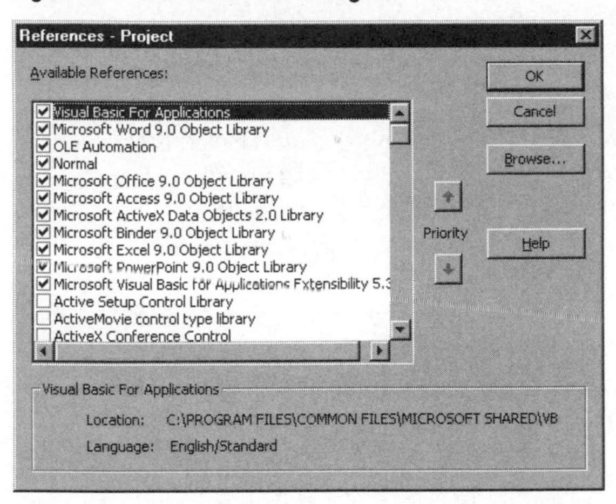

The example shown in Figure 4.3 includes references to most of the Microsoft Office applications. In your custom solutions, however, you need only reference the application that contains the objects you want to manipulate by using Automation. Including unnecessary references will increase the time it takes for your solution to load and will consume some additional memory resources.

Note You can use another Office application's objects (or the objects exposed by any other application or component that supports Automation) without setting a reference in the **References** dialog box by using the **CreateObject** or **GetObject** function and declaring object variables as the generic **Object** type. If you use this technique, the objects in your code will be late-bound, and as a result you will not be able to use design-time tools such as automatic statement completion or the Object Browser, and your code will not run as fast. For more information about using the **CreateObject** and **GetObject** functions, see "Using the CreateObject and GetObject Functions" later in this chapter.

Tip Because the **Application** object of every Office 2000 application includes accessor properties to work with some of the shared Office components such as the **Assistant** and **FileSearch** objects, you can work with these objects without having a reference to the Microsoft Office 9.0 object library. You may want to do this if your application must load quickly. However, when you are using a shared Office component without a reference to the Microsoft Office 9.0 object library, your code can't use enumerated constants; if it does, an error will be displayed. For example, when you are using the **Assistant** object with a reference to the Microsoft Office 9.0 object library, you can use a line of code such as the following to animate the Office Assistant:

```
Application.Assistant.Animation = msoAnimationGreeting
```

To use the same line of code without a reference to the Microsoft Office 9.0 office library, you must use the actual value of the **msoAnimationGreeting** constant, which is 2, as in the following line of code:

```
Application.Assistant.Animation = 2
```

To determine the values for constants such as **msoAnimationGreeting**, you must temporarily establish a reference to the Microsoft Office 9.0 office library and use the Object Browser to look up the numeric values of the constants you want work with. Using the numeric values will make your code less readable, and Microsoft doesn't guarantee that the same value will be used in future versions of Microsoft Office, so code written in this manner may not work correctly in future versions of Office. The VBA projects for all Office applications except Access include a reference to the Microsoft Office 9.0 office library by default. Therefore, if you want to prevent a reference to the Microsoft Office 9.0 office library from being loaded when your solution is opened, you must remove the reference in your solution's VBA project.

When you refer to an object in code, VBA determines what type of object it is by searching the type libraries selected in the **References** dialog box in the order in which they are displayed. If an object has the same name in two or more referenced type libraries, VBA uses the definition provided by the type library listed higher in the **Available References** list. To change the order in which the libraries are searched, you can use the **Priority** buttons to move the type libraries (except for the Visual Basic for Applications and the host application's type library) up or down the list. However, a better way to eliminate ambiguous object references is to fully qualify type declarations by including the programmatic identifier in front of the object name; for example, `Dim docNew As Word.Document`. Qualifying type declarations by using the programmatic identifier eliminates a potential source of errors and also makes your code more self-documenting.

If you have established a reference to an application or component's type library, you can learn about the exposed objects by using the Object Browser and the Help system. For more information about using the Object Browser, see "Using the Object Browser" earlier in this chapter.

Declaring Object Variables

Before one application can work with the objects exposed by another application's type library, it must first determine what information is contained in that type library. The process of querying the objects, methods, and properties exposed by another application is called *binding*. VBA programming in Office applications supports two kinds of binding: *early binding* and *late binding*. How and when binding occurs can have a great impact on how your solution performs.

If you establish a reference to the application's or component's type library, you can use early binding. When early binding is used, VBA retrieves information at design time about the application's objects directly from the type library, thus allowing you to declare object variables as specific types. For example, if you establish a reference to the Microsoft Word 9.0 object library when you are working with Word documents, you can declare object variables by using data types that are specific to Word, such as the **Documents** or **Document** types. Early binding reduces the amount of communication that needs to occur when your solution is running, thereby enhancing your solution's performance.

Late binding queries the application you are automating at run time, which allows you to declare object variables by using the generic **Object** or **Variant** data type. In general, late binding is useful if you are writing generic code to run against any of several applications and won't know the type of object you are working with until run time. Note that the additional overhead of querying an application at run time can slow down the performance of your solution.

Note Some applications and components that support Automation support only late binding. All Office 2000 applications and most contemporary applications that support Automation support both early and late binding. However, scripting languages such as VBScript and JavaScript don't support early binding because they don't support references or specific object data types (for example, in VBScript only the **Variant** data type is supported).

Early-Bound Declarations

Early binding allows you to declare an object variable as a programmatic identifier, or class name, rather than as an **Object** or a **Variant** data type. The programmatic identifier of an application is stored in the Windows registry as a subkey below the \HKEY_CLASSES_ROOT subtree. For example, the programmatic identifier for Access is "Access.Application"; for Excel it is "Excel.Application."

When you are using early binding, you can initialize the object variable by using the **CreateObject** or **GetObject** function or by using the **New** keyword if the application supports it. All Office 2000 applications can be initialized by using the **New** keyword. Because the Outlook 2000 programming environment for Outlook items supports only scripting, you can't use early binding declarations of any sort in its VBScript programming environment; however, you can use early binding in VBA code in a local Outlook VBA project or COM add-in, or in Automation code that works with Outlook from another host application.

Early binding is the friendly name for what C programmers call virtual function table binding, or vtable binding. In order to use early binding, the host application must establish a reference to a type library (.tlb) or an object library (.olb), or an .exe, .dll, or .ocx file that contains type information about the objects, methods, properties, and events of the application or service you want to automate.

In the following code fragment, an **Application** variable is declared by using the programmatic identifier for Word (**Word.Application**) and a new instance of Word is created by using the **Set** statement with the **New** keyword:

```
Dim wdApp As Word.Application
Set wdApp = New Word.Application
```

If the code following these lines doesn't set the **Application** object's **Visible** property to **True**, the new instance of Word will be hidden. All Office applications are hidden by default when they are automated from another application.

Use early binding whenever possible. Early binding has the following advantages:

- **Syntax checking** When you use early binding, VBA checks the syntax of your statements against the syntax stored in the object library during compilation rather than checking it at run time, so that you can catch and address errors at design time. For example, VBA can determine if you are using valid properties or methods of an object, and if you are passing valid arguments to those properties and methods.
- **Support for statement-building tools** When you use early binding, the Visual Basic Editor supports features that make writing code much easier and less prone to errors, such as automatic listing of an object's properties and methods, and pop-up tips for named arguments.
- **Support for built-in constants** When you use early binding, your code can refer to the built-in constants for method arguments and property settings because this information is available from the type library at design time. If you use late binding, you must define these constants in your code by looking up the values in the application's documentation.
- **Better performance** Performance is significantly faster with early binding than with late binding.

Late-Bound Declarations

Late binding allows you to declare a variable as an **Object** or a **Variant** data type. The variable is initialized by calling the **GetObject** or **CreateObject** function and specifying the application's programmatic identifier. For example, in the following code fragment, an **Object** variable is declared and then set to an instance of Access by using the **CreateObject** function:

```
Dim objApp As Object
Set objApp = CreateObject("Access.Application")
```

Late binding is the friendly name for what C programmers used to call IDispatch binding, and was the first method of binding implemented in applications that can control other applications through Automation. For this reason, you can use late binding to maintain backward compatibility with older applications. However, late binding uses a lot of overhead; it is faster than dynamic data exchange (DDE), but slower than early binding.

Tip DDE is a protocol that was established before OLE for exchanging data between Windows applications. There is no need to use DDE to exchange data between Office applications because of their support for Automation. However, you may have to use DDE from some other application that doesn't support Automation code in order to work with data from an Office application. For more information about using DDE, search the Visual Basic Reference Help for the Office application you want to work with.

The **CreateObject** function must also be used to work with objects from any Automation component from script. This is because scripting has no method of establishing references to type libraries to support early binding.

Creating an Object Variable to Automate Another Office Application

Working with the objects in another Office application through VBA code is very similar to using code to work with the objects within the code's host application. In most cases, you begin by creating an object variable that points to the **Application** object representing the Office application that contains the objects you want to work with. In general, you create an early-bound object variable by using the **New** keyword. However, there are limited circumstances where you may choose to use the **CreateObject** or **GetObject** function to create an object variable. For more information, see "Using the CreateObject and GetObject Functions" later in this chapter.

When you write VBA code in an application that manipulates objects within that same application, the reference to the **Application** object is implicit. When you are automating another application, the reference to the **Application** object generally must be explicit. The following two examples illustrate this difference. The first example contains VBA code intended to be run in Word. The second example contains VBA code intended to be run from another Office application (or any application that supports Automation through VBA). For the second example to work, a reference must be set to the Microsoft Word 9.0 object library in the application the code is run from.

```
Sub CodeRunningInsideWord()
   Dim docNew As Word.Document

   ' Add new document to Documents collection.
   Set docNew = Documents.Add
   ' Type text into document.
   Selection.TypeText "Four score and seven years ago"
   ' Display document name and count of words, and then close document without
   ' saving changes.
   With docNew
      MsgBox "'" & .Name & "' contains " & .Words.Count & " words."
      .Close wdDoNotSaveChanges
   End With
   Set docNew = Nothing
End Sub
```

The CodeRunningInsideWord procedure is available in the modSetObjVariable module in Automating&IDE.doc in the Samples\CH04 subfolder on the companion CD-ROM.

```
Sub CodeRunningOutsideWord()
   Dim wdApp    As Word.Application
   Dim docNew   As Word.Document

   ' Create new hidden instance of Word.
   Set wdApp = New Word.Application
   ' Create a new document.
   Set docNew = wdApp.Documents.Add
   ' Add text to document.
   wdApp.Selection.TypeText "Four score and seven years ago"
   ' Display document name and count of words, and then close
   ' document without saving changes.
   With docNew
      MsgBox "'" & .Name & "' contains " & .Words.Count & " words."
      .Close wdDoNotSaveChanges
   End With
   wdApp.Quit
   Set wdApp = Nothing
End Sub
```

The CodeRunningOutsideWord procedure is available in the modGetRecords module in AutomatingWord.xls in the Samples\CH04 subfolder on the companion CD-ROM.

In most cases, you will create an object variable that refers to the top-level object representing the application you want to access through Automation, the **Application** object. Once you have the reference to the **Application** object, you use additional references to that object's child objects to navigate to the object or method you want to manipulate. You assign object variables to child objects by using a method of a higher-level object with the **Set** statement. However, Excel and Word also allow you to create a top-level reference to certain child objects of the **Application** object. For this reason, it is possible to rewrite the previous CodeRunningOutsideWord procedure to start from a reference to a Word **Document** object, like this:

```
Sub CodeRunningOutsideWord2()
   Dim docNew As Word.Document

   Set docNew = New Word.Document
   Set docNew = Documents.Add
   ' The following line uses the Application property to access the
   ' implicit instance of the Word Application object.
   docNew.Application.Selection.TypeText "Four score and seven years ago"
   With docNew
      MsgBox "'" & .Name & "' contains " & .Words.Count & " words."
      .Close wdDoNotSaveChanges
   End With
   docNew.Application.Quit
   Set docNew = Nothing
End Sub
```

The CodeRunningOutsideWord2 procedure is available in the modGetRecords module in AutomatingWord.xls in the Samples\CH04 subfolder on the companion CD-ROM.

Similarly, Excel allows you to create a top-level reference starting from the **Workbook** object. You can do this in either of two ways:

- By using the **Excel.Sheet** class name to create a workbook that contains a single worksheet.

  –or–

- By using the **Excel.Chart** class name to create a workbook that contains a worksheet with an embedded Chart object and another worksheet that contains a default data set for the chart.

To create a **Workbook** object either way, you must use the **CreateObject** function, because the **Excel.Sheet** and **Excel.Chart** class names don't support the **New** keyword. For example, to automate Excel starting with a top-level reference to a **Workbook** object that contains a single worksheet, use code like this:

```
Dim wbkSheet As Excel.Workbook
Set wbkSheet = CreateObject("Excel.Sheet")
```

To automate Excel starting with a top-level reference to a **Workbook** object that contains a worksheet with a chart and another worksheet containing a default data set for the chart, use code like this:

```
Dim wbkChart As Excel.Workbook
Set wbkChart = CreateObject("Excel.Chart")
```

When you are automating Word starting from a **Document** object or automating Excel starting from a **Workbook** object, an implicit reference is created to the **Application** object. If you need to access properties and methods of the **Application** object, you can use the **Application** accessor property of the **Document** or **Workbook** objects. While using the **Document** or **Workbook** objects as top-level objects may reduce the amount of code you have to write somewhat, in most cases your code will be easier to understand and more consistent if you start from a reference to the **Application** object.

The following table shows all the top-level Office objects you can reference and their class names.

Object type	Class name
Access **Application**	**Access.Application**
Office **Binder**	**OfficeBinder.Binder**
Excel **Application**	**Excel.Application**
Excel **Workbook**	**Excel.Sheet** **Excel.Chart**
FrontPage **Application**	**FrontPage.Application**
Outlook **Application**	**Outlook.Application**

Object type	Class name
PowerPoint **Application**	**PowerPoint.Application**
Word **Application**	**Word.Application**
Word **Document**	**Word.Document**

You can see the complete object models for each Office application in the "Object Model Diagrams" appendix.

Automating the Visual Basic Editor

In addition to using code to work with other Office applications, you can also use Automation code to work with the objects exposed by the Visual Basic Editor's object model. You can use the Visual Basic Editor's object model to work with the objects in its user interface, such as its windows and command bars, which allows you to develop add-ins to customize and extend the Visual Basic Editor's user interface. Additionally, you can use the Visual Basic Editor's object model to work with your VBA project itself to add and delete references, to set and read project properties, and to work with the components that make up your project, such as standard modules, class modules, and UserForms. This feature allows you to write code to maintain references, to document and set properties for projects, and to work with existing components and add new ones.

To work with the Visual Basic Editor's objects, first you must establish a reference to its type library, which is named Microsoft Visual Basic for Applications Extensibility 5.3. To write code to work with the Visual Basic Editor, you must initialize a variable to work with the Visual Basic Editor's top-level object, the **VBE** object. However, you can't reference the **VBE** object directly. This is because the Visual Basic Editor isn't an independent application or service; it's running as part of the host application's process. To initialize an object variable to work with the Visual Basic Editor, you must use the **VBE** accessor property of the host application's **Application** object. The following example shows how to initialize an object variable to work with the Visual Basic Editor:

```
Dim objVBE As VBIDE.VBE

Set objVBE = Application.VBE
```

To see code samples that use the Visual Basic Editor's object model to display VBA project property and component information, see modProjectInfo in Automating&IDE.doc in the Samples\CH04 subfolder on the companion CD-ROM. For information about creating COM add-ins for the Visual Basic Editor, see Chapter 11, "Add-ins, Templates, Wizards, and Libraries." For an overview of working with the Visual Basic Editor's object model, see the *Visual Basic Language Developer's Handbook* by Ken Getz and Mike Gilbert (Sybex, 1999).

Automating the Visual Basic Editor (*continued*)

Note The Access **Application** object provides a **References** collection and **Reference** object that allow you to work with references in an Access VBA project without requiring you to establish a reference to the Microsoft Visual Basic for Applications Extensibility 5.3 type library. To view a code sample, see the ReferenceInfo procedure in the modReferences module in Startup.mdb in the Samples\CH04 subfolder on the companion CD-ROM. For more information about the Access **References** collection, search the Microsoft Access Visual Basic Reference Help index for "References collection."

Using the Set Statement and the New Keyword

You start Automation code by declaring object variables with a specific object type that represents the top-level object and then declaring any child objects you want to reference. You then create an instance of the top-level object by using the **Set** statement and the **New** keyword. However, the **New** keyword can't be used to create a new instance of a child object. To create an instance of a child object, use the appropriate method of the parent object along with the **Set** statement.

In the following example, the top-level Excel **Application** object variable is assigned by using the **Set** statement and the **New** keyword. The object variable representing the **Workbook** child object is assigned by using the parent object's **Add** method and the **Set** statement.

```
Sub CreateExcelObjects()
   Dim xlApp          As Excel.Application
   Dim wkbNewBook     As Excel.Workbook
   Dim wksSheet       As Excel.Worksheet
   Dim strBookName    As String

   ' Create new hidden instance of Excel.
   Set xlApp = New Excel.Application
   ' Add new workbook to Workbooks collection.
   Set wkbNewBook = xlApp.Workbooks.Add
   ' Specify path to save workbook.
   strBookName = "c:\my documents\xlautomation.xls"
   ' Loop through each worksheet and append " - By Automation" to the
   ' name of each sheet. Close and save workbook to specified path.
   With wkbNewBook
      For Each wksSheet In .Worksheets
         wksSheet.Name = wksSheet.Name & " - By Automation"
      Next wksSheet
      .Close SaveChanges:=True, FileName:=strBookName
   End With

   Set wkbNewBook = Nothing
   XlApp.Quit
   Set xlApp = Nothing
End Sub
```

The CreateExcelObjects procedure uses three Excel object variables, but only the first two are instantiated by using the **Set** statement. You do not need to use the **Set** statement to create an object variable that will be used only inside a **For...Each** loop. The CreateExcelObjects procedure is available in the modSetObjVariable module in Automating&IDE.doc in the Samples\CH04 subfolder on the companion CD-ROM.

In the next example, the top-level Outlook **Application** object is created by using the **Set** statement and the **New** keyword. The **MailItem** child object variable is created by using the **Application** object's **CreateItem** method. The **Recipient** child object is created by using the **Add** method of the **MailItem** object's **Recipients** collection.

```
Sub CreateOutlookMail()
   Dim olApp                  As Outlook.Application
   Dim olMailMessage          As Outlook.MailItem
   Dim olRecipient            As Outlook.Recipient
   Dim blnKnownRecipient      As Boolean

   ' Create new instance of Outlook or open current instance.
   Set olApp = New Outlook.Application
   ' Create new message.
   Set olMailMessage = olApp.CreateItem(olMailItem)
   ' Prompt for message recipient, attempt to resolve address, and
   ' then send or display.
   With olMailMessage
      Set olRecipient = .Recipients.Add(InputBox("Enter name of message recipient", _
         "Recipient Name"))
      blnKnownRecipient = olRecipient.Resolve
      .Subject = "Testing mail by Automation"
      .Body = "This message was created by VBA code running " _
         & "Outlook through Automation."
      If blnKnownRecipient = True Then
         .Send
      Else
         .Display
      End If
   End With
   Set olMailMessage = Nothing
   olApp.Quit
   Set olApp = Nothing
End Sub
```

The CreateOutlookMail procedure is available in the modSetObjVariable module in Automating&IDE.doc in the Samples\CH04 subfolder on the companion CD-ROM. Note that at the end of this procedure, each object variable is destroyed by explicitly setting it equal to the **Nothing** keyword. For more information about destroying object variables, see "Shutting Down an Object Created by Using Automation" later in this chapter.

Tip You can also use the **New** keyword to create a new instance of the object at the same time you declare its object variable. For example:

```
Dim olApp As New Outlook.Application
```

If you do this, there is no need to use a **Set** statement to instantiate the object. However, this technique is not recommended because you have no control over when the object variable is created. For example, if your code needs to test to see if an object exists by using a statement such as `If olApp Is Nothing Then`, this test will return **True** if you have created an instance of the object in the **Dim** statement. Additionally, you may not need to use an object except at the user's request. If you create an instance of the object by using **New** in the **Dim** statement, the object will be created even if it isn't used. To maintain control over when an object is created, don't use the **New** keyword in the **Dim** statement, and instantiate the object by using a **Set** statement at the point in your code where you need to use the object.

Single-Use vs. Multi-Use Applications

Whether you return a reference to a new instance of the **Application** object or an existing instance depends on whether the application's default behavior is as a *single-use* or a *multi-use* application. A single-use application causes a new instance of that application to be created whenever an object variable is instantiated in any host application. For example, Microsoft Word is a single-use application, so the following code creates a new instance of Microsoft Word regardless of how many instances of Word may already be running:

```
Dim wdApp As Word.Application
Set wdApp = New Word.Application
```

A multi-use application allows host applications to share the same instance of the application. The next example creates a new instance of Microsoft Outlook only if Outlook is not running when the code is executed. Since Outlook is a multi-use application, if Outlook is already running when this code is run, the object variable points to the currently running instance.

```
Dim olApp As Outlook.Application
Set olApp = New Outlook.Application
```

The following table shows the default behavior for each Office application.

Application	Application type
Access	Single-use
Binder	Single-use
Excel	Single-use
FrontPage	Single-use
Outlook	Multi-use
PowerPoint	Multi-use
Word	Single-use

You can use the **GetObject** function to create an object variable that references a currently running instance of a single-use application.

If you create an object variable that points to a multi-use application (Outlook or PowerPoint) and an instance of the application is already running, any method you use to create the object variable will return a reference to the running instance. For example, if Outlook is already running, the following lines of code all return a reference to the same instance of Outlook:

```
Dim olApp1 As Outlook.Application
Dim olApp2 As Outlook.Application
Dim olApp3 As Outlook.Application

Set olApp1 = New Outlook.Application
Set olApp2 = CreateObject("Outlook.Application")
Set olApp3 = GetObject(, "Outlook.Application")
```

Using the CreateObject and GetObject Functions

You can use the **Set** statement with the **CreateObject** and **GetObject** functions to create a top-level object variable that represents an Office application. These functions should be used only in those situations where the **New** keyword does not provide the functionality you need.

You use the **CreateObject** function to create a top-level object variable that represents an Office application in the following two situations:

- The Office application for which you want to create an Application object is not available on the local computer but is available on some other computer on your network. For example, you can run VBA code that prints reports from an Access database that is located on a network server even though Access is not installed on the computer from which the code is run. If Access is installed on the network server, you can create an Access Application object that runs on the server by specifying the name of the server in the **CreateObject** function's optional *servername* argument. For example:

  ```
  Dim objAcApp As Object
  Set objAcApp = CreateObject("Access.Application", "MyServer1")
  ```

  The *servername* argument of the **CreateObject** function is the same as the machine name portion of a share name. Therefore, for a share named \\MyServer1\Public, the *servername* argument is "MyServer1".

  To successfully run an Office application as a remote server, you must configure Distributed Component Object Model (DCOM) settings on the computer that is acting as a server, and also possibly on the client computers. To configure DCOM, run the Distributed COM Configuration utility (Dcomcnfg.exe) from the **Run** box on the **Startup** menu. For more information about configuring DCOM, search the Microsoft Technical Support Web site (http://support.microsoft.com/support) for "Configure DCOM."

- The **CreateObject** function is also useful when you are not sure if the Office application you want to automate will be installed on the computer that runs your code. The following example illustrates how to use the **CreateObject** function to make sure an application is available for Automation:

```
Sub CreateObjectExample()
   Dim objApp As Object

   Const ERR_APP_NOTFOUND As Long = 429

   On Error Resume Next

   ' Attempt to create late-bound instance of Access application.
   Set objApp = CreateObject("Access.Application")
   If Err = ERR_APP_NOTFOUND Then
      MsgBox "Access isn't installed on this computer. " _
         & "Could not automate Access."
      Exit Sub
   End If
   With objApp
      ' Code to automate Access here.
      .Quit
   End With
   Set objApp = Nothing
End Sub
```

  The CreateObjectExample procedure is available in the modSetObjVariable module in Automating&IDE.doc in the Samples\CH04 subfolder on the companion CD-ROM. Note that the **Application** object variable in this procedure is declared by using the **Object** data type and is late-bound to the application by using the **CreateObject** function. The code must be written this way because if an object variable is declared as a specific **Application** object type and that application is not present, the code will break.

Note The **CreateObject** function also must be used to work with objects from any Automation component from script. This is because scripting has no method of establishing references to type libraries to support early binding. However, for security reasons, you wouldn't typically use the **CreateObject** function from script to create an instance of an Office application.

You can use the **GetObject** function in these situations:

- You need to create a reference to a running instance of an application. For example, the following code creates a reference to the running instance of Access. If Access is not running when the code executes, a **Set** statement is used to create an object variable for the Access **Application** object.

```
Sub GetObjectExample()
   Dim acApp As Access.Application

   Const ERR_APP_NOTRUNNING As Long = 429

   On Error Resume Next

   ' Attempt to reference running instance of Access.
   Set acApp = GetObject(, "Access.Application")
   ' If Access isn't running, create a new instance.
   If Err = ERR_APP_NOTRUNNING Then
      Set acApp = New Access.Application
   End If
   With acApp
      ' Code to automate Access here.
   End With
   ' If instance of Access was started by this code,
   ' shut down application.
   If Not acApp.UserControl Then
      acApp.Quit
      Set acApp = Nothing
   End If
End Sub
```

The GetObjectExample procedure is available in the modSetObjVariable module in Automating&IDE.doc in the Samples\CH04 subfolder on the companion CD-ROM.

Note If multiple instances of the application you want to automate are running, there is no way to guarantee which instance the **GetObject** function will return. For example, if two sessions of Access are running and you use the **GetObject** function to retrieve an instance of Access from code running in Excel, there's no way to guarantee which instance of Access will be used.

There are few circumstances where it makes sense to use the **GetObject** function to return a reference to a running instance of an Office application. If a user opened the running instance, you would rarely want your code to be manipulating the objects in that instance of the application. However, when you use the **Shell** function to start an Access application (so that you can supply a password and workgroup information file to open a secured database), it does make sense to work with the running instance of Access by using the **GetObject** function to return a reference to the instance of Access that you started. To see an example of how to use the **GetObject** function to open a secured Access database, see the GetSecureDb procedure in the modSetObjVariable module in Automating&IDE.doc in the Samples\CH04 subfolder on the companion CD-ROM.

Note You cannot use the **GetObject** function to return a reference to a running instance of the Office Binder.

- You also use the **GetObject** function when you need to open an Office file and return a reference to the host application object at the same time. The following example shows how to use the **GetObject** function to open an Access database from disk and return a reference to the Access application. When HTML is passed as the value for the *lngRptType* argument, the procedure creates a Web page from a report and displays that page in a Web browser.

```
Function GetReport(Optional lngRptType As opgRptType) As Boolean
   ' This function outputs a report in the format specified by
   ' the optional lngRptType argument. If lngRptType is specified,
   ' the report is automatically opened in the corresponding
   ' application.
   ' lngRptType can be any of the following constants defined
   ' by Enum opgRptType in the Declarations section of this
   ' module:
   '    XLS = output to Excel
   '    RTF = output to Rich Text Format
   '    SNAPSHOT = output to Access snapshot report format
   '    HTML = output to HTML
   ' If lngRptType is not specified, the report is opened in
   ' Access and displayed in Print Preview.

   Dim acApp            As Access.Application
   Dim strReportName    As String
   Dim strReportPath    As String

   Const SAMPLE_DB_PATH As String = "c:\program files\" _
      & "microsoft office\office\samples\northwind.mdb"

   strReportName = "Alphabetical List of Products"
   strReportPath = "c:\my documents\"
   ' Start Access and open Northwind Traders database.
```

```
        Set acApp = GetObject(SAMPLE_DB_PATH, "Access.Application")
        With acApp
           ' Output or display in specified format.
           With .DoCmd
              Select Case lngRptType
                 Case XLS
                 .OutputTo acOutputReport, strReportName, _
                    acFormatXLS, strReportPath & "autoxls.xls", True
                 Case RTF
                 .OutputTo acOutputReport, strReportName, _
                    acFormatRTF, strReportPath & "autortf.rtf", True
                 ' Snapshot Viewer must be installed to view snapshot
                 ' output.
                 Case SNAPSHOT
                 .OutputTo acOutputReport, strReportName, _
                    acFormatSNP, strReportPath & "autosnap.snp", True
                 Case HTML
                 .OutputTo acOutputReport, strReportName, _
                    acFormatHTML, strReportPath & "autohtml.htm", _
                    True, "NWINDTEM.HTM"
                 Case Else
                 acApp.Visible = True
                 .OpenReport strReportName, acViewPreview
              End Select
           End With
           ' Close Access if this code created current instance.
           If Not .UserControl Then
              acApp.Quit
              Set acApp = Nothing
           End If
        End With
     End Function
```

The GetReport procedure is available in the modSetObjVariable module in Automating&IDE.doc in the Samples\CH04 subfolder on the companion CD-ROM.

Working with Documents That Contain Startup Code

Using Automation to open a document does not prevent a document's startup code from running. Startup code can be defined in various ways in Office applications, as explained in the following table.

Application	Startup code location
Word	Startup code is contained in the event procedures for the Open or New events in the ThisDocument module of a document or template.
Excel	Startup code is contained in the event procedure for the Open event in the ThisWorkbook module of a workbook or template.
Outlook	Startup code is contained in the event procedures for the Startup event in the ThisOutlookSession of the local Outlook VBA project.

Application	Startup code location
Access	If you create an Access macro named AutoExec, this macro's actions will run on startup. You can also place startup code in the event procedure for the startup form's Open event. To specify a form to be opened on startup, use the **Startup** command on the **Tools** menu.

Note PowerPoint and FrontPage documents don't have a way to define startup code.

Because startup code may display message boxes or modal forms that act as dialog boxes, these message or dialog boxes may prevent your code from proceeding until a user closes or responds to them. If you have startup code in an Excel workbook or Access database that you don't want to run if the document is opened programmatically from another application, you can often use the **UserControl** property of the **Application** object to determine how a document is being opened and then act accordingly. If you can't use the **UserControl** property, you may need to use a **SendKeys** statement to send keystrokes to close the message or dialog box.

In Excel, the **UserControl** property will return **False** only when the document or workbook is opened from Automation by using a hidden instance of the Excel **Application** object (`Application.Visible = False`). For example, the following code defined in an Excel workbook's Open event procedure will run only if the workbook is opened by a user or a visible instance of the Excel **Application** object. If you open the workbook by using a hidden instance of the Excel **Application** object from code running in another application, the message box won't be displayed.

```
Private Sub Workbook_Open()
   Dim strMsg As String

   strMsg = "This message was triggered by this workbook's " & _
         "Open event." & vbCrLf & _
         "It won't be displayed if this workbook " & _
         "is opened by using a hidden" & vbCrLf & _
         "instance of the Excel Application object " & _
         "from Automation code."

   ' If opened through Automation by using a hidden instance,
   ' the UserControl property will be False.
   If Application.UserControl = True Then
      MsgBox strMsg
   End If
End Sub
```

The Workbook_Open procedure is available in the ThisWorkbook module in AutomatingWord.xls in the Samples\CH04 subfolder on the companion CD-ROM.

Note In Word 2000 and Word 97, there is no way to prevent Open event code from running with the **UserControl** property. If Word is visible to the user, or if you call the **UserControl** property of a Word **Application** or **Document** object from within a Word code module, this property will always return **True**. However, you can still use the Word **UserControl** property from Automation code (that creates a hidden instance of Word) running from another application to determine if a document was opened programmatically or by the user.

In Access, you don't have to check or keep track of whether the instance of the **Application** object is hidden or visible because the **UserControl** property is **False** whenever the application is started from code. To control whether code in the startup form's Open event is executed, Access provides a *Cancel* argument for the Open event. As shown in the following example, you can set the *Cancel* argument to **True** to keep a startup form from opening if you open the database by using Automation code:

```
Private Sub Form_Open (Cancel As Integer)
   ' If database is opened from Automation,
   ' cancel the Open event of the form.
   If Application.UserControl = False Then
      Cancel = True
   Else
   ' Any startup code that needs to run when the
   ' database is opened by a user goes here.
   End If
End Sub
```

The Form_Open procedure is available in the Form_frmStartup module in Startup.mdb in the Samples\CH04 subfolder on the companion CD-ROM.

You can also use the **UserControl** property of the Access **Application** object to control whether actions in a database's AutoExec macro will run when the database is opened from another program by using Automation. To do this, you must enter `Application.UserControl = True` in the **Condition** column for each action you want to cancel. (To display the **Condition** column, click **Conditions** on the **View** menu.) To see an example of an AutoExec macro that cancels an action when the database is opened through Automation, open Startup.mdb in the Samples\CH04 subfolder on the companion CD-ROM and then open the AutoExec macro in Design view.

Tip You can also use COM add-ins to implement a startup form or code. COM add-ins support events that you can use to determine how an application was loaded before connecting the add-in. For more information about COM add-ins, see Chapter 11, "Add-ins, Templates, Wizards, and Libraries."

Shutting Down an Object Created by Using Automation

A local variable is normally destroyed when the procedure in which it is declared is finished executing. However, it is good programming practice to explicitly destroy an application-level object variable used to automate another application by setting it equal to the **Nothing** keyword. Doing this frees any remaining memory used by the variable. For some **Application** objects, you may also have to use the object's **Quit** method to completely destroy an object variable and free up the memory it is using. As a general rule, it's safest to do both: Use the **Quit** method and then set the object variable equal to the **Nothing** keyword.

Note For the **OfficeBinder** object, use the **Close** method instead of the **Quit** method and then set the object variable equal to the **Nothing** keyword.

To see examples of how to destroy application-level object variables, see the code in the CreateExcelObjects and CreateOutlookMail procedures in the modSetObjVariable module in Automating&IDE.doc in the Samples\CH04 subfolder on the companion CD-ROM.

There may be situations where you need to determine if the instance of an application you are working with was created by your code before shutting it down. Generally, you can inspect the **UserControl** property of the **Application** object to determine if your code opened the current instance. However, there are cases where the value of the **UserControl** property can change from **False** to **True** as your code executes. For example, if you start Excel through Automation, make it visible, and allow the user to interact with this instance, such as by typing something in a cell, the **UserControl** property will return **True** even though your code started the instance. To handle this situation, assign the value of the **UserControl** property to a variable right after you create the instance of the **Application** object, and use this variable to test the value of the **UserControl** property before closing the application, as shown in the following example:

```
Sub GetObjectXL()
   Dim xlApp              As Excel.Application
   Dim blnUserControl     As Boolean

   Const ERR_APP_NOTRUNNING As Long = 429

   ' Set blnUserControl to True as default.
   blnUserControl = True
   On Error Resume Next
   ' Attempt to open current instance of Excel.
   Set xlApp = GetObject(, "Excel.Application")
   ' If no instance, create new instance.
   If Err = ERR_APP_NOTRUNNING Then
      Set xlApp = New Excel.Application
      ' Store current state of UserControl property.
      blnUserControl = xlApp.UserControl
   End If
```

```
    With xlApp
        ' Code to automate Excel here.
        ' Check original value of UserControl property.
        If blnUserControl = False Then
            xlApp.Quit
            Set xlApp = Nothing
        End If
    End With
End Sub
```

The GetObjectXL procedure is available in the modSetObjVariable module in Automating&IDE.doc in the Samples\CH04 subfolder on the companion CD-ROM.

Note PowerPoint, Outlook, and FrontPage have no method of determining if an instance of the **Application** object has been started by a user or program. For information about how the **UserControl** property works in Word, see the previous section, "Working with Documents That Contain Startup Code."

Where to Go from Here

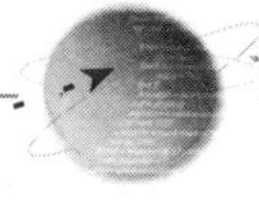

For additional information about the subjects discussed in this chapter, see the following sources.

Visual Basic for Applications

Visual Basic for Applications Web site
(http://msdn.microsoft.com/vba/)

VBA Objects Web site
(http://www.inquiry.com/objects/)

Getz, Ken, and Mike Gilbert. *Visual Basic Language Developer's Handbook.* Alameda, CA: Sybex, 1999.

VBScript

Chapter 12, "Using Web Technologies"

Microsoft Scripting Technologies Web site
(http://msdn.microsoft.com/scripting/)

Application-Specific Automation Examples

Chapter 5, "Working with Office Applications"

Byrne, Randy. *Building Applications with Microsoft Outlook 2000.* Redmond, WA: Microsoft Press, 1999.

Microsoft Office Developer Forum Web site
(http://www.microsoft.com/officedev/)

Automating Shared Office Components

Chapter 6, "Working with Shared Office Components"

Microsoft Office Developer Forum Web site
(http://www.microsoft.com/officedev/)

Creating Your Own Classes and Objects

Chapter 9, "Custom Classes and Objects"

Automating and Extending Applications by Using Add-ins

Chapter 11, "Add-ins, Templates, Wizards, and Libraries"

Microsoft Office Developer Forum Web site
(http://www.microsoft.com/officedev/)

Configuring DCOM Settings

Microsoft Technical Support Web site
(http://support.microsoft.com/support)

Object Model Diagrams

"Object Model Diagrams" appendix

VBA Objects Web site
(http://www.inquiry.com/objects/)

Code Samples

The code samples shown in this chapter, along with additional examples demonstrating similar techniques, can be copied from the files in the Samples\CH04 subfolder on the companion CD-ROM.

CHAPTER 5

Working with Office Applications

As an Office developer, you are probably well versed in at least one of the Microsoft Office applications. However, when you need to build a solution based on an Office application that you are not familiar with, you may find it difficult to get started because each Office application exposes an object model with hundreds of different objects, collections of objects, properties, methods, and events.

This chapter is designed to give you an introduction to the objects that you will use most often in each of the Office applications. This introduction should give you the head start you will need to become immediately productive when you are working with Visual Basic for Applications (VBA) in any Office application or when you are driving another application through Automation (formerly called OLE Automation).

Note For information about working with events and event procedures in Office applications, see Chapter 4, "Understanding Office Objects and Object Models." For information about deploying solutions based on Office applications, see Chapter 2, "Designing and Deploying Office Solutions."

Contents

Working with Microsoft Access Objects

Working with Microsoft Access objects primarily means working with **Form**, **Report**, and **DataAccessPage** objects and the controls they contain. You can use these powerful Access objects to format and display data and allow the user to add or edit data in a database. In addition, Access exposes many other objects you can use to work with your Access application; among the most important are the **CurrentProject**, **CurrentData**, **CodeProject**, **CodeData**, **Screen**, and **DoCmd** objects and the **Modules** and **References** collections. This section presents an overview of how to work with Access objects by using VBA.

Note You can view the entire Access object model in the "Object Model Diagrams" appendix. You can also use the Object Browser and Microsoft Access Visual Basic Reference Help to learn more about individual objects, properties, methods, and events. For more information about using VBA to work with an Office application's object model, see Chapter 4, "Understanding Office Objects and Object Models."

Tables and relationships, the data in tables, and queries are managed and maintained by a database engine. For .mdb-type databases, Access uses the Microsoft Jet database engine. For .adp-type databases, Access uses the Microsoft SQL Server database engine or any other ActiveX Data Objects (ADO) data source. You programmatically work with tables, data in tables, or queries by using ADO or Data Access Objects (DAO). For information about using ADO and DAO to work with data in Office applications, see the chapters in Part 3, "Working with Data in Office Solutions."

Working with the Access Developer Solutions Sample Database

The coding techniques discussed in this section, along with many other techniques, are demonstrated and documented in the Developer Solutions sample database (Solutions9.mdb) and its accompanying Help file (Solutn80.hlp). You can find this database and Help file in the Samples\CH05 subfolder on the companion CD-ROM.

The Developer Solutions sample database, along with some of the code samples used in this section, depends on the existence of the Northwind Traders sample database (Northwind.mdb) that is installed with Microsoft Access 2000. The Northwind Traders sample database is installed in the C:\Program Files \Microsoft Office\Office\Samples subfolder by default.

Understanding the Access Application Object

The **Application** object is the top-level object in the Access object model. It provides properties and methods you can use to create and work with other Access objects. It also provides several built-in functions you can use to work with the objects in your database. In essence, the **Application** object serves as the gateway to all other Access objects.

Setting Application Options

Application-wide options are available through the **Options** dialog box and the **Startup** dialog box. The commands to open these dialog boxes are located on the **Tools** menu. You can use the **Options** dialog box to specify or determine application-wide settings, such as whether the status bar is displayed, the new database sort order, and the default record-locking settings. You use the **Startup** dialog box to specify or determine settings such as which form opens automatically when your database opens and your database application's title and icon. The following sections discuss how you can use VBA to access all of these settings.

Working with the Options Dialog Box Settings

You use the **Application** object's **SetOption** and **GetOption** methods to specify or determine the settings in the **Options** dialog box. Both methods use a string argument that identifies the option you want to access. The **SetOption** method takes an additional argument representing the value you want to set. For example, the following code displays a message box that indicates whether datasheet gridlines are turned on:

```
MsgBox "Horizontal Gridlines On = " & _
   CBool(GetOption("Default Gridlines Horizontal")) & vbCrLf _
   & "Vertical Gridlines On = " & CBool(GetOption("Default Gridlines Vertical"))
```

The next example illustrates how you can use the **SetOption** method to specify a new default database folder:

```
SetOption "Default Database Directory", "C:\NewMDBs"
```

To see a list of all the string arguments used to access settings in the **Options** dialog box, search the Microsoft Access Visual Basic Reference Help index for "options, setting," open the topic "Set Startup Properties and Options in Code," and then jump to the topic "Set Options from Visual Basic."

The value returned by the **GetOption** method and the value you pass to the **SetOption** method as the *setting* argument depend on the type of option you are using. The following table establishes some guidelines for **Options** dialog box settings.

If the option is	Then the value of the option is
A text box	A string or numeric value
A check box	An integer that will be **True** (-1) (selected) or **False** (0) (not selected)
An option button in an option group, or an item in a combo box or a list box	An integer corresponding to the item's position in the option group or list (starting with 0 for the first item, 1 for the second item, and so on)

Important If you use the **SetOption** method to change a user's **Options** dialog box settings, be sure to restore those settings when your code is finished executing or when your application ends. Otherwise, the settings you specify will be applied to any database the user opens. Note that the settings in the **Options** dialog box are stored in the Windows registry in the \HKEY_CURRENT_USER\Software\Microsoft\Office\9.0\Access\Settings subkey. As a result, changes to these settings will not persist if the database is run on a different machine.

Understanding Startup Properties

You use startup properties to customize how a database application appears when it is opened. You work with startup properties differently than you do the settings in the **Options** dialog box. Each option in the **Startup** dialog box has a corresponding Access property, but you won't find these properties in the Object Browser. In a new database, the startup properties do not exist until a user makes a change to the default settings in the **Startup** dialog box.

To set these properties programmatically for an .mdb-type database, you must first add each property to the **Properties** collection of the **Database** object. This is true whether you are using DAO or ADO. In other words, even without a reference to DAO, you still use the **Properties** collection of the **Database** object to work with these properties. In an .adp-type database, startup properties are stored in the **Properties** collection of the **CurrentProject** object.

In the following sample, the AddCustomProperty sample procedure is used to set the **AppTitle** property in an .mdb-type database. Note that if the property does not exist when the AddCustomProperty procedure is called, the property is created and appended to the **Properties** collection of the **Database** object.

```
Const TEXT_VALUE As Integer = 10
If AddCustomProperty("AppTitle", TEXT_VALUE, "MyDatabase") Then
   ' Property added to collection.
End If

Function AddCustomProperty(strName As String, _
                           varType As Variant, _
                           varValue As Variant) As Boolean
   ' The following generic object variables are required
   ' when there is no reference to the DAO 3.6 object library.
   Dim objDatabase As Object
   Dim objProperty As Object

   Const PROP_NOT_FOUND_ERROR = 3270

   Set objDatabase = CurrentDb
   On Error GoTo AddProp_Err
   objDatabase.Properties(strName) = varValue

   AddCustomProperty = True

AddProp_End:
   Exit Function

AddProp_Err:
   If Err = PROP_NOT_FOUND_ERROR Then
      Set prpProperty = objDatabase.CreateProperty(strName, varType, varValue)
      objDatabase.Properties.Append objProperty
      Resume
   Else
      AddCustomProperty = False
      Resume AddProp_End
   End If
End Function
```

The AddCustomProperty procedure is available in the modSolutionsUtilities module in the Solutions9.mdb file in the Samples\CH05 subfolder on the companion CD-ROM.

Important Changes you make to any of the startup properties by using VBA will be available programmatically but will not take effect until the next time the database is opened.

For more information about setting startup properties, search the Microsoft Access Visual Basic Reference Help index for "startup options, setting," open the Help topic "Set Startup Properties and Options in Code," and then jump to "Set Startup Properties from Visual Basic."

Working with Built-in Access Functions and Methods

The Access **Application** object contains several functions and methods you can use to work with data or Access objects or the application itself. These functions and methods appear in the Object Browser as methods of the **Application** object, although they may be referred to as "functions." These functions and methods can be used within Access or from another application by using Automation.

Calling Built-in Access Functions and Methods Without Using an Application Object Variable

To use Automation, you usually have to create an instance of the **Application** object, but you can call built-in Access functions and methods of the **Application** object from other Office applications without first creating an Access **Application** object variable. The only requirements are that you set a reference to the Microsoft Access 9.0 object library in the calling application's VBA project, and that you call the function or method by using the **Access** qualifier, as illustrated in the following example. For example, you could use the following VBA code to call the built-in Access **Eval** function to evaluate a string expression contained in a Microsoft Word bookmark:

```
Dim rngResults As Word.Range
Set rngResults = ActiveDocument.Bookmarks("MathMark").Range
rngResults.Text = Access.Eval(rngResults.Text)
```

Note Direct calls to built-in Access functions and methods, like the one illustrated in the preceding example, automatically create a new instance of Access that remains in memory until the document containing the code that called the function or method is closed. If you want more control over when the instance of Access is created and destroyed, create it by using the **New** keyword or the **CreateObject** or **GetObject** function, and close it by setting the **Application** object variable equal to **Nothing**. For more information about the **New** keyword and the **CreateObject** and **GetObject** functions, see Chapter 4, "Understanding Office Objects and Object Models."

The following table summarizes some of the Access functions and methods available to you from the **Application** object and descriptions of how they might be used.

Function or method	Description
Domain aggregate functions	A domain is simply a set of records defined by a table or query. You use domain aggregate functions to get statistical information about a set of records; for example, to count the number of records or to determine the sum of values in a particular field. These functions use a naming convention that begins with a capital "D"; for example, **DAvg**, **DCount**, **DLookup**, **DSum**, and so on. You can use these functions in VBA code, in a query expression, or in a calculated control on a form or report.
Eval function	You use this function to evaluate a string expression that results in a text string or numeric value. The **Eval** function uses a single argument that either is a string expression that returns a value or is the name of a built-in or user-defined function that returns a string. You can use the **Eval** function in a calculated control, a query expression, a macro, or VBA code.
GUIDFromString and **StringFromGUID** functions	You use these functions to convert a globally unique identifier (GUID) to a **String** value or a **String** value to a GUID. A GUID is a 16-byte value used to uniquely identify an object.
hWndAccessApp method	You can use this method to determine the handle (a unique **Long Integer** value) assigned by Microsoft Windows to the main Access window. You can use the **hWnd** property to determine the handle assigned by Microsoft Windows to an Access Form or Report window.
HyperlinkPart function	The **HyperlinkPart** function returns information about data stored in a field that has the Hyperlink data type; this information is similar to the information contained in the properties of a **Hyperlink** object. You can use this function in VBA code, a query expression, or a calculated control.
LoadPicture method	This method loads a graphic file stored on disk into the **Picture** property of a control. You use this method to set or change the **Picture** property of a control at run time.
Nz function	You use the **Nz** function to evaluate a value and return a specified value if the evaluated value is **Null**. This function is useful when you are assigning values from a field in a recordset to a control that cannot use **Null** values.
SysCmd method	This is the Swiss army knife of Access methods. It can perform a variety of tasks depending on the value of the **acSysCmdAction** constant supplied in its *action* argument. For example, you can use this method to display a progress meter or text in the status bar, return information about Access (such as the directory where Msaccess.exe is located), or to get information about an Access object (such as whether a form is open).

For more information about these functions and methods, search for them by name in the Microsoft Access Visual Basic Reference Help index.

Note In addition to working with built-in Access methods and functions, you can use the **Application** object's **Run** method to call custom procedures stored in an Access database.

Other Objects, Properties, and Methods of the Application Object

This section presents an overview of some of the Access objects you will use most often when you are using VBA to work with Access. For complete documentation about all objects in the Access object model and their methods and properties, search the Microsoft Access Visual Basic Reference Help index for the name of the item you want more information about.

Creating, Opening, and Closing an Access Application

You can create a new database, or open and close an existing database, from within Access or by using Automation from another application. The methods discussed in this section are typically used in Automation from another application. If your code is running inside Access, the code typically works with the currently open database, and using these methods is not necessary.

Note If you are working in another application and you need to access only the data in a database (tables or queries), and not objects such as forms or reports, you use ADO to access the data you need. For more information about using ADO and DAO to work with data in Office applications, see the chapters in Part 3, "Working with Data in Office Solutions."

You use the **NewCurrentDatabase** method to create a new .mdb-type database. You use the **OpenCurrentDatabase** and **CloseCurrentDatabase** methods to open and close an existing .mdb-type database. The following sample is designed to be run from any Office application. It opens the Northwind Traders sample database and prints the portion of the Product Catalog report specified in the **OpenReport** method:

```
Sub PrintReport(strCategoryName As String)
   Dim acApp      As Access.Application
   Dim strDBPath  As String

   Const DB_PATH As String = _
      "c:\program files\microsoft office\office\samples\northwind.mdb"

   Set acApp = New Access.Application
   With acApp
      .OpenCurrentDatabase DB_PATH
      ' Print the Product Catalog report.
      .DoCmd.OpenReport "Catalog", acViewNormal, , _
         "CategoryName = '" & strCategoryName & "'"
   End With
   acApp.Quit
   Set acApp = Nothing
End Sub
```

The PrintReport procedure is available in the modAccessPrintExample module in ExcelSamples.xls file in the Samples\CH05 subfolder on the companion CD-ROM.

You use the **NewAccessProject**, **OpenAccessProject**, or **CreateAccessProject** method to open or create an .adp-type database. The **NewAccessProject** method creates a new .adp-type database and causes it to become active, whereas the **CreateAccessProject** method only creates an .adp file on disk. You use the **OpenAccessProject** method to open an existing .adp-type database and the **CloseCurrentDatabase** method to close an .adp-type database.

Once you create a new database or have a database open, you can use other methods of the **Application** object to create new Access objects. For example, you use the **CreateForm** and **CreateControl** methods to create forms and controls on forms. You use the **CreateReport** and **CreateReportControl** methods to create reports and controls on reports. You use the **CreateDataAccessPage** method to create data access pages. To programmatically add controls to a data access page, you must use script or the Dynamic HTML (DHTML) object model to work with the HTML directly.

Note Although the methods discussed above let you programmatically create a database and the objects it contains, these methods are typically used only in wizards or add-ins. Normally, you create the database and its objects through the Access user interface and then work with these objects programmatically by using VBA code run from Access or another Office application. For more information about creating and using wizards and add-ins, see Chapter 11, "Add-Ins, Templates, Wizards, and Libraries."

Understanding the CurrentData and CurrentProject Objects

In previous versions of Access, you can use DAO objects and their methods and properties to get information about forms, reports, macros, tables, fields, relationships, and queries. For example, you can use **Document** objects to get information about the tables and queries in a database. There are separate **Container** objects representing forms, reports, scripts (Access macros), tables (tables and queries), and modules. Each of these **Container** objects contains a collection of **Document** objects representing all the objects of the specified type in the current database. Each **Document** object contains only summary information about each object and does not provide access to the properties of the object or the data it contains. You use DAO **Recordset** objects to work with the data in a table or query, and you use members of the **Forms** or **Reports** collection to work with forms and reports themselves.

However, in Access 2000, DAO is no longer the default programmatic way to interact with data and objects that contain data; therefore, Access 2000 has two new objects—**CurrentData** and **CurrentProject**—that contain collections of **AccessObject** objects, which are used in place of the **Container** and **Document** objects available through DAO in previous versions.

Access 2000 uses the **CurrentData** object to store collections of **AccessObject** objects that are administered by the database engine; for example, tables and queries in .mdb-type databases, and database diagrams, stored procedures, tables, and views in .adp-type databases. Information about each collection of objects is stored in a collection where each object is represented as an **AccessObject** object.

For example, information about tables is contained in the **AllTables** collection and information about views is stored in the **AllViews** collection. To access the **CurrentData** object, you use the **CurrentData** property of the **Application** object. When code is running in an add-in or library database, you would use the **CodeData** object to refer to the objects managed by the add-in or library database. The **CodeData** property of the **Application** object returns the **CodeData** object.

Note **AccessObject** objects contain information about the objects that contain data, but do not provide access to the data itself. To work with data, you use ADO or DAO. For more information about using ADO and DAO to work with data, see the chapters in Part 3, "Working with Data in Office Solutions."

You use the **CurrentProject** property of the **Application** object to get information about the Access objects in a database, such as data access pages, forms, macros, modules, and reports. The **CurrentProject** property of the **Application** object returns the **CurrentProject** object, which contains collections of **AccessObject** objects as well as information about the name, path, and connection of the database itself. For example, the **AllForms** collection contains information about all the forms in a database, and the **AllReports** collection contains information about all the reports in the database. When code is running in an add-in or library database, the **CodeProject** object contains the collections of **AccessObject** objects in the add-in or library database. The **CodeProject** property of the **Application** object returns the **CodeProject** object.

An **AccessObject** object exposes the following properties you can use to get information about an object: **IsLoaded**, **Name**, **Parent**, **Properties**, and **Type**. These properties are described in the following table.

AccessObject property	Description
IsLoaded	A **Boolean** value indicating whether the object is currently loaded. This property is **True** when an object is open in any view.
Name	A **String** value representing the name of the object.
Parent	Returns the parent object for the specified object. For example, the parent of an item in the **AllForms** collection is the **AllForms** collection object. The parent of the **CurrentProject** object is the **Application** object.
Properties	Returns an **AccessObjectProperties** collection, which contains all the custom properties associated with a particular **AccessObject** object. The **Properties** collection can store **String** or **Long Integer** values only.
Type	A **Long Integer** value representing one of the objects specified by the **acObjectType** intrinsic constants.

Note Collections of **AccessObject** items are indexed beginning with a value of 0 for the first item in the collection, 1 for the second item, and so on.

The following sample shows how you can use the **IsLoaded** property to determine if a form, report, or data access page is currently loaded:

```
With CurrentProject
   Select Case intObjectType
      Case acForm
         IsObjectOpen = .AllForms(strObjName).IsLoaded
      Case acReport
         IsObjectOpen = .AllReports(strObjName).IsLoaded
      Case acDataAccessPage
         IsObjectOpen = .AllDataAccessPages(strObjName).IsLoaded
      Case Else
         Err.Raise ERR_INVALIDOBJTYPE
   End Select
End With
```

The `intObjectType` variable would be passed to a procedure as an argument of type `acObjectType`.

The next sample illustrates how to add custom properties to a form:

```
Sub AddCustomFormProperty(strFormName As String, _
                          strPropName As String, _
                          varPropValue As Variant)
   ' This procedure illustrates how to add custom
   ' properties to the Properties collection that
   ' is associated with an AccessObject object.

   With CurrentProject.AllForms(strFormName).Properties
      .Add strPropName, varPropValue
   End With
End Sub
```

The AddCustomFormProperty procedure is available in the modSolutionsUtilities module in Solutions9.mdb in the Samples\CH05 subfolder on the companion CD-ROM.

Working with the Screen Object

Other Office applications have properties that return a reference to active objects. For example, Word has the **ActiveDocument** property to determine which document currently has the focus. Excel has properties to return the active **Workbook**, **Worksheet**, **Cell**, **Chart**, and **Window** objects. Similarly, PowerPoint has the **ActivePresentation** property to determine the active presentation.

In Access, you use the **Screen** object to work with the object or control that currently has the focus. The **Screen** object has properties that return a reference to the currently active control (on a form or report), data access page, datasheet, form, or report. These properties are useful in code that operates against an object and needs to know only the type of object. For example, the following line of code hides the currently active form:

```
Screen.ActiveForm.Visible = False
```

The next example shows how you can use the **Screen** object to determine which cell in a datasheet is selected:

```
MsgBox "The selected item is located at: Row " _
   & Screen.ActiveDatasheet.SelTop & ", Column " _
   & Screen.ActiveDatasheet.SelLeft
```

The **Screen** object also has properties you can use to work with the previously active control and the mouse pointer.

Important If you try to refer to an object by using properties of the **Screen** object and there is no object of that type currently active, an error occurs.

Working with the DoCmd Object

The **DoCmd** object allows you to carry out various Access commands by using VBA. These commands are called *actions* when they are used in Access macros and are called methods of the **DoCmd** object when they are carried out in code.

Note In other Office applications, the term "macro" is synonymous with a VBA procedure. In Access, macros are completely different from the VBA code you write in a procedure. For more information about Access macros, search the Microsoft Access Help index for "macros, overview," and then open the topic "Macros: What they are and how they work."

Two of the most common tasks that require methods of the **DoCmd** object are opening and closing Access objects. To open an Access object, you use the **DoCmd** object's **Open*Object*** method, where ***Object*** represents the name of the object you want to open. For example, you use the **OpenForm** method to open a form, the **OpenReport** method to open a report, and the **OpenQuery** method to open a query. All of the **Open*Object*** methods take arguments that specify the object to open and how to display the object. For example, the following code opens the Customers form as read-only in Form view (**acNormal**) and specifies that only customers in the USA be shown:

```
DoCmd.OpenForm FormName:="Customers", View:=acNormal, _
   WhereCondition:="Country = 'USA'", DataMode:=acFormReadOnly
```

You can use the **OpenReport** method to open a report in Design view or Print Preview, or you can specify that the report be printed, as in the following example:

```
DoCmd.OpenReport ReportName:="CustomerPhoneList", _
   View:=acViewNormal, WhereCondition:="Country = 'USA'"
```

Note When you use the **acViewNormal** constant in the *view* argument of the **OpenReport** method, the report is not displayed but is printed to the default printer.

You use the **DoCmd** object's **Close** method to close an Access object. You can use the optional arguments of the **Close** method to specify the object to close and whether to save any changes. The following example closes the Customers form without saving changes:

```
DoCmd.Close acForm, "Customers", acSaveNo
```

Note All the arguments of the **Close** method are optional. If you use the method without specifying arguments, the method closes the currently active object.

You can use the **DoCmd** object's **RunCommand** method to run commands that appear on an Access menu or toolbar that do not have separate methods exposed in the Access object model. The **RunCommand** method uses a collection of enumerated constants to represent available menu and toolbar commands. For more information about the **RunCommand** method, search the Microsoft Access Visual Basic Reference Help index for "RunCommand method."

Working with the Modules Collection

The **Modules** collection contains a **Module** object representing each module that is currently opened for editing. The **Module** object may represent a standard or class module that is currently open in the Visual Basic Editor or a module associated with a form or report that is open in Design view. You can use the methods and properties of a **Module** object to get information about the code contained in the module or to insert procedures or lines of code. The objects in this collection are typically used by code running in an add-in or wizard.

For more information about the **Modules** collection and **Module** objects, search the Microsoft Access Visual Basic Reference Help index for "Modules collection" or "Module object."

Working with the References Collection

The **References** collection contains **Reference** objects representing each reference in the **References** dialog box (**Tools** menu in the Visual Basic Editor) to another project or object library. A new Access database contains four references by default. You can add or remove references by using the **References** dialog box or by using methods of the **References** collection in VBA code.

For more information about the **References** collection and **Reference** objects, search the Microsoft Access Visual Basic Reference Help index for "References collection" or "Reference object."

Working with Reports, Forms, and Data Access Pages

Microsoft Access provides three objects you can use to display data to the user: reports, forms, and data access pages. Although these objects have many similar features, they are used in different ways.

Note This section discusses working with forms, reports, and data access pages, but not the data underlying them. For more information about creating a relational database and using ADO and DAO to work with the data stored in a database, see the chapters in Part 3, "Working with Data in Office Solutions."

You use reports to display formatted data. The user cannot edit or add data to a report. Reports can be viewed in the database where they were created or printed. You can also save reports as snapshot files so they can be viewed outside an Access application. For more information about working with snapshot files, search the Microsoft Access Help index for "report snapshots."

You can also use forms to display data to users. But the real power of forms comes from their ability to collect data from users or let users add new records or edit existing records. Forms can also be printed or saved as reports or data access pages.

Note Although Microsoft Access hosts VBA just like the other Office applications, it uses its own built-in forms package. UserForms are not available in Access.

Data access pages combine the features of forms and reports so that you can display data to users and let users interact with data through Microsoft Internet Explorer version 5 or later. (You can also use other Web browsers to display data access pages, but users will not be able to work with the data directly.) Although you design data access pages by using Access, you save them to disk as separate files designed to be used in a Web browser, which means users can work with Access data from within an Access database or over an intranet or the Internet. Data access pages can contain data in an Access database (.mdb file) or Access project (.adp file).

Access forms, reports, and data access pages have numerous properties, methods, and events you can use to specify how the object will look and behave. A complete discussion of all properties, methods, and events is beyond the scope of this section. For information about a specific property, method, or event, search the Microsoft Access Visual Basic Reference Help index for the name of the item you want information about.

You can use the **Application** object's **CreateForm**, **CreateReport**, and **CreateDataAccessPage** methods to programmatically create forms, reports, and data access pages. You can also add controls to these objects through VBA code, but unless you are building an add-in or a wizard, you typically create these objects by using the Access user interface and then display them from code. When you display an object, you can use various properties of the object to specify the records it will contain.

Referring to Open Objects

The **Application** object has properties that return collections of open Access objects. The **Reports** property returns a reference to the **Reports** collection that contains all currently open reports. The **Forms** property returns a reference to the **Forms** collection that contains all currently open forms. The **DataAccessPages** property returns a reference to the **DataAccessPages** collection that contains all currently open data access pages. You specify a member of a collection by using its name or its index value in the collection. You typically use the index valuc only when iterating through all the members of a collection because the index value of an item can change as items are added to or removed from the collection. For example, the following sample uses the form's name to reference the open Customers form:

```
Dim rstCustomers As ADODB.Recordset
Set rstCustomers = Forms("Customers").Recordset
```

The next example closes and saves all open data access pages by looping through the **DataAccessPages** collection:

```
For intPageCount = DataAccessPages.Count - 1 To 0 Step -1
   DoCmd.Close acDataAccessPage, _
      DataAccessPages(intPageCount).Name, acSaveYes
Next intPageCount
```

The **Forms**, **Reports**, and **DataAccessPages** collections contain only open objects. To determine if an object is open, you can use the **IsLoaded** property of an item in the **AllForms**, **AllReports**, or **AllDataAccessPages** collections, or you can use the **SysCmd** method with the **acSysCmdGetObjectState** constant. You can also use the **CurrentView** property to determine if a form is open in Design, Form, or Datasheet view or if a data access page is open in Design or Page view. The following procedure uses the **SysCmd** method and the **CurrentView** property to determine if a form is open in Form or Datasheet view:

```
Function IsLoaded(ByVal strFormName As String) As Boolean
   ' Returns True if the specified form is open in Form view or Datasheet view.

   Const OBJ_STATE_CLOSED = 0
   Const DESIGN_VIEW = 0

   If SysCmd(acSysCmdGetObjectState, acForm, strFormName) <> OBJ_STATE_CLOSED Then
      If Forms(strFormName).CurrentView <> DESIGN_VIEW Then
         IsLoaded = True
      End If
   End If
End Function
```

The IsLoaded procedure is available in the modIsLoaded module in Solutions9.mdb in the Samples\CH05 subfolder on the companion CD-ROM.

The Data Behind Forms and Reports

Most of the forms you create will be designed to display or collect data. Forms can display data for viewing, editing, or input. Forms are also used to create dialog boxes that collect information from a user, but do not display data. Reports display static data only, and aren't used to edit or collect data.

The source of the data behind a form or report is specified by the object's **RecordSource** property. The **RecordSource** property can be a table, query, or SQL statement. You can display subsets of the data contained in the object's **RecordSource** property by using the **Filter** property to filter the data or by using the *wherecondition* argument of the **OpenForm** or **OpenReport** method to specify a subset of data. Once you have specified a record source for a form or report, you can use the field list (in form or report Design view) to drag fields from the object's source of data to the object.

If you set the **RecordSource** property by using VBA, you can use the name of an existing table or query, or an SQL statement. The easiest way to create an SQL statement to use in code, whether from within an Access module or another Office application, is to use the Access query design grid to create a query that displays the appropriate records. Once the query contains the records you want, click **SQL View** on the **View** menu and copy the SQL string that defines your query. You can then paste the SQL string into your VBA code and replace any hard-coded criteria with variables that will contain the data you want to use as criteria.

The following figure (Figure 5.1) shows a query created in the query design grid that selects all fields from the Customers table for the customer named B's Beverages.

Figure 5.1 Specifying Criteria in the Query Design Grid

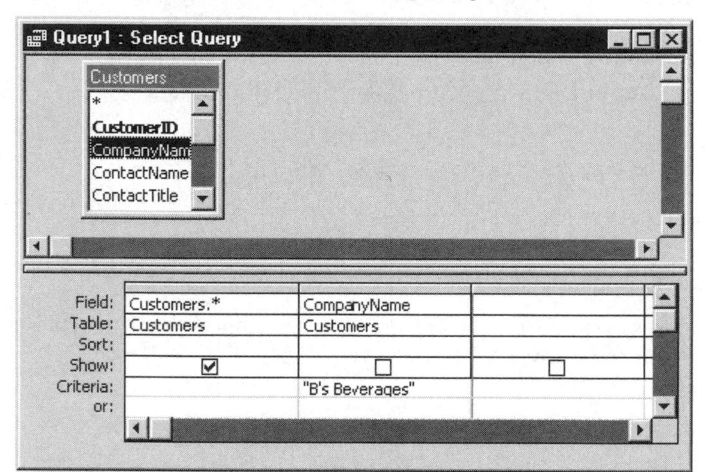

The SQL view for this query contains the following SQL statement:

```
SELECT * FROM Customers WHERE CompanyName = "B's Beverages";
```

You can modify this SQL statement for use in the following VBA procedure so that it will display a single customer record for any company passed in the `strCompanyName` variable:

```
Option Explicit
Dim frmTempForm As Form

Sub ShowCustomerRecord(strCompanyName As String)
   Dim strSQL As String

   strSQL = "SELECT * FROM Customers WHERE CompanyName = " _
      & """" & strCompanyName & """"
   Set frmTempForm = New Form_Customers
   With frmTempForm
      .RecordSource = strSQL
      .Visible = True
   End With
End Sub
```

The ShowCustomerRecord procedure is available in the modRecordsetCode module in Solutions9.mdb in the Samples\CH05 subfolder on the companion CD-ROM.

Specifying String Criteria by Using Variables in Code

When you specify criteria for a query, filter, or *wherecondition* argument from code, you typically use a variable. For example, you could specify the *wherecondition* argument of the **OpenReport** method like this:

```
DoCmd.OpenReport ReportName:="CustomerPhoneList", _
   WhereCondition:="Country = " & "'" & strCountry & "'"
```

When the criteria used is a string, the variable can be surrounded with single quotation marks ('). However, if the value of the variable contains a single quotation mark, this technique will not work. For example, if you are searching for records that match the criteria `"CompanyName = 'B's Beverages'"`, you will encounter errors. If there is any chance that a variable will contain a value that itself contains a single quotation mark, you should surround the variable with two sets of double quotation marks ("), as shown in the following example:

```
DoCmd.OpenReport ReportName:="Invoice", _
   WhereCondition:="CompanyName = " & """" & strCountry & """"
```

For more information about using quotation marks in strings, search the Microsoft Access Visual Basic Reference Help index for "quotation marks," and then open the topic "Quotation Marks in Strings."

When you are working with forms, you can also use the new **Recordset** property to specify the **Recordset** object that contains the form's or subform's records. The following example illustrates how to change the source of data for a currently open form:

```
Sub ChangeRecordsetProperty()
   Dim frmNewRecords    As Form
   Dim rstNewRecordset  As New ADODB.Recordset

   Call ShowCustomerRecord("B's Beverages")
   Stop ' View Customers form containing 1 record.

   Set frmNewRecords = Forms(Forms.Count - 1)
   rstNewRecordset.Open "SELECT * FROM Customers", _
      CurrentProject.Connection, adOpenKeyset, adLockOptimistic
   Set frmNewRecords.Recordset = rstNewRecordset
   Stop ' View Customers form containing 91 records.
End Sub
```

The ChangeRecordsetProperty procedure is available in the modRecordsetCode module in Solutions9.mdb in the Samples\CH05 subfolder on the companion CD-ROM.

The **Recordset** property of forms is new in Access 2000. You use the **Recordset** property to specify or determine the **Recordset** object representing a form's source of data. The recordset represented by the **Recordset** property is a read-only recordset. If you need to programmatically work with the data contained in the records displayed in a form, you will need to use the DAO **RecordsetClone** property or the ADO **Clone** method to create a second recordset that you can manipulate with VBA code. The **Recordset** property can be accessed only by using VBA code and can be used to bind multiple forms to a single recordset or to synchronize multiple forms or multiple **Recordset** objects. When you change a form's **Recordset** property, you must use the **Set** statement, as illustrated in the preceding code sample.

Note Changing a form's **Recordset** property may also change the **RecordSource**, **RecordsetType**, and **RecordLocks** properties. In addition, other data-related properties may also be overridden; for example, the **Filter**, **FilterOn**, **OrderBy**, and **OrderByOn** properties may all be affected when you change the **Recordset** property of a form.

To see sample code that displays different Access reports depending on the criteria supplied by the user, see the ShowAccessReports.doc file in the Samples\CH05 subfolder on the companion CD-ROM.

Working with Controls on Forms and Reports

Although forms, reports, and data access pages are the objects you use to present or gather data from users, it is really the controls on these objects that do all the work. Access contains a wide variety of built-in controls that you can use on these objects.

Forms, reports, and data access pages all use controls to display information or to allow the user to interact with the object or the data it contains. Forms and reports have a **Controls** property that returns a collection of all the controls on the object. For more information about working with controls on data access pages, see Chapter 12, "Using Web Technologies."

Controls Collections for Forms and Reports

You can refer to a control on a form or report as a member of the **Controls** collection or by using the name of the control itself. For example, the following lines of code illustrate three ways to return the **RowSource** property setting for a combo box control on a form. Since the **Controls** property is the default property of a **Form** object, you can refer to the control's name without explicitly specifying the **Controls** property, as shown in the second and third examples that follow:

```
strSource = Forms("SalesTotals").Controls("cboSelectSalesPerson").RowSource
strSource = Forms("SalesTotals")!cboSelectSalesPerson.RowSource
strSource = Forms!SalesTotals!cboSelectSalesPerson.RowSource
```

Note The **!** operator is used to refer to user-defined items, such as forms, reports, and controls on Access forms or reports.

You can also use the **Controls** property to work with all the controls on a form or report. For example, the following code loops through all the controls on a form and sets the **Text** property for each text box control to a zero-length string (""):

```
Sub ClearText(frmCurrent As Form)
   Dim ctlCurrent As Control

   For Each ctlCurrent In frmCurrent.Controls
      If ctlCurrent.ControlType = acTextBox Then
         ctlCurrent.Value = ""
      End If
   Next ctlCurrent
End Sub
```

The ClearText procedure is available in the modSolutionsUtilities module in the Solutions9.mdb file in the Samples\CH05 subfolder on the companion CD-ROM.

You can pass the **Form** object to the ClearText procedure by using the **Me** property. The **Me** property returns an object representing the form, report, or class module where code is currently running. For example, you could call the ClearText procedure from a form by using the following syntax:

```
Call ClearText(Me)
```

Certain controls on forms and reports also have a **Controls** collection. For example, the option group control may contain a **Controls** collection representing option button, toggle button, check box, or label controls in the option group. The tab control has a **Pages** collection containing a **Page** object for each page in the tab control. Each **Page** object also has a **Controls** collection representing all the controls on a page in a tab control.

Subform and Subreport Controls

Forms and reports can also contain subform or subreport controls that contain another form or report. These controls allow you to display related records from another form or report within a main form or report. A common example of this is a Customers form that contains a subform containing customer orders. You use the **SourceObject** property of the subform or subreport control to specify the form or report that will be displayed in the control.

The form or report in the subform or subreport control can share a common field, known as the *linking field*, with the records displayed in the main form or report. The linking field is used to synchronize the records between the subform or subreport and the main form or report; for example, if the record sources for an Orders subform and a Customers main form both contain a CustomerID field, this would be the common field that links the two forms. To specify the linking field, you use the **LinkChildFields** property of the subform or subreport control and **LinkMasterFields** property of the main form or report. However, the easiest way to create a linked subform or subreport is to open the main form or report in Design view, drag the appropriate form or report from the Database window to the main form or report, and then release the mouse button.

You use the **Form** property of a subform control to refer to controls on a subform. You use the **Report** property of a subreport control to refer to controls on a subreport. The following examples illustrate how to get the value of a control on a subform or subreport by using VBA. The first two lines show alternative ways to reference a control named Quantity on a subform. The last line shows how to use the **RecordCount** property to get the number of records contained in the recordset associated with a subreport control:

```
lngOrderQuantity = Forms("CustomerOrders").Controls("SubForm1").Form!Quantity
lngOrderQuantity = Forms!CustomerOrders!SubForm1.Form!Quantity

lngNumProducts = Reports!SuppliersAndProducts!SubReport1.Form.Recordset.RecordCount
```

List Box and Combo Box Controls on Forms

List box and combo box controls are very powerful and versatile tools for displaying information and allowing the user to interact with the data displayed on a form. These controls work differently in Access than list box and combo box controls in other Office applications and it is important to understand these differences if you want to use these controls effectively.

If you are used to working with these controls in other applications, the most important difference is how you add items to and remove items from these controls. In other applications, these controls have **AddItem** and **RemoveItem** methods to add and remove items. These methods are not supported for Access list and combo box controls. Instead, you use combinations of **RowSource** and **RowSourceType** properties to specify the data that appears in a list box or combo box control. The relationship between the **RowSource** property setting and the **RowSourceType** property setting is illustrated in the following table.

RowSourceType property setting	RowSource property setting
Table/Query	Table name, query name, or SQL statement
Value List	Semicolon-delimited list of values
Field List	List of field names from a table, query, or SQL statement
User-defined function	No value specified

For more information about setting the **RowSourceType** and **RowSource** properties to fill a list box or combo box control, search the Microsoft Access Visual Basic Reference Help index for "RowSource property" or "RowSourceType property."

If you are creating list box or combo box controls through the Access user interface, you can take advantage of the List Box Wizard and the Combo Box Wizard to set the various properties needed to display data in these controls. To use these wizards, make sure the **Control Wizards** tool in the toolbox is pressed in, then click the **List Box** or **Combo Box** tool in the toolbox, and then click the place on the form where you want the control to appear. Follow the instructions displayed by the wizard.

You can set the properties of a list box or combo box control without using the wizard by using the control's property sheet or VBA. You use the **ControlSource** property to bind a list box or combo box control to a field in the recordset specified in the form's **RecordSource** property. As mentioned earlier, you use the **RowSource** property in combination with the **RowSourceType** property to specify the source of data for the list box or combo box control.

The **BoundColumn** property specifies which column in the record source specified by the **RowSource** property will contain the value of the list box or combo box control. If a list box or combo box control does not have a **ControlSource** property setting, you can set the **BoundColumn** property to 0. When you do this, the **Value** property of the control will contain the row number of the selected row specified by the **RowSource** property. The row number of the selected row is the same as the value of the control's **ListIndex** property. The **ColumnCount** and **ColumnWidths** properties specify which columns are displayed in the control.

The following sample fills a combo box control with data from an SQL statement, specifies which column in the SQL statement specified by the **RowSource** property will contain the value for the control, and uses the **ColumnWidths** property to specify which columns are displayed in the control:

```
With Me!cboEmployees
   .RowSource = "SELECT EmployeeID, FirstName, " _
      & "LastName FROM Employees ORDER BY LastName"
   .RowSourceType = "Table/Query"
   .BoundColumn = 1
   .ColumnCount = 3
   .ColumnWidths = "0in;.5in;.5in"
   .ColumnHeads = False
   .ListRows = 5
End With
```

The preceding code fills a combo box with data from 3 fields (columns) from each record (row) in the Employees table, as specified by the **RowSource** property. The **BoundColumn** property is set to the first field in the Employees table; in this case, EmployeeID. When an item is selected from the combo box, the value of the EmployeeID field will be the control's value and is the value saved to the field specified by the **ControlSource** property. Note that the first column in the **ColumnWidths** property is set to 0 inches. This hides the bound column (EmployeeID) from the user when the combo box's drop-down list is displayed. The user sees only the FirstName and LastName fields, and these fields are displayed in .5-inch wide columns. Note also that the **ColumnHeads** property is set to **False**, meaning that the names of the FirstName and LastName fields are not shown in the control's drop-down list. And finally, the **ListRows** property is set to 5, specifying that the control's drop-down list will display only 5 records at a time.

Using a User-Defined Function to Fill a List Box or Combo Box Control

You can specify a user-defined function as the **RowSourceType** property setting for a list box or combo box control. The function you use for this property setting has to meet specific criteria in order to work correctly because the function is called repeatedly as Access fills the control with data. For more information about creating and using user-defined functions to fill a list box or combo box control, search the Microsoft Access Visual Basic Reference Help index for "RowSourceType property," then open the "RowSourceType, RowSource Properties" topic, and then use the See Also jump to open the "RowSourceType Property (User-Defined Function) — Code Argument Values" topic. To see a sample procedure used to fill a combo box control, see the AddAllToList procedure in the modSolutionsUtilities module in Solutions9.mdb in the Samples\CH05 subfolder on the companion CD-ROM.

Adding New Values to a Combo Box Control

You use the **LimitToList** property to specify whether a user can add new values to a bound combo box from the user interface when the form is in Form view or Datasheet view. When this property is set to **True** (the default), the user can't add new items to the combo box. If the **BoundColumn** property is set to any column other than 1, Access will automatically set the **LimitToList** property to **True**. When this property is set to **False**, new values are added to the underlying record source specified by the **RowSource** property.

When the **LimitToList** property is set to **True**, any attempt to add a new item to a combo box control will cause the NotInList event to occur. You can add code to the NotInList event procedure to handle the attempt to add new data to the control. This event procedure uses the NewData and Response arguments to represent the new data the user has tried to enter and the response you want to provide to the attempt to add new data. Setting the Response argument to one of the following built-in constants specifies how you want to respond to the attempt to add data to the control: **acDataErrAdded**, **acDataErrContinue**, or **acDataErrDisplay**. For example, the following sample illustrates one way to add new data to a combo box control:

```
Private Sub CategoryID_NotInList(NewData As String, _
                                 Response As Integer)

   If MsgBox("Do you want to add '" _
      & NewData & "' to the items in this control?", _
      vbOKCancel, "Add New Item?") = vbOK Then

      ' Remove new data from combo box so control can be requeried
      ' after the AddNewData form is closed.
      DoCmd.RunCommand acCmdUndo

      ' Display form to collect data needed for the new record.
      DoCmd.OpenForm "AddNewData", acNormal, , , acAdd, acDialog, NewData
```

```
      ' Continue without displaying default error message.
      Response = acDataErrAdded
   Else
      Response = acDataErrContinue
   End If
End Sub
```

The CategoryID control's NotInList event procedure is available in the Form_EnterOrEditProducts module in Solutions9.mdb in the Samples\CH05 subfolder on the companion CD-ROM.

For more information about how to use the NotInList event procedure, search the Microsoft Access Visual Basic Reference Help index for "NotInList event."

Enabling Multiple Selections in a List Box Control

To allow users to make multiple selections from a list box control, you set the **MultiSelect** property. When the **MultiSelect** property is set to Simple (2) or Extended (1), the **Value** property of the control is **Null**. You work with multiple selections in a list box control by using the **Selected**, **ItemsSelected**, and **Column** properties.

Working with Data Access Pages

Data access pages are new to Access 2000. Data access pages are HTML documents comprised of HTML code, HTML intrinsic controls, and ActiveX controls. Data access pages rely on DHTML and are designed to work best with Internet Explorer version 5 or later. (You can also use other Web browsers to display data access pages, but users will not be able to work with the data directly.)

A data access page can be a simple HTML document or can include data-bound controls that let users use a Web browser to interact with data stored in a database. Access provides a WYSIWYG design environment for creating data access pages and a means for deploying those pages and any necessary supporting files to a Web server, network server, or local file system. In addition, you can view and use data access pages within Access itself.

You may be tempted to think of data access pages as HTML documents that combine the best features of forms and reports for display on the Web, but that would be a very narrow definition. Data access pages do support much of the functionality you are used to in Access forms and reports, but they also provide a completely new way to interact with data from within an Access database or on the Web. These objects allow users to use a Web browser to work with data in an interactive manner and in a way that has never been possible before. Data access pages are like forms in that you can use them to view, edit, or delete existing records and you can also use them to add new records to an underlying record source. They are like reports in that you can sort and filter records as well as group records according to criteria you specify. In addition, while a page is displayed, you can manipulate the records that are displayed and change how the records are displayed.

You can create data access pages from scratch in Access or you can base them on existing HTML pages created by using some other HTML authoring tool. Only those pages created or modified within the Access design environment will be visible in the **Pages** object list in the Database window. This means that if you edit an HTML document in Access, a link to that document is created, even if you later use another tool to make additional changes. In addition, because the data access pages that appear in the Database window are links to the files stored on disk, you can delete a page in the Database window without deleting the file from disk. Unlike other objects in an Access database, data access pages are stored on disk as .htm files that are separate from the Access database in which they are created.

Creating a data access page in Access is similar to creating a form or report. Data access pages have their own object list in the Database window, and when they are opened in Design view, they have a toolbox and property sheet. The toolbox contains tools for inserting the HTML intrinsic controls, such as the text box, label, list box, and command button controls. In addition, the toolbox contains tools for inserting controls that are useful only on data access pages, such as the expand, bound HTML, and scrolling text controls. The toolbox also contains tools for inserting the Microsoft Office Web Component controls on a data access page. For more information about the Office Web Components, see Chapter 12, "Using Web Technologies."

To see examples of data access pages, see the Solutions9.mdb file in the Samples\CH05 subfolder on the companion CD-ROM. The modDataAccessPageCode module in this database contains most of the VBA code that works with data access pages. You can use the DataAccessPages form to display the data access pages within the sample database.

Note Because Access does not use the shared Office components related to **Script** objects or **HTMLProject** objects, you can't use these objects to work with scripts or the HTML code in data access pages through VBA code. To work with scripts or the HTML code in an Access **DataAccessPage** object, you use the Microsoft Script Editor or a **DataAccessPage** object's **Document** property, which returns the Web browser's **document** object for an HTML page. For more information about working with shared Office components, see Chapter 6, "Working with Shared Office Components." For more information about working with the **document** object, see Chapter 12, "Using Web Technologies."

Creating, Saving, and Closing Data Access Pages

You will typically create data access pages in the data access page design environment in Access. However, there may be circumstances where you want to use VBA code to display a data access page within Access or to programmatically output a page to a separate location, such as a Web server on your local intranet.

You create a data access page programmatically by using the **Application** object's **CreateDataAccessPage** method. You can use the **CreateDataAccessPage** method to work with an existing HTML page as a data access page or to create a new, blank page. For example, the following code illustrates how to use this method to create a new page called BlankDAP.htm:

```
Application.CreateDataAccessPage FileName:="c:\WebPages\BlankDAP.htm" _
   CreateNewFileName:=True
```

The **CreateDataAccessPage** method creates a new blank page by default and adds a link to that page in the **Pages** object list in the Database window. If the file specified in the ***FileName*** argument already exists when the method is called and the ***CreateNewFileName*** argument is set to **True** (the default), an error occurs. If you set the method's ***CreateNewFileName*** argument to **False**, the ***FileName*** argument must contain the path and name of an existing file. If the file does not exist, an error occurs. If the ***FileName*** argument contains the path and file name of a file for which there is already a link in the **Pages** object list in the Database window, a new, uniquely named link is created that points to the same file on disk. If you provide a name but do not specify the path to a new file, the page is created in the current directory.

You can determine the path and file name for pages that appear in the **Pages** object list in the Database window by using the read-only **FullName** property of the **AccessObject** object that represents a particular data access page. For example, the following code prints the **Name** and **FullName** properties for each page in the current database:

```
Dim objDAP As AccessObject

For Each objDAP In CurrentProject.AllDataAccessPages
Debug.Print "The '" & objDAP.Name & _
   "' is located at: " & objDAP.FullName
Next objDAP
```

When you call the **CreateDataAccessPage** method, Access creates a temporary file on disk. To permanently save the page and create a pointer to it from the **Pages** object list in the Database window, you must use the **Save** method or the **Close** method of the **DoCmd** object.

The following code fragment illustrates how you could create a new data access page, work with the HTML in the page, and then create a link to the page and permanently save it to disk. The procedure also illustrates one way to use an error trap to handle files that already exist.

```
Function CreateDAP(strFileName As String) As Boolean
   ' This procedure illustrates how to create a data access
   ' page, work with the HTML in the page, and then save the page.
   ' The procedure also shows how to use an error trap to avoid
   ' the error that ocurrs if strFileName already exists.
   Dim dapNewPage As DataAccessPage

   Const DAP_EXISTS As Long = 2023

   On Error GoTo CreateDAP_Err
   ' Create the new page.
   Set dapNewPage = Application.CreateDataAccessPage(strFileName, True)

   ' Use the Document property to return the Internet Explorer 5
   ' document object, and then use the objects on the page to
   ' work with the HTML in the page.
   With dapNewPage.Document
      .All("HeadingText").innerText = "This page was created programmatically!"
      .All("HeadingText").Style.display = ""
      .All("BeforeBodyText").innerText = "When you work " _
         & "with the HTML in a data access page, you " _
         & "must use the document property of the page " _
         & "to get to the HTML. "
         .All("BeforeBodyText").Style.display = ""
   End With

   ' Close the page and save all changes.
   DoCmd.Close acDataAccessPage, dapNewPage.Name, acSaveYes

   CreateDAP = True

CreateDAP_End:
   Exit Function
CreateDAP_Err:
   If Err = DAP_EXISTS Then
      ' The file specified in strFileName already exists,
      ' so replace it with this new page.
      If MsgBox("'" & strFileName & "' already exists. Do you want to " _
         & "replace it with a new, blank page?", vbYesNo, _
         "Replace existing page?") = vbYes Then
         Set dapNewPage = Application.CreateDataAccessPage(strFileName, False)
         Resume Next
      Else
         CreateDAP = False
         Resume CreateDAP_End
      End If
   Else
      CreateDAP = False
      Resume CreateDAP_End
   End If
End Function
```

The CreateDAP procedure is available in the modDataAccessPageCode module in Solutions9.mdb in the Samples\CH05 subfolder on the companion CD-ROM.

Note When you create a new data access page, the **display** property of the **style** object for the HeadingText and BeforeBodyText elements is set to None by default. The preceding example also illustrates how to change this setting so the text you insert is visible when the page is viewed.

The CreateDAP procedure uses the data access page's **Document** property to return the Internet Explorer 5 **document** object and then sets properties of elements in the page. This procedure also uses the **innerText** property of an HTML element to specify the text that appears in the element. For more information about working with the Internet Explorer 5 object model, see Chapter 12, "Using Web Technologies."

Opening and Working with Data Access Pages

Although data access pages are designed to be viewed in a browser, you can display data access pages in Access to let users view and work with data just like they do with forms and reports.

To open an existing data access page for which a link exists in the **Pages** object list in the Database window, you use the **DoCmd** object's **OpenDataAccessPage** method. You use the ***View*** argument of the **OpenDataAccessPage** method to specify whether to view the page in Design view or Page view. The following example illustrates how to open the Employees page in Page view:

```
DoCmd.OpenDataAccessPage "Employees", acDataAccessPageBrowse
```

To determine whether a page is currently open in Page view or Design view, you use a **DataAccessPage** object's **CurrentView** property.

The **DataAccessPages** collection contains all currently open data access pages. You can access an open page as a member of this collection and gain access to the properties and methods of the page itself as well as any controls on the page. The following sample code opens the Employees page in Design view, applies a theme, adds some text to the main heading, and then displays the page to the user:

```
With DoCmd
   .Echo False
   .OpenDataAccessPage "Employees", acDataAccessPageDesign
   With DataAccessPages("Employees")
      .ApplyTheme "Blends"
      .Document.All("HeadingText").innerText = "Today is " _
         & Format(Date, "mmmm d, yyyy"
   End With
   .OpenDataAccessPage "Employees", acDataAccessPageBrowse
   .Echo True
End With
```

Important To save the changes you make to a data access page, you must make sure the page is in Design view, and then use the **DoCmd** object's **Save** method to save changes. If you programmatically make changes to a page while it is in Page view, those changes will be lost as soon as you call the **Save** method. To see an example of how you can make changes to the text in a data access page regardless of the current view, see the DAPInsertText procedure in the modDataAccessPageCode module in Solutions9.mdb in the Samples\CH05 subfolder on the companion CD-ROM.

To get information about the pages in your database, including whether a page is currently open, you use the **CurrentProject** object's **AllDataAccessPages** collection. To specify or determine property settings for a page or controls on a page, you use the properties of a **DataAccessPage** object. The following sample uses both techniques to print information about data access pages to the Immediate window:

```
Sub DAPGetPageInfo()
   ' This procedure prints information about the data access pages
   ' in this database to the Immediate window.
   Dim objCurrentDAP    As AccessObject
   Dim strPageInfo      As String

   Const DAP_DESIGNVIEW As Integer = 0
   Const DAP_PAGEVIEW   As Integer = 1

   Debug.Print "There are "; CurrentProject.AllDataAccessPages.Count _
      & " data access pages in this database."
   For Each objCurrentDAP In CurrentProject.AllDataAccessPages
      Debug.Print objCurrentDAP.Name & ":"
      Debug.Print vbTab & "File name: " & objCurrentDAP.FullName
      If objCurrentDAP.IsLoaded <> True Then
         Debug.Print vbTab & "The '" & objCurrentDAP.Name _
            & "' page is not currently open."
      Else
         Select Case DataAccessPages(objCurrentDAP.Name).CurrentView
            Case DAP_DESIGNVIEW
               Debug.Print vbTab & "The '" & objCurrentDAP.Name _
                  & "' page is open in Design view."
            Case DAP_PAGEVIEW
               Debug.Print vbTab & "The '" & objCurrentDAP.Name _
                  & "' page is open in Page view."
         End Select
      End If
   Next objCurrentDAP
End Sub
```

Note that the **DataAccessPages** collection contains **DataAccessPage** objects, whereas the **AllDataAccessPages** collection contains **AccessObject** objects. The DAPGetPageInfo procedure is available in the modDataAccessPageCode module in Solutions9.mdb in the Samples\CH05 subfolder on the companion CD-ROM.

When you work with data access pages inside Access, you can use VBA code, in a form for example, to specify or determine property settings of the page or controls on a page. In the next example, the SimplePageExample page is opened and the **DataEntry** property of the page's **Data Source** control is set to **True** so the page can be used only to enter new records:

```
Private Sub cmdSimpleDAPDataEntry_Click()
   With DoCmd
      .Echo False
      .OpenDataAccessPage "SimplePageExample", _
         acDataAccessPageBrowse
      DataAccessPages("SimplePageExample").Document _
         .All("MSODSC").DataEntry = True
      .Echo True
   End With
End Sub
```

Note The ActiveX control that binds controls on a page to an underlying data source is the Microsoft Office **Data Source** control (MSODSC). This control is included in every data access page you create but is not visible on the page itself. In the preceding example, the **DataEntry** property of the MSODSC is set to **True**. As you can see, the control is created by using an **id** property setting of `"MSODSC"`, and you use this **id** property to specify that the control is a member of the **all** collection in the data access page's **Document** object.

Caution Although the HTML underlying the MSODSC is available, you should never modify the HTML directly either in Access or in any HTML authoring tool. To set properties of the MSODSC, you must use its property sheet in the Microsoft Script Editor or use VBScript code in the data access page itself.

To open the SimplePageExample page so that it displays all records, you would use the following code:

```
DoCmd.OpenDataAccessPage "SimplePageExample", acDataAccessPageBrowse
```

You can also use the Microsoft Script Editor to add to a page script that runs when the page is displayed or in response to events that occur on the page. The script you add to a page is part of the page itself and can run when the page is displayed in Access or in a Web browser. For more information about working with scripting event procedures in an HTML page, see Chapter 12, "Using Web Technologies."

Using the Microsoft Script Editor with Data Access Pages

The Microsoft Script Editor is an editor and debugger that you can use to work with the HTML code and script in a data access page. This section describes how to use the Script Editor with data access pages. For general information about using the Script Editor, see Chapter 12, "Using Web Technologies."

When you view a data access page in the Script Editor, you see color-coded HTML code and script in the page. In addition, depending on the controls you have placed on the page, you may also see icons representing some controls. For example, the **Data Source** control is displayed as an icon. You can see the HTML and XML code underlying a control's icon by right-clicking the icon in the Script Editor and clicking **Always View As Text** on the shortcut menu.

When you create a new data access page, the page contains a two-dimensional section, represented by a <DIV> tag in the HTML code that uses the CLASS attribute `MSOShowDesignGrid` and a default ID attribute of `SectionUnbound`. When you add data-bound controls to this section of the page, Access automatically changes the ID attribute to reflect the controls you are using. For example, if you drag the Customers table to this section, Access changes the ID attribute to `HeaderCustomers`. You can place controls anywhere within the two-dimensional section just like you can on a form or report. Outside of this section, controls cannot be positioned in this manner.

When you create event procedures, the Script Editor does not insert the event procedure arguments when they are required. You must insert these yourself. For example, every event associated with the **Data Source** control requires a single *dscEventInfo* argument. If you double-click the Current event for the **Data Source** control (MSODSC) in the Script Editor's Script Outline window, the following script block is inserted in your page:

```
<SCRIPT Language=vbscript FOR=MSODSC EVENT=Current>
<!--
-->
</SCRIPT>
```

You must add the event's argument or arguments by adding parentheses and a name for the argument or arguments. It does not matter what name you use for each argument, and it does not matter if the argument is actually used in your script. You must supply all the arguments to the event, even if your code does not use them, or the code will not work. For example, here is the corrected event handler for the **Data Source** control's Current event:

```
<SCRIPT Language=vbscript FOR=MSODSC EVENT=Current(EventInfo)>
<!--
-->
</SCRIPT>
```

For information about how to use the Script Editor to debug script in a data access page, see Chapter 8, "Error Handling and Debugging."

Security Considerations for Data Access Pages

Because data access pages are designed to work both within and outside Access databases, security issues pertaining to data access pages require special attention. Understanding these issues requires an understanding of database security as well as Internet Explorer security. For more information about securing data access pages, see Chapter 18, "Securing Access Databases."

Working with Microsoft Excel Objects

The Microsoft Excel object model contains several dozen objects that you can manipulate through VBA code. Almost anything you can do with Excel from its user interface, you can do by manipulating its objects through VBA. In addition, you can do things through VBA that can't be done through the user interface.

When you use VBA to work with Excel objects, either from within Excel itself or from another Office application, you have access to every part of Excel. The objects you will work with include cells, ranges, sheets, workbooks, charts, and more. In other words, every element in Excel can be represented by an object that you can manipulate through VBA.

This section will explore those objects, methods, and properties you will use most often and give you some insight into how to work with Excel objects. There are four Excel objects you will work with more than any others: the **Application** object, the **Workbook** object, the **Worksheet** object, and the **Range** object. Understanding when and how to use these objects will go a long way toward helping you understand how to work with Excel objects through VBA.

This section discusses some of the more common methods and properties you will use when working with Excel objects, but by no means does it discuss all available properties, methods, or events.

Note You can view the entire Excel object model in the "Object Model Diagrams" appendix. You can also use the Object Browser and Microsoft Excel Visual Basic Reference Help to learn more about individual objects, properties, methods, and events. For more information about using VBA to work with an Office application's object model, see Chapter 4, "Understanding Office Objects and Object Models."

Understanding the Excel Application Object

The Excel **Application** object is the top-level object in Excel's object model. You use the **Application** object to determine or specify application-level properties or execute application-level methods. The **Application** object is also the entry point into the rest of the Excel object model.

When you work with properties and methods of the **Application** object by using VBA from within Excel, the **Application** object is available to you by default. This is known as an implicit reference to the object. If you work with Excel objects from another Office application, you must create an object variable representing the Excel **Application** object. This is known as an explicit reference to the object. For example, the following two procedures return the name of the currently active **Worksheet** object. The ShowNameFromInsideXL procedure is designed to work from within Excel and uses an implicit reference to the **Application** object. In other words, it references the **ActiveSheet** property of the **Application** object without explicitly referencing the **Application** object itself. The ShowNameFromOutsideXL procedure is designed to be run from outside Excel and so must use an explicit reference to the **Application** object.

```
Sub ShowNameFromInsideXL()
   MsgBox "'" & ActiveSheet.Name & "' is the currently active worksheet."
End Sub

Sub ShowNameFromOutsideXL()
   Dim xlApp As Excel.Application

   Const XL_NOTRUNNING As Long = 429

   On Error GoTo ShowName_Err
   Set xlApp = GetObject(, "Excel.Application")
   MsgBox "'" & ActiveSheet.Name & "' is the currently active worksheet."
   xlApp.Quit
   Set xlApp = Nothing

ShowName_End:
   Exit Sub
ShowName_Err:
   If Err = XL_NOTRUNNING Then
      ' Excel is not currently running.
      Set xlApp = New Excel.Application
      xlApp.Workbooks.Add
      Resume Next
   Else
      MsgBox Err.Number & " - " & Err.Description
   End If
   Resume ShowName_End
End Sub
```

The ShowNameFromInsideXL and ShowNameFromOutsideXL procedures are available in the modExcelSamples module in ExcelSamples.xls in the Samples\CH05 subfolder on the companion CD-ROM.

Shortcuts to Active Objects

Like other Office application object models, the Excel **Application** object exposes several properties you can use to work with a currently active Excel object. For example, you will often write VBA procedures designed to work with information in the currently selected cell, or with the currently active worksheet. The **Application** object exposes the **ActiveCell**, **ActiveChart**, **ActivePrinter**, **ActiveSheet**, **ActiveWindow**, and **ActiveWorkbook** properties, which you can use to return a reference to the currently active cell, chart, printer, sheet, window, or workbook. The following examples illustrate various ways you might use some of these properties:

```
' ActiveWorkbook property example:
Function SaveBookAs(strFileName As String) As Boolean
   ActiveWorkbook.SaveAs ActiveWorkbook.Path & "\" & strFileName
End Function

' ActiveCell property example:
Function CustomFormatCell()
   With ActiveCell
      If IsNumeric(.Text) And .Formula < 0 Then
         With .Font
            .Bold = True
            .Italic = True
         End With
         .Borders.Color = 255
      End If
   End With
End Function

' ActiveSheet property example:
Function ChangeName(strNewName As String) As Boolean
   ActiveSheet.Name = strNewName
End Function
```

The SaveBookAs, CustomFormatCell, and ChangeName procedures are available in the modExcelSamples module in ExcelSamples.xls in the Samples\CH05 subfolder on the companion CD-ROM.

In addition to the **ActiveWorkbook** property, you can use the **Application** object's **Workbooks** and **Worksheets** properties to return equivalent Excel objects. The **Workbooks** property returns the **Workbooks** collection that contains all the currently open **Workbook** objects. The **Worksheets** property returns the **Sheets** collection associated with the currently active workbook. The following example uses the **Workbooks** property to determine if a workbook is already open, and if not, to open it:

```
Function OpenBook(strFilePath As String) As Boolean
   ' This procedure checks to see if the workbook
   ' specified in the strFilePath argument is open.
   ' If it is open, the workbook is activated. If it is
   ' not open, the procedure opens it.
   Dim wkbCurrent    As Excel.Workbook
   Dim strBookName   As String

   On Error GoTo OpenBook_Err

   ' Determine the name portion of the strFilePath argument.
   strBookName = NameFromPath(strFilePath)
   If Len(strBookName) = 0 Then Exit Function
   If Workbooks.Count > 0 Then
      For Each wkbCurrent In Workbooks
         If UCase$(wkbCurrent.Name) = UCase$(strBookName) Then
            wkbCurrent.Activate
            Exit Function
         End If
```

```
        Next wkbCurrent
    End If
    Workbooks.Open strBookName
    OpenBook = True

OpenBook_End:
    Exit Function
OpenBook_Err:
    OpenBook = False
    Resume OpenBook_End
End Function
```

In the preceding example, the OpenBook procedure calls a custom procedure named NameFromPath that returns the file name portion of the full path and file name passed to the OpenBook procedure in the *strFilePath* argument. The OpenBook and NameFromPath procedures are available in the modExcelSamples module in ExcelSamples.xls in the Samples\CH05 subfolder on the companion CD-ROM.

Understanding the Workbook Object

In the Excel object model, the **Workbook** object appears just below the **Application** object. The **Workbook** object represents an Excel .xls or .xla workbook file. You use the **Workbook** object to work with a single Excel workbook. You use the **Workbooks** collection to work with all currently open **Workbook** objects.

You can also use the **Application** object's **ActiveWorkbook** property to return a reference to the currently active workbook. The **Workbooks** collection has a **Count** property you can use to determine how many visible and hidden workbooks are open. By default, Excel typically has one hidden workbook named Personal.xls. The Personal.xls workbook is created by Excel as a place to store macros. If the hidden Personal.xls workbook is the only open workbook, the **ActiveWorkbook** property returns **Nothing**, but the **Workbooks** collection's **Count** property returns 1. The **Workbooks** collection's **Count** property will return 0 only when there are no hidden or visible open workbooks.

Creating, Saving, Opening, and Closing Workbook Objects

You create a new **Workbook** object by using the **Workbooks** collection's **Add** method. The **Add** method not only creates a new workbook, but also immediately opens the workbook as well. The **Add** method also returns an object variable that represents the new workbook just created. The new workbook will contain the number of worksheets specified in the **Sheets in new workbook** box on the **General** tab of the **Options** dialog box (**Tools** menu). You can also specify the number of sheets a new workbook will have by using the **Application** object's **SheetsInNewWorkbook** property.

You can save a new workbook by using the **Workbook** object's **SaveAs** method and specifying the name of the workbook you want to save. If a workbook by that name already exists, an error occurs. Once a workbook has been saved by using the **SaveAs** method, additional changes are saved by using the **Workbook** object's **Save** method. You can also save a copy of an existing workbook with a different file name by using the **SaveCopyAs** method. You can supply a file name to be used with the **SaveAs** or **SaveCopyAs** method, or you can use the **Application** object's **GetSaveAsFileName** method to let the user supply the name to be used to save the workbook. If the user clicks **Cancel** in the **Save As** dialog box, the **GetSaveAsFileName** method returns **False.**

Before you save a new workbook by using the **SaveAs** method, the **Workbook** object's **Name** property setting is a value assigned by Excel, such as Book1.xls. After you save the workbook, the **Name** property contains the name you supplied in the ***Filename*** argument of the **SaveAs** method. The **Name** property is read-only; to change the name of a workbook, you must use the **SaveAs** method again, and pass a different value in the ***Filename*** argument.

Note A **Workbook** object's **FullName** property contains the object's path and file name, whereas the **Path** property contains only the saved path to the current workbook. Before a new workbook is saved, the **FullName** property has the same as the **Name** property, and the **Path** property has no value.

The **Workbooks** collection's **Open** method opens an existing workbook. When you open a workbook by using the **Open** method, it also becomes the active workbook. You can supply a file name to be used with the **Open** method, or you can use the **Application** object's **GetOpenFileName** method to let the user select the workbook to open. If the user clicks **Cancel** in the **Open** dialog box, the **GetOpenFileName** method returns **False**.

You use a **Workbook** object's **Close** method to close an open workbook. To specify whether pending changes to the workbook should be saved before the object is closed, you use the ***SaveChanges*** argument. If the ***SaveChanges*** argument is omitted, the user is prompted to save pending changes. You can also use the **Close** method of the **Workbooks** object to close all open workbooks. If there are unsaved changes to any open workbook when this method is used, the user is prompted to save changes. If the user clicks **Cancel** in this **Save** dialog box, an error occurs. You can suppress this **Save** dialog box by setting the **Application** object's **DisplayAlerts** property to **False** before executing the **Close** method. When you use the **Workbooks** object's **Close** method in this manner, any unsaved changes to open workbooks are lost. After the **Close** method has run, remember to set the **DisplayAlerts** property to **True**.

Important The Auto_Open and Auto_Close procedures are ignored when a workbook is opened or closed by using the **Open** or **Close** methods. You can force these procedures to run by using the **Workbook** object's **RunAutoMacros** method. The VBA code in a workbook's Open and BeforeClose event procedures will be executed when the workbook is opened or closed by using the **Open** or **Close** methods.

The following example illustrates how to create a new workbook and specify the number of worksheets it will have:

```
Function CreateNewWorkbook(Optional strBookName As String = "", _
                           Optional intNumSheets As Integer = 3) As Workbook
   ' This procedure creates a new workbook file and saves it by using the path
   ' and name specified in the strBookName argument. You use the intNumsheets
   ' argument to specify the number of worksheets in the workbook;
   ' the default is 3.
   Dim intOrigNumSheets       As Integer
   Dim wkbNew                 As Excel.Workbook

   On Error GoTo CreateNew_Err

   intOrigNumSheets = Application.SheetsInNewWorkbook
   If intOrigNumSheets <> intNumSheets Then
      Application.SheetsInNewWorkbook = intNumSheets
   End If
   Set wkbNew = Workbooks.Add
   If Len(strBookName) = 0 Then strBookName = Application.GetSaveAsFilename
   wkbNew.SaveAs strBookName
   Set CreateNewWorkbook = wkbNew
   Application.SheetsInNewWorkbook = intOrigNumSheets

CreateNew_End:
   Exit Function
CreateNew_Err:
   Set CreateNewWorkbook = Nothing
   wkbNew.Close False
   Set wkbNew = Nothing
   Resume CreateNew_End
End Function
```

The CreateNewWorkbook procedure is available in the modExcelSamples module in ExcelSamples.xls in the Samples\CH05 subfolder on the companion CD-ROM.

Important A **Workbook** object's **Saved** property is a **Boolean** value indicating whether the workbook has been saved. The **Saved** property will be **True** for any new or opened workbook where no changes have been made and **False** for a workbook that has unsaved changes. You can set the **Saved** property to **True**. Doing this prevents the user from being prompted to save changes when the workbook closes but does not actually save any changes made since the last time the workbook was saved by using the **Save** method.

A Note About Working with Workbooks Through Automation

When you are using Automation to edit an Excel workbook, keep the following in mind.

Creating a new instance of Excel and opening a workbook results in an invisible instance of Excel and a hidden instance of the workbook. Therefore, if you edit the workbook and save it, the workbook is saved as hidden. The next time the user opens Excel manually, the workbook is invisible and the user has to click **Unhide** on the **Window** menu to view the workbook.

To avoid this behavior, your Automation code should unhide the workbook before editing it and saving it. Note that this does *not* mean Microsoft Excel itself has to be visible.

Understanding the Worksheet Object

Most of the work you will do in Excel will be within the context of a worksheet. A worksheet contains a grid of cells you can use to work with data and hundreds of properties, methods, and events you can use to work with the data in a worksheet.

To work with the data contained in a worksheet, in a cell or within a range of cells, you use a **Range** object. The **Worksheet** and **Range** objects are the two most basic and most important components of any custom solution you create within Excel. For more information about the **Range** object, see "Understanding the Range Object" later in this chapter.

The **Workbook** object's **Worksheets** property returns a collection of all the worksheets in the workbook. The **Workbook** object's **Sheets** property returns a collection of all the worksheets and chart sheets in the workbook.

Each Excel workbook contains one or more **Worksheet** objects and can contain one or more chart sheets as well. Charts in Excel are either embedded in a worksheet or contained on a chart sheet. You can have only one chart on a chart sheet, but you can have multiple charts on a worksheet. Each embedded chart on a worksheet is a member of the **Worksheet** object's **ChartObjects** collection. **Worksheet** objects are contained in the **Worksheets** collection, which you can access by using the **Workbook** object's **Worksheets** property. When you use VBA to create a new workbook, you can specify how many worksheets it will contain by using the **Application** object's **SheetsInNewWorkbook** property.

Referring to a Worksheet Object

Because a **Worksheet** object exists as a member of a **Worksheets** collection, you refer to a worksheet by its name or its index value. In the following example, both object variables refer to the first worksheet in a workbook:

```
Sub ReferToWorksheetExample()
   ' This procedure illustrates how to programmatically refer to
   ' a worksheet.
   Dim wksSheetByIndex  As Excel.Worksheet
   Dim wksSheetByName   As Excel.Worksheet

   With ActiveWorkbook
      Set wksSheetByIndex = Worksheets(1)
      Set wksSheetByName = Worksheets("Main")
      If wksSheetByIndex.Index = wksSheetByName.Index Then
         MsgBox "The worksheet indexed as #" _
            & wksSheetByIndex.Index & vbCrLf _
            & "is the same as the worksheet named '" _
            & wksSheetByName.Name & "'", vbOKOnly, "Worksheets Match!"
      End If
   End With
End Sub
```

The ReferToWorksheetExample procedure is available in the modExcelSamples module in ExcelSamples.xls in the Samples\CH05 subfolder on the companion CD-ROM.

Note You can also use the **Application** object's **ActiveSheet** property to return a reference to the currently active worksheet in the currently active workbook.

You can use the VBA **Array** function to work with multiple worksheets at the same time, as shown in the following example:

```
Sub ReferToMultipleSheetsExample()
   ' This procedure shows how to programmatically refer to
   ' multiple worksheets.
   Dim wksCurrent As Excel.Worksheet

   With ActiveWorkbook.Worksheets(Array("Employees", "Sheet2", "Sheet3"))
      .FillAcrossSheets (Worksheets("Employees").UsedRange)
   End With
   Stop
   ' The worksheets named "Sheet2" and "Sheet3" should now
   ' contain the same table that is found on the "Employees"
   ' sheet. Press F5 to clear the contents from these worksheets.
   For Each wksCurrent In ActiveWorkbook _
      .Worksheets(Array("Sheet2", "Sheet3"))
      wksCurrent.UsedRange.Clear
   Next wksCurrent
End Sub
```

The ReferToMultipleSheetsExample procedure is available in the modExcelSamples module in ExcelSamples.xls in the Samples\CH05 subfolder on the companion CD-ROM.

You can specify or determine the name of a worksheet by using its **Name** property. To change the name of a new worksheet, you first add it to the **Worksheets** collection and then set the **Name** property to the name you want to use.

Adding, Deleting, Copying, and Moving a Worksheet Object

You can add one or more worksheets to the **Worksheets** collection by using the collection's **Add** method. The **Add** method returns the new **Worksheet** object. If you add multiple worksheets, the **Add** method returns the last worksheet added to the **Worksheets** collection. If the ***Before*** or ***After*** arguments of the **Add** method are omitted, the new worksheet is added before the currently active worksheet. The following example adds a new worksheet before the active worksheet in the current collection of worksheets:

```
Dim wksNewSheet As Excel.Worksheet

Set wksNewSheet = Worksheets.Add
With wksNewSheet
   ' Work with properties and methods of the
   ' new worksheet here.
End With
```

You use the **Worksheet** object's **Delete** method to delete a worksheet from the **Worksheets** collection. When you try to programmatically delete a worksheet, Excel will display a message (alert); to suppress the message, you must set the **Application** object's **DisplayAlerts** property to **False**, as illustrated in the following example:

```
Function DeleteWorksheet(strSheetName As String) As Boolean
   On Error Resume Next

   Application.DisplayAlerts = False
   ActiveWorkbook.Worksheets(strSheetName).Delete
   Application.DisplayAlerts = True
   ' Return True if no error occurred;
   ' otherwise return False.
   DeleteWorksheet = Not CBool(Err.Number)
End Function
```

The DeleteWorksheet procedure is available in the modExcelSamples module in ExcelSamples.xls in the Samples\CH05 subfolder on the companion CD-ROM.

Important When you set the **DisplayAlerts** property to **False**, always set it back to **True** before your procedure has finished executing, as shown in the preceding example.

You can copy a worksheet by using the **Worksheet** object's **Copy** method. To copy a worksheet to the same workbook as the source worksheet, you must specify either the ***Before*** or ***After*** argument of the **Copy** method. You move a worksheet by using the **Worksheet** object's **Move** method. For example:

```
Worksheets("Sheet1").Copy After:=Worksheets("Sheet3")
Worksheets("Sheet1").Move After:=Worksheets("Sheet3")
```

The next example illustrates how to move a worksheet so that it is the last worksheet in a workbook:

```
Worksheets("Sheet1").Move After:=Worksheets(Worksheets.Count)
```

Important When you use either the **Copy** or the **Move** method, if you do not specify the ***Before*** or ***After*** argument, Excel creates a new workbook and copies the specified worksheet to it.

Understanding the Range Object

In Excel, the **Range** object is the most powerful, dynamic, and often-used object. Once you develop a full understanding of the **Range** object and how to use it effectively in VBA procedures, you will be well on your way to harnessing the power of Excel.

The Excel **Range** object is somewhat unique in terms of objects. In most cases, an "object" is a thing with some clearly identifiable corollary in the Excel user interface. For example, a **Workbook** object is recognizable as an .xls file. In a workbook, the collection of **Worksheet** objects is represented in the user interface by separate tabbed sheets. But the **Range** object is different. A range can be a different thing in different circumstances. A **Range** object can be a single cell or a collection of cells. It can be a single object or a collection of objects. It can be a row or column, and it can represent a three-dimensional collection of cells that span multiple worksheets. In addition, unlike other objects that exist as objects and as members of a collection of objects, there is no **Ranges** collection containing all **Range** objects in a workbook or worksheet. It is probably easiest to think of the **Range** object as your handle to the thing you want to work with.

Because the **Range** object is such a fundamental entity within Excel, you will find that many different properties and methods return a **Range** object that you can use to work with the data in your custom solution. The following sections discuss some basic aspects of **Range** objects and many of the ways you can return a **Range** object from a built-in property or method.

The Range Property

You will use the **Range** property to return a **Range** object in many different circumstances. The **Application** object, the **Worksheet** object, and the **Range** object all have a **Range** property. The **Application** object's **Range** property returns the same **Range** object as that returned by the **Worksheet** object. In other words, the **Application** object's **Range** property returns a reference to the specified cell or cells on the active worksheet. The **Range** property of the **Range** object has a subtle difference that it is important to understand. Consider the following example:

```
Dim rng1 As Range
Dim rng2 As Range
Dim rng3 As Range

Set rng1 = Application.Range("B5")
Set rng2 = Worksheets("Sheet1").Range("B5")
Set rng3 = rng2.Range("B5")
```

The three **Range** objects do not all return a reference to the same cell. In this example, `rng1` and `rng2` both return a reference to cell B5. But `rng3` returns a reference to cell C9. This difference occurs because the **Range** object's **Range** property returns a reference *relative* to the specified cell. In this case, the specified cell is B5. Therefore, the "B" means that the reference will be one column to the right of B5, and the "5" means the reference will be the fifth row below the row specified by B5. In other words, the **Range** object's **Range** property returns a reference to a cell that is *n* columns to the right and *y* rows down from the specified cell.

You will typically use the **Range** property to return a **Range** object, and then use the properties and methods of that **Range** object to work with the data in a cell or group of cells. The following table contains several examples illustrating usage of the **Range** property.

To do this	Use this code
Set the value of cell A1 on Sheet1 to 100	`Worksheets("Sheet1").Range("A1").Value = 100`
Set the value for a group of cells on the active worksheet	`Range("B2:B14").Value = 10000`
Set the formula for cell B15 on the active worksheet	`Range("B15").Formula = "=Sum(B2:B14)"`
Set the font to bold	`Range("B15").Font.Bold = True`
Set the font color to green	`Range("B15").Font.Color = RGB(0, 255, 0)`
Set an object variable to refer to a single cell	`Set rngCurrent = Range("A1")`
Set an object variable to refer to a group of cells	`Set rngCurrent = Range("A1:L1")`
Format all the cells in a named range	`Range("YTDSalesTotals").Font.Bold = True`

To do this	Use this code
Set an object variable to a named range	`Set rngCurrent = Range("NovemberReturns")`
Set an object variable representing all the used cells on the Employees worksheet	`Set rngCurrent = Worksheets("Employees").UsedRange`
Set an object variable representing the group of related cells that surround the active cell	`Set rngCurrent = ActiveCell.CurrentRegion`
Set an object variable representing the first three columns in the active worksheet	`Set rngCurrent = Range("A:C")`
Set an object variable representing rows 3, 5, 7, and 9 of the active worksheet	`Set rngCurrent = Range("3:3, 5:5, 7:7, 9:9")`
Set an object variable representing multiple noncontiguous groups of cells on the active sheet	`Set rngCurrent = Range("A1:C4, D6:G12, I2:L7")`
Remove the contents for all cells within a specified group of cells (B5:B10) while leaving the formatting intact	`Range("B5", "B10").ClearContents`

As you can see from the examples in the preceding table, the ***Cell*** argument of the **Range** property is either an A1-style string reference or a string representing a named range within the current workbook.

You will also use the **Range** property to return **Range** objects as arguments to other methods in the Excel object model. When you use the **Range** property in this way, make sure you fully qualify the **Worksheet** object to which the **Range** property applies. Failing to use fully qualified references to the **Range** property in arguments for Excel methods is one of the most common sources of error in range-related code.

The ActiveCell and Selection Properties

The **ActiveCell** property returns a **Range** object representing the currently active cell. When a single cell is selected, the **ActiveCell** property returns a **Range** object representing that single cell. When multiple cells are selected, the **ActiveCell** property represents the single active cell within the current selection. When a cell or group of cells is selected, the **Selection** property returns a **Range** object representing all the cells within the current selection.

To understand how the **ActiveCell** and **Selection** properties relate to one another, consider the case where a user selects cells A1 through F1 by clicking cell A1 and dragging until the selection extends over cell F1. In this case, the **ActiveCell** property returns a **Range** object that represents cell A1. The **Selection** property returns a **Range** object representing cells A1 through F1.

When you work with Excel's user interface, you typically select a cell or group of cells and then perform some action on the selected cell or cells, such as entering a value for a single cell or formatting a group of cells. When you use VBA to work with cells, you don't need to make a selection before performing some action on a cell or group of cells. Instead, you need only return a **Range** object representing the cell or cells you want to work with. For example, to enter "January" as the value for cell A1 by using the user interface, you would select cell A1 and type **January**. The following sample performs the same action in VBA:

```
ActiveSheet.Range("A1").Value = "January"
```

Using VBA to work with a **Range** object in this manner does not change the selected cells on the current worksheet. However, you can make your VBA code act upon cells in the same way as a user working through the user interface by using the **Range** object's **Select** method to select a cell or range of cells and then using the **Range** object's **Activate** method to activate a cell within the current selection. For example, the following code selects cells A1 through A6 and then makes cell A3 the active cell:

```
With ActiveSheet
   .Range("A1:A6").Select
   .Range("A3").Activate
End With
```

When you use the **Select** method to select multiple cells, the first cell referenced will be the active cell. For example, in the preceding sample, after the **Select** method is executed, the **ActiveCell** property returns a reference to cell A1, even though cells A1 through A6 are selected. After the **Activate** method is executed in the next line of code, the **ActiveCell** property returns a reference to cell A3 while cells A1 through A6 remain selected. The next example illustrates how to return a **Range** object by using the **ActiveCell** property or the **Selection** property:

```
Dim rngActiveRange As Excel.Range

' Range object returned from the Selection property.
Set rngActiveRange = Selection
Call PrintRangeInfo(rngActiveRange)
' Range object returned from the ActiveCell property.
Set rngActiveRange = ActiveCell
Call PrintRangeInfo(rngActiveRange)
```

The PrintRangeInfo custom procedure called in the preceding example prints information about the cell or cells contained in the **Range** object passed in the argument to the procedure. This procedure is available in the modExcelSamples module in ExcelSamples.xls in the Samples\CH05 subfolder on the companion CD-ROM.

> **The Macro Recorder and the Selection Object**
>
> When you are learning to work with the Excel object model, it is often helpful to turn on the macro recorder and carry out the steps you want to accomplish and then examine the VBA code that results to see which objects, properties, and methods are used. You should be aware, however, that in many cases the macro recorder records your actions from the perspective of a user interacting with the user interface. This means that the **Selection** object, the **Select** method, and the **Activate** method are used over and over.
>
> Once you get a solid grasp on the most efficient way to work with Excel objects, you will find yourself rewriting or restructuring the VBA code written by the macro recorder to use the **Range** object instead.

Using the CurrentRegion and UsedRange Properties

There are many circumstances where you will write code to work against a range of cells but at the time you write the code you will not have information about the range. For example, you may not know the size or location of a range or the location of a cell in relation to another cell. You can use the **CurrentRegion** and **UsedRange** properties to work with a range of cells whose size you have no control over. You can use the **Offset** property to work with cells in relation to other cells where the cell location is unknown. For more information about the **Offset** property, see "Using the Offset Property" later in this chapter.

As shown in Figure 5.2, the **Range** object's **CurrentRegion** property returns a **Range** object representing a range bounded by (but not including) any combination of blank rows and blank columns or the edges of the worksheet.

Figure 5.2 The Ranges Returned by the ActiveCell and CurrentRegion Properties

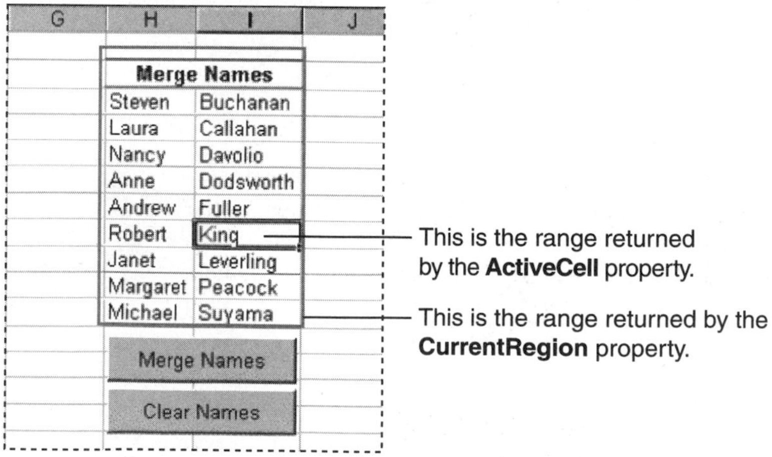

G	H	I	J
	Merge Names		
	Steven	Buchanan	
	Laura	Callahan	
	Nancy	Davolio	
	Anne	Dodsworth	
	Andrew	Fuller	
	Robert	King	
	Janet	Leverling	
	Margaret	Peacock	
	Michael	Suyama	
	Merge Names		
	Clear Names		

This is the range returned by the **ActiveCell** property.

This is the range returned by the **CurrentRegion** property.

The **CurrentRegion** property can return many different ranges on a single worksheet. This property is useful for operations where you need to know the dimensions of a group of related cells, but all you know for sure is the location of a cell or cells within the group. For example, when the active cell is inside a table of cells, you could use the following line of code to apply formatting to the entire table:

```
ActiveCell.CurrentRegion.AutoFormat xlRangeAutoFormatAccounting4
```

You could also use the **CurrentRegion** property to return a collection of cells. For example:

```
Dim rngCurrentCell As Excel.Range

For Each rngCurrentCell In ActiveCell.CurrentRegion.Cells
   ' Work with individual cells here.
Next rngCurrentCell
```

Every **Worksheet** object has a **UsedRange** property that returns a **Range** object representing the area of a worksheet that is being used. The **UsedRange** property represents the area described by the farthest upper-left and farthest lower-right nonempty cells on a worksheet and includes all cells in between. For example, imagine a worksheet with entries in only two cells: A1 and G55. The worksheet's **UsedRange** property would return a **Range** object containing 385 cells between and including A1 and G55.

You might use the **UsedRange** property together with the **SpecialCells** method to return a **Range** object representing all cells on a worksheet of a specified type. For example, the following code returns a **Range** object that includes all the cells in the active worksheet that contain a formula:

```
Dim rngFormulas As Excel.Range
Set rngFormulas = ActiveSheet.UsedRange.SpecialCells(xlCellTypeFormulas)
```

If you examine the sample code in the ExcelSamples.xls file in the Samples\CH05 subfolder on the companion CD-ROM, you will find many procedures that use the **CurrentRegion** and **UsedRange** properties to define ranges.

Using the Cells Property

You use the **Cells** property to loop through a range of cells on a worksheet or to refer to a range by using numeric row and column values. The **Cells** property returns a **Range** object representing all the cells, or a specified cell, in a worksheet. To work with a single cell, you use the **Item** property of the **Range** object returned by the **Cells** property to specify the index of a specific cell. The **Item** property accepts arguments specifying the row or the row and column index for a cell.

Since the **Item** property is the default property of the **Range** object, it is not necessary to explicitly reference it. For example, the following **Set** statements both return a reference to cell B5 on Sheet1:

```
Dim rng1 As Excel.Range
Dim rng2 As Excel.Range

Set rng1 = Worksheet("Sheet1").Cells.Item(5, 2)
Set rng2 = Worksheet("Sheet1").Cells(5, 2)
```

The row and column index arguments of the **Item** property return references to individual cells beginning with the first cell in the specified range. For example, the following message box displays "G11" because that is the first cell in the specified **Range** object:

```
MsgBox Range("G11:M30").Cells(1,1).Address
```

The following procedure illustrates how you would use the **Cells** property to loop through all the cells in a specified range. The OutOfBounds procedure looks for values that are greater than or less than a specified range of values and changes the font color for each cell with such a value:

```
Function OutOfBounds(rngToCheck As Excel.Range, _
                     lngLowValue As Long, _
                     lngHighValue As Long, _
                     Optional lngHighlightColor As Long = 255) As Boolean
   ' This procedure illustrates how to use the Cells property
   ' to iterate through a collection of cells in a range.
   ' For each cell in the rngTocheck range, if the value of the
   ' cell is numeric and it falls outside the range of values
   ' specified by lngLowValue to lngHighValue, the cell font
   ' is changed to the value of lngHighlightColor (default is red).
   Dim rngTemp         As Excel.Range
   Dim lngRowCounter   As Long
   Dim lngColCounter   As Long

   ' Validate bounds parameters.
   If lngLowValue > lngHighValue Then
      Err.Raise vbObjectError + 512 + 1, _
         "OutOfBounds Procedure", _
         "Invalid bounds parameters submitted: " _
            & "Low value must be lower than high value."
      Exit Function
   End If

   ' Iterate through cells and determine if values
   ' are outside bounds parameters. If so, highlight value.
   For lngRowCounter = 1 To rngToCheck.Rows.Count
      For lngColCounter = 1 To rngToCheck.Columns.Count
```

```
            Set rngTemp = rngToCheck.Cells(lngRowCounter, lngColCounter)
            If IsNumeric(rngTemp.Value) Then
               If rngTemp.Value < lngLowValue Or rngTemp.Value > lngHighValue Then
                  rngTemp.Font.Color = lngHighlightColor
                  OutOfBounds = True
               End If
            End If
         Next lngColCounter
      Next lngRowCounter
   End Function
```

The OutOfBounds procedure is available in the modExcelSamples module in ExcelSamples.xls in the Samples\CH05 subfolder on the companion CD-ROM.

You can also use a **For Each...Next** statement to loop through the range returned by the **Cells** property. The following code could be used in the OutOfBounds procedure to loop through cells in a range:

```
' Iterate through cells and determine if values
' are outside bounds parameters. If so, highlight value.
For Each rngTemp in rngToCheck.Cells
   If IsNumeric(rngTemp.Value) Then
      If rngTemp.Value < lngLowValue Or rngTemp.Value > lngHighValue Then
         rngTemp.Font.Color = lngHighlightColor
         OutOfBounds = True
      End If
   End If
Next rngTemp
```

Using the Offset Property

You can use the **Offset** property to return a **Range** object with the same dimensions as a specified **Range** object but offset from the specified range. For example, you could use the **Offset** property to create a new **Range** object adjacent to the active cell to contain calculated values based on the active cell.

The **Offset** property is useful in circumstances where you do not know the specific address of the cells you will need to work with, but you do know where the cell is located *in relation to* other cells you need to work with. For example, you may have a command bar button in your custom solution that fills the active cell with the average of the values in the two cells immediately to the left of the active cell:

```
ActiveCell.Value = (ActiveCell.Offset(0, -2) + ActiveCell.Offset(0, -1)/2)
```

For an example that illustrates how to use the **Offset** property to create full names out of a column of first names and a column of last names, see the MergeNamesExample procedure in the modExcelSamples module in ExcelSamples.xls in the Samples\CH05 subfolder on the companion CD-ROM.

Working with Microsoft FrontPage Objects

Microsoft FrontPage is new to the Office suite of applications and is available in Microsoft Office 2000 Premium. FrontPage is a powerful and popular application used to create, deploy, and manage Web sites. You can also use FrontPage to create individual Web pages or modify existing Web pages.

FrontPage 2000 now supports the Visual Basic Editor and VBA. In addition, to enable you to work with the various parts of a FrontPage-based web or a Web page, FrontPage now exposes a complete object model that you can use either from within a FrontPage VBA project or from another application through Automation. The new VBA language elements replace the FrontPage 98 language elements. To ensure backward compatibility, the FrontPage 98 language elements are included as hidden elements in the FrontPage 2000 object model, but these language elements are not recommended for use in FrontPage 2000.

Note You can view the FrontPage object model in the "Object Model Diagrams" appendix. You can also use the Object Browser and Microsoft FrontPage Visual Basic Reference Help to learn more about individual objects, properties, methods, and events. For more information about using VBA to work with an Office application's object model, see Chapter 4, "Understanding Office Objects and Object Models."

Although all Office applications support VBA, it is used a bit differently in FrontPage and Outlook than it is in the other Office applications. FrontPage and Outlook support a single VBA project that is associated with a running instance of the application. The other Office applications let you associate a VBA project with each Office document. For example, you can have several workbooks open in Excel at one time, and each workbook can have its own VBA project that contains modules, class modules, and UserForms. In FrontPage, you can have several webs or Web pages open at one time, but there is only one VBA project. The FrontPage VBA project is stored in a file named Microsoft FrontPage.fpm in the following locations:

- **Microsoft Windows** If user profiles have been set up for multiple users, Microsoft FrontPage.fpm is stored in the C:\Windows\Profiles*UserName*\Application Data \Microsoft\FrontPage\Macros subfolder. If user profiles have not been set up, Microsoft FrontPage.fpm is stored in the C:\Windows\Application Data\Microsoft \FrontPage\Macros subfolder.
- **Microsoft Windows NT Workstation and Microsoft Windows NT Server** The Microsoft FrontPage.fpm file is stored in the C:\Winnt\Profiles*UserName* \Application Data\Microsoft\FrontPage\Macros subfolder.

This section discusses how to work with commonly used FrontPage objects and their related methods and properties, but it does not provide a complete discussion of the FrontPage object model. You can get more information about the objects, methods, and properties in the FrontPage object model by using Microsoft FrontPage Visual Basic Reference Help in the C:\Program Files\Microsoft Office\Office\1033 \Vbafp4.chm file.

Note The path to the Vbafp4.chm Help file reflects the language ID folder (1033) for U.S. English language support in Office. The language ID folder below C:\Program Files \Microsoft Office\Office differs for each language.

Understanding the FrontPage Object Model

Microsoft FrontPage is designed to work with Web sites. A Web site can exist on a local intranet or on a server on the World Wide Web. There are several different metaphors you can use when envisioning a Web site. For example, you can think of a Web site as a collection of windows showing different parts of the Web site in an open instance of FrontPage. Or, you might think of a Web site as a collection of files on disk, organized in folders, all of which are organized under one main folder that contains the entire web. Finally, you could think of a Web site as the relationship between pages that exists as a result of the navigation structure between the pages.

When you have one or more Web sites open in FrontPage, the **Webs** collection contains a **Web** object representing each open Web site. Each **Web** object has a **WebWindow** object that represents the main application window containing the web. The **WebWindow** object looks like a separate instance of FrontPage; for example, each **WebWindow** object has its own FrontPage icon on the Windows taskbar. Each **WebWindow** object has a **PageWindows** collection that contains a **PageWindow** object for each open Web page. And each **PageWindow** object has a **Document** property that returns the DHTML **document** object for a Web page in the FrontPage web. For more information about the **document** object, see "Understanding the Page Object Model" later in this chapter.

When you first open FrontPage, you see a blank Web page open in Page view. You can use the **Normal**, **HTML**, and **Preview** tabs along the bottom of the page to edit the page in different ways or to preview it in your Web browser. The FrontPage menu bar and toolbars appear above the page, and the FrontPage **Views** bar appears along the left side of the page. At this point, FrontPage contains a single blank document only. There is no open Web site, and as a result, the **Webs** collection object's **Count** property returns zero. In addition, the **WebWindows** collection contains a single **WebWindow** object, and the **PageWindows** collection contains one **PageWindow** object that contains the blank page.

Each of these objects and collections has methods and properties you can use to work with the object. For example, the **PageWindow** object has a **Document** property you can use to work with the HTML elements contained in the Web page and an **IsDirty** property you can use to determine if the page has been changed. In addition, the **PageWindow** object has an **ApplyTheme** method you can use to apply a FrontPage theme to the page and **Save** and **SaveAs** methods you can use to save the page.

FrontPage-based webs exist on disk as a collection of files organized in folders. The base for the web is the root folder in the directory structure. For example, if you created a web called MyPersonalWeb on your hard disk, the root folder for the web could be C:\MyWebs\MyPersonalWeb. Under the MyPersonalWeb folder would be all the directories that make up your Web site. For example, when you use FrontPage to create a Web site based on the Personal Web template, FrontPage creates nine subfolders for the web that contain supporting files, such as images and style sheets.

The file structure of a web as it exists on disk is also available through the object model. Each folder in the web is represented by a **WebFolder** object. The **RootFolder** property returns the root **WebFolder** object in the web. The **WebFolders** collection contains a **WebFolder** object for each folder in the web. Each **WebFolder** object has, among others, a **Folders** property and a **Files** property. The **Folders** property returns a **WebFolders** collection for all the subfolders under a folder. The **Files** property returns a **WebFiles** collection that contains a **WebFile** object for each file in a folder.

The navigation structure of a Web site starts with a home page that can branch off to other pages in the Web site. In FrontPage, you can programmatically move through the navigation structure of a Web site by using **NavigationNode** objects. A **NavigationNode** object represents a node in the navigation structure of a Web site. The **NavigationNodes** collection contains all the **NavigationNode** objects in a Web site. You start navigation at the home page by using the **HomeNavigationNode** property, which returns the **NavigationNode** object for the Web site's home page. Each **NavigationNode** object has a **Children** property that returns the **NavigationNodes** collection representing all of the pages you can navigate to from a **NavigationNode** object. You use the **Move** method to move among **NavigationNode** objects in the **NavigationNodes** collection returned by the **Children** property. You use the **Next** and **Prev** properties to return the next or previous **NavigationNode** object.

Whether you use windows, files, or navigation nodes to move among objects in FrontPage will depend on what you are trying to accomplish.

Understanding the Application Object

The **Application** object is the top-level object in the FrontPage object model. It represents FrontPage itself and provides access to all of the objects in the FrontPage object model. If you are automating FrontPage from another Office application, you should set a reference to the Microsoft FrontPage 4.0 Page Object Reference library by clicking **References** on the **Tools** menu in the Visual Basic Editor in the application you are working from. You can then write code to instantiate an **Application** object variable, as shown in the following example:

```
Dim fpApp As FrontPage.Application

Set fpApp = New FrontPage.Application
```

To create a FrontPage **Application** object without setting a reference to the FrontPage 4.0 Page Object Reference library, you can use the **CreateObject** function.

If you are writing VBA code from within the FrontPage VBA project, you can refer to the **Application** object directly without creating an object variable.

From the **Application** object, you can reach any other object in the FrontPage object model. In addition, the properties, methods, and events of the **Application** object are also *global properties* that you can use to return currently active objects. A global property is a property that you can use to return an object without having to refer to the **Application** object or any top-level objects. The global properties that represent active objects in FrontPage are **ActiveDocument**, **ActivePageWindow**, **ActiveWeb**, and **ActiveWebWindow**. The following examples illustrate how you can work with these properties and the objects they represent:

```
' Apply the classic theme to the active document and specify
' vivid colors and active graphics.
ActiveDocument.ApplyTheme "classic", fpThemeVividColors + fpThemeActiveGraphics

' Locate the HelpInformation.htm file in the currently active web.
Dim wflCurrentFile As WebFile

Set wflCurrentFile = ActiveWeb.LocateFile("HelpInformation.htm")
If Not wflCurrentFile Is Nothing Then
   With wflCurrentFile
      ' Code to work with found file here.
   End With
End If

' Check to see if the page in the active page window has changed and,
' if so, save it to disk.
With ActivePageWindow
   If .IsDirty Then
      .Refresh SaveChanges:=True
   End If
End With
```

```
' Display a message showing the window captions for all open
' documents in the active web window.
Dim pgeCurr       As PageWindow
Dim strCaptions   As String

If ActiveWebWindow.PageWindows.Count > 0 Then
   For Each pgeCurr In ActiveWebWindow.PageWindows
      strCaptions = strCaptions & pgeCurr.Caption & vbCrLf
   Next pgeCurr
   If Len(strCaptions) > 0 Then
      MsgBox "The following pages are currently open:" & vbCrLf & strCaptions
   End If
End If
```

The **Application** object also exposes properties that you can use to get information about the current machine, such as the user's name, the version of FrontPage, the language settings, and the registry values, among others. You can use the **System** property to return the **System** object, which provides information about the operating system and screen resolution. In addition, you can use the **ProfileString** property of the **System** object to read and write FrontPage registry values.

In addition to getting information about the current machine, the **Application** object provides ten application-level events that you can use to run VBA code when the events occur.

Understanding the Page Object Model

When you write script to work with the HTML elements in a Web page you are working with the page through the DHTML **document** object model. FrontPage exposes nearly all of the methods and properties of this object model through the FrontPage Page object model. To see the restrictions of the Page object model, search the Microsoft FrontPage Visual Basic Reference Help index for "object model," and then open the "Exploring the FrontPage Object Model" topic.

In FrontPage, you can use VBA code to work with the HTML elements in a Web page. You use the **Document** property or the **ActiveDocument** property to return a DHTML **document** object. Once you have the **document** object, you have access to all HTML elements contained in a Web page. For more information about working with the DHTML object model, see Chapter 12, "Using Web Technologies." You can get documentation for all of the objects, properties, and methods of the DHTML object model in the Htmlref.chm file located in the C:\Program Files \Microsoft Visual Studio\Common\IDE\IDE98\MSE\1033 subfolder.

Note The path to the Htmlref.chm Help file reflects the language ID folder (1033) for U.S. English language support in Office. The language ID folder below C:\Program Files \Microsoft Visual Studio\Common\IDE\IDE98\MSE differs for each language.

Working with Microsoft Outlook Objects

You can create custom Outlook objects and manipulate those objects from within Outlook or from another application. This section discusses how to manipulate Outlook objects by using VBA code from within Outlook or from another Office application by using Automation. The Microsoft Outlook object model exposes Outlook objects, which you can use to gain programmatic access to Outlook functionality. Before you use VBA to access Outlook objects, methods, or properties from another application, you must first set a reference to the Microsoft Outlook 9.0 object library by clicking **References** on the **Tools** menu in the Visual Basic Editor.

Note You can view the entire Outlook object model in the "Object Model Diagrams" appendix. You can also use Microsoft Outlook Visual Basic Reference Help to learn more about individual objects, properties, methods, and events. For more information about using VBA to work with an Office application's object model, see Chapter 4, "Understanding Office Objects and Object Models."

Understanding the Application and NameSpace Objects

When you manipulate Outlook objects, you always start with the **Application** object. If you are using VBA in Outlook, there is a reference to the Outlook object library set by default. If you are using Automation to work with Outlook objects from another application, you must first set a reference to the Outlook 9.0 object library by using the **References** dialog box in the application you are working from. If you have set a reference to the Outlook 9.0 object library, you create a new instance of an Outlook **Application** object by using the **New** keyword as follows:

```
Dim olApp As Outlook.Application

Set olApp = New Outlook.Application
```

If you have not set a reference to the Outlook 9.0 object library, you must use the **CreateObject** function. There can only be one instance of Outlook available at one time. Therefore, when Outlook is not running, the **New** keyword (or the **CreateObject** function) creates a new, hidden, instance of Outlook. If an instance of Outlook is already running, then using the **New** keyword (or the **CreateObject** function) returns a reference to the running instance. For more information about using the **New** keyword or the **CreateObject** function, see Chapter 4, "Understanding Office Objects and Object Models."

You use the **Application** object's **CreateItem** method to create a new Outlook item. You access existing Outlook items by using the **NameSpace** object.

All the sample procedures discussed in this section use global object variables to represent the **Application** object and the **NameSpace** object. Each procedure first checks to see if the **Application** object variable has been created and, if not, calls the InitializeOutlook procedure to instantiate the global **Application** and **NameSpace** object variables. For example:

```
' Declare global Outlook Application and NameSpace variables.
' These are declared as global variables so that they need not
' be re-created for each procedure that uses them.
Public golApp        As Outlook.Application
Public gnspNameSpace As Outlook.NameSpace

Function InitializeOutlook() As Boolean
   ' This function is used to initialize the global Application and
   ' NameSpace variables.

   On Error GoTo Init_Err

   Set golApp = New Outlook.Application           ' Application object.
   Set gnspNameSpace = golApp.GetNamespace("MAPI") ' Namespace object.

   InitializeOutlook = True

Init_End:
   Exit Function
Init_Err:
   InitializeOutlook = False
   Resume Init_End
End Function
```

The InitializeOutlook procedure is available in the modOutlookCode module in OutlookSamples.mdb in the Samples\CH05 subfolder on the companion CD-ROM.

You use an **olItemType** constant as the **CreateItem** method's single argument to specify whether you want to create a new appointment, contact, distribution list, journal entry, mail message, note, posting to a public folder, or task. The **CreateItem** method returns an object of the type specified in the **olItemType** constant; you can then use this object to set additional properties of the item. For example, the following procedure creates a new mail message and sets the recipients, attachments, subject, and message text by using the information passed to the procedure as arguments:

```
Function CreateMail(astrRecip As Variant, _
                    strSubject As String, _
                    strMessage As String, _
                    Optional astrAttachments As Variant) As Boolean
   ' This procedure illustrates how to create a new mail message
   ' and use the information passed as arguments to set message
   ' properties for the subject, text (Body property), attachments,
   ' and recipients.
```

```
   Dim objNewMail          As Outlook.MailItem
   Dim varRecip            As Variant
   Dim varAttach           As Variant
   Dim blnResolveSuccess   As Boolean

   On Error GoTo CreateMail_Err

   ' Use the InitializeOutlook procedure to initialize global
   ' Application and NameSpace object variables, if necessary.
   If golApp Is Nothing Then
      If InitializeOutlook = False Then
         MsgBox "Unable to initialize Outlook Application "
            & "or NameSpace object variables!"
         Exit Function
      End If
   End If

   Set golApp = New Outlook.Application
   Set objNewMail = golApp.CreateItem(olMailItem)
   With objNewMail
      For Each varRecip In astrRecip
         .Recipients.Add varRecip
      Next varRecip
      blnResolveSuccess = .Recipients.ResolveAll
      For Each varAttach In astrAttachments
         .Attachments.Add varAttach
      Next varAttach
      .Subject = strSubject
      .Body = strMessage
      If blnResolveSuccess Then
         .Send
      Else
         MsgBox "Unable to resolve all recipients. Please check " _
            & "the names."
         .Display
      End If
   End With

   CreateMail = True

CreateMail_End:
   Exit Function
CreateMail_Err:
   CreateMail = False
   Resume CreateMail_End
End Function
```

The preceding procedure also illustrates how to use a **MailItem** object's **Recipients** and **Attachments** properties to return the respective collection objects and then add one or more recipients or attachments to a mail message. The CreateMail procedure is available in the modOutlookCode module in OutlookSamples.mdb in the Samples\CH05 subfolder on the companion CD-ROM.

For an example of a procedure you can use to create any new Outlook item, see the CreateNewOutlookItem procedure in the modOutlookCode module in OutlookSamples.mdb in the Samples\CH05 subfolder on the companion CD-ROM.

You use the **Application** object's **GetNameSpace** method to instantiate an object variable representing a recognized data source. Currently, Outlook supports the `"MAPI"` message store as the only valid **NameSpace** object. To see an example of how to use the **GetNameSpace** method to create a **NameSpace** object variable, see the InitializeOutlook procedure earlier in this section.

If Outlook is not running when you create a **NameSpace** object variable, the user will be prompted for a profile if the user's mail services startup setting is set to **Prompt for a profile to be used**. Startup settings are on the **Mail Services** tab of the **Options** dialog box (**Tools** menu). You can use the **NameSpace** object's **Logon** method to specify a profile programmatically. Profiles are stored in the Windows registry under the \HKEY_CURRENT_USER\Software\Microsoft\Windows Messaging Subsystem \Profiles subkey.

Working with Outlook Folders and Items

You can think of the **NameSpace** object as the gateway to all existing Outlook folders. By default, Outlook creates two top-level folders representing all public folders and all mailbox folders. Mailbox folders contain all Outlook built-in and custom folders. Each folder is a **MAPIFolder** object. **MAPIFolder** objects can contain subfolders (which are also **MAPIFolder** objects), as well as individual Outlook item objects, such as **MailItem** objects, **ContactItem** objects, **JournalItem** objects, and so on.

Note In Outlook, an "item" is the object that holds information (similar to files in other applications). Items include mail messages, appointments, contacts, tasks, journal entries, and notes.

Once you have created a **NameSpace** object variable, you can access the top-level folder for any built-in Outlook item by using the **NameSpace** object's **GetDefaultFolder** method. For example, the following code sample returns a reference to the ContactItems folder:

```
Dim fldContacts As Outlook.MAPIFolder
Set fldContacts = gnspNameSpace.GetDefaultFolder(olFolderContacts)
```

You can also return a reference to any folder by using the name of the folder. For example, the following procedure returns a reference to the folder in the current user's mailbox whose name is specified in the *strFolderName* argument:

```
Function GetFolderByName(strFolderName As String) As Outlook.MAPIFolder
   ' This procedure illustrates how to return a MAPIFolder
   ' object representing any folder in the mailbox folders
   ' collection whose name is specified by the strFolderName
   ' argument.
   Dim fldMain As Outlook.MAPIFolder
```

```
   On Error Resume Next

   ' Use the InitializeOutlook procedure to initialize global
   ' Application and NameSpace object variables, if necessary.
   If golApp Is Nothing Then
      If InitializeOutlook = False Then
         MsgBox "Unable to initialize Outlook Application " _
            & "or NameSpace object variables!"
         Exit Function
      End If
   End If

   Set fldMain = gnspNameSpace.Folders(GetMailboxName()).Folders(strFolderName)
   If Err = 0 Then
      Set GetFolderByName = fldMain
   Else
      ' Note: The most likely cause of an error here is that
      ' the folder specified in strFolderName could not be found.
      Set GetFolderByName = Nothing
   End If
End Function
```

You may recall that the **NameSpace** object has at least two top-level folders representing all public folders and the user's mailbox. The preceding procedure uses the GetMailboxName procedure to return the name of the mailbox folder. The GetMailboxName and GetFolderByName procedures are available in the modOutlookCode module in OutlookSamples.mdb in the Samples\CH05 subfolder on the companion CD-ROM.

Once you return a reference to a folder in the user's mailbox, that folder may contain additional folders, individual Outlook items, or both. The GetFolderInfo procedure in the modOutlookCode module in OutlookSamples.mdb in the Samples\CH05 subfolder on the companion CD-ROM illustrates how to iterate through all the subfolders and items within a folder and retrieve information about the items contained in a folder or subfolder.

```
Sub GetFolderInfo(fldFolder As Outlook.MAPIFolder)
   ' This procedure prints to the Immediate window information
   ' about items contained in a folder.
   Dim objItem           As Object
   Dim dteCreateDate     As Date
   Dim strSubject        As String
   Dim strItemType       As String
   Dim intCounter        As Integer

   On Error Resume Next

   If fldFolder.Folders.Count > 0 Then
      For Each objItem In fldFolder.Folders
         Call GetFolderInfo(objItem)
      Next objItem
   End If
```

```
      Debug.Print "Folder '" & fldFolder.Name & "' (Contains " _
         & fldFolder.Items.Count & " items):"
      For Each objItem In fldFolder.Items
         intCounter = intCounter + 1
         With objItem
            dteCreateDate = .CreationTime
            strSubject = .Subject
            strItemType = TypeName(objItem)
         End With
         Debug.Print vbTab & "Item #" & intCounter & " - " _
            & strItemType & " - created on " _
            & Format(dteCreateDate, "mmmm dd, yyyy hh:mm am/pm") _
            & vbCrLf & vbTab & vbTab & "Subject: '" _
            & strSubject & "'" & vbCrLf
   Next objItem
End Sub
```

The GetFolderInfo procedure examines a folder for subfolders and calls itself recursively until there are no subfolders remaining. It then prints information about the items contained in the folder or subfolder to the Immediate window. Note that the `objItem` object variable is declared by using the **Object** data type so that the procedure can work with any Outlook item.

To work with a single item or subset of items in a folder, you use the **Restrict** method, which returns a collection of objects that match the criteria specified in the method's single argument. For example, the following procedure uses the **Restrict** method to create a collection of Outlook **ContactItem** objects that match the name supplied in the *strLastName* argument:

```
Function GetItemFromName(strLastName As String, _
                         Optional strFirstName As String = "", _
                         Optional strCompany As String = "") As Boolean
   ' This procedure returns an Outlook ContactItem that matches the
   ' criteria specified in the arguments passed to the procedure.
   Dim fldFolder             As Outlook.MAPIFolder
   Dim objItemsCollection    As Object
   Dim objItem               As Object
   Dim strCriteria           As String
   Dim objMatchingItem       As Object

   On Error GoTo GetItem_Err

   ' Use the InitializeOutlook procedure to initialize global
   ' Application and NameSpace object variables, if necessary.
   If golApp Is Nothing Then
      If InitializeOutlook = False Then
         MsgBox "Unable to initialize Outlook Application " _
            & "or NameSpace object variables!"
         Exit Function
      End If
   End If
```

```
   Set fldFolder = gnspNameSpace.GetDefaultFolder(olFolderContacts)

   If Len(strLastName) = 0 And Len(strFirstName) = 0 Then
      If Len(strCompany) > 0 Then
         strCriteria = "[Company] = '" & strCompany & "'"
      End If
   Else
      strCriteria = IIf(Len(strFirstName) = 0, _
         "[LastName] = '" & strLastName & "'", _
         "[LastName] = '" & strLastName & _
         "' AND [FirstName] = '" & strFirstName & "'")
   End If
   Set objItemsCollection = fldFolder.Items.Restrict(strCriteria)
   If objItemsCollection.Count > 0 Then
      If objItemsCollection.Count = 1 Then
         For Each objItem In objItemsCollection
            Set objMatchingItem = _
               gnspNameSpace.GetItemFromID(objItem.EntryId)
            objMatchingItem.Display
            GetItemFromName = True
            Exit Function
         Next objItem
      Else
         GetItemFromName = False
         Exit Function
      End If
   End If

   GetItemFromName = True

GetItem_End:
   Exit Function
GetItem_Err:
   GetItemFromName = False
   Resume GetItem_End
End Function
```

The GetItemFromName procedure is available in the modOutlookCode module in OutlookSamples.mdb in the Samples\CH05 subfolder on the companion CD-ROM.

When you are using the **Restrict** method, you use Outlook field names within brackets to specify criteria for a search. You can join multiple criteria by using operators such as **And**, **Or**, and **Not**. For example, the following sample returns all the mail items sent in the last 7 days that are unread and marked as highly important:

```
Dim fldMail     As Outlook.MAPIFolder
Dim itmItems    As Outlook.Items

strCriteria = "[SentOn] > '" & (Date - 7) _
   & "' And [UnRead] = True And [Importance] = High"

Set fldMail = gnspNameSpace.GetDefaultFolder(olFolderInbox)
Set itmItems = fldMail.Items.Restrict(strCriteria)
```

The following example comes from the GetOutlook procedure in the modGetAddressCode module in NorthwindContacts.dot in the Samples\CH05 subfolder on the companion CD-ROM. This line illustrates how to return all the Outlook **ContactItem** items that contain a value in the Business Address field:

```
Set objContacts = fldContacts.Items.Restrict("[BusinessAddress] <> '" & strZLS & "'")
```

The NorthwindContacts.dot sample file is a Word template that retrieves contacts from the Outlook Contacts folder and then displays the contacts in a UserForm. When the user selects a contact from the form, the contact name and address information is inserted in an address block in a letter.

Note The NorthwindContacts.dot sample file also illustrates how to collect contact information from a database so that the user can insert name and address information into a letter.

Understanding the Explorer and Inspector Objects

The **Explorer** object represents what you would recognize as the Outlook user interface. For example, when you open Microsoft Outlook, you are working in the Outlook **Explorer** object. A window that contains a specific Outlook item, such as a mail message or a contact, is an Outlook **Inspector** object.

You can open these objects programmatically and display items for the user. You can also use the **ActiveExplorer** and **ActiveInspector** methods of the **Application** object to return a programmatic reference to the **Explorer** or **Inspector** object that the user is currently working with.

If you want to use VBA to add, remove, or manipulate command bars in Outlook, you start with a reference to the **Explorer** or **Inspector** object that contains the command bar you want to use and then use the object's **CommandBars** property to return a reference to the object's **CommandBars** collection. For example, the following code illustrates how to get a reference to the **CommandBars** collection for the active **Explorer** object:

```
Dim cbrExplorerBars As CommandBars
Set cbrExplorerBars = ActiveExplorer.CommandBars
```

You can use the GetExplorerInfo and GetInspectorInfo procedures to see sample code that uses the **Explorer** and **Inspector** objects to get information about what is displayed in the active Outlook **Explorer** and **Inspector** objects, including information about built-in and custom command bars. These procedures are available in the modOutlookExplorerAndInspector module in OutlookSamples.mdb in the Samples\CH05 subfolder on the companion CD-ROM. Figure 5.3 illustrates the kind of information you can get from an **Explorer** object.

Figure 5.3 Information Returned by the GetExplorerInfo Procedure

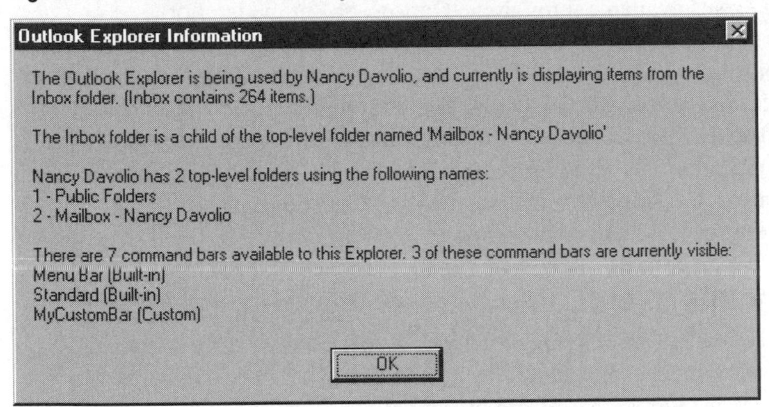

Understanding VBA in Outlook

Developers have wanted to use VBA in Outlook since Outlook was first released. Outlook 2000 now supports both the VBA language and the Visual Basic Editor found in all other Office applications.

Outlook supports a single VBA project that is associated with a particular user and a running instance of the application. The other Office applications (except FrontPage) let you associate a VBA project as code behind an individual Office document. Since Outlook has no "document" like the other Office applications, VBA code is associated only with the application.

Note The closest thing to a "document" in Outlook is an Outlook item (for example, a mail message, an appointment item, or a task). As in previous versions of Outlook, you use VBScript to write code behind an Outlook item.

The Outlook VBA project is stored in a file named VbaProject.OTM in the following locations:

- **Microsoft Windows** If user profiles have been set up for multiple users, VbaProject.OTM is stored in the C:\Windows\Profiles*UserName*\Application Data \Microsoft\Outlook subfolder. If user profiles have not been set up, VbaProject.OTM is stored in the C:\Windows\Application Data\Microsoft\Outlook subfolder.
- **Microsoft Windows NT Workstation and Microsoft Windows NT Server** The VbaProject.OTM file is stored in the C:\Winnt\Profiles*UserName* \Application Data\Microsoft\Outlook subfolder.

You use VBA in Outlook to customize the application by working with the objects, methods, properties, and events available through the Outlook object model. For example, you can add code to application-level events to process messages, add custom command bar controls to call custom VBA procedures, or create Component Object Model (COM) add-ins by using the Visual Basic Editor to debug the add-in as it is being developed and tested. You can access the Visual Basic Editor just like you do in any other Office application, by pointing to **Macro** on the **Tools** menu, and then clicking **Visual Basic Editor**. For information about creating COM add-ins, see Chapter 11, "Add-ins, Templates, Wizards, and Libraries."

Understanding Events in Outlook

There are two classes of events in Outlook, and you work with each class differently. The first class represents item-level events that are associated with a particular Outlook item. For example, an Outlook **MailItem** object has events such as Open, Close, Forward, and Send. As in previous versions of Outlook, you use VBScript code within the item itself to handle these item-level events.

The second class of events supported in Outlook represents application-level events. Because these events are associated with the application itself, or with top-level objects within the application, such as folders or the Outlook Bar, you can use VBA code to handle these events.

Application-Level Events

When you create a new VBA project in Word or Excel, the project contains, by default, a class module bound to the application's current document. For example, Word creates a module for the **ThisDocument** object and Excel creates a module for the **ThisWorkbook** object. In Outlook, because you use VBA to work with the application, the VBA project contains a class module called **ThisOutlookSession**, which is pre-bound to the Outlook **Application** object. As a result, all application-level events are available to you in the Visual Basic Editor's **Procedures** drop-down list when you click the **Application** object in the **Object** drop-down list.

There are six events associated with the **Application** object that you can use to run custom VBA procedures. For example, you could use the Startup event to call custom procedures to customize the Outlook workspace or to create or display custom command bars or command bar controls. You could use the NewMail event procedure to call custom procedures that implement your own rules for handling incoming mail. These events are somewhat self-explanatory, and you can get complete documentation for each event by searching the Microsoft Outlook Visual Basic Reference Help index for the name of the event.

Other Outlook Events

Working with the event procedures exposed by other Outlook objects is identical to creating event procedures in the other Office applications and requires a few more steps than are required when you are working with **Application** object events. First, you must declare an object variable by using the **WithEvents** keyword in the ThisOutlookSession module (or in another class module) for each object you want to work with. Second, you must add the VBA code to the event procedure that you want to run when the event occurs. Finally, you must initialize the object variables that you have created.

For example, the following VBA code illustrates how to create an object variable that represents the Outlook Bar in the ThisOutlookSession module:

```
Dim WithEvents obpOutlookBar As Outlook.OutlookBarPane
```

Once you declare an object variable as shown in the previous example, the variable name appears in the **Object** drop-down list in the class module's Code window. When you select this variable from the **Object** list, you can select the object's available event procedures by using the **Procedure** drop-down list. For example, the **OutlookBarPane** object shown earlier exposes the BeforeGroupSwitch and BeforeNavigate events.

```
Private Sub opbOutlookBar_BeforeNavigate(ByVal Shortcut As OutlookBarShortcut, _
      Cancel As Boolean)
   If Shortcut.Name <> "Inbox" Then
      Msgbox "Sorry, you only have permission to access the Inbox."
      Cancel = True
   End If
End Sub
```

Now you need to initialize the object variable. You can do this in two places: in the **Application** object's Startup event procedure, so that the variable is always available, or in a custom procedure you create for the purpose of initializing object variables. The following code shows how to initialize the object variable by using the Startup event procedure:

```
Private Sub Application_Startup()
   Set opbOutlookBar = Application.ActiveExplorer.Panes("OutlookBar")
End Sub
```

To determine how to instantiate an object variable, search the Microsoft Outlook Visual Basic Reference Help index for the name of the object you want to work with. For example, the Help topic for the **OutlookBarPane** object shows that the object is a member of the **Panes** collection and also that you use the string `"OutlookBar"` to identify the object within the collection.

You can get more information about the objects, methods, and properties in the Outlook object model by using Microsoft Outlook Visual Basic Reference Help in the C:\Program Files\Microsoft Office\Office\1033\Vbaoutl9.chm file.

Note The path to the Vbaoutl9.chm Help file reflects the language ID folder (1033) for U.S. English language support in Office. The language ID folder below C:\Program Files \Microsoft Office\Office differs for each language.

Working with Microsoft PowerPoint Objects

This section discusses how to use VBA to manipulate Microsoft PowerPoint objects, methods, properties, and events. Just like other Office applications, you begin automating PowerPoint by using the **Application** object. From the **Application** object you can open an existing **Presentation** object or create a new presentation. Each **Presentation** object contains one or more **Slide** objects and each **Slide** object can contain **Shape** objects that represent text, graphics, tables, and other items found on a slide.

Note You can view the entire PowerPoint object model in the "Object Model Diagrams" appendix. You can also use the Object Browser and Microsoft PowerPoint Visual Basic Reference Help to learn more about individual objects, properties, methods, and events. For more information about using VBA to work with an Office application's object model, see Chapter 4, "Understanding Office Objects and Object Models."

Understanding the PowerPoint Application Object

When you write VBA code to work with PowerPoint, you begin with the **Application** object. If you are writing VBA code within PowerPoint, the **Application** object is created for you. If you are automating PowerPoint from some other application, you first create a PowerPoint **Application** object variable and then create an instance of PowerPoint. Unlike the other Office applications (except Outlook), there can be only one instance of PowerPoint running at a time. If an instance of PowerPoint is running and you use the **New** keyword or the **CreateObject** or **GetObject** function to instantiate a PowerPoint object variable, that object variable will point to the currently running instance of PowerPoint. This single instance of the **Application** object can contain any number of open **Presentation** objects. For more information about using the **New** keyword or the **CreateObject** and **GetObject** functions, see Chapter 4, "Understanding Office Objects and Object Models."

Microsoft PowerPoint's **Application** object has properties you can use to access shared Office components such as command bars and the Office Assistant. In addition, the **Application** object has properties that return the currently active presentation or window, or information about the printer. The PPTShowApplicationInfo procedure illustrates how you might use properties of the **Application** object. This procedure is available in the modPPTCode module in PowerPointTools.ppt in the Samples\CH05 subfolder on the companion CD-ROM. Figure 5.4 displays the message box created by the PPTShowApplicationInfo procedure.

Figure 5.4 Information Returned by the PPTShowApplicationInfo Procedure

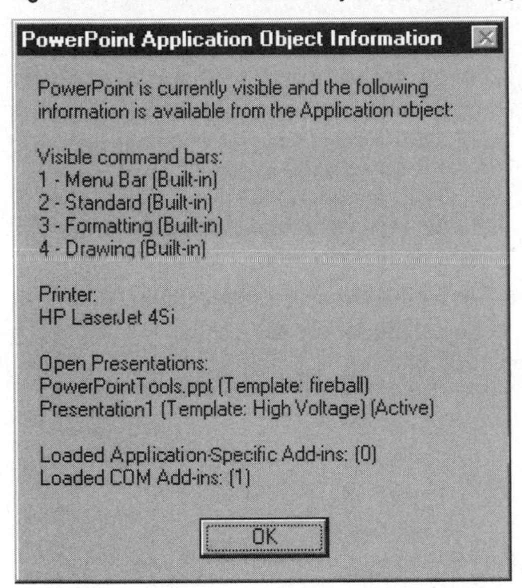

Working with the Presentation Object

When you are working with PowerPoint objects through VBA, you typically work with a **Presentation** object and the slides it contains.

Working with Open Presentations

You create a reference to an open presentation in two ways: by using the **Application** object's **ActivePresentation** property or by accessing a **Presentation** object as a member of the **Presentations** collection. There are three ways you can access a **Presentation** object through the **Presentations** collection:

- By using the presentation's file name.
- By using the **Caption** property setting of the **Window** object that contains the presentation.
- By using the presentation's index value. PowerPoint presentations are indexed in the order in which they are opened.

The following examples illustrate the different ways to set a reference to an open presentation:

```
Dim prsPres As PowerPoint.Presentation

' Use the ActivePresentation property.
Set prsPres = ActivePresentation
```

```
' Use the presentation's file name.
Set prsPres = Presentations("PowerPointTools.ppt")

' Use the Caption property setting of the Window
' object that contains the presentation.
Set prsPres = Presentations("PowerPointTools")

' Use the presentation's index value in the collection.
Set prsPres = Presentations(1)
```

Working with Existing Presentations

You can also use the **Presentations** collection's **Open** method to open a presentation saved to disk and create a reference to that presentation at the same time. The following example opens the PowerPointTools.ppt presentation:

```
Dim ppApp   As PowerPoint.Application
Dim prsPres As PowerPoint.Presentation

Set ppApp = New PowerPoint.Application
Set prsPres = ppApp.Presentations.Open("c:\opg\samples\ch05\PowerPointTools.ppt")
With prsPres
   ' Code to manipulate presentation and its
   ' contents goes here.
End With
```

Creating a New Presentation

There are two ways you can create a PowerPoint presentation:

- By using the **Open** method of the **Application** object. You can use any file format recognized by PowerPoint in the **Open** method's ***FileName*** argument. For example, if the ***FileName*** argument specifies a Word document in outline view, the outline will be converted to a new presentation with a slide representing each paragraph that has the Heading 1 style in the document.
- By using the **Presentations** collection's **Add** method. For example:

```
Dim ppApp   As PowerPoint.Application
Dim prsPres As PowerPoint.Presentation

Set ppApp = New PowerPoint.Application
With ppApp
   Set prsPres = .Presentations.Add(msoFalse)
   With prsPres
      ' Code here to add and format slides in
      ' the new presentation.
   End With
End With
```

Note The ***WithWindow*** argument of the **Add** and **Open** methods accepts a **Boolean** value that specifies whether the **Window** object that contains the presentation will be visible. (The default is **True**.) Although the Auto List Members drop-down list for the **Add** method's ***WithWindow*** argument contains five enumerated constants, you should use only the **msoTrue** or **msoFalse** constants.

When you use VBA to create a new presentation, it exists in memory but will not be saved to disk until you use the **Presentation** object's **SaveAs** method. (Use the **Save** method to save changes to a presentation that has already been saved to disk.) The following procedure creates a new **Presentation** object and immediately saves the presentation by using the name supplied in the *strPresName* argument. It then returns the new **Presentation** object to the calling procedure.

```
Function PPTCreatePresentation(ppApp As PowerPoint.Application, _
                              strPresName As String) As PowerPoint.Presentation
   ' This procedure illustrates how to use the SaveAs method to
   ' save a new presentation as soon as it is created.
   ' Note that in this example, the new Presentation object
   ' is not visible.

   On Error GoTo PPTCreate_Err

   Set PPTCreatePresentation = ppApp.Presentations.Add(msoFalse)
   If InStr(strPresName, "\") = 0 Then
      strPresName = "c:\" & strPresName
   End If
   PPTCreatePresentation.SaveAs strPresName
PPTCreate_End:
   Exit Function
PPTCreate_Err:
   Select Case Err
      Case Err <> 0
         Set PPTCreatePresentation = Nothing
   End Select
   Resume PPTCreate_End:
End Function
```

The PPTCreatePresentation procedure is available in the modPPTCode module in PowerPointTools.ppt in the Samples\CH05 subfolder on the companion CD-ROM.

Formatting a Presentation

You use a PowerPoint template to apply a consistent look to an entire presentation. A PowerPoint template is a presentation saved with a .pot extension that contains master slides and may contain regular slides. To see the difference, compare the master-slide-only templates found in C:\Program Files\Microsoft Office\Templates\Presentation Designs with the templates found in C:\Program Files\Microsoft Office\Templates \Presentations. Templates that contain slides typically include boilerplate text that you can replace with your own text to make a custom presentation.

Master slides specify the basic layout and formatting for the title slide in a presentation as well as regular slides, handouts, and notes. When you use the **ApplyTemplate** method, you specify the template that contains the master slides that contain the layout and formatting you want to apply to your presentation. For example, the following sample code applies the Fireball.pot template to the currently active presentation:

```
With ActivePresentation
   .ApplyTemplate FileName:="c:\program files\microsoft office\" _
      & "templates\presentation designs\fireball.pot"
End With
```

You can also use VBA to create or manipulate master slides directly. Each **Presentation** object has a property that returns the available master slide that contains the formatting you want to use. You use the **Presentation** object's **TitleMaster**, **SlideMaster**, **HandoutMaster**, and **NotesMaster** properties to return a **Slide** object that represents the master slide you want to work with. Any changes you make to the layout or formatting of a master slide are applied to all slides of the specified type in the current presentation. For example, the following sample adds the CompanyLogo.bmp image to the background of the title master slide:

```
ActivePresentation.TitleMaster _
   .Shapes.AddPicture(Filename:="c:\CompanyLogo.bmp", _
   Left:=100, Top:=200, Width:=400, Height:=300)
```

The master properties are useful when you want to apply changes to all slides based on a master, rather than applying changes one slide at a time. If you have an image or other formatting you want to appear on all slides in a presentation, make the change to the appropriate master slide.

Running a Slide Show from a Presentation

You use properties of the **SlideShowSettings** object to specify how you want a slide show to appear and which slides to include in the show. You use the **SlideShowSettings** object's **Run** method to start the slide show. You access the **SlideShowSettings** object by using the **Presentation** object's **SlideShowSettings** property. These objects and properties are most useful if you want to create and run a PowerPoint presentation from another Office application. For example, the following code is from the PresentationView sample procedure, and it is used in Microsoft Word to take a Word outline and display it as a PowerPoint presentation. The slide show runs automatically, and when it is finished, it returns the focus to the Word document from which the macro was run.

```
Set prsPres = ppApp.Presentations.Open(strOutlineFileName)
' Format the presentation and set the slide show timings.
With prsPres
   .ApplyTemplate strTemplate
   With .Slides.Range.SlideShowTransition
      .AdvanceTime = intShowSlide
      .AdvanceOnTime = msoTrue
   End With
   ' Run the slide show, showing each slide once,
   ' and then end the show and close the presentation.
   With .SlideShowSettings
      .AdvanceMode = ppSlideShowUseSlideTimings
      .ShowType = ppShowTypeSpeaker
      .StartingSlide = 1
      .EndingSlide = prsPres.Slides.Count
      Set objCurrentShow = .Run.View
      Do Until objCurrentShow.State = ppSlideShowDone
         DoEvents
      Loop
   End With
End With
```

The PresentationView procedure is available in the modRunPPtPresentation module in PowerPointSamples.dot in the Samples\CH05 subfolder on the companion CD-ROM.

Working with PowerPoint Slides

Every PowerPoint presentation (with the exception of some templates) is a collection of slides. Each slide can contain text or graphics and may include animation effects. The **Presentation** object has a **Slides** property that returns the **Slides** collection, which you use to add new slides to or access an existing slide in a presentation. Each slide is represented in the collection by a **Slide** object.

Working with the Slides Collection

You primarily use the **Slides** collection to add new slides to a presentation or to access a specific slide within a presentation. You use the **Slides** collection's **Add** method to add a new slide to a collection. You use arguments of the **Add** method to specify the location of the slide in the **Slides** collection and the slide's layout. The following example shows how you would add a new blank slide to the end of the current **Slides** collection:

```
Dim sldNewSlide         As PowerPoint.Slide
Dim lngLastSlideAdded   As Long

With ActivePresentation
   Set sldNewSlide = .Slides.Add(.Slides.Count + 1, ppLayoutBlank)
   With sldNewSlide
      ' Add code to set properties of the slide here.
      lngLastSlideAdded = .SlideID
   End With
End With
```

You can add existing slides, or data that can be converted to slides, to a presentation by using the **Slides** collection's **InsertFromFile** method. For example, you could create a new presentation that used the opening and closing slides from a company presentation template and then used a Word outline to create the slides that make up the body of the presentation:

```
Dim ppApp   As New PowerPoint.Application
Dim prsPres As PowerPoint.Presentation

With ppApp
   Set prsPres = .Presentations.Add
   With prsPres
      .ApplyTemplate "c:\corp\corpPresentations.pot"
      .Slides.InsertFromFile "c:\PPTOutline.doc", 1
   End With
End With
```

To locate a slide within the collection, you use the **Slides** collection's **FindBySlideID** method. Each slide in a PowerPoint presentation has a **SlideID** property that is a **Long Integer** value that uniquely identifies the slide regardless of its location in the **Slides** collection. When you add to or delete slides from a collection, a slide's index value may change, but its **SlideID** property will always be the same. The first code sample in this section illustrates how to save the **SlideID** property to a variable so that it may be used again to locate the slide. The following sample shows how to locate a slide by using the **Long Integer** value representing the **SlideID** property:

```
Function FindSlide(lngID As Long) As PowerPoint.Slide
   ' This procedure returns the slide whose SlideID property value
   ' matches lngID. If no match is found, the return value of the
   ' procedure is  = Nothing.
   On Error Resume Next
   Set FindSlide = ActivePresentation.Slides.FindBySlideID(lngID)
End Function
```

The FindSlide procedure is available in the modPPTCode module in PowerPointTools.ppt file in the Samples\CH05 subfolder on the companion CD-ROM.

Working with Slide Objects

By default, PowerPoint names slides by using the convention Slide*n*, where *n* is a number representing the location of the slide at the time it was added to the **Slides** collection. You can specify your own name for a slide by setting the **Slide** object's **Name** property.

There are four ways to access a **Slide** object in the **Slides** collection:

- By using an index value representing the location of the slide in the **Slides** collection.
- By using the slide's name.

- By using the slide's **SlideID** property with the **Slides** collection's **FindBySlideID** method, as discussed in "Working with the Slides Collection" earlier in this chapter.
- By using the **SlideIndex** property of the **SlideRange** object from the PowerPoint **Selection** object to return the currently selected slide; however, using the **SlideIndex** property in this manner may return an error if more than one slide is selected.

The following code sample illustrates three ways to return the third **Slide** object in the current presentation and a way to return the currently selected slide:

```
Dim sldCurrentSlide As PowerPoint.Slide
' Using the slide's index value.
Set sldCurrentSlide = ActivePresentation.Slides(3)

' Using the slide's name.
Set sldCurrentSlide = ActivePresentation.Slides("Slide3")

' Using the FindBySlideID method, where lngSlide3 contains the SlideID
' property for the third slide.
Set sldCurrentSlide = ActivePresentation.Slides.FindBySlideID(lngSlide3)

' Using the SlideIndex property to return the currently selected slide.
' This sample shows how to determine if a single slide is currently selected.
If ActiveWindow.Selection.SlideRange.Count = 1 Then
   Set sldCurrentSlide = ActivePresentation _
      .Slides(ActiveWindow.Selection.SlideRange.SlideIndex)
End If
```

If you want to work with a group of **Slide** objects, perhaps to apply consistent formatting to the slides, you can use the **Slides** collection's **Range** method. The **Range** method returns a **SlideRange** object representing one or more **Slide** objects in a presentation.

If you use the **Range** method without an argument, the method returns a **SlideRange** object that contains all the **Slide** objects in a presentation. To see an example of this, see the PresentationView procedure in the modRunPPtPresentation module in PowerPointSamples.dot in the Samples\CH05 subfolder on the companion CD-ROM.

You use the **Range** method's ***Index*** argument to specify one or more **Slide** objects to include in the **SlideRange** object returned by the method. If the argument is a single integer, the method returns a **SlideRange** object for the **Slide** object whose index value matches the integer. For example, the following sample returns a **SlideRange** object representing the third slide in the current presentation:

```
Dim sldCurrSlide As PowerPoint.SlideRange
Set sldCurrSlide = ActivePresentation.Slides.Range(3)
```

In addition to using the ***Index*** argument, you can also use the VBA **Array** function as an argument to the **Range** method in order to return a **SlideRange** object containing multiple **Slide** objects. The **Array** function uses a comma-delimited list of values to be included in the array. When used as an argument to the **Range** method, the comma-delimited list should contain the index values or names of the slides you want to include in the **SlideRange** object returned by the method. The following sample shows how to use the **Array** function to return a **SlideRange** object containing the first four slides with even-numbered index values:

```
Dim sldCurrSlides As PowerPoint.SlideRange
Set sldCurrSlides = ActivePresentation.Slides.Range(Array(2,4,6,8))
```

The next sample illustrates how to use the **Array** function to return a **SlideRange** object that is a collection of specific named slides in a presentation:

```
Dim sldCurrSlides As PowerPoint.SlideRange

Set sldCurrSlides = ActivePresentation.Slides _
   .Range(Array("CostOfGoods", "SalesTotals", "Benefits", "Forecast"))
With sldCurrSlides
   ' Set properties common to all slides in this collection.
End With
```

Note You can also use the **Array** function as an argument to the **Range** method for a **Shapes** collection in order to return a collection of specified **Shape** objects as a **ShapeRange** object. For more information about working with shapes, see the next section, "Working with Shapes on Slides."

Working with Shapes on Slides

Just as a PowerPoint presentation consists of a collection of slides, a PowerPoint slide typically consists of one or more **Shape** objects. Whether a slide contains a picture, a title, text, an OLE object, an AutoShape, or other content, everything on the slide is a **Shape** object.

You can refer to a **Shape** object on a slide in two ways:

- By using the value of the shape's index in the collection of shapes on the slide. A shape will have an index value equal to its position in the **Shapes** collection at the time it was added to the collection.
- By using the name of the shape. You can specify the name of a **Shape** object by setting its **Name** property. By default, PowerPoint sets the name of a shape at the time it is added to a slide. The naming convention is *shapetype n*, where *shapetype* is the type of shape added and *n* is a number representing 1 plus the number of shapes on the slide when the current shape was added. For the first shape added to a slide, *n* = 2. To find out more about the types of shapes available in PowerPoint, search the Microsoft PowerPoint Visual Basic Reference Help index for "Shapes collection object."

To work with multiple shapes on a slide, you use the **Range** method of the **Shapes** collection. The **Range** method returns a **ShapeRange** object containing the shapes specified in the method's argument. If no ***Index*** argument is supplied, the **Range** method returns a **ShapeRange** object containing all the shapes on a slide. To specify multiple shapes, you can use the VBA **Array** function. For more information about using the **Array** function to specify multiple items, see the discussion of the **Array** function in the previous section, "Working with Slide Objects."

Adding Shapes to Slides

Typically, you use the **Add** method of a collection object to add an item to the collection. For example, to add a slide to a PowerPoint presentation, you use the **Presentation** object's **Slides** collection's **Add** method. However, adding shapes to a slide is a little different. The PowerPoint object model provides a different method for each shape you can add to a slide. For example, the following sample inserts a new slide at the end of the current presentation and uses two methods of the **Shapes** collection to add shapes to the slide. The **AddTextEffect** method is used to add a WordArt shape and the **AddTextbox** method is used to add a text box shape:

```
Sub AddTestSlideAndShapes()
   ' Illustrate how to add shapes to a slide and then
   ' center the shapes in relation to the slide and
   ' each other.
   Dim sldNewSlide      As PowerPoint.Slide
   Dim shpCurrShape     As PowerPoint.Shape
   Dim lngSlideHeight   As Long
   Dim lngSlideWidth    As Long

   With ActivePresentation
      ' Determine height and width of slide.
      With .PageSetup
         lngSlideHeight = .SlideHeight
         lngSlideWidth = .SlideWidth
      End With
      ' Add new slide to end of presentation.
      Set sldNewSlide = .Slides.Add(.Slides.Count + 1, ppLayoutBlank)
      With sldNewSlide
         ' Specify a background color for the slide.
         .ColorScheme = ActivePresentation.ColorSchemes(3)
         ' Add a WordArt shape by using the AddTextEffect method.
         Set shpCurrShape = .Shapes.AddTextEffect(msoTextEffect16, _
            "Familiar Quotations", "Tahoma", 42, msoFalse, msoFalse, 100, 100)
         ' Locate the WordArt shape at the middle of the slide, near the top.
         With shpCurrShape
            .Left = (lngSlideWidth - .Width) / 2
            .Top = (lngSlideHeight - .Height) / 8
         End With
         ' Add a Textbox shape to the slide and add text to the shape.
         Set shpCurrShape = .Shapes _
            .AddTextbox(msoTextOrientationHorizontal, 100, 100, 500, 500)
```

```
            With shpCurrShape
               With .TextFrame.TextRange
                  .Text = "'If not now, when? If not us, who?'" _
                     & vbCrLf & "'There is no time like the present.'" _
                     & vbCrLf & "'Ask not what your country can do for you, " _
                     & "ask what you can do for your country.'"
                  With .ParagraphFormat
                     .Alignment = ppAlignLeft
                     .Bullet = msoTrue
                  End With
                  With .Font
                     .Bold = msoTrue
                     .Name = "Tahoma"
                     .Size = 24
                  End With
               End With
               ' Shrink the Textbox to match the text it now contains.
               .Width = .TextFrame.TextRange.BoundWidth
               .Height = .TextFrame.TextRange.BoundHeight
               .Left = (lngSlideWidth - .Width) / 2
               .Top = (lngSlideHeight - .Height) / 2
            End With
         End With
      End With
End Sub
```

The AddTestSlideAndShapes procedure is available in the modShapeCode module in Shapes.ppt in the Samples\CH05 subfolder on the companion CD-ROM.

To see an example of how to determine the types of **Shape** objects a slide contains as well as some of the properties of a particular shape, you can use the GetShapeInfo procedure. The GetShapeInfo procedure is available in the modShapeCode module in Shapes.ppt in the Samples\CH05 subfolder on the companion CD-ROM.

Positioning Shapes on Slides

When you add a shape to a slide, the method you use typically requires you to specify values to establish the dimensions of the shape. In some cases, as with the **AddTextEffect** method (illustrated in the AddTestSlideAndShapes procedure shown earlier in "Adding Shapes to Slides"), you specify values for the **Left** and **Top** properties of the shape (the height and width of the shape is determined by the text it contains). In other cases (as with the **AddTextbox** method, also illustrated in the AddTestSlideAndShapes procedure), you must specify values for the **Shape** object's **Left**, **Top**, **Width**, and **Height** properties.

The height and width of shapes are specified in pixels. The default slide size is 720 pixels wide and 540 pixels high. The center of a slide is 360 pixels from the left edge of the slide and 270 pixels from the top of the slide. You can center any shape horizontally by using the formula (*SlideWidth* - *ShapeWidth*) / 2. You can center any shape vertically by using the formula (*SlideHeight* - *ShapeHeight*) / 2. You can programmatically specify or determine the height and width setting for the slides in a presentation by using the **Presentation** object's **PageSetup** property to return a **PageSetup** object, and then use the **PageSetup** object's **SlideHeight** and **SlideWidth** properties. This technique is also illustrated in the AddTestSlideAndShapes procedure shown earlier.

To position one or more shapes on a slide either in relation to the slide or to other shapes on the slide, you can use the **Align** or **Distribute** methods of a **ShapeRange** object.

Working with Text in a Shape

Much of what you do with shapes on slides involves adding or modifying text. In addition to the Textbox shape, many other **Shape** objects can contain text. For example, you can add text to many of the AutoShape **Shape** objects.

All shapes that support text have a **TextFrame** property you can use to return a **TextFrame** object. You can determine if a shape supports the use of a text frame by using the **Shape** object's **HasTextFrame** property. Each **TextFrame** object has a **HasText** property you can use to determine if the text frame contains text.

The **TextFrame** object has a **TextRange** property you use to return a **TextRange** object. You use the **TextFrame** object's **Text** property to specify or determine the text within a frame. You use the properties and methods of the **TextRange** object to work with the text associated with a PowerPoint shape. To see an example of how to use these properties to add text to the text frame of a text box shape, see the AddTestSlideAndShapes procedure shown in "Adding Shapes to Slides," earlier in this chapter.

Note Placeholder shapes contain default text that is visible from the PowerPoint user interface, but is not available programmatically. When you set the **Text** property of a Placeholder shape's **TextRange** object, the default text is replaced with the text you specify.

There is one **Shape** object that contains text but does not use the **TextFrame** or **TextRange** objects. The **TextEffect** property returns a **TextEffectFormat** object that contains the properties and methods used to work with WordArt shapes. You add WordArt shapes to a slide by using the **Shapes** collection's **AddTextEffect** method. The text of the WordArt shape and the location of the shape are specified in the arguments to the **AddTextEffect** method. You use the **TextEffectFormat** object's **Text** property to read or change the text in a WordArt shape. For example, the following code changes the text of an existing WordArt shape on the first slide of the current presentation:

```
With ActivePresentation
   strExistingText = .Slides(1).TextEffect.Text
   If Len(strNewText) <= Len(strExistingText) Then
      .Slides(1).TextEffect.Text = strNewText
   End If
End With
```

Note that this code checks to make sure the new text is not longer than the existing text. This step is required because a WordArt shape does not automatically resize itself to accommodate new text. Alternatively, you could capture the properties of the existing WordArt shape, then delete it and replace it with a new WordArt shape that uses the same properties as the old shape.

To see an example that shows how to add WordArt shapes to a slide, see the AddTestSlideAndShapes procedure shown in "Adding Shapes to Slides" earlier in this chapter.

Working with Microsoft Word Objects

In Word, the fundamental working object is a document and everything is part of the document. When you are using VBA to work with Word, a **Document** object represents an open document, and all **Document** objects are contained in the **Application** object's **Documents** collection. Because each **Document** object is based on a template, each document has an **AttachedTemplate** property.

A document is a collection of characters arranged into words, words are arranged into sentences, sentences are arranged into paragraphs, and so on. Therefore, each **Document** object has a **Characters** collection, a **Words** collection, a **Sentences** collection, and a **Paragraphs** collection. Furthermore, each document has a **Sections** collection of one or more sections, and each section has a **HeadersFooters** collection that contains the headers and footers for the section. In addition, some or all of the text in the document may have certain formatting attributes set, and paragraphs may have built-in or custom styles applied.

Note You can view the entire Word object model in the "Object Model Diagrams" appendix. You can also use the Object Browser and Microsoft Word Visual Basic Reference Help to learn more about individual objects, properties, methods, and events. For more information about using VBA to work with an Office application's object model, see Chapter 4, "Understanding Office Objects and Object Models."

Understanding Application-Level Objects

Application-level objects are the **Application** object itself and its properties, methods, options (**Options** dialog box), and global dialog boxes (built-in dialog boxes)—in other words, these are objects that can affect more than one document at a time or are accessed and manipulated independent of the currently active **Document** object.

Working with the Application Object

Every time you write VBA code in Word, or write code to automate Word from some other application, you begin with the **Application** object. If you are working in Word, the **Application** object is created for you and you can use the **Application** property to return a reference to the Word **Application** object. If you are automating Word from some other application, you must create a Word **Application** object variable and then create an instance of Word.

From the **Application** object, you can access all the other objects exposed by the application as well as properties and methods unique to the **Application** object itself. For information about using other objects exposed by the Word **Application** object, see "The Document Object" later in this chapter.

To access properties and methods of the **Application** object, you use the following syntax:

Application.*PropertyName*

Application.*MethodName* (*arg1*, *arg2*, *argN*)

You can access child objects of the **Application** object by using the following syntax:

Application.*ObjectName*

–or–

ObjectName

You don't need to use the **Application** property in this context because these objects are global. To see an application's global members, open the Object Browser and click **<globals>** in the **Classes** list. The global items will be displayed in the **Members of** list.

To see examples of accessing properties and methods of the **Application** object, see the ApplicationObjectExample procedure, which is available in the modApplicationObject module in WordOptions.doc in the Samples\CH05 subfolder on the companion CD-ROM.

Working with the Settings in the Options Dialog Box

The **Options** dialog box contains many settings that let you customize the way Word looks and behaves. You can view this dialog box by clicking **Options** on the **Tools** menu. To programmatically access the settings in this dialog box, you use the **Options** object or the **View** object of a **Window** object. You can also access these settings through the **Dialog** object that represents the tab in the **Options** dialog box that contains the setting you want to manipulate.

Note For information about using built-in Word dialog boxes to perform actions other than the built-in behavior, see "Working with Word Dialog Boxes" later in this chapter.

Using the Options Object

The **Options** object contains many properties that represent items in the **Options** dialog box. For example, the **Options** object's **ReplaceSelection** property setting is equivalent to the **Typing replaces selection** setting on the **Edit** tab of the **Options** dialog box. The easiest way to identify which properties of the **Options** object represent settings on a tab in the **Options** dialog box is to record a macro that changes a setting and then examine the property settings Word records. For example, the **Print** tab of the **Options** dialog box contains fourteen settings. Two settings (**Print PostScript over text** and **Print data only for forms**) apply only to the active document and are therefore properties of the **Document** object. The remaining settings represent properties of the **Options** object. A macro that records a change to a setting on the **Print** tab would create, in part, the following list of **Options** object properties:

```
With Options
   .UpdateFieldsAtPrint = False
   .UpdateLinksAtPrint = False
   .DefaultTray = "Use printer settings"
   .PrintBackground = True
   .PrintProperties = False
   .PrintFieldCodes = False
   .PrintComments = True
   .PrintHiddenText = True
   .PrintDrawingObjects = True
   .PrintDraft = False
   .PrintReverse = False
   .MapPaperSize = True
End With
```

If you change the settings of **Options** object properties, make sure you return each setting to its original value when you are finished. Many of these properties are global application-level settings, and you may be making changes that the user would not want persisted. The following example illustrates how to return **Options** object properties to their original settings when a procedure that changes those properties ends:

```
Sub PrintAllDocInfo()
   ' This procedure illustrates how to use the Options object
   ' to change certain settings, print a document, and then
   ' return the settings to their original state.
   Dim blnProps      As Boolean
   Dim blnFields     As Boolean
   Dim blnComments   As Boolean
   Dim blnHidden     As Boolean

   With Options
      ' Save the existing property settings.
      blnProps = .PrintProperties
      blnFields = .PrintFieldCodes
      blnComments = .PrintComments
      blnHidden = .PrintHiddenText
```

```
        ' Set properties to True and print document.
        .PrintProperties = True
        .PrintFieldCodes = True
        .PrintComments = True
        .PrintHiddenText = True
        Application.PrintOut
        ' Return properties to original settings.
        .PrintProperties = blnProps
        .PrintFieldCodes = blnFields
        .PrintComments = blnComments
        .PrintHiddenText = blnHidden
    End With
End Sub
```

To try the PrintAllDocInfo procedure, open the WordOptions.doc sample file in the Samples\CH05 subfolder on the companion CD-ROM and print a copy of the document. Then run the PrintAllDocInfo procedure in the modOptionsDialog module and compare the printed output between the two versions of the document.

Using the View Object and the Dialog Object

The **View** object lets you determine or specify all the attributes of a **Window** object. For example, you can run the following code sample from the Immediate window in the Visual Basic Editor to determine whether hidden text is displayed in the current document:

```
? ActiveWindow.View.ShowHiddenText
```

Note that although many of the **View** object properties map directly to settings in the **Options** dialog box, they do not necessarily map to settings on the **View** tab of that dialog box.

You use the **Dialogs** collection to access a **Dialog** object that represents a tab in the **Options** dialog box. For example, if you execute the following code from the Immediate window, it prints the current setting for the **Typing replaces selection** check box on the **Edit** tab of the **Options** dialog box:

```
? CBool(Dialogs(wdDialogToolsOptionsEdit).ReplaceSelection)
```

Working with Word Dialog Boxes

You can create your own custom dialog boxes by using UserForms, but before you do, you should determine whether you can simply appropriate the functionality of one of Word's more than two hundred built-in dialog boxes.

From VBA, you access any of Word's built-in dialog boxes through the **Dialogs** collection. The **Dialogs** collection is a global object, so you can reference it without specifying the **Application** property. For example, you can run the following code from the Immediate window to return the number of dialog boxes in the **Dialogs** collection:

```
? Dialogs.Count
```

To work with a particular dialog box, you create an object variable declared **As Dialog** and use one of the **wdWordDialog** constants to specify the dialog box you want to reference. For example, the following code creates a reference to the **Spelling and Grammar** dialog box:

```
Dim dlgSpell As Dialog
Set dlgSpell = Dialogs(wdDialogToolsSpellingandGrammar)
```

Once you instantiate a **Dialog** object variable in this way, you can easily determine or specify the various dialog box settings. To determine the settings available from a built-in dialog box, search the Microsoft Word Visual Basic Reference Help index for "built-in Word dialog boxes," and then open the topic "Built-in dialog box argument lists." This Help topic lists the available settings for each dialog box. When you refer to one of these settings in VBA, you can reference it as a property of the dialog box. For example, you can refer to the **All** setting on the **View** tab of the **Options** dialog box by using the **ShowAll** property:

```
MsgBox "The 'All' setting on the View tab is currently set to " _
   & CBool(Dialogs(wdDialogtoolsOptionsView).ShowAll)
```

Dialog box properties are typically set from the user interface by using check box controls, combo box controls, or text box controls. Check box controls contain the value 1 when they are selected and 0 when they are not selected. Combo box controls contain the index value of the item selected, beginning at 0 for the first item in the control. Text box controls contain a **String** value representing the text in the control.

You also have control over how a dialog box is displayed and when changes to settings take effect. When you display a dialog box from the Word user interface and change a setting, the change usually takes effect as soon as you click the dialog box's **OK** button, although some dialog box settings take effect immediately. When you use VBA to display a dialog box, you can control how the dialog box behaves by using either the **Dialog** object's **Show** method or its **Display** method. If you use the **Show** method, the dialog box behaves just as it does when Word displays it. The **Display** method simply displays the dialog box and you must use additional VBA code to take further action in response to any selections made in the dialog box by the user. Both methods also return a value representing whether the user clicked **OK**, **Cancel**, **Close**, or some other button in the dialog box. For more information about using these methods to display built-in Word dialog boxes, search the Microsoft Word Visual Basic Reference Help index for "built-in Word dialog boxes," and then open the topic "Displaying built-in Word dialog boxes."

Modifying Built-in Commands

One simple but very powerful method you can use to customize the way Word works is to run your own VBA procedure in place of a built-in procedure. Doing this lets you customize the behavior of Word in any way you can imagine.

There is no limit to the kinds of things you can do and the kinds of built-in behaviors you can change. You could save documents created by using your custom template to a different directory than documents created by using Normal.dot. You could modify the **File New** command to create custom document properties for every new document. You could display your own custom dialog box instead of the Word dialog box normally displayed in response to a menu command. You could also let the built-in command run and then detect whether a user made certain selections from a Word dialog box.

The first thing you have to do is figure out which procedure Word runs to perform a built-in action. This is easy to do for all built-in menu commands. If you press ALT+CTRL+PLUS SIGN (+) on the numeric keypad (not the PLUS SIGN on the keyboard) and then click the menu item you want to investigate, Word displays the **Customize Keyboard** dialog box, which shows the name of the built-in procedure in the **Commands** list. For example, in Figure 5.5, you can see that Word runs the FileSaveAs procedure whenever a user clicks **Save As** on the **File** menu.

Figure 5.5 The Customize Keyboard Dialog Box

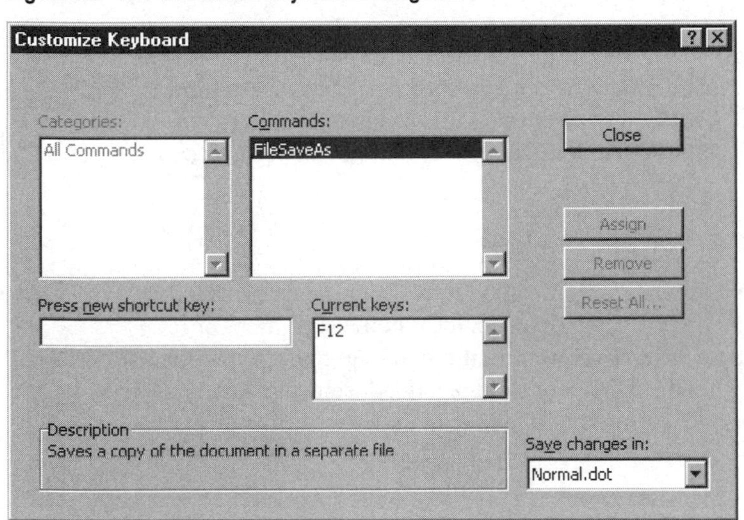

There are three ways you can substitute your own procedure for a built-in Word procedure:

- In any standard module, create a VBA procedure that uses the same name as the procedure you want to replace. For example, if you create a procedure named FileSaveAs, Word will run your procedure instead of the built-in FileSaveAs procedure whenever the built-in procedure would normally be called.

- Create a module and name it by using the name of the built-in command you want to replace. Then add a subroutine named Main() to the module and add your custom code to that procedure. The modToolsOptions module in the WordOptions.doc sample file in the Samples\CH05 subfolder on the companion CD-ROM contains an example of this technique.
- Create a new procedure by using the **Macros** dialog box. To do this, point to **Macro** on the **Tools** menu, and then click **Macros**. In the **Macros** dialog box, click **Word Commands** in the **Macros in** list. The **Macro name** list will then display the hundreds of built-in Word procedures. You can learn something about what these procedures do by clicking a procedure name in the list and reading its description in the **Description** box at the bottom of the dialog box. When you locate the command you want to modify, click it and then use the **Macros in** list to select the template or document in which to save the procedure. Then click the **Create** button to create a new VBA procedure that uses the same name as the built-in command.

The Document Object

The **Document** object is just below the **Application** object in Word's object model and is at the heart of Word programming. When you open a new document from the user interface, you create a new **Document** object. Each document you create or open is added to the **Documents** collection, and the document that has the focus is called the active document.

Working with the Document Object

You can reference a **Document** object as a member of the **Documents** collection by using either its index value (where 1 is the first document in the collection) or its name. In addition, you can use the **ActiveDocument** property to return a reference to the document that currently has the focus. For example, if a document named Policies.doc is the only open document, the following three object variables will all point to Policies.doc:

```
Dim docOne     As Word.Document
Dim docTwo     As Word.Document
Dim docThree   As Word.Document

Set docOne = Documents(1)
Set docTwo = Documents("Policies.doc")
Set docThree = ActiveDocument
```

You will rarely refer to a document by using its index value in the **Documents** collection because this value can change for a given document as other documents are opened and closed. Typically, you will use the **ActiveDocument** property or a **Document** object variable created by using the **Documents** collection's **Add** method or **Open** method. The following example shows how you can use the **ActiveDocument** property to add an address to the document that currently has the focus:

```
Sub AddOPGAddress()
   With ActiveDocument
      .Envelope.Insert Address:="The OPG Team" _
         & vbCrLf & "One Microsoft Way" & vbCrLf _
         & "Redmond, WA  98052", ReturnAddress:= _
         "One Happy Customer" & vbCrLf & _
         "77 Pine Bough Lane" & vbCrLf & _
         "Any Town, USA 12345"
   End With
End Sub
```

The next example illustrates how to instantiate a **Document** object variable by using the **Documents** collection's **Open** method. After the **Document** object variable is set, the code calls the procedure from the prior example to add an envelope and then the envelope and the document are printed. Finally, the document is closed and all changes are saved.

```
Dim docPolicy As Word.Document

Set docPolicy = Documents.Open("c:\my documents\policies.doc")
With docPolicy
   Call AddOPGAddress
   .Envelope.PrintOut
   .PrintOut
   .Close SaveChanges:=True
End With
```

Note The document opened by using the **Open** method or the document created by using the **Add** method will also be the currently active document represented by the **ActiveDocument** property. If you want to make some other document the active document, use the **Document** object's **Activate** method.

Opening, Creating, Saving, and Closing New Documents

You use the **Documents** collection's **Open** method to open an existing document. The ***FileName*** argument can include the full path to the file or the file name alone. If the file specified in the ***FileName*** argument does not include the full path to the document, Word looks for the document in the current directory. If Word can't find the file by using the file path and file name specified in the ***FileName*** argument, an error occurs. The last code sample in the preceding section, "Working with the Document Object," illustrates how to use the **Documents** collection's **Open** method to return a reference to an existing file.

Instead of using a hard-coded path and file name, you can use the **FileSearch** object to make sure the file exists before trying to open it. You can also create a **Dialog** object that represents the **File Open** dialog box and use it to let the user select the file name to use as the ***FileName*** argument of the **Open** method.

You create a new document by using the **Documents** collection's **Add** method. The **Add** method can accept up to two optional arguments. You use the ***Template*** argument to specify the template on which to base the new document. If you leave this argument blank, the new document is based on the Normal.dot template. The ***NewTemplate*** argument is a **Boolean** value that specifies whether to create the new document as a template. The following example creates a new document based on the Normal.dot template:

```
Dim docNew As Word.Document

Set docNew = Documents.Add
With docNew
   ' Add code here to work with the new document.
End With
```

The method you use to save a document depends on whether the document is new or has already been saved. To save an existing document, you use the **Document** object's **Save** method. To save a new document, you use the **Document** object's **SaveAs** method and specify a file name in the method's ***FileName*** argument. If you use the **Save** method on a new document, Word displays the **Save As** dialog box to prompt the user to give the document a name.

You can also save a new document as soon as it is created by using the **Add** method and the **SaveAs** method together as follows:

```
Documents.Add.SaveAs FileName:="c:\my documents\fastsave.doc"
Set docNew = Documents("fastsave.doc")
```

If you use the **Documents.Add.SaveAs** syntax, you will not be able to set a **Document** object variable at the same time you use the **Add** method. Instead, you can refer to the newly created document by using the **ActiveDocument** property or by using the document's name in the **Documents** collection, as shown in the preceding example.

To close a document, you use the **Document** object's **Close** method. If there are changes to the document and you do not specify the ***SaveChanges*** argument, Word prompts the user to save changes. To prevent this prompt from appearing, use either the **wdDoNotSaveChanges** or the **wdSaveChanges** built-in constant in the **Close** method's ***SaveChanges*** argument. To close all open documents at once, use the **Documents** collection's **Close** method and either the **wdDoNotSaveChanges** or the **wdSaveChanges** constant in the ***SaveChanges*** argument.

Working with Document Content

Once you've got a document to work with, most of the tasks you'll want to perform with VBA will involve working with the text in the document or manipulating the objects contained in the document. Documents contain words, sentences, paragraphs, sections, headers and footers, tables, fields, controls, images, shapes, hyperlinks and more. All of these objects (and more) are available to you through VBA. This section will not cover all the objects a document exposes, just those that you are most likely to use on a regular basis.

The starting point for much of what you do to the contents of a document will be to specify a part of the document and then to do something to it. This may involve, for example, adding or removing text or formatting words or characters. The two objects you will use to accomplish much of this work are the **Range** object and the **Selection** object.

The Range Object

A **Range** object represents a contiguous area in a document, defined by a starting character position and an ending character position. The contiguous area can be as small as the insertion point or as large as the entire document. It can also be, but does not have to be, the area represented by the current selection. You can define a **Range** object that represents a different area than the current selection. You can also define multiple **Range** objects in a single document. The characters in a **Range** object include nonprinting characters, such as spaces, carriage returns, and paragraph marks.

Note The area represented by the current selection is contained in the **Selection** object. For information about using the **Selection** object, see "The Selection Object" later in this chapter.

A **Range** object is similar to a Word bookmark in that they both define a specific area within a document. However, unlike a bookmark, a **Range** object exists only so long as the code that creates it is running. In addition, when you insert text at the end of a range, Word automatically expands the range to include the new text. When you insert text at the end of a bookmark, Word does not expand the bookmark to include the new text. For more information about bookmarks, see "Working with Bookmarks" later in this chapter.

Creating, Defining, and Redefining a Range

You typically create a **Range** object by declaring an object variable of type **Range** and then instantiating that variable by using either the **Document** object's **Range** method or the **Range** property of another object, such as a **Character**, **Word**, **Sentence**, or **Selection** object. For example, the following code creates two **Range** objects that both represent the second sentence in the active document.

```
Public Sub GetRangeExample()
   ' This example shows how the Range method and the Range
   ' property both return the same characters.

   Dim rngRangeMethod    As Word.Range
   Dim rngRangeProperty    As Word.Range

   With ActiveDocument
      If .Sentences.Count >= 2 Then
            Set rngRangeMethod = .Range(.Sentences(2).Start, _
                .Sentences(2).End)
            Set rngRangeProperty = .Sentences(2)
      End If
   End With

   Debug.Print rngRangeMethod.Text
   Debug.Print rngRangeProperty.Text
End Sub
```

The GetRangeExample procedure is available in the modRangeCode module in WordSamples.doc in the Samples\CH05 subfolder on the companion CD-ROM.

When you use the **Range** method to specify a specific area of a document, you use the method's ***Start*** argument to specify the character position where the range should begin and you use the ***End*** argument to specify where the range should end. The first character in a document is at character position 0. The last character position is equal to the total number of characters in the document. You can determine the number of characters in a document by using the **Characters** collection's **Count** property. As shown in the preceding example, you can also use the **Start** and **End** properties of a **Bookmark**, **Selection**, or **Range** object to specify the **Range** method's ***Start*** and ***End*** arguments. You can set the ***Start*** and ***End*** arguments to the same number. In this case, you create a range that does not include any characters.

You can set or redefine the contents of a **Range** object by using the object's **SetRange** method. You can specify or redefine the start of a range by using the **Range** object's **Start** property or its **MoveStart** method. Likewise, you can specify or redefine the end of a range by using the **Range** object's **End** property or its **MoveEnd** method.

The following example begins by using the **Content** property to create a **Range** object that covers the entire contents of a document. It then changes the **End** property to specify that the end of the range will be at the end of the first sentence in the document. It then uses the **SetRange** method to redefine the range to cover the first paragraph in the document. Finally, it uses the **MoveEnd** method to extend the end of the range to the end of the second paragraph in the document. At each step in the example, the number of characters contained in the range is printed to the Immediate window.

```
Public Sub RedefineRangeExample1()
   ' This procedure illustrates how to use various properties
   ' and methods to redefine the contents of a Range object.
   ' See also the RedefineRangeExample2 procedure.
   Dim rngSample As Range

   Set rngSample = ActiveDocument.Content

   With rngSample
      Debug.Print "The range now contains " & .Characters.Count _
            & " characters."
      .End = ActiveDocument.Sentences(1).End
      Debug.Print "The range now contains " & .Characters.Count _
            & " characters."
      .SetRange Start:=0, End:=ActiveDocument.Paragraphs(1).Range.End
      Debug.Print "The range now contains " & .Characters.Count _
            & " characters."
      .MoveEnd Unit:=wdParagraph, Count:=1
      Debug.Print "The range now contains " & .Characters.Count _
            & " characters."
   End With
End Sub
```

The RedefineRangeExample1 procedure is available in the modRangeCode module in WordSamples.doc in the Samples\CH05 subfolder on the companion CD-ROM.

You can also redefine a **Range** object by using the object's **Find** property to return a **Find** object. The following example illustrates the use of the **Find** property to locate text within the active document. If the text is found, the **Range** object is automatically redefined to contain the text that matched the search criteria.

```
With rngRangeText.Find
   .ClearFormatting
   If .Execute(FindText:=strTextToFind) Then
      Set RedefineRangeExample2 = rngRangeText
   Else
      Set RedefineRangeExample2 = Nothing
   End If
End With
```

For more information about using the **Find** object, see "The Find and Replacement Objects" later in this chapter.

Many Word objects have a **Range** property that returns a **Range** object. You use an object's **Range** property to return a **Range** object under circumstances where you need to work with properties or methods of the **Range** object that are not available from the object itself. For example, the following code uses the **Range** property of a **Paragraph** object to return a **Range** object that is used to format the text in the first paragraph in a document:

```
Dim rngPara As Range

Set rngPara = ActiveDocument.Paragraphs(1).Range
With rngPara
   .Bold = True
   .ParagraphFormat.Alignment = wdAlignParagraphCenter
   .Font.Name = "Arial"
End With
```

After you identify the **Range** object, you can apply methods and properties of the object to modify the contents of the range or get information about the range. You use the **Range** object's **StoryType** property to determine where in the document the **Range** is located. For more information about the **StoryType** property, see "Knowing Where You Are" later in this chapter.

Watch Your Code Work

There are two important debugging tips you can use when writing VBA code that manipulates text. One is to make all nonprinting characters visible. This lets you see exactly what is happening to all characters as your code executes. The other tip is to have your code select objects before manipulating them. This creates a visual corollary between the object your code is manipulating and what is happening on screen.

To view all nonprinting characters, click **Options** on the **Tools** menu, click the **View** tab, and then select the **All** check box under **Formatting Marks**.

You can use the **Range** object's **Select** method to highlight its text, making it easier to see what the code is doing. To deselect the range, use the **Range** object's **Collapse** method. When you have finished debugging your code, remove the **Select** method code. If your code manipulates the **Selection** object, the object's text is highlighted by default. For more information about the **Selection** object, see "The Selection Object" later in this chapter.

Working with Text in a Range Object

You use a **Range** object's **Text** property to specify or determine the text the range contains. For example, the following code first displays the text within a **Range** object, then changes it and displays the new text, and finally restores the original text:

```
Public Sub ChangeTextSample()
   ' This procedure illustrates how to use the Range object's Text
   ' property to copy and paste text into a document while
   ' maintaining the original paragraphs.
   '
```

```
   ' When the rngText variable is instantiated, it includes all of
   ' the text in the first paragraph in the active document plus the
   ' paragraph mark at the end of the paragraph. Note how the new
   ' text in the strNewText variable includes a paragraph mark
   ' (vbCrLf) to replace the mark removed when the orginal text was
   ' replaced.
   Dim rngText              As Range
   Dim strOriginalText      As String
   Dim strNewText           As String

   strNewText = "Now is the time to harness the power of VBA in Word." _
      & "This text is replacing the original text in the first " _
      & "paragraph. This is all done using only the Text property " _
      & "of the Range object!" _
      & vbCrLf

   Set rngText = ActiveDocument.Paragraphs(1).Range
   With rngText
      MsgBox .Text, vbOKOnly, "This is the original text."
      strOriginalText = .Text
      .Text = strNewText
      MsgBox .Text, vbOKOnly, "This is the new text inserted in paragraph 1."
      .Text = strOriginalText
      MsgBox "The original text is restored."
   End With
End Sub
```

In this example, the **Range** object's **Text** property is used to specify the text that appears in the document. The ChangeTextSample procedure is available in the modRangeCode module in WordSamples.doc in the Samples\CH05 subfolder on the companion CD-ROM. To see examples of simple procedures that use the **Range** object to replace text, or portions of text, in a document, open the WordSamples.doc sample file and click the buttons on the Range Examples menu of the Working with Word Objects toolbar.

Knowing Where You Are

You can use the **Range** object's **StoryType** property to determine where the range is located. Stories are distinct areas of a document that contain text. You can have up to 11 story type areas in a document, representing areas such as document text, headers, footers, footnotes, comments, and more. You use the **StoryRanges** property to return a **StoryRanges** collection. The **StoryRanges** collection contains **Range** objects representing each story in a document.

A new Word document contains a single story, called the Main Text story, which represents the text in the main part of the document. Even a blank document contains a character, a word, a sentence, and a paragraph.

You do not expressly add new stories to a document but rather, Word adds them for you when you add text to a portion of the document represented by one of the 11 story types. For example, if you add footnotes, Word adds a Footnotes story. If you add comments, Word adds a Comments story to the document.

You use the **Range** property to return a **Range** object representing each story in a document. For example, the following code prints the text associated with the Main Text story and the Comments story:

```
Dim rngMainText      As Word.Range
Dim rngCommentsText  As Word.Range

Set rngMainText = ActiveDocument.StoryRanges(wdMainTextStory)
Set rngComments = ActiveDocument.StoryRanges(wdCommentsStory)
Debug.Print rngMainText.Text
Debug.Print rngComments.Text
```

To work with a code sample that shows how to access all **StoryRanges** collection members and their related properties, see the StoryRangeTest procedure in the modRangeCode module in WordSamples.doc in the Samples\CH05 subfolder on the companion CD-ROM.

Understanding Paragraph Marks—They're Not Just Carriage Returns

When you work with text programmatically, it is important to understand how Word handles paragraph marks. At a basic level, a Word document is nothing more than a vast collection of characters. We tend to think of documents as collections of words, sentences, and paragraphs, but basically all you really have are characters. Each character has a specific job to do. Some characters are letters, spaces, or tabs. Some characters are paragraph marks or page breaks.

Paragraph marks play a unique and sometimes misunderstood role in Word documents. A paragraph consists of a paragraph mark and all text that precedes the mark up to, but not including, a previous paragraph mark. In addition—and this is the important part—a paragraph mark *contains* all the information about how the paragraph is formatted.

When you copy a word, sentence, or paragraph and you include a paragraph mark, all the formatting information contained in the paragraph mark is also copied and applied to the paragraph when it is pasted in another location.

If you want to copy text from within one paragraph and paste it into another paragraph but do not want to copy the paragraph formatting as well, make sure that you do not copy the paragraph mark adjacent to the text you copy.

Every blank Word document contains a single paragraph mark that constitutes a **Character** object, a **Word** object, a **Sentence** object, and a **Paragraph** object all at the same time. However, the **Statistics** tab of the **Properties** dialog box (**File** menu) reports that there are no characters, words, sentences, or paragraphs in a blank document. This difference highlights an important aspect of Word that you will need to consider when manipulating these objects programmatically. To see a procedure that illustrates these differences, see the WhatIsInThisDocument procedure in the modRangeCode module in WordSamples.doc in the Samples\CH05 subfolder on the companion CD-ROM.

In the ChangeTextSample procedure shown in "Working with Text in a Range Object" earlier in this chapter, note how the text in the `strNewText` variable uses the **vbCrLf** built-in constant to create a paragraph mark at the end of the text that will replace the existing text in paragraph 1 of the active document. This is done to prevent the new text from becoming part of the second paragraph.

When you create a **Range** object that represents a **Character**, **Word**, or **Sentence** object and that object falls at the end of a paragraph, the paragraph mark is automatically included within the range. Moreover, the **Range** object will include all additional subsequent empty paragraph marks. For example, in a document where the first paragraph consists of three sentences, the following code creates a **Range** object that represents the last sentence in the first paragraph:

```
Set rngCurrentSentence = ActiveDocument.Sentences(3)
```

Because the `rngCurrentSentence` **Range** object refers to the last sentence in the first paragraph, that paragraph mark (and any additional empty paragraph marks) will be included in the range. If you then set the **Text** property of this object to a text string that didn't end with a paragraph mark, the first and second paragraphs in the document would be deleted.

When you write VBA code that manipulates text in a Word document, you need to account for the presence of a paragraph mark in your text. There are two basic techniques you can use to account for paragraph marks when you are cutting and pasting text in **Range** objects:

- Include a new paragraph mark (represented by the **vbCrLf** constant) in the text to be inserted in the document. This technique is illustrated in the ChangeTextSample procedure shown in "Working with Text in a Range Object" earlier in this chapter.
- Exclude the final paragraph mark from a **Range** object. The following code sample shows how to change the contents of a **Range** object to exclude the final paragraph mark. The example uses the **Chr$()** function with character code 13 to represent a paragraph mark.

```
Function IsLastCharParagraph(ByRef rngTextRange As Word.Range, _
                             Optional blnTrimParaMark As Boolean = _
                             False) As Boolean
    ' This procedure accepts a character, word, sentence, or
    ' paragraph Range object as the first argument and returns True
    ' if the last character in the range is a paragraph mark, and
    ' False if it is not. The procedure also accepts an optional
    ' Boolean argument that specifies whether the Range object
    ' should be changed to eliminate the paragraph mark if it
    ' exists. When the blnTrimParaMark argument is True, this
    ' procedure calls itself recursively to strip off all trailing
    ' paragraph marks.
    Dim strLastChar As String
```

```
      strLastChar = Right$(rngTextRange.Text, 1)
      If InStr(strLastChar, Chr$(13)) = 0 Then
         IsLastCharParagraph = False
         Exit Function
      Else
         IsLastCharParagraph = True
         If Not blnTrimParaMark = True Then
               Exit Function
         Else
            Do
               rngTextRange.SetRange rngTextRange.Start, _
                  rngTextRange.Start + rngTextRange.Characters.Count - 1
               Call IsLastCharParagraph(rngTextRange, True)
            Loop While InStr(rngTextRange.Text, Chr$(13)) <> 0
         End If
      End If
   End Function
```

In this example, the **Count** property of the **Range** object's **Characters** collection is used to redefine the **Range** object's end point. The IsLastCharParagraph procedure is available in the modRangeSimpleCode module in WordSamples.doc in the Samples\CH05 subfolder on the companion CD-ROM.

Inserting Text in a Range

You use the **Range** object's **InsertBefore** or **InsertAfter** methods to add text to an existing **Range** object. In fact, there is an entire class of methods, with names that begin with "Insert," that you can use to manipulate a **Range** object. For complete information about all the **Range** object's properties and methods, search the Microsoft Word Visual Basic Reference Help index for "Range object."

Note All the methods and properties discussed in this section also apply when you are working with text in the **Selection** object. For more information about the **Selection** object, see "The Selection Object" later in this chapter.

It's useful to have a procedure that combines the **Range** object's **InsertBefore** and **InsertAfter** methods with the **Text** property. Having such a procedure creates a single place to handle much of the work you will do when manipulating text programmatically. The InsertTextInRange procedure in the clsManipulateText module in WordSamples.doc in the Samples\CH05 subfolder on the companion CD-ROM is just such a procedure. The InsertTextInRange procedure is contained in a class module and is exposed as a method of the class to make it even easier to use in any Word solution you develop. For more information about creating custom class objects, see Chapter 9, "Custom Classes and Objects."

You can call the InsertTextInRange procedure any time you need to add text to a **Range** object. In other words, the procedure is useful any time you want to programmatically make any changes to existing text in a Word document.

The InsertTextInRange procedure uses two required arguments and one optional argument. The *strNewText* argument contains the text you want to add to the **Range** object specified in the *rngRange* argument. The *intInsertMode* optional argument specifies how the new text will be added to the range. The values for this argument are one of three custom enumerated constants that specify whether to use the **InsertBefore** method, the **InsertAfter** method, or the **Text** property to replace the existing range text.

```
Public Function InsertTextInRange(strNewText As String, _
                                  Optional rngRange As Word.Range, _
                                  Optional intInsertMode As opgTextInsertMode = _
                                  Replace) As Boolean
   ' This procedure inserts text specified by the strNewText
   ' argument into the Range object specified by the rngRange
   ' argument. It calls the IsLastCharParagraph procedure to
   ' strip off trailing paragraph marks from the rngRange object.

   Call IsLastCharParagraph(rngRange, True)

   With rngRange
      Select Case intInsertMode
         Case 0 ' Insert before text in range.
            .InsertBefore strNewText
         Case 1 ' Insert after text in range.
            .InsertAfter strNewText
         Case 2 ' Replace text in range.
            .Text = strNewText
         Case Else
      End Select
      InsertTextInRange = True
   End With
End Function
```

Note that the IsLastCharParagraph procedure is used to strip off any final paragraph marks before inserting text in the range. The IsLastCharParagraph procedure is discussed in "Understanding Paragraph Marks—They're Not Just Carriage Returns" earlier in this chapter.

The Selection Object

When you use the Word user interface to work with a document, you typically select (highlight) text and then do something to the text, such as formatting it, typing new text, or moving it to another location. The **Selection** object represents the currently selected text in a Word document. The **Selection** object is always present in a document; if no text is selected, it represents the insertion point. Unlike the **Range** object, there can only be one **Selection** object at a time. You can use the **Selection** object's **Type** property to get information about the state of the current selection. For example, if there is no current selection, the **Selection** object's **Type** property returns **wdSelectionIP**. The **Type** property will return one of nine different values represented by the **wdSelectionType** enumerated constants.

You access a **Selection** object by using the **Selection** property. This property is available from the **Application**, **Window**, and **Pane** objects. However, since the **Selection** property is global, you can refer to it without referencing another object first. For example, the following sample code illustrates how you use the **Selection** property to get information about the currently selected text:

```
Sub SelectionCurrentInfo()
   Dim strMessage As String

   With Selection
      If .Characters.Count > 1 Then
         strMessage = "The Selection object in '" & ActiveDocument.Name _
            & "' contains " & .Characters.Count & " characters, " _
            & .Words.Count & " words, " & .Sentences.Count _
            & " sentences, and " & .Paragraphs.Count _
            & " paragraphs."
         MsgBox strMessage
      End If
   End With
End Sub
```

The SelectionCurrentInfo procedure is available in the modRangeSimpleCode module in WordSamples.doc file in the Samples\CH05 subfolder on the companion CD-ROM.

The Selection Object vs. the Range Object

In many ways, the **Selection** object is like a **Range** object. The **Selection** object represents an arbitrary portion of a document. It has properties that represent characters, words, sentences, paragraphs, and other objects in a Word document. The main difference is that when you use the **Range** object, it's not necessary to first select the text. In addition, there can only be one **Selection** object at a time, but the number of **Range** objects you can create is unlimited.

The **Selection** object and the **Range** object have many common methods and properties, and it is easy to return a **Range** object from a **Selection** object or to create a **Selection** object from a **Range** object. However, most things you can do with a **Selection** object, you can do even faster with a **Range** object. There are two main reasons for this:

- The **Range** object typically requires fewer lines of code to accomplish a task.
- Manipulating a **Range** object does not incur the overhead associated with Word having to move or change the selection "highlight" in the active document.

The Selection Object vs. the Range Object (*continued*)

In addition, you can do much more with a **Range** object than you can with a **Selection** object:

- You can manipulate a **Range** object without changing what the user has selected in the document. Practically speaking, you could save the original selection by using a **Range** object variable, manipulate the **Selection** object programmatically, and then use the saved **Range** object's **Select** method to display the original selection, but there is rarely a good reason to show the user that the selection is changing. Some WordBasic developers relied on changing the selection to indicate to the user that the code is still running (and the machine has not locked up). But this is not the right way to convey information to a user. An operation that takes a long time to execute should signal its progress by using a progress meter or by posting status messages to the status bar.
- You can maintain multiple **Range** objects in your code, and, where necessary, store those objects in a custom **Collection** object. You cannot do these two things by using only the **Selection** object.

For more information about differences between how the **Selection** and **Range** objects work, see "The Find and Replacement Objects" later in this chapter.

When it comes to manipulating text, the **Selection** and **Range** objects have many methods and properties in common—for example, all the **Insert*Name*** methods and the **Text** property discussed in "Working with Text in a Range Object" earlier in this chapter. However, the **Selection** object has a unique set of methods for manipulating text. These are the **TypeText**, **TypeParagraph**, and **TypeBackspace** methods. You use these methods to enter or remove text and insert paragraph marks in a **Selection** object. In order to get the results you expect, there are a few things you need to understand about the **Type*Name*** methods.

With the exception of the **InsertParagraph** and **InsertFile** methods, which remove selected text, the **Insert*Name*** methods let you work with a selection without deleting existing text. In contrast, the **Type*Name*** methods may delete existing text, depending on the value of the **Options** object's **ReplaceSelection** property.

When the **ReplaceSelection** property is **True**, using any of the **Type*Name*** methods results in the currently selected text being replaced. When the **ReplaceSelection** property is **False**, the **TypeText** and **TypeParagraph** methods behave just like the **InsertBefore** method: The text or paragraph mark is inserted at the beginning of the current selection. When the **ReplaceSelection** property is **False**, the **TypeBackspace** method behaves the same as the **Collapse** method of a **Range** or **Selection** object when the **wdCollapseStart** constant is specified in the ***Direction*** argument. The **Collapse** method collapses a range or selection so that its starting point and ending point are the same.

Knowing when to use a **Range** object, when to use a **Selection** object, and when to use both objects together gives you many powerful and flexible options when you are working with the objects in a Word document. This section has given examples showing how to use both objects individually and together. For another example showing how these objects work well together, see the SearchAndReturnExample procedure in "The Find and Replacement Objects" later in this chapter. In addition, there are several procedures in the WordSamples.doc sample file in the Samples\CH05 subfolder on the companion CD-ROM that illustrate a wide variety of circumstances where these objects work well together.

Working with Bookmarks

In many ways, a **Bookmark** object is similar to a **Selection** or **Range** object in that it represents a contiguous area in a document. It has a starting position and an ending position and it can be as small as the insertion point or as large as the entire document. However, a **Bookmark** object differs from a **Selection** or **Range** object because you can give the **Bookmark** object a name and it does not go away when your code stops running or when the document is closed. In addition, although bookmarks are normally hidden, you can make them visible by setting the **View** object's **ShowBookmarks** property to **True**.

You use bookmarks to mark a location in a document or as a container for text in a document. The following examples illustrate these uses:

- You could use bookmarks to mark areas in a document that will contain data supplied by the user or obtained from an outside data source. For example, a business letter template may have bookmarks marking the locations for name and address information. Your VBA code could obtain the data from the user or from a database and then insert it in the correct locations marked by bookmarks. Once a location is marked, navigating to that location is as simple as navigating to the bookmark. You can determine if a document contains a specific bookmark by using the **Bookmarks** collection's **Exists** method. You display a location marked by a bookmark by using the **Bookmark** object's **Select** method. Once a bookmark is selected, the **Selection** object and the **Bookmark** object represent the same location in the document.
- If you have a document that contains boilerplate text that you need to modify in certain circumstances, you could use VBA code to insert different text in these specified locations depending on whether certain conditions were met. You can use a **Bookmark** object's **Range** property to create a **Range** object, and then use the **Range** object's **InsertBefore** method, **InsertAfter** method, or **Text** property to add or modify the text within a bookmark.

Once you understand the subtleties associated with adding or changing text through VBA code, working with bookmarks can be a powerful way to enhance your custom solutions created in Word.

You add a bookmark by using the **Bookmarks** collection's **Add** method. You specify where you want the bookmark to be located by specifying a **Range** or **Selection** object in the **Add** method's ***Range*** argument. When you use the **InsertBefore** method, the **InsertAfter** method, or the **Text** property, a **Range** object automatically expands to incorporate the new text. As you will see in the next few examples, a bookmark does not adjust itself as easily, but making a bookmark as dynamic as a range is a simple exercise.

When you use the **Range** object's **InsertBefore** method to add text to a bookmark, the text is added to the start of the bookmark and the bookmark expands to include the new text. For example, if you had a bookmark named CustomerAddress on the following text (the brackets appear when the **ShowBookmarks** property is set to **True**)

[Seattle, WA 12345]

you could add the street address to this bookmark by using the following VBA code:

```
Dim rngRange As Word.Range

Set rngRange = ActiveDocument.Bookmarks("CustomerAddress").Range
rngRange.InsertBefore "1234 Elm Drive  #233" & vbCrLf
```

As you might expect, the bookmark expands to include the additional address information:

[1234 Elm Drive #233
Seattle, WA 12345]

Now suppose you want to use the **InsertAfter** method to add text to the end of a bookmark that contains the street address, and you want to add the city, state, and zip code information by using this code:

```
Dim rngRange As Word.Range

Set rngRange = ActiveDocument.Bookmarks("CustomerAddress").Range
rngRange.InsertAfter vbCrLf & "Seattle, WA  12345"
```

Note that when you use the **InsertAfter** method to add text to the end of a bookmark, the bookmark does not automatically expand to include the new text:

[1234 Elm Drive #233]
Seattle, WA 12345

This behavior could create problems if you were unaware of it. But now you are aware of it, and the solution is quite easy. The first part of the solution results from the benefits achieved when you use the **Selection** and **Range** objects together. The second part results from another aspect of bookmarks that you need to know: When you add a bookmark to a document in which the bookmark already exists, the original bookmark is deleted (but not the text it contained) when the new bookmark is created.

The following sample code uses the **InsertAfter** method to add text to the end of the CustomerAddress bookmark. It then uses the **Range** object's **Select** method to create a **Selection** object covering all the text you want to bookmark. Finally, it uses the **Bookmarks** collection's **Add** method to add a new bookmark that has the same name as the original bookmark and then uses the **Selection** object's **Range** property to specify the location of the bookmark:

```
Dim rngRange As Word.Range

Set rngRange = ActiveDocument.Bookmarks("CustomerAddress").Range
With rngRange
   .InsertAfter vbCrLf & "Seattle, WA  12345"
   .Select
End With
ActiveDocument.Bookmarks.Add "CustomerAddress", Selection.Range
```

If you use the **Range** object's **Text** property to replace the entire contents of a bookmark, you run into a similar problem: The text in the bookmark is replaced, but in the process, the bookmark itself is deleted. The solution to this problem is the same solution we used for the **InsertAfter** method in the preceding example. You insert the new text, use the **Range** object's **Select** method to select the text, and then create a new bookmark that has the same name as the original bookmark.

To see complete examples showing a custom class that handles adding text to bookmarks, see the modBookmarkCode module in WordSamples.doc in the Samples\CH05 subfolder on the companion CD-ROM. You can also open the WordSamples.doc file and use the bookmark examples from the Working with Word Objects toolbar.

The Find and Replacement Objects

Among the most frequently used commands in the Word user interface are the **Find** and **Replace** commands on the **Edit** menu. These commands let you specify the criteria for what you want to locate. They are both really the same thing, with the **Replace** command's functionality being just an extension of the **Find** command's functionality. In fact, you may have noticed that **Find**, **Replace**, and **Go To** appear on different tabs of the same dialog box—the **Find and Replace** dialog box.

Much of the VBA code you write in Word involves finding or replacing something in a document. There are several techniques you can use to locate text or other elements in a document; for example, using the **GoTo** method or the **Select** method. Typically, you use the **Find** object to loop through a document looking for some specific text, formatting, or style. To specify what you want to use to replace the item you found, you use the **Replacement** object, which you can access by using the **Replacement** property of the **Find** object.

The **Find** object is available from both the **Selection** object and the **Range** object; however, it behaves differently depending on whether it is used from the **Selection** object or the **Range** object. Searching for text by using the **Find** object is one of those situations where the **Selection** and **Range** objects can be used together to accomplish more than either object can its own. For examples that use the **Range** and **Selection** objects together to find text or other items, see the procedures in the modFindAndReplace module in WordSamples.doc in the Samples\CH05 subfolder on the companion CD-ROM.

The following list describes differences between the behavior of the **Range** object and the **Selection** object when you are searching for an item in a document:

- When you are using the **Selection** object, your search criteria are applied only against the currently selected text.
- When you are using the **Selection** object, if an item matching the search criteria is found, the selection changes to highlight the found item, as illustrated by the following example, which uses the **Find** object to search within the currently selected text:

```
With Selection.Find
   .ClearFormatting
   strFindText = InputBox("Enter the text you want to find.", _
      "Find Text")
   If Len(strFindText) = 0 Then Exit Sub
   .Text = strFindText
   If .Execute = True Then
      MsgBox "'" & Selection.Text & "'" _
         & " was found and is now highlighted."
   Else
      MsgBox "The text could not be located."
   End If
End With
```

- When you are using the **Find** object off of the **Range** object, the definition of the **Range** object changes when an item matching the search criteria is found. Failing to account for this change in the definition of the **Range** object can cause all kinds of debugging headaches. The following code sample illustrates how the **Range** object is redefined:

```
Dim rngText    As Word.Range
Dim strToFind  As String

Set rngText = ActiveDocument.Paragraphs(3).Range
With rngText.Find
   .ClearFormatting
   strToFind = InputBox("Enter the text you want to find.", _
      "Find Text")
   If Len(strFindText) = 0 Then Exit Sub
   .Text = strFindText
```

```
      If .Execute = True Then
         MsgBox "'" & strToFind & "'" & " was found. " _
            & "As a result, the Range object has been " _
            & "redefined and now covers the text: " _
            & rngText.Text
      Else
         MsgBox "The text could not be located."
      End If
   End With
```

Regardless of whether you are using the **Find** object with the **Range** object or the **Selection** object, you need to account for the changes that occur to the object when the search is successful. Because the object itself may point to different text each time the search is successful, you may need to account for this and you may also need to keep track of your original object so that you can return to it once the search has been completed.

The following sections provide additional details regarding searching for and replacing items in a Word document.

Specifying and Clearing Search Criteria

You specify the criteria for a search by setting properties of the **Find** object. There are two ways to set these properties. You can set individual properties of the **Find** object and then use the **Execute** method without arguments. You can also set the properties of the **Find** object by using the arguments of the **Execute** method. The following two examples execute identical searches:

```
' Example 1: Using properties to specify search criteria.
With Selection.Find
   .ClearFormatting
   .Forward = True
   .Wrap = wdFindContinue
   .Text = strToFind
   .Execute
End With

' Example 2: Using Execute method arguments to specify search criteria.
With Selection.Find
   .ClearFormatting
   .Execute FindText:=strToFind, _
      Forward:=True, Wrap:=wdFindContinue
End With
```

The **Find** object's search criteria are cumulative, which means that unless you clear out the criteria from a previous search, new criteria are added to the criteria used in the previous search. You should get in the habit of always using the **ClearFormatting** method to remove formatting from the criteria from a previous search before specifying the criteria for a new search. The **Find** object and the **Replacement** object each has its own **ClearFormatting** method. When you are performing a find and replace operation, you need to use the **ClearFormatting** method of both objects, as illustrated in the following example:

```
With Selection.Find
   .ClearFormatting
   .Text = strToFind
   With .Replacement
      .ClearFormatting
      .Text = strReplaceWith
   End With
   .Execute Replace:=wdReplaceAll
End With
```

Finding All Instances of the Search Criteria

When you use the **Execute** method as shown in the preceding examples, the search stops at the first item that matches the specified criteria. To locate all items that match the specified criteria, use the **Execute** method inside a loop, as shown in the following example:

```
Public Sub SearchAndReturnExample()
   ' This procedure shows how to use the Execute method inside
   ' a loop to locate multiple instances of specified text.
   Dim rngOriginalSelection   As Word.Range
   Dim colFoundItems          As New Collection
   Dim rngCurrent             As Word.Range
   Dim strSearchFor           As String
   Dim intFindCounter         As Integer

   If (Selection.Words.Count > 1) = True Or _
         (Selection.Type = wdSelectionIP) = True Then
      MsgBox "Please select a single word or part or a word. " _
         & "This procedure will search the active document for " _
         & "additional instances of the selected text."
         Exit Sub
   End If

   Set rngOriginalSelection = Selection.Range
   strSearchFor = Selection.Text

   ' Call custom procedure that moves the insertion point to the
   ' start of the document.
   Call GoToStartOfDoc

   With Selection.Find
      .ClearFormatting
      .Forward = True
      .Wrap = wdFindContinue
      .Text = strSearchFor
      .Execute
      Do While .Found = True
         intFindCounter = intFindCounter + 1
         colFoundItems.Add Selection.Range, CStr(intFindCounter)
         .Execute
      Loop
   End With

   rngOriginalSelection.Select
```

```
   If MsgBox("There are " & intFindCounter & " instances of '" _
         & rngOriginalSelection & "' in this document." & vbCrLf & vbCrLf _
         & "Would you like to loop through and display all instances?", _
         vbYesNo) = vbYes Then
      intFindCounter = 1
      For Each rngCurrent In colFoundItems
         rngCurrent.Select
         MsgBox "This is instance #" & intFindCounter
         intFindCounter = intFindCounter + 1
      Next rngCurrent
   End If

   rngOriginalSelection.Select
End Sub
```

The preceding example also illustrates how to use a **Collection** object to store the matching items as **Range** objects. In this example, the user is given the option of viewing all matching items, but you could use the same technique to work with the found items as a group. The SearchAndReturnExample procedure is available in the modFindAndReplace module in WordSamples.doc in the Samples\CH05 subfolder on the companion CD-ROM.

Replacing Text or Other Items

To replace one item with another, you must specify a setting for the ***Replace*** argument of the **Execute** method. You can specify the replacement item by using either the **Text** property of the **Replacement** object or the ***ReplaceWith*** argument of the **Execute** method. To delete an item by using this technique, use a zero-length string (**""**) as the replacement item. The following example replaces all instances of the text specified by the *strFind* argument with the text specified in the *strReplace* argument:

```
Sub ReplaceText(strFind As String, _
                strReplace As String)
   Application.ScreenUpdating = False
   ActiveDocument.Content.Select
   With Selection.Find
      .ClearFormatting
      .Forward = True
      .Wrap = wdWrapContinue
      .Execute FindText:=strFind, _
         Replace:=wdReplaceAll, ReplaceWith:=strReplace
   End With
End Sub
```

The ReplaceText procedure is available in the modFindAndReplace module in WordSamples.doc in the Samples\CH05 subfolder on the companion CD-ROM.

Restoring the User's Selection After a Search

In most cases, when you finish a search operation, you should return the selection (or the insertion point if there was no previous selection) to where it was when the search began. You do this by saving the state of the **Selection** object before you begin a search, and then restoring it when the search is completed, as shown in the following example:

```
Sub SimpleRestoreSelectionExample()
   Dim rngStartMarker   As Word.Range
   Dim strToFind        As String

   Set rngStartMarker = Selection.Range
   strToFind = InputBox("Enter the text to find.", "Find Text")
   With Selection.Find
      .ClearFormatting
      .Text = strToFind
      If .Execute = True Then
         MsgBox "'" & strToFind & "'" & " was found and is " _
            & "currently highlighted. Click OK to restore your " _
            & "original selection."
      Else
         MsgBox "'" & strToFind & "'" & " was not found."
      End If
   End With
   rngStartMarker.Select
End Sub
```

The SimpleRestoreSelectionExample procedure is available in the modFindAndReplace module in WordSamples.doc file in the Samples\CH05 subfolder on the companion CD-ROM.

Where to Go from Here

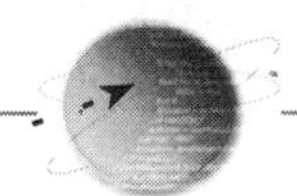

For additional information about the subjects discussed in this chapter, see the following resources.

Microsoft Office Objects and Object Models

Chapter 4, "Understanding Office Objects and Object Models"

"Object Model Diagrams" appendix

Microsoft Outlook

Byrne, Randy. *Building Applications with Microsoft Outlook 2000*. Redmond, WA: Microsoft Press, 1999.

Customizing Command Bars and Working with the Office Assistant

Chapter 6, "Working with Shared Office Components"

Using ADO and DAO to Work with Data in Office Applications

Part 3, "Working with Data in Office Solutions"

Creating and Using Wizards and Add-ins

Chapter 11, "Add-Ins, Templates, Wizards, and Libraries"

Working with Microsoft Office Web Components

Chapter 12, "Using Web Technologies"

Working with the Internet Explorer Object Model

Chapter 12, "Using Web Technologies"

Working with Scripting Event Procedures in an HTML Page

Chapter 12, "Using Web Technologies"

Working with Shared Office Components

Chapter 6, "Working with Shared Office Components"

Securing Data Access Pages

Chapter 18, "Securing Access Databases"

Creating Custom Class Objects

Chapter 9, "Custom Classes and Objects"

Code Samples

The code samples shown in this chapter, along with additional examples demonstrating similar techniques, can be copied from the files in the Samples\CH05 subfolder on the companion CD-ROM.

CHAPTER 6

Working with Shared Office Components

Microsoft Office includes a set of shared objects available in all Office applications that help you search for files, use the Office Assistant, manipulate command bars, read and write document properties, read and write script, and hook add-ins to your Office solution. Because these objects are shared among all Office applications, it is easy to write code that uses these objects and that will run without modification from within any Office application or custom Office solution.

Note Although **COMAddIn** objects are a shared Office component in the Microsoft Office 9.0 object library, they are not discussed in this chapter. For information about how to create and use **COMAddIn** objects, see Chapter 11, "Add-ins, Templates, Wizards, and Libraries."

You can use these objects to customize the appearance of your application, create custom toolbars and menu bars in code, perform custom file searches, or customize the Office Assistant to respond to the user's actions.

Note Object model diagrams for all the shared Office components discussed here are available in the "Object Model Diagrams" appendix.

Contents

Referencing Shared Office Components

Every Office application includes *accessor properties* that provide access to the shared Office components. For example, an Office application's **Assistant** property returns a reference to the **Assistant** object, the **FileSearch** property returns a reference to the **FileSearch** object, and the **Scripts** property returns a reference to the **Scripts** collection. From within any Office application, you can return a reference to a shared component object by using the appropriate accessor property; you don't need to use the **New** keyword to create an object variable that references the shared Office component.

Important All Office applications, except Microsoft Access, include a reference to the Microsoft Office 9.0 object library by default. Before you can work with shared Office components in Access, you must first manually set a reference to the Microsoft Office 9.0 object library.

As with any object model, before you can work with an object, you must either set an object variable to the object you want to work with or use the host application's accessor property. For example, the following code fragments illustrate using the accessor property (in these cases, the **FileSearch**, **Assistant**, and **CommandBars** accessor properties are used) to access various shared Office components.

```
With Application.FileSearch
   .NewSearch
   .LookIn = "C:\My Documents"
   .FileName = "*.doc"
   If .Execute() > 0 Then
      ' Work with found files here.
   End If
End With

Dim objAssistant As Assistant

Set objAssistant = Application.Assistant
With objAssistant
   .On = True
   .Visible = True
   .Animation = msoAnimationCharacterSuccessMajor
End With

Dim cbrCustomBar As CommandBar

Set cbrCustomBar = Application.CommandBars(strCBName)
With cbrCustomBar.Controls(strCtlName)
   .Enabled = Not .Enabled
End With
```

Important To set a reference to a shared Office component from outside an Office application, you must still use the accessor property of an Office application. For example, to set a reference to the **FileSearch** object from a Microsoft Visual Basic application, you could set a reference to the Word **Application** object and then use the Word **FileSearch** property to return a reference to the **FileSearch** object. For example:

```
Dim wdApp As Word.Application

Set wdApp = New Word.Application
With wdApp.FileSearch
```

Working with the FileSearch Object

The **FileSearch** object exposes a programmatic interface to all the functionality of the Office **File Open** dialog box, including the features found in the **Advanced Find** dialog box, which is available from the **Open** dialog box. You can use the objects, methods, and properties of the **FileSearch** object to search for files or collections of files based on criteria you supply.

Note If Microsoft Fast Find is enabled, the **FileSearch** object can use Fast Find indexes to speed up its searching capabilities.

The Basics of File Searching

The following code fragment is from the CustomFindFile procedure, available in the modGeneralCode module in ExcelExamples.xls in the Samples\CH06 subfolder on the companion CD-ROM. This fragment illustrates how to use an application's **FileSearch** property to return a reference to the **FileSearch** object. Because the **FileSearch** object is shared among all Office applications, this code will work without modification from within any Office application:

```
Function CustomFindFile(strFileSpec As String)
   Dim fsoFileSearch   As FileSearch
   .
   .
   .
   Set fsoFileSearch = Application.FileSearch
   With fsoFileSearch
      .NewSearch
      .LookIn = "c:\"
      .FileName = strFileSpec
      .SearchSubFolders = False
      If .Execute() > 0 Then
         For Each varFile In .FoundFiles
            strFileList = strFileList & varFile & vbCrLf
         Next varFile
      End If
   End With
   MsgBox strFileList
   .
   .
   .
End Function
```

The **FileSearch** object has two methods and several properties you can use to build custom file-searching functionality into your custom Office solutions. The previous example uses the **NewSearch** method to clear any previous search criteria and the **Execute** method to carry out the search for the specified files. The **Execute** method returns the number of files found, and also supports optional parameters that let you specify the sort order, the sort type, and whether to use only saved Fast Find indexes to perform the search. You use the **FoundFiles** property to return a reference to the **FoundFiles** object that contains the names of all matching files found in your search.

Important You must use the **NewSearch** method to clear any search criteria from previous searches; otherwise, the new search criteria will be added to the existing search criteria.

You use the **LookIn** property to specify what directory to begin searching in and the **SearchSubFolders** property to specify whether the search should extend to subfolders of the directory specified in the **LookIn** property. The **FileName** property supports wildcard characters and a semicolon-delimited list of file names or file-type specifications.

For more information about using the methods and properties of the **FileSearch** object, search the Microsoft Office Visual Basic Reference Help index for "FileSearch object."

Using Advanced File-Searching Features

You get programmatic access to the advanced features of the **FileSearch** object by using its **PropertyTests** collection. These features correspond to the options available in the **Advanced Find** dialog box, which is available through the Office **File Open** dialog box.

Figure 6.1 The Advanced Find Dialog Box

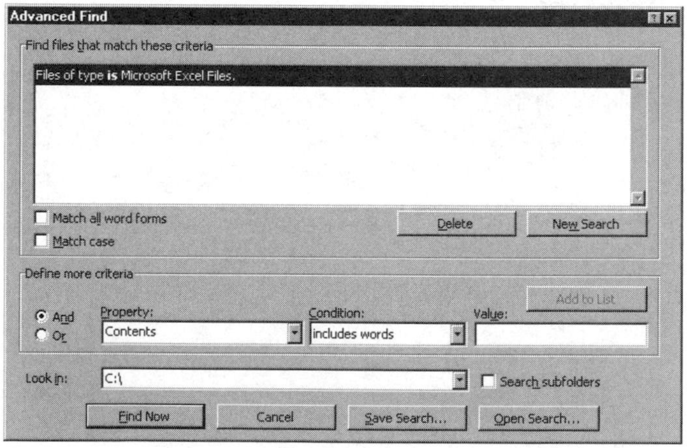

The **PropertyTests** collection contains the criteria for a file search. Some of these criteria may have been specified by properties of the **FileSearch** object itself while others must be added to the **PropertyTests** collection by using its **Add** method.

In the following example, one of the file-search criteria added to the **PropertyTests** collection corresponds to the **Contents** setting in the **Property** box and another corresponds to the **includes words** setting in the **Condition** box in Figure 6.1.

```
Set fsoFileSearch = Application.FileSearch
With fsoFileSearch
   .NewSearch
   .FileName = strFileName
   .LookIn = strLookIn
   .SearchSubFolders = blnSearchSubDir
   .PropertyTests.Add "Contents", msoConditionIncludes, strFindThisText
   If .Execute(msoSortByFileName, msoSortOrderAscending, True) > 0 Then
      For Each varFile In .FoundFiles
         cboFoundCombo.AddItem varFile
      Next varFile
   Else
      cboFoundCombo.AddItem "No Matching Files Located!"
   End If
   cboFoundCombo.ListIndex = 0
   Beep
   Beep
   Beep
End With
```

The preceding code fragment is part of the FindFiles procedure, which is available in the modAdvancedFileSearchObject module in FileSearch.xls in the Samples\CH06 subfolder on the companion CD-ROM.

Creating Reusable File-Search Code

Searching for files is something you may do over and over again in any number of different Office solutions. This makes the **FileSearch** object a great candidate for encapsulation in a class module that could be used in any Office solution that requires file-searching capabilities.

The ExcelExamples.xls sample file in the Samples\CH06 subfolder on the companion CD-ROM shows one way to use a custom class that uses the **FileSearch** object. The sample file uses the dialog box in Figure 6.2 to gather information about a search from the user.

Figure 6.2 Dialog Box Used to Gather Custom Search Criteria

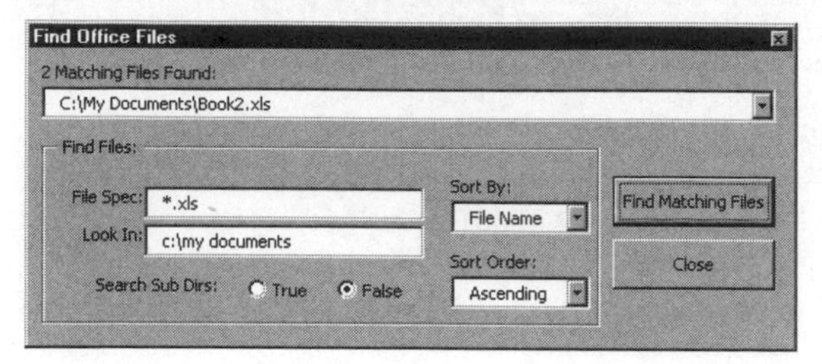

The Find Office Files dialog box is shown immediately after executing a search for files with an ".xls" extension in the "c:\my documents" directory. Code behind the Find Matching Files command button uses a global variable named `objFileInfo` to call the GetFileList method of the custom clsGetFileInfo class as follows:

```
Sub UpdateFileList()
   ' If the file-search specifications are valid, update
   ' the files contained in the form's combo box with a current
   ' list of matching files.

   Dim varFoundFiles As Variant
   Dim varFile       As Variant

   varFoundFiles = objFileInfo.GetFileList

   If IsArray(varFoundFiles) Then
      With Me
         .cboMatchingFiles.Clear
         For Each varFile In varFoundFiles
            .cboMatchingFiles.AddItem varFile
         Next varFile
         .cboMatchingFiles.ListIndex = 0
         .lblFilesFound.Caption = CStr(objFileInfo.MatchingFilesFound) _
            & " Matching Files Found:"
      End With
   Else
      MsgBox "No files matched the specification: '" & Me.txtFileSpec & "'"
   End If
End Sub
```

The UpdateFileList procedure is available in the frmFindFileDialog module in ExcelExamples.xls in the Samples\CH06 subfolder on the companion CD-ROM.

The class contains several properties used to set the properties of the **FileSearch** object. It also exposes the GetFileList method that returns an array containing all files that match the specified criteria.

```
Public Function GetFileList() As Variant
   ' This function returns an array of files that match the criteria
   ' specified by the SearchPath and SearchName properties. If the
   ' SearchSubDirs property is set to True, the search includes
   ' subdirectories of SearchPath.

   Dim intFoundFiles As Integer
   Dim astrFiles()   As String
   Dim fsoFileSearch As FileSearch

   Set fsoFileSearch = Application.FileSearch
   With fsoFileSearch
      .NewSearch
      .LookIn = p_strPath
      .FileName = p_strName
      .FileType = msoFileTypeAllFiles
      .SearchSubFolders = p_blnSearchSubs

      If .Execute(p_intSortBy, p_intSortOrder) > 0 Then
         p_intFoundFiles = .FoundFiles.Count
         ReDim astrFiles(1 To .FoundFiles.Count)
            For intFoundFiles = 1 To .FoundFiles.Count
               astrFiles(intFoundFiles) = .FoundFiles(intFoundFiles)
            Next intFoundFiles
            GetFileList = astrFiles
      Else
         GetFileList = ""
      End If
   End With
End Function
```

The GetFileList procedure is available in the clsGetFileInfo module in ExcelExamples.xls in the Samples\CH06 subfolder on the companion CD-ROM.

For more information about creating and using custom class modules in your Office solutions, see Chapter 9, "Custom Classes and Objects."

Working with the Office Assistant

You can use the Office Assistant to animate characters that interact with your users, provide context-sensitive help, highlight parts of your user interface, collect information from users, or otherwise provide a "social" interface to your application that many users find interesting and fun to use. The Office Assistant character is drawn onscreen without an enclosing window and can interact with other elements of the application interface, pointing out controls or directing the user's attention to specific sections of a document.

Note The Office Assistant is not available in Microsoft FrontPage.

You use the objects, methods, and properties of the **Assistant** object to programmatically control the Office Assistant, the Office Assistant balloon, and all the items inside the balloon.

Microsoft Agent ActiveX Control vs. the Office Assistant

The Office Assistant is based on the Microsoft Agent ActiveX control. Many of the Agent control's methods and properties are exposed through the Assistant's object model. You can use the Agent control in Office applications, on Web pages, or in any environment that supports ActiveX controls.

There are some circumstances where you would use the Agent control instead of the **Assistant** object to provide Office Assistant services:

- You want to use features of the Agent that are available only through the control. For example, the Agent's speech-recognition capabilities.
- You want to use the Agent control in an Office application where the Assistant object is not available. For example, if you have an Access run-time application on a machine that does not have Office installed, you can use the Agent control to provide the full range of Assistant services without accessing the Assistant's object model.
- You want to use the Agent to provide Assistant-like services on a Web page. The Agent control is added to HTML pages by using the <OBJECT> tag and is manipulated by using script.

For more information about using the Agent control, see the Microsoft Agent Web site at http://www.microsoft.com/intdev/agent.

Programming the Office Assistant

Programming the Assistant is a matter of setting an object variable to the **Assistant** object and then accessing the properties and methods you need to make the assistant do what you want. You can make the Assistant visible, move it to different locations on the screen, specify the animation you want to run, and display Assistant balloons containing text and controls.

One important thing to remember when you programmatically manipulate the properties of the Assistant is that the user may have set various Assistant properties that you should preserve. Any time you manipulate the Assistant, you should save the properties that existed before you began and then restore those properties when you are finished. For example, if the user normally has the Assistant turned off and you programmatically turn it on to perform some task, you should make sure you turn it off when you are finished using it. For an example of how to use a class module to preserve Assistant settings and restore them when your code is finished, see the TestSaveAssistProperties procedure in the modAssistantCode module in AssistantSamples.dot in the Samples\CH06 subfolder on the companion CD-ROM.

In previous versions of Microsoft Office, the Assistant is either visible and available or not visible and unavailable, but the Assistant can never be completely turned off. In Microsoft Office 2000, the Assistant has an **On** property that affects whether the Assistant is available at all.

You use the Assistant's **On** and **Visible** properties to determine its initial state. When the **On** property is set to **False**, the **Visible** property is **False** and any attempt to programmatically manipulate the Assistant (except for a call to the Assistant's **Help** method) is ignored and no error is raised. When the **On** property is set to **True**, the Assistant will be either visible or hidden depending on the **Visible** property's setting.

Note When the **On** property's value is changed from **False** to **True**, the **Visible** property is set to **True**.

The following example demonstrates how to save the initial settings for the **On** and **Visible** properties, how to make the Assistant visible, and a simple animation technique:

```
Sub SimpleAnimation()
   ' This procedure shows simple Assistant animation
   ' techniques. It calls the Wait procedure between
   ' animations to give the animation time to complete.

   Dim blnAssistantVisible    As Boolean
   Dim blnAssistantOn         As Boolean

   With Application.Assistant
      blnAssistantOn = .On
      blnAssistantVisible = .Visible

      If Not blnAssistantOn Then
         .On = True
      ElseIf Not blnAssistantVisible Then
         .Visible = True
      End If
      .Animation = msoAnimationCheckingSomething
      Call Wait(5000)
      .Animation = msoAnimationEmptyTrash
      Call Wait(7000)
      .Animation = msoAnimationCharacterSuccessMajor
      Call Wait(5000)
      If (Not blnAssistantOn) Or (Not blnAssistantVisible) Then
         .On = blnAssistantOn
         .Visible = blnAssistantVisible
      End If
   End With
End Sub
```

The SimpleAnimation procedure is available in the modAssistantCode module in AssistantSamples.dot in the Samples\CH06 subfolder on the companion CD-ROM.

Note The Wait procedure used in the previous example is a subroutine that uses a custom class object to wait the number of milliseconds specified in the procedure's argument. When you are stringing Assistant animations together, this procedure is needed in order to give one animation time to finish before another animation begins. To see the Wait procedure and the custom class object it uses, see the modAssistantCode module in AssistantSamples.dot in the Samples\CH06 subfolder on the companion CD-ROM. For more information about custom class objects, see Chapter 9, "Custom Classes and Objects."

The Assistant's **FileName** property specifies the animated character that is displayed when the Assistant is visible. Character files use an ".acs" extension, and several characters are supplied with Office. You can also create your own character files by using the Microsoft Agent ActiveX control's character editor. For more information about the Agent control and the character editor, see the Microsoft Agent Web site at http://www.microsoft.com/intdev/agent.

Characters you create should be stored in the host application's folder or in the C:\Windows\Application Data\Microsoft\Office\Actors subfolder; if multiple users work on the same machine and user profiles have been set up on the machine, store your characters in the host application's folder or in the C:\Windows\Profiles *UserName*\Application Data\Microsoft\Office\Actors subfolder. For more information about setting up user profiles, search the Microsoft Windows Help index for "user profiles."

You specify which character is displayed by setting the Assistant's **FileName** property to the name of the .acs file for the character you want to use. For example, the following procedure changes the character to the name of the character specified in the *strCharName* argument:

```
Function ChangeCharacter(strCharName As String) As Integer
   ' This procedure changes the existing Assistant
   ' character to the character specified in the
   ' strCharName argument. The procedure's return
   ' values are set by using constants defined in the
   ' Declarations section of this module.

   With Application.Assistant
      If UCase(.FileName) = UCase(strCharName) Then
         ChangeCharacter = ASST_CHAR_SAMECHAR
         Exit Function
      End If
      .FileName = strCharName
      ChangeCharacter = ASST_CHAR_CHANGED
   End With
End Function
```

The ChangeCharacter procedure is available in the modAssistantCode module in AssistantSamples.dot in the Samples\CH06 subfolder on the companion CD-ROM.

Note If you are using a character supplied by Office, you don't need to include the full path to the .acs file you want to use. When you set the **FileName** property, Visual Basic for Applications (VBA) will look for the file in the host application's folder and then in the C:\Windows \Application Data\Microsoft\Office\Actors subfolder and, if it exists, in the C:\Windows\Profiles *UserName*\Application Data\Microsoft\Office\Actors subfolder. If your character files are located somewhere other than the three locations discussed here, you must set the **FileName** property by using the full path to the file. If the file can't be found, a message is displayed. If the user clicks **OK**, the same file-search sequence is executed again. If the user clicks **Cancel**, the attempt to change the **FileName** property is ignored and no error occurs.

Working with Balloon Objects

The Assistant's **Balloon** object enables the Assistant to communicate with and get feedback from your users. **Balloon** objects are designed to let you create a simple interface for user interaction. They are not designed to replace complex dialog boxes.

Balloon objects can contain text that can be plain, underlined, or displayed in different colors. In addition, **Balloon** objects can contain labels or check boxes, certain icons, and bitmaps. Only one **Balloon** object can be visible at a time, but you can create multiple **Balloon** objects in code and use them when needed. For an example of how to create multiple **Balloon** objects, see the CreateMultipleBalloons procedure in the modAssistantCode module in AssistantSamples.dot in the Samples\CH06 subfolder on the companion CD-ROM. For an example of how to display multiple preformatted messages stored in a database, see the ShowBalloonTour procedure in the modAssistantCode module.

You create a **Balloon** object by using the Assistant's **NewBalloon** property. Once you have created the new **Balloon** object, you can set its properties and then display it by using the **Balloon** object's **Show** method. The following two simple procedures illustrate many of the features of **Balloon** objects discussed so far. The TestCreateSimpleBalloon procedure creates two formatted strings used to specify the balloon **Heading** and **Text** properties. The procedure then creates the balSimple **Balloon** object by calling the CreateSimpleBalloon procedure and passing in the heading and text strings. CreateSimpleBalloon sets several other "default" properties for this balloon and then returns the new **Balloon** object to the calling procedure where it is displayed by using the **Show** method.

```
Sub TestCreateSimpleBalloon()
   Dim balSimple          As Balloon
   Dim strMessage         As String
   Dim strHeading         As String
   Dim blnAssistVisible As Boolean

   strHeading = "This is a simple balloon."
   strMessage = "When you have finished reading this message, click OK to proceed." _
      & vbCrLf & "{cf 249}This text is red." & vbCrLf & "{cf 252}This text is blue." _
      & vbCrLf & "{cf 0}This text has a {ul 1}word{ul 0} that is underlined." _
      & vbCrLf & "This text is plain."
   blnAssistVisible = Application.Assistant.Visible

   Set balSimple = CreateSimpleBalloon(strMessage, strHeading)

   If Not blnAssistVisible Then
      Call ShowAssistant
   End If
   With balSimple
      .Show
   End With
   Application.Assistant.Visible = blnAssistVisible
End Sub

Function CreateSimpleBalloon(strText As String, _
                             strHeading As String) As Office.Balloon

   Dim balBalloon As Balloon

   With Application.Assistant
      Set balBalloon = .NewBalloon
      With balBalloon
         .BalloonType = msoBalloonTypeButtons
         .Button = msoButtonSetOK
         .Heading = strHeading
         .Icon = msoIconTip
         .Mode = msoModeModal
         .Text = strText
      End With
      Set CreateSimpleBalloon = balBalloon
   End With
End Function
```

The TestCreateSimpleBalloon and CreateSimpleBalloon procedures are available in the modAssistantCode module in AssistantSamples.dot in the Samples\CH06 subfolder on the companion CD-ROM.

Note that the `strMessage` variable contains a string that includes embedded brackets such as `{cf 252}`, `{cf 0}`, `{ul 1}`, and `{ul 0}`. You use the **{cf** *value***}** brackets to specify the color of the text that follows the bracket. You use the **{ul** *value***}** brackets to specify where text underlining begins and ends. For more information about specifying text color and underlining text in **Balloon** objects, search the Microsoft Office Visual Basic Reference Help index for "Text property."

If you run the sample code, you will notice that the code stops executing while the **Balloon** object is displayed. This is because the balloon's **Mode** property specifies that the balloon is modal. You can also display modeless **Balloon** objects. For more information about modeless balloons, see "Modeless Balloons and the Callback Property" later in this chapter.

Using Balloon Controls

You add labels or check box controls to a **Balloon** object by using the **Balloon** object's **Labels** or **Checkboxes** property, respectively. (Note that label controls in **Balloon** objects are similar to option button controls.) You specify the text associated with a label or check box by using the control's **Text** property. You specify a single control by using an index number between 1 and 5, which represents the number of the label or check box control in the balloon. For example, the following sample shows one way to use label controls in a **Balloon** object:

```
With balBalloon
   .Button = msoButtonSetNone
   .Heading = "Balloon Object Example One"
   .Text = "Select one of the following " _
      & .Labels.Count & " options:"
   .Labels(1).Text = "VBA is a powerful programming language."
   .Labels(2).Text = "Office is a great development environment."
   .Labels(3).Text = "The Assistant is cool!"
   .Labels(4).Text = "Balloon objects are easy to use."

   ' Show the balloon.
   intRetVal = .Show

   ' Save the selection made by the user.
   If intRetVal > 0 Then
      strChoice = "{cf 4}" & .Labels(intRetVal).Text & "{cf 0}"
   Else
      strChoice = ""
   End If
End With

Set balBalloon = Assistant.NewBalloon
With balBalloon
   .Text = "You selected option " & CStr(intRetVal) & ": '" _
      & strChoice & "'"
   .Show
End With
```

The preceding code fragment is part of the BalloonLabelControls procedure, which is available in the modAssistantTour module in AssistantTour.mdb in the Samples\CH06 subfolder on the companion CD-ROM.

Note that when the balloon is displaying label controls, you don't need to also have **OK** or **Cancel** buttons because the balloon is dismissed as soon as any label control is selected, and the user can select only one control at a time. This is not the case when you use check box controls. The user can select more than one check box before dismissing the balloon, so your code should account for multiple selections. The next example shows one way to display check box controls and then identify the selections made by the user:

```
With balBalloon
   .Button = msoButtonSetOK
   .Heading = "Balloon Object Example Two"
   .Text = "How many of the following " _
      & .Checkboxes.Count & " statements do you agree with?"
   .Checkboxes(1).Text = "VBA is a powerful programming language."
   .Checkboxes(2).Text = "Office is a great development environment."
   .Checkboxes(3).Text = "The Assistant is cool!"
   .Checkboxes(4).Text = "Balloon objects are easy to use."
   ' Save the selection made by the user.
   intRetVal = .Show
   ' Construct the string to display to the user based on the
   ' user's selections.
   For Each chkBox In .Checkboxes
      If chkBox.Checked = True Then
         strChoice = strChoice & "{cf 4}" & chkBox.Text & "{cf 0}" & "' and '"
      End If
   Next chkBox
   ' Remove the trailing "' and '" from strChoice.
   If Len(strChoice) <> 0 Then
      strChoice = Left(strChoice, Len(strChoice) - 7)
   End If
End With

' Create new Balloon object and display the user's choices.
Set balBalloon = Assistant.NewBalloon
With balBalloon
   If intRetVal > 0 Or Len(strChoice) > 0 Then
      .Text = "You selected '" & strChoice & "'."
   Else
      .Text = "You didn't make a selection."
   End If
   .Show
End With
```

The preceding code fragment is part of the BalloonCheckBoxControls procedure, which is available in the modAssistantTour module in AssistantTour.mdb in the Samples\CH06 subfolder on the companion CD-ROM.

Modeless Balloons and the Callback Property

When you display a modeless balloon, the user is able to use your application while the balloon is displayed. You specify that a balloon is modeless by setting the **Mode** property to the built-in constant **msoModeModeless**.

When you create a modeless balloon you must also set its **Button** property to something other than **msoButtonSetNone** and its **Callback** property to the name of a procedure to call when the user clicks a button in the modeless balloon. The procedure named in the **Callback** property must accept three arguments: a **Balloon** object, a long integer representing the button selected (**msoBalloonButtonType** values or a number representing the button clicked when the **BalloonType** property is set to **msoBalloonTypeButtons**), and a long integer representing the **Balloon** object's **Private** property.

You use the **Private** property to assign a value to a **Balloon** object that uniquely identifies it to the procedure named in the **Callback** property. You could use this property in a single generic callback procedure that is called from multiple modeless balloons. For example, the BalloonSamples.xls sample file in the Samples\CH06 subfolder on the companion CD-ROM contains a five-step tour of a Northwind Company spreadsheet that uses a collection of modeless balloons representing each step in the tour. All five **Balloon** objects name the BalloonCallBackProc procedure in their **Callback** property setting. Each **Balloon** object uses a unique value in its **Private** property setting, and the BalloonCallBackProc procedure uses this value and the value of the button clicked by the user (`lngBtnRetVal`) to identify which balloon has called the procedure and which button was clicked. The **Balloon** objects that call this procedure all specify a **Private** property by using a module-level constant (`BALLOON_ONE`, `BALLOON_TWO`, and so on) that indicates in which step of the tour they are called. Each balloon has a Close button and either a Next button, a Back button, or both, depending on the balloon's location in the tour. This single procedure is designed to handle all selections made in all balloons:

```
Function BalloonCallBackProc(balBalloon As Balloon, _
                             lngBtnRetVal As Long, _
                             lngPrivateBalloonID As Long)

    ' This procedure is specified in the Callback property
    ' setting for all five balloons used in the Modeless
    ' Balloon Demo. These balloons are created in the AddBalloon
    ' procedure and stored in the mcolModelessBalloons collection.

    Const BUTTON_BACK As Long = -5
    Const BUTTON_NEXT As Long = -6

    ' Close current balloon.
    balBalloon.Close
```

```
    Select Case lngPrivateBalloonID + lngBtnRetVal
        Case BALLOON_ONE + BUTTON_NEXT
            ' User clicked first balloon, Next button.
            Call ShowModelessBalloon(CStr(BALLOON_TWO))
        Case BALLOON_TWO + BUTTON_NEXT
            Call ShowModelessBalloon(CStr(BALLOON_THREE))
        Case BALLOON_TWO + BUTTON_BACK
            Call ShowModelessBalloon(CStr(BALLOON_ONE))
        Case BALLOON_THREE + BUTTON_NEXT
            Call ShowModelessBalloon(CStr(BALLOON_FOUR))
        Case BALLOON_THREE + BUTTON_BACK
            Call ShowModelessBalloon(CStr(BALLOON_TWO))
        Case BALLOON_FOUR + BUTTON_NEXT
            Call ShowModelessBalloon(CStr(BALLOON_FIVE))
        Case BALLOON_FOUR + BUTTON_BACK
            Call ShowModelessBalloon(CStr(BALLOON_THREE))
        Case BALLOON_FIVE + BUTTON_BACK
            Call ShowModelessBalloon(CStr(BALLOON_FOUR))
        Case Else
            ' User clicked Close button.
            Set mcolModelessBalloons = Nothing
    End Select
End Function
```

The BalloonCallBackProc procedure is available in the modTutorial module in BalloonSamples.xls in the Samples\CH06 subfolder on the companion CD-ROM.

This is just one example of the kinds of things you can do with modeless **Balloon** objects. You have a great deal of flexibility over what you can do with a balloon and a great deal of programmatic control over how your users interact with the balloons you create. You can use the Object Browser to get a complete listing of all the **Balloon** object's properties and methods. You can use the Microsoft Office Visual Basic Reference Help index to get more information about these properties and methods.

Working with Command Bars

Microsoft Office applications all share the same technology for creating menus and toolbars, and this technology is available to you through the command bars object model. In Microsoft Office applications, there are three kinds of **CommandBar** objects: toolbars, menu bars, and pop-up menus. Pop-up menus are displayed in three ways: as menus that drop down from menu bars, as submenus that cascade off menu commands, and as shortcut menus. Shortcut menus (also called "right-click menus") are menus that appear when you right-click something.

Since the command bars object model is shared among all Office applications, you can write code to manipulate command bars that can be used in any Office application or custom solution you develop. This section will occasionally discuss using the **Customize** dialog box, but will emphasize programmatically creating, deleting, and manipulating **CommandBar** objects.

Note You can create and modify menus and toolbars in your custom Office solutions through the host application's user interface by pointing to **Toolbars** on the **View** menu, and then clicking **Customize**. The functionality of the **Customize** dialog box differs slightly between Office applications. For more information about creating and customizing command bars by using the **Customize** dialog box, search the Help index for "toolbars, creating" in the Office application used to create your command bar.

Everything you can do in a host application by using the **Customize** dialog box you can also do by using VBA code. In addition, there are some things you can do only by using VBA code. For example, there is no way to copy a command bar from the **Customize** dialog box.

Understanding how to work with command bars in Office applications requires that you understand not only what they have in common across all applications (the command bars object model) but also how they differ within each application. The differences are covered in the next section; the similarities are covered in "Manipulating Command Bars and Command Bar Controls with VBA Code" later in this chapter.

Understanding Application-Specific Command Bar Information

Despite sharing a common object model, each Office application stores command bar information in a different location and, in some cases, implements command bars in a different way. The primary difference is how and where each Office application stores custom command bars.

Note When you make changes to any of the built-in command bars in an Office application, information about those changes is stored in the Windows registry on a per-user basis. Information about the visibility and location of built-in and custom command bars is stored in the registry as well.

Each Office application stores its command bars either with the Office document that contains the command bars, or in an application-specific file. One important result of this is that command bars cannot be shared between Office documents of different types although they can be shared among documents of the same type. You can't create a command bar in Word and then copy that command bar to an Access application and use it there.

With the exception of Access, all Office applications store command bar information in specific locations, the path to which depends on whether user profiles have been set up for multiple users on the computer where the command bars are created. For more information about setting up user profiles, search the Microsoft Windows Help index for "user profiles."

For application-specific information about command bars, see the next five sections in this chapter.

Microsoft Access Command Bars

The command bars you create in Access are stored with the database in which they are created. If you want to create command bars that are available to more than one database, you must create them in an add-in database and reference that database from each database application where you want the command bars to be available. For more information about creating add-ins, see Chapter 11, "Add-ins, Templates, Wizards, and Libraries."

Built-in command bars and information about them, for example their visibility and location, is stored in the Windows registry.

The location of information about command bars in an Access database is not dependant upon whether user profiles have been set up for multiple users.

Microsoft Excel Command Bars

Excel lets you store command bars with an individual workbook or in the Excel workspace. Workspace command bars are saved in a file named Excel.xlb. If user profiles have been set up for multiple users, Excel.xlb is stored in the C:\Windows \Profiles*UserName*\Application Data\Microsoft\Excel subfolder. If user profiles have not been set up, Excel.xlb is stored in the C:\Windows\Application Data\Microsoft \Excel subfolder.

You can copy command bars from the workspace to a workbook by using the **Attach Toolbars** dialog box (click **Attach** on the **Toolbars** tab of the **Customize** dialog box). You cannot copy command bars to a workbook by using VBA code. After you have copied a command bar to a workbook, you can delete it from the workspace by clicking **Delete** on the **Toolbars** tab of the **Customize** dialog box or by using the **Delete** method of the **CommandBars** collection.

Important When you open a workbook, Excel copies the workbook's custom command bars that do not already exist in the workspace to the workspace. These copied command bars are not deleted from the workspace when you close your workbook. If you want custom command bars to be available only when your workbook is open, you must programmatically delete them from the workspace when your workbook closes. When you delete a command bar in this fashion, you are removing only the workspace copy, not the workbook copy. The workbook copy will be again copied to the workspace the next time your custom application opens. If you do not delete the workspace copy and the workspace copy of the command bar is modified by the user, the workbook copy will not be recopied to the workspace when your workbook is reopened.

You can't use VBA to copy a workspace command bar to a workbook or to delete a workbook command bar from a workbook. The only way to delete a custom command bar from a workbook is to use the **Delete** button in the **Attach Toolbars** dialog box.

If a control on the workspace copy of the command bar calls code that exists in a workbook and the workbook is not open when the control is used, the workbook is immediately opened and made visible.

Command bars that you create to distribute with a custom application should be stored in the application's workbook or template.

Microsoft FrontPage Command Bars

In FrontPage, you can create custom command bars that will be available in the FrontPage workspace. In other words, custom command bars are generally available and are not linked to a specific FrontPage-based web. FrontPage command bars are saved in a file named CmdUI.PRF. If user profiles have been set up for multiple users, CmdUI.PRF is stored in the C:\Windows\Profiles*UserName*\Application Data \Microsoft\FrontPage\State subfolder. If user profiles have not been set up, CmdUI.PRF is stored in the C:\Windows\Application Data\Microsoft\FrontPage\State subfolder.

Microsoft Outlook Command Bars

In Outlook, command bars are stored in the Outlook workspace in the Outcmd.dat file. If user profiles have been set up for multiple users, the Outcmd.dat file is stored in the C:\Windows\Profiles*UserName*\Application Data\Microsoft\Outlook subfolder. If user profiles have not been set up, the Outcmd.dat file is stored in the C:\Windows \Application Data\Microsoft\Outlook subfolder.

Microsoft PowerPoint Command Bars

In PowerPoint, custom command bars are stored only in the application workspace in a file named PPT.pcb. If user profiles have been set up for multiple users, the PPT.pcb file is stored in the C:\Windows\Profiles*UserName*\Application Data\Microsoft \PowerPoint subfolder. If user profiles have not been set up, the PPT.pcb file is stored in the C:\Windows\Application Data\Microsoft\PowerPoint subfolder.

Note Command bars are not visible while a PowerPoint presentation is running. Therefore, changes you make to PowerPoint command bars are limited to those that are available in the design-time environment.

Microsoft Word Command Bars

When you create a command bar in Word, you have the option of storing that command bar in the Normal.dot template, in a separate template, or in the currently active document. If the command bar is stored with the Normal.dot template, it will be available to any document, even if the document is based on a different template. If the command bar is stored with the currently active document and that document is a template, the command bar will be available for any document created based on that template. If the command bar is stored with a document, it will be available only when that document is open.

In Word, custom command bars are stored in the Normal.dot file by default. If user profiles have been set up for multiple users, this file is stored in the C:\Windows \Profiles*UserName*\Application Data\Microsoft\Templates subfolder. If user profiles have not been set up, the Normal.dot file is stored in the C:\Windows \Application Data\Microsoft\Templates subfolder. Command bars created in other documents or in document templates are stored with that document or template.

When you create custom solutions based on Word, it is typical to store your code in a custom document template so that the code is available to documents created based on your template. You should also store any custom command bars in the template on which your custom solution documents are based. If you need to have your command bars available to documents based on more than one template, you can store them in a global template or add-in. For more information about templates and add-ins, see Chapter 11, "Add-ins, Templates, Wizards, and Libraries."

Note It is not a good practice to store your code or command bars in a user's Normal.dot file. Many users or system administrators protect the Normal.dot file from modifications in order to prevent the file from being infected by a virus or to keep the file from growing to an unreasonable size. Since you can never be sure that Normal.dot will be available for modifications, you should use your own custom template or add-in to distribute your code.

When you create custom command bars in Word by using the **Customize** dialog box, you specify where the command bar is stored by using the **Save In** box on the **Commands** tab of the **Customize** dialog box. When you create a custom command bar in Word by using VBA code, you specify where it is stored by using the **CustomizationContext** property of the **Application** object.

Manipulating Command Bars and Command Bar Controls with VBA Code

The command bars object model exposes a wealth of objects, collections, properties, and methods that you can use to show, hide, and modify existing command bars and command bar controls, and create new ones. You can also specify a VBA procedure to run when a user clicks a command bar button or to respond to events triggered by a command bar or command bar control. The following sections provide a broad overview of the kinds of things you can do in your custom Office solutions and how to accomplish them.

Note Many of the examples in this section refer to the "Menu Bar" **CommandBar** object. This is the name of the main menu bar in Word, PowerPoint, and Access. The main menu bar in Excel is called "Worksheet Menu Bar." To experiment with sample code that refers to the "Menu Bar" **CommandBar** object in Excel, simply change the reference from "Menu Bar" to "Worksheet Menu Bar."

Getting Information About Command Bars and Controls

Each Office application contains dozens of built-in command bars and can contain as many custom command bars as you choose to add. Each command bar can be one of three types: menu bar, toolbar, or pop-up menu. All of these command bar types can contain additional command bars and any number of controls. To get a good understanding of the command bars object model, it's often best to start by examining the various command bars and controls in an existing application.

You can use the following procedure to print (to the Debug window) information about any command bar and its controls:

```
Function CBPrintCBarInfo(strCBarName As String) As Variant
   ' This procedure prints (to the Debug window) information
   ' about the command bar specified in the strCBarName argument
   ' and information about each control on that command bar.

   Dim cbrBar                         As CommandBar
   Dim ctlCBarControl                 As CommandBarControl
   Const ERR_INVALID_CMDBARNAME       As Long = 5

   On Error GoTo CBPrintCBarInfo_Err

   Set cbrBar = Application.CommandBars(strCBarName)

   Debug.Print "CommandBar: " & cbrBar.Name & vbTab & "(" _
      & CBGetCBType(cbrBar) & ")" & vbTab & "(" _
      & IIf(cbrBar.BuiltIn, "Built-in", "Custom") & ")"
   For Each ctlCBarControl In cbrBar.Controls
      Debug.Print vbTab & ctlCBarControl.Caption & vbTab & "(" _
         & CBGetCBCtlType(ctlCBarControl) & ")"
   Next ctlCBarControl

CBPrintCBarInfo_End:
   Exit Function
CBPrintCBarInfo_Err:
   Select Case Err.Number
      Case ERR_INVALID_CMDBARNAME
         CBPrintCBarInfo = "'" & strCBarName & _
            "' is not a valid command bar name!"
      Case Else
         CBPrintCBarInfo = "Error: " & Err.Number _
            & " - " & Err.Description
   End Select
   Resume CBPrintCBarInfo_End
End Function
```

The CBPrintCBarInfo procedure is available in the modCommandBarCode module in CommandBarSamples.mdb in the Samples\CH06 subfolder on the companion CD-ROM.

You call this procedure in the Visual Basic Editor's Immediate window by using the name of a command bar as the only argument. For example, if you execute the following command from the Immediate window:

```
? CBPrintCBarInfo("Web")
```

You will see a listing of all the controls and their control types on the Microsoft Office Web built-in toolbar, as shown in Figure 6.3.

Figure 6.3 Listing of Web Toolbar Controls

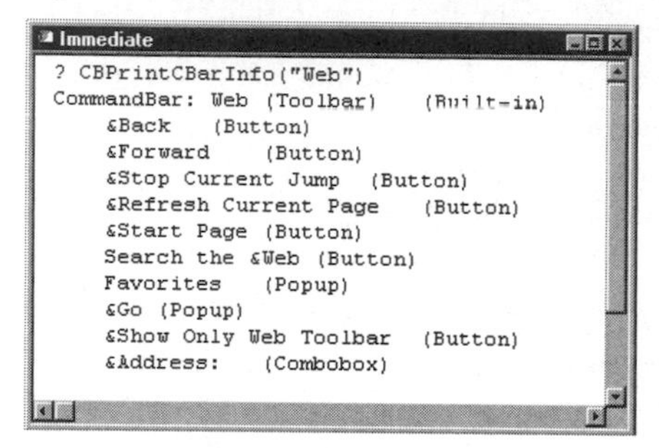

When a control type is shown as "Popup," as with the **Favorites** control above, the control itself is a command bar. You can get a listing of the controls on a pop-up menu command bar by calling the CBPrintCBarInfo procedure and passing in the name of the pop-up menu as the *strCBarName* argument. For example:

```
? CBPrintCBarInfo("Favorites")
```

Note that the CBPrintCBarInfo procedure calls two other custom procedures to get the command bar type and the control type. To get information about every command bar of any type in an application, you can use the PrintAllCBarInfo procedure. You can view and test all the command bar related custom procedures in the CommandBarSamples.mdb file in the Samples\CH06 subfolder on the companion CD-ROM.

Note To refer to a member of the **CommandBars** collection, use the name of the **CommandBar** object or an index value that represents the object's location in the collection. The controls on a command bar are members of the **CommandBar** object's **Controls** collection. To refer to a control in the **Controls** collection, use the control's **Caption** property or an index value that represents the control's location within the collection. All collections are indexed beginning with 1.

Creating a Command Bar

You can create toolbars by using the **Customize** dialog box or by using VBA code in any Office application. In Access, you can also create menu bars and pop-up menus by using the **Customize** dialog box. However, in all other Office applications, you must use VBA code to create menu bars or pop-up menus.

You create a custom command bar by using the **CommandBars** collection's **Add** method. The **Add** method creates a toolbar by default. To create a menu bar or pop-up menu, use the **msoBarMenuBar** or **msoBarPopup** constant in the **Add** method's ***Position*** argument. The following code sample illustrates how to create all three types of **CommandBar** objects:

```
Dim cbrCmdBar     As CommandBar
Dim strCBarName   As String

' Create a toolbar.
strCBarName = "MyNewToolbar"
Set cbrCmdBar = Application.CommandBars.Add(Name:=strCBarName)

' Create a menu bar.
strCBarName = "MyNewMenuBar"
Set cbrCmdBar = Application.CommandBars _
   .Add(Name:=strCBarName, Position:=msoBarMenuBar)

' Create a pop-up menu.
strCBarName = "MyNewPopupMenu"
Set cbrCmdBar = Application.CommandBars _
   .Add(Name:=strCBarName, Position:=msoBarPopup)
```

The CBCreateCommandBar procedure, available in the modCommandBarCode module in CommandBarSamples.mdb in the Samples\CH06 subfolder on the companion CD-ROM, illustrates one way that you can use a single procedure to create all three command bar types.

After you have created a command bar, you still need to add any controls that you want and set the command bar's **Visible** property to **True**. For more information about adding controls to command bars, see "Working with Command Bar Controls" later in this chapter.

Hiding and Showing a Command Bar

You hide or show a toolbar by using the **CommandBar** object's **Visible** property. When you display a toolbar, you can specify where it will appear on the screen by using the **Position** property. For example, the following code sample takes three arguments: the name of a toolbar, a Boolean value indicating whether it should be visible or hidden, and a value matching an **msoBarPosition** constant specifying where on the screen the toolbar should be displayed. The sample code also illustrates how to use the **CommandBar** object's **Type** property to make sure the specified command bar is a toolbar:

```
Function CBToolbarShow(strCBarName As String, _
                       blnVisible As Boolean, _
                       Optional lngPosition As Long = msoBarTop) As Boolean

   ' This procedure displays or hides the command bar specified in the
   ' strCBarName argument according to the value of the blnVisible
   ' argument. The optional lngPosition argument specifies where the
   ' command bar will appear on the screen.
```

```
    Dim cbrCmdBar As CommandBar

    On Error GoTo CBToolbarShow_Err

    Set cbrCmdBar = Application.CommandBars(strCBarName)

    ' Show only toolbars.
    If cbrCmdBar.Type > msoBarTypeNormal Then
       CBToolbarShow = False
       Exit Function
    End If
    ' If Position argument is invalid, set to the default
    ' msoBarTop position.
    If lngPosition < msoBarLeft Or lngPosition > msoBarMenuBar Then
       lngPosition = msoBarTop
    End If

    With cbrCmdBar
       .Visible = blnVisible
       .Position = lngPosition
    End With

    CBToolbarShow = True

CBToolbarShow_End:
    Exit Function
CBToolbarShow_Err:
    CBToolbarShow = False
    Resume CBToolbarShow_End
End Function
```

The CBToolbarShow procedure is available in the modCommandBarCode module in CommandBarSamples.mdb in the Samples\CH06 subfolder on the companion CD-ROM.

You display a custom menu bar by setting its **Visible** property to **True** and setting the existing menu bar's **Visible** property to **False**. To see an example of a procedure that displays a menu bar, see the CBMenuBarShow procedure in the modCommandBarCode module in the CommandBarSamples.mdb file in the Samples\CH06 subfolder on the companion CD-ROM.

Copying a Command Bar

You must use VBA code to copy an existing command bar. You create a copy of a command bar by creating a new command bar of the same type as the one you want to copy, and then use the **CommandBarControl** object's **Copy** method to copy each control from the original command bar to the new command bar. The following procedure illustrates how to use VBA to copy an existing command bar:

```
Function CBCopyCommandBar(strOrigCBName As String, _
                          strNewCBName As String, _
                          Optional blnShowBar As Boolean = False) As Boolean

   ' This procedure copies the command bar named in the strOrigCBName
   ' argument to a new command bar specified in the strNewCBName argument.

   Dim cbrOriginal      As CommandBar
   Dim cbrCopy          As CommandBar
   Dim ctlCBarControl   As CommandBarControl
   Dim lngBarType       As Long

   On Error GoTo CBCopy_Err

   Set cbrOriginal = CommandBars(strOrigCBName)

   lngBarType = cbrOriginal.Type
   Select Case lngBarType
      Case msoBarTypeMenuBar
         Set cbrCopy = CommandBars.Add(Name:=strNewCBName, Position:=msoBarMenuBar)
      Case msoBarTypePopup
         Set cbrCopy = CommandBars.Add(Name:=strNewCBName, Position:=msoBarPopup)
      Case Else
         Set cbrCopy = CommandBars.Add(Name:=strNewCBName)
   End Select

   ' Copy controls to new command bar.
   For Each ctlCBarControl In cbrOriginal.Controls
      ctlCBarControl.Copy cbrCopy
   Next ctlCBarControl

   ' Show new command bar.
   If blnShowBar = True Then
      If cbrCopy.Type = msoBarTypePopup Then
         cbrCopy.ShowPopup
      Else
         cbrCopy.Visible = True
      End If
   End If
   CBCopyCommandBar = True
CBCopy_End:
   Exit Function
CBCopy_Err:
   CBCopyCommandBar = False
   Resume CBCopy_End
End Function
```

The CBCopyCommandBar procedure is available in the modCommandBarCode module in CommandBarSamples.mdb in the Samples\CH06 subfolder on the companion CD-ROM.

Notes

- This procedure won't work if you pass in the name of an existing command bar in the *strNewCBName* argument, because that argument represents the name of the new command bar.
- If you copy a pop-up menu and set the *blnShowBar* argument to **True**, the pop-up menu will be displayed at the current location of the mouse pointer. For more information about displaying pop-up menus, search the Microsoft Office Visual Basic Reference Help index for "ShowPopup method."

Deleting a Command Bar

You can delete toolbars and menu bars from the **Customize** dialog box or by using VBA. You can delete pop-up menus only by using VBA. Use the **Delete** method of the **CommandBars** collection to remove an existing command bar from the collection. The following procedure illustrates one way to delete a **CommandBar** object:

```
Function CBDeleteCommandBar(strCBarName As String) As Boolean
   On Error Resume Next
   Application.CommandBars(strCBarName).Delete
End Function
```

The CBDeleteCommandBar procedure is available in the modCommandBarCode module in CommandBarSamples.mdb in the Samples\CH06 subfolder on the companion CD-ROM.

Note that an error will occur if *strCBarName* is not the name of an existing command bar. The procedure uses the **On Error Resume Next** statement to ignore this error because if an error occurs, it means there is nothing to delete.

Preventing Users from Modifying Custom Command Bars

There may be circumstances when you want to make sure that users of your custom solution can't delete or disable your custom command bars by using the **Customize** dialog box. The easiest, but least secure, way to keep users from modifying your custom command bars is to disable the command bars and make sure they are visible only when absolutely necessary. You disable a command bar by setting its **Enabled** property to **False**. You hide a command bar by setting its **Visible** property to **False**. However, hiding a command bar does nothing to prevent users from getting to the bar through the **Customize** dialog box.

To completely restrict access to your custom command bars, you must restrict all access to the **Customize** dialog box. This dialog box can be accessed in three ways: by pointing to **Toolbars** on the **View** menu and then clicking **Customize**; by right-clicking any command bar and then clicking **Customize** on the shortcut menu; and by clicking **Customize** on the **Tools** menu.

All Office applications use the Toolbar List pop-up command bar to provide access to built-in and custom command bars. The Toolbar List command bar appears when you click **Toolbars** on the **View** menu or when you right-click any command bar. If you set the **Enabled** property of the Toolbar List command bar to **False** as shown in the following line of code, a user will not be able to open the **Customize** dialog box from either of these access points:

```
CommandBars("Toolbar List").Enabled = False
```

Note Because of the way the Toolbar List command bar is constructed, you cannot disable any of its commands. The only way to disable commands on this command bar is to disable the entire command bar.

Because you can also open the **Customize** dialog box by clicking **Customize** on the **Tools** menu, you will need to disable this command as well in order to completely restrict access to your custom command bars. The following procedure illustrates how to disable all access to the **Customize** dialog box:

```
Sub AllowCommandBarCustomization(blnAllowEnabled As Boolean)
   ' This procedure allows or prevents access to the command bars
   ' Customize dialog box according to the value of the blnAllowEnabled
   ' argument.
   CommandBars("Tools").Controls("Customize...").Enabled = blnAllowEnabled
   CommandBars("Toolbar List").Enabled = blnAllowEnabled
End Sub
```

The AllowCommandBarCustomization procedure is available in the modCommandBarCode module in CommandBarSamples.mdb in the Samples\CH06 subfolder on the companion CD-ROM.

Working with Personalized Menus

Personalized menus are a new feature in Office 2000 that let you see a collapsed subset of menu items that you use most often. You specify whether personalized menus are enabled by pointing to **Toolbars** on the **View** menu, clicking **Customize**, clicking the **Options** tab, and then selecting the **Menus show recently used commands first** check box. Personalized menus are turned on by default.

Note The personalized menus feature doesn't apply to shortcut menus.

You can turn on personalized menus for all command bars in an application or for individual command bars only. You can use the **CommandBars** collection's **AdaptiveMenus** property to specify whether personalized menus are on or off for all command bars. You use a **CommandBar** object's **AdaptiveMenu** property to specify whether that object's menus are displayed as personalized menus.

You use a **CommandBarControl** object's **Priority** property to specify whether a control on a menu will be visible when personalized menus are on. When you add a custom **CommandBarControl** object to a command bar, it will be visible by default. If you set a control's **Priority** property to 1, the control will always be visible. If you set the **Priority** property to 0, the control will initially be visible but may be hidden by the host application if it is not used regularly. When a control is hidden, it is still available on the menu, but you must expand the menu to see it.

The **CommandBarControl** object's **IsPriorityDropped** property specifies whether a control is currently displayed. When this property is set to **True**, the control is hidden. Selecting a control that has its **IsPriorityDropped** property set to **True** changes the property setting to **False**, which makes the control visible the next time its menu is displayed.

The host application may change the **IsPriorityDropped** property setting if the control is not used again within a certain time period. For more information about how long a control remains visible, search the Microsoft Office Visual Basic Reference Help index for "IsPriorityDropped property."

The following procedure turns personalized menus on or off for all command bars or a single command bar according to the value of the *blnState* argument:

```
Function SetPersonalizedMenuState(blnState As Boolean, _
                                  Optional cbrBar As CommandBar = Nothing)
   ' This procedure sets the AdaptiveMenus property to the value of the
   ' blnState argument. If a CommandBar object is supplied in the cbrBar
   ' argument, the AdaptiveMenu property for that command bar is set to
   ' the value of the blnState argument.
   On Error Resume Next
   If cbrBar Is Nothing Then
      Application.CommandBars.AdaptiveMenus = blnState
   Else
      cbrBar.AdaptiveMenu = blnState
   End If
End Function
```

The following procedure changes the setting of the **Priority** property for a menu item:

```
Function PromoteMenuItem(cbrBar As CommandBar, _
                         strItemCaption As String)
   ' This procedure changes the Priority property setting for the
   ' cbrBar command bar control whose Caption property setting
   ' matches the value of the strItemCaption argument.
   Dim ctlMenuItem As CommandBarControl

   On Error Resume Next
   If cbrBar.AdaptiveMenu = False Then Exit Function
   Set ctlMenuItem = cbrBar.Controls(strItemCaption)
   With ctlMenuItem
      If .Priority <> 1 Then
         .Priority = 1
      End If
   End With
End Function
```

The SetPersonalizeMenuState and PromptMenuItem procedures are available in the modCommandBarCode module in CommandBarSamples.mdb in the Samples\CH06 subfolder on the companion CD-ROM.

Working with Images on Command Bar Buttons

Every built-in command bar button has an image associated with it. You can use these images on your own command bar buttons as long as you know the **FaceId** property value of the built-in button that contains the image. The values for the **FaceId** property range from zero (no image) to the total number of button images used in the host application (typically a few thousand). One easy way to browse the available button images is to build a toolbar, add some buttons, and assign **FaceId** property values to those buttons. The buttons display the image associated with the specified **FaceId** property value. The modCommandBarCode module in CommandBarSamples.mdb in the Samples\CH06 subfolder on the companion CD-ROM contains the CBShowButtonFaceIDs procedure, which accepts starting and ending **FaceId** property values and builds a toolbar that displays all the specified images. For example, to see button images with values from 200 to 299, you would call CBShowButtonFaceIDs from the Immediate window like this:

```
? CBShowButtonFaceIDs(200, 299)
```

And the button images would display as shown in Figure 6.4.

Figure 6.4 A Collection of Built-in Toolbar Icons

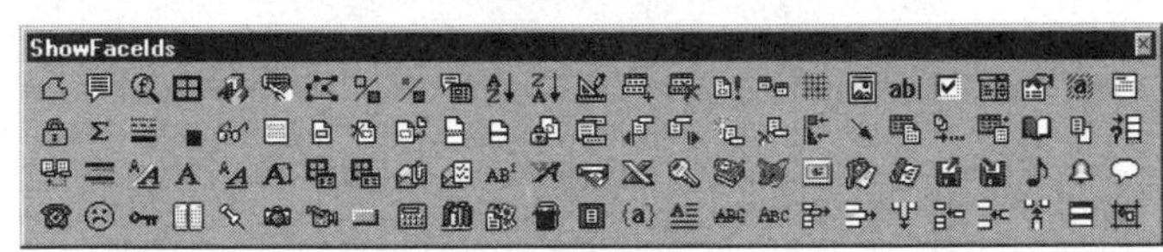

You can see the value of the **FaceId** property for any image on the command bar by resting your mouse pointer on the image until the value appears in the button's ToolTip.

Another way to copy the image from one command bar button to another is to use the **FindControl** method of the **CommandBars** collection to determine the value of the **FaceId** property for the image you want to copy. You can then use the **CommandBarControl** object's **CopyFace** and **PasteFace** methods to copy the image to a new control. The following sample code illustrates how to use these methods to paste the icon associated with an existing command bar button to a new command bar button.

```
Private Sub CBCopyIconDemo()
   ' This procedure demonstrates how to copy the image associated
   ' with a known toolbar button to a new toolbar button. This example
   ' copies the image associated with the "Contents and Index" control
   ' on the Help menu to a new command bar control.

   Dim cbrNew                 As CommandBar
   Dim ctlNew                 As CommandBarControl
   Const ERR_CMDBAR_EXISTS    As Long = 5

   On Error Resume Next
   Set cbrNew = CommandBars.Add("TestCopyFaceIcon")
   If Err = ERR_CMDBAR_EXISTS Then
      Call CBDeleteCommandBar("TestCopyFaceIcon")
      Set cbrNew = CommandBars.Add("TestCopyFaceIcon")
   ElseIf Err <> 0 Then
      Exit Sub
   End If
   On Error GoTo 0
   Set ctlNew = cbrNew.Controls.Add(msoControlButton)
   Call CBCopyControlFace("Help", "Contents and Index")

   With ctlNew
      .PasteFace
   End With
   cbrNew.Visible = True
End Sub
```

The CBCopyIconDemo procedure is available in the modCommandBarCode module in CH06_2.mdb in the Samples\CH06 subfolder on the companion CD-ROM.

This procedure calls two other custom procedures. The CBDeleteCommandbar procedure was discussed in the previous section and is used to delete the command bar if it already exists. The CBCopyControlFace procedure copies the image of the specified control to the Clipboard:

```
Function CBCopyControlFace(strCBarName As String, _
                           strCtlCaption As String)

   ' This procedure uses the CopyFace method to copy the image associated
   ' with the control specified in the strCtlCaption argument to the Clipboard.

   Dim ctlCBarControl As CommandBarControl

   Set ctlCBarControl = CommandBars.FindControl(msoControlButton, _
      CBGetControlID(strCBarName, strCtlCaption))
   ctlCBarControl.CopyFace
End Function
```

The CBCopyControlFace procedure is available in the modCommandBarCode module in CommandBarSamples.mdb in the Samples\CH06 subfolder on the companion CD-ROM.

The CBCopyControlFace procedure uses the CBGetControlID procedure as the ***Id*** argument for the **FindControl** method. CBGetControlID returns the **Id** property for the specified control by using the following line:

```
CBGetControlID = Application.CommandBars(strCBarName) _
   .Controls(strControlCaption).ID
```

The **CommandBar** object also supports a **FindControl** method that searches for the specified control only on the **CommandBar** object itself.

To see these procedures working together, place the insertion point (cursor) anywhere in the CBCopyIconDemo procedure and use the F8 key to step through the code. Try changing the command bar name and control name to copy different images to the new control.

Working with Command Bar Controls

Each **CommandBar** object has a **CommandBarControls** collection, which contains all the controls on the command bar. You use the **Controls** property of a **CommandBar** object to refer to a control on a command bar. If the control is of the type **msoControlPopup**, it also will have a **Controls** collection representing each control on the pop-up menu. Pop-up menu controls represent menus and submenus and can be nested several layers deep, as shown in the second example below.

In this example, the code returns a reference to the **New** button on the **Standard** toolbar:

```
Dim ctlCBarControl As CommandBarControl

Set ctlCBarControl = Application.CommandBars("Standard").Controls("New")
```

Here the code returns a reference to the **Macros...** control on the **Macro** pop-up menu on the **Tools** menu on the "Menu Bar" main menu bar:

```
Dim ctlCBarControl As CommandBarControl

Set ctlCBarControl = Application.CommandBars("Menu Bar").Controls("Tools") _
   .Controls("Macro").Controls("Macros...")
```

Because each pop-up menu control is actually a **CommandBar** object itself, you can also refer to them directly as members of the **CommandBars** collection. For example, the following line of code returns a reference to the same control as the previous example:

```
Set ctlCBarControl = Application.CommandBars("Macro") _
   .Controls("Macros...")
```

Once you have a reference to a control on a command bar, you can access all available properties and methods of that control.

Note When you refer to a command bar control by using the control's **Caption** property, you must be sure to specify the caption exactly as it appears on the menu. For example, in the previous code sample, the reference to the control caption "Macros..." requires the ellipsis (...) so that it matches how the caption appears on the menu.

Adding Controls

To add a control to a command bar, use the **Add** method of the **Controls** collection, specifying which type of control you want to create. You can add controls of the following type: button (**msoControlButton**), text box (**msoControlEdit**), drop-down list box (**msoControlDropdown**), combo box (**msoControlComboBox**), or pop-up menu (**msoControlPopup**).

The following example adds a new menu to the "Menu Bar" command bar and then adds three controls to the menu:

```
Private Sub CBAddMenuDemo()
   ' Illustrates adding a new menu and filling it with controls. Also
   ' illustrates deleting a menu control from a menu bar.
   '
   ' In Microsoft Excel, the main menu bar is named "Worksheet Menu Bar"
   ' rather than "Menu Bar".

   Dim strCBarName   As String
   Dim strMenuName   As String
   Dim cbrMenu       As CommandBarControl

   strCBarName = "Menu Bar"
   strMenuName = "Custom Menu Demo"

   Set cbrMenu = CBAddMenu(strCBarName, strMenuName)

   ' Note: The following use of the MsgBox function in
   ' the OnAction property setting will work only with
   ' command bars in Microsoft Access. In the other Office
   ' applications, you call built-in VBA functions for the
   ' OnAction property setting. To call a built-in VBA
   ' function from a command bar control in the other Office
   ' applications, you must create a custom procedure that
   ' uses the VBA function and call that custom procedure in
   ' the OnAction property setting.
   Call CBAddMenuControl(cbrMenu, "Item 1", _
      "=MsgBox('You selected Menu1 Control 1.')")
   Call CBAddMenuControl(cbrMenu, "Item 2", _
      "=MsgBox('You selected Menu1 Control 2.')")
   Call CBAddMenuControl(cbrMenu, "Item 3", _
      "=MsgBox('You selected Menu1 Control 3.')")
```

```
   ' The menu should now appear to the right of the
   ' Help menu on the menu bar. To see how to delete
   ' a menu from a menu bar, press F8 to step through
   ' the remaining code.
   Stop
   Call CBDeleteCBControl(strCBarName, strMenuName)
End Sub
```

The CBAddMenuDemo procedure is available in the modCommandBarCode module in CommandBarSamples.mdb in the Samples\CH06 subfolder on the companion CD-ROM.

Note that the CBAddMenuDemo procedure calls three other procedures: CBAddMenu, CBAddMenuControl, and CBDeleteCBControl. CBAddMenu returns the new pop-up menu as a **CommandBarControl** object. In addition, if the command bar specified by the *strCBarName* argument does not exist, CBAddMenu creates it. CBAddMenuControl adds a button control to the menu created by CBAddMenu and sets the control's **OnAction** property to the code to run when the button is clicked. CBDeleteCBControl just removes the menu created in the CBAddMenu procedure. CBAddMenu and CBAddMenuControl are shown below:

```
Function CBAddMenu(strCBarName As String, _
                   strMenuName As String) As CommandBarControl

   ' Add the menu named in strMenuName to the
   ' command bar named in strCBarName.

   Dim cbrBar          As CommandBar
   Dim ctlCBarControl  As CommandBarControl

   On Error Resume Next
   Set cbrBar = CommandBars(strCBarName)
   If Err <> 0 Then
      Set cbrBar = CommandBars.Add(strCBarName)
      Err = 0
   End If

   With cbrBar
      Set ctlCBarControl = .Controls.Add(msoControlPopup)
      ctlCBarControl.Caption = strMenuName
   End With
   Set CBAddMenu = ctlCBarControl
End Function

Function CBAddMenuControl(cbrMenu As CommandBarControl, _
                          strCaption As String, _
                          strOnAction As String) As Boolean

   ' Add a button control to the menu specified in cbrMenu and set
   ' its Caption and OnAction properties to the values specified in
   ' the strCaption and strOnAction arguments.
```

```
    Dim ctlCBarControl As CommandBarControl

    With cbrMenu
        Set ctlCBarControl = .Controls.Add(msoControlButton)
        With ctlCBarControl
            .Caption = strCaption
            .OnAction = strOnAction
            .Tag = .Caption
        End With
    End With
End Function
```

The CBAddMenu and CBAddMenuControl procedures are available in the modCommandBarCode module in CommandBarSamples.mdb in the Samples\CH06 subfolder on the companion CD-ROM.

You normally set the **OnAction** property to the name of a procedure to run when the button is clicked. In the example above, however, the **OnAction** property is set by using a string that contains the built-in VBA **MsgBox** function and the text to display in the message box. For an example that illustrates how to have multiple command bar controls of different types call the same procedure, see the CreateCustomCommandbar and MoveRecord procedures in the modEmployeesCmdBar module in the CommandBarSamples.mdb sample file in the Samples\CH06 subfolder on the companion CD-ROM. When multiple command bar controls use the same **OnAction** property setting, you can use the **ActionControl** property and the **Parameter** property to determine which command bar button is calling the procedure. You can also use VBA code that executes in response to **CommandBar** and **CommandBarControl** events. For more information about these events, see "Working with Command Bar Events" later in this chapter.

To see an example of what you can do with the **OnAction**, **Parameter**, and **ActionControl** properties, open the Employees form in the CommandBarSamples.mdb sample file in the Samples\CH06 subfolder on the companion CD-ROM and navigate among the available records by using the two custom toolbar buttons and the combo box control. This example illustrates how to add a **CommandBarComboBox** object to a command bar, populate it with information stored in a database, and execute code in response to a user's selection from the combo box control.

You can easily add any built-in command bar control to a command bar by using the **Id** property of the built-in control. The following procedure illustrates a technique to add a built-in control to a command bar.

```
Function CBAddBuiltInControl(cbrDestBar As CommandBar, _
                             strCBarSource As String, _
                             strCtlCaption As String) As Boolean

    ' This procedure adds the built-in control specified in
    ' strCtlCaption from the strCBarSource command bar to the
    ' command bar specified by cbrDestBar.
```

```
   On Error GoTo CBAddBuiltInControl_Err

   If CBDoesCBExist(strCBarSource) <> True Then
      CBAddBuiltInControl = False
      Exit Function
   End If

   cbrDestBar.Controls.Add ID:=CBGetControlID(strCBarSource, strCtlCaption)
   CBAddBuiltInControl = True

CBAddBuiltInControl_End:
   Exit Function
CBAddBuiltInControl_Err:
   CBAddBuiltInControl = False
   Resume CBAddBuiltInControl_End
End Function
```

The CBAddBuiltInControl procedure is available in the modCommandBarCode module in CommandBarSamples.mdb in the Samples\CH06 subfolder on the companion CD-ROM.

This procedure uses the CBGetControlID procedure to find the **Id** property of the desired control. The CBGetControlID procedure was also used in the "Working with Images on Command Bar Buttons" section earlier in this chapter. To see this procedure used to build a command bar that uses built-in controls, use the F8 key to step through the code in the CBAddBuiltInCtlDemo procedure, available in the modCommandBarCode module in the CommandBarSamples.mdb file in the Samples\CH06 subfolder on the companion CD-ROM.

Note When you specify a control's **Id** property, you also specify the action the control will take when it is selected and, if applicable, the image that appears on the face of the control. To add a control's image without its built-in action, you specify only the **FaceId** property. For more information about using the **FaceId** property, see "Working with Images on Command Bar Buttons" earlier in this chapter.

Showing and Enabling Controls

You specify whether a command bar control appears on a command bar by using its **Visible** property. You specify whether a command bar control appears enabled or disabled (grayed out) by using its **Enabled** property. For example, the following two lines of code could be used to toggle the **Visible** and **Enabled** properties of the named controls:

```
Application.CommandBars("Menu Bar").Controls("Edit").Enabled = _
   Not Application.CommandBars("Menu Bar").Controls("Edit").Enabled

Application.CommandBars("Formatting").Controls("Font").Visible = _
   Not Application.CommandBars("Formatting").Controls("Font").Visible
```

When a command bar control's **Enabled** property is **False**, the control appears on the command bar but is disabled and cannot be manipulated.

To see sample procedures that you can use to toggle the **Visible** or **Enabled** properties of any command bar control, see the CBCtlToggleVisible and CBCtlToggleEnabled procedures in the modCommandBarCode module in the CommandBarSamples.mdb file in the Samples\CH06 subfolder on the companion CD-ROM.

Indicating the State of a Command Bar Control

Many menu commands or toolbar buttons are used to toggle the state of some part of an application from one condition to another. For example, in Office applications, the **Bold** button and the **Align Left** button will appear pressed in or not pressed in, depending on the formatting applied to text at the current selection. You can achieve this same effect with your custom command bar button controls by setting the **State** property to one of the **msoButtonState** constants.

Note The **State** property is read-only for built-in command bar controls.

The following procedure shows how to toggle the **State** property of a custom command bar button control:

```
Function CBCtlToggleState(strCBarName As String, _
                          strCtlCaption As String) As Boolean

   ' Toggle the State property of the strCtlCaption control
   ' on the strCBarName command bar. The State property is
   ' read-only for built-in controls, so if strCtlCaption
   ' is a built-in control, return False and exit the procedure.

   Dim ctlCBarControl As CommandBarControl

   On Error Resume Next

   Set ctlCBarControl = Application.CommandBars(strCBarName).Controls(strCtlCaption)

   If ctlCBarControl.BuiltIn = True Then
      CBCtlToggleState = False
      Exit Function
   End If

   If ctlCBarControl.Type <> msoControlButton Then
      CBCtlToggleState = False
      Exit Function
   End If

   ctlCBarControl.State = Not ctlCBarControl.State

   If Err = 0 Then
      CBCtlToggleState = True
   Else
      CBCtlToggleState = False
   End If
End Function
```

The CBCtlToggleState procedure is available in the modCommandBarCode module in CommandBarSamples.mdb in the Samples\CH06 subfolder on the companion CD-ROM.

Working with Command Bar Events

You can use command bar event procedures to run your own code in response to an event. You can also use these event procedures to substitute your own code for the default behavior of a built-in control. The **CommandBars** collection and the **CommandBarButton** and **CommandBarComboBox** objects expose the following event procedures that you can use to run code in response to an event:

- The CommandBars collection supports the OnUpdate event, which is triggered in response to changes made to an Office document that may affect the state of any visible command bar or command bar control. For example, the OnUpdate event occurs when a user changes the selection in an Office document. You can use this event to change the availability or state of command bars or command bar controls in response to actions taken by the user.

  Important The OnUpdate event can be triggered repeatedly in many different contexts. Any code you add to this event that does a lot of processing or performs a number of actions may affect the performance of your solution.

- The **CommandBarButton** control exposes a Click event that is triggered when a user clicks a command bar button. You can use this event to run code when the user clicks a command bar button.
- The **CommandBarComboBox** control exposes a Change event that is triggered when a user makes a selection from a combo box control. You can use this method to take an action depending on what selection the user makes from a combo box control on a command bar.

To expose these events, you must first declare an object variable in a class module by using the **WithEvents** keyword. The following code, entered in the Declarations section of a class module, creates object variables representing the **CommandBars** collection, three command bar buttons, and a combo box control on a custom toolbar:

```
Public WithEvents colCBars          As Office.CommandBars
Public WithEvents cmdBold           As Office.CommandBarButton
Public WithEvents cmdItalic         As Office.CommandBarButton
Public WithEvents cmdUnderline      As Office.CommandBarButton
Public WithEvents cboFontSize       As Office.CommandBarComboBox
```

Once you use the **WithEvents** keyword to declare an object variable in a class module, the object appears in the **Object** box in the Code window, and when you select it, the object's events are available in the **Procedure** box. For example, if the clsCBarEvents class module contained the previous code, you could select the colCBars, cmdBold, cmdItalic, cmdUnderline, and cboFontSize objects from the **Object** drop-down list and each object's event procedure template would be added to your class module as follows:

```
Private Sub colCBars_OnUpdate()
   ' Insert code you want to run in response to selection changes in an
   ' Office document.
End Sub

Private Sub cmdBold_Click (ByVal Ctrl As Office.CommandBarButton, _
                           CancelDefault As Boolean)
   ' Insert code you want to run in response to this event.
End Sub

Private Sub cmdItalic_Click (ByVal Ctrl As Office.CommandBarButton, _
                             CancelDefault As Boolean)
   ' Insert code you want to run in response to this event.
End Sub

Private Sub cmdUnderline_Click (ByVal Ctrl As Office.CommandBarButton, _
                                CancelDefault As Boolean)
   ' Insert code you want to run in response to this event.
End Sub

Private Sub cboFontSize_Change (ByVal Ctrl As Office.CommandBarComboBox)
   ' Insert code you want to run when a selection is made in a combo box.
End Sub
```

You add to the event procedures the code that you want to run when the event occurs.

Note If you set the variable for a command bar control object to a built-in command button, you can set the Click event's *CancelDefault* argument to **True** to prevent the button's default behavior from occurring. This behavior is useful if you are developing an add-in and want code to run instead of, or in addition to, the application code that runs when a built-in button is clicked.

After you have added code to the event procedures, you create an instance of the class in a standard or class module and use the **Set** statement to link the control events to specific command bar controls. In the following example, the InitEvents procedure is used in a standard module to link clsCBarEvents object variables to specific command bar controls on the Formatting Example toolbar:

```
Option Explicit
Dim clsCBClass As New clsCBEvents

Sub InitEvents()
    Dim cbrBar As Office.CommandBar

    Set cbrBar = CommandBars("Formatting Example")
    With cbrBar
        Set clsCBClass.cmdBold = .Controls("Bold")
        Set clsCBClass.cmdItalic = .Controls("Italic")
        Set clsCBClass.cmdUnderline = .Controls("Underline")
        Set clsCBClass.cboFontSize = .Controls("Set Font Size")
    End With
    Set clsCBClass.colCBars = CommandBars
End Sub
```

The InitEvents procedure is available in the modStartupCode module in CommandBarEvents.doc in the Samples\CH06 subfolder on the companion CD-ROM.

Once the InitEvents procedure runs, the code you placed in the command bar's and command bar controls' event procedures will run whenever the related event occurs.

To see an example that uses a class module to link command bar and command bar control events in order to specify and determine text formatting information, see the CommandBarEvents.doc file in the Samples\CH06 subfolder on the companion CD-ROM.

For more information about using the **WithEvents** keyword, see Chapter 9, "Custom Classes and Objects." For more information about using command bar events in add-in applications, see Chapter 11, "Add-ins, Templates, Wizards, and Libraries."

Working with Document Properties

Every file created by a Microsoft Office application supports a set of built-in document properties. In addition, you can add your own custom properties to an Office document either manually or through code. You can use document properties to create, maintain, and track information about an Office document such as when it was created, who the author is, where it is stored, and so on. In addition, when you save an Office document as an HTML file, all of the document properties are written to the HTML file within <XML> tag pairs. This enables you to use document properties to track or index files according to properties you specify, regardless of what format you use to save the file. To see an example of how built-in and custom document properties are saved as HTML, see DocumentProperties.htm in the Samples\CH06 subfolder on the companion CD-ROM.

Note Microsoft Office uses the term "document" to represent any file created by using an Office application.

You can view and set built-in and custom document properties by clicking **Properties** on the **File** menu. (In Access, click **Database Properties** on the **File** menu.)

Figure 6.5 The Document Properties Dialog Box

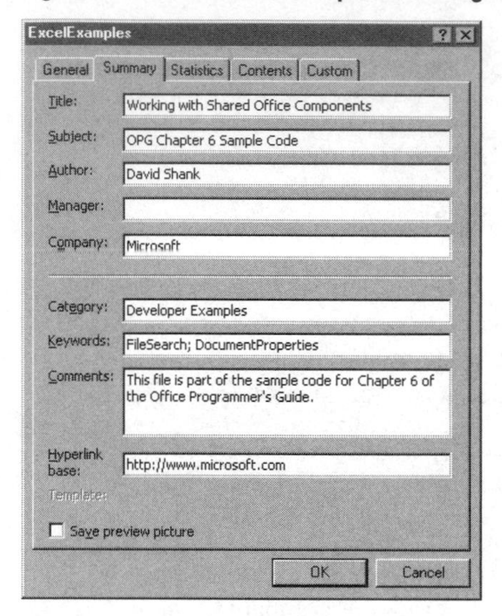

The built-in and custom document properties are stored in the shared Office component called the **DocumentProperties** collection. Each individual property is represented in that collection by a **DocumentProperty** object.

Document Properties in Microsoft Access, Microsoft FrontPage, and Microsoft Outlook

Access does not use the **DocumentProperties** collection to store the built-in and custom properties displayed in its **Database Properties** dialog box. You can access these properties by using Data Access Objects (DAO) in an .mdb-type database. For more information about database properties, search the Microsoft Access Visual Basic Reference Help index for "database properties."

FrontPage also does not use the **DocumentProperties** collection to store the built-in and custom properties displayed in its **Page Properties** dialog box (**File** menu). In FrontPage, built-in and custom properties are stored in the **MetaTags** and **Properties** collections of a **WebFile** object. For more information about working with the FrontPage object model, see Chapter 5, "Working with Office Applications."

Outlook does not provide a **Document Properties** dialog box from the **File** menu like the other Office applications do.

You access the **DocumentProperties** collection by using the **BuiltInDocumentProperties** and **CustomDocumentProperties** properties of an Office document. For an example that prints all built-in and custom document properties for an Office document to the Immediate window, see the PrintAllDocProperties procedure in the modDocumentPropertiesCode module in the ExcelExamples.xls file in the Samples\CH06 subfolder on the companion CD-ROM.

Note The **BuiltInDocumentProperties** property returns a collection that contains properties that may apply only to certain Office applications. If you try to return the value of these properties in the wrong context, an error occurs. The sample code shows how to trap this error and continue to identify all the properties that are valid in a given context.

The following code sample shows how to determine the value of a built-in document property. The GetBuiltInProperty procedure accepts an Office document object (**Workbook**, **Document**, or **Presentation**) and a property name and returns the value of the built-in property, if available:

```
Function GetBuiltInProperty(objDoc As Object, _
                            strPropname As String) As Variant

   ' This procedure returns the value of the built-in document
   ' property specified in the strPropName argument for the Office
   ' document object specified in the objDoc argument.

   Dim prpDocProp    As DocumentProperty
   Dim varValue      As Variant

   Const ERR_BADPROPERTY   As Long = 5
   Const ERR_BADDOCOBJ     As Long = 438
   Const ERR_BADCONTEXT    As Long = -2147467259

   On Error GoTo GetBuiltInProp_Err

   Set prpDocProp = objDoc.BuiltInDocumentProperties(strPropname)
   With prpDocProp
      varValue = .Value
      If Len(varValue) <> 0 Then
         GetBuiltInProperty = varValue
      Else
         GetBuiltInProperty = "Property does not currently have a value set."
      End If
   End With

GetBuiltInProp_End:
   Exit Function
GetBuiltInProp_Err:
   Select Case Err.Number
      Case ERR_BADDOCOBJ
         GetBuiltInProperty = "Object does not support BuiltInProperties."
      Case ERR_BADPROPERTY
         GetBuiltInProperty = "Property not in collection."
```

```
        Case ERR_BADCONTEXT
            GetBuiltInProperty = "Value not available in this context."
        Case Else
    End Select
    Resume GetBuiltInProp_End:
End Function
```

The GetBuiltInProperty procedure is available in the modDocumentPropertiesCode module in ExcelExamples.xls in the Samples\CH06 subfolder on the companion CD-ROM.

Note For a complete list of built-in document properties, search the Microsoft Office Visual Basic Reference Help index for "DocumentProperty object."

You can determine the value of an existing custom document property by using the same techniques as those illustrated in the previous code example. The only difference is that you would use the Office document's **CustomDocumentProperties** collection to return the **DocumentProperty** object you were interested in.

You use the **Add** method of the **CustomDocumentProperties** collection to add a custom **DocumentProperty** object to the **DocumentProperties** collection. When you add a custom property, you specify its name, data type, and value. You can also link a custom property to a value in the Office document itself. When you add linked properties, the value of the custom property changes when the value in the document changes. For example, if you add a custom property linked to a named range in an Excel spreadsheet, the property will always contain the current value of the data in the named range.

The following procedure illustrates how to add both static and linked custom properties to the **DocumentProperties** collection. It is essentially a wrapper around the **Add** method of the **DocumentProperties** collection that includes parameter validation and deletes any existing custom property before adding a property that uses the same name.

```
Function AddCustomDocumentProperty(strPropName As String, _
                                   lngPropType As Long, _
                                   Optional varPropValue As Variant = "", _
                                   Optional blnLinkToContent As Boolean = False, _
                                   Optional varLinkSource As Variant = "") _
                                   As Long

    ' This procedure adds the custom property specified in the strPropName
    ' argument. If the blnLinkToContent argument is True, the custom
    ' property is linked to the location specified by varLinkSource.
    ' The procedure first checks for missing or inconsistent input parameters.
    ' For example, a value must be provided unless the property is linked, and
    ' when you are using linked properties, the source of the link must be provided.

    Dim prpDocProp As DocumentProperty
```

```
   ' Validate data supplied in arguments to this procedure.
   If blnLinkToContent = False And Len(varPropValue) = 0 Then
      ' No value supplied for custom property.
      AddCustomDocumentProperty = ERR_CUSTOM_LINKTOCONTENT_VALUE
      Exit Function
   ElseIf blnLinkToContent = True And Len(varLinkSource) = 0 Then
      ' No source provided for LinkToContent scenario.
      AddCustomDocumentProperty = ERR_CUSTOM_LINKTOCONTENT_LINKSOURCE
      Exit Function
   ElseIf lngPropType < msoPropertyTypeNumber Or _
         lngPropType > msoPropertyTypeFloat Then
      ' Invalid value for data type specifier. Must be one of the
      ' msoDocProperties enumerated constants.
      AddCustomDocumentProperty = ERR_CUSTOM_INVALID_DATATYPE
      Exit Function
   ElseIf Len(strPropName) = 0 Then
      ' No name supplied for new custom property.
      AddCustomDocumentProperty = ERR_CUSTOM_INVALID_PROPNAME
      Exit Function
   End If

   Call DeleteIfExisting(strPropName)

   Select Case blnLinkToContent
      Case True
         Set prpDocProp = ActiveWorkbook.CustomDocumentProperties _
            .Add(Name:=strPropName, LinkToContent:=blnLinkToContent, _
            Type:=lngPropType, LinkSource:=varLinkSource)
            ActiveWorkbook.Save
      Case False
         Set prpDocProp = ActiveWorkbook.CustomDocumentProperties. _
            Add(Name:=strPropName, LinkToContent:=blnLinkToContent, _
            Type:=lngPropType, Value:=varPropValue)
   End Select
End Function
```

The AddCustomDocumentProperty procedure is available in the modDocumentPropertiesCode module in ExcelExamples.xls in the Samples\CH06 subfolder on the companion CD-ROM.

Important When you programmatically add a custom property to the **DocumentProperties** collection and the property is linked to a value in the underlying Office document, you must use the document's **Save** method, as illustrated above, before the property value will be correctly reflected for the new **DocumentProperty** object.

Working with Scripts

You can use the **Scripts** collection and the **Script** object to programmatically access script, or insert script into a cell or range in an Excel worksheet, a PowerPoint slide, or a Word document or Word **Selection** object. In addition, if you use an Office application to open an HTML page, any script contained in that page will be available through the **Scripts** collection.

Note Microsoft Access and Microsoft Outlook do not use this shared Office component. In Access, you can create an HTML page by using the **DataAccessPage** object, but you cannot use VBA to programmatically access script by using the Office script object model within Access. For more information about creating and manipulating Web pages in Access, see Chapter 5, "Working with Office Applications," and Chapter 12, "Using Web Technologies."

Every **Script** object that is inserted in an Office document includes a **Shape** object of the type **msoScriptAnchor**. In Excel and PowerPoint, these shapes are added to the **Worksheet** or **Slide** object's **Shapes** collection. In Word, these shapes are added to a document's **InLineShapes** collection.

If you want to write script in a document you create in an Office application, use the Microsoft Script Editor. On the other hand, if you want to add script to an Office document programmatically, from an add-in for example, use the objects, properties, and methods of the script object model discussed here. For more information about creating add-ins, see Chapter 11, "Add-ins, Templates, Wizards, and Libraries."

Understanding Script Object Properties

The **Scripts** collection contains all the **Script** objects in an Office document. A **Script** object represents a <SCRIPT> tag pair, its attribute settings, and all the text contained between the tag pair. An Office document or an HTML page can contain several script blocks and each script block can contain any number of procedures. For example, the following HTML code contains three script blocks. The first block initializes an array representing the days of the week, the second block contains a procedure that executes when the page loads, and the third block contains the WriteDay and WriteDate procedures that create a part of the text that is displayed on the page itself.

```
<HTML>
<HEAD>
<TITLE>Office Programmer's Guide Chapter 6</TITLE>
<SCRIPT LANGUAGE="VBSCRIPT" ID="scrDayArray">
<!--
   Option Explicit
   Dim arrDays(6)
   Dim strDay
```

```
   arrDays(0) = "Sunday"
   arrDays(1) = "Monday"
   arrDays(2) = "Tuesday"
   arrDays(3) = "Wednesday"
   arrDays(4) = "Thursday"
   arrDays(5) = "Friday"
   arrDays(6) = "Saturday"
-->
</SCRIPT>
<SCRIPT LANGUAGE="VBSCRIPT" ID="scrShowDay">
<!--
   Option Explicit
   Function ShowDayMessage()
      Dim intDay
      Dim strDayOfWeek

      intDay = WeekDay(Date())
      strDayOfWeek = arrDays(intDay - 1)
      MsgBox "Today is " & strDayOfWeek
      Call WriteDay(strDayOfWeek)
      Call WriteDate()
   End Function
-->
</SCRIPT>
</HEAD>

<BODY ONLOAD="ShowDayMessage()">
<H2>Office Programmer's Guide Chapter 6:</H2>
<H3>Shared Office Components</H3>
<HR>

<DIV ID=DayText>
<!-- Day and date text is inserted here. -->
</DIV>

<SCRIPT LANGUAGE="VBSCRIPT" ID="scrWriteDay">
<!--
   Option Explicit
   Function WriteDay(strDay)
      DayText.innerText = "Today is " & strDay
   End Function

   Function WriteDate()
      Dim strDay
      Dim strNum

      strDay = Day(Date())
      If Len(strDay) = 2 Then
         If left(strDay, 1) = 1 Then
            strNum = 0
         Else
            strNum = Right(strDay, 1)
         End If
```

```
        Else
           strNum = strDay
        End If
        Select Case CInt(strNum)
           Case 1
              strDay = strDay & "st"
           Case 2
              strDay = strDay & "nd"
           Case 3
              strDay = strDay & "rd"
           Case else
              strDay = strDay & "th"
        End Select

        DayText.innerText = DayText.innerText & _
           ", the " & strDay & " day of the month."
     End Function
-->
</SCRIPT>
</BODY>
</HTML>
```

The HTML code and script in the previous example is from the ScriptSamples.doc file in the Samples\CH06 subfolder on the companion CD-ROM. (There is also an HTML version in the ScriptSamples.htm file.) If you open this document in Word and then open the Immediate window in the Visual Basic Editor, you can use the **Scripts** collection and **Script** object to discover the information you can get using the collection and object properties, as shown in Figure 6.6.

Figure 6.6 Listing of Various Script Properties

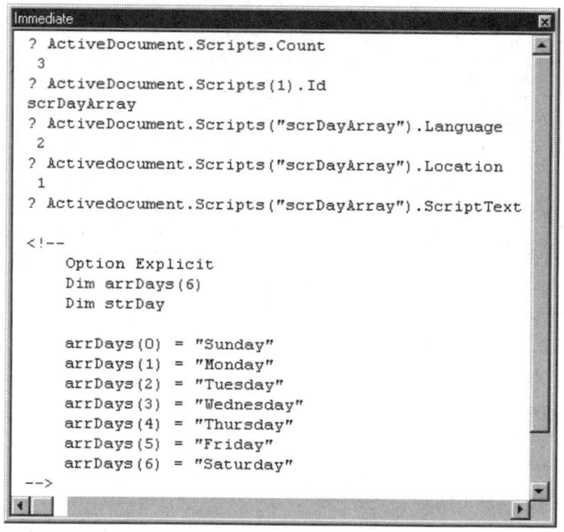

```
Immediate
? ActiveDocument.Scripts.Count
 3
? ActiveDocument.Scripts(1).Id
scrDayArray
? ActiveDocument.Scripts("scrDayArray").Language
 2
? Activedocument.Scripts("scrDayArray").Location
 1
? Activedocument.Scripts("scrDayArray").ScriptText

<!--
    Option Explicit
    Dim arrDays(6)
    Dim strDay

    arrDays(0) = "Sunday"
    arrDays(1) = "Monday"
    arrDays(2) = "Tuesday"
    arrDays(3) = "Wednesday"
    arrDays(4) = "Thursday"
    arrDays(5) = "Friday"
    arrDays(6) = "Saturday"
-->
```

You access a **Script** object within the **Scripts** collection by using either the index for the object within the collection, or the value of the object's ID attribute. If a <SCRIPT> tag has an ID attribute, the value of that attribute becomes the value of the **Script** object's **Id** property. If the <SCRIPT> tag does not have an ID attribute setting, an index value is the only way to locate the **Script** object within the **Scripts** collection.

When a document that contains script is opened in an Office application, script blocks are added to the **Scripts** collection in the order in which they appear in the document. When you add a **Script** object to a document, the new object is added at the end of the collection of **Script** objects, regardless of the value of the object's **Location** property. However, once the document is closed and reopened, that same script will appear in the **Scripts** collection in the order in which it appears in the document.

Since a **Script** object's index position within the **Scripts** collection can change between the time the object is added and the time the document is saved and reopened, it is never a good idea to try to locate a specific **Script** object within the **Scripts** collection by using its index position in the collection. Instead, you should make a habit of specifying an **Id** property value when creating a **Script** object and using that **Id** property value to locate the **Script** object within the **Scripts** collection. It is useful to use the index when you are looping through all the **Script** objects in a document, however.

Important If a <SCRIPT> tag in a document uses the same ID attribute as another <SCRIPT> tag, the **Scripts** collection will contain only the first **Script** object that uses the duplicate ID attribute. Any other tags that use the same ID attribute will not be included in the collection.

The **Script** object's **Location** property returns a long integer representing an **msoScriptLocation** constant that specifies whether the script is located in the <HEAD> element or the <BODY> element of the HTML code. If you don't specify a value for this argument, the default location is within the <BODY> element. Similarly, the **Language** property returns a long integer representing an **msoScriptLanguage** constant that specifies the LANGUAGE attribute of the <SCRIPT> tag. If you don't specify a value, the default is VBScript, except in Access, where it is JavaScript.

Important The **Script** object's **ScriptText** property returns everything between the <SCRIPT> tags, but not the <SCRIPT> tags themselves. You must account for this when you are using the **Script** object's **Add** method to programmatically add your own script to a document. For more information about adding **Script** objects, see the following section, "Adding and Removing Script from a Document."

Adding and Removing Script from a Document

You add script to a document by using the **Scripts** collection's **Add** method. The **Add** method uses optional arguments that let you specify the script's location, language, ID attribute, additional <SCRIPT> tag attributes, and the script to be contained within the <SCRIPT> tags. The **Add** method also automatically generates HTML comment tags (`<!--` and `-->`) around your script so that browsers that do not recognize script can ignore it. If you use the **Add** method without specifying any of the method's arguments, you create an empty <SCRIPT> tag pair that looks like this:

```
<SCRIPT ID="" LANGUAGE="VBScript">
<!--

-->
</SCRIPT>
```

You use the ***Anchor*** argument of the **Add** method to specify where the **Script** object should be located in a document.

- In Word, if you don't specify a value for the ***Anchor*** argument, the **Script** object is inserted at the current location of the insertion point (cursor). You can also add a **Script** object to a **Selection** object or an **InLineShape** object. When you specify a **Selection** object in the ***Anchor*** argument, the **Script** object is inserted at the end of the **Selection** object. When you specify an **InLineShape** object in the ***Anchor*** argument, the **Script** object is inserted before the paragraph marker for the paragraph that is the anchor point for the shape. You can't add a **Script** object to a **Range** object in Word.
- In Excel, if you don't specify a value for the ***Anchor*** argument, the **Script** object is inserted in the currently active cell. You can also add a **Script** object to a **Range** object by specifying the **Range** object in the ***Anchor*** argument. You cannot add a **Script** object to a **Shape** object in Excel. If you do specify a **Shape** object in the ***Anchor*** argument, the argument is ignored and the **Script** object is inserted in the currently active cell.
- In PowerPoint, you can only add a **Script** object to a **Slide** object. If you specify a **Shape** object in the ***Anchor*** argument, the argument is ignored and the **Script** is inserted in the specified **Slide** object.

Note To see the **Shape** objects that are inserted when script is added to an Office document, point to **Macro** on the **Tools** menu, and then click **Show All Script Anchors**.

The following procedure uses the **Scripts** collection's **Add** method to add a <SCRIPT> tag pair and some Microsoft Visual Basic Scripting Edition (VBScript) code to the <HEAD> element of the current Word document:

```
Function AddScriptToDocumentDemo()
   ' This procedure illustrates how to use the Scripts collection
   ' to add VBScript code to an Office document.
   Dim strScriptCode As String
   Dim scrArrayScript As Script

   On Error Resume Next

   Set scrArrayScript = ActiveDocument.Scripts("scrDayArray")
   If Err = 0 Then
      ' The script is already in the document so no
      ' need to add it again.
      Exit Function
   End If

   strScriptCode = vbTab & "Option Explicit" & vbCrLf & vbTab _
      & "Dim arrDays(6)" & vbCrLf & vbTab _
      & "arrDays(0) = " & """Sunday""" & vbCrLf & vbTab _
      & "arrDays(1) = " & """Monday""" & vbCrLf & vbTab _
      & "arrDays(2) = " & """Tuesday""" & vbCrLf & vbTab _
      & "arrDays(3) = " & """Wednesday""" & vbCrLf & vbTab _
      & "arrDays(4) = " & """Thursday""" & vbCrLf & vbTab _
      & "arrDays(5) = " & """Friday""" & vbCrLf & vbTab _
      & "arrDays(6) = " & """Saturday"""

   With Application.ActiveDocument
      .Scripts.Add Location:=msoScriptLocationInHead, _
         Language:=msoScriptLanguageVisualBasic, ID:="scrDayArray", _
         ScriptText:=strScriptCode
   End With
End Function
```

The AddScriptToDocumentDemo procedure in the modAddScript module in ScriptSamples.doc in the Samples\CH06 subfolder on the companion CD-ROM recreates the first script block shown in the HTML and script examples at the beginning of this section.

You can remove all the script and <SCRIPT> tags from a document by using the **Scripts** collection's **Delete** method. You remove a single script from the **Scripts** collection by using the **Script** object's **Delete** method.

Working with the HTMLProject Object

The **HTMLProject** object is the top-level object representing the HTML code in an Office document. It is the equivalent of the top-level project branch in the Microsoft Script Editor Project Explorer when it contains an Office document. The **HTMLProject** object has properties you can use to determine the current state of an Office document and to access individual **HTMLProjectItem** objects, and methods you can use to save the current project or document.

For example, you can tell if a document is currently opened in the Microsoft Script Editor and if the HTML code that exists in the Script Editor is the same as what is contained in the document. If the HTML code is out of sync, you can programmatically synchronize the HTML code before manipulating the document's contents. You can add HTML to a document programmatically or load it from a file saved on disk. You can also use the objects contained within the **HTMLProject** object and their properties and methods to manipulate the HTML code or add script to the HTML code.

Note The **HTMLProject** object is not available in Microsoft Access, Microsoft FrontPage, or Microsoft Outlook. To manipulate the HTML code in an Access **DataAccessPage** object, you use the object's **Document** property. To work with the HTML code in a page in FrontPage, you use the HTML tab in the FrontPage design environment.

The **HTMLProject** object's **HTMLProjectItems** property returns a collection of all of the **HTMLProjectItem** objects in the project. The default number of **HTMLProjectItem** objects in an Office application will depend on the kind of Office document you are working with. The following table shows the default number of **HTMLProjectItem** objects in a new Office document.

Application	Default number of HTMLProjectItem objects
Excel	5 items (Book, Tab, Sheet1, Sheet2, Sheet3)
PowerPoint	2 items (SlideMaster, Slide1)
Word	1 item (Document Web Page)

You reference an **HTMLProject** object by using the **HTMLProject** property of an Office document. For example, the following code illustrates how to return a reference to the top-level **HTMLProject** object in each Office application:

```
' Create Word reference:
Dim prjWord As Word.HTMLProjectItem
Set prjWord = ActiveDocument.HTMLProject

' Create PowerPoint reference:
Dim prjPPT As PowerPoint.HTMLProjectItem
Set prjPPT = ActivePresentation.HTMLProject

' Create Excel reference:
Dim prjXL As Excel.HTMLProjectItem
Set prjXL = ActiveWorkbook.HTMLProject
```

Once you have created a reference to the **HTMLProject** object, you then use the **HTMLProjectItems** property to access individual **HTMLProjectItem** objects. In the following example, the IsHTMLProjectDirty procedure can be used to determine if the **HTMLProject** object in an Office document is "dirty" (contains changes). You use the *blnRefreshProject* argument to specify whether to refresh, or synchronize, the HTML code with the source Office document.

```
Function IsHTMLProjectDirty(objOffDoc As Object, _
                            blnRefreshProject As Boolean) As Boolean
   ' This procedure determines if the HTMLProject object
   ' in the document represented by the objOffDoc argument
   ' is dirty and, if so, refreshes the project according
   ' to the value of the blnRefreshProject argument.

   Dim prjProject As HTMLProject

   On Error GoTo IsHTMLDirty_Err

   Set prjProject = objOffDoc.HTMLProject
   With prjProject
      ' The Office document will be locked as soon as any
      ' changes are made to the HTML code in the document.
      If .State = msoHTMLProjectStateDocumentLocked Then
         IsHTMLProjectDirty = True
         If blnRefreshProject = True Then
            ' Merge the changes to the HTML code with the
            ' underlying Office document.
            .RefreshDocument
         End If
      Else
         IsHTMLProjectDirty = False
      End If
   End With

IsHTMLDirty_End:
   Exit Function

IsHTMLDirty_Err:
   Select Case Err
      Case Is > 0
         IsHTMLProjectDirty = False
         Resume IsHTMLDirty_End
   End Select
End Function
```

The IsHTMLProjectDirty procedure is available in the modScripting module in HTMLProjectSamples.doc in the Samples\CH06 subfolder on the companion CD-ROM.

You could use the preceding procedure to determine the state of any Office document by using the **ActiveWorkbook**, **ActivePresentation**, or **ActiveDocument** property in the first argument.

Once you have a reference to an **HTMLProjectItem** object, you can work directly with the HTML code in the document by using the object's **Text** property. For example, you can run the following code from the Immediate window to print all of the HTML code in a Word document:

```
? ActiveDocument.HTMLProject.HTMLProjectItems(1).Text
```

You can change the HTML code in an Office document by using the **LoadFromFile** method or by setting the **Text** property to the HTML code you want to use. The following example illustrates how to replace the HTML code in a Word document with the HTML code contained in a file on disk:

```
ActiveDocument.HTMLProject.HTMLProjectItems(1).LoadFromFile = "c:\MyHTMLFile.htm"
```

In many cases you will want to leave the existing HTML code in a document unchanged, but you will want to insert additional HTML code or script to give the document additional functionality when viewed in a Web browser. In the following example, the AddHTMLAndScriptExample procedure inserts within the first section of a Word document HTML code that includes formatted text, a command button, and script that executes when the command button is clicked. The formatted text and command button are contained in text returned by the GetText procedure and the script that executes when the command button is clicked is returned by the GetScript procedure. The InsertHTMLText procedure inserts the HTML code and script in an existing document just after the location specified by the procedure's second argument.

```
Sub AddHTMLAndScriptExample(objOffDoc As Object)
   Dim itmPrjItem    As HTMLProjectItem
   Dim strNewText    As String
   Dim strNewScript  As String
   Dim strNewHTML As String

   strNewText = GetText()
   strNewScript = GetScript()

   Set itmPrjItem = objOffDoc.HTMLProject.HTMLProjectItems(1)

   With itmPrjItem
      strNewHTML = .Text
      Call InsertHTMLText(strNewHTML, "<div class=""Section1"">", strNewText _
         & vbCrLf & strNewScript)
      .Text = strNewHTML
   End With
End Sub
```

To see all the code associated with this procedure, see the modScripting module in HTMLProjectSamples.doc in the Samples\CH06 subfolder on the companion CD-ROM.

Where to Go from Here

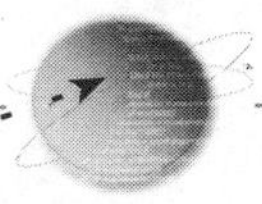

For additional information about the subjects discussed in this chapter, see the following resources.

Working with Software Assistants

Developing for Microsoft Agent. Redmond, WA: Microsoft Press, 1998.

Microsoft Agent Web site
(http://www.microsoft.com/intdev/agent)

Working with Command Bars

Microsoft Knowledge Base article: "*Command Bar Wizard Available on MSL*," Q172300 (http://support.microsoft.com/support)

Using Document Properties in Microsoft Access

Search the Microsoft Access Visual Basic Reference Help index for "database properties."

Creating and Using Add-ins

Chapter 11, "Add-ins, Templates, Wizards, and Libraries"

Working with Objects and Collections

Chapter 4, "Understanding Office Objects and Object Models"

Working with Script in Office Documents

Chapter 12, "Using Web Technologies"

Code Samples

The code samples shown in this chapter, along with additional examples demonstrating similar techniques, can be copied from the files in the Samples\CH06 subfolder on the companion CD-ROM.

CHAPTER 7

Getting the Most Out of Visual Basic for Applications

As a developer, your goal is to write code that's fast, efficient, easy to read and maintain, and if possible, reusable. To do so, you need a solid working knowledge of Visual Basic for Applications (VBA)—what features the language includes, and what you can do with it.

As you develop solutions, you'll find that there are a number of operations that you need to perform repeatedly—parsing a file path, for example, or returning all the files in a directory. Rather than rewriting these routines every time you need them, you can begin building an arsenal of procedures that solve common problems. This chapter gives you a head start by providing functions that perform some often-needed operations on strings, numbers, dates and times, files, and arrays. It also explains the key aspects of each procedure and covers fundamental VBA programming issues so that you can continue to expand your code arsenal yourself. You can use these procedures not only in VBA code but also in Microsoft Visual Basic Scripting Edition (VBScript) code in HTML documents.

Contents

Working with Strings

A set of alphanumeric characters—what could be simpler? Strings are basic in concept, but getting the information you need from them can be a different story. The following sections cover the key things you need to know about working with strings and provide some functions that you can reuse within your solutions.

Comparing Strings

You can compare strings to determine whether they contain equivalent characters and how they differ if they do not match. When you compare two strings, you're actually comparing the ANSI value of each character to the value of the corresponding character in the other string. You can specify whether you want to make comparisons case-sensitive or whether you want to ignore the case and simply compare the strings' characters.

Specifying the String-Comparison Setting for a Module

The **Option Compare** statement determines how strings are compared within a module. There are three settings for the **Option Compare** statement:

- **Option Compare Binary** String comparisons are case-sensitive. **Option Compare Binary** is the default string-comparison setting for all the Office applications except Microsoft Access, for which **Option Compare Database** is the default.
- **Option Compare Text** String comparisons are case-insensitive. To make case-insensitive string comparison the default method for a module, add this statement to the module's Declarations section.
- **Option Compare Database** String comparisons depend on the sort order for the specified locale; the default sort order is case-insensitive. The **Option Compare Database** setting is available only for Access databases. Note that when you create a new module in Access, the **Option Compare Database** statement is automatically inserted in the module's Declarations section. If you delete the **Option Compare Database** statement, the default string-comparison setting for the module is **Option Compare Binary**.

  Important If you're writing code in Access that you may want to export to another VBA host application, you should explicitly specify string comparisons as binary or text-based in the line that performs the comparison. Because the **Option Compare Database** setting is available only in Access, the code will not compile when you import it into another application unless you remove this setting. If you have explicitly specified the string-comparison method for each line that performs comparisons, you can export the code and be confident that string comparisons will continue to work as expected after you remove the **Option Compare Database** setting.

Tip To change the sort order for a database, click **Options** on the **Tools** menu, click the **General** tab, and then change the **New Database Sort Order** setting. After you change this setting, any new database you create will perform text comparisons based on the new sort order; changing this option has no effect on existing databases.

Comparing Strings by Using Comparison Operators

Since you're actually comparing ANSI values when you compare two strings, you can use the same comparison operators that you would use with numeric expressions—greater than (>), less than (<), equal to (=), and so on. In addition to these numeric comparison operators, you can also use the **Like** operator, which is specifically for use in comparing strings, including strings that contain wildcard characters.

Using Comparison Operators

When you use comparison operators such as the greater than (>) and less than (<) operators to compare two strings, the result you get depends on the string-comparison setting for the module. Consider the following example:

```
"vba" > "VBA"
```

If the string-comparison setting is **Option Compare Binary**, the comparison returns **True**.

When VBA performs a binary text comparison, it compares the binary values for each corresponding position in the string until it finds two that differ. In this example, the lowercase letter "v" corresponds to the ANSI value 118, while the uppercase letter "V" corresponds to the ANSI value 86. Since 118 is greater than 86, the comparison returns **True**.

Note For tables of ANSI values and the characters they represent, search the Visual Basic Reference Help index for "ANSI."

If the string-comparison setting is **Option Compare Text**, `"vba" > "VBA"` returns **False**, since the strings are equivalent apart from case.

In an Access database, if the string-comparison setting is **Option Compare Database** and the **New Database Sort Order** option is set to **General** (the default setting), the string comparison is case-insensitive and the example returns **False**.

Using the Like Operator

You can perform wildcard string comparisons by using the **Like** operator. The following table shows the wildcard characters supported by VBA.

Wildcard	Represents	Example
*	Any number of characters	**t*** matches any word beginning with "t."
?	Any single character	**t??t** matches any four-letter word beginning and ending with "t."
#	Any single digit (0–9)	**1#3** matches any three-digit number beginning with "1" and ending with "3."
[*charlist*]	Any single character in *charlist*	**[a-z]** matches any letter that falls between "a" and "z" (case-sensitivity depends on **Option Compare** setting).
[!*charlist*]	Any single character not in *charlist*	**[!A-Z]** excludes the uppercase alphabetic characters (case-sensitivity depends on **Option Compare** setting).

You can use the **Like** operator to perform data validation or wildcard searches. For example, suppose you want to ensure that a user has entered a telephone number in the format *nnn-nnn-nnnn*. You can use the **Like** operator to check that the entry is valid, as the following procedure does:

```
Function ValidPhone(strPhone As String) As Boolean
   ' This procedure checks that the passed-in value is
   ' a valid, properly formatted telephone number.

   ValidPhone = strPhone Like "###-###-####"
End Function
```

This procedure compares characters in a string to make sure that certain positions contain numeric characters. In order to return **True**, all characters must be digits between 0 and 9 or hyphens, and the hyphens must be present at the correct position in the string. This procedure is available in the modStrings module in VBA.mdb in the Samples\CH07 subfolder on the companion CD-ROM.

Overriding the Default String-Comparison Setting

To perform a string comparison within a procedure and override the string-comparison setting for the module, you can use the **StrComp** function. The **StrComp** function takes two strings as arguments, along with a *compare* argument, which you can use to specify the type of comparison. The possible settings for the *compare* argument are **vbBinaryCompare**, **vbTextCompare**, and (in Access) **vbDatabaseCompare**. If you omit this argument, the **StrComp** function uses the module's default comparison method.

The following table lists the possible return values for the **StrComp** function.

If	Then StrComp returns
string1 < *string2*	-1
string1 = *string2*	0
string1 > *string2*	1
string1 **Or** *string2* **Is Null**	**Null**

For example, running the following code from the Immediate window prints "1", indicating that the ANSI value of the first character in the first string is greater than the ANSI value of the first character in the second string:

```
? StrComp("vba", "VBA", vbBinaryCompare)
```

On the other hand, if you specify text-based string comparison, this code prints "0", indicating that the two strings are identical:

```
? StrComp("vba", "VBA", vbTextCompare)
```

Other VBA string functions that perform string comparison also provide a *compare* argument that you can use to override the default string-comparison setting for that function call. For example, the **InStr** and **InStrRev** functions both have a *compare* argument.

Calculating String Length

Often you need to know the length of a string in order to parse its contents. You can use the **Len** function to calculate the length of a string:

```
Dim lngLen As Long
lngLen = Len(strText)
```

When VBA stores a string in memory, it always stores the length of the string in a long integer at the beginning of the string. The **Len** function retrieves this value and is therefore quite fast.

The **Len** function is useful when you need to determine whether a string is a zero-length string (""). Rather than comparing the string in question to a zero-length string to determine whether they're equivalent, you can simply check whether the length of the string is equal to 0. For example:

```
If Len(strText) > 0 Then
   ' Perform some operation here.
End If
```

Searching a String

When you need to know whether a string contains a particular character or group of characters, you can search the string by using one of two functions. The traditional candidate for this job is the **InStr** function, which you can use to find one string within another. The **InStr** function compares two strings, and if the second string is contained within the first, it returns the position at which the substring begins. If the **InStr** function doesn't find the substring, it returns 0.

The **InStr** function takes an optional argument, the *start* argument, in which you can specify the position to begin searching. If you omit this argument, the **InStr** function starts searching at the first character in the string.

The newest version of VBA includes a function called **InStrRev**, which behaves in the same way as the **InStr** function, except that it begins searching at the end of the string rather than at the beginning. As with the **InStr** function, you can specify a starting position for the **InStrRev** function; it will search backward through the string beginning at that point. If you know that the substring you're looking for probably falls at the end of the string, the **InStrRev** function may be a better option. For example, the **InStrRev** function makes it easier to parse a file path and return just the file name. The next section, "Returning Portions of a String," shows an example of how to use the **InStrRev** function.

Note Both the **InStr** and **InStrRev** functions return the same value when they locate the same substring. Although the **InStrRev** function begins searching at the right side of the string, it counts characters from the left side, as does the **InStr** function. For example, calling either the **InStr** or **InStrRev** function to search the string "C:\Temp" for the substring "C:\" returns 1. However, if the substring appears more than once, and you haven't specified a value for the *start* argument, the **InStr** function returns the position of the first instance and the **InStrRev** function returns the position of the last instance.

The following procedure counts the occurrences of a particular character or group of characters in a string. To call the procedure, you pass in the string, the substring that you're looking for, and a constant indicating whether the search should be case-sensitive.

The possible constant values are specified by the built-in enumerated constants in **vbCompareMethod**, which groups the three VBA string-comparison constants (**vbBinaryCompare**, **vbDatabaseCompare**, and **vbTextCompare**). If you declare an argument as type **vbCompareMethod**, VBA lists the constants in that grouping when you call the procedure. This is a convenient way to remember what values an argument takes. You can also define your own enumerated constants and use them as data types. For more information about creating enumerated constants, see Chapter 9, "Custom Classes and Objects."

The following CountOccurrences procedure uses the **InStr** function to search for the specified text and return the value of the position at which it first occurs; for example, if it's the third character in the string, the **InStr** function returns 3. This value is stored in a temporary variable so that the value can be maintained after the next call to the **InStr** function. The procedure increments the counter variable, which keeps track of the number of occurrences found, and then sets the starting position for the next call to the **InStr** function. The new starting position is the position at which the search text was found, plus the length of the search string. By setting the start position in this manner, you ensure that you don't locate the same substring twice when you're searching for text that's more than one character in length.

```
Function CountOccurrences(strText As String, _
                          strFind As String, _
                          Optional lngCompare As VbCompareMethod) As Long

   ' Count occurrences of a particular character or characters.
   ' If lngCompare argument is omitted, procedure performs binary comparison.

   Dim lngPos      As Long
   Dim lngTemp     As Long
   Dim lngCount    As Long

   ' Specify a starting position. We don't need it the first
   ' time through the loop, but we'll need it on subsequent passes.
   lngPos = 1
   ' Execute the loop at least once.
   Do
      ' Store position at which strFind first occurs.
      lngPos = InStr(lngPos, strText, strFind, lngCompare)
      ' Store position in a temporary variable.
      lngTemp = lngPos
      ' Check that strFind has been found.
      If lngPos > 0 Then
         ' Increment counter variable.
         lngCount = lngCount + 1
         ' Define a new starting position.
         lngPos = lngPos + Len(strFind)
      End If
   ' Loop until last occurrence has been found.
   Loop Until lngPos = 0
   ' Return the number of occurrences found.
   CountOccurrences = lngCount
End Function
```

This procedure is available in the modStrings module in VBA.mdb in the Samples\CH07 subfolder on the companion CD-ROM.

Calling this function from the Immediate window as follows returns "3":

```
? CountOccurrences("This is a test", "t", vbTextCompare)
```

Returning Portions of a String

To work with part of a string's contents, you need to parse the string. You can use the **InStr** or **InStrRev** function to find the position at which to begin parsing the string. Once you've located that position, you can use the **Left**, **Right**, and **Mid** functions to do the job. The **Left** and **Right** functions return a specified number of characters from either the left or right portion of the string. The **Mid** function is the most flexible of the parsing functions—you can specify a starting point anywhere within the string, followed by the number of characters you want to return.

Note Some of the VBA string functions come in two varieties, one that returns a string, and one that returns a string-type **Variant** value. The names of the functions that return a string include a dollar sign ("$"); for example, **Chr$**, **Format$**, **LCase$**, **Left$**, **LTrim$**, **Mid$**, **Right$**, **RTrim$**, **Space$**, **Trim$**, and **UCase$**. The functions that return a string-type **Variant** value have no dollar sign; for example, **Chr**, **Format**, **LCase**, **Left**, **LTrim**, **Mid**, **Right**, **RTrim**, **Space**, **Trim**, and **UCase**. The string-returning functions are faster; however, you'll get an error if you call them with a value that is **Null**. The functions that return a string-type **Variant** value handle **Null** values without an error. Code examples in this chapter use the string-returning functions where appropriate.

The following procedure parses a file path and returns one of the following portions: the path (everything but the file name), the file name, the drive letter, or the file extension. You specify which part of the string you want to return by passing a constant to the *lngPart* argument. The *lngPart* argument is defined as type **opgParsePath**, which contains custom enumerated constants declared in the modPublicDefs module in VBA.mdb in the Samples\CH07 subfolder on the companion CD-ROM.

Note that this procedure uses the **InStrRev** function to find the last path separator, or backslash (\), in the string. If you used the **InStr** function, you'd have to write a loop to make sure that you'd found the last one. With the **InStrRev** function, you know that the first backslash you find is actually the last one in the string, and the characters to the right of it must be the file name.

```
Function ParsePath(strPath As String, _
                   lngPart As opgParsePath) As String

   ' This procedure takes a file path and returns
   ' the path (everything but the file name), the
   ' file name, the drive letter, or the file extension,
   ' depending on which constant was passed in.

   Dim lngPos           As Long
   Dim strPart          As String
   Dim blnIncludesFile  As Boolean
```

```
   ' Check that this is a file path.
   ' Find the last path separator.
   lngPos = InStrRev(strPath, "\")
   ' Determine whether portion of string after last backslash
   ' contains a period.
   blnIncludesFile = InStrRev(strPath, ".") > lngPos

   If lngPos > 0 Then
      Select Case lngPart
         ' Return file name.
         Case opgParsePath.FILE_ONLY
            If blnIncludesFile Then
               strPart = Right$(strPath, Len(strPath) - lngPos)
            Else
               strPart = ""
            End If
         ' Return path.
         Case opgParsePath.PATH_ONLY
            If blnIncludesFile Then
               strPart = Left$(strPath, lngPos)
            Else
               strPart = strPath
            End If
         ' Return drive.
         Case opgParsePath.DRIVE_ONLY
            strPart = Left$(strPath, 3)
         ' Return file extension.
         Case opgParsePath.FILEEXT_ONLY
            If blnIncludesFile Then
               ' Take three characters after period.
               strPart = Mid(strPath, InStrRev(strPath, ".") + 1, 3)
            Else
               strPart = ""
            End If
         Case Else
            strPart = ""
      End Select
   End If
   ParsePath = strPart

ParsePath_End:
   Exit Function
End Function
```

This procedure is available in the modStrings module in VBA.mdb in the Samples\CH07 subfolder on the companion CD-ROM.

Calling this function as follows from the Immediate window returns "Test.txt":

```
? ParsePath("C:\Temp\Test.txt", opgParsePath.FILE_ONLY)
```

Working with Strings as Arrays

It may be hard to believe, but some of the most exciting new features in VBA in Microsoft Office 2000 are the new functions for working with strings as arrays. These functions can turn once-lengthy string-manipulation procedures into just a few lines of code. And in many cases, they're faster than using loops and string-parsing techniques to work with the contents of a very large string.

Note If you're unfamiliar with arrays or you need a quick refresher course, see "Understanding Arrays" later in this chapter.

The Split Function

The **Split** function takes a string and converts it into an array of strings. By default, it divides the string into elements by using the space character as a delimiter, so that if you pass in a sentence, each element of the array contains a word. For example, if you pass this string to the **Split** function

```
"This is a test"
```

you'll get an array that contains the following four elements:

```
"This"
"is"
"a"
"test"
```

You can specify that the **Split** function split the string based on a different delimiter by passing in the *delimiter* argument.

Once you've split a string into an array, it's easy to work with the individual elements. The **Split** function sizes the array for you, so you don't have to worry about maintaining the array's size.

The following example uses the **Split** function to count the number of words in a string. The procedure takes a string and returns a long integer indicating the number of words found. Since the string is divided into elements at the space between each word, each element of the resulting array represents a word. To determine the number of words, you simply need to determine the number of elements in the array. You can do this by subtracting the lower bound from the upper bound and adding 1.

```
Function CountWords(strText As String) As Long
   ' This procedure counts the number of words in a string.

   Dim astrWords() As String

   astrWords = Split(strText)
   ' Count number of elements in array -- this will be the
   ' number of words.
   CountWords = UBound(astrWords) - LBound(astrWords) + 1
End Function
```

This procedure is available in the modStrings module in VBA.mdb in the Samples\CH07 subfolder on the companion CD-ROM.

The Join Function

After you've finished processing an array that's been split, you can use the **Join** function to concatenate the elements of the array together into a single string again. The **Join** function takes an array of strings and returns a concatenated string. By default it adds a space between each element of the string, but you can specify a different delimiter.

The following procedure uses the **Split** and **Join** functions together to trim extra space characters from a string. It splits the passed-in string into an array. Wherever there is more than one space within the string, the corresponding array element is a zero-length string. By finding and removing these zero-length string elements, you can remove the extra white space from the string.

In order to remove zero-length string elements from the array, the procedure must copy the non-zero-length string elements into a second array. The procedure then uses the **Join** function to concatenate the second array into a whole string.

Because the second array isn't created by the **Split** function, you need to size it manually. It's easy to do, however—you can size it initially to be the same size as the first array, then resize it after you've copied in the non-zero-length string elements.

```
Function TrimSpace(strInput As String) As String
   ' This procedure trims extra space from any part of
   ' a string.

   Dim astrInput()   As String
   Dim astrText()    As String
   Dim strElement    As String
   Dim lngCount      As Long
   Dim lngIncr       As Long

   ' Split passed-in string.
   astrInput = Split(strInput)

   ' Resize second array to be same size.
   ReDim astrText(UBound(astrInput))

   ' Initialize counter variable for second array.
   lngIncr = LBound(astrInput)
   ' Loop through split array, looking for
   ' non-zero-length strings.
   For lngCount = LBound(astrInput) To UBound(astrInput)
      strElement = astrInput(lngCount)
      If Len(strElement) > 0 Then
         ' Store in second array.
         astrText(lngIncr) = strElement
         lngIncr = lngIncr + 1
      End If
```

```
    Next
    ' Resize new array.
    ReDim Preserve astrText(LBound(astrText) To lngIncr - 1)

    ' Join new array to return string.
    TrimSpace = Join(astrText)
End Function
```

This procedure is available in the modStrings module in VBA.mdb in the Samples\CH07 subfolder on the companion CD-ROM.

To test the TrimSpace procedure, try calling it from the Immediate window with a string like the following:

```
? TrimSpace("  This  is    a  test  ")
```

Tip To see the elements in each array while the code is running, step through the procedure, and use the Locals window to view the values contained in each variable.

The Filter Function

The **Filter** function searches a string array for all elements that match a given text string. The **Filter** function takes three arguments: a string array, a string containing the text to find, and a constant specifying the string-comparison method. It returns a string array containing all the matches that it finds.

You can use the **Filter** function to determine whether a particular element exists in an array. An example, the ConvertToProperCase procedure, appears in "Converting Strings" later in this chapter.

When working with the **Filter** function, you may notice that it returns a particular element even if only part of the element matches the search text. In other words, if your search text is the letter "e," and the array you're searching contains the element "test," the array returned by the **Filter** function will contain the element "test."

Given this behavior, you might be tempted to use the **Filter** function to rewrite the CountOccurrences procedure shown earlier in this chapter. Before doing so, bear in mind that the CountOccurrences procedure counts every occurrence of a particular character in a string, even if there is more than one occurrence in a word. When you are using the **Filter** function, on the other hand, you can count an occurrence only once per element, even if the character occurs twice within a single element in the array.

For examples that demonstrate the **Filter** function, see "Converting Strings" and "Searching an Array" later in this chapter.

Finding and Replacing Text Within a String

VBA provides another new function, the **Replace** function, that makes it easy to find and replace all occurrences of a substring within a string. The **Replace** function takes six arguments: the string to be searched, the text to find within the string, the replacement text, what character to start at, how many occurrences to replace, and a constant indicating the string-comparison method. You don't even have to write a loop to use the **Replace** function—it automatically replaces all the appropriate text for you with one call.

For example, suppose you want to change the criteria for an SQL statement based on some condition in your application. Rather than re-creating the SQL statement, you can use the **Replace** function to replace just the criteria portion of the string, as in the following code fragment:

```
strSQL = "SELECT * FROM Products WHERE ProductName Like 'M*' ORDER BY ProductName;"
strFind = "'M*'"
strReplace = "'T*'"

Debug.Print Replace(strSQL, strFind, strReplace)
```

Running this code fragment prints this string to the Immediate window:

```
SELECT * FROM Products WHERE ProductName Like 'T*' ORDER BY ProductName;
```

Wildcard Search and Replace

The **Replace** function greatly simplifies string search-and-replace operations, but it doesn't enable you to perform wildcard searches. Here's another place where the **Split** and **Join** functions come in handy.

The ReplaceWord procedure shown below takes three mandatory arguments: a string to be searched, the word to find within the string, and the replacement text. When you call this procedure, you can include wildcard characters in the string that you pass for the *strFind* argument. For example, you might call the ReplaceWord procedure from the Immediate window with these parameters:

```
? ReplaceWord("There will be a test today", "t*t", "party")
```

The procedure splits the *strText* argument into an array, then uses the **Like** operator to compare each element of the array to *strFind*, replacing the elements that match the wildcard specification.

```
Function ReplaceWord(strText As String, _
                     strFind As String, _
                     strReplace As String) As String

   ' This function searches a string for a word and replaces it.
   ' You can use a wildcard mask to specify the search string.

   Dim astrText() As String
   Dim lngCount   As Long

   ' Split the string at specified delimiter.
   astrText = Split(strText)

   ' Loop through array, performing comparison
   ' against wildcard mask.
   For lngCount = LBound(astrText) To UBound(astrText)
      If astrText(lngCount) Like strFind Then
         ' If array element satisfies wildcard search,
         ' replace it.
         astrText(lngCount) = strReplace
      End If
   Next
   ' Join string, using same delimiter.
   ReplaceWord = Join(astrText)
End Function
```

This procedure is available in the modStrings module in VBA.mdb in the Samples\CH07 subfolder on the companion CD-ROM.

Converting Strings

To convert text in a string from one case to another, you can use the VBA **StrConv** function. The **StrConv** function converts a string to lowercase, uppercase, or proper case (initial capital letters). It takes a string and a constant that specifies how to convert the string. For example, the following code fragment converts a string to proper case:

```
Debug.Print StrConv("washington, oregon, and california", vbProperCase)
```

Running this code prints the following text to the Immediate window:

```
Washington, Oregon, And California
```

Note The **StrConv** function performs other string conversions as well. For example, it converts a string from Unicode to ANSI, or vice versa. For more information about the **StrConv** function, search the Visual Basic Reference Help index for "StrConv function."

Most likely, you'll be about three-fourths satisfied with this result—you probably want "washington," "oregon," and "california" to be capitalized, but not "and." The word "and" is a minor word that isn't capitalized according to grammatical convention, unless it's the first word in the sentence. Unfortunately, VBA doesn't know which words to convert and which to leave alone, so it converts everything.

If you want VBA to omit the minor words, you can define those words in a file or a table, and perform a comparison against the file or table when you convert each word. The following procedure, ConvertToProperCase, does just that—it takes a string, splits it into individual words, compares each word against a list in a text file, and converts all non-minor words to proper case.

The ConvertToProperCase procedure calls another procedure, the GetMinorWords procedure. This procedure reads a text file containing a list of minor words and returns an array of strings containing each word in the text file. The ConvertToProperCase procedure then uses the **Filter** function to compare each word in the string to be converted against the list of words contained in the array of minor words. If a word doesn't appear in the list, then it's converted to proper case. If it does appear, it's converted to lowercase.

```
Function ConvertToProperCase(strText As String) As String
   ' This function takes a string and converts it to proper
   ' case, except for any minor words.

   Dim astrText()     As String
   Dim astrWords()    As String
   Dim astrMatches()  As String
   Dim lngCount       As Long

   ' Return array containing minor words.
   astrWords = GetMinorWords

   ' Split string into array.
   astrText = Split(strText)

   ' Check each word in passed-in string against array
   ' of minor words.
   For lngCount = LBound(astrText) To UBound(astrText)
      ' Filter function returns array containing matches found.
      ' If no matches are found, upper bound of array is less than
      ' lower bound. Store result returned by Filter function in a
      ' String array, then compare upper bound with lower bound.
      astrMatches = Filter(astrWords, astrText(lngCount))
      If UBound(astrMatches) < Lbound(astrMatches) Then
         ' If word in string does not match any word in array
         ' of minor words, convert word to proper case.
         astrText(lngCount) = StrConv(astrText(lngCount), vbProperCase)
      Else
         ' If it does match, convert it to lowercase.
         astrText(lngCount) = StrConv(astrText(lngCount), vbLowerCase)
      End If
   Next

   ' Join the string.
   ConvertToProperCase = Join(astrText)
End Function
```

This procedure is available in the modStrings module in VBA.mdb in the Samples\CH07 subfolder on the companion CD-ROM.

The ConvertToProperCase procedure calls the GetMinorWords procedure, which opens the text file that contains the list of minor words, gets a string containing all the words in the list, splits the string into an array, and returns the array. GetMinorWords calls another procedure, the GetLikelyDelimiter procedure, which finds the first likely delimiter character in the text file. Both of these procedures, as well as the text file that contains the list of minor words, appear in the modStrings module in VBA.mdb in the Samples\CH07 subfolder on the companion CD-ROM.

Note In order to call the ConvertToProperCase procedure, you must set a reference to the Microsoft Scripting Runtime object library. For more information about this object library, see "Working with Files" later in this chapter.

Working with Numbers

Almost every procedure you write in VBA uses numeric values in some way. For optimal performance and efficiency, and for accuracy in calculations, it's important to understand the different numeric data types and when to use which.

Numeric Types in VBA

There are several different numeric data types in VBA, and each is appropriate for a different use. The following sections discuss the numeric data types.

The Integer Data Types

Three data types in VBA can represent integers, or whole numbers: the **Integer**, **Long**, and **Byte** data types. Of these, the **Integer** and **Long** types are the ones you're most likely to use regularly.

The **Integer** and **Long** data types can both hold positive or negative values. The difference between them is their size: **Integer** variables can hold values between -32,768 and 32,767, while **Long** variables can range from –2,147,483,648 to 2,147,483,647. Traditionally, VBA programmers have used integers to hold small numbers, because they required less memory. In recent versions, however, VBA converts all integer values to type **Long**, even if they're declared as type **Integer**. So there's no longer a performance advantage to using **Integer** variables; in fact, **Long** variables may be slightly faster because VBA does not have to convert them.

The **Byte** data type can hold positive values from 0 to 255. A **Byte** variable requires only a single byte of memory, so it's very efficient. You can use a **Byte** variable to hold an **Integer** value if you know that value will never be greater than 255. However, the **Byte** data type is typically used for working with strings. For some string operations, converting the string to an array of bytes can significantly enhance performance.

For more information about byte arrays, see the *Visual Basic Language Developer's Handbook* by Ken Getz and Mike Gilbert (Sybex, 1999).

The Boolean Data Type

The **Boolean** data type is a special case of an integer data type. The **Boolean** data type can contain **True** or **False**; internally, VBA stores the value of **True** as –1, and the value of **False** as 0.

You can use the **CBool** function to convert any numeric value to a **Boolean** value. When another numeric data type is converted to a **Boolean** value, any nonzero value is equivalent to **True**, and zero (0) is equivalent to **False**. For example, `CBool(7)` returns **True**, and `CBool(5 + 2 - 7)` returns **False**, since it evaluates to `CBool(0)`.

The following procedure determines whether a number is even. The procedure uses the **Mod** operator to determine whether a number can be divided by 2 with no remainder. If a number is even, dividing by 2 leaves no remainder; if it's odd, dividing by 2 leaves a remainder of 1:

```
Function IsEven(lngNum As Long) As Boolean
   ' Determines whether a number is even or odd.

   If lngNum Mod 2 = 0 Then
      IsEven = True
   Else
      IsEven = False
   End If
End Function
```

Note For more information about the **Mod** operator, see "Using the Mod Operator" later in this chapter, or search the Visual Basic Reference Help index for "Mod operator."

Another way to write this procedure is to convert the result of an expression to a **Boolean** value and then use the **Not** keyword to toggle its value, as shown in the following example. If the *lngNum* argument is odd, then it must be nonzero; converting *lngNum* to a **Boolean** value yields **True**. Since the procedure must return **False** if the value is odd, using the **Not** keyword to toggle the **Boolean** value gives the correct result.

```
Function IsEven(lngNum As Long) As Boolean
   ' Determines whether a number is even or odd.

   IsEven = Not CBool(lngNum Mod 2)
End Function
```

Note that the revised IsEven procedure condenses a five-line **If...Then** statement into a single line of code. If you're using an **If...Then** statement to set a value to **True** under one condition and to **False** under another, as the IsEven procedure does, you can condense the **If...Then** statement by modifying its condition to return **True** or **False**. However, the revised procedure may be somewhat harder to understand. The revised IsEven procedure is available in the modNumbers module in VBA.mdb in the Samples\CH07 subfolder on the companion CD-ROM.

The Floating-Point Data Types

VBA provides two floating-point data types, **Single** and **Double**. The **Single** data type requires 4 bytes of memory and can store negative values between -3.402823×10^{38} and $-1.401298 \times 10^{-45}$ and positive values between 1.401298×10^{-45} and 3.402823×10^{38}. The **Double** data type requires 8 bytes of memory and can store negative values between $-1.79769313486232 \times 10^{308}$ and $-4.94065645841247 \times 10^{-324}$ and positive values between $4.94065645841247 \times 10^{-324}$ and $1.79769313486232 \times 10^{308}$.

The **Single** and **Double** data types are very precise—that is, they allow you to specify extremely small or large numbers. However, these data types are not very accurate because they use floating-point mathematics. Floating-point mathematics has an inherent limitation in that it uses binary digits to represent decimals. Not all the numbers within the range available to the **Single** or **Double** data type can be represented exactly in binary form, so they are rounded. Also, some numbers can't be represented exactly with any finite number of digits—pi, for example, or the decimal resulting from 1/3.

Because of these limitations to floating-point mathematics, you may encounter rounding errors when you perform operations on floating-point numbers. Compared to the size of the value you're working with, the rounding error will be very small. If you don't require absolute accuracy and can afford relatively small rounding errors, the floating-point data types are ideal for representing very small or very large values. On the other hand, if your values must be accurate—for example, if you're working with money values—you should consider one of the scaled integer data types.

The Scaled Integer Data Types

The two scaled integer data types, **Currency** and **Decimal**, provide a high level of accuracy. These are also referred to as fixed-point data types. They are not as precise as the floating-point data types—that is, they can't represent numbers as large or as small. However, if you can't afford rounding errors, and you don't require as many decimal places as the floating-point data types provide, you can use the scaled integer data types. Internally, the scaled integer types represent decimal values as integers by multiplying them by a factor of 10.

The **Currency** data type uses 8 bytes of memory and can represent numbers with fifteen digits to the left of the decimal point and four to the right, in the range of –922,337,203,685,477.5808 to 922,337,203,685,477.5807.

The **Decimal** data type uses 12 bytes of memory and can have between 0 and 28 decimal places. The **Decimal** data type is a **Variant** subtype; in order to use the **Decimal** data type, you must declare a variable of type **Variant**, and then convert it by using the **CDec** function.

The following example shows how to convert a **Variant** variable to a **Decimal** variable. It also demonstrates how using the **Decimal** data type can minimize the rounding errors inherent in the floating-point data types.

```
Sub DoubleVsDecimal()
   ' This procedure demonstrates how using the
   ' Decimal data type can minimize rounding errors.

   Dim dblNum     As Double
   Dim varNum     As Variant
   Dim lngCount   As Long

   ' Increment values in loop.
   For lngCount = 1 To 100000
      dblNum = dblNum + 0.00001
      ' Convert value to Decimal using CDec.
      varNum = varNum + CDec(0.00001)
   Next

   Debug.Print "Result using Double: " & dblNum
   Debug.Print "Result using Decimal: " & varNum
End Sub
```

The procedure prints these results to the Immediate window:

```
Result using Double: 0.999999999998084
Result using Decimal: 1
```

The DoubleVsDecimal procedure is available in the modNumbers module in VBA.mdb in the Samples\CH07 subfolder on the companion CD-ROM.

A Note About Division

Any time you use the floating-point division operator (/), you're performing floating-point division, and your return value will be of type **Double**. This is true whether your dividend and divisor are integer, floating-point, or fixed-point values. It's true whether or not your result has a decimal portion.

For example, running the following code from the Immediate window prints "Double":

```
? TypeName(2.34/5.9)
```

So does this code, even though the result is an integer:

```
? TypeName(9/3)
```

Since all floating-point division returns a floating-point value, you can't ever be certain that your result is accurate to every decimal place, even if you're performing division on **Decimal** or **Currency** values. There will always be an inherent possibility of rounding errors, although they're likely to be small.

If you're dividing integers, or if you don't care about the decimal portion of the result, you can use the integer division operator (\). Integer division is faster than floating-point division, and the result is always an **Integer** or **Long** value, either of which requires less memory than a **Double** value. For example, running this code from the Immediate window prints "Integer":

```
? TypeName(9\3)
```

Conversion, Rounding, and Truncation

When you convert a decimal value to an integer value, VBA rounds the number to an integer value. How it rounds depends on the value of the digit immediately to the right of the decimal place—digits less than 5 are rounded down, while digits greater than 5 are rounded up. If the digit is 5, then it's rounded down if the digit immediately to the left of the decimal place is even, and up if it's odd. When the digit to be rounded is a 5, the result is always an even integer.

For example, running the following line of code from the Immediate window prints "8," because VBA rounds down when the number immediately to the left of the decimal is even:

```
? CLng(8.5)
```

However, this code prints "10," because 9 is odd:

```
? CLng(9.5)
```

If you want to discard the decimal portion of a number, and return the integer portion, you can use either the **Int** or **Fix** function. These functions simply truncate without rounding. For example, `Int(8.5)` returns 8, and `Int(9.5)` returns 9. The **Int** and **Fix** functions behave identically unless you're working with negative numbers. The **Int** function rounds to the lower negative integer, while the **Fix** function rounds to the higher one.

For example, the following code evaluates to "–8":

```
? Fix(-8.2)
```

Using the **Int** function, on the other hand, yields "–9":

```
? Int(-8.2)
```

Note The **Int** and **Fix** functions always return a **Double** value. You may want to convert the result to a **Long** value before performing further operations with it.

VBA includes a new rounding function called **Round**, which you can use to round a floating-point or fixed-point decimal to a specified number of places. For example, the following code rounds the number 1.2345 to 1.234:

```
? Round(1.2345, 3)
```

Although the **Round** function is useful for returning a number with a specified number of decimal places, you can't always predict how it will round when the rounding digit is a 5. How VBA rounds a number depends on the internal binary representation of that number. If you want to write a rounding function that will round decimal values according to predictable rules, you should write your own. For more information, see the *Visual Basic Language Developer's Handbook* by Ken Getz and Mike Gilbert (Sybex, 1999).

Formatting Numeric Values

VBA provides several functions that you can use to format numbers, including the **FormatNumber**, **FormatCurrency**, **FormatPercent**, and **Format** functions. Each of these functions returns a number formatted as a string.

The **FormatNumber** function formats a number with the comma as the thousands separator. You can specify the number of decimal places you want to appear. For example, calling the following code from the Immediate window prints "8,012.36":

```
? FormatNumber(8012.36)
```

The **FormatCurrency** function formats a number with a dollar sign, including two decimal places by default. Calling this code from the Immediate window prints "$10,456.45":

```
? FormatCurrency(10456.45)
```

The **FormatPercent** function formats a number as a percentage, including two decimal places by default. For example, calling this code from the Immediate window prints “80.00%”:

```
? FormatPercent(4/5)
```

If you need finer control over the formatting of a number, you can use the **Format** function to specify a custom format. For example, to display leading zeros before a number, you can create a custom format that includes placeholders for each digit. If a digit is absent, a zero appears in that position. The following procedure shows an example that returns a formatted string complete with leading zeros:

```
Function FormatLeadingZeros(lngNum As Long) As String
   ' Formats number with leading zeros.

   FormatLeadingZeros = Format$(lngNum, "00000")
End Function
```

The FormatLeadingZeros procedure is available in the modNumbers module in VBA.mdb in the Samples\CH07 subfolder on the companion CD-ROM.

For more information about creating custom formats, search the Visual Basic Reference Help index for “Format function.”

Using the Mod Operator

The **Mod** operator divides two numbers and returns the remainder. It’s useful when you need to determine whether two numbers divide evenly, or how close they come to dividing evenly. The **Mod** operator always returns an **Integer** or **Long** value, even when you divide floating-point or fixed-point numbers.

For example, the IsFactor procedure takes two arguments, a number and a potential factor, and returns **True** if the second argument is indeed a factor of the first. The procedure uses the **Mod** operator to determine whether one value divides evenly into the other.

```
Function IsFactor(lngNum As Long, _
                  lngFactor As Long) As Boolean

   ' Determines whether one number is a factor of another number.

   IsFactor = Not CBool(lngNum Mod lngFactor)
End Function
```

The IsFactor procedure is available in the modNumbers module in VBA.mdb in the Samples\CH07 subfolder on the companion CD-ROM.

Performing Calculations on Numeric Arrays

Many mathematical functions operate on a variable set of numbers. For example, you can take the median, or middle value, of a set of any size. Since you won't know how many numbers the set will contain while you're writing code to find the median, you can't create a procedure with a set number of arguments. Instead, you can use a dynamic array to store an indeterminate number of values and perform an operation on them.

The following procedure takes a parameter array and returns the median of the values in the array. A parameter array encompasses a variable number of arguments that are passed to a procedure as an array. The **ParamArray** keyword specifies a parameter array, which must be defined as type **Variant**.

The Median procedure calls another procedure, IsNumericArray, which determines whether the array contains any non-numeric elements before the Median procedure attempts to find the median. It then calls the QuickSortArray procedure, which sorts the array. Finally, it determines whether the array contains an even or odd number of elements. If the number of elements is odd, the middle element in the sorted array is the median. If the number of elements is even, the median is the average of the two midmost elements.

```
Function Median(ParamArray avarValues() As Variant) As Double
   ' Return the median of a set of numbers.

   Dim lngCount   As Long
   Dim varTemp    As Variant

   ' Store array in temporary variable.
   varTemp = avarValues()

   ' Check whether array is numeric.
   If IsNumericArray(varTemp) Then
      ' Determine how many elements are in array.
      lngCount = UBound(varTemp) - LBound(varTemp) + 1
      ' Sort the array.
      QuickSortArray varTemp
      ' Determine whether array contains an odd or even number of elements.
      If IsEven(lngCount) Then
         ' If even, need to find the two middle elements and
         ' return the average of their values.
         ' Remember we're working with a zero-based array!
         Median = (varTemp(lngCount / 2 - 1) + varTemp(lngCount / 2)) / 2
      Else
         ' If odd, need to find the middle element.
         Median = varTemp(Int(lngCount / 2))
      End If
   Else
      ' Return -1 if array isn't numeric.
      Median = -1
   End If
End Function
```

This procedure is available in the modNumbers module in VBA.mdb in the Samples\CH07 subfolder on the companion CD-ROM.

To test the Median procedure, try calling it with an even set of numbers, then with an odd set of numbers, as follows:

```
? Median(45, 67, 23, 89, 52, 101)
```

To make sure it's working properly, you can check it against the Excel **Median** worksheet function. Note that the Excel **Median** function can take no more than 30 arguments, while the procedure shown here can take any number of arguments.

You could also modify this procedure to take an array, rather than a parameter array. The parameter array is somewhat easier to test in isolation, but a procedure that takes an array may be more practical for use within your code. For example, you may have a procedure that fills an array with numeric data from a data source, which you can then pass to the Median procedure to determine the median of the set of numbers, without having to pass each value as an argument to the procedure.

The strategy shown here for finding the median also works for other operations that take an indeterminate number of values, such as finding the average or standard deviation, or performing other statistical calculations.

Working with Dates and Times

VBA provides a data type for storing date and time values, the **Date** data type. Convenient as the **Date** data type is, manipulating date values in VBA can still be tricky. To easily work with dates, you need to understand how VBA stores date values internally.

Note The Microsoft Office 2000 applications all support dates beyond the year 2000. However, there are some issues you need to take into account in order to design your application so that it properly handles both twentieth and twenty-first century dates. An extensive discussion of these issues is available on the Microsoft Year 2000 Resource Center Web site at http://www.microsoft.com/technet/topics/year2k/default.htm.

The Date Data Type

VBA provides the **Date** data type to store date and time values. The **Date** data type is an 8-byte floating-point value, so internally it's the same as the **Double** data type. The **Date** data type can store dates between January 1, 100, and January 1, 9999.

VBA stores the date value in the integer portion of the **Date** data type, and the time value in the decimal portion. The integer portion represents the number of days since December 30, 1899, which is the starting point for the **Date** data type. Any dates before this one are stored as negative numbers; all dates after are stored as positive values. If you convert a date value representing December 30, 1899, to a double, you'll find that this date is represented by zero.

The decimal portion of a date represents the amount of time that has passed since midnight. For example, if the decimal portion of a date value is .75, three-quarters of the day has passed, and the time is now 6 P.M.

Because the integer portion of a date represents number of days, you can add and subtract days from one date to get another date.

Getting the Current Date and Time

Three functions in VBA can tell you exactly when it is: the **Now**, **Date**, and **Time** functions. The **Now** function returns both the date and time portions of a **Date** variable. For example, calling the **Now** function from the Immediate window returns a value like this one:

```
2/23/98 6:16:47 PM
```

The **Date** function returns the current date. You can use it if you don't need to know the time. The **Time** function returns the current time, without the date.

Formatting a Date

You can use predefined formats to format a date by calling the **FormatDateTime** function, or you can create a custom format for a date by using the **Format** function.

The following procedure formats a date by using both built-in and custom formats:

```
Sub DateFormats(Optional dteDate As Date)
   ' This procedure formats a date using both built-in
   ' and custom formats.

   ' If dteDate argument has not been passed, then
   ' dteDate is initialized to 0 (or December 30, 1899,
   ' the date equivalent of 0).
   If CLng(dteDate) = 0 Then
      ' Use today's date.
      dteDate = Now
   End If

   ' Print date in built-in and custom formats.
   Debug.Print FormatDateTime(dteDate, vbGeneralDate)
   Debug.Print FormatDateTime(dteDate, vbLongDate)
   Debug.Print FormatDateTime(dteDate, vbShortDate)
   Debug.Print FormatDateTime(dteDate, vbLongTime)
   Debug.Print FormatDateTime(dteDate, vbShortTime)
   Debug.Print Format$(dteDate, "ddd, mmm d, yyyy")
   Debug.Print Format$(dteDate, "mmm d, H:MM am/pm")
End Sub
```

The DateFormats procedure is available in the modDateTime module in VBA.mdb in the Samples\CH07 subfolder on the companion CD-ROM.

Date Delimiters

When you work with date literals in your code, you need to indicate to VBA that a value is a date. If you don't, VBA may think you're performing subtraction or floating-point division.

For example, if you run the following fragment, the value that VBA assigns to the **Date** variable is not April 5, 1998, but 4 divided by 5 divided by 98. Because you're assigning it to a **Date** variable, VBA converts the number to a date, and prints "12:11:45 AM" to the Immediate window:

```
Dim dteDate As Date
dteDate = 4 / 5 / 98
Debug.Print dteDate
```

To avoid this problem, you must include delimiters around the date. The preferred date delimiter for VBA is the number sign (#). You can also use double quotation marks, as you would for a string, but doing so requires VBA to perform an extra step to convert the string to a date. If you rewrite the fragment as follows to include the date delimiter, VBA prints "4/5/98" to the Immediate window:

```
Dim dteDate As Date
dteDate = #4/5/98#
Debug.Print dteDate
```

Assembling a Date

To work with a date in code, you sometimes need to break it down into its component parts—that is, its day, month, and year. Once you've done this, you can perform a calculation on one element, and then reassemble the date. To break a date into components, you can use the **Day**, **Month**, and **Year** functions. Each of these functions takes a date and returns the day, month, or year portion, respectively, as an **Integer** value. For example, `Year(#2/23/98#)` returns "1998."

To reassemble a date, you can use the **DateSerial** function. This function takes three integer arguments: a year, a month, and a day value. It returns a **Date** value that contains the reassembled date.

Often you can break apart a date, perform a calculation on it, and reassemble it all in one step. For example, to find the first day of the month, given any date, you can write a function similar to the following one:

```
Function FirstOfMonth(Optional dteDate As Date) As Date

   ' This function calculates the first day of a month, given a date.
   ' If no date is passed in, the function uses the current date.

   If CLng(dteDate) = 0 Then
      dteDate = Date
   End If

   ' Find the first day of this month.
   FirstOfMonth = DateSerial(Year(dteDate), Month(dteDate), 1)
End Function
```

The FirstOfMonth procedure takes a date or, if the calling procedure doesn't pass one, uses the current date. It breaks the date into its component year and month, and then reassembles the date using 1 for the *day* argument. Calling this procedure with the *dteDate* argument #2/23/98# returns "2/1/98".

The following procedure uses the same strategy to return the last day of a month, given a date:

```
Function LastOfMonth(Optional dteDate As Date) As Date

   ' This function calculates the last day of a month, given a date.
   ' If no date is passed in, the function uses the current date.

   If CLng(dteDate) = 0 Then
      dteDate = Date
   End If

   ' Find the first day of the next month, then subtract one day.
   LastOfMonth = DateSerial(Year(dteDate), Month(dteDate) + 1, 1) - 1
End Function
```

Both of these procedures are available in the modDateTime module in VBA.mdb in the Samples\CH07 subfolder on the companion CD-ROM.

VBA also provides functions that you can use to disassemble and reassemble a time value in the same manner. The **Hour**, **Minute**, and **Second** functions return portions of a time value; the **TimeSerial** function takes an hour, minute, and second value and returns a complete time value.

Getting Part of a Date

The previous section showed how to return the year, month, and day from a date. You can get other information about a date as well, such as what quarter or week it falls in, or what day of the week it is.

The **Weekday** function takes a date and returns a constant indicating on what day of the week it falls. The following procedure takes a date and returns **True** if the date falls on a workday—that is, Monday through Friday—and **False** if it falls on a weekend.

```
Function IsWorkday(Optional dteDate As Date) As Boolean
   ' This function determines whether a date
   ' falls on a weekday.

   ' If no date passed in, use today's date.
   If CLng(dteDate) = 0 Then
      dteDate = Date
   End If

   ' Determine where in week the date falls.
   Select Case Weekday(dteDate)
      Case vbMonday To vbFriday
         IsWorkday = True
      Case Else
         IsWorkday = False
   End Select
End Function
```

This procedure is available in the modDateTime module in VBA.mdb in the Samples\CH07 subfolder on the companion CD-ROM.

In addition to the individual functions that return part of a date—**Year**, **Month**, **Day**, and **Weekday**—VBA includes the **DatePart** function, which can return any part of a date. Although it may seem redundant, the **DatePart** function gives you slightly more control over the values you return, because it gives you the option to specify the first day of the week and the first day of the year. For this reason, it can be useful when you're writing code that may run on systems in other countries. In addition, the **DatePart** function is the only way to return information about what quarter a date falls into.

Adding and Subtracting Dates

To add an interval to a given date, you must use the **DateAdd** function, unless you're adding days to a date. As mentioned earlier, since the integer portion of a **Date** variable represents the number of days that have passed since December 30, 1899, adding integers to a **Date** variable is equivalent to adding days.

By using the **DateAdd** function, you can add any interval to a given date: years, months, days, weeks, quarters. The following procedure finds the anniversary of a given date; that is, the next date on which it occurs. If the anniversary has already occurred this year, the procedure returns the date of the anniversary in the next year.

```
Function Anniversary(dteDate As Date) As Date
   ' This function finds the next anniversary of a date.
   ' If the date has already passed for this year, it returns
   ' the date on which the anniversary occurs in the following year.

   Dim dteThisYear As Date

   ' Find corresponding date this year.
   dteThisYear = DateSerial(Year(Date), Month(dteDate), Day(dteDate))
   ' Determine whether it's already passed.
   If dteThisYear < Date Then
      Anniversary = DateAdd("yyyy", 1, dteThisYear)
   Else
      Anniversary = dteThisYear
   End If
End Function
```

This procedure is available in the modDateTime module in VBA.mdb in the Samples\CH07 subfolder on the companion CD-ROM.

To find the interval between two dates, you can use the **DateDiff** function. The interval returned can be any of several units of time: days, weeks, months, years, hours, and so on.

The following example uses the **DateDiff** function to return the day number for a particular day of the year. The procedure determines the last day of the last year by using the **DateSerial** function, and then subtracts that date from the date that was passed in to the procedure.

```
Function DayOfYear(Optional dteDate As Date) As Long

   ' This function takes a date as an argument and returns
   ' the day number for that year. If the dteDate argument is
   ' omitted, the function uses the current date.

   ' If dteDate argument has not been passed, dteDate is
   ' initialized to 0 (or December 30, 1899, the date
   ' equivalent of 0).
   If CLng(dteDate) = 0 Then
      ' Use today's date.
      dteDate = Date
   End If

   ' Calculate the number of days that have passed since
   ' December 31 of the previous year.
   DayOfYear = Abs(DateDiff("d", dteDate, _
      DateSerial(Year(dteDate) - 1, 12, 31)))
End Function
```

Calling this procedure with the value of #2/23/98# returns “54.”

This procedure is available in the modDateTime module in VBA.mdb in the Samples\CH07 subfolder on the companion CD-ROM.

Calculating Elapsed Time

You can use the **DateAdd** and **DateDiff** functions to calculate the time that has elapsed between two dates, and then, with a little additional work, present that time in the desired format. For example, the following procedure calculates a person's age in years, taking into account whether his or her birthday has already occurred in the current year.

Using the **DateDiff** function to determine the number of years between today and a birthdate doesn't always give a valid result because the **DatcDiff** function rounds to the next year. If a person's birthday hasn't yet occurred, using the **DateDiff** function will make the person one year older than he or she actually is.

To remedy this situation, the procedure checks to see whether the birthday has already occurred this year, and if it hasn't, it subtracts 1 to return the correct age.

```
Function CalcAge(dteBirthdate As Date) As Long

   Dim lngAge As Long

   ' Make sure passed-in value is a date.
   If Not IsDate(dteBirthdate) Then
      dteBirthdate = Date
   End If

   ' Make sure birthdate is not in the future.
   ' If it is, use today's date.
   If dteBirthdate > Date Then
      dteBirthdate = Date
   End If

   ' Calculate the difference in years between today and birthdate.
   lngAge = DateDiff("yyyy", dteBirthdate, Date)
   ' If birthdate has not occurred this year, subtract 1 from age.
   If DateSerial(Year(Date), Month(dteBirthdate), Day(dteBirthdate)) > Date Then
      lngAge = lngAge - 1
   End If
   CalcAge = lngAge
End Function
```

This procedure is available in the modDateTime module in VBA.mdb in the Samples\CH07 subfolder on the companion CD-ROM.

Working with Files

With the advent of the Microsoft Scripting Runtime object library, you can work with drives, folders, and files as objects.

The Microsoft Scripting Runtime Object Library

When you install the Office 2000 applications, one of the object libraries installed on your system is the Microsoft Scripting Runtime object library. This object library contains objects that are useful from either VBA or script, so it's provided as a separate library.

The objects in the Scripting Runtime library provide easy access to the file system, and make reading and writing to a text file much simpler than it is in previous versions.

By default, no reference is set to this library, so you must set a reference before you can use it. If **Microsoft Scripting Runtime** does not appear in the **References** dialog box (**Tools** menu), you should be able to find it in the C:\Windows\System subfolder as Scrrun.dll.

The top-level objects in the Scripting Runtime object library are the **Dictionary** object and the **FileSystemObject** object. To use the **Dictionary** object, you create an object variable of type **Dictionary**, then set it to a new instance of a **Dictionary** object:

```
Dim dctDict As Dictionary

Set dctDict = New Dictionary
```

To use the other objects in the Scripting Runtime library in code, you must first create a variable of type **FileSystemObject**, and then use the **New** keyword to create a new instance of the **FileSystemObject**, as shown in the following code fragment:

```
Dim fsoSysObj As FileSystemObject

Set fsoSysObj = New FileSystemObject
```

You can then use the variable that refers to the **FileSystemObject** to work with the **Drive**, **Folder**, **File**, and **TextStream** objects.

The following table describes the objects contained in the Scripting Runtime library.

Object	Collection	Description
Dictionary		Top-level object. Similar to the VBA **Collection** object.
Drive	**Drives**	Refers to a drive or collection of drives on the system.
File	**Files**	Refers to a file or collection of files in the file system.
FileSystemObject		Top-level object. Use this object to access drives, folders, and files in the file system.

Object	Collection	Description
Folder	**Folders**	Refers to a folder or collection of folders in the file system.
TextStream		Refers to a stream of text that is read from, written to, or appended to a text file.

Returning Files from the File System

Once you've created a new instance of the **FileSystemObject**, you can use it to work with drives, folders, and files in the file system.

The following procedure returns the files in a particular folder into a **Dictionary** object. The GetFiles procedure takes three arguments: the path to the directory, a **Dictionary** object, and an optional **Boolean** argument that specifies whether the procedure should be called recursively. It returns a **Boolean** value indicating whether the procedure was successful.

The procedure first uses the **GetFolder** method to return a reference to a **Folder** object. It then loops through the **Files** collection of that folder and adds the path and file name for each file to the **Dictionary** object. If the *blnRecursive* argument is set to **True**, the GetFiles procedure is called recursively to return the files in each subfolder.

```
Function GetFiles(strPath As String, _
                  dctDict As Dictionary, _
                  Optional blnRecursive As Boolean) As Boolean

   ' This procedure returns all the files in a directory into
   ' a Dictionary object. If called recursively, it also returns
   ' all files in subfolders.

   Dim fsoSysObj     As FileSystemObject
   Dim fdrFolder     As Folder
   Dim fdrSubFolder  As Folder
   Dim filFile       As File

   ' Return new FileSystemObject.
   Set fsoSysObj = New FileSystemObject

   On Error Resume Next
   ' Get folder.
   Set fdrFolder = fsoSysObj.GetFolder(strPath)
   If Err <> 0 Then
      ' Incorrect path.
      GetFiles = False
      GoTo GetFiles_End
   End If
   On Error GoTo 0
```

```
   ' Loop through Files collection, adding to dictionary.
   For Each filFile In fdrFolder.Files
      dctDict.Add filFile.Path, filFile.Path
   Next filFile

   ' If Recursive flag is true, call recursively.
   If blnRecursive Then
      For Each fdrSubFolder In fdrFolder.SubFolders
         GetFiles fdrSubFolder.Path, dctDict, True
      Next fdrSubFolder
   End If

   ' Return True if no error occurred.
   GetFiles = True

GetFiles_End:
   Exit Function
End Function
```

You can use the following procedure to test the GetFiles procedure. This procedure creates a new **Dictionary** object and passes it to the GetFiles procedure.

```
Sub TestGetFiles()
   ' Call to test GetFiles function.

   Dim dctDict As Dictionary
   Dim varItem As Variant

   ' Create new dictionary.
   Set dctDict = New Dictionary
   ' Call recursively, return files into Dictionary object.
   If GetFiles(GetTempDir, dctDict, True) Then
      ' Print items in dictionary.
      For Each varItem In dctDict
         Debug.Print varItem
      Next
   End If
End Sub
```

Both of these procedures are available in the modFiles module in VBA.mdb in the Samples\CH07 subfolder on the companion CD-ROM.

You can also use the Office **FileSearch** object, discussed in Chapter 6, “Working with Shared Office Components,” to find a file or group of files. The **FileSearch** object has certain advantages in that you can search subfolders, search for a particular file type, or search the contents of a file by simply setting a few properties.

On the other hand, the Microsoft Scripting Runtime object library allows you to work with individual files or folders as objects that have their own methods and properties. For example, the ChangeFileAttributes procedure in the following section, “Setting File Attributes,” alters file attributes by setting the **Attributes** property for each **File** object in the **Files** collection of a particular **Folder** object.

Setting File Attributes

The **File** object and **Folder** object provide an **Attributes** property that you can use to read or set a file or folder's attributes, as shown in the following example.

The ChangeFileAttributes procedure takes four arguments: the path to a folder, an optional constant that specifies the attributes to set, an optional constant that specifies the attributes to remove, and an optional argument that specifies that the procedure should be called recursively.

If the folder path passed in is valid, the procedure returns a **Folder** object. It then checks to see if the *lngSetAttr* argument was provided. If so, it loops through all the files in the folder, appending the new attribute or attributes to each file's existing attributes. It does the same for the *lngRemoveAttr* argument, except in this case it removes the specified attributes if they exist for files in the collection.

Finally, the procedure checks whether the *blnRecursive* argument has been set to **True**. If so, it calls the procedure for each file in each subfolder of the *strPath* argument.

```
Function ChangeFileAttributes(strPath As String, _
                              Optional lngSetAttr As FileAttribute, _
                              Optional lngRemoveAttr As FileAttribute, _
                              Optional blnRecursive As Boolean) As Boolean

   ' This function takes a directory path, a value specifying file
   ' attributes to be set, a value specifying file attributes to be
   ' removed, and a flag that indicates whether it should be called
   ' recursively. It returns True unless an error occurs.

   Dim fsoSysObj      As FileSystemObject
   Dim fdrFolder      As Folder
   Dim fdrSubFolder   As Folder
   Dim filFile        As File

   ' Return new FileSystemObject.
   Set fsoSysObj = New FileSystemObject

   On Error Resume Next
   ' Get folder.
   Set fdrFolder = fsoSysObj.GetFolder(strPath)
   If Err <> 0 Then
      ' Incorrect path.
      ChangeFileAttributes = False
      GoTo ChangeFileAttributes_End
   End If
   On Error GoTo 0
```

```
   ' If caller passed in attribute to set, set for all.
   If lngSetAttr Then
      For Each filFile In fdrFolder.Files
         If Not (filFile.Attributes And lngSetAttr) Then
            filFile.Attributes = filFile.Attributes Or lngSetAttr
         End If
      Next
   End If

   ' If caller passed in attribute to remove, remove for all.
   If lngRemoveAttr Then
      For Each filFile In fdrFolder.Files
         If (filFile.Attributes And lngRemoveAttr) Then
            filFile.Attributes = filFile.Attributes - lngRemoveAttr
         End If
      Next
   End If

   ' If caller has set blnRecursive argument to True, then call
   ' function recursively.
   If blnRecursive Then
      ' Loop through subfolders.
      For Each fdrSubFolder In fdrFolder.SubFolders
         ' Call function with subfolder path.
         ChangeFileAttributes fdrSubFolder.Path, lngSetAttr, lngRemoveAttr, True
      Next
   End If
   ChangeFileAttributes = True

ChangeFileAttributes_End:
   Exit Function
End Function
```

Both of these procedures are available in the modFiles module in VBA.mdb in the Samples\CH07 subfolder on the companion CD-ROM.

Logging Errors to a Text File

The Scripting Runtime object library simplifies the code required to read from and write to a text file. To use the new objects to write to a text file, you return an object that refers to a new or existing file, and then use the **OpenAsTextStream** method to open it for input or output. The **OpenAsTextStream** method has an ***IOMode*** argument, which you can set to indicate whether you want to read from the file, write to it, or append to it.

The **OpenAsTextStream** method returns a **TextStream** object, which is the object you use to work with the text in the file. To read a line, for example, you can use the **TextStream** object's **ReadLine** method; to write a line, you can use the **WriteLine** method. When you're finished working with the file, you can use the **Close** method to close it.

The following procedure logs an error to a text file. It takes two arguments: an *ErrObject* argument, which is a reference to the **Err** object that contains the current error, and an optional *strProcName* argument, which specifies the procedure in which the error occurred.

The LogError procedure writes to a text file in the C:\Windows\Temp folder. To determine where the Windows Temp folder is, it calls another procedure, the GetTempDir procedure. This procedure makes a call to the Windows application programming interface (API) to determine the Temp folder. Windows can't boot without a designated Temp folder, so you can be certain that the Temp folder will always be available.

The LogError procedure is meant to be used to log multiple errors. The first time the procedure is called, no log file exists, so it must create one. On each subsequent call, the procedure must open the existing log file. The simplest way to do this is to look for the name of the file that you're expecting, and if it's not there, handle the error and create the file.

Unfortunately, when the procedure is first called and the error occurs, the existing information in the **Err** object is cleared and the information for the new error takes its place. Since there's only one **Err** object available in VBA, the error information that you passed to the procedure is lost when a new error occurs. Therefore, the first thing that the procedure does is to store the error number and description of the error in variables.

Once the procedure has a reference to the text file, it opens it for appending, and then writes the error information to the file line by line.

```
Sub LogError(errX As ErrObject, _
             Optional strProcName As String)

   ' This procedure logs errors to a text file. It is used in
   ' this chapter to log synchronization errors.
   '
   ' Arguments:
   '   errX: A variable that refers to the VBA Err object.

   Dim fsoSysObj  As FileSystemObject
   Dim filFile    As File
   Dim txsStream  As TextStream
   Dim lngErrNum  As Long
   Dim strPath    As String
   Dim strErrText As String

   Set fsoSysObj = New FileSystemObject

   ' Store error information.
   lngErrNum = errX.Number
   strErrText = errX.Description
   ' Clear error.
   errX.Clear
```

```
   ' Return Windows Temp folder.
   strPath = GetTempDir
   If Len(strPath) = 0 Then
      GoTo LogError_End
   End If

   On Error Resume Next
   ' See if file already exists.
   Set filFile = fsoSysObj.GetFile(strPath & APP_ERROR_LOG)
   ' If not, then create it.
   If Err <> 0 Then
      Set filFile = fsoSysObj.CreateTextFile(strPath & APP_ERROR_LOG)
   End If
   On Error GoTo 0

   ' Open file as text stream for reading.
   Set txsStream = filFile.OpenAsTextStream(ForAppending)
   ' Write error information and close.
   With txsStream
      .WriteLine lngErrNum
      .WriteLine strErrText
      If Len(strProcName) > 0 Then .WriteLine strProcName
      .WriteLine Now
      .WriteBlankLines 1
      .Close
   End With

LogError_End:
   Exit Sub
End Sub
```

The LogError procedure calls the GetTempDir procedure, which returns the path to the C:\Windows\Temp folder by calling the **GetTempPath** function in the Windows API. For more information about working with the Windows API, see Chapter 10, "The Windows API and Other Dynamic-Link Libraries."

To try the LogError procedure, you can call the following procedure. This procedure suspends error handling, then uses the **Raise** method of the **Err** object to force an error. It then passes the **Err** object to the **LogError** procedure, along with the name of the procedure that caused the error.

```
Sub TestLogError()
   ' This procedure tests the LogError function.

   On Error Resume Next
   ' Raise an error.
   Err.Raise 11
   ' Log it.
   LogError Err, "TestLogError"
End Sub
```

Both of these procedures are available in the modFiles module in VBA.mdb in the Samples\CH07 subfolder on the companion CD-ROM.

The Dictionary Object

The **Dictionary** object is a data structure that can contain sets of pairs, where each pair consists of an item, which can be any data type, and a key, which is a unique **String** value that identifies the item. The **Dictionary** object is similar in some ways to the VBA **Collection** object; however, the **Dictionary** object offers certain features that the **Collection** object lacks, including:

- The **Exists** method. You can use this method to determine whether a particular key, and its corresponding item, exist in a **Dictionary** object. The **Exists** method makes it simpler and more efficient to search a **Dictionary** object than to search a **Collection** object.
- The **CompareMode** property. Setting this property specifies the text-comparison mode for the **Dictionary** object, so that you can search for a key in either a case-sensitive or case-insensitive manner. By default, it's set to **BinaryCompare**, which means that the **Exists** method will return **True** only if it finds a binary match. There's no way to specify a text-comparison mode for a key that retrieves an item from a **Collection** object.
- The **Key** property. This property enables you to return the key for a particular item in the dictionary. An item in a **Collection** object also has a key, which you can use to retrieve that item; however, there's no way to retrieve the key itself.
- The **RemoveAll** method. This method removes all items in the **Dictionary** object. A **Collection** object, on the other hand, has no method for removing all items at once, although setting the **Collection** object to **Nothing** has the same effect.

The primary advantage of the **Dictionary** object over the **Collection** object is the fact that it's easier to search a **Dictionary** object for a given item. Despite this advantage, the **Dictionary** object does not entirely replace the **Collection** object. The **Collection** object is useful in some situations where the **Dictionary** object is not. For example, if you're creating a custom object model, you can use a **Collection** object to store a reference to a custom collection, but you can't use a **Dictionary** object to do this. For more information about creating custom object models, see Chapter 9, "Custom Classes and Objects."

The modDictionary module, which is available in the VBA.mdb sample file in the Samples\CH07 subfolder on the companion CD-ROM, contains code examples that compare the **Dictionary** and **Collection** objects. The GetFiles procedure and TestGetFiles procedure in "Returning Files from the File System" earlier in this chapter also demonstrate uses of the **Dictionary** object. For information about searching a dictionary for an item, see "Searching a Dictionary" later in this chapter.

For more information about the **Dictionary** object, see the VBScript documentation on the Microsoft Scripting Technologies Web site at http://msdn.microsoft.com /scripting/default.htm.

Understanding Arrays

An array is a variable that can contain multiple values. Arrays are useful when you need to store a number of values of the same type, but you don't know how many, or you don't want to create individual variables to store them all.

For example, suppose you need to store a numeric value for every day of the year. You could declare 365 separate numeric variables, but that would be a lot of work. Instead, you can create an array to store all the data in one variable. The array itself is a single variable with multiple elements; each element can contain one piece of data.

You can use loops, together with a couple of special functions for working with arrays, to assign values to or retrieve values from the various elements of an array.

Creating Arrays

You can create two types of arrays in VBA—fixed-size arrays and dynamic arrays. A fixed-size array has a fixed number of elements, and is useful only when you know exactly how many elements your array will have while you're writing the code. Most of the time you'll create dynamic arrays.

Arrays can be of any data type. The data type for an array specifies the data type for each element of the array; for example, each element of an array of type **Long** can contain a **Long** value. The following code fragment declares an array variable of type **Long**:

```
Dim alngNum() As Long
```

Note You don't have to include the parentheses when you refer to an array variable, except when you declare it, resize it, or refer to an individual element. However, you may want to include the parentheses everywhere to make it clear that the variable is an array.

Once you've declared a dynamic array variable, you can resize the array by using the **ReDim** statement. To resize the array, you provide a value for the upper bound, and optionally, for the lower bound. The upper and lower bound of an array refer to the beginning and ending indexes for the array.

You must specify the upper bound for the array when you resize it. The lower bound is optional, but it's a good idea to include it, so that it's obvious to you what the lower bound of the array is:

```
' This array contains 100 elements.
ReDim alngNum(0 To 99)
```

If you don't include the lower bound, it's determined by the **Option Base** setting for the module. By default, the **Option Base** setting for a module is 0. You can set it to 1 by entering `Option Base 1` in the Declarations section of the module.

If you are using the **ReDim** statement on an array that contains values, those values may be lost when the array is resized. To ensure that any values in the array are maintained, you can use the **Preserve** keyword with the **ReDim** statement, as follows:

```
ReDim Preserve alngNum(0 To 364)
```

Resizing an array with the **Preserve** keyword can be slow, so you want to do it as infrequently as possible. A good way to minimize use of the **Preserve** keyword in your code is to estimate the amount of data you need to store and size the array accordingly. If an error occurs because you haven't made the array large enough, you can resize it within the error handler as many times as necessary. Once you're through working with the array, if it's larger than you need, you can resize it to make it only large enough to contain the data it currently has. The example in "Returning an Array from a Function" later in this chapter demonstrates this technique.

Arrays and Variants

A **Variant** variable can store an array. For example, the following code fragment assigns an array of type **String** to a **Variant** variable:

```
Dim astrItems(0 To 9)    As String
Dim varItems             As Variant

varItems = astrItems
```

When a static array is initialized, or when a dynamic array is redimensioned, each element is initialized according to its type. In other words, **String** type elements are initialized to zero-length strings, **Integer** and **Long** type elements are initialized to zero (0), and **Variant** type elements are initialized to **Empty**. The point is that in the preceding example, it's not necessary to fill the array in order to work with it. By simply declaring an array of ten elements as type **String**, we've created an array containing ten zero-length strings.

An array of type **Variant** can store any data type in any of its elements. For example, a **Variant** type array can have one element of type **String**, one element of type **Long**, and another of type **Date**. It can even store a **Variant** variable that contains another array.

A **Variant** type array can also store an array of objects. If you know that an array will store only objects, you can declare it as type **Object** rather than as type **Variant**. And if you know that an array of objects will contain only one type of object, you can declare the array as that object type.

Tip You may want to consider using a **Collection** or **Dictionary** object to store groups of objects in a single variable, rather than creating an array of objects. The advantage to using an array over a **Collection** or **Dictionary** object is that it's easy to sort. But if you're storing objects, you probably don't care about the sort order. Since a **Collection** or **Dictionary** object resizes itself automatically, you don't have to worry about keeping track of its size, as you do with an array.

Assigning One Array to Another

If two dynamic arrays have the same data type, you can assign one array to another. Assigning one array to another of the same type is quick because the first array is simply pointed to the memory location that stores the second array. This feature is new to this version of VBA; it's not available in previous versions.

For example, the following code fragment assigns one string array to another:

```
Dim astr1() As String
Dim astr2(0 To 9) As String

astr1 = astr2
```

Important This type of assignment works only for dynamic arrays of the *same* type. The two arrays must both be dynamic arrays, and they must be declared as the exact same type: if one is type **String**, the other must be type **String**. It can't be type **Variant** or any other data type. If you want to assign one array's elements to an array of a different type, you must create a loop and assign each element one at a time.

Returning an Array from a Function

The previous example assigned one array variable to another. Based on this example, you might guess that you can also call a procedure that returns an array and assign that to another array, as in the following code fragment:

```
Dim astr1() As String

astr1 = ReturnArray
```

To return an array, a procedure must have a return value type of the array's data type, or of type **Variant**. The advantage to declaring a procedure to return a typed array versus a **Variant** value is that you don't need to use the **IsArray** function to ensure that the procedure indeed returned an array. If a procedure returns a value of type **Variant**, you may need to check its contents before performing array operations.

The ReturnArray procedure prompts the user for input and creates an array of the resulting values, resizing the array as needed. Note that to return an array from a procedure, you simply assign the array to the name of the procedure.

```
Function ReturnArray() As String()
   ' This function fills an array with user input, then
   ' returns the array.

   Dim astrItems()   As String
   Dim strInput      As String
   Dim strMsg        As String
   Dim lngIndex      As Long
```

```
    On Error GoTo ReturnArray_Err

    strMsg = "Enter a value or press Cancel to end:"

    lngIndex = 0

    ' Prompt user for first item to add to array.
    strInput = InputBox(strMsg)
    If Len(strInput) > 0 Then
       ' Estimate size of array.
       ReDim astrItems(0 To 2)
       astrItems(lngIndex) = strInput
       lngIndex = lngIndex + 1
    Else
       ' If user cancels without adding item,
       ' don't resize array.
       ReturnArray = astrItems
       GoTo ReturnArray_End
    End If

    ' Prompt user for additional items and add to array.
    Do
       strInput = InputBox(strMsg)
       If Len(strInput) > 0 Then
          astrItems(lngIndex) = strInput
          lngIndex = lngIndex + 1
       End If
    ' Loop until user cancels.
    Loop Until Len(strInput) = 0

    ' Resize to current value of lngIndex - 1.
    ReDim Preserve astrItems(0 To lngIndex - 1)

    ReturnArray = astrItems

ReturnArray_End:
    Exit Function

ReturnArray_Err:
    ' If upper bound is exceeded, enlarge array.
    If Err = ERR_SUBSCRIPT Then ' Subscript out of range.
       ' Double the size of the array.
       ReDim Preserve astrItems(lngIndex * 2)
       Resume
    Else
       MsgBox "An unexpected error has occurred!", vbExclamation
       Resume ReturnArray_End
    End If
End Function
```

To test the ReturnArray procedure, you can run the GetArray procedure, available in the modArrays module in VBA.mdb in the Samples\CH07 subfolder on the companion CD-ROM.

When you call a procedure that returns an array, you need to take into account the case in which the returned array does not contain any elements. For example, in the preceding ReturnArray procedure, if you cancel the input box the first time that it appears, the array returned by the procedure contains no elements. The calling procedure needs to check for this condition. The best way to do this is to define a procedure such as the following one, which takes an array and checks the upper bound. If the array contains no elements, checking the upper bound causes a trappable error.

```
Function IsArrayEmpty(varArray As Variant) As Boolean
   ' Determines whether an array contains any elements.
   ' Returns False if it does contain elements, True
   ' if it does not.

   Dim lngUBound As Long

   On Error Resume Next
   ' If the array is empty, an error occurs when you
   ' check the array's bounds.
   lngUBound = UBound(varArray)
   If Err.Number <> 0 Then
      IsArrayEmpty = True
   Else
      IsArrayEmpty = False
   End If
End Function
```

The IsArrayEmpty procedure is available in the modArrays module in VBA.mdb in the Samples\CH07 subfolder on the companion CD-ROM.

Note The VBA **Split** and **Filter** functions can also return an array that contains no elements. Checking the upper or lower bounds on an array returned by either of these procedures does not cause an error, however. When the **Split** or **Filter** function returns an array containing no elements, the lower bound of that array is 0, and the upper bound is –1. Therefore, to determine whether the returned array contains any elements, you can check for the condition where the upper bound of the array is less than the lower bound. For an example, see the ConvertToProperCase procedure in the "Converting Strings" section earlier in this chapter.

Passing an Array to a Procedure

You can declare an array in one procedure, and then pass the array to another procedure to be modified. The procedure that modifies the array doesn't necessarily need to return an array. Arrays are passed by reference, meaning that one procedure passes to the other a pointer to the array's location in memory. When the second procedure modifies the array, it modifies it at that same memory location. Therefore, when execution returns to the first procedure, the array variable refers to the modified array.

Note For more information about passing values by reference, see "Tips for Defining Procedures in VBA" later in this chapter.

Sorting Arrays

Sorting an array is an iterative process that requires a fairly sophisticated algorithm. An example of a common sorting algorithm, the QuickSort algorithm, appears in the QuickSortArray procedure in the modArrays module in VBA.mdb in the Samples\CH07 subfolder on the companion CD-ROM.

A full explanation of the QuickSort algorithm is beyond the scope of this book. The QuickSort algorithm is explained in thorough detail in the *Visual Basic Language Developer's Handbook* by Ken Getz and Mike Gilbert (Sybex, 1999)—a good place to start if you're looking for more information about sorting arrays.

In brief, the QuickSort algorithm works by using a divide-and-sort strategy. It first finds the middle element in the array, then works its way from the rightmost element to the middle, and from the leftmost element to the middle, comparing elements on both sides of the middle value and swapping their values if necessary. Once this part of the sort is complete, the values on the right side are all greater than those on the left, but they're not necessarily in order. The procedure then looks at the values on the left side by using the same strategy—finding a middle value and swapping elements on both sides. It does this until all the elements on the left side have been sorted, and then it tackles the right side. The procedure calls itself recursively and continues executing until the entire array has been sorted.

Searching an Array

When you need to determine whether a particular item exists in an array, how do you do it? You can loop through the array, checking each element, until you find what you need. However, this method, though obvious, is inefficient. The following sections present alternative ways to search an array.

Using the Filter Function to Search String Arrays

The **Filter** function, described earlier in this chapter in "Working with Strings as Arrays," makes it easy to search a string array if you simply need to know whether an item exists in the array. The **Filter** function takes a string array and a string containing the search text. It returns a one-dimensional array containing all the elements that match the search text.

One potential disadvantage of using the **Filter** function to search an array is that it doesn't return the index of the elements of the array that match the search text. In other words, the **Filter** function tells you whether an element exists in an array, but it doesn't tell you where.

Another potential problem with using the **Filter** function to search an array is that there's no way to specify whether the search text should match the entire element, or whether it need only match a part of it. For example, if you use the **Filter** function to search for an element matching the letter "e," the **Filter** function returns not only those elements containing only "e," but also any elements containing larger words that include "e."

The following procedure augments the capabilities of the **Filter** function in order to search an array and returns only elements that match exactly. The FilterExactMatch procedure takes two arguments: a string array to search and a string to find. It uses the **Filter** function to return an array containing all elements that match the search string, either partially or entirely. It then checks each element in the filtered array to verify that it matches the search string exactly. If the element does match exactly, it's copied to a third string array. The function returns this third array, which contains only exact matches.

```
Function FilterExactMatch(astrItems() As String, _
                          strSearch As String) As String()

   ' This function searches a string array for elements
   ' that exactly match the search string.

   Dim astrFilter()  As String
   Dim astrTemp()    As String
   Dim lngUpper      As Long
   Dim lngLower      As Long
   Dim lngIndex      As Long
   Dim lngCount      As Long

   ' Filter array for search string.
   astrFilter = Filter(astrItems, strSearch)

   ' Store upper and lower bounds of resulting array.
   lngUpper = UBound(astrFilter)
   lngLower = LBound(astrFilter)

   ' Resize temporary array to be same size.
   ReDim astrTemp(lngLower To lngUpper)

   ' Loop through each element in filtered array.
   For lngIndex = lngLower To lngUpper
      ' Check that element matches search string exactly.
      If astrFilter(lngIndex) = strSearch Then
         ' Store elements that match exactly in another array.
         astrTemp(lngCount) = strSearch
         lngCount = lngCount + 1
      End If
   Next lngIndex

   ' Resize array containing exact matches.
   ReDim Preserve astrTemp(lngLower To lngCount - 1)

   ' Return array containing exact matches.
   FilterExactMatch = astrTemp
End Function
```

This procedure is available in the modArrays module in VBA.mdb in the Samples\CH07 subfolder on the companion CD-ROM.

Using a Binary Search Function to Search Numeric Arrays

The **Filter** function works well for searching string arrays, but it's inefficient for numeric arrays. To use the **Filter** function for a numeric array, you have to convert all of the numeric elements to strings, an extra step that impairs performance. Then you must perform string-comparison operations, when numeric comparisons are much faster.

Although it's more involved, the binary-search algorithm performs efficient searching on a sorted array—whether numeric or string. The binary-search algorithm divides a set of values in half, and determines whether the value being sought lies in the first half or the second half. Whichever half contains the value is kept, and the other half is discarded. The remaining half is then again divided in half, and the process repeats until it either arrives at the sought value, or determines that it's not in the set. Note that the array must be sorted in order for this algorithm to work.

A detailed discussion of the binary-search algorithm is beyond the scope of this book. However, an example appears in the BinarySearch procedure in the modArrays module in VBA.mdb in the Samples\CH07 subfolder on the companion CD-ROM. For an in-depth discussion of the binary-search algorithm, see the *Visual Basic Language Developer's Handbook* by Ken Getz and Mike Gilbert (Sybex, 1999).

Searching a Dictionary

Strictly speaking, a **Dictionary** object is not an array, but it's similar. Both are data structures that can store multiple values. The **Dictionary** object has certain advantages over an array: you can use object programming constructs such as **For Each...Next** and **With...End With** statements to work with it, and you don't have to worry about sizing it, as you do an array.

If you use a **Dictionary** object instead of an array to store a set of data, you can quickly check whether a particular item exists in the dictionary by calling the **Exists** method of the **Dictionary** object and passing it the key for the item you want. However, the **Exists** method doesn't provide any information regarding where the item is within the dictionary or how many times it occurs.

An advantage of using the **Exists** method with a **Dictionary** object, rather than using the **Filter** function with an array, is that the **Exists** method returns a **Boolean** value, while the **Filter** function returns another array. If you don't need to know how many times the search item occurs, using the **Dictionary** object may simplify your code.

Tips for Defining Procedures in VBA

When you're defining a **Function** or **Sub** procedure, you have options available to you that can make your code more extensible or more flexible. The following sections discuss how to extend your procedures by using optional arguments, using parameter arrays to pass a variable number of arguments, and passing arguments by value and by reference.

Using Optional Arguments

Optional arguments are arguments that aren't required in order for a procedure to be compiled and run. Many built-in functions and methods take optional arguments. Adding optional arguments to user-defined procedures is an easy way to add functionality without updating all the code that calls those procedures. In addition, if you declare arguments that aren't always needed as optional, you can minimize resource use by passing only those arguments that are necessary for a given procedure call.

To define an optional argument in a user-defined procedure, use the **Optional** keyword. You can have as many optional arguments as you want, but once you denote one argument as optional, any arguments that follow it in the argument list must also be optional, as shown in this procedure definition:

```
Function SomeProc(strRequired1 As String, _
                  strRequired2 As String, _
                  Optional lngOpt1 As Long, _
                  Optional blnOpt2 As Boolean)
```

Within the body of the procedure, you need a way to check whether the optional argument was passed in. In many cases, if an optional argument hasn't been passed in, you may want it to have a default value. If the calling procedure doesn't provide a value for an optional argument, the optional argument is automatically initialized in the same way it would be if it were a variable—string arguments are initialized to a zero-length string, numeric arguments to zero (0), **Boolean** arguments to **False**, and so on.

You can override this default initialization by providing a different default value for the optional argument in the procedure definition. The value you provide becomes the default value when the calling procedure fails to pass a value for the optional argument. The following procedure definition sets the default value for an argument of type **Long** to 1, and for an argument of type **Boolean** to **True**:

```
Function SomeProc(strRequired1 As String, _
                  strRequired2 As String, _
                  Optional lngOpt1 As Long=1, _
                  Optional blnOpt2 As Boolean=True)
```

As you can see, an argument of any data type but **Variant** will always have a value, and it may not be possible to determine within the procedure whether the value was passed in or whether it's the default value. If you need to know whether the argument was passed in, define the optional argument as type **Variant**. Then, use the **IsMissing** function within the procedure to determine whether the argument has been passed in, as shown in the following procedure:

```
Sub TestIsMissing(varTest As Variant)
   If IsMissing(varTest) Then
      Debug.Print "Missing"
   Else
      Debug.Print varTest
   End If
End Sub
```

The **IsMissing** function works only with the **Variant** data type; since any other data type will always have a default initialization value, the **IsMissing** function will return **False** regardless of whether a value has been passed for the argument.

Using Parameter Arrays

You can pass an array of arguments to a procedure by using a parameter array. The advantage to using a parameter array is that you don't need to know at design time how many arguments will be passed to a procedure—you can pass a variable number of arguments when you call it.

To define a parameter array, use the **ParamArray** keyword followed by an array of type **Variant**, as shown in the following procedure definition:

```
Function SomeProc(ParamArray avarItems() As Variant)
```

A parameter array must always be an array of type **Variant**, and it must always be the last argument in the argument list.

To call a procedure that includes a parameter array, pass in a set of any number of arguments, as shown here:

```
? SomeProc("red", "yellow", "blue", "green", "orange")
```

Within the body of the procedure, you can work with the parameter array as you would with any other array.

For an example of a procedure that takes a parameter array, see the Median procedure in "Performing Calculations on Numeric Arrays" earlier in this chapter.

Passing Arguments by Value or by Reference

When you define a procedure, you have two choices regarding how arguments are passed to it: by reference or by value. When a variable is passed to a procedure by reference, VBA actually passes the variable's address in memory to the procedure, which can then modify it directly. When execution returns to the calling procedure, the variable contains the modified value.

When an argument is passed by value, VBA passes a copy of the variable to the procedure. The procedure then modifies the copy, and the original value of the variable remains intact; when execution returns to the calling procedure, the variable contains the same value that it had before being passed.

By default, VBA passes arguments by reference. To pass an argument by value, precede the argument with the **ByVal** keyword in the procedure definition, as shown here:

```
Function SomeProc(strText As String, _
                  ByVal lngX As Long) As Boolean
```

If you want to explicitly denote that an argument is passed by reference, you can preface the argument with the **ByRef** keyword in the argument list. It's not necessary to use the **ByRef** keyword since passing by reference is VBA's default behavior.

Passing by reference can be useful as long as you understand how it works. For example, you must pass arrays by reference; you'll get a syntax error if you try to pass an array by value. Because arrays are passed by reference, you can pass an array to another procedure to be modified, and then continue working with the modified array in the calling procedure.

You can see how this works by running the TestQuickSort procedure, available in the modArrays module in VBA.mdb in the Samples\CH07 subfolder on the companion CD-ROM. TestQuickSort calls the QuickSortArray procedure in the same module. Even if you don't completely understand how the QuickSortArray procedure works, you can see that it takes an array (or a **Variant** variable containing an array) as an argument, and that it's a **Sub** procedure, so it doesn't return a value. When you pass an array to the QuickSortArray procedure, it receives the memory location for the array and sorts the array. Once it's finished, TestQuickSort can continue working with the sorted array.

The danger in passing by reference lies in the fact that you may unwittingly allow another procedure to modify a value that you have passed it. To prevent this from happening, either pass the argument by value or use a temporary variable to store an argument, and then modify the temporary variable.

For the most part, VBA programmers pass arguments by value when calling functions in the Windows API; many API calls require that an argument be passed by value. For more information about calling the Windows API, see Chapter 10, "The Windows API and Other Dynamic-Link Libraries." For more information about passing by value and by reference, see the *Visual Basic Language Developer's Handbook* by Ken Getz and Mike Gilbert (Sybex, 1999).

Optimizing VBA Code

The following sections contain some tips for optimizing your VBA code. These are only a few of the many optimizations you can make; for more ideas, see the resources listed in "Where to Go from Here" at the end of this chapter.

Declaring Variables

The following points provide suggestions for ways to streamline your memory requirements and speed up performance when you are using variables:

- To conserve memory resources, always declare all your variables with specific data types. When you declare a variable without a specific data type, VBA creates a variable of type **Variant**, which requires more memory than any of the other data types.
- Be aware of how much memory each data type requires and what range of values it can store. Always use a smaller data type if possible, except in the case where using a smaller data type will force an implicit conversion. For example, since variables of type **Integer** are converted to variables of type **Long**, it makes sense to declare variables that will store integer values as type **Long** instead of as type **Integer**.
- Avoid using floating-point data types unless you really need them. Even though it's larger, the **Currency** data type is faster than the **Single** data type because the **Currency** data type doesn't use the floating-point processor.
- If you refer to an object more than once within a procedure, create an object variable and assign to it a reference to the object. Because the object variable stores the object's location in memory, VBA won't have to look up the location again.
- Declare object variables as specific types rather than as type **Object** so that you can take advantage of early binding.

Mathematical Operations

The following points provide suggestions for ways to speed up operations on numbers:

- When performing division on integers, use the integer division operator (\) rather than the floating-point division operator (/), which always returns a value of type **Double** regardless of the types of the numbers being divided.

- Keep in mind that any time you use a **Single** or **Double** value in an arithmetic expression with integer values, the integers are converted to **Single** or **Double** values, and the final result is a **Single** or **Double** value. If you're performing several operations on a number that is the result of an arithmetic operation, you may want to explicitly convert the number to a smaller data type.

String Operations

The following points provide suggestions for ways to enhance the performance of string operations:

- Minimize concatenation operations when you can. You can use the **Mid** function on the left side of the equal sign to replace characters within the string, rather than concatenating them together. The drawback to using the **Mid** function is that the replacement string must be the same length as the substring you are replacing.

```
Dim strText As String

strText = "this is a test"
Mid(strText, 11, 4) = "tent"
Debug.Print strText
```

- VBA provides a number of intrinsic string constants that you can use to replace function calls. For example, you can use the **vbCrLf** constant to represent a carriage return/linefeed combination within a string, rather than using `Chr(13) & Chr(10)`.
- String-comparison operations are slow. You can sometimes avoid them by converting a character in the string to an ANSI value. For example, this code checks whether the first character in a string is a space:

```
If Asc(strText) = 32 Then
```

  The previous code is faster than the following:

```
If Left(strText, 1) = " " Then
```

Loops

The following points provide suggestions for ways to save resources when you are executing loops:

- Analyze your loops to see whether you are needlessly repeating memory-intensive operations. For example, are there any variables that you can set outside the loop, rather than within it? Are you performing a conversion procedure each time through the loop that could be done outside the loop?

- Consider whether you need to loop only until a certain condition is met. If so, you may be able to exit the loop early. For example, suppose you are performing data validation on a string that should not contain numeric characters. If you have a loop that checks each character in a string to determine whether the string contains any numeric characters, you can exit the loop as soon as you find the first numeric character.
- If you need to refer to an element of an array within a loop, create a temporary variable that stores the element's value rather than referring to it within the array. Retrieving values from an array is slower than reading a variable of the same type.

Where to Go from Here

For additional information about the subjects discussed in this chapter, see the following resources. If a file name is listed, that file is located in the Appendixes folder on the companion CD-ROM, unless otherwise noted.

Working with VBA

Getz, Ken, and Mike Gilbert. *Visual Basic Language Developer's Handbook.* Alameda, CA: Sybex, 1999.

Useful VBA Sample Code

For samples and how-to articles that may provide interesting code, search the Visual Basic for Applications section of the Microsoft Knowledge Base for "VBA." The Knowledge Base is available at http://support.microsoft.com/support.

Optimizing VBA Code

Balena, Francesco. "88 Optimization Tips." *Visual Basic Programmer's Journal* 7, no. 14 (December 1997): 28–41.

Working with Class Modules

Chapter 9, "Custom Classes and Objects"

Working with VBScript

Microsoft Scripting Technologies Web site (http://msdn.microsoft.com/scripting/default.htm)

Calling the Windows API

Chapter 10, "The Windows API and Other Dynamic-Link Libraries"

Creating and Using Add-ins

Chapter 11, "Add-ins, Templates, Wizards, and Libraries"

Preparing Your Code for the Year 2000

Microsoft Year 2000 Resource Center Web site
(http://www.microsoft.com/technet/topics/year2k/default.htm)

Code Samples

The code samples shown in this chapter, along with additional examples demonstrating similar techniques, can be copied from the files in the Samples\CH07 subfolder on the companion CD-ROM.

CHAPTER 8

Error Handling and Debugging

All code contains errors of one kind or another and how you deal with errors may be the most important part of a well-designed application. There are two categories of errors: those you can prevent, which are called development errors, and those you can't prevent but can trap, which are called run-time errors.

Development errors are either syntax errors or logic errors. Syntax errors occur from typographical errors, missing punctuation, or improper use of a language element; for example, forgetting to properly terminate an **If...Then...Else** statement. Logic errors are more commonly referred to as "bugs." These errors occur when code executes without causing an error, but does not produce the results intended. You eliminate development errors by "debugging" your code. There are a wide variety of tools that can help you debug script and Visual Basic for Applications (VBA) code.

Run-time errors are errors that occur while the application is running. These are errors where otherwise correct code fails due to invalid data or system conditions that prevent the code from executing (for example, lack of available memory or disk space). You handle run-time errors by writing error handlers and by writing procedures that can validate program or environmental conditions in appropriate circumstances.

Successfully debugging code is more of an art than a science. The best results come from writing understandable and maintainable code and using the available debugging tools. When it comes to successful debugging, there is no substitute for patience, diligence, and a willingness to test relentlessly, using all the tools at your disposal.

Writing good error handlers is a matter of anticipating problems or conditions that are beyond your immediate control and that will prevent your code from executing correctly at run time. Writing a good error handler should be an integral part of the planning and design of a good procedure. It requires a thorough understanding of how the procedure works and how the procedure fits into the overall application. And, of course, writing good procedures is an essential part of building solid Microsoft Office solutions.

Contents

Writing Error-Free Code

When you write VBA code, or script in an HTML page, it is not a question of "if" the code will contain errors but "when" those errors will be introduced and how many there will be. No matter how careful you are or how much experience you have, errors will occur. There are some things you can do to make sure errors are kept to a minimum.

The best way to reduce errors and minimize the amount of debugging you'll need to do is to follow the guidelines discussed in Chapter 3, "Writing Solid Code." If you have written maintainable code, you have also written code that is going to be much easier to debug.

Make sure that you use the **Option Explicit** statement in every module. The **Option Explicit** statement forces you to declare all variables before you use them in code. This simple step eliminates undeclared variables, which cause some of the most common, and often difficult to detect, errors in code. When you are writing Microsoft Visual Basic Scripting Edition (VBScript) code, insert `Option Explicit` as the first line after the first <SCRIPT> tag on the HTML page.

Avoid using the **Variant** data type unless you are declaring a variable and you truly do not know what kind of data it may contain at run time. Variants are slow, they take up a lot of memory, and using them when not absolutely necessary can create hard-to-find bugs in your code.

Always declare variables as a group at the beginning of each procedure and always declare each variable on a separate line. This will prevent you from inadvertently declaring a **Variant** variable. For example, the following line creates two **Variant** variables and one **String** variable, which is not what the developer intended:

```
Dim strFirstName, strLastName, strCompanyName As String
```

When you are creating VBA object variables, explicitly reference the object the variable represents rather than declaring the variable by using a **Variant** or **Object** data type. For example:

```
Dim xlSheet        As Excel.Worksheet
Dim cboUserNames   As ComboBox
```

When you are creating procedures that accept arguments that must fall within a specified range of data, validate the data before using it in the procedure. If an argument uses a value that represents a built-in enumerated constant, you won't have to validate the argument if you declare its data type by using the name of the enumerated constant class. If a procedure uses optional arguments, make sure that you supply the default value for each argument and make sure that the data supplied falls within the desired range. For example, the following procedure shows how to validate the data in an argument. If the data is invalid, the **Raise** method of the **Err** object is used to pass error information back to the calling procedure.

```
Function ErrorExample3(strTextToCheck As String) As Boolean

   ' This procedure illustrates using the Err.Raise method
   ' along with the vbObjectError constant to define and
   ' raise a custom error and return that error to the
   ' calling procedure. The CUSTOM_ERROR constant is defined
   ' in the Declarations section of the module by using the
   ' vbObjectError constant.

   Dim strTemp              As String
   Const CUSTOM_ERR_DESC    As String = "The argument passed to " & "ErrorExample3" _
                               & " is invalid - a zero-length string is not" _
                               & " permitted."

   If Len(strTextToCheck) = 0 Then
      Err.Raise CUSTOM_ERROR, "ErrorExample3", CUSTOM_ERR_DESC
      ErrorExample3 = False
   Else
      ' Continue processing successful case here.
      ErrorExample3 = True
      strTextToCheck = "This procedure executed successfully!"
   End If
End Function
```

The ErrorExample3 procedure is available in the modErrorCode module in ErrorHandlers.dot in the Samples\CH08 subfolder on the companion CD-ROM.

Note When debugging, you can also use the **Assert** method of the **Debug** object to test the validity of the supplied data. For more information about using the **Assert** method, see "Using Assertions" later in this chapter.

Test each procedure as soon as it is written to make sure that it does what it is supposed to do and, if necessary, validates data submitted in arguments. If your application uses data supplied by the user, make sure you test for unexpected input values. For example, if you expect a user to enter a numeric value in a text box control, what happens if the user enters text in that control instead?

Make sure you know that your code actually works. When an error occurs in a procedure, you know that your code does not work given the input data that caused the error. But it does not follow that if an error does not occur, you are safe to assume that your code does work. While debugging your code, use assertions to test for conditions that should exist at specific points in your code. For example, you can use assertions to test the validity of inputs to procedures. For more information about assertions, see "Using Assertions" later in this chapter.

When you locate a problem in your code, make sure you understand its nature and extent (errors in code are not always what they appear to be) and then fix it immediately. Avoid flagging errors or questionable code with the intent to come back and fix them later. You may never get back to it and what needs to be done will never be clearer in your mind than when you are creating the procedure.

When you do make a change to your code, use a comment to document the change. Consider commenting out old code but leaving it in a procedure until you're certain the new code works correctly.

Be aware that changing code in one place can introduce additional bugs somewhere else. When debugging code, never make more than one change to a procedure without retesting it and all related procedures after each change.

Debugging Code

VBA provides several debugging tools that help analyze how code operates and help locate errors in your code. There is no magic to properly debugging your code and no correct series of steps that always leads to the discovery of errors. Instead, there are some very powerful tools that let you closely examine what is happening in your code so that you can figure out where and when things are going wrong.

This section covers some of the tools you will use repeatedly when debugging your code. You may need to know exactly where an error occurs in a series of nested procedure calls or when a variable is being changed from one value to another. The tool that works best will depend on what you are trying to accomplish.

For more information about debugging VBA code in general, search the Visual Basic for Applications Reference Help index for "debugging" and "debugging code."

VBA Debugging Tools

VBA and the Visual Basic Editor contain many tools you can use to help debug your code. Some of the tools are available when you are actually writing your code; these are known as design-time tools. Other tools are used when your code is running; these are known as run-time tools, and they let you break into, examine, and step through running code to determine what is happening. Experienced Office developers use all of these tools at one time or another in the development process.

This section presents a brief overview of the available tools. For more information about any of the specific debugging tools, search the Visual Basic for Applications Reference Help index for the name of the tool.

Design-Time Tools

The Visual Basic Editor has several features that can help you debug your code. You specify whether these features are turned on by clicking **Options** on the **Tools** menu, clicking the **Editor** tab, and then selecting the features you want under **Code Settings**. Turning on all these settings can make it easier to debug code. The **Require Variable Declaration** option is probably the most important because, when it is selected, the **Option Explicit** statement is inserted in the first line of any module you create, including those for forms, reports, and Office documents. The **Option Explicit** statement forces you to declare every variable you use and prevents one of the most common sources of hard-to-find bugs: misspelled variable names.

The **Auto Syntax Check** option specifies whether the Visual Basic Editor will check each line of code for errors as soon as you have finished writing the code. If this option is not selected, the Visual Basic Editor will still check the syntax of all your code before you can compile or run it.

The **Auto Data Tips** option specifies whether you can view the data contained in a variable while in break mode by resting the mouse pointer on the variable name.

The **Options** dialog box contains another important set of options that can make debugging easier. On the **General** tab, there is an **Error Trapping** section where you can specify what will happen when an error occurs in your code.

You will want to select different options in the **Error Trapping** section depending on where you are in the debugging process. The default setting is **Break on Unhandled Errors**. This setting makes it easier to debug error handlers because you can step through the code as it enters the error handler in all circumstances.

Most of the time you will want to select the **Break on Unhandled Errors** option. However, when you are debugging code in class modules, you will want to select the **Break in Class Module** option so that you can identify the offending line of code in the class module. Otherwise, an error in a class module will cause code to break in the procedure that called the class module rather in the class module itself. If your application has no class modules, selecting **Break in Class Module** has the same effect as selecting **Break on Unhandled Errors**.

For more information about the options available in the **Options** dialog box, click the tab that contains the option you are interested in, and then click the **Help** button.

Viewing Code After Errors in Microsoft Access

In previous versions of Access you could prevent users from entering break mode when errors occurred by clearing the **Allow Viewing Code After Error** check box in the **Startup** dialog box (**Tools** menu). This setting did not actually secure code modules, but the option to view code was disabled when errors were encountered so that code can't be viewed easily. Because of changes in how VBA is integrated into Access 2000, the option to view code when errors are encountered is no longer available. However, you can prevent all unauthorized users from viewing your code under any circumstances by locking your application's VBA project. For more information about locking a VBA project, see "Protecting Your Solution's VBA Code" in Chapter 17, "Securing Office Documents and Visual Basic for Applications Code."

Run-Time Tools

The VBA run-time debugging tools are designed to give you a snapshot of what is happening in your code at any point. You use these tools together to let you take a closer look at what your code is doing at any point in time. The following table contains a list of all the tools available to you and a short description of when they are useful.

Tool	Description
Breakpoints	Breakpoints let you stop program execution on any line of executable code. Once execution has stopped, you can use one or more of the other available tools to investigate your code. A breakpoint will stop your code on the line of code that will be executed next. Once your code encounters a breakpoint, it is in break mode and remains in break mode until you press F5 to continue execution.
Step modes	You can use the four step modes to start execution of a subroutine or to continue execution after it has stopped at a breakpoint. The four available modes are Step Into, Step Over, Step Out, and Run To Cursor. Using any of these modes to step through code does not take the code out of break mode.

Tool	Description
Locals window	This extremely powerful and often overlooked tool provides a snapshot view of the values of all variables, constants, objects, and properties of objects currently in scope when code is in break mode.
Watch expressions	Watch expressions let you monitor the value of any variable, property, object, or expression as your code executes. They also let you specify that your code should enter break mode upon some condition; for example, if an expression is true or if the value of a variable changes. If you don't need to continually monitor a value, you can use the **Quick Watch** dialog box to quickly check the value of a variable or expression.
Immediate window	This window is an extremely versatile tool that you should be using constantly to debug and test your code. All **Debug.Print** statements are output to the Immediate window. When your code is in break mode, the Immediate window has the same scope as the procedure in which the breakpoint is located. This allows you to test and change the value of variables. You can also use the Immediate window to call procedures and test them by using different data without having to run your application from the beginning.
Call stack	This stack contains a list of all active procedures when code is in break mode. This list can help you trace the execution of your code and highlight the possible location of errors in currently active procedures.

For more information about any of the debugging tools, search the Visual Basic for Applications Reference Help index for the name of the specific tool.

Script Debugging Tools

The Microsoft Script Debugger provides a comprehensive debugging environment for working with both client- and server-side script in HTML pages and Active Server pages (ASP). The Script Debugger works with VBScript and Microsoft JScript. It provides all of the debugging tools described in the previous section, with the exception of watch expressions. However, you cannot use the **Print** method of the **Debug** object to output information to the Script Debugger's Immediate window.

The Microsoft Script Debugger and its supporting documentation are available from the Microsoft Scripting Technologies Web site at http://msdn.microsoft.com/scripting/.

You can debug the script you add to an Office document by using the debugging capabilities of the Microsoft Script Editor. For more information about using the Script Editor to work with the HTML code and script in an Office document, see Chapter 12, "Using Web Technologies." For information about using the Script Editor with data access pages, see Chapter 5, "Working with Office Applications."

To enable script debugging in the Script Editor, click **Options** on the **Tools** menu, and then click **Debugger** in the hierarchical view of options. Select the **Just-In-Time debugger** and **Attach to programs running on this machine** check boxes. Once these options have been selected, errors in script will generate a message box that gives you the option of opening the Script Editor's debugger.

You can use the Script Editor to set breakpoints in your script. These breakpoints work just like they do when you are debugging VBA code in the Visual Basic Editor. The Script Editor also has the following debugging windows that you can use to work with script: Immediate, Locals, Watch, Threads, and Call Stack. These windows give you views into your running script in the same way that they let you debug VBA code when they are used in the Visual Basic Editor. There is one difference you need to be aware of however. In the Script Editor, the script debugger is not as tightly integrated with the host application as the VBA debugger is in Office applications. This means that the Immediate and Watch windows in the Script Editor are not active unless your script is stopped at a breakpoint. In other words, you can't set up a Watch variable in the Script Editor and watch its value change as your script executes.

You should remember to close the script debugger each time you are finished debugging or each time you return to running your script. This is because each time you open the debugger, a new instance of the Script Editor is created. If you don't close these instances, you can end up with a lot of open windows on your desktop. To avoid opening and closing the script debugger, you can create a debug log file to record errors that occur on a page while a script is running. You can also open a separate window to display the logged error information. To see an example of script that displays error information in a separate window as script is running, see the LogScriptErrors.htm file in the Samples\CH08 subfolder on the companion CD-ROM.

Additional Debugging Techniques

The techniques discussed here can be used in conjunction with the tools discussed in the previous section to give you an even more powerful arsenal for finding and fixing errors in your code.

Understanding Conditional Compilation

You can use conditional compilation to selectively include blocks of debugging code by testing for the value of a conditional compilation constant. If the constant is **True**, the debugging code is included. To do this, you specify a conditional compilation constant by using the **#Const** directive. You then test for the value of this constant within a procedure by using the **#If...Then...#Else** directive within a procedure. For example, the following procedure uses the value of the FLAG_DEBUG conditional compilation constant to determine if the conditional constant is set to **True**. If the constant is set to **True**, the **Assert** method of the **Debug** object is used to test the validity of the procedure's input parameters. For example:

```
Sub OutputString(strMessage As String, _
                 Optional intOutputType As Integer = 0)

   Dim intFileNum As Integer

   #If FLAG_DEBUG = True Then
      ' Test validity of strMessage.
      Debug.Assert Len(strMessage) > 0
```

```
        ' Test validity of intOutputType.
        Debug.Assert intOutputType >= 0 and intOutputType <= 3
        Stop
    #End If

    Select Case intOutputType
        Case 0
    .
    .
    .
End Sub
```

The OutputString procedure is available in the modErrorCode module in ErrorHandlers.dot in the Samples\CH08 subfolder on the companion CD-ROM.

For more information about using the **Assert** method of the **Debug** object, see the next section, "Using Assertions."

Using conditional compilation is really a shortcut for commenting out entire blocks of code depending on a global setting. Without the ability to use the constant as a flag to direct program flow, you would have to litter your code with commented-out calls to alternative procedures. If you always use conditional compilation constants to test alternative procedures, then you have an easy way to turn on and off calls to the designated procedures and an easy way to find the code that you ultimately decide to remove. The cost of using this technique is that you must give a great deal of thought to how your code is constructed and called. Although this may mean a little more work, it results in the kind of manageable, maintainable, and reusable code that is discussed in Chapter 3, "Writing Solid Code."

Using Assertions

It is easy to tell when code is broken because an error occurs. It is often harder to tell that your code is using or creating invalid data. Just because a procedure runs without generating an error does not mean that there are no bugs in that procedure.

You use assertions to test for certain conditions in your code. Using an assertion is like making a statement about some condition in your code. If the statement is true, nothing happens. If the statement is false, your code enters break mode with the line containing the false statement highlighted. Using assertions to test the validity of expressions or variables in your code is like adding custom rules to VBA itself that will cause the code to stop executing if one of the rules is violated.

The VBA **Debug** object has an **Assert** method that you can use to test the truth of a condition or statement in your code. Using the **Assert** method is similar to setting a watch expression that will break when some statement is true. If you are using the **Assert** method, the break will occur when the statement asserted is false.

Although the **Assert** method is a valuable tool for debugging and testing your code, it is not very useful in a distributed application because it forces execution to stop when an assertion is false. Eventually you will remove the **Debug.Assert** statements and replace them with error handlers. After your code has been debugged and thoroughly tested, you can remove the assertions by searching your project for **Debug.Assert** and deleting those lines from your final code. For more information about handling errors, see "Handling Errors" later in this chapter.

Creating Custom Assertions

In some circumstances you may not want to break into your code each time an assertion fails. For example, you may want to log assertion information to a file and use an error handler to handle any errors that result from the bad data. With a little bit of planning, you can create code to use while debugging that will let you handle assertions according to a flag you pass to a general routine. For example, the following procedure accepts arguments representing an assertion expression to test, the text of the assertion expression, the calling procedure's name, and a flag indicating how to display or log a failed assertion:

```
Function CustomAssertError(varExpression As Variant, _
                           strExpression As String, _
                           strCallingProc As String, _
                           Optional intOutputType As Integer = 0) As Boolean

   Dim intFileNum       As Integer
   Dim strErrorMessage  As String
   Const DEBUG_LOGFILE  As String = "c:\CustomAssertLog.txt"

   #If FLAG_DEBUG = True Then
      If varExpression = False Then
         strErrorMessage = "ASSERTION FAILURE! " & Now() & vbCrLf _
            & "The expression: " & vbCrLf & "'" & strExpression & "'" _
            & vbCrLf & "Called from: " & vbCrLf & "'" & strCallingProc _
            & "'" & vbCrLf & "failed!"

         Select Case intOutputType
            Case 0
               ' Display in message box.
               MsgBox strErrorMessage
            Case 1
               ' Write to Debug window.
               Debug.Print strErrorMessage
            Case 2
               ' Write to text file on disk.
               intFileNum = FreeFile
               Open DEBUG_LOGFILE For Append As #intFileNum
               Write #intFileNum, strErrorMessage
               Close #intFileNum
            Case Else
               Stop
         End Select
      End If
   #End If
End Function
```

To experiment with the different ways to call the CustomAssertError procedure, examine the TestCustomAssertError procedure; both of these procedures are available in the modErrorCode module in ErrorHandlers.dot in the Samples\CH08 subfolder on the companion CD-ROM.

Handling Errors

When an error occurs in a procedure that does not have error handling enabled, VBA responds by displaying an error message and terminating the application. While this behavior may be acceptable when you are writing and debugging code, it is never acceptable when your users are running your application.

A hallmark of the well-written application is its ability to anticipate and handle any error that may occur. In the best of cases, you have designed the error handler to anticipate the error and recover from it quickly and transparently to the user. No developer, no matter how diligent or experienced, will anticipate every error that can occur. In the worst case, the well-designed error handler will gracefully terminate the application and perhaps record information about the error to an error log.

You do not need an error handler in every procedure you write, and every error handler you write need not operate the same way. The key to effective error handling is knowing when to trap an error and what to do with it once you've caught it.

Whether you are handling errors in VBA or in script behind an HTML page, there are two basic tools you can use. One is the **On Error** statement, which you use to "enable" error handling in a procedure. The other is the **Err** object, which contains information about an error that has already occurred.

When a run-time error occurs, your error handler may be able to fix the error directly or give the user a chance to fix the error. If your error handler is unable to fix the error so that the code can continue to execute, it should allow the program to fail gracefully.

Once execution has passed to the error-handling routine, your code must determine which error has occurred and either fix the error or raise the error back to the calling procedure. If an error occurs within an error handler, VBA will handle the error (because error handling is no longer enabled), unless you call another procedure to handle such errors. You may consider writing a generic error-handling routine that can be used to handle errors generated within error handlers. VBA can have only one error handler active at a time in any procedure, but it can have more than one error handler active within the current procedure stack.

Basic Error Handling

Effective error-handling code can be quite simple or very sophisticated. It can create an error trap or handle errors in-line. It may display a message to the user or log information about the error to a file. But no matter how an error handler is implemented, the basic components of every error handler are the same. An error handler consists of code that does all of the following:

- Specifies what to do if an error occurs
- Handles the error that has occurred
- Specifies how program execution is to continue

The **On Error** statement is used to specify the first component. The **Resume** statement is used to specify the third component. The second component represents the code you write to handle any errors that occur.

The basic format for how an error trap is included in a procedure is as follows (the use of italics indicates the location of placeholders for elements you would specify in a real procedure):

```
Function ProcedureName(ArgumentList) As DataType
   ' Procedure comments.
   ' Declare local variables and constants.

   On Error GoTo ProcedureName_Err
   ' Procedure code.
   .
   .
   .
   ProcedureName = True (or some other return value)
ProcedureName_End:
   ' Cleanup code that closes open files and sets object variables = Nothing.
   Exit Function
ProcedureName_Err:
   ProcedureName = False
   Select Case Err.Number
      Case AnticipatedError#1
         ' Handle error #1.
      Case AnticipatedError#2
         ' Handle error #2.
      Case UnAnticipatedErrors
         ' Handle unanticipated error.
      Case Else
         ' Handle unforseen circumstances.
   End Select
   Resume ProcedureName_End
End Function
```

For an example of this simple error-handling format used in a procedure that generates and then handles a series of anticipated errors, see the SimpleErrorHandler procedure available in the modErrorCode module in ErrorHandlers.dot in the Samples\CH08 subfolder on the companion CD-ROM.

Another common error-handling technique is to attempt an operation that you know will generate a specific error if some condition is not met. In this case you can use in-line error handling to attempt the operation and then test for the presence of the known error. For example, when you are using Automation to access the objects in another Office application, there are times when you will want to use an existing instance of the application. Only if there is no existing instance do you want to create a new instance. The following code fragment shows how to use in-line error handling to create a new instance of Microsoft Excel only if there is no instance currently open:

```
On Error Resume Next
Set xlApp = GetObject(, "Excel.Application")
If Err = ERR_EXCEL_NOTRUNNING Then
   Set xlApp = CreateObject("Excel.Application")
End If

On Error GoTo ProcedureName_Err
```

Note that the **On Error Resume Next** statement is used to turn on in-line error handling. A test for the anticipated error comes immediately after the code that may cause the error. (In this example, a constant was created that contained the value of the anticipated error.) Finally, the procedure's regular error trap is re-enabled to handle any additional errors.

In some cases, you know an error may occur but you don't intend to handle it at all; instead, you plan to ignore it. For example, if your application tries to delete its custom command bar when it terminates, you will want to ignore errors that occur if the user has already deleted the command bar:

```
Private Sub Workbook_BeforeClose(Cancel As Boolean)
   ' Remove the custom command bar created when
   ' this application started. Ignore any error
   ' generated if it has already been deleted.

   On Error Resume Next

   CommandBars("CustomAppCmdbar").Delete
End Sub
```

For more examples of basic error-handling techniques, see ErrorHandlers.dot in the Samples\CH08 subfolder on the companion CD-ROM.

Getting Information About an Error

You can't handle an error until you know something about it. Where you get information about an error depends on what caused it. The two main sources of information about errors are the VBA **Err** object and the ActiveX Data Objects (ADO) **Error** object. The VBA **Err** object provides information about VBA errors. The ADO **Error** object and **Errors** collection provide information about data-provider errors that occur when ADO objects are being used to access data. Errors that occur in ADO itself, as opposed to the data provider, are reported to the VBA **Err** object.

The VBA Err Object

When an error occurs, VBA uses the **Err** object to store information about that error. The **Err** object can only contain information about one error at a time. Each time an error occurs, any existing information in the **Err** object is replaced with information about the new error.

The properties of the **Err** object contain information such as the error number, description, and source. The **Err** object's **Raise** method is used to generate errors, and its **Clear** method is used to remove any existing error information.

To see a variety of examples that illustrate how to use the VBA **Err** object, use the F8 key to step through the code in the CallErrorExamples procedure, available in the modErrorCode module in ErrorHandlers.dot in the Samples\CH08 subfolder on the companion CD-ROM.

For more information about the VBA **Err** object, search the Visual Basic for Applications Reference Help index for "Err object."

The ADO Error Object and Errors Collection

Any operation involving ADO objects can generate one or more errors from the data provider. Each error resulting from an ADO operation creates an **Error** object that is added to the **Connection** object's **Errors** collection. If another ADO operation generates one or more errors, the **Errors** collection is cleared, and a new set of **Error** objects is placed in the **Errors** collection.

When an ADO error occurs, the VBA **Err** object contains the error number for the first object in the **Errors** collection. The values of the **Number** and **Description** properties of the first **Error** object in the **Errors** collection should match the values of the **Number** and **Description** properties of the VBA **Err** object.

Notes

- If there is no valid **Connection** object, the VBA **Err** object is the only source for information about ADO errors.
- Some ADO methods can also generate warnings that are returned as members of the **Errors** collection but will not affect a program's execution.

To see a variety of examples that illustrate how to use the ADO **Error** object and **Errors** collection, use the F8 key to step through the code in the ADOErrorExample1 procedure, available in the modErrorCode module in ErrorHandlers.dot in the Samples\CH08 subfolder on the companion CD-ROM.

For more information about the ADO **Error** object and **Errors** collection, search the ADO Help index for "Error object" and "Errors collection."

Returning Information About an Error

There are two ways of returning information about an error. The traditional VBA style is to raise the error in a procedure, either by leaving out an error handler so that the VBA error is returned to the calling procedure or by using the **Raise** method of the **Err** object. The other way to return error information uses the Windows application programming interface (API) style, where an error value is assigned to one of the procedure's parameters. For an example of using an API-style return value to get information about an error, see the ErrorExample2 procedure, available in the modErrorCode module in ErrorHandlers.dot in the Samples\CH08 subfolder on the companion CD-ROM.

If you use the API style of returning error information, the calling procedure must use in-line error handling to identify whether an error has occurred. If you use the traditional VBA style, the calling procedure can use either in-line error handling or an error handler. Neither way is inherently better than the other. The important point to remember is to adopt a style that works for you and to use it consistently.

Error Handling in Class Modules

You use class modules to create custom objects. When an error occurs in your class module, you do not want the error message to be raised in your class module, but rather you want to define a custom error and raise that error in the class module and send the error back to the calling procedure.

You can define custom errors by creating custom error numbers and assigning custom error descriptions. You then use the **Raise** method of the **Err** object to raise the custom error. You can use error numbers for your own errors in the range **vbObjectError** + 512 to **vbObjectError** + 65536. You can assign custom error values and associated error descriptions by using module-level constants in your class module and then use those values when raising errors to be returned to the calling procedure.

The sample code in ErrorRaise.dot in the Samples\CH08 subfolder on the companion CD-ROM contains a class module, clsMailMessage, that defines a custom object used to add a simple mail-messaging component to any Office application. Constants are used to define custom error numbers and descriptions, as shown in the following example.

```
' Custom error constants:
Private Const CUSTOM_ERR_SOURCE       As String = "clsMailMessage Object"
Private Const CUSTOM_ERR_ERRNUMBASE   As Long = vbObjectError + 512

' Invalid MailType custom errors:
Private Const CUSTOM_ERR_INVALID_MAILTYPE _
   As Long = CUSTOM_ERR_ERRNUMBASE + 1
Private Const CUSTOM_ERR_INVALID_MAILTYPE_DESC _
   As String = "MailItem Type argument must be 1 (olTo), 2 (olCC), or 3 (olBCC)."

' Unable to initialize Outlook errors:
Private Const CUSTOM_ERR_OUTLOOKINIT_FAILED _
   As Long = CUSTOM_ERR_ERRNUMBASE + 2
Private Const CUSTOM_ERR_OUTLOOKINIT_FAILED_DESC _
   As String = "Could not initialize Microsoft Outlook."

' Unable to send mail errors:
Private Const CUSTOM_ERR_SENDMAIL_FAILED _
   As Long = CUSTOM_ERR_ERRNUMBASE + 3
Private Const CUSTOM_ERR_SENDMAIL_FAILED_DESC _
   As String = "Unable to send mail message."
```

Procedures within the class module use these values as arguments to the **Raise** method of the **Err** object to raise custom errors. For example, the following procedure raises a custom error if an invalid value is passed to the procedure in the *intType* argument:

```
Public Function MailAddRecipient(strName As String, _
                                 Optional intType As Integer = olTo) As Boolean

   ' This procedure adds a recipient name and MailItem object type specifier
   ' to the p_strRecipients() array. This array is used in the CreateMail
   ' function to add recipients to the MailItem object's Recipients collection.

   Static intToCntr As Integer

   ' Validate intType argument.
   If intType > 3 Or intType < 1 Then
      ' Raise error: Type argument must be olTo (or 1),
      ' olCC (or 2), or olBCC (or 3) only.
      Err.Raise Number:=CUSTOM_ERR_INVALID_MAILTYPE, _
         Source:=CUSTOM_ERR_SOURCE, _
         Description:=CUSTOM_ERR_INVALID_MAILTYPE_DESC
      MailAddRecipient = False
      Exit Function
   End If

   ReDim Preserve p_strRecipients(1, intToCntr)

   p_strRecipients(0, intToCntr) = strName
   p_strRecipients(1, intToCntr) = intType

   intToCntr = intToCntr + 1
End Function
```

The MailAddRecipient procedure is available in the clsMailMessage module in ErrorRaise.dot in the Samples\CH08 subfolder on the companion CD-ROM.

Note You cannot use the **Raise** method to return an error to the calling procedure if you have error handling turned on in the procedure where the error occurs. If error handling is on, you need to use the **Raise** method again within the class module error handler.

Handling Script Errors

You have limited run-time error-handling options with script behind an HTML page, and the conditions that generate errors can differ depending on the scripting language you use. For example, in VBScript, dividing by zero results in a run-time error. In JScript it does not.

In VBScript you are limited to basic in-line error handling using the **On Error Resume Next** statement. You can suppress default error messages but you can't specify your own error-handling code to run when an error occurs. After you have trapped and handled an error, you use the **Clear** method of the **Err** object to clear out the error information.

In JScript you can handle errors by using the **window** object's onerror event handler. The onerror event passes three arguments to the specified error-handling function: the error message itself, the URL representing the source of the error, and a number representing the line where the error occurred.

There are also special circumstances you should keep in mind when writing script and script-error handlers.

Script in an HTML page is not interpreted until the script is executed, which occurs at the earliest when an HTML page is loaded. This means that the language interpreter will not catch any syntax errors until the page is actually loaded.

Subtle logic errors can result from the required use of **Variant** variables with different data subtypes. For example, the statement `"10" = 10` evaluates to **True**.

Script in the <HEAD> portion of the page is interpreted before script in the <BODY> portion of the page. A run-time error can occur if script in the <HEAD> portion of a page references elements within the <BODY> portion of a page and the script executes before the page is completely loaded.

Web pages consist of a number of different components that may be downloaded at different times. Because of this, you can't always be sure that an element of your page referenced in script is going to be available when the script executes. For example, if you use framesets, objects, images, linked style sheets, applets, or plug-ins, you must verify that the component is available before performing operations that depend on the component.

Handling VBScript Run-Time Errors

Although VBScript provides the **Err** object and that object exposes the same methods and properties available in the VBA **Err** object, writing error handlers using VBScript is not the same as in VBA. The primary limitation is due to the limited functionality of the **On Error** statement in VBScript. In VBScript you can't branch to an error handler by using the familiar `On Error GoTo ErrorHandler` syntax. You can only enable error handling in VBScript by using the `On Error Resume Next` syntax.

The following code excerpt shows the error-handler portion of the script in ScriptErrors.htm in the Samples\CH08 subfolder on the companion CD-ROM. The script performs simple division and then immediately checks to see if an error occurred and responds accordingly:

```
intResult = intNumerator/intDenominator

' Check for errors as a result of the division.
If Err <> 0 Then
   Select Case Err.Number
      Case DIVIDE_BY_ZERO
         If Len(txtDenominator.Value) = 0 Then
            strErrorResultText = "Missing!"
         Else
            strErrorResultText = "'" & txtDenominator.Value & "'"
         End If
         strErrorMessage = "Error: " & Err.Number & _
            vbCrLf & vbCrLf & "The value you entered in the " _
            & "text box was: " & strErrorResultText
         txtDenominator.Focus
      Case Else
         strErrorMessage = "Error: " & Err.Number & _
            vbCrLf & vbCrLf & "Unrecognized error!"
   End Select
   MsgBox strErrorMessage, CRITICAL_ERROR + MSGBOX_OKONLY, _
      "Error Type = " & Err.Description
End If
```

Handling JScript Run-Time Errors

In JScript, you can use the **window** object's onerror event to trap an error and respond accordingly. The onerror event is triggered when an error occurs anywhere on an HTML page. The onerror event passes three arguments to the function specified by the `window.onerror =` *`functionname`*`;` line. The arguments are the error message itself, the URL representing the source of the error, and a number representing the line where the error occurred. For example:

```
<SCRIPT LANGUAGE = "JavaScript">
   function BadFunction(){
      This.badcode.willnot.work = 1000
   }

   function ForceError(msg, url, lno) {
      alert("Error Occurred! Handled by Generic Error Handler" + "\n" +
         "Error: " + msg + "\n" + "URL: " + url + "\n" +
         "Line Number: " + lno);

      return true;
   }

   window.onerror = ForceError;
</SCRIPT>
```

Note how returning **True** in the error-handler procedure forces the default message box not to appear. To see the entire sample, see JScriptErrors.htm in the Samples\CH08 subfolder on the companion CD-ROM.

For more information about scripting HTML and ASP pages by using VBScript or JScript, see the Microsoft Scripting Technologies Web site at http://msdn.microsoft.com/scripting/.

Logging Errors

Logging errors is the process of recording information about an error. You can use error-logging techniques to help debug your application. And even though you hope that most bugs are removed from your code before you deploy your application to your users, you may consider using error-logging techniques in "finished" applications as well.

One powerful option to consider is to create your own error-logging object class that you can use in any application by simply adding the class module that contains the error-logging code to your project. For more information about creating custom objects, see Chapter 9, "Custom Classes and Objects."

The sample code in the modErrorCode module in ErrorHandlers.dot in the Samples\CH08 subfolder on the companion CD-ROM illustrates several techniques for displaying and logging errors.

The ADOErrorExample1 procedure contains several lines of code that generate errors. When an error occurs in this procedure, the error handler calls the HandleErrorMessage procedure and passes the ADO **Errors** collection, the VBA **Err** object, and an integer specifying how the error information is to be recorded. The procedure can record errors by using a message box, the Debug window, a text file, or a database.

The HandleErrorMessage procedure is not necessarily the best way to handle error logging in your own applications, but rather is presented to illustrate the variety of techniques you can use.

One of the most interesting aspects of the HandleErrorMessage procedure is how it handles multiple errors passed to it in the ADO **Errors** collection. The techniques illustrated in the HandleErrorMessage procedure show how to retrieve all the error information from all the **Error** objects in the collection as well as information contained in the VBA **Err** object for the same error.

Where to Go from Here

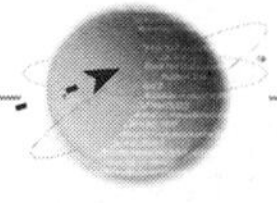

For additional information about the subjects discussed in this chapter, see the following resources.

Debugging VBA Code

Maguire, Steve. *Writing Solid Code.* Redmond, WA: Microsoft Press, 1993.

McConnell, Steve. *Code Complete*. Redmond, WA: Microsoft Press, 1993.

Chapter 3, "Writing Solid Code"

Debugging and Error Handling in Script

Microsoft Scripting Technologies Web site (http://msdn.microsoft.com/scripting/)

Error Handling and the Windows Installer

Chapter 2, "Designing and Deploying Office Solutions"

Chapter 4, "Understanding Office Objects and Object Models"

Code Samples

The code samples shown in this chapter, along with additional examples demonstrating similar techniques, can be copied from the files in the Samples\CH08 subfolder on the companion CD-ROM.

CHAPTER 9

Custom Classes and Objects

Are you ready to take your Visual Basic for Applications (VBA) programming skills to a new level? If you've never used class modules to build custom objects before, this chapter covers the concepts that you need to understand to design, build, and use custom objects with their own methods and properties. If you've been building your own objects for some time now, this chapter also covers some exciting new additions to the VBA language in Microsoft Office 2000: the ability to add custom events to your objects, and the ability to extend your objects by implementing interfaces. In addition to describing how to use VBA to build custom objects, this chapter provides an introduction to the basics of using script to create reusable custom objects for Web pages.

Contents

Why Build Your Own Objects?

If you have any experience with programming in VBA, you probably have heard that you can use class modules to create custom objects, with their own methods, properties, and events. If you're like many VBA programmers, you also may be wondering why you would ever want to, when you've been getting along just fine without custom objects.

In and of themselves, custom objects don't add new functionality to your code. There's nearly always another way to arrive at the same result that doesn't involve creating objects. What they can do is make complex operations appear simpler, sophisticated solutions more self-documenting and maintainable, and procedures that required hours of coding time more reusable, both for yourself and for other programmers. In fact, creating a custom object is an ideal way to package your code for other VBA programmers to use, because rather than figuring out how to call your code, they can work with your custom object much as they would with any built-in object.

As an analogy, think of a car. It's made up of complex mechanical systems working together to get you where you're going. Although there are those who like to tinker under the hood, most people don't want to think about how the car works. They're content to press on the gas pedal, without considering the fuel lines, filters, fuel-injection system, cylinders, and pistons that respond to that simple action. Even most mechanics don't want to think about those things every time they drive. The gas pedal, brake, steering wheel, and gearshift provide an *interface* for the driver, hiding the complexity that's actually at work in the system. Although it wouldn't be very practical, you can imagine a car that would run only if the driver pumped the fuel through the lines, mixed a certain ratio of gasoline and air together, and instructed the pistons to drive up and down at a certain rate.

Coding without objects doesn't make your life that difficult, of course. The point is that effort invested in simplicity can pay off for yourself and others in the long term. Once you've created and tested an object, you can treat it as a "black box" and forget about the code that makes the object behave the way it does.

You can build entire custom object models that involve complex code behind the scenes, but that present a relatively simple and intuitive object syntax to the programmer. This is, in fact, what all of the Office and VBA object models do for you—they take complex operations and package them into easy-to-use objects, methods, properties, and events. When you set the **Visible** property of a Microsoft Excel object to **False**, for example, you don't have to worry about how VBA, Excel, and Windows cooperate to hide the object. You can focus on the larger-scale goals of building your solution.

Naturally, simplicity and reusability come at a price. Creating custom objects and object models requires a different, perhaps even revolutionary, way of thinking than the sort of programming you may be accustomed to doing in VBA. It can take time to get the hang of it. In the long run, though, coding with objects can make you a better programmer by increasing your efficiency, honing your design skills, and making it easier to reuse your code.

When Should You Create Custom Objects?

The following sections outline some situations in which it makes sense to create your own objects.

Reducing Code Complexity

Any time you find yourself writing code for a complex operation that you may need to use more than once, consider building an object. Remember that the object itself doesn't have to do anything new or profound; simplicity that will save you time in the future is sufficient justification. For example, if you're building a solution that involves displaying data from a Microsoft Access database on an Excel worksheet, you may want to create a combo box that can bind to data in the database. Rather than doing all the binding work every time you need such a combo box, you can create a new object that has all the functionality of a combo box but also has methods and properties for binding data. For an example that shows how to build such an object, see the ListComboWiz.xla sample add-in in the Samples\CH11 subfolder on the companion CD-ROM. This sample add-in includes a custom BoundList object and BoundLists collection, which are used to create data-bound list and combo boxes on an Excel worksheet.

Calling Dynamic-Link Library (DLL) Functions

Calls to the Windows application programming interface (API) and other DLLs lend themselves to being encapsulated in class modules. Creating a class module that handles DLL calls is sometimes called "wrapping" the DLL. Since DLL calls are often complicated, you can write the code to call a DLL function from within a class module, and use it in the future without having to remember the details of calling the DLL function directly. For example, you might create a System object with properties and methods that call various API functions internally to set and return information about the operating system. The System.xls sample file, found in the Samples\CH10 subfolder on the companion CD-ROM, wraps some system-related API calls.

Building Custom Data Structures

A custom object can act as a *data structure*, which is a group of related data stored as a unit. For example, you might create a Server object, with properties such as UNCPath and Available, and methods such as SaveFile, and use this object to manage operations between your solution and a network server. Of course, you could also store this kind of data in a database; it depends on the needs of your solution. If you're working with small data structures, using a custom object may provide better performance.

Building Component Object Model (COM) Add-ins and Application-Specific Add-ins

If you're building a COM add-in, you'll work with the class module provided by the add-in designer. You may want your add-in to provide custom events; at the very least, you may want an event procedure to run in response to the click of a command bar button, which involves some of the concepts discussed later in this chapter.

Custom objects can be useful in application-specific add-ins as well. They're a good way to add new functionality to a document. For example, the ListComboWiz.xla sample add-in mentioned earlier in this section copies the BoundList and BoundLists classes, which are used to rebind the lists, to an Excel workbook, and then uses these classes in code that runs when the workbook opens.

For more information about creating COM add-ins and application-specific add-ins, see Chapter 11, "Add-ins, Templates, Wizards, and Libraries."

Creating Custom Object Models

You can create a custom object model to represent relationships between different parts of your application. Your custom object model can include objects and collections, just like any built-in object model does. The key to creating a custom object model is that you can use a class module to represent a collection. Since a collection is just an object that groups other objects of a particular type, you can write code within a class module so that the class module acts as a collection.

This chapter does not delve extensively into creating custom object models. The "Designing Object Models" section later in this chapter provides some suggestions and considerations for designing an object model. Two sample files on the companion CD-ROM, ListComboWiz.xla and EnumWindows.xls, include examples of custom object models. Additionally, the "Where to Go from Here" section at the end of this chapter points to resources that provide greater detail about creating object models.

Using the Sample Files

Some of the sample files discussed in this chapter are shared between this chapter and Chapters 3, 10, and 11. Each sample is included on the companion CD-ROM only once, so some of the samples cited here can be found in the Samples\CH10 or Samples\CH11 subfolder rather than in the Samples\CH09 subfolder. The following table indicates the location of each sample file referred to in this chapter.

Sample file	Location	Description
DataComboBox.xls	Samples\CH09	Demonstrates a custom event added to a combo box
EnumWindows.xls	Samples\CH10	Calls API functions to enumerate open windows and create custom objects representing them
Library.xls	Samples\CH09	Implements an interface to create a simple library application
ListComboWiz.xla	Samples\CH11	Creates bound list box or combo box on an Excel worksheet
Queries.xls	Samples\CH09	Implements an interface to create a simple SQL parsing application
ScriptGoodFormatting.htm	Samples\CH03	Shows how to call procedures in a Microsoft Scripting Component (scriptlet)
Scriptlet.htm	Samples\CH03	Contains script procedures that behave like methods and properties
System.xls	Samples\CH10	Wraps system-related Windows API functions

Basic Class Concepts

In case you're not yet familiar with using class modules to build custom objects, this section covers the basics of adding a class to your project, creating an instance of a class in memory, and constructing properties and methods.

What Is a Class?

A *class* is a definition for an object. It contains information about how an object should behave, including its name, methods, properties, and events. It's not actually an object itself, in that it doesn't exist in memory. When code runs that refers to a class, a new *instance* of the class, an *object*, is created in memory. Although there is only one class, multiple objects of the same type can be created in memory from that class.

You can think of a class as an object "on paper"—that is, it provides the blueprint for an object, but has no substance in memory itself. Any number of objects can be created from this blueprint. A useful analogy is that a class is like a cookie cutter, and the objects are like cookies. Each cookie may have slightly different characteristics, but all are cut from the same cookie cutter. Similarly, each object created from a class has the same *members*: its properties, methods, and events. But each object behaves as an independent entity; for example, one object's properties may be set to different values than those of another object of the same type.

A VBA project can contain two different varieties of class modules: basic class modules, which don't have any kind of user interface associated with them, and class modules that are associated with a form or another component. Class modules that are associated with a form, for example, are identical to basic class modules, except that they exist in memory only when that form exists in memory. Examples of objects that have associated class modules are UserForms, Access forms and reports, the Microsoft Word **ThisDocument** object, and the Excel **ThisWorkbook** and **Sheet*N*** objects. This chapter will focus on using basic class modules to create objects that don't have an associated component.

Adding a Class Module

To add a class module to your VBA project, click **Class Module** on the **Insert** menu in the Visual Basic Editor. Then name the class module by setting its **Name** property in the Properties window. Keep in mind that the class module will be treated as an object, so use a name that suggests the object's functionality. The name that you assign to the class module will also be the name under which it appears in the **Classes** list in the Object Browser.

If you've been following this book's naming convention for standard modules, you can forgo the three-letter prefix here. It's best to name an object intuitively. For example, the class in the ListComboWiz.xla sample file that represents a list box or combo box that's bound to data is named BoundList in order to imply its functionality.

Creating a New Instance of a Class

To work with a custom object from code, you first create a new instance of the class that defines the object. When you create a new instance of a class, the object defined by the class is created in memory.

You can create a new instance of a class from within any type of module. Create an object variable of type *ClassName*, and then use the **New** keyword to assign a new instance of that class to the object variable.

For example, the following code creates a new instance of a custom class named System and assigns it to an object variable of type `System`:

```
' Declare an object variable of type System.
Dim sysLocal As System

' Create a new instance of the System class and assign it to the object variable.
Set sysLocal = New System
```

You can also declare the object variable and assign a new instance of the class all in one step, as shown in the following code fragment:

```
Dim sysLocal As New System
```

The first method of declaring an object variable is generally preferable because you have control over when the new instance of the class is created in memory and thus more control over when memory resources are consumed. You're less likely to introduce unexpected bugs when your code controls the creation of the instance. In addition, when you're building a custom object model, you often need to perform certain operations at the time that an object is created, so it's critical to know where in your code that will happen. If you use the second method, VBA creates the object in memory the first time that you refer to it, so you can't check to see whether it is equal to **Nothing**; performing this check creates the object if it doesn't already exist.

The Instancing Property

You may notice that a class module has an additional property in the Properties window, the **Instancing** property. This property specifies whether the class module should be visible from another project when you've set a reference to the project that contains the class module. The property has two settings, Private, which is the default setting, and PublicNonCreatable. If you set the **Instancing** property to Private, a project that sets a reference to your project will not be able to view that class module in the Object Browser, nor will it be able to work with an instance of the class. If you set it to PublicNonCreatable, a project that sets a reference to your project can see the class module in the Object Browser. The referencing project can work with an instance of the class, but only if the referenced project has first created that instance. The referencing project can't actually create the instance itself.

Matters of Scope

When designing a custom object, you should think carefully about the object's scope and lifetime within the project, as well as that of its properties and methods. The following sections outline some things to consider when deciding how to scope object variables and procedures.

Object Variable Scope

When you create a new instance of a class and assign it to an object variable, that instance exists in memory until the object variable goes out of scope, or until you explicitly set it to **Nothing** in your code. This is an important issue to consider when designing custom objects, because it's easy to leave objects lying around in memory, tying up resources unnecessarily.

The scope of an object variable depends on where you've declared it. If you declare it in the Declarations section of a standard module, it exists from the time code begins running in the project until the project is reset or the file containing the project is closed. If you declare it within a procedure, it exists until the procedure has finished executing. If you declare it in the Declarations section of a class module, it exists for the lifetime of an instance of that class.

When creating a hierarchical object model, you typically want top-level objects or collections to have a global scope, so you should declare the object variables to represent them as public module-level variables in a standard module. That way the object variables will be available throughout the project for the lifetime of the project. Of course, you have to assign to them an instance of a class before you can use them.

For example, the ParentWindows collection is the top-level object in the EnumWindows.xls sample file, which is available in the Samples\CH10 subfolder on the companion CD-ROM. The object variable that represents the ParentWindows collection is declared at the module level in a standard module, so that the variable is available to all procedures in the project as soon as code in the project begins running.

If your object model includes an object or collection that belongs to another object or collection, you'll want the lower-level object to exist only after the higher-level object has been created. For example, each ParentWindow object in the ParentWindows collection represents an open application window in the system. Each ParentWindow object has a collection of ChildWindow objects that contains the child windows belonging to the ParentWindow object, if there are any. Since you don't know what window a ChildWindow object will represent until you've created its parent, and since you may have several different collections of ChildWindow objects, you don't want to declare the object variable for the ChildWindows collection globally. Instead, declare a private module-level object variable to represent the ChildWindows collection within the ParentWindow class module. Each instance of the ParentWindow class can then maintain its own ChildWindows collection.

If your project includes objects that don't form an object model, you may simply want to create an instance of the class locally within a procedure, as you need it. For example, the System object in the System.xls sample file, which is available in the Samples\CH10 subfolder on the companion CD-ROM, is an object that you may only use once in a while within a procedure to return the path to the Windows folder. In that case, it makes sense to create the System object variable within the procedure that requires it, and destroy it as soon as you're finished using it.

As with any other variable, you should try to scope object variables that point to custom objects as narrowly as possible in order to optimize performance and to reduce the risk of bugs that may be introduced by having to manage global variables.

For more information about designing an object model, see "Designing Object Models" later in this chapter.

Member Scope

The set of public variables, methods, properties, and events described in a class module define the *interface* for an object. The interface consists of the object members that are available to a programmer who's using the object from code.

A class module can also include private members that are not available to a programmer working with the object. You can create private variables, methods, properties, and events that are used by other procedures within the class module but are not part of the object's public interface. Additionally, constants, user-defined types, and **Declare** statements within a class module must always be private.

By default, **Sub**, **Function**, and **Property** procedures within a class module are public. Variables declared with the **Dim** statement, on the other hand, are private. It's a good idea to preface variable declarations and procedure definitions with either the **Public** or **Private** keyword, so that it's clear to you or any other developer looking at the class which elements are intended to be public or private.

You can also declare a **Sub**, **Function**, or **Property** procedure with the **Friend** keyword. The **Friend** keyword makes a procedure private to the project: The procedure is available to any code running within the project, but it's not available to a referencing project. For more information about the **Friend** keyword, search the Visual Basic Reference Help index for "Friend keyword."

Creating Simple Properties with Variables

A property sets and stores a characteristic of an object. The simplest way to create a property for a custom object is to add a public module-level variable to the class module. This variable behaves as a property of the object—you can set its value, and then retrieve the value later. A module-level variable in a class module exists as long as an instance of the class exists in memory, so you can count on the property being available for the lifetime of the object.

For example, the following line of code is all that you need to create a property named FirstName within a hypothetical class named Customer:

```
Public FirstName As String
```

To set this property, create a new instance of the Customer class and provide a value for the property, as shown in the following code fragment:

```
Dim cstCust As New Customer

cstCust.FirstName = "Maria"
```

The property that you create in this manner is always read-write, and there's no way to run other code when you set or return the property's value. Although this is an easy way to create a property when you're first beginning to program with class modules, you'll often find that you want to run code when a property is set or retrieved, or that you need to make certain properties read only. If you need more control over the property, you can create a **Property** procedure, discussed in "Creating Scalar Properties" later in this chapter.

Creating Methods

A method performs an action on or with an object. Any public **Sub** or **Function** procedure that you add to a class module becomes a method of the object. If a method is a **Sub** procedure, it doesn't return a value; if it is a **Function** procedure, it returns a value.

For example, the following procedure is the Multiply method for a hypothetical object named Calculator:

```
Public Function Multiply(ParamArray avarOperands() As Variant) As Variant
   ' Multiplies the set of numbers passed in to the procedure.
   Dim lngCount   As Long
   Dim dblResult  As Double
   Dim varElement As Variant

   ' Initialize result to 1, since multiplying by 0 would
   ' return 0.
   dblResult = 1
   ' Loop through parameter array, from lower bound to upper
   ' bound.
   For lngCount = LBound(avarOperands) To UBound(avarOperands)
      ' Store value of element.
      varElement = avarOperands(lngCount)
      ' Check whether element is numeric.
      If IsNumeric(varElement) Then
         ' Multiply result by element.
         dblResult = dblResult * varElement
      Else
         ' Return Null if any element is not numeric.
         Multiply = Null
         GoTo Multiply_End
      End If
   Next
```

```
   Multiply = dblResult

Multiply_End:
   Exit Function
End Function
```

To call this method, create a new object of type Calculator, and pass in the values that you want to multiply, as shown in the following code fragment:

```
Dim calCalc As New Calculator

Debug.Print calCalc.Multiply(2.5, 2.5, 2.5)
```

Creating Property Procedures

As mentioned previously, public module-level variables in a class module function as properties of an object. However, they're not very sophisticated. If you need to run code in order to set or return a property's value, or you want to make a property read-only, you can create a **Property** procedure. There are three types of **Property** procedures: **Property Get**, **Property Let**, and **Property Set** procedures. The **Property Get** procedure returns the current value of a property, whereas the **Property Let** procedure sets the value. The **Property Set** procedure assigns an object to an object property.

To create a read-write property, you need to include a pair of **Property** procedures in the class module. Both procedures must have the same name. If the property stores and returns a *scalar* value, such as a numeric, text, or date value, you use a **Property Let** procedure to set the value and a **Property Get** procedure to retrieve it. If the property stores and returns a reference to an object, you use the **Property Set** procedure to store the reference and the **Property Get** procedure to return it.

You can also create read-only, write-only, and write-once properties. The following table outlines which property procedures you need for each type.

Type of property	Procedures needed
Read-write, scalar	**Property Let, Property Get**
Read-write, object	**Property Set, Property Get**
Read-only, scalar	**Property Get**
Read-only, object	**Property Get**
Write-only, scalar	**Property Let**
Write-once, scalar	**Property Let**, including code to determine whether property has been set previously, **Property Get**
Write-once, object	**Property Set**, including code to determine whether object property has been set previously, **Property Get**

Creating Scalar Properties

The properties that you use to return information about a characteristic of an object are usually scalar properties. For example, a Name property most likely sets or returns a **String** value, an Age property sets or returns a numeric value, and a Birthdate property sets or returns a **Date** value. The following sections discuss how to create scalar properties.

Property Let Procedures

A **Property Let** procedure sets the value for a scalar property. The **Property Let** procedure takes one argument, which is the value that the property is to store. Note that since it sets a value, rather than returning one, the **Property Let** procedure doesn't have a return value.

The **Property Let** procedure doesn't do all of the work for you—if you want to store the value that's passed into the **Property Let** procedure, you have to actually store the value that you pass into the procedure yourself. You can store it in a private module-level variable. For example, the following **Property Let** procedure sets the LastName property for a hypothetical Customer object:

```
' Declare private module-level variable to store value.
Private p_strLastName As String

Public Property Let LastName(strLastName As String)
   ' Store value of argument in module-level variable.
   p_strLastName = strLastName
End Property
```

When you work with the Customer object from code in another module, you can set the LastName property as follows:

```
Dim cstCust As Customer

Set cstCust = New Customer
cstCust.LastName = "Andrews"
```

This line of code passes the value `"Andrews"` to the **Property Let** LastName procedure. The procedure then assigns this value to the module-level variable `p_strLastName`.

You don't always have to store a property value in a module-level variable. In some cases, you may use the **Property Let** procedure to affect some aspect of the application or system. For example, the following **Property Let** procedure sets the minute portion of the local system time. To do so, it calls the Windows API **SetLocalTime** function:

```
Public Property Let Minute(intMinute As Integer)
   ' Retrieve current time so that all values will be current.
   ' Then set minute portion of local time.

   GetLocalTime sysSystemTime
   sysSystemTime.wMinute = intMinute
   SetLocalTime sysSystemTime
End Property
```

There's no point in storing the value of the Minute property in a module-level variable; if you retrieve the property value several minutes later, the stored value will be inaccurate. The following section describes how to retrieve the value of the Minute property by calling the Windows API **GetLocalTime** function.

This procedure is available in the System class module in System.xls, available in the Samples\CH10 subfolder on the companion CD-ROM. To see how the **Property** procedure works, run the SetLocalSystemTime procedure in the modSystemInfo module in the sample project. This procedure creates a new instance of the System class and sets the Hour, Minute, and Second properties to update the local system time.

For more information about calling the **SetLocalTime** function and other API functions, see Chapter 10, "The Windows API and Other Dynamic-Link Libraries."

Property Get Procedures

A **Property Get** procedure returns the value of a property through the procedure's return value. Note that the **Property Get** procedure complements the **Property Let** procedure: The **Property Get** procedure has a return value, but takes no argument. Note also that the argument passed to the **Property Let** procedure must have the same data type as the return value of the **Property Get** procedure.

To return a property value by using a **Property Get** procedure, you must retrieve the value for the property from within the **Property Get** procedure. Assuming that the corresponding **Property Let** procedure has already stored the value assigned to the property in a module-level variable, you would read the value of this variable from within the **Property Get** procedure, and assign it as the return value for the **Property Get** procedure. For example, the following **Property Get** procedure is the companion procedure to the **Property Let** LastName procedure shown in the previous section. It retrieves the value of the `p_strLastName` variable and assigns it to the name of the property:

```
Public Property Get LastName As String
   ' Retrieve value stored in module-level variable.
   LastName = p_strLastName
End Property
```

When you work with the Customer object from code in another module, you can retrieve the value of the LastName property as follows:

```
Dim cstCust As Customer

Set cstCust = New Customer
Debug.Print cstCust.LastName
```

Note If the property hasn't already been set, the `p_strLastName` variable doesn't yet have a value; therefore, the **Property Get** procedure for the LastName property returns an empty string.

In the **Property** procedures for the LastName property, you can see that both procedures use the `p_strLastName` variable. The **Property Let** procedure writes a value to the variable, and the **Property Get** procedure reads the value from it.

There may be situations in which you need to ensure that a **Property Get** procedure returns the most up-to-date information from the system or application. In this case, you don't want to store the property value in a variable. Instead, you should call a function that always returns current information.

For example, the **Property Get** Minute procedure is the companion procedure to the **Property Let** Minute procedure shown in the previous section. If you stored the value set by the **Property Let** Minute procedure in a variable, and then used the **Property Get** procedure to retrieve the value several minutes later, it would be out-of-date and incorrect. Instead, you can call the Windows API **GetLocalTime** function from within the **Property Get** procedure to retrieve the current local time for the system, and then return the minute portion, as shown:

```
Public Property Get Minute() As Integer
   ' Retrieve current time, then return minute.

   GetLocalTime sysSystemTime
   Minute = sysSystemTime.wMinute
End Property
```

This **Property** procedure is available in the System class module in System.xls, which is available in the Samples\CH10 subfolder on the companion CD-ROM. To see how the **Property** procedure works, run the DisplayLocalSystemTime procedure in the modSystemInfo module in the sample project. This procedure creates a new instance of the System class and displays a dialog box that shows the local system time.

Creating Object Properties

The **Property Set** procedure behaves like the **Property Let** procedure, except that you use it to assign an object reference to an object property. You can then use a corresponding **Property Get** procedure to return the object reference.

There are a couple of cases in which it's useful to create an object property. When you want to create a new object that provides all the properties, methods, and events of an existing object, plus additional ones that you've defined, you can create an object property that returns a reference to the existing object. In addition, when you create an object model that has a hierarchy—the object contains other objects or collections—you must create an object property in order to access a lower-level object in the hierarchy.

Wrapping a Built-in Object

You can use the **Property Set** procedure to create an object that *wraps* an existing built-in object; that is, it contains unique properties and methods, and also provides access to all the built-in properties and methods of the existing object. In this way you can add additional properties, methods, and events to a built-in object.

For example, the ListComboWiz.xla add-in in the Samples\CH11 subfolder on the companion CD-ROM contains the BoundList class, which can represent a list box or combo box on an Excel worksheet. List boxes and combo boxes on a worksheet differ from those on UserForms; they are ActiveX controls that belong to the **OLEObjects** collection of the **Worksheet** object. The BoundList custom object contains some custom properties and methods, and also provides access to all the properties and methods of the **OLEObject** class that's built into Excel. What makes this possible is an object property that sets and returns a reference to an object of type **OLEObject**, which refers to the list box or combo box on the worksheet. This property maintains the reference to the **OLEObject** object for the BoundList class.

The following example shows the **Property Set** and **Property Get** procedures for the ActiveXControl object property of the BoundList class. The ActiveXControl object property requires both a **Property Set** procedure and a **Property Get** procedure. The **Property Set** procedure stores a reference to an object of type **OLEObject** in a private module-level variable, `p_oleCtl`. The **Property Get** procedure returns that reference.

```
Private p_oleCtl As OLEObject

Property Set ActiveXControl(oleCtl As OLEObject)
   If p_oleCtl Is Nothing Then
      Set p_oleCtl = oleCtl
   End If
End Property

Property Get ActiveXControl() As OLEObject
   Set ActiveXControl = p_oleCtl
End Property
```

You can name this property whatever you want; in this case it's named ActiveXControl because it sets and returns a reference to an ActiveX control on a worksheet.

Note that the **Property Set** procedure makes the ActiveXControl property a write-once property. The **Property** procedure checks whether the private object variable that stores the reference to the **OLEObject** object already points to a valid object. If it does, the property has already been set and won't be set again. The write-once property ensures that the reference to the **OLEObject** object is set only once, when it is first added to the BoundLists collection.

In the ListComboWiz.xla add-in, the ActiveXControl property is set in the Add method of the BoundLists class. First, the Add method creates a new instance of the BoundList class. Then, in one line of code, it uses the built-in **Add** method of the **OLEObjects** collection to add a new **OLEObject** object (the new list box or combo box) to the worksheet, and assigns a reference to this **OLEObject** object to the ActiveXControl property of the BoundList object. Setting the ActiveXControl property passes the reference to the new **OLEObject** object to the **Property Set** procedure for the ActiveXControl property. The ActiveXControl property stores the reference to the **OLEObject** object, to be maintained for the lifetime of that BoundList object.

In essence, the Add method of the custom BoundLists collection wraps the built-in **Add** method of the **OLEObjects** collection, and the ActiveXControl property wraps the built-in **OLEObject** object. The code within the custom objects still uses the **OLEObject** object and **OLEObjects** collection to control a list box or combo box on a worksheet. A programmer working with the BoundList object and BoundLists collection, however, sees only the properties and methods of those custom objects, rather than the internal code that's managing **OLEObject** objects.

The Add method for the BoundLists collection is shown here. Also shown is the `opgListType` custom enumeration, which provides the constants that specify whether to create a list box or a combo box; one of these constants is passed to the procedure for the *lngListType* argument:

```
Enum opgListType
   COMBO_BOX
   LIST_BOX
End Enum

Public Function Add(strListName As String, _
                    lngListType As opgListType) As BoundList
   ' Add new BoundList object to BoundLists collection and return reference to object.
   ' This procedure not only creates the BoundList object but also creates a new
   ' OLEObject on the worksheet and returns a reference to it, which is then
   ' assigned to the ActiveXControl property of the new BoundList object. The BoundList
   ' object "wraps" the OLEObject object.
   Dim objBndLst As BoundList

   Set objBndLst = New BoundList
```

```
    ' Create either a list box or a combo box.
    Select Case lngListType
       Case opgListType.LIST_BOX
          Set objBndLst.ActiveXControl = _
             ActiveSheet.OLEObjects.Add(ClassType:="Forms.ListBox.1", _
             Link:=False, DisplayAsIcon:=False, Left:=100, _
             Top:=100, Width:=150, Height:=150)
       Case opgListType.COMBO_BOX
          Set objBndLst.ActiveXControl = _
             ActiveSheet.OLEObjects.Add(ClassType:="Forms.ComboBox.1", _
             Link:=False, DisplayAsIcon:=False, Left:=100, _
             Top:=100, Width:=150, Height:=25)
    End Select

    ' Name the new list.
    objBndLst.ListName = strListName

    ' Add BoundList object to BoundLists collection.
    p_colLists.Add objBndLst, objBndLst.ListName

    ' Return added object.
    Set Add = objBndLst
End Function
```

Once the ActiveXControl property has been set, you can use it to access the properties and methods of the **OLEObject** corresponding to the list box or combo box. For example, the following code fragment returns the height of the first bound list in the BoundLists collection to the Immediate window:

```
? BoundLists.Item("Combo1").ActiveXControl.Height
```

Note The Item property of the BoundLists collection is a custom property that's used to return a reference to a BoundList object in the collection. Because the custom BoundLists collection is created from a class module, it does not have a default **Item** property like built-in collections do. When you build a class to represent a collection, you must implement the Item property yourself, and to return a reference to an object in the collection, you must explicitly refer to the Item property. In addition, you can't use the **For Each...Next** statement to loop through a collection that is built from a custom class; instead, you must use a **For...Next** loop and maintain a counter variable that acts as an index into the collection.

Accessing Objects in a Custom Object Model

If you create an object model that has a hierarchical organization, you must include object properties to access the lower-level members of the object model. For example, in the EnumWindows.xls example, located in the Samples\CH10 subfolder on the companion CD-ROM, every ParentWindow object has a ChildWindows collection. To work with the ChildWindows collection, you must return a reference to it that's associated with the ParentWindow object. The sample uses an object property within the ParentWindow object to do this, the ChildWindows property. The ChildWindows property has the same name as the collection it returns, which simplifies its use and makes the custom object model consistent with the built-in object models in Office 2000.

Here are the **Property Set** and **Property Get** procedures for the ChildWindows property of the ParentWindow object. Note that the **Property Set** procedure takes an argument of type `ChildWindows`, and the **Property Get** procedure returns a reference to a ChildWindows collection.

```
Public Property Set ChildWindows(colChildWindows As ChildWindows)
   ' This property sets a reference to the ParentWindow
   ' object's ChildWindows collection.
   ' Write-once property.

   If p_colChildWindows Is Nothing Then
      ' Assign reference to passed-in object to private
      ' module-level variable.
      Set p_colChildWindows = colChildWindows
   End If
End Property

Public Property Get ChildWindows() As ChildWindows
   ' This property returns a reference to the ParentWindow
   ' object's ChildWindows collection.

   ' Return reference to ChildWindows collection stored in
   ' private module-level variable.
   Set ChildWindows = p_colChildWindows
End Property
```

The **Property Set** procedure is a write-once property. For each instance of the ParentWindow class, you can set the ChildWindows property only once, although you can return it as many times as you want. Since every ParentWindow object has a ChildWindows collection, whether or not it contains any elements, the ChildWindows property is set in the Class_Initialize event procedure of the ParentWindow class. From the perspective of the programmer using the ParentWindow object, the ChildWindows property is read-only; because the property is set in the Class_Initialize event procedure, the property returns a reference to the ChildWindows collection as soon the object has been created.

Note that every property that is read-only must be set somewhere within your code. The difference between a read-write property and a read-only property is whether the property can be set by the programmer who's using the object, or whether it can only be set internally, by your code.

The line of code that sets the ChildWindows property is shown in the following example, taken from the Class_Initialize event procedure:

```
' Create a new ChildWindows collection and assign it
' to the ParentWindow object's ChildWindows property.
Set Me.ChildWindows = New ChildWindows
```

This statement creates a new instance of the ChildWindows collection. Rather than assigning the reference directly to an object variable, the statement assigns it to the ChildWindows property of the ParentWindow object. The ChildWindows property takes care of handling the reference to the parent window's ChildWindows collection.

After the object property has been set, it returns a reference to the collection, so that you can use it to traverse the object hierarchy. For example, the following line of code prints the value of the first child window's Caption property to the Immediate window:

```
? ParentWindows.Item(1).ChildWindows.Item(1).Caption
```

Creating Events and Event Procedures

As a VBA programmer, you understand how to handle form and control events. If you've programmed in Word or Excel, you may also have taken advantage of events on the **ThisDocument**, **ThisWorkbook**, or **Sheet*N*** objects. These event procedures are simple to create—you just open the class module and construct the event procedure from the **Object** and **Procedure** drop-down lists in the Code window.

There are two additional ways to handle events from VBA code in an Office application. You can create event procedures for certain objects that provide built-in events but that don't have associated class modules. You can also create custom events for your own classes.

Creating Event Procedures for Built-in Events by Using the WithEvents Keyword

The objects for which you've commonly written event procedures—UserForms, Access forms and reports, and the **ThisDocument**, **ThisWorkbook**, and **Sheet*N*** objects —have one thing in common: They all have an associated class module. Some other objects in the Office 97 and Office 2000 object models also provide built-in events, but they don't have associated class modules. For example, if you look at the Object Browser in the Visual Basic Editor in Excel 2000, you'll see that the Excel **Application** object has several events listed as its members—NewWorkbook, WorkbookOpen, and SheetChange, to name a few. Examples of other Excel objects that provide events include the **Chart**, **OLEObject**, and **QueryTable** objects. The Word **Application** object and the Microsoft PowerPoint **Application** object also provide events.

You can create event procedures for these events in a generic class module. Though the class module isn't associated with the object by default, it can contain event procedures for an object that has events.

If you consider event procedures in a form module, you may realize that those event procedures exist only for a particular instance of the form. For example, UserForm1 and UserForm2 are separate instances of an object of type **UserForm**. Both have an Initialize event, which occurs only when that form is loaded. The Initialize event procedure for UserForm1 runs only when UserForm1 is loaded, not when UserForm2 is loaded, and vice versa.

The same holds true for events on objects that don't have associated modules—an event occurs for a particular instance of an object. More specifically, it occurs for an instance of an object that you've indicated should respond to events, not for any other instance.

To indicate that an instance of an object should respond to events, you declare a module-level object variable of that type by using the **WithEvents** keyword in a class module. This keyword notifies VBA that you want to respond to events for the instance that is assigned to that object variable. You can use the **WithEvents** keyword only with objects that support events, and only in a class module.

For example, the following line of code in a class module declares a private object variable of type **Excel.Application** to respond to events:

```
Private WithEvents xlApp As Excel.Application
```

Once you've declared an object variable to respond to events, that object variable appears in the **Object** box in the class module's Code window, and its events appear in the **Procedures** box in the Code window. To create an event procedure stub, click the object name and event name in these boxes. The Visual Basic Editor inserts an event procedure stub for you that looks like the following:

```
Private Sub xlApp_NewWorkbook(ByVal Wb As Excel.Workbook)

End Sub
```

At this point, you've created an object variable that has associated events, and an event procedure. The object variable doesn't yet point to anything, however. You need to assign a reference to it, which you can do in the Initialize event procedure for the class module. The Initialize event occurs as soon as a new instance of the class is created, so if you assign a reference to the object variable here, you can always be sure it will exist when you need it.

In this case, you want the object variable to point to the current instance of the application:

```
Private Sub Class_Initialize()
   Set xlApp = Application
End Sub
```

Finally, you need to create a new instance of the class in order to trigger the Initialize event and load the event-ready **Application** object variable into memory. Insert a new standard module, and declare a private module-level object variable that will point to the instance of the class. For example, if the class is named XLEvents, you can declare the following object variable:

```
Private p_evtEvents As XLEvents
```

You must declare this object variable at the module level, so that it will remain in memory until the project is closed or reset, since this object variable points to the class that contains the event-ready object and its event procedures. Otherwise, the object will no longer respond to events once the variable has gone out of scope.

Next, add the procedure that creates the new instance of the class in a standard module:

```
Public Sub InitXLEvents()
   Set p_evtEvents = New XLEvents
End Sub
```

After you run this procedure, any code you've added to the **Application** object's event procedures will run when the corresponding **Application** object event occurs.

Note that you have to run the InitXLEvents procedure each time you open Excel in order to make the **Application** object event-ready. It's not possible to define events for the **Application** object once and for all.

Note If you think about the events that are available to you for objects such as the Excel **Application** object, you may realize that there's no way to use some of them consistently from within their own application. For example, the Excel **Application** object has an OpenWorkbook event. But in order to run a procedure like InitXLEvents, you're going to need to open a workbook. So there's no way to trap the event for the first workbook that's opened, although after you run InitXLEvents, the event will occur when subsequent workbooks are opened.

It makes more sense to use the OpenWorkbook event in the context of a COM component that supports Automation (formerly OLE Automation). For example, you can write an application in Word that includes the class and standard modules described above. You have to make two changes—you must set a reference to the Excel object library, and you need to use the **New** keyword to create a new instance of the Excel **Application** object, rather than returning the current instance. When you create a new instance of the **Application** object from Automation by calling the InitXLEvents procedure or one like it, Excel loads without opening a workbook. The **Application** object is now event-ready, and the OpenWorkbook event will occur as soon as you open a workbook through Automation.

Adding Events to Custom Classes

You can also include your own events in custom classes, and create event procedures that run when those events occur. Creating a custom event is somewhat more complex than creating an event procedure for a built-in event, because your code has to *raise* the custom event in response to something that happens within the code.

Understanding Custom Events

When you raise an event, you cause its event procedure to run. For the built-in events you're accustomed to working with, this is the job of the application; for example, when you click a button on a form in a Microsoft Access application, VBA in Access calls the button's Click event procedure and runs any code that's in it. However, when you create a custom event, the application doesn't know when your event is supposed to occur; you have to specify that in your code. Then you—or other developers who are using your custom object—have to create the event procedure and write the code that runs when the event is raised.

The most important thing to understand about custom events is that your code has to cause them to occur. They don't automatically occur in response to something that the user or system does, although you can write code that does cause an event to occur in this manner. The class module that contains a custom event must also include a public method that raises the event. This method raises the event by calling the **RaiseEvent** statement and passing in any arguments defined for the event. These arguments are in turn passed in to the event procedure that runs in response to the event.

In order for the event to occur, some code outside the class module must call the method that raises the event. For example, code in a form that runs when a command button is clicked might create a new instance of the custom class, assign it to an object variable that has been declared by using the **WithEvents** keyword, and then call the method that raises the event. When the event occurs, the event procedure in the form's module runs, if the event procedure exists.

Of course, an event can occur without any code responding to it. Events are occurring all the time, in the operating system and in your applications, and code runs in response to some events but not to others. To run code in response to an event that is occurring in an instance of a class, you must create an event procedure that is associated with that instance, as described in "Creating Custom Events" later in this chapter.

When Do You Need to Create a Custom Event?

In many cases, it's not absolutely necessary to create a custom event—you can call a procedure to do the same thing. On the other hand, creating an event for a custom object can improve the object's flexibility and reusability. If you call a method rather than raising an event, the method will run the same way every time, no matter what code is working with the object. If you raise an event, the programmer who's using the object can decide how to respond to the event and can use the same object in different scenarios. Imagine, for example, if a command button ran the same code every time the user clicked it, instead of providing an event procedure to run whatever code the programmer chooses. Command buttons wouldn't be nearly as useful!

Here are some cases where you'll need to create an event rather than use a procedure:

- When you implement an interface in multiple classes, and you want to maintain common code within the class that provides the interface, but you also need to provide some customization within each individual class. For more information about implementing an interface, see "Extending Objects Through Interfaces" later in this chapter. For an example of an event that allows you to customize code within classes that implement the same interface, see the SetSQL event in the BaseQuery class module in the Queries.xls sample file, available in the Samples\CH09 subfolder on the companion CD-ROM.
- When you want to trap the messages that Windows sends to an application. Windows messages are similar to events—Windows alerts an application when the application gets or loses the focus, for example, and the application can respond accordingly. In some cases you may want your VBA code to take notice of certain Windows messages and respond to them. To do this you need to employ an advanced technique called *subclassing*, which allows your VBA code to look at a window's messages and take some action before the window's normal code is called. You can correlate particular messages to custom events that you create in your code. For more information about subclassing, see "Where to Go from Here" at the end of this chapter.
- When two or more objects, components, or applications need to know that an event has occurred in an instance of a class that both are aware of. When an event occurs for an instance of a class, every variable that points to that instance in memory is notified of the event, and any event procedure that is tied to that instance runs. For example, if you have two forms that both have a variable pointing to a single instance of a Timer object, and the Timer object has an event that occurs when the timer is stopped, both forms will be notified of the event and will run the corresponding event procedure if it exists.

Creating Custom Events

The sample code in this section is taken from the DataComboBox.xls sample, which is available in the Samples\CH09 subfolder on the companion CD-ROM. This sample includes a custom event named ItemAdded on a custom object named DataComboBox. Since creating and responding to a custom event requires code in several places, it may be useful for you to study and run this sample while reading this section.

The DataComboBox object wraps a combo box on a form in order to provide an additional event, the ItemAdded event, which the MSForms **ComboBox** control doesn't have. When the user enters a new item and chooses to add it to the list, the ItemAdded event occurs. The programmer can use the ItemAdded event procedure to run validation code before adding the item to the list. For example, the ItemAdded event procedure in the sample file checks to see whether the item already exists in the list. If it does, the event is cancelled and the item is not added.

To define a custom event in a class module, use the **Event** keyword. An event may be public or private and must be declared at the module level. It can have any number of arguments, but it can't return a value. The following statement defines the ItemAdded event in the DataComboBox class:

```
Public Event ItemAdded(strValue As String, _
                       blnCancel As Boolean)
```

After you've defined the event in the DataComboBox class module, you can declare a private module-level variable of type `DataComboBox`, declared by using the **WithEvents** keyword, in the module of the frmDataCombo form:

```
Private WithEvents mdcbCombo As DataComboBox
```

This declaration notifies VBA that the instance of the DataComboBox class that this variable points to will respond to events. Once you've added this variable declaration to the form's module, you can create the mdcbCombo_ItemAdded event procedure stub by using the module's **Object** and **Procedure** drop-down lists:

```
Private Sub mdcbCombo_ItemAdded(strValue As String, _
                                blnCancel As Boolean)
   ' Code that runs when event occurs.
End Sub
```

When the form loads, the code creates a new instance of the DataComboBox object and sets its custom ComboBox property, which is an object property, to point to the cboData combo box on the form:

```
Private Sub UserForm_Initialize()
   ' Create new instance of DataComboBox object.
   Set mdcbCombo = New DataComboBox

   ' Set ComboBox property of DataComboBox object
   ' to point to combo box on form.
   Set mdcbCombo.ComboBox = Me.cboData
End Sub
```

Note that the ComboBox object property is the key to wrapping the built-in **ComboBox** object within a custom class, as was discussed earlier in this chapter in "Creating Object Properties." The ComboBox property provides access to all the properties and methods of the built-in **ComboBox** object.

At this point, the event has been defined in the class module, and the form is set up to respond to the event when it occurs. The next step is to write the procedure that raises the event. This procedure must be in the same module in which the event is defined, namely the DataComboBox class module.

It's reasonable that a combo box would know how to add an item that the user has entered in the text portion of the combo box. There's no built-in way to do this for an MSForms **ComboBox** control, however, so the DataComboBox class provides one, a method named AddDataItem. When the form calls this method on an instance of the class, the method raises the ItemAdded event, giving the programmer an opportunity to respond through the event procedure and handle the event as needed. After the event procedure runs, if the event was not cancelled, the AddDataItem method adds the new item to the list.

Here's the code for the AddDataItem method. Note that the **RaiseEvent** statement raises the ItemAdded event and passes values for its arguments. When this line executes, the event procedure defined in the form's module runs.

```
Public Function AddDataItem(strValue As String)
   ' Raises ItemAdded event when user chooses to add
   ' item. If item already exists in list, event is
   ' cancelled. Otherwise new item is added to list.
   Dim blnCancel As Boolean

   ' Initialize Boolean variable.
   blnCancel = False

   ' Raise ItemAdded event, passing in new value
   ' and Boolean variable. Boolean variable is passed
   ' by reference, so event procedure may alter its
   ' value.
   RaiseEvent ItemAdded(strValue, blnCancel)

   ' If ItemAdded event is cancelled, then exit.
   ' Otherwise add new item to list.
   If blnCancel = False Then
      Me.ComboBox.AddItem strValue
   End If
End Function
```

Finally, there must be code that calls the AddDataItem method. In the sample file, this method is called from the Click event procedure of the cmdAdd command button:

```
Private Sub cmdAdd_Click()
   Dim strValue As String

   ' Store value that's been typed into combo box.
   strValue = Me.cboData.Text

   ' Call AddDataItem method of DataComboBox object.
   mdcbCombo.AddDataItem strValue
End Sub
```

In summary, a command button's Click event procedure in the form's module calls the AddDataItem method of the DataComboBox object. The AddDataItem method raises the ItemAdded event, which in turn calls the combo box's ItemAdded event procedure in the form's module.

The ItemAdded event procedure in this example checks to make sure that the item doesn't already exist in the list and cancels the add operation if it does. You could put whatever code you wanted here, though, and it could be different code for different forms. For example, the ItemAdded event could include code to convert the entry to proper case, or it could trim additional spaces from the text entered, or it could write the entry to a database.

Extending Objects Through Interfaces

Suppose that in the process of designing your solution, you decide that you want to create several objects that are closely related, and in fact require at least some of the same properties and methods. Also, in the future, you might need to add more objects that are related to these, and you'd like to make the process as easy as possible for yourself down the road. You can *implement an interface* that defines the properties and methods that these objects have in common.

As noted earlier, an interface is the set of properties, methods, and events that define an object's characteristics and behavior. Every object has an interface, whether it's a built-in or custom object. When you implement an interface in a class module, you take advantage of another object's interface to provide some or all of the properties and methods for that class. In this way you can extend your objects, relate them according to their functionality, and maximize your code's reusability. You can implement interfaces to take advantage of *polymorphism*. Polymorphism refers to the ability to create objects that have specific individual functionality, but that share something in common with a more general object.

Note If you've programmed in object-oriented programming languages, you may be familiar with the concepts of polymorphism and *inheritance*. Inheritance refers to the ability of a class to derive members (and their functionality) from other classes. By implementing an interface, you can achieve polymorphism. However, interfaces don't provide true inheritance, because a class can implement only those members that are defined within an interface that it implements. For example, if Class B implements the interface for Class A, and Class C implements the interface for Class B, Class C must implement all the members of Class B, but it cannot directly implement members of Class A. In true inheritance, objects can derive characteristics from an entire hierarchy of other objects. For example, if Class B inherits from Class A, and Class C inherits from Class B, and so on, Class E can selectively derive all or some characteristics from Classes A, B, C, and D.

As a conceptual example of polymorphism, consider **Control** objects. There are several different control classes. For example, **CommandButton** controls are created from the **CommandButton** class, and **TextBox** controls are created from the **TextBox** class. You can create a variable of type **CommandButton** and assign to it a reference to a **CommandButton** control. You can do the same with a variable of type **TextBox**. You can't, however, assign a reference to a **TextBox** control to a variable of type **CommandButton**—you'll get an error if you try it.

On the other hand, both types of controls also have the more general type **Control**. If you create a variable of type **Control**, you can assign a reference to either a command button or a text box to the variable. This flexibility is indispensable in cases where you need to enumerate through all the controls on a form and set their **Visible** properties to **True**, for example. When you know what type of control your code will work with, it's better to create a variable of the more specific type, but when you don't know ahead of time, you can create a variable of type **Control**.

The samples discussed in this section implement custom interfaces similar to the way that individual controls support the same **Control** class interface. There are a couple of ways to do this. The following sections discuss both ways in the context of examples. First, though, the next section covers some of the basics of implementing interfaces.

Interface Basics

Fundamentally, implementing an interface requires two components. One component defines the interface, and the other implements it.

The component that defines the interface can come from a variety of places. It can be a class module in your project or in a referenced project. It can be a referenced component, such as a DLL. It can even be a built-in class. You can implement any interface contained in a type library, as long as that interface supports Automation. The component that implements the interface is a class module in a VBA project.

This section assumes that you're designing your own interface, and that you're creating it in a class module in the same VBA project that contains the classes in which you're implementing it. The examples shown here are designed in this way: One class module in the project defines the interface, and one or more class modules implement it.

Note that if the component that provides the interface is not part of your project, you must set a reference to its type library before you can implement it within a class in the project.

To notify VBA that you want to implement an interface, you use the **Implements** keyword, followed by the name of the interface (which is simply the name of the class that defines the interface). For example, the Library.xls sample file, found in the Samples\CH09 subfolder on the companion CD-ROM, contains a class named LibraryItem, which defines the LibraryItem interface. To implement the LibraryItem interface in another class named Periodical, you would type the following line in the Declarations section of the Periodical class:

```
Implements LibraryItem
```

After you enter this line, when you click the **Object** drop-down list in the module's Code window, you'll see that LibraryItem appears in the list of available objects, and all the properties and methods defined for the interface appear in the **Procedure** drop-down list. For example, if the LibraryItem class includes a property named CheckedOut, the **Property Let** and **Property Get** procedures for the CheckedOut property appear in the list. When you select the **Property Get** procedure from the list, a procedure stub like the following one is added to the class module:

```
Private Property Get LibraryItem_CheckedOut() As Boolean

End Property
```

Note that the name of the interface you've implemented precedes the name of the property itself. Also note that the procedure stub created is denoted as private. This means that the LibraryItem_CheckedOut property does not form part of the Periodical object's own interface; it won't appear in the list of available properties for an object of type `Periodical`. Instead, the CheckedOut property will appear in the list of available properties for an object of type `LibraryItem`.

An important thing to understand when you implement an interface is that an interface is like a contract. When you implement an interface in a class module, you agree to include all of the interface's public members in the class module. Every procedure that appears in the **Procedure** list must be included in the class module before your project will compile, and each procedure must contain either code or a comment. For example, the LibraryItem interface has four read-write properties: Name, AllowCheckOut, ItemType, and CheckedOut. Each class that implements the LibraryItem interface must include the **Property Let** and **Property Get** procedures for each of these four properties.

Even if you don't need a particular procedure in your class module, you still have to include it in order to implement the interface. If you omit a procedure that's provided by the interface, the VBA project won't compile.

Only those members of the interface that are public are visible to the class module that's implementing the interface. In other words, only the public members of the interface are part of the contract, and only they can be implemented by other class modules. The class that describes the interface can include private members, but these members won't be part of the interface.

Implementing an Abstract Interface

One way to design an interface is to create a class that describes **Sub**, **Function**, and **Property** procedure definitions, including arguments and return types, without adding any code to the procedures. This is referred to as an *abstract interface*. The advantage to implementing an abstract interface is that the class that implements it can include whatever code you want in the procedures it provides. Two classes that implement the same method can contain entirely different code within that method.

The sample file Library.xls, found in the Samples\CH09 subfolder on the companion CD-ROM, implements an abstract interface. The solution models a simple library system, which adds and catalogs different library holdings, and checks them out to patrons. There are four custom classes that represent different library items: Fiction, Nonfiction, Periodical, and Reference. The project also contains a class module named LibraryItem, which provides an abstract interface to the other classes. You may want to study and run this example while reading this section.

The four different objects that the library offers are all similar, but not identical. Fiction and Nonfiction objects can be checked out, while Periodical and Reference objects can't. But the objects are similar enough to share certain common properties. And as the library expands and adds new types of holdings, such as Audio or Film, those new holdings will also have common properties. All of these objects implement the LibraryItem interface, which supplies the common properties that each object needs to have. Within each object's class module, a property procedure can contain custom code tailored to that object's needs.

The interface described by the LibraryItem class defines four read-write properties: Name, ItemType, AllowCheckOut, and CheckedOut. The Name property is a simple public module-level variable; the others are paired **Property Let** and **Property Get** procedures. Because this is an abstract interface, none of the **Property** procedures contains any code.

The LibraryItem class also contains a public enumeration that defines numeric constants that represent each of the four existing object types. In the interest of organization, the enumeration appears in the LibraryItem class; however, it could also be defined in a standard module. The enumeration itself does not form part of the interface.

The Fiction, Nonfiction, Periodical, and Reference objects all implement the LibraryItem interface, so each of them has its own property procedures for each property defined by the interface. You can customize these procedures according to the needs of the object. For example, the AllowCheckOut property indicates whether a particular item can be checked out. For Fiction and Nonfiction objects, this property should return **True**. For Periodical and Reference objects, it should return **False**. Compare the LibraryItem_AllowCheckOut property procedures for the Fiction and Periodical classes:

```
' AllowCheckOut property for Fiction object.
Private Property Get LibraryItem_AllowCheckOut() As Boolean
   ' Fiction can be checked out.
   LibraryItem_AllowCheckOut = True
End Property

' AllowCheckOut property for Periodical object.
Private Property Get LibraryItem_AllowCheckOut() As Boolean
   ' Don't allow periodical to be checked out.
   LibraryItem_AllowCheckOut = False
End Property
```

Although it's practical for both Fiction and Periodical objects to have an AllowCheckOut property, it's not practical for both properties to return the same value.

The real power of implementing an abstract class becomes apparent when you begin using the objects to construct an application. The library system needs to be designed to handle any type of holding, and yet to distinguish between different types at the same time. Since the LibraryItem class is implemented in all four of the specific classes, an item of type `LibraryItem` can represent any of those objects, just as a **Control** object can represent any type of control generically.

The concepts of implementing an abstract class are more important than the details of the library solution, so the discussion here will focus on explaining the concepts. When the user clicks the Catalog New Items button on the switchboard form (frmLibrary), another form loads (frmCatalog). This form allows the user to enter a name for a new library holding and select the type of holding from a combo box. When the user clicks the Catalog button, a new object of the appropriate type is created and added to the collection.

Here's the code that creates a new library item in the cmdCatalog_Click event procedure. Note that this code fragment calls the AddLibraryItem procedure, passing in the name of the library item and its type, and returns a reference to an object that is assigned to a variable of type `LibraryItem`:

```
Dim colItem As LibraryItem

Set colItem = AddLibraryItem(Me.txtItemName, Me.cboItemType.ListIndex)
```

Next, take a look at the AddLibraryItem procedure. This procedure examines the value passed in for the *lngType* argument and creates a new object of type `Reference`, `Fiction`, `Nonfiction`, or `Periodical`. It then adds this reference to a global VBA **Collection** object in order to store it. Finally, the procedure returns a reference to the new object. Since the procedure's return type is declared as type `LibraryItem`, it is this type of object that is returned to the calling procedure and assigned to a variable of type `LibraryItem`:

```
Public Function AddLibraryItem(strName As String, _
                               lngType As opgItemType) As LibraryItem
   ' This function creates a library item of the specified type,
   ' sets its Name property, adds it to the collection,
   ' and returns a reference to the object.
   ' Note that a variable of type LibraryItem is used to store the
   ' reference, even though the code creates a specific object type.
   ' In a more sophisticated solution, you would probably include
   ' this method in a collection class as the Add method.

   Dim colNew As LibraryItem

   ' Determine what type of library item this is and
   ' create a new object of the appropriate type.
   Select Case lngType
      Case opgItemType.ITEM_REFERENCE
         Set colNew = New Reference
      Case opgItemType.ITEM_FICTION
         Set colNew = New Fiction
      Case opgItemType.ITEM_NONFICTION
         Set colNew = New NonFiction
      Case opgItemType.ITEM_PERIODICAL
         Set colNew = New Periodical
   End Select

   ' Set object's Name property.
   colNew.Name = strName

   ' Add new object to collection, specifying its name as
   ' the key for the item. The key can be used to retrieve
   ' the item from the collection.
   gcolLibItems.Add colNew, strName

   ' Return reference to new object.
   Set AddLibraryItem = colNew
End Function
```

As you can see from this procedure, implementing the LibraryItem interface in the Reference, Fiction, Nonfiction, and Periodical classes means that a reference to any of those objects can be assigned to a variable of type `LibraryItem`. You don't need to know ahead of time exactly which object your code will be dealing with. When you set or return a property on the LibraryItem object, the property procedure for the appropriate object runs.

For example, the following event procedure determines whether an item can be checked out, and if so checks it out by setting the CheckedOut property to **True**. All of the available object types have an AllowCheckOut property. For Fiction and Nonfiction objects, this property returns **True**. For Periodical and Reference objects, it returns False. Without knowing exactly which type of object the `colLibItem` variable refers to, you can check the property and respond appropriately:

```
Private Sub cmdCheckOut_Click()
   ' Attempt to check out library item.

   Dim colLibItem    As LibraryItem
   Dim strMsg        As String

   ' Locate item in collection and return reference to it.
   ' Assign reference to variable of type LibraryItem.
   ' Note that although the object has a specific type,
   ' you don't need to know what it is to use it.
   ' Value of selected text in combo box is same as
   ' item's key in collection. The key can be used to retrieve
   ' the item from the collection.
   Set colLibItem = gcolLibItems.Item(cboItems.Text)

   ' Check whether this item can be checked out.
   If colLibItem.AllowCheckOut Then
      If colLibItem.CheckedOut Then
         ' If item is already checked out, apologize.
         strMsg = "Sorry, this item is already checked out."
      Else
         ' Otherwise, check out and give return date.
         colLibItem.CheckedOut = True
         strMsg = "Item is checked out to you; due back " & Date + 14
      End If
   Else
      ' If item can't be checked out, apologize.
      strMsg = "Sorry, this item can't be checked out."
   End If

   ' Display message.
   MsgBox strMsg
End Sub
```

You can also add properties or methods that are not part of the interface to any object. For example, you could add a Volume property to the Periodical and Reference classes to set and return the volume number for the object. To set that property, however, you need to use an object of type `Periodical` or `Reference`, because the Volume property is not part of the LibraryItem interface. To determine whether the type of object you're working with is a Periodical or Reference object, you can use the **If TypeOf** construct. For example, the following procedure sets the volume number if the object passed in is a Periodical or Reference object:

```
Public Sub SetVolume(colItem As LibraryItem, _
                     strVolNum As String)
   ' Declare object variables of specific types.
   Dim perItem As Periodical
   Dim refItem As Reference

   ' Use Is TypeOf... construct to check whether
   ' library item is a periodical.
   If TypeOf colItem Is Periodical Then
      ' Assign library item reference to object variable
      ' of type Periodical.
      Set perItem = colItem
      ' Set Volume property on Periodical object.
      perItem.Volume = strVolNum
   Else
      ' Check whether library item is reference material.
      If TypeOf colItem Is Reference Then
         ' Assign library item reference to object variable
         ' of type Reference.
         Set refItem = colItem
         ' Set Volume property on Reference object.
         refItem.Volume = strVolNum
      Else
         ' Library item must be fiction or nonfiction.
         MsgBox "You can't enter a volume label for " _
            & "a fiction or nonfiction item."
      End If
   End If
End Sub
```

Note You could also implement the Volume property shown in the previous example as part of the LibraryItem interface, and simply not add any code to it for the Fiction and Nonfiction classes. This may be a better approach, because then you don't need to use the **If TypeOf** construct or create an additional object variable.

Implementing a Nonabstract Class

The abstract interfaces discussed in the previous section impose a discipline on a set of related objects. Each class contains the same properties and methods, at a minimum, and each class must provide the code that runs for a given property or method, which is desirable if the objects behave differently. In some cases, however, every object in the set may behave in exactly the same manner for a given property. In this case, you can implement an interface that contains the desired code in the **Property** procedure, and call that **Property** procedure from the corresponding property for each object.

For example, every class in the Library.xls sample implements the Name property for the object in an identical way. Each time you add a new type of object, you need to implement the Name property again. You can save yourself a little effort by moving the code for the Name property into the LibraryItem interface itself. Of course, each class must still implement the Name property. Instead of storing and retrieving the value itself, however, each class can delegate that task to the LibraryItem interface. In order to call code in the LibraryItem class, each class must contain a private variable of type `LibraryItem`, which can be initialized in the Class_Initialize event procedure:

```
Private p_colLibItem As LibraryItem

Private Sub Class_Initialize()
   Set p_colLibItem = New LibraryItem
End Sub
```

To delegate to the LibraryItem interface, the class must set and retrieve the Name property on this object of type `LibraryItem`:

```
Private Property Let LibraryItem_Name(ByVal RHS As String)
   ' Store name.
   p_colLibItem.Name = RHS
End Property

Private Property Get LibraryItem_Name() As String
   ' Return name.
   LibraryItem_Name = p_colLibItem
End Property
```

The only difference between implementing the Name property by delegating it to the LibraryItem interface and implementing it individually in each class module is that rather than storing a value in a module-level variable that's private to that class, you're storing a value in the Name property of a LibraryItem object, which in turn stores the value in its own private module-level variable.

Finally, note that when a class implements an interface, all the members that it implements are automatically denoted as private. This means that the implemented properties and methods in the Fiction, Nonfiction, Periodical, and Reference classes don't appear as part of the available interfaces for those objects. The implemented properties and methods appear on a variable of type `LibraryItem` only, which is fine if you're using variables of type `LibraryItem` to represent all of the other objects, as is done in the Library.xls sample.

If you want to define a public interface for each object, however, you can create a public property or method that calls the code that's in the private member. For example, if you wanted the Name property to be publicly available on an object, you could write a public Name property procedure that calls the private procedure supplied by the implemented interface, as shown in the following example:

```
Public Property Let Name(strName As String)
   LibraryItem_Name = strName
End Property

Public Property Get Name As String
   Name = LibraryItem_Name
End Property
```

You have a great deal of flexibility in how you define an interface. It can be fully abstract, nonabstract, or a combination of the two. Often a combination of the two types can be useful. For those members that share the same code, you can group that code in the interface. For those that don't, you can implement the code separately in each class.

For more examples of classes that implement abstract and nonabstract interfaces, see the Queries.xls sample file, available in the Samples\CH09 subfolder on the companion CD-ROM.

Designing Object Models

Designing a custom object model can be a tricky business. If you dive in and start coding right away, you may find yourself realizing in the middle of your development process that your design is less than ideal. It pays to take some time to think through an object model, and even draw diagrams and make notes by hand. You may also want to study other object models to understand how they were constructed. When you design an object model, you are taking abstract processes and imposing concrete relationships upon them. In essence, you are creating artificial conceptual divisions for your code.

This section includes some suggestions to get you started on object model design. Two of the sample files on the companion CD-ROM, EnumWindows.xls and ListComboWiz.xla, include custom object models that demonstrate the basic concepts of object model design. A complete discussion of the intricacies of object model design, however, is beyond the scope of this book. For other books that delve more deeply into this subject, see "Where to Go from Here" at the end of this chapter.

Planning the Object Model

Begin by determining how many objects and collections you need and naming all of them. You may find it helpful to draw the objects and collections in a hierarchical diagram that shows the relationships between them.

List as many of the properties, methods, and events for each object and collection that you can. Denote which properties can be simple module-level variables, which require **Property** procedures, and which are object properties. Also indicate whether properties should be read-write, read-only, write-only, or write-once.

Creating Collection Classes

You can represent a collection with a class module, and use the collection to organize objects of the same type. By convention, a collection class is usually given the plural name of the object that it contains; for example, the BoundLists collection contains BoundList objects.

Collection classes usually contain a Count property, for counting the number of objects in the collection, and an Item property, which returns a reference to an object in the collection by its index or key value. Most collection classes also contain an Add method, which adds a new object to the collection and returns a reference to it, and a Remove method, which removes an item from the collection.

You should consider how a top-level collection or object is to be initialized. Somewhere in your project there must be a line of code that creates an instance of the top-level collection or object. From there all other objects can be created from within your object model. If the collection will contain objects that may already exist or are saved with the file, such as bound list boxes or combo boxes, the collection will probably have to be initialized when the solution loads. If the collection provides objects on demand, it may not have to be initialized until the objects are needed.

You should also consider how objects are to be added to a collection. Does this happen based on user or programmatic input, or based on some change in the state of the system, or both? And do objects need to be added when the solution is first loaded? For example, the ListComboWiz.xla sample application, available in the Samples\CH11 subfolder on the companion CD-ROM, includes two custom classes, one that represents a bound list box or combo box and one that represents a collection of these objects. The collection needs to add any existing bound lists when the solution opens, and new bound lists need to be added when the user creates them. The Collection object is initialized in the Workbook_Open event, and existing objects are added to the collection in the Class_Initialize event for the Collection object.

Relating Objects with Object Properties

If an object contains a collection or another object, you need to create an object property that returns a reference to the object or collection that it contains. The object property should have the same name as the object or collection. For example, suppose a ParentWindow object contains a ChildWindows collection. In this case, you would create a ChildWindows property of the ParentWindow object to return a reference to that object's ChildWindows collection.

If an object belongs to another object, you may want to add a Parent property that returns a reference to the parent object. To do so, you need to define the Parent property in the class module for the child object, and set the Parent property in the class module for the parent object, after the child object has been created. For an example, see the Parent property of the ChildWindows collection in EnumWindows.xls, which is available in the Samples\CH10 subfolder on the companion CD-ROM.

Important When you implement a Parent property for an object that belongs to another object or collection, you run the risk of creating circular references. A circular reference exists when a parent object maintains a reference to a child object, and the child object, through its Parent property, maintains a reference to the parent object. The problem with this circular reference is that an object is not destroyed until the last remaining reference to it is destroyed. When you attempt to destroy the parent object by setting the reference to it to **Nothing**, the parent object will not actually be destroyed because each of its child objects still maintain a reference to the parent object.

For example, in the EnumWindows.xls sample file, a ParentWindow object maintains a reference to its collection of ChildWindows objects through the ChildWindows object property. A ChildWindows collection maintains a reference to its ParentWindow object through its Parent property. Setting a ParentWindow object to **Nothing** does not destroy the reference to the ParentWindow object that is maintained by the ChildWindows collection's Parent property. To truly destroy a Parent object, you must also destroy the references maintained by the Parent property.

One way to solve the problem of circular references is to include a TearDown method on the parent object. This method should set all of the parent object's object properties to **Nothing** so that any references maintained indirectly through these object properties are destroyed. After you call the TearDown method on the parent object, you can set the parent object to **Nothing**. As long as there are no additional references to the parent object in your code, setting the parent object to **Nothing** will destroy the parent object in memory.

Sharing Code by Using Interfaces

If two or more objects share common functionality, consider whether you can implement an interface that the objects can share. That way you can consolidate your code by moving common code to the interface.

Creating Custom Objects for Web Pages

There are two ways to create objects for Web pages that are similar to custom objects created in VBA: by creating scriptlets, and by using Microsoft Internet Explorer 5 behaviors. The following sections describe both of these technologies briefly and point to additional resources.

Dynamic HTML (DHTML) Scriptlets

You can create custom reusable objects for Web pages by using *DHTML scriptlets*. DHTML scriptlets are Web pages in which script procedures have been written according to certain conventions so that these procedures behave like methods and properties of the scriptlet. Scriptlets are supported in Internet Explorer version 4.0 and later. You can build scriptlets in either Microsoft Visual Basic Scripting Edition (VBScript) or Microsoft JScript.

Scriptlets can be script only, or they can have a user interface component in addition to script. You can include a scriptlet in the HTML for other pages in order to add the functionality that the scriptlet provides to those pages. By building scriptlets, you can componentize the process of developing Web pages in much the same way that you componentize solutions with custom objects in VBA.

For example, the scriptlet included in the Samples\CH03 subfolder on the companion CD-ROM, Scriptlet.htm, includes code that returns the current month name, day of month, and year. The file ScriptGoodFormatting.htm, also in the Samples\CH03 subfolder, refers to this scriptlet in order to display a digital clock on the Web page.

You refer to a scriptlet in an <OBJECT> tag in the HTML code for the page in which you want to use it. The following HTML code, taken from ScriptGoodFormatting.htm, shows how to refer to the Scriptlet.htm sample file. Note that the DATA attribute contains the name of the scriptlet file, Scriptlet.htm; this is comparable to the name of a class in VBA. The name for the scriptlet, as it is referred to within the script in ScriptGoodFormatting.htm, is `scrltDateCode`; this name is comparable to the variable that you use to represent an instance of a class in VBA.

```
<OBJECT ID="scrltDateCode"
STYLE=  "position:absolute;
      width:0;
      height:0;"
      type="text/x-scriptlet"
      data="Scriptlet.htm">
</OBJECT>
```

The scriptlet file itself, Scriptlet.htm, contains script procedures that behave like methods and properties. The following procedure defines the GetYear property for the scriptlet:

```
Function public_get_GetYear()
' Return the current year.
   public_get_GetYear = Year(Date())
End Function
```

Once the scriptlet has been included in a Web page by using the <OBJECT> tag, script in that Web page can call methods and properties of the scriptlet. For example, the following script fragment from ScriptGoodFormatting.htm returns the value of the scriptlet's GetYear property and stores it in a variable.

```
Dim strCurrentYear

strCurrentYear = scrltDateCode.GetYear
```

For more information about creating and using scriptlets, see Chapter 12, "Using Web Technologies," and see the Microsoft Scripting Technologies Web site at http://msdn.microsoft.com/scripting/.

DHTML Behaviors

Internet Explorer 5 supports *DHTML behaviors*. DHTML behaviors are lightweight, reusable components that encapsulate specific functionality or behavior on a page. You apply a behavior to a standard HTML element on a page to enhance that element's default functionality. Once you have defined a custom DHTML behavior, you or other people on your Web development team can easily apply the behavior to achieve custom interactive effects across multiple pages, without having to write script.

Internet Explorer 5 implements several default behaviors. For example, the **saveFavorite** behavior saves the current state of a page when it is added to the **Favorites** list. You can use the **saveFavorite** default behavior to save information that a user has added to a Web page prior to saving it in the user's **Favorites** list. If your Web page provides stock information, for example, you might use the **saveFavorite** behavior to allow the user to save selected stock symbols with the user's page.

You can also create custom DHTML behaviors by using scriptlets. For example, you can create a behavior that affects a list item on a Web page, so that when the user rests the mouse pointer on the list item, the item changes color. To apply this behavior to a Web page, you refer to the file containing the behavior within a <STYLE> tag. The following example applies the behavior defined in a file named Hilite.sct to two list items in an HTML file:

```
<BODY><UL>
<LI STYLE="behavior:url(hilite.sct)">Item1
</UL></BODY>

<BODY><UL>
<LI STYLE="behavior:url(hilite.sct)">Item2
</UL></BODY>
```

The scriptlet that defines the behavior must implement certain tags that Internet Explorer recognizes in order to associate the behavior with an HTML element. For more information about creating and using behaviors, see the Microsoft Site Builder Workshop Web site at http://www.microsoft.com/workshop/default.asp, and see Chapter 12, "Using Web Technologies."

Where to Go from Here

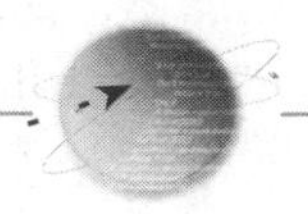

For additional information about the subjects discussed in this chapter, see the following resources.

Creating Object Models in VBA

Getz, Ken, and Mike Gilbert. *Visual Basic Language Developer's Handbook.* Alameda, CA: Sybex, 1999.

Stearns, Dave. "The Basics of Programming Model Design." MSDN Online Web site at http://msdn.microsoft.com/developer/news/devnews/julaug98/basicpmd.htm.

Creating and Implementing Interfaces

Microsoft Visual Basic 6.0 Programmer's Guide. Redmond, WA: Microsoft Press, 1998. (An online version of this book is included with Visual Basic 6.0 and is also available on the MSDN Online Web site at http://msdn.microsoft.com/developer/.)

Wrapping API Functions

Chapter 10, "The Windows API and Other Dynamic-Link Libraries"

Appleman, Dan. *Dan Appleman's Visual Basic 5.0 Programmer's Guide to the Win32 API.* Indianapolis, IN: Macmillan Computer Publishing, 1998.

MSDN Online Web site
(http://msdn.microsoft.com/developer/)

Subclassing Windows Messages

Bockmann, Christopher J., Lars Klander, and Lingyan Tang. *Visual Basic Programmer's Library.* Las Vegas, NV: Jamsa Press, 1998.

Creating COM Add-ins and Application-Specific Add-ins

Chapter 11, "Add-ins, Templates, Wizards, and Libraries"

Creating and Using DHTML Scriptlets

Chapter 12, "Using Web Technologies"

Microsoft Scripting Technologies Web site
(http://msdn.microsoft.com/scripting/)

Creating and Using DHTML Behaviors

Chapter 12, "Using Web Technologies"

Microsoft Site Builder Workshop Web site
(http://www.microsoft.com/workshop/default.asp)

Code Samples

The code samples shown in this chapter, along with additional examples demonstrating similar techniques, can be copied from the files in the Samples\CH03, Samples\CH09, Samples\CH10, and Samples\CH11 subfolders on the companion CD-ROM.

CHAPTER 10

The Windows API and Other Dynamic-Link Libraries

One of the most powerful features of Visual Basic for Applications (VBA) is its extensibility. You can extend your applications by calling functions in the Microsoft Windows application programming interface (API) and other dynamic-link libraries (DLLs). As a VBA programmer, you'll find that most of the functions in the Windows API are available to you, meaning that you not only have control over your solution, but you also have potential control over a significant portion of the operating system. And once you've learned how to use VBA to call a DLL function, you can call functions in almost any DLL, so that you can take advantage of technologies that are typically the domain of C/C++ programmers. This chapter introduces some of the concepts behind calling DLL functions from VBA and includes examples to get you started.

Contents

API Basics

This chapter covers some of the basics of calling the Windows API. You can apply the skills you learn in calling the Windows API to calling DLL functions in other DLLs as well.

The Windows API is a complex set of functions. This chapter doesn't cover absolutely everything that you need to know in order to call any function, but it aims to give you a starting point and directs you to other resources if you find that you need to know more.

What Is an API?

API stands for *application programming interface*. An API is simply a set of functions that you can use to work with a component, application, or operating system. Typically an API consists of one or more DLLs that provide some specific functionality.

DLLs are files that contain functions that can be called from any application running in Windows. At run time, a function in a DLL is *dynamically linked* into an application that calls it. No matter how many applications call a function in a DLL, that function exists in only a single file on the disk, and the DLL is created only once in memory.

The API you've probably heard about most frequently is the Windows API, which includes the DLLs that make up the Windows operating system. Every Windows application interacts with the Windows API directly or indirectly. The Windows API ensures that all applications running under Windows will behave in a consistent manner.

Note As the Windows operating system has evolved, several versions of the Windows API have been published. Windows 3.1 uses the Win16 API. The Windows NT, Windows 95, and Windows 98 platforms use the Win32 API. This chapter focuses on functions included in the Win32 API that are available to the Windows NT, Windows 95, and Windows 98 platforms.

There are other published APIs available in addition to the Windows API. For example, the Mail Application Programming Interface (MAPI) is a set of DLLs that can be used to write e-mail applications.

APIs are traditionally written for C and C++ programmers who are building Windows applications, but the functions in a DLL can be called by other programming languages, including VBA. Because most DLLs are written and documented primarily for C/C++ programmers, calling a DLL function may differ somewhat from calling a VBA function. In order to work with an API, you need to understand how to pass arguments to a DLL function.

Warning Calling the Windows API and other DLL functions can be hazardous to the health of your application. When you call a DLL function directly from your code, you're bypassing some of the safety mechanisms that VBA normally provides for you. If you make a mistake in defining or calling a DLL function (as all programmers eventually do), you may cause an application error (also referred to as a general protection fault, or GPF) in your application. The best strategy is to save your project before you run your code, and to make sure that you understand the principles behind calls to DLL functions.

Why Use VBA to Call the Windows API?

VBA is a powerful tool for building Windows applications. With VBA, however, you have control over only a small portion of the operating system, the part that is available through the functions and objects exposed directly to VBA in your application. The Windows API includes functions to control the most minute aspects of the operating system. You can extend and fine-tune your VBA applications by calling functions in the Windows API from VBA.

For example, VBA provides functions that read from and write to a portion of the registry reserved for VBA applications. You can use these functions—**GetSetting**, **GetAllSettings**, **SaveSetting**, and **DeleteSetting**—to maintain information about your application between sessions. However, these functions permit you to work with only one subkey in the registry, namely the \HKEY_CURRENT_USER\Software\VB and VBA Program Settings subkey. If you want to store or retrieve information from any other part of the registry, you must use the Windows API.

Because the Windows API provides such granular control over the operating system, you may need to call several functions to accomplish a single task. There are several different API functions for manipulating the registry, which you use in conjunction with each other. For example, to assign a new value to a registry subkey, you can use the **RegOpenKeyEx** function, which opens an existing subkey for reading or writing values. Then you can use the **RegSetValueEx** function to set the new value for that subkey, followed by the **RegCloseKey** function to close the subkey.

The API functions for manipulating the Windows Clipboard may also be useful to you as a VBA programmer. VBA doesn't provide an object for working with the Clipboard, but you can create your own by wrapping the Clipboard API functions in a class module to create a simple, reusable object representing the Windows Clipboard. You may need to use several functions together to accomplish a single task. For example, the **OpenClipboard** function opens the Clipboard for examination and prevents other applications from modifying the Clipboard content. The **GetClipboardData** function returns data that's saved to the Clipboard, and the **CloseClipboard** function closes the Clipboard, making it again available to other applications.

Note Each of the Office 2000 applications provides a **Clipboard** toolbar that you can use to store up to 12 items. You can also work with the items stored by the **Clipboard** toolbar programmatically through the command bar object model. The last item copied to the **Clipboard** toolbar is the one stored in the Windows Clipboard.

Other useful API functions are demonstrated in the sample applications referred to in this chapter. The IniFile.xls sample demonstrates how to read from and write to an initialization (.ini) file.

The System.xls sample contains a custom class named System, which has a number of properties that set and return general information about the operating system. For example, you can determine the current display resolution. You can set and retrieve the local system time, and return the paths to the Windows folder and the Windows temporary folder. You can expand this sample to provide further information about the system.

The EnumWindows.xls sample contains code for working with windows. This sample creates a collection of custom objects representing application windows that are open and visible in the operating system. You can use the API functions for working with windows to determine which applications are currently running and which one is currently active. You can set or retrieve the size of a window, return its caption, make its caption flash, make it the active window, minimize the window, and so on.

These sample files are available in the Samples\CH10 subfolder on the companion CD-ROM.

API Resources

In order to call functions in the Windows API, or any API for that matter, you'll need documentation describing the available functions, how to declare them in VBA, and how to call them. Two helpful resources are:

- The Win32API.txt file included in Microsoft Office 2000 Developer and in Microsoft Visual Basic. The Win32API.txt file contains VBA **Declare** statements for most of the functions in the Windows API. You can use the API Viewer add-in that's also included in Office 2000 Developer to locate and copy the **Declare** statement that you need. For information about installing and using the API Viewer add-in, see the apiload.txt file that's included with Office 2000 Developer. The API Viewer application that's included with Microsoft Visual Basic provides the same functionality, except that it's a stand-alone application.

  The first time you run the API Viewer application, it loads the Win32API.txt file. This text file can be exported to a Microsoft Access database (.mdb file), which speeds the process of loading and scrolling the API data. The companion CD-ROM includes a custom version of the exported database, OPG_Win32API.mdb, available in the Samples\CH10 folder. This database contains forms and queries you can use to search for API functions containing particular keywords.

- The Microsoft Platform SDK, which contains complete documentation for the Windows API. It is available free of charge on the Microsoft Developer Network site at http://msdn.microsoft.com/developer/.

For other sources of information about the Windows API and other APIs published by Microsoft, see "Where to Go from Here" at the end of this chapter.

Accessing Functions in a DLL

Before you can call a function in a DLL from VBA, you must provide VBA with information about where that function is and how to call it. There are two ways to do this: by setting a reference to the DLL's type library, or by using a **Declare** statement in a module.

Setting a reference to a DLL's type library is the easiest way to work with functions in the DLL. Once you set the reference, you can call the DLL function as though it were part of your project. There are a couple of caveats, however. First of all, setting references to multiple type libraries can affect your application's performance. Secondly, not all DLLs provide type libraries. Although you can set a reference to a DLL that doesn't provide a type library, you can't call functions in that DLL as though they were part of your project.

Note that the DLLs that form the Windows API don't provide type libraries, so you can't set references to them and call their functions. To call a function in the Windows API, you must include a **Declare** statement in the Declarations section of a module in your project.

A **Declare** statement is a definition that tells VBA where to find a particular DLL function and how to call it. The easiest way to add a **Declare** statement to your code is to use the API Viewer add-in, which contains **Declare** statements for most of the functions in the Windows API, as well as the constants and type definitions that some functions require.

Anatomy of a Declare Statement

Here's an example of the **Declare** statement for the **GetTempPath** function, which returns the path to the Windows temporary folder (by default, C:\Windows\Temp):

```
Private Declare Function GetTempPath Lib "kernel32" _
        Alias "GetTempPathA" (ByVal nBufferLength As Long, _
        ByVal lpBuffer As String) As Long
```

The **Declare** keyword alerts VBA that you want to include the definition for a DLL function in your project. A **Declare** statement in a standard module can be public or private, depending on whether you want the API function to be available to only a single module or to the entire project. In a class module, a **Declare** statement must be private.

The name of the function that follows the **Function** keyword is the name that you use to call the function from VBA. This name can be identical to the name of the API function itself, or you can use the **Alias** keyword within the **Declare** statement to indicate that you intend to call the function by a different name (an *alias*) in VBA.

In the above example, the name of the API function in the DLL is **GetTempPathA**, and the name by which you would call it from VBA is **GetTempPath**. Note that the actual name of the DLL function appears after the **Alias** keyword. Note also that **GetTempPath** is the name that the Win32API.txt file uses to alias the function, but you could change this to be any name you wanted.

Here are a few reasons why you might want to use an alias within a **Declare** statement:

- Some API function names begin with an underscore character (_), which is not legal in VBA. In order to call the function from VBA, you will need to use an aliased name.
- Because an alias allows you to name a DLL function anything you want to, you can make the function name conform to your own naming standards within VBA.
- Because API functions are case-sensitive, and VBA functions are not, you can use an alias to change the case of a function name.
- Some DLL functions have arguments that can take different data types. The VBA **Declare** statements for these functions define these arguments as type **Any**. Calling a DLL function with arguments declared as **Any** can be perilous because VBA does not perform any data type checking for you. If you want to avoid the hazards of passing arguments as **Any**, you can declare multiple versions of the same DLL function, each with a different name and a different data type.
- The Windows API contains two versions of all functions that take string arguments: an ANSI version and a Unicode version. The ANSI version has an "A" suffix, as shown in the above example, while the Unicode version has a "W" suffix. Although VBA uses Unicode internally, it converts all strings to ANSI strings before calling a function in a DLL, so you'll usually use the ANSI version when calling a Windows API function from VBA. The API Viewer add-in automatically aliases all functions that take string arguments so that you can call the function without including the "A" suffix.

The **Lib** keyword specifies which DLL contains the function. Note that the name of the DLL is contained in a string within the **Declare** statement. If the DLL specified after the **Lib** keyword is not found on the user's system, a call to the function will fail with run-time error number 48, "Error in loading DLL." Because you can handle this error in your VBA code, you can write robust code that deals with the error gracefully.

Note This is not an issue if you're calling a function in one of the basic Windows DLLs, as those DLLs must be present in order for your application to load.

The following table describes the most commonly used DLLs in the Windows API.

DLL	Contains
Kernel32.dll	Low-level operating system functions, such as those for memory management and resource handling
User32.dll	Windows management functions, such as those for message handling, timers, menus, and communications
GDI32.dll	The Graphics Device Interface (GDI) library, which contains functions for device output, such as those for drawing, display context, and font management

Most DLLs, including those in the Windows API, are written in C/C++. Passing arguments to a DLL function therefore requires some understanding of the arguments and data types expected by a C/C++ function, which differ in several ways from those expected by a VBA function. For more information about passing arguments, see the following section, "Calling DLL Functions."

Also, many arguments to DLL functions are passed by value. By default, arguments in VBA are passed by reference, so it's imperative that you include the **ByVal** keyword in the function definition when the DLL function requires that an argument be passed by value. Omitting the **ByVal** keyword in a function definition may cause an application error in some cases. In other cases the VBA run-time error number 49, "Bad DLL calling convention," may occur.

Passing an argument by reference passes the memory location of that argument to the procedure being called. If the procedure modifies that argument's value, it modifies the only copy of that argument, so when execution returns to the calling procedure, the argument contains the modified value.

Passing an argument to a DLL function by value, on the other hand, passes a copy of the argument. This prevents that function from modifying the contents of the actual argument; the function operates on a copy of the argument instead. When execution returns to the calling procedure, the argument contains the same value it did before the other procedure was called.

Because passing by reference allows an argument to be modified in memory, if you incorrectly pass an argument by reference, the DLL function may overwrite memory that it should not, causing an error or otherwise unexpected behavior. Windows maintains many values that should not be overwritten. For example, Windows assigns to every window a unique 32-bit identifier called a *handle*. Handles are always passed to API functions by value, because if Windows were to modify a window's handle, it would no longer be able to track that window.

Note Although the **ByVal** keyword appears in front of some arguments of type **String**, strings are always passed to Windows API functions by reference. For more information about passing strings, see "Returning Strings from DLL Functions" later in this chapter.

For more information about passing arguments by value or by reference, see "Passing Arguments by Value or by Reference" in Chapter 7, "Getting the Most Out of Visual Basic for Applications."

Constants and User-Defined Types

In addition to the **Declare** statement for a DLL function, some functions require that you define constants and types for use with that function. You include constant and user-defined type definitions in the Declarations section of a module, along with the **Declare** statements for the functions that require them.

How do you know which constants and user-defined types a function requires? Again, you need to look at documentation for the function. The Win32API.txt file contains definitions for the constants and user-defined types that accompany the functions it includes. You can use the API Viewer add-in to locate these constants and user-defined types and copy them to paste into your code. Unfortunately, the constants and user-defined types are not associated in any way with the **Declare** statements that require them, so you'll still need to check the documentation for the DLL function to determine which constants and types go with which **Declare** statements.

Defining Constants for DLL Functions

A function may require that you pass a constant to indicate what information you want the function to return. For example, the **GetSystemMetrics** function takes any one of 75 constants, each specifying a different aspect of the operating system. The information returned by the function depends on which constant you passed to it. To call **GetSystemMetrics**, you don't need to include all 75 constants—you can simply include the ones you're going to use.

Note It's a good idea to define constants rather than simply passing in the values that they represent. Microsoft ensures that the constants will remain the same in future versions, but there are no guarantees for the constant values themselves.

The constants required by a DLL function are often cryptic in nature, so you'll need to consult documentation for the function to determine what constant to pass in order to return a particular value.

The following example includes the **Declare** statement for the **GetSystemMetrics** function and two of the constants that it can take, then shows how to call **GetSystemMetrics** from within property procedures to return the height of the screen in pixels:

```
Declare Function GetSystemMetrics Lib "User32" (ByVal nIndex As Long) As Long

Const SM_CXSCREEN As Long = 0
Const SM_CYSCREEN As Long = 1

Public Property Get ScreenHeight() As Long
   ' Return screen height in pixels.

   ScreenHeight = GetSystemMetrics(SM_CYSCREEN)
End Property

Public Property Get ScreenWidth() As Long
   ' Return screen width in pixels.

   ScreenWidth = GetSystemMetrics(SM_CXSCREEN)
End Property
```

These procedures are available in the System class module in System.xls, available in the Samples\CH10 folder on the companion CD-ROM.

Creating User-Defined Types for DLL Functions

A *user-defined type* is a data structure that can store multiple related variables of different types. It corresponds to a structure in C/C++. In some cases you pass an empty user-defined type to a DLL function, and the function fills in the values for you; in other cases you fill the user-defined type from VBA, and pass it to the DLL function.

You can think of a user-defined type as a chest of drawers. Each drawer can contain different types of items, but together they can be treated as a single chest of related items. And you can retrieve an item from any drawer without worrying about the items stored in any other drawer.

To create a user-defined type, use the **Type…End Type** statement. Within the **Type…End Type** statement, list each element that is to contain a value, along with its data type. An element of a user-defined type can be an array.

The following code fragment shows how to define the RECT user-defined type, which you use with several Windows API functions that manage rectangles on the screen. For example, the **GetWindowRect** function takes a data structure of type RECT, and fills it with information about a window's left, top, right, and bottom positions.

```
Type RECT
      Left   As Long
      Top    As Long
      Right  As Long
      Bottom As Long
End Type
```

In order to pass a user-defined type to a DLL function, you must create a variable of that type. For example, if you were planning to pass a user-defined type of type RECT to a DLL function, you could include a variable declaration such as the following in the module:

```
Private rectWindow As RECT
```

You can refer to an individual element within the user-defined type as shown in the following code fragment:

```
Debug.Print rectWindow.Left
```

For more information about passing user-defined types to DLL functions, see "Passing User-Defined Types" later in this chapter.

Understanding Handles

Another important concept that you need to understand before calling functions in DLLs is that of the *handle*. A handle is simply a 32-bit positive integer that Windows uses to identify a window or another object, such as a font or bitmap.

In Windows, a window can be many different things. In fact, almost anything that you can see on the screen is in a window, and most things that you can't see are also in windows. A window can be a bounded rectangular area of the screen, like the application windows that you're accustomed to. A control on a form, such as a list box or scroll bar, may also be a window, although not all types of controls are windows. The icons that appear on your desktop, and the desktop itself, are windows.

Because all of these types of objects are windows, Windows can treat them similarly. Windows gives every window a unique handle, and uses the handle to work with that window. Many API functions return handles or take them as arguments.

Windows assigns a handle to a window when it is created and frees the handle when the window is destroyed. Although the handle remains the same for the lifetime of the window, there is no guarantee that a window will have the same handle if it is destroyed and recreated. Therefore, if you store a handle in a variable, keep in mind that the handle will no longer be valid if the window is destroyed.

The **GetActiveWindow** function is an example of a function that returns a handle to a window—in this case, the application window that's currently active. The **GetWindowText** function takes a handle to a window and returns that window's caption if it has one. The following procedure uses **GetActiveWindow** to return a handle to the active window, and **GetWindowText** to return its caption:

```
Declare Function GetActiveWindow Lib "user32" () As Long
Declare Function GetWindowText Lib "user32" Alias "GetWindowTextA" _
   (ByVal Hwnd As Long, ByVal lpString As String, ByVal cch As Long) As Long

Function ActiveWindowCaption() As String
   Dim strCaption As String
   Dim lngLen     As Long

   ' Create string filled with null characters.
   strCaption = String$(255, vbNullChar)
   ' Return length of string.
   lngLen = Len(strCaption)

   ' Call GetActiveWindow to return handle to active window,
   ' and pass handle to GetWindowText, along with string and its length.
   If (GetWindowText(GetActiveWindow, strCaption, lngLen) > 0) Then
      ' Return value that Windows has written to string.
      ActiveWindowCaption = strCaption
   End If
End Function
```

The **GetWindowText** function takes three arguments: the handle to a window, a null-terminated string into which the window's caption will be returned, and the length of that string. For more information about passing strings to DLL functions, see "Returning Strings from DLL Functions" later in this chapter.

The ActiveWindowCaption procedure shown in the previous example is available in the modActiveWindowCaption module in MiscAPIFunctions.xls in the Samples\CH10 subfolder on the companion CD-ROM.

Calling DLL Functions

Although calling DLL functions is in many ways similar to calling VBA functions, there are differences that may make DLL functions confusing at first. This section addresses how arguments are typed and prefixed in DLL functions, how to return a string, how to pass a data structure, what return values you can expect, and how to retrieve error information.

Argument Data Types

The data types used in C/C++, and the notation used to describe them, differ from those used in VBA. The following table describes some of the common data types used in DLL functions and their VBA equivalents. This list is not all-inclusive, so if you encounter a data type not described here, check one of the reference sources listed in "Where to Go from Here" at the end of this chapter.

C/C++ data type	Hungarian prefix	Description	VBA equivalent
BOOL	b	8-bit **Boolean** value. Zero indicates **False**; nonzero indicates **True**.	**Boolean** or **Long**
BYTE	ch	8-bit unsigned integer	**Byte**
HANDLE	h	32-bit unsigned integer that represents a handle to a Windows object	**Long**
int	n	16-bit signed integer	**Integer**
long	l	32-bit signed integer	**Long**
LP	lp	32-bit long pointer to a C/C++ structure, string, function, or other data in memory	**Long**
LPZSTR	lpsz	32-bit long pointer to a C-type null-terminated string	**Long**

Although you should be familiar with these data types and their prefixes, the Win32API.txt file mentioned earlier contains **Declare** statements ready for use in VBA. If you use these **Declare** statements in your code, the function arguments are already defined with the correct VBA data types.

For the most part, as long as you've defined and passed the correct data types, calling DLL functions works the same way as calling VBA functions. The exceptions are discussed in the following sections.

Returning Strings from DLL Functions

DLL functions don't return strings in the same way that VBA functions do. Because strings are always passed to DLL functions by reference, the DLL function can modify the value of the string argument. Rather than returning a string as the return value for the function, as you would probably do in VBA, a DLL function returns a string into an *argument* of type **String** that was passed to the function. The actual return value for the function is often a long integer specifying the number of bytes that were written into the string argument.

A DLL function that takes a string argument gets a *pointer* to the location of that string in memory. A pointer is just a memory address that indicates where the string is stored. So when you pass a string to a DLL function from VBA, you're passing the DLL function a pointer to your string in memory. The DLL function then modifies the string that's stored at that address.

To call a DLL function that writes to a **String** variable, you need to take additional steps to format the string properly. First of all, the **String** variable must be a *null-terminated string*. A null-terminated string ends in a special null character, which is specified by the VBA constant **vbNullChar**.

Secondly, a DLL function can't change the size of a string once it has been created. Therefore, you need to make sure that the string that you pass to a function is large enough to hold the entire return value. When you pass a string to a DLL function, you'll usually need to specify the size of the string that you've passed in another argument. Windows keeps track of the length of the string to ensure that it doesn't overwrite any memory that the string is using.

A good way to pass a string to a DLL function is to create a **String** variable and use the **String$** function to fill it with null characters, making it large enough to hold the string that the function returns. For example, the following code fragment creates a string 144 bytes long and filled with null characters:

```
Dim strTempPath As String

strTempPath = String$(144, vbNullChar)
```

If you don't know the length of the string when you pass it to the DLL function, you can use the **Len** function to determine it.

The **GetTempPath** function, which retrieves the path to the Windows temporary folder, is an example of a DLL function that returns a **String** value. It takes two arguments—a null-terminated **String** variable and a numeric variable containing the string's length—and modifies the string so that it contains the path, for example, "C:\Temp\".

Note In order to boot, Windows requires that a temporary folder exist, so this function should always return a path to that folder. If for some reason it doesn't, **GetTempPath** returns zero.

The following procedure retrieves the path to the Windows temporary folder by calling the **GetTempPath** function:

```
Declare Function GetTempPath Lib "kernel32" Alias "GetTempPathA" _
   (ByVal nBufferLength As Long, ByVal lpBuffer As String) As Long

Property Get GetTempFolder() As String
   ' Returns the path to the user's Temp folder. To boot, Windows
   ' requires that a temporary folder exist, so this should always
   ' safely return a path to one. Just in case, though, check the
   ' return value of GetTempPath.

   Dim strTempPath As String
   Dim lngTempPath As Long

   ' Fill string with null characters.
   strTempPath = String(144, vbNullChar)
   ' Get length of string.
   lngTempPath = Len(strTempPath)
   ' Call GetTempPath, passing in string length and string.
   If (GetTempPath(lngTempPath, strTempPath) > 0) Then
      ' GetTempPath returns path into string.
      ' Truncate string at first null character.
```

```
      GetTempFolder = Left(strTempPath, _
         InStr(1, strTempPath, vbNullChar) - 1)
   Else
      GetTempFolder = ""
   End If
End Property
```

The GetTempFolder property procedure is available in the System class module in System.xls in the Samples\CH10 subfolder on the companion CD-ROM.

Figure 10.1 shows how the `strTempPath` string appears in memory when it is passed to the **GetTempPath** function, and how it appears after the function call is complete.

Figure 10.1 Returning a String from a DLL Function

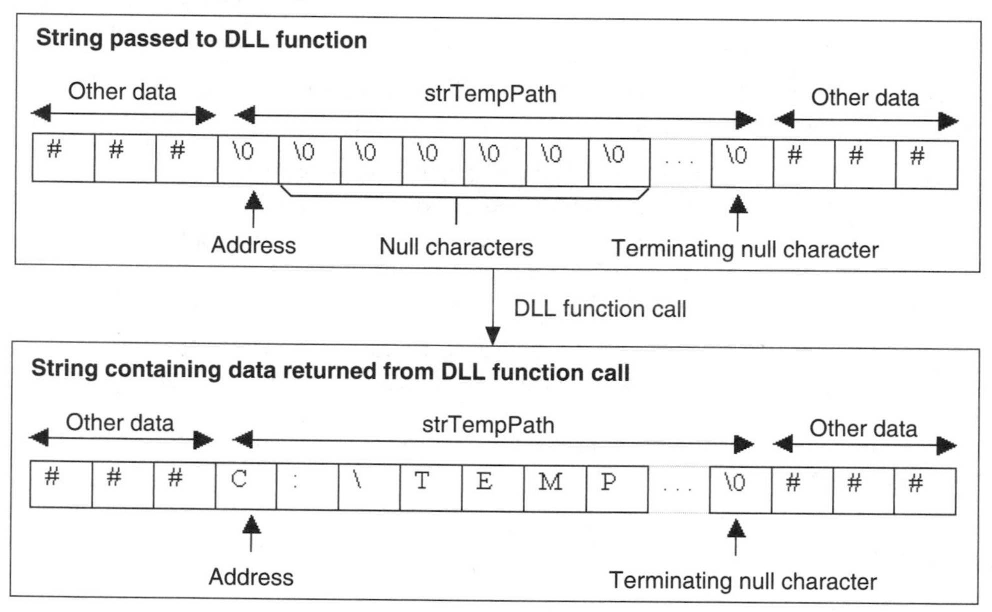

Note that the string is filled with null characters when it is passed to the function. The function writes the returned **String** value, "C:\Temp\", into the first part of the **String** variable, and the rest remains padded with null characters, which you can then truncate by using the **Left** function.

The actual return value for the GetTempPath function is the number of characters that have been written into the **String** variable. If the returned string is "C:\Temp\", the **GetTempPath** function returns 8.

Note that it's only necessary to pass in a null-terminated string and its size if you're returning a string from a function. If the function does not return a string into a string argument, but instead takes a string that provides information to the function, you can simply pass in a normal VBA **String** variable.

Passing User-Defined Types

Many DLL functions require that you pass in a data structure by using a predefined format. When calling a DLL function from VBA, you pass a user-defined type that you've defined according to the function's requirements.

You can figure out when you need to pass a user-defined type and which type definition you need to include in your code by looking at the **Declare** statement for the function. An argument requiring a data structure is always declared as a *long pointer*: a 32-bit numeric value that points to the data structure in memory. The conventional prefix for a long pointer argument is "lp". In addition, the data type for the argument will be the name of the data structure.

For example, take a look at the **Declare** statements for the **GetLocalTime** and **SetLocalTime** functions:

```
Private Declare Sub GetLocalTime Lib "kernel32" (lpSystem As SYSTEMTIME)
Private Declare Function SetLocalTime Lib "kernel32" (lpSystem As SYSTEMTIME) As Long
```

Both functions take an argument of type SYSTEMTIME, a data structure that contains date and time information. Here's the definition for the SYSTEMTIME type:

```
Private Type SYSTEMTIME
      wYear          As Integer
      wMonth         As Integer
      wDayOfWeek     As Integer
      wDay           As Integer
      wHour          As Integer
      wMinute        As Integer
      wSecond        As Integer
      wMilliseconds As Integer
End Type
```

To pass the data structure to a function, you must declare a variable of type SYSTEMTIME, as in the following example:

```
Private sysLocalTime As SYSTEMTIME
```

When calling **GetLocalTime**, you pass a variable of type SYSTEMTIME to the function, and it fills the data structure with numeric values indicating the current local year, month, day, day of week, hour, minute, second, and millisecond. For example, the following **Property Get** procedure calls **GetLocalTime** to return a value indicating the current hour:

```
Public Property Get Hour() As Integer
   ' Retrieve current time, then return hour.

   GetLocalTime sysLocalTime
   Hour = sysLocalTime.wHour
End Property
```

When calling **SetLocalTime**, you also pass a variable of type SYSTEMTIME, but you first provide values for one or more of the elements of the data structure. For example, the following **Property Let** procedure sets the hour value for the local system time. First, it calls **GetLocalTime** to retrieve the most current values for the local time into the data structure, `sysSystem`. Then it updates the value of the `sysLocalTime.wHour` element of the data structure with the value of the argument passed to the property procedure. Finally, it calls **SetLocalTime**, passing in the same data structure, which contains the values retrieved by **GetLocalTime** plus the new hour value.

```
Public Property Let Hour(intHour As Integer)
   ' Retrieve current time so that all values will be current,
   ' then set hour portion of local time.

   GetLocalTime sysLocalTime
   sysLocalTime.wHour = intHour
   SetLocalTime sysLocalTime
End Property
```

The **Hour** property procedures are available in the System class module in System.xls in the Samples\CH10 subfolder on the companion CD-ROM.

Note The **GetLocalTime** and **SetLocalTime** functions are similar to the **GetSystemTime** and **SetSystemTime** functions. The primary difference is that the **GetSystemTime** and **SetSystemTime** functions express time as Greenwich mean time. For example, if your local time is 12:00 midnight, and you live on the West Coast, Greenwich mean time is 8:00 A.M., an eight-hour difference. The **GetSystemTime** function returns the current time as 8:00 A.M., while **GetLocalTime** returns 12:00 midnight.

For more information about creating property procedures in class modules, see Chapter 9, "Custom Classes and Objects."

Using the Any Data Type

Some DLL functions have an argument that can take more than one type of data. In the **Declare** statement for a DLL function, such an argument is declared as type **Any**. VBA allows you to pass any data type to this argument. However, the DLL function may be designed to accept only two or three different types of data, so passing in the wrong type of data may cause an application error.

Normally when you compile your code in a VBA project, VBA performs type-checking on the values that you pass for each argument. That is, it ensures that the data type of the value passed in matches the data type for the argument in the function definition. If you define an argument as type **Long**, for example, and you attempt to pass in a value of type **String**, a compile-time error occurs. This holds true whether you're calling a built-in VBA function, a user-defined function, or a DLL function. When you declare an argument as type **Any**, however, no type-checking occurs, so you should be cautious when passing a value to an argument of this type.

Note Some DLL functions have an argument that can accept either a string or a null pointer to a string. A null pointer to a string is a special pointer that instructs Windows to ignore a given argument. It is different from a zero-length string (""). In early versions of VBA, programmers must either declare such an argument as type **Any**, or declare two versions of the DLL function, one that defines the argument as type **String** and one that defines it as type **Long**. VBA now includes the **vbNullString** constant, which represents a null pointer to a string, so that you can declare the argument as type **String**, and pass in the **vbNullString** constant for the case in which you need to pass in a null pointer. For more information about passing a null pointer from VBA, search the Microsoft Developer Network site at http://msdn.microsoft.com/developer/ for the keyword "vbNullString."

For an example of a DLL function that uses the **Any** data type, see the section "Displaying Help by Using the HtmlHelp API" in Chapter 13, "Adding Help to Your Custom Solution."

Retrieving Error Information Following DLL Function Calls

Run-time errors that occur in DLL functions behave differently from run-time errors in VBA in that no error message box is displayed. When a run-time error occurs, the DLL function returns some value that indicates that an error occurred, but the error does not interrupt VBA code execution.

Some functions in the Windows API store error information for run-time errors. If you're programming in C/C++, you can use the **GetLastError** function to retrieve information about the last error that occurred. From VBA, however, **GetLastError** may return inaccurate results. To get information about a DLL error from VBA, you can use the **LastDLLError** property of the VBA **Err** object. The **LastDLLError** property returns the number of the error that occurred.

Note In order to use the **LastDLLError** property, you need to know which error numbers correspond with which errors. This information is not available in the Win32API.txt file, but is available free of charge in the Microsoft Platform SDK, available on the Microsoft Developer Network site at http://msdn.microsoft.com/developer/.

The following example shows how you can use the **LastDLLError** property after you've called a function in the Windows API. The PrintWindowCoordinates procedure takes a handle to a window and calls the **GetWindowRect** function. **GetWindowRect** fills the RECT data structure with the lengths of the sides of the rectangle that make up the window. If you pass an invalid handle, an error occurs, and the error number is available through the **LastDLLError** property.

```
Declare Function GetWindowRect Lib "user32" (ByVal hwnd As Long, _
                                             lpRect As RECT) As Long

Type RECT
      Left   As Long
      Top    As Long
      Right  As Long
      Bottom As Long
End Type

Const ERROR_INVALID_WINDOW_HANDLE       As Long = 1400
Const ERROR_INVALID_WINDOW_HANDLE_DESCR As String = "Invalid window handle."

Sub PrintWindowCoordinates(hwnd As Long)
   ' Prints left, right, top, and bottom positions of a window in pixels.

   Dim rectWindow As RECT

   ' Pass in window handle and empty the data structure.
   ' If function returns 0, an error occurred.
   If GetWindowRect(hwnd, rectWindow) = 0 Then
      ' Check LastDLLError and display a dialog box if the error
      ' occurred because an invalid handle was passed.
      If Err.LastDllError = ERROR_INVALID_WINDOW_HANDLE Then
         MsgBox ERROR_INVALID_WINDOW_HANDLE_DESCR, _
            Title:="Error!"
      End If
   Else
      Debug.Print rectWindow.Bottom
      Debug.Print rectWindow.Left
      Debug.Print rectWindow.Right
      Debug.Print rectWindow.Top
   End If
End Sub
```

The PrintWindowCoordinates procedure is available in the modWindowCoordinates module in MiscAPIFunctions.xls in the Samples\CH10 subfolder on the companion CD-ROM.

To get the coordinates for the active window, you can return the handle of the active window by using the **GetActiveWindow** function, and pass that result to the procedure defined in the previous example. To use **GetActiveWindow**, include the following **Declare** statement:

```
Declare Function GetActiveWindow Lib "user32" () As Long
```

In the Immediate window, type the following:

```
? PrintWindowCoordinates(GetActiveWindow)
```

To generate an error message, call the procedure with a random long integer.

Wrapping DLL Functions

If you call DLL functions frequently, you may want to simplify the process by encapsulating those functions within class modules. By creating a property or method that calls one or more DLL functions, you can work with DLL functions in an object-oriented manner more typical of VBA. And because declaring and calling DLL functions can be a difficult and error-prone experience, packaging calls to DLL functions in reusable objects can save you from having to repeat this experience every time you need to call the API.

When you encapsulate DLL function calls in a class module, you're actually defining a VBA interface for those functions. This is often called "wrapping" a function. You don't change the function itself, but you provide an easier way to call it. Although it can be a little more work to wrap DLL functions, you'll benefit in the long term if you call the functions repeatedly.

To see a simple example of a class that wraps DLL functions, take a look at the System class module in System.xls, available in the Samples\CH10 subfolder on the companion CD-ROM. This class wraps some of the functions discussed earlier in this chapter, including the **GetLocalTime**, **SetLocalTime**, and **GetTempPath** functions. You can create a new instance of the System class and use the resulting object to set or retrieve certain information about the system.

The **Property Get** procedure for each of the Year, Month, Day, Hour, Minute, and Second properties calls the **GetLocalTime** function, which returns the current value for each portion of the local time into the SYSTEMTIME data structure. To make sure that the value returned by the **Property Get** procedure is current, **GetLocalTime** is called each time the **Property Get** procedure runs.

The **Property Let** procedure for each property also calls **GetLocalTime** to ensure that the values in the data structure are current. It then updates the appropriate element of the structure and passes the entire structure to **SetLocalTime** to change the local system time.

The **Property Get** and **Property Let** procedures for the Hour property are shown in "Passing User-Defined Types" earlier in this chapter.

Once you've created an object-oriented interface for DLL functions, you can create a new instance of the wrapper class and work with its properties and methods. The following example uses the Hour, Minute, and Second properties of the System object to display the local system time in a dialog box.

```
Sub DisplayLocalSystem()
   Dim sysLocal As System
   Dim strMsg   As String
   Dim dteTime  As Date

   ' Create new instance of System class.
   Set sysLocal = New System

   With sysLocal
      ' Return date value by using Hour, Minute, and
      ' Second properties of System object.
      dteTime = TimeSerial(.Hour, .Minute, .Second)
      strMsg = "The current local system time is: " _
         & CStr(dteTime)
      MsgBox strMsg
   End With
End Sub
```

This procedure is available in the modDisplaySystem module in System.xls in the Samples\CH10 subfolder on the companion CD-ROM.

You can expand the System class to contain other system-related properties and methods. For example, you might add additional properties that call the **GetSystemMetrics** function with different constants.

For more information about creating custom objects, see Chapter 9, "Custom Classes and Objects."

Using Callback Functions

Some DLL functions need to call a function in your code in order to run. When a function in a DLL calls a function in your code, your function is referred to as a *callback* function.

What Is a Callback Function?

To call most DLL functions from VBA, you write a VBA function that calls the DLL function, and you're done. To call a function that requires a *callback function*, however, you write a VBA function that calls the DLL function, and the DLL function then calls another VBA function, the callback function, that you've defined in your project. You never call the VBA callback function directly; the DLL function calls it for you. The diagram in Figure 10.2 provides a conceptual overview of how a callback function works.

Figure 10.2 DLL Function and Callback Function

Typical DLL function

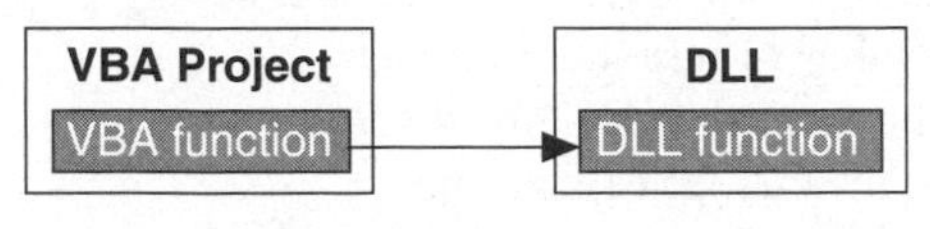

DLL function requiring callback function

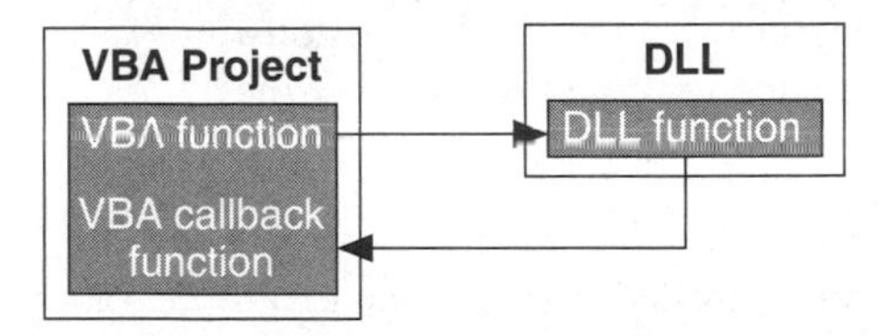

The DLL functions that require callback functions are often functions that must execute some action repeatedly. For example, the **SetTimer** API function requires a callback function each time a specified interval elapses. You might use it to update a clock on a form every second, or to display a form every hour. This is a simple task in Microsoft Access, which provides a Timer control for use on Access forms. The other Office applications, however, don't have Timer controls. You can use the **SetTimer** function to create a timer.

Other DLL functions that require callback functions are the enumeration functions, which enumerate through a group of Windows objects: **EnumWindows**, **EnumPrinters**, **EnumFontFamilies**, and so on. For example, the **EnumWindows** function enumerates through all of the existing windows and calls the callback function for each window. You can use the **EnumWindows** callback function to perform an operation on each available window, such as getting the window's caption text or determining its location on the screen. Procedures that call the **EnumWindows** function can be found in the EnumWindows.xls sample file, available in the Samples\CH10 subfolder on the companion CD-ROM.

Creating a Callback Function

You can determine whether a DLL function requires a callback function by looking at its arguments and reading the documentation for the function. An argument that takes a pointer to a callback function is a long pointer, usually prefaced with the prefix "lp". Also, the name of the argument usually ends in "Func", indicating that it takes a pointer to a function. For example, take a look at the **Declare** statement for the **EnumWindows** function. The *lpEnumFunc* argument indicates that the function requires a callback function.

```
Declare Function EnumWindows Lib "user32" (ByVal lpEnumFunc As Long, _
                                           ByVal lngParam As Long) As Long
```

So how do you know what the callback function should look like? The answer is in the documentation for the function. Each callback function has different arguments. Unfortunately, although information about DLL functions requiring callbacks is available in Win32API.txt, information about creating the callback functions themselves is not.

The Microsoft Platform SDK, available on the Microsoft Developer Network site at http://msdn.microsoft.com/developer/, contains information about all DLL functions that require callbacks and their corresponding callback functions, and is probably the best source for this information. However, in order to use it, you need to be able to interpret C/C++ documentation and translate it to VBA.

You can name the callback function whatever you want to; the suggested name is usually the name of the DLL function, followed by "Proc". For example, the suggested name for the callback function of the **EnumWindows** function is EnumWindowsProc. Note that you can have more than one callback function for the same DLL function.

Here's the C/C++ definition for the EnumWindowsProc function, as described in the Platform SDK:

```
BOOL CALLBACK EnumWindowsProc(
   HWND hwnd, // handle to parent window
   LPARAM lParam // application-defined value
);
```

Translated to VBA, this function becomes:

```
Function EnumWindowsProc(ByVal hwnd As Long, ByVal lParam As Long) As Long
End Function
```

The *hwnd* argument is a handle to a window. The *lParam* argument is an application-defined argument that can be any data type. The value that you pass to the *lParam* argument for the **EnumWindows** function is also the value passed to the *lParam* argument of the EnumWindowsProc function. You don't have to define *lParam* as a **Long**; you can define it as another type if you know that you will be passing in, say, a **ListBox** control, or an array. Also, you don't have to pass any value to *lParam* at all.

Callback functions usually return a **Long** value—nonzero for success, zero for failure. To continue enumerating, a callback function must return **True**, so you must explicitly set the return value to **True** within the function. Setting it to **False** halts the enumeration. The function will run until it either finishes enumerating or returns **False**.

Important Be careful when defining the callback function. You must include the **ByVal** keyword where necessary, and you must include the return value for the function. Also, the function must be declared exactly according to the documentation. If you don't define the function correctly, your solution will most likely cause an application error when you try to run it.

When you call the **EnumWindows** function, this function calls the EnumWindowsProc function in your VBA project for each existing window, passing in the window's handle and whatever value is contained in the *lParam* argument. You can add whatever code you want within the callback function.

The following example shows a callback function for the **EnumWindows** function. This callback function, EnumWindowsProc, adds each visible parent window to the ParentWindows collection, a custom collection of ParentWindow objects. In order to add windows to the collection, the collection object is passed into the callback function in the *lParam* argument. The procedure calls two other functions: the **IsWindowVisible** API function, which determines whether a given window is visible, and the GetWindowCaption procedure, which in turn calls the **GetWindowText** API function to return the window's caption.

Note Parent windows are primary application windows; child windows are windows that exist within parent windows. A separate DLL function, **EnumChildWindows**, exists for enumerating child windows within parent windows. The EnumWindows.xls sample file demonstrates both functions.

```
Function EnumWindowsProc(ByVal hWnd As Long, ByVal lParam As Object) As Long
   ' Add all visible windows to ParentWindows collection.
   ' This is the callback function called by EnumWindows.
   '
   ' The hWnd argument provides a handle to a specific window each time
   ' the callback function runs.
   ' The lParam argument can take any data that the user wants to pass to
   ' the function. In this case, it is defined as type Object, so that
   ' the EnumWindows function can pass in a reference to the ParentWindows
   ' collection.
   '
   ' You could use this function to return both visible and non-visible
   ' windows by removing the code that calls the IsWindowVisible function.

   Dim strCaption As String
   Dim pwnNew As ParentWindow

   ' Check whether this window is visible.
   If IsWindowVisible(hWnd) Then
      ' Add new ParentWindow object to ParentWindows collection.
      Set pwnNew = lParam.Add(hWnd)
      ' Call function to enumerate child windows.
      EnumChildWindows hWnd, AddressOf EnumChildWindowsProc, _
         pwnNew.ChildWindows
   End If

   ' Return True to continue enumerating windows.
   ' Function will stop running when all windows have been
   ' enumerated.
   EnumWindowsProc = True
End Function
```

The EnumWindowsProc callback function is available in the modEnumWindows module in EnumWindows.xls in the Samples\CH10 subfolder on the companion CD-ROM. This procedure is used to create objects in a small custom object model. The ParentWindows collection contains ParentWindow objects, which refer to individual visible windows. The address of the EnumWindowsProc function is passed to the **EnumWindows** function, which is called from the Class_Initialize event procedure for the ParentWindows collection, so that the existing windows are immediately added to the collection.

Once the ParentWindows collection has been initialized, you can refer to a ParentWindow object within the collection by its index or by its key, which is the window's handle. Use the Item property of the ParentWindows collection to refer to a member of the collection. For example, the following code fragment prints the caption of the third ParentWindow object in the ParentWindows collection:

```
Debug.Print ParentWindows.Item(3).Caption
```

Calling a Callback Function

In previous versions of VBA, it is not possible to use callback functions, because there is no way to tell the DLL function which of your own functions you want to call. In order to call a callback function, a DLL function needs a pointer to the callback function's address in memory. Previous versions of VBA do not support pointers to functions. VBA now supports the **AddressOf** operator, which enables you to pass the address of a VBA function to a DLL.

The Class_Initialize procedure in the ParentWindows collection calls the **EnumWindows** function, passing the address of EnumWindowsProc for the *lpEnumFunc* argument, and a reference to the ParentWindow object itself (using the **Me** keyword) for the *lParam* argument. Note that the **AddressOf** operator is followed by the name of the callback function, without any arguments:

```
Private Sub Class_Initialize()

   ' Create new instance of private collection object.
   Set mcolParents = New Collection

   ' Add visible parent windows to collection.
   ' Pass Me as reference to ParentWindows collection.
   EnumWindows AddressOf EnumWindowsProc, Me
End Sub
```

The ParentWindows Class_Initialize event procedure is available in the ParentWindows class module in EnumWindows.xls in the Samples\CH10 subfolder on the companion CD-ROM.

Where to Go from Here

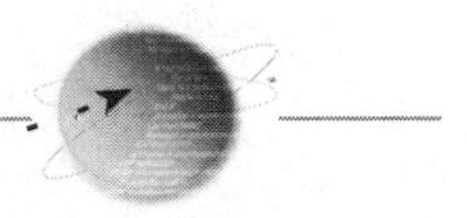

For additional information about the subjects discussed in this chapter, see the following resources.

Windows API Reference

Microsoft Platform SDK, available free of charge through the Microsoft Developer Network Web site (http://msdn.microsoft.com/developer/)

Calling the Windows API from VBA

Appleman, Dan. *Dan Appleman's Visual Basic 5.0 Programmer's Guide to the Win32 API*. Indianapolis, IN: Macmillan Computer Publishing, 1998.

O'Brien, Timothy, Steven Pogge, and Geoffrey White. *Microsoft Access 97 Developer's Handbook*. Redmond, WA: Microsoft Press, 1997.

Getz, Ken, and Mike Gilbert. *Visual Basic Language Developer's Handbook*. Alameda, CA: Sybex, 1999.

Bockmann, Christopher J., Lars Klander, and Lingyan Tang. *Visual Basic Programmer's Library*. Las Vegas, NV: Jamsa Press, 1998.

Microsoft Visual Basic 6.0 Programmer's Guide. Redmond, WA: Microsoft Press, 1998. (An online version of this book is included with Visual Basic 6.0 and is also available on the MSDN Online Web site at http://msdn.microsoft.com/developer/.)

Code Samples

The code samples shown in this chapter, along with additional examples demonstrating similar techniques, can be copied from the files in the Samples\CH10 subfolder on the companion CD-ROM.

CHAPTER 11

Add-ins, Templates, Wizards, and Libraries

Creating a Microsoft Office solution is about enhancing and extending powerful applications that you and your users already have on your desktops. You can take advantage of the features in Microsoft Word, Microsoft Excel, Microsoft PowerPoint, Microsoft Access, Microsoft FrontPage, and Microsoft Outlook, and all the time and resources Microsoft has invested in developing and testing these applications, to quickly and easily build a solution that meets your users' needs without requiring a lot of training and support.

One way to provide users with a custom solution is to build an *add-in*. An add-in extends an application by adding functionality that isn't in the core product itself. If you're a frequent user of Excel or Access, you may already be familiar with some of the add-ins that these applications include. For example, the Linked Table Manager in Access is an add-in that was built in Visual Basic for Applications (VBA).

There are two different types of add-ins. *Component Object Model (COM) add-ins* are a new technology available to Microsoft Office 2000. You can build a COM add-in that works in more than one of the Office 2000 applications. One of the sample COM—add-ins included in this chapter performs the same task in Word, Excel, or PowerPoint—it displays thumbnail graphics and inserts the selected one in the current document. Of course, the code that inserts the graphic in Word isn't the same code that inserts it in Excel. But a great deal of the code is shared, and it all exists in the same file.

The other type of add-in you can create is an *application-specific add-in*. You can create application-specific add-ins in Office 2000 as well as in previous versions of Office. An application-specific add-in works in only one application. They're easier to build and distribute than COM add-ins, so if your solution is for only one application, you may decide to build an application-specific add-in.

In addition, in order to create COM add-ins, you need either Microsoft Visual Basic or Microsoft Office 2000 Developer; if you don't have either of these, the only type of add-in that you can create is an application-specific add-in.

Another way to distribute a custom Office solution is to create a *template*. A template provides the user with a basis for creating a new document. For example, a Word template might include the basic information and layout for a standard report so that an employee can create a new document based on the template and simply fill in the required information.

In addition to the add-ins and templates mentioned above, you can also create two specialized kinds of add-ins: *wizards* and *code libraries*. Wizards are add-ins that walk users through a complex process step-by-step. Code libraries are add-ins in which you can store frequently used procedures and generic code. By setting a reference to a code library, you can call procedures stored within that library from your current VBA project.

Contents

What Is a COM Add-in?

COM add-ins are an exciting addition to Office 2000. You can create a single COM add-in that's available to any of the Office applications—Word, Excel, Access, PowerPoint, Outlook, or FrontPage. You can also create add-ins for the Visual Basic Editor. By building COM add-ins, you can extend the functionality of your Office-based applications without adding complexity for the user.

A COM add-in is a dynamic-link library (DLL) that is specially registered so that it can be loaded by the Office 2000 applications. You can build COM add-ins with Microsoft Visual Basic version 5.0 or later, or any of the Office 2000 applications in Microsoft Office 2000 Developer. You can also create COM add-ins with Microsoft Visual C++ or Microsoft Visual J++. A discussion of these tools is beyond the scope of this book; for more information about them, see the Microsoft Developer Network Web site at http://msdn.microsoft.com/developer/.

Note A COM add-in can also be an ActiveX .exe file. This chapter focuses on creating COM add-ins as DLLs because they generally provide better performance than .exe files do.

Using the Image Gallery Sample Project

Some of the information about COM add-ins presented in this chapter may be easier to follow if you have a working COM add-in project to examine. For this reason, you may want to take time now to copy the files for the Image Gallery sample project from the Samples\CH11\ImageGallery subfolder on the companion CD-ROM to your computer.

ImageGallery.vbp is a sample Microsoft Visual Basic 6.0 project that demonstrates the fundamentals of creating COM add-ins for Office 2000 applications. The Image Gallery add-in can be used from Word, Excel, or PowerPoint. It prompts the user to select a folder in the file system, and then displays thumbnails for the image files contained in that folder, of types bitmap (.bmp), Microsoft Windows metafile (.wmf), GIF (.gif), and JPEG (.jpg). When the user selects a thumbnail and clicks Insert, the graphic is inserted in the document, worksheet, or presentation in which he or she is working.

The Image Gallery project includes the components listed in the following table.

Component name	Description
frmImageGallery	Form that prompts the user to select a folder containing graphics and insert an image in a document
modSharedCode	Procedures that are called from all the add-in designers
modFormFunctions	Procedures called from event procedures in the form's module
dsrImageExcel	Add-in designer for the Excel version of the add-in
dsrImagePpt	Add-in designer for the PowerPoint version of the add-in
dsrImageWord	Add-in designer for the Word version of the add-in

Before you can try the Image Gallery add-in, you must register it on your computer. Copy ImageGallery.dll from the Samples\CH11\ImageGallery subfolder on the companion CD-ROM to your computer. On the Windows Start menu, click **Run**, and type the following command line to register the DLL, where *path* is the path to which you've copied ImageGallery.dll:

Regsvr32 *path***\ImageGallery.dll**

If you have Visual Basic 6.0, you can also open the ImageGallery.vbp project in Visual Basic 6.0 and click **Make ImageGallery.dll** on the **File** menu to make the DLL. This process registers the DLL and also adds information to the registry necessary for Office to recognize this COM add-in.

COM Add-ins vs. Application-Specific Add-ins

In the previous and current versions of Word, Excel, Access, and PowerPoint, you can use VBA to create add-ins specific to each of those applications. For example, you can create an add-in for Word that builds a custom report from a selected database, and another add-in for Excel that performs a similar task. You save the Word add-in as a Word template file (*.dot), and the Excel add-in as an Excel add-in file (*.xla). Despite the fact that the two add-ins share some common code, you have to create two separate add-ins in order to add functionality to both applications.

Note Outlook and FrontPage do not provide any way to create application-specific add-ins by using VBA.

A COM add-in, on the other hand, can share some add-in functionality and code across applications. The COM add-in project contains a component for each application in which it will run and is also registered for each application. Usually a COM add-in contains some code that is common across all applications and some that is specific to each application. For example, if you build a COM add-in to create a custom report in Word or Excel from a database, the code that accesses the database and retrieves a set of data can be shared. Once you've retrieved the data, you need to work with the Word object model to write the data to Word, and with the Excel object model to write the data to Excel.

The following table lists both types of add-ins and their file extensions.

Add-ins	File extensions	Available to
Word add-ins (application-specific)	.dot, .wll, .wiz	Word only
Excel add-ins (application-specific)	.xla, .xll	Excel only
PowerPoint add-ins (application-specific)	.ppa, .pwz	PowerPoint only
Access add-ins (application-specific)	.mda, .mde	Access only
Exchange Client extensions (application-specific)	.dll	Outlook and Microsoft Exchange clients only
COM add-ins	.dll	Word, Excel, Access, PowerPoint, Outlook, and FrontPage

Note Prior to Visual Basic 4.0, DLLs could not be created in Visual Basic. Developers used Visual C++ or a comparable language to create DLLs. The .wll and .xll add-in file formats refer to DLLs created in C++ specifically as add-ins for Word and Excel, before these applications included VBA. Likewise, the only add-ins available for the previous version of Microsoft Outlook were Exchange Client extensions, which are DLLs created only in C/C++. Although more recent versions of Word, Excel, and Outlook still support these custom add-ins, you no longer need to create .wll and .xll files or Exchange Client extensions in order to build a sophisticated add-in.

COM add-ins and application-specific add-ins also differ in terms of how the user views and installs available add-ins. In all Office 2000 applications, available COM add-ins are displayed in the **COM Add-ins** dialog box. This dialog box is the same across all Office applications.

Viewing the List of Available COM Add-ins

By default, there's no menu item or toolbar button to display the **COM Add-ins** dialog box, but you can easily display it.

▶ To add a menu item or toolbar button for the COM Add-ins dialog box

1. In the Office 2000 application, click **Customize** on the **Tools** menu.
2. Click the **Commands** tab.
3. In the **Categories** list, click **Tools**.
4. In the **Commands** list, click **COM Add-ins**. You may have to scroll through the list to find it.
5. Drag the **COM Add-ins** command to a toolbar or a menu.
6. Close the **Customize** dialog box.

Note In Microsoft Outlook 2000, you can also access the **COM Add-ins** dialog box by clicking **Options** on the **Tools** menu, clicking the **Other** tab, and then clicking **Advanced Options**. In the **Advanced Options** dialog box, click **COM Add-ins**.

When you click the **COM Add-ins** toolbar button or menu item, the **COM Add-ins** dialog box appears, showing the list of available COM add-ins. You can load (connect) or unload (disconnect) an add-in by selecting the check box next to it. Loading a COM add-in loads it into memory so that you can work with it. Unloading an add-in removes it from memory; you can't use the add-in until you load it again.

You can add a new COM add-in to the list by clicking **Add** and locating the add-in. Clicking **Add** and selecting an add-in that doesn't appear in the list registers the add-in DLL if it's not already registered, and adds the add-in to the list of available COM add-ins for an Office application. If you've copied the Image Gallery sample add-in to your computer, you can locate ImageGallery.dll and add it to the list of available COM add-ins in Word, Excel, or PowerPoint.

To remove a COM add-in from the list, select it and click **Remove**. Removing an add-in deletes the registry key that contains the add-in's name and load behavior. The registry contains information about a COM add-in in two places. Like any other DLL, the add-in's DLL is registered as a unique object on the system. Additionally, information about the add-in is placed in another section of the registry in order to notify Office applications that the add-in exists, and it's this section that's deleted when you remove an add-in from the list. The DLL itself remains registered, and if you add the add-in to the list again, the add-in's informational section is re-created in the registry.

Notes

- You can add only DLLs that are COM add-ins to the list of available add-ins in the **COM Add-ins** dialog box. Moreover, you can add only COM add-ins that are registered for the application you're working in. For example, if you're working in Access, you can't add a COM add-in that's registered only for Word and Excel.
- You can also create COM add-ins for the Visual Basic Editor. Loading and unloading a COM add-in for the Visual Basic Editor is slightly different than doing so for COM add-ins in the host application's user interface. For more information about working with COM add-ins for the Visual Basic Editor, see "Building COM Add-ins for the Visual Basic Editor" later in this chapter.

Viewing Available Application-Specific Add-ins

Application-specific add-ins are displayed in other dialog boxes, which differ slightly between applications. In Word, this is the **Templates and Add-ins** dialog box; in Excel and PowerPoint, it's the **Add-ins** dialog box; in Access, it's the Add-in Manager.

Each dialog box has buttons to add or remove add-ins from the list of application-specific add-ins, and a check box to indicate whether the add-in is loaded. As with COM add-ins, the application-specific add-in must be loaded into memory before it can be used.

Building COM Add-ins for Office Applications

COM add-ins aren't difficult to create, but there are several steps involved. The following sections outline these steps.

What You Need

To create a COM add-in, you need either of the following:

- Visual Basic 5.0 or later
- Office 2000 Developer

The companion CD-ROM provides a template project, COM Add-In.vbp, for creating a COM add-in in Visual Basic 6.0. This template project is available in the Samples\CH11\VB_COM_AddIn subfolder. The template project supplies the files you need to create a COM add-in, as well as the code that forms the basis of any add-in.

The COM Add-In.vbp project provides you with the following:

- An *add-in designer*. An add-in designer is a component that helps you to create and register a COM add-in. You can modify an add-in designer to create your COM add-in and hook it into an application's user interface. For more information about add-in designers, see "Working with Add-in Designers" later in this chapter.
- A reference to the IDTExtensibility2 type library. The Visual Basic 6.0 template project sets a reference to this type library, contained in the file Msaddndr.dll. The IDTExtensibility2 library supplies the events you can use to run code when your add-in is connected to or disconnected from the hosting application.

Note This chapter focuses on creating COM add-ins in Visual Basic 6.0. The process of creating COM add-ins in Visual Basic 5.0 or with Office 2000 Developer differs in several ways that may not be fully explained in this chapter. For more information about creating add-ins in Visual Basic 5.0, see the documentation for Visual Basic 5.0. For more information about creating COM add-ins with Office 2000 Developer, see the documentation for Office 2000 Developer.

Getting Started

The template project helps you to begin building a COM add-in in Visual Basic 6.0. It provides the key components and code that you need to get your add-in working.

Note To begin using the template project, copy the project from the Samples\Ch11\VB_COM_AddIn subfolder on the companion CD-ROM to the C:\Program Files\Microsoft Visual Studio\VB98\Template\Projects folder of your Visual Basic 6.0 installation. Copying the template project to this location will ensure that the template appears in the Visual Basic 6.0 **New Project** dialog box.

▶ To begin building a COM add-in in Visual Basic 6.0

1. Run Visual Basic 6.0.
2. In the **New Project** dialog box, click **COM Add-in**. This creates a new template project containing a form with OK and Cancel buttons, an add-in designer named AddInDesigner1, and a reference to the IDTExtensibility2 library.
3. Rename the project, form, and add-in designer by changing their **Name** property settings in the Properties window. Give them meaningful names that are appropriate to the add-in that you're creating.
4. Save the project, form, and add-in designer files.

The form and the add-in designer both contain code that serves as a basis for your add-in. You can also build a COM add-in by creating a new DLL project in Visual Basic 6.0 and adding the add-in designer yourself. Adding the designer automatically sets a reference to the IDTExtensibility2 library. For more information about adding an add-in designer to a project, see "Creating COM Add-ins for Multiple Applications" later in this chapter.

Notes

- The add-in designer is not supported in Visual Basic 5.0. To build a COM add-in in Visual Basic 5.0, create a new ActiveX DLL project, and use a basic class module in place of an add-in designer. The user interface component of an add-in designer specifies data that is written to the registry when the add-in DLL is registered. You must add this data to the registry yourself if you're building a COM add-in in Visual Basic 5.0.
- Although Visual Basic 5.0 and Visual Basic 6.0 both supply a template project named AddIn, these template projects can be used only to create add-ins for Visual Basic, not to create COM add-ins for the Office 2000 applications.

Working with Add-in Designers

An add-in designer is a file included with the template project that helps you create and register your COM add-in. You can create a COM add-in without including an add-in designer, but it simplifies the process of creating and registering the add-in. You can use an add-in designer to specify important information for your COM add-in: its name and description, what application it is to run in, and how it loads in that application.

Like forms in a Visual Basic project, an add-in designer (shown in Figure 11.1) has a user interface component and an associated class module. The user interface component is never visible to the user when the add-in is running, however; it's visible only to the developer at design time. You can think of the add-in designer as a sort of dialog box where you specify settings for an add-in.

Figure 11.1 An Add-in Designer for Visual Basic 6.0

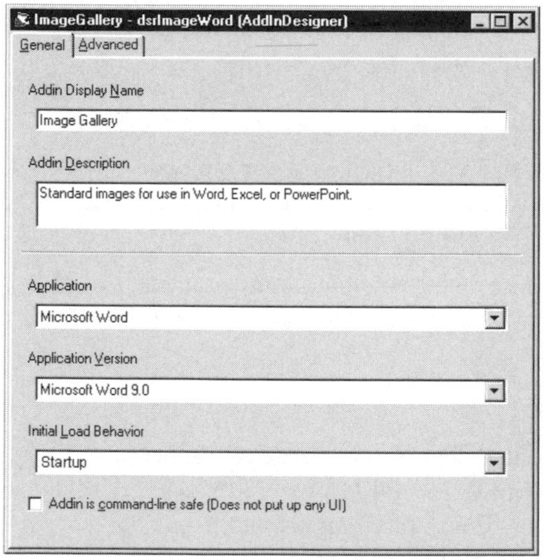

The class module contains the events that occur when the add-in is loaded or unloaded. You can use these events to integrate the add-in into the application.

When you create the add-in DLL, Visual Basic 6.0 uses the information you've given to the add-in designer to properly register the DLL as a COM add-in. Visual Basic 6.0 writes the add-in's name, description, and initial load behavior setting to the registry. The add-in's host application reads these registry entries and loads the add-in accordingly.

Creating COM Add-ins for Multiple Applications

Each add-in designer in your project creates an add-in that can run in only one application. To create a COM add-in that's available to more than one application, you create a new add-in designer for each application that you want to use the add-in, and then customize the add-in designer for each application.

For example, suppose that you want to create an add-in for Word and PowerPoint that creates an organizational chart from a table in a database and inserts the chart into the document or slide. You would begin by making sure there is an add-in designer for Word and one for PowerPoint.

▶ To add a new add-in designer

1 On the **Project** menu in Visual Basic 6.0, click **Add Add-in Class**.

  If the **Add Add-in Class** command does not appear on the **Project** menu, click **Components** on the **Project** menu to open the **Components** dialog box. Click the **Designers** tab, and select the **Add-in Class** check box.

2 Change the add-in designer's **Name** property setting in the Properties window. It may be helpful to indicate in the name of the add-in designer which designer goes with which application. For example, the add-in designer for Excel in the Image Gallery project is named dsrImageExcel.

3 Save the add-in designer file.

Important When you add an add-in designer to your project, you must make sure that the **Public** property for the add-in designer is set to **True**. This property appears in the Visual Basic 6.0 Properties window. If this property is set to **False** for an add-in designer that appears in the project, the COM add-in will not be registered for the host application designated by that add-in designer.

Essentially, each add-in designer in the Visual Basic project represents a separate add-in that can run in only one Office application. The resulting DLL can contain multiple add-ins that share forms, modules, and class modules, but are targeted for different applications.

Note If your COM add-in will run in more than one application, it's a good idea to set the threading model for the project to **Apartment Threaded**. Apartment threading can enhance the performance of add-ins that run in more than one application and that involve lengthy operations. You can set the threading model on the **General** tab of the **Project Properties** dialog box, available on the **Project** menu in Visual Basic 6.0. For more information about threading models, refer to the Visual Basic 6.0 documentation.

Configuring an Add-in Designer

To open an add-in designer, double-click it in the Project Explorer, or right-click it and then click **View Object** on the shortcut menu.

To create your add-in, you first need to fill out the options on the **General** tab of the add-in designer. The following table explains each option.

Option	Description
Add-in Display Name	The name that will appear in the **COM Add-ins** dialog box in an Office 2000 application. The name you supply should be descriptive to the user. If the name is to come from a resource file specified in the **Satellite DLL Name** box on the **Advanced** tab, it must begin with a number sign (#), followed by an integer specifying a resource ID within the file.
Add-in Description	Descriptive text for a COM add-in, available from VBA in the **Description** property of the **COMAddIn** object. If the description is to come from a resource file specified in the **Satellite DLL Name** box on the **Advanced** tab, it must begin with a number sign (#), followed by an integer specifying a resource ID within the file.
Application	The application in which the add-in will run. This list displays applications that support COM add-ins.
Application Version	The version of the application in which the add-in will run.
Initial Load Behavior	The way that the add-in will load in the Office 2000 application. The list of possible settings comes from the registry. For more information, see the following section, "Specifying Load Behavior."
Add-in is command-line safe (does not put up any UI)	Does not apply to COM add-ins running in Office 2000 applications.

The **Advanced** tab of the add-in designer allows you to specify a file containing localized resource information for the add-in and to specify additional registry data. The following table describes the options available on the **Advanced** tab.

Option	Description
Satellite DLL Name	The name of a file containing localized (translated) resources for an add-in; the file must be located in the same directory as the add-in's registered DLL.
Registry Key for Additional Add-in Data	The registry subkey to which additional data is to be written.
Add-in Specific Data	The names and values to be stored in the registry subkey. Only **String** and **DWORD** type values are permitted.

Specifying Load Behavior

When a COM add-in has been properly registered, it's available to whatever applications are specified in the add-in designers that the project contains. The registered COM add-in's display name appears in the **COM Add-ins** dialog box; if it doesn't, click **Add** to browse for the add-in and add it to the list.

Selecting the check box next to an add-in in the **COM Add-ins** dialog box loads (connects) the add-in and makes it available to the user; clearing the check box unloads (disconnects) the add-in, and it can't be run.

As the developer, you specify when a COM add-in should be loaded. You do this in the **Initial Load Behavior** list in the add-in designer. You can specify that an add-in be loaded in one of the following ways:

- Only when the user loads it in the **COM Add-ins** dialog box, or when VBA code loads it by setting the **Connect** property of the corresponding **COMAddIn** object.
- Every time the application starts.
- The first time the application starts, so that it can create a toolbar button or menu item for itself. After that, the add-in is loaded only when the user requests it by clicking the menu item or button.

The following table describes the different settings for the Initial Load Behavior setting.

Initial Load Behavior setting	Behavior
None	The COM add-in is not loaded when the application boots. It can be loaded in the **COM Add-ins** dialog box or by setting the **Connect** property of the corresponding **COMAddIn** object.

Initial Load Behavior setting	Behavior
Startup	The add-in is loaded when the application boots. Once the add-in is loaded, it remains loaded until it is explicitly unloaded.
Load on Demand	The add-in is not loaded until the user clicks the button or menu item that loads the add-in, or until a procedure sets its **Connect** property to **True**. In most cases you won't set the initial load behavior to **Load on Demand** directly; you'll set it to **Load at Next Startup Only**, and it will automatically be set to **Load on Demand** on subsequent boots of the host application.
Load at Next Startup Only	After the COM add-in has been registered, it loads as soon as the user runs the host application for the first time, and it creates a button or menu item for itself. The next time the user boots the application, the add-in is loaded on demand—that is, it doesn't load until the user clicks the button or menu item associated with the add-in.

Writing Code in the Add-in Designer

After you've specified general information for a COM add-in in the add-in designer, you can begin writing code in the designer's class module. To view the add-in designer's class module, right-click the add-in designer in the Project Explorer, and then click **View Code** on the shortcut menu.

Code that's in the add-in designer handles the add-in's integration with the host application. For example, code that runs when the add-in is loaded or unloaded resides in the add-in designer's module. If the add-in contains forms, the add-in designer may also contain code to display the forms.

Implementing the IDTExtensibility2 Library

A COM add-in has events that you can use to run code when the add-in is loaded or unloaded, or when the host application has finished starting up or shutting down. In order to use these events, you must *implement* the IDTExtensibility2 library, which provides a programming interface for integrating COM add-ins with their host applications. When you implement the IDTExtensibility2 library within a class module, the library makes a set of new events available to the module. These are the events that you need to control your COM add-in.

If you've created your add-in project from the template, the IDTExtensibility2 library has already been implemented for you in the add-in designer's class module. If you're creating the COM add-in from scratch, use the following procedure.

▶ To manually implement the IDTExtensibility2 library in Visual Basic 6.0

1. Set a reference to the library by clicking **References** on the **Project** menu and then selecting the check box next to **Microsoft Add-in Designer**. If this library doesn't appear in the list, you can add it by clicking **Browse** and finding the file Msaddndr.dll. By default this file is located in the C:\Program Files\Common Files \Designer subfolder.
2. In the Declarations section of the add-in designer's class module, add the following code:

   ```
   Implements IDTExtensibility2
   ```

3. In the Code window, click **IDTExtensibility2** in the **Object** box. This creates the OnConnection event procedure stub.
4. Create event procedure stubs for the four remaining event procedures by clicking them in the **Procedure** box in the Code window.
5. Add code or a comment to each of the five event procedures.

   Important You must include the event procedure stub for each event provided by the IDTExtensibility2 interface. If you omit any of the event procedures, your project will not compile. If you're not adding code to an event procedure stub, it's a good idea to add a comment; a single apostrophe (') is sufficient.

For more information about the **Implements** keyword and implementing libraries in a class module, see Chapter 9, "Custom Classes and Objects."

Working with the IDTExtensibility2 Event Procedures

The IDTExtensibility2 library provides five events that you can use to manipulate your add-in and the host application: OnConnection, OnDisconnection, OnAddInsUpdate, OnStartupComplete, and OnBeginShutdown. The following sections describe each of these event procedures.

Note If you don't have Visual Basic 6.0, you can try the sample add-in in Word, Excel, or PowerPoint, and then view the code in the add-in's modules by opening them in a text editor such as Notepad.

The OnConnection Event

The OnConnection event occurs when the COM add-in is loaded (connected). An add-in can be loaded in one of the following ways:

- The user starts the host application and the add-in's load behavior is specified to load when the application starts.
- The user loads the add-in in the **COM Add-ins** dialog box.
- The **Connect** property of the corresponding **COMAddIn** object is set to **True**. For more information about the **COMAddIn** object, search the Microsoft Office Visual Basic Reference Help index for "COMAddIn object."

The OnConnection event procedure takes four arguments, described in the following table.

Argument	Type	Description
Application	**Object**	Provides a reference to the application in which the COM add-in is currently running.
ConnectMode	Custom **Long**	A constant that specifies how the add-in was loaded.
AddInInst	**Object** (**COMAddIn**)	A **COMAddIn** object that refers to the instance of the class module in which code is currently running. You can use this argument to return the programmatic identifier for the add-in.
Custom()	**Variant**	An array of **Variant** type values that provides additional data. The numeric value of the first element in this array indicates how the host application was started: from the user interface (1); by embedding a document created in the host application in another application (2); or through Automation (3).

The constants for the *ConnectMode* argument are grouped in the **ext_ConnectMode** enumeration. These constants are described in the following table.

Constant	Description
ext_cm_AfterStartup	Add-in was loaded after the application started, or by setting the **Connect** property of the corresponding **COMAddIn** object to **True**.
ext_cm_CommandLine	Does not apply to building COM add-ins for Office 2000 applications.
ext_cm_External	Does not apply to building COM add-ins for Office 2000 applications.
ext_cm_Startup	Add-in was loaded on startup.

If you're building a COM add-in that will run in more than one host application, you may find that you call the same code from each add-in designer's OnConnection event. For example, you may create a new command bar button in the OnConnection event procedure in the same way within each add-in designer. If so, it's more efficient to create a public procedure in a standard module and call it from within the OnConnection event procedure for each add-in designer than to include the same code in each add-in designer.

The following example shows the OnConnection event procedure as it appears in the dsrImageWord add-in designer in the Image Gallery sample project, located in the Samples\CH11\ImageGallery subfolder on the companion CD-ROM. The OnConnection event procedure calls the CreateAddInCommandBarButton procedure in the modSharedCode module. This procedure creates a new command bar button and returns a reference to it. The OnConnection event procedure then assigns this reference to a private event-ready variable of type **CommandBarButton**.

```
' Event-ready variable declared in add-in designer's module.
Private WithEvents p_ctlBtnEvents     As Office.CommandBarButton

Private Sub IDTExtensibility2_OnConnection(ByVal Application As Object, _
   ByVal ConnectMode As AddInDesignerObjects.ext_ConnectMode, _
   ByVal AddInInst As Object, _
   custom() As Variant)

   ' Call shared code to create new command bar button
   ' and return a reference to it. Assign reference to
   ' event-ready CommandBarButton object declared with
   ' WithEvents within this module.

   Set p_ctlBtnEvents = CreateAddInCommandBarButton(Application, _
      ConnectMode, AddInInst)
End Sub

' Public function in modSharedCode module.
Public Function CreateAddInCommandBarButton(ByVal Application As Object, _
   ByVal ConnectMode As AddInDesignerObjects.ext_ConnectMode, _
   ByVal AddInInst As Object) As Office.CommandBarButton

   ' This procedure assigns a reference to the Application
   ' object passed to the OnConnection event to a global
   ' object variable. It then creates a new command bar
   ' button and returns a reference to the button to the
   ' OnConnection event procedure. The advantage to putting
   ' this code in a public module is that if you have more
   ' than one add-in designer in the project, you can call
   ' this procedure from each of them rather than duplicating
   ' the code.
```

```
    Dim cbrMenu              As Office.CommandBar
    Dim ctlBtnAddIn          As Office.CommandBarButton

    On Error GoTo CreateAddInCommandBarButton_Err

    ' Return reference to Application object and store it
    ' in public variable so that other procedures in add-in
    ' can use it.
    Set gobjAppInstance = Application

    ' Return reference to command bar.
    Set cbrMenu = gobjAppInstance.CommandBars(CBR_NAME)

    ' Add button to call add-in from command bar, if it doesn't
    ' already exist.
    ' Constants are declared at module level.
    ' Look for button on command bar.
    Set ctlBtnAddIn = cbrMenu.FindControl(Tag:=CTL_KEY)
    If ctlBtnAddIn Is Nothing Then
       ' Add new button.
       Set ctlBtnAddIn = cbrMenu.Controls.Add(Type:=msoControlButton, _
          Parameter:=CTL_KEY)
       ' Set button's Caption, Tag, Style, and OnAction properties.
       With ctlBtnAddIn
          .Caption = CTL_CAPTION
          .Tag = CTL_KEY
          .Style = msoButtonCaption
          ' Use AddInInst argument to return reference
          ' to this add-in.
          .OnAction = PROG_ID_START & AddInInst.ProgId _
             & PROG_ID_END
       End With
    End If

    ' Return reference to new commandbar button.
    Set CreateAddInCommandBarButton = ctlBtnAddIn

CreateAddInCommandBarButton_End:
    Exit Function

CreateAddInCommandBarButton_Err:
    ' Call generic error handler for add-in.
    AddInErr Err
    Resume CreateAddInCommandBarButton_End
End Function
```

The CreateAddInCommandBarButton procedure first performs a critical step: it assigns the object passed to the procedure in the *Application* argument to a public module-level object variable. This object variable persists as long as the COM add-in is loaded, so that any other procedures in the module can determine in what application the add-in is currently running. A public module-level variable declared in a standard module in a COM add-in remains in existence from the time the add-in is loaded to the time it is unloaded.

This procedure also contains code that creates a new menu item on the **Tools** menu of the host application the first time the add-in is loaded. Before creating the new menu item, the procedure checks to see whether the item already exists; if it does, the procedure returns a reference to the existing menu item rather than creating a new one. The OnConnection event procedure then assigns the reference returned by the CreateAddInCommandBarButton procedure to a variable (`p_ctlBtnEvents`) that's been declared by using the **WithEvents** keyword, so that the menu item's Click event procedure will be triggered when the user clicks the new menu item. For more information about creating a menu item for a COM add-in, see "Hooking a COM Add-in Up to a Command Bar Control" later in this chapter. For more information about using the **WithEvents** keyword to sink command bar events, see Chapter 6, "Working with Shared Office Components," and Chapter 9, "Custom Classes and Objects."

The OnDisconnection Event

The OnDisconnection event occurs when the COM add-in is unloaded. You can use the OnDisconnection event procedure to run code that restores any changes made to the application by the add-in and to perform general clean-up operations.

An add-in can be unloaded in one of the following ways:

- The user clears the check box next to the add-in in the **COM Add-ins** dialog box.
- The host application closes. If the add-in is currently loaded when the application closes, it is unloaded. If the add-in's load behavior is set to **Startup**, it is reloaded when the application starts again.
- The **Connect** property of the corresponding **COMAddIn** object is set to **False**.

The OnDisconnection event procedure takes two arguments, described in the following table.

Argument	Type	Description
RemoveMode	Custom **Long**	A constant that specifies how the add-in was unloaded.
Custom()	**Variant**	An array of **Variant** type values that provides additional data. The numeric value of the first element in this array indicates how the host application was started: from the user interface (1); by embedding a document created in the host application in another application (2); or through Automation (3).

The following table lists the available constants for the **RemoveMode** method, which are grouped in the **ext_DisconnectionMode** enumeration.

Constant	Description
ext_dm_HostShutdown	Add-in was unloaded when the application was closed.
ext_dm_UserClosed	Add-in was unloaded when the user cleared the corresponding check box in the **COM Add-ins** dialog box, or when the **Connect** property of the corresponding **COMAddIn** object was set to **False**.

The following code shows the OnDisconnection event procedure as it appears in the dsrImageWord designer in the Image Gallery project, located in the Samples\CH11 \ImageGallery subfolder on the companion CD-ROM. The OnDisconnection event procedure calls the RemoveAddInCommandBarButton procedure located in the modSharedCode module. If the user unloads the add-in, the add-in's menu command is deleted; otherwise it's maintained for the next time the user starts the application:

```
Private Sub IDTExtensibility2_OnDisconnection(ByVal _
   RemoveMode As AddInDesignerObjects.ext_DisconnectMode, _
   custom() As Variant)

   ' Call common procedure to disconnect add-in.
   RemoveAddInCommandBarButton RemoveMode
End Sub

Function RemoveAddInCommandBarButton(ByVal _
   RemoveMode As AddInDesignerObjects.ext_DisconnectMode)

   ' This procedure removes the command bar button for
   ' the add-in if the user disconnected it.

   On Error GoTo RemoveAddInCommandBarButton_Err

   ' If user unloaded add-in, remove button. Otherwise,
   ' add-in is being unloaded because application is
   ' closing; in that case, leave button as is.
   If RemoveMode = ext_dm_UserClosed Then
      On Error Resume Next
      ' Delete custom command bar button.
      gobjAppInstance.CommandBars(CBR_NAME).Controls(CTL_NAME).Delete
      On Error GoTo RemoveAddInCommandBarButton_Err
   End If

RemoveAddInCommandBarButton_End:
   Exit Function

RemoveAddInCommandBarButton_Err:
   AddInErr Err
   Resume RemoveAddInCommandBarButton_End
End Function
```

The OnStartupComplete Event

The OnStartupComplete event occurs when the host application completes its startup routines, in the case where the COM add-in loads at startup. If the add-in is not loaded when the application loads, the OnStartupComplete event does not occur, even when the user loads the add-in in the **COM Add-ins** dialog box. When this event does occur, it occurs after the OnConnection event.

You can use the OnStartupComplete event procedure to run code that interacts with the application and shouldn't be run until the application has finished loading. For example, if you want to display a form that gives users a choice of documents to create when they start the application, you can put that code in the OnStartupComplete event procedure.

The OnBeginShutdown Event

The OnBeginShutdown event occurs when the host application begins its shutdown routines, in the case where the application closes while the COM add-in is still loaded. If the add-in is not currently loaded when the application closes, the OnBeginShutdown event does not occur. When this event does occur, it occurs before the OnDisconnection event.

You can use the OnBeginShutdown event procedure to run code when the user closes the application. For example, you can run code that saves form data to a file.

The OnAddInsUpdate Event

The OnAddInsUpdate event occurs when the set of loaded COM add-ins changes. When an add-in is loaded or unloaded, the OnAddInsUpdate event occurs in any other loaded add-ins. For example, if add-ins A and B are both currently loaded, and add-in C is then loaded, the OnAddInsUpdate event occurs in add-ins A and B. If C is unloaded, the OnAddInsUpdate event occurs again in add-ins A and B.

If you have an add-in that depends on another add-in, you can use the OnAddInsUpdate event procedure in the dependent add-in to determine whether the other add-in has been loaded or unloaded.

Note The OnStartupComplete, OnBeginShutdown, and OnAddInsUpdate event procedures each provide only a single argument, the *Custom()* argument, which is an empty array of **Variant** type values. This argument is ignored in COM add-ins for Office 2000 applications.

Hooking a COM Add-in Up to a Command Bar Control

If your COM add-in has a user interface, it needs to be integrated with the host application in some way so that the user can interact with it. For example, the user interface for your COM add-in most likely includes a form. At some point, code in the add-in needs to be run in order to display the form.

One way to integrate your add-in with an application's user interface is to include code in the OnConnection event procedure that creates a new command bar control (toolbar button or menu item) in the host application. When your add-in is loaded, the user can click the button or menu item to work with the add-in.

The critical aspect of integrating an add-in through a command bar control is the process of setting up the *event sink*. You must create a command bar control that is event-ready so that its Click event is triggered when the user clicks the control. You can use the **WithEvents** keyword to create an event-ready command bar control.

If you set the load behavior for your add-in to **Load at Next Startup Only**, you also need to set the **OnAction** property for the command bar control. If you don't set the **OnAction** property, the add-in will load the first time the application starts. The next time you start the application, however, the load behavior for the add-in will be set to **Load on Demand**, and the command bar control that you've created for the add-in won't load the add-in unless the **OnAction** property has been set.

Even if your add-in is not demand-loaded, it's a good idea to set this property in your code in case you later change the load behavior for the add-in. The syntax for setting the **OnAction** property for a COM add-in is

ctlButton.**OnAction = "!<***ProgID***>"**

where *ctlButton* is the **CommandBarButton** object and *ProgID* is the *programmatic identifier* for the add-in. The programmatic identifier is the subkey that's created for the add-in in the Windows registry. Each add-in designer or class module that implements the IDTExtensibility2 library in the COM add-in project adds its own programmatic identifier to the registry, beneath the AddIns subkey for the host application in which it will run. The programmatic identifier for a COM add-in consists of the name of the project followed by the name of the add-in designer or class module. For example, the programmatic identifier for the ImageGallery add-in for Word is ImageGallery.dsrImageWord.

To return the programmatic identifier for an add-in, you can use the *AddInInst* argument that's passed to the OnConnection event procedure. This argument provides a reference to the add-in designer or class module in which code is currently running. The *AddInInst* argument is an object of type **COMAddIn**, which has a **ProgId** property that returns the programmatic identifier. Note that you need to concatenate the **!<** and **>** delimiters before and after the programmatic identifier string to properly set the **OnAction** property.

Important If your add-in will run in Word, you also need to set the **Tag** property for the **CommandBarButton** object to a unique **String** value. This ensures that the command bar button will respond to the Click event and load the add-in for each new document window that the user opens. Because the **Tag** property provides you with additional information about the control, it's a good idea to set the **Tag** property for a command bar button that loads a COM add-in in any host application.

▶ To create a command bar control that displays the add-in's form

1 In the add-in designer's module, use the **WithEvents** keyword to declare a module-level variable of type **CommandBarButton**. This creates an event-ready **CommandBarButton** object.

2 In the same module, create the Click event procedure stub for the **CommandBarButton** object by clicking the name of the object variable in the **Object** box and then clicking **Click** in the **Procedure** box.

3 Write code within the event procedure stub to open the form when the Click event occurs.

4 In the OnConnection event procedure, check to see whether the command bar control already exists, and return a reference to it if it does. If it doesn't exist, create the new command bar control and return a reference to it. You need to check whether the command bar control exists so that you don't create a new control each time your code runs.

5 When you create the new command bar control, set the **Tag** property for the **CommandBarButton** object to a unique string. This is necessary only for COM add-ins running in Word, but it's recommended for COM add-ins running in any host application.

6 When you create the new command bar control, set the **OnAction** property for the command bar control if the COM add-in is to be demand-loaded. If you fail to set the **OnAction** property, the command bar button will load the add-in the first time the application starts, but will not load the add-in when the application is closed and reopened.

7 Within the OnConnection event procedure, assign the reference to the command bar control to the event-ready **CommandBarButton** object variable.

8 Add code to the OnDisconnection event to remove the command bar control when the add-in is unloaded.

The add-in designer in the COM add-in template project includes code that performs all these steps to create a menu item on the **Tools** menu. By default, the template project has a reference set to the Microsoft Office 9.0 object library so that you can work with Office command bars.

For more information about using the **WithEvents** keyword and sinking events, see Chapter 9, "Custom Classes and Objects." For more information about working with command bars and their events, see Chapter 6, "Working with Shared Office Components."

Working with Host Application Object Models

There are a few things to keep in mind as you add forms and other components to your COM add-in. First of all, your COM add-in is like a separate application running inside an Office 2000 application. Therefore, you need to set references to any object libraries you want to work with from within the COM add-in's project. If your add-in will be run in more than one application, you can use the OnConnection event procedure to determine which application your add-in is currently running in and then selectively run code that works with that application's objects.

To figure out in which application the add-in is currently running, use the object supplied by the *Application* argument of the OnConnection event procedure. Assign this object variable to a global object variable. In the code that interacts with the host application, check to see which application you're working with, and use that application's object model to perform the task.

A DLL is loaded into memory only once, but each application that accesses the DLL gets its own copy of the DLL's data, stored in a separate space in memory. Therefore, you can use global variables in a COM add-in without worrying about data being shared between two applications that are using the COM add-in at the same time. For example, the Image Gallery sample add-in can run simultaneously in Word, Excel, and PowerPoint. When Word loads the add-in, the OnConnection event occurs and a reference to the Word **Application** object is stored in a global variable of type **Object**. If Excel then loads the add-in, the OnConnection event occurs and a reference to the Excel **Application** object is also stored in a global variable of type **Object**, but in a different space in memory. Within the code for the add-in, you can use the **If TypeOf…End If** construct to check which application's **Application** object the variable points to. The Click event procedure for the cmdInsert button in frmImageGallery in the Image Gallery project, located in the Samples\CH11 \ImageGallery subfolder on the companion CD-ROM, uses this approach:

```
' Global object variable, declared in modSharedCode module.
Public gobjAppInstance As Object

Private Sub cmdInsert_Click()
   ' Insert selected image.
   ' Check which object variable has been initialized.
   If TypeOf gobjAppInstance Is Word.Application Then
      ' Insert into Word.
      Word.Selection.InlineShapes.AddPicture FileName:= _
         img(mlngSel).Tag, LinkToFile:=False, _
         SaveWithDocument:=True
   ElseIf TypeOf gobjAppInstance Is Excel.Application Then
      gobjAppInstance.ActiveSheet.Pictures.Insert img(mlngSel).Tag
   ElseIf TypeOf gobjAppInstance Is Powerpoint.Application Then
      gobjAppInstance.ActiveWindow.Selection.SlideRange.Shapes.AddPicture _
         FileName:=img(mlngSel).Tag, LinkToFile:=msoFalse, _
         SaveWithDocument:=msoCTrue, Left:=100, Top:=100
   End If
End Sub
```

Debugging a COM Add-in

When you're developing a COM add-in in Visual Basic, you can debug the add-in by putting the project into run mode. With the project in run mode, you can load and use the COM add-in from within an Office 2000 application to test and debug it by using any of the Visual Basic debugging tools.

▶ To debug a COM add-in in Visual Basic 6.0

1. Open the add-in project in Visual Basic 6.0.
2. Place any desired breakpoints, **Stop** statements, or watches in the code.
3. On the **Run** menu, click **Start with Full Compile**. This compiles your project, alerting you to any compilation errors, and then puts the project into run mode.
4. Open the intended host application for the COM add-in. If you've set the add-in's load behavior to **Startup** or **Load at Next Startup Only**, the add-in loads as soon as you start the application. If the add-in's load behavior is set to **None** or **Load on Demand**, open the **COM Add-ins** dialog box and select the check box next to your add-in to load it.

When the add-in loads, the OnConnection event occurs. You can now enter break mode in the add-in project in Visual Basic 6.0 and debug the code.

Making the DLL

When you've debugged your COM add-in to your satisfaction, you can make it into a DLL. In Visual Basic, click **Make** ***projectname*****.dll** on the **File** menu. The **Make Project** dialog box appears; note that you can enter a name for the DLL that's different from the suggested name. The process of making the DLL registers it on the local machine.

When you make the DLL in Visual Basic 6.0, the information in the add-in designer is used to add a subkey to the Windows registry, indicating which applications can host the add-in. The COM add-in then appears in the **COM Add-ins** dialog box in those applications for which it is registered.

When you make the DLL in Visual Basic 5.0, you must add a subkey to the registry to indicate that the DLL is an add-in so that it will appear in the **COM Add-ins** dialog box. The following section describes the information that you need to add to the registry.

Add-in Registration

Before you can use a COM add-in in an Office 2000 application, the add-in DLL must be registered, like any other DLL on the computer. The DLL's class ID is registered beneath the \HKEY_CLASSES_ROOT subtree in the registry. The DLL can be registered on a user's computer by using a setup program like the ones created by the Visual Basic 6.0 Package and Deployment Wizard, or by running the Regsvr32.exe command-line utility that's included with Windows. Adding a COM add-in by using the **COM Add-ins** dialog box also registers the DLL if it was created with Visual Basic 6.0.

Registering the DLL beneath the \HKEY_CLASSES_ROOT subtree informs the operating system of its presence, but additional information must be added to the registry in order for the add-in to be available to an Office 2000 application. This is the information that you can specify in the add-in designer—the add-in's name, description, target application, target application version, and initial load behavior. The add-in designer ensures that this application-specific information is written to the correct place in the registry at the same time that the add-in DLL is registered. The **COM Add-ins** dialog box displays the information contained in the subkey for the corresponding Office 2000 application.

Since Visual Basic 5.0 does not support the add-in designer, if you're developing in Visual Basic 5.0, you have to add the additional information to the registry yourself on each computer where the add-in is installed.

This subkey must be added to the following registry subkey, where *appname* is the name of the application in which the add-in will run:

\HKEY_CURRENT_USER\SOFTWARE\Microsoft\Office*appname*\AddIns

The new subkey itself must be the programmatic identifier of the COM add-in, which consists of the name of the project followed by the name of the class module or add-in designer. For example, the registry subkey for the Image Gallery add-in for Word would be ImageGallery.dsrImageWord.

The following table describes the entries that you can add beneath this subkey. Only the LoadBehavior entry is required; the others are optional.

Name	Type	Value
Description	**String**	Name to appear in **COM Add-ins** dialog box
FriendlyName	**String**	String returned by **Description** property
LoadBehavior	**DWORD**	Integer indicating load behavior: 0 (**None**), 3 (**Startup**), 9 (**Load on Demand**), or 16 (**Load At Next Startup Only**)

For more information about registering an add-in created in Visual Basic 5.0, see "Distributing COM Add-ins Created with Visual Basic 5.0" later in this chapter.

Distributing COM Add-ins

If you're planning to distribute your COM add-in to other users, you need to install all the necessary files on each user's system and register the add-in. How you do this depends on the environment in which you're developing the add-in.

Distributing COM Add-ins Created with Visual Basic 6.0

If you're developing in Visual Basic 6.0, the easiest way to distribute a COM add-in is to include the add-in designer in the add-in project, and then create a setup program for the add-in. The user can install and register the add-in by running the setup program.

To create the setup program, run the Visual Basic 6.0 Package and Deployment Wizard on the add-in project. When the user runs the setup program, all the files required for the add-in to run will be copied to the user's computer and registered.

For more information about using the Visual Basic 6.0 Package and Deployment Wizard, see the documentation included with Visual Basic 6.0.

Distributing COM Add-ins Created with Visual Basic 5.0

To create a setup program for an add-in created with Visual Basic 5.0, you have a couple of options:

- You can create a custom setup program that copies the DLL to the user's computer, registers it by calling Regsvr32.exe, and writes the additional subkeys needed for a COM add-in to the Windows registry. For more information about creating a custom setup program, see Chapter 2, "Designing and Deploying Office Solutions."
- You can run the Visual Basic 5.0 Setup Wizard on the add-in project. The Visual Basic 5.0 Setup Wizard will create a setup program that installs and registers the add-in DLL and any other necessary files. However, since the Visual Basic 5.0 add-in doesn't contain the add-in designer, you must take additional steps to add a subkey to the registry on the user's machine so that the COM add-in appears in the **COM Add-ins** dialog box.

There are two ways to write information to the registry when a setup program runs:

- Use the Visual Basic 5.0 Setup Toolkit to modify the setup project, and call the functions that write the new subkey to the registry when the setup program runs.
- Include a .reg file with the setup program that contains the necessary registry information, and modify the Setup.lst file created by the Visual Basic 5.0 Setup Wizard so that the information in the .reg file is transferred to the user's registry.

An in-depth discussion of these techniques is beyond the scope of this book. For more information, see the documentation included with Visual Basic 5.0.

COM Add-ins and Security

You can specify security settings for Office 2000 applications in the Office 2000 **Security** dialog box, available by pointing to **Macro** on the **Tools** menu and then clicking **Security**. The **Security Level** tab includes a check box, **Trust all installed add-ins and templates**. If this box is selected, Office 2000 applications will load all COM add-ins, application-specific add-ins, and templates in trusted folders without checking to see whether they have valid digital signatures from trusted sources. For more information about trusted folders, see Chapter 2, “Designing and Deploying Office Solutions,” and Chapter 17, “ Securing Office Documents and Visual Basic for Applications Code.”

If this check box is not selected, the Office 2000 application checks to see whether the add-in or template has been digitally signed by a trusted source before loading it. If it has, the add-in will be loaded under any security level. If it has not been signed, if it has not been signed by a trusted source, or if the signature has been invalidated, the add-in will not load under high security. Under medium security, users will be warned that the add-in may not be safe. Under low security, the add-in will load and run without prompting the user.

To digitally sign a COM add-in DLL, you need to obtain a *digital certificate* from a certificate authority, and you need to run the Signcode.exe utility included with the Microsoft Internet Client Software Development Kit (SDK) on the COM add-in DLL. A digital certificate identifies the developer of a component as a trusted source. For more information about digitally signing a DLL, search the Microsoft Developer Network Web site, at http://msdn.microsoft.com/developer/, for “digital signing.” For more information about security for VBA projects and digital signatures, including how to obtain a digital certificate and the Internet Client SDK, see Chapter 17, “Securing Office Documents and Visual Basic for Applications Code.”

You can use the **COMAddIn** object and the **COMAddIns** collection to control COM add-ins from VBA code that is running within the host application. For example, you can load an add-in programmatically when a user clicks a button to access a particular feature. Or, you can load an add-in from VBA when you open an application through Automation (formerly called OLE Automation).

The Microsoft Office 9.0 object library supplies the **COMAddIn** object and the **COMAddIns** collection. The **Application** object for each Office 2000 application—Word, Excel, PowerPoint, Access, FrontPage, and Outlook—has a **COMAddIns** property, which returns a reference to the **COMAddIns** collection. For any application, the **COMAddIns** collection contains only those COM add-ins that are registered for that application. The **COMAddIns** collection in Excel, for example, contains no information about **COMAddIn** objects in Word.

The **Connect** property of a **COMAddIn** object sets or returns the load status of the add-in. Setting this property to **True** loads the add-in, while setting it to **False** unloads it.

The **ProgId** property returns the name of the registry subkey that stores information about the COM add-in. The registry subkey takes it name from the COM add-in's programmatic identifier, which consists of the name of the add-in project followed by the name of the add-in designer or class module that's actually supplying the add-in for a particular application. For example, when it's properly registered, the Image Gallery sample add-in for Excel has the following value for its **ProgId** property:

ImageGallery.dsrImageExcel

The name of the add-in project is ImageGallery, and the name of the add-in designer for the Excel version of the add-in is dsrImageExcel.

You can use an add-in's **ProgId** property value to return a reference to the add-in from the **COMAddIns** collection, as shown in the following code fragment, which prints the current value of the Excel Image Gallery COM add-in's **Connect** property:

```
Debug.Print Excel.Application.COMAddIns("ImageGallery.dsrImageExcel").Connect
```

You can use the **COMAddIn** object and **COMAddIns** collection to get information about available COM add-ins from code running in an Office 2000 application. You can also use it to load and unload add-ins from code running in the add-in host application, or from code that is performing an Automation operation on the host application from another application.

If you're concerned about the performance of your application, you may want to load an add-in only at certain times. You can control this by loading and unloading it through VBA code.

The following code uses Automation to launch Word from another application, such as Excel, and load the Image Gallery add-in. To run this code from another application, remember to first set a reference to the Word object library.

```
Function LoadWordWithImageGallery() As Boolean
   ' Loads Word and connects Image Gallery add-in.
   ' If Image Gallery add-in is not available, procedure
   ' fails silently and returns False.

   Dim wdApp      As Word.Application
   Dim comAddIn   As Office.comAddIn

   ' Create instance of Word and make visible.
   Set wdApp = New Word.Application
   wdApp.Visible = True
   ' Add new document.
   wdApp.Documents.Add
```

```
    ' Return reference to COM add-in, checking for error
    ' in case it doesn't exist.
    On Error Resume Next
    ' Set reference to COM add-in by using its ProgId property value.
    Set comAddIn = wdApp.ComAddIns("ImageGallery.dsrImageWord")
    If Err.Number = 0 Then
        ' Connect add-in.
        comAddIn.Connect = True
        ' Perform other operations here.
        ' .
        ' .
        ' .
        LoadWordWithAddIn = True
    Else
        ' Return False if error occurred.
        LoadWordWithAddIn = False
    End If

    ' Enter break mode here to verify that add-in is loaded.
    Stop

    ' Quit Word.
    wdApp.Quit
    Set wdApp = Nothing
End Function
```

The LoadWordWithImageGallery procedure is available in the modAddInObjects module in AddInObjects.xls in the Samples\CH11 subfolder on the companion CD-ROM.

For more information about the **COMAddIn** object and the **COMAddIns** collection, search the Microsoft Office Visual Basic Reference Help index for "COMAddIn object" and "COMAddIns collection."

Building COM Add-ins for the Visual Basic Editor

By creating COM add-ins for the Visual Basic Editor, you can customize your development environment and work with components in a VBA project from code. For example, you can build a code wizard that walks a programmer through a series of steps and then builds a procedure. Or you can build a code analyzer that determines how many times and from where a procedure is called. Creating COM add-ins for the Visual Basic Editor is one way to make your own job easier!

When you create a COM add-in for the Visual Basic Editor, it appears in all instances of the Visual Basic Editor. You can't, for example, create a COM add-in that appears only in the Visual Basic Editor in Word; it will also appear in the Visual Basic Editor in Access, Excel, PowerPoint, FrontPage, and any other VBA host applications on the computer where the COM add-in DLL is registered.

Note also that you can create multiple add-ins in a single DLL. Each add-in designer in the add-in project represents a separate add-in. For example, you can create a single DLL that contains a suite of add-ins for developers, and the developers can load just the add-ins they want to use.

To control the Visual Basic Editor from the code inside an add-in, you use the Microsoft Visual Basic for Applications Extensibility 5.3 library. This object library contains objects that represent the parts of a VBA project, such as the **VBProject** object and the **VBComponent** object. The top-level object in the VBA Extensibility library object model is the **VBE** object, which represents the Visual Basic Editor itself. For more information about this object library, use context-sensitive Help (F1) in the Object Browser. For a diagram of its objects, see the "Object Model Diagrams" appendix.

Note Don't confuse the VBA Extensibility library with the IDTExtensibility2 library. Although their names are similar, the VBA Extensibility library provides objects that you can use to work with the Visual Basic Editor from an add-in while it is running, and the IDTExtensibility2 library provides events that are triggered when the add-in is connected or disconnected. In addition, don't confuse the VBA Extensibility library with the Microsoft Visual Basic 6.0 Extensibility library, which is used for creating add-ins in Microsoft Visual Basic.

To see a sample COM add-in for the Visual Basic Editor, copy the DevTools project from the Samples\CH11\DevTools subfolder on the companion CD-ROM to your computer. The DevTools sample project includes two simple add-ins that work with objects in the VBA Extensibility library. The Insert Procedure Template add-in found in this project inserts a new procedure skeleton into a selected code module, complete with scoping, arguments, a return value, and simple error handling. The PathFinder add-in saves you from having to type long file paths—you can use it to navigate to the file you're interested in, and then copy a string containing the file path.

Creating a COM Add-in for the Visual Basic Editor

For the most part, creating a COM add-in for the Visual Basic Editor is similar to creating one for an Office 2000 application. COM add-ins for the Visual Basic Editor also include either the add-in designer or a class module that implements the IDTExtensibility2 library. You can begin with the COM add-in template project.

One key difference to note is that the initial load behavior setting for a COM add-in for the Visual Basic Editor differs from that of a COM add-in for an Office application. A COM add-in for the Visual Basic Editor can have one of two initial load behaviors: **None**, meaning that the add-in is not loaded until the user loads it, or **Startup**, meaning that the add-in is loaded when the user opens the Visual Basic Editor.

▶ To create a COM add-in in Visual Basic 6.0 for the Visual Basic Editor

1. Create a new COM add-in project and modify the add-in designer so that the **Application** box is set to **VBE** and the **Application Version** box is set to **VBE 6.0**. Set the initial load behavior for the add-in to either **None** or **Startup**.
2. Set a reference to the Microsoft Visual Basic for Applications Extensibility 5.3 library. The file Vbe6ext.olb contains this object library; if the object library doesn't appear in the list of available references, it is installed by default in C:\Program Files\Common Files\Microsoft Shared\VBA\VBA6. The name of the library as it appears in the Object Browser is VBIDE.
3. In the add-in designer's class module, implement the IDTExtensibility2 library as described in "Implementing the IDTExtensibility2 Library" earlier in this chapter. Make sure that each event procedure contains code or a comment.
4. The OnConnection event procedure passes in the *Application* argument, which contains a reference to the instance of the Visual Basic Editor in which the add-in is running. You can use this object to work with all other objects in the VBA Extensibility library. To do so, create a public module-level object variable of type **VBIDE.VBE**, and assign the object referenced by the *Application* argument to this variable.
5. Within the OnConnection event procedure, you can optionally include code to hook the add-in's form up to a command bar control in the Visual Basic Editor. You can work with the Visual Basic Editor's command bars by using the **CommandBars** property of the **VBE** object.
6. Build any forms or other components to be included in the project.
7. Place a breakpoint in the OnConnection event procedure, and then click **Start with Full Compile** on the **Run** menu.
8. In a VBA host application, such as Excel, open the Visual Basic Editor, click **Add-in Manager** on the **Add-ins** menu, and select your add-in from the list. Select the **Loaded/Unloaded** check box to load the add-in, if it's not set to load on startup.
9. Debug the add-in. When you've debugged it to your satisfaction, end the running project in Visual Basic 6.0, and make the add-in's DLL by clicking **Make *projectname*.dll** on the **File** menu.

You can use the same strategies to distribute COM add-ins for the Visual Basic Editor as you use to distribute COM add-ins for the Office 2000 applications. For more information, see "Distributing COM Add-ins" earlier in this chapter.

Working with the Microsoft Visual Basic for Applications Extensibility 5.3 Library

The VBA extensibility library provides objects that you can use to work with the Visual Basic Editor and any VBA projects that it contains. From an add-in created in Visual Basic 6.0, you can return a reference to the **VBE** object, the top-level object in the VBA Extensibility library, through the *Application* argument of the OnConnection event procedure. This argument provides a reference to the instance of the Visual Basic Editor in which the add-in is running.

The **VBProject** object refers to a VBA project that's open in the Visual Basic Editor. A **VBProject** object has a **VBComponents** collection, which in turn contains **VBComponent** objects. A **VBComponent** object represents a component in the project, such as a standard module, class module, or form. Because a **VBComponent** object can represent any of these objects, you can use its **Type** property to determine which type of module you're currently working with.

For example, suppose you have a variable named `vbeCurrent`, of type **VBIDE.VBE**, that represents the instance of the Visual Basic Editor in which the add-in will run. The following code fragment prints the names and types of all components in the active project to the Immediate window:

```
Dim vbcComp As VBIDE.VBComponent

For Each vbcComp In vbeCurrent.ActiveVBProject.VBComponents
    Debug.Print vbcComp.Name, vbcComp.Type
Next vbcComp
```

A **VBComponent** object has a **CodeModule** property that returns a **CodeModule** object, which refers to the code module associated with that component. You can use the methods and properties of the **CodeModule** object to manipulate the code in that module on a line-by-line basis. For example, you can insert lines by using the **InsertLines** method, or perform find and replace operations by using the **Find** and **Replace** methods.

To work with command bars in the Visual Basic Editor, use the **CommandBars** property of the **VBE** object to return a reference to the **CommandBars** collection.

For more information about working with the VBA Extensibility library, search the Visual Basic Reference Help index for "VBProject object."

Building Application-Specific Add-ins

For some solutions, creating an application-specific add-in is easier and more convenient than building a COM add-in. The following sections discuss creating application-specific add-ins for Word, Excel, PowerPoint, and Access.

Note For more information about developing add-ins for systems that are using user profiles, see Chapter 2, "Designing and Deploying Office Solutions."

Word Add-ins

You can add functionality to a Word solution by creating a Word-specific add-in (also sometimes referred to as a global template). Add-ins are good for adding generic functionality to the Word environment. For example, you might create a Word add-in that contains common tools for working with Word documents. The user can use any of these tools with his or her documents by clicking the toolbars and menu commands that the add-in provides.

To see a list of currently available Word add-ins, click **Templates and Add-ins** on the **Tools** menu. The currently loaded add-ins appear checked in the **Global templates and add-ins** list in the **Templates and Add-ins** dialog box.

A Word add-in is similar to a Word template in that both add-ins and templates have the .dot file extension. However, add-ins and templates contribute different functionality to a Word document. For more information about templates and how they differ from add-ins, see "Word Templates" later in this chapter.

The Samples\CH11 subfolder on the companion CD-ROM contains an add-in called UsefulTools.dot. This template contains four tools that may be helpful to a Word user: Tile Vertical, which tiles multiple windows vertically; Navigate Bookmarks, which lists all bookmarks in the document and allows the user to navigate easily to a bookmark; Global Print, which prints all the .doc files in a specified folder; and Global Replace, which replaces a string of text in all documents in a specified folder. Each of these tools is available through a button on the UsefulTools toolbar that is saved with the add-in. To make these tools available to your own Word documents, load the add-in in the **Global templates and add-ins** list in the **Templates and Add-ins** dialog box.

Creating a Word Add-in

You should create an add-in when:

- Your solution doesn't require boilerplate text or custom styles.
- You want to make some functionality available to any document the user creates, through toolbar buttons, menu commands, or macros.

▶ To create a Word add-in

1. Create a new document template. (For information about creating a document template, see "Word Templates" later in this chapter.)
2. Add code to the add-in and create a new toolbar with buttons that call your code when they are clicked.
3. Compile the project by clicking **Compile Project** on the **Debug** menu in the Visual Basic Editor.
4. If you want, protect the project from viewing as described in "Securing an Access, Excel, PowerPoint, or Word Add-In's VBA Project" later in this chapter.
5. Save the template as type Document Template with the .dot extension. By default, a Word add-in is saved to C:\Windows\Application Data\Microsoft\Templates; if you're using user profiles, the default path is C:\Windows\Profiles*UserName*\Application Data\Microsoft\Templates. To change the default path for templates, click **Options** on the **Tools** menu. Click the **File Locations** tab, click **User templates** in the **File types** list, and then click **Modify**. If you want the add-in to load automatically when you start Word, save the add-in to the Word Startup folder, as discussed in the following section, "Loading a Word Add-in."

Note You can also modify the default location for workgroup templates in the **Options** dialog box. Workgroup templates are templates that you share on a network with other users.

Loading a Word Add-in

You can load an add-in in one of three ways:

- Manually, by clicking **Templates and Add-ins** on the **Tools** menu, and then selecting the check box next to the template's name in the **Global templates and add-ins** list. If the add-in doesn't appear in the list, click **Add** to locate it. Once an add-in is loaded, it is available to each new document that is created, until you clear the check box in the **Global templates and add-ins** list in the **Templates and Add-ins** dialog box.
- Automatically when Word starts, by saving the template file in the Word Startup folder on your computer. The default path to this folder is C:\Windows\Application Data\Microsoft\Word\Startup; if you're using user profiles, the default path is C:\Windows\Profiles*UserName*\Application Data\Microsoft\Word\Startup. You can change this path in the **Options** dialog box.

- Programmatically, by doing one of the following:
  - Calling the **Add** method of the **AddIns** collection and passing in the add-in's file name. By default, the **Add** method adds the add-in to the **AddIns** collection, if it's not there already, and loads the add-in. If the add-in is in the **AddIns** collection, it will appear in the **Global templates and add-ins** list in the **Templates and Add-ins** dialog box. To add the add-in to the collection without loading it, pass in **False** for the optional ***Install*** argument.
  - Setting the **Installed** property of the corresponding **AddIn** object to **True**. When you try to set this property, an error will occur if the add-in has not already been added to the collection.

If an error occurs in a loaded add-in, you can't debug the add-in's code while it's loaded or view or modify its project. To view or change the code that is in the add-in's project, open it directly in Word.

Running Code When a Word Add-in Is Loaded or Unloaded

To automatically run code when an add-in is loaded, create a **Sub** procedure named AutoExec in a standard module in the add-in project. Any code within this procedure runs when the add-in is loaded. To run code when an add-in is unloaded, add a **Sub** procedure named AutoExit. If you close and reopen Word while an add-in is loaded, the AutoExec procedure runs when you reopen Word.

Note The Document_Open event procedure doesn't run when a document is loaded as an add-in. It runs only when the document is opened directly in Word.

Excel Add-ins

You can build an Excel add-in to add tools or commands to a user's Excel environment. To load an Excel add-in, click **Add-ins** on the **Tools** menu and select the add-in from the list, or browse to find it if it doesn't appear in the list.

Once the add-in has been loaded, any toolbars or menu items that it includes appear in Excel. An add-in remains loaded until the user unloads it or until Excel is closed, so tools in the add-in are available to all open workbooks. When the user closes Excel, the add-in is unloaded. It will be reloaded again when Excel is opened only if the add-in is saved to the XLStart folder. For more information, see "Loading an Excel Add-in" later in this chapter.

Several characteristics distinguish an Excel add-in from a typical workbook file:

- An add-in has the file extension .xla to indicate that it is an add-in.
- When you save a workbook as an Excel add-in, the workbook window is made invisible and cannot be viewed. You can use the invisible workbook and worksheets for storing calculations or data that your add-in requires while it is running.

- Users can't use the SHIFT key to bypass events that are built into the add-in. This feature ensures that any event procedures you've written in the add-in will run at the proper time.
- Excel messages (alerts) are not displayed by code running in an add-in. In a standard workbook file, messages appear to verify that the user wants to perform an operation that may result in data loss, such as deleting a worksheet or closing an unsaved workbook file. In an add-in, you can perform such operations without the messages being displayed.

The Samples\CH11 subfolder on the companion CD-ROM contains an Excel add-in named ListComboWiz.xla. This add-in provides a wizard for creating a list box or combo box on a worksheet that displays data from a table in a database.

For information about when to create an Excel add-in and when to create an Excel template, see "Excel Templates" later in this chapter.

Creating an Excel Add-in

You create an Excel add-in by creating a workbook, adding code and custom toolbars and menu items to it, and saving it as an Excel add-in file.

▶ To create an Excel add-in

1. Create a new workbook, add code to it, and create any custom toolbars or menu bars.
2. On the **File** menu, click **Properties**. In the ***DocumentName*** **Properties** dialog box, click the **Summary** tab, and then use the **Title** box to specify the name for your add-in, as you want it to appear in the **Add-ins** dialog box.
3. Compile the add-in project by clicking **Compile VBA Project** on the **Debug** menu in the Visual Basic Editor.
4. If you want, protect the project from viewing as described in "Securing an Access, Excel, PowerPoint, or Word Add-In's VBA Project" later in this chapter.
5. Save the add-in workbook as type Microsoft Excel Add-in, which has the extension .xla. By default, Excel add-ins are saved to the C:\Windows\Application Data \Microsoft\AddIns subfolder or, if the system is using user profiles, to the C:\Windows\Profiles*UserName*\Application Data\Microsoft\AddIns subfolder. This folder is where Excel looks for add-ins when you browse for a new add-in in the **Add-ins** dialog box. However, if you want the add-in to load automatically when you start Excel, save the add-in to the XLStart folder, as discussed in the following section, "Loading an Excel Add-in."

Important When you're creating an Excel add-in, pay close attention to the context in which your code is running. When you want to return a reference to the add-in workbook, use the **ThisWorkbook** property, or refer to the workbook by name. To refer to the workbook that's currently open in Excel, use the **ActiveWorkbook** property, or refer to the workbook by name.

Once you've saved the add-in, you can reopen it in Excel to make changes to the project. The saved add-in no longer has a visible workbook associated with it, but when you open it, its project is available in the Visual Basic Editor.

Saving the add-in workbook as an Excel add-in sets the **IsAddIn** property of the corresponding **Workbook** object to **True**. You can set this property for the **ThisWorkbook** object in the Properties window in the Visual Basic Editor; setting it to **False** makes the workbook visible again.

You can debug an Excel add-in while it's loaded. When you load an add-in, its project appears in the Project Explorer in the Visual Basic Editor. If the project is protected, you must enter the correct password in order to view its code.

Loading an Excel Add-in

You can load an Excel add-in in one of three ways:

- Manually, by selecting the check box next to the name of the add-in in the **Add-ins** dialog box on the **Tools** menu.
- Automatically when Excel starts, by saving the add-in to the C:\Windows \Application Data\Microsoft\Excel\XLStart subfolder, or, if the system is using user profiles, to the C:\Windows\Profiles*UserName*\Application Data\Microsoft\Excel \XLStart subfolder. You can change the location of the XLStart subfolder on the **General** tab of the **Options** dialog box (**Tools** menu).
- Programmatically, by using the **Add** method of the **AddIns** collection to add the add-in to the list of available add-ins, and then by setting the **Installed** property of the corresponding **AddIn** object to **True**.

For example, the following procedure loads an add-in by first checking whether it is in the **AddIns** collection and adding it if it is not. The procedure then sets the add-in's **Installed** property to **True**. To call this procedure, pass in the path and file name of the add-in that you want to add:

```
Function Load_XL_AddIn(strFilePath As String) As Boolean
   ' Checks whether add-in is in collection, and
   ' then loads it. To call this procedure, pass
   ' in add-in's path and file name.

   Dim addXL         As Excel.AddIn
   Dim strAddInName  As String

   On Error Resume Next
   ' Call ParsePath function to return file name only.
   strAddInName = ParsePath(strFilePath, FILE_ONLY)
   ' Remove extension from file name to get add-in name.
   strAddInName = Left(strAddInName, Len(strAddInName) - 4)
   ' Attempt to return reference to add-in.
   Set addXL = Excel.AddIns(strAddInName)
```

```
   If Err <> 0 Then
      Err.Clear
      ' If add-in is not in collection, add it.
      Set addXL = Excel.AddIns.Add(strFilePath)
      If Err <> 0 Then
         ' If error occurs, exit procedure.
         Load_XL_AddIn = False
         GoTo Load_XL_AddIn_End
      End If
   End If
   ' Load add-in.
   If Not addXL.Installed Then addXL.Installed = True
   Load_XL_AddIn = True

Load_XL_AddIn_End:
   Exit Function
End Function
```

The Load_XL_AddIn procedure is available in the modAddInObjects module in AddInObjects.xls in the Samples\CH11 subfolder on the companion CD-ROM.

Running Code Automatically When an Excel Add-in Is Loaded or Unloaded

To automatically run code when an Excel add-in is loaded, you have two choices:

- Create a **Sub** procedure named Auto_Open in a standard module in the add-in project. Any code within this procedure runs when the add-in is loaded. To run code when an add-in is unloaded, add a procedure named Auto_Close.

  –or–

- Add code to the add-in workbook's Open event procedure. The code in this procedure also runs when an add-in is loaded, and it runs before the Auto_Open procedure runs.

Keep in mind that if you want an add-in to load automatically when Excel starts up, you must save it in the C:\Windows\Application Data\Microsoft\Excel\XLStart subfolder or, if the system is using user profiles, in the C:\Windows\Profiles *UserName*\Application Data\Microsoft\Excel\XLStart subfolder. If the add-in is not saved in this folder, it is not loaded when Excel starts, and neither the Auto_Open nor Workbook_Open procedure will run.

PowerPoint Add-ins

PowerPoint add-ins are similar to Excel add-ins. You build a PowerPoint add-in to provide additional functionality to users while they're developing or running a PowerPoint slide presentation. In most cases, the user works with your add-in by clicking a toolbar button or menu item that you've included with the add-in.

For information about when to create a PowerPoint add-in and when to create a PowerPoint template, see "PowerPoint Templates" later in this chapter.

Creating a PowerPoint Add-in

To create a PowerPoint add-in, you create a new presentation and add code and custom toolbars. Then you save your presentation as both a presentation file (.ppt) and a PowerPoint add-in (.ppa).

▶ To create a PowerPoint add-in

1. Create a new presentation and add code to its VBA project, and create any custom toolbars or menu bars.
2. When you've tested and debugged the code, compile the project by clicking **Compile VBA Project** on the **Debug** menu.
3. If you want, protect the project from viewing as described in "Securing an Access, Excel, PowerPoint, or Word Add-In's VBA Project" later in this chapter.
4. Save the project as a PowerPoint presentation, with the extension .ppt, and then save the project as a PowerPoint add-in, which has the extension .ppa. By default, PowerPoint add-ins are saved to the same folder as Excel add-ins: the C:\Windows \Application Data\Microsoft\Addins subfolder or, if the system is using user profiles, the C:\Windows\Profiles*UserName*\Application Data\Microsoft\AddIns subfolder. This folder is where PowerPoint looks for add-ins when you browse for a new add-in in the **Add-ins** dialog box (**Tools** menu).

   Important Once you save the project as a PowerPoint add-in, you can no longer view the VBA project, not even in break mode, nor can you view the slides associated with it. Therefore, you should also save your PowerPoint add-in as a standard presentation, in case you need to make changes to it and resave it as an add-in.

Loading a PowerPoint Add-in

You can load a PowerPoint add-in in any of the following ways:

- Manually, by clicking **Add-ins** on the **Tools** menu. The **Available Add-ins** list displays the available add-ins; you can add add-ins to the list by clicking **Add New** and locating the add-in file. Any add-in that is currently loaded has an "x" next to its name. To unload an add-in, select it and click **Unload**. You can use an add-in only when it is loaded.
- Automatically when PowerPoint starts, by setting the **AutoLoad** property of the **AddIn** object to **True**. The next time you start PowerPoint, the add-in is loaded and the **Loaded** property is set to **True**.
- Programmatically, by setting the **Loaded** property of the corresponding **AddIn** object to **True**.

Running Code Automatically When a PowerPoint Add-in Is Loaded or Unloaded

To automatically run code when an add-in is loaded, create a **Sub** procedure named Auto_Open in a standard module in the add-in project. Any code within this procedure runs when the add-in is loaded. To run code when an add-in is unloaded, add a procedure named Auto_Close.

If you close PowerPoint while an add-in is loaded, the Auto_Open procedure will run when you reopen PowerPoint, since the add-in is reloaded on startup.

Adding and Removing Command Bars for Word, Excel, and PowerPoint Add-ins

If the user runs your add-in by clicking a command bar control (toolbar button or menu item), you can include code to display or create the command bar and control when the add-in loads, and hide or remove the command bar and control when it unloads. Although it may seem like more effort, creating and destroying the command bar from within your code gives you greater control over when the command bar is displayed than simply storing the command bar in the add-in file.

To create the command bar when the add-in is loaded, add code to the procedure that runs when the add-in is loaded: AutoExec for Word, or Auto_Open for Excel and PowerPoint. First check whether the command bar already exists. If it does not, create it and add a button that runs a **Sub** procedure, as shown in the following example:

```
Private Const CBR_INSERT As String = "Insert Info Wizard"
Private Const CTL_INSERT As String = "Insert Info"
Sub AutoExec()
   Dim cbrWiz     As CommandBar
   Dim ctlInsert  As CommandBarButton
   On Error Resume Next
   ' Determine whether command bar already exists.
   Set cbrWiz = CommandBars(CBR_INSERT)
   ' If command bar does not exist, create it.
   If cbrWiz Is Nothing Then
      Err.Clear
      Set cbrWiz = CommandBars.Add(CBR_INSERT)
      ' Make command bar visible.
      cbrWiz.Visible = True
      ' Add button control.
      Set ctlInsert = cbrWiz.Controls.Add
      With ctlInsert
         .Style = msoButtonCaption
         .Caption = CTL_INSERT
         .Tag = CTL_INSERT
         ' Specify procedure that will run when button is clicked.
         .OnAction = "ShowForm"
      End With
   End If
End Sub
```

To delete the command bar when the add-in is unloaded, add code to the procedure that runs when the add-in is unloaded: AutoExit for Word, or Auto_Close for Excel and PowerPoint. The following procedure deletes the command bar created in the previous example:

```
Sub AutoExit()
   On Error Resume Next
   ' Delete command bar, if it exists.
   CommandBars(CBR_INSERT).Delete
End Sub
```

The AutoExec and AutoExit procedures shown in the preceding examples are available in the modWizard module in InsertInfo.dot in the Samples\CH11 subfolder on the companion CD-ROM.

Controlling Word, Excel, and PowerPoint Add-ins from Code

Word, Excel, and PowerPoint all have an **AddIns** collection that contains **AddIn** objects that correspond to application-specific add-ins. You can use these **AddIn** objects and the **AddIns** collections to control the behavior of application-specific add-ins from VBA.

Note that the **AddIns** collection and the **COMAddIns** collection are two separate collections. Both are returned by a property of the **Application** object: the **AddIns** property for application-specific add-ins, and the **COMAddIns** property for COM add-ins. However, the Office 9.0 object library provides the **COMAddIns** collection, while the **AddIns** collection is part of the host application's object model.

Although the **AddIn** objects and the **AddIns** collections for Word, Excel, and PowerPoint are similar, they each have different properties and methods. For example, each **AddIn** object has a read/write property that you can set to load or unload the add-in. In Word and Excel, this is the **Installed** property; in PowerPoint, it is the **Loaded** property.

The following code displays information about PowerPoint add-ins in a message box:

```
Sub DisplayPptAddins()
   ' This procedure displays information about add-ins currently
   ' registered and/or loaded in PowerPoint. To determine which
   ' add-ins are registered, VBA looks for add-ins in the registry.

     Dim lngNumAddIns   As Long
     Dim addPpt         As AddIn

     ' Used to build the dialog box.
     Dim strPrompt      As String
     Dim strRegistered  As String
     Dim strLoaded      As String
     Dim strTitle       As String
```

```
    ' Get the total number of add-ins.
    lngNumAddIns = PowerPoint.AddIns.Count

    Select Case lngNumAddIns
      Case 0
        ' No add-ins registered.
        strTitle = "No Add-ins"
        strPrompt = "You currently have no PowerPoint" _
           & " add-ins registered."
      Case 1
        ' One add-in registered.
        strTitle = "One Add-in Registered"
        strPrompt = addPpt.FullName
     Case Is > 1
        ' Set up the title for the dialog box.
        strTitle = lngNumAddIns & " Add-ins Registered"

        ' Determine which add-ins are loaded and/or registered.
        strLoaded = "Loaded: " & vbCrLf
        strRegistered = vbCrLf & "Registered: " & vbCrLf

        ' Loop through the AddIns collection.
        For Each addPpt In PowerPoint.AddIns
           ' Check Loaded property.
           If addPpt.Loaded = msoTrue Then
             strLoaded = strLoaded & vbCrLf & addPpt.FullName _
               & vbCrLf
           Else
             strRegistered = strRegistered & vbCrLf _
               & addPpt.FullName & vbCrLf
           End If
        Next addPpt

        ' Combine the loaded add-ins list with registered
        ' add-ins list.
        strPrompt = strLoaded & strRegistered
    End Select

    ' Display the dialog box.
    MsgBox strPrompt, vbInformation, strTitle
End Sub
```

The DisplayPptAddins procedure is available in the modEnumAddIns module in AddInObjects.ppt in the Samples\CH11 subfolder on the companion CD-ROM.

For more information about using the **AddIn** object and **AddIns** collection, search the VBA host application's (Word, Excel, or PowerPoint) Visual Basic Reference Help index for "AddIn Object" and "AddIns collection."

Microsoft Access Add-ins

You can build add-ins for Access to help users manage and analyze their databases. Access includes several add-ins, which are written in VBA. For example, the Linked Table Manager is an add-in that handles the updating of linked tables when the database containing the source tables is moved or renamed. The wizards included with Access are also add-ins.

Access add-ins have the file extension .mda or .mde. A user can open an .mda file and look at the code, unless you've secured the modules by using either user-level security or project-level security. When you create an .mde file, however, all VBA source code is removed. The .mde contains only compiled VBA pseudocode, which can't be viewed by the user. Creating an .mde file is therefore the best way to secure your code, if you're concerned about protecting your source code. For more information about .mda and .mde files, search the Microsoft Access Help index for "MDE files." For more information about securing Access database applications, see Chapter 18, "Securing Access Databases."

When you write code that will run in an Access add-in, use caution when referring to the current database. If you want to refer to the add-in database in which code is currently running, use the **CodeProject** or **CodeData** object to return a reference to this database. If you want to refer to the database that's currently open in Access, use the **CurrentProject** or **CurrentData** object.

Creating Menu Add-ins for Access

The simplest Access add-in is a menu add-in. A menu add-in calls a procedure in another database, perhaps a database that's serving as a code library. For example, a simple menu add-in might call a procedure that generates a report containing information about the various objects in the current database, such as the date they were created and their descriptions. Menu add-ins appear when you point to **Add-ins** on the **Tools** menu.

▶ To create a menu add-in

1. Add a subkey to the registry that specifies the name of the file containing the procedure and the name of the procedure itself. Menu add-ins are listed beneath the following subkey in the registry:

   \HKEY_LOCAL_MACHINE\SOFTWARE\Microsoft\Office\Access\Addins \Menu Add-ins

2. To specify the command that should appear on the **Add-ins** submenu of the **Tools** menu, create a new subkey beneath the add-in's subkey. For example, naming this subkey **&Analyze Database Objects** would result in a command named **Analyze Database Objects** on the **Add-ins** submenu.

3 To hook up the menu command to the add-in, add two entries (in this case, **String** values) beneath the command's subkey, one named Expression and one named Library. Set the value of the Library entry to the path and file name of the database that contains the procedure that provides an entry point to the add-in. Set the value of the Expression entry to the name of the procedure itself. For example, if the procedure is named AnalyzeDatabaseObjects and it resides in a database named CodeLib.mda, you would set these entries as follows:

   Expression: "=AnalyzeDatabaseObjects()"

   Library: "C:\Windows\Application Data\Microsoft\AddIns\CodeLib.mda"

After you've added these keys, the new add-in command will appear on the **Add-ins** submenu of the **Tools** menu the next time you open Access.

Note If you need to distribute your Access menu add-in to users, create an installable add-in as described in the next section, "Creating Installable Add-ins for Access," so that the add-in is properly registered on users' machines.

Creating Installable Add-ins for Access

You can also create add-ins that the user can load (install) or unload (uninstall) by using the Add-in Manager. The Add-in Manager can load the following types of add-ins:

- Menu add-ins, like those described in the previous section.
- Object wizards, which help the user create a new table, query, form, data access page, or report. Access includes a number of built-in object wizards, which are available in the **New Table**, **New Query**, **New Form**, **New Data Access Page**, and **New Report** dialog boxes. An object wizard that you create will also appear in one of these dialog boxes.
- Control wizards, which help the user to add either an Access control or an ActiveX control to a form, report, or data access page. A control wizard runs only if the **Control Wizards** tool in the toolbox is pressed in. When this button is pressed in, clicking a control in the toolbox and dropping it onto a form, report, or data access page launches the wizard that is associated with that control.
- Builders, which help the user to set a property for an object in the database, usually through a dialog box. When a builder is available for a particular property, the **Build** button (the small button with the ellipsis [...]) appears next to that property's name in the property sheet.

In order to load or unload one of these add-ins, the Add-in Manager relies on the presence of a table within the add-in, called the USysRegInfo table. The USysRegInfo table provides information that the Add-in Manager writes to the registry. Access uses this registry information to launch the add-in in response to an action taken by the user.

Note The USysRegInfo table is a system table and is therefore usually hidden. To view system tables, click **Options** on the **Tools** menu, click the **View** tab, and then select the **System objects** check box.

You must create the USysRegInfo table; it's not automatically created for you when you create a new .mda file. The USysRegInfo table must contain the four fields described in the following table.

Field	Field type	Description
Subkey	Text	The name of the subkey that contains the registry information for the add-in
Type	Number	The type of value to create beneath the subkey: subkey (0), **String** (1), or **DWORD** (4)
ValName	Text	The name of the registry entry to be created
Value	Text	The value to be stored in the registry entry defined by the ValName field

Each record in the USysRegInfo table describes a subkey or value that is to be added to the registry for a particular add-in. The table can contain information for multiple add-ins.

For each add-in, the USysRegInfo table must contain a minimum of three records: one to create the subkey for the add-in, one to add the Library entry, and one to add the Expression entry. Note that these are the same values required to create a menu add-in, as described in the previous section. You can add other records to store additional values in the registry. For example, you might add a record that creates a registry entry that indicates where a bitmap file required by the add-in is stored.

In the Subkey field, you can use the "HKEY_CURRENT_ACCESS_PROFILE *AddInType**AddInName*" string to create the new registry entry. The Add-in Manager uses this string to determine the location on the user's machine of Access-specific information in the registry so that Access can create the entry for the add-in in the appropriate place. If the user started Access with the **/profile** command-line option, this string ensures that the registry entry is created beneath the specified Access user profile; otherwise, the entry is created under the \HKEY_LOCAL_MACHINE \SOFTWARE\Microsoft\Office\9.0\Access*AddInType* subkey in the registry. For more information about starting Access from the command line with the **/profile** option, search the Microsoft Access Help index for "user profiles."

Note A user profile that you use to start Access from the command line is not the same thing as a user profile that's defined for logging on to the operating system. An Access user profile applies only to Access, and only when you start Access from the command line. A user profile defined for the operating system applies to every application on the system, and is used to maintain system data for individual users.

You can also use the "HKEY_LOCAL_MACHINE\SOFTWARE\Microsoft\Office\9.0\Access*AddInType*" string to specify that the registry entries for the add-in should always be created under this registry subtree and that Access user profiles are to be ignored. Note that in this case you need to include the full registry path to the add-in's subkey.

Figure 11.2 shows the USysRegInfo table included in the sample add-in, Create Procedures Table (ProcTable.mda), available in the Samples\CH11 subfolder on the companion CD-ROM. You can import this table into your own add-in to give you a start on creating a USysRegInfo table.

Figure 11.2 Sample USysRegInfo Table

Subkey	Type	ValName	Value
HKEY_CURRENT_ACCESS_PROFILE \Menu Add-ins\&Create Procedures Table	0		
HKEY_CURRENT_ACCESS_PROFILE \Menu Add-ins\&Create Procedures Table	1	Library	|ACCDIR\ProcTable.mda
HKEY_CURRENT_ACCESS_PROFILE \Menu Add-ins\&Create Procedures Table	1	Expression	=AddProcsToTable()

For more information about creating the USysRegInfo table for the various types of add-ins, see USysReg.doc in the Appendixes folder on the companion CD-ROM.

Securing an Access, Excel, PowerPoint, or Word Add-in's VBA Project

If you want to protect your code and prevent users from changing it, you can set a password for the add-in's VBA project. To set the project password, click **VBAProject Properties** on the **Tools** menu in the Visual Basic Editor. On the **Protection** tab, select the **Lock project for viewing** check box, and then enter a password and confirm it.

For more information about securing VBA projects, see Chapter 17, "Securing Office Documents and Visual Basic for Applications Code." For more information about securing Access databases, see Chapter 18, "Securing Access Databases."

Creating Templates

So far this chapter has discussed creating different types of add-ins to add tools to Office 2000 applications. In some cases, your solution may require that you also give users a framework within which to complete common tasks. A template can provide such a framework. Within a template, you can include boilerplate text and graphics, custom styles, toolbars and menu items, macros, and VBA codc.

Word Templates

Word is ideal for creating custom word-processing solutions. You can take advantage of Word's power to easily create nicely formatted invoicing, reporting, and form letter applications, to name just a few.

Every Word document has an associated VBA project. However, code that you write in one document isn't easily available to other documents. If you're creating a solution in Word, it makes sense to create a custom document template and distribute that template to your users. That way, a number of different documents can call the code in the template. The same holds true for custom styles, toolbars, and recorded macros.

To further illustrate the advantages of packaging code in a template, consider the New event for a Word **Document** object. This event occurs when you create a new document from a template. The Document_New event procedure itself must reside in the template project; there's no reason to use it in a regular Word document (.doc file), since you can't create a new document from another document.

For more information about when to create a template and when to create an add-in, see "Word Document Templates vs. Word Add-ins (Global Templates)" later in this chapter.

The following sections briefly discuss the different templates you can use to distribute a Word solution.

The Normal Template

The Normal template (Normal.dot) is loaded automatically when you start Word. By default, new documents are based on the Normal template. Even if you attach another template to a document, any styles, text, AutoText entries, command bars, recorded macros, or code included in the Normal template are available to any document open in Word. If you look at the Project Explorer in the Visual Basic Editor, you'll see that the Normal template always appears.

Although you can customize the Normal template, it's not necessarily the best way to distribute a solution to users, because replacing their own Normal template may inconvenience them. They'll lose any custom settings or macros they may have created. Moreover, many users and system administrators restrict access to the Normal template, so you may not be able to replace or modify it anyway.

A better way to distribute solutions is to create either a custom document template or an add-in (global template) that can be loaded in addition to the Normal template. Which one should you use? If you want to build a solution that allows users to create new documents based on an existing document, and that can include text and custom styles, use a custom document template. If you want to add toolbars, menu commands, or macros that are available to every document the user opens, create an add-in. Once an add-in is loaded, it is available to every document that the user opens until the add-in is unloaded.

Custom Document Templates

One way to build a solution in Word is to create a custom template on which a user bases new documents. The template that's attached to a document is specified in the **Document template** box in the **Templates and Add-ins** dialog box (**Tools** menu). A document can have only one document template. Even when a document template is attached to a document, however, the Normal template remains loaded.

You should create a custom document template when:

- Your solution requires that some boilerplate text or fields be included in the document when it is created.
- You want to make custom styles available to each document the user creates.
- Your solution includes custom toolbars or menus that the user can use while working with documents based on the template.
- You want to call VBA procedures in the template from code running in a document that is based on the template.

Custom document templates are good for ensuring that all users have a consistent set of styles and tools for working on a particular project. For example, if your team is writing a book, you can create a document template that the writers use as the basis for each chapter.

Creating a Custom Document Template

To create a custom document template, click **New** on the **File** menu, click the **General** tab, click **Blank Document**, and then click **Template** under **Create New**.

You can write code in the template's VBA project. You can also add text, styles, and custom toolbars to the template. By default, the template is saved with the .dot extension, in the C:\Windows\Application Data\Microsoft\Templates folder; if user profiles are being used, the default folder is C:\Windows\Profiles*UserName*\Application Data\Microsoft\Templates.

Note By default, custom command bars are saved in Normal.dot. To save a command bar with a custom document template, create the command bar by clicking **Customize** on the **Tools** menu, clicking the **Toolbars** tab, and then clicking **New**. In the **New Toolbar** dialog box, click the document template's name in the **Make toolbar available to** list.

Creating a New Document Based on a Word Template

To create a new document based on your custom template, click **New** on the **File** menu to open the **New** dialog box. Your template should appear on the **General** tab, or on one of the other tabs if you saved it in a subfolder of the Templates folder. Click the template and then click **OK**.

You can also attach a custom template to an existing document. Doing so won't add any text that's in the template to your document, but any code, styles, and toolbars in the template will be available to your document. On the **Tools** menu, click **Templates and Add-ins**, and then click **Attach** to find and attach your document template.

If you look at the VBA project for a document that has a custom document template attached, you'll see that three projects appear in the Project Explorer in the Visual Basic Editor: the document's project, the custom template's project, and the Normal template's project. You can write code in any of these projects. In addition, you can call a procedure in the Normal template or in the custom template from a procedure in the document's project.

Note When you create a document based on a template, that template appears in the document's References folder in the Project Explorer. If you open the **References** dialog box by clicking **References** on the **Tools** menu, you'll see that the template appears checked in the list of available references. Attaching a template to a Word document sets a reference to the template's VBA project, making the code that's in that template available to any procedure in the document.

Word includes a number of document templates that you can look at for tips on creating your own. If you've installed them, you can find these templates in the C:\Program Files\Microsoft Office\Templates\1033 folder of your Office 2000 installation.

Note The 1033 subfolder beneath the Templates folder indicates the language ID for U.S. English language support. The language ID folder below C:\Program Files\Microsoft Office\Templates differs for each language. Templates you create yourself should be stored in the C:\Windows\Application Data\Microsoft\Templates folder or in a user profile-specific location. For more information about template deployment, see Chapter 2, "Designing and Deploying Office Solutions."

Word Document Templates vs. Word Add-ins (Global Templates)

Word add-ins and document templates both have the same file extension, the .dot extension. In fact, you can use a template as an add-in, or an add-in as a template.

So what's the difference between the two? The best way to use a Word template is as the basis for new documents. For example, you might create an invoicing template that employees could use to create customer invoices. When users create a new document based on the template, some of the information is available to them already—the name of your company, the date, and so forth. All they need to do is enter the customer name and the items purchased.

An add-in, on the other hand, provides custom tools that employees can use to work with all of their Word documents, like the custom features provided in the UsefulTools.dot add-in described earlier. An add-in extends Word's functionality in a way that can be tightly integrated with Word itself. When you load an add-in, it remains loaded for each document opened in Word, until you explicitly unload it.

The following table summarizes the differences between Word templates and add-ins.

Custom document template	Add-in
A document template has the .dot file extension.	An add-in has the .dot file extension.
You can attach only one template to a document. (The Normal template is always loaded whether or not there is an attached template.)	You can load multiple add-ins at the same time.
A template is attached to a document at the time the document is created, or after the document is created by clicking the **Attach** button in the **Templates and Add-ins** dialog box (**Tools** menu) and selecting the template.	An add-in is loaded by selecting the corresponding check box in the **Global templates and add-ins** list in the **Templates and Add-ins** dialog box.
A template can be used by any document, but it must be attached to each individual document.	Once loaded, an add-in is available to all documents.
A template adds toolbar buttons, menu items, macros, styles, or boilerplate text to a specific document.	An add-in adds toolbar buttons, menu items, or macros to the Word environment. It doesn't display any boilerplate text or contain any custom styles.
The attached template can be accessed from VBA by using the **AttachedTemplate** property of a **Document** object. Templates are available in the **Templates** collection. The **Templates** collection contains the Normal template, the attached template (if any), and any loaded add-ins.	Add-ins in the **Global templates and add-ins** list, whether loaded or not, can be accessed from VBA through the Word **AddIns** collection. Add-ins can also be accessed through the **Templates** collection.
A reference to the template's VBA project is automatically set when you attach a template to a document. Therefore, you can call procedures in the template's project from the document's project.	No reference is set to an add-in's VBA project when it is loaded. Therefore, although you can call procedures in the add-in project through toolbars, menu items, or macros, you cannot directly call a procedure in an add-in's project from code running in a document unless you explicitly set a reference to the add-in's project.

Excel Templates

Excel templates differ from Word templates in that when you create a new workbook based on a template, your workbook is actually a copy of that template. In Word, creating a document based on a template loads two VBA projects—one for the template, and one for the document. In Excel, only one project is loaded: the project associated with the new workbook.

Use an Excel template when you want to distribute a custom spreadsheet solution that has an Excel user interface component. For example, you might create a reporting template that's formatted in a standardized fashion, with embedded graphics, so that any reports users create with the template have the same look.

To create a new Excel template, create a new workbook and add the elements that you want to include in the template, such as code, custom dialog boxes, custom worksheet and chart layouts, toolbars, and recorded macros. Save the template file in the C:\Windows\Application Data\Microsoft\Templates folder with the .xlt extension; if user profiles are being used, save the template in the C:\Windows\Profiles*UserName*\Application Data\Microsoft\Templates folder.

To create a new workbook based on a custom template, run Excel and click **New** on the **File** menu. If you saved your template in the Templates folder, it appears on the **General** tab of the **New** dialog box. Click the template, and then click **OK**.

Excel includes sample templates that you can install to familiarize yourself with how templates work and to get ideas for creating your own templates.

PowerPoint Templates

Like an Excel template, when you create a new PowerPoint presentation based on a template, the new presentation is a copy of the template. Only one VBA project is loaded for the new presentation, but it includes all the components that you've defined in the presentation template.

Use a PowerPoint template when you need a custom solution for building presentations. A presentation template makes it easy for your users to build attractive slide presentations and saves them time laying out the presentation or looking for the right graphics. You can also include content in the template, such as information about departmental contacts, for example, or placeholders for quarterly sales information in a financial presentation. And you can include instructions that guide the user in completing the presentation.

To create a PowerPoint template, create a new presentation, add any text, graphics, buttons, toolbars, custom dialog boxes, and code, and save the presentation in the C:\Windows\Application Data\Microsoft\Templates folder with a .pot extension; if user profiles are being used, save the template in the C:\Windows\Profiles*UserName*\Application Data\Microsoft\Templates folder.

To create a new presentation based on your custom template, run PowerPoint and click **New** on the **File** menu. Click your template in the **New Presentation** dialog box, and then click **OK**.

PowerPoint includes a number of custom templates that you can use and modify. The templates that appear on the **Design Templates** tab of the **New Presentation** dialog box contain only formatted backgrounds. The templates that appear on the **Presentations** tab also contain text and placeholders for information, navigation buttons, and instructions for completing the presentation. For example, the Corporate Financial Overview presentation provides a template for a financial presentation that can be customized and used repeatedly.

Access Templates

Templates in Access are different from templates for any other Office 2000 application. Instead of creating a template for a database (.mdb) file, you can create default templates for the forms and reports stored in a database, so that when you create a new form or report, it is automatically based on the default template. You can create a template for a form or a report in one of two ways:

- Create the form or report that you want to be the template, and save it with the name Normal to replace the default template.

  –or–

- Create the form or report that you want to be the template and save it with whatever name you want. On the **Tools** menu, click **Options**, click the **Forms/Reports** tab, and then type the name of your template in the **Form Template** or **Report Template** box.

Note Access saves the settings for the **Form Template** and **Report Template** options in your Access workgroup information file, not in your user database (the .mdb file). When you change an option setting, the change applies to any database you open or create. To see the name of the template that is currently used for new forms or reports, click **Options** on the **Tools** menu, and then click the **Forms/Reports** tab.

To use your templates in other databases, copy or export the templates to them. If your templates are not in a database, Access uses the Normal template for any new forms and reports you create. However, the names of your templates appear in the **Form Template** and **Report Template** options in every database in your database system, even if the templates are not in every database.

Creating Wizards

A wizard is a template or add-in that walks a user through a series of steps to create a new document, spreadsheet, presentation, database, Web application, or some object within any of those applications. Typically, when users launch a wizard, they are presented with a series of information-gathering forms, and once they have entered all the necessary information in a form, the wizard creates the new component.

The advantage of using a wizard to deliver a solution is that it's easy to use, and you can include detailed instructions on each frame of the wizard. For example, Word includes a Letter Wizard that gathers information from the user and then creates a new letter based on that information. The wizard saves the user from having to lay the letter out correctly and from having to think about where the information goes in the final document. The Word letter templates provide the same result as the Letter Wizard, but the user has to figure out where each bit of information in the letter goes and navigate around the document to insert it.

This chapter has already discussed how to create templates and add-ins. Once you understand how to build these, creating wizards is fairly intuitive. The following sections provide some additional information that may help you with the process.

Common Characteristics of Wizards

You can create a wizard by using any of the following:

- A Word, Excel, or PowerPoint template
- A Word, Excel, PowerPoint, or Access application-specific add-in
- A COM add-in for Office 2000 applications or for the Visual Basic Editor

Which you choose depends on the level of complexity of your wizard, which application or applications you want it to run in, and how you want to distribute it to your users. A template or application-specific add-in is the simplest solution. A COM add-in may be more complex because the add-in DLL and any dependent files must be properly registered on the user's computer. For more information about which to choose, see "COM Add-ins vs. Application-Specific Add-ins" earlier in this chapter.

Some other common characteristics of wizards include:

- A form or set of forms that gathers information from the user and that appears when the user launches the wizard
- Navigation buttons (such as the standard Next, Previous, Cancel, and Finish buttons) that allow the user to move back and forth between pages

- The ability to launch the wizard either from a command bar control or by creating a new document based on the wizard
- An optional special file extension

As you can see, wizards don't significantly differ from add-ins or templates.

Tip Rather than creating a new form for each page of your wizard, you can create a multipage control on a form, with a unique control layout on each page. Then, when the user clicks the Next or Previous button, move the focus to the appropriate page. This way you don't need to recreate the form background and buttons for each page of the wizard. Also, you don't have to manage the opening and closing of multiple forms. For ideas regarding how to do this, see ListComboWiz.xla in the Samples\CH11 subfolder on the companion CD-ROM.

Word Wizards

Word includes several wizards that are installed optionally; the Letter Wizard, the Memo Wizard, and the Résumé Wizard are a few examples. These files have the extension .wiz, but they are Word templates, so you can open them in Word and view their VBA projects. They're located in the C:\Program Files\Microsoft Office \Templates\1033 folder.

To create an application-specific wizard for Word, first create a Word template that contains any boilerplate text, plus the wizard forms and code. The wizard should include code that displays a form as soon as the user launches the wizard.

Next, determine how users will launch the wizard. If they will launch the wizard from a command bar control, you can add the control programmatically from code running in a Word add-in.

▶ To design a wizard that is launched from a command bar control

1. Add the AutoExec procedure to a standard module in the wizard's project, and include the code to create the control in that procedure.
2. In the code that creates the control, set the control's **OnAction** property to the name of a procedure in the wizard project that displays the starting form for your wizard. For information about setting the **OnAction** property, search the Microsoft Word Visual Basic Reference Help index for "OnAction property."
3. Add the AutoExit procedure, and include code to remove the control when the wizard is unloaded so that the user doesn't see the control unless the wizard is loaded.
4. Load your wizard as an add-in in any of the ways described in "Loading a Word Add-in" earlier in this chapter.

If the user will launch the wizard by creating a new document, you don't need a command bar control or the AutoExec or AutoExit procedures.

▶ To design a wizard that is launched by creating a new document

1. In the wizard's VBA project, open the ThisDocument module.
2. Create the Document_New event procedure by clicking **Document** in the **Object** box and **New** in the **Procedure** box.
3. Within this event procedure, call the procedure that displays the wizard's starting form.
4. Copy the wizard template to the C:\Windows\Application Data\Microsoft\Templates folder, or if user profiles are being used, to the C:\Windows\Profiles*UserName*\Application Data\Microsoft\Templates folder, and change the file's extension to .wiz. Confirm this change when Windows prompts you to do so.

When users create a new document by clicking **New** on the **File** menu, they'll see your wizard displayed in the **New** dialog box. Clicking the wizard and then clicking **OK** creates a new document and runs the Document_New event procedure, which displays the wizard's starting form.

Excel Wizards

An Excel wizard is simply a template or add-in. There's no special file format that indicates that an Excel file is a wizard. To create an Excel wizard, follow the guidelines discussed in "Excel Templates" and "Excel Add-ins" earlier in this chapter.

The List Box/Combo Box Wizard, available as ListComboWiz.xla in the Samples\CH11 subfolder on the companion CD-ROM, is a good example of an Excel wizard. This add-in guides users through the process of creating a list box or combo box on an Excel worksheet based on a table in an Access database.

PowerPoint Wizards

PowerPoint includes the Auto Content Wizard, which automatically generates a presentation with generic content based on information that the user entered in the wizard. Unfortunately, you can't view the VBA project associated with the Auto Content Wizard, because it's saved as a PowerPoint add-in.

The presentations created by the Auto Content Wizard are based on the presentation templates included with PowerPoint. You could create a new presentation based on one of these templates and achieve the same result. Again, the advantage to using the wizard is that it enters some of the information into the presentation for you.

To create a custom PowerPoint wizard, follow the instructions for building a PowerPoint add-in described in "PowerPoint Add-ins" earlier in this chapter. Remember to save your presentation as a .ppt file in case you need to re-create the add-in.

If you want the user to be able to create a new presentation based on your wizard, copy the wizard to the C:\Windows\Application Data\Microsoft\Templates folder, or if user profiles are being used, to the C:\Windows\Profiles*UserName*\Application Data \Microsoft\Templates folder, and change its extension to .pwz. When users click **New** on the **File** menu in PowerPoint, they can click your wizard in the **New Presentation** dialog box, and then click **OK** to launch the wizard and create a new presentation.

Access Wizards

An Access wizard is an add-in that can be integrated into the Access user interface. You can create a table, query, form, or report wizard, which appears in the list of options in the **New Table**, **New Query**, **New Form**, or **New Report** dialog box. For example, you can design a wizard to help users build complex queries, such as update queries.

You can also create control wizards, which are launched when users create new controls on a form or report. Users can disable control wizards by toggling the state of the **Control Wizards** tool in the toolbox.

You can add a USysRegInfo table to a wizard database and use the Add-in Manager to install wizards. The registry subkeys that you must create to register a wizard, however, are different from those you create to register an add-in. For more information about creating these subkeys, see USysReg.doc in the Appendixes folder on the companion CD-ROM. For more information about creating Access add-ins, see "Microsoft Access Add-ins" earlier in this chapter.

Building Reusable Code Libraries

Once you've been writing VBA code for any length of time, you'll find that you need to perform certain operations regularly. For example, you may often need to parse a file path and return just the name of the file. Or you may need to write procedures to log errors to a text file. Rather than re-creating these procedures each time you need them, you can store them in a code library and reuse them in other VBA projects.

There are two ways that you can create a reusable code library:

- By creating a DLL in Visual Basic 4.0 or later
- By creating an application-specific template or add-in

Whatever method you choose, you must always set a reference from the VBA project to the file containing the code library. Even if the file is a template or add-in, the procedures it contains will not be available to your VBA project unless you set a reference to it. Once you do set a reference to a code library, you can call its procedures from your VBA project.

The Samples\CH11\CodeLib subfolder on the companion CD-ROM contains examples of both types of code libraries. These sample code libraries contain procedures from Chapter 7, "Getting the Most Out of Visual Basic for Applications," plus some additional procedures that you may find useful. The files that contain code libraries are CodeLib.dll, which can be used from any VBA host application, and CodeLib.dot, which can be used only from Word.

Creating a DLL That Acts as a Code Library

DLLs make ideal code libraries, because they are small and fast. The disadvantage to using a DLL is that you must make certain it is properly registered on the user's machine.

▶ To create a DLL that acts as a code library

1. Create a new DLL project in Microsoft Visual Basic.
2. Create a new class module in the project.
3. Set the class module's **Instancing** property to **GlobalMultiUse**. This ensures that your procedures will be visible to any project that wants to use them and that they will behave as global procedures.
4. Set references to any object libraries required by your code.
5. Add the procedures you want in your code library to the class module as public **Function** and **Sub** procedures.
6. Change the project's name to the name you want for your code library by clicking **Properties** on the **Project** menu and entering a new value for the **Project Name** property.
7. Make the DLL.

To use the code library from a VBA project, set a reference to the DLL. To set a reference to a DLL, click **References** on the **Tools** menu, and use the **Browse** button to locate the DLL. After the reference has been added, the Object Browser will display information about the procedures in the code library.

If your code library is large, you may not want to load it with your project. Rather than setting a reference to the DLL, you can use the **Declare** statement to declare references to individual procedures in the DLL.

Creating an Application-Specific Template or Add-in That Acts as a Code Library

If you don't have Microsoft Visual Basic or don't want to create a DLL, you can create an application-specific template or add-in that contains reusable code for that application.

For example, if you have a set of procedures that you call regularly from code in Word, you can create a template that contains these procedures and set a reference to it from any Word VBA project that needs to use those procedures. To set a reference to a template (or any file that contains a VBA project), click **References** on the **Tools** menu, and use the **Browse** button to locate the template file.

Note that simply loading a global template in the **Templates and Add-ins** dialog box doesn't allow you to call the code that the template contains, except through a command bar control. You must set a reference to the template in order to call code in the template, even if the template is already loaded.

This solution allows you to keep application-specific code in an application-specific template, which doesn't have to be registered in the Windows registry, so it may be an easier solution to implement than a DLL. However, application-specific templates are larger than most DLLs and take longer to load, so your solution may be somewhat slower.

Where to Go from Here

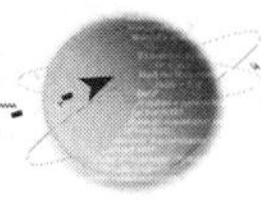

For additional information about the subjects discussed in this chapter, see the following resources. If a file name is listed, that file is located in the Appendixes folder on the companion CD-ROM, unless otherwise noted.

Creating Add-ins and DLLs in Microsoft Visual Basic

Microsoft Visual Basic 6.0 Programmer's Guide. Redmond, WA: Microsoft Press, 1998. (An online version of this book is included with Visual Basic 6.0 and is also available on the MSDN Online Web site at http://msdn.microsoft.com/developer/.)

McKinney, Bruce. *Hardcore Visual Basic, Second Edition*. Redmond, WA: Microsoft Press, 1997.

Cornell, Gary, and Dave Jezak. *Core Visual Basic 6*. Upper Saddle River, NJ: Prentice Hall PTR, 1998.

Microsoft Developer Network Web site (http://msdn.microsoft.com/developer/)

Implementing Libraries in a Class Module

Chapter 9, "Custom Classes and Objects"

Working with the Visual Basic for Applications Extensibility Library

Getz, Ken, and Mike Gilbert. *Visual Basic Language Developer's Handbook*. Alameda, CA: Sybex, 1999.

Creating COM Add-ins with Visual C++ and Visual J++

MSDN Online Web site
(http://msdn.microsoft.com/developer/)

Creating Application-Specific Templates and Add-ins

Boctor, David. *Microsoft Office 2000/Visual Basic Fundamentals*. Redmond, WA: Microsoft Press, 1999.

Getz, Ken, Paul Litwin, and Mike Gilbert. *Access 2000 Developer's Handbook, Volume 1: Desktop Edition*. Alameda, CA: Sybex, 1999.

"Creating the USysRegInfo Table for a Microsoft Access 2000 Add-in" (USysReg.doc)

Using the WithEvents Keyword to Sink Command Bar Events

Chapter 9, "Custom Classes and Objects"

Chapter 6, "Working with Shared Office Components"

Securing VBA Projects and Working with Digital Signatures

Chapter 17, "Securing Office Documents and Visual Basic for Applications Code"

Securing Access Databases

Chapter 18, "Securing Access Databases"

Deploying Templates and Add-ins

Chapter 2, "Designing and Deploying Office Solutions"

Useful Tips and Sample Code

The following Web sites contain many useful articles about creating add-ins and wizards:

The Microsoft Office Developer Forum Web site
(http://www.microsoft.com/OfficeDev/)

The Microsoft Knowledge Base
(http://support.microsoft.com/support)

Code Samples

The code samples shown in this chapter, along with additional examples demonstrating similar techniques, can be copied from the files in the Samples\CH11 subfolder on the companion CD-ROM. Additional sample files for this chapter are located in the Samples\CH11\CodeLib, Samples\CH11\DevTools, and Samples\CH11\ImageGallery subfolders. The template project discussed in this chapter can be found in the Samples\CH11\VB_COM_AddIn subfolder.

CHAPTER 12

Using Web Technologies

The applications in the Microsoft Office suite have always focused on making it easy to create powerful documents. But these documents haven't always been that easy to share with large groups of people. In the last few years, the popularity of the Internet and corporate intranets has exploded because they make it so easy to disseminate information to a wide audience. As a result, Microsoft Office 2000 has been designed to seamlessly integrate Office desktop productivity with the ability of the Internet and corporate intranets to share information.

The Web technologies integrated into Office 2000 give developers like you a host of new features you can use to create custom solutions that take full advantage of Web-based information sharing and collaboration. You can think of Office 2000 as an easily accessible set of Web-publishing tools that enable users to manage information instead of documents.

To help you make use of these Web technologies, this chapter includes an overview of the document object model that lies behind Web pages and introduces scripting in Office documents and the new Microsoft Script Editor. It also introduces Dynamic HTML (DHTML), cascading style sheets, and other tools and techniques you can use to create powerful Office documents for the Web.

Along with these features, the chapter also describes how to use two new Web-related features of Office 2000: Microsoft Office Web Components and Microsoft Office Server Extensions. The Office Web Components make it easy to create Web pages that let users view and manipulate data in ways never before possible, and Microsoft Office Server Extensions allow users to create threaded discussions associated with Web pages and Office documents.

Obviously, there is much to learn when it comes to Web technologies, and the material in this chapter is only a beginning.

Starting with what you know about Office and Visual Basic for Applications (VBA), this chapter helps you apply your existing knowledge in ways that will make you immediately productive. If you have already created Web-based solutions, some of what is covered in the first section of this chapter may already be familiar to you, so you may want to go directly to the sections about the Office Web Components and Office Server Extensions.

Contents

Understanding DHTML, Cascading Style Sheets, and Scripting

Even if you are an experienced Office and VBA developer, you might approach this subject with a little apprehension. If you have no experience with using DHTML or adding script to Web pages, this section heading alone may be somewhat intimidating. But there is good news here: Working with Web technologies is remarkably similar to working with Office objects through VBA. Therefore, this chapter provides an introduction to using these Web technologies by building on your existing knowledge of VBA.

Note The sample files that accompany this chapter contain examples of the various tools and techniques discussed in this section and elsewhere in this chapter. To gain additional understanding of how the subjects discussed here apply to Office documents, you should examine the files in the Samples\CH12 subfolder on the companion CD-ROM to see how they were built. This chapter also uses a number of the HTML sample files in the Samples\CH05 subfolder.

DHTML, through the document object model, provides an application programming interface (API) for working with HTML elements and cascading style sheet information. You can write script against the objects on a page to work with the data they contain as well as with their location and appearance. Writing script to manipulate the objects in a Web page is really no different from writing VBA code to manipulate the objects in an Office document.

The document object model supports a data-binding architecture that allows you to programmatically sort or filter data displayed on the page without requiring additional trips to the server. The document object model also supports Microsoft Scripting Components (scriptlets), which are lightweight, reusable objects that encapsulate code or a user-interface component. Scriptlets are created by using HTML code and script (either Microsoft Visual Basic Scripting Edition [VBScript] or Microsoft JScript).

To add script to an Office document, you use the Microsoft Script Editor. To open the Script Editor from inside an Office document, point to **Macro** on the **Tools** menu, and then click **Microsoft Script Editor**. For more information about working with the Script Editor, see "Scripting in Office Applications" later in this chapter.

VBScript vs. JScript

Although Microsoft Internet Explorer supports the use of VBScript code, JScript code, or both in a Web page, this chapter focuses primarily on working with VBScript code for three reasons:

- VBScript is a subset of VBA, which means that you already know how to use this scripting language because of your familiarity with VBA. In many cases, you can paste VBA code directly into a Web page and have it run unchanged.
- There is not room in this chapter to completely document either scripting language, so the discussion will focus on the one you are already familiar with.
- VBScript is a lot easier to learn and a great deal easier to use than JScript. A simple example will illustrate why: JScript is a case-sensitive language and VBScript is not. If you are used to writing VBA code, you are used to writing **If** statements beginning with a capital "I." And if you inadvertently use a lowercase "I," the Visual Basic Editor capitalizes it for you. Since VBScript is case-insensitive, you can begin an **If** statement either way. JScript, on the other hand, requires an **If** statement begin with a lowercase "i." If you use a capital "I" in JScript, your script simply won't run. Debugging code is hard enough without having to worry about whether incorrect capitalization is causing a problem.

The only time you may not be able to use VBScript code in a Web page is for code used to detect the type of browser being used to view the page. VBScript code works in all versions of Internet Explorer 3.0 or later. However, VBScript code works in Netscape Navigator only by using a plug-in. Since JScript code runs in both browsers, you will want to write script that detects the browser type in JScript. To see an example of a scriptlet that uses a combination of VBScript and JScript code to return information about the browser being used to view a page, see the BrowserVersion.htm file in the Samples\CH12 subfolder on the companion CD-ROM.

Note Many of the techniques discussed in this chapter involve technologies designed to work best with Internet Explorer version 4.01 or later. In particular, some of the DHTML features discussed in this chapter may not be fully functional when they are viewed in another browser. However, the DHTML features discussed here are designed to degrade gracefully when you use a browser that does not fully support all features. Typically, this means that interactive features are inoperable and the content is displayed as static data on the page.

A complete discussion of Web technologies is beyond the scope of this chapter, and these technologies are well documented in other resources. For a list of those resources, see "Where to Go from Here" at the end of this chapter.

Working with DHTML and the DHTML Object Model

DHTML is based on the document object model developed by the World Wide Web Consortium (W3C) and is designed to give developers a way to create *dynamic Web pages*. A dynamic Web page is one where the page's structure, style, or content can be changed after the page is loaded in the browser without having to request a new page from a Web server. By using DHTML, you can create a page that can interact with the user without using additional controls and without requiring multiple trips to a server to update the page.

DHTML uses standard HTML tags to render and manipulate content on a page. It also includes a comprehensive object model that exposes every element on a page as an object that can be manipulated by calling its methods or setting its properties. In other words, everything you see (and many things you can't see) when you look at a page in a browser is an object that can be manipulated by using script. To see the complete DHTML object model, see the "Object Model Diagrams" appendix.

DHTML and Scripting Documentation

The material presented in this section is intended to give you an overview of DHTML and scripting from an Office developer's perspective. You can find complete documentation and lots of sample code for DHTML, the DHTML object model, VBScript, and JScript in the following subfolder on your machine after you install Microsoft Office 2000:

C:\Program Files\Microsoft Visual Studio\Common\IDE\IDE98\MSE\1033

The DHTML and DHTML object model references are in the Htmlref.chm Help file, the complete VBScript reference is in the Vbscrip5.chm Help file, and the complete JScript reference is in the Jscript5.chm Help file. You can also find a wealth of information about using DHTML on the Microsoft Site Builder Workshop Web site at http://www.microsoft.com/workshop/author/default.asp.

Note The path to the Htmlref.chm, Vbscrip5.chm, and Jscript5.chm Help files reflects the language ID folder (1033) for U.S. English language support in Office. The language ID folder below C:\Program Files\Microsoft Visual Studio\Common\IDE\IDE98\MSE differs for each language.

Working with Objects and Collections

What does it mean to say that every element on a Web page is exposed as an object in the DHTML object model? In HTML code, an *element* is the portion of a page represented by an HTML tag. A page contains an object for each HTML tag or *tag pair*. A tag pair consists of the opening and closing tags for an element, such as <BODY> and </BODY>.

For example, in the following simple page, there are eight objects. These objects consist of the following element tags and the text they enclose: <HTML>, <HEAD>, <TITLE>, <BODY>, <CENTER>, <H1>, and <P>.

```
<HTML>
<HEAD>
   <TITLE>
      A Simple Page
   </TITLE>
</HEAD>
<BODY>
   <CENTER>
      <H1>
         This is the heading on a simple page.
      </H1>
   </CENTER>
   <P>
      This is the first paragraph on a simple page.
   </P>
   <P>
      This is the second paragraph on a simple page.
   </P>
</BODY>
</HTML>
```

Important Some HTML tags, such as the <BR> tag or the <P> tag, work with or without a closing tag. However, if you want to use DHTML to work with the contents of an element, you should always use both the opening and the closing element tags and specify the ID attribute for the tag. For information about tags you can use to enclose items for the purpose of creating objects that you can work with through DHTML, see "Working with <DIV> and <SPAN> Tags" later in this chapter.

Collections in the DHTML object model are similar to collections of objects exposed by an Office application. You can retrieve an item from a collection by specifying its name or the index number that corresponds to the position of the item in the collection. Collection indexes are zero-based, so the first item in a collection always has an index number of zero.

In the DHTML object model, the **document** object represents the HTML page that is displayed in the browser or in a particular frame of a frameset. The **document** object exposes several collections that represent elements on a page, and one collection, called **all**, that represents all the objects on a page. This discussion covers only the **all** collection.

Capitalization of Object, Collection, Method, and Property Names in HTML Code

VBA objects, collections, methods, and properties use names that begin with a capital letter and use capitals for the first letter of concatenated names; for example, **ActiveDocument** and **MoveNext**.

DHTML objects, collections, methods, and properties always begin with a lowercase letter; for example, **document**, **all**, and **setTimeout**.

Note When you create a data access page in Microsoft Access, the VBA **DataAccessPage** object representing the page has a **Document** property that returns the DHTML **document** object. You can use VBA to work with the HTML code in a data access page by accessing the DHTML object model for the page through this property. For more information about data access pages, see "Working with the Office Web Components" later in this chapter or see Chapter 5, "Working with Office Applications."

One difference between collections in the DHTML object model and collections in Office applications is the property you use to determine the total number of items in a collection. In VBA, you use a collection's **Count** property to determine the number of items in a collection. In DHTML, you use a collection's **length** property to determine the number of items in a collection. The following VBScript code displays a message box showing the number of objects in the Web page in which the script is run:

```
MsgBox "This page contains " & document.all.length & " DHTML objects."
```

A Web page can have multiple elements of the same type. For example, you might have a page with ten paragraphs of text where each paragraph is contained in a <P></P> tag pair. You can use the **tags** method of the **all** collection to return a subcollection of items of the same type. The **tags** method returns the members of the **all** collection that have the same **tagName** property value that is specified in the method's *sTag* argument. For example, the following VBScript code can be used to create a new collection of objects representing all the <P> objects on the current page. The sample code then specifies new text to appear in the third paragraph and underlines all the new text:

```
Dim colParagraphs
Dim objSinglePara

Set colParagraphs = document.all.tags("P")
Set objSinglePara = colParagraphs(2)
objSinglePara.innerText = "This is brand new text!"
objSinglePara.style.textDecoration = "underline"
```

When you know a page will contain objects that you want to manipulate from script, you can uniquely identify an object by using its **id** property. You can set the **id** property by specifying the ID attribute within the tag itself. The attribute for an element usually has a corresponding property in the DHTML object model. For example, all the following <P> elements within the body of the page are specifically identified by using the ID attribute:

```
<BODY>
   <CENTER>
      <H1>
         This is the heading on a simple page.
      </H1>
   </CENTER>
   <P ID="para1">
      This is the first paragraph on a simple page.
   </P>
   <P ID="para2">
      This is the second paragraph on a simple page.
   </P>
</BODY>
```

When you add a control to a page by using the toolbox for a data access page in Access or the toolbox in the Script Editor, a default ID attribute is added automatically. The following example shows the HTML element representing a command button that has been created by using the toolbox for a data access page:

```
<BUTTON ID=Command0 STYLE="HEIGHT: 0.57in; LEFT: 1in; POSITION: absolute;
TOP: 0.31in; WIDTH: 3.06in" tabIndex=1 TITLE=Command0>Command0</BUTTON>
```

You can use the **id** property to return a reference to an object in the **all** collection. For example, the following VBScript procedure shows how to change the text associated with a particular element. The ChangeElementText procedure uses the **id** property specified by the *strID* argument to return a reference to the specified object:

```
' Call the ChangeElementText procedure.
ChangeElementText "para2", "I am the new text in the second paragraph."

Sub ChangeElementText(strID, strNewText)
   Dim objElement

   Set objElement = document.all(strID)
   If Len(objElement.innerText) > 0 Then
      objElement.innerText = strNewText
   End If
End Sub
```

You can see the ChangeElementText procedure work in an HTML page by opening the SimpleObjectReference.htm file in the Samples\CH12 subfolder on the companion CD-ROM. The preceding example illustrates how to use a DHTML object's **innerText** property to work with the text associated with an object. If you use the same ID attribute for multiple tags, the **all** collection will return a collection of all elements that share the same ID attribute. For example, in a page where five elements all have an ID attribute of "MyElement", the following myObject variable will contain a collection of those five items:

```
myObject = document.all("MyElement")
```

When you have uniquely identified an object on a page by specifying its ID attribute, you can also directly refer to the element in script without going through the **all** collection. For example, the following two lines are equivalent for an element that has an ID attribute of "myElement":

```
MsgBox document.all("myElement").innerText
MsgBox myElement.innerText
```

For more information about working with the text or the HTML code associated with an object, see the following section, "Understanding Dynamic Content."

Understanding Dynamic Content

To understand how to create and work with dynamic content in a Web page, you need to know how to identify and manipulate the specific objects on the page. In the previous section, you learned to use the **id** property to uniquely identify an object on a page. In this section, you will learn how to use the <DIV> and <SPAN> tags to turn any part of a page, portion of text, or part of another object into an object. You will also learn about the handful of properties and methods you will use to manipulate the content of an object.

Working with <DIV> and <SPAN> Tags

Most HTML element tags have a very specific purpose. For example, the <IMG> image tag embeds an image or video clip in a page, the <A> anchor tag designates a hyperlink, and the <P> paragraph tag designates a paragraph. Each of these tags represents an object on a Web page. The <DIV> and <SPAN> tags, on the other hand, are container tags that you can use to create objects out of any other HTML element or content on a page. The difference between <DIV> and <SPAN> is simply that the <DIV> tag forces a break in the flow of the page structure and the <SPAN> tag does not. Therefore, you use a <DIV> tag to set off any arbitrary part of the page as an object, and you use a <SPAN> tag to designate any arbitrary inline part of the page as an object.

An example will highlight the difference between these tags and illustrate how they can be used. Imagine you create a page containing a display area and some text. The text contains words representing the colors you can use in the display area, and you want the color of the display area to change when the user clicks the words in the text. You would use a <DIV> tag to specify the display area and <SPAN> tags to surround the words in the text that you want to work with as objects. The following HTML sample code illustrates how to use these tags to create DHTML objects:

```
<BODY>
<H2>Office Programmer's Guide Chapter 12:
<BR> Using Web Technologies
</H2>
<HR>
This page contains a <SPAN id=color1 class=boldBlack>black</SPAN>
square. You can change the color of this square to
<SPAN ID=colorRed CLASS=boldRed>red</SPAN>,
<SPAN ID=colorBlue CLASS=boldBlue>blue</SPAN>, or
<SPAN ID=colorGreen CLASS=boldGreen>green</SPAN>
by clicking the name of the color in this sentence.

<DIV
   ID=displayedText
   STYLE="BACKGROUND-COLOR: black; HEIGHT: 100px; LEFT: 150; POSITION: absolute;
      TOP: 180; WIDTH: 100px">
   <SPAN STYLE="COLOR: white">I am text in the box!</SPAN>
</DIV>
</BODY>
```

The Web page created from this HTML code would look like Figure 12.1.

Figure 12.1 Using <DIV> and <SPAN> Tags to Create Objects on a Page

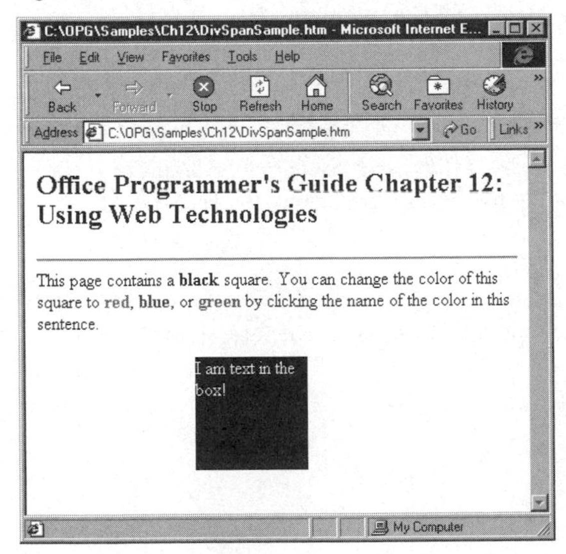

The <SPAN> and <DIV> tags are extremely useful when you need to create an object you can work with in script from any part of a Web page. You can view the page illustrated in Figure 12.1 by opening the DivSpanSample.htm file in the Samples\CH12 subfolder on the companion CD-ROM. For another example that uses this same technique, see RollOverSample.htm in the same subfolder.

Manipulating Text and HTML Code

You can use certain properties and methods of DHTML objects to determine or specify the text or the HTML code the object contains. The properties you will use most often are the **innerText**, **outerText**, **innerHTML**, and **outerHTML** properties. The methods you will use most often are the **insertAdjacentText**, **insertAdjacentHTML**, and **createTextRange** methods.

Important Changes you make to a page by using these properties and methods do not change the HTML code for a page as it exists on disk. They only change the HTML code as it exists in the browser. If the page is refreshed, the page's original HTML code is used to redisplay the page.

Working with Text

The **innerText** and **outerText** properties return the same information and so operate the same when you are trying to identify the text contained within an HTML element. The difference between the two properties appears when you set them. The **innerText** property replaces the text between the opening and closing element tags of an object. For example, replacing the **innerText** property of the `para1` object changes the HTML code in the page as follows:

```
document.all("para1").innerText = "I am the new text!"

' The preceding line changes the HTML code for the para1 object as follows:
' Original HTML code
<P ID=para1>Old innerText is here.</P>
' New HTML code
<P ID=para1>I am the new text!</P>
```

The **outerText** property replaces the text and the HTML tags surrounding the text. For example, replacing the **outerText** property of the `para1` object changes the HTML code in the page as follows:

```
document.all("para1").outerText = "I am the new text!"

' The preceding line changes the HTML code for the para1 object as follows:
' Original HTML code
<P ID=para1>Old innerText is here.</P>
' New HTML code
I am the new text!
```

In the preceding example, not only is the text replaced, but also the original `para1` object is removed from the HTML code in the page. Although there may be times when this is useful, you will typically use the **innerText** property and leave the surrounding element tags intact. For an example that illustrates the differences between these properties, see the InnerAndOuter.htm file in the Samples\CH12 subfolder on the companion CD-ROM.

You use the **insertAdjacentText** method to add to the existing text in an element. This method uses two arguments to specify where text should be inserted. The first argument, *sWhere*, uses a constant to specify where the new text should be inserted: before the element itself (**beforeBegin**), before the existing text in the element (**afterBegin**), at the end of the existing text (**beforeEnd**), or after the element itself (**afterEnd**). The second argument, *sText*, is the new text to insert. For an example that illustrates the effect of adding text to an element by using each of the four described constants, see the InsertAdjacent.htm file in the Samples\CH12 subfolder on the companion CD-ROM.

You can also use the **textRange** object to work with the text in certain elements in a Web page. The **textRange** object represents text in an HTML element. You create a **textRange** object by using the **createTextRange** method. For more information about the **textRange** object, look up the object and its related method in the "Objects" section of the "Document Object Model Reference" in the C:\Program Files\Microsoft Visual Studio\Common\IDE\IDE98\MSE\1033\Htmlref.chm file.

Note The path to the Htmlref.chm Help file reflects the language ID folder (1033) for U.S. English language support in Office. The language ID folder below C:\Program Files \Microsoft Visual Studio\Common\IDE\IDE98\MSE differs for each language.

Working with HTML Code

You use the **innerHTML** property to work with the HTML-formatted text inside an object. You use the **outerHTML** property to work with the HTML tags of the object itself. For example, the following VBScript code uses the **innerHTML** property to change the text in the `para1` object so that the word "this" appears as bold text instead of italic text:

```
document.all("para1").innerHTML = "I am the text in <B>this</B> element."

' The preceding line changes the innerHTML for the para1 object as follows:
' Original HTML code
<P ID=para1>I am the text in <I>this</I> element.</P>
' New HTML code
<P ID=para1>I am the text in <B>this</B> element.</P>
```

The next example replaces the **outerHTML** property of the `para1` object, and actually changes the element from a paragraph to an image, while keeping the `para1` ID attribute setting:

```
document.all("para1").outerHTML = _
   "<IMG ID=para1 SRC='picture.gif' WIDTH=150 HEIGHT=200>"

' The preceding line changes the outerHTML for the para1 object as follows:
' Original outerHTML
<P ID=para1>Old innerText is here.</P>
' New outerHTML
<IMG ID=para1 SRC='picture.gif' WIDTH=150 HEIGHT=200>"
```

If you add a new element by using the **outerHTML** property, the element that is replaced is no longer a part of the page. If that element was identified by an **id** property and referenced by other script in the page, the script will no longer work. You will typically use the **innerHTML** property and leave the surrounding element tags intact. For an example that illustrates the differences between these properties, see the InnerAndOuter.htm file in the Samples\CH12 subfolder on the companion CD-ROM.

You use the **insertAdjacentHTML** method to add to the existing HTML code in an element. The method uses two arguments to specify where HTML code should be inserted. This method works in exactly the same way as the **insertAdjacentText** method discussed in the previous section, "Working with Text," only you use it to add HTML code instead of text to an element. To see how the different arguments work, see the discussion of the **insertAdjacentText** method in the previous section.

Understanding Dynamic Styles

Formatting HTML elements in a Web page is a lot like using styles to format text in a Microsoft Word document. The information about what style should be applied to an element can be contained within the element tag itself, within <STYLE> tags in the document, or within an external style sheet that is included in a Web page by reference. The technology through which styles are applied to the elements in a page is called cascading style sheets. This is an extremely powerful technology you can use to format the appearance of elements in a Web page.

Note The term "cascading" in cascading style sheets refers to how the cascading style sheets technology resolves conflicts when more than one style tries to apply formatting to the same element at the same time. When multiple styles conflict, the most specific style is applied.

For an example of a page that uses custom style classes defined in the <STYLE> tag of a Web page, see the DivSpanSample.htm and RollOverSample.htm files in the Samples\CH12 subfolder on the companion CD-ROM. For a more complete cascading style sheets discussion and reference, see the "Dynamic Styles" and the "CSS Attributes Reference" sections in the C:\Program Files\Microsoft Visual Studio \Common\IDE\IDE98\MSE\1033\Htmlref.chm file.

Note The path to the Htmlref.chm Help file reflects the language ID folder (1033) for U.S. English language support in Office. The language ID folder below C:\Program Files \Microsoft Visual Studio\Common\IDE\IDE98\MSE differs for each language.

Understanding Events

An *event* is something that happens in response to an action, such as clicking a button or moving the mouse. In a Web page, an *event handler* is a script procedure that runs in response to an event. If you have used VBA, you are probably very familiar with the concept of events and event handlers. This section introduces you to events in the DHTML object model and gives a brief overview of how to work with them by using script in a Web page.

To write script that responds to events in a Web page, you can write an event handler for an object in the page, or you can take advantage of *event bubbling* in DHTML to create a global event handler. The DHTML object model exposes an **event** object that has a **srcElement** property that you can use to return the object that triggered an event. In addition, when an event occurs in a Web page, the VBScript **me** property returns a reference to the object in which the event occurred. When an event occurs in an object on a Web page, the event will "bubble up" through each parent object until it reaches the **document** object.

Here's how event bubbling works: Everything you see on a Web page displayed in a browser is part of the **document** object. Therefore, any object on the page is a child object of, at least, the **document** object. You can have objects nested several levels deep. For example, in the following HTML code, there is a `word1` word object nested in a `sent2` sentence object, which is nested in a `para1` paragraph object, which is nested in the `body` object, which is nested in the **document** object. The HTML code has been formatted to make it easier to identify the nested levels in this page:

```
<BODY ID=body>
<H2>Office Programmer's Guide Chapter 12:
<BR> Using Web Technologies
</H2>
<HR>
<P ID=para1>
   <SPAN ID=sent1>
      This is text in the first paragraph on this page.
   </SPAN>
   <SPAN ID=sent2>
      This sentence is itself an object on this page and
      it contains this
      <SPAN ID=word1>
         <B>word</B>,
      </SPAN>
      which is also an object on this page.
   </SPAN>
</P>
</BODY>
```

If a user viewing this page in a browser clicked the `word1` object, a click event would occur for that object. If that event is not handled, or the event is handled but the **event** object's **cancelBubble** property is not set to **True**, that event will continue to bubble up through every parent object until it reaches the **document** object level. In the HTML code shown above, an uncancelled click event would bubble up to the **document** object through the following sequence of events:

word1 onclick ⇒ sent2 onclick ⇒ para1 onclick ⇒ body onclick ⇒ document onclick

For an example of a page that illustrates event bubbling and how to handle or cancel the bubbling of the click event at any level, see the EventBubbling.htm file in the Samples\CH12 subfolder on the companion CD-ROM.

The EventBubbling.htm file also illustrates several of the other properties discussed in this section. It shows how to use the VBScript **me** property to identify an object on a page, and it shows how to use the **srcElement** property of the **event** object to identify the object that is the source of an event in a document-level global event handler. It also shows how to use the **event** object's **cancelBubble** property to prevent an event from bubbling up further through a document.

There are three ways to tie an event procedure directly to an object on a Web page:

- The most common method is to create a subroutine within a script block by using the form **Sub** *objectid*_**on***eventname*(). For example, the following code from the EventBubbling.htm file shows the `word1` object's click event procedure:

  ```
  <SCRIPT LANGUAGE = VBScript>
  <!--
  Sub word1_onclick()
     If MsgBox("The object with the id = " & me.id _
           & " was just clicked. Do you want to cancel event" _
           & " bubbling?", vbYesNo, "Cancel Event Now?") = vbYes Then
        window.event.cancelBubble = True
     End If
  End Sub
  -->
  </SCRIPT>
  ```

  If, instead of using the click event, you want to write script to run when the mouse pointer moves over an object on a page, you could create the following mouseOver event procedure for an object with an **id** property value of `menuItem`:

  ```
  Sub menuItem_onmouseOver()
     ' Add VBScript code for mouseOver event here.
  End Sub
  ```

- A second way to create an event procedure for an object is to use the **For** and **Event** keywords within the <SCRIPT> tag itself. For example, here is another way to create a script block to run code for the onclick event of the `word1` object shown earlier:

```
<SCRIPT LANGUAGE = VBScript For=word1 Event=onclick>
<!--
   If MsgBox("The object with the id = " & me.id _
         & " was just clicked. Do you want to cancel event" _
         & " bubbling?", vbYesNo, "Cancel Event Now?") = vbYes Then
      window.event.cancelBubble = True
   End If
-->
</SCRIPT>
```

The disadvantage to using this technique is that you must create separate <SCRIPT> tag blocks for each event procedure you want in the page. If you use the first technique illustrated earlier with the `menuItem` object's mouseOver event procedure, you can add as many event procedures as you want inside a single <SCRIPT> tag block.

Note You must use this technique when you are using VBScript code to create event handlers in data access pages. In addition, if you are adding VBScript code to an existing Web page, you also need to insert the following <META> tag at the top of the page:

```
<META Name=VBSForEventHandlers Value=True>
```

- A third way to create an event procedure for an object is to call a custom procedure directly from an object's element tag. For example, if in the mouseOver event you were only going to call the MyCustomFunction procedure, you could do it in one of two ways. You could create the menuItem_onmouseOver() event procedure as shown earlier and then call MyCustomFunction from that procedure, or you could include the event as an attribute of the object's element tag and indicate that you want to call the MyCustomFunction procedure. For example:

```
<SPAN ID=menuItem onmouseOver="MyCustomFunction()">
Menu Item One
</SPAN>
```

To see a simple example that uses all three methods discussed here to handle the onclick event for an object, see the ClickTest.htm file in the Samples\CH12 subfolder on the companion CD-ROM.

For examples of pages that use both specific event handlers and a global event handler that takes advantage of the **srcElement** property, see the EventBubbling.htm, RollOverSample.htm, and DataSourceControl.htm files (or any of the many sample files discussed later in this chapter in "Working with the Office Web Components") in the Samples\CH12 subfolder on the companion CD-ROM.

For more information about working with the DHTML object model, see the C:\Program Files\Microsoft Visual Studio\Common\IDE\IDE98\MSE\1033 \Htmlref.chm file.

Note The path to the Htmlref.chm Help file reflects the language ID folder (1033) for U.S. English language support in Office. The language ID folder below C:\Program Files \Microsoft Visual Studio\Common\IDE\IDE98\MSE differs for each language.

Scripting in Office Applications

In the past, scripting in Office applications was confined to manipulating Microsoft Outlook objects and controls from within an Outlook form. And in one sense this is still the case. You can still use script to work with Outlook objects from within the Outlook application. You still use VBA to work with the objects exposed by Office applications.

What has changed is that you can now use Office applications to create Office documents designed to be viewed with a Web browser. The ability to add script to an Office document from within an Office application is part of the seamless integration with the Internet that Office 2000 was designed to achieve. This section discusses working with the Microsoft Script Editor and using scriptlets. For additional scripting information, see "Working with DHTML and the DHTML Object Model" earlier in this chapter.

Complete coverage of scripting in Web pages is beyond the scope of this book. This section presents an overview of scripting in Office applications in order to help you understand how, when, and why you add script to a document and the Office technologies available to help you work with script. All the script examples in this section are written in VBScript. You can get a complete scripting reference, including the complete VBScript language reference and a VBScript tutorial, in the Htmlref.chm and Vbscrip5.chm files in the C:\Program Files\Microsoft Visual Studio\Common \IDE\IDE98\MSE\1033 subfolder.

Note The path to the Htmlref.chm and Vbscrip5.chm Help files reflects the language ID folder (1033) for U.S. English language support in Office. The language ID folder below C:\Program Files\Microsoft Visual Studio\Common\IDE\IDE98\MSE differs for each language.

Working with the Microsoft Script Editor

The Microsoft Script Editor has been added to the Office applications so you can work with the HTML code, DHTML objects, and script in an Office document from within an Office application. To open the Script Editor, point to **Macro** on the **Tools** menu, and then click **Microsoft Script Editor**.

Note The Microsoft Script Editor is not used in Microsoft Outlook. To work with script in Outlook, you use the Outlook Script Editor. For more information about using the Outlook Script Editor, see "Working with the Outlook Object Model" in Chapter 4, "Understanding Office Objects and Object Models."

The Script Editor was designed to work much like the Visual Basic Editor. Unlike the Visual Basic Editor, there is a single instance of the Script Editor open at one time, which means that you can use the Script Editor's Project Explorer to access every open Office document that also has the Script Editor open.

When you view an Office document in the Script Editor, you will see the HTML and XML code that constitute the Office document when it is rendered as a Web page.

Understanding XML Code in Office Documents

When you view an Office document in the Script Editor or any other HTML editor, you may see a great deal of information you do not recognize as part of a typical HTML document. Most likely, you are looking at the Extensible Markup Language (XML) elements the Office application has added to the document. You can identify the XML code in an Office document as the information between the <XML> tags.

The XML data that appears by default in an Office document depends on the application used to create the document. In Microsoft Excel, Microsoft PowerPoint, and Word, the XML data is used to preserve document-specific information, such as document properties or option settings, so that the page can be accurately rendered as an Office document when it is opened in an Office application. In an Access data access page, XML data is used to supply data to the hidden Microsoft Office **Data Source** control (MSODSC). It should never be necessary for you to manipulate the XML code that appears in an Office document when it is viewed in an HTML editor.

Caution You should never manipulate the XML code associated with a **Data Source** control in an Access data access page.

A complete discussion of XML is beyond the scope of this chapter. You can find a complete discussion of XML on the Microsoft Site Builder Workshop Web site at http://www.microsoft.com/workshop/c-frame.htm#/xml/default.asp.

Understanding the Script Editor's User Environment

In the Script Editor, you work with the HTML code and script in an Office document by using the **Source** tab at the bottom of the editor window. You can see the results of your work on the page by using the **Quick View** tab instead of having to switch back to the host Office application or viewing the document in a Web browser.

Note The Script Editor also displays a **Design** tab, but Design view is not enabled when you are working with an Office document.

In addition to the tabs for switching between different views of the document, the left side of the editor window allows you to access a toolbox, an HTML Outline window, and a Script Outline window. As when you are working with UserForms in the Visual Basic Editor, you use the toolbox in the Script Editor to add controls to the HTML code in the page. To see the hierarchy of HTML objects on a page, you use the HTML Outline window; to see the various DHTML objects in a document, you use the Script Outline window. Much like the Visual Basic Editor, the Script Editor's Source view includes a color-coded view of the HTML code in a document along with drop-down lists that display the available objects and their related methods and properties.

Note For complete documentation about the Script Editor's user environment, click **Contents** on the **Help** menu in the Script Editor.

Using the Script Editor to Add Event Procedures

The Script Outline window makes it easy to add event procedures to an Office document. For example, to add an event procedure for the **document** object's onclick event, click the "+" sign next to the **document** object in the Script Outline window and then double-click **onclick**. The Script Editor inserts a VBScript <SCRIPT> block in the document and adds the onclick event procedure, as shown in Figure 12.2.

Figure 12.2 Script Outline View in the Microsoft Script Editor

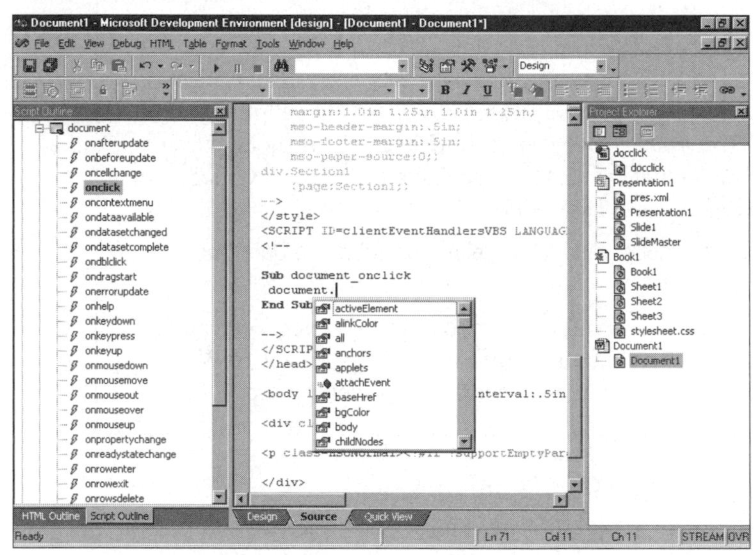

There is one very important difference between what happens when you use the Script Editor to add event procedures and what happens when you use the Visual Basic Editor to add event procedures to Office documents: The Script Editor does not add the parentheses or the required arguments (if any) at the end of the event procedures.

For event procedures that do not require arguments, the absence of the empty parentheses does not prevent the script from running when the page is viewed in a browser. However, for event procedures that do require arguments, their absence prevents the script from running even if the code in the procedure does not use the missing arguments. If you are unaware of this, the missing arguments can cause you some headaches when you are trying to debug your script.

It is up to you do determine which event procedures require additional arguments and what those arguments are. Once you determine this information, you add the arguments by hand. You can find complete documentation for an event procedure related to an object in that object's Help file or by using the Object Browser. The following event procedure for the **Spreadsheet** control's Calculate event is an example of an event procedure that requires an argument that is not added by the Script Editor:

```
Sub Spreadsheet1_Calculate(EventInfo)
   document.all("txtTotal").value = formatNumber(document _
      .all("Spreadsheet1").Range("A7").value, 2, TristateTrue, TristateTrue)
End Sub
```

The parentheses and the *EventInfo* argument in the preceding example were added by hand. The argument information was obtained by viewing the Help topic for the Calculate event in the **Spreadsheet** control's Help file. In this example, *EventInfo* is the actual name for the argument as it appears in the Help file, but this argument could have been named anything. You are not required to use the same name for an argument as long as there are placeholders provided for each argument.

Understanding Scriptlets and Behaviors

A scriptlet is a lightweight, reusable Component Object Model (COM) component that consists of HTML code and script and is created according to certain conventions. A *behavior* is a lightweight component that encapsulates specific functionality. When applied to an HTML element, a behavior enhances the element's default behavior.

Scriptlets and behaviors are very similar in that they both contain script in a separate document that exposes functionality that can be used in a Web page. They differ in that behaviors are STYLE attributes that point to a separate file containing script that is called in response to an event associated with an HTML element. Scriptlets, on the other hand, can be used for almost anything you can do with script in a Web page.

Scriptlets are supported in Internet Explorer 4.0 or later, and behaviors are supported in Internet Explorer version 5 or later. Deciding when to use a scriptlet and when to use a behavior depends on what you are trying to accomplish and what browser you are writing for. If your users are running Internet Explorer 4.*x*, scriptlets are your only choice. If you want to create a self-contained component for use in HTML, a DHTML scriptlet makes sense. If you want to add a lightweight component to be used as a STYLE attribute, a behavior is a good choice.

Creating Scriptlets

A scriptlet is an HTML code file that has either an .sct or an .htm extension. You can create scriptlets by using HTML code and VBScript code, JScript code, or both, and you can create them in any HTML editor. You can also create scriptlets by using the Microsoft Scriptlet Wizard. If you have worked with the Class Builder in Microsoft Visual Basic version 5.0 or 6.0, you are already familiar with how this wizard works. The wizard takes you through the steps required to create the basic HTML code required for a scriptlet, along with a sample container file containing the HTML code required to reference the scriptlet from another Web page. You can download the Scriptlet Wizard from the Microsoft Scripting Technologies Web site at http://msdn.microsoft.com/scripting/.

What Kind of Scriptlet Should I Create?

There are two basic types of scriptlets: those that have a user interface (DHTML scriptlets) and those that do not (code-only scriptlets). Scriptlets that have a user interface are encapsulated script and DHTML code and are designed to display their user interface in another HTML page. For example, you could create a scriptlet that displays a digital clock or a calendar. The display elements and all the code necessary to make the display work properly are encapsulated within the scriptlet so that it can be used again and again just like any other COM component.

Scriptlets without a user interface are Web pages in which script procedures have been written so that these procedures behave like methods and properties of an object. This type of scriptlet is analogous to a custom object created from a VBA class module. Like a class module, the scriptlet contains a number of procedures, some of which are exposed to other objects as methods or properties and others that are accessible only by other procedures within the scriptlet itself.

The reasons for creating reusable objects that contain script are the same as the reasons for creating reusable objects through VBA. For a complete discussion of the benefits of reusable code objects, see Chapter 9, "Custom Classes and Objects." For a complete discussion of scriptlets, see the Scriptlet Technology Web site at http://msdn.microsoft.com/developer/sdk/inetsdk/help/scriptlets/scrlt.htm.

Working with DHTML Scriptlets

A DHTML scriptlet is a Web page that exposes a user interface that can be used from another Web page. To create a DHTML scriptlet, you simply create a Web page that displays the user interface you want to save as a scriptlet. You then add any script necessary to make the user interface fully functional. That is all there is to it. For example, the following sample shows all the HTML code and script required to create and display a digital clock on a page:

```
<HTML>
<HEAD>
<SCRIPT LANGUAGE="VBScript">
<!--
Sub InitDigiTimer
   ' Specify that the MoveTime procedure should be
   ' called at 1-second intervals.
   window.setInterval "MoveTime", 1000
End Sub

Function MoveTime()
   document.all("displayTime").innerText = time()
End Function

Sub window_onload()
   InitDigiTimer
End Sub
-->
</SCRIPT>
</HEAD>
```

```
<BODY>
<DIV  ID=displayTime
      STYLE="position:absolute;
             width: 120;
             height: 20;
             border:solid;
             border-color:lightblue;
             border-left-width:thin;
             border-right-width:thin;
             background-color:darkblue;
             color:yellow;
             text-align:center;
             font-family:arial;
             font-weight:bold">
</DIV>
</BODY>
</HTML>
```

Figure 12.3 shows how this HTML code is rendered in the browser.

Figure 12.3 Digital Clock Scriptlet

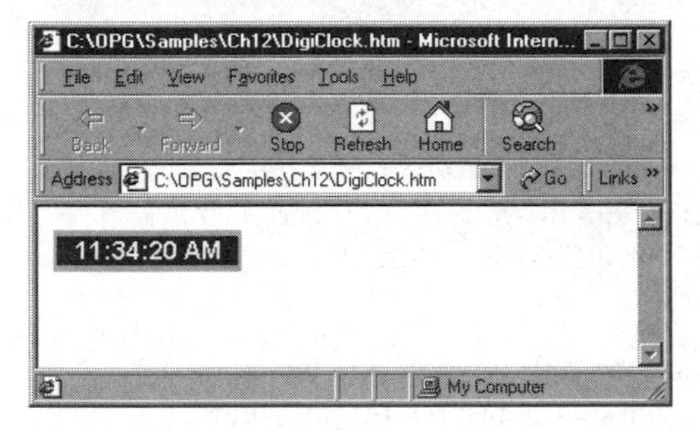

When you use this file as a scriptlet, only the clock and its related formatting appear in the container Web page. For example, you could name this file DateTime.htm and use it as a scriptlet from another Web page by inserting the following <OBJECT> tag in the container page:

```
<OBJECT  ID="scrltCode2"
         STYLE=  "position:absolute;
                  width:150;
                  height:40;"
         TYPE="text/x-scriptlet"
         DATA="DateTime.htm">
</OBJECT>
```

The only mandatory <OBJECT> tag attributes to create a DHTML scriptlet are TYPE and DATA. The TYPE attribute setting will always be `"text/x-scriptlet"`. The DATA attribute should always contain the path and name of the file you are referencing as a scriptlet. If you want to change the design of the clock, you need only change the settings for the STYLE attribute in the DateTime.htm file. You can position the clock anywhere on the container page by enclosing the <OBJECT> tags shown above in <DIV> tags with STYLE attribute settings indicating precisely where on the page you want the clock to appear.

Working with Code-Only Scriptlets

There are two ways to create this kind of scriptlet. You can create an HTML file with <SCRIPT> tags to contain your custom procedures, or you can use the Scriptlet Wizard. In either case, you are creating a basic template with procedures that represent the public properties and methods of the object along with any private procedures available only to other procedures in the scriptlet object itself.

The following sample illustrates the HTML code and script for a very simple (no provision is made for handling errors) code-only scriptlet named GetRecords.htm. This scriptlet is designed to return an ActiveX Data Objects (ADO) **Recordset** object to the calling function in the container Web page. The GetRecords.htm file is available in the Samples\CH12 subfolder on the companion CD-ROM.

You create properties for the scriptlet by adding the **get_** (read) or **put_** (write) prefix to the property name in the **Function** procedure. If you create both **get_** and **put_** procedures for a property, the property will be read/write. Using only one of the two designators creates a read-only or write-only property. Procedures created with the **get_** and **put_** designators are analogous to the **Property Get** and **Property Let** procedures used in a VBA class module. You specify default values for properties by setting each property to some value at the top of the script block, before the procedures are defined.

You create public methods for the scriptlet by adding the **public_** prefix to the name of the method in the **Function** procedure. Procedures that do not use the **public_** prefix will be available only to other procedures within the scriptlet and will not be visible from the container Web page.

```
<HTML>
<HEAD>
<TITLE>GetRecords Scriptlet</TITLE>
</HEAD>

<SCRIPT LANGUAGE="VBScript">
<!--
' Initialize properties to their default values.
Dim p_provider
Dim p_databasePath

p_provider = "Microsoft.Jet.OLEDB.4.0"
p_databasePath = "c:\program files\microsoft office\office\samples\northwind.mdb"
```

```
Function get_provider()
   get_provider = p_provider
End Function
Function put_provider(newValue)
   p_provider = newValue
End Function

Function get_databasePath()
   get_databasePath = p_databasePath
End Function

Function put_databasePath(newValue)
   p_databasePath = newValue
End Function

Function public_GetRecordset(strSQL)
   Dim rstRecordset
   Dim cnnConnection

   Set cnnConnection = CreateObject("ADODB.Connection")
   cnn.Provider = p_provider
   cnn.Open p_databasePath

   Set rstRecords = CreateObject("ADODB.Recordset")
   rstRecords.Open strSQL, cnn, 1, 3
   Set public_GetRecordset = rstRecords
End Function
-->
</SCRIPT>

<BODY>
</BODY>
</HTML>
```

In the container Web page, you create a reference to this scriptlet by using an <OBJECT> tag as shown earlier for DHTML scriptlets:

```
<OBJECT
   ID="NWIND"
   STYLE="  position:absolute;
            width:0;
            height:0;
            top:0;
            left:0;"
   TYPE="text/x-scriptlet"
   DATA="GetRecords.htm">
</OBJECT>
```

The <OBJECT> tag is using an ID attribute setting of `"NWIND"`, and you use this identifier when calling procedures in the scriptlet. For example, you would use the following script in the container Web page to call the custom GetRecordset method of the referenced scriptlet.

```
<SCRIPT LANGUAGE="VBScript">
<!--
Sub DisplayCustomerInfo()
   Dim strCountry
   Dim strSQL
   Dim rstRecords

   strCountry = document.all("txtCustomerCountry").value
   strSQL = "SELECT * FROM Customers WHERE Country = '" & strCountry & "'"
   Set rstRecords = NWIND.GetRecordset(strSQL)
   ' Work with the returned records here.
End Sub
-->
</SCRIPT>
```

This scriptlet is useful and flexible enough to work against any number of data sources. All you have to do is specify a different data source by setting the properties and then return matching records defined by your `strSQL` variable. As you can see from the preceding example, using scriptlets can be a very powerful technique for encapsulating related script procedures into reusable objects.

How Scriptlets and Web Browser Security Interact

In a security-aware host such as Internet Explorer 4.0 or later, a scriptlet and any controls contained within it are subject to Internet Explorer security. To set the security level in Internet Explorer, click **Internet Options** on the **View** menu (version 4.0*x*) or the **Tools** menu (version 5 or later), and then click the **Security** tab.

On a user's machine, the security level for the zone containing the scriptlet's server must be set to either **Medium** or **Low**. If the security setting is **High**, the scriptlet will not be downloaded to the user's computer. If custom security settings are specified for a zone by clicking **Custom Level** on the **Security** tab in the **Internet Options** dialog box, both **Script ActiveX controls marked safe for scripting** and **Initialize and script ActiveX controls not marked as safe** must be set to either **Prompt** or **Enable**.

The same guidelines apply to any controls that the scriptlet contains, including other scriptlets, especially if the scriptlet contains controls that reside on a server in a different zone.

Therefore, when you distribute an application that uses a scriptlet, make sure that users set the security settings in their copy of Internet Explorer to the correct level to allow them to use your scriptlets.

For more information about the security settings in Internet Explorer, see Internet Explorer Help.

Understanding Behaviors

Scriptlets and behaviors provide a way to create reusable components you can use on a Web page. They allow you to encapsulate and reuse blocks of code and to separate the script in a page from its content. There are two types of behaviors you can use with your Web pages: custom behaviors and built-in behaviors.

Custom Behaviors

Custom behaviors are integrated with Internet Explorer through an *interface handler*. Internet Explorer provides the Behavior Handler (a type of interface handler) as the way a behavior scriptlet can communicate with the page that references it. The Behavior Handler allows the behavior scriptlet to expose custom events, access the containing page's DHTML object model, and receive notification when an event has occurred in the containing page. For complete information about the Behavior Handler, see the Behavior Handler Reference at http://www.microsoft.com/workshop/components/scriptoid/reference/behavior.asp.

The basic parts of a custom behavior scriptlet are <SCRIPTLET> tags, <IMPLEMENTS> tags, and <SCRIPT> tags, which are saved in a file that has an .sct extension. The <IMPLEMENTS> tag uses a TYPE attribute of `"Automation"`. The <SCRIPT> tags contain the script you want to associate with the behavior.

```
<SCRIPTLET>
<!--
   <IMPLEMENTS Type="Behavior">
   </IMPLEMENTS>
   <SCRIPT Language="VBScript">
      ' Add your script here.
-->
   </SCRIPT>
</SCRIPTLET>
```

Once you have created this basic framework, you can use DHTML objects and methods to create custom events, synchronize with events generated by an element in the containing page, or expose custom properties and methods. The following example serves to illustrate the concepts behind creating a custom behavior scriptlet. This behavior uses the **attachEvent** method to monitor events from the containing page and execute script when the specified events occur:

```
<SCRIPTLET>
   <IMPLEMENTS Type="Behavior">
   </IMPLEMENTS>
   <SCRIPT Language="VBScript">
<!--
      Dim previousColor

      attachEvent("onmouseOver", event_onmouseOver)
      attachEvent("onmouseOut", event_onmouseOut)
```

```
      Function event_onMouseOver()
         previousColor = style.color
         style.color = "red"
      End Function

      Function event_onMouseOut()
         style.color = previousColor
      End Function
-->
   </SCRIPT>
</SCRIPTLET>
```

When this behavior is connected to an HTML element as a STYLE attribute, the script it contains runs in response to the mouseOver and mouseOut events. When the mouse pointer moves over the element, the element color is changed to red and the element's original color is saved in the `previousColor` variable. When the mouse pointer moves off the element, the original color is restored. You can add this behavior to an HTML element by specifying the behavior scriptlet as a STYLE attribute of the element, as shown in the following example:

```
<HTML>
<TITLE>Behavior Demo</TITLE>
<HEAD>
<STYLE>
   .HiLite {behavior:url(hilite.sct)}
</STYLE>
</HEAD>
<BODY>
This word is <SPAN style=hilite>CAPITALIZED</SPAN>. Move the mouse pointer over it to
change its color.
</BODY>
</HTML>
```

Built-in Behaviors

You can also take advantage of the built-in, or default, behaviors included with Internet Explorer. These behaviors are available directly from the browser; you can use them without writing any additional external components yourself. The behaviors implemented by Internet Explorer are listed in the following table.

Built-in behavior	Description
anchor	Enables browser navigation to a folder view.
clientCaps	Provides information about the capabilities Internet Explorer supports, as well as a means to install browser components on demand.
download	Provides a means to download a file and notify a callback function when the download is complete.
homePage	Contains information about a user's home page.
httpFolder	Contains script features that enable browser navigation to a folder view.
saveFavorite	Allows the current state of a page to be saved when it is added to Favorites.

Built-in behavior	Description
saveHistory	Allows the current state of the page to be saved when the user navigates away from the page.
saveSnapshot	Allows persistence of information (form values, styles, dynamically updated content, and script variable values) when a page is saved locally.
userData	Allows persistence of information across sessions by writing data to XML storage.

You reference a built-in behavior by using the behavior's name and `#default#`*`BehaviorName`* as the value for the *url* argument, as shown in the following example:

```
<HTML>
<TITLE>Built-in Behavior Demo</TITLE>
<HEAD>
<STYLE>
   .saveFavorite {behavior:url(#default#savefavorite)}
</STYLE>
</HEAD>
<BODY>
<INPUT class=saveFavorite type=text width=35 value="I am a text box.">
</BODY>
</HTML>
```

For more information about built-in behaviors, see Chapter 9, "Custom Classes and Objects," the Component Development section of the Microsoft Site Builder Workshop Web site at http://www.microsoft.com/workshop/default.asp, and the DHTML Behaviors section of the Microsoft Site Builder Workshop Web site at http://www.microsoft.com/workshop/c-frame.htm#/workshop/author/default.asp.

Working with the Office Web Components

Microsoft Office 2000 applications support HTML code as a native file format, making all Office documents "Web-ready" by default. Publishing an Office document to the Web is now as easy as saving a file to your computer's hard disk.

However, publishing an Office document to the Web is only half the challenge. When you are working with worksheets or databases, much of the value of these documents is the ability to interact with the data they display. Allowing users to interact with the data in an Office document when it is viewed in a Web browser is a key aspect of publishing powerful and useful views of the data displayed by an Office document. Being able to interact with the data allows users to get the information that they think is important, not just the information that the document's publisher thinks is important.

Web browsers do not provide a way to sort, filter, change, or recalculate the data displayed in the browser. The Microsoft Office Web Components provide the means to let you publish Office documents to the Web while preserving the interactivity the documents have when they are viewed in their native applications. The Office Web Components are a collection of ActiveX controls designed to let you publish fully interactive worksheets, charts, PivotTable reports, and databases to the Web.

When users view a Web page that contains an Office Web Component, they can interact with the data displayed in that document right in Internet Explorer. Users can sort, filter, add, or change data, expand and collapse detail views, work with PivotTable lists, and chart the results of their changes. In addition, the Office Web Components are fully programmable, which lets you create rich, interactive content for Web-based solutions.

Important The Office Web Components work only in Internet Explorer 4.01 or later. Office Web Components on Access data access pages work only in Internet Explorer 5 or later. In addition, you get the most complete functionality with all of the Office Web Component controls in Internet Explorer 5 or later. To view and work with any of thc Office Web Components, users must either have Office 2000 installed, or if your company has an Office 2000 site license, they must download the Office Web Components from your corporate intranet.

The following table describes the Office Web Components and lists the ActiveX control and object that correspond to each component.

Office Web Component	ActiveX control	Object	Description
Spreadsheet Component	**Spreadsheet**	**Spreadsheet**	This component provides a recalculation engine, a full function library, and a simple worksheet user interface for use on Web pages.
Chart Component	**Chart**	**ChartSpace**	This component displays a graphical representation of data from a **Spreadsheet**, **PivotTable List**, or **Data Source** control. When bound to other controls on a page, the **Chart** control updates instantly in response to changes made to the bound controls.
PivotTable Component	**PivotTable List**	**PivotTable**	This component allows users to sort, group, filter, outline, and manipulate data from a worksheet, database, or multidimensional data cube.
(None)	**Data Source**	**DataSourceControl**	This control manages communication between a Web page or controls on the page and the source of data for the page. This control provides the reporting engine behind data access pages as well as the **PivotTable List** control.

All of the Office Web Components expose an object model and are fully programmable by using VBA within an Office application or by using VBScript or JScript code in a Web page. In addition, since the Office Web Components are ActiveX controls, they can be used in any environment that supports ActiveX controls, including all the programming tools in Microsoft Visual Studio.

You can use the Object Browser to view the objects, methods, and properties associated with the Office Web Components. To display these items in the Object Browser, you must set a reference to the Microsoft Office Web Components 9.0 object library (Msowc.dll), which is in the C:\Program Files\Microsoft Office\Office folder.

You can insert an Office Web Component control in a Web page in several ways:

- In Excel, you can use the Publish as Web Page feature to export Excel charts, worksheets, and PivotTable reports to a Web page.

  Note Not only can you export data from Excel to an Office Web Component control on a Web page, but the **Spreadsheet** and **PivotTable List** controls also support exporting data from the control to Excel by clicking **Export to Excel** on the control's toolbar.

- In Access, you can add an Office Web Component control to a data access page by clicking the **Office Chart**, **Office Spreadsheet**, or **Office PivotTable** tool in the toolbox and then clicking the place on the page where you want the control to appear.
- In FrontPage, you can add a **Chart**, **Spreadsheet**, or **PivotTable List** control to a FrontPage document by pointing to **Component** on the **Insert** menu, and then clicking **Office Chart**, **Office Spreadsheet**, or **Office PivotTable**.
- In a Web page, you can insert an Office Web Component control by adding an <OBJECT> tag for the control to the page and then specifying the control's class identifier (CLSID) as the setting for the CLASSID attribute.

The CLSIDs for the Office Web Component controls and all the objects and related methods and properties for each control are documented in the Msowcvba.chm Help file, which is located in the C:\Program Files\Microsoft Office\Office\1033 subfolder.

Note The path to the Msowcvba.chm Help file reflects the language ID folder (1033) for U.S. English language support in Office. The language ID folder below C:\Program Files \Microsoft Office\Office differs for each language.

Understanding the Spreadsheet Control

The **Spreadsheet** control is an ActiveX control that lets you add the functionality of a worksheet to a Web page. You can also place a hidden instance of this control on a page and use it as a powerful recalculation engine that works with other visible controls on a page. You can think of this control as a way to take the power behind an Excel worksheet and transfer it to a Web page.

You can insert the **Spreadsheet** control on a Web page in several ways. However, the easiest and most useful way to create a page that uses the **Spreadsheet** control is by using Microsoft Excel or Microsoft Access.

Using Microsoft Excel to Create a Spreadsheet Control

In Excel, you do your work on a worksheet, and when you have the sheet looking and working the way you want, you use the **Publish as Web Page** dialog box to specify how you want the sheet to appear in Internet Explorer. You get to the **Publish as Web Page** dialog box by clicking **Save as Web Page** on the **File** menu and then clicking the **Publish** button.

The SalesScenario.xls file in the Samples\CH12 subfolder on the companion CD-ROM contains a worksheet with a simple interactive scenario calculator. The **Publish as Web Page** dialog box for this worksheet is shown in Figure 12.4.

Figure 12.4 The Publish as Web Page Dialog Box

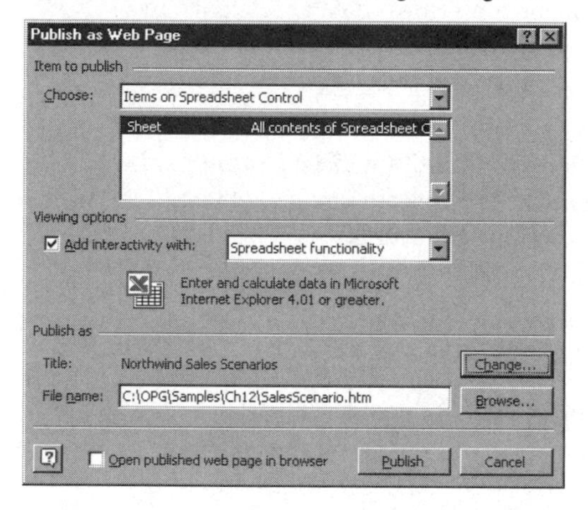

Note Unlike what is shown in Figure 12.4, when you are using the **Publish as Web Page** dialog box, you most likely will be publishing to an HTTP address in the **File name** box.

If you specify interactivity by selecting **Spreadsheet functionality** under **Viewing options** in the **Publish as Web Page** dialog box, Excel creates a Web page (shown in Figure 12.5) that contains a **Spreadsheet** control that displays your calculator. Anyone who views this page (SalesScenario.htm in the Samples\CH12 subfolder on the companion CD-ROM) in Internet Explorer can use the calculator as if it were still an Excel worksheet.

Figure 12.5 The SalesScenario.htm File

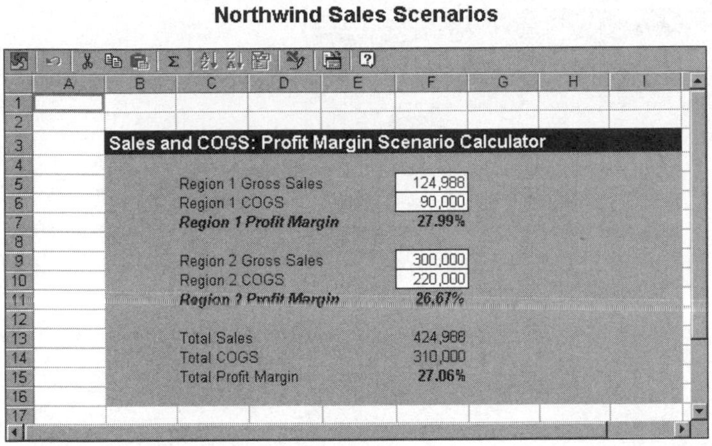

Northwind Sales Scenarios

Sales and COGS: Profit Margin Scenario Calculator

Region 1 Gross Sales	124,988
Region 1 COGS	90,000
Region 1 Profit Margin	***27.99%***
Region 2 Gross Sales	300,000
Region 2 COGS	220,000
Region 2 Profit Margin	***26.67%***
Total Sales	424,988
Total COGS	310,000
Total Profit Margin	**27.06%**

In Figure 12.5, only the cells with a white background can be edited. To achieve this effect in Excel, you select the cells you want users to be able to edit and then set the **Locked** property for the cells to **False**. To do this, select the cells, click **Cells** on the **Format** menu, click the **Protection** tab, and then clear the **Locked** check box. Once you have unlocked the cells you want to edit, you protect the rest of the worksheet by pointing to **Protection** on the **Tools** menu, and then clicking **Protect Sheet**. When you publish the worksheet as a Web page, those protection settings will be preserved in the **Spreadsheet** control.

The **Publish as Web Page** dialog box lets you specify what to publish. In the preceding example, the entire worksheet was published. Publishing the entire sheet results in the scroll bars you see in Figure 12.5. You can eliminate the scroll bars by clicking **Range of Cells** in the **Choose** box in the **Publish as Web Page** dialog box and then specifying the range of cells or a named range in the following box.

You can specify a title for your **Spreadsheet** control by clicking the **Change** button in the **Publish as Web Page** dialog box. Clicking this button opens the **Set Title** dialog box.

In the following figure (Figure 12.6), a range of cells was saved as a **Spreadsheet** control from an Excel worksheet (MortgageCalc.xls in the Samples\CH12 subfolder on the companion CD-ROM) to create a mortgage payment calculator. A title for the control was added by using the **Set Title** dialog box. As in the previous example, worksheet and cell protection was used to specify that only the cells in the shaded area can be edited.

Figure 12.6 Spreadsheet Control Containing Mortgage Calculator

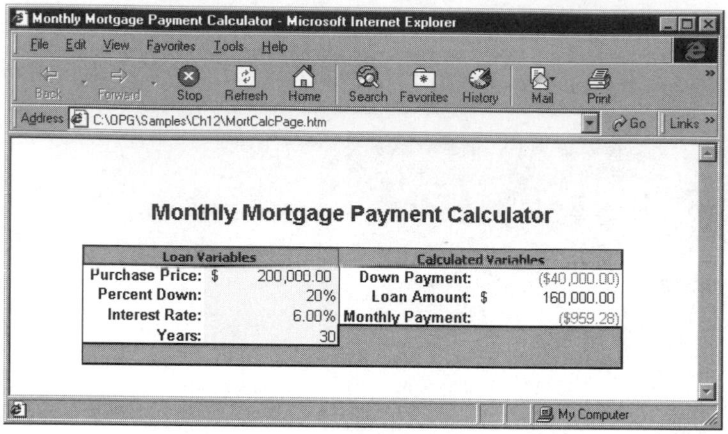

The MortCalcPage.htm page is in the Samples\CH12 subfolder on the companion CD-ROM.

Using Microsoft Access to Create a Spreadsheet Control

In Microsoft Access, you can add a **Spreadsheet** control to a data access page by opening the data access page in Design view, clicking the **Office Spreadsheet** tool in the toolbox, and then clicking the place on the page where you want the control to appear. The **Spreadsheet** control can be displayed and used like a worksheet, or it can be hidden and used as a recalculation engine that is tied to visible controls on the page.

To create a reference in a cell of the **Spreadsheet** control that gets data from another control on the page, you enter a formula that references the control by using the following syntax:

=document.*controlname***.value**

For example, in a data access page with two controls named Value1 and Value2, the following formulas could be used to add the values from the two controls:

```
Cell A1 formula: =document.Value1.value
Cell A2 formula: =document.Value2.value
Cell A3 formula: =SUM(A1:A2)
```

The HiddenRecalcExample.htm sample file in the Samples\CH12 subfolder on the companion CD-ROM uses seven visible text box controls and a hidden **Spreadsheet** control. The **Spreadsheet** control pulls the values from the first six controls into cells A1 through A6 and calculates the sum of those values in cell A7. The values from the text box controls are entered in the hidden **Spreadsheet** control by using the formulas shown earlier. The total of the values entered in the control is calculated in cell A7 and this total is then transferred to the visible txtTotal text box control by using the **Spreadsheet** control's Calculate event procedure:

```
Sub Spreadsheet1_Calculate(EventInfo)
   document.all("txtTotal").value = _
      formatNumber(document.all("Spreadsheet1").Range("A7").Value, _
      2, TristateTrue, TristateTrue)
End Sub
```

There are two ways to transfer a value from a cell on a **Spreadsheet** control to another control on a data access page. The first way is to use the **Spreadsheet** control's Calculate event, as shown in the previous example. The second way is to set the other control's **ControlSource** property to the cell in the **Spreadsheet** control you want to use. For example:

```
=document.all("Spreadsheet1").Range("A7").Value
```

Working with the Spreadsheet Component's Object Model

Whether you are using VBA or VBScript code, working with the **Spreadsheet** control's object model is surprisingly similar to working with a worksheet in Excel. In fact, since both object models support an **ActiveSheet** property (the **Spreadsheet** control can contain only a single worksheet), you may find that some code written to work with Excel's **Worksheet** object (and its related objects, properties, and methods) will work exactly the same way when it is run against a **Spreadsheet** control. For example, Figure 12.7 shows a Web page (ConvertToScript.htm in the Samples\CH12 subfolder on the companion CD-ROM) that was created from an Excel worksheet that originally contained VBA code.

Figure 12.7 An HTML Version of an Excel Worksheet That Used VBA Code

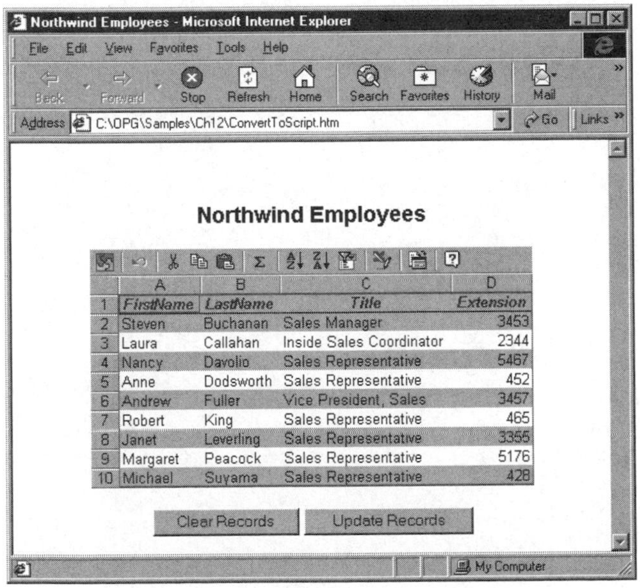
Northwind Employees - Microsoft Internet Explorer
File Edit View Favorites Tools Help
Back Forward Stop Refresh Home Search Favorites History Mail
Address C:\OPG\Samples\Ch12\ConvertToScript.htm
Go Links
Northwind Employees
A B C D
1 FirstName LastName Title Extension
2 Steven Buchanan Sales Manager 3453
3 Laura Callahan Inside Sales Coordinator 2344
4 Nancy Davolio Sales Representative 5467
5 Anne Dodsworth Sales Representative 452
6 Andrew Fuller Vice President, Sales 3457
7 Robert King Sales Representative 465
8 Janet Leverling Sales Representative 3355
9 Margaret Peacock Sales Representative 5176
10 Michael Suyama Sales Representative 428
Clear Records
Update Records
My Computer

The ConvertToScript.htm sample file was created to show how easy it is to convert Excel VBA code that inserts data into a worksheet to VBScript code that inserts the same data into a **Spreadsheet** control on a Web page. This sample file was created by using the **Publish as Web Page** dialog box to publish the Employees worksheet in the ExcelSamples.xls file (located in the Samples\CH05 subfolder on the companion CD-ROM) as the ConvertToScript.htm file. The two **CommandButton** controls on the worksheet were replaced with HTML intrinsic command button controls. The VBA code was copied from the Excel VBA project and pasted into the Web page in the command buttons' onclick event procedures. The VBA code did have to be modified somewhat to account for the different way that VBScript handles some of the language elements, but it is essentially the same.

The following code samples illustrate the similarity between the VBA code and the VBScript code used to make these samples work. The first code sample is VBA code from the GetEmployeeData procedure in ExcelSamples.xls. The second code sample is VBScript code from the cmdUpdate button's onclick event procedure. You can use the comments in the example to compare the VBA code to the VBScript code required to do the same task.

```
' VBA Code Sample
' The wksEmployees variable is a VBA object variable that points
' to a worksheet in Excel's current workbook.

' Create Recordset object and fill it with
' records from the Northwind sample database.
strSQL = "SELECT FirstName, LastName, Title, Extension " _
   & "FROM Employees ORDER BY LastName"
With rstEmployees
   .Open strSQL, CONN_STRING & DB_PATH, adOpenKeyset, adLockOptimistic

   ' Remove the existing values from the control.
   wksEmployees.UsedRange.Clear

   ' Add the field names as column headers.
   For Each fldCurrent In .Fields
      intIRow = intIRow + 1
      wksEmployees.Cells(1, intIRow).Value = fldCurrent.Name
   Next fldCurrent

   ' Fill the control with data from the database.
   varData = .GetRows(.RecordCount)
   For intIRow = 1 To .RecordCount
      For intICol = 0 To UBound(varData)
         wksEmployees.Cells(intIRow + 1, intICol + 1).Value _
            = varData(intICol, intIRow - 1)
      Next intICol
   Next intIRow
End With
```

```
' VBScript Code Sample
' The Spreadsheet1 object is the ID of the Spreadsheet control on this page.
' You specify the name of an object in script by using the value of the
' ID attribute of the control you want to work with.

' Create Recordset object and fill it with
' records from the Northwind sample database.
Set rstEmployees = CreateObject("ADODB.Recordset")
strSQL = "SELECT FirstName, LastName, Title, Extension "
strSQL = strSQL & "FROM Employees ORDER BY LastName"
rstEmployees.Open strSQL, cnnConnection, 3, 1

' Remove the existing values from the control.
Spreadsheet1.ActiveSheet.Cells(1,1).Select
Spreadsheet1.ActiveSheet.UsedRange.Clear

' Add the field names as column headers.
For fldCurrent = 0 to rstEmployees.Fields.Count - 1
   intIRow = intIRow + 1
   Spreadsheet1.ActiveSheet.Cells(1, intIRow).Value = _
      rstEmployees.Fields(fldCurrent).Name
Next

' Fill the control with data from the database.
varData = rstEmployees.GetRows(rstEmployees.RecordCount)
For intIRow = 1 To rstEmployees.RecordCount
   For intICol = 0 To UBound(varData)
      Spreadsheet1.ActiveSheet.Cells(intIRow + 1, intICol + 1).Value = _
         varData(intICol, intIRow - 1)
   Next
Next
```

As you can see from the preceding example, you use script to work with individual cells in the **Spreadsheet** control in exactly the same way that you work with cells by using VBA code in Microsoft Excel.

For complete documentation of the **Spreadsheet** control's object model, see the Msowcvba.chm Help file, which is located in the C:\Program Files\Microsoft Office \Office\1033 subfolder.

Note The path to the Msowcvba.chm Help file reflects the language ID folder (1033) for U.S. English language support in Office. The language ID folder below C:\Program Files \Microsoft Office\Office differs for each language.

Understanding the Chart Control

The **Chart** control is an ActiveX control that lets you create a two-dimensional graphical representation of data displayed in a Web page in Internet Explorer 4.01 or later. You get the most complete functionality with this control, and all of the Office Web Component controls, by using Internet Explorer 5 or later.

The **Chart** control can be bound to a **Spreadsheet** control, a **Data Source** control, a **PivotTable List** control, an ADO recordset, or any ActiveX control that supports data binding. You can bind the chart to a local data source (data stored in the HTML code in the page itself) or to a remote data source (data stored in a Microsoft Access or SQL Server database, for example). As data changes in the data source, the **Chart** control automatically updates, scales, and sizes itself appropriately.

You can insert a **Chart** control in a Web page in several ways:

- In Excel, you can add a **Chart** control to a Web page by using the Chart Wizard to create a chart and then using the **Publish as Web Page** dialog box to create a Web page that contains the chart.
- In Access, you can add a chart to a data access page by clicking the **Office Chart** tool in the toolbox and then clicking the place on the page where you want the chart to appear. This launches the Microsoft Office Chart Wizard, which steps you through the process of connecting the chart to a data source.
- In FrontPage, you can add a **Chart** control to a page by pointing to **Component** on the **Insert** menu, and then clicking **Office Chart**. This inserts an empty **Chart** control on the page, but unlike in Access, the Microsoft Office Chart Wizard is not launched. To bind the control to data, you use VBScript code in the Web page. For an example, see DataSourceControl.htm in the Samples\CH12 subfolder on the companion CD-ROM.
- You can also insert a **Chart** control directly in a web page by adding an <OBJECT> tag for the control to the page and specifying the control's CLSID as the setting for the CLASSID attribute. You can then use VBA or VBScript code to work with the chart programmatically.

The CLSID for the **Chart** control and all the objects and related methods and properties for the control are documented in the Msowcvba.chm Help file, which is located in the C:\Program Files\Microsoft Office\Office\1033 subfolder.

Note The path to the Msowcvba.chm Help file reflects the language ID folder (1033) for U.S. English language support in Office. The language ID folder below C:\Program Files \Microsoft Office\Office differs for each language.

Supplying Data to a Chart Control

You can supply data to the **Chart** control by linking, or *binding*, the chart to a data source (bound data), or by programmatically providing data directly to the chart (literal data). Both methods are discussed in this section.

Creating a Data-Bound Chart Control

When you create a **Chart** control in Microsoft Excel or Microsoft Access, the Microsoft Office Chart Wizard is used to help you link the chart to its source of data.

Using Microsoft Excel to Create a Chart Control

The easiest way to create a data-bound **Chart** control is to create the chart by using Excel and then the **Publish as Web Page** dialog box to specify that the Web page should have interactivity with chart functionality. For more information about using the **Publish as Web Page** dialog box, see "Using Microsoft Excel to Create a Spreadsheet Control" earlier in this chapter. When you use this technique to create a **Chart** control, both the chart and the data it is based on are published to the Web page. The data for the chart is saved in a **Spreadsheet** control.

Once you have created a **Chart** control by using the **Publish as Web Page** dialog box, you can further customize the page in Access by using the data access page designer. For example, you could open the page by using the **Edit Web page that already exists** object in the **Pages** object list in the Database window. You could then hide the **Spreadsheet** control and add text box controls tied to the **Spreadsheet** control that would allow a user to change the data supplied to the chart and see those changes immediately displayed in the **Chart** control.

For an example of a chart published from Excel and modified in Access, see the SimpleChartExample.htm file in the Samples\CH12 subfolder on the companion CD-ROM.

Using Microsoft Access to Create a Chart Control

You can create a **Chart** control on a data access page in Access by clicking the **Office Chart** tool in the toolbox and then clicking the place on the page where you want the control to appear. Once you have placed the control on the page, the Microsoft Office Chart Wizard walks you through the steps necessary to bind the chart to a table or query in the database or to a **PivotTable List** control on the same data access page. Unlike the **Chart** control that is created by using the **Publish as Web Page** dialog box in Excel, the **Chart** control created in Access does not place a **Spreadsheet** control on the page. Instead, the chart is linked directly to a data source in the database, and the chart displays the most current data from the underlying data source. When the data access page is viewed in Internet Explorer, the chart always displays the most recent data from the database. However, if the data in the database changes while the page is being viewed in Internet Explorer, the change is not immediately reflected in the **Chart** control on the Web page, unless the user viewing the data in Internet Explorer refreshes the page.

Programmatically Providing Data to a Chart Control

The **Chart** control exposes a wide variety of objects you can use to specify how the chart will display data when it is viewed in Internet Explorer. Manipulating these objects programmatically allows you to customize the behavior of the control.

If you want to write code to manipulate the **Chart** control when it is viewed in Internet Explorer, you must do so by using VBScript or JScript code. If you are going to display the page as a data access page within Access, you can write VBA code to manipulate the **Chart** control's objects. If you are in the process of learning to work with script in a Web page, you may find it easier to write VBA code in Access and then revise that code to run as VBScript code in the page when the page is displayed in Internet Explorer.

The Developer Solutions (Solutions9.mdb) sample database in the Samples\CH05 subfolder on the companion CD-ROM contains a number of data access pages that you can examine to see how these pages are constructed and how they work when viewed in Internet Explorer. In addition, the Developer Solutions database contains the DataAccessPages form (shown in Figure 12.8), which shows how to use VBA code to work with data access pages within Access. The DataAccessPages form and its related code illustrate how to use VBA code to fill a **Chart** control with data from an ADO data source.

Figure 12.8 Form to Launch Data Access Pages from Within Access

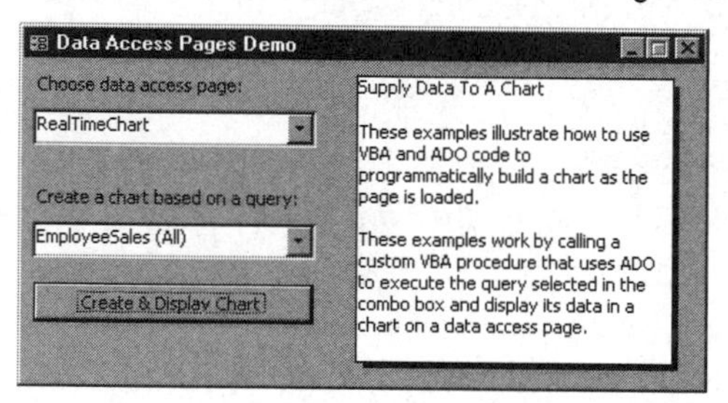

In the DataAccessPages form, the VBA code in the Click event procedure for the Create & Display Chart command button calls the BuildCustomChart procedure, passing it both the name of the query to use as the data source for the chart and the text that appears as the chart heading. The following code sample shows the portion of the BuildCustomChart procedure that executes the query and adds the data to the **Chart** control:

```
' Execute the query supplied in the strQueryName argument
' and format the data to be charted as a tab-delimited string.
rstRecords.Open Source:=strQueryName, _
   ActiveConnection:=CurrentProject.Connection
With rstRecords
   .MoveFirst
   Do While Not .EOF
      varCategories = varCategories & .Fields(0).Value & vbTab
      varValues = varValues & .Fields(1).Value & vbTab
      .MoveNext
   Loop
End With
' Remove trailing tab character.
varCategories = Left$(varCategories, Len(varCategories) - 1)
varValues = Left$(varValues, Len(varValues) - 1)
```

```
' Fill the chart with data.
With dapPage.Document.ChartSpace1
   .Clear
   .Charts.Add
   .Charts(0).SeriesCollection.Add
   .Charts(0).SeriesCollection(0).Caption = strCaption
   .Charts(0).SeriesCollection(0).SetData .Constants.chDimCategories, _
      .Constants.chDataLiteral, varCategories
   .Charts(0).SeriesCollection(0).SetData .Constants.chDimValues, _
      .Constants.chDataLiteral, varValues
   ' Create a bar chart.
   .Charts(0).Type = .Constants.chChartTypeBarClustered
   ' Format the bottom chart axis values as currency.
   .Charts(0).Axes(.Constants.chAxisPositionBottom).NumberFormat = "$#,##0"
End With
```

For more information about programmatically filling a **Chart** control with data, see the next section, "Working with the Chart Component's Object Model."

Working with the Chart Component's Object Model

When you are working with the **Chart** control, the top-level object in the object model is the **ChartSpace** object, which represents the chart itself. The control has a collection of **Chart** objects contained in the **Charts** collection. You add a **Chart** object to a **Chart** control by using the **Add** method of the **Charts** collection. You specify the type of chart (bar, line, pie, and so on) by using the **Chart** object's **Type** property.

You fill a chart with data designated in one or more series; each series consists of categories and values. For example, to fill a chart with data about employee sales, you could add a series that charts employee names as the categories and sales amounts as the values. Each series in the chart is represented by a **SeriesCollection** object. You specify the data to be used for the desired categories and values by using the **SeriesCollection** object's **SetData** method. You can then specify various properties of the **SeriesCollection** object by using its properties. For a complete example that charts employee sales, see the BuildChart procedure in the EmployeeSalesSummary.htm file in the Samples\CH12 subfolder on the companion CD-ROM.

The EmployeeSalesSummary.htm sample file illustrates how you can use VBScript code to create and manipulate a **Chart** control on a Web page. Figure 12.9 shows this sample file displayed in Internet Explorer.

Figure 12.9 Using a Chart Control on a Web Page

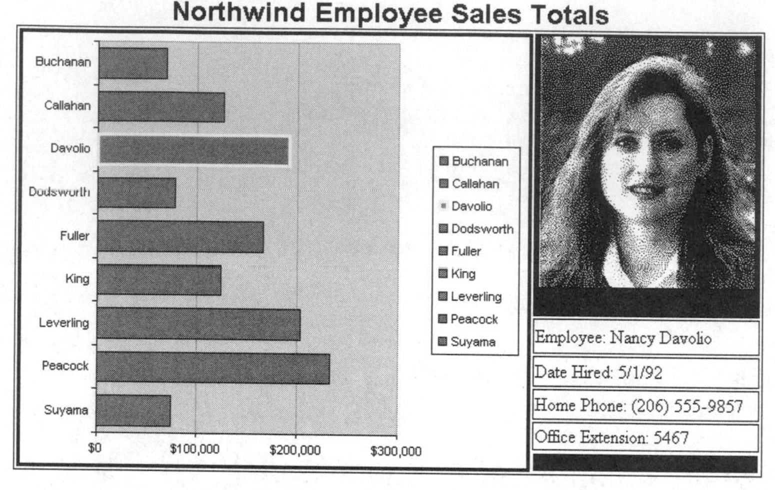

The VBScript code in this .htm file builds the **Chart** control in a very similar manner to that shown in the BuildCustomChart procedure in "Programmatically Providing Data to a Chart Control" earlier in this chapter. The interesting part of the EmployeeSalesSummary sample is that it illustrates how to manipulate the chart and related data displayed on the page depending on how the user interacts with the chart. In this example, as the user moves the mouse pointer over different bars on the chart, the employee's picture and related information is displayed in the area to the right of the chart.

What makes this example work is VBScript code in the **Chart** control's MouseMove event procedure. The code in the event procedure detects the bar on the chart that the mouse pointer is over, retrieves the corresponding employee's record from the database, and then displays the employee's information on the page. As shown in the following procedure, the **RangeFromPoint** method of the **ChartSpace** object is used to determine which bar on the chart is currently under the mouse pointer:

```
Sub ChartSpace1_MouseMove(lngMousePosition)
   Dim objSelection

   On Error Resume Next

   Set objSelection = _
      ChartSpace1.RangeFromPoint(lngMousePosition.x, lngMousePosition.y)

   ' If the mouse pointer is not over one of the bars in the
   ' chart, exit the procedure.
   If TypeName(objSelection) <> "WCPoint" Then Exit Sub

   ' Display data for selected employee in display area to the
   ' right of the chart.
   SetEmployeeInfo objSelection.Index
```

```
   ' Format the border of the previous bar on the chart.
   If Not(gLastSelection Is Nothing) Then
      gLastSelection.Border.Weight = 1
      gLastSelection.Border.Color = "Black"
   End If

   ' Highlight the current bar on the chart and save the object
   ' just highlighted so it can be identified when the selection
   ' changes again.
   objSelection.Border.Weight = 3
   objSelection.Border.Color = "Yellow"
   Set gLastSelection = objSelection

   On Error GoTo 0

   Set objSelection = Nothing
End Sub
```

The VBScript code in the MouseMove event procedure calls the SetEmployeeInfo procedure. The SetEmployeeInfo procedure retrieves the employee record from the Northwind sample database (Northwind.mdb) and displays that information on the Web page.

```
Sub SetEmployeeInfo(intEmployee)
   Dim rstSingleRecord
   Dim strSQL

   If Len(intEmployee) > 0 Then
      ' If this is the same employee that is already highlighted,
      ' then leave now. There is no need to replace the current
      ' information.
      If strCurrentName = gastrNames(intEmployee) Then Exit Sub

      strCurrentName = gastrNames(intEmployee)

      ' Create a new ADO Recordset object containing a single record
      ' for the employee named in the strCurrentName variable.
      Set rstSingleRecord =  CreateObject("ADODB.Recordset")
      strSQL = "SELECT * FROM Employees WHERE LastName = '" & strCurrentName & "'"
      rstSingleRecord.Open strSQL, gcnnConnection, 3, 1

      ' Fill the remaining cells in the table with additional information
      ' about the selected employee.
      strEmployeeName.innerText = "Employee: " _
         & rstSingleRecord("FirstName") & " " & rstSingleRecord("LastName")
      strHireDate.innerText = "Date Hired: " & rstSingleRecord("HireDate")
      strPhoneNumber.innerText = "Home Phone: " & rstSingleRecord("HomePhone")
      strExtension.innerText = "Office Extension: " & rstSingleRecord("Extension")
      imgEmployeePicture.src = strPhotoPath & Trim(strCurrentName) & ".gif"
   End If

   Set rstSingleRecord = Nothing
End Sub
```

For complete documentation of the **Chart** control's object model, see the Msowcvba.chm Help file, which is located in the C:\Program Files\Microsoft Office \Office\1033 subfolder.

Note The path to the Msowcvba.chm Help file reflects the language ID folder (1033) for U.S. English language support in Office. The language ID folder below C:\Program Files \Microsoft Office\Office differs for each language.

Understanding the PivotTable List Control

The **PivotTable List** control lets users analyze data displayed on a Web page in Internet Explorer 5. This control combines the list features of Excel (sort, AutoFilter, and outline) with the auto-summarizing features of PivotTable reports into a single ActiveX control that runs in Internet Explorer. Therefore, a PivotTable list on a Web page is roughly equivalent to a PivotTable report in an Excel worksheet.

With the **PivotTable List** control, users can easily transform their view of data by using the mouse or simple keyboard commands. Although the author of the data determines the initial view of the data when the page is first viewed in Internet Explorer, users are free to use the dynamic run-time features of the **PivotTable List** control to manipulate and analyze the data in any way they choose. Once users have customized the data in a **PivotTable List** control, they can save that view of the data and share it with others.

A PivotTable list is the best way for Office users to get dynamic reporting and data analysis by using Internet Explorer. Using the **PivotTable List** control to work with data on a Web page allows users to merge the ability to create and report on data in an Access database with the ability to analyze data in Excel.

Creating a PivotTable List Control

You can insert a **PivotTable List** control in a Web page in several ways:

- In Excel, you add a **PivotTable List** control to a Web page by creating a list or PivotTable report in Excel and then using the **Publish as Web Page** dialog box to save the data in a **PivotTable List** control on a Web page.

  For more information about using the **Publish as Web Page** dialog box, see "Using Microsoft Excel to Create a Spreadsheet Control" earlier in this chapter. For information about creating and working with PivotTable reports in Excel, see Chapter 15, "Retrieving and Analyzing Data."
- In Access, you can add a **PivotTable List** control to a data access page by dragging a table or query from the field list to the page. This creates a **PivotTable List** control populated with data from the table or query in the open database.
- In FrontPage, you can add an unbound **PivotTable List** control to a page by pointing to **Component** on the **Insert** menu, and then clicking **Office PivotTable**. To bind the control to data, you use VBScript code in the Web page.

- In a Web page, you can insert a **PivotTable List** control by adding an <OBJECT> tag for the control to the page and specifying the control's CLSID as the setting for the CLASSID attribute. You can then use VBA or VBScript code to fill the control programmatically when the page loads.

The CLSID for the **PivotTable List** control and all the objects and related methods and properties for the control are documented in the Msowcvba.chm Help file, which is located in the C:\Program Files\Microsoft Office\Office\1033 subfolder.

Note The path to the Msowcvba.chm Help file reflects the language ID folder (1033) for U.S. English language support in Office. The language ID folder below C:\Program Files \Microsoft Office\Office differs for each language.

Working with the PivotTable Component's Object Model

The **PivotTable List** control is represented in the object model by the **PivotTable** object. You use the **DataSource** property to specify the source of the data to be displayed in the control. Typically this property setting will consist of an ADO data source or another one of the Office Web Component controls.

The **PivotTable** object has two child objects: the **PivotData** object and the **PivotView** object. The **PivotData** object represents the data in a **PivotTable List** control, and the **PivotView** object represents a specific view of the data in the **PivotTable List** control. In the following example, the **ActiveView** property is used to return the **PivotView** object so that various properties of the object can be specified.

The following code sample illustrates how to create a simple list by using the **PivotTable List** control. The list is filled with customer data from an ADO data source, in this case, the Northwind sample database.

```
Sub InitializeList(pt)
   strProvider = "Microsoft.Jet.OLEDB.4.0"
   strDBPath = "c:\program files\microsoft office\office\samples\Northwind.mdb"

   strSQL = "SELECT * FROM Customers"
   strTitle = "Customers of the Northwind Company"

   Set cnnConnection = CreateObject("ADODB.Connection")
   cnnConnection.Provider = strProvider
   cnnConnection.Open strDBPath

   ' Set the connection string.
   pt.ConnectionString = cnnConnection.ConnectionString
   pt.CommandText = strSQL

   set view = pt.ActiveView

   ' Automatically add all result columns to the detail area.
   view.AutoLayout
```

```
    ' Set the title.
    view.Titlebar.Caption = strTitle

    ' Hide the drop areas.
    view.RowAxis.Label.Visible = False
    view.ColumnAxis.Label.Visible = False

    ' Set detail maximum width so that it doesn't have detail scroll bars.
    view.DetailMaxHeight = 32000
    view.DetailMaxWidth = 32000

    ' Turn off AutoFit.
    pt.AutoFit = False
    pt.Width = "100%"
    pt.Height = "65%"

    ' Disallow grouping.
    pt.AllowGrouping = False
End Sub
```

The InitializeList procedure is available in the PivotListSimpleListExample.htm file in the Samples\CH12 subfolder on the companion CD-ROM. This same view of the Northwind customer data could have easily been created in a data access page by simply dragging the Customers table from the field list to the page in Design view.

For complete documentation of the **PivotTable List** control's object model, see the Msowcvba.chm Help file, which is located in the C:\Program Files\Microsoft Office \Office\1033 subfolder.

Note The path to the Msowcvba.chm Help file reflects the language ID folder (1033) for U.S. English language support in Office. The language ID folder below C:\Program Files \Microsoft Office\Office differs for each language.

Understanding the Data Source Control

The **Data Source** control is best understood as the reporting engine behind data access pages, **PivotTable List** controls, and data-bound **Chart** controls. The **Data Source** control has no visual representation. It is designed to manage the connection to the underlying data source and deliver records to be displayed by other controls on a Web page.

The **Data Source** control relies on ADO for connections to relational data sources such as Microsoft Access, Microsoft SQL Server, or Oracle databases. Although the **Data Source** control can provide data to the **PivotTable List** control, the **Data Source** control cannot be bound to multidimensional data sources; transformations of relational data to multidimensional data are managed by the PivotTable Service.

Note If you are creating a PivotTable list from a relational data source, the PivotTable Service is used to create a multidimensional data cube from the relational data bound to the **Data Source** control. This data cube is then used by the **PivotTable List** control. For multidimensional data sources, the **PivotTable List** control relies upon an OLE DB for online analytical processing (OLAP) provider. The PivotTable Service is the OLE DB for OLAP provider for Microsoft SQL Server OLAP Services.

You can use the **Data Source** control to do the following:

- Associate a **DataSourceControl** object with a database connection.
- Add a record (row) source (table, view, stored procedure, or SQL statement) to a **Data Source** control.
- Provide an ADO recordset to data-consuming objects on a Web page. These objects include the Internet Explorer built-in controls that can be data bound, such as the TEXT or SELECT control, and all of the other Office Web Component controls.
- Build SQL commands to request data from relational data sources.
- Construct hierarchical (shaped) **Recordset** objects from one or more data providers by using the services of the Microsoft Data Shaping Service for OLE DB service provider.
- Persist data in an Office Web Component to a file or load data from a file to an Office Web Component.

Note Although you can work directly with the **Data Source** control, in many cases you will not need to. For example, when you create an Access data access page and add fields to the page by dragging them from the field list, Access automatically adds a properly configured **Data Source** control to the page.

Working with the Data Source Control's Object Model

You specify the source for the data in the **Data Source** control by setting the control's **ConnectString** property. You then add one or more recordset definitions by using the **AddNew** method of the **RecordsetDefs** collection. The following example illustrates how to initialize the **Data Source** control and then use it to provide data to a **Chart** control:

```
Sub CreateChart()
   Dim cnnConnection
   Dim strSQL

   Set cnnConnection = CreateObject("ADODB.Connection")
   cnnConnection.Provider = "Microsoft.Jet.OLEDB.4.0"
   cnnConnection.Open "c:\opg\samples\ch05\solutions9.mdb"
   DataSourceControl1.ConnectionString = cnnConnection.ConnectionString
```

```
    strSQL = "SELECT DISTINCTROW Employees.LastName, "
    strSQL = strSQL & "Sum(OrderDetailsExtended.ExtendedPrice) AS [Order Amount] "
    strSQL = strSQL & "FROM Employees "
    strSQL = strSQL & "INNER JOIN (Products "
    strSQL = strSQL & "INNER JOIN (Orders "
    strSQL = strSQL & "INNER JOIN OrderDetailsExtended "
    strSQL = strSQL & "ON Orders.OrderID = OrderDetailsExtended.OrderID) "
    strSQL = strSQL & "ON Products.ProductID = OrderDetailsExtended.ProductID) "
    strSQL = strSQL & "ON Employees.EmployeeID = Orders.EmployeeID "
    strSQL = strSQL & "GROUP BY Employees.LastName;"

    DataSourceControl1.RecordsetDefs.AddNew strSQL, dscCommandText, "EmployeeSales"

    ChartSpace1.DataSource = DataSourceControl1
    ChartSpace1.DataMember = "EmployeeSales"
    ChartSpace1.Charts.Add
    ChartSpace1.Charts(0).Type = ChartSpace1.Constants.chChartTypeBarClustered
    ChartSpace1.Charts(0).SetData ChartSpace1.Constants.chDimCategories, 0, "LastName"
    ChartSpace1.Charts(0).SetData ChartSpace1.Constants.chDimValues, 0, "Order Amount"
End Sub
```

You can add multiple recordsets to the control and then use VBScript code to specify which recordset to display. The DataSourceControl.htm file in the Samples\CH12 subfolder on the companion CD-ROM contains VBScript code that illustrates how to programmatically work with many of the properties and methods of the **Data Source** control.

For complete documentation of the **Data Source** control's object model, see the Msowcvba.chm Help file, which is located in the C:\Program Files\Microsoft Office \Office\1033 subfolder.

Note The path to the Msowcvba.chm Help file reflects the language ID folder (1033) for U.S. English language support in Office. The language ID folder below C:\Program Files \Microsoft Office\Office differs for each language.

Working with Office Server Extensions

When you install Microsoft Office 2000, the **Discuss** command is added to the **Explorer Bar** submenu of the **View** menu in Internet Explorer 5. This feature lets you add *threaded discussions* to a Web page that appear when the page is viewed in Internet Explorer. Threaded discussions are comments added to the page or to an element on the page that can be seen and responded to by others who share the same discussion server.

To enable discussions, you point to **Explorer Bar** on the **View** menu, and then click **Discuss**. In addition, a **Web Discussions** command is added to the **Online Collaboration** submenu of the **Tools** menu in Word, Excel, and PowerPoint. Clicking the **Discuss** command in Internet Explorer, or the **Web Discussions** command any of the listed Office applications, displays the **Discussions** toolbar at the bottom of the application window. The version of the **Discussions** toolbar that is displayed in Internet Explorer 5 is shown in Figure 12.10.

Figure 12.10 The Discussions Toolbar as It Is Displayed in Internet Explorer 5

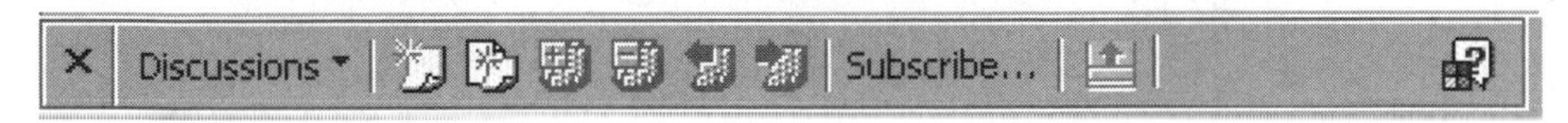

You can use the commands on this toolbar to add a discussion server, specify what information will be displayed for a discussion, or subscribe to a particular Web page, Office document on a Web server, or folder on a Web server. Subscribing to an item lets you specify when and how you will be notified of changes to the item.

You use the Microsoft Office Server Extensions 1.0 object library to programmatically work with discussion servers or discussions on a page. The Office Server Extensions object library contains objects, methods, and properties you can use to create and work with discussions on a page. The following sections provide the information you need to work with discussions by using VBA code.

The Office Server Extensions Object Model

You work with the objects in the Office Server Extensions object model by first setting a reference to the Microsoft Office Server Extensions 1.0 object library (Owsdsc.dll). The object model is very simple and straightforward and the methods and properties of the objects map directly to the objects and settings available from the **Discussions** toolbar.

For a graphical representation of the Office Server Extensions object model, see the "Object Model Diagrams" appendix. For complete documentation of the Office Server Extensions object model, see the Owsvba.chm Help file, which is located in the C:\Program Files\Microsoft Office\Office\1033 subfolder.

Note The path to the Owsvba.chm Help file reflects the language ID folder (1033) for U.S. English language support in Office. The language ID folder below C:\Program Files \Microsoft Office\Office differs for each language.

Understanding the Global Object

Because the **Global** object is the top-level object in the Office Server Extensions object model, it is not necessary to explicitly reference the **Global** object when you are using its methods or properties. The **Global** object exposes two properties and two methods. The **DiscussionServers** property returns the **DiscussionServers** collection, and the **CurrentUserName** property contains the user name of the person currently logged on to the machine. The **OpenDiscussions** method returns the **Discussions** collection for the document specified by its ***URL*** argument, and the **AddOfficeServerSubscription** method is used to add a subscription to a document. This method uses several arguments that map directly to the settings in the **Document Subscription** dialog box that appears when you click the **Subscribe** button on the **Discussions** toolbar.

Understanding Discussion Servers

The **DiscussionServers** collection contains all the **DiscussionServer** objects that represent each discussion server registered on your machine. You can also view this collection in the **Select a discussion server** box in the **Discussion Options** dialog box (shown in Figure 12.11). A **DiscussionServer** object is used to store discussion items for any document. Typically, a workgroup would agree to use a specific discussion server so that all members of the group will be able to see each other's comments.

Figure 12.11 The Discussion Options Dialog Box

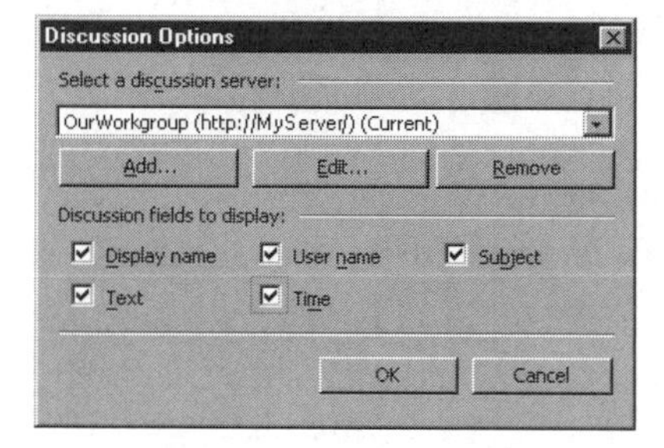

You use the **DiscussionServers** collection's **Add** method to add a new **DiscussionServer** object to the list of discussion servers registered on your machine. The **Add** method requires values for both the ***ServerName*** and the ***FriendlyName*** arguments. These arguments map directly to the settings you provide in the **Add or Edit Discussion Servers** dialog box, which you open by clicking the **Add** or **Edit** button in the **Discussion Options** dialog box. The default discussion server is represented by the `DiscussionServers(1)` **DiscussionServer** object. You can make any **DiscussionServer** object the default by using the object's **SetAsDefault** method, which re-sorts the collection of **DiscussionServer** objects. You remove a **DiscussionServer** object by using the object's **Delete** method.

The following code shows how to determine the number of discussion servers registered on the current machine:

```
Sub DisplayDiscussionServerInfo()
   Dim strCountMessage     As String
   Dim strServerInfo       As String
   Dim dscCurrentServer    As DiscussionServer

   strCountMessage = "There are " & OSE.DiscussionServers.Count _
      & " discussion servers registered on this machine." & vbCrLf
   If OSE.DiscussionServers.Count > 0 Then
      For Each dscCurrentServer In OSE.DiscussionServers
         With dscCurrentServer
            strServerInfo = strServerInfo & "Name = " & .FriendlyName _
               & ", Address = " & .ServerAddress & "." & vbCrLf
         End With
      Next dscCurrentServer
   Else
      strServerInfo = ""
   End If
   MsgBox strCountMessage & strServerInfo
End Sub
```

Understanding Discussions

The **Discussions** collection contains all the **Discussion** objects associated with each level of discussion on a page. In turn, each **Discussion** object may have a **Discussions** collection that contains the **Discussion** objects related to that level of discussion.

A **Discussion** object represents an entry in a discussion. Each **Discussion** object has properties and methods you can use to specify the information that appears in the discussion and how and when changes are made to a discussion. Several of these properties map directly to settings you can specify in the **Discussion fields to display** section of the **Discussion Options** dialog box shown in Figure 12.11 earlier in this chapter.

You add a **Discussion** object to a **Discussions** collection by using the **Discussions** collection's **Add** method. You remove a **Discussion** object from a **Discussions** collection by using the **Discussion** object's **Delete** method.

The following code illustrates one technique you can use to get some basic information about the number of top-level discussions on a page:

```
Sub DisplayDiscussionInfo(strURL As String)
   Dim colDiscussions  As Discussions
   Dim dscCurrent      As Discussion
   Dim strMessage      As String

   Set colDiscussions = OSE.OpenDiscussions(strURL)
   If colDiscussions.Count = 0 Then
      strMessage = "The page '" & strURL _
         & "' has no discussions."
   Else
```

```
      strMessage = "The page '" & strURL _
         & "' has " & colDiscussions.Count _
         & " discussions." & vbCrLf & vbCrLf
      For Each dscCurrent In colDiscussions
         With dscCurrent
            strMessage = strMessage _
               & "The top-level discussion number " _
               & .Index & " " _
               & IIf(.Discussions.Count > 0, "has one or more", _
               "does not have") & " replies." & vbCrLf
         End With
      Next dscCurrent
   End If
   MsgBox strMessage
End Sub
```

Each **Discussion** object in the **Discussions** collection represents a message in a discussion thread. If a page has a single message, the **Discussions** collection will contain a single **Discussion** object representing that message. If there are replies to a message, the **Discussion** object's **Discussions** property will return the collection of all replies to that message. This pattern is repeated for every **Discussion** object in a thread that has replies. Figure 12.12 illustrates the relationship between a **Discussions** collection and the **Discussion** objects it contains.

Figure 12.12 Relationship Between Discussions Collections and Discussion Objects

```
⊟ This is the first message in a thread
   ⊟ This is a reply to the first message
      This is a reply to a reply
      This is another reply to a reply
   ⊟ This is another reply to the first message in a thread
      This is a reply to a reply
```

The **Discussions** collection for this page contains one **Discussion** object. That **Discussion** object's **Discussions** property would return a **Discussions** collection containing two **Discussion** objects, and so on. The following code sample illustrates how you would refer to the message titled "This is another reply to a reply." In this example, the `colDiscussions` variable represents the **Discussions** collection returned by the **OpenDiscussions** method:

```
With colDiscussions(1).Discussions(1).Discussions(2)
   MsgBox .Subject & " added to page at: " & .Timestamp
End With
```

Understanding Subscriptions

You use subscriptions to specify the time and type of notification to send when changes occur to the discussions in a document or to any document within a specified folder. For example, the following code creates a subscription to a Web page. The subscription specifies that an e-mail message should be immediately sent to user@host.domain.com when a discussion item is inserted or deleted on the specified Web page:

```
strURL = "http://www.microsoft.com/officedev/topten.htm"
strMailTo = "user@host.domain.com"
AddOfficeServerSubscription FileURL:=strURL, _
   NotifyWhen:=oseNotifyWhenDiscussionAnything, _
   MailTo:=strMailTo, MailTime:=oseMailImmediately
```

In this instance, an e-mail message is generated whenever a discussion item is added to or deleted from the Topten.htm page. This VBA code has the same effect as opening the **Document Subscription** dialog box and entering the values shown in Figure 12.13.

Figure 12.13 The Document Subscription Dialog Box

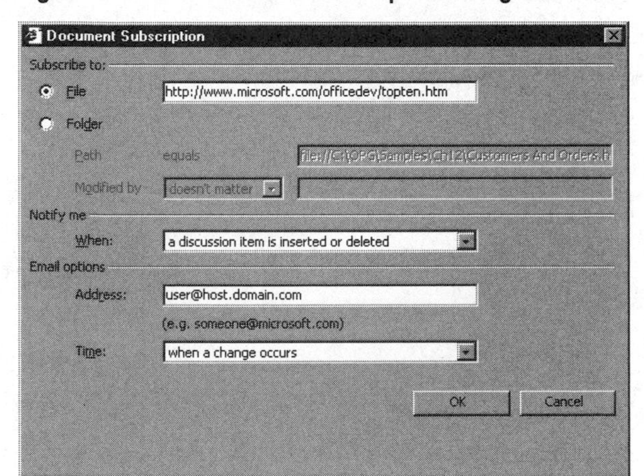

Although you can add a subscription programmatically, there is no way to work with existing subscriptions by using VBA code.

Where to Go from Here

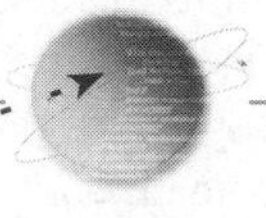

For additional information about the subjects discussed in this chapter, see the following resources.

Using Scriptlets

Chapter 3, "Writing Solid Code"

Chapter 9, "Custom Classes and Objects"

Scriptlet Technology Web site (http://msdn.microsoft.com/developer/sdk/inetsdk/help/scriptlets/scrlt.htm)

Isaacs, Scott. *Inside Dynamic HTML.* Redmond, WA: Microsoft Press, 1997.

Scriptlet Wizard on Microsoft Scripting Technologies Web site (http://msdn.microsoft.com/scripting/)

Working with Script and HTML Code in Office Applications

Chapter 6, "Working with Shared Office Components"

DHTML

Isaacs, Scott. *Inside Dynamic HTML.* Redmond, WA: Microsoft Press, 1997.

HTML Reference Help (C:\Program Files\Microsoft Visual Studio \Common\IDE\IDE98\MSE\1033\Htmlref.chm)

Chapter 9, "Custom Classes and Objects"

Microsoft Site Builder Workshop Web site (http://www.microsoft.com/workshop/default.asp)

Simpson, Alan. *Official Microsoft Internet Explorer 4 Site Builder Toolkit.* Redmond, WA: Microsoft Press, 1998.

XML

Microsoft Site Builder Workshop Web site (http://www.microsoft.com/workshop/default.asp)

Creating and Securing Data Access Pages

Chapter 5, "Working with Office Applications"

Chapter 18, "Securing Access Databases"

Creating PivotTable Reports

Chapter 15, "Retrieving and Analyzing Data"

Working with VBScript

Microsoft Scripting Technologies Web site (http://msdn.microsoft.com/scripting/)

Visual Basic Scripting Help (C:\Program Files\Microsoft Visual Studio \Common\IDE\IDE98\MSE\1033\Vbscrip5.chm)

Working with JScript

Microsoft Scripting Technologies Web site (http://msdn.microsoft.com/scripting/)

JScript Help (C:\Program Files\Microsoft Visual Studio\Common\IDE \IDE98\MSE\1033\Jscript5.chm)

Code Samples

The code samples shown in this chapter, along with additional examples demonstrating similar techniques, can be copied from the files in the Samples\CH05 and Samples\CH12 subfolders on the companion CD-ROM.

CHAPTER 13

Adding Help to Your Custom Solution

Adding online Help to your Microsoft Office solution can reduce the amount of time required to train and support users of your solutions. By using the tools provided with Microsoft HTML Help Workshop or your favorite HTML editor, you can author topics for a Help system by using the same tools and technologies used to create Web pages—including hyperlinks, ActiveX controls, scripting, and Dynamic HTML (DHTML) support. You can then compile your topics into a single file and display them by using the same viewer that is used to display Help in Microsoft Office 2000.

By using standard properties and methods, you can integrate Help topics and context-sensitive Help into your solution's custom dialog boxes, error messages, and forms. If you want even more control over how HTML Help is displayed and integrated into your solution, you can work directly with HtmlHelp application programming interface (API) calls from your Visual Basic for Applications (VBA) code.

If you purchased Microsoft Office 2000 Developer or the *Microsoft Office 2000 Resource Kit* (Microsoft Press, 1999), you can use the Answer Wizard Software Development Kit (SDK) to integrate your own Help topics with those returned to users in Office 2000 by the Microsoft Office Assistant.

You can also use the navigation functionality of the HTML Help ActiveX control, such as a hierarchical table of contents or an index, on Web pages independently of using the HTML Help Viewer.

Contents

What Is Microsoft HTML Help?

Microsoft HTML Help is Microsoft's next-generation online Help authoring system. It is designed for use by authors or developers who create Help for software programs, multimedia titles, intranets, extranets, or the Internet. Topics in an HTML Help online Help system are authored as standard HTML files, which you can create with the editor in HTML Help Workshop or with any other HTML authoring tool, such as Microsoft Word or Microsoft FrontPage.

The HTML Help Viewer uses the layout engine components of Microsoft Internet Explorer (Shdocvw.dll hosting Mshtml.dll) to display Help topics. As a result, Microsoft HTML Help topics can use the same technologies supported by Internet Explorer, such as HTML (including DHTML when the layout engine components for Internet Explorer version 4.0 or later are installed), ActiveX controls and documents, Java applets, scripting, HTML image formats (.jpeg, .gif, .png), and even video and audio.

Redistributing HTML Help Components

To display HTML Help, a user's computer must have both HTML Help components and Microsoft Internet Explorer layout engine components installed. If you are creating an Access run-time application and installing it on a computer that does not have Office 2000 installed, the components necessary to display HTML Help may not available. All the components necessary to display HTML Help are installed with any of the following:

- Microsoft Office 2000
- Microsoft Internet Explorer version 4.0 or later
- Microsoft Windows 98

If none of these are available on a user's computer, you will need to redistribute some or all of the components necessary to display HTML Help.

If users have Internet Explorer version 3.02 installed, and the HTML Help system you are distributing doesn't require DHTML or other functionality supported only by Internet Explorer 4.0 or later, you can use the HTML Help Update component (Hhupd.exe) to redistribute HTML Help. In this case, if you use Hhupd.exe to install HTML Help, HTML Help will use the layout engine components of Internet Explorer 3.02. The HTML Help Update component is available from the HTML Help Web site at http://www.microsoft.com/workshop/author/htmlhelp/default.asp.

Redistributing HTML Help Components (*continued*)

If the Help system you are distributing requires functionality available only from the layout engine components of Internet Explorer 4.0 or later, users must install the appropriate version of Internet Explorer in order to install both HTML Help and the necessary layout engine components. If you need to redistribute and install Internet Explorer, you can do so by using the Microsoft Internet Explorer Administration Kit (IEAK). For information about obtaining this kit, see the Internet Explorer Administration Kit Web site at http://ieak.microsoft.com/.

HTML Help Tools and Features

You create an HTML Help online Help system by using the tools provided with HTML Help Workshop. To download and install these tools, go to the HTML Help Web site at http://www.microsoft.com/workshop/author/htmlhelp/default.asp. Third-party tools are also available for authoring and compiling HTML Help files. Information about third-party tools is also available on the HTML Help Web site.

HTML Help consists of the following tools:

- HTML Help Workshop (Hhw.exe), a Help authoring tool with an easy-to-use graphical interface for creating Help project files, HTML topic files, contents files, index files, and everything else you need to put together a Help system or Help Web site.
- The HTML Help ActiveX control (HHCtrl.ocx), for inserting features such as Help navigation and secondary window functionality into an HTML file.
- The HTML Help Java applet (HHCtrl.class and associated .class files), for inserting Help navigation and secondary window functionality into an HTML page when you want to use a Java applet instead of an ActiveX control.
- The Microsoft HTML Help Image Editor (Flash.exe), a tool for creating screenshots; converting, editing, and viewing image files; and browsing thumbnail images.
- The HTML Help Authoring Guide, an online guide for using HTML Help Workshop and designing a Help system, plus a complete HtmlHelp API reference for developers and an HTML tag reference for authors.
- The HTML Help Viewer program (Hh.exe), which displays and runs your Help system. Topics displayed in the HTML Help Viewer can use the HTML Help ActiveX control so that any navigational elements such as a table of contents, index, full-text search, or related topic jumps specified by the author will be part of the Help system.

Along with these tools, HTML Help provides two important features:

- The ability to convert existing Windows Help files to HTML Help files.
- The ability to compress your HTML files while compiling them into a single file. This feature greatly reduces the amount of disk space required for your HTML files and simplifies distribution. A compiled HTML Help file (.chm) plays the same role as a compiled Windows Help file (.hlp).

What Kinds of Help Systems Can You Create?

You can use HTML Help to create two types of Help systems. You can:

- Create a compiled Help file that is viewed by using the HTML Help Viewer. This is typically the way HTML Help is used to provide help for an Office solution. For more information about using HTML Help in Office solutions, see "Adding Help to Your Office Solution" later in this chapter.
- Create Web pages that use the HTML Help ActiveX control or the HTML Help Java applet to implement navigation and secondary window features to display HTML pages and other documents from a Web browser. If you provide the appropriate value for the CODEBASE attribute when you are inserting the HTML Help ActiveX control in a Web page, the control can be installed and downloaded if it isn't already installed when a user opens the Web page. This method can be used to run a locally installed Help system, but it is more typically used to create general-purpose Web sites. For more information about using HTML Help to create a Web site, see "Using HTML Help to Author a Web Site" later in this chapter.

Displaying HTML Help

HTML Help supports many of the same features as Microsoft WinHelp 4.0 and uses a similar development model with a Help project file to combine topic, contents, index, image, and other source files into one compiled HTML Help file. You can also use many of the same HTML Help features available in a compiled HTML Help file by using either the HTML Help ActiveX control or the HTML Help Java applet to display your Help system from a Web browser.

You can use HTML Help to display Help topics for users in a variety of ways:

- By using the free-standing HTML Help Viewer
- By using customized windows called within an Office solution
- From a Web site, by using the HTML Help ActiveX control (for Internet Explorer) or the HTML Help Java applet (for browsers that support Java)

Note HTML Help also allows you to author context-sensitive pop-up Help for user-interface elements. However, Office 2000 applications don't support context-sensitive Help that has been authored by using HTML Help. To create context-sensitive Help for Office solutions, you must use WinHelp 4.0 (.hlp) files. For more information about authoring and implementing context-sensitive Help for Office solutions, see "Displaying Help in Forms and Documents" later in this chapter.

The HTML Help Viewer

The HTML Help Viewer is the default display method for all compiled HTML Help files and is used to display Help topics in Office 2000 applications. The HTML Help Viewer features a three-paned window as shown in Figure 13.1.

Figure 13.1 The HTML Help Viewer

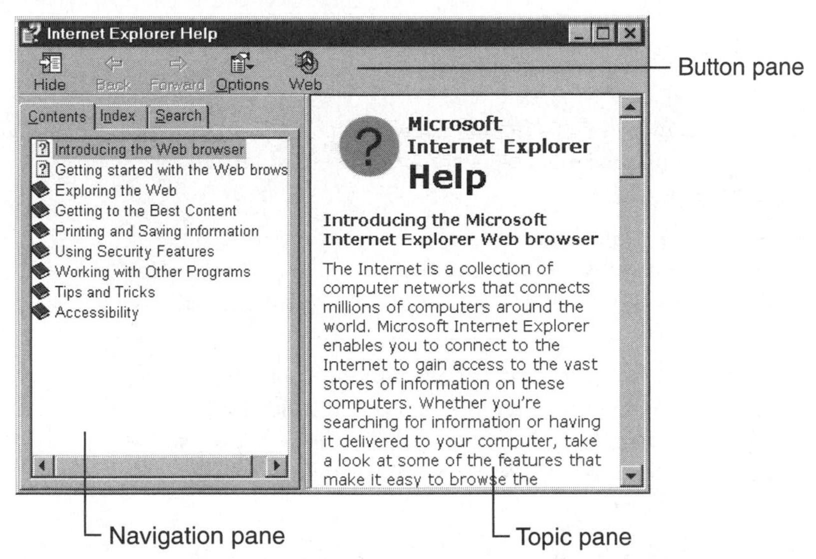

The topic pane of the HTML Help Viewer is an embedded instance of the Internet Explorer layout engine (Shdocvw.dll hosting Mshtml.dll) and can display any content supported by Internet Explorer, including Office document formats (Microsoft Word, Microsoft Excel, and Microsoft PowerPoint). The navigation pane can include a variety of different ways of accessing Help topics, including a table of contents, an index, and a full-text search tab. The button pane contains a toolbar that by default contains the following buttons.

Button	Description
Hide/Show	Allows users to display or hide the navigation pane.
Back	Displays the previous topic.
Print	Prints individual topics or groups of topics from the **Contents** tab.
Options	Displays a menu that provides keyboard accessibility to button commands and other options.

You can use HTML Help Workshop to customize the window definition of the default HTML Help Viewer window to add **Forward**, **Stop**, **Refresh**, **Home**, and **Locate** (to manually synchronize a topic to the contents) buttons to the button pane. You can also define up to two custom buttons to jump to URLs you specify. Figure 13.1 shows an example of a customized button pane.

Custom Help Windows

If you are distributing compiled HTML Help files, you can use HTML Help Workshop to customize the appearance of the default HTML Help Viewer window, or you can create additional custom window definitions that change the window's size, position, background color, and other attributes. You can also embed a Help window directly within the user interface of your solution. These are the types of windows you can create or customize:

- The HTML Help Viewer window, which by default is displayed as the three-paned window described in the previous section. Its appearance can be customized by creating a custom window definition.
- A secondary window is a custom window in which you assign topics to display. You can customize a secondary window to be as full-featured as the HTML Help Viewer or to have fewer features; for example, to display as a single pane without the toolbar.
- An embedded topic window that is nested in an application; for example, as a window displayed on a tab in a dialog box. To implement an embedded window, an application must use calls to the HtmlHelp API. The docked Help window used to display Help in Office 2000 applications is an example of an embedded Help window.

You create window definitions and specify the default window type for your Help system in an HTML Help project file (.hhp). You can also specify custom window types to be used when you are displaying topics from the contents or index, and when you are linking to other topics by using the HTML Help ActiveX control.

If you develop your solution in Excel or PowerPoint, you can display your solution's Help topics in the same docked window used by the Office 2000 Help system. To do this, the default window type in your HTML Help project file must be defined with the same name as one of the window types used by the Office Help system. For more information about how to display custom Help topics in an Office application's Help window, see "Displaying Custom Help Topics in an Office Application's Help Window" later in this chapter.

Working with the HTML Help ActiveX Control

Many of the features available in HTML Help are implemented through the HTML Help ActiveX control (HHCtrl.ocx). The HTML Help ActiveX control is used to provide navigation features (such as a table of contents), to display secondary windows and pop-up definitions, and to provide other features. The HTML Help ActiveX control can be used from topics in a compiled Help system as well as from HTML pages displayed in a Web browser. The functionality provided by the HTML Help ActiveX control will run in the HTML Help Viewer or in any browser that supports ActiveX technology, such as Internet Explorer (version 3.01 or later). Some features provided by the HTML Help ActiveX control are available only when it is used from a compiled HTML Help file (.chm) that is displayed by using the HTML Help Viewer.

The most commonly used features supported by the HTML Help ActiveX control are:

- Table of contents (displayed in a tree control)
- Index
- Secondary windows (available only from a .chm file displayed in the HTML Help Viewer)
- The ability to size and position windows (available only from a .chm file displayed in the HTML Help Viewer)
- Pop-up definitions
- Context-sensitive Help (available only from a .chm file displayed in applications that support this functionality)
- Shortcut buttons to run other programs (available only from a .chm file displayed in the HTML Help Viewer)
- Related Topics links
- Training card Help (step-by-step interactive help that is available only from a .chm file displayed in the HTML Help Viewer)
- Splash screen

The best way to insert the HTML Help ActiveX control in an HTML file is by opening the HTML file in HTML Help Workshop and clicking **HTML Help Control** on the **Tags** menu. A wizard appears that lets you choose what kind of command to use with the control and helps you define other parameters to apply to that command. When you click **Finish**, the wizard inserts the appropriate <OBJECT> and <PARAM> tags in the HTML file.

For example, the following HTML fragment inserts an instance of the HTML Help ActiveX control that creates a Related Topics button to display a dialog box that lists two topics:

```
<OBJECT ID=HHCtrl TYPE="application/x-oleobject"
        CLASSID="clsid:adb880a6-d8ff-11cf-9377-00aa003b7a11"
        CODEBASE="HHCtrl.ocx#Version=4,73,8259,0"
        WIDTH=12
        HEIGHT=12>

    <PARAM NAME="Command" VALUE="Related Topics">
    <PARAM NAME="Button" VALUE="Text:Related Topics">
    <PARAM NAME="Item1" VALUE="First topic;topic1.htm">
    <PARAM NAME="Item2" VALUE="Second topic;topic2.htm">
</OBJECT>
```

Note Unlike many ActiveX controls, the HTML Help ActiveX control can be inserted only in HTML files. Even though the HTML Help ActiveX control is available as the **HHCtrl** object in the list of controls that you can add to the Toolbox in Office applications, if you try to insert the control in a form or document, an error message is displayed. The version number shown in the previous sample HTML code for the CODEBASE attribute (`Version=4,73,8259,0`) is the current version of the control at the time of this writing. When you insert an HTML Help ActiveX control by using HTML Help Workshop, the version number will reflect the version of the control that is installed on your computer.

Once you have the <OBJECT> tag for an instance of the HTML Help ActiveX control inserted in an HTML page, you can use Microsoft JScript or Microsoft Visual Basic Scripting Edition (VBScript) to work with the control. For example, the following HTML fragment uses an instance of HHCtrl.ocx and the control's **TextPopup** method in JScript to create a text pop-up:

```
<OBJECT ID=HHCtrl TYPE="application/x-oleobject"
        CLASSID="clsid:adb880a6-d8ff-11cf-9377-00aa003b7a11"
        CODEBASE="HHCtrl.ocx#Version=4,73,8259,0">
</OBJECT>

<P>This is a
<A HREF=JavaScript:HHCtrl.TextPopup(MyText,"Verdana,10",9,9,-1,-1)>
pop-up</A>.
</P>
<SCRIPT>MyText="This is how a text pop-up window looks."
</SCRIPT>
```

If you prefer to use VBScript, you can create an identical text pop-up by replacing `JavaScript` in the <A HREF> tag with `VBScript` like this:

```
<A HREF=VBScript:HHCtrl.TextPopup(MyText,"Verdana,10",9,9,-1,-1)>
pop-up</A>
```

For more information about using script with the HTML Help ActiveX control, see the HTML Help ActiveX Control Reference Web site at http://www.microsoft.com /workshop/author/htmlhelp/hharef.asp.

The HTML Help ActiveX Control vs. the HTML Help Java Applet

Although the HTML Help Java applet provides much of the same functionality as the HTML Help ActiveX control, the Java applet is more useful when it is used on a Web site than when it is used in a compiled HTML Help file. The Java applet does not provide as many features as the ActiveX control does, and it loads the table of contents and index more slowly than the ActiveX control does. However, the Java applet allows your Web site to use HTML Help navigation features and still be compatible with browsers that don't support ActiveX controls. For more information about working with the Java applet, see "Working with the HTML Help Java Applet" later in this chapter.

Deploying HTML Help

You can deploy the files that make up your HTML Help online Help system in any of the following ways:

- As a set of HTML files compiled into one or more locally installed compiled HTML Help files (.chm)
- As a set of locally installed HTML files to be accessed through the Windows file system
- As a set of HTML files to be accessed through an intranet, an extranet, or the Internet
- A combination of these formats

The advantage of using compiled HTML Help files is that you can install a single file or small set of files on each user's local drive that can be accessed without a network connection. Additionally, compiled HTML Help files use disk space much more efficiently than uncompiled HTML files, particularly on hard disks that have been formatted with the FAT file system. For this reason, using locally installed HTML files is not generally recommended unless you want to be able to access your HTML files from outside your HTML Help online Help system.

The advantage of supplying the Help topics as a Web site is that you can update and add new Help topics from a single central location; however, providing Help this way requires that users have network access to your Web site. Moreover, certain features of HTML Help, such as full-text search, are available only when you are using compiled HTML Help files.

You can also provide Help topics through a combination of both standard and compiled HTML formats, most typically in the form of a locally installed compiled HTML Help file with jumps from individual topics or the table of contents to Web pages on an intranet, an extranet, or the Internet. In addition, you can display an HTML page contained in a compiled HTML Help file from Internet Explorer by using an appropriately formatted URL. For information about how to do this, see "Using a URL to Open a Page in a Compiled HTML Help File" later in this chapter.

Adding Help to Your Office Solution

You can display Help topics to assist users of your Office solutions in the following ways.

Object or area	Kinds of Help you can provide
Documents	Help topics that are displayed by clicking a Help button or a command bar control
UserForms	Context-sensitive Help for controls
	Help topics that are displayed by clicking a Help button or pressing F1
Access forms and reports	Context-sensitive Help for controls
	Help topics that are displayed by clicking a Help button or pressing F1
Command bars	Context-sensitive Help for command bar controls
	Help topics that are displayed by clicking a command bar control
Office Assistant	Help topics that are displayed by clicking a button in the Help balloon or (if you have the Answer Wizard SDK and create the necessary files) by querying the Office Assistant
VBA code	Help topics that are displayed by using the **Help** method of the **Application** object
	Help topics that are displayed by clicking the Help button, when you are using the **InputBox** and **MsgBox** functions
	Help topics for custom error messages, when you are using the **Raise** method of the **Err** object
	Context-sensitive Help topics for custom properties and methods you define in class modules (displayed through the Object Browser or by pressing F1 in a code module)
	Help topics that are displayed by using HtmlHelp API calls
Script	Help topics that are displayed by using the commands and methods of the HTML Help ActiveX control

The following sections provide details and pointers on how to add Help to your Office solution in all of these ways.

Maintaining Backward Compatibility with Office 97 Applications

If your solution needs to maintain backward compatibility with Office 97 applications, you should supply all Help authored and compiled as WinHelp 4.0 files by using Microsoft Help Workshop or some other WinHelp 4.0 authoring tool. The standard properties and methods available to display Help in Office 97 applications don't support using HTML Help files to display context-sensitive Help or standard Help topics.

However, you can display standard Help topics (but not context-sensitive Help) in Office 97 applications from HTML Help files if you create a function declaration to call the HtmlHelp API directly to display the topic. For information about using the HtmlHelp API to display a standard Help topic, see "Displaying Help by Using the HtmlHelp API" later in this chapter.

For information about creating WinHelp 4.0 files, see the Help system in Microsoft Help Workshop. Microsoft Help Workshop can be downloaded for free from the Microsoft Technical Support Web site at http://support.microsoft.com/download/support/mslfiles/hcwsetup.exe.

The Kinds of Help You Can Use

You can create three kinds of Help for your Office solutions:

- Context-sensitive pop-up Help to describe your solution's interface elements. (This kind of Help is sometimes referred to as *What's This Help*.)

  You can create context-sensitive Help for dialog boxes created by using UserForms or Access forms. This type of Help is displayed either by clicking the question mark button in the title bar of a dialog box and then clicking a control, or by moving the focus to a control and then pressing SHIFT+F1. A small borderless pop-up window appears next to the clicked control.

  You can also create context-sensitive Help for command bar controls. Context-sensitive Help for command bar controls is displayed either by pressing SHIFT+F1 and then clicking the control, or by clicking **What's This?** on the **Help** menu before clicking the control.

  Important While HTML Help does provide the ability to author and display pop-up windows for context-sensitive Help, UserForms, Access forms, and command bars in Office 2000 do not support using HTML Help files for context-sensitive Help. If you want to add context-sensitive Help for interface elements in your Office 2000 solution, you must author and compile your topics as WinHelp 4.0 (.hlp) files by using Microsoft Help Workshop or some other WinHelp 4.0 authoring tool.

- Standard Help topics that can be displayed by clicking a Help button in a dialog box or form, or by clicking a control on a command bar.

  Clicking a Help button in a dialog box or form displays a Help topic in a separate Help window. You can also associate a Help topic with the Help button displayed in dialog boxes created by using the **InputBox** and **MsgBox** functions, and you can provide Help topics for custom errors returned by using the **Raise** method. Similarly, you can provide a menu item or toolbar button on a command bar to display a Help topic.

- Standard Help topics that can be displayed from the Object Browser to document the properties and methods you define in custom class modules.

Creating a Help File to Use with an Office Solution

Office 2000 applications can display standard Help topics authored and compiled by using either HTML Help (.chm) or WinHelp 4.0 (.hlp). Context-sensitive Help for Office 2000 solutions must be authored by using WinHelp 4.0. You can download the tools required to author and compile both HTML Help and WinHelp 4.0 from the following locations:

- To download and install the tools used to create HTML Help files, go to the HTML Help Web site at http://www.microsoft.com/workshop/author/htmlhelp/default.asp.
- To download and install Microsoft Help Workshop, used to create WinHelp 4.0 files, go to the Microsoft Technical Support Web site at http://support.microsoft.com/download/support/mslfiles/hcwsetup.exe.

Jumping from a WinHelp Topic to an HTML Help Topic

Because Office 2000 applications require you to use WinHelp 4.0 topics to author context-sensitive Help, you may sometimes need to jump from a WinHelp 4.0 topic to an HTML Help topic. You author a jump from any WinHelp 4.0 topic to an HTML Help topic by using the **ExecFile** macro. For example, a jump in a WinHelp 4.0 file that is formatted like the following example opens the first page in the compiled HTML Help file that is installed for Internet Explorer 4.0 or later:

```
Internet Explorer
Help!ExecFile(hh,its:c:\windows\help\iexplore.chm::/iexplore_welcome.htm)
```

The first argument passed to the **ExecFile** macro, **hh**, refers to the program to run, Hh.exe, the HTML Help Viewer. The second argument is the URL to open a page in a .chm file as described in "Using a URL to Open a Page in a Compiled HTML Help File" later in this chapter.

Creating HTML Help Topics

The top-level steps for using HTML Help Workshop to create a Help system are as follows:

- Create a Help project file (.hhp) to manage your topics, art, contents (.hhc), index (.hhk), and other source files, and to define the on-screen appearance of your Help system.
- Author Help topic files in HTML. If you want to use the same styles as Microsoft Office Help topics, use the Office.css cascading style sheet file in the Samples\CH13\Help Source subfolder on the companion CD-ROM.
- Create a table of contents file for easy navigation to Help topics. (Optional)
- Create an index file for indexing Help topics. (Optional)
- Create window definitions to define each kind of window in which you want to display Help information. (Optional if you only want to use the default HTML Help Viewer window)
- Define and assign information types for custom grouping of topics for different audiences, such as beginning or advanced users, or to display different sets of topics for different versions or installations of your solution. (Optional)
- Compile your Help file. (Optional if you are using the HTML Help ActiveX control or the HTML Help Java applet from a Web site)

For detailed information about each of these steps, see the Help index in HTML Help Workshop.

Creating Context IDs

To display Help topics in Office solutions by using standard properties or the **Help** method of the **Application** object, your compiled Help file must have a numeric value, called a *context ID*, for each topic you want to display. This is true for both context-sensitive Help and standard Help topics, and whether you are using a compiled HTML Help file or a WinHelp 4.0 file.

Creating Context IDs for WinHelp 4.0 Files

For WinHelp 4.0 files, the process of mapping context IDs is the same for both context-sensitive pop-up Help and standard Help topics.

▶ To create and map context IDs in a WinHelp 4.0 Help file

1. Use Word to create a document, inserting a page break between each topic.
2. On the **Insert** menu, click **Footnote** to add a footnote to the first paragraph in each topic. In the **Footnote and Endnote** dialog box, click **Custom mark** and type **#** as the footnote symbol. As the footnote text, type a unique string called a *topic ID* for each topic; for example, **HelpTopic1**.
3. Save the document as a Rich Text Format file (.rtf).
4. Use Microsoft Help Workshop to create a Help project file that specifies this .rtf file as your topic file, and then either manually map each topic ID to a unique numeric context ID or create a C header file to do this.
5. Compile your Help file.

For more information about creating WinHelp files, see the Help system in Microsoft Help Workshop.

Creating Context IDs for HTML Help Files

In Office applications, HTML Help files can be used only for standard Help topics, and the process of mapping context IDs in HTML Help files is different than that used for WinHelp 4.0 files. In HTML Help, Help topics that will be displayed in the HTML Help Viewer or a Help window are authored by using a separate HTML file for each topic. After you have authored your Help topics, you will want to create jumps between them. To do this, instead of using a topic ID to specify the topic to jump to as is done for WinHelp 4.0 files, you author a standard HTML hyperlink that specifies the HTML file name of the topic. For example, the following <A> (anchor) tag creates a jump to the topic authored in the Options.htm file:

```
<A HREF="Options.htm">Options</A>
```

To retain compatibility with applications that expect context IDs, HTML Help requires you to perform two steps to create numeric context IDs for each topic file you want to display:

1. Create a C header file that maps an arbitrary topic ID text string to a numeric context ID.
2. Map each topic ID from the header file to the actual HTML file name of the topic you want to display. In HTML Help Workshop, this is called *aliasing* topic IDs to HTML file names. You can do this manually through the HTML Help Workshop user interface, or by creating a text file with an .h extension.

The following procedures assume you have already created Help topics for your HTML Help file.

▶ **To create a C-style header file to map topic IDs to context IDs**

1 Create a new text file in HTML Help Workshop or in your favorite text editor.

2 For each topic you want to create a context ID for, enter a line in this format:

#define *topic_id nnnn // comment*

The string constant after **#define** is the topic ID and the number following it is the context ID. Each topic ID and context ID must be unique within your Help project. The "//" comment introducer and comment text are optional.

3 Save the text file with your other HTML Help source files and make sure it is named with an .h extension.

4 In HTML Help Workshop, open your Help project file, click the **HtmlHelp API Information** button on the **Project** tab, and then on the **Map** tab, click **Header File** and specify the header file.

After you have created your header file and specified it for your Help project file, you must alias each of the topic ID strings in the header file. You can do this manually or by including a text file that defines each alias. Before doing this, you should print out or open a copy of the map header file you created in the previous procedure so that you can view the names of each topic ID string.

▶ **To manually alias topic IDs to context IDs**

1 Open your Help project file in HTML Help Workshop.

2 Click the **HtmlHelp API Information** button on the **Project** tab, and then click the **Alias** tab.

3 To manually specify the alias for each topic ID string, click **Add**, type the topic ID string you want to alias in the first box, and then select the HTML file that contains the topic in the second box.

▶ **To alias topic IDs to context IDs by using a text file**

1 Create a text file and enter a line in this format for each topic ID you want to alias to an HTML file:

topic_id=filename.**htm ;** *comment*

The *topic_id* string constant is the topic ID from the mapping header file, and the file name following the equal sign (=) is the HTML file name of the topic you want to display. The ";" comment introducer and comment text that follows are optional.

2 Save the text file, making sure it has an .h extension.

3 Open your Help project file in HTML Help Workshop.

4 Click the **HtmlHelp API Information** button on the **Project** tab, and then click the **Alias** tab.

5 Click **Include** and specify the text file you just created.

Once you have mapped context IDs to the topic IDs in your compiled WinHelp 4.0 and HTML Help files, you use the appropriate context IDs in the design-time settings of forms and controls, and in your program code to display the correct Help topic.

For more information about creating HTML Help files, see the Help system in HTML Help Workshop.

Displaying Custom Help Topics in an Office Application's Help Window

Built-in Help in Office 2000 applications is displayed in a docked window on the right side of the application window. If you are displaying a custom Help topic from Excel or PowerPoint by using the **Help** method of the **Application** object, you can also display your Help topic in this same window. This isn't possible in Word and Access because they require you to use a call to the HtmlHelp API to display a custom Help topic. Custom Help topics in Word and Access are always displayed in floating windows as defined by the window type specified in the HtmlHelp API call. If you prefer not to display your Excel or PowerPoint solution's Help in a docked window, you can use the HtmlHelp API to display the Help topic as described in "Displaying Help by Using the HtmlHelp API" later in this chapter.

To display a custom Help topic in an Office application's docked Help window, the compiled HTML Help file for your Help project must have a default window definition that is named either MSO_Small or MSO_Large. If you want, you can define toolbar buttons that are different from those in the standard Help window, but changes to other details of the window definition, such as the window's size and placement, will be ignored. The Help topic window will automatically be sized and placed in the application's docked Help window.

In addition to naming the default window definition, the window type's *notification ID* (referred to as **idNotify** in the HtmlHelp API) must be set to a nonzero value. This setting is not available in HTML Help Workshop's user interface. In order to make this setting for your Help project, you must edit the Help project file (.hhp) with a text editor and add a nonzero value at the end of your window definition. For example, the default window definition in the Sample.hhp file included in the Samples\CH13 \Help Source subfolder on the companion CD-ROM looks like this:

```
[WINDOWS]
MSO_Small="Sample Help","Toc.hhc","Sample.hhk","home.htm",,,,,,0x2121,
200,0x300e,[0,0,445,514],,,,,,,1
```

The arbitrary value 1 was added to the end of the MSO_Small definition in order to specify a nonzero value for **idNotify**. After you change this value, make sure that this window definition is also specified as the default window (for example, `Default Window=MSO_Small`) in the [OPTIONS] section of the .hhp file, and then compile your Help file.

In addition to defining the window type as described above, you must also make sure the Office Assistant is displayed, or your Help topic will not be displayed in the docked Help window. If the Office Assistant isn't displayed, your topic will be displayed with the navigation pane expanded to show the **Contents**, **Answer Wizard**, and **Index** tabs. To make sure the Office Assistant is displayed, the code that displays your topic should set the **Visible** property of the **Assistant** object to **True** before it opens your topic.

Specifying the Path to Your Solution's Help File

To display Help for your solution, you must specify the path to the Help file that contains the topics you want to display. If you know where Help will be installed for your solution, you can hard-code the complete path to the file. However, if the exact path to your Help file isn't known, you must determine a way for your solution to find your Help file at run time. The simplest way to do this is to install your solution and Help file in the same folder, and then use the **Path** property of the application that is running to determine what folder the document or database was opened from. For example, this fragment of code uses the **ActiveWorkbook** property to return the current Excel **Workbook** object and the **Path** property to determine its location, and then appends the name of the Help file:

```
ActiveWorkbook.Path & "\sample.chm"
```

You can use the **Path** property the same way by using the **ActiveDocument** property or the **Document** object in Word, the **ActivePresentation** property or the **Presentation** object in PowerPoint, or the **CurrentProject** object in Access.

Displaying Help in Forms and Documents

In UserForms and Access forms, you can display context-sensitive Help for interface elements and you can display standard Help topics from a Help button on the form. You can also display Help from a form's command bar by adding a toolbar button or menu item that displays a Help topic. In Word, Excel, and PowerPoint documents, you can display Help by using the Toolbox to insert a Help button in the document.

The method you use to implement context-sensitive Help in forms is very similar across all Office applications. Although the methods used for UserForms and Access forms differ slightly, essentially you specify property settings to identify the Help file that contains context-sensitive Help and then specify the context ID of the context-sensitive Help topic to display for each control.

The method you use to implement a Help button on a form or document depends on which Office application is hosting the form or document. In all cases, you run code triggered by the Click event of the Help command button, but the method used to call the Help topic differs depending on the application. In Excel and PowerPoint, you can use the **Help** method of the **Application** object to display a custom Help topic. In Word, the **Help** method of the **Application** object allows you to display only built-in

Help, and Access has no such method. For this reason, implementing a Help button in both Word and Access requires you to use an API call to the HTML Help or WinHelp engine to display the Help topic. If you prefer to use the same method for displaying Help topics regardless of the application (for example, if you want to create code that will run in all four applications), you must use an API call to the Help engine.

Displaying Context-Sensitive Help in UserForms

Implementing context-sensitive Help for interface elements in UserForms is the same regardless of which Office application the form will be used with.

▶ To define context-sensitive Help for UserForms

1. Create a WinHelp 4.0 Help file that contains the Help topics you want to display. For more information about creating a Help file, see "Creating a Help File to Use with an Office Solution" earlier in this chapter.
2. Open the Visual Basic Editor in the application you are working with.
3. In the Project Explorer, right-click the name of the VBA project for the document you are working with, and then click **Project Properties**.
4. In the **Help File Name** box, specify the full path and name of the Help file that contains context-sensitive Help topics.

   If you don't want to include the full path to the Help file, omit steps 3 and 4 and add code to the form's Initialize event that specifies the path by using the **HelpFile** and **Path** properties of the document. For example:

   ```
   Dim strHelpPath As String

   strHelpPath = ActiveDocument.Path & "\samplepopups.hlp"

   ActiveDocument.VBProject.HelpFile = strHelpPath
   ```

   Note You can specify only one Help file per VBA project. If you want to define context-sensitive Help for more than one UserForm or for class modules in the project, the Help file you specify must contain Help topics for all of these items.

5. Open the UserForm you want to work with, and set the form's **WhatsThisButton** and **WhatsThisHelp** properties to **True**.
6. For each control that you want to display context-sensitive Help for, set the control's **HelpContextID** property to the context ID of the Help topic you want to display for that control.

Displaying Context-Sensitive Help in Access Forms

Implementing context-sensitive Help for interface elements in Access forms is similar to the process of defining context-sensitive Help for UserForms, except the form and control properties you set are slightly different. In addition, you can specify different Help files for each form, and specify the window type in which to display the topic. To display the topic in a full WinHelp 4.0 Help window, enter the context ID as a positive value; that is, enter it exactly as it is defined in your .hlp file. To display the topic in a small borderless pop-up window that appears adjacent to the interface element, precede the context ID with a minus sign (–). Note that this does not mean you need to use negative values for context IDs when authoring your .hlp file; you need only precede the authored value with a minus sign.

▶ To define context-sensitive Help for Access forms

1. Create a WinHelp 4.0 Help file that contains the Help topics you want to display. For more information about creating a Help file, see "Creating a Help File to Use with an Office Solution" earlier in this chapter.
2. Open the form you want to work with in Design view and display the form's property sheet. To do this, click **Select Form** on the **Edit** menu, and then click **Properties** on the **View** menu.
3. Click the **Other** tab, and then set the **HelpFile** property to the full path and name of the Help file that contains context-sensitive Help topics.

   If you don't want to include the full path to the Help file, omit steps 2 and 3 and add code to the form's Load event that specifies the path by using the form's **HelpFile** property and the **CurrentProject** object's **Path** property. For example:

   ```
   Dim strHelpPath As String

   strHelpPath = CurrentProject.Path & "\samplepopups.hlp"

   Me.HelpFile = strHelpPath
   ```
4. In the form's property sheet, click the **Format** tab, set the **MinMaxButtons** property to **None**, and set the **WhatsThisButton** property to **Yes**.
5. For each control that you want to display context-sensitive Help for, set the control's **HelpContextID** property to the context ID of the topic you want to display for that control. To display the topic in a borderless pop-up window, precede the context ID with a minus sign (–).

Creating a Help Button

In Excel and PowerPoint, you can use the **Help** method of the **Application** object to display a custom Help topic. But in Word and Access, you must use a call to the HtmlHelp or WinHelp API. In either case, implementing a Help button in a UserForm, Access form, or document is simply a matter of adding a command button to the form or document and defining a line of code to specify the Help file and context ID of the topic you want to display.

To use the **Help** method of the **Application** object in Excel, you would add a line like the following to the Help button's Click event procedure:

```
Application.Help ActiveWorkbook.Path & "\sample.chm", 2001
```

In PowerPoint, you would use the same line, but you'd use the **ActivePresentation** property to access the current path. For example:

```
Application.Help ActivePresentation.Path & "\sample.chm", 2001
```

For more information about using the **Help** method of the **Application** object, see "Displaying Help by Using the Help Method" later in this chapter.

To use the HtmlHelp API to display a Help topic, you must include a function declaration to use the HtmlHelp API in the Declarations section of a form, class, or standard module, and then add a line of code like the following to the Help button's Click event procedure:

```
Call HtmlHelp(0, ActiveDocument.Path &"\sample.chm", HH_HELP_CONTEXT, ByVal 2001&)
```

For more information about using a call to the HtmlHelp API to display a Help topic, see "Displaying Help by Using the HtmlHelp API" later in this chapter.

Displaying Help from Command Bars

In much the same way as forms, you can display both context-sensitive Help for custom command bar controls, and also call a standard Help topic when a user clicks a toolbar button or menu item. The same restrictions for displaying context-sensitive Help also apply to displaying standard Help topics: In Excel and PowerPoint, you can use the **Help** method of the **Application** object; in Word and Access, you must call the Help engine directly by using an API call.

Displaying Context-Sensitive Help for Command Bar Controls

To implement context-sensitive Help for a command bar control, you set the control's **HelpFile** property to the name of the Help file that contains the context-sensitive Help topic, and set the **HelpContextID** property to the context ID of the topic you want to display. There is no need to do this for built-in command bar controls used in custom command bars because they already have context-sensitive Help topics associated with them.

In all Office applications, you can set the **HelpFile** and **HelpContextID** properties by using VBA code. In Access, you can also set these properties through the user interface by clicking **Customize** on the **Tools** menu. The following code fragment sets these properties for a command bar control:

```
With ctlCBarControl
   .Caption = "M&y Help"
   .BeginGroup = True
   .FaceId = 0
   .OnAction = "DisplayHelp"
   .HelpFile = strAppPath & "\samplepopups.hlp"
   .HelpContextID = 1004
   .Visible = True
End With
```

Displaying a Standard Help Topic from a Toolbar Button or Menu Item

Displaying a Help topic when a user clicks a toolbar button or menu item is similar to creating a Help button for a form. However, command bar controls don't provide a Click event, so you must first create a **Sub** or **Function** procedure that displays the Help topic, and then set the control's **OnAction** property to the name of that procedure. The same restrictions apply when you are creating a procedure to display a Help topic as when you are creating a Help button: You can use the **Help** method of the **Application** object to display a custom Help topic only in Excel and PowerPoint, but you must use an API call to HTML Help to display a custom Help topic in Word and Access.

For more information about creating command bars and command bar controls, see Chapter 6, "Working with Shared Office Components."

Using the Office Assistant to Display Help

You can use the Office Assistant to display a balloon that allows users to access custom Help topics. If you have the Answer Wizard SDK, you can also integrate your custom Help topics with the built-in Help topics provided with Office.

Displaying Help Topics from an Office Assistant Balloon

You can use the Assistant to display a balloon containing buttons and labels that users can click to open custom Help topics. As with other methods of displaying custom Help topics, you can use the **Help** method of the **Application** object to display a custom Help topic in Excel and PowerPoint, but you must use an API call to HTML Help to display a custom Help topic in Word and Access.

The following procedure can be used from Excel or PowerPoint (if you replace `ActiveWorkbook.Path` with `ActivePresentation.Path`) to display a Help balloon with labels and buttons for two topics:

```
Sub HelpFromAssistant()
   Dim intTopic       As Integer
   Dim blnVisible     As Boolean
   Dim strMsg         As String

   blnVisible = Assistant.Visible

   ' Determine if the Assistant is already visible.
   If blnVisible = False Then
      With Assistant
         .Visible = True
         .Animation = msoAnimationIdle
      End With
   Else
      Assistant.Animation = msoAnimationIdle
   End If

   ' Display Help balloon with two buttons and store user's
   ' selection in intTopic.
   With Assistant.NewBalloon
      .BalloonType = msoBalloonTypeButtons
      .Heading = "Displaying Help Topics"
      .Text = "Select a topic:"
      .Labels(1).Text = "Topic One"
      .Labels(2).Text = "Topic Two"
      .Button = msoButtonSetCancel
      .Mode = msoModeModal
      intTopic = .Show
   End With

   ' Determine which button the user clicked and display the Help
   ' topic. This code works only in Excel 2000 because it refers to
   ' a .chm file. Replace with a WinHelp 4.0 .hlp file if you also
   ' need this code to run in Excel 97.
   Select Case intTopic
      Case 1
         Application.Help ActiveWorkbook.Path & "\sample.chm", 2001
      Case 2
         Application.Help ActiveWorkbook.Path & "\sample.chm", 2002
   End Select
End Sub
```

The HelpFromAssistant procedure is available in the modHTMLHelp module in ExcelHelp.xls in the Samples\CH13 subfolder on the companion CD-ROM.

The same code can be used from Word or Access if you replace the calls to the **Help** method of the **Application** object with calls to the HtmlHelp API to display the topics. For Word, the **Select Case** statements would look like this:

```
Select Case intTopic
   Case 1
      Call HtmlHelp(0, ActiveDocument.Path & "\sample.chm", HH_HELP_CONTEXT, _
         ByVal 2001&)
   Case 2
      Call HtmlHelp(0, ActiveDocument.Path & "\sample.chm", HH_HELP_CONTEXT, _
         ByVal 2002&)
End Select
```

In Access, you would use the **Path** property of the **CurrentProject** object to display a topic from a compiled HTML Help file located in the same folder as the current database. For example:

```
Call HtmlHelp(0, CurrentProject.Path & "\sample.chm", HH_HELP_CONTEXT, ByVal 2001&)
```

For more information about working with the Office Assistant, see Chapter 6, "Working with Shared Office Components."

Using the Assistant with Access Run-Time Applications

If you are creating an Access run-time application and installing it on a computer that does not have Office installed, the **Assistant** object is not available. However, the Office Assistant is based on the Microsoft Agent ActiveX control, which is freely distributable. For Access run-time applications, you can use the Agent control to provide the full range of Assistant services without accessing the Assistant's object model. For more information about using the Agent control, see the Microsoft Agent Web site at http://www.microsoft.com/intdev/agent.

If Office is not installed on the computer where your Access run-time application will be used, you may also need to install HTML Help components. For more information, see the "Redistributing HTML Help Components" sidebar earlier in this chapter.

Creating an Answer Wizard Index to Display Custom Help Topics from the Office Assistant

If you purchased Office 2000 Developer or the *Microsoft Office 2000 Resource Kit* (Microsoft Press, 1999), you can use the Microsoft Answer Wizard Builder available with the Answer Wizard SDK to create a custom Answer Wizard index with references to your custom Help topics. When this custom Answer Wizard index is installed with your solution, if a user asks a question that applies to your solution, your custom Help topics will be displayed along with those built-in Help topics returned by the Office Assistant. This way of integrating Help topics is most appropriate for Office solutions that are deployed as add-ins. For information about the Answer Wizard SDK, see the *Microsoft Office 2000 Resource Kit* (Microsoft Press, 1999) or Office 2000 Developer.

The Microsoft Office 9.0 object library provides methods for the **AnswerWizard** and **AnswerWizardFiles** objects that allow developers to control when a custom Answer Wizard index is used by the Office Assistant to return custom Help topics. For information about these objects and methods, search the Microsoft Office Visual Basic Reference Help index for "AnswerWizard object" and "AnswerWizardFiles object."

Displaying Help from VBA Code

As mentioned earlier in this chapter, there are two ways to display a custom Help topic from code. In Excel and PowerPoint, you can use the **Help** method of the **Application** object, but in Word and Access you must use an API call to HTML Help or to WinHelp to display the Help topic. For this reason, if you need to use the same code across applications, you must use an API call. The following sections describe how to do both, and also detail how to display Help topics from the **InputBox** and **MsgBox** functions, how to display Help topics when error messages are displayed, and how to associate Help topics with properties and methods in class modules.

Displaying Help by Using the Help Method

The **Help** method of the **Application** object can be used from Excel and PowerPoint to display a custom Help topic. You can invoke the **Help** method from practically any context, but it is most commonly used to display a Help topic from a command button or from a menu item or toolbar button. You use the following syntax to call the **Help** method

expression.**Help**(*HelpFile, HelpContextID*)

where *expression* returns an **Application** object, *HelpFile* is the name of either a .chm or .hlp file, and *HelpContextID* is the context ID of the topic you want to display. The *HelpFile* argument must include the full path to the file.

For example, the following code fragment opens the Help file Sample.chm in the current folder of the active Excel workbook and displays the topic mapped to context ID 2001:

```
Application.Help ActiveWorkbook.Path & "\sample.chm", 2001
```

While you can't display a custom Help topic by using the **Help** method of the **Application** object in Word, you can use it to display built-in Help. For more information about how to do this, search the Microsoft Word Visual Basic Reference Help index for "Help method."

Displaying Help by Using the HtmlHelp API

Because the current implementation of the HTML Help ActiveX control can't be inserted in a form and doesn't provide Component Object Model (COM) interfaces, you must call its API directly if you need to use features beyond those supported by the methods and properties available in VBA. Because Word and Access don't currently provide a built-in method for displaying custom Help topics, you must use the HtmlHelp API to display a custom Help topic in those applications.

Before you can use an API call from VBA code, you must create a function declaration in the Declarations section of a form, class, or standard module. The HtmlHelp API requires a single function declaration that looks like this:

```
Declare Function HtmlHelp Lib "HHCtrl.ocx" Alias "HtmHelpA" _
   (ByVal hwndCaller As Long, _
   ByVal pszFile As String, _
   ByVal uCommand As Long, _
   dwData As Any) As Long
```

This declaration uses the ANSI version of the **HtmlHelp** function exported by HHCtrl.ocx. For more information about using API calls from VBA, see Chapter 10, "The Windows API and Other Dynamic-Link Libraries."

The arguments of the **HtmlHelp** function provide the following functionality.

Argument	Description
hwndCaller	A handle to an application window or **Null**. This window handle may be used as a parent, owner, or message recipient for HTML Help, depending on how it is used. In VBA, instead of setting this to **vbNullString**, set it to **0** (zero).
pszFile	File to display; optionally also specifies which window type to display it in, delimited with the right angle bracket character (*filename>windowtype*). If you omit the window type, the **HtmlHelp** function will use the default window type specified in the HTML Help project file. For *uCommand* values that don't require a source file, *pszFile* can be **Null**, or **0** (zero), in VBA. However, a compiled HTML Help file is typically specified.
uCommand	The action to perform; see the remainder of this section for examples of how to display a Help topic by using either the HH_HELP_CONTEXT or HH_DISPLAY_TOPIC command.
dwData	Specifies additional data depending on the value of *uCommand*. Note that in this declaration this argument is declared **As Any**, because this argument accepts several different data types. You must be careful to pass the correct data type or risk an invalid page fault (also known as general protection fault [GPF]).

The **HtmlHelp** function supports a broad variety of HTML Help functionality and provides detailed control unavailable through other programmatic means. The rest of this section describes how to use the **HtmlHelp** function to display a custom Help topic. For more information about using other commands with the *uCommand* argument, see the HtmlHelp API Reference in the Help system for HTML Help Workshop.

To make using the **HtmlHelp** function from VBA simpler, in addition to the function declaration, you should also declare the following constants to pass as the *uCommand* argument:

```
Const HH_DISPLAY_TOPIC = &H0
Const HH_HELP_CONTEXT = &HF
```

The constants in the following table are used to specify which *uCommand* command to use with the **HtmlHelp** function to display a Help topic.

uCommand command	Description
HH_DISPLAY_TOPIC	Displays a Help topic by passing the name of the HTML file that contains the topic as the *dwData* argument.
HH_HELP_CONTEXT	Displays a Help topic by passing the mapped context ID for the topic as the *dwData* argument.

The command you choose to use depends on whether you have mapped context IDs for each topic as described earlier in this chapter in "Creating a Help File to Use with an Office Solution." If you haven't created context IDs, you must use the HH_DISPLAY_TOPIC command. If you have created context IDs, you can use either command.

When you are using either command from an Office application, you should pass 0 (zero) as the *hwndCaller* argument so that HTML Help will display the Help topic in *sibling mode*. Sibling mode (shown in Figure 13.2) causes HTML Help to display Help topics in a separate top-level overlapped Help window that is displayed alongside the calling application. The user can freely switch between the application and the Help window.

Figure 13.2 Sibling Mode

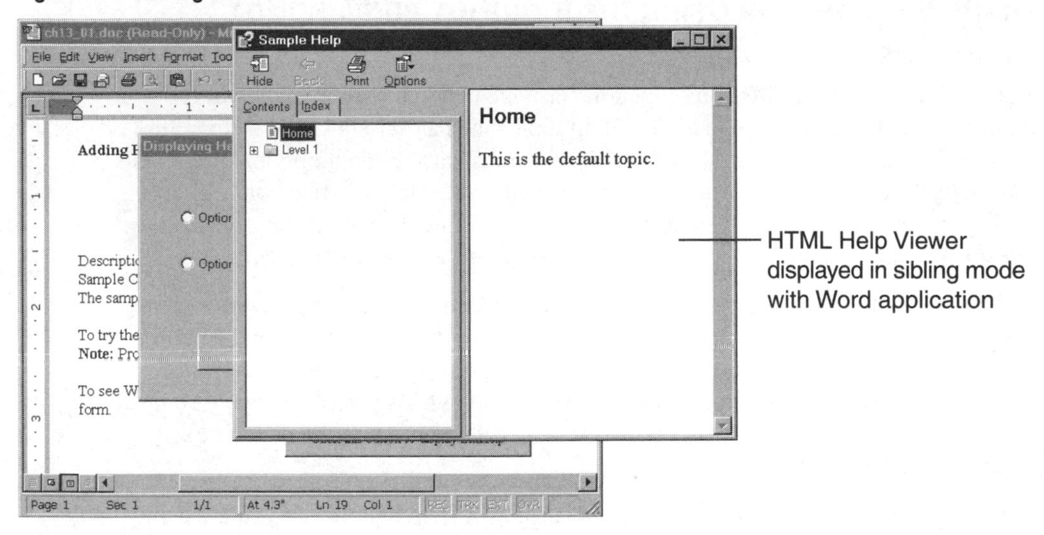

The following line of code shows how to display a Help topic by using the HH_DISPLAY_TOPIC command:

```
Call HtmlHelp(0, "c:\help\Sample.chm", HH_DISPLAY_TOPIC, By Val "Topic1.htm")
```

This code will display the topic authored in Topic1.htm, which is compiled in the Sample.chm file. Because no window type was specified for the *pszFile* argument, the topic will be displayed by using the default window type specified in the HTML Help project file that was used when the Help file was compiled.

The following line of code shows how to display a Help topic by using the HH_HELP_CONTEXT command:

```
Call HtmlHelp(0, "c:\help\Sample.chm>mso_small", HH_DISPLAY_TOPIC, By Val 2001&)
```

This code will display the topic specified by the mapped context ID 2001 in the Sample.chm file. The ampersand (&) following the context ID is required to specify that the value being passed to the **HtmlHelp** function is a **Long** data type. The topic will be displayed by using the mso_small window type specified in the *pszFile* argument. In order for this line of code to work correctly, the mso_small window type must be specified in the HTML Help project file that was used when the Help file was compiled.

Displaying Help by Using the InputBox and MsgBox Functions

Both the **InputBox** and **MsgBox** functions provide optional ***helpfile*** and ***context*** arguments that can be use to display a Help topic when a user clicks the Help button or presses F1. To display a custom Help topic, you must specify both optional arguments. The ***helpfile*** argument is a string value that specifies the Help file that contains the topic you want to display. This argument can accept either a .chm or .hlp file. The ***context*** argument specifies the mapped context ID of the topic to display.

If you specify the ***helpfile*** and ***context*** arguments when you are using the **InputBox** function, a Help button will automatically be added to the dialog box created by the **InputBox** function. If you specify the ***helpfile*** and ***context*** arguments when you are using the **MsgBox** function, you must also specify the **vbMsgBoxHelpButton** built-in constant in the ***buttons*** argument in order to add a Help button to the dialog box created by the **MsgBox** function.

The following code fragment shows how to display a Help topic when you are using the **InputBox** function:

```
InputBox Prompt:="Enter data", _
         HelpFile:=strAppPath & "\sample.chm", _
         Context:="2001"
```

The following line of code shows how to display a Help topic when you are using the **MsgBox** function:

```
MsgBox Prompt:= "You must enter a valid date.", _
       Buttons:=vbMsgBoxHelpButton, _
       HelpFile:= strAppPath & "\sample.chm", _
       Context:= "2002"
```

The **InputBox** and **MsgBox** functions allow you to display a Help topic contained in a compiled HTML Help file in all Office applications, including Word and Access. There is no need to use the HtmlHelp API to display a Help topic in a .chm file when you are using these functions in Word and Access.

Displaying Help for Custom Error Messages

The **Raise** method of the **Err** object has optional ***helpfile*** and ***helpcontext*** arguments that set the **HelpFile** and **HelpContext** properties of the **Err** object to the specified Help file name and context ID when your custom error is triggered. If the error trap in your procedure then passes these values to the **MsgBox** function, you can add a Help button to call additional Help from your error message dialog box. The following code example shows how to do this:

```
Sub ShowErrorHelp()
   Dim strAppPath As String

   strAppPath = ActiveDocument.Path

   On Error GoTo ShowErrorHelp_Err
   Err.Raise Number:=vbObjectError + 1234, _
             Source:="Sub ShowErrorHelp", _
             Description:="This error has a reason.", _
             HelpFile:=strAppPath & "\sample.chm", _
             HelpContext:=2003

ShowErrorHelp_End:
   Exit Sub

ShowErrorHelp_Err:
   MsgBox Prompt:=Err.Description, _
          Buttons:=vbMsgBoxHelpButton, _
          HelpFile:=Err.HelpFile, _
          Context:=Err.HelpContext
   Resume ShowErrorHelp_End
End Sub
```

The ShowErrorHelp procedure is available in the modHTMLHelp module in the WordHelp.doc in the Samples\CH13 subfolder on the companion CD-ROM.

The ***helpfile*** and ***helpcontext*** arguments of the **Raise** method support using a compiled HTML Help file in all Office applications, including Word and Access. There is no need to use the HtmlHelp API to display a Help topic in a .chm file when you are using the **Raise** method to return a Help file name and context ID in Word and Access.

Displaying Help for Properties and Methods in Class Modules

You can also add Help information for the custom properties and methods in your class modules. If you do so, Help can be displayed for these properties and methods by pressing F1 when they are viewed in the Object Browser or used in a procedure. This feature is useful if you will be distributing your applications to other developers.

▶ To provide Help for properties and methods in a class module

1 Create a Help file that contains the topics you want to display and maps each topic to a numeric context ID. For more information about creating a Help file, see "Creating a Help File to Use with an Office Solution" earlier in this chapter.

2 Open the Visual Basic Editor in the application you are working with.

3 In the Project Explorer, right-click the name of the VBA project for the document you are working with, and then click ***projectname*** **Properties**.

4 In the **Help File Name** box, specify the name of the Help file that contains the Help topics. If you don't include the full path, Help will be displayed as long as the Help file is installed in the same folder as your solution.

   Note You can specify only one Help file per VBA project. If you want to define context-sensitive Help for more than one class module or for UserForms in the project, the Help file you specify must contain topics for all of these items.

5 Open the Object Browser, and then click the name of your class module in the **Classes** box.

6 In the **Members Of** box, right-click a property or method, and then click **Properties**.

7 In the **Member Options** dialog box, type the context ID of the topic to display in the **Help Context ID** box. You can also type a description that will display in the Object Browser in the **Description** box.

8 Repeat steps 6 and 7 for each property and method in your class module.

The WordHelp.doc file in the Samples\CH13 subfolder on the companion CD-ROM contains a class module (clsTimerClass) that has Help topics associated with its properties and methods. In addition, the modTimerHelp module demonstrates how to display these Help topics from a procedure.

Using HTML Help to Author a Web Site

There are two ways to use HTML Help functionality when authoring Web sites. You can:

- Use the HTML Help ActiveX control or the HTML Help Java applet to implement navigation to documents on your Web site by using a hierarchical table of contents tree control or an index.
- Use HTML Help Workshop to create a compiled HTML Help file, and then create URLs to display HTML pages from the compiled HTML Help file in Internet Explorer.

To implement navigation by using the HTML Help ActiveX or the HTML Help Java applet, you first create the HTML files and other documents you want to use from your Web site. Then you use HTML Help Workshop to create table of contents and index files to navigate to your documents. Finally, you insert the control or applet in a Web page and use it to display the table of contents and index you created. Typically a Web site authored by using the HTML Help ActiveX control or Java applet uses a custom frameset to produce similar functionality to the freestanding HTML Help Viewer.

Displaying an HTML page from a compiled HTML Help file simply requires you to format the appropriate URL to open and display the HTML file.

Using HTML Help Features from a Custom Frameset

Framesets are a way of specifying multiple independent regions, called frames, within a browser window. Each frame in a frameset displays a separate HTML document. You can have frames that scroll and resize, depending on how you author the frameset. You assign each frame a name, so that links from one frame can jump to another frame.

After you have created a frameset, you add the HTML Help ActiveX control or the HTML Help Java applet (discussed in the following section) to the frames that you want to have HTML Help functionality. For example, one frame can use the HTML Help ActiveX control to display a table of contents that, when clicked, displays an HTML page or Office document in an adjoining frame.

You can use the HTML Help ActiveX control to add the following functionality to HTML pages displayed in your frameset:

- A table of contents
- An index
- Related topic links
- A splash screen
- Pop-up windows that display simple text strings without formatting

Figure 13.3 shows an example of a frameset in which the HTML Help ActiveX control is used to display a contents or index pane in the left frame.

Figure 13.3 A Frameset Authored by Using the HTML Help ActiveX Control

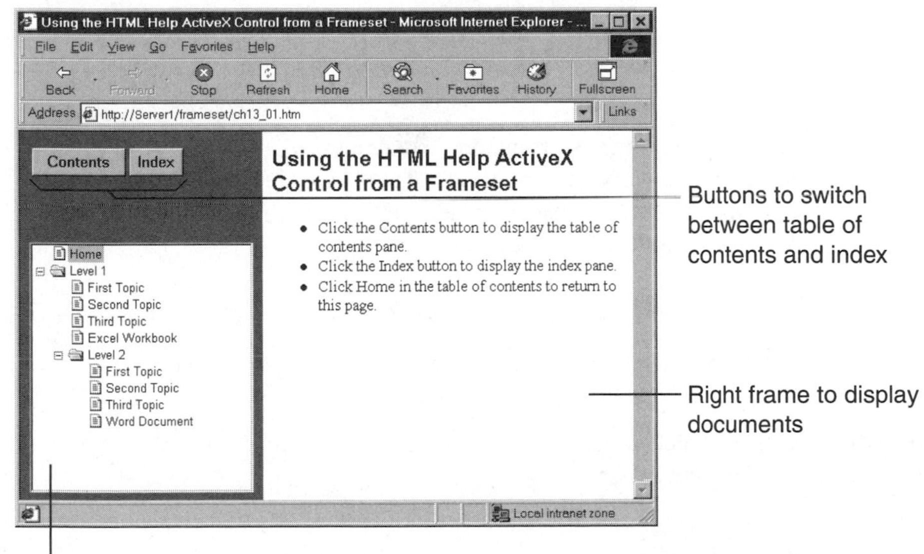

You can author the HTML files that make up the topics for an HTML Help frameset in whatever editor you choose, but to insert the HTML Help ActiveX control in your pages, it is recommended that you use the **HTML Help Control** command on the **Tags** menu of HTML Help Workshop. For more information about using the HTML Help ActiveX control, see "Working with the HTML Help ActiveX Control" earlier in this chapter.

You should author the files used to create the table of contents (.hhc) and index (.hhk) in HTML Help Workshop, but once you understand their format, you can update and modify them by using a text editor, if you want. The .hhc and .hhk files themselves (not a compiled HTML Help file that contains compiled versions of them) must be copied to your Web site in order to support a table of contents and index. Unlike a compiled index, an HTML Help index file used on a Web site can't merge keywords from other indexes or use keyword links (KLinks).

To view a sample frameset that uses the HTML Help ActiveX control to display a table of contents and index for navigation to HTML files and Office documents, see HTMLHelpActiveX.htm in the Samples\CH13\Frameset subfolder on the companion CD-ROM.

Working with the HTML Help Java Applet

If you need to have compatibility with browsers that don't support ActiveX controls, you can add HTML Help functionality to Web pages by using the HTML Help Java applet.

You can use the HTML Help Java applet to add the following HTML Help features to HTML pages displayed in your frameset:

- A table of contents
- An index
- Related Topics links

Note that the HTML Help Java applet doesn't support displaying text pop-up windows. To create similar functionality, you can use the JavaScript **alert** method of the **window** object to display a dialog box that contains a text string. For example, the following JavaScript displays a simple pop-up message:

```
<P>This is a <A HREF='JavaScript:alert("This a JavaScript message.")'
TITLE="This is a JavaScript message.">pop-up</A>.</P>
```

The TITLE attribute of the <A> tag provides a pop-up window for browsers that support this functionality.

To use the HTML Help Java applet from an HTML page, insert an <APPLET> tag similar to the one in the following example:

```
<APPLET CODE=HHCtrl.class
        ALIGN="baseline"
        WIDTH=240
        HEIGHT=270
        NAME=HHCtrl
        ARCHIVE="HHCtrl.zip">

   <PARAM NAME="Cabbase" VALUE="HHCtrl.cab">
   <PARAM NAME="Command" VALUE="Contents">
   <PARAM NAME="Item1" VALUE="hh_toc_java.hhc">
</APPLET>
```

The CODE attribute specifies HHCtrl.class, which is the name of the Java class used to load the HTML Help Java applet. Netscape Navigator uses the ARCHIVE attribute to specify a .zip file that contains Java class files. In this case, HHCtrl.zip contains all the Java class files required by the HTML Help Java applet. Similarly, the Cabbase parameter is used by Microsoft Internet Explorer to specify the name of a compressed archive that contains Java class files, in this case in the .cab file format. A copy of HHCtrl.cab is installed in the C:\Program Files\HTML Help Workshop\Java subfolder when you install HTML Help Workshop. You can create your own .zip archive by compressing all the .class files included in the Java subfolder.

The Command parameter is used to specify the kind of HTML Help functionality to be used with this instance of the HTML Help Java applet. You can specify the following commands.

Command	Description
Contents	Specifies that a table of contents will be displayed based on the information supplied in the HTML Help table of contents file specified in the Item1 parameter (normally an .hhc file). The specified file must reside in the same folder as the document containing the applet. You must also include a copy of cntimage.gif (from the C:\Program Files \HTML Help Workshop\Java folder created when you install HTML Help Workshop) to display folder and document icons in the table of contents tree view.
Index	Specifies that an index will be displayed based on the information supplied in the HTML Help index file specified in the Item1 parameter (normally an .hhk file). The specified file must reside in the same folder as the document containing the applet.
Related Topics	Specifies that a dialog box listing related topics will be displayed based on the information supplied in one or more Item*n* parameters in this format: <PARAM NAME="Item*n*" VALUE="*TopicTitle*;*TopicFile*.htm">

You can see additional parameters supported by the Contents, Index, and Related Topics commands by opening an HTML file in HTML Help Workshop, and then clicking **HTML Help Control** on the **Tags** menu. A wizard that is used to insert the HTML Help ActiveX control appears. You can select the **Table of Contents**, **Index**, or **Related Topics** command from this wizard to insert an <OBJECT> tag for the selected command. Most of the parameters supported by the <OBJECT> tag for the HTML Help ActiveX control can be used with the corresponding command for the HTML Help Java applet.

To view a sample frameset that uses the HTML Help Java applet to display a table of contents and index for navigation to HTML files and Office documents, see HTMLHelpJava.htm in the Samples\CH13\Frameset subfolder on the companion CD-ROM.

Using a URL to Open a Page in a Compiled HTML Help File

You can use a URL to open an HTML page in a compiled HTML Help file from Internet Explorer or an Office hyperlink. The kind of URL you use depends on which version of Internet Explorer users have installed, and whether the compiled HTML Help file is being opened directly from the file system or from an HTTP server.

When you are using Internet Explorer versions 3.*x* or later, you can open a specific HTML page contained in a compiled HTML Help file from the file system by using a URL in this format:

mk:@MSITStore:*path**filename***.chm::***page***.chm**

When you are using Internet Explorer versions 4.*x* or later, you can open an HTML page in a compiled HTML Help file from the file system by using a URL in this format:

its:*path**filename***.chm::/***page***.chm**

For example, you can open the first page in the compiled HTML Help file installed for the Internet Explorer 4.*x* or later Help system by using this URL:

```
its:c:\windows\help\iexplore.chm::/iexplore_welcome.htm
```

When you are using Internet Explorer 4.*x* or later, you can open a page in a compiled HTML Help file located on an HTTP server by using a URL in this format:

its:http://*serverpath*/*filename***.chm::/***page***.htm**

Where to Go from Here

For additional information about the subjects discussed in this chapter, see the following sources.

HTML Help

HTML Help Web site (http://www.microsoft.com/workshop/author/htmlhelp/default.asp)

HTML Help ActiveX Control Reference Web site (http://www.microsoft.com/workshop/author/htmlhelp/hharef.asp)

Steve Wexler. *Official Microsoft HTML Help Authoring Kit*. Redmond, WA: Microsoft Press, 1998.

WinHelp 4.0

Microsoft Windows 95 Help Authoring Kit. Redmond, WA: Microsoft Press, 1995.

Microsoft Help Workshop (download from the Microsoft Technical Support Web site at http://support.microsoft.com/download/support/mslfiles/hcwsetup.exe)

Answer Wizard SDK

Microsoft Office 2000 Resource Kit Web site (http://www.microsoft.com/office/ork/)

Microsoft Office 2000 Resource Kit. Redmond, WA: Microsoft Press, 1999.

Code Samples

The code samples shown in this chapter, along with sample Help files, can be copied from the files in the Samples\CH13 subfolder on the companion CD-ROM. Additional sample files for this chapter are located in the Samples\CH13\Frameset and Samples\CH13\Help Source subfolders.

Part Three

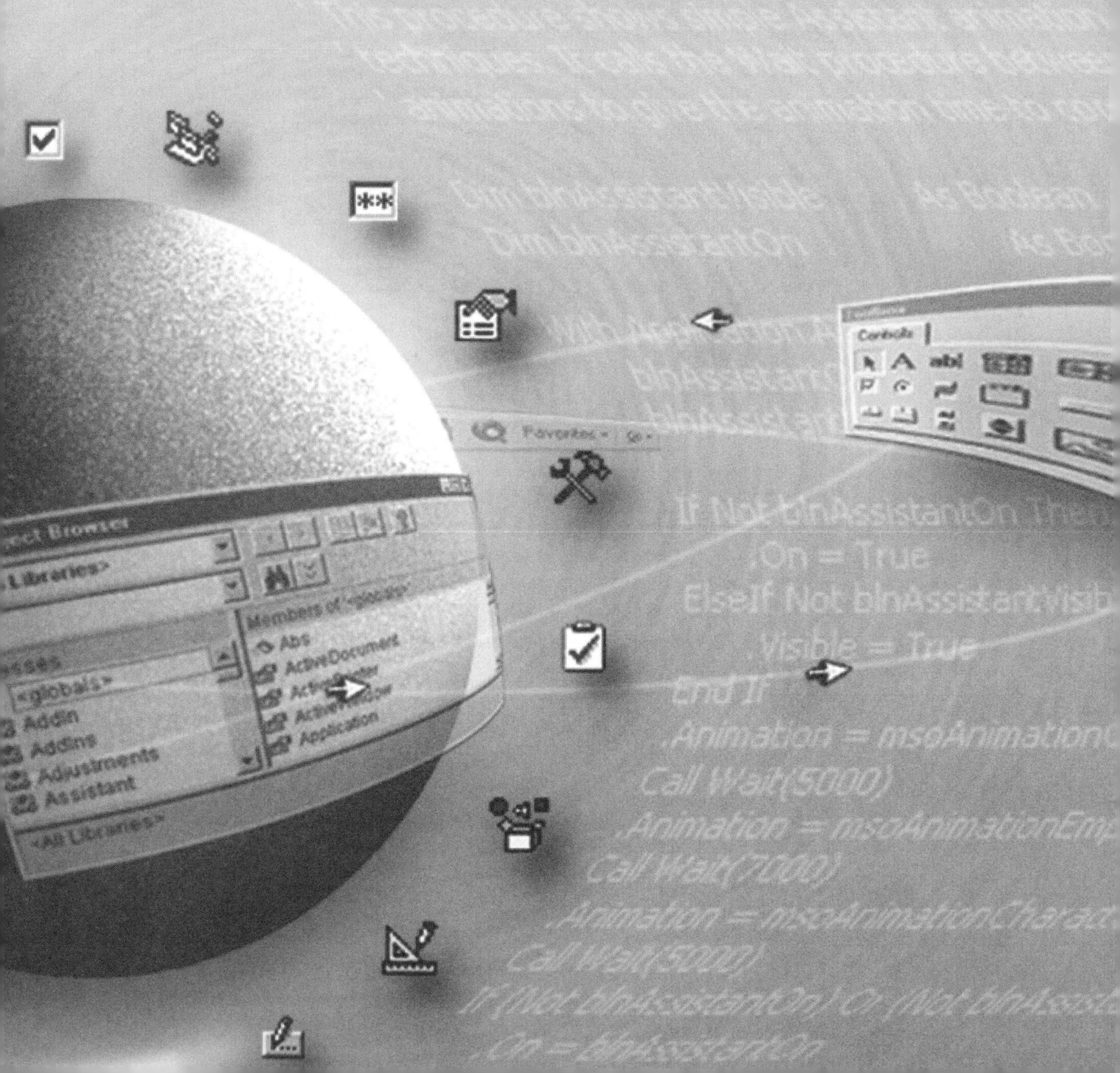

Dim blnAssistantOn
.On = True
Visible = True
End If
Call Wait(5000)
Call Wait(7000)
Controls
Favorites
Abs
ActiveDocument
Application
<globals>
Addin
Addins
Adjustments
Assistant
<All Libraries>

Working with Data in Office Solutions

The chapters in this part cover the fundamentals of accessing and working with data, analyzing and presenting data, and working with multiuser database applications.

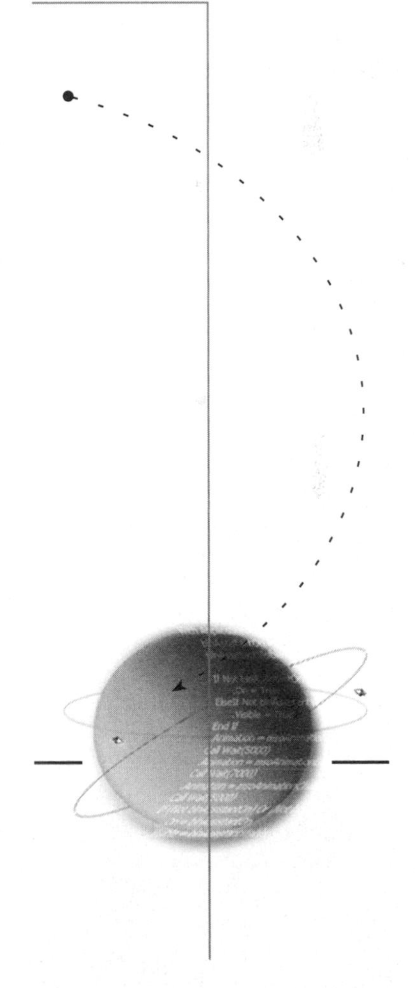

The first chapter in this part, Chapter 14, "Working with the Data Access Components of an Office Solution," provides an overview of the data access technologies supported by the Microsoft Office 2000 applications. The primary focus of this chapter is on using ActiveX Database Objects (ADO) and Data Access Objects (DAO) code to work with data stored in Microsoft Access databases, but it also includes information about working with data in Microsoft Excel workbooks and Microsoft Outlook folders, as well as in other sources, such as Microsoft SQL Server databases, HTML tables, dBASE files, Lotus 1-2-3 spreadsheets, and tabular text files.

The second chapter in this part, Chapter 15, "Retrieving and Analyzing Data," describes some of the tools and techniques available in Office 2000 for retrieving, analyzing, and presenting data in a manner that makes it easy to understand. This chapter describes the query-building tools available in Access and Excel and covers the basics of creating SQL statements. It also describes how to create reports in Microsoft Office solutions, how to sort and filter data, and how to work with PivotTable and PivotChart reports.

The third chapter in this part, Chapter 16, "Multiuser Database Applications," provides an overview of the tools and technologies available in Microsoft Office for creating multiuser database solutions. This chapter focuses on the three multiuser database architectures you can use with Microsoft Access to create desktop application-based solutions: file-server, client/server, and replication architectures. The fourth database architecture, Web-based database solutions, is covered in Chapter 5, “Working with Office Applications,” and Chapter 12, “Using Web Technologies,” in Part 2, “Developing Office Solutions.” Chapter 16 covers issues such as managing record locking, using transactions, and optimizing file-server solutions. It also provides an overview of how to create client/server solutions by using the new tools available in Access 2000, and how to use database replication in your Access database solutions.

CHAPTER 14

Working with the Data Access Components of an Office Solution

The primary role of many Microsoft Office solutions is to turn raw data into usable information. This can entail managing data from a broad variety of sources, including data stored in Office applications, such as Microsoft Access databases, Microsoft Excel workbooks, or Microsoft Outlook folders, as well as in other sources, such as Microsoft SQL Server databases, HTML tables, dBASE files, Lotus 1-2-3 spreadsheets, or tabular text files. This chapter describes the data access technologies supported by Office applications, and provides an introduction to using ActiveX Database Objects (ADO) code to work with your data.

Contents

Microsoft Office Data Access Technologies

Historically, Microsoft Office applications have supported a broad variety of data formats and data access technologies. Microsoft Office 2000 is no exception to this trend. However, all Microsoft products that support data access are converging on a new data access strategy called Universal Data Access. The primary technologies that are used to implement Universal Data Access are the low-level data access component architecture, called OLE DB, and the higher-level programming interface to OLE DB, ActiveX Data Objects (ADO). ADO can be used from any programming language that complies with the Component Object Model (COM), which for Office solution development includes Visual Basic for Applications (VBA), Visual Basic Scripting Edition (VBScript), and Microsoft JScript, and may also include Microsoft Visual C++ and Microsoft Visual J++ if those languages are used to develop COM add-ins or ActiveX controls.

Microsoft Office 2000 installs the OLE DB components and the latest version of ADO, ADO 2.1. ADO supports a broader array of data sources than the Data Access Objects (DAO) programming model provided in previous versions of Office. However, Office 2000 applications continue to provide support for DAO through the Microsoft DAO 3.6 object library, so you can run existing solutions that use DAO, or create new solutions that use DAO as well. You can also use both ADO and DAO code in your solution if you want. For more information about converting DAO code to ADO and co-existence issues, see "Choosing ADO or DAO for Working with Access Databases" later in this chapter.

OLE DB and ADO

ADO is Microsoft's new high-level programming interface to a broad variety of data sources. ADO is designed as an easy-to-use, application-level programming interface to Microsoft's newest and most powerful data access technology, OLE DB.

OLE DB is Microsoft's system-level data access interface to data across the organization. OLE DB is an open specification designed to build on the success of Open Database Connectivity (ODBC) by providing an open standard for accessing an even broader variety of data. Whereas ODBC was created to access only relational databases, OLE DB is designed for both relational and nonrelational data sources, including mainframe and hierarchical databases; e-mail and file system stores; text, graphical and geographical data; custom business objects; and more.

OLE DB consists of a collection of COM interfaces to various database management system services. These interfaces define the underlying architecture for the creation of software components that implement these services. As an Office solution developer, the primary thing you need to know about OLE DB is that it provides access to a particular data source by using a COM component called a *data provider*, which is often referred to as an *OLE DB provider*. You can think of an OLE DB provider as being much like an ODBC driver for a particular data source, with two exceptions: OLE DB providers can support access to a broader variety of data sources, and similar ADO code can be used to work with data exposed by any OLE DB provider. If the system your solution is running on has the appropriate OLE DB provider installed (as well as the core ADO and OLE DB components, which are installed by Office or by downloading and installing the Microsoft Data Access Components [MDAC] from the Universal Data Access Web site at http://www.microsoft.com/data/), your solution can use ADO code to work with the data exposed by that provider.

The primary providers you will be working with as an Office developer are the Microsoft Jet 4.0 OLE DB Provider and the Microsoft OLE DB Provider for SQL Server:

- The Microsoft Jet 4.0 OLE DB Provider is used to work with the Microsoft Jet database engine, which provides access to data in Access databases as well as providing database access to the installable Indexed Sequential Access Method (I-ISAM) data supported by Jet: tabular data stored in Excel workbooks, Outlook or Microsoft Exchange mail stores, dBASE tables, Paradox tables, Lotus 1-2-3 spreadsheets, text, and HTML files.
- Microsoft OLE DB Provider for SQL Server provides access to databases stored on Microsoft SQL Server versions 6.5 and 7.0.

In addition, for data sources that don't currently have OLE DB providers, you can use the Microsoft OLE DB Provider for ODBC drivers to access data made available by the broad range of ODBC relational database drivers available today. For more information about the data formats supported by Office 2000 and the OLE DB providers installed with Office 2000, see FormatsAndProviders.doc in the Appendixes folder on the companion CD-ROM.

The ADO programming model supports key features for building desktop, client/server, and Web-based applications, including the following:

- Independently created objects. Unlike DAO or Remote Data Objects (RDO), you no longer have to navigate through a hierarchy to create objects because most ADO objects can be independently created. This allows you to create and track only the objects you need, and also results in fewer ADO objects and thus a smaller memory footprint.
- Batch updating, which helps improve performance by locally caching changes to data, then writing them all to the server in a single update.

  Note Although the Microsoft Jet 4.0 OLE DB Provider supports batch updating, there is no need to use batch updating with Access databases to improve performance because the Jet database engine runs locally—you won't see a performance gain when performing batch updates against an Access database. However, you should see a performance gain when performing batch updates against a SQL Server database because SQL Server's query processor can optimize and perform multiple SQL statements in a single operation on the server without requiring additional network round-trips.
- Support for stored procedures with in/out parameters and return values against a SQL Server database.
- Different cursor types, including the potential for support of back-end–specific cursors. For information about cursor types, see "Working with Records" later in this chapter.

- Support for limits on the number of returned records and other query goals for performance tuning.

  Note The ADO **MaxRecords** property of a **Recordset** object, which is designed to limit the number of returned records, is not supported by the Microsoft Jet 4.0 OLE DB Provider or the Microsoft Access ODBC driver. However, if you require this functionality, you can use the TOP *n* predicate in a Jet SQL statement, or set the **TopValues** property of a query that is saved in an Access database.

- Support for multiple recordsets returned from stored procedures or batch statements.

  Note Multiple recordsets can be returned for SQL Server databases. Access databases can't return multiple recordsets because Jet SQL statements don't support multiple SELECT statements.

- Free-threaded objects for efficient Web server applications.

Choosing ADO or DAO for Working with Access Databases

Although ADO provides access to a broader variety of data sources than DAO, and even exposes some features of the Jet 4.0 database engine that aren't available from DAO, there are some limitations to using ADO against Access databases that require you to continue to use DAO:

- In the Access object model, the new **Recordset** property of a **Form** object can be used to request or specify a **Recordset** object for the data being browsed in a form. If you request the **Recordset** object for the current form in an Access database, Access always returns a DAO **Recordset** object. Therefore, you must continue to use DAO code to work with the **Recordset** object that is returned.
- When you use the **Recordset** property to set the **Recordset** object of a **Form** object to a **Recordset** object you created, if you set the **Form** object to an ADO **Recordset** object, the data will be read-only. If you want the data to be writable, you must set the **Form** object to a DAO **Recordset** object.
- To read and set database properties in an Access database, and to read and set certain table properties, such as the **Description** and **Filter** properties, you must continue to use DAO code.

- It's not possible to exchange information between ADO and DAO code. For example, if a DAO procedure returns a **Recordset** object, there is no way to translate or pass that DAO **Recordset** object to ADO code, and vice versa—an ADO **Recordset** object can't be read by or translated to DAO. However, this doesn't mean that ADO can't work with saved database objects, such as tables and queries, that were created with DAO, and vice versa. But it does mean that although ADO and DAO can coexist in the same project, you can't use ADO code to work with objects returned by preexisting DAO code. You must either continue to use DAO code, or rewrite those procedures by using ADO code.

For more information about working with the **Recordset** property of an Access **Form**, and working with database properties, see Chapter 5, "Working with Office Applications." For more information about working with table properties, see "Creating and Modifying Access Tables" later in this chapter.

If you are updating an existing DAO data access component, or developing new data access components that will only be working with Access databases or other data sources supported by the I-ISAM drivers of the Jet database engine, you can continue to use DAO by establishing a reference to the Microsoft DAO 3.6 object library. All DAO code written for DAO 3.5 (with the exception of code that defines user-level security for code modules in Access 2000 databases) will continue to work with DAO 3.6.

There are only a small number of Jet database engine features that require ADO: *passive shutdown*, a setting that allows you to exclude all new connections and exclude current users once they exit the database; *access to a schema rowset* that lists all the users who are currently logged into the database; and *control over page- or record-level locking*. For information about these features, see Chapter 16, "Multiuser Database Applications." If you don't require access to these Jet engine features and don't require other ADO-specific features, you can safely continue to write code that uses DAO until you encounter these requirements.

If you are creating new data access components, you should consider using ADO for its advanced features, simplified object model, and support for multiple data sources. In particular, ADO is a good choice if you are developing an Access database solution that will later be upgraded to SQL Server—you can write your ADO code to minimize the number of changes that will be required to work against a SQL Server database. In addition, ADO is a good choice for developing new data access components that work with SQL Server, multidimensional data, and Web applications.

The following table summarizes most of the functionality that is available when using Data Access Objects (DAO) and how that functionality compares to what is available in the Microsoft ActiveX Data Objects 2.1 (ADO), Microsoft ADO Extensions for DDL and Security 2.1 (ADOX), and Microsoft Jet and Replication Objects 2.1 (JRO) object models.

Note Unlike DAO, ADO and ADOX objects can perform the marked actions in databases other than Jet, as long as the providers for those databases support that action.

Functionality	DAO	ADO[1]	ADOX[2]	JRO (.mdb only)
Create **Recordset** objects	X	X		
Create new databases	X		X[3]	
Edit database properties	X			
Edit start-up properties	X	X[4]		
Create custom database properties	X			
Create tables	X		X	
Set and edit table properties	X		X[5]	
Set and edit field properties	X		X	
Create table relationships	X		X[3]	
Support for new Jet 4.0 SQL commands and syntax[6]		X	X	
Support for new Jet 4.0 **Decimal** data type			X	
Support for **Compression** attribute for field data			X	
Create and edit saved queries that are accessible only through code[6]			X[3]	
Create and edit saved queries that are accessible from both the Access Database window and code	X			
Compact/encrypt database	X			X[7]
Refresh cache	X			X[7]
Make database replicable	X			X[8]
Make database replicas	X			X[8]
Synchronize replicas	X			X[8]
Synchronize replicas with SQL Server replicas				X[8]
Support for connection control to prevent current users from reopening a shared database after they exit		X		
Retrieve a **Recordset** object that lists information about users in a shared database		X		
Programmatic control over using page- or record-level locking for **Recordset** objects and SQL DML statements		X		

[1] Uses the **Connection** object to reference to database.

[2] Uses the Catalog object to reference database.

[3] Only available when working with Access database files (.mdb). Future versions of the SQL Provider may provide this functionality when working with SQL Server views from Access project files (.adp).

[4] Only available when working with Access project files (.adp).

[5] Limited support. For more information about which table properties are supported, see "Setting Additional Table Properties" later in this chapter.

[6] The native Jet 4.0 SQL has been extended to support more ANSI 92 SQL commands and syntax. These commands and syntax are only supported when they are run from ADO code. They aren't supported by DAO or from the SQL View window in Access. However, at the time of this writing, no stored queries created with ADOX, regardless of whether they use these commands and syntax, can be viewed or run from the Access Database window. For more information, see "Creating and Modifying Stored Queries" later in this chapter.

[7] Uses the **JetEngine** object to reference database.

[8] Uses the **Replica** object to reference database.

This chapter provides an overview of ADO and focuses on using ADO to create data access components that use the Microsoft Jet 4.0 OLE DB Provider to work with Access databases, with information about when DAO is required. DAO conversion issues and coexistence techniques are covered in "Using ADO to Work with Access Databases" later in this chapter. Using ADO for multiuser database applications is covered in Chapter 16, "Multiuser Database Applications." For more information about using DAO, see Microsoft DAO 3.6 Help and the *Microsoft Jet Database Engine Programmer's Guide, Second Edition* (Microsoft Press, 1997).

ADO Basics

ADO enables you to write an application to access and manipulate data in a database server through an OLE DB data provider. ADO's primary benefits are high speed, ease of use, low memory overhead, and a small disk footprint.

ADO Component Libraries

Office 2000 installs the Microsoft Data Access Components (MDAC) version 2.1, which includes OLE DB components, a set of OLE DB providers, and six ADO components, each of which has its own set of functionality and corresponding object model. To minimize the memory use of your solution, you can reference only the ADO components your solution requires. It is beyond the scope of this chapter to discuss each of these components in detail, but the following table lists each ADO component and provides a brief description of its use.

ADO component	Description	Object library name and ProgID
Microsoft ActiveX Data Objects 2.1	The core ADO functionality that allows you to open a connection to a data source, send commands (such as SQL statements), work with records, and handle any errors returned by providers. **Note** The component file for ADO 2.1 is named Msado15.dll. By default, this file is installed in the C:\Program Files\Common Files\System\ADO subfolder. This file's name is the same as for previous versions of ADO (back to ADO 1.5) in order to retain compatibility with older solutions. If you need to manually establish a reference to the ADO 2.1 library, you must reference the Msado15.dll file. Office 2000 also installs a type library file named Msado20.tlb in the same folder, but you shouldn't manually reference this file because it is installed to maintain backward compatibility with ADO 2.0 solutions.	Microsoft ActiveX Data Objects 2.1 Library ADODB
Microsoft ActiveX Data Objects Recordset 1.5	A lightweight version of ADO that contains only the functionality of the ADO **Recordset** object. This version of ADO is typically used only from script in a Web page to minimize memory requirements.	Microsoft ActiveX Data Objects Recordset 1.5 Library ADOR
Microsoft ActiveX Data Objects Extensions for Data Definition Language and Security 2.1	Extensions to the base ADO functionality that allow you to perform data definition language (DDL) functions such as creating databases, and creating, modifying, or deleting tables, views (queries), stored procedures, indexes, and relationships. Also includes security objects to maintain security on user and group accounts, and to grant and revoke permissions on objects.	Microsoft ADO Ext. 2.1 for DDL and Security ADOX
Microsoft ActiveX Data Objects Multi-dimensional 1.0	Extends ADO to include objects specific to multidimensional data on online analytical processing (OLAP) servers, such as the OLAP extensions to SQL Server 7.0, which are named Microsoft SQL Server OLAP Services. Multidimensional data is conceptually similar to standard Excel PivotTable reports, with the option of supplying additional dimensions, using large data sets, and enabling more complete analysis. For more information about working with multidimensional data, search the ADO Help index for "Microsoft ADO MD Programmer's Reference."	Microsoft ActiveX Data Objects (Multi-dimensional) 1.0 ADOMD

ADO component	Description	Object library name and ProgID
Microsoft Remote Data Services 2.1	Primarily used in Web-based, 3-tier applications, for example, as a component running on Internet Information Server (IIS) that is accessed from Active Server Pages (ASP) script running on a Web page to retrieve or update data. For more information about the Remote Data Services component, search the ADO Help index for "Remote Data Service Developer's Guide."	Microsoft Remote Data Services 2.1 Library RDS
Microsoft Jet and Replication Objects 2.1	Extensions to ADO to perform functions specific to the Jet database engine: compacting and encrypting databases, refreshing data from the cache, and creating and maintaining replicated databases.	Microsoft Jet and Replication Objects 2.1 Library JRO

Note For detailed information about each of these ADO components, see ADO Help. You can view ADO Help from the Visual Basic Editor by searching for ADO keywords. In all Office applications that support the Visual Basic Editor, you can view ADO Help for collections, properties, methods, and events, but not all objects, by clicking an ADO keyword in your code and pressing F1, or by highlighting an ADO class or member in the Object Browser and pressing F1. Even if the message "Keyword Not Found" or "No Help Available" is displayed when you press F1 to display Help for some objects, you can still get help by searching ADO Help.

To view ADO conceptual and tutorial topics, after displaying a topic, click the **Show** button to display the contents for ADO Help; however, authored index entries for ADO Help aren't available when you browse Help from within Office applications. To display ADO Help in the stand-alone HTML Help viewer, which includes access to authored index entries from the **Index** tab, open the Ado210.chm file directly from the C:\Program Files\Common Files\System\ADO folder.

When you create a new Access database file (.mdb) or Access project file (.adp), the only reference that is automatically established when you create new modules or code behind forms and reports is to the Microsoft ActiveX Data Objects 2.1 object library. If you want to use the Microsoft ActiveX Data Objects 2.1 object library from other Office applications, or use any other ADO component libraries from other Office applications, you use the **References** command (**Tools** menu) to establish a reference manually.

When you use any ADO component from VBScript or JScript, you also need to use the ***#include*** statement to specify an additional file in your source code to provide the constants that define the enumerations used by ADO. For VBScript, specify the adovbs.inc file; for Jscript, specify the adojavas.inc file. By default, both of these files are installed in the C:\Program Files\Common Files\System\ADO folder. For information about using scripting in Office 2000 applications, see Chapter 12, "Using Web Technologies."

The following sections provide an overview of the base ADO 2.1 and ADO 2.1 Extensibility objects and an introduction to working with them.

ADO Objects

Although ADO objects can be created outside the scope of a hierarchy, the objects exist within hierarchical relationships, as shown in the Microsoft ActiveX Data Objects 2.1 Object Model in the "Object Model Diagrams" appendix.

The four primary ADO objects—the **Connection**, **Command**, **Recordset**, and **Field** objects—each has a **Properties** collection that is used to expose *dynamic properties* or *provider-specific properties* on these objects. Properties in these collections are required for provider-specific settings that aren't available through standard ADO properties and methods. For more information about provider-specific properties, see "Provider-Specific Properties Collections" later in this chapter.

The following sections provide a brief overview of these objects; each one is discussed in greater detail later in this chapter or in other chapters.

The Connection Object

The **Connection** object is the top-level object in the ADO hierarchy. It represents the connection made to the data source through the OLE DB data provider, and handles all communication between your solution and a data source. Unlike the **Connection** object in DAO's ODBCDirect or in Remote Data Objects (RDO), you don't have to instantiate an ADO **Connection** object before you create other objects such as the **Command** or **Recordset** object. This lets you create temporary objects and associate them with a **Connection** object as needed.

You open and close a **Connection** object by using the **Open** and **Close** methods. Additionally, **Connection** objects provide transaction support by using the **BeginTrans**, **CommitTrans**, and **RollbackTrans** methods. Use transactions when you want to save or cancel a series of changes made to the source data as a single unit. For example, if you are transferring money between two accounts, you want to make sure that both debiting and crediting operations occur. By making these changes within a transaction, you ensure that either all or none of the changes go through. This chapter discusses opening and working with **Connection** objects; however, working with transactions is discussed in Chapter 16, "Multiuser Database Applications."

The Command Object

The **Command** object represents an SQL statement, stored procedure, or any other command that can be processed by the data source. The **Command** object is similar to a DAO temporary **QueryDef** object, including a **Parameters** collection that can accept input and output parameters. You can execute a command string on a **Connection** object (by using the **Execute** method) or pass a query string as part of opening a **Recordset** object (as the **Source** property), without explicitly creating a **Command** object. The **Command** object is most useful when you want to define query parameters, or execute a stored procedure that returns output parameters. You can also use a **Command** object in conjunction with the ADO **Views** and **Procedures** collections to store queries in your database. For information about using the **Command** object to work with stored queries, see "Creating and Modifying Stored Queries" later in this chapter. For information about using the **Command** object to open a parameter query, see "Opening a Query That Has Parameters" later in this chapter.

The Recordset Object

The **Recordset** object represents a set of records returned from a query, and a cursor into those records. You can open a **Recordset** object without explicitly opening a **Connection** object by passing a connection string to the **Recordset** object's **Open** method. However, if you create and open a **Connection** object, you can open multiple **Recordset** objects on the same connection. The **Recordset** object contains a **Fields** collection that contains **Field** objects, each of which represents a single column of data within a **Recordset** object. For information about using the **Recordset** object, see "Working with Records" later in this chapter.

The Error Object

The **Error** object contains extended error information about an error condition raised by the OLE DB provider. Because a single statement can generate one or more errors, the **Errors** collection can contain more than one **Error** object at a time, and all of them can result from the same incident. For information about using the ADO **Error** object, see "The ADO Error Object and Errors Collection" in Chapter 8, "Error Handling and Debugging."

Note Jet database engine error numbers aren't returned by the **Number** property of either the VBA **Err** object or the ADO **Error** object. To retrieve Jet error numbers from ADO, you must use the **SQLState** property of the ADO **Error** object instead.

Provider-Specific Properties Collections

The ADODB **Connection**, **Command**, **Recordset**, and **Field** objects, and the **Parameters** collection each include a **Properties** collection. Additionally, the ADOX **Table**, **Column**, and **Index** objects also have **Properties** collections. Each object or collection's **Properties** collection exposes both standard ADO properties and properties that are specific to the provider. The ADO **Properties** collections provide an extensibility mechanism that allows an OLE DB provider to expose additional properties that are not defined by ADO itself. The properties in an ADO **Properties** collection are often referred to as *dynamic properties* because they can change depending on the state or functionality of the object they are associated with.

Some provider-specific properties are used to set or read properties that may be required to work with the particular data source exposed by the provider. For example, to access a secured Access database, you may be required to specify the workgroup information file that contains the security accounts used for that database. Because ADO has no built-in property for this purpose, when you open a **Connection** object by using the Microsoft Jet 4.0 OLE DB Provider, the **Properties** collection exposes a **Jet OLE DB:System Database** property that you can use to specify the workgroup information file. You can also use some properties in an ADO object's **Properties** collection to determine whether the current object supports an ADO feature (for example, to determine whether a **Recordset** object supports transactions or updating).

You access properties in the **Properties** collection as you do most VBA collections: by using the **Item** method to reference the property by its ordinal position in the collection,

```
Connection.Properties.Item(0)
```

or by specifying its name:

```
Connection.Properties.Item("Jet OLE DB:System Database") = _
   "\\MyComputer\MyShare\MySystem.mdw"
```

Because the **Item** method is the default method of an ADO collection, you can omit it as shown in the following functionally equivalent code fragments:

```
Connection.Properties(0)

Connection.Properties("Jet OLE DB:System Database") = _
   "\\MyComputer\MyShare\MySystem.mdw"
```

Further, the accessor property to the **Properties** collection itself is the default property for the **Connection**, **Command**, and **Recordset** objects, so you can omit it as well:

```
Connection(0)

Connection("Jet OLE DB:System Database") = _
   "\\MyComputer\MyShare\MySystem.mdw"
```

However, for clarity's sake, the sample code in this chapter includes the name of the **Properties** collection to make it obvious when a provider-specific property is being set or read.

You can examine the entire contents of a **Properties** collection by looping through it with a **For Each...Next** loop. The following sample procedure shows how to print the contents of the **Properties** collection for the **Connection** to the current database. This code sample uses the **Connection** property of the **CurrentProject** object to return a **Connection** object for the current database, which will work only when this code is running within an Access database. For more information about the **Connection** property of the **CurrentProject** object, see "Connecting to the Current Access Database by Using ADO" later in this chapter.

```
Sub PrintConnectionProperties()
   Dim cnnDb   As ADODB.Connection
   Dim prpProp As ADODB.Property

   ' Use connection to the current database.
   Set cnnDB = CurrentProject.Connection

   For Each prpProp in cnnDB.Properties
      Debug.Print prpProp.Name & "=" & prpProp.Value
   Next

   Set cnnDB = Nothing
End Sub
```

The PrintConnectionProperties procedure can be found in the PrintProperties module of the DataAccess.mdb sample file, which is available in the Samples\CH14 subfolder on the companion CD-ROM.

The values of the properties in an ADO **Properties** collection are dynamic—that is, they will be different before and after the parent object is opened, and they depend on how the object is opened or initialized. For example, the values of properties in a **Recordset** object's **Properties** collection differ depending on the arguments passed to its **Open** method.

In most cases, properties in an ADO **Properties** collection become read-only after the parent object is opened. For this reason, if you need to set a provider-specific property, typically your code should set the property's value before it opens the parent object. For example, when it is running against the Microsoft Jet provider, the **Properties** collection of the **Connection** object provides a **Jet OLEDB:System database** property that can be used to specify the workgroup information file (system database), which defines the user and group accounts to use when you are working with an Access database that has been secured with user-level security. This property can only be set before you use the **Open** method to open the **Connection** object. After a **Connection** object is open, the **Jet OLEDB:System database** property becomes read-only. All properties in an ADO **Properties** collection can be referenced by name, as shown in the following code fragment, which sets the **Jet OLEDB:System database** property in a **Connection** object before it opens a database.

```
Dim cnn As ADODB.Connection
Set cnn = New ADODB.Connection

With cnn
   .Provider = "Microsoft.Jet.OLEDB.4.0"
   ' Set path to workgroup information file.
   .Properties("Jet OLE DB:System Database") = _
      "\\MyComputer\MyShare\MySystem.mdw"
   .Open "\\MyComputer\MyShare\MyDatabase.mdb"
End With
```

For more information about properties specific to the Microsoft Jet 4.0 OLE DB Provider, see ADOProperties.doc in the Appendixes folder on the companion CD-ROM.

Using ADO Connection Strings

When you use ADO, you can often specify property settings several different ways: by setting built-in properties and arguments, by setting properties that use an object's **Properties** collection, or by passing in the value as part of a *connection string*. The basic format of a connection string is a series of keyword and value pairs separated by semicolons. The keyword is separated from the value by an equals sign (=), as shown in the following format:

keyword1=value;keyword2=value;keyword3=value

The values passed for connection string keywords must be formatted as strings and can contain spaces within the value. For example, the following is a valid keyword and value pair:

```
Jet OLE DB:Database Password=My Password
```

However, if the value contains single-quote ('), double-quote ("), or semicolon (;) characters, the value must be surrounded with either double quote or single quote characters, as shown in the following example for the password **My's Password**:

```
Jet OLE DB:Database Password="My's Password"
```

If the value contains both single- and double-quote characters, the quote character used to surround the entire value must be doubled each time it occurs within the value string, as shown in the following example for the password **My's"Password**:

```
Jet OLE DB:Database Password="My's""Password"
```

The following code fragment shows a specific example that passes a connection string to the ***ConnectionString*** argument of the **Open** method of the **Connection** object to specify the OLE DB provider to use, the database to open, and the workgroup information file (system database) to use for security accounts:

```
cnnDB.Open "Provider=Microsoft.Jet.OLEDB.4.0;Data Source=C:\MyDb.mdb;" & _
   "Jet OLE DB:System Database=C:\MySystemDB.mdw"
```

You can also set the same properties and values from the previous example by using the ADO **Provider** property and **Properties** collection, as shown in the following code fragment:

```
With cnnDB
   .Provider = "Microsoft.Jet.OLEDB.4.0"
   .Properties("Jet OLE DB:System Database") = "C:\MySystemDB.mdw"
   .Open "C:\MyDb.mdb"
End With
```

Each method has equivalent results, so you can use whatever method you prefer. Most of the code examples in this chapter use the latter method to avoid formatting problems with long connection strings and to make it easier to see which properties are being set. However, some ADO component object models, such as the Microsoft ActiveX Data Objects Extensions for DDL and Security 2.1 (ADOX) and the Microsoft Jet and Replication Objects 2.1 (JRO) object libraries, require you to use connection strings to set certain properties. For example, ADOX doesn't have a **Provider** property, so if you aren't working with a **Connection** object that was previously opened by using ADO 2.1, you must specify the provider by using the `Provider=` keyword in a connection string. Similarly, the JRO **CompactDatabase** method requires you to pass connection strings for its ***SourceConnection*** and ***DestConnection*** arguments.

Using ADO to Work with Access Databases

This section covers how to use ADO to perform some of the more common data access programming tasks for Access databases. Because the DAO programming model has been used for many years to work with Access databases and is familiar to many Office developers, this section describes the mapping between many DAO objects, properties, and methods and those in ADO. It also highlights areas where there are differences between apparently similar methods or properties. It is beyond the scope of this chapter to provide in-depth detail on particular ADO and DAO objects, properties, or methods. Refer to the online documentation provided with DAO and ADO for specific details.

There are three distinct ADO object models that together provide the functionality found in DAO. These three models are known as:

- Microsoft ActiveX Data Objects 2.1 (ADODB)
- Microsoft ActiveX Data Objects Extensions for DDL and Security 2.1 (ADOX)
- Microsoft Jet and Replication Objects 2.1 (JRO)

ADO functionality was divided among these three models because there are many applications that will need only a subset of the full set of functionality. By selecting only the object models required for a given task, you are only required to load into memory the objects necessary for that task.

Each of these three ADO object models corresponds to the following sets of functionality.

- **Data Manipulation** The Microsoft ActiveX Data Objects 2.1 (ADODB) object model enables your client applications to access and manipulate data in a database server through any OLE DB provider. In particular, to work with Access databases (.mdb files), you should use the Microsoft Jet 4.0 OLE DB Provider.

- **Data Definition and Security** The ADO Extensions for DDL and Security 2.1 (ADOX) object model contains objects, properties, and methods for creating and modifying the structure of databases, tables, and queries. ADOX also lets you create and modify user and group accounts for databases secured with user-level security, and grant and revoke permissions on objects. The ADOX object model is designed to work with any OLE DB provider that supports its interfaces. At the time of this writing, you can use ADOX for data definition in both Access and SQL Server databases; however, you can use ADOX to work with security only in Access databases. This chapter discusses the Data Definition Language (DDL) features of ADOX. For information about the security features of ADOX, see Chapter 18, "Securing Access Databases."

  The top-level object in the ADOX object model is the **Catalog** object. It provides access to the **Tables**, **Views**, and **Procedures** collections, which are used to work with the structure of the database, and also provides the **Users** and **Groups** collections, which are used to work with security. Each **Catalog** object is associated with only one **Connection** to an underlying data source.

  The ADOX model differs somewhat from the DAO model. DAO has a **Workspace** object that defines a session for a user but does not define the data source. The DAO **Workspace** object is also the container for the **Users** and **Groups** collections that are needed to work with security accounts. In DAO, a **Workspace** may be created and security information may be retrieved or modified without opening a database. When you work with the ADOX **Catalog** object, you must specify a connection to a database before you have access to security information.

- **Replication and Jet Engine Services** The Microsoft Jet and Replication Objects 2.1 (JRO) object model contains objects, properties, and methods that let you create, modify, and synchronize replicas. It is designed specifically for use with the Microsoft Jet 4.0 OLE DB Provider. Unlike ADO and ADOX, JRO can't be used with data sources other than Access databases.

  The top-level object in the JRO object model is the **Replica** object. The **Replica** object is used to create new replicas, retrieve and modify properties of an existing replica, and to synchronize changes with other replicas. This differs from DAO, where the **Database** object is used for these tasks.

  The JRO object model also contains the freestanding **JetEngine** object, which provides access to two Jet database engine-specific features: compacting databases and refreshing data from the cache for connections to any kind of Access database.

  This chapter discusses only some of the features of the **JetEngine** object. For information about the replication features of JRO, see Chapter 16, "Multiuser Database Applications."

Referencing ADO Object Libraries

In general, for all VBA code, you should qualify object names by preceding them with the object library's ProgID to correctly resolve references to identically named objects in two or more referenced object libraries. If you include references to both ADO and DAO object libraries in your VBA project, it is absolutely necessary to qualify object names. This is because DAO and ADO include several objects with the same names. For example, both models include a **Recordset** object, so if you are using both DAO and ADO references, the following code is ambiguous:

```
Dim rstCustomers As Recordset object
```

To specify which object library you want to use, include the object library's ProgID in front of the object name:

```
Dim rstADO As ADODB.Recordset
Dim rstDAO As DAO.Recordset
```

If the ProgID qualifier is omitted, VBA will use the object from the first object library in the **References** dialog box list, and your code may not function properly.

Microsoft Jet 4.0 OLE DB Provider Property Values

The Microsoft Jet 4.0 OLE DB Provider defines a number of property values for provider-specific features. Because they are provider-specific values, ADO does not expose them via its built-in enumeration values or constants. To make it easier to work with these values in a VBA development environment, you can define global constants or VBA **Enum** statements for these values. Many of the following sections contain tables of values for properties specific to the Microsoft Jet 4.0 OLE DB Provider that you can set when you work with or create ADO objects. For an example of code that uses this technique, see the GetJetConnection procedure in "Opening an Access Database by Using ADO" later in this chapter.

Opening an Access Database by Using ADO

To open an Access database by using ADO, you use the **Connection** object. Because you need to use the Jet database engine to open an Access database, you must set the **Provider** property to specify that ADO use the Microsoft Jet 4.0 OLE DB provider before it opens the **Connection** object. By default, the Microsoft Jet 4.0 OLE DB Provider opens a connection to a database in shared-access mode (**Mode = adModeShareDenyNone**). The following procedure establishes a connection to the database specified by the ***strDBPath*** argument in shared-access mode.

```
Sub OpenDBShared (strDBPath As String)
   Dim cnnDB As ADODB.Connection

   ' Initialize Connection object
   Set cnnDB = New ADODB.Connection
   ' Specify Microsoft Jet 4.0 Provider and then open the
   ' database specified in the strDBPath variable.
   With cnnDB
      .Provider = "Microsoft.Jet.OLEDB.4.0"
      .Open strDBPath
      ' Code to work with database goes here.
   End With

   ' Close Connection object and destroy object variable.
   cnnDB.close
   Set cnnDB = Nothing
End Sub
```

Note Prior to ADO 2.0 (which was released with Microsoft Visual Studio® 6.0 and on the Web as part of MDAC 2.0), there was no Microsoft Jet OLE DB Provider. All code written to work against ADO 1.5 used the Microsoft OLE DB Provider for ODBC (which is used by default in ADO) and the Microsoft Access ODBC driver. For this reason, you may see code such as the following code fragment used to open an Access database:

```
Set cnn = New ADODB.Connection
strCnn = "driver={Microsoft Access Driver (*.mdb)};dbq=c:\Nwind.mdb"
cnn.Open strCnn
```

Although code that specifies the Microsoft OLE DB Provider for ODBC and the Microsoft Access ODBC driver will continue to work under ADO 2.1, there is no reason to continue to use this method of opening an Access database. The Microsoft Jet 4.0 OLE DB Provider exposes more functionality of the Jet Database engine, and provides better performance than do the Microsoft OLE DB Provider for ODBC and the Microsoft Access ODBC driver.

By default, both DAO and ADO using the Jet OLE DB provider open a database for shared, updatable access. However, there may be times when you want to open the database exclusively or in read-only mode. To do this, you need to explicitly specify the mode used to open the database with the **Mode** property of the **Connection** object before you open it. The following code fragment shows how to open a database in shared, read-only mode by using ADO.

```
Set cnnDB = New ADODB.Connection
With cnnDB
   .Provider = "Microsoft.Jet.OLEDB.4.0"
   .Mode = adModeRead
   .Open strDBPath
End With
```

There are a number of Microsoft Jet 4.0 OLE DB Provider-specific properties that you may want or need to set when you open an Access database. For example, if the database is secured by using a database password, you need to use the **Jet OLEDB:Database Password** property to specify the password used to open the database. The following code fragment shows how to specify a password by using the **Properties** collection of the **Connection** object.

```
cnnDB.Properties("Jet OLEDB:Database Password") = "OpenSesame"
```

The following table lists a few of the provider-specific initialization properties that you can set by using the **Properties** collection of the **Connection** object or the ***ConnectionString*** argument of the **Open** method when you use the Microsoft Jet 4.0 OLE DB Provider.

Property	Description
Jet OLEDB:Registry Path	The path to the registry subkey to use for Jet database engine settings. This value can be changed to a secondary location to store registry values for a particular application that are not shared with other applications that use Jet on the machine. Don't include HKEY_LOCAL_MACHINE as part of this subkey. For example, the setting for the default location for Access 2000 is: SOFTWARE\Microsoft\Office\9.0\Access\Jet\4.0\Engines
Jet OLEDB:System database	The location of the Jet workgroup information file (system database) to use for authenticating users who open a database secured by using user-level security. Setting this property overrides the value set in the registry or the corresponding **SystemDB** value entry if the **Jet OLEDB:Registry Path** property is used. This setting can include the path to the file.
Jet OLEDB:Database Password	The password used to open the database when the database has a database password set. Note that this is not the same as the ***Password*** argument of the **Open** method, which is used in conjunction with the ***UserID*** argument to specify the user account and password to open a database secured by using user-level security.
Jet OLEDB:Engine Type	A **Long** value (Read/Write) that specifies which Jet database engine I-ISAM driver to use to access this database or file format. When you create a new database by using the **Create** method of the ADOX **Catalog** object, this value can be used to specify the format for the new database. Once a database has been opened, this property can be read to determine what file version or format is open. For a list of all engine types, see ADOProperties.doc in the Appendixes folder on the companion CD-ROM.

For a complete list of initialization properties, see ADOProperties.doc in the Appendixes folder on the companion CD-ROM. In addition to initialization properties, the Microsoft Jet provider exposes settings called *session properties* that can be used to optimize the performance of the Microsoft Jet database engine. For information about session properties, see "Provider-Specific ADO Connection Object Session Properties" in ADOProperties.doc in the Appendixes folder on the companion CD-ROM.

The following sample procedure specifies the **Mode** property by using the built-in ADO **ConnectModeEnum** enumeration, and provides several optional arguments to specify database password, workgroup information file (system database), user ID, user password, and the engine type (which is specified with the user-defined `opgJetEngineType` enumeration in the JetOLEDBConstants module) when you create a **Connection** object to open an Access database.

```
Function GetJetConnection(strPath As String, _
                          lngMode As ADODB.ConnectModeEnum, _
                          Optional strDBPwd As String, _
                          Optional strSysDBPath As String, _
                          Optional strUserID As String, _
                          Optional strUserPwd As String _
                          Optional lngEngineType As opgJetEngineType) _
                          As ADODB.Connection
   Dim cnnDB As ADODB.Connection

   Set cnnDB = New ADODB.Connection
   With cnnDB
      .Provider = "Microsoft.Jet.OLEDB.4.0"
      .Mode = lngMode
      .Properties("Jet OLEDB:Database Password") = strDBPwd
      .Properties("Jet OLEDDB:System Database") = strSysDBPwd
      .Properties("Jet OLEDDB:Engine Type") = lngEngineType
      .Open ConnectionString:=strPath, _
            UserID:=strUserID, _
            Password:=strUserPwd
   End With

   Set GetJetConnection = cnnDB
End Function
```

The GetJetConnection procedure can be found in the OpenDatabase module of the DataAccess.mdb sample file, which is available in the Samples\CH14 subfolder on the companion CD-ROM.

Connecting to a Database by Using a Data Link File

You can also save OLE DB connection information to a *data link* file and use that file to open a data source. A data link file is similar to a File DSN (data source name) that is created by using the ODBC Data Source Administrator, except that a data link defines OLE DB connection information, instead of ODBC connection information. To create a data link file, right-click in a folder, and then click **Microsoft Data Link** on the **New** submenu. Double-click the file to display the **Data Link Properties** dialog box, click the **Provider** tab, and then select **Microsoft Jet 4.0 OLE DB Provider**. Click the **Connection** tab to define basic connection information, and use the **Advanced** or **All** tab if you want to define additional settings.

To use the **Open** method of the **Connection** object to a database by using a data link file, pass the location of the data link file in the **File Name** property to the ***ConnectionString*** argument as shown in the following line of code:

```
cnnDB.Open "File Name=C:\DataLinks\MyDataLink.udl"
```

Connecting to the Current Access Database by Using ADO

When you open an Access database by using the Access user interface, Access 2000 automatically establishes an ADO **Connection** object for you. To work with the current database by using ADO code that is running in the current database, you use the **Connection** property of the Access **CurrentProject** object. The following code sample shows how to access the **Connection** object for the current database and print its connection string to the Immediate pane.

```
Sub PrintCurrentConnectString()
   Dim cnnDB As ADODB.Connection

   ' Get connection to current database.
   Set cnnDB = CurrentProject.Connection
   Debug.Print cnnDB.ConnectionString
   Set cnnDB = Nothing
End Sub
```

The PrintCurrentConnectString procedure can be found in the OpenDatabase module in the DataAccess.mdb sample file, which is available in the Samples\CH14 subfolder on the companion CD-ROM.

By using this same technique, you can set a **Connection** object to **CurrentProject.Connection** and then pass that **Connection** to other ADO objects to open them. For example, you can pass a **Connection** object as the ***ActiveConnection*** argument of the **Open** method of a **Recordset** object to open that **Recordset** object by using a connection to the current database. As an example of this technique, the following code fragment opens a **Recordset** object on a table in the current database by using the current connection.

```
Set cnn = CurrentProject.Connection

Set rst = New ADODB.Recordset
With rst
' Open table-type Recordset object.
.Open Source:=strTblName, _
      ActiveConnection:=cnn, _
      CursorType:=adOpenKeyset, _
      LockType:=adLockOptimistic, _
      Options:adCmdTableDirect
' Code to work with Recordset object goes here.
End With
```

Note If you use the **CurrentProject.Connection** setting in an Access project file (.adp), it always returns a connection that uses the MSDataShape OLE DB provider. The MSDataShape OLE DB provider behaves differently than does a direct connection through the Microsoft OLE DB Provider for SQL Server. For more information about these differences, see "Using the Connection Property of the CurrentProject Object in an Access Project" in Chapter 16, "Multiuser Database Applications."

Opening Other Database File Formats by Using the Microsoft Jet 4.0 OLE DB Provider

The Microsoft Jet database engine can be used to access data in other database file formats, data in Excel and Lotus spreadsheets, and textual data stored in tabular format through installable ISAM drivers. In order to open external formats supported by the Jet database engine by using ADO and the Microsoft Jet 4.0 OLE DB Provider, you specify the database type by using the **Extended Properties** property of the **Connection** object. The following procedure shows how to open a Microsoft Excel 97 or 2000 spreadsheet.

```
Sub OpenExcelDatabase(strDBPath As String)
   Dim cnnDB As ADODB.Connection

   Set cnnDB = New ADODB.Connection

   ' Specify Excel 8.0 by using the Extended Properties
   ' property, and then open the Excel file specified by
   ' strDBPath.
   With cnnDB
   .Provider = "Microsoft.Jet.OLEDB.4.0"
   .Properties("Extended Properties") = "Excel 8.0"
   .Open strDBPath
    Debug.Print .ConnectionString
    .Close
   End With
   Set cnnDB = Nothing
End Sub
```

The OpenExcelDatabase procedure can be found in the OpenDatabase module of the DataAccess.mdb sample file, which is available in the Samples\CH14 subfolder on the companion CD-ROM.

For a list of **Extended Properties** property settings for all database types supported by the Microsoft Jet 4.0 database engine, see "Extended Properties Property Settings" in ADOProperties.doc in the Appendixes folder on the companion CD-ROM.

Creating, Modifying, and Viewing the Structure of an Access Database by Using ADO

The ADO Extensions for DDL and Security (ADOX) object model contains objects, properties, and methods for creating, modifying, and viewing the structure of databases, tables, and queries. ADOX has been written to work with any OLE DB provider that supports its interfaces. The following sections describe how to use ADOX to create and modify Access databases, tables, and queries.

Creating an Access Database

To create a database by using ADOX, you use the **Create** method of the **Catalog** object. The following code example creates a new Access database.

```
Sub CreateAccessDatabase(strDBPath As String)
   Dim catNewDB As ADOX.Catalog
   Set catNewDB = New ADOX.Catalog

   catNewDB.Create "Provider=Microsoft.Jet.OLEDB.4.0;" & _
                   "Data Source=" & strDBPath

   Set catNewDB = Nothing
End Sub
```

The CreateAccessDatabase procedure can be found in the CreateDatabase module in the DataAccess.mdb sample file, which is available in the Samples\CH14 subfolder on the companion CD-ROM.

When you use the DAO **CreateDatabase** method to create a database, the ***Locale*** argument is used to specify the database's *collating order,* which is the character set that will be used to determine how values in the database are sorted. To create a database that supports sorting for English, German, French, Portuguese, Italian, and Modern Spanish, the DAO **CreateDatabase** method uses the **dbLangGeneral** setting. In the previous ADOX code sample, the collating order is not explicitly specified. The default collating order for the Microsoft Jet 4.0 OLE DB Provider is equivalent to the DAO **dbLangGeneral** setting. To specify different collating orders when you use ADOX to create a database, set the ADO **Locale Identifier** property in the ***ConnectString*** argument of the **Create** method. For example, the following code fragment sets the **Local Identifier** property to 1036, which creates a database that uses the French language collating order.

```
catNewDB.Create "Provider=Microsoft.Jet.OLEDB.4.0;" & _
                "Locale Identifier=1036;" & _
                "Data Source=" & strDBPath
```

For information about the values you can use for the **Locale Identifier** property, see "Locale Identifier Property Settings" in ADOProperties.doc in the Appendixes folder on the companion CD-ROM.

Listing the Tables in an Access Database

In ADOX, the **Table** object represents a table and the **Tables** collection provides access to information about all tables in the database. You can use the **Tables** collection to list all tables within a database. However, the **Tables** collection may also contain **Table** objects that aren't actual tables in your Access database. For example, a query that returns records but doesn't have parameters (what is known as a *select query* in Access) is considered a **View** object in ADOX, and is also included in the **Tables** collection. The ADOX **Tables** collection also includes linked tables and system tables. You can distinguish between different kinds of **Table** objects by using the **Type** property. The following table lists the possible string values returned for the **Type** property when you use ADO with the Microsoft Jet 4.0 OLE DB Provider.

Type	Description
ACCESS TABLE	The table is an Access system table.
LINK	The table is a linked table from a non-ODBC data source.
PASS-THROUGH	The table is a linked table from an ODBC data source.
SYSTEM TABLE	The table is a Microsoft Jet system table.
TABLE	The table is a standard table.
VIEW	The table is a query that has no parameters and returns records.

The following procedure shows how to print the names of all tables in the database.

```
Sub ListAccessTables(strDBPath As String)
   Dim catDB   As ADOX.Catalog
   Dim tblList As ADOX.Table

   Set catDB = New ADOX.Catalog
   ' Open the catalog.
   cat.ActiveConnection = "Provider=Microsoft.Jet.OLEDB.4.0;" & _
                          "Data Source=" & strDBPath

   ' Loop through all the tables, but not queries,
   ' and print their names and types.
   For Each tblList In catDB.Tables
      If tblList.Type <> "VIEW" Then
         Debug.Print tblList.Name & vbTab & tblList.Type
      End If
   Next

   Set catDB = Nothing
End Sub
```

Alternatively, you can use the ADO **OpenSchema** method to return a **Recordset** object that contains information about the tables in the database. When you use this method, you can restrict the list of tables returned on the basis of **Type** as well as **Name** properties. In general, it is faster to use the **OpenSchema** method rather than loop through the ADOX **Tables** collection, because ADOX must incur the overhead of creating objects for each element in the collection. The following procedure shows how to use the **OpenSchema** method to print the same information as the previous ADOX example.

```
Sub ListAccessTables2(strDBPath)
   Dim cnnDB   As ADODB.Connection
   Dim rstList As ADODB.Recordset

   Set cnnDB = New ADODB.Connection

   ' Open the connection.
   With cnnDB
      .Provider = "Microsoft.Jet.OLEDB.4.0"
      .Open strDBPath
   End With

   ' Open the tables schema rowset.
   Set rstList = cnnDB.OpenSchema(adSchemaTables)

   ' Loop through the results and print the
   ' names and types in the Immediate pane.
   With rstList
      Do While Not .EOF
         If .Fields("TABLE_TYPE") <> "VIEW" Then
            Debug.Print .Fields("TABLE_NAME") & vbTab & _
               .Fields("TABLE_TYPE")
         End If
         .MoveNext
      Loop
   End With
   cnnDB.Close
   Set cnnDB = Nothing
End Sub
```

The ListAccessTables and ListAccessTables2 procedures can be found in the CreateDatabase module in the DataAccess.mdb sample file, which is available in the Samples\CH14 subfolder on the companion CD-ROM.

Creating and Modifying Access Tables

You can view, create, and modify the structure of Access databases by using ADOX objects, methods, and properties. The following sections provide details on how to do this.

Tip You can use a transaction to “wrap” a set of changes you make to the structure of a database; by using the transaction as a wrapper around the changes, you ensure that all work is performed as a single unit. For information about how to use transactions, see “Using Transactions” in Chapter 16, “Multiuser Database Applications.”

Creating a Table

To create a table by using ADOX, follow these steps:

1. Open a **Catalog** object on the database you want to add a table to.
2. Create a new **Table** object.
3. Use the **Append** method of the **Columns** collection to add the field definitions (**Column** objects) to the **Columns** collection of the new **Table** object.
4. Append the new **Table** object to the **Tables** collection of the **Catalog** object.

It is not necessary to use the **Create** method to create **Column** objects for the field definitions before you append them to the **Columns** collection. The **Append** method can be used to both create and append the **Column** object. The following procedure creates a table named Contacts by using ADOX.

```
Sub CreateAccessTable(strDBPath As String)
   Dim catDB  As ADOX.Catalog
   Dim tblNew As ADOX.Table

   Set catDB = New ADOX.Catalog
   ' Open the catalog.
   catDB.ActiveConnection = "Provider=Microsoft.Jet.OLEDB.4.0;" & _
      "Data Source=" & strDBPath

   Set tblNew = New ADOX.Table
   ' Create a new Table object.
   With tblNew
      .Name = "Contacts"
      ' Create fields and append them to the
      ' Columns collection of the new Table object.
      With .Columns
         .Append "FirstName", adVarWChar
         .Append "LastName", adVarWChar
         .Append "Phone", adVarWChar
         .Append "Notes", adLongVarWChar
      End With
   End With

   ' Add the new Table to the Tables collection of the database.
   catDB.Tables.Append tblNew

   Set catDB = Nothing
End Sub
```

The CreateAccessTable procedure can be found in the CreateDatabase module in the DataAccess.mdb sample file, which is available in the Samples\CH14 subfolder on the companion CD-ROM.

The data type names for DAO fields are different from ADOX names. The following table shows how the data types in the Access user interface and DAO map to the ADOX data types.

Access user interface data type	DAO data type	ADOX data type
Yes/No	**dbBoolean**	**adBoolean**
Number (FieldSize = Byte)	**dbByte**	**adUnsignedTinyInt**
Currency	**dbCurrency**	**adCurrency**
Data/Time	**dbDate**	**adDate**
Number (FieldSize = Decimal)	**dbDecimal**	**adDecimal**
Number (FieldSize = Double)	**dbDouble**	**adDouble**
Number or **AutoNumber** (FieldSize = Replication ID)	**dbGUID**	**adGUID**
Number (FieldSize = Integer)	**dbInteger**	**adSmallInt**
Number or **AutoNumber** (FieldSize = LongInteger)	**dbLong**	**adInteger**
OLE Object	**dbLongBinary**	**adLongVarBinary**
Memo	**dbMemo**	**adLongVarWChar**
Number (FieldSize = Single)	**dbSingle**	**adSingle**
Text	**dbText**	**adVarWChar**
Hyperlink	**dbMemo**, plus DAO **Attributes** property set to **dbHyperlinkField**	**adLongVarWChar**, plus ADOX provider-specific **Column** property set to **Jet OLEDB:Hyperlink**

Setting Additional Field Attributes and Properties

In addition to specifying the data type for a field, you may also wish to specify other attributes of a field, such as whether the field is auto-incrementing (the **AutoNumber** data type in the Access user interface) or will be used to store active hyperlinks (the **Hyperlink** data type in the Access user interface). When you create an auto-incrementing or hyperlink field by using DAO, you add the appropriate constant to the field's **Attributes** property. To create the same fields in ADOX, you set the appropriate property in the **Properties** collection of the **Column** object that is used to create the field. The following code shows how to create an auto-incrementing field with ADOX, by setting the field's **AutoIncrement** property to **True**.

```
Sub CreateAutoNumberField(strDBPath As String)
   Dim catDB As ADOX.Catalog
   Dim tbl   As ADOX.Table

   Set catDB = New ADOX.Catalog
   ' Open the catalog.
   catDB.ActiveConnection = "Provider=Microsoft.Jet.OLEDB.4.0;" & _
      "Data Source=" & strDBPath

   Set tbl = New ADOX.Table
   With tbl
      .Name = "Contacts"
      Set .ParentCatalog = catDB
      ' Create fields and append them to the
      ' Columns collection of the new Table object.
```

```
        With .Columns
            .Append "ContactId", adInteger
            ' Make the ContactId field auto-incrementing.
            .Item("ContactId").Properties("AutoIncrement") = True
            .Append "CustomerID", adVarWChar
            .Append "FirstName", adVarWChar
            .Append "LastName", adVarWChar
            .Append "Phone", adVarWChar, 20
            .Append "Notes", adLongVarWChar
        End With
    End With

    ' Add the new Table to the Tables collection of the database.
    catDB.Tables.Append tbl

    Set catDB = Nothing
End Sub
```

The CreateAutoNumberField procedure can be found in the CreateDatabase module in the DataAccess.mdb sample file, which is available in the Samples\CH14 subfolder on the companion CD-ROM.

The following table maps DAO **Attributes** property constants for fields to ADO provider-specific **Column** properties for auto-incrementing fields, as well as others.

Access user interface data type	DAO Attributes property constant	ADOX provider-specific Column property
AutoNumber	**dbAutoIncrField**	**AutoIncrement** Set to **True**
Default for **Numeric** fields; not available from the user interface for **Text** fields	**dbFixedField**	**ColumnAttributes** Set to **adColFixed**
Hyperlink	**dbHyperlinkField**	**Jet OLEDB:Hyperlink** Set to **True**. (Only for **Memo** fields—**adLongVarWChar** data type)
N/A	**dbSystemField**	**N/A**
Default for **Text** fields	**dbVariableField**	**ColumnAttributes** Set to **Not adColFixed**

For information about additional field properties that you can set by using the **Properties** collection of an ADOX **Column** object, see "The Properties Collection of the Column Object" in ADOProperties.doc in the Appendixes folder on the companion CD-ROM.

Setting Additional Table Properties

You can also set a number of table-level properties, such as the **Description** property, which you can use to provide descriptive information about the table, and the **ValidationRule** property, which you can use to enter an expression that specifies the requirements for data entered into a record. The following table lists the three provider-specific table properties, exclusive of those used to create linked tables, that can be defined by using the **Properties** collection of an ADOX **Table** object.

Access/DAO Table property	Provider-specific property for Microsoft Jet 4.0 OLE DB Provider
Hidden	**Jet OLEDB:Table Hidden In Access**
ValidationRule	**Jet OLEDB:Table Validation Rule**
ValidationText	**Jet OLEDB:Table Validation Text**

To see a code example that creates a table validation rule, see the CreateTableWithValidationRule procedure in the CreateDatabase module in DataAccess.mdb, which is available in the Samples\CH14 subfolder on the companion CD-ROM.

You must establish a reference to the Microsoft DAO 3.6 object library and use DAO code to programmatically set these remaining table properties: **Description**, **Filter**, **OrderBy**, **LinkChildFields**, **LinkMasterFields**, **SubdatasheetExpanded**, **SubdatasheetName**, and **SubdatasheetHeight**. For information about working with these properties, search Microsoft Access Help.

Creating a Linked Table

Linking a table from an external database allows you to read data, update and add data (in most cases), and create queries that use the table, in the same way as you would with a table native to the database. With the Microsoft Jet database engine, you can create links to tables in Access databases as well as other data formats supported by Microsoft Jet's installable ISAM drivers (Excel, dBase, Paradox, Exchange/Outlook, Lotus WKS, Text, and HTML) and ODBC drivers.

ADO and ADOX distinguish between tables that are linked from native Access database tables and installable ISAMs, and those linked by using ODBC drivers. If you use the ADO **OpenSchema** method and specify **adSchemaTables** as the ***QueryType*** argument to return a **Recordset** object that describes a database's tables, the TABLE_TYPE field returns "LINK" for linked Access tables and linked installable ISAM tables; however, it returns "PASS-THROUGH" for tables linked by using ODBC drivers. This is also true for the ADOX **Table** object's **Type** property. This is equivalent to using the DAO **Attributes** property with the read-only **dbAttachedTable** and **adAttachedODBC** constants.

Creating a Linked Access Table

To create a linked Access table by using ADOX and the Microsoft Jet 4.0 OLE DB Provider, you must specify the path to the external data source and the name of the external table. To do this, you need to specify the provider-specific **Jet OLEDB:Link Datasource** and **Jet OLEDB:Remote Table Name** properties. Additionally, to create a linked table for any kind of data source table by using ADOX, you must set the **Jet OLEDB:Create Link** property to **True**.

The following example shows how to link a table in another Access database.

```
Sub CreateLinkedAccessTable(strDBLinkFrom As String, _
                            strDBLinkTo As String, _
                            strLinkTbl As String, _
                            strLinkTblAs As String)
   Dim catDB   As ADOX.Catalog
   Dim tblLink As ADOX.Table

   Set catDB = New ADOX.Catalog
   ' Open a Catalog on the database in which to create the link.
   catDB.ActiveConnection = "Provider=Microsoft.Jet.OLEDB.4.0;" & _
      "Data Source=" & strDBLinkFrom

   Set tblLink = New ADOX.Table
   With tblLink
      ' Name the new Table and set its ParentCatalog property to the
      ' open Catalog to allow access to the Properties collection.
      .Name = strLinkTblAs
      Set .ParentCatalog = catDB

      ' Set the properties to create the link.
      .Properties("Jet OLEDB:Create Link") = True
      .Properties("Jet OLEDB:Link Datasource") = strDBLinkTo
      .Properties("Jet OLEDB:Remote Table Name") = strLinkTbl
   End With

   ' Append the table to the Tables collection.
   catDB.Tables.Append tblLink

   Set catDB = Nothing
End Sub
```

The CreateLinkedAccessTable procedure can be found in the CreateDatabase module in the DataAccess.mdb sample file, which is available in the Samples\CH14 subfolder on the companion CD-ROM.

Notice that it is not necessary to define the table structure for the linked table. The Microsoft Jet engine will automatically create the appropriate fields based on the definition of the table in the external data source.

Creating a Linked External Table

Even though ADO and ADOX distinguish between tables that are linked by using Jet I-ISAM drivers and tables linked from ODBC data sources, the method you use to create any linked external table is the same. To create a linked external table by using ADOX and the Microsoft Jet 4.0 OLE DB Provider, you must use the provider-specific **Jet OLEDB:Link Provider String** property to specify a Microsoft Jet connection string that tells how to connect to the external table. For I-ISAM tables, the connection string specifies the I-ISAM type and the path to the external data source. For ODBC tables, the connection string specifies the ODBC connection string that is necessary to connect to the data source. You then use the provider-specfic **Jet OLEDB:Remote Table Name** property to specify the name of the source table, which varies for the type of data you are linking to. For example, for an Excel worksheet, the source table can refer to an entire worksheet, a named range, or an unnamed range, whereas for Microsoft Exchange or Outlook, the source table refers to a folder in the mail storage. Just as when you create a linked Access table, you must also set the **Jet OLEDB:Create Link** property to **True**. The following code sample can be used to create a linked table for any I-ISAM or ODBC data source.

```
Sub CreateLinkedExternalTable(strTargetDB As String, _
                              strProviderString As String, _
                              strSourceTbl As String, _
                              strLinkTblName As String)
   Dim catDB   As ADOX.Catalog
   Dim tblLink As ADOX.Table

   Set catDB = New ADOX.Catalog
   ' Open a Catalog on the database in which to create the link.
   catDB.ActiveConnection = "Provider=Microsoft.Jet.OLEDB.4.0;" & _
                            "Data Source=" & strTargetDB

   Set tblLink = New ADOX.Table
   With tblLink
      ' Name the new Table and set its ParentCatalog property to the
      ' open Catalog to allow access to the Properties collection.
      .Name = strLinkTblAs
      Set .ParentCatalog = catDB

      ' Set the properties to create the link.
      .Properties("Jet OLEDB:Create Link") = True
      .Properties("Jet OLEDB:Link Provider String") = strProviderString
      .Properties("Jet OLEDB:Remote Table Name") = strLinkTbl
   End With

   ' Append the table to the Tables collection.
   catDB.Tables.Append tblLink

   Set catDB = Nothing
End Sub
```

The CreateLinkedExternalTable procedure can be found in the CreateDatabase module in the DataAccess.mdb sample file, which is available in the Samples\CH14 subfolder on the companion CD-ROM.

To use this procedure, you need to format the correct Jet connection string for the ***strProviderString*** argument to establish a connection to the external data source. You also need to specify the correct string for the ***strSourceTbl*** argument to identify the source table, such as the Exchange folder or Excel range you want to link to. The following sections describe how to create a Jet connection string and specify the source table for Excel, HTML, Microsoft Exchange or Outlook, and ODBC data sources.

Tip An easy way to determine the Jet connection string required to link an external data source is to create a linked table by using the Access user interface (**File** menu, **Get External Data** submenu, **Link Tables** command). Then open the linked table in Design view and display the **Table Properties** dialog box (**View** menu, **Properties** command). The **Description** property of a linked table shows the connection string used to link the table. You can display a long connection string by clicking in the **Description** property and then pressing SHIFT+F2.

Basic Jet I-ISAM Connection String Syntax

To specify the data source you want to open, all Jet I-ISAM drivers accept a connection string that uses the same basic syntax:

"*identifier*;*source*;*options*"

The ***identifier*** argument is a keyword that specifies the type of file being opened. This is the same string that is used with the **Extended Properties** property of the **Connection** object when you open an external data source. For example, **Excel 8.0** is used when you open an Excel 97 or Excel 2000 workbook. For a list of **Extended Properties** property settings for all database types supported by the Microsoft Jet 4.0 database engine, see "Extended Properties Property Settings" in ADOProperties.doc in the Appendixes folder on the companion CD-ROM.

The ***source*** argument contains a drive letter or transfer protocol (either http:// or ftp://), a fully qualified path, and the file name of the file you want to open. The ***source*** argument always begins with **DATABASE=**.

The ***options*** argument is used to specify additional, optional arguments to the I-ISAM driver, such as a password, or to indicate whether the first row specified in a spreadsheet file contains column header information. Multiple arguments are separated by semicolons.

Linking Excel Workbooks

The connection string to open an Excel worksheet has this format

"*identifier*;**DATABASE=**{*drive*:**\|FTP://|HTTP://**}*path**filename*.**xls** [;**HDR=**{**Yes**|**No**}]"

where *identifier* is the appropriate data source identifier for the version of Excel you want to open (see "Extended Properties Property Settings" in ADOProperties.doc in the Appendixes folder on the companion CD-ROM for a complete list); *drive*, *path* and *filename* point to the specific data source file; and **HDR** indicates whether the first row contains headers (set to **Yes** to use the first row as field names, or set to **No** to use the first row as data).

The ***strSourceTbl*** argument of the CreateLinkedExternalTable procedure specifies the data you want to link and passes that value to the **Jet OLEDB:Remote Table Name** property. When you link a Microsoft Excel 5.0, 7.0 (95), 8.0 (97), or 9.0 (2000) workbook, you can specify a subset of the available data. You can link a single worksheet, a named range anywhere in the workbook, or an unnamed range in a single worksheet. The following table lists the syntax you use to specify the desired subset of data.

To access this object	Use this syntax
Entire worksheet in a workbook file	*sheetname*$ where *sheetname* is the name of the worksheet. **Important** You must follow the worksheet name with a dollar sign ($). The dollar sign character appended to the sheet name tells the I-ISAM driver that you're referencing the entire sheet, rather than just a range on the sheet.
Named range of cells in a worksheet or workbook file	*namedrange* where *namedrange* is the name previously assigned to the range in Microsoft Excel.
Unnamed range of cells in a single worksheet in a workbook file	*sheetname*$*range* For example, to access cells A1 through D12 in a worksheet named 1996 Sales, you would use the following in the ***source*** argument: **1996 Sales$A1:D12**.

For example, to use the CreateLinkedExternalTable procedure to create a table that is linked to data on a worksheet named "Products" in an Excel workbook named Products.xls and treat the first row as field names, you can use a line of code like this:

```
CreateLinkedExternalTable _
   "C:\Program Files\Microsoft Office\Office\Samples\Northwind.mdb", _
   "Excel 8.0;DATABASE=C:\Products.xls;HDR=YES", "Products$","LinkedXLS"
```

Linking HTML Tables

Hypertext Markup Language (HTML) is a standard for presenting information over an intranet or the Internet. HTML files are text files that contain tags that specify how information in the file is displayed. You can use the HTML table tags (<TD> and </TD>) to embed one or more tables in an HTML file. The Microsoft Jet HTML I-ISAM driver can access information in HTML files that is formatted as tabular data or data in HTML files that is formatted as list data.

The Microsoft Jet HTML I-ISAM driver reads the data in the HTML table and chooses the data type for the data in the table columns by interpreting the data contained in the table cells. For example, if any of the data in a column is text, the I-ISAM driver interprets the column data type as text, with a field size of 255 characters. If the data in a column is numeric, the I-ISAM driver interprets the column data type as **Long** or **Double**, depending on whether most of the values are integer or floating point. If the data in a column is a combination of numeric and text values, the column data type is interpreted as text.

You can force the Microsoft Jet HTML I-ISAM driver to interpret column data as a specific data type by creating a Schema.ini file that contains information about the data type for each column of data. For more information about Schema.ini files, see Microsoft Access Help.

The connection string to open an HTML table has this format

"HTML Import;DATABASE={*drive*:\|**FTP://**|**HTTP://**}*path\filename* [**;HDR=**{**Yes**|**No**}]**"**

where *drive* is the letter of the disk drive on a local computer; *path* and *filename* point to the data source file; and **HDR** indicates whether the first row contains headers, instead of data. The path node delimiters can be either backslashes (\) or forward slashes (/).

The ***strSourceTbl*** argument of the CreateLinkedIISAMTable procedure specifies the source table you want to link. For an HTML table, the table is identified by the name surrounded by <CAPTION> tags (if they exist) within the HTML file that contains the data you want to link. If the table does not have a caption, and it is the only table in the file, use the title of the HTML file to refer to the table. If more than one table exists and none of the tables has a caption, you refer to them sequentially as Table1, Table2, and so on. The I-ISAM driver interprets these references as the first unnamed table in the HTML file, the second unnamed table in the HTML file, and so on.

For example, to use the CreateLinkedExternalTable procedure to create a table that is linked to a table named "Sales" in Sales_1.html and treat the first row in the table as field names, you can use a line of code like this:

```
CreateLinkedExternalTable _
   "C:\Program Files\Microsoft Office\Office\Samples\Northwind.mdb", _
   "HTML Import;DATABASE=C:\Sales_1.html;HDR=YES","Sales","LinkedHTML"
```

Linking Outlook/Exchange Folders

The Microsoft Exchange I-ISAM driver lets you access Microsoft Exchange and Outlook data stored remotely on a Microsoft Exchange server or data stored locally in offline folder (.ost), personal folder (.pst), or personal address book (.pab) files.

Using the Microsoft Exchange I-ISAM driver to access Microsoft Exchange and Outlook data is primarily useful for reading information from message folders, public folders, address books, and other items. You can't modify any existing items. And, while it is possible to write new items to Microsoft Exchange and Outlook message stores, not all fields are available or updatable, which limits your ability to create some items.

The following table contains a description of the required and optional elements used to create the *identifier*, *source*, and *options* portions of a connection string for a Microsoft Exchange or Outlook external data source.

Element	Description
Identifier	**Exchange 4.0** (required). The setting works with Microsoft Exchange 4.*x*, 5.0, and Outlook data.
Source table path	**MAPILEVEL=***storage*|*folderpath* (required). The *storage* entry is the exact name of a mailbox on a server, a personal folder, or public folder as it appears in the Outlook Folder List; and *folderpath* is the path to the folder immediately above the folder you want to connect to. The *storage* entry and the pipe character (|) are always required. The *folders* entry is required to access folders below the top-level of folders within *storage*. When you are listing nested folders, separate each folder name with a backslash (\) (for example, "Mailbox – Pat Smith|Inbox\Big Project").
Source table type	**TABLETYPE=0** (for folders) (default) **TABLETYPE=1** (for address books; required)
Database name	**DATABASE=***path* (required). The *path* entry is the fully resolved path and file name to a Microsoft Access database (.mdb) in which to store system tables used by the driver (usually the current database).
Profile name	**PROFILE=***profile* (optional; if not specified, the default profile is used). The *profile* entry is the name of the Microsoft Exchange or Outlook profile to use.
Password	**PWD=***password* (optional; not required if your network logon password is passed to your Microsoft Exchange server). The *password* entry is the Microsoft Exchange or Outlook logon password.

Strung together, the connection string to open a Microsoft Exchange or Outlook data source has this format:

"Exchange 4.0;MAPILEVEL= *storage|folderpath*;**TABLETYPE=**{0|1};
➥ **DATABASE=***path*;[**PROFILE=***profile*;**PWD=***password*;]"

The ***strSourceTbl*** argument of the CreateLinkedISAMTable procedure specifies the source table you want to link. For a Microsoft Exchange or Outlook item, this is the name of the folder you want to connect to as it appears in the Outlook Folder List.

For example, to use the CreateLinkedExternalTable procedure to first create a table that is linked to a folder named "Big Project" that is a subfolder of the Inbox folder, and then name the linked table "LinkedExchange," you can use a line of code like this:

```
CreateLinkedExternalTable _
   "C:\Program Files\Microsoft Office\Office\Samples\Northwind.mdb", _
   "Exchange 4.0;MAPILEVEL=Mailbox - Pat Smith|Inbox;TABLETYPE=0;" & _
   "DATABASE=C:\Program Files\Microsoft Office\Office\Samples\Northwind.mdb;" _
   ,"Big Project","LinkedExchange"
```

Linking ODBC Tables

The connection string to open an ODBC table has this format:

"ODBC;*connectstring***"**

where *connectstring* is the connection string required to connect to an ODBC data source. For example, the ODBC connection string to connect to the Pubs sample database on SQL Server might look something like this:

```
"DSN=Publishers;;UID=sa;PWD=;DATABASE=pubs"
```

Other ODBC data sources will have different formats. A simple way to create an ODBC connection string is to create an SQL pass-through query in Access. Clicking the **Build** button of the **ODBCConnectStr** property in the **Query Properties** dialog box for an SQL pass-through query starts a wizard that walks you through creating an ODBC connection string. For more information about creating an SQL pass-through query, search Microsoft Access Help.

The ***strSourceTbl*** argument of the CreateLinkedExternalTable procedure specifies the source table you want to link to. For an ODBC table, this is the name of the table in the database on the ODBC server you want to link to.

For example, to use the CreateLinkedExternalTable procedure to create a table that is linked to the table named "dbo.Authors" in the Pubs sample database on SQL Server, and name the linked table "LinkedODBC," you can use a line of code like this:

```
CreateLinkedExternalTable _
   "C:\Program Files\Microsoft Office\Office\Samples\Northwind.mdb", _
   "ODBC;DSN=Publishers;UID=sa;PWD=;DATABASE=pubs;", _
   "dbo.Authors","LinkedODBC"
```

The user ID and password from the connection string for a linked ODBC table aren't saved by default, which means users will be prompted for this information whenever they (or your code) open the table. If you want to save the user ID and password as part of the connection string, set the provider-specific **Jet OLEDB:Cache Link Name/Password** property to **True**. In DAO, this is equivalent to adding the **dbAttachSavePWD** constant to the table's **Attributes** property.

For a list of all the provider-specific properties that can be used when you create linked tables, see ADOProperties.doc in the Appendixes folder on the companion CD-ROM.

Refreshing Links for Linked Tables

If the data source for a linked table is renamed or moved, you need to refresh the connection information used to establish the link. To refresh the link, update the connection string for the table by using the provider-specific **Jet OLEDB:Link Datasource** property, and then reestablish the link by setting the provider-specific **Jet OLEDB:Create Link** property to **True**. The following code example shows how to refresh the links for tables linked to another Access database.

```
Sub RefreshLinks(strDBLinkFrom As String, _
                 strDBLinkSource As String)
   Dim catDB   As ADOX.Catalog
   Dim tblLink As ADOX.Table

   Set catDB = New ADOX.Catalog
   ' Open a catalog on the database in which to refresh links.
   catDB.ActiveConnection = "Provider=Microsoft.Jet.OLEDB.4.0;" & _
      "Data Source=" & strDBLinkFrom

   For Each tblLink In catDB.Tables
      ' Check to make sure table is a linked table.
      If tblLink.Type = "LINK" Then
         tblLink.Properties("Jet OLEDB:Link Datasource") = strDBLinkSource
         tblLink.Properties("Jet OLEDB:Create Link") = True
      End If
   Next

   catDB = Nothing
End Sub
```

The RefreshLinks procedure can be found in the CreateDatabase module in the DataAccess.mdb sample file, which is available in the Samples\CH14 subfolder on the companion CD-ROM.

Creating and Modifying Indexes

The process for creating an index is essentially the same in ADOX as it is in DAO. To create an index, you append fields to an **Index** object's **Columns** collection, and then append the **Index** object to the **Table** object's **Indexes** collection.

However, there are differences in behavior between the **Index** objects in these two models. DAO has two properties, **Required** and **IgnoreNulls**, that together determine whether or not **Null** values can be inserted for fields in the index, and whether or not index entries will be created when some of the fields in a multicolumn index contain **Nulls**. By default, both of these properties are **False,** indicating that **Null** values are allowed in the index, and that an index entry will be added even if the entry contains **Nulls**. This differs from ADOX, which has a single property, **IndexNulls**, for this purpose. By default, the **IndexNulls** property is set to **adIndexNullsDisallow**, which indicates that **Null** values aren't allowed in the index, and that no index entry will be added if a field in the index contains a **Null**. The table below shows the mapping from the DAO **Required** and **IgnoreNulls** properties to the ADOX **IndexNulls** property.

DAO Required and IgnoreNulls settings	ADO IndexNulls settings	Result
Required = True **IgnoreNulls =True** or **False**	**adIndexNullsDisallow**	A **Null** value isn't allowed in the index field; no index entry added.
Required = False **IgnoreNulls = True**	**adIndexNullsIgnore**	A **Null** value is allowed in the index field; but no index entry added.
Required = False **IgnoreNulls = False**	**adIndexNullsAllow**	A **Null** value is allowed in the index field; index entry added.

Note ADOX also provides the **adIndexNullsAllowAny** constant for setting the **IndexNulls** property, but this setting returns an error if you try to use it to create an index in an Access database.

The following code sample shows how to create an index by using ADOX.

```
Sub CreateIndex(strDbPath As String, _
                strTblToIdx As String, _
                strIdxName As String, _
                strIdxField As String, _
                lngIndexNulls As ADOX.AllowNullsEnum, _
                lngSortOrder As ADOX.SortOrderEnum)
   Dim catDB As ADOX.Catalog
   Dim tbl   As ADOX.Table
   Dim idx   As ADOX.Index

   Set catDB = New ADOX.Catalog
   ' Open a catalog on the database in which to create the index.
   catDB.ActiveConnection = "Provider=Microsoft.Jet.OLEDB.4.0;" & _
                            "Data Source=" & strDbPath
   Set tbl = New ADOX.Table
   Set tbl = catDB.Tables(strTblToIdx)

   ' Create Index object and append table columns to it.
   Set idx = New ADOX.Index
   With idx
      .Name = strIdxName
      .IndexNulls = lngIndexNulls
      .Columns.Append strIdxField
      .Columns(strIdxField).SortOrder = lngSortOrder
   End With

   ' Append the Index object to the Indexes collection of the Table object.
   tbl.Indexes.Append idx

   Set catDB = Nothing
End Sub
```

For example, to use the CreateIndex procedure to create an index on the Country field in the Employees table that is sorted in ascending order and allows nulls, you can use a line of code like this:

```
CreateIndex _
   "C:\Program Files\Microsoft Office\Office\Samples\Northwind.mdb", _
   "Employees", "CountryIndex", "Country", "adIndexNullsIgnore","adSortAscending"
```

The same process can be used to create an index that will used as the table's primary key. To do this, set the **PrimaryKey** property of the **Index** object to **True** before appending it to the table's **Indexes** collection.

The CreateIndex procedure can be found in the CreateDatabase module in the DataAccess.mdb sample file, which is available in the Samples\CH14 subfolder on the companion CD-ROM.

Creating Relationships and Integrity Constraints

In a *relational database*, a relationship is created between a *foreign key* in one table and typically a *primary key* (or some other field that contains unique values) in another table. For simplicity's sake, we'll assume that the foreign key and primary key are both single fields, but it is possible that either or both can be made up of more than one field. To get a handle on the tables that contain the foreign and primary keys, we'll use the term *foreign table* for the table that contains the foreign key, and the term *related table* for the table that contains the primary key.

A foreign table is most typically on the "many" side of a relationship. For example, in the Northwind sample database there is a one-to-many relationship between the Categories table and the Products table, so the Categories table is the related table and the Products table is the foreign table, and the relationship is established between the primary key field in the Categories table, CategoryID, and the foreign key field in the Products table, which is also named CategoryID.

To create a relationship by using ADOX, you use a **Key** object to create an object that defines the relationship by specifying the related table and key fields. You then open a **Table** object on the foreign table and add the new **Key** object to the **Keys** collection of the table. The following code sample shows how to create a relationship by using ADOX.

```
Sub CreateRelationship(strDBPath As String, _
                       strForeignTbl As String, _
                       strRelName As String, _
                       strFTKey As String, _
                       strRelatedTbl As String, _
                       strRTKey As String)
   Dim catDB As ADOX.Catalog
   Dim tbl   As ADOX.Table
   Dim key   As ADOX.Key
```

```
    Set catDB = New ADOX.Catalog
    ' Open the catalog.
    catDB.ActiveConnection = "Provider=Microsoft.Jet.OLEDB.4.0;" & _
       "Data Source =" & strDBPath

    Set key = New ADOX.Key
    ' Create the foreign key to define the relationship.
    With Key
       ' Specify name for the relationship in the Keys collection.
       .Name = strRelName
       ' Specify the related table's name.
       .RelatedTable = strRelatedTbl
       .Type = adKeyForeign
       ' Add the foreign key field to the Columns collection.
       .Columns.Append strFTKey
       ' Specify the field the foreign key is related to.
       .Columns(strFTKey).RelatedColumn = strRTKey
    End With

    Set tbl = New ADOX.Table
    ' Open the table and add the foreign key.
    Set tbl = catDB.Tables(strForeignTbl)
    tbl.Keys.Append key

    Set catDB = Nothing
End Sub
```

For example, to use this procedure to create the relationship described above between the Categories and Products tables in the Northwind database, you can use a line of code like this:

```
CreateRelationship _
   "c:\Program Files\Microsoft Office\Office\Samples\Northwind.mdb", _
   "Products","CategoriesProducts","CategoryID","Categories","CategoryID"
```

The CreateRelationship procedure can be found in the CreateDatabase module in the DataAccess.mdb sample file, which is available in the Samples\CH14 subfolder on the companion CD-ROM.

The **Key** object also supports two additional properties that are used to define whether related records will be automatically updated or deleted if the value in the primary key in the related table is changed. These features of the Jet database engine are called *cascading updates* and *cascading deletions*. By default, cascading updates and deletions are not active when you create a new relationship. To turn on cascading updates for the relationship, set the **UpdateRule** property for the **Key** object to **adRICascade**; to turn on cascading deletions for the relationship, set the **DeleteRule** property for the **Key** object to **adRICascade**.

Note When you use OLE DB, there is no way to create a relationship that is not enforced, therefore there is no equivalent in ADOX to the DAO **dbRelationDontEnforce** setting of the DAO **Attributes** property of a **Relation** object. Also, ADOX and the Microsoft Jet 4.0 OLE DB Provider don't provide a way to specify the default join type that will be used in the Access query Design view window, as can be done by using the **dbRelationRight** and **dbRelationLeft** settings of the **Attributes** property.

Creating and Modifying Stored Queries

Although it is possible to create and modify a stored query in an Access database by using ADOX, if you do so your query won't be visible in the Access Database window or any other part of the Access user interface—for example, you can't set the **RecordSource** property of a form to a query created with ADOX, or import a query created with ADOX into another database. However, you can still run stored queries created by using ADOX from ADO code.

This is so because the Microsoft Jet 4.0 database engine can run in two modes: one mode that supports the same Jet SQL commands used in previous versions of Access, and another new mode that supports the new Jet SQL commands and syntax that are more compliant with the ANSI SQL-92 standard.

For these reasons, you should use ADOX to create queries only in a database that you will use as a code library, or in a solution that doesn't expose the Database window to users.

For information about how to create stored queries by using ADOX code, see ADOCreateQueries.doc in the Appendixes folder on the companion CD-ROM. ADOCreateQueries.doc also contains additional information about using the new Jet 4.0 SQL commands and syntax. If you need to use code to create stored queries that are available from the Access user interface, you must use the DAO **CreateQueryDef** method to do so. For information about how to do so, see Microsoft DAO 3.6 Help or the *Microsoft Jet Database Engine Programmer's Guide, Second Edition* (Microsoft Press, 1997).

You can still use the new Jet 4.0 SQL commands and syntax in ADO code that is running against the Microsoft Jet 4.0 OLE DB Provider. Because ADO opens a new connection to the database, ADO is always able to open this connection while using the mode of the Jet database engine that supports the new commands. However, you can't use the new Jet 4.0 SQL commands and syntax from DAO code because DAO isn't able to open the database while using a mode that supports these commands. For information about how to run SQL commands without using a stored query, see the following section, "Running a Temporary Query."

Running a Temporary Query

ADO provides a variety of ways to run a query without using a stored query. Queries of all types are specified by using the Structured Query Language (SQL). Queries can be of two basic types: queries that return a set of records, and queries that don't return a set records. Queries that don't return a set of records can be further divided into two types: Data Definition Language (DDL) queries, which create database objects or alter the structure of a database, and Data Manipulation Language (DML) queries, which perform bulk operations on a set of records, such as adding, updating, or deleting a set of records.

For information about how to run a temporary query that returns records, see "Working with Records" later in this chapter.

To run a temporary query that doesn't return records, such as DDL or DML SQL statements, you can use the **Execute** method of either the ADO **Command** object or the ADO **Connection** object. The primary differences between these two methods are as follows:

- To use a **Command** object to execute a query, you set the **CommandText** property of the object to the SQL statement you want to run, and then set the **ActiveConnection** property of the object to a connection string or an open **Connection** object that specifies the data source you want to run against. Once this is done, to run the command you use the **Execute** method. If you want to run the same command against a different data source, you can set the **Command** object's **ActiveConnection** property to **Nothing**, and then reset the **ActiveConnection** property to a new data source.
- To use a **Connection** object to execute a query, you open the **Connection** object, and then run the **Execute** method by passing in the SQL statement you want to run as the ***CommandText*** argument. As long as you don't close the connection, you can use the **Execute** method again to run additional SQL statements against the connection.

Also, for both methods, the **CommandText** property or the ***CommandText*** argument can refer to the name of a stored query, a stored procedure, or a table. For information about how to do that, see ADO Help.

The following procedure shows how to use the **Command** object to run an SQL statement.

```
Sub RunSQLCommand(strDBPath As String, _
                  strSQL As String)
   Dim cmd        As ADODB.Command
   Dim strConnect As String

   strConnect = "Provider=Microsoft.Jet.OLEDB.4.0;Data Source=" & strDBPath

   Set cmd = New ADODB.Command
   With cmd
      .CommandText = strSQL
      .ActiveConnection = strConnect
      .Execute
   End With

   Set cmd = Nothing
End Sub
```

For example, the new IDENTITY command in Jet SQL allows you to specify a starting value and an increment value when creating an **AutoNumber** field (which you can't do while using the Access 2000 user interface). You could use the following line of code with the RunSQLCommand procedure to create a table with an **AutoNumber** field that starts with a value of 10 for the first record and increments 5 for each new record:

```
RunSQLCommand "c:\Program Files\Microsoft Office\Office\Samples\Northwind.mdb", _
   "CREATE TABLE MyTable(MyCounter IDENTITY (10, 5), FirstName CHAR, LastName CHAR)"
```

The RunSQLCommand procedure can be found in the CreateDatabase module in the DataAccess.mdb sample file, which is available in the Samples\CH14 subfolder on the companion CD-ROM. The CreateDatabase module also contains the RunSQLConnection procedure that demonstrates how to execute an SQL statement by using the **Execute** method of a **Connection** object.

For more information about the new Jet SQL commands, see the "Overview of What's New" topic in the Jetsql40.chm Help file. By default, this Help file is installed in the C:\Program Files\Microsoft Office\Office\1033 folder.

Working with Records

One of the primary functions of a data access solution is working with records. The ADO object model supports a rich set of features for organizing, sorting, searching, updating, adding, and deleting data from a broad variety of data sources. The **Recordset** object alone provides 23 methods and 23 properties that give you a great deal of control over records in a database. In addition to these methods and properties, you can use the methods and properties of the **Recordset** object's **Fields** collection and the **Field** object to work with data at the field level. This section describes how to work with records and fields by using the ADO **Recordset** and **Field** objects.

Tip You can use a transaction to "wrap" a set of changes you make to the structure of a database; by using the transaction as a wrapper around the changes, you ensure that all work is performed as a single unit. For information about how to use transactions, see "Using Transactions" in Chapter 16, "Multiuser Database Applications."

Recordset Object Basics

To work with records in a database by using Visual Basic or VBScript code, you use ADO **Recordset** objects. A **Recordset** object represents the records from a single table or the set of records returned by executing a command, such as an SQL string, an Access query, or a SQL Server stored procedure.

You can open a **Recordset** object in ADO by using any of these three methods:

- The **Execute** method of the **Connection** object
- The **Execute** method of the **Command** object
- The **Open** method of the **Recordset** object

The syntax for each of these methods is as follows:

Set *recordset* = *connection*.**Execute** ([*CommandText*, [*RecordsAffected*, [*Options*]]])
Set *recordset* = *command*.**Execute** ([*RecordsAffected*, [*Parameters*, [*Options*]]])
recordset.**Open** [*Source*, [*ActiveConnection*, [*CursorType*, [*LockType*, [*Options*]]]]]

Although using the **Execute** method of the **Connection** or **Command** object returns a **Recordset** object, these methods are primarily intended for executing commands (typically SQL strings) that don't return records; queries that are called *action queries* in Access. When they are used to return a set of records, they create only **Recordset** objects of the Forward-only, Read-only cursor type, and there is no way to specify any other cursor type. Because of this limitation, we will not discuss using the **Execute** method of the **Connection** or **Command** object for opening **Recordset** objects for the purpose of creating a client-side set of records. For information about cursor types, see "Specifying Cursor Types" later in this chapter.

However, a **Command** object can be passed to the **Open** method of the **Recordset** object as the ***Source*** argument. This can be useful in two ways:

- You can use the **Prepared** property of the **Command** object to optimize and precompile the command. If you will be using the **Command** object more than once within the scope of your procedure, this will optimize the performance of your procedure.
- A **Command** object is required if you want to supply parameters to a query that can be reused efficiently.

These applications of the **Command** object are discussed later in this chapter. The following sections discuss how to use the **Open** method of the **Recordset** object, which provides more options and greater flexibility when you open **Recordset** objects.

Using the Open Method of a Recordset Object

The syntax for the **Open** method of an ADO **Recordset** object is as follows:

recordset.**Open** *Source*, *ActiveConnection*, *CursorType*, *LockType*, *Options*

As is true for other Visual Basic methods, you can pass each of the arguments of the **Open** method as either a positional argument or a named argument. Additionally, each of the arguments of the **Open** method (except for the ***Options*** argument) can also be specified by setting the corresponding properties of the **Recordset** object before invoking the **Open** method. For example, the following code fragment specifies the database connection and cursor type by setting the **ActiveConnection** and **CursorType** properties before opening the **Recordset** object, and then passes the name of the data source to the **Open** method as a named argument.

```
cnn = CurrentProject.Connection
Set rst = New ADODB.Recordset
With rst
   .ActiveConnection = cnn
   .CursorType = adOpenKeyset
   .Open Source:= "Employees"
End With
```

Neither method is better than the other; you can use either method or both together.

The following table briefly describes each of the arguments of the **Open** method.

Argument	Description
Source	Optional. A valid **Command** object variable name, an SQL statement, a table name, a query name (Access), a stored procedure name (SQL Server), or the file name of a **Recordset** object previously saved by using the **Save** method of the **Recordset** object.
ActiveConnection	Optional. A valid **Connection** object variable name, a String containing connection string parameters, or if you are creating a **Recordset** object associated with the current Access database, you can pass **CurrentProject.Connection** for this argument.
CursorType	Optional. A constant that determines the type of cursor that the provider should use when it opens the **Recordset** object.
LockType	Optional. A constant that determines what type of locking (concurrency) the provider should use when it opens the **Recordset** object.
Options	Optional. A constant that indicates how the provider should evaluate the ***Source*** argument if it represents something other than a **Command** object, or that the **Recordset** object should be restored from a file where it was previously saved.

Details on how to use each of these arguments are provided in the following sections.

Specifying the Records to Work With

When you open a **Recordset** object, you use the ***Source*** argument of the **Open** method to specify the set of records you want to open. The ***Source*** argument can be a valid **Command** object variable name that executes a command that returns records, an SQL statement, or a table name. If you are connecting to an Access database file, you can also pass the name of a query that returns records, or if you are connecting to a SQL Server database, you can pass the name of a stored procedure that returns rows.

If you pass anything other than a **Command** object, you must also use the ***ActiveConnection*** argument of the **Open** method to specify how to connect to the database.

Before you pass a **Command** object as the ***Source*** argument, its **ActiveConnection** property or argument must already be set to a valid **Connection** object or connection string. If you pass a **Command** object in the ***Source*** argument and also pass an ***ActiveConnection*** argument, an error occurs.

The following code fragment passes a string variable that contains the name of a table as the ***Source*** argument.

```
rst.Open Source:=strSourceTable
```

Connecting a Recordset Object Variable

When you use some OLE DB providers (such as the Microsoft Jet 4.0 and SQL Server OLE DB providers), you can create **Recordset** objects independently of a previously defined **Connection** object by using the ***ActiveConnection*** argument of the **Open** method to pass a connection string. ADO still creates a **Connection** object, but it doesn't assign that object to an object variable. For example, the following code fragment opens a **Recordset** object by passing a connection string to the **Open** method.

```
Dim rstFieldData As ADODB.Recordset
Dim strConnect   As String
Dim strSQL       As String

strConnect = "Provider=Microsoft.Jet.OLEDB.4.0;" _
   & "Data Source=C:\Program Files\Microsoft Office\Office\Samples\Northwind.mdb;"
strSQL = "SELECT * FROM Customers WHERE Region = 'WA'"

Set rstFieldData = New ADODB.Recordset
' Specify the cursor type and lock type, and then
' open the Recordset object by passing criteria and the
' connection string to the Open method.
With rstFieldData
   .CursorType = adOpenForwardOnly
   .LockType = adLockReadOnly
   .Open Source := strSQL, _
      ActiveConnection := strConnect, _
      Options:= adCmdText
End With
```

Important Note that the WHERE clause in the SQL statement in the previous example uses single-quote marks (') around the value specified in the criterion (Region = 'WA'). When you use DAO, a WHERE clause can have double-quote marks (") around a value, but in ADO you must use single-quote marks when specifying criteria. Additionally, if your criteria contain field names that have the same name as SQL keywords, you must surround the field name with square brackets ([ ]). For example, if the field name for the criterion in the previous example had been named Where, the criterion in the WHERE clause would have to look like this:

```
WHERE [Where] = 'WA'
```

However, if you plan on opening more than one **Recordset** object over the same connection, you will get better performance and use fewer resources if you explicitly create and open a **Connection** object and then pass this object variable to the **Open** method. This ensures that the **Connection** object is created only once. If you open your **Recordset** objects by passing a connection string, ADO creates a new **Connection** object for each new **Recordset** object, even if you pass the same connection string. The previous sample rewritten to pass a **Connection** object looks like this:

```
Dim cnnConnect   As ADODB.Connection
Dim rstFieldData As ADODB.Recordset
Dim strConnect   As String
Dim strSQL       As String

strConnect = "Provider=Microsoft.Jet.OLEDB.4.0;" _
   & "Data Source=C:\Program Files\Microsoft Office\Office\Samples\Northwind.mdb;"
Set cnnConnect = New ADODB.Connection
cnnConnect.Open strConnect

strSQL = "SELECT * FROM Customers WHERE Region = 'WA'"

Set rstFieldData = New ADODB.Recordset
With rstFieldData
   .CursorType = adOpenForwardOnly
   .LockType = adLockReadOnly
   .Open Source := strSQL, _
      ActiveConnection := cnnConnect, _
      Options := adCmdText
End With
```

Specifying Cursor Types

At any given time, a **Recordset** object can only refer to one record within the set as the *current record*. The software functionality that lets you work programmatically with a set of records is referred to as a *cursor*. You can think of a cursor as a device that you can use to scroll through a set of records in a database to read, add, delete, or update records. There are four types of cursors for **Recordset** objects in ADO: Dynamic, Keyset, Static, and Forward-only.

The functionality available to each of the cursor types depends on how the cursor manages *currency* and *membership*.

Currency is a measure of how current the data is that is displayed for records available to the cursor. The data displayed by Dynamic and Keyset cursor types are regularly updated to reflect changes that have been made by other users or processes. The data displayed in Static and Forward-only cursor types represents a snapshot of the data made at the time the **Recordset** object was opened; however, it is possible to force an update of one or more records in these cursor types by using the **Resync** method.

Membership describes whether the set of records available to a cursor automatically reflects any newly added or deleted records. New additions or deletions are available to the Dynamic cursor type, so its membership is not fixed. New additions or deletions are not reflected in the Keyset, Static, and Forward-only cursor types, so their membership is fixed. You can manually refresh all of the data in these cursor types by using the **Requery** method, which is equivalent to closing and then reopening the **Recordset** object.

To specify the cursor type, set the **CursorType** property of a **Recordset** object before you open it. For example, the following code fragment creates a **Recordset** object and sets its cursor type to open as a Keyset cursor.

```
Dim rst As ADODB.Recordset

Set rst = New ADODB.Recordset
rst.CursorType = adOpenKeyset
```

You can also specify a cursor type by passing the ***CursorType*** argument to the **Open** method of a **Recordset** object, as shown in the following code fragment.

```
Dim rst As ADODB.Recordset

Set rst = New ADODB.Recordset
rst.Open _
   Source:=strSourceTable, _
   ActiveConnection:=cnn, _
   CursorType:=adOpenKeyset
```

If you don't specify a cursor type, ADO opens a Forward-only cursor by default.

Note Some providers don't support all cursor types, so check the documentation for the provider. For information about the cursor types supported by the Microsoft Jet 4.0 OLE DB Provider, see "ADO Equivalents to DAO Recordset Types" later in this chapter.

The following table describes the features of each cursor type and lists the constants you can use to set or read the **CursorType** property.

Cursor type	Constant	Description
Dynamic	**adOpenDynamic**	Reflects any new additions, changes, and deletions made by other users, and allows all types of movement through the **Recordset** object that don't rely on bookmarks; allows bookmarks if the provider supports them. This cursor type isn't supported by the Microsoft Jet 4.0 OLE DB Provider.
Keyset	**adOpenKeyset**	Behaves like a Dynamic cursor, except that it doesn't contain any new or deleted records added by other users. Any data changes made by other users to the records available when the **Recordset** object was opened will still be visible. A Keyset cursor always supports bookmarks and therefore allows all types of movement through the **Recordset** object.
Static	**adOpenStatic**	Provides a static, but updatable, copy of a set of records. Always allows bookmarks and therefore allows all types of movement through the **Recordset** object. Any additions, changes, or deletions by other users will not be visible until the **Resync** method is called. This is the only type of cursor allowed when you open a client-side (ADOR) **Recordset** object.
Forward-only	**adOpenForwardOnly**	Behaves identically to a Static cursor except that it only allows you to scroll forward through records. This improves performance in situations where you need to make only a single pass through a **Recordset** object. (Default) **Note** The **RecordCount** property for a forward-only **Recordset** object always returns –1 because ADO can't determine the number of records in a forward-only **Recordset** object. To get a valid count of records when using a **Recordset** object to work with an Access database, you must use either a Keyset cursor or a Static cursor.

Specifying Locking

The **LockType** property or argument specifies what kind of locking is used while you edit records in the **Recordset** object. *Locking* is used to regulate what other users in a multiuser database can do with a record while it is being edited. If you don't set the **LockType** property, read-only locks will be used by default, which will prevent you from editing records. To edit the data in a **Recordset** object, you must set the **LockType** property before you open it, or else you must pass the ***LockType*** argument to the **Open** method. The **LockType** property is read/write before a **Recordset** object is opened (or after it is closed), and read-only while it is open. The following table lists the constants you can use to set or read the **LockType** property and describes how each lock functions when you are editing records.

Constant	Description
adLockReadOnly	Read-only—you cannot edit the data. (Default)
adLockPessimistic	Pessimistic locking, record by record—the provider does what is necessary to ensure successful editing of the records, usually by locking records at the data source as soon as you start editing records. No other users can read or edit the data until you either save changes with the **Update** method or cancel them with the **CancelUpdate** method.
adLockOptimistic	Optimistic locking, record by record—the provider locks records only when you call the **Update** method. Other users can read, edit, and save changes to the same record while you have it open.
adLockBatchOptimistic	Optimistic batch updates—required for batch update mode as opposed to immediate update mode.

The following addition to the previous code example specifies optimistic locking, so that the **Recordset** object can be edited.

```
rst.Open _
   Source:=strSourceTable, _
   ActiveConnection:=cnn, _
   CursorType:=adOpenKeyset, _
   LockType:=adLockOptimistic
```

Some OLE DB providers may not support all lock types. If a provider cannot support the requested **LockType** setting, it will substitute another type of locking. To determine the actual locking functionality available in a **Recordset** object, you can use the **Supports** method with **adUpdate** and **adUpdateBatch** constants. For more information about the **Supports** method, see "Determining Cursor Features" later in this chapter.

For a more detailed discussion of locking and other multiuser database issues, see Chapter 16, "Multiuser Database Applications."

Optimizing the Evaluation of the Source Argument

If you pass something other than a **Command** object in the ***Source*** argument to the **Open** method of the **Recordset** object, you can use the ***Options*** argument to optimize evaluation of the ***Source*** argument. If you don't specify the ***Options*** argument, you may experience diminished performance, because ADO must make calls to the provider to determine if the ***Source*** argument is an SQL statement, a stored procedure, or a table name. If you know what type of object or command you're using for the ***Source*** argument, setting the ***Options*** argument instructs ADO to jump directly to the relevant code. You can use one of the following constants to specify the ***Options*** argument.

Constant	Description
adCmdText	Indicates that the provider should evaluate the ***Source*** argument as a textual definition of a command.
adCmdTable	Indicates that ADO should generate an SQL query to return all records from the table named in the ***Source*** argument.
adCmdTableDirect	Indicates that the provider should return all records from the table named in the ***Source*** argument.
adCmdStoredProc	Indicates that the provider should evaluate the ***Source*** argument as a stored procedure.
adCmdUnknown	Indicates that the type of command in the ***Source*** argument is not known.
adCmdFile	Indicates that a persisted (saved) **Recordset** object should be restored from the file named in the ***Source*** argument.
adAsyncExecute	Indicates that the ***Source*** argument should be executed asynchronously.
adAsyncFetch	Indicates that after the initial quantity specified in the **CacheSize** property is fetched, any remaining records should be fetched asynchronously.

The following addition to the previous code sample ensures that the ***Source*** argument is evaluated as a table name.

```
rst.Open _
   Source:=strSourceTable, _
   ActiveConnection:=cnn, _
   CursorType:=adOpenDynamic, _
   LockType:=adLockOptimistic, _
   Options:=adCmdTableDirect
```

The default for the ***Options*** argument is **adCmdFile** if no connection is associated with the **Recordset** object. This will typically be the case for saved **Recordset** objects.

Specifying the Cursor Location

ADO also supports two kinds of cursor engines: the *server cursor engine* and the *client cursor engine*. The location of the cursor engine determines certain aspects of the functionality of ADO **Recordset** objects.

To specify which cursor engine to use, you use the **CursorLocation** property of the **Recordset** or **Connection** object. Set the **CursorLocation** property to **adUseServer** to use the server cursor engine, and to **adUseClient** to use the client cursor engine. To specify the cursor engine for a **Recordset** object, you must set the **CursorLocation** property before opening the **Recordset** object. If you set the **CursorLocation** property of a **Connection** object, any **Recordset** object you open while using that **Connection** object will inherit that connection's setting. By default, when opening a **Connection** object for an Access database, the **CursorLocation** property is **adUseServer**.

To determine which cursor engine to use—client or server—you should know the following:

- The *server cursor engine* is provided by the OLE DB provider and the database engine itself, which for Access databases means the Microsoft Jet 4.0 OLE DB Provider and the Microsoft Jet database engine. For SQL Server databases it means the Microsoft SQL Server OLE DB Provider and either SQL Server or the Microsoft Data Engine (MSDE). In both cases, the database engine builds a set of keys, called a *keyset*, which is stored locally for Access databases and on the server for SQL Server databases. The database engine then uses the keyset to retrieve and scroll through the records in the database.
- The *client cursor engine* is an OLE DB service component that buffers and copies the specified records to a temporary table that is stored locally in memory, or on disk, if the number of records is sufficiently large. If you make changes to field data, or call the **AddNew** or **Delete** method on a client-side cursor, ADO automatically generates the appropriate SQL UPDATE, INSERT, and DELETE statements and sends them to the database engine when you update the **Recordset** object.

A cursor generated by the server cursor engine is often called a *server-side cursor,* and a cursor generated by the client cursor engine is called a *client-side cursor*. The differences between them are as follows:

- The features provided by server-side cursors are specific to the database engine and OLE DB provider you are using. For Access databases, a **Recordset** object that uses a server-side cursor is generally more likely to be updatable than a client-side cursor, and when the database is shared by multiple users, a server-side cursor can show changes made by other users.
- You can think of a client-side cursor as an updatable snapshot. By specifying the **adBatchOptimistic** constant for the ***LockType*** argument of the **Open** method of a **Recordset** object that is using a client-side cursor, you can use the **UpdateBatch** method to send updates to the database as a batch. Because the client cursor engine is an OLE DB service provider, the features provided by client-side cursors are fairly consistent across all data sources and OLE DB providers.

As a general rule, you should use server-side cursors for working with Access databases, and client-side cursors when working with SQL Server databases. However, although using client-side cursors with Access databases generates additional overhead to cache records and doesn't expose all of the functionality of the Jet database engine, you still may want to use client-side cursors with Access databases if you are working with a remote database, or if you need to ensure uniformity of behavior when working with multiple data sources.

ADO Equivalents to DAO Recordset Types

The combined ***CursorType***, ***LockType***, and ***Options*** arguments of the ADO **Open** method determine the type of ADO **Recordset** object that is returned. The table below shows how the ***Type*** and ***Options*** arguments of the DAO **OpenRecordset** method can be mapped to ADO **Recordset Open** method argument settings when you use ADO and the Microsoft Jet 4.0 OLE DB Provider to work with Access databases.

DAO arguments		ADO arguments		
Type	*Options*	*CursorType*	*LockType*	*Options*
dbOpenDynaset		**adOpenKeyset**	**adLockOptimistic**	
dbOpenSnapshot		**adOpenStatic**	**adLockReadOnly**	
dbOpenSnapshot	**dbForwardOnly**	**adOpenForwardOnly**	**adLockReadOnly**	
dbOpenTable		**adOpenKeyset**	**adLockOptimistic**	**adCmdTableDirect**

Not all of the possible combinations of ADO **Recordset** ***CursorType*** and ***LockType*** arguments are listed above, because the Microsoft Jet 4.0 OLE DB Provider doesn't support all combinations of the ***CursorType*** and ***LockType*** arguments. Additionally, the setting of the **CursorLocation** property for the **Recordset** object, which specifies whether to use the server cursor engine or the client cursor engine, also determines the kind of functionality available to the **Recordset** object. If your ADO code uses a combination of **CursorLocation** property and ***CursorType*** and ***LockType*** argument settings that aren't supported by the Microsoft Jet 4.0 OLE DB Provider, it will then return a **Recordset** object that it does support.

The table below describes the results you can expect for all combinations of the ***CursorType*** and ***LockType*** arguments when using the Microsoft Jet 4.0 OLE DB Provider with server-side cursors (**CursorLocation = adUseServer**).

CursorType	*LockType*	Results
adOpenForwardOnly	**adLockReadOnly**	You can only scroll forward one record at a time. If you try to scroll backwards, ADO will requery the **Recordset** object and start from the beginning. You can't update data.
adOpenForwardOnly	**adLockOptimistic** **adLockPessimistic** **adBatchOptimistic**	For all other lock types, a Keyset cursor is returned.
adOpenStatic	**adLockReadOnly**	The **Recordset** object contains a scrollable, read-only snapshot of your data. You can't see changes made by other users.
adOpenStatic	**adLockOptimistic** **adLockPessimistic** **adBatchOptimistic**	For all other lock types, a Keyset cursor is returned.

CursorType	*LockType*	Results
adOpenKeyset	**adLockReadOnly**	The **Recordset** object has a read-only, scrollable cursor. You can see updates and deletions, but not insertions made by other users. If the **Recordset** object is opened by specifying a table name for the ***Source*** argument and the **adCmdTableDirect** constant for the ***Options*** argument, you will be able to use the **Index** property to use table indexes for scrolling and searching for records.
adOpenKeyset	**adLockOptimistic**	The **Recordset** object has an updatable, scrollable cursor. You can see updates and deletions, but not insertions made by other users. The record is not locked to save updates to the current record until the **Update** method is called, or when you move to a different record. If the **Recordset** object is opened by specifying a table name for the ***Source*** argument and the **adCmdTableDirect** constant for the ***Options*** argument, you will be able to use the **Index** property to use table indexes for scrolling and searching for records.
adOpenKeyset	**adBatchOptimistic**	The **Recordset** object has an updatable, scrollable cursor. When using server-side cursors, the batch size is limited to one record. This makes this type of **Recordset** object functionally similar to the previous entry, except that updates to the current record aren't automatically saved if you move to a different record without calling the **UpdateBatch** method. The updated record is not locked until the **UpdateBatch** method is called. If the **Recordset** object is opened by specifying a table name for the ***Source*** argument and the **adCmdTableDirect** constant for the ***Options*** argument, you will be able to use the **Index** property to use table indexes for scrolling and searching for records.
adOpenKeyset	**adLockPessimistic**	The **Recordset** object has an updatable, scrollable cursor. You can see updates and deletions, but not insertions made by other users. The record is locked when the first field is modified. If the **Recordset** object is opened by specifying a table name for the ***Source*** argument and the **adCmdTableDirect** constant for the ***Options*** argument, you will be able to use the **Index** property to use table indexes for scrolling and searching for records.
adOpenDynamic	**adLockReadOnly**	Dynamic cursors are not supported for Access databases by the server cursor engine. A Static cursor is returned instead.
adOpenDynamic	**adLockOptimistic** **adLockPessimistic** **adBatchOptimistic**	Dynamic cursors are not supported for Access databases by the server cursor engine. If you request a Dynamic cursor for all other lock types, you will receive a Keyset cursor. However, ADO uses different methods to manipulate the **Recordset** object if you open it by using the ***adOpenDynamic*** argument for the ***CursorType*** argument. This may result in improved performance when scrolling large numbers of records compared to an explicitly requested Keyset cursor.

CursorType	*LockType*	Results
Not specified	**adLockReadOnly**	If you don't specify the ***CursorType*** argument, a Static cursor is returned.
Not specified	**adLockOptimistic** **adLockPessimistic** **adBatchOptimistic**	If you don't specify the ***CursorType*** argument for all other lock types, a Keyset cursor is returned.

If you use the Microsoft Jet 4.0 OLE DB Provider with client-side cursors (**CursorLocation** = **adUseClient**), the provider doesn't support Forward-only (**adOpenForwardOnly**), Keyset (**adOpenKeyset**), or Dynamic (**adOpenDynamic**) cursors. If you attempt to set the ***CursorType*** argument to any of these settings, the provider will return a static (**adOpenStatic**) cursor. For client-side cursors, the only ***CursorType*** setting supported is a static (**adOpenStatic**) cursor. The following table describes the results you can expect when using each of the ***LockType*** settings with a static cursor from the client cursor engine.

LockType	Results
adLockReadOnly	The **Recordset** object contains a scrollable snapshot of your data. You will not see updates, insertions, or deletions made by other users unless you use the **Requery** method.
adLockOptimistic	The **Recordset** object contains a scrollable, updatable snapshot of your data. Changes are made on a record-by-record basis.
adBatchOptimistic	The **Recordset** object contains a scrollable, updatable snapshot of your data. Changes can be grouped into batches and processed all at once by using the **UpdateBatch** method.
adLockPessimistic	Pessimistic locks are not supported by the client cursor engine. An Optimistic lock is used instead.

Determining Cursor Features

You can use the ADO **Supports** method to determine what types of functionality are supported when you open a **Recordset** object against the current OLE DB provider. The **Supports** method returns a Boolean value that indicates whether the provider supports the features identified by the various ***CursorOptions*** constants. For example, the **adAddNew** constant is used to determine if the current **Recordset** object supports your using the **AddNew** method for adding new records.

Note Although the **Supports** method may return **True** for a given functionality, it does not guarantee that the OLE DB provider can make the feature available under all circumstances. The **Supports** method simply tells whether or not the provider can support the specified functionality, assuming that certain conditions are met. For example, the **Supports** method may indicate that a **Recordset** object supports updates even though the cursor is based on a multi-table join, some fields of which are not updatable.

For more information about the **Supports** method, see ADO Help. For an example of a procedure that lists the features supported by any OLE DB provider, see the ProviderSupports procedure in the OpenRecordset module in the DataAccess.mdb sample file, which is available in the Samples\CH14 subfolder on the companion CD-ROM.

Opening a Forward-Only, Read-Only Recordset Object

The following code demonstrates how to open a forward-only, read-only **Recordset** object.

```
Sub OpenReadOnlyRecordset(strDBPath As String, _
                          strSQL As String)
   Dim cnn As ADODB.Connection
   Dim rst As ADODB.Recordset
   Dim fld As ADODB.Field

   Set cnn = New ADODB.Connection
   ' Open the connection.
   With cnn
      .Provider = "Microsoft.Jet.OLEDB.4.0"
      .Open strDBPath
   End With

   Set rst = New ADODB.Recordset
   With rst
      ' Open a forward-only, read-only Recordset object.
      .Open Source:= strSQL, _
         ActiveConnection:= cnn, _
         CursorType:=adOpenForwardOnly, _
         LockType:=adLockReadOnly

      ' Display the records in the Debug window.
      Do While Not .EOF
         For Each fld In .Fields
            Debug.Print fld.Value & ";";
         Next
         Debug.Print
         .MoveNext
      Loop

      'Close the Recordset.
      .Close
   End With

   ' Close connection and destroy object variables.
   cnn.Close
   Set rst = Nothing
   Set cnn = Nothing
End Sub
```

For example, to use this procedure to open the Customers table in the Northwind database and return only customers from Washington State, you can use a line of code like this:

```
OpenReadOnlyRecordset _
   "c:\Program Files\Microsoft Office\Office\Samples\Northwind.mdb", _
   "SELECT * FROM Customers WHERE Region = 'WA'"
```

The OpenReadOnlyRecordset procedure can be found in the OpenRecordset module in the DataAccess.mdb sample file, which is available in the Samples\CH14 subfolder on the companion CD-ROM.

In the ADO code above, the **Recordset** object is opened and then the data in the **Recordset** object is printed to the Immediate pane by moving through each record in the **Recordset** object and then iterating through each field in the **Fields** collection.

This can be rewritten to use the **Recordset** object's **GetString** method to print the data to the Immediate pane. The **GetString** method returns a formatted, delimited string that contains some or all of the records in the **Recordset** object. If you use the **GetString** method, the **Do While** loop in the previous example could be replaced with the single line:

```
Debug.Print rst.GetString(StringFormat:=adClipString, _
                          ColumnDelimeter:=";", _
                          RowDelimeter:=vbCrLf)
```

Note The ***ColumnDelimeter*** and ***RowDelimeter*** named arguments are intentionally misspelled because this is how they are defined in the ADO object library.

This method is useful for populating grids and other controls that allow you to pass in a formatted string representing the data. The **GetString** method is also faster than looping through the **Recordset** object and generating the string.

Updating Data in a Recordset Object

The following code demonstrates how to open a scrollable, updatable **Recordset** object and modify the data in a record.

```
Sub UpdateRecordset(strDBPath As String, _
                    strSQL As String, _
                    strUpdateFld As String, _
                    strUpdateValue As String)
   Dim cnn As ADODB.Connection
   Dim rst As ADODB.Recordset

   Set cnn = New ADODB.Connection
   ' Open the connection.
   With cnn
      .Provider = "Microsoft.Jet.OLEDB.4.0"
      .Open strDBPath
   End With
```

```
    Set rst = New ADODB.Recordset
    With rst
       ' Open the Recordset object.
       .Open Source:= strSQL, _
          ActiveConnection:= cnn, _
          CursorType:= adOpenKeyset, _
          LockType:= adLockOptimistic

       ' Update the specified field for the current record.
       .Fields(strUpdateFld).Value = strUpdateValue

       ' Save the changes you made to the current record in the Recordset object.
       .Update

       ' Close the Recordset object.
       .Close
    End With

    ' Close connection and destroy object variables.
    cnn.Close
    Set rst = Nothing
    Set cnn = Nothing
End Sub
```

For example, to use this procedure to open the Customers table in the Northwind database, retrieve the record for the Around the Horn company, and update the ContactName to "Jane New," you can use a line of code like this:

```
UpdateRecordset "c:\Program Files\Microsoft Office\Office\Samples\Northwind.mdb", _
   "SELECT * FROM Customers WHERE CustomerId = 'AROUT'", _
   "ContactName", "Jane New"
```

The UpdateRecordset procedure can be found in the OpenRecordset module in the DataAccess.mdb sample file, which is available in the Samples\CH14 subfolder on the companion CD-ROM.

ADO and DAO code for updating data in a **Recordset** object is very similar. The major difference between the two examples above is that DAO requires that you put the **Recordset** object into an editable state by using the **Edit** method, whereas ADO does not require that you explicitly indicate that you want to be in edit mode. In both DAO and ADO, you can verify the edit status of the current record by checking the **EditMode** property.

One difference between DAO and ADO to be aware of is the behavior when you update a record and then move to another record without calling the **Update** method. In DAO, any changes made to the current record are lost when you move to another record without first calling the **Update** method. In ADO, on the other hand, the changes to the current record are automatically saved when you move to a new record. You can explicitly discard changes to the current record with both DAO and ADO by using the **CancelUpdate** method.

Opening a Recordset Object by Using a Saved Query

Saved queries that return records in an Access database may have parameters (a parameter query) or not have parameters (an Access select query). The following sections describe how to use an ADO **Recordset** object to work with each kind of saved query.

Opening a Query That Has No Parameters and Returns Records

To open a **Recordset** object by using a saved query that returns records and has no parameters, pass the query's name as the ***source*** argument to the **Open** method of the **Recordset** object, as shown in the following example.

```
Sub RunSavedQuery(strDBPath As String, _
                  strQryName As String)
   Dim cnn As New ADODB.Connection
   Dim rst As New ADODB.Recordset
   Dim fld As ADODB.Field

   ' Open the connection.
   Set cnn = New ADODB.Connection
   With cnn
      .Provider = "Microsoft.Jet.OLEDB.4.0"
      .Open strDBPath
   End With

   Set rst = New ADODB.Recordset
   With rst
      ' Open the query by using a forward-only, read-only Recordset object.
      .Open Source:= strQryName, _
         ActiveConnection:= cnn, _
         CursorType:=adOpenForwardOnly, _
         LockType:=adLockReadOnly

      ' Display the records in the Debug window.
      Do While Not .EOF
         For Each fld In .Fields
            Debug.Print fld.Value & ";";
         Next
         Debug.Print
         .MoveNext
      Loop

      'Close the Recordset object.
      .Close
   End With

   Close connection and destroy object variables.
   cnn.Close
   Set rst = Nothing
   Set cnn = Nothing
End Sub
```

For example, to use a **Recordset** object to open the Products Above Average Price query in the Northwind database, you can use a line of code like this:

```
RunSavedQuery _
   "c:\Program Files\Microsoft Office\Office\Samples\Northwind.mdb", _
   "[Products Above Average Price]"
```

Note that with ADO, if the query name contains spaces, you must use either square brackets ([ ]) or the accent grave character (`) around the name.

The RunSavedQuery procedure can be found in the OpenRecordset module in the DataAccess.mdb sample file, which is available in the Samples\CH14 subfolder on the companion CD-ROM.

Opening a Query That Has Parameters

One way of running a query that has parameters (or a "parameter query") is to use ADOX code to retrieve the query as a **Command** object from the database's **Procedures** collection, and then specify the parameters by using the **Command** object's **Parameters** collection. The following procedure shows how to do this.

```
Sub RunParamQuery(strDBPath As String, _
                  strQryName As String, _
                  strParamName1 As String, _
                  varParamValue1 As Variant, _
                  strParamName2 As String, _
                  varParamValue2 As Variant)
   Dim cnn As ADODB.Connection
   Dim cat As ADOX.Catalog
   Dim cmd As ADODB.Command
   Dim rst As New ADODB.Recordset
   Dim fld As ADODB.Field

   ' Open the connection.
   Set cnn = New ADODB.Connection
   With cnn
      .Provider = "Microsoft.Jet.OLEDB.4.0"
      .Open strDBPath
   End With

   ' Open the catalog.
   Set cat = New ADOX.Catalog
   cat.ActiveConnection = cnn
```

```
    ' Get the Command object from the Procedures collection.
    Set cmd = New ADODB.Command
    Set cmd = cat.Procedures(strQryName).Command

    ' Specify the parameter values.
    With cmd
       .Parameters(strParamName1) = varParamValue1
       .Parameters(strParamName2) = varParamValue2
    End With

    Set rst = New ADODB.Recordset
    With rst
       ' Open the Command by using a forward-only, read-only Recordset object.
       .Open Source:= cmd, _
          CursorType:=adOpenForwardOnly, _
          LockType:=adLockReadOnly

       ' Display the records in the Debug window.
       Do While Not .EOF
          For Each fld In rst.Fields
             Debug.Print fld.Value & ";";
          Next
          Debug.Print
          .MoveNext
       Loop

       ' Close the Recordset object.
       .Close
    End With

    ' Close connection and destroy object variables.
    cnn.Close
    Set rst = Nothing
    Set cnn = Nothing
End Sub
```

For example, to use a **Recordset** object to open the Employee Sales by Country query in the Northwind database and pass in parameter values, you can use a line of code like this:

```
RunParamQuery "c:\Program Files\Microsoft Office\Office\Samples\Northwind.mdb", _
   "Employee Sales by Country","[Beginning Date]",#8/1/96#,"[Ending Date]",#8/31/96#
```

The RunParamQuery procedure can be found in the OpenRecordset module in the DataAccess.mdb sample file, which is available in the Samples\CH14 subfolder on the companion CD-ROM.

You can use fewer lines of code by specifying the parameter values with the ***Parameters*** argument of the **Command** object's **Execute** method. The following lines of code

```
' Specify the parameter values.
With cmd
   .Parameters(strParamName1) = varParamValue1
   .Parameters(strParamName2) = varParamValue2
End With

Set rst = New ADODB.Recordset
With rst
   ' Open the Command by using a forward-only, read-only Recordset object.
   .Open Source:= cmd, _
      CursorType:=adOpenForwardOnly, _
      LockType:=adLockReadOnly
```

can be replaced by these lines:

```
Set rst = New ADODB.Recordset
' Execute the Command, passing in the values for the parameters.
Set rst = cmd.Execute Parameters:=Array(varParamValue1, varParamValue2)
```

You can also run a parameter query without using any ADOX code by connecting a **Command** object to the database, and then setting its **CommandText** property to the query's name. In this case, you'll also need to set the provider-specific **Jet OLEDB:Stored Query** property of the Microsoft Jet 4.0 OLE DB Provider to **True** to indicate that the command text is the name of a stored query. By default, the Microsoft Jet 4.0 OLE DB Provider evaluates the **CommandText** as an SQL string. In the previous examples that use ADOX code, this was not necessary because a query is automatically recognized as a stored query when it is retrieved from the **Procedures** or **Views** collection. The following procedure shows a complete example of how to run a parameter query without using ADOX code.

```
Sub RunParamQueryNoADOX(strDBPath As String, _
                        strQryName As String, _
                        varParamValue1 As Variant, _
                        varParamValue2 As Variant)
   Dim cnn As ADODB.Connection
   Dim cmd As ADODB.Command
   Dim rst As ADODB.Recordset
   Dim fld As ADODB.Field

   ' Open the connection
   Set cnn = New ADODB.Connection
   With cnn
      .Provider = "Microsoft.Jet.OLEDB.4.0"
      .Open strDBPath
   End With
```

```
    ' Create the command
    Set cmd = New ADODB.Command
    Set cmd.ActiveConnection = cnn
    With cmd
       .Properties("Jet OLEDB:Stored Query") = True
       .CommandText = strQryName
    End With

    ' Execute the command and pass in the values for the parameters.
    Set rst = New ADODB.Recordset
    Set rst = cmd.Execute(Parameters:=Array(varParamValue1, varParamValue2))

    With rst
       ' Display the records in the Immediate pane.
       Do While Not rst.EOF
          For Each fld In .Fields
             Debug.Print fld.Value & ";";
          Next
          Debug.Print
          .MoveNext
       Loop

       ' Close the Recordset object.
       .Close
    End With

    ' Close connection and destroy object variables.
    cnn.Close
    Set rst = Nothing
    Set cnn = Nothing
End Sub
```

To use this procedure to open the Employee Sales by Country query in the Northwind database, you don't need to pass in the parameter names, just the parameter values, like this:

```
RunParamQueryNoADOX _
   "c:\Program Files\Microsoft Office\Office\Samples\Northwind.mdb", _
   "Employee Sales by Country",#8/1/96#,#8/31/96#
```

The RunParamQueryNoADOX procedure can be found in the OpenRecordset module in the DataAccess.mdb sample file, which is available in the Samples\CH14 subfolder on the companion CD-ROM.

Performing Bulk Operations

The **Execute** method of the ADO **Connection** object can be used to run queries that return records, as well as queries that issue SQL statements to perform actions such as updating or deleting multiple records, or that create a table from records read from other tables. These kinds of queries are often called *bulk operations* or *action queries*. The following code example demonstrates how to execute a bulk operation in ADO.

```
Sub RunBulkOpQuery(strDBPath As String, _
                   strSQL As String)
   Dim cnn         As ADODB.Connection
   Dim lngAffected As Long

   ' Open the connection.
   Set cnn = New ADODB.Connection
   With cnn
      .Provider = "Microsoft.Jet.OLEDB.4.0"
      .Open strDBPath
   End With

   ' Execute the query.
   cnn.Execute CommandText:=strSQL, _
               RecordsAffected:=lngAffected, _
               Options:=adExecuteNoRecords

   Debug.Print "Records Affected = " & lngAffected

   ' Close connection and destroy object variables.
   cnn.Close
   Set cnn = Nothing
End Sub
```

For example, to use this procedure to update records in the Customers table in the Northwind database that have "USA" in the Country field to read "United States," you can use a line of code like this:

```
RunBulkOpQuery "c:\Program Files\Microsoft Office\Office\Samples\Northwind.mdb", _
   "UPDATE Customers SET Country = 'United States'" _
    & "WHERE Country = 'USA'"
```

The RunBulkOpQuery procedure can be found in the OpenRecordset module in the DataAccess.mdb sample file, which is available in the Samples\CH14 subfolder on the companion CD-ROM.

Finding Records in a Recordset Object

Both DAO and ADO have two mechanisms for locating a record in a **Recordset** object: the **Find** and **Seek** methods. With both methods you specify criteria to be used to locate a matching record. In general, for equivalent types of searches, the **Seek** method provides better performance than the **Find** method, because the **Seek** method uses an underlying index to locate the record. For this reason, you can only use the **Seek** method on **Recordset** objects that are based on a table (opened by using the ***Options*** argument set to **adCmdTableDirect**) that has an associated index.

Using the Find Method

DAO includes four "Find" methods: **FindFirst**, **FindLast**, **FindNext**, and **FindPrevious**. The method you use is determined by where you want to start searching (from the beginning, end, or current record) and the direction you want to search (forward or backward). However, ADO has a single **Find** method. When you use ADO's **Find** method, the search always starts from the current record. The **Find** method has a ***SearchDirection*** argument that allows you to specify the search direction, and a ***SkipRows*** argument that specifies an offset from the current record from which to begin searching. The following table shows how to map the four DAO **Find** methods to the equivalent functionality in the ADO **Find** method.

DAO method	ADO Find method argument settings	
	SkipRows	*SearchDirection*
FindFirst	0	**adSearchForward** (If not currently positioned on the first record, use the **MoveFirst** method before you use the **Find** method.)
FindLast	0	**adSearchBackward** (If not currently positioned on the last record, use the **MoveLast** method before you use the **Find** method.)
FindNext	1	**adSearchForward**
FindPrevious	1	**adSearchBackward**

DAO and ADO require a different syntax for locating records based on a **Null** value. In DAO if you want to find a record that has a **Null** value you use this syntax:

```
"Region Is Null"
```

And if you want to find a record that does not have a **Null** value for that field, you use this syntax:

```
"Region Is Not Null"
```

ADO, however, does not recognize the VBA **Is** operator. You must use the = or <> operators instead. So the equivalent ADO criteria would be:

```
"Region = Null"
```

–or–

```
"Region <> Null"
```

So far, each of the criteria shown in the examples has been based on a value of a single field. However, with DAO **Find** methods, the ***Criteria*** argument is like the WHERE clause in an SQL statement and can contain multiple fields and comparison operators within the criteria. This is not the case with the ADO **Find** method. The ADO **Find** method's ***Criteria*** argument is a string that contains a single field name, comparison operator, and value to use in the search. If you need to find a record based on multiple fields, use the **Filter** property (see "Filtering and Sorting Data in a Recordset Object" later in this chapter) to create a view of the **Recordset** object that contains only those records that match the criteria.

DAO and ADO also behave differently if no record that meets the specified criteria is found. The DAO **Find** and **Seek** methods set the **NoMatch** property to **True** and the current record is not defined. If the ADO **Find** and **Seek** methods don't find a record that meets the criteria, the current record is positioned after the end of the **Recordset** object if you are searching forward (**EOF = True**), or before the beginning of the **Recordset** object if you are searching backward (**BOF = True**). Use the **BOF** or **EOF** property as appropriate to determine whether or not a match was found.

The following example demonstrates how to locate a record by using the ADO **Find** method.

```
Sub FindRecord(strDBPath As String, _
               strTable As String, _
               strCriteria As String, _
               strDisplayField As String)
   Dim cnn As ADODB.Connection
   Dim rst As ADODB.Recordset

   ' Open the connection.
   Set cnn = New ADODB.Connection
   With cnn
      .Provider = "Microsoft.Jet.OLEDB.4.0"
      .Open strDBPath
   End With

   Set rst = New ADODB.Recordset
   With rst
      ' Open the table by using a scrolling Recordset object.
      .Open Source:= strTable, _
            ActiveConnection:= cnn, _
            CursorType:=adOpenKeyset, _
            LockType:=adLockOptimistic

      ' Find the first record that meets the criteria.
      .Find Criteria:=strCriteria, SearchDirection:=adSearchForward
```

```
      ' Make sure record was found (not at end of file).
      If Not .EOF Then
         ' Print the first record and all remaining
         ' records that meet the criteria.
         Do While Not .EOF
            Debug.Print .Fields(strDisplayField).Value
            ' Skip the current record and find next match.
            .Find Criteria:=strCriteria, SkipRecords:=1
         Loop
      Else
         MsgBox "Record not found"
      End If
      ' Close the Recordset object.
      .Close
   End With

   ' Close connection and destroy object variables.
   cnn.Close
   Set rst = Nothing
   Set cnn = Nothing
End Sub
```

For example, to use this procedure to find records in the Customers table in the Northwind database that have "USA" in the Country field, you can use a line of code like this:

```
FindRecord "c:\Program Files\Microsoft Office\Office\Samples\Northwind.mdb", _
   "Customers","Country='USA'","CustomerID"
```

The FindRecord procedure can be found in the OpenRecordset module in the DataAccess.mdb sample file, which is available in the Samples\CH14 subfolder on the companion CD-ROM.

Using the Seek Method

Because the ADO **Seek** method uses an index, it is a good idea to specify an index before you search. However, if you don't specify an index, the Jet database engine will use the primary key index.

If you need to specify a value for more than one field, use the VBA **Array** function to pass those values to the ***KeyValues*** argument of the **Seek** method. If you only need to specify one value, it is not necessary to use the **Array** function.

As with the **Find** method, you use the **BOF** or **EOF** property (depending on the search direction) to determine whether or not a matching record was found.

The following example shows how to locate a record by using the ADO **Seek** method.

```
Sub SeekRecord(strDBPath As String, _
               strIndex As String, _
               strTable As String, _
               varKeyValues As Variant, _
               strDisplayField As String)
   Dim cnn As ADODB.Connection
   Dim rst As ADODB.Recordset

   ' Open the connection.
   Set cnn = New ADODB.Connection
   With cnn
      .Provider = "Microsoft.Jet.OLEDB.4.0"
      .Open strDBPath
   End With

   Set rst = New ADODB.Recordset
   With rst
      ' Select the index used to order the data in the Recordset object.
      .Index = strIndex

   ' Open the table by using a scrolling Recordset object.
      .Open Source:= strTable, _
            ActiveConnection:= cnn, _
            CursorType:=adOpenKeyset, _
            LockType:=adLockOptimistic, _
            Options:=adCmdTableDirect

   ' Find the order where OrderId = 10255 and ProductId = 16.
      .Seek KeyValues:=varKeyValues, SeekOption:=adSeekFirstEQ

   ' If a match is found, print the value of the specified field.
      If Not .EOF Then
         Debug.Print .Fields(strDisplayField).Value
      End If

   ' Close the Recordset object.
      .Close
   End With

   ' Close connection and destroy object variables.
   cnn.Close
   Set rst = Nothing
   Set cnn = Nothing
End Sub
```

For example, to use the PrimaryKey index to find records in the Order Details table in the Northwind database where the OrderID field is 10255 and ProductID is 16 and display the value in the Quantity field, you can use a line of code like this:

```
SeekRecord "c:\Program Files\Microsoft Office\Office\Samples\Northwind.mdb", _
   "PrimaryKey", "Order Details", Array(10255,16), "Quantity"
```

The SeekRecord procedure can be found in the OpenRecordset module in the DataAccess.mdb sample file, which is available in the Samples\CH14 subfolder on the companion CD-ROM.

Using Bookmarks

A *bookmark* is a system-generated value that uniquely identifies each record in a scrolling **Recordset** object. The **Bookmark** property of the **Recordset** object specifies the value of the current record. You can use the **Bookmark** property to store the bookmark of the current record and then return to that record from any other record in the **Recordset** object. To store the bookmark for a record, move to that record, and then assign the value of the **Bookmark** property to a **Variant** variable. To return to the bookmarked record after moving to a different record, set the **Bookmark** property to the value of that variable.

If you use the **Clone** method to create a copy of a **Recordset** object, the **Bookmark** property settings for the original and cloned **Recordset** objects are identical and you can use them interchangeably. However, you can't use bookmarks from different **Recordset** objects interchangeably, even if they were created from the same source or command.

The following procedure shows how you can use a bookmark to save the current record position and then return to it from any record in the **Recordset** object.

```
Sub BookmarkRecord()
   Dim rst         As ADODB.Recordset
   Dim strMessage  As String
   Dim intCommand  As Integer
   Dim varBookmark As Variant

   ' Open Recordset object with data from Employees table.
   Set rst = New ADODB.Recordset
   With rst
      .Open Source:="SELECT LastName, FirstName FROM Employees " & _
            "ORDER BY LastName", _
            ActiveConnection:=CurrentProject.Connection, _
            CursorType:=adOpenStatic, _
            Options:=adCmdText
      .MoveFirst
```

```
      Do While True
         ' Display information about current
         ' record and get user input.
         strMessage = _
            "Employee: " & !FirstName & " " & !LastName & vbCr & _
            "(record " & .AbsolutePosition & _
            " of " & .RecordCount & ")" & vbCr & vbCr & _
            "Enter command:" & vbCr & _
            "1 = Next" & vbCr & _
            "2 = Previous" & vbCr & _
            "3 = Set Bookmark" & vbCr & _
            "4 = Go to Bookmark"
         intCommand = Val(InputBox(strMessage))

         Select Case intCommand
            ' Move forward, trapping for EOF.
            Case 1
               .MoveNext
               If .EOF Then
                  MsgBox "You tried to move past the last record." & _
                     vbCr & "Try again."
                  .MoveLast
               End If
            ' Move backward, trapping for BOF.
            Case 2
               .MovePrevious
               If .BOF Then
                  MsgBox "You tried to move past the first record." & _
                     vbCr & "Try again."
                  .MoveFirst
               End If
            ' Store the bookmark of the current record.
            Case 3
               varBookmark = .Bookmark
            ' Go to the record indicated by the stored bookmark.
            Case 4
               If IsEmpty(varBookmark) Then
                  MsgBox "No Bookmark set!"
               Else
                  .Bookmark = varBookmark
               End If
            Case Else
               Exit Do
         End Select
      Loop
      .Close
   End With
   Set rst = Nothing
End Sub
```

The BookmarkRecord procedure can be found in the OpenRecordset module in the DataAccess.mdb sample file, which is available in the Samples\CH14 subfolder on the companion CD-ROM.

Filtering and Sorting Data in a Recordset Object

The following sections describe how to filter and sort data in an ADO **Recordset** object.

Filtering Records

The DAO and ADO **Filter** properties are used slightly differently:

- In DAO, the **Filter** property is used to specify a filter to be applied to any subsequently opened **Recordset** objects that are based on the **Recordset** object to which you have applied the filter. You must essentially create a clone of the original **Recordset** object in order to filter the data.
- In ADO, the **Filter** property applies directly to the **Recordset** object on which you set the filter. The ADO **Filter** property allows you to create a temporary view that can be used to locate a particular record or set of records within the current **Recordset** object. When a filter is applied to the current **Recordset** object, the **RecordCount** property reflects just the number of records available after you apply the filter. The filter can be removed by setting the **Filter** property to **adFilterNone**.

The following example shows how to filter a **Recordset** object by using the ADO **Filter** property.

```
Sub FilterRecordset(strDBPath As String, _
                    strTable As String, _
                    strFilter As String, _
                    strDisplayField As String)
   Dim cnn As ADODB.Connection
   Dim rst As ADODB.Recordset

   ' Open the connection.
   Set cnn = New ADODB.Connection
   With cnn
      .Provider = "Microsoft.Jet.OLEDB.4.0"
      .Open strDBPath
   End With

   Set rst = New ADODB.Recordset
   With rst
      ' Open the table by using a scrolling Recordset object.
      .Open Source:= strTable, _
            ActiveConnection:= cnn, _
            CursorType:=adOpenKeyset, _
            LockType:=adLockOptimistic

      ' Filter the Recordset object.
      .Filter = strFilter
```

```
        ' Print the records.
        Do While Not .EOF
           Debug.Print .Fields(strDisplayField).Value
           .MoveNext
        Loop

        ' Close the Recordset object.
        .Close
    End With

    ' Close connection and destroy object variables.
    cnn.Close
    Set rst = Nothing
    Set cnn = Nothing
End Sub
```

To use this procedure to filter a **Recordset** object opened on the Customers table in the Northwind database to include only those customers in the U.S. that have a fax number and display the values in the CustomerID field, you can use a line of code like this:

```
FilterRecordset "c:\Program Files\Microsoft Office\Office\Samples\Northwind.mdb", _
   "Customers", "Country='USA' And Fax<>Null", "CustomerID"
```

The FilterRecordset procedure can be found in the OpenRecordset module in the DataAccess.mdb sample file, which is available in the Samples\CH14 subfolder on the companion CD-ROM.

Sorting Records

Like the **Filter** property, the DAO and ADO **Sort** properties differ in that the DAO **Sort** method applies to subsequently opened **Recordset** objects, and for ADO it applies only to the current **Recordset** object.

The Microsoft Jet 4.0 OLE DB Provider doesn't support the **IViewFilter** or **IViewSort** OLE DB interfaces that ADO uses to filter and sort **Recordset** objects. For the **Filter** property, ADO will automatically call the client cursor engine to perform the filtering. However, for the **Sort** method, you must explicitly specify that you want to use the client cursor engine by setting the **CursorLocation** property to the **adUseClient** constant before you open the **Recordset** object. The client cursor engine will copy all of the records in the **Recordset** object to a cache on your local machine and will build temporary indexes in order to perform the sorting. In many cases, you will get better performance by re-executing the query used to open the **Recordset** object and by specifying an SQL WHERE or ORDER BY clause as appropriate.

The following example shows how to sort a **Recordset** object by using the ADO **Sort** property.

```
Sub SortRecordset(strDBPath As String, _
                  strTable As String, _
                  strSort As String, _
                  strDisplayField As String)
   Dim cnn As ADODB.Connection
   Dim rst As ADODB.Recordset

   ' Open the connection.
   Set cnn = New ADODB.Connection
   With cnn
      .Provider = "Microsoft.Jet.OLEDB.4.0"
      .Open strDBPath
   End With

   Set rst = New ADODB.Recordset
   With rst
      ' Specify client-side cursor.
      .CursorLocation = adUseClient

      ' Open the table by using a scrolling Recordset object.
      .Open Source:= strTable, _
            ActiveConnection:= cnn, _
            CursorType:=adOpenKeyset, _
            LockType:=adLockOptimistic

      ' Sort the Recordset object.
      .Sort = strSort

      ' Print the records.
      Do While Not .EOF
         Debug.Print .Fields(strDisplayField).Value
         .MoveNext
      Loop

      ' Close the Recordset object.
      .Close
End With

   ' Close connection and destroy object variables.
   cnn.Close
   Set rst = Nothing
   Set cnn = Nothing
End Sub
```

For example, to use this procedure to sort a **Recordset** object opened on the Customers table in the Northwind database by the Country and Region fields and display the values in the CustomerID field, you can use a line of code like this:

```
SortRecordset "c:\Program Files\Microsoft Office\Office\Samples\Northwind.mdb", _
   "Customers","Country, Region", "CustomerID"
```

The SortRecordset procedure can be found in the OpenRecordset module in the DataAccess.mdb sample file, which is available in the Samples\CH14 subfolder on the companion CD-ROM.

Where to Go from Here

For additional information about the subjects discussed in this chapter, see the following sources.

Database Design

Hernandez, Michael J. *Database Design for Mere Mortals*. Reading, MA: Addison-Wesley Developers Press, 1997.

Roman, Steven. *Access Database Design and Programming*. Sebastopol, CA: O'Reilly & Associates, 1997.

Data Access Objects (DAO)

Microsoft Jet Database Engine Programmer's Guide, Second Edition. Redmond, WA: Microsoft Press, 1997.

Microsoft Office Developer Forum Web site (http://www.microsoft.com/officedev/)

Universal Data Access Strategy

Microsoft Universal Data Access Web site (http://www.microsoft.com/data/)

OLE DB

Microsoft OLE DB Web site (http://www.microsoft.com/data/oledb/)

ActiveX Data Objects (ADO)

Microsoft ActiveX Data Objects Web site
(http://www.microsoft.com/data/ado/)

Vaughn, William R. *Hitchhiker's Guide to Visual Basic and SQL Server, Sixth Edition*. Redmond, WA: Microsoft Press, 1998.

Microsoft Office Developer Forum Web site
(http://www.microsoft.com/officedev/)

Using ADO with MDB Files and the Microsoft Jet Database Engine

Microsoft Jet Database Engine Programmer's Guide, Third Edition. Redmond, WA: Microsoft Press, 1999.

Microsoft ActiveX Data Objects Web site
(http://www.microsoft.com/data/ado/)

Code Samples

The code samples shown in this chapter, along with additional examples that demonstrate similar techniques, can be copied from the files in the Samples\CH14 subfolder on the companion CD-ROM.

CHAPTER 15

Retrieving and Analyzing Data

Nearly any solution that stores data also needs to retrieve, analyze, and present the data in a manner that makes the data easy to understand. Although there are quick and simple ways to present data, such as in a Microsoft Access report, you may need to design a custom reporting component for your application if you want to create flexible or dynamic reports. There are so many ways to retrieve data and create reports that deciding on the best format for a report can be a challenging task. This chapter discusses some of the options available to you for creating reports in Microsoft Office solutions.

Contents

Retrieving Data from a Data Source

The first step in creating a report is determining where the data is located and how to retrieve it. In an Office 2000 solution, your data can come from a variety of places—a relational database such as an Access or SQL Server database, a spreadsheet, a text file, a MAPI store (such as a Microsoft Exchange data source), or a table on a Web page, to name a few. For more information about the types of data sources you can access from an Office solution, see Chapter 14, "Working with the Data Access Components of an Office Solution."

In some cases, a table in your data source contains exactly the data that you want to present. In most cases, however, you need to create a query to retrieve the data you want from a data source. Queries that you create in Office 2000 applications are expressed as statements in Structured Query Language (SQL), which is a universal language for data access from relational data sources.

You can construct an SQL statement by typing it directly into your code. For complex SQL statements, however, you may want to use a tool that allows you to construct the query visually and then copy the corresponding SQL statement. Office 2000 contains several tools that you can use to create SQL statements that you can copy into your code. You can use these tools to create saved queries or temporary queries.

Query-Building Tools

The following sections describe tools you can use to build queries in Office 2000.

Access Query Tools

The Microsoft Access query wizards (Simple Query Wizard, Crosstab Query Wizard, Find Duplicates Query Wizard, and Find Unmatched Query Wizard) step you through the process of creating commonly used queries. After you've created a query by using one of the wizards, you can open it in Design view, and then view it in SQL view.

The Access query design grid provides a simple visual tool for building saved queries. You can create a query in the query design grid and display the result set in Datasheet view to test it. Access generates the corresponding SQL statement for the query, which you can copy from the query's SQL view.

From Visual Basic for Applications (VBA) code, you can use the ActiveX Data Objects (ADO) data definition language (DDL) to create saved SELECT queries. You can also create temporary and saved queries in an Access database by using the Data Access Objects (DAO) **QueryDef** object. For more information about creating queries programmatically, see Chapter 14, "Working with the Data Access Components of an Office Solution."

Note You can also create saved SQL pass-through, union, and data definition queries in Access. These are SQL-specific queries, however, so you can't use the query design grid; you must type the SQL statement directly into SQL view.

For more information about using the Access query tools, search the Microsoft Access Help index for "queries, creating."

Excel Query Tools

Microsoft Excel includes Microsoft Query, a tool similar to the Access query design grid, which you can use to create queries and return the result sets to an Excel worksheet. You can also save queries created in Microsoft Query as database queries (.dqy). Within the Microsoft Query grid, click **SQL** on the **View** menu to view or edit the SQL statement that's associated with the query shown in the grid.

Note The syntax for an SQL string shown in SQL view in the Access query design grid is not identical to that of the SQL string shown in SQL view in Microsoft Query for the same query. In other words, you can't copy an SQL string from Access into Microsoft Query, or vice versa, without making minor modifications. You need to change brackets([ ]) to accent grave characters (`), which are found on the same key as the tilde (~). Also, a query that you create in Microsoft Query may include the path to the database within the SQL statement, which isn't allowed in Access.

You can also create a saved Web query (.iqy) in Excel. A Web query extracts data from text or tables on a Web page and imports that data into Excel. A Web query does not have a corresponding SQL statement because it pulls data directly from a Web page without modification. However, Web queries are useful for displaying data from a Web page in Excel, especially if that data is updated frequently. For example, some of the sample Web queries included with Excel 2000 retrieve stock quotes from the Microsoft Investor Web site. To try one of the sample Web queries, click **Get External Data** on the **Data** menu in Excel, then click **Run Saved Query** and select a Web query from the **Run Query** dialog box. To create a new Web query, click **Get External Data** on the **Data** menu, and then select **New Web Query**. In the **New Web Query** dialog box, enter the address for the Web page that contains the data you want.

Note A Web query (.iqy) file is a text file that specifies the URL of the Web page containing the data, any data to be posted, and options indicating how the data is to be retrieved and formatted. You can edit a Web query file in a text editor such as Notepad.

You can create a third type of saved query in Excel 2000, an online analytical processing (OLAP) query (.oqy). An OLAP query returns data from any OLE DB for OLAP provider, such as Microsoft SQL Server OLAP Services, which provides rapid, sophisticated data analysis on large volumes of data. For information about OLAP queries, see the Universal Data Access Web site at http://www.microsoft.com/data/. For information about Microsoft SQL Server OLAP Services, see the Microsoft SQL Server OLAP Services Web site at http://www.microsoft.com/sql/olap/.

Writing SQL Statements

When you create a report, you usually want to display data without affecting the data itself. The SQL statement that you construct to retrieve the data will therefore usually be a SELECT statement. The following table describes the common types of SELECT queries.

Query type	Description	Example
Simple SELECT	Selects specified fields (columns) from one or more tables.	`SELECT ProductID, ProductName FROM Products;`
Totals	Groups data at table level or at group level; may summarize data with SQL aggregate functions.	`SELECT Title, Min(BirthDate) AS MinOfBirthDate FROM Employees GROUP BY Title;`
INNER JOIN	Joins two tables on a field that both have in common; results include only records (rows) for which both tables share a common value in the joined field.	`SELECT CategoryName, ProductName FROM Categories INNER JOIN Products ON Categories.CategoryID = Products.CategoryID ORDER BY CategoryName;`
LEFT OUTER JOIN and RIGHT OUTER JOIN	Joins two tables on a field that both have in common; results include all records from one table and only records from the other table where the joined fields are equal. Useful for finding unmatched records in two tables.	`SELECT Employees.LastName, Orders.OrderID FROM Employees LEFT JOIN Orders ON Employees.EmployeeID = Orders.EmployeeID ORDER BY Employees.LastName;`
UNION	Returns combined result set including records from two tables that have common fields.	`SELECT City, CompanyName, ContactName FROM Customers UNION SELECT City, CompanyName, ContactName FROM Suppliers ORDER BY City, CompanyName;`
Crosstab	Summarizes tabular data in a columnar format.	`TRANSFORM Sum([Order Details].[UnitPrice]*[Quantity]) AS Total SELECT OrderID FROM Products INNER JOIN [Order Details] ON Products.ProductID = [Order Details].ProductID GROUP BY OrderID PIVOT ProductName;`
TOP N, TOP N PERCENT	Retrieves the top *n* or *n* percent of values, based on the order in which the records are sorted.	`SELECT TOP 10 PERCENT UnitsInStock, ProductID, ProductName FROM Products ORDER BY UnitsInStock;`
Parameter	Prompts user to enter parameters for query that are used to restrict the result set.	`SELECT ProductName, UnitPrice FROM Products WHERE ProductName Like [Enter first part of product name:] & "*" ORDER BY ProductName;`

For more information about designing SQL statements, search the Microsoft Access Help index for “SQL statements.”

Presenting Data in Office Solutions

Most solutions that manage data include some way of presenting that data in reports. By creating reports, you can turn raw data into usable information.

There are lots of different ways to present data in an Office solution. How you build reports depends on how your solution is designed and where the data is stored. For example, suppose that Access forms the basis for your solution, so that users interact with data through Access forms and data access pages. However, your users may prefer to view and manipulate data in Excel so that they can create custom reports with maximum flexibility. In that case, you may want to export data from Access to Excel. On the other hand, if your data is stored in an Access or SQL Server database but your solution is Excel-based, you probably want to write code in Excel to display the data.

When you design a custom report, you should ask yourself these two questions:

- Should the data in the report be static or dynamic?

  A static report is not linked to the data source. In order to display updated data, you must re-create a static report. This approach is fine for data that does not change frequently, or reports that are re-created only occasionally, such as weekly or monthly. One advantage to a static report is that it's easy to alter the report's data source. For example, you can enhance the report by adding additional fields before you re-create it. Or perhaps you need to allow the user to choose which fields are to be included in the report each time it is created.

  A dynamic report remains linked to the data source, and the user can view updated data by refreshing the report. Dynamic reports are easy to create, but you need to ensure that the data source will be available when the user refreshes the report. If you change the structure of a dynamic report's data source (for example, by adding a new field), you need to re-create the report. Refreshing a report will not display new fields added to the underlying query.

- Should the report be read-only, or should users be able to manipulate the data?

  If the data to be displayed in a report is fairly simple, you can present it as a read-only report—that is, a report that the user can view but not modify after it's been created. Read-only reports include Access reports, report snapshots, and objects saved as HTML. Of course, you can write code that sorts, filters, or otherwise customizes a read-only report as it is being created. A customer phone list is an example of a report that could be a read-only report.

  If the data to be presented is more complex, you may want to create a report that users can manipulate to display the data the way that they want it. Excel is an ideal tool for this—you can build a report including data lists, PivotTable reports, and charts, all of which the user can alter in the Excel user interface.

The following sections outline some common approaches for presenting data in an Office solution.

Building Custom Reports in Access

If your data is stored in an Access database, or in an Access table that is linked to another data source, you have several options for presenting data from within Access or on a Web page. Access reports are the obvious choice, but if they don't meet your needs, you can also create report snapshots, static or dynamic Web pages, and subforms within forms.

Keep in mind that it's also fairly straightforward to create a report in Excel from data that's stored in Access, if you want to present data in a spreadsheet format. "Building Custom Reports for External Data in Excel" later in this chapter discusses creating custom reports in Excel.

Creating Access Reports

If your data is stored in an Access database and you want to create a report that displays dynamic data, an Access report is a simple solution. The data in an Access report is refreshed each time you reopen the report. You can also format Access reports easily, so they make excellent printed reports. However, an Access report is read-only; users cannot manipulate, analyze, or filter the data in the report. If your solution requires that users be able to manipulate the data in novel ways, consider another type of report.

You can create an Access report from VBA code by using the **CreateReport** method, and then add controls to the report by using the **CreateReportControl** method. The following **Property Let** procedure creates an Access report from a table or query.

```
Private Property Let CustomReport_Source(RHS As String)
   ' Create report based on specified data source.
   Dim txtNew     As Access.TextBox
   Dim lblNew     As Access.Label
   Dim rstSource  As ADODB.Recordset
   Dim fldData    As ADODB.Field
   Dim lngTop     As Long
   Dim lngLeft    As Long

   lngLeft = 0
   lngTop = 0

   ' Set report's RecordSource property.
   Me.Report.RecordSource = RHS
   ' Open recordset on specified record source.
   Set rstSource = New ADODB.Recordset
   rstSource.Open "SELECT * FROM [" & RHS & "];", _
      CurrentProject.Connection, adOpenForwardOnly
   ' Create corresponding label and text box controls for each field.
```

```
   For Each fldData In rstSource.Fields
      ' Create new text box control and size to fit data.
      Set txtNew = CreateReportControl(Me.Report.Name, acTextBox, _
         acDetail, , fldData.Name, lngLeft + 1500, lngTop)
      txtNew.SizeToFit
      ' Create new label control and size to fit data.
      Set lblNew = CreateReportControl(Me.Report.Name, acLabel, acDetail, _
         txtNew.Name, fldData.Name, lngLeft, lngTop, 1400, txtNew.Height)
      lblNew.SizeToFit
      ' Increment top value for next control.
      lngTop = lngTop + txtNew.Height + 25
   Next

CustomReport_Source_End:
   On Error Resume Next
   rstSource.Close
   Set rstSource = Nothing
   Exit Property
End Property
```

This procedure is available in the AccessReport class module of the NorthwindReports.mdb sample file, which is available in the Samples\CH15 subfolder on the companion CD-ROM.

For more information about creating and formatting Access reports, search the Microsoft Access Help index for "reports."

Creating a Report Snapshot from an Access Report

You can save Access reports as HTML files (.htm). However, an Access report saved as HTML doesn't retain all of its formatting. If you want to view a formatted Access report in a Web page, save it as a report snapshot file (.snp), and then use the Snapshot Viewer ActiveX control (Snapview.ocx) to embed the report snapshot in a Web page. You can also view a report snapshot file in the Snapshot Viewer, which is included with Microsoft Access, and which can be downloaded free of charge from the Microsoft Office Developer Forum Web site at http://www.microsoft.com/officedev/index/snapshot.htm. Users who don't have Access can use the Snapshot Viewer to view Access reports.

A report snapshot displays only static data. To update the data in a report snapshot, you must re-create the report snapshot file from the report.

To create a report snapshot from VBA, use the **OutputTo** method of the Access **DoCmd** object, passing in the constant **acFormatSNP** for the *outputformat* argument. For example, the following line of code creates a report snapshot file from an Access report named Invoice:

```
DoCmd.OutputTo acOutputReport, "Invoice", acFormatSNP, _
   CurrentProject.Path & "\Invoice.snp"
```

Note You can also use the **OutputTo** method to output data from Access to a number of other formats, which may be useful for creating custom reports. For more information, search the Microsoft Access Visual Basic Reference Help index for "OutputTo method."

For more information about creating report snapshot files, search the Microsoft Access Help index for "report snapshots."

Creating Web Pages from Access Objects

You can create either static or dynamic reports for the Web from Access. The following sections outline ways to create either type.

Creating Static Web Pages

To create a static Web page from Access, you have three options:

- You can export a table or query as an HTML file by using the **TransferText** method of the **DoCmd** object:

  ```
  DoCmd.TransferText acExportHTML, , "Products", "Products.htm"
  ```

- You can output a table, query, form, or report as an HTML file by using the **OutputTo** method of the **DoCmd** object:

  ```
  DoCmd.OutputTo acOutputTable, "Products", acFormatHTML, _
     "Products.htm"
  ```

- You can output a report as a report snapshot, and then embed the report snapshot in a data access page by using the Snapshot Viewer ActiveX control. See the previous section, "Creating a Report Snapshot from an Access Report," for more information about report snapshots, and the following section, "Creating Dynamic Web Pages," for more information about data access pages.

Note Although data access pages may be dynamically linked to a data source, a report snapshot is always a static report, even when it is embedded in a data access page.

Creating Dynamic Web Pages

To create a dynamic Web page from Access, you can create a data access page. Data access pages combine the features of forms and reports so that you can display data to users and let users interact with data through Microsoft Internet Explorer version 5 or later. (You can also use other Web browsers to display data access pages, but users will not be able to work with the data directly.)

To create a data access page from VBA, use the **CreateDataAccessPage** method. To programmatically add controls to a data access page, use script or the Dynamic HTML (DHTML) object model to work with the HTML code directly. For more information about building and working with data access pages, see Chapter 5, "Working with Office Applications," and Chapter 12, "Using Web Technologies."

Using Subforms to Create Filterable Reports in an Access Database

Access reports and report snapshots can be filtered and sorted only when they are being created. If you want the user to be able to filter on one or two specific fields, you can use a subform within an Access form to make a tabular report. You can also use a combo box to present the filter criteria to the user, and filter the data in the subform according to the user's choice in the combo box.

For an example of a form that uses a subform to create a filterable report, see the frmProductsByCategory form in the NorthwindReports.mdb sample file, which is available in the Samples\CH15 subfolder on the companion CD-ROM.

Building Custom Reports for External Data in Excel

Excel makes an excellent reporting tool for data stored in an external data source because it provides so many features for analyzing data and presenting it in different configurations. You can import data into Excel from an Access database, a SQL Server database, or any OLE DB data source. Once you get your data into Excel, you can sort, filter, and perform calculations on it. You can also save it as a Web page.

Data in Excel can be static or dynamic, depending on whether it's linked to the data source. You can display data in Excel in the following ways:

- In a list in a worksheet. A list presents data in rows and columns, like a table. A list can display static or dynamic data.
- In a chart. A chart can be embedded in a worksheet, or it can exist on a chart sheet. A chart is dynamically linked to a list in Excel; the list may or may not be dynamically linked to an external data source.
- In a PivotTable report or PivotChart report. A PivotTable report is dynamically linked to either a list in Excel, an external data source, or another PivotTable report. A PivotChart report, in turn, is dynamically linked to a PivotTable report. PivotTable reports are discussed in greater detail later in this chapter, in "Working with PivotTable and PivotChart Reports."
- In a Web page. A Web page can display static data or dynamic data, depending on whether it's linked to the data source.

The following sections describe different ways to create custom list reports in Excel.

Importing Static Data from an Access Database into Excel

If your solution is based in Excel, you can write code in Excel to import static data from an Access database. Once you've defined an SQL statement that returns the records you want from the database, you can open a recordset, and then use the **CopyFromRecordset** method to copy data from a recordset into a range on an Excel worksheet. The recordset may be either an ADO or a DAO recordset.

The **CopyFromRecordset** method simply copies data into a worksheet. To update the worksheet after the data has changed, you must copy the data to the worksheet again; there is no dynamic link to the data. The following code fragment creates an ADO recordset and copies the data in the recordset into a range on a worksheet.

```
Dim cnnConnect As New ADODB.Connection
Dim rstData    As New ADODB.Recordset
Dim lngReturn  As Long

' Open ADO connection.
cnnConnect.Open strConnect
' Open Recordset object.
rstData.Open strSQL, cnnConnect, adOpenForwardOnly
' Copy data from recordset and store return value.
lngReturn = rngDest.CopyFromRecordset(rstData)
```

This code fragment is taken from the InsertStaticData procedure in the modStaticReport module in the Northwind.xls sample file, which is available in the Samples\CH15 subfolder on the companion CD-ROM.

Note When you display data from an Access database in Excel, any *lookup fields* in the source table or query will display their underlying numeric values, rather than the text values that you usually see in Access. A lookup field is one that stores a numeric value but displays a text value. Access uses the numeric value to "look up" the text value to display. To display the corresponding text value for a lookup field, you need to create an SQL statement that performs an inner join on the lookup field and retrieves the text value that it represents.

Exporting Static Data from an Access Database into Excel

If your solution is based in Access, you can use the **TransferSpreadsheet** method of the Access **DoCmd** object to export a table or query to an Excel worksheet, as shown in the following procedure:

```
Sub ExportDataToExcel(strTableName, _
                      strFileName As String, _
                      blnHasFieldNames As Boolean)
   ' Exports a table or query as static data to Excel.

   DoCmd.TransferSpreadsheet acExport, acSpreadsheetTypeExcel9, _
      strTableName, strFileName, blnHasFieldNames
End Sub
```

The **TransferSpreadsheet** method in Access provides a quick way to get data from an Access database into Excel. However, it's limited in its flexibility. Because using the **TransferSpreadsheet** method creates a static report, you must re-create the report in order to update the data. Also, you must pass a table or saved query to the **TransferSpreadsheet** method—you can't create a query on the fly by passing in an SQL statement. If you want to create a dynamic report to display Access data in Excel, use Automation (formerly OLE Automation) from Access to create a query table or PivotTable report within an Excel workbook, as discussed in the following section.

Creating Dynamic Reports with Query Tables in Excel

The **CopyFromRecordset** and **TransferSpreadsheet** methods are fine for importing or exporting external data that doesn't change frequently. However, if you're creating reports in Excel to present data that needs to be updated often, you may want to create a query table. A query table is a table in an Excel worksheet that's linked to an external data source, such as a SQL Server database, a Microsoft Access database, a Web page, or a text file. To retrieve the most up-to-date data, the user can refresh the query table.

Creating a Query Table by Using a Database Query

Excel creates a query table in a worksheet when you create a new database query and returns the data to that worksheet. To create a new database query from the Excel user interface, click **Get External Data** on the **Tools** menu, and then click **New Database Query**. In the **Choose Data Source** dialog box, select an existing data source or create a new one. You can then use either the Query Wizard or the Microsoft Query grid to create the database query and return the data to a worksheet. Once you've retrieved the data, click **Refresh** on the **Tools** menu to refresh the query table.

To create a new query table from VBA, use the **Add** method of the **QueryTables** collection. The **QueryTables** collection belongs to a **Worksheet** object and contains all of the **QueryTable** objects for that worksheet. Once you've created a new query table, you must use the **Refresh** method of the **QueryTable** object to display data in the query table. If you don't use the **Refresh** method, the query table will not display any data. The following example creates a query table on a new worksheet.

```
Function CreateQueryTable(strConnect As String, _
                          strSQL As String) As Boolean
   ' Create query table from external data source.
   ' Takes a valid ADO connection string and a
   ' valid SQL SELECT statement.

   Dim cnnConnect As ADODB.Connection
   Dim rstData    As ADODB.Recordset
   Dim qtbData    As Excel.QueryTable
   Dim wksNew     As Excel.Worksheet

   On Error GoTo CreateQueryTable_Err

   ' Open connection on data source.
   Set cnnConnect = New ADODB.Connection
   cnnConnect.Open strConnect

   ' Open Recordset object on connection.
   Set rstData = New ADODB.Recordset
   rstData.Open strSQL, cnnConnect, adOpenForwardOnly

   ' Add new worksheet.
   Set wksNew = ThisWorkbook.Worksheets.Add
```

```
    ' Create query table in new worksheet.
    Set qtbData = _
       wksNew.QueryTables.Add(rstData, wksNew.Range("A1"))

    ' Refresh query table to display data.
    qtbData.Refresh

    CreateQueryTable = True

CreateQueryTable_End:
    On Error Resume Next
    rstData.Close
    Set rstData = Nothing
    Exit Function

CreateQueryTable_Err:
    CreateQueryTable = False
    MsgBox "Error: " & Err.Number & vbCrLf & Err.Description
    Resume CreateQueryTable_End
End Function
```

The CreateQueryTable procedure appears in the modQueryTables module in the Northwind.xls sample file, which is available in the Samples\CH15 subfolder on the companion CD-ROM.

If your solution is an Access-based solution, and you want to create dynamic reports in Excel, you can use Automation to create a query table or PivotTable report in Excel from code running in Access. Using Automation gives you more control over the process of transferring data from a database to Excel. You can also use Automation to format the report, filter data, create charts, and so on, so that the user simply clicks a button in Access to bring up a formatted report in Excel.

Creating a Query Table by Using a Web Query

You can also create a query table from data on a Web page. In this case, you specify one of the following for the ***Connection*** argument of the **Add** method of the **QueryTables** collection: either a Web page address, or the path and file name of a saved Web query (.iqy). The following code fragment creates a query table by using a saved query that pulls stock quotes from the Microsoft Investor Web site.

```
' Add new worksheet.
Set wksNew = ThisWorkbook.Worksheets.Add
' Create query table from saved Web query.
Set qtbQuote = wksNew.QueryTables.Add(Connection:= _
    "FINDER;C:\Program Files\Microsoft " _
    & "Office\Office\Queries\Microsoft " _
    & "Investor Stock Quotes.iqy", Destination:=Range("A1"))
' Set query table properties and retrieve data.
With qtbQuote
    .Name = "Microsoft Investor Stock Quotes_1"
    .FieldNames = True
    .PreserveFormatting = False
    .RefreshStyle = xlInsertDeleteCells
```

```
    .SaveData = True
    .AdjustColumnWidth = True
    .RefreshPeriod = 0
    .WebSelectionType = xlEntirePage
    .WebFormatting = xlWebFormattingAll
    .WebPreFormattedTextToColumns = True
    .WebConsecutiveDelimitersAsOne = True
    .WebSingleBlockTextImport = False
    .Refresh BackgroundQuery:=False
End With
```

This code fragment is taken from the RetrieveStockQuotes procedure, which appears in the modStockQuotes module in the StockQuotes.xls sample file, which is available in the Samples\CH15 subfolder on the companion CD-ROM.

Creating Web Pages to Display Excel Data

To create a Web page to display data from Excel, save all or part of an Excel workbook as HTML. You can create either a static report or a dynamic report on a Web page. The report may also be either read-only or interactive.

For a sample procedure that publishes data from an Excel workbook to a Web page, see the PublishDataToWebPage procedure in the modPublish module in the Northwind.xls sample file, available in the Samples\CH15 subfolder on the companion CD-ROM. For more information about creating dynamic Web pages, see Chapter 12, "Using Web Technologies."

Creating Static Reports in Word

For data analysis, Excel is the obvious choice, but there may be times when you want to display data in Microsoft Word—for example, if you're preparing a memo that contains sales information from an Access database.

Getting Data into Word

To write data to a Word document from an Access database, you can save an Access table, query, form, or report as a Rich Text Format file (.rtf) or an HTML file and open it in Word. From Excel, you can save a worksheet as a text file (.txt) or an HTML file.

The following code fragment writes data from an Access saved query to an RTF file. The data is automatically displayed in a table in the RTF file.

```
DoCmd.OutputTo acOutputQuery, "Current Product List", acFormatRTF, _
    "Current Product List.rtf"
```

Manipulating Data in Word

To perform a simple operation on the data in a Word table, such as finding the sum or average of the values in a column, you can insert the appropriate formula in a table cell. For example, the following code fragment prints the average of a column of numbers to a new row in the table.

```
' Return reference to first table in document.
Set tblData = ThisDocument.Tables(1)
With tblData
   ' Add row to end of table.
   .Rows.Add
   ' Store number of rows.
   lngRowCount = .Rows.Count
   ' Specify formula for cell in first column of last row.
   .Columns(1).Cells(lngRowCount).Formula "=Average(Above)"
End With
```

If you're performing complex calculations, consider embedding an Excel worksheet in a Word document rather than adding a formula to a Word table.

Sorting and Filtering Data

The purpose of a report is to present data efficiently, so that persons viewing the report can quickly find the information they need. Sorting and filtering are two important aspects of efficient data presentation.

Sorting Data in Access

The key to sorting data in an Access database is to define a query that specifies the sort order. You can do this by setting the **Sort** field in the query design grid to **Ascending** or **Descending**, or by including an ORDER BY clause in the SQL statement. You can ensure that you always display sorted data in a form, report, or data access page by specifying a sorted query as the record source.

You can speed up sort and find operations by defining indexes on Access tables. An index can be based on a single field or on multiple fields. The index can enforce certain rules for a field or set of fields, such as whether the indexed field contains unique values, whether to ignore **Null** values, and whether the index includes the primary key for the table. The primary key is a special type of index that uniquely identifies each record in the table.

You can add an index to a table by using the table design view in Access, or create it programmatically, through ADO or DAO. For more information about indexes, see Chapter 14, "Working with the Data Access Components of an Office Solution," or search the Microsoft Access Help index for "indexes."

Filtering Data in Access

To filter data in an Access form or report by using VBA, set the **Filter** and **FilterOn** properties of the form or report. The **Filter** property specifies the criteria on which to filter, and the **FilterOn** property activates the filter. The following procedure filters a subform based on the user's selection in a combo box.

```
Private Sub cboCategories_AfterUpdate()
   ' Filter subform after value in combo box is updated.
   Dim lngCategoryID As Long

   ' Store value selected in combo box.
   lngCategoryID = cboCategories.Value

   ' Filter subform.
   With sfmProducts.Form
      ' If value is anything but "(All)", filter on that value.
      If lngCategoryID > 0 Then
         .Filter = "[CategoryID]=" & lngCategoryID
         .FilterOn = True
      ' If value is "(All)", remove filter.
      Else
         .FilterOn = False
      End If
   End With
End Sub
```

This procedure appears in the frmProductsByCategory form module in the NorthwindReports.mdb sample file, which is available in the Samples\CH15 subfolder on the companion CD-ROM.

Sorting Data in Excel

To sort data in Excel by using VBA, use the **Sort** method on a range or PivotTable report. You can specify up to three columns on which to sort. Keep in mind that if your data is organized in rows—that is, if the data in the first cell of a row is in some way associated with the data in other cells in that row—you must sort on the entire range or PivotTable report in order to maintain the integrity of row data. To ensure that you're sorting on the entire data range, use the **CurrentRegion** or **UsedRange** property to return a range representing the whole block of data.

Filtering Data in Excel

The easiest way to filter data in Excel is by using the **AutoFilter** command on the **Data** menu (click **Filter**, then click **AutoFilter**). The **AutoFilter** command creates drop-down boxes for each column of a range of data. Each drop-down box contains all of the values that appear in that column, and you can filter on any of them.

To toggle the AutoFilter feature from VBA, apply the **AutoFilter** method to the range of data that you want to filter. If the AutoFilter feature is already on, applying the **AutoFilter** method will turn it off, and vice versa, so it's a good idea to check the value of the **AutoFilterMode** property before applying the method to determine whether the AutoFilter feature is on or off.

You can also use the **AutoFilter** method with an alternative syntax to filter the range on specific criteria. The syntax takes four arguments: ***Field***, ***Criteria1***, ***Operator***, and ***Criteria2***. Use the ***Field*** argument to specify the number of the column to filter, and the ***Criteria1*** argument to specify a single criterion. Use the ***Operator*** and ***Criteria2*** arguments to specify an additional criterion.

Note The number that you specify for the ***Field*** argument must take into account any hidden fields that precede it in the worksheet. For example, if column 2 is hidden, you must still specify 3 to filter on column 3.

The following code fragment filters and sorts data on a specified column.

```
' Return reference to worksheet.
Set wksWorksheet = ThisWorkbook.Worksheets(strWksName)
' Store result range for query table.
Set rngRange = wksWorksheet.QueryTables(varIndex).ResultRange

' Check whether AutoFilter is off.
If wksWorksheet.AutoFilterMode = False Then
   ' Turn AutoFilter on.
   rngRange.AutoFilter
End If

' Show all data in worksheet, in case a filter was
' in effect when procedure began running.
' Suppress the error that occurs if all data is already showing.
On Error Resume Next
wksWorksheet.ShowAllData
On Error GoTo FilterAndSortQueryTable_Err

' Filter on specified criteria.
rngRange.AutoFilter lngField, strCriteria1, lngOperator, strCriteria2

' Sort on same column that was filtered.
rngRange.Sort rngRange.Columns(lngField), lngOrder
```

This code fragment is taken from the FilterAndSortQueryTable procedure in the modFilterSort module in the Northwind.xls sample file, which is available in the Samples\CH15 subfolder on the companion CD-ROM.

You can also use the **AdvancedFilter** method to filter data in Excel. For more information, search the Microsoft Excel Visual Basic Reference Help index for "AdvancedFilter method."

Sorting Data in a Word Table

To sort the data in a Word table by using VBA, use the **Sort** method of the **Table** object to specify how the table should be sorted. You can specify up to three fields (columns) on which to sort. For each field participating in the sort operation, you can specify the data type of the field (numeric, alphanumeric, date, and so on) and the sort order for the field (ascending or descending). The following procedure sorts data in a single column of a table.

```
Sub SortSingleColumn(tblTable As Word.Table, _
                     strFieldNum As String, _
                     lngSortFieldType As WdSortFieldType, _
                     lngSortOrder As WdSortOrder)
   ' Sort on a single column of a table.

   With tblTable
      ' Select table.
      .Select
      ' Sort as specified.
      .Sort ExcludeHeader:=True, FieldNumber:=strFieldNum, _
         SortFieldType:=lngSortFieldType, _
         SortOrder:=lngSortOrder
   End With
End Sub
```

The SortSingleColumn procedure can be found in the ThisDocument module in SortTable.doc, which is available in the Samples\CH15 subfolder on the companion CD-ROM.

Working with PivotTable and PivotChart Reports

PivotTable and PivotChart reports are powerful tools for presenting and analyzing data. A user can manipulate a single PivotTable report to display the same data in dozens of different ways. Until you get the hang of them, however, PivotTable reports can be confusing. The following sections introduce the basics of PivotTable reports, then describe how to build and control them by using VBA.

Understanding PivotTable Reports

PivotTable reports provide a means to view a single set of data in a variety of configurations. Like a query, a PivotTable report can answer a question about a data set: Which customers provided the most sales for the first quarter of this year? In which country was a particular product most popular last year? How well did a particular sales representative do in Europe for the past two years?

If you're skilled at building queries, you can answer each of these questions with a separate query. The advantage of the PivotTable report, however, is that once you've defined the data set, you can "pivot" the data to answer all of these questions with a single data set. For most users, this is easier and more intuitive than building a query, especially when the PivotTable report combines data from multiple tables. It's also easy to build PivotChart reports from PivotTable reports and publish the data to a Web page. And, because PivotTable data is cached in memory, PivotTable reports provide extremely fast querying.

The simple PivotTable report in Figure 15.1 answers the question, "In which countries have customers purchased the product Sasquatch Ale so far during 1998, and what are the sales figures?" You could easily modify this PivotTable report to answer the same question for other products, or to view sales for a different year, or to view sales only for European countries.

Figure 15.1 PivotTable Report Showing Sales Data for a Product, by Country, for a Single Year

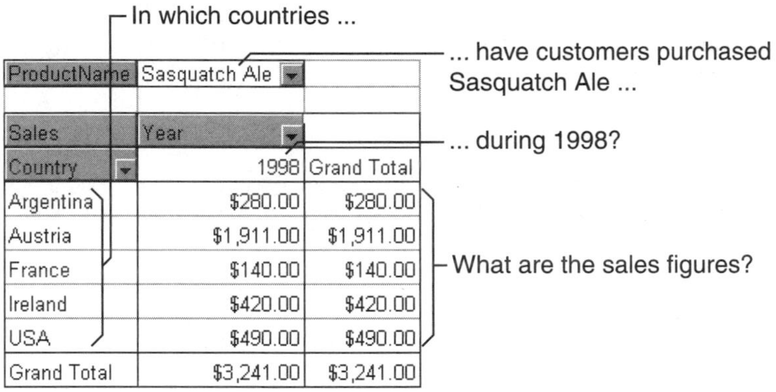
In which countries ...
... have customers purchased Sasquatch Ale ...
... during 1998?
What are the sales figures?
ProductName
Sasquatch Ale
Sales
Year
Country
1998
Grand Total
Argentina
$280.00
$280.00
Austria
$1,911.00
$1,911.00
France
$140.00
$140.00
Ireland
$420.00
$420.00
USA
$490.00
$490.00
Grand Total
$3,241.00
$3,241.00

Not every question about a data set can be answered by a PivotTable report. Because the data fields in a PivotTable report are always calculated fields, PivotTable reports are ideal for summarizing numeric data, such as sales data. You can display the sum; the count of data items; the average, minimum, and maximum values; and the product, standard deviation, or variance of a set of values. You can also define custom-calculated fields to add to a PivotTable report. However, you can't display text in the data area of a PivotTable report. For example, you can't use a PivotTable report to display a grid of text values such as "True," "False," or "Unknown" (although you could represent these values numerically and provide a key). If you need to display text, consider creating a query in a database, displaying the data as a list in Excel, or using a grid control to display the data on a form.

You create and manipulate PivotTable reports in Excel. Although Access includes the PivotTable Wizard, which you can use to create an embedded PivotTable report in a form, you can't edit a PivotTable report directly within Access. When you choose to edit the PivotTable report, Access launches Excel so that you can edit the PivotTable report within Excel.

In order to create a useful PivotTable report, you need to understand and define the set of data that should appear in the table. Depending on where your data is stored, this may be the most difficult part of creating a PivotTable report. If your data is stored in an Excel worksheet or worksheets, you can define a range or ranges as the data source for the PivotTable report. If your data is stored in an external database, you need to define a query that extracts the data that you want. See "Creating a PivotTable Report from an External Data Source" later in this chapter for more information.

For example, if you want to create a PivotTable report that displays sales data by quarter, you need to base the table on a query that groups records by quarter. A well-designed database is more likely to store the date that a given order was taken than the quarter, because you can easily build a query that displays the data by quarter if you've stored the date. However, you need to create this query before you can display quarterly information in the PivotTable report.

The following SQL statement defines calculated fields that parse the order date from the Northwind Orders table to return the quarter and year in which the order was taken.

```
SELECT
   Orders.OrderID,
   DatePart('q',[OrderDate]) AS Quarter,
   Year([OrderDate]) AS [Year]
FROM Orders;
```

Although PivotTable reports are fairly easy to use once you understand the concepts behind them and the data they contain, they may still be confusing to many users. As a developer, you can simplify PivotTable reports for users by providing a set of options for viewing PivotTable report data. For example, you might create a solution that includes a form for users who need to look at just a few variations of PivotTable report data, and configure the PivotTable report for them based on which option they choose. The Northwind.xls sample file in the Samples\CH15 subfolder on the companion CD-ROM includes a form that demonstrates ways to control user interaction with a PivotTable report.

PivotTable Report Structure

A PivotTable report consists of four areas where you can display fields: the row area, column area, data area, and page area. Figure 15.2 shows each of these areas, and the following sections describe them.

Figure 15.2 Four Areas of a PivotTable Report

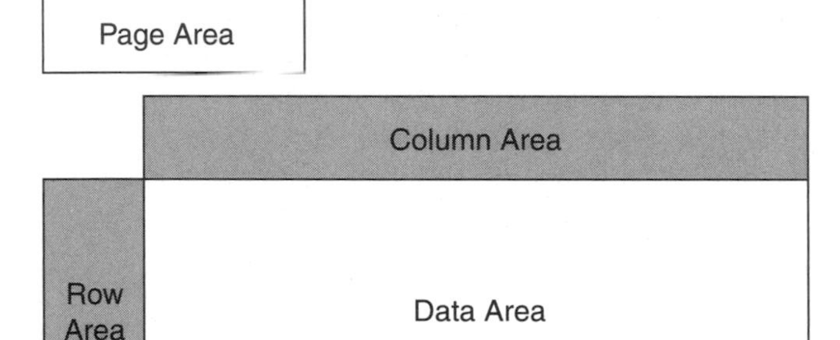

Row Area and Column Area

The row and column areas usually display the fields that are most critical for your query. For example, if you want the PivotTable report to answer the question, "Which countries generated the most sales for the first quarters of 1996, 1997, and 1998?", the PivotTable report needs to display both a list of countries and the data for the first quarter of each of those years. Because you want to display data by country for the first quarter, add the Country field to the row area, add the Year field to the column area, and add the Quarter field to the column area to the right of the Year field.

Whether you put a given field in the row area or in the column area is up to you; the resulting data in the PivotTable report will be the same. However, it makes sense to arrange individual fields within an area hierarchically, so that you can group data in the way that's easiest to read. For example, if you're adding a Country field and a City field, add the Country field first, then add the City field to the right of it, so that data is grouped first by country, then by cities within those countries.

Figure 15.3 points out the row and column fields in a PivotTable report. As you can see, the Country field is in the first position in the row area, and the City field is in the second position. This way, the data is grouped first by country, then by city.

Figure 15.3 PivotTable Report Showing Sales Data for All Products, by City, for Selected Countries, for Multiple Years

Data field — Row fields — Column field

ProductName	(All)				
Sales		Year			
Country	City	1996	1997	1998	Grand Total
Austria	Graz	$15,568.06	$48,096.26	$41,210.65	$104,874.97
	Salzburg	$10,033.28	$9,305.58	$3,790.00	$23,128.86
Germany	Aachen	$533.60	$420.00	$2,809.61	$3,763.21
	Berlin		$2,022.50	$2,250.50	$4,273.00
	Brandenburg	$1,661.40	$9,664.21	$19,582.77	$30,908.38
	Cunewalde	$11,950.08	$61,109.90	$37,217.31	$110,277.29
	Frankfurt a.M.	$3,105.37	$13,076.12	$3,079.90	$19,261.39
	Köln	$1,504.65	$8,254.26	$2,737.28	$12,496.19
	Leipzig	$1,200.80	$3,596.40	$245.00	$5,042.20
	Mannheim		$1,079.80	$2,160.00	$3,239.80
	München	$9,748.04	$11,829.78	$5,078.74	$26,656.56
	Münster	$1,863.40	$2,004.34	$910.40	$4,778.14
	Stuttgart	$3,839.80	$4,262.82	$1,485.80	$9,588.42
Grand Total		$61,008.48	$174,721.97	$122,557.96	$358,288.41

Values in data field

Data Area

The data area displays the data that you want to analyze with the PivotTable report; it answers the questions that you ask about the data. You can think of the data in a cell in the data area of a PivotTable report as the intersection between values in the row and column fields. For example, the data in one cell in Figure 15.3 shows that sales in Salzburg, Austria for 1996 were $10,033.28.

The name of the data field appears in the upper left corner of the PivotTable report, as shown in Figure 15.3. By default the field name includes the aggregate function that is being performed on the data—for example, "Sum of Sales"—but you can name the PivotTable field whatever you want.

As mentioned previously, the data area must contain numeric data. However, you can perform additional calculations on this data, to find the sum, average, and so on. You can also create a *calculated field* to perform calculations on data. For example, you can multiply the Quantity and UnitPrice fields together to display the total value for a group of orders in the PivotTable report. You can also use calculated fields to perform projections on the data. For example, you can create a calculated field to answer the question, "How will profits be affected if sales in Germany increase by 10% for the upcoming year?"

Page Area

Although you must add fields to the row, column, and data areas of a PivotTable report, adding fields to the page area is optional. Page fields can add an additional level to your data analysis. For example, suppose you've laid out the PivotTable report to display quarterly sales information by country for three years. The data that appears in a cell in the PivotTable report represents the sales of all products for a given country during a given quarter. But you may want to look at the sales numbers for just one particular product. Assuming that your data source contains a ProductName field, you can add that field to the page area.

In the row and column fields, you can look at data for any number of values. For example, if the Country field is in the column area, you can look at data for one country, or ten countries, or all of the countries listed in the database by clicking the drop-down box on the Country field and selecting or unselecting the countries you're interested in. In a page field, however, you can look at data either for one value or for all values. For example, you can view data in the PivotTable report for all products, or you can view data for one product at a time.

Page fields are advantageous when you want to look at data in the PivotTable report for only one value in a given field. For example, suppose you want to view only sales for Brazil in the PivotTable report. If you add the Country field to the page area, and add the City field to the column area, you can select Brazil from the Country field's list to view sales data for Brazil by city, as shown in Figure 15.4.

Note If you compare figures 15.3 and 15.4, you may notice that the ProductName field appears as a page field in Figure 15.3 but not in Figure 15.4. Nonetheless, the data area in Figure 15.4 displays sales figures for all products, even though the ProductName field is not included in the PivotTable report. If you include a page field and set its value to `"(All)"`, the effect on the PivotTable report is the same as if you had omitted the page field in the first place. In other words, adding a page field to a PivotTable report does not affect the data that is displayed in the report unless you specify a value from the page field on which to filter the data.

Figure 15.4 PivotTable Report Showing Sales Data for All Products in a Single Country for Multiple Years

Page field

Country	Brazil			
Sales	Year			
City	1996	1997	1998	Grand Total
Campinas		$8,008.79	$405.35	$8,414.14
Resende	$517.80	$4,415.15	$1,135.25	$6,068.20
Rio de Janeiro	$5,974.70	$13,808.95	$32,173.33	$51,956.98
São Paulo	$13,656.32	$15,708.30	$11,121.84	$40,486.46
Grand Total	$20,148.82	$41,941.19	$44,835.77	$106,925.78

Note If you hide PivotTable items in a row or column field, and then move the field to the page area, the hidden PivotTable items will not appear in the drop-down list for the page field.

Creating PivotTable Reports

The easiest way to create a PivotTable report is with the PivotTable Wizard. The wizard allows you to create a PivotTable report from data in one or more Excel ranges, an external data source, or an existing PivotTable report.

For many solutions, you may not need to create a PivotTable report in VBA—you can create a PivotTable report by using the wizard and then manipulate the data either through the Excel user interface or from VBA code. If you're using Excel as a reporting tool, however, you may find it useful to create a PivotTable report from code. The following sections describe how to create a PivotTable report from a range on an Excel worksheet, another PivotTable report, and an external data source.

Creating a PivotTable Report from an Excel Range or Another PivotTable Report

To create a PivotTable report from an Excel range or another PivotTable report, you can use the **PivotTableWizard** method of a **Worksheet** or **PivotTable** object. The **PivotTableWizard** method allows you to specify multiple characteristics of the PivotTable report as arguments to the method.

All of the arguments of the **PivotTableWizard** method are optional, but you'll probably want to specify values for at least the ***SourceType*** and ***SourceData*** arguments. To create a PivotTable report from an Excel range, specify **xlDatabase** for the ***SourceType*** argument, and the range containing the data for the ***SourceData*** argument. To create a PivotTable report from an existing PivotTable report, specify **xlPivotTable** for the ***SourceType*** argument, and set a reference to an existing PivotTable report for the ***SourceData*** argument.

Note When you call the **PivotTableWizard** method, you can't mix named and positional arguments. You must pass in all arguments either by name or by position.

The following code fragment creates a PivotTable report from the data range in a worksheet.

```
' Return used data range on Order Details Extended worksheet.
Set wksData = ThisWorkbook.Worksheets(ORDER_DETAILS_EXTENDED)
Set rngData = wksData.UsedRange

' Create PivotTable report. Start at cell B5 so there is enough
' room for page fields.
Set pvtTable = wksData.PivotTableWizard(SourceType:=xlDatabase, _
   SourceData:=rngData, TableDestination:=wksPivot.Range("B5"))
```

Note Calling the **PivotTableWizard** method creates a PivotTable report, but doesn't add any fields to the table, so you won't see any data in the PivotTable report until you add them. You can add fields either by dragging them from the **PivotTable** toolbar or by setting the **Orientation** property of the **PivotField** object that corresponds to a given field.

The preceding code fragment is taken from the CreatePivotTableFromXLRange procedure in the modPivotTable module in the Northwind.xls sample file, which is available in the Samples\CH15 subfolder on the companion CD-ROM.

For an example of creating a PivotTable report from an existing PivotTable report, see the CreatePivotTableFromPivotTable procedure in the modPivotTable module of the Northwind.xls sample file, which is available in the Samples\CH15 subfolder on the companion CD-ROM.

Creating a PivotTable Report from an External Data Source

To create a PivotTable report from an external data source, such as an Access or SQL Server database, you specify **xlExternal** for the ***SourceType*** argument of the **PivotTableWizard** method, and a single-element, two-dimensional array for the ***SourceData*** argument. The first element of the array should contain the connection string for the data source, and the second element should contain the SQL statement to retrieve the data.

Creating the Connection String

The connection string must be a valid Open Database Connectivity (ODBC) connection string. For example, the following constant defines an ODBC connection string for the Northwind sample database that is installed with Access:

```
Public Const ODBC_CONNECT As String = "ODBC;" _
   & "DBQ=C:\Program Files\Microsoft Office\Office\Samples\Northwind.mdb;" _
   & "Driver={Microsoft Access Driver (*.mdb)};"
```

Defining the SQL Statement

If your data is coming from a relational data source that is properly normalized, you'll almost certainly have to define a query with multiple joined tables in order to get the data you want in the PivotTable report. By definition, a PivotTable report displays data from more than one table. For example, suppose you're creating a PivotTable report from the Northwind sample database to display information about sales by customer, customer city or customer country, and product or category. You'll need to create a query that includes the Customers, Products, Categories, and Order Details tables, at a minimum.

As noted earlier, lookup fields in an Access database can be problematic when you move data to Excel, because Excel displays only the stored numeric value, not the text value that appears in Access. In order to retrieve the text value, you must define a query containing inner joins between tables. If your query includes more than two tables, the SQL statement for such a query quickly becomes complex.

If the SQL statement has 255 or fewer characters, you can use it as-is as the second element of the two-dimensional array. If it's a longer string, however, you must either parse the string into 255-character segments, or create a saved query in the data source, if it supports saved queries, and base the SQL statement included in the array on that query.

If you choose to parse the SQL string into 255-character segments, you can simply add each segment as an additional element in the array, as long as the first element is the connection string. When you pass the array as the ***SourceData*** argument, Excel concatenates the strings together to form the complete SQL string. For example, the following line of code creates the array for the ***SourceData*** argument from four strings that include contiguous segments of the SQL statement:

```
varSource = Array(strConnect, strSQL1, strSQL2, strSQL3, strSQL4)
```

Parsing the SQL string into 255-character segments can be a hassle. If your data is in an Access database and you build the SQL statement in the Access query design grid, it's easiest to create a saved query in the database and use a simple SQL statement to retrieve data from that query. For example, the following code fragment creates a saved query based on a lengthy SQL string in an Access database. It then creates the two-dimensional array containing the connection string and a second SQL string that retrieves records from the saved query.

```
' Create new query in Northwind and append to Views collection.
' This is one way to handle the problem of passing an SQL string
' longer than 255 characters.
' Open new ADO connection.
Set cnnNwind = New ADODB.Connection
cnnNwind.Open ADO_CONNECT_STRING
Set catDb = New ADOX.Catalog
' Open catalog on data source.
Set catDb.ActiveConnection = cnnNwind
' Create new command.
Set cmdQuery = New ADODB.Command
' Specify SQL string as command text.
cmdQuery.CommandText = REGIONAL_SALES_SQL

' Before appending new view, delete query with the
' same name, if it exists.
On Error Resume Next
catDb.Views.Delete QUERY_NAME
On Error GoTo 0

' Append new view.
catDb.Views.Append QUERY_NAME, cmdQuery

' Create array containing connection string and SQL string.
varSource = Array(ODBC_CONNECT_STRING, "SELECT * FROM " & QUERY_NAME)

' Create PivotTable report. Start at cell B8 so there is enough room
' for page fields.
Set pvtTable = wksPivot.PivotTableWizard(xlExternal, varSource, _
   wksPivot.Range("B8"))
```

This code fragment is taken from the CreatePivotTableFromMDB procedure in the modPivotTable module in the Northwind.xls sample file, which is available in the Samples\CH15 subfolder on the companion CD-ROM.

Adding Fields to a PivotTable Report

When you first create a PivotTable report, no data is displayed because all of the fields in the PivotTable data source are hidden. You need to add fields to the PivotTable report in order to display data. You must add one or more row, column, and data fields; page fields are optional. The **PivotField** object represents a field that's available in the PivotTable data source. The **PivotFields** collection belongs to a **PivotTable** object.

To display a PivotTable field in a PivotTable report, set the **Orientation** property of the corresponding **PivotField** object to a constant that specifies where in the table you want to add the field: **xlRowField**, **xlColumnField**, **xlDataField**, or **xlPageField**. To remove a field from a PivotTable report, set the **Orientation** property to **xlHidden**. If you're adding more than one field to an area of a PivotTable report, you can use the **Position** property to specify the order in which the fields are arranged. The following code fragment adds seven fields to a PivotTable report.

```
With pvtTable
   ' Specify row field.
   .PivotFields("Country").Orientation = xlRowField
   ' Specify column fields. Specify their relative positions
   ' in the table -- year should come before quarter.
   With .PivotFields("Year")
      .Orientation = xlColumnField
      .Position = 1
   End With
   With .PivotFields("Quarter")
      .Orientation = xlColumnField
      .Position = 2
   End With
   ' Specify page fields.
   .PivotFields("CategoryName").Orientation = xlPageField
   .PivotFields("ProductName").Orientation = xlPageField
   .PivotFields("LastName").Orientation = xlPageField
   ' Specify data field.
   .PivotFields("ProductPrice").Orientation = xlDataField
   ' Format data region as currency.
   .DataBodyRange.NumberFormatLocal = "$#,##0.00"
   .
   .
   .
End With
```

This code fragment is taken from the CreatePivotTableFromMDB procedure in the modPivotTable module in the Northwind.xls sample file, which is available in the Samples\CH15 subfolder on the companion CD-ROM.

Working with PivotTable fields

The **PivotFields** collection contains all of the fields available in the PivotTable's data source. If you need to refer to a PivotTable field in a particular area of a PivotTable report, it's often easier to use one of the properties in the following table, which define subsets of the **PivotFields** collection.

Property	Description
ColumnFields	Returns collection of fields in column area
DataFields	Returns collection of fields in data area
HiddenFields	Returns collection of fields that are not displayed in the PivotTable report
PageFields	Returns collection of fields in page area
RowFields	Returns collection of fields in row area
VisibleFields	Returns collection of fields that are displayed in the PivotTable report

For example, in order to determine whether a particular field is visible in a PivotTable report, you need to determine whether it is in the subset of visible fields. The following code fragment checks whether the City and Country fields are currently visible in a PivotTable report by first suppressing error handling, and then attempting to return a reference to each field within the **VisibleFields** subset of the **PivotFields** collection. If no error occurs, the field is visible and the check box is set to **True**. If an error occurs, the field is not visible and the check box is set to **False**.

```
' Determine whether City and Country fields
' are visible by attempting to return a
' reference to them and checking for the error.
With p_pvtTable
   ' The VisibleFields property returns the
   ' collection of fields visible in the
   ' PivotTable report.
   On Error Resume Next
   Set pvfCity = .VisibleFields("City")
   If Err = 0 Then chkByCity = True
   Err.Clear
   Set pvfCountry = .VisibleFields("Country")
   If Err = 0 Then chkByCountry = True
   Err.Clear
   .
   .
   .
End With
```

This code fragment is taken from the UserForm_Initialize event procedure for the frmPivotOptions form in the Northwind.xls sample file, which is available in the Samples\CH15 subfolder on the companion CD-ROM.

Using VBA to Manipulate PivotTable Reports

Each PivotTable field contains a set of values from the corresponding field in the data source. These are the values that you manipulate to display subsets of data.

In VBA, each PivotTable field has a **PivotItems** collection. A **PivotItem** object represents a value that appears in a PivotTable field. For example, the **PivotItems** collection of a field named Quarter probably contains four **PivotItem** objects, which have respective values of 1, 2, 3, and 4.

You can only work with fields that are displayed in the PivotTable report. To display a page field item, set the **CurrentPage** property for the **PivotField** object. A page field can display either a single value or all values. To display a single value, set the **CurrentPage** property to that value. To display all pivot items for a page field, set the **CurrentPage** property to `"(All)"`. For example, if you have a page field named Employees, you can display sales data for a single employee by setting the **CurrentPage** property to the employee's last name, "Smith." To display sales data for all employees, set the **CurrentPage** property to `"(All)"`.

To display an item in a row, column, or data field, set that **PivotItem** object's **Visible** property to **True**. You can loop through the **PivotField** object's collection of **PivotItems** and set the **Visible** property of each to **True** to display all pivot items. The following procedure displays all items in a particular PivotTable field.

```
Private Sub cmdShowAll_Click()
   ' Makes all pivot items for specified field visible.

   Dim pvfField As PivotField
   Dim pviItem  As PivotItem

   ' Return reference to selected PivotTable field.
   Set pvfField = p_pvtTable.PivotFields(cboShowAll.Value)

   ' Determine PivotTable field orientation.
   Select Case pvfField.Orientation
      Case xlHidden
         MsgBox "Field is not visible in PivotTable report!"
      Case xlPageField
         ' If page field, set CurrentPage property to "(All)".
         pvfField.CurrentPage = "(All)"
      Case Else
         ' If row, column, or data field, make all
         ' pivot items visible.
         For Each pviItem In pvfField.PivotItems
            pviItem.Visible = True
         Next
   End Select
End Sub
```

This procedure appears in the module for the frmPivotOptions form, which is available in the Samples\CH15 subfolder on the companion CD-ROM. The form includes a combo box that displays all available PivotTable fields; the user can select a field from the combo box and click the cmdShowAll button to display all items for that PivotTable field.

Formatting PivotTable Data

To format an area of a PivotTable report, you can return a range that represents that particular area, and apply formatting to the range. For example, if you're displaying sales information in the data area of a PivotTable report, you probably want to format those cells with a Currency format. You can use the **DataBodyRange** property of a **PivotTable** object to return a reference to the data range. The following line of code sets the **NumberFormatLocal** property for a PivotTable's data range.

```
ThisWorkbook.ActiveSheet.PivotTables(1).DataBodyRange.NumberFormatLocal = _
   "$#,##0.00"
```

Some other useful properties that return PivotTable ranges are the **RowRange**, **ColumnRange**, **PageRange**, **TableRange1** and **TableRange2** properties.

Creating PivotChart Reports

You can create a PivotChart report that's associated with a PivotTable report so that users can view data in a graph as well as in a table. A PivotTable report and PivotChart report are linked, so that pivoting on data in the PivotTable report updates the PivotChart report, and vice versa.

To create a PivotChart report from code, you add a new chart to the workbook and call the **SetSourceData** method of the chart, passing in a reference to the PivotTable range. You can use the **TableRange1** and **TableRange2** properties to return ranges representing part or all of the PivotTable report. The **TableRange1** property returns a range representing the PivotTable report but excluding page fields; the **TableRange2** property returns a range representing the entire PivotTable report, including page fields.

The following code creates a PivotChart report from a worksheet named Regional Sales.

```
Private Sub cmdChart_Click()
   Dim chtNew        As Excel.Chart
   Dim lngWksCount   As Long

   ' Count number of worksheets in workbook and add chart to end.
   lngWksCount = ThisWorkbook.Sheets.Count
   ' Add new chart.
   Set chtNew = _
      ThisWorkbook.Charts.Add(After:=ThisWorkbook.Sheets(lngWksCount))
   With chtNew
      .Name = REGIONAL_SALES & " Chart"
      ' Set chart's data source to be PivotTable report.
```

```
      chtNew.SetSourceData _
         Source:=Sheets(REGIONAL_SALES).PivotTables(1).TableRange2
      ' Set chart type.
      chtNew.ChartType = xlColumnClustered
   End With
End Sub
```

This procedure appears in the module for the frmPivotOptions form, which is available in the Samples\CH15 subfolder on the companion CD-ROM. The form includes a button that the user can click to create a PivotChart report.

Where to Go from Here

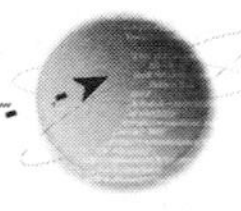

For additional information about the subjects discussed in this chapter, see the following resources. If a file name is listed, that file is located in the Appendixes folder on the companion CD-ROM, unless otherwise noted.

Retrieving Data from External Data Sources

Microsoft Jet Database Engine Programmer's Guide, Third Edition. Redmond, WA: Microsoft Press, 1999.

Creating PivotTable Reports

Wells, Eric, and Steve Harshberger. *Microsoft Excel 97 Developer's Handbook*. Redmond, WA: Microsoft Press, 1997.

Microsoft Office Developer Forum Web site, Excel articles (http://www.microsoft.com/ExcelDev/)

OLAP, OLE DB for OLAP, and OLAP Queries

Universal Data Access Web Site (http://www.microsoft.com/data/)

Microsoft SQL Server OLAP Services (http://www.microsoft.com/sql/olap/)

Data Sources

Chapter 14, "Working with the Data Access Components of an Office Solution"

Working with Data Access Pages

Chapter 5, "Working with Office Applications"

Chapter 12, "Using Web Technologies"

Creating Dynamic Web Pages

Chapter 12, "Using Web Technologies"

Creating Indexes Programmatically

Chapter 14, "Working with the Data Access Components of an Office Solution"

Code Samples

The code samples shown in this chapter, along with additional examples demonstrating similar techniques, can be copied from the files in the Samples\CH15 subfolder on the companion CD-ROM.

CHAPTER 16

Multiuser Database Solutions

Microsoft Office provides a broad array of tools and technologies for creating multiuser database solutions. Specifically, Microsoft Access provides tools and features for creating multiuser database solutions by using four different database architectures: file-server, client/server, replication, and Web-based data access pages. This chapter deals with the first three types; Web-based solutions (including data access pages) are addressed in Chapter 5, "Working with Office Applications" and Chapter 12, "Using Web Technologies."

Although Access is the primary focus of multiuser database features, other Office applications also provide data access and reporting features, such as Excel's Microsoft Query tool, PivotTable reports, and PivotChart reports, all of which can be connected to a variety of database back-ends, including an Access database, a SQL Server database, or an online analytical processing (OLAP) server, such as the Microsoft SQL Server OLAP Services. Additionally, you can create Web-based multiuser solutions using the Office Web components available when you publish pages from Excel or FrontPage. All Office applications that support Visual Basic for Applications (VBA) programming also provide access to data when you use ActiveX Data Objects (ADO) and Data Access Objects (DAO) from VBA code.

Note The discussions about code and code examples used throughout this section refer to ADO unless noted otherwise. Features that require DAO are noted as exceptions. DAO code written for multiuser database solutions in previous versions of Access should continue to work in most cases, as long as your project contains a reference to the Microsoft DAO 3.6 object library. For detailed information about using DAO code, see DAO 3.6 Help and the *Microsoft Jet Database Engine Programmer's Guide, Second Edition* (Microsoft Press, 1997).

Contents

Multiuser Database Solution Architectures

Microsoft Access provides four main ways of working with a database that is shared among multiple users on a network:

- **File-server solutions** Solutions that share an Access database (.mdb) that is placed on a network share so that it can be shared by multiple users.
- **Client/server solutions** Solutions that use a client application, for example, an Access project file (.adp) containing forms and code that connects to a remote database server, such as SQL Server, to share data between multiple users. Copies of the client application are distributed to all users so that they can access the server database from their own computer.
- **Database replication solutions** Solutions that use database replication to share an Access database among multiple users. *Database replication* is the process of sharing data or database design changes between copies of an Access database in different locations without having to redistribute copies of the entire database. Replication involves producing one or more copies, called *replicas*, of a single original database, called the *Design Master*. Together, the Design Master and its replicas are called a *replica set*. By performing a process called *synchronization,* changes to objects and data are distributed to all members of the replica set. Changes to the design of objects can only be made in the Design Master, but changes to data can be made from any member of the replica set.

  Note SQL Server also provides replication features that use a different "publish and subscribe" model. For more information about SQL Server replication features, see SQL Server Books Online.

- **Web-based database solutions** Solutions that use one or more Web pages as the front-end client application connected to a shared Access or SQL Server database.

This chapter provides an overview of the first three Access database solution architectures listed above, the tools Access provides for creating multiuser database solutions, and discussions of multiuser database solution design and implementation issues.

File-Server Solutions

In a file-server environment, a multiuser database solution that is based on Access consists of the following components:

- One or more Access database files (.mdb) residing on the network server
- A locking information file (.ldb) for each database
- A workgroup information file (.mdw) residing either on the network server or on each user's workstation
- A copy of the Access application and the Jet database engine running on the local workstation(s)

System Components and Multiuser Settings

The following sections briefly describe the purpose of the locking information file, the workgroup information file, multiuser settings that control how shared Access databases behave, page-level vs. record-level locking, and running a system on a peer-to-peer network.

The Locking Information File

When a database is opened in shared mode, it's necessary to address issues of *concurrency*, that is, the simultaneous availability of the same sets of data and objects to multiple users. This is done through a locking information file (.ldb), which stores information about any records that are locked in a shared database.

When the first user opens a database in shared mode, the Jet database engine automatically creates a locking information file in the same folder as the database. The Jet database engine then uses this same locking file to manage locking for each subsequent user who opens the same database. One locking information file is created for each Access database (.mdb) that is opened in shared mode. The Jet database engine gives the file the same name as the database that was opened, but with an .ldb file name extension. The Jet database engine deletes the .ldb file for a database when the last user closes the database.

For more information about the locking information file and Jet database engine locking architecture, see "Understanding Microsoft Jet Locking," by Kevin Collins, which is available in the Microsoft Office Developer Forum Web site at http://www.microsoft.com/officedev/.

The Workgroup Information File

In addition to a locking information file, Access 2000 creates a workgroup information file (.mdw), also known as the *system database*. (The default file created when Access 2000 is installed is named System.mdw.) This file is a Microsoft Jet database that stores information about the users, groups, and passwords for a secured database, and its location in multiuser environments is important. The workgroup information file can be placed on the local workstation or shared on a network drive. However, if it's stored locally, you must take the steps necessary to update it when security settings change. For more information about workgroup information files, see Chapter 18, "Securing Access Databases."

Note In versions of Access prior to Access 97, the workgroup information file is used to store various options that the user can set. It also stores the most recently used (MRU) list of databases opened. In Microsoft Access 2000, settings in the user's **Options** dialog box (**Tools** menu, **Options** command) and MRU information are stored in the Windows registry in the HKEY_CURRENT_USER\Software\Microsoft\Office\9.0\Access\Settings subkey on each user's computer.

Multiuser Settings

To control how Microsoft Jet behaves in a multiuser environment, you can use a variety of Windows registry entries. You can change these entries by using the Registry Editor (Regedit.exe for Windows 95 and Windows NT Workstation 4.0) to edit values in the HKEY_LOCAL_MACHINE\SOFTWARE\Microsoft\Jet\4.0\Engines\Jet 4.0 subkey for Jet-specific settings, or in HKEY_CURRENT_USER\SOFTWARE\Microsoft\Office\9.0\Access\Settings for Access-specific settings. The following settings are also available in the Access user interface, either on the **Advanced** tab of the **Options** dialog box (**Tools** menu), or programmatically through the **SetOption** method of the Access **Application** object.

- **Default open mode** Determines how the database is to be opened if no explicit options are specified. You can specify explicit options when you open the database directly, through the DAO **OpenDatabase** method or the ADO **Open** method (**Connection** object). If the database is to be used in a multiuser environment, set this option to **Shared**. This setting corresponds to the Default Open Mode for Databases entry in the Access Settings subkey in the registry.
- **Default record locking** Specifies how records are to be locked when they are edited from table and query datasheets. This setting is also inherited as a default setting for the **RecordLocks** property when you create a new form, but you can override this setting for any form in the database by setting the form's **RecordLocks** property yourself. The three settings correspond to the locking modes that

Microsoft Jet defines. **No Locks** corresponds to *optimistic* locking, **Edited Record** corresponds to *pessimistic* locking, and **All Records** corresponds to *recordset* locking. This setting corresponds to the Default Record Locking entry in the Access Settings subkey in the registry.

- **Number of update retries** Specifies how many times Access tries to save a changed record that is locked before displaying an error message. This sets the Number of Update Retries entry in the Access Settings subkey in the registry.
- **Update retry interval** Specifies the number of milliseconds Access waits before trying again to save a changed record that is locked by another user. This setting corresponds to the Update Retry Interval (msec) entry in the Access Settings subkey in the registry.
- **ODBC refresh interval** Specifies how often (in seconds) Access refreshes a form with updates to the current set of records from Open Database Connectivity (ODBC) data sources. The refreshed data doesn't show new records added by other users, or remove records deleted by other users. To display all updates, additions, and deletions, you must requery the form by pressing SHIFT+F9, or you can use the **Requery** method from code. This setting corresponds to the ODBC Refresh Interval (sec) entry in the Access Settings subkey in the registry.
- **Refresh interval** Specifies how often (in seconds) Access refreshes a form with updates to the current set of records from native Microsoft Jet data sources. The refreshed data will not show new records added by other users, or remove records deleted by other users. To display all updates, additions, and deletions, you must requery the form by pressing SHIFT+F9, or you can use the **Requery** method from code. It should be noted that this setting performs the same function as the PageTimeout entry for Microsoft Jet in the registry. In Access, both the RefreshInterval and the PageTimeout entries are in effect at the same time. This setting corresponds to the Refresh Interval (sec) entry in the Access Settings subkey in the registry.
- **Open databases using record-level locking** Specifies whether record-level or page-level locking mode is used when opening databases on a per-user basis. For more information, see "Page-Level Locking vs. Record-Level Locking" later in this chapter. This setting corresponds to the Use Row Level Locking entry in the Access Settings subkey in the registry.

For the most flexibility, you can temporarily modify Microsoft Jet engine–specific settings in VBA code by using the DAO **SetOption** method of the **DBEngine** object, or from ADO by setting Microsoft Jet 4.0 OLE DB Provider-specific session properties of the **Connection** object. For information about the DAO **SetOption** method, search the DAO Help index for "SetOption method." For information about setting ADO provider-specific session properties, see ADOProperties.doc in the Appendixes folder on the companion CD-ROM.

Page-Level Locking vs. Record-Level Locking

When a user edits a record in a shared database, you can prevent conflicts with other users by locking the data while it is being edited. When data is locked, any number of users can read it, but only one user can make changes to it.

In previous versions of the Jet database engine (version 3.5*x* and earlier), locking a record locks one *page* of data. For previous versions of the Jet database engine, a page is equal to 2K (2048 bytes) of data within the database file; for the current version, Jet 4.0, a page is 4K (4096 bytes) of data. (The size was doubled to accommodate storing data as Unicode characters, which occupy 2 bytes instead of the 1 byte used by previous characters.) Locking at the page-level can lock multiple records if the combined length of two or more records is smaller than the size of a page; this prevents other users from editing any records on that page until the user is finished editing the record that caused the entire page to be locked. Page locking generally results in better performance, but can reduce the ability of other users to edit data.

A new feature of Jet 4.0 is the ability to lock individual records rather than pages. In Access, this is controlled by the **Open databases using record-level locking** setting on the **Advanced** tab of the **Options** dialog box (**Tools** menu). By default, this setting is selected (on), which means two users can update or delete two different records that are located on the same page within the database (which isn't possible when you use pessimistic locking under page-level locking). The locking mode that is in effect is determined by the first user to open a database. If the first user has the **Open databases using record-level locking** setting selected, all users who subsequently open that database will use record-level locking whether they have the setting selected or not. Conversely, if the first user to open a database has the **Open databases using record-level locking** setting cleared, all users who subsequently open that database will use page-level locking.

When record-level locking is on, data edited through Access forms and datasheets will use record-level locking. Also, **Recordset** objects opened by using the DAO **OpenRecordset** method, and any ADO methods (when you use the Microsoft Jet 4.0 OLE DB provider) that open or return a **Recordset** object will use record-level locking. However, any SQL Data Manipulation Language (DML) queries—that is, queries that add, delete, or modify records—that are run from ADO (when you use the Microsoft Jet 4.0 OLE DB Provider), DAO, or the Access query user interface will use page-level locking. Page-level locking is used for SQL DML statements to improve performance when you are working with many records. However, even when record-level locking is turned on, it is not used for updates to values in memo fields and values in fields that are indexed—they still require page-level locking.

You can't programmatically override record locking settings for DAO **Recordset** objects, Access forms and datasheets, or SQL DML statements run from the Access query user interface.

When you use ADO with the Microsoft Jet 4.0 OLE DB Provider to work with an Access database, you can set the provider-specific **Jet OLEDB:Database Locking Mode** property of the **Connection** object before opening a database, and then set the provider-specific **Jet OLEDB:Locking Granularity** property of the **Recordset** object used to execute SQL DML statements or to work with methods that open or return a **Recordset** object. For information about the **Jet OLEDB:Database Locking Mode** and **Jet OLEDB:Locking Granularity** properties, see ADOProperties.doc in the Appendixes folder on the companion CD-ROM.

Running on Peer-to-Peer Networks

Microsoft Jet supports most file-server and peer-to-peer networks that work on personal computers. However, the performance of a multiuser database system running on a peer-to-peer network may suffer, depending on how the computer that's serving as a file-server is being used. If a workstation that contains a shared database is also being used to run desktop applications, there will be increased levels of disk and network I/O, which will affect performance. Also, if a user runs another application that locks the system, all users sharing the database will lose their connections to the database. This can compromise the integrity of the database. For the best performance and stability on peer-to-peer networks, make sure that a workstation containing a shared database is dedicated solely to that purpose.

Location of Solution Components

Because network file access is typically slower than local disk access, you might want to improve performance by storing some of your solution's components on the local workstation. With most network operating systems, you have a great deal of flexibility for controlling where various components of your multiuser solution reside. For this discussion, components are grouped into two categories:

- **Static components** The parts of your solution that don't change often. The dynamic-link libraries (.dll) and executable files (.exe) that make up Access and the Jet database engine are examples of static components. Components in your solution itself, such as forms, reports, and program code, are also static components.
- **Active components** The files that contain the actual data that your solution's users access in a multiuser environment. These can include Access databases, external database files such as Microsoft FoxPro® database files, or ODBC databases stored on database servers.

Because static components don't often change, they are ideal candidates for workstation storage. In this scenario, you install Access and the Jet database engine components on the local workstation along with your solution's static objects. Active components, such as your solution's data files, are stored on the network server. To do this with an Access database, you split your database solution into a back-end database that contains only tables, and a front-end database that contains your solution's queries, forms, reports, macros, and modules, and then create links to the tables in the back-end database. Details about how this is done are provided in the following section, "The Two-Database Approach." When you store static components on local workstations, you optimize performance; the tradeoff is that you have to worry about updating objects on local workstations when the solution's design changes.

In situations where you would like greater control over modification of static components, or where user workstations don't have sufficient disk space, static components can be stored on the network. This has the obvious effect of increasing network traffic and reducing application performance, but it also minimizes administrative issues.

The Two-Database Approach

When developing multiuser database solutions with Access, you may find it helpful to split your objects into two databases. This approach offers many advantages. These two databases are known as the *front-end* database and the *back-end* database.

The front-end database has three basic characteristics:

- It contains non-data objects, such as saved queries, forms, reports, macros, and modules. It can also contain additional objects created by the user for personal use.
- It serves as an area for managing temporary objects. Most multiuser solutions perform some type of data access that is temporary in nature: creating tables with transient data, for example.
- You distribute a copy for each user to run from his or her workstation.

The back-end database contains the tables that hold your solution's data. The tables in this database are accessed by your solution through links in the front-end database. Figure 16.1 illustrates the two-database approach.

Figure 16.1 The Two-Database Approach

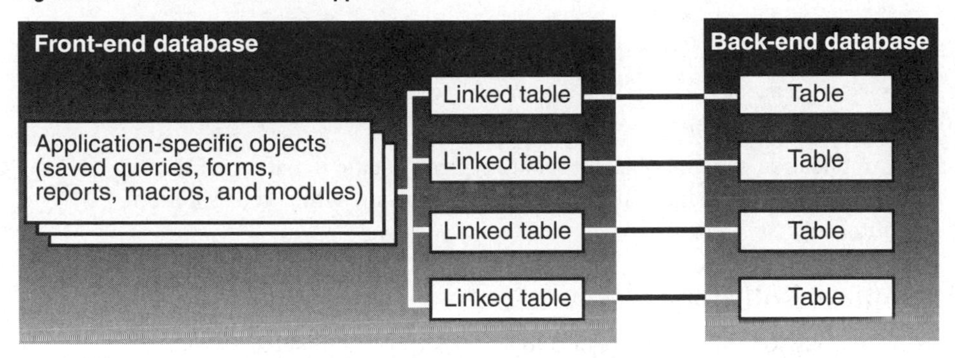

If you know from the beginning that you intend to split your solution into two database files, you can develop it with this in mind. Or you can keep tables and objects together in the same file and split them only when you're finished with development and are ready to distribute the solution. The easiest way to split a solution after creating its objects is to use the Database Splitter Wizard.

▶ To split an Access solution after creating its objects

1 On the **Tools** menu, point to **Add-ins**, and then click **Database Splitter**.

2 Follow the instructions in the dialog boxes that appear.

The Database Splitter Wizard creates a new, empty back-end database. It moves all tables in the current database to the new back-end database, preserving table relationships and properties. The current database is now the front-end database. The wizard then links each table in the back-end database to the front-end database. For information about linking tables by using ADO code, see Chapter 14, "Working with the Data Access Components of an Office Solution."

The links used by linked tables in the front-end database are based on the location of the back-end database. If users move the back-end database to a different location, the links will fail. If the current links are broken, you can automate the process of linking tables for your users by prompting them for the path to the back-end database when they start your solution. Then you can refresh the links to your solution's tables. For an example of how to do this, see the RefreshLinks procedure in Chapter 14, "Working with the Data Access Components of an Office Solution" (the procedure can also be found in the CreateDatabase module in the DataAccess.mdb sample file, which is available in the Samples\CH14 subfolder on the companion CD-ROM).

The advantages of using the two-database approach in a multiuser environment are as follows:

- By storing the front-end database on the user's workstation, there is no contention for temporary objects, such as creating a temporary table, because only one user has the front-end database open.
- By storing application-specific objects that are typically static in nature on the user's workstation, the amount of network traffic that occurs while your solution runs is minimized.

Self-Updating Solutions

Moving some of your solution's components to a user's workstation creates some administrative concerns. For example, when you need to modify a static object in your solution, such as the design of a form or code, you must have mechanisms in place for updating all affected components on each individual workstation.

This problem can be minimized by building your solution so that it checks for latest versions upon startup. For example, your solution's startup code can check the modification dates of static objects in the local database by using the DAO **LastUpdated** property (there is no comparable method of getting this information for all objects in a database when you use ADO) and comparing them to dates in a central database located on the server. Whenever a newer date is found on a server object, you can use code to automatically import the latest version of the object, keeping the local database up-to-date.

In Access 2000, the **CurrentDb** method of the **Application** object can be used to return a DAO **Database** object that refers to the current database. The **CurrentDb** method establishes a hidden reference to the DAO 3.6 object library. That is, when you use the **CurrentDb** method, you don't have to explicitly establish the reference by using the **References** command (**Tools** menu). You can then use the **Database** object to navigate down through the DAO object hierarchy to reference the object you want to check. For example, the following line of code returns the last time the Categories form in the Northwind sample database was updated:

```
Application.CurrentDb.Containers("Forms").Documents("Categories") _
   .LastUpdated
```

For more information about using the **CurrentDb** method and DAO, search the Microsoft Access Visual Basic Reference Help index for "CurrentDb method."

Note It is possible to use the **DateModified** property of the ADOX **Tables, Views**, and **Procedures** collections to return dates for tables and queries, but not for other Access database objects.

You can also use database replication features to keep objects up-to-date by synchronizing them. For example, you can create replicas of the front-end database and distribute them to users. Then if you make changes to the original Design Master of the front-end database, you can synchronize the replicas to distribute updated objects. For more information about replication, see "Database Replication Solutions" later in this chapter.

Handling Locking Conflicts

When working in a single-user environment, your solution doesn't encounter conflicting requests for resources. Because only one user is accessing data at a time, you can reasonably assume that the needed data will always be exclusively available. In a multiuser environment, on the other hand, multiple users may be accessing data at the same time, so the only reasonable assumption is that conflicts will occur when two or more users try to change the same data.

You can prevent such conflicts by making sure that only one user at a time can change data. To protect shared data in this way, you can lock data while a user edits it. When data is locked, any number of users can read it, but only one user can make changes to it.

There are two techniques you can use to lock data in your multiuser solution: (1) bound forms and (2) VBA code that makes direct updates to data in ADO or DAO **Recordset** objects. When you use bound forms, Access performs certain aspects of locking automatically. Alternatively, you can write your own locking procedures in VBA; this approach gives you more control over your solution's locking behavior. Both techniques are discussed below.

Locking Shared Data with Bound Forms

The easiest way to create a multiuser database solution is to create forms that are bound to tables or queries. You control how Access locks data by setting multiuser options and form properties.

Selecting a Locking Strategy

When you share data with bound forms, you can specify how Access locks records in a form. There are three locking strategies to choose from:

- **No locks** Access doesn't attempt to lock the record you're editing until the moment you save changes to the record. This strategy ensures that records can always be edited, but it can create editing conflicts between users if both users try to save changes to the same record. This method is sometimes called *optimistic locking*.

- **Edited record** Access attempts to lock the record or page that contains the record you're editing as soon as you start editing. This strategy ensures that you can always finish making changes that you start. This method is sometimes called *pessimistic locking*.
- **All records** Access locks all records in the underlying table or query of the form that contains the record you're editing for the entire time you have the form open. This strategy is very restrictive, so choose it only when you know you're the only person who needs to edit records at any given time. This method is sometimes called *exclusive locking*.

To set the default locking strategy for all new forms in the database, as well as for all editing performed while using Access datasheets, select one of these options in the **Default record locking** group on the **Advanced** tab of the **Options** dialog box (**Tools** menu). Note that this setting only determines the default for new forms. If you want to set the locking strategy for an individual form, set the form's **RecordLocks** property to one of these settings, which will override the setting of the **Default record locking** group in the **Options** dialog box. You can specify a locking strategy for one, many, or all forms in a database by setting the **RecordLocks** property of the **Form** object in code. For more information about the **RecordLocks** property, search the Microsoft Access Visual Basic Reference Help index for "RecordLocks property."

In addition to specifying a locking strategy, you can set other multiuser options that help you avoid locking conflicts with other users, as described in "Multiuser Settings" earlier in this chapter.

When you share data while using bound forms, Access displays standard messages when locking conflicts occur.

Locking Shared Data by Using Recordset Objects in VBA

Although bound forms are one way to create a multiuser solution, they don't provide the flexibility that VBA procedures do. When you write your own locking procedures and run them from unbound forms, you can adapt your locking strategy to handle conflicts among users in a way that's most suitable for your situation—something that isn't possible with bound forms.

Levels of Locking

There are four different levels at which you can lock data in **Recordset** objects:

- **Exclusive mode** To prevent all other users from using the entire database. This is the most restrictive level.
- **Recordset locking** To lock a **Recordset** object's underlying table.
- **Page-level locking** To lock the entire 4096-byte (4K) page where the data that is being edited resides.
- **Record-level locking** To lock only the current record that is being edited.

Note Whether records are to be locked by using page- or record-level locking is determined when the database is opened by using the **Open databases using record-level locking** setting on the **Advanced** tab of the **Options** dialog box (**Tools** menu). From ADO code, page- or record-level locking can also be controlled by setting the provider-specific **Jet OLEDB:Database Locking Mode** property of the **Connection** object, and the provider-specific **Jet OLEDB:Locking Granularity** property of the **Recordset** object. For more information, see "Page-Level Locking vs. Record-Level Locking" earlier in this chapter.

To determine at which level you want to lock objects in your solution, you must decide the level of *concurrency* that you need. Concurrency is the ability of more than one transaction to access the same data at the same time. For example, if you want the objects to be available as often as possible to as many users as possible, a high-concurrency strategy would dictate that you use page- or record-level locking, which is the least restrictive level. However, if your solution requires guaranteed access to most or all of the data in the database, you may opt for exclusive mode. This ensures that your solution has the database open exclusively so it can't be shared by other users.

The four levels aren't mutually exclusive. Many multiuser solutions use all four levels at different times. For example, in an order-entry system in which you want many order takers to have access to data simultaneously, you can use page- or record-level locking to lock data in the Orders table. You can use recordset locking at the end of the day to lock a summary table and update it with summary data. Finally, you can use exclusive mode each night to lock the entire database while you compact the database.

Using Exclusive Mode

Exclusive mode is the most restrictive way you can lock data. It prevents all other users from opening the database; therefore, it denies all users access to all data in the database. This is useful for performing administrative or bulk changes to the database, such as repair or compacting operations, or for making changes to the design of the database.

When you access a database in a single-user environment, you typically open it in exclusive mode. This may provide better performance because the Jet database engine doesn't have to lock and unlock objects or refresh its cache. To allow multiple users to open the database, users must not use exclusive mode to open the database or other users will be locked out. If you want multiple users to share data with your solution, make sure none of them open your solution's database in exclusive mode. You can use security features in Access to deny most users Open Exclusive permission. The database administrator should have Open Exclusive permission to perform such tasks as compacting and repairing the database. For information about setting permissions, see Chapter 18, "Securing Access Databases."

You can use code to open a database in exclusive mode. To do so when using ADO, set the **Mode** property of the **Connection** object you are using to open the database to **adModeShareExclusive**. The following procedure opens the specified Access database in exclusive mode and checks for errors to determine if the operation was successful. Note that the **For Each...Next** loop that displays any errors uses the **SQLState** property of the ADO **Error** object to retrieve the Jet error number. When you use ADO, the **Number** property of the VBA **Err** object doesn't return the Jet error number.

```
Sub OpenDBExclusive (strDBPath As String)
   Dim cnnDB      As ADODB.Connection
   Dim errCurrent As ADODB.Error

   ' Initialize Connection object.
   Set cnnDB = New ADODB.Connection

   ' Specify Microsoft Jet 4.0 provider and then try
   ' to open the database specified in the strDBPath
   ' variable in exclusive mode.
   On Error Resume Next
   With cnnDB
      .Provider = "Microsoft.Jet.OLEDB.4.0"
      .Mode = adModeShareExclusive
      .Open strDBPath
   End With

   If Err <> 0 Then
      ' If errors occur, display them.
      For Each errCurrent In ADODB.Errors
         Debug.Print "Error " & errCurrent.SQLState _
            & ": " & errCurrent.Description
      Next
   Else
      ' No errors: You have exclusive access.
      Debug.Print "The database is open in exclusive mode."
   End If

   ' Close Connection object and destroy object variable.
   cnnDB.close
   Set cnnDB = Nothing
End Sub
```

The OpenDBExclusive procedure can be found in the OpenDatabase module of the MultiuserDatabase.mdb sample file, which is available in the Samples\CH16 subfolder on the companion CD-ROM.

Using ADO to open an Access database in exclusive mode has the same effect as selecting the **Open Exclusive** button in the **Open** dialog box (**File** menu). If one user already has the database open for write access, and another user tries to open the database in exclusive mode, a locking error occurs. The second user can't open the database in exclusive mode until the first user closes it. For information about determining which users have a shared database open, see "Identifying Users" later in this chapter.

Using Read-Only Mode

If you open the database for a user in shared mode with read-only access by setting the **Mode** property of the **Connection** object to **adModeRead** when opening the database, any other user can read the database, but the current user can't write to it. You may want to do this to prevent the current user from changing data or the design of objects in the database without establishing user-level security. Using ADO to open an Access database in read-only mode has the same effect as selecting the **Open Read-Only** button in the **Open** dialog box (**File** menu).

Note Opening a database in read-only mode doesn't prevent locking conflicts, because other users can still open the database in shared, read/write mode.

The Access **Open** dialog box (**File** menu) also includes an **Open Exclusive Read Only** button. Clicking this allows you to open the database in both read-only and exclusive modes. This prevents other users from opening the database, and also prevents you (the current user) from making changes to the database. If you want to use code to open the database in exclusive, read-only mode, set the **Mode** property to both the **adModeShareExclusive** and **adModeRead** constants by combining them with the plus (+) operator, as shown in the following line of code:

```
cnnDB.Mode = adModeShareExclusive + adModeRead
```

Opening the Database in Shared Mode

If you want to implement any other form of locking, you must open your database in shared mode. When a database is opened in shared mode, multiple users can simultaneously access the database and the Jet database engine handles conflicts between users.

You can use code to open a database in shared mode. When using ADO with the Microsoft Jet 4.0 OLE DB Provider, the **Open** method of the **Connection** object opens the database in shared mode by default. To open the database explicitly in shared mode, set the **Mode** property to **adModeShareDenyNone**. The following procedure opens the specified database in shared mode and checks for errors to determine if the operation was successful.

```
Sub OpenDBShared (strDBPath As String)
   Dim cnnDB As ADODB.Connection
   Dim errCurrent As ADODB.Error

   ' Initialize Connection object
   Set cnnDB = New ADODB.Connection

   ' Specify Microsoft Jet 4.0 provider and then try to open
   ' the database specified in the strDBPath variable in shared
   ' mode.
   On Error Resume Next
   With cnnDB
      .Provider = "Microsoft.Jet.OLEDB.4.0"
      .Mode = adModeShareDenyNone
      .Open strDBPath
   End With

   If Err <> 0 Then
      ' If errors occur, display them.
      For Each errCurrent In ADODB.Errors
         Debug.Print "Error " & errCurrent.SQLState _
            & ": " & errCurrent.Description
      Next
   Else
      ' No errors: You have shared access.
      Debug.Print "The database is open in shared mode."
   End If

   ' Close Connection object and destroy object variable.
   cnnDB.close
   Set cnnDB = Nothing
End Sub
```

The OpenDBShared procedure can be found in the OpenDatabase module of the MultiuserDatabase.mdb sample file, which is available in the Samples\CH16 subfolder on the companion CD-ROM.

Using ADO to open a database in shared mode has the same effect as selecting the **Open** button in the **Open** dialog box (**File** menu).

Checking for Errors

When you are setting locks in code with any level of locking, it's important that you handle any errors that occur. In Access, you don't check to see if a lock can be set before you set it. Instead, you try the operation and then check to see if it succeeded.

The typical approach to locking is a four-step process:

1. Turn off error handling.
2. Attempt the operation.
3. Check to see if an error occurred. If so, handle the error based on the error number.
4. Turn on error handling.

This approach works well because you don't have to anticipate every possible error before trying to set a lock; you handle the error only if it occurs. When writing multiuser code, you should handle the error by displaying a message and giving the user an opportunity to retry the operation.

The most common error you'll encounter when you use exclusive mode is error number 3006, "Database <*name*> is exclusively locked." This error occurs when you try to open a database that is currently open in exclusive mode by another user. To respond to the error, wait until the other user has finished working with the database and then try the operation again. For more information about error handling, see Chapter 8, "Error Handling and Debugging."

Using Recordset Locking

You use exclusive mode to lock an entire database. You use *recordset locking,* on the other hand, to specify locking for an entire table in a shared database. You can specify a *read lock* to prevent other users from reading records in the table, a *write lock* to prevent other users from editing records in the table, or both. ADO and OLE DB don't currently support this kind of locking, so you must use DAO code if you require recordset locking. Recordset locking applies only to DAO table- and dynaset-type **Recordset** objects; it can't be used with DAO snapshot-type or forward-only–type **Recordset** objects, because these are inherently read-only objects. To implement recordset locking, Microsoft Jet places shared table-read and shared table-write locks.

After you open the database in shared mode, you can implement recordset locking by specifying either of the **dbDenyRead** and **dbDenyWrite** constants in the ***Options*** argument of the DAO **OpenRecordset** method. You can also combine both constants by using the plus (+) operator if you want to apply both read and write locks to the table.

▶ To open a DAO Recordset object with recordset locking

1. Open the **Recordset** object's database in shared mode.
2. Determine the type of recordset locking you want to use.
3. Open the **Recordset** object by using the **OpenRecordset** method and set the ***Options*** argument to specify the type of locking that you want.
4. Close the **Recordset** object when you're finished performing operations on the data to release any locks on the **Recordset** object.

For example, the following code locks a table by opening it with the **dbDenyWrite** and **dbDenyRead** constants specified in the ***Options*** argument of the **OpenRecordset** method. For the duration of the procedure, no other users can access this table. If an error occurs when you try to open the table, the function returns **Nothing**. This procedure requires the DAOOpenDBShared procedure, which attempts to open a database in shared mode and handles errors if it can't. The DAOOpenDBShared and

DAOOpenTableExclusive procedures can be found in the RecordsetLocking module of the MultiuserDatabase.mdb sample file, which is available in the Samples\CH16 subfolder on the companion CD-ROM.

```
Function DAOOpenTableExclusive(strDbPath As String, _
                               strRstSource As String) As DAO.Recordset
   Dim dbs As DAO.Database
   Dim rst As DAO.Recordset

   ' Open the database in shared mode by calling the
   ' DAOOpenDBShared function.
   Set dbs = DAOOpenDBShared(strDbPath)

   ' Check whether database was successfully opened in shared mode.
   ' If it was, open specified table exclusively.
   If Not dbs Is Nothing Then
      Set rst = dbs.OpenRecordset(strRstSource, _
         dbOpenTable, dbDenyRead + dbDenyWrite)
      ' Check whether recordset was opened successfully. If it was,
      ' return the Recordset object; otherwise return Nothing.
      If Not rst Is Nothing Then
         Set DAOOpenTableExclusive = rst
      Else
         Set DAOOpenTableExclusive = Nothing
      End If
   Else
      Set OpenTableExclusive = Nothing
   End If
End Function
```

Important You must also use DAO code to work with the **Recordset** object returned by this procedure. You can't use ADO code to work with DAO objects, and vice versa.

Note If you open a **Recordset** object without specifying any value for the ***Options*** argument, Microsoft Jet uses record locking by default. It opens the **Recordset** object in shared mode and locks only the data that's being edited in the current record.

For more information about opening a **Recordset** object by using DAO, see DAO 3.6 Help and the *Microsoft Jet Database Engine Programmer's Guide, Second Edition* (Microsoft Press, 1997).

Checking for Errors with Recordset Locking

As with opening databases in exclusive mode, setting locks on **Recordset** objects can cause errors if the lock fails. You should use the four-step process described in the previous section: Turn off error handling, attempt the operation, check for errors and handle any that occur, and finally, turn on error handling.

The most common error in recordset locking is error number 3262, "Couldn't lock table *<name>*; currently in use by user *<name>* on machine *<name>*." This error occurs when you try to use the **OpenRecordset** method on an object that can't be locked. There is usually another user who has the same table or tables locked in a way that prevents your action. To respond to the error, wait a short period of time and try the operation again.

Using Page-Level and Record-Level Locking

Whereas opening a database in exclusive mode locks the entire database, and recordset locking locks one or more individual tables, page- or record-level locking locks only the page or record containing the record that is currently being edited. This is the least restrictive level of locking. When you use page- or record-level locking, other users can read data from the locked page or record, but they can't change it. Record-level locking is the default for ADO and DAO **Recordset** objects. Page-level locking is the default for SQL DML statements (bulk operations such as UPDATE, DELETE, and INSERT INTO statements) that use ADO **Command** objects or DAO **QueryDef** objects.

When working with **Recordset** objects that lock data at the page or record level, you must specify which type of locking you want to use. There are two of types of locking available when you use page- and record-level locking: *pessimistic locking* and *optimistic locking*.

You can set the type of locking for an ADO **Recordset** object by specifying either the **adLockPessimistic** or the **adLockOptimistic** constant in the ***LockType*** argument of the **Open** method of the **Recordset** object. You can't change the type of locking after you open an ADO **Recordset** object as you can with a DAO **Recordset** object by setting its **LockEdits** property.

Pessimistic Locking

With pessimistic locking, a record (or the page the record resides on) is locked once you begin editing the record. In ADO you don't use the **Edit** method to start an editing operation as you do in DAO. To edit a field's value in ADO, you simply change the **Value** property of a **Field** object. The record or page remains locked until you save your changes to the record by moving to a new record or by using the **Update** method. If you aren't using batch updating, you must use the **CancelUpdate** method to cancel the edit before moving to a new record.

The main advantage of pessimistic locking is that after you have obtained a lock, you know that you won't encounter any locking conflicts as long as the record is locked. Additionally, pessimistic locking is the only way to guarantee that your solution reads the most current data, because one user can't change a record after another user has started to edit it.

The disadvantage to using pessimistic locking when you are using page-level locking is that the entire page is locked for the duration of the procedure. Therefore, other users can't change any records on that page until the lock is released. However, by default, both ADO and DAO **Recordset** objects use record-level locking, so this is only an issue if you override the default setting.

▶ To use pessimistic locking in your code

1. Implement pessimistic locking by setting the ***LockType*** argument of the **Open** method of the **Recordset** object to **adLockPessimistic** when you open the **Recordset** object.
2. Move to the record that you're interested in.
3. Edit the record by specifying changes to **Field** objects. When you use pessimistic locking, ADO attempts to lock the record as soon as you start editing the first **Field** object. If the lock fails, try again.
4. When the record is locked, make your changes to the record.
5. Save your changes to the record by moving to a new record or by using the **Update** method. After your changes are saved, the lock is released.

Optimistic Locking

With optimistic locking, a record or page is locked only when you try to save the changes to the record by moving to a new record or by using the **Update** method. Because the lock is applied only when your solution tries to update the record, you minimize the time the lock is in place; this is the main advantage of optimistic locking.

The disadvantage of optimistic locking is that when you are editing a record, you can't be sure that the update will succeed. Your attempt to update the record with your edits will fail if another user updates the record first.

▶ To use optimistic locking in your code

1. Implement optimistic locking by setting the ***LockType*** argument of the **Open** method of the **Recordset** object to **adLockOptimistic** when you open the **Recordset** object.
2. Move to the record that you're interested in.
3. Edit the record by specifying changes to **Field** objects. When you use optimistic locking, this doesn't lock the record.
4. Save your changes to the record by moving to a new record or by using the **Update** method. This attempts to lock the record.
5. Check to see if the **Update** method succeeded. If it didn't, try again.

It's possible for the **Update** method to fail in optimistic locking. For example, if one user has a **Recordset** object open with pessimistic locking, and another user tries to update data on the same page by using optimistic locking, the second user's attempt to update will fail.

Note Optimistic locking turns into pessimistic locking when transactions are used. Because a transaction locks data so that users can't change it until the transaction is committed, pessimistic locking is used even though the ***LockType*** argument may have been set to **adLockOptimistic**. For more information about transactions, see "Using Transactions" later in this chapter.

Checking for Errors with Record-Level and Page-Level Locking

When you use record- or page-level locking, before proceeding, your code must check to see if the attempted lock succeeded. As with exclusive mode and recordset locking, you should turn off error handling, attempt the operation, check for errors and handle any that occur, and finally, turn on error handling.

The following table describes the three most common errors that your solution may encounter when you use record- or page-level locking. These errors are returned by the Jet Database engine.

Error number and text	Cause and suggested response
3218 "Could not update; currently locked."	This error occurs when a user tries to save a record that is locked by another user. To handle this error, program your solution to wait for a short period of time, and then try to save the record again. Or, you can display a message that explains the problem and give users the opportunity to try the operation again.
3197 "The database engine stopped the process because you and another user are attempting to change the same data at the same time."	This error occurs if another user has changed the data since the current user started trying to update the record. When this error is triggered depends on the locking mode you are using: • If you are using pessimistic locking, this error occurs when the current user attempts to start editing the record after the other user has saved changes to the record. • If you are using optimistic locking, this error occurs when the user attempts to save changes by using the **Update** method after the other user has already saved changes to the record. In either situation, to handle this error, program your solution to display a message that informs the user that someone else has changed the data. You may want to display the current data and give users the choice of whether to overwrite the other user's changes or cancel their own edits.
3260 "Couldn't update; currently locked by user *<name>* on machine *<name>*."	This error occurs when a user attempts to edit a record and the current record (or if you are using page-level locking, the page it is on) is locked. If you are using page-level locking, this error also occurs when a user uses the **AddNew** method or the **Update** method to save a record on a locked page. This situation can occur when the user is trying to save a new record or when optimistic locking is in place and another user locks the page. To handle this error, program your solution to wait for a short period of time, and then try to save the record again. Or, you can inform users of the problem and allow them to indicate whether or not they want to retry the operation.

Record-Level or Page-Level Locking Code Example

You can write a procedure that tries to lock a record, checks to see if an error occurred, and responds to it regardless of the type of error. Alternatively, you can write a procedure that identifies the specific error that occurs and responds to it. The following procedure tries to edit a record. If a locking error occurs, the procedure tries to identify the error and responds accordingly. If an unidentified error occurs, the procedure displays a message and exits the function.

```
Function UpdateUnitsInStock(strProduct As String, _
                            intUnitsInStock As Integer,_
                            intMaxTries As Integer) As Boolean
   Dim strConnect    As String
   Dim cnn           As ADODB.Connection
   Dim rstProducts   As ADODB.Recordset
   Dim blnError      As Boolean
   Dim intCount      As Integer
   Dim intLockCount  As Integer
   Dim intChoice     As Integer
   Dim intRndCount   As Integer
   Dim intI          As Integer
   Dim strMsg        As String

   Const MULTIUSER_EDIT As Integer = 3197
   Const RECORD_LOCKED As Integer = 3218
   Const NWIND_PATH As String = "C:\Program Files\Microsoft " _
      "Office\Office\Samples\Northwind.mdb"

   On Error GoTo UpdateUnitsInStockError

   ' Format connection string to open database.
   strConnect = "Provider=Microsoft.Jet.OLEDB.4.0;Data Source=" & NWIND_PATH

   ' Open database.
   Set cnn = New ADODB.Connection
   cnn.Open strConnect

   ' Open the Products table for editing by using pessimistic locking.
   Set rstProducts = New ADODB.Recordset
   rstProducts.Open "Products", cnn, adOpenKeyset, _
      adLockOptimistic, adCmdTableDirect

   With rstProducts
      .Find Criteria:="ProductName = " & "'" & strProduct & "'", _
           SkipRecords:=0, _
           SearchDirection:=adSearchForward

      If .EOF Then
         MsgBox "Record not found."
         UpdateUnitsInStock = False
         GoTo UpdateUnitsInStockExit
      End If
```

```
      ' Attempt to edit the record. If a lock error occurs, the
      ' error handler will attempt to resolve it. Because this
      ' procedure uses pessimistic locking, errors are generated
      ' when you begin to edit a record. If you used optimistic
      ' locking, lock errors will occur when you update a record.

      ![UnitsInStock] = intUnitsInStock
      .Update
      UpdateUnitsInStock = True
   End With

UpdateUnitsInStockExit:
   On Error Resume Next
   rstProducts.Close
   Set rstProducts = Nothing
   Exit Function

UpdateUnitsInStockError:
   ' Check the SQLState property of the first Error object in
   ' the Errors collection to retrieve the Jet error number.
   Select Case cnn.Errors(0).SQLState

      Case MULTIUSER_EDIT
         ' Data in the recordset has changed since it was opened.
         ' Display current value to user and provide option to overwrite.

         strMsg = "The record was changed by another user since you opened it." _
            & vbCr & "The value of UnitsInStock is now: " _
            & rstProducts.Fields("UnitsInStock").OriginalValue & vbCr _
            & " Save anyway?"
         intChoice = MsgBox(strMsg, vbYesNo + vbQuestion)
         If intChoice = vbYes Then
            Resume
         Else
            UpdateUnitsInStock = False
            Resume UpdateUnitsInStockExit
         End If

      Case RECORD_LOCKED
         ' The record is locked.
         intLockCount = intLockCount + 1
         ' Tried to get the lock twice already. Let the user cancel or retry.
         If intLockCount > 2 Then
            intChoice = MsgBox(Err.Description & " Retry?", _
               vbYesNo + vbQuestion)
            If intChoice = vbYes Then
               intLockCount = 1
            Else
               UpdateUnitsInStock = False
               Resume UpdateUnitsInStockExit
            End If
         End If
```

```
            ' Yield to Windows.
            DoEvents
            ' Delay a short random interval, making it longer each
            ' time the lock fails.
            intRndCount = intLockCount ^ 2 * Int(Rnd * 3000 + 1000)
            For intI = 1 To intRndCount
            Next intI
            Resume                  ' Try the edit again.
         Case Else                  ' Unanticipated error.
            MsgBox "Error " & cnn.Errors(0).SQLState & ": " _
                  & Err.Description, vbOKOnly, "ERROR"
            UpdateUnitsInStock = False
            Resume UpdateUnitsInStockExit

   End Select
End Function
```

The UpdateUnitsInStock procedure can be found in the RecordLocking module of the MultiuserDatabase.mdb sample file, which is available in the Samples\CH16 subfolder on the companion CD-ROM.

Note that the code specifies a random interval to retry the operation. This is an important technique for making sure that two users who are trying to update the same record don't end up in a deadlock situation where the code keeps trying to lock the record at the same time. By introducing a random element into the timing loop, you can minimize the chances of a deadlock.

Testing a Record for Locking Status

You may want to check to see if a record is locked without actually locking its page or pages. The following procedure attempts to edit the current record to determine if it is locked.

```
Function IsRecordLocked(strProduct) As Boolean
   Dim rst          As ADODB.Recordset
   Dim strConnect As String
   Dim cnn          As ADODB.Connection
   Dim strSQL       As String
   On Error GoTo RecordLockedError

   Const NWIND_PATH As String = "C:\Program Files\Microsoft " _
      & "Office\Office\Samples\Northwind.mdb"
   ' Format connection string to open database.
   strConnect = "Provider=Microsoft.Jet.OLEDB.4.0;Data Source=" & NWIND_PATH

   ' Open database.
   Set cnn = New ADODB.Connection
   cnn.Open strConnect

   ' Format SQL statment to open Recordset object on the specified record.
   strSQL = "SELECT Products.ProductName,Products.UnitsInStock FROM " _
      & "Products WHERE Products.ProductName ='" & strProduct & "';"
```

```
   ' Open the Products table for editing by using pessimistic locking.
   Set rst = New ADODB.Recordset
   With rst
      .Open strSQL, cnn, adOpenKeyset, _
         adLockPessimistic, adCmdText

      ' If no record is found, display message, return False, and exit.
      If .EOF Then
         MsgBox "Record not found."
         IsRecordLocked = False
         GoTo IsRecordLockedExit
      End If

      ' Attempt to edit a value in the record. If this succeeds,
      ' return False; otherwise an error will be triggered.
      ![UnitsInStock] = 999
      IsRecordLocked = False
   End With

IsRecordLockedExit:
   rst.CancelUpdate
   rst.Close
   Set rst = Nothing
   cnn.Close
   Set cnn = Nothing
   Exit Function

RecordLockedError:
   Select Case cnn.Errors(0).SQLState
      ' Record is locked.
      Case 3260
         IsRecordLocked = True
         GoTo IsRecordLockedExit
      Case Else
         Resume Next
   End Select
End Function
```

The IsRecordLocked procedure can be found in the RecordLocking module of the MultiuserDatabase.mdb sample file, which is available in the Samples\CH16 subfolder on the companion CD-ROM.

Using Transactions

Defined as a "logical unit of work," a *transaction* is one of the features common to most database management systems. By wrapping multiple database operations into a single unit, transactions offer the developer the ability to enforce data integrity by making sure multiple operations can be treated by the engine as an "all or nothing" proposition, thereby never allowing the database to end up in an inconsistent state.

The most common example of transaction processing involves a bank's automated teller machine. The processes of dispensing cash and then debiting the user's account are considered to constitute a logical unit of work and are therefore wrapped in a transaction: The cash is not dispensed unless the system is also able to debit the account. By using a transaction, the entire operation either succeeds or fails. This maintains the consistent state of the ATM database.

Transactions can be defined by what are known as the *ACID* properties. The following attributes of transactions make up the ACID acronym:

- *Atomic* denotes that transactions are all-or nothing operations. Each operation wrapped in a transaction must be successful for all operations to be committed.
- *Consistent* denotes that a transaction enables data operations to transform the database from one consistent state to another, even though at any point during the transaction the database may be inconsistent.
- *Isolated* denotes that all transactions are "invisible" to other transactions. That is, no transaction can see another transaction's updates to the database until the transaction is committed.
- *Durable* denotes that after a transaction is committed, its updates survive—even if there is a subsequent system crash.

Important File-server databases, such as the Jet database engine, can't guarantee durable transactions. There are currently no file-server–based database engines that can fully support this criterion of true transactions. For example, a database connected to a file server can't be expected to fully support the durability rule if the file server crashes before a transaction has had time to commit its changes. If you require true transaction support with respect to durability, you should investigate the use of a client/server database engine such as SQL Server or the Microsoft Data Engine (MSDE).

Note The behavior of transactions with Microsoft Jet databases differs in other respects from the behavior of Microsoft SQL Server and MSDE.

Using Transactions in Your Solutions

To provide transactions when you use ADO with the Microsoft Jet 4.0 provider, you use the **BeginTrans**, **CommitTrans** and **RollbackTrans** methods of the **Connection** object. The basic syntax is shown in the following table.

Method	Operation
connection.**BeginTrans**	Begins the transaction.
connection.**RollbackTrans**	Undoes the transaction.
connection.**CommitTrans**	Posts the transaction, writing its updates to the permanent database objects.

The following example changes the job title of all sales associates in the Employees table of the Northwind database. After the **BeginTrans** method starts a transaction that isolates all of the changes made to the Employees table, you can choose to use the **CommitTrans** method to save the changes, or you can use the **RollbackTrans** method to undo changes that you saved within the transaction by using the **Update** method.

```
Sub ChangeTitle()
   Dim cnn          As ADODB.Connection
   Dim strConnect   As String
   Dim strSQL       As String

   Const conFilePath As String = "C:\Program Files\Microsoft " _
      & "Office\Office\Samples\Northwind.mdb"

   ' Format connection string.
   strConnect = "Provider=Microsoft.Jet.OLEDB.4.0;Data Source=" & conFilePath

   ' Open Connection object.
   Set cnn = New ADODB.Connection
   cnn.Open strConnect

   ' Format SQL statement to update records.
   strSQL = "UPDATE Employees SET Title = " _
      & "'Sales Associate' WHERE Title = 'Sales Representative'"

   ' Begin transaction.
   cnn.BeginTrans

   ' Execute SQL statement.
   cnn.Execute strSQL

   ' Prompt user to save changes or roll back.
   ' Note that this is being done for demonstration
   ' purposes. In an actual solution, you shouldn't
   ' leave a transaction waiting for a user's response
   ' because all affected records are locked until
   ' the user responds.
   If MsgBox("Save all changes?", vbQuestion + vbYesNo) = vbYes Then
      ' Commit transaction.
      cnn.CommitTrans
   Else
      ' Roll back transaction.
      cnn.RollbackTrans
   End If

   ' Close Connection object and destroy object variable.
   cnn.Close
   Set cnn = Nothing
End Sub
```

The ChangeTitle procedure can be found in the Transactions module of the MultiuserDatabase.mdb sample file, which is available in the Samples\CH16 subfolder on the companion CD-ROM.

Note In DAO, because the scope of transactions is determined by the **Workspace** object, transactions are global to the workspace, not to a specific database or set of records. If you perform operations on more than one database or set of records within a DAO **Workspace** object's transaction, the **CommitTrans** and **RollbackTrans** methods affect all the objects that were changed while using that connection during the transaction. However, this concern doesn't apply when using transactions against an ADO **Connection** object with an Access database, because an ADO **Connection** object can open only one database at a time. It is possible to create a transaction that spans multiple **Connection** objects when using ADO with the Microsoft Transaction Server transaction processor, but the Microsoft Jet 4.0 OLE DB Provider doesn't support this functionality.

Another common use of transactions in multiuser environments is to make sure users don't see an incomplete view of shared data as it's being changed. For example, assume your solution is running code that is updating data, and another user is simultaneously running a report on that data. If you don't wrap your updates in a transaction, the user running the report could receive inconsistent data if some records have been updated by your code, and some have not been. If you wrap your updates in a transaction, however, the other user can't receive inconsistent data because all records are updated at once.

Try not to keep a transaction open too long. All locks that result from your edits with the transaction are kept in place until the transaction is committed or rolled back. This can diminish the concurrency of your multiuser solution. If your transaction needs to process many records, break up the operation into a series of smaller transactions.

Managing Transactions

When you are using ADO code with a Microsoft Jet 4.0 provider to perform transactions, the Jet database engine manages your transactions. The Jet database engine uses sophisticated algorithms to enhance transaction performance, reliability, and usability. This section discusses topics related to how the engine manages transactions.

The Temporary Database

Almost all database-transaction systems store intermediate changes in a temporary log file instead of writing them directly to the database. Microsoft Jet uses a similar mechanism in that it buffers all transaction activity to a temporary database. When the transaction is committed, the contents of the temporary database are merged into the real database. If you use the **RollbackTrans** method to cancel the transaction, the engine frees the pages in the temporary database.

The Jet database engine doesn't create the temporary database until it has to. It uses whatever cache memory is available to store changes to data. After the cache is exhausted, the engine creates the temporary database and starts to write changes there.

The Jet database engine creates the temporary database in the directory specified by the TEMP environment variable of the workstation. If the available disk space for the temporary database is exhausted during a transaction, a trappable run-time error occurs. If you attempt to commit the transaction after this error occurs, the engine will commit an indeterminate number of changes, possibly leaving the database in an inconsistent state. To ensure a consistent database state, you usually should roll back the transaction when this error occurs.

Although the temporary database is an Access database, it's used internally by the engine only. It can't be opened from other applications. After a transaction is complete, the engine frees the pages in the temporary database.

Nesting Transactions

When you use the Microsoft Jet 4.0 OLE DB Provider with ADO, you can have up to five levels of transactions per **Connection** object active at any one time by nesting combinations of the **BeginTrans** and **CommitTrans** methods or the **RollbackTrans** method. If you nest transactions, you must make sure you commit or roll back the current transaction before trying to commit or roll back a transaction at a higher level of nesting.

If you want to have transactions with overlapping, non-nested scopes, you can open additional **Connection** objects and manage other transactions within those new connections.

When a Transaction Is Rolled Back by the Engine

If you close a **Connection** object, any uncommitted transactions that were within the scope of that connection are automatically rolled back. Microsoft Jet never automatically commits any transactions you have started. You should be aware of this behavior when you write your code. Never assume that the engine is going to commit your transaction for you.

Transactions on External Data Sources

The Jet database engine only supports transactions against Access databases (including databases from previous versions of Access) and ODBC data sources. For example, if your database has linked Excel or dBASE tables, any transactions on those objects are ignored. This means that the transaction will not fail or generate a run-time error, but it won't actually do anything, either. Note that even though Microsoft Jet 2.*x* and 3.*x* databases (Access 2.0, 95, and 97 databases) are opened by Microsoft Jet 4.0 as external ISAM databases, the engine does support transactions on those databases.

However, you may be able to use ADO code to perform transactions against other data sources by using a different OLE DB provider. For example, if you need to write code to work directly with a SQL Server database, you can use ADO code with the Microsoft OLE DB Provider for SQL Server (Provider=SQLOLEDB) to perform transactions. For more information about available OLE DB providers, see http://www.microsoft.com/data/oledb/products/product.htm.

Regardless of the OLE DB provider you are using, you can check the value of the provider-specific **Transaction DDL** property in the **Properties** collection of the **Connection** object to determine whether the object supports transactions. A value of 0 indicates that the object doesn't support transactions. The value for **Transaction DDL** on a **Connection** object that uses the Microsoft Jet 4.0 OLE DB Provider to connect to an Access database is 16, which indicates that both SQL Data Definition Language (DDL) and Data Manipulation Language (DML) statements can be used within a transaction, but DDL statements that modify tables or indexes will lock those objects until the transaction finishes. This means you won't be able to execute multiple statements if a subsequent SQL statement needs to place a lock on an object that has already been locked by a previous statement. The table below describes all possible values of the **Transaction DDL** property.

Transaction DDL value	Description
0	Transactions are not supported.
1	Transactions can only contain DML statements. DDL statements within a transaction cause an error.
2	Transactions can only contain DML statements. DDL statements within a transaction cause the transaction to be committed.
4	Transactions can only contain DML statements. DDL statements within a transaction are ignored.
8	Transactions can contain DDL and DML statements in any order.
16	Transactions can contain both DML and DDL statements that modify tables or indexes, but modifying a table or index within a transaction causes the table or index to be locked until the transaction completes. This means you won't be able to execute additional statements that affect the tables or indexes once they are locked.

Other File-Server Solution Issues

Up to this point, locking has been covered as the main multiuser issue for file-server solutions. It is not, however, the only issue. When designing a file-server solution for multiuser access, you should keep in mind several additional factors. This section covers these factors.

Refreshing Collections

Any time you are working with collections it is a good idea to use the **Refresh** method to refresh the contents of the collection before working with it. For example, if your procedure works with a collection, calls a procedure that adds or deletes objects from the collection, and then returns and works with the collection again, the contents of the collection often won't be current unless you've refreshed it. This problem can be compounded even further in a multiuser setting, because other users may be modifying collections by adding new objects to the database, or deleting existing objects. The following code fragment loops through the **Table** objects in a **Tables** collection. By using the **Refresh** method to force ADO to reinventory the database and update the **Tables** collection with the most recent changes, it ensures that the contents of the **Tables** collection are current.

```
Set cat = New ADOX.Catalog
cat.ActiveConnection = CurrentProject.Connection

' Refresh the collection before proceeding.
cat.Tables.Refresh

For Each tbl In cat.Tables
   If tbl.Type = "TABLE"
      Debug.Print tbl.Name
Next tbl
```

This code fragment is from the ShowAllTables procedure, which can be found in the MultiuserIssues module of the MultiuserDatabase.mdb sample file, available in the Samples\CH16 subfolder on the companion CD-ROM.

Requerying Data

If your multiuser solution presents data to the user in a visual form, such as in a window or form, you may want to update the user's view with the most current data. Although this functionality is automatically available to solutions that use the Access objects and user interface, when working with data while using VBA, you must explicitly requery data to get the most current view of other users' changes.

When you use the **Requery** method with DAO, you must first determine if the **Recordset** object supports the **Requery** method by checking the value of the **Restartable** property of the **Recordset** object. If the value is **True**, you can refresh the **Recordset** object's contents by using the **Requery** method. If the **Recordset** object doesn't support the **Requery** method, you must open the **Recordset** object again with the **Open** method.

When you use the **Requery** method with ADO, you don't have to check the **Recordset** object to see if it is restartable. The **Requery** method in ADO handles this automatically; if the **Recordset** isn't restartable, **Requery** will reopen the **Recordset** instead.

The following code illustrates how to requery a **Recordset** object by using ADO. The OpenRecordsetForRequery procedure opens a Keyset cursor **Recordset** object on the Orders table and then requeries it.

```
Sub OpenRecordsetForRequery()
   Dim rst        As ADODB.Recordset
   Dim strConnect As String

   Const conFilePath As String = _
      "C:\Program Files\Microsoft Office\Office\Samples\Northwind.mdb"

   ' Format connection string to open database.
   strConnect = "Provider=Microsoft.Jet.OLEDB.4.0;Data Source=" _
      & conFilePath

   ' Open Recordset object.
   Set rst = New ADODB.Recordset
   With rst
      .Open "Orders", strConnect, adOpenKeyset, adLockOptimistic, _
         adCmdTable
      ' Requery Recordset object.
      .Requery
   End With

   rst.Close
   Set rst = Nothing
End Sub
```

The OpenRecordsetForRequery procedure can be found in the MultiuserIssues module of the MultiuserDatabase.mdb sample file, which is available in the Samples\CH16 subfolder on the companion CD-ROM.

In general, most **Recordset** objects are restartable, which means they can be requeried. The exceptions are **Recordset** objects based on pass-through queries and on crosstab queries that contain variable-length fields. These types of **Recordset** objects can't be requeried and must be reopened to get the most current state of the data. To determine if a **Recordset** object is restartable from ADO, check the **Quick Restart** property in the **Properties** collection of the **Recordset** object.

Identifying Users

In your multiuser solution, you may want to programmatically identify the user who is currently logged on to the system. This is useful for administrative functions such as storing the user's name with edited records to create an audit trail. Several methods are available to achieve this functionality. One involves Microsoft Jet user-level security, another uses the ADO **OpenSchema** method to retrieve information about the users in the database.

Checking a User's Logon ID

When you establish user-level security for your database, you force the user to log on to your solution with a predefined user name and password. From ADO code, the user name is then available to your solution through the **User ID** property of the **Connection** object. The following procedure writes the user's name and the current date and time to fields in a table named AuditTrail in the current database.

```
Sub WriteAuditTrail()
   Dim rst As ADODB.Recordset
   Dim cnn As ADODB.Connection

   Set cnn = CurrentProject.Connection

   ' Open AuditTrail table.
   Set rst = New ADODB.Recordset
   rst.Open "AuditTrail", cnn, adOpenKeyset, adLockOptimistic, adCmdTableDirect
   With rst
      ' Add new record.
      .AddNew
      ' Write name of current user to table.
      !UserLastModified = cnn.Properties("User ID")
      ' Write time to table.
      !DateLastModified = Now
      .Update
   End With
End Sub
```

The WriteAuditTrail procedure can be found in the MultiuserIssues module of the MultiuserDatabase.mdb sample file, which is available in the Samples\CH16 subfolder on the companion CD-ROM.

For more information about user-level security, see Chapter 18, "Securing Access Databases."

Retrieving User Information with the OpenSchema Method

ADO and the Microsoft Jet 4.0 OLE DB Provider also supply a way to retrieve information about which users are in the database by using a *schema query*. ADO provides schema queries to furnish a variety of information about a database. You use the ADO **OpenSchema** method to run a schema query and return values to a **Recordset** object, which you can then use to read the information. For details about using the **OpenSchema** method, search the ADO Help index for "OpenSchema method."

To run a schema query that returns information about the users who currently have a shared Access database open, you must specify the **adProviderSpecific** constant for the *Schema* argument of the **OpenSchema** method, and pass a globally unique identifier (GUID) value that identifies the query to the Jet provider as the ***SchemaID*** argument. The following code demonstrates how to do this.

```
Sub OpenJetUserInfo(strDbPath As String)
   Dim cnn        As ADODB.Connection
   Dim rst        As ADODB.Recordset
   Dim fld        As ADODB.Field
   Dim strConnect As String

   ' Format connection string to open database.
   strConnect = "Provider=Microsoft.Jet.OLEDB.4.0;Data Source=" & strDbPath

   Set cnn = New ADODB.Connection
   cnn.Open strConnect

   ' Open user information schema query.
   Set rst = cnn.OpenSchema(Schema:=adSchemaProviderSpecific, _
      SchemaID:="{947bb102-5d43-11d1-bdbf-00c04fb92675}")

   ' Print user information to the Immediate pane.
   With rst
      Do Until .EOF
         For Each fld In .Fields
            Debug.Print fld.Name, fld.Value
         Next fld
         .MoveNext
         Debug.Print
      Loop
   End With
End Sub
```

The OpenJetUserInfo procedure can be found in the MultiuserIssues module of the MultiuserDatabase.mdb sample file, which is available in the Samples\CH16 subfolder on the companion CD-ROM.

The following table describes the information contained in each column returned by the schema query.

Column	Description
COMPUTER_NAME	The name of the user's computer as specified when you click the Network icon in the Control Panel.
LOGIN_NAME	The user name used to log onto the database if the database has been secured by using user-level security. Otherwise the default value will be Admin.
CONNECTED	**True**, if there is a corresponding user lock in the lock file (.ldb).
SUSPECTED_STATE	**True**, if the user has left the database in a suspect state; for example, if the user didn't exit the database normally due to loss of power or a system failure. Otherwise the value in this column will be **Null**.

Connection Control

The Jet 4.0 database engine provides a new feature called *connection control*, which prevents users from connecting to a database. This feature is also called *passive shutdown* because when connection control is invoked, users who are currently connected to the database remain unaffected until they disconnect. This capability is useful if you need to acquire exclusive access to a database to perform maintenance operations, such as compacting the database, or make updates to the database's design.

When connection control is invoked, users who are currently connected to a database remain unaffected until they disconnect from the database. At that point they will be unable to reconnect to the database until the user who invoked connection control revokes it or closes his or her connection to the database.

The following scenarios provide examples of how the connection control feature works. Assume there are five users in the database and that user five has invoked connection control on the database:

- **Scenario 1** User six tries to connect to the database, but is denied access, and an error message is returned stating that user five is preventing the database from being opened.
- **Scenario 2** User one closes the database and tries to reconnect to the database, but is denied access, and an error message is returned stating that user five is preventing the database from being opened.
- **Scenario 3** User five closes the database. User six tries to open the database and is successful. This is because connection control only persists while the user who invoked it remains connected to the database.
- **Scenario 4** Users one through four exit the database. User five uses the ADO **OpenSchema** method to retrieve a list of users in the database and determines that no other users are in the database. User five compacts the database, closes the database, and connection control is automatically revoked.

To use connection control, set the **Jet OLEDB:Connection Control** provider-specific property on an ADO **Connection** object. The **Jet OLEDB:Connection Control** property is a **Long** value that can be set to 1 to invoke connection control, or to 2 (the default value) to revoke connection control. The following procedure either invokes or revokes connection control for the current Access database, based on the value of the `opgConnectionControl` enumeration, which can be either INVOKE_CONTROL (which equals 1) or REVOKE_CONTROL (which equals 2).

```
Sub ConnectionControl(lngState As opgConnectionControl)
   CurrentProject.Connection. _
      Properties("Jet OLEDB:Connection Control") = lngState
End Sub
```

The ConnectionControl procedure can be found in the MultiuserIssues module of the MultiuserDatabase.mdb sample file, which is available in the Samples\CH16 subfolder on the companion CD-ROM.

Optimizing Multiuser Solutions

In most scenarios, the very act of sharing a database across a network incurs a substantial performance penalty. Few networks in the world supply "across the wire" performance that approaches local disk access performance. Given this, your biggest tasks in optimizing your multiuser solution are minimizing network traffic and identifying and eliminating bottlenecks in your local area network (LAN). Most of the following suggestions are based on the supposition that decreasing network traffic has the most positive effect on your solution's performance.

Minimizing Network Traffic for Data

Most of the optimizations you perform for data access in a single-user environment create equal, if not greater, improvements in multiuser environments. When you optimize a single-user solution, you're concerned only with that solution's performance on a local machine. When you optimize a multiuser solution, reductions in network traffic help not only the individual user, but all users of the solution.

For example, consider the case in which your solution must search for a record in a table that has no indexes. In this scenario, the database engine must perform a *sequential scan* of the entire table to find a match. This means that the entire table must be sent from the server to the workstation's copy of the engine. If the table is large, this can be quite a lengthy operation. The problem is further compounded because the user running the search is waiting a long time for a response, and the high volume of network traffic is in turn slowing down other users. This situation can be alleviated by adding indexes to the table for the fields your solution searches on. However, keep in mind that having many indexes may actually cause increased network traffic and may reduce concurrency and efficient performance when many users are adding, deleting, or updating records because indexes must be updated to reflect these changes.

In another example, assume that your solution uses a set of tables containing lookup data that represents postal codes or lists of part numbers—data that doesn't change often. By moving this type of data to the local workstation, you can eliminate network access that may be made hundreds of times during the solution's typical execution.

Minimizing Network Traffic for Static Objects

As discussed earlier in this chapter, the location of objects in a multiuser solution has a direct effect on the solution's performance. Consider splitting your database into front-end and back-end databases, as described in "The Two-Database Approach" earlier in this chapter. This will move static objects to each user's local drive.

Minimizing Network Bottlenecks

Finally, investigate bottlenecks occurring on your LAN that are due to hardware. You may want to try the following:

- **Segment the LAN into subnets.** Typically, a server has only one network interface card (NIC) with many nodes connected to it. To reduce this bottleneck, add multiple NICs to the server and spread the nodes across those segments. This is probably the cheapest and biggest performance improvement because it substantially reduces collisions on the wire and gives each station a larger slice of bandwidth to communicate with the server.
- **Add a better NIC to the server.** Practically all Pentium systems now come with slots for the Peripheral Component Interconnect (PCI) bus. By using PCI NICs you can experience significantly faster throughput while keeping the central processing unit (CPU) usage lower. Also, many PCI NICs offer a multiported design, thus allowing you to do multiple segments from one PCI NIC. An example of this is a server with two PCI slots that uses two four-port PCI NICs. This creates 8 segments that go to 36 nodes to reduce collisions on the wire and increase the bandwidth that is available to each node when it is communicating with the server. This would allow you to focus on performance issues that are software-related instead of hardware-related.

  Another option with PCI NICs is the 100 MB Ethernet standard. Although the 100 MB hubs required to accompany the 100 MB NICs are expensive, they do provide an alternative to finding workarounds for performance issues over the wire, and they can use existing cabling.
- **Add faster disk drives and host adapters to the server.** Again, moving to PCI- or Extended Industry Standard Architecture (EISA) -based host adapters can have a significant impact on performance. To eliminate this bottleneck, one approach is to configure the server to use an EISA SCSI RAID controller using eight 1-GB Small Computer System Interface (SCSI) drives. This increases performance because the EISA card reduces CPU processing by handling some processing itself, and because the Redundant Array of Inexpensive Disks (RAID) configuration allows reads and writes to be spread across the eight disk drives, thus reducing contention issues when multiple users try to access a drive. This is probably the most expensive solution, but it makes a big performance improvement over a one-ISA-card, one-disk solution.

Client/Server Solutions

In previous versions of Access, the only way to create a client/server solution is to create an .mdb file with linked tables that use an ODBC driver to link to a database server such as SQL Server. This kind of client/server solution also requires Access to load the Jet database engine to open the database and open the linked tables, which creates additional memory overhead. Although Access 2000 continues to support client/server solutions that use linked tables, it also supports a new file format and data access architecture that allows you to create a client application that connects to a SQL Server 6.5 (with Service Pack 5) or SQL Server 7.0 database through OLE DB without loading the Jet database engine. To do this, you create an *Access project file,* which is saved by using an .adp extension. An Access project can store forms, reports, macros, and VBA modules locally in your client solution file and use the OLE DB connection to display and work with the tables, views, relationships, and stored procedures that are stored on SQL Server. You create the forms, reports, macros, and VBA modules in an Access project by using most of the same tools and wizards you use to create these objects in Access databases. This allows you to quickly develop client/server solutions that work directly against a SQL Server back end.

Note Even though an Access project file uses an OLE DB connection to connect to a database, it can't use just any OLE DB provider to make this connection. It can only use the Microsoft OLE DB Provider for SQL Server, and can only connect to SQL Server 6.5 (with Service Pack 5) and SQL Server 7.0 databases. This is because the database creation and design tools in Access 2000 can only support SQL Server 6.5 or 7.0 databases.

Access also allows you to create new SQL Server databases, and provides a variety of visual tools to create and modify the design of tables, views, stored procedures, triggers, and database diagrams on your database server. The tables, views, and stored procedures you create, as well as SQL SELECT statements, are all valid data sources for Access forms, reports, and data access pages.

In addition to providing you with the ability to create and design client/server solutions from scratch, Access 2000 also includes the Upsizing Wizard, which allows you to convert an existing Access database to a client/server solution by creating a new SQL Server back-end database linked to an Access client front-end application.

File-Server vs. Client/Server

What is a client/server solution? A useful way to understand it is to describe the differences between the underlying system architectures of file-server and client/server solutions. In a file-server solution, when your solution needs data, Access and the Jet database engine (which are running locally on a user's workstation) determine how to directly access the network drive, which files should be read, and what data to retrieve.

Because retrieving data from the database file may require a series of requests and responses that must be sent between the server and the workstation, network traffic is increased. For example, to edit a record on a file-server database, the Jet database engine must read an index, retrieve the data, read and write to the *locking file* (a file that is used to coordinate requests to edit records between multiple users), and then update the index and the database itself. Figure 16.2 illustrates the file-server system.

Figure 16.2 A Typical File-Server System

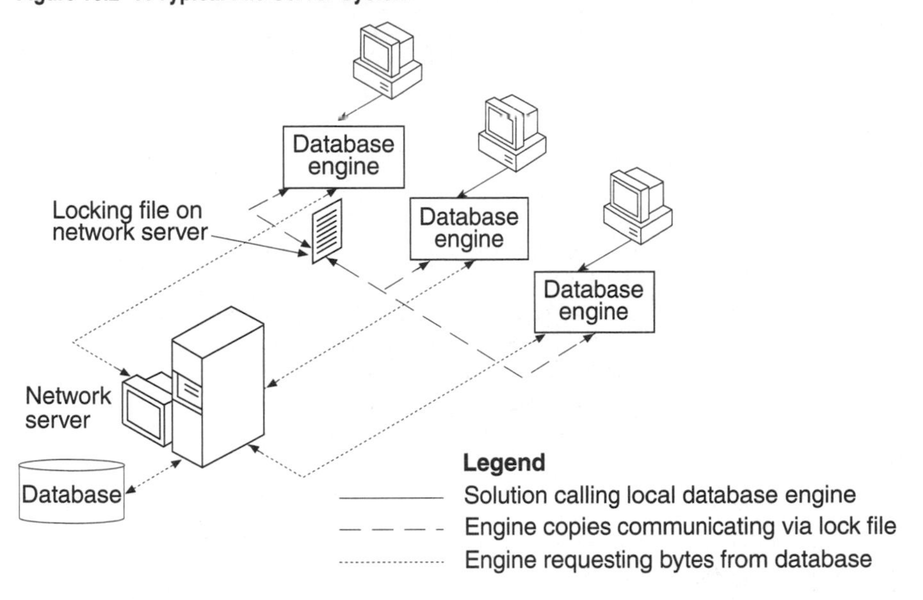

A multiuser database system within a file-server environment is made up of:

- A database that resides on a network file server running an operating system such as Microsoft Windows NT Server or Novell NetWare.
- One or more users accessing the database from a workstation's application software.

In a client/server system, the network database server processes all requests for data on the server itself. The solution running on a user's workstation doesn't request data at the file level, but sends a high-level request to the server to execute a specific query and return its results. The primary advantage of this technique is that network traffic is reduced because only the result set of the query is returned to the workstation, as shown in Figure 16.3.

Figure 16.3 A Typical Client/Server System

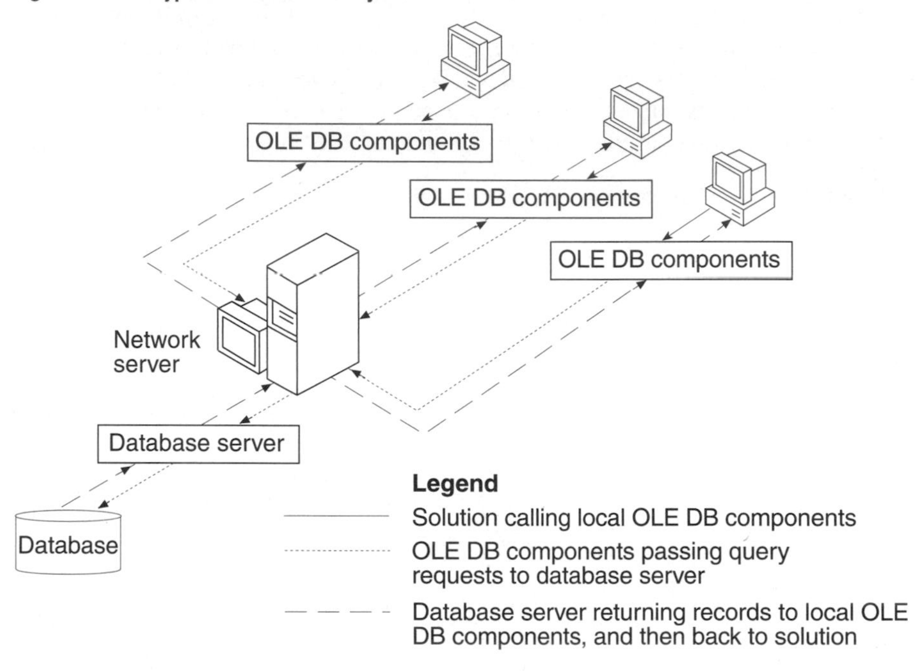

A client/server system is typified by:

- A back-end database residing on the server, and controlled and maintained by the server software, such as Microsoft SQL Server.
- One or more users running a local client application, such as an Access project (.adp), which requests data from the server through an interface such as an OLE DB data provider.

The performance and simplicity of a file-server architecture make it ideal for small- to moderate-sized solutions. The primary deciding factor when choosing whether to use a file-server or client/server architecture is the number of users who will be working with your solution. As an absolute limit, an Access database can handle up to 255 simultaneous users, but if users of your solution will be frequently adding and updating data, an Access file-server is generally best for a maximum of about 25 to 50 users.

A file-server database also has inherent limitations because it is maintained as a file in the file system. By isolating all database files under the control of a database server, the client/server architecture can provide advanced features that can't be furnished by a file-server architecture. For example:

- **Online backup** Use an automatic scheduler to back up your database without having to exclude users from the database.
- **Durable transactions** SQL Server logs transactions so that updates made within a transaction can always be recovered or rolled back if either the client or the server computer fails. This allows the SQL Server database to fulfill all four requirements of true ACID transactions, as described earlier in this chapter in "Using Transactions."
- **Better reliability and data protection** If either a workstation or file server fails while an Access database (.mdb) file is being written to, the database may be damaged. You can usually recover a damaged database by using the **CompactDatabase** method from either DAO or Microsoft Jet and Replication Objects (JRO), but you must have all users close the database before doing so. This rarely happens with a server database such as Microsoft SQL Server.
- **Faster query processing** Because an Access database (.mdb) is a file-server system, it must load the Jet database engine locally to process queries on the client. For large databases, this can involve moving a lot of data over the network. In contrast, SQL Server runs queries on the server, which is typically a much more powerful computer than client workstations. Running queries on the server increases the load on the server more than an Access file-server solution, but can reduce the network traffic substantially—especially if users are selecting a small subset of the data.
- **Advanced hardware support** Uninterruptible power supplies, hot swappable disk drives, and multiple processors can all be added to the server with no changes to the client workstations.

Another factor you need to consider when choosing whether to use a file-server solution or a client/server solution is the amount of data your solution will be required to work with. In Access 2000, an Access database can handle up to 2 gigabytes of data per .mdb file. If you really need to, you can effectively create even larger databases by using linked tables to several different .mdb files. However, SQL Server has a much higher limit, and is much less prone to data corruption.

If your solution needs to handle more users or requires the reliability of a database server, consider creating a client/server solution that employs an Access project as the client application and a server back-end database such as Microsoft SQL Server. For more information about building Access client/server solutions, see "Client/Server Solutions" earlier in this chapter.

Note Access project files also support creating databases by using Microsoft Data Engine (MSDE). For more information about using MSDE to develop databases, see "Using Microsoft Data Engine" later in this chapter.

Microsoft Access Client/Server Tools

Access provides a variety of tools that you can use to create SQL Server 6.5 and 7.0 databases and to work with the design of the database objects contained within them. You can also use the Upsizing Wizard to convert an existing Access database solution into an Access client/server solution.

Creating an Access Project

You can create an Access project to work with an existing SQL Server 6.5 or 7.0 database, or you can run the Microsoft SQL Server Database Wizard to create a new, empty SQL Server database and then use Access visual design tools to create database objects. You can also use the Microsoft Data Engine (MSDE) running locally to create and run databases that are compatible with SQL Server. For information about using MSDE, see "Using Microsoft Data Engine" later in this chapter.

To create an Access project file to work with an existing SQL Server database, on the **File** menu, click **New**, and then double-click **Project (Existing Database)**. On the **Connection** tab of the **Data Link Properties** dialog box, specify the server's name, logon information, and the database to open, and then click **OK**. Access will create a new project file connected to the database and display its objects in the Database window.

To create a new SQL Server database by using the Microsoft SQL Server Database Wizard, on the **File** menu, click **New**, and then double-click **Project (New Database)**. Follow the directions in the wizard to specify the server that will create the database and other settings required to create a new database. When you click **Finish**, Access will create a new project file connected to the database and display an empty Database window. Use Access database design tools to create your database tables, views, and stored procedures.

Important You can only use an Access project file to connect to existing databases or create new databases on Microsoft SQL Server 6.5 (with Service Pack 5), Microsoft SQL Server 7.0, or Microsoft Data Engine (MSDE). MSDE can be installed from the Microsoft Office 2000 CD-ROM. For more information about using MSDE, see "Using Microsoft Data Engine" later in this chapter.

Working with the Objects in a SQL Server Database from Access

The database window for an Access project displays options to work with the following objects contained in the SQL Server database back-end:

- **Tables** You can create and modify tables stored in a SQL Server database. By using the Design view, you can add or modify columns (fields), define their properties (such as data types), and set default values. You can also define additional properties of the tables, such as *check constraints* (which are similar to

Access validation rules), and indexes, by displaying the table's **Properties** dialog box. And, you can create one or more *triggers,* which are actions that are performed whenever a record is added, updated, or deleted. Triggers are defined by using Transact-SQL statements. To add a trigger to a table, right-click the table in the Database window, and then click **Triggers**.

- **Views** You can create and modify *views* that are stored in a SQL Server database. A view is essentially the same thing as an Access select query. That is, a query that returns records from one or more tables by using an SQL SELECT statement. You define views in Design view by using visual tools that are very similar to those available in the query Design view for Access databases. However, queries that require argument aren't defined as views, but as stored procedures. Additionally, queries that perform bulk operations, such as Access action queries, are also defined as stored procedures on SQL Server.
- **Database diagrams** Database diagrams provide a graphic display of the tables and relationships in your database that is similar to the Relationships window for Access databases. In addition to allowing you create, edit, or delete relationships between tables, you can also create, edit, or delete tables and table column definitions. To work with database objects that aren't graphically represented in the diagram, such as indexes and constraints, you can display the table's **Properties** dialog box. When you save a database diagram, the database is updated to match your diagram. You can create more than one database diagram to work with subsets of your database's design.
- **Stored procedures** In a SQL Server database, a *stored procedure* is a precompiled collection of SQL statements and optional control-of-flow statements stored under a name and processed as a unit. A stored procedure can be executed with one call from an application; and allows user-declared variables, conditional execution, and other powerful programming features. Stored procedures can contain program flow, business logic, and queries against the database. They can accept arguments, output parameters, return single or multiple result sets, and return values. You can use stored procedures for any purpose for which you would use SQL statements, with these advantages:
  - You can execute a series of SQL statements in a single stored procedure.
  - You can reference other stored procedures from within your stored procedure, which can simplify a series of complex statements.
  - The stored procedure is compiled on the server when it is created, so it executes faster than individual SQL statements.

Stored procedures can be used for a broad variety of functions, much like VBA procedures, but their functionality is specific to SQL Server and the Transact-SQL language. They are similar to Access action queries, but they can perform a much broader array of actions against the database and the server itself.

Working with Access Objects in an Access Project

You can use most of the same design tools as those available for an Access database to work with forms, reports, data access pages, macros, and VBA modules in an Access project file. To create any of these objects, open the Database window, select the type of object you want to create, and then click **New**.

In addition to the Design views for creating forms and reports from scratch, Access projects provide the following wizards for creating forms and reports: the Form Wizard, the AutoForm wizards, the Report Wizard, the AutoReport wizards, and the Label Wizard. A form's or report's **RecordSource** property can be set to tables, views, and any stored procedures or SQL statements that return a single set of records. When you use a stored procedure as the record source for a form or report, you can use the form's **InputParameters** property to specify the source for the stored procedure's input arguments. For information about setting the **InputParameters** property, search the Microsoft Access Visual Basic Reference Help index for "InputParameters property."

Data access pages support the same design tools for both Access databases and SQL Server back-end databases: the Data access page Design view, the Page Wizard, and the Microsoft Script Editor. For more information about working with data access pages, see Chapter 5, "Working with Office Applications," Chapter 12, "Using Web Technologies," and the Microsoft Access Help index (search for "data access pages").

Macros provide additional actions and action arguments to allow you to create macros that work with SQL Server objects. The same Visual Basic Editor is used from Access projects to create VBA code.

Using the Connection Property of the CurrentProject Object in an Access Project

When you use the **Connection** property of the **CurrentProject** object in an Access database (.mdb), Access returns a connection that uses the Microsoft Jet 4.0 OLE DB Provider. However, when you use the **Connection** property of the **CurrentProject** object in an Access project (.adp), Access doesn't return a direct connection to the SQL Server database. Instead it uses the Microsoft Data Shaping Service for OLE DB, which is an OLE DB service component that runs on top of a data provider. For Access project files, the data provider used in conjunction with the Microsoft Data Shaping Service for OLE DB is the Microsoft OLE DB Provider for SQL Server. This is required because updates to data in forms in an Access project require the Shaping Service. This also is a requirement if you use the **Recordset** property of a form in an Access project to programmatically specify the form's data source. For more information about using the **Recordset** property of a form in an Access project, see "The Form Recordset Property" later in this chapter.

The fact that the **Connection** property returns a **Connection** object that uses the Microsoft Data Shaping Service for OLE DB does have certain consequences:

- **Recordset** objects always use the client-side cursor engine (**CursorLocation=adUseClient**). Even if you set the **CursorLocation** property of a **Recordset** object to **adUseServer** prior to creating a **Recordset** object by using the **Execute** method of a **Connection** object, the **Execute** method of a **Command** object, or the **Open** method of a **Recordset** object, you will always get a client-side cursor.

  Note For more information about cursors and cursor engines, see Chapter 14, "Working with the Data Access Components of an Office Solution."

- **Recordset** objects always use a Static cursor (**CursorType=adOpenStatic**), regardless of what you set the **CursorType** property to when opening the **Recordset** object.
- You can set the **LockType** property of a **Recordset** object to the **adLockOptimistic**, **adLockBatchOptimistic**, or **adLockReadOnly** constants. If you set the **LockType** to **adLockPessimistic**, it gets converted silently to **adLockOptimistic**. As with **Recordset** objects created with other connections, if you don't specify the **LockType** property, it will be set to **adLockReadOnly** by default.
- A **Connection** object established by using the Microsoft Data Shaping Service for OLE DB doesn't support all ADOX operations that a **Connection** object established by using a direct connection through the Microsoft OLE DB Provider for SQL Server would provide. In particular, operations on the **Properties** collection of the **Column** object are not supported.

  Note The ADOX **Views**, **Users**, and **Groups** collections are not supported against SQL Server when you use connections through either the Microsoft Data Shaping Service for OLE DB or the Microsoft OLE DB Provider for SQL Server.

- The **Properties** collection of a **Connection** object doesn't support the same properties as a direct connection. For example, the **DBMS Version** property is not supported.
- If the **CommandType** property of a **Command** object isn't specified, the connection will not try again to open the **Command** object as a table if the **CommandText** property doesn't refer to a stored procedure. You can avoid this problem either by specifying an SQL statement to open the table (for example, `"SELECT * FROM Authors"`), or by explicitly specifying the **CommandType** as **adCmdTable** when opening the **Command** object, as shown in the following code fragment.

```
Dim rst As New ADODB.Recordset
Dim cmd As New ADODB.Command

' Specify properties of the Command object.
With cmd
   .ActiveConnection = CurrentProject.Connection
   .CommandText="authors"
   .CommandType=adCmdTable
End With

' Open the Recordset object by using the Command object.
Set rst=cmd.Execute
```

You can also avoid this and any other limitations that you might encounter when using Microsoft Data Shaping Service for OLE DB by creating a separate connection that doesn't use the Shaping Service. You can do this by using the **BaseConnectionString** property of the **CurrentProject** object. The **BaseConnectionString** property returns a connection string that specifies the Microsoft OLE DB Provider for SQL Server (Provider=SQLOLEDB.1). The following code fragment shows how to open a **Connection** object by using the **BaseConnectionString** property.

```
Dim cnn As New ADODB.Connection
Dim rst As New ADODB.Recordset

cnn.ConnectionString = CurrentProject.BaseConnectionString
cnn.Open

Set rst = cn.Execute("authors")
```

For more information about the features of the Microsoft Data Shaping Service for OLE DB, search ADO Help for "data shaping."

The Form Recordset Property

In an Access project file you can use the **Recordset** property of an Access **Form** object to specify an ADO **Recordset** object that will be used as the form's record source. If you want the record source to be updatable, you must specify that the **Connection** object used to open the **Recordset** object is using the Microsoft Data Shaping Service for OLE DB. To do this, you must set the **Provider** property in the connection string that is used to open the **Connection** object to **MSDataShape**. Additionally, you need to specify that the **Data Provider** property in the connection string is using the Microsoft OLE DB Provider for SQL Server (Data Provider=SQLOLEDB), and other properties are set as described in the following table.

Connection string property	Description
Provider	This property must be set to **MSDataShape** to specify the Microsoft Data Shaping Service for OLE DB.
Data Provider	This property must be set to **SQLOLEDB** to specify the Microsoft OLE DB Provider for SQL Server. If you use any other OLE DB provider, it will return a read-only connection.
Data Source	This property specifies the server name, which is the same as the network name of the computer on which SQL Server is running. To view this name, open the Control Panel on the computer, click the **Network** icon, and read the **Computer Name** on the **Identification** tab.
Initial Catalog	This property specifies the name of the database to open.
User ID	If you are using SQL Server Authentication, use this property to specify the user account name (such as "sa", the default user account). Don't set this property if you are using Windows NT Authentication.
Password	If you are using SQL Server Authentication, use this property to specify the password for the user account specified with the **User ID** property. Don't set this property if you are using Windows NT Authentication.
Trusted_Connection	If you are using Windows NT Authentication instead of SQL Server Authentication, set this property to **Yes**.

For example, the following code fragment opens an ADO **Recordset** object directly by passing a connection string to the ***ActiveConnection*** argument of the **Open** method. It then assigns the **Recordset** property of the current form to that **Recordset** object.

```
Dim rst        As ADODB.Recordset
Dim strConnect As String
Dim strSQL     As String

strConnect = "Provider=MSDataShape;Data Provider=SQLOLEDB;" _
   & "User ID=sa;Password="";Data Source=MyServer;" _
   & "Initial Catalog=NorthwindCS"

strSQL = "SELECT ContactName, CompanyName, Address, City _
   FROM Customers WHERE (Region = 'SP')

Set rst = New ADODB.Recordset
With rst
         .Open Source:=strSQL, _
         ActiveConnection:=strConnect, _
         LockType:=adLockOptimistic
End With

Set Me.Recordset = rst
```

As noted in "Using the Connection Property of the CurrentProject Object in an Access Project," a connection established through the Microsoft Data Shaping Service for OLE DB always uses the client-side cursor engine (**CursorLocation=adUseClient**) and returns a Static cursor (**CursorType=adOpenStatic**). Additionally, you can only set the **LockType** property to one of these constants: **adLockOptimistic**, **adLockBatchOptimistic**, and **adLockReadOnly**; setting the property to **adLockPessimistic** will return **adLockOptimistic**.

For more information about opening ADO **Recordset** objects, see Chapter 14, "Working with the Data Access Components of an Office Solution."

Limiting the Number of Records Returned for a Form

The navigation buttons on a form in an Access project include a **Cancel Query** button that a user can use to stop downloading data from the server to the Access project record cache if this operation is taking too long. There is also a **Maximum Record Limit** button that allows the user to specify the maximum number of records that will be cached. The default value is 10,000. You can change the default value used for all new forms and for datasheets by setting **Default max records** on the **Advanced** tab of the **Options** dialog box (**Tools** menu). You can set this value on a per-form basis by setting the **MaxRecords** property of the form in Design view. You can also limit the number of records displayed in a form by specifying a filter that uses the **ServerFilter** and **ServerFilterByForm** properties. For information about how to use the **ServerFilter** and **ServerFilterByForm** properties, search the Microsoft Access Visual Basic Reference Help index for "ServerFilter property" and "ServerFilterByForm property."

Converting an Access Database with the Upsizing Wizard

You can use the Upsizing Wizard to convert an existing Access database (.mdb) to a client/server solution. The Upsizing Wizard creates a new SQL Server database structure by re-creating the structure of your Access tables (including indexes, validation rules, defaults, and relationships), and then copying your data into the new SQL Server database. Additionally, the Upsizing Wizard will attempt to re-create your queries as SQL Server views and stored procedures.

You can choose to upsize only your database structure and data, or, after creating the SQL Server back-end database, you can choose to create an Access front-end client application. The Upsizing Wizard can create the front-end client application in either of two ways:

- By keeping the current Access database file (.mdb) and adding linked tables that connect to the upsized tables on SQL Server. Your existing forms, reports, and data access pages will use the new linked tables as their data sources.

- By creating a new Access project file (.adp) and copying the forms, reports, data access pages, macros, and modules from the current Access database, and then connecting that Access project file to the upsized tables on SQL Server. The copied forms, reports, and data access pages that refer to the local database will be converted to use the new upsized SQL Server tables, views, and stored procedures as their data sources through the .adp file's connection to the server. Data access pages that refer to databases other than the current database will be unchanged after upsizing.

It's important to note that running the Upsizing Wizard isn't necessarily a perfect process. There are differences and potential incompatibilities between Access and SQL Server databases, such as differences in SQL dialects and data types. Although the wizard can handle many of these differences and still convert objects correctly, it can't handle all differences, and so may encounter problems while creating your new database and client application. If the Upsizing Wizard encounters a problem during the upsizing process, it won't halt the process. It records the error and continues working with the next object. After the upsizing process is complete, the wizard will display a report that shows details of the process, such as the name and size of the new database, the selections you made while running the wizard, and any errors it encountered.

For details about how to run the Upsizing Wizard, search the Microsoft Access Help index for "Upsizing Wizard." For information about differences between Access and SQL Server SQL syntax and how the Upsizing Wizard handles these differences, see the "Comparison of Microsoft Access and SQL Server syntax" topic in Microsoft Access Help.

Database Design Considerations Before Upsizing

Before upsizing a solution to SQL Server, there are several important design issues you should take into consideration. The following tips describe the most common issues and strategies.

- If you are upsizing to an Access database (.mdb) linked to SQL Server, design forms so that the form doesn't require data to be retrieved from the server during the form-opening process. Instead, add a command button to the form to fetch data to populate the form. You may want to save the last set of form data in a local table, then load the form from the saved data the first time the user opens the form. If you are upsizing to an Access project file (.adp) linked to SQL Server, you can't save data to local tables in the file, but you can limit the number of records that are opened at one time by using the **MaxRecords**, **ServerFilter**, and **ServerFilterByForm** properties of the form after your database is upsized.

- Use an ADO **Recordset** object with a client-side, Static cursor that specifies read-only locking (**CursorLocation = adUseClient**, **CursorType = adOpenStatic**, and **LockType = adLockReadOnly**) if you don't need to update the server tables. For forms, you can achieve the same result by setting the form's **RecordsetType** property to **Snapshot**. If you do need to update server tables, use an ADO client-side cursor (**CursorLocation = adUseClient**) with a Static cursor (**CursorType = adOpenStatic**) and use batch optimistic locking (**LockType = adLockBatchOptimistic**) so that you can perform batch updates by using the **BatchUpdate** method. For forms, you can achieve a similar result by setting the form's **RecordsetType** property to **Updatable Snapshot**.
- Minimize the number of items in server-populated combo boxes. Use an ADO **Recordset** object with a Forward-only cursor for server-populated combo boxes. It's important to remember that as database sizes increase, certain solutions may become unworkable. For instance, a combo box of 30 records is reasonable for a user to browse and pick from. When the list of possibilities numbers in the hundreds, using a combo box becomes awkward.
- If combo box data changes infrequently, maintain a local copy of the server data that populates the combo boxes. If you are using an Access database (.mdb) linked to SQL Server, you can save data in local tables. If you are using an Access project (.adp), you can't store local tables, but you can use the **Save** method of the ADO **Recordset** object to save server data to a local file. You can't use the saved **Recordset** file directly as the setting for the combo box's **RowSource property**, but you can use the **Open** method of the ADO **Recordset** object to open the file, loop through the **Recordset** object to generate a text string formatted as a value list, and then populate the combo box from that list. Include only the field(s) you need for the combo box in the table. For local Access tables, you can create an index on the local table to speed population of the combo box. Provide the user with a simple means of replacing the local data with current data from the server. Alternatively, you can populate a combo box by setting the **RowSourceType** and **RowSource** properties of the combo box to use a stored procedure or an SQL statement to select the values to display.
- If decision-support application users need to compare multiple sets of data, consider storing the data returned by the server in temporary local tables or files. Provide a form in which the user can elect to either use the previously stored data or run a new query. Adding the ability to quickly compare results of successive queries is especially important in applications that process financial information.
- Adhere to server-based naming restrictions from the beginning. The Upsizing Wizard corrects many common mistakes in this regard, but not all. In order to ensure a painless migration to the back end, it is best to adhere to the following SQL Server restrictions from the beginning:

- For SQL Server 6.5, names must be 30 characters or less. For SQL Server 7.0, this limit has been expanded to a maximum of 128 characters.
- The first character must be a letter or the "at" sign (@).
- The remaining characters may be numbers, letters, the dollar sign ($), the number sign (#), or the underscore (_).
- For SQL Server 6.5, no spaces are allowed. For SQL Server 7.0, spaces are allowed, but the name must be surrounded by double quotation marks (") or square brackets ([ ]).
- The name must not be a Transact-SQL keyword. SQL Server reserves both the uppercase and lowercase versions of keywords. For information about Transact-SQL keywords, see the *Transact-SQL Reference* in the Microsoft Access Help or in SQL Server Books Online.

Converting Your Solution's Code to ADO

The Upsizing Wizard doesn't convert your Access solution's code. Code that works directly with Access objects should continue to work, but you will need to convert any DAO code that works with tables and queries to ADO code. For an overview of using ADO, see Chapter 14, "Working with the Data Access Components of an Office Solution." For additional references on using ADO, see the following section, "Programming in Access Client/Server Solutions."

Programming in Access Client/Server Solutions

Programming in Access client/server solutions is very similar to programming in Access database solutions. Most of the features of the Access object model when used in Access project files are the same as, or similar to, the features available when programming in Access database files.

The following additional methods of the **DoCmd** object have been added to open Access project views, stored procedures, and database diagrams: **OpenView**, **OpenStoredProcedure**, and **OpenDiagram**. Also, a number of the other methods of the **DoCmd** object have different behaviors and arguments to accommodate the differences in Access project objects. For information about these changes, search the Microsoft Access Visual Basic Reference Help index for "DoCmd object."

For information about working with Access objects, see Chapter 5, "Working with Office Applications." For information about working with Access reports, see Chapter 15, "Retrieving and Analyzing Data." For details on the differences in the functionality of Access methods, properties, and events between Access project files and Access databases, search the Microsoft Access Visual Basic Reference Help index for the method, property, and event names.

To work directly with the objects stored in a SQL Server database from an Access project, you should use ADO code. For an introduction to using ADO code, see Chapter 14, "Working with the Data Access Components of an Office Solution." For detailed information about using ADO code, see ADO Help. For information about using ADO to work with SQL Server 7.0, see the "Building SQL Server Applications" book in the SQL Server Books Online that is installed with SQL Server 7.0. The Microsoft Access Help also includes two components of SQL Server documentation: Transact-SQL Reference Help and SQL Server Error Messages. For information about using ADO and other data access object models to work with SQL Server 6.5 and 7.0, see the *Hitchhiker's Guide to Visual Basic and SQL Server, Sixth Edition*, by William R. Vaughn (Microsoft Press, 1998).

Managing Client/Server Solution Security

An Access project file can't use the same user-level security features that an Access database file can. The data and other objects stored on your SQL Server can be fully secured by using SQL Server's security features. To secure server-side objects, use SQL Server's SQL Server Enterprise Manager, Transact-SQL statements, or the **SQL Server Security** dialog box in Access (**Tools** menu, **Security** submenu, **Database Security** command). For information about securing SQL Server databases, see SQL Server Books Online, or click the **Help** button in the Access **SQL Server Security** dialog box and the **Help** button in the properties dialog boxes displayed from the main dialog box.

To secure the objects stored in your Access project file, Access provides three features:

- **Startup options** You can set options in the **Startup** dialog box (**Tools** menu, **Startup** command) to restrict access to default menus and toolbars, the Database window, and special keys. You can then set the **AllowBypassKey** property to **False** to prevent users from holding down the SHIFT key to override these options. For more information about setting startup options, see Chapter 18, "Securing Access Databases."
- **Locking your VBA project** You can secure VBA code in an Access project by locking your VBA project with a password. For information about locking a VBA project, see Chapter 17, "Securing Office Documents and Visual Basic for Applications Code."
- **Saving as an .ade file** To secure the design of forms, reports, and VBA code in your Access project file, you can save the file as an .ade file. Saving as an .ade removes your Access project's VBA source code and prevents users from changing the design of forms and reports. For information about removing your Access project's VBA source code, see Chapter 18, "Securing Access Databases."

SQL Server Replication

Replication is an important and powerful technology for distributing data and stored procedures across an enterprise. The replication technology in Microsoft SQL Server allows you to make duplicate copies of your data, move those copies to different locations, and automatically synchronize the data so that all copies have the same data values. Replication can be implemented between databases on the same server or between different servers connected by LANs, WANs, or the Internet.

The replication model used in SQL Server 7.0 continues to build on the "publish and subscribe" metaphor introduced by earlier versions of SQL Server. Replication in SQL Server 7.0 also supports:

- Replication to heterogeneous databases. Databases that provide 32-bit ODBC drivers or OLE DB providers, such as Microsoft Access and Oracle, can be part of your replication design.
- Programmatic interfaces for replicating data from heterogeneous databases.

For more information about SQL Server replication, see SQL Server Books Online. For information about synchronizing between an Access replicated database and SQL Server see "Synchronizing Changes with a Microsoft SQL Server Database" in JROReplication.doc in the Appendixes folder on the companion CD-ROM.

Using Microsoft Data Engine

Microsoft Data Engine (MSDE) is a new technology that provides local data storage compatible with Microsoft SQL Server 7.0. You can also use MSDE as a remote data storage solution. You can think of MSDE as a client/server database engine alternative to the file-server Microsoft Jet database engine. MSDE runs under Windows NT 4.0 or later and Windows 95 or later. It is designed and optimized for use on smaller computer systems, such as a single-user computer or small-workgroup server.

MSDE doesn't limit the number of users who can connect to its database, but is optimized for five users. For a larger numbers of users, you should use SQL Server 7.0. Databases created with MSDE are 100 percent compatible with SQL Server 7.0 and support many of the features of SQL Server 7.0, including most Transact-SQL commands. MSDE also logs transactions, which means that if anything should go wrong during a write to an MSDE database, such as a disk error, network failure, or power failure, MSDE will recover from its transaction log and revert to its last consistent state. This gives MSDE databases greater reliability than Microsoft Jet (.mdb) databases, which don't log transactions.

Because MSDE is based on the same database engine as SQL Server, most Access projects or client/server applications can run unchanged on either version. However, unlike SQL Server 7.0, MSDE has a 2-gigabyte database size limit, supports up to 2 processors for Symmetrical Multiprocessing (SMP), and in a replicated database environment cannot be a replication publisher for transactional replication (although it can act as a replication subscriber for both transactional and merge replication, and as a replication publisher for merge replication).

Compared with using Access with a Microsoft Jet database (.mdb), using MSDE does require more memory. The minimum supported configuration for running MSDE is a Pentium 166 with 32 MB of RAM. MSDE does manage its memory usage dynamically, so that it will react to operating system pressure on memory resources to allocate as much memory as it can effectively use, but will stop allocating memory and even, if needed, give back memory to ensure that other applications have memory available. However, if your solution requires the minimum usage of memory resources, you should use Access with a Microsoft Jet database.

When to Use MSDE

Consider using MSDE as a desktop database alternative to an Access database in the following ways:

- As a small-workgroup server database. You can develop your solutions by using an Access project connected to MSDE, anticipating that your workgroup and its business requirements may grow over time, eventually needing the full functionality of SQL Server 7.0 running on a larger network server.
- As a replication subscriber in a SQL Server replicated database environment. For example, you may have mobile users working in the field who access and update MSDE on laptops or disconnected computers, but then periodically connect to the Master SQL Server database to reconcile changes.
- To easily develop and test an Access project or client/server application on a personal computer or workstation. You would then modify the Access project connection information to connect to a SQL Server database on a remote server for final testing and production.

Installing MSDE

Although MSDE is not installed by default in Microsoft Office 2000 or Microsoft Access 2000, you can install MSDE from the CD-ROM by running Setupsql.exe, which is located in the SQL\x86\Setup folder.

Once you install MSDE on your computer, on Windows 95 or later, you may need to start the **SQL Server Service Manager** (double-click the MSSQLServer icon on the task bar and click **Start/Continue**). MSDE starts automatically on Windows NT Workstation 4.0 or later; you may want to automatically start MSDE on Windows 95 or later by selecting the **Auto-start server when OS starts** check box on the **SQL Server Service Manager** dialog box.

Installing MSDE also installs the Data Transformation Services Wizard, which allows you to import and export data by using OLE DB providers or ODBC drivers to transform and validate data. To run the Data Transformation Services Wizard after installing MSDE, on the **Start** menu, click **Programs**, point to **MSDE**, and then click **Import and Export Data**. You can also use the Data Transformation Services Wizard to transfer objects and data between MSDE and SQL Server 7.0. For example, if you use Access and MSDE to create a prototype of a client/server solution, you can use the Data Transformation Services Wizard to transfer the back-end objects and data from MSDE to SQL Server 7.0. For additional information about using the Data Transformation Services Wizard, see the DTS Import and Export Wizards Help file (Dtswiz70.chm), which is installed by default in your C:\Windows\Help folder.

Database Replication Solutions

Database replication is the process of sharing data or database design changes between databases in different locations without having to copy the entire database. Replication involves copying a database so that two or more copies of a single database remain synchronized. The original database is called a *Design Master* and each copy of the database is called a *replica*. Together, the Design Master and the replicas make up a *replica set*. There is only one Design Master in a replica set. The Design Master is the only member of the replica set in which you can make design changes to the objects in the database. Each member of the replica set contains a common set of replicable objects, such as tables, queries, forms, reports, macros, or modules. Each member of the replica set can also contain nonreplicated—or local—tables and queries. In previous versions of Access, you can create any database object and save it locally in any member of a replica set, but in Access 2000, the only objects that can be kept as local objects are tables and queries. In Access 2000, you can create new forms, reports, macros, and modules only in the Design Master, and those objects will be replicated to other members of the replica set. This is due to a change in the way Access 2000 stores Access-specific objects.

Synchronization is the process of ensuring that every copy of the database contains the same objects and data. When you synchronize the replicas in a replica set, only the data that has changed is updated. You can also synchronize changes made to the design of the objects in the Design Master.

If you design your solutions for multiple users, then database replication, in the appropriate circumstances, can improve the way your users share data. By using database replication, you can make copies of a database so that two or more users can work on their own copy of the database at the same time and each user's changes are passed on to other members of the replica set through synchronization.

Why Use Database Replication?

Imagine that a client has asked you to develop a contact-management solution that the company's field sales staff can use to monitor sales and orders. Each sales representative has a laptop computer that can be connected to the company's network.

A traditional approach to building this solution is to separate the tables from the other objects in the database so that the data can reside in a back-end database on a network server, or on the Internet or an intranet, while the queries, forms, reports, macros, and modules reside in a separate front-end database on the user's computer. The objects in the front-end database are based on tables that are linked to the back-end database. When sales representatives want to retrieve or update information in the database, they use the front-end database.

Database replication enables you to take a new approach to building this solution by creating a single database that contains both the data and objects, and then making replicas of the database for each sales representative. You can make replicas for each user and synchronize each replica with the Design Master on a network server. Sales representatives update the replicas on their computers during the course of a work session, and users synchronize their replicas with the Design Master on the server as needed.

In addition, you can choose to replicate only a portion of the data in the Design Master, and you can replicate different portions for different users by creating *partial replicas*. In the scenario involving sales representatives who use replica databases, each individual salesperson typically needs only the sales data related to his or her own territory. Replicating all sales data for all sales representatives would involve unnecessary processing and duplication of data. By using partial replicas, you can duplicate only the data that each salesperson actually needs. A complete set of data is still contained in the Design Master, but each replica handles only a subset of that data.

When to Choose Database Replication

Database replication is well suited to business solutions that need to:

- **Share data among remote offices.** You can use database replication to create copies of a corporate database to send to each satellite office across a wide area network (WAN). Each location enters data in its replica, and all remote replicas are synchronized with the replica at corporate headquarters. Individual replicas can maintain local tables that contain information not included in the other replicas in the set.

- **Share data among dispersed users.** New information that is entered in the database while sales representatives are out of the office can be synchronized any time the sales representatives establish an electronic link with the corporate network. As part of their workday routine, sales representatives can dial in to the network, synchronize the replica, and work on the most current version of the database.

  Because only the incremental changes are transmitted during synchronization, the time and expense of keeping up-to-date information are minimized. By using partial replicas, you can synchronize only specified parts of the data.

- **Make server data more accessible.** If your solution doesn't need to have immediate updates to data, you can use database replication to reduce the network load on your primary server. Introducing a second server with its own copy of the database improves response time. You determine the schedule for synchronizing the replicas, and you can adjust that schedule to meet the changing needs of your users. Replication requires less centralized administration of the database while offering greater access to centralized data.

- **Distribute solution updates.** When you replicate your solution, you automatically replicate not only the data in your tables, but also your solution's objects. If you make changes to the design of the database, the changes are transmitted during the next synchronization; you don't have to distribute complete new versions of the software.

- **Back up data.** At first glance, database replication might appear to be very similar to copying a database. However, while replication initially makes a complete copy of the database, thereafter it simply synchronizes that replica's objects with the original objects at regular intervals. This copy can be used to recover data if the original database is destroyed. Furthermore, users at any replica can continue to access the database during the entire backup process.

- **Provide Internet or intranet replication.** You can configure an Internet or intranet server to be used as a hub for propagating changes to participating replicas.

When Database Replication Should Not Be Used

Although database replication can solve many of the problems inherent in distributed-database processing, it is important to recognize that there are situations in which replication is less than ideal. You may not want to use replication if:

- **There are large numbers of record updates at multiple replicas.** Solutions that require frequent updates of existing records in different replicas are likely to have more record conflicts than solutions that simply insert new records in a database. Record conflicts occur when any changes are made to the same record by users at different locations at the same time. Solutions with many record conflicts require more administrative time because the conflicts must be resolved manually. This is true even if different fields are updated within the same record.

- **Data consistency is critical at all times.** Solutions that rely on information being correct at all times, such as funds transfers, airline reservations, and the tracking of package shipments, usually use a transaction method. Although transactions can be processed within a replica, there is no support for processing transactions across replicas. The information exchanged between replicas during synchronization is the result of the transaction, not the transaction itself.

For more information about replication, see the Microsoft Access and Microsoft Replication Manager Help files, and see the white paper "Database Replication in Microsoft Jet" (RepJet.doc), located in the Appendixes folder on the companion CD-ROM.

Implementing Database Replication

You can implement Microsoft Jet database replication by using the following:

- Microsoft Access menu commands
- Briefcase replication in Windows 95, Windows 98, or Windows NT 4.0
- Microsoft Replication Manager
- Data Access Objects (DAO) programming
- Jet Replication Objects (JRO) programming

The first three replication tools provide an easy-to-use visual interface, while the last two enable programmers to build replication directly into their solution's code.

Partial replicas are available only by using the Partial Replica Wizard in Microsoft Access (**Tools** menu, **Replication** submenu, **Partial Replica Wizard** command) or through DAO or JRO programming.

Replication can be used on a variety of computer networks, including Microsoft Windows 95 and Windows 98 peer-to-peer networks, Microsoft Windows NT Server or Workstation version 4.0 or later networks, and Novell NetWare versions 3.*x*, 4.*x* and 5.*x* network servers.

For information about implementing replication in Access, search the Microsoft Access Help index for "replication." The Replication Manager ships in the Microsoft Office 2000 Developer package; for information about using it, see Help after installing Microsoft Office 2000 Developer. For information about using DAO programming to implement replication, see the *Microsoft Jet Database Engine Programmer's Guide, Second Edition* (Microsoft Press, 1997). For information about using JRO to implement replication, see JROReplication.doc, located in the Appendixes folder on the companion CD-ROM.

Where to Go from Here

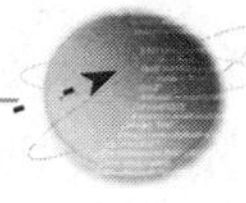

For additional information about the subjects discussed in this chapter, see the following sources. If a file name is listed, that file is located in the Appendixes folder on the companion CD-ROM, unless otherwise noted.

Database Design

Hernandez, Michael J. *Database Design for Mere Mortals*. Reading, MA: Addison-Wesley Developers Press, 1997.

Data Access Objects (DAO)

Microsoft Jet Database Engine Programmer's Guide, Second Edition. Redmond, WA: Microsoft Press, 1997.

Microsoft Office Developer Forum Web site (http://www.microsoft.com/officedev/)

ActiveX Data Objects (ADO)

Microsoft ActiveX Data Objects Web site (http://www.microsoft.com/data/ado/)

Microsoft Office Developer Forum Web site (http://www.microsoft.com/officedev/)

ADO properties (ADOProperties.doc)

Using ActiveX Data Objects with MDB Files and the Microsoft Jet Database Engine

Microsoft Jet Database Engine Programmer's Guide, Third Edition. Redmond, WA: Microsoft Press, 1999.

Henry, Alyssa. "Migrating from DAO to ADO (Using ADO with the Microsoft Jet OLE DB Provider)." Microsoft ActiveX Data Objects Web site at http://www.microsoft.com/data/ado/.

Microsoft SQL Server

Microsoft SQL Server Web site (http://www.microsoft.com/sql/)

SQL Server Books Online

Using ActiveX Data Objects with SQL Server

Vaughn, William R. *Hitchhiker's Guide to Visual Basic and SQL Server, Sixth Edition*. Redmond, WA: Microsoft Press, 1998.

SQL Server Books Online, *Building SQL Server Applications*.

SQL Server Replication

SQL Server Books Online, *Replication*.

Microsoft Jet Replication

Dove, Debra. "Database Replication in Microsoft Jet." (RepJet.doc)

Microsoft Jet Database Engine Programmer's Guide, Second Edition. Redmond, WA: Microsoft Press, 1997.

Code Samples

The code samples shown in this chapter, along with additional examples that demonstrate similar techniques, can be copied from the files in the Samples\CH16 subfolder on the companion CD-ROM.

Part Four

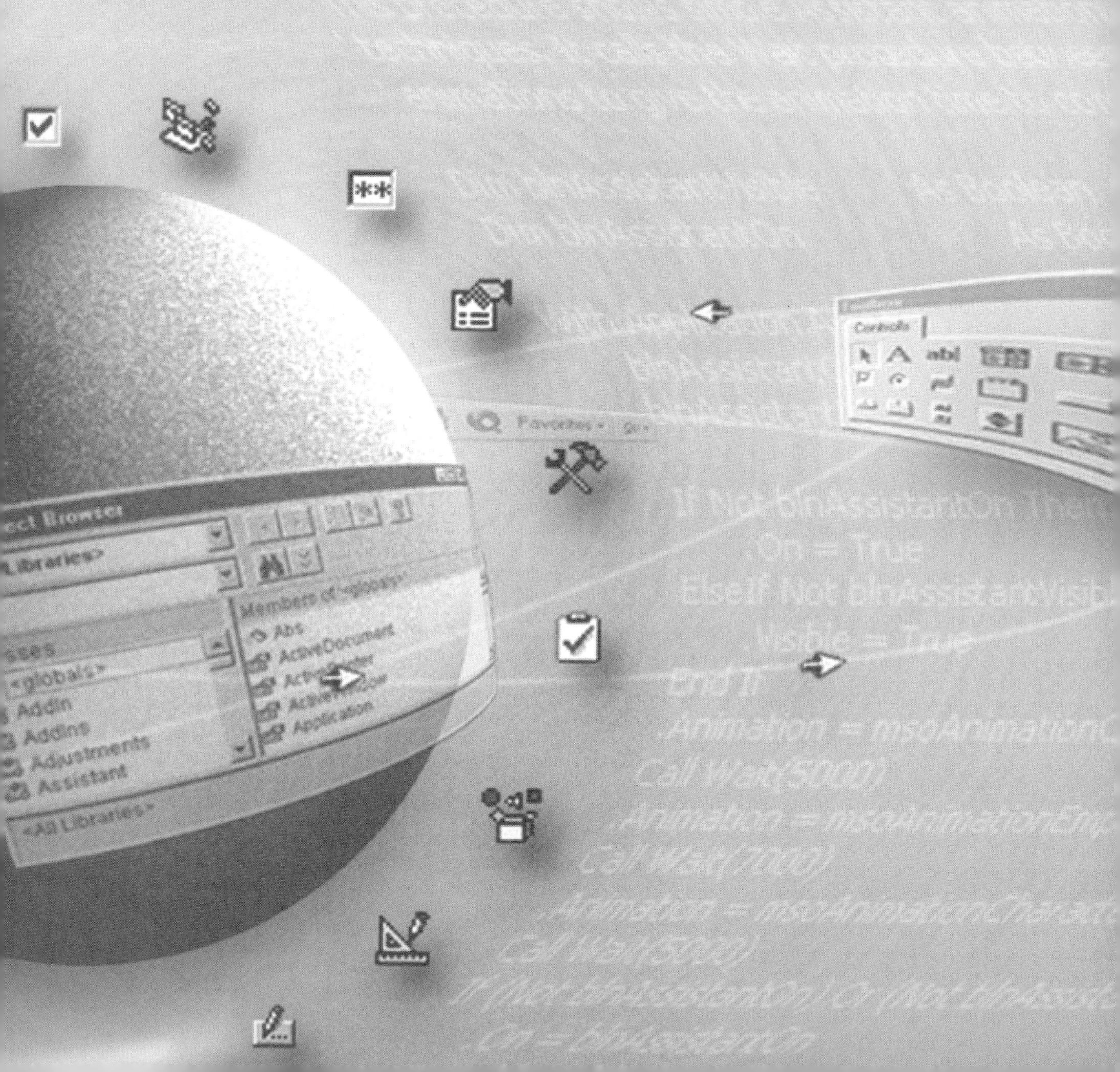

Controls
Favorites
Members of '<globals>'
Abs
ActiveDocument
Application
<globals>
AddIn
AddIns
Adjustments
Assistant
<All Libraries>
On = True
Call Wait(5000)

Securing Office Solutions

In an age where large amounts of information are being shared faster and further than ever before, security is a growing concern for both solution developers and customers alike. There are several different aspects to security: the security of your intellectual property; the security of the data in your solution; and the integrity of the code in your solution.

Chapter 17, "Securing Office Documents and Visual Basic for Applications Code," explains how to secure your VBA code so that your intellectual property cannot be abused or altered. Additionally, this chapter discusses ways to protect Microsoft Office documents from users who do not have viewing privileges for the data in the document.

Chapter 17 also addresses how developers and customers can ensure protection from macro viruses by entering into trusted relationships. Using Microsoft's new Authenticode technology, developers can digitally sign the VBA projects in their solutions to indicate to users that the developer has been approved as a trusted source. Customers can then determine whether they want to run solutions that have not been signed by a trusted source.

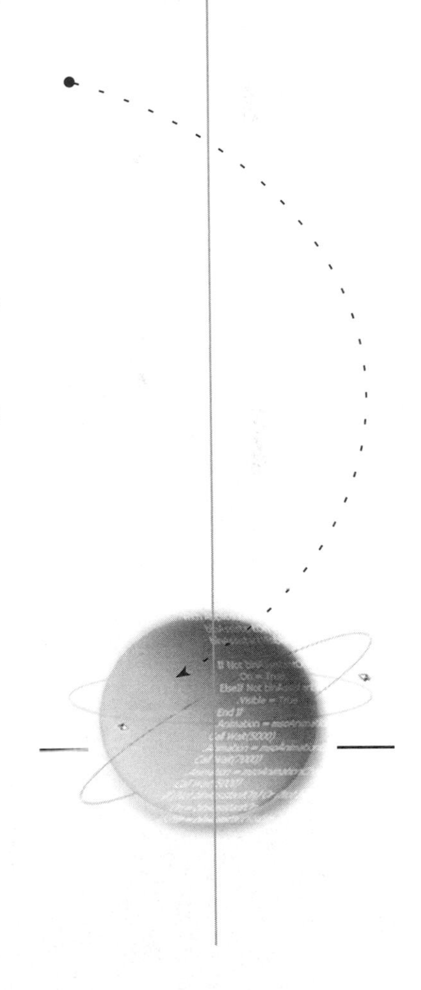

Chapter 18, "Securing Access Databases," discusses the additional security options available to you for a Microsoft Access-based solution. To protect your intellectual property, you can save an Access database in a manner that converts all of the VBA code to pseudocode, a form that cannot be read by people.

Chapter 18 also discusses the two options for protecting the data in your Access solution. The simplest way to protect the data in your database is to set a database password. A more complex, but also more flexible approach, is to use the sophisticated user-level security system in Access. This system allows you to set different levels of security on various objects for different users.

Finally, Chapter 18 explores security issues for data access pages, including preventing unauthorized users from viewing data in the database, preventing access by malicious scripts, controlling access by authorized users, and protecting the HTML pages themselves on the server.

CHAPTER 17

Securing Office Documents and Visual Basic for Applications Code

Security can mean many things depending on your perspective. If your solution contains or provides access to sensitive information, such as legal documents or payroll records, you will need to control access to this information. In this chapter, this is referred to as providing *access security* for your solution.

If you are retaining the ownership of the Visual Basic for Applications (VBA) code you develop, an additional aspect of access security is protecting the intellectual property value of your code. In this case, you need to prevent unauthorized access to your solution's code.

Developers, administrators, and users are all concerned with the reliability of a Microsoft Office solution. Part of ensuring the reliability of your solution is making sure that users can't alter its code or design in any way that will keep it from working. In this chapter, this is referred to as providing *integrity security* for your solution. This chapter discusses how to preserve the integrity of code in your solution by restricting access to the code.

With the advent of macro viruses, you also need to assure users and administrators that they can trust macros (VBA code) contained in any Office documents that are part of your solution. Microsoft Word, Microsoft Excel, Microsoft PowerPoint, and Microsoft Outlook now allow anti-virus software to scan documents as they are being opened. Additionally, Word, Excel, PowerPoint, and Outlook incorporate Microsoft Authenticode technology, which allows developers to digitally sign the VBA projects in their solutions and allows users to set security settings to automatically enable only macros from trusted sources.

This chapter discusses how to address these access security and virus security issues for Word, Excel, PowerPoint, and Outlook. It also discusses how to secure VBA code, which applies to Microsoft FrontPage and Microsoft Access as well. For more information about addressing security issues in Access, see Chapter 18, "Securing Access Databases."

Contents

Providing Access Security for Office Documents

You can provide access security for Office documents in three ways:

- In Word and Excel, you can set passwords that are required before any user can open or modify the document. Similarly, in Access, you can set a password that is required to open a database; for information about setting a database password, see Chapter 18, "Securing Access Databases." PowerPoint, Outlook, and FrontPage don't provide password protection for documents.
- For all Office documents, you can use the file-system access-control features of operating systems and Web servers to control what users can do with documents.
- In Word, Excel, Access, FrontPage, Outlook, and PowerPoint, you can control access to VBA code by setting a password that is required to view the code in the Visual Basic Editor.

Using Passwords to Protect Access to Word and Excel Documents

One way of controlling access to information in Word and Excel documents is by setting passwords that are required to open or modify the document. The **Save As** dialog box (**File** menu) and **SaveAs** method in Word and Excel provide the option to assign either of two passwords: a password that is required to open a document, and a password that is required to modify the document after it is opened. When you set either open or modify passwords, the password and the contents of the document are encrypted to secure the contents of the document and password. Word and Excel use the RC4 symmetric encryption algorithm to perform this encryption.

Using passwords can have certain drawbacks; for example, users can forget passwords and thus lose access to their documents. For this reason, tools are available for Microsoft Office 2000 that allow administrators to disable the user interface for setting document passwords. For information about how administrators can disable passwords, see the *Microsoft Office 2000 Resource Kit* (Microsoft Press, 1999).

However, disabling the password user interface doesn't prevent you from using VBA code to set and remove passwords. Nonetheless, before developing a solution that depends on document passwords, you should determine if users or system administrators want to use password protection. If using passwords is not desirable, you can use file-system features to control access to documents. For more information about using file-system access control for Office documents, see "Using File-System Access Control to Protect Access to Documents" later in this chapter.

Note Although the **Protect** and **Unprotect** methods in Word and Excel sound similar to the features discussed in this section, they correspond to the **Protect Document** command (Word) and **Protection** submenu commands (Excel) on the **Tools** menu. These methods are used to protect the design of certain elements of a document after it is opened.

▶ To set open or modify passwords in Word or Excel

1 Open the document or workbook you want to secure.

2 On the **File** menu, click **Save As**.

3 In the **Save As** dialog box, click the **Commands and Settings** button, and then click **General Options** (Word) or **Options** (Excel).

4 Type a password to open or modify the document, and then click **OK**.

5 Confirm the password, and then click **Save**.

Important Open and modify passwords in Word and Excel are case-sensitive. When you open a protected document, you must use the exact case you used when setting the password. If you lose or forget the password, there is no way to open the document. When password-protecting documents, be sure to write down the password and keep it in a physically secured location.

You can set open and modify passwords in code by using the **SaveAs** method in Word or Excel. The following example shows how to use the **SaveAs** method to set open and modify passwords in Word:

```
Function SetPwd(strNoPwdFile As String, _
                strPwdFile As String, _
                Optional strOpenPwd As String, _
                Optional strModPwd As String) As Boolean

   ' This function requires the following arguments:
   ' strNoPwdFile - The path to a document without a password.
   ' strPwdFile   - The path and name to save the password-
   '                protected document.
   '
```

```
    ' This function accepts the following optional arguments:
    ' strOpenPwd    - A case-sensitive password required to open
    '                 the document.
    ' strModPwd     - A case-sensitive password required to modify
    '                 the document.

    On Error GoTo SetPwd_Err

    Documents.Open FileName:=strNoPwdFile
    With ActiveDocument
       .SaveAs FileName:=strPwdFile, _
               Password:=strOpenPwd, _
               WritePassword:=strModPwd
       .Close
    End With
    SetPwd = True

SetPwd_End:
   Exit Function

SetPwd_Err:
   MsgBox "Error #: " & Err.Number & vbCrLf _
      & Err.Description
   Resume SetPwd_End
End Function
```

The SetPwd procedure is available in the modCh17 module in WordPasswords.dot in the Samples\CH17 subfolder on the companion CD-ROM.

To use the SetPwd procedure, you must supply the path to a document that has no password, the path and name to save the password-protected document under, and the text of the passwords you want to set.

Once you password-protect a document, if you want to open it with code, you must pass the same case-sensitive password to the ***PasswordDocument*** or ***WritePasswordDocument*** arguments of the **Open** method, as shown in the following code fragment:

```
Documents.Open FileName:=strPwdFile, _
          PasswordDocument:=strOpenPwd, _
          WritePasswordDocument:=strModPwd
```

This code fragment is from the OpenPwd2 procedure, available in the modCh17 module in WordPasswords.dot in the Samples\CH17 subfolder on the companion CD-ROM.

If you hard-code passwords into your code, you should secure access to the code itself in order to preserve the secrecy of a document's password. For information about securing access to code, see "Protecting Your Solution's VBA Code" later in this chapter. If the user of your solution will know the password, you can prompt the user to enter the password in either of two ways. You can display your own dialog box to prompt the user to enter the password, or you can use the Word **Password** dialog boxes. For information about how to create your own password dialog box, see "Controlling Macro Execution with a Password" later in this chapter.

To use the Word **Password** dialog boxes, don't pass passwords to the **Open** method; instead, handle any errors based on a user's response. When a password-protected document is opened, if you don't pass a password to the **Open** method, Word will automatically display the **Password** dialog box for each defined password. For an example of how to use the Word **Password** dialog boxes, see the OpenPwd2 procedure, available in the modCh17 module in WordPasswords.dot in the Samples\CH17 subfolder on the companion CD-ROM.

To clear a password from code, open the document by passing the correct passwords, and then use the **SaveAs** method to set either the ***Password*** or ***WritePassword*** arguments to a zero-length string (""), as shown in the following code fragment:

```
With ActiveDocument
   .SaveAs FileName:=strNoPwdFile, _
           Password:="", _
           WritePassword:=""
   .Close
End With
```

This code fragment is from the ClearPwd procedure, available in the modCh17 module in WordPasswords.dot in the Samples\CH17 subfolder on the companion CD-ROM.

You can view complete code samples in WordPasswords.dot in the Samples\CH17 subfolder on the companion CD-ROM.

In Excel, you use similar code to set and clear file passwords by using the ***Password*** and ***WriteResPassword*** arguments of the **Open** and **SaveAs** methods of the **Workbook** object. For code samples, see ExcelPasswords.xls in the Samples\CH17 subfolder on the companion CD-ROM.

Using File-System Access Control to Protect Access to Documents

Using open or modify passwords to provide access security for Word and Excel documents has certain drawbacks. For example, users can set and then forget passwords, and thus permanently lose access to their documents.

For this reason, many solution providers prefer to work with a network system administrator to provide access security by locating sensitive files on a network server and then using network or operating system file-system security features, such as logon authentication and file permissions, to set and override access permissions for individuals and groups. For example, you could place a Word template in a read-only folder so that users can run macros in the template, but not modify them.

While file servers are currently the most common way to provide controlled access to files, many Web servers and Web-site management applications also allow administrators and users to control read, write, and modify access to their files. For example, Microsoft Internet Information Services and FrontPage provide support for controlling access to files. For more information, see your Web server or Web-site management software documentation.

Using Operating System Access Control

You can control access to files and folders by using Microsoft Windows NT Server, Microsoft Windows NT Workstation, Microsoft Windows 95, or Microsoft Windows 98. Under Windows NT Workstation and Windows NT Server, you can control access to local folders on an NTFS-formatted hard disk and to shared folders; with Windows 95 and 98, you can control access only to shared folders.

Windows NT Workstation and Windows NT Server

You can control access to folders in Windows NT Server and Windows NT Workstation by setting access permissions. Additionally, if the files are located on an NTFS-formatted hard disk, you can define access permissions for individual files. Under both Windows NT Server and Windows NT Workstation, you can define access permissions for folders and files that are shared across a network, as well as folders and files on local NTFS-formatted drives that are shared by multiple users logging on to the same computer by using different local user account names.

To set access permissions for a folder located on an NTFS-formatted hard disk in Windows NT Server and Windows NT Workstation, right-click the folder, click **Properties** on the shortcut menu, and then click **Permissions** on the **Security** tab. You can share the folder on a network by using the settings on the **Sharing** tab, but leave the **Permissions** settings on the **Sharing** tab at their default (**Everyone–Full Control**), and make final permission settings by using the **Permissions** button on the **Security** tab. Permissions settings made by using the **Security** tab override settings made on the **Sharing** tab.

To set access permissions for an individual file located on an NTFS-formatted hard disk, right-click the file, click **Properties** on the shortcut menu, and then click **Permissions** on the **Security** tab.

If you are setting permissions for a file that needs to run code, such as a copy of Normal.dot or a template containing macros in a protected folder, you must provide at least Read permissions. If your solution creates additional files, such as log files, you must provide at minimum the Add & Read permission. If your solution uses an Access add-in that you want to install in a protected folder, you must also provide at least Add, Read, and Write permissions, because even if you aren't adding data to an .mdb file, users must be able to create and write to an .ldb file before the .mdb file can be opened.

For more information about setting access permissions in Windows NT Server version 4.0 and Windows NT Workstation version 4.0, search the Help index for "permissions." You can also find more information about setting access permissions in Windows NT Server 4.0 in the *Windows NT Server Concepts and Planning* guide, Chapter 4, "Managing Shared Resources and Resource Security."

Other network operating systems, such as Novell NetWare, provide similar features to control access to files. For information about how to control access to files with these network operating systems, refer to the documentation for these products.

Windows 95 and Windows 98

You can control access to folders that are shared across a peer-to-peer or server based network in Windows 95 and Windows 98. Before you can do this in Windows 95 and 98, you must use the **Network** icon in Control Panel to enable file sharing by clicking the **File and Print Sharing** button on the **Configuration** tab. You can use options on the **Access Control** tab to determine whether to use share-level (password) or user-level (users and groups) access control for shared folders. The user-level access control option is available only if the computer is connected to a network server where user accounts reside, such as a Windows NT domain controller. In Windows 95 and 98, there is no way to control access to folders on local drives that are shared by multiple users logging on to the same computer by using different user account names.

To set access permissions for a folder shared across a network in Windows 95 or 98, right-click the folder in Windows Explorer or My Computer, and then click **Sharing** on the shortcut menu. Click **Shared As**, and then define access permissions for the folder. For more information about setting access permissions in Windows 95 and 98, search the Microsoft Windows Help index for "permissions."

Protecting Your Solution's VBA Code

By default, the VBA code in a Word, Excel, FrontPage, Access, Outlook, or PowerPoint solution can be accessed by anyone who knows how to open the Visual Basic Editor. In the absence of any access security, any such user can open and alter your solution's code, potentially breaking it, or a malicious user or macro virus could add code that performs pranks or compromises the security of files and settings on a user's computer. There are four ways to control access to the VBA code in your solution:

- You can set a password that is required before the VBA code in a document, template, or database can be viewed. This is called locking your document's VBA project. Your VBA code will still run, but can only be viewed by a user who knows the correct password.

- To provide the highest level of security for your VBA code, use Microsoft Visual Basic version 6.0 to create a Component Object Model (COM) add-in. Because the VBA code in a COM add-in is compiled as a dynamic-link library (DLL), it can't be modified without access to the source code used to originally create it. Application-specific add-ins are not compiled; you must use the same protections as templates and documents.
- In Access, you can save an .mdb or .adp file as a file type that contains only compiled VBA code without the source code. For .mdb files, this file type is called an .mde file; for .adp files, this file type is called an .ade file. VBA code in these file types still runs, but there is no way to view or modify the code.
- You can use file-system access-control features to control what users can do with documents and templates.

This section discusses how to lock your solution's VBA project. For information about how to create COM add-ins, see Chapter 11, "Add-ins, Templates, Wizards, and Libraries." For more information about Access .mde and .ade files, see Chapter 18, "Securing Access Databases." For information about controlling access to files, see "Using File-System Access Control to Protect Access to Documents" earlier in this chapter.

Locking Your Solution's VBA Project

You can prevent users from viewing code by locking each VBA project associated with your solution. To lock a project, you define a password that must be entered before a user can view the project in the Visual Basic Editor. You can lock the VBA project in Word, Excel, Access, PowerPoint, Outlook, and FrontPage. This section covers the procedure for locking a VBA project for all of these applications. For more information about security in Access, see Chapter 18, "Securing Access Databases."

You can lock the VBA project contained within a document, template, or database. For Outlook, you can lock the VBA project for the local session of Outlook, which is stored in the VbaProject.OTM file. Similarly, for FrontPage, you can lock the VBA project for the local session of FrontPage, which is stored in the Microsoft FrontPage.fpm file. You can lock only an entire VBA project, not individual components within the project. This means that when you lock a VBA project, you are controlling access to all standard modules (including the default ThisDocument, ThisWorkbook, and ThisOutlookSession modules for Word, Excel, and Outlook, respectively), all class modules, and all UserForms contained by the project.

Important VBA project passwords are case-sensitive. To view a locked VBA project, you must use the exact case you used when setting the password. If you lose or forget the password, there is no way to view the locked VBA project. When password-protecting a VBA project, be sure to write down the password and keep it in a physically secured location.

▶ To lock a VBA project for viewing

1. Open the document, template, or database that contains the VBA project you want to protect. For Outlook or FrontPage, start Outlook or FrontPage on the computer that contains the VBA project you want to protect.
2. Open the Visual Basic Editor.
3. In the Project Explorer, right-click the project you want to protect, and then click ***ProjectName*** **Properties** on the shortcut menu.
4. On the **Protection** tab, select the **Lock project for viewing** check box, enter and confirm the password, and then click **OK**.

The next time you open the document, the password you set will be required to view code in the project.

Important You can set a password without selecting the **Lock project for viewing** check box, but doing so only controls access to the **Project Properties** dialog box itself. If you set a password without selecting the **Lock project for viewing** check box, users will be able to view and modify your code.

There is no way to programmatically specify a password for a locked VBA project. If you write code that attempts to work with components in a locked VBA project, the Visual Basic Editor will display a dialog box to prompt the user for the correct password. If the user specifies the correct password, your code will continue to run. If the user doesn't specify the correct password, a trappable error will be returned.

To determine if a VBA project is locked, set a reference to the Microsoft Visual Basic for Applications Extensibility 5.3 object library, and then inspect the **Protection** property of the VBA project. The following example shows how to check the **Protection** property of the VBA project in a Word document.

```
Function IsWordProjectLocked(strDocPath As String) As Boolean
   Dim vbpProj As VBIDE.VBProject
   Dim docProj As Word.Document

   ' Open document.
   Set docProj = Documents.Open(strDocPath)

   ' Set reference to document's VBA project.
   Set vbpProj = docProj.VBProject

   ' Check Protection property of VBA project.
   If vbpProj.Protection = vbext_pp_locked Then
      IsWordProjectLocked = True
   Else
      IsWordProjectLocked = False
   End If
End Sub
```

The IsWordProjectLocked procedure is available in the IsProjectLocked module in CheckProject.dot in the Samples\CH17 subfolder on the companion CD-ROM.

Controlling Macro Execution with a Password

Under some circumstances you may want to provide controlled access to a procedure in your solution. For example, suppose you have a procedure that only you or some authorized user, such as an administrator, should be allowed to run. You can control access to this procedure by creating a simple password logon dialog box that passes the entered password to a procedure that checks the password before continuing. In the simplest case, you use an **If** statement that checks a hard-coded password against the password entered by the user. If you do this, you should lock the VBA project so that users can't easily view the code to discover the password.

You can prompt for the password by using the VBA **InputBox** function, but if you want to create a typical input box that is masked to prevent others from seeing the password entered, you need to use a UserForm. You can set the **PasswordChar** property of a **TextBox** control on a UserForm to the character you want to use to mask the input; for example, an asterisk (*). For an example of how to prompt for a password and mask the input, see the frmGetPwd UserForm and the CallGetPwd procedure, available in the modGetPwd module in PasswordDialog.dot in the Samples\CH17 subfolder on the companion CD-ROM. To run the sample code, place the insertion point (cursor) in the CallGetPwd procedure and step through it by pressing the F8 key.

Protecting Office Documents from Macro Viruses

In recent years, a new kind of computer virus has emerged that uses application macro languages, such as VBA, to produce viruses that are associated with documents. For example, one of the first macro viruses was the Word Concept (also called Prank) macro virus that forced documents to be saved as templates. In Word, macro viruses typically transmit themselves by adding code to Word's default template, Normal.dot, which then copies code to each document you open or create to continue the replication process. Excel macro viruses perform similar operations, copying themselves to Personal.xls or some hidden location and replicating themselves to other workbooks when they are opened or created. At their most benign, a macro virus may perform a "prank" such as altering the text on the application title bar or displaying a message, but a macro virus is capable of doing anything that can be performed from VBA, such as renaming and deleting files.

For more information about macro viruses and anti-virus software, see the International Computer Security Association (ICSA) Web site at http://www.icsa.net/. Microsoft recommends using anti-virus software that is certified by this association. For information about anti-virus products that are certified by the ICSA, see http://www.icsa.net/services/consortia/anti-virus/certified_products.shtml.

For more information about macro viruses, see the Microsoft Office Anti-Virus Center Web site at http://officeupdate.microsoft.com/Articles/antivirus.htm.

In Office 97, Word, Excel, and PowerPoint provide the ability to a display a dialog box that warns users before opening a document that contains macros. The dialog box allows the user to enable or disable macros before opening the document. Because the effectiveness of this dialog box depends on the user's familiarity with the document being opened, an unfamiliar Office solution that depends on macros will be effectively broken if the user chooses to disable its macros when it is opened.

In Office 2000, Word, Excel, PowerPoint, and Outlook provide the following additional anti-virus features:

- Support for third-party anti-virus software. (This feature does not apply to Outlook.)
- Microsoft Authenticode technology to allow developers to *digitally sign* the VBA projects in their solutions by using a *digital certificate*.

These features aren't available in Access and FrontPage because solutions developed for these products typically must be installed in some formal fashion before they are run. For example in corporate sites, an Access or FrontPage solution is typically distributed by installing from an IT group-approved network share. This form of installation implies a trust relationship between users, developers, and administrators. Additionally, in Access, you can create an .mde or .ade file that contains compiled VBA code without the source code, thus making it impossible for malicious users to add or alter code in these types of files.

Using Third-Party Anti-Virus Software

Word, Excel, and PowerPoint now support a new application programming interface (API) that allows third-party anti-virus software to scan and disinfect a document, as well as the template it is based on and any installed add-ins, as the document is opened. For more information about anti-virus software that supports this new API, see the Microsoft Office Anti-Virus Center Web site at http://officeupdate.microsoft.com/Articles/antivirus.htm.

Using Digital Certificates to Produce Trusted Solutions

Office 2000 uses Microsoft Authenticode technology to allow developers to digitally sign VBA projects in their documents, templates, and add-ins by using a digital certificate that identifies the developer as a trusted source. In conjunction with this ability, Word, Excel, PowerPoint, and Outlook have security-level settings similar to those in Microsoft Internet Explorer, which allow users to identify code produced by trusted sources and ensure that signed code hasn't been altered.

To produce a trusted solution, you need to obtain and install a digital certificate that you can use to digitally sign the VBA projects in Word, Excel, PowerPoint, and Outlook solutions to identify them as your work. When opening a signed document, Microsoft Office applications can verify a digital signature to determine if the signed VBA project has been altered in any way, and automatically disable macros that might have been altered by a macro virus.

Note Digital signing works with Office installations only on computers that also have Internet Explorer version 4.0 or later installed. The digital-signing and signature-verification features in Microsoft Office will not work at all on computers that have Internet Explorer versions 3.*x* or earlier, any version of Netscape Navigator, or any other browser installed. If a user attempts to digitally sign a VBA project on such computers, a message informs the user that this feature is not available without Internet Explorer 4.0 or later installed. When opening any document that contains macros (signed or not) on such computers, the Office application displays a standard macro virus dialog box that allows the user to choose whether to enable or disable macros before opening the document.

The following sections discuss the concepts and technology behind digital signing and how Word, Excel, PowerPoint, and Outlook use this technology to identify a trusted solution.

What Are Digital Certificates?

You can think of a digital certificate as the electronic counterpart of an ID card, such as a driver's license or passport. The validity of a digital certificate is based on similar systems to those used to issue physical ID cards. You provide information about yourself to a trusted public body call a *certification authority*, such as VeriSign, Inc. or Thawte Consulting. The certification authority validates your information and then issues your digital certificate. The digital certificate contains information about who the certificate was issued to, as well as the certifying authority that issued it. Additionally, some certifying authorities may themselves be certified by a hierarchy of one or more certifying authorities, and this information is also part of the certificate. When a digital certificate is used to sign documents and software, this ID information is stored with the signed item in a secure and verifiable form so that it can be displayed to a user to establish a trust relationship.

Digital certificates use a cryptographic technology called *public-key cryptography* to sign software publications and to verify the integrity of the certificate itself. Public key cryptography uses a matched pair of encryption and decryption keys called a *public key* and a *private key*. The public-key cryptography algorithms perform a one-way transformation of the data they are applied to, so that data that is encrypted with one key can only be decrypted by the other key. Additionally, each key uses a sufficiently large value to make it computationally infeasible to derive a private key from its corresponding public key. For this reason, a public key can be made widely available without posing a risk to security.

To further reduce the possibility that someone will derive a private key from its public key, the certifying authority timestamps the key pair so that they must be replaced periodically, and provides an additional mechanism to assure that a signature was applied before the certificate expired. Any signature applied during the active lifetime of the digital certificate will remain valid for an unlimited time (unless the signed item is tampered with or the signature is removed). Any signature applied after the digital certificate expires is invalid.

To understand how public-key cryptography works, it helps to first describe how it is used to encrypt email messages. To do this, the sender obtains the recipient's public key from a directory service and uses it to encrypt the message before sending it. When the message is received, the recipient uses his or her private key to decrypt the message. As long as the private key is kept secure, no other user can decrypt the message and the recipient is assured that the transmission hasn't been tampered with.

A similar system is used to digitally sign documents and software, but instead of encrypting the entire file, first the file is passed through a one-way hashing algorithm to produce what is called a *message digest*. The message digest is a unique value that can be thought of as a "digital fingerprint" of the file. Microsoft Office uses the MD5 hashing algorithm to produce a message digest. Producing a message digest increases the efficiency of the process of creating and later verifying the signature for larger documents and software files. The message digest is then encrypted by using the signer's private key to produce the digital signature that is attached to the file.

To verify the integrity of the file, the application opening the file first uses the same hashing function to produce a message digest of the file. It then decrypts the signature attached to the file by using the signer's public key to recover the message digest produced when the file was originally signed. The two message digests are compared, and if any part of the file has been modified or corrupted, the digests will not match and the contents of the file can't be trusted. The verification process will fail regardless of how the file was modified—whether through corruption, a macro virus, or programmatic changes made by an add-in or Office solution. The verification process will also fail if the file wasn't signed with a valid certificate; that is, if the certificate had expired, or had been forged, altered, or corrupted. If another user modifies the VBA project, the Office 2000 application removes the current signature and prompts the user to re-sign the VBA project; if the user doesn't sign the VBA project or signs it with another certificate, the file may fail the verification process.

Important While the previous description describes the process used to digitally sign both documents and software, Office 2000 applications provide only the ability to sign VBA projects contained within documents. Office 2000 applications don't provide the ability to sign documents themselves to ensure that text and other contents (other than macros) haven't been altered. However, Microsoft Outlook does provide the ability to digitally sign and encrypt the contents of messages. For more information about signing and encrypting messages in Outlook, search the Microsoft Outlook Help index for "security."

For a summary of the digital-signing process, see Figure 17.1.

Figure 17.1 Overview of the Digital-Signing Process

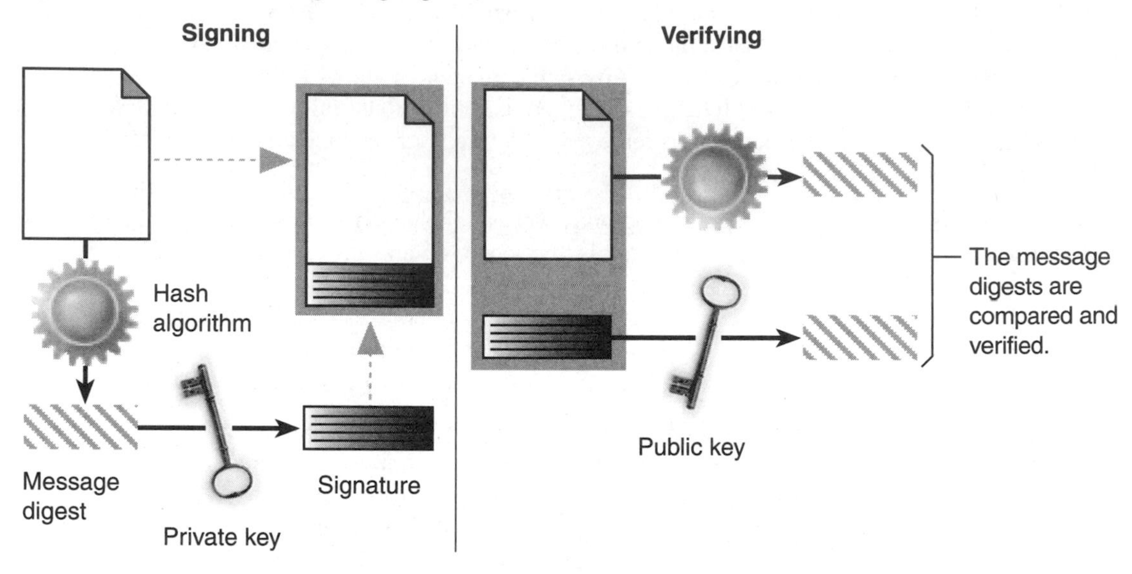

This same digital-signing process is also used within the digital certificate itself to identify it as being produced by the certifying authority and to ensure that the certificate has not been altered or forged.

For added security, a digital certificate has an expiration date that is enforced by the certification authority. Typically a digital certificate expires one year from the time it was issued. The reason for doing this is to greatly reduce the possibility that a malicious individual could derive a signature's private key from its public key. While deriving a private key from a public key is extremely unlikely because of the vast number of possible combinations that would need to be calculated for large key values, it is still not theoretically impossible. Additionally, adding an expiration date limits the lifetime of the certificate in the event that it is stolen. The certificate's expiration date ensures that any signature made after a certificate expires is invalid.

If the certification authority that issued the certificate provides a *timestamping service*, a hash of the code to be signed is sent over an Internet or intranet connection to a timestamping server maintained by the certification authority to be verified. If the code is being signed within the valid lifetime of the signature, a timestamp is added to the signature, and the signature will remain valid even after the certificate expires. If the certification authority that issues your digital certificate doesn't support timestamping, all signatures made with your certificate become invalid after the certificate expires.

For more information about digital signing and Microsoft Authenticode technology, see the Microsoft Authenticode Technology page of the Microsoft Security Advisor Web site at http://www.microsoft.com/security/tech/authenticode/default.asp.

Signing a VBA Project

To digitally sign VBA projects in your solution, you must first obtain a digital certificate for software publishing. There are three ways of getting a digital certificate:

- Create a digital certificate for your own use. Such a certificate would only be used to sign macros for your own use or for sharing within a small workgroup.
- Obtain a digital certificate from your organization's internal certification authority. Some organizations and corporations may choose to have a security administrator or group act as its own certification authority and produce or distribute digital certificates by using tools such as Microsoft Certificate Server. Microsoft Certificate Server can function as a stand-alone certificate authority or as part of an existing certificate authority hierarchy.
- Obtain a digital certificate from a commercial certification authority such as VeriSign, Inc.

Note Depending on how digital signing is administered in an organization, you may not be allowed to create your own digital certificate or sign your own documents. Typically in this scenario only solutions signed with approved certificates will be allowed to run. In this case, you need to submit your solution to an administrator to have it signed before it can be distributed.

Creating Your Own Digital Certificate

When the security level is set to High in your Office 2000 application, only signed macros from trusted sources can be run; the macros in all other documents are disabled. If you want to use the High security setting for macros you write yourself, you either need to obtain a certificate from a certification authority as described later in this section, or create a digital certificate for your own use. For information about setting the security level for your Office 2000 applications, see "Setting the Security Level" later in this chapter.

To create a digital certificate for your own use, you run the Create Digital Certificate utility (Selfcert.exe) and enter information about yourself that will be stored in the certificate. Because a digital certificate created in this fashion isn't issued by a formal certification authority, a digital certificate created this way is called a *self-signed certificate* and VBA projects signed by using such a certificate are referred to as *self-signed projects*. Depending on how Office 2000 digital-signature features are being used in your organization, you may be prevented from using such a certificate, or other users may not be able to trust macros in self-signed projects.

Before you can create a self-signed certificate, you must install the Create Digital Certificate utility (Selfcert.exe), which isn't installed if you select **Typical** during the Office 2000 installation.

▶ To install the Create Digital Certificate utility

1. In the Control Panel, double-click **Add/Remove Programs**.
2. On the **Install/Uninstall** tab, click **Microsoft Office 2000**, and then click **Add/Remove**.
3. In the **Microsoft Office 2000 Maintenance Mode** dialog box, click the **Add or Remove Features** button.
4. Expand **Office Tools** and set **Digital Signature for VBA Projects** to **Run from My Computer**.
5. Click **Update Now**.

   Selfcert.exe will be installed in the same folder as the Office 2000 applications, which by default is the C:\Program Files\Microsoft Office\Office folder.

▶ To create a self-signed digital certificate

1. Run Selfcert.exe from My Computer or Windows Explorer.
2. In the **Your name** box, type your name and any other identifying information you want associated with this certificate, and then click **OK**.

   Selfcert.exe will create and install a self-signed certificate that you can use to sign VBA projects on the current computer. To create a self-signed certificate to use on another computer, run Selfcert.exe again on that computer.

Important In most cases, a self-signed certificate created with Selfcert.exe should be used only for personal use or for testing purposes. To use Microsoft Office macro-virus protection features in the most secure fashion possible, you and your organization should sign VBA projects only with certificates issued by a certification authority. If you sign a VBA project by using a self-signed certificate, if security is set to **Medium** or **High**, the first time you open the document containing the signed VBA project, the **Security Warning** dialog box is displayed, indicating that the certificate used to sign the VBA project hasn't been issued by a certification authority and shouldn't be trusted. Obviously, you can safely trust a VBA project you have signed yourself by using a self-signed certificate, and if you do so the **Security Warning** dialog box won't be displayed the next time you open the document. However, as a general security policy an organization should either lock the trusted sources list to prevent users from trusting any certificates other than those provided by administrators or should strongly discourage users from trusting VBA projects signed with self-signed certificates.

Requesting a Digital Signature from Your Organization

Depending on how Office 2000 digital-signature features are being used in your organization, you may be able to obtain a digital certificate from your organization's internal certification authority. Your organization's publication process may not allow you to sign documents containing macros yourself. In this case, an administrator would sign a document that contains macros for you by using an approved certificate. For more information about your organization's policy, contact your network administrator or IT department.

Obtaining a Digital Signature from a Commercial Certification Authority

To obtain a digital certificate from a commercial certification authority, you or your organization must submit an application.

Depending on your status as a developer, you should apply for either a Class 2 or Class 3 digital certificate for software publishers:

- A Class 2 digital certificate is designed for people who publish software as individuals. This class of digital certificate provides assurance as to the identity of the individual publisher.
- A Class 3 digital certificate is designed for companies and other organizations that publish software. This class of digital certificate provides greater assurance about the identity of the publishing organization. Class 3 digital certificates are designed to represent the level of assurance provided today by retail channels for software. An applicant for a Class 3 digital certificate must also meet a minimum financial stability level based on ratings from Dun & Bradstreet Financial Services.

When you receive your digital certificate, you will be given instructions on how to install it on the computer you use to sign your Office solutions.

Backing Up or Transferring a Digital Certificate to Another Computer

If you have Microsoft Internet Explorer 5 installed, you can back up or transfer your digital certificate to another computer. To do this, you use the Certificate Manager to export or import your certificate.

▶ To use the Certificate Manager to export or import a digital certificate

1. Right-click the **Internet Explorer** icon on your desktop, and then click **Properties** on the shortcut menu.
2. On the **Content** tab, click **Certificates**. This displays the **Certificate Manager** dialog box, which lists all the certificates installed on your computer. Your personal certificates are listed on the **Personal** tab.
3. Do one of the following:
   - To export a certificate, select the certificate in the list, and then click **Export**. This starts the Certificate Manager Export Wizard. Follow the instructions in the wizard's dialog boxes to save your certificate to a file.

     Note In order to use a personal digital certificate to sign VBA projects, your digital certificate must include a private key. When exporting a personal digital certificate, be sure to choose to include its private key.
   - To import a certificate, click **Import**. This starts the Certificate Manager Import Wizard. Follow the instructions in the wizard's dialog boxes to install a certificate that has been saved to a file.

Signing Your VBA Project

Once you have your digital certificate installed, you can sign the VBA projects associated with Word, Excel, and PowerPoint documents, templates, and add-ins. For Outlook, you can sign the VBA project that is associated with the installation of Outlook on a particular computer, or if user profiles are in use, for a particular user on that computer. You should do this only after your solution has been tested and is ready for deployment, because any time code in a signed VBA project is modified in any way, its digital signature is removed. However, modifying the contents of the document other than the VBA code won't invalidate the signature on a VBA project contained within the document. This is because only the VBA project is signed, not the entire document. If you want to prevent users of your solution from accidentally modifying your VBA code and invalidating your signature, lock the VBA project before signing it. For information about how to lock a VBA project, see "Locking Your Solution's VBA Project" earlier in this chapter.

Note Locking your VBA project doesn't prevent another user from replacing the digital signature with another signature. This is allowed so that a system administrator or end user can replace a current signature with an approved signature or re-sign a document after a previous signature expires.

Similarly, if you produce an add-in that adds code to a document's VBA project, your code should determine if the project is digitally signed and notify the user of the consequences of modifying a signed project before continuing. For more information, see "Using Code and Objects in a Signed VBA Project from Automation" later in this chapter.

Important You can't sign VBA projects in Excel workbooks that contain Excel 4.0 macro sheets (XLM). If you try to sign a workbook that contains XLM macros, an error message is displayed. You must remove all XLM macros before you can sign the workbook.

▶ To digitally sign a VBA project

1. Open the document or template that contains the VBA project you want to sign. For Outlook, open Outlook on the computer that contains the VBA project you want to sign. If user profiles are in use, log on as the user whose Outlook VBA project you want to sign.
2. Open the Visual Basic Editor.
3. In the Project Explorer, select the project you want to sign.
4. On the **Tools** menu, click **Digital Signatures**.
5. Do one of the following:
   - If you haven't previously selected a digital certificate, or want to use another one, click **Choose**, select the certificate, and click **OK** twice.
   - Click **OK** to use the current certificate.

Note If a VBA project has been signed previously, clicking **Choose** and selecting a new digital certificate replaces the previous signature. To remove a signature from a previously signed project, click **Remove**.

Using Signed Office VBA Projects

In Microsoft Office, digital signatures are used in conjunction with a user's security settings and a list of known and verified certificates called *trusted sources.* The user's security level and the trusted sources list are maintained on the user's computer, but can be subject to an administrator's control. To provide the most administrative control over the use of digital signatures, an administrator can lock the user's security setting so that it can't be changed. Typically this would be used to force the setting to High so that only macros in signed VBA projects can be run. Additionally, an administrator can populate the trusted sources list with approved certificates and lock the list to prevent users from adding any new trusted sources.

For more information about how administrators can control the use of Office digital-signing features and security settings, see the *Microsoft Office 2000 Resource Kit* (Microsoft Press, 1999).

The security settings in Word, Excel, PowerPoint, and Outlook work similarly to those available in Internet Explorer. Office 2000 provides three security settings that affect documents containing macros:

- **High** Only macros that are signed by using a trusted certificate are allowed to run automatically; all unsigned macros are disabled without notification. If macros have been signed with a signature that isn't in the trusted sources list, a dialog box is displayed. What a user can do at this point depends on what choices the system administrator has made:
  - If the system administrator has not locked the trusted sources list, a user can choose to add the current signature to the trusted sources list when opening a signed, but not previously trusted document.
  - If the system administrator has locked the trusted sources list after adding trusted signatures, a user can't add new signatures to the trusted sources list, and only macros signed by using existing trusted certificates can be run.
  - If the system administrator has locked the trusted sources list without adding any trusted signatures, no macros can be run.
- **Medium** Only macros that are signed by using a trusted certificate are allowed to run automatically, and the same administrative restrictions described for the High setting apply when new signatures are added to the trusted sources list. However, under the Medium setting, a user can choose to enable macros whether or not they have been signed.
- **Low** The user receives no warnings; all documents are opened and all macros are enabled. This setting is recommended only if users have anti-virus software installed and don't want to use digital signatures.

Setting the Security Level

To set security settings, point to **Macro** on the **Tools** menu, and then click **Security** to display the dialog box shown in Figure 17.2.

Figure 17.2 The Security Dialog Box

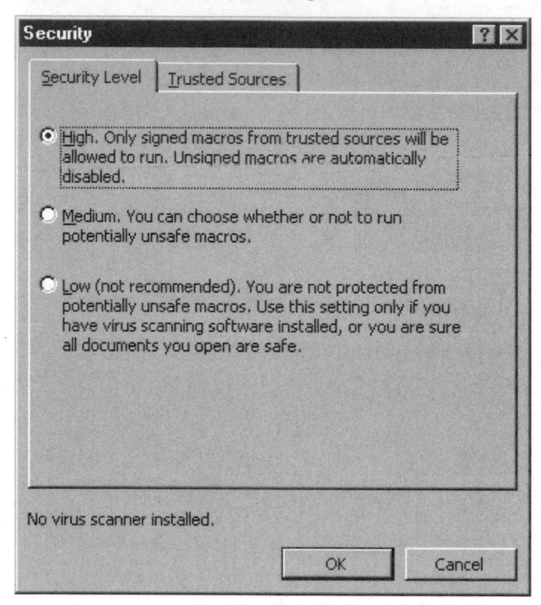

The following table summarizes how macro-virus protection works under each setting on the **Security Level** tab with various types of documents and signature-verification results. Under all settings, if anti-virus software is installed and the document contains macros, the document is scanned for known viruses before it is opened and verified.

Type of document and verification result	High	Medium	Low
No macros.	Document is opened.	Document is opened.	Document is opened.
Unsigned macros.	Macros are automatically disabled without notification and the document or Outlook application is opened.	User is prompted to enable or disable macros.	No prompt. Macros are enabled.
Signed macros from a trusted source. Verification succeeds.	Macros are automatically enabled and the document or Outlook application is opened.	Macros are automatically enabled and the document or Outlook application is opened.	No prompt or verification. Macros are enabled.

Type of document and verification result	High	Medium	Low
Signed macros from an unknown author. Verification succeeds.	A dialog box is displayed with information about the certificate. Macros can be enabled only if the user chooses to trust the author and certifying authority by selecting the **Always trust macros from this author** check box in the **Security Warning** dialog box. A network administrator can lock the trusted sources list and prevent the user from adding the author to the list and enabling the document's or Outlook VBA project's macros.	A dialog box is displayed with information about the certificate. The user is prompted to enable or disable macros. Optionally, the user can choose to trust the author and certifying authority by selecting the **Always trust macros from this author** check box in the **Security Warning** dialog box.	No prompt or verification. Macros are enabled.
Signed macros from any author. Verification fails, possibly due to a virus.	User is warned of a possible virus. Macros are automatically disabled.	User is warned of a possible virus and macros are automatically disabled.	No prompt or verification. Macros are enabled.
Signed macros from any author. Verification not possible because public key is missing or incompatible encryption methods were used.	User is warned that verification is not possible. Macros are automatically disabled.	User is warned that verification is not possible. User is prompted to enable or disable macros.	No prompt or verification. Macros are enabled.
Signed macros from any author. The signature was made after the certificate had expired or been revoked.	User is warned that the signature has expired or been revoked. Macros are automatically disabled.	User is warned that the signature has expired or been revoked. User is prompted to enable or disable macros.	No prompt or verification. Macros are enabled.

Identifying Trusted Sources

The **Trusted Sources** tab in the **Security** dialog box lists all digital certificates that have been previously accepted by a user or that have been previously installed by a network administrator. A user doesn't add trusted sources directly to this dialog box, but can add a new certificate to the list by selecting the **Always trust macros from this author** check box the first time he or she opens a signed document from a new source. An administrator can lock the trusted sources list so that no new sources can be added to the list by users. Therefore, only macros signed by using approved certificates currently in the list will run.

The **Trusted Sources** tab also contains a **Trust all installed add-ins and templates** check box, which is selected by default. When this check box is selected, macros in all add-ins and templates in all of the locations in following table are ignored by security-level checks because it is assumed that these add-ins and templates are already trusted. This includes all templates and add-ins that are installed by Microsoft Office.

Installation location	Notes
C:\Program Files\Microsoft Office\Templates *LanguageIDSubfolder*	For U.S. English language installations, the language ID subfolder is named 1033.
C:\Windows\Application Data\Microsoft \Templates	This folder is used only when Windows 95 or 98 is being used and user profiles aren't enabled.
C:*WindowsFolder*\Profiles*UserName* \Application Data\Microsoft\Templates	This folder is used with Windows NT Workstation or Windows NT Server, or when Windows 95 or 98 is being used and user profiles are enabled.
C:\Windows\Application Data\Microsoft \AddIns	This folder is used only when Windows 95 or 98 is being used and user profiles aren't enabled.
C:*WindowsFolder*\Profiles*UserName* \Application Data\Microsoft\AddIns	This folder is used with Windows NT Workstation or Windows NT Server, or when Windows 95 or 98 is being used and user profiles are enabled.
C:\Program Files\Microsoft Office\Office \Library	This folder is used for add-ins installed by Microsoft Office.
C:\Program Files\Microsoft Office\Office \AddIns	This folder is used for add-ins installed by Microsoft Office.
C:\Program Files\Microsoft Office\Office \Startup	This folder is used for Word templates only.
C:\Program Files\Microsoft Office\Office \XLStart	This folder is used for Excel workbooks and add-ins only.
The Excel alternate startup file location	You can specify this location in the **Alternate startup file location** box on the **General** tab in the **Options** dialog box (**Tools** menu).

If you want to require that all add-ins and templates be signed, clear the **Trust all installed add-ins and templates** check box.

Important In Excel, if you clear the **Trust all installed add-ins and templates** check box and the security level is set to **Medium** or **High**, users will be prompted to enable any add-in that contains XLM macros (Excel version 4.0 macros) that is being loaded from the locations listed in the preceding table. Users are prompted to enable these add-ins because workbooks and add-ins that contain XLM macros can't be signed. This behavior also applies to some add-ins that are installed for Excel 2000, such as the Analysis ToolPak and Solver add-ins.

Note Selecting the **Trust all installed add-ins and templates** check box has no effect on templates in Excel. Installed Excel templates containing code can't be trusted by default.

If users or administrators want to require that installed add-ins and templates also be evaluated based on the security-level setting, they can clear the **Trust all installed add-ins and templates** check box. In this case, assuming the security level is set to High, only macros in installed templates and add-ins that have been signed will be run. Application-specific add-ins (.dot, .xla, and .ppa) created in Office 2000 applications can be signed by using the **Digital Signatures** command on the **Tools** menu in the Visual Basic Editor, but COM add-ins (add-ins created as a COM DLL) must be signed by using the Signcode.exe utility provided with the Microsoft Internet Client Software Development Kit (SDK). For information about downloading or ordering the Microsoft Internet Client SDK, see http://msdn.microsoft.com/developer/sdk/inetsdk /asetup/default.htm. Installed templates or add-ins created in previous versions of Microsoft Office must be opened and signed in their corresponding Office 2000 applications before they can be run. Additionally, an administrator can lock the **Trust all installed add-ins and templates** check box setting to prevent users from changing it.

Opening Signed Documents in Office 97

Word 2000, Excel 2000, and PowerPoint 2000 documents share the same file formats as the corresponding Office 97 applications, so documents produced with Office 2000 applications can be opened in Office 97 without conversion. Digitally signed documents from Office 2000 can be opened in their corresponding Office 97 applications and most VBA code will be run; however, to protect the digital signature, the VBA project will be locked. There is no way to override or provide a password for this lock in an Office 97 application. To view or modify the VBA code in a digitally signed document, it must be opened in the corresponding Office 2000 application.

While most VBA code will run under Office 97, code that uses Office 2000-specific VBA properties, methods, objects, and keywords will not run—not due to digital-signing features, but simply because new VBA features aren't supported by previous versions of VBA.

Using Code and Objects in a Signed VBA Project from Automation

Signing a VBA project does not prevent you from running code or working with objects contained in that project from Automation (formerly known as OLE Automation) code. The warnings and dialog boxes that are displayed to users when they open signed documents from an Office 2000 application's user interface are disabled when a signed document is opened and worked with from code.

However, if you use code to add or change code in a signed document, those modifications will invalidate the digital signature and cause the document to be flagged as suspect the next time it is opened from an Office 2000 application's user interface. There is no way to prevent modifications to the project from invalidating the signature (doing so would create a security hole), but you can detect the presence of a signature, so that you can display a message that allows the user to choose whether to continue. This message should also inform the user that if he or she continues, the document must be re-signed before it can be trusted. Similarly, you may want to use VBA to scan a set of documents to determine if their VBA projects haven't been signed before distributing them.

To detect the presence of a digital signature in Word, Excel, and PowerPoint, check the **VBASigned** property of the corresponding document object. For example, to reference the **VBASigned** property, use a line of code in this form

```
object.VBASigned
```

where *object* is a reference to a **Document** object (Word), a **Workbook** object (Excel) or a **Presentation** object (PowerPoint). If the **VBASigned** property is **True**, the VBA project associated with the document is digitally signed; if the **VBASigned** property is **False**, the document hasn't been signed. The following procedure detects a digital signature in a Word document by checking the value of the **VBASigned** property of the document:

```
Public Function IsWordProjectSigned(strDocPath As String) As Boolean
   Dim docProj As Word.Document

   ' Open document.
   Set docProj = Documents.Open(strDocPath)

   ' Check VBASigned property of document.
   If docProj.VBASigned Then
      IsWordProjectSigned = True
   Else
      IsWordProjectSigned = False
   End If
End Function
```

The IsWordProjectSigned procedure is available in the IsProjectSigned module in CheckProject.dot in the Samples\CH17 subfolder on the companion CD-ROM.

Where to Go from Here

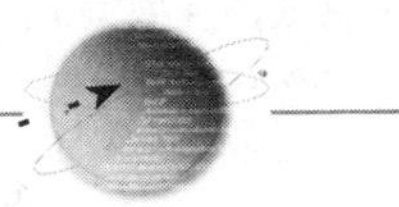

For additional information about the subjects discussed in this chapter, see the following sources.

General Security Issues

Microsoft Security Advisor Web site (http://www.microsoft.com/security/)

Securing Access Databases

Chapter 18, "Securing Access Databases"

Windows File System Security

Microsoft Windows 95 Resource Kit. Redmond, WA: Microsoft Press, 1995.

Microsoft Windows 98 Resource Kit. Redmond, WA: Microsoft Press, 1998.

Microsoft Windows NT Workstation Resource Kit. Redmond, WA: Microsoft Press, 1996.

Microsoft Windows NT Server Resource Kit. Redmond, WA: Microsoft Press, 1996.

Disabling User Passwords

Microsoft Office 2000 Resource Kit Web site (http://www.microsoft.com/office/ork/)

Microsoft Office 2000 Resource Kit. Redmond, WA: Microsoft Press, 1999.

Controlling the Use of Office Digital-Signing Features and Security Settings

Microsoft Office 2000 Resource Kit Web site (http://www.microsoft.com/office/ork/)

Microsoft Office 2000 Resource Kit. Redmond, WA: Microsoft Press, 1999.

Macro Viruses

Microsoft Office Anti-Virus Center Web site (http://officeupdate.microsoft.com/Articles/antivirus.htm)

International Computer Security Association (ICSA) Web site (http://www.icsa.net/services/consortia/anti-virus/certified_products.shtml)

Creating COM Add-ins and Application-Specific Add-ins

Chapter 11, "Add-ins, Templates, Wizards, and Libraries"

Signcode.exe Utility for Signing COM Add-ins

Microsoft Internet Client SDK Web site
(http://msdn.microsoft.com/developer/sdk/inetsdk/asetup/default.htm)

Code Samples

The code samples shown in this chapter, along with additional examples demonstrating similar techniques, can be copied from the files in the Samples\CH17 subfolder on the companion CD-ROM.

CHAPTER 18

Securing Access Databases

Establishing security for your Microsoft Access database file (.mdb) or project file (.adp) protects intellectual property such as your solution's structure and programming code. It also prevents your solution's users from inadvertently changing object designs or code in a way that would cause your solution to stop working. If your .mdb file also contains data, establishing security protects sensitive data regardless of what program is used to access your database file. This chapter discusses techniques you can use to secure your Access solution.

Contents

Protecting an Access Solution

There are several reasons why it may be important to protect the data and features in an Access solution. For example, your solution may use objects that took you a great deal of time to design. Perhaps you or the users of your solution need to control access to sensitive information. Or, to reduce maintenance for your solution, you may want to prevent users from inadvertently breaking your solution by changing code or objects on which the solution depends. Consider implementing some form of security to control what a user, or group of users, can do with the objects and data in your solution.

Access provides four methods of protecting your solution. All of these methods apply to .mdb files, and some of these methods also apply to .adp files. The most powerful and flexible method of protecting the data and objects in an .mdb file is called *user-level security*, which is discussed later in this chapter. However, establishing and maintaining user-level security is a relatively complex process that may exceed your situation's requirements. As alternatives or adjuncts to user-level security, Access provides the following three methods you can use to protect your solution:

- Using startup options to restrict access to default menus and toolbars, the Database window, and special keys (both .mdb and .adp files)
- Setting a password to control opening the database (.mdb only)
- Saving your solution in a format that removes Microsoft Visual Basic source code and prevents changes to the design of forms, reports, and modules (both .mdb and .adp)

Access also provides database encryption for .mdb files that you can use to prevent unauthorized users from viewing the objects in your solution with a disk editor or other utility program. You can use encryption in conjunction with all methods of protecting your Access database solution.

The strategy you use depends on how your solution will be used and the extent of security required to protect its objects. The following sections discuss these options.

Note You can also use the security features of your operating system to control access to .mdb, .adp, and data access page files. For more information about how to do this, see "Using File-System Access Control to Protect Access to Documents" in Chapter 17, "Securing Office Documents and Visual Basic for Applications Code."

Using Startup Options

In an environment where a high level of security isn't required, you can use startup options to restrict access to default menus and toolbars, the Database window, and special keys. To perform the following procedure, your solution must have a startup form and a custom menu bar that contains only the commands you want available. This method can be used for both .mdb and .adp files. You can also use startup options in conjunction with other forms of security.

▶ To use startup options to protect your solution

1. On the **Tools** menu, click **Startup**.
2. Click **Advanced** to display the rest of the dialog box.
3. In the **Display Form** box, click the name of your startup form.
4. In the **Menu Bar** box, click the name of your menu bar.
5. Clear the following check boxes: **Allow Full Menus**, **Allow Default Shortcut Menus**, **Display Database Window**, **Allow Built-in Toolbars**, **Allow Toolbar/Menu Changes**, and **Use Access Special Keys**.

6 In Visual Basic for Applications (VBA), set the **AllowBypassKey** property to **False**. This prevents users from using the SHIFT key to bypass the settings in the **Startup** dialog box. For information about how to set the **AllowBypassKey** property, search the Microsoft Access Visual Basic Reference Help index for "AllowBypassKey property." You can also set the startup options and properties used in this procedure (as well as other startup options and properties) from VBA code. For information about how to do this, search the Microsoft Access Visual Basic Reference Help index for "Startup properties."

Note A user can bypass this method of security by setting the database's **AllowBypassKey** property back to **True**, but that user would need to understand how to create the appropriate line of VBA code to do so.

Setting a Database Password

Adding a database password is an easy way to prevent unauthorized users from opening your solution. Use this approach when you need to control which users can open your solution, but not what they do after providing the correct database password. This method can be used only with .mdb files.

▶ To set a database password

1. Close the database. If the database is being shared on a network, make sure no other users have it open.
2. Make a backup copy of your database and store it in a secure place.
3. On the **File** menu, click **Open**.
4. Navigate to the folder that contains the database and select it in the file list, click the arrow next to the **Open** button, and then click **Open Exclusive**.
5. On the **Tools** menu, point to **Security**, and then click **Set Database Password**.
6. In the **Password** box, type the password. Passwords are case-sensitive.
7. In the **Verify** box, type the password again to confirm it, and then click **OK**.

The password is now set. Each time a user tries to open the database, a dialog box appears that requests the database password.

Caution Write down your database password and keep it in a safe place. If your database password is lost or forgotten, you won't be able to open your database or retrieve the information it contains.

Do not use a database password if you plan to replicate the database. You can't synchronize a replicated database if a database password has been set. Defining user-level security permissions doesn't interfere with replica synchronization.

When you set a database password, the **Set Database Password** command changes to **Unset Database Password**. To clear a database password, open the database in exclusive mode, click **Unset Database Password** on the **Security** submenu (**Tools** menu), type the correct password in the **Password** box, then confirm it in the **Verify** box.

Important Considerations When Using a Database Password

Take the following items into consideration when you use a database password:

- Setting a database password doesn't prevent someone from using a disk editor or other utility program to read your data without opening the database. To prevent this as well, encrypt your database. For more information about encrypting a database, see "Encrypting a Database" later in this chapter.
- Any user who knows the database password and has access to the **Unset Database Password** command can change or clear the password, unless you remove the Administer permission on the database for all users and groups except the database administrator. Similarly, if you want to prevent users from setting a password on a database, remove the Administer permission on the database for those users or groups. By default, the Users group, the Admins group, and the creator (owner) of the database all have Administer permission on the database. For more information about permissions, see "Permissions" later in this chapter. Additionally, tools are available for Microsoft Office 2000 that allow system administrators to disable the user interface for setting database and document passwords. For information about how administrators can disable the password user interface, see the *Microsoft Office 2000 Resource Kit* (Microsoft Press, 1999).

  Note You can remove the Administer permission without establishing user-level security, but any user who knows how to do so can restore the Administer permission by using the **User and Group Permissions** command on the **Security** submenu (**Tools** menu). If you want to make sure that no unauthorized user can set, clear, or change a database password, you must establish user-level security in addition to removing the Administer permission.

- If you use a password to protect an Access database containing tables that are linked to another database, Access stores the password when the link is established. This means that any user who can open the database that contains the link can open the linked table. Additionally, Access stores the password in an unencrypted form. If this will compromise the security of the password-protected database, you should not use a database password to protect the database. Instead, you should establish user-level security to control access to sensitive data in that database. For more information about user-level security, see "Access User-Level Security" later in this chapter.

Working with Database Passwords in VBA Code

As an alternative to using the Access user interface to work with database passwords, you can use Data Access Objects (DAO) and ActiveX Data Objects (ADO) in VBA code.

Important If you use code to open a database and a user later sets a database password without your being aware of it, your code will no longer be able to open the database. Your code should always check to see if the attempt to open a database has succeeded. The code should also provide error handling in case it encounters a password-protected database.

Setting, Changing, or Clearing a Database Password in Code

Unfortunately there is no way to set, change, or clear a database password by using ADO code. It is possible to set, change, or clear a database password when you are compacting a database by using the **CompactDatabase** method of the Microsoft Jet and Replication Objects 2.1 object library; however the **CompactDatabase** method requires you to create a second copy of the database to do so.

A simpler method of setting, changing, or clearing a database password is to use the **NewPassword** method of the DAO **Database** object. To work with the **NewPassword** method, you must set a reference to the Microsoft DAO 3.6 object library. Before you can work with a database password, you must be able to open the database in exclusive mode. To open a database by using exclusive access with DAO, set the *Options* argument of the **OpenDatabase** method to **True**. The following procedure opens a database in exclusive mode, and sets, changes, or clears a database password depending on what values you pass to it for the *strOldPwd* and *strNewPwd* arguments:

- To set a database password for a database that currently has no password, pass a zero-length string ("") for *strOldPwd* and the password you want to set for *strNewPwd*.
- To change a database password, pass the current password for *strOldPwd* and the new password for *strNewPwd*.
- To clear a database password, pass the current database password for *strOldPwd* and a zero-length string for *strNewPwd*.

```
Function SetDBPassword(strDBPath As String, _
                       strOldPwd As String, _
                       strNewPwd As String)
   ' This procedure sets a new password or changes an existing
   ' password.

   Dim dbsDB       As DAO.Database
   Dim strOpenPwd As String

   ' Create connection string by using current password.
   strOpenPwd = ";pwd=" & strOldPwd
```

```
    ' Open database for exclusive access by using current password. To
    ' get exclusive access, you must set the Options argument to True.
    Set dbsDB = OpenDatabase(Name:=strDBPath, _
                             Options:=True, _
                             ReadOnly:=False, _
                             Connect:=strOpenPwd)

    ' Set or change password.
    With dbsDB
       .NewPassword strOldPwd, strNewPwd
       .Close
    End With

    Set dbsDB = Nothing
 End Function
```

The SetDBPassword procedure is available in the modSecurity module in AccessSecurity.mdb in the Samples\CH18 subfolder on the companion CD-ROM.

Opening a Password-Protected Database with ADO

To open an Access password-protected database by using ADO code, you specify the password by using the provider-specific **Jet OLEDB:Database Password** property. You can specify the **Jet OLEDB:Database Password** property by using the **Properties** collection of the **Connection** object, or as part of the connection string passed to the **Open** method of the **Connection** object. For example, the following procedure opens a password-protected database:

```
Function OpenProtectedDB(strDBPath As String, _
                         strPwd As String)
   Dim cnnDB As ADODB.Connection

   Set cnnDB = New ADODB.Connection

   ' Open database for shared (by default), read/write access, and
   ' specify database password.
   With cnnDB
      .Provider = "Microsoft.Jet.OLEDB.4.0"
      .Properties("Jet OLEDB:Database Password") = strPwd
      .Mode = adModeReadWrite
      .Open strDBPath
   End With
   ' Code to work with database goes here.
   cnnDB.Close
   Set cnnDB = Nothing
End Function
```

The OpenProtectedDB procedure is available in the modSecurity module in AccessSecurity.mdb in the Samples\CH18 subfolder on the companion CD-ROM.

Saving Your Solution Without VBA Source Code

If your primary security concern is protecting your VBA code and the design of your forms and reports, you can save your .mdb as an *MDE (.mde) file*, or your .adp as an *ADE (.ade) file*. An .mde file is an Access database file with all modules compiled and all editable source code removed. Likewise, an .ade file is an Access project file with all modules compiled and all editable source code removed. You can also save a database as an .mde or .ade file in conjunction with other forms of security.

Saving your database as an .mde or .ade file creates a separate copy of your database that contains no VBA source code and that is smaller than the original database. Your code is compiled and continues to run, but it can't be viewed or edited. Additionally, users can't view or modify the design of forms, reports, and modules in an .mde or .ade file. Users can still view and modify the design of your database's relationships, tables, queries, and macros after you have saved the database as an .mde file; however, you can establish user-level security if you want to protect the design of these objects. Similarly, saving an .adp file as an .ade file doesn't protect the design of database diagrams, tables, views, stored procedures, and macros, but you can establish security on the server itself to protect all of these objects except macros.

Saving your database as an .mde or .ade file also prevents the following actions:

- Creating forms, reports, or modules.
- Adding or deleting references to object libraries or databases by using the **References** command on the **Tools** menu.
- Using the Object Browser.
- Changing code by using the properties or methods of the Access or VBA object models (because .mde and .ade files contain no source code).
- For .mde files, importing or exporting forms, reports, macros, or modules. However, tables and queries can be imported from or exported to non-.mde databases. Any tables or queries in an .mde database can be imported into another database, but no forms, reports, macros, or modules can be imported into another database. For .ade files, only tables can be imported from or exported to non-.ade databases.

If you need to modify the design of forms, reports, or modules in a database saved as an .mde or .ade file, you must open the original .mdb or .adp file, modify the items, and then save it as an .mde or .ade file again. Saving an .mdb that contains tables as an .mde file creates complications when you are reconciling different versions of the data if you need to modify the design of the solution later. For this reason, saving a database as an .mde file is most appropriate for the front end of an solution that has been split into a front-end/back-end database, in which the back end contains only tables and the front end contains the remaining objects. An .adp can only be a front-end (client) to server tables, database diagrams, views, and stored procedures. That is, it can only contain connections to these objects, so this isn't an issue with an .adp file saved as an .ade file. For more information about splitting databases, see "The Two-Database Approach" in Chapter 16, "Multiuser Database Applications."

Note The process of saving a database as an .mde or .ade file compiles all modules and compacts the destination database, so there is no need to perform these steps before saving a database as an .mde or .ade file.

▶ To save a database as an .mde or .ade file

1 Open the Access database (.mdb) or project (.adp) file you want to work with. If the Access database (.mdb) is being shared on a network, make sure no other users have it open.

2 On the **Tools** menu, point to **Database Utilities**, and then click **Make MDE File** or **Make ADE File**.

3 In the **Save MDE As** or **Save ADE As** dialog box, specify a file name and the location where you want to save the file, and then click **Save**.

   Your original file is unchanged and a new copy is saved as an .mde or .ade file by using the file name and location you specified.

Caution Be sure to keep your original Access database (.mdb) or project file (.adp) in a safe place. If you need to modify the design of forms, reports, or modules in your file, you must open the original file, modify the objects, and then save the file again as an .mde or .ade file. Also, databases saved as .mde or .ade files in Access 2000 cannot be opened or converted in later versions of Access. To convert or open it in later versions of Access, you must use the original file.

Note Saving as an .mde or .ade file doesn't create a run-time version of the file. To use an .mde or .ade file, users must have Access 2000 installed. Alternatively, if you have Microsoft Office 2000 Developer, you can save an .mde file, and then use the Packaging and Deployment Wizard to create a setup program that installs the run-time version of Access and your .mde file. Note that the run-time version of Access can't be used to open .adp or .ade files; however, you can use the Packaging and Deployment Wizard to create a setup program to distribute .adp or .ade files to users who already have the full version of Access installed.

Using Other Forms of Security with an Access Solution That Will Be Saved as an .Mde or .Ade File

Saving an .mdb file as an .mde file is a good way to protect the code and the design of forms and reports in your solution, and it doesn't require users to log on or require you to create and manage the user accounts and permissions required by user-level security. However, an .mde file doesn't control how users access your solution's tables, queries, and macros. If you want more control over these database objects, you should establish user-level security before you save your database as an .mde file. User-level security will be preserved in the new .mde file. Alternatively, you can split your .mdb into a front-end/back-end database and establish user-level security for your front-end database to protect access to queries and macros, and also for your back-end database to protect access to your back-end tables. In this case, you would save only your front-end database as an .mde file to protect the design of forms, reports, and code.

However, saving your database as an .mde file prevents all users (including database administrators) from modifying the design of forms, reports, and modules. If this is too restrictive and you require additional control and flexibility in these areas, you shouldn't save your database as an .mde file—you should establish user-level security instead.

Once you have secured your .mdb with user-level security, if you want to save it as an .mde file, you must meet the following requirements:

- Before starting Access, you must use the Workgroup Administrator program (Wrkgadm.exe, installed by default in the C:\Program Files\Microsoft Office\Office \1033 subfolder) or the **/wrkgrp** command-line option to join the workgroup information file (.mdw) that was in use when the database was created.

  Note The path to Wrkgadm.exe reflects the language ID folder (1033) for U.S. English language support in Office. The language ID folder below C:\Program Files\Microsoft Office \Office differs for each language.

- Your user account must have Open/Run and Open Exclusive permissions for the database itself.
- Your user account must have Modify Design or Administer permission for any tables in the database, or you must be the owner of any tables in the database.
- Your user account must have Read Design permission for all objects in the database.

You can also use a database password to control who can open an .mde file, but you must set the password in the original database before you save it as an .mde file. The database password will be preserved in the new .mde database.

Similarly, saving an .adp as an .ade file doesn't control how users access the tables, views, stored procedures, and database diagrams in the SQL Server database that your .ade file is connected to. To protect access there, you must establish security for those objects on your server by using the SQL Server Enterprise Manager, the properties and methods of the **Group** and **User** objects in ADO code, the GRANT and REVOKE statements in Transact-SQL, or security management system stored procedures such as sp_addrole and sp_addrolemember.

Saving a Replicated Database as an .Mde File

A replicated database (either a replica or Design Master) cannot be saved as an .mde file; however, once a database is saved as an .mde file, it can be replicated. To save a replicated database as an .mde file, you must first remove replication system fields, tables, and properties. For more information, search the Microsoft Access Help index for "replicated databases, making regular." For more information about database replication, see Chapter 16, "Multiuser Database Applications."

Saving .Mdb or .Adp Files That Reference Other Files as .Mde or .Ade Files

If you try to save an .mdb or .adp file that references another .mdb, .adp, or add-in database (.mda) as an .mde or .ade file, Access displays an error message and doesn't let you complete the operation. To save an .mdb or .adp file that references another file, you must save all files in the chain of references as .mde or .ade files, starting from the first file referenced. After saving the first file as an .mde or .ade file, you must then use the **References** dialog box (**Tools** menu, **References** command) to update the reference in the next file to point to the new .mde or .ade file before saving it as an .mde or .ade file, and so on.

For example, if Database1.mdb references Database2.mdb, which references Database3.mda, you would proceed as follows:

1. Save Database3.mda as Database3.mde.
2. Open Database 2.mdb and change its reference to point to the new Database3.mde.
3. Save Database2.mdb as Database2.mde.
4. Open Database1.mdb and change its reference to point to the new Database2.mde.
5. Save Database1.mdb as Database1.mde.

Access User-Level Security

User-level security is the most flexible and secure method of protecting the sensitive data, code, and design of objects in an Access database. In addition, user-level security is the only form of Access security that allows you to establish different levels of access to sensitive data and objects. User-level security for Access databases is provided through the Microsoft Jet database engine. Because all access to an .mdb file is accomplished through Microsoft Jet regardless of what program is being to used to open the database, user-level security is enforced whether Access or some other program is used to access the database.

Microsoft Jet provides a robust and powerful security model that gives you a great deal of control over users' access to your Access solution and the data it contains. Because of its flexibility, the model is somewhat more complicated than those provided by other desktop databases. Indeed, security is one of the more commonly misunderstood aspects of Access and is usually incorrectly implemented by developers who lack a cohesive understanding of its workings. The following section contains detailed information, structured in a way that helps you understand the model before you implement security.

User-Level Security Support in Access 2000

If you are familiar with user-level security in previous versions of Access, you should be aware of the following differences in Access 2000:

- **User-Level Security No Longer Supported for Modules** In previous versions of Access, user-level security can be used with VBA modules. In Access 2000, the entire VBA project for an .mdb or .adp file, which contains all modules (stand-alone modules, modules behind forms and reports, and class modules), must be secured by setting a password, or by saving the database as an .mde or .ade file, which removes VBA source code. For information about setting a password for a VBA project, see Chapter 17, "Securing Office Documents and Visual Basic for Applications Code." For information about saving a database as an .mde or .ade file, see "Saving Your Solution Without VBA Source Code" earlier in this chapter.
- **User-Level Security Not Supported for Access Project Files** Microsoft Jet user-level security can't be used with Access project (.adp or .ade) files. To secure access to the tables, views, stored procedures, and database diagrams in the SQL Server database that your .adp or .ade file is connected to, you must establish security for those objects on your server by using the SQL Server Enterprise Manager, the properties and methods of the **Group** and **User** objects in ADO code, the GRANT and REVOKE statements in Transact-SQL, or security management system stored procedures such as sp_addrole and sp_addrolemember. To secure access to the VBA code in an .adp file, you must password-protect its VBA project, or remove your VBA source code by saving your .adp file as an .ade file. To secure access to the design of forms and reports in an .adp file, you can either set startup options as described in "Using Startup Options" earlier in this chapter, or save your .adp file as an .ade file. The only way to secure access to macros in an Access project file is by setting startup options.

User-Level and Share-Level Security

Microsoft Jet provides both *share-level* and *user-level security*. In share-level security systems, passwords are associated with specific objects, not with users. Any user who knows the password for an object can access that object. Microsoft Jet provides a simple form of share-level security: the ability to password-protect the opening of a database. Add a password to your database when all you want to do is prevent unauthorized users from opening your solution and you're not concerned about what authorized users do once they're inside. For more information about using database passwords, see "Setting a Database Password" earlier in this chapter.

If you need more control, for example, to prevent users from modifying the design of your tables and queries, Microsoft Jet also provides user-level security. With user-level security, users are *authenticated* when they start Microsoft Jet, before any database is opened. (A user is authenticated by logging on to the system with a name and a password, which are compared to a database of user account information that is called a *workgroup information file* or *system database*.) After the user is authenticated, the system determines the user's level of access to a database and the objects it contains by comparing the user's identification to a set of object permissions that have been defined for that object by the solution's administrator. Different users can have different levels of permissions for the same objects.

Microsoft Jet user-level security functions as follows: Administrators assign specific permissions for a database and the objects it contains to users and groups. When a user starts up a session of the Jet database engine in a secure environment, the user logs on, entering a user name and password. The password's function is to authenticate the user, not to give access to any particular objects. Microsoft Jet then reads the current workgroup information file to determine all the groups the user belongs to, and stores that information internally. Every time the user tries to perform an action such as opening a database, browsing a table, or modifying a query, Microsoft Jet first checks to see if the user, or *any* of the groups to which the user belongs, has the necessary permissions to perform this action. If the user or groups the user belongs to have sufficient permissions, Microsoft Jet performs the action. If not, Microsoft Jet returns an error message indicating that permission is denied, and the operation fails.

Advantages of User-Level Security

To see the advantages of user-level security, consider this example: Suppose you have a Salary table and two groups of people who use that table—managers who can update the table and workers who can view, but not update, the table. In a user-level system such as one created with the Jet database engine, you can assign update permissions for the Salary table to the managers group and read permissions to the workers group. Then you add each user in your system into one of these two groups.

Once this is done, users log on with their user account name and password. They need perform no other action to use the solution. They are granted the appropriate level of access to objects on the basis of the permissions settings stored with each object, and their group membership as established when logging on to the system. The users manage their own passwords, and their passwords are used to verify their identity rather than to identify a permission for an object.

In a share-level system, two passwords would be required to implement this scheme: an update password and a read password, both applied directly to the Salary table. In this scenario, you would have to provide the passwords directly to the appropriate people. This becomes even more complicated if you have to change a password; you must have administrative mechanisms in place to make sure that all users get their appropriate updated passwords. Also, any time a user is moved from the managers group to the workers group, the password for the managers group must be changed to maintain security.

You can see that even in this simple scenario, the administrative overhead associated with share-level security can be substantial. When you imagine a real solution with many tables, users, and groups, you can quickly see that share-level security is a cumbersome solution.

Elements of the User-Level Security Model

To establish user-level security, the Jet database engine uses a set of elements that, taken as a whole, describe the model. The four elements that make up the model are:

- **The user of your solution** This may be a real person or a process running on a computer.
- **The group** A group is a collection of users who require the same level of access to a set of objects. Users can belong to more than one group.
- **The SystemDB or workgroup information file** This is a Microsoft Jet database that stores the definitions of users, groups, and passwords.
- **Your database** The database contains your solution's objects, along with the permissions settings for each object for each user and group.

Figure 18.1 illustrates how these elements relate.

Figure 18.1 The Microsoft Jet Security Model

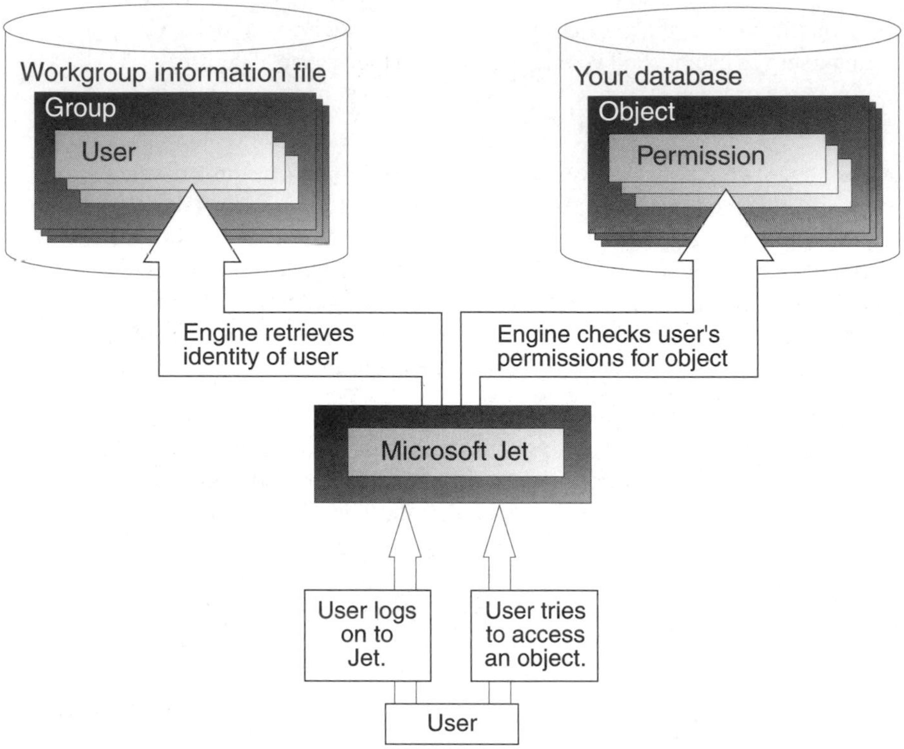

Workgroup information file
Group
User
Your database
Object
Permission
Engine retrieves identity of user
Engine checks user's permissions for object
Microsoft Jet
User logs on to Jet.
User tries to access an object.
User

Users and Groups

Microsoft Jet defines users of your solution in two ways: as individual users, or as groups of users.

Note Users and groups share the same namespace in Microsoft Jet: You can't have a user and group with the same name.

If you've never built or administered a user-level security system before, it's important to understand that there is no such thing as a permission on an object that exists by itself. Permissions on objects are always granted to specific users or predefined groups of users. That is, a permission exists only in the dual context of a user or group *and* the object it applies to.

The Security Identifier

After a user logs on, the Jet database engine uses a special number to identify that user. This number, called a *security identifier (SID)* is a machine-readable value that varies in length and will be 128 bytes at most. Microsoft Jet creates an SID when a user or group is created. When a user requests access to objects, Microsoft Jet uses the user's or group's SID for identification. The user's name and password are not used. The name and password are used only for authentication—the process of verifying a person's identity. From then on, Microsoft Jet uses the SID to determine a user's access to objects.

The Personal Identifier

To generate an SID, the Jet database engine uses a *personal identifier (PID)*. This value is a variable-length string that you specify when you create a user or group. The user or group name and PID are fed to the encryption program that generates the SID for that account. If you feed the same user name and PID back into the encryption program, you get the same SID. This gives you the ability to re-create user accounts if your workgroup information file (system database) becomes corrupted or is lost.

Figure 18.2 Creating Security Identifiers

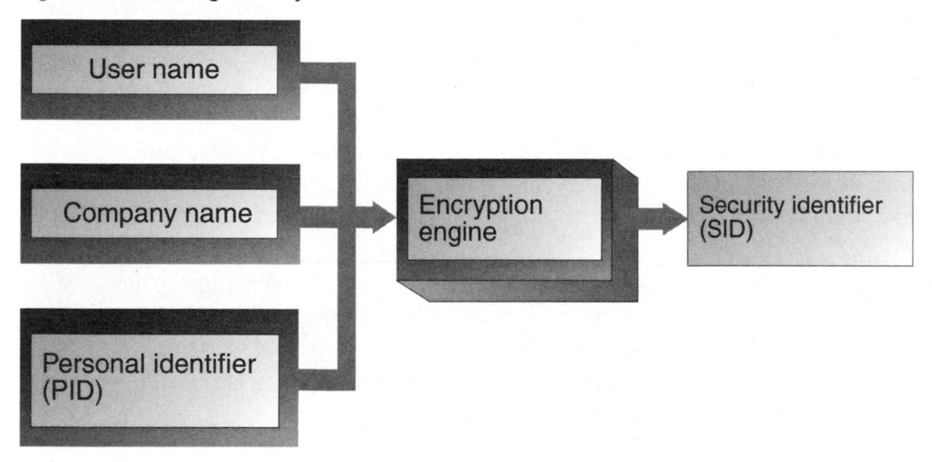

The Default User Account

Microsoft Jet defines a default user account named "Admin." Before user-level security is established, all users are implicitly logged on as the Admin user. Unfortunately, the Admin user is not very well named, as this user has no particular administrative characteristics. Because most users are logged on as Admin without ever knowing it, and because by default all users have permissions for the objects they create, any object owned by the Admin user or for which the Admin user has explicit permissions is unsecured. Think of the Admin user as the default User account or, for those familiar with Windows NT Server or Windows NT Workstation security, the Everybody account.

Understanding how the SIDs of these default accounts are generated helps you understand how the security model works. The Admin user's SID is identical across all installations of the Jet database engine. Even if no one in your workgroup is using the Admin account (because you have defined a password for it), all objects owned by Admin, or for which Admin has explicit permissions, are still open to anyone who is using Microsoft Jet. This is one of the most common misunderstandings regarding Microsoft Jet security. Fortunately, once you understand the problem, it's easily prevented: Make sure that Admin has no explicit permissions and owns no objects. The User-Level Security Wizard makes this easy.

Microsoft Jet also creates two accounts, Creator and Engine, that are used internally. These accounts are not accessible by users.

Default Groups

Microsoft Jet defines two default groups for you: the Admins group and the Users group.

The Admins Group

The Admins group is designed to hold user accounts for people who are the true administrators of the workgroup. They manage user and group membership and have the power to clear users' passwords. Members of the Admins group that was in use when you created the database always have permission to grant permissions on any object in that database. For example, if user Bob is a member of the Admins group, he may not have permissions to open a particular table, but he will be able to grant himself permission to open that table, even if he doesn't own the table. The Admins groups of other workgroup information files don't have this privilege. An Admins group should have at least one member at all times.

Caution Although Microsoft Jet allows you to delete the last member of the Admins group, this is not advised, because only the object's owner has irrevocable permissions for that object. If that owner's account ever becomes corrupted or deleted, and cannot be re-created because you don't have that user's name and PID, there is *no way* to recover the permissions for that object. In other words, there is no member of the Admins group to fall back on.

The SID of the Admins group is unique for each workgroup information file and is generated when the file is created. When you use the Workgroup Administrator or the User-Level Security Wizard to create the workgroup information file, this SID is generated by encrypting three strings that you enter: user name, organization name, and *workgroup ID (WID)*. When you install Access, a workgroup information file is created. The default name of this file is System.mdw. However, only the user's name and the company name (provided during installation) are used to generate the SID for the Admins group of the default workgroup information file. Therefore, you shouldn't use this default workgroup information file to secure your database, because these two names are available from the **About Microsoft Access** command on the **Help** menu.

If you use the default workgroup information file, unauthorized users trying to breach security could re-create an identical Admins account by using the Workgroup Administrator to create a new file with these values, and then adding themselves to the Admins group.

When establishing user-level security, use the Workgroup Administrator or the User-Level Security Wizard to create a new workgroup information file, making sure to enter a workgroup ID value that is known only to you. This ensures that the new workgroup information file contains an Admins group with a unique, secure SID. For information about using the User-Level Security Wizard, see "Running the User-Level Security Wizard" later in this chapter.

The Users Group

The Users Group is the default group for new users. By definition, all users of your database are members of the Users group. Any permissions assigned explicitly to the Users group are available to all users in all installations of Microsoft Jet. By default, the Users group has full permissions for all newly created objects. This is the main mechanism the Jet database engine uses to "hide" security for solutions that don't need it. Even though Microsoft Jet security is always "on," if you don't need its functionality and don't want your users to have to log on and worry about permissions, Microsoft Jet ensures that you don't have to worry about security by making all users members of the Users group and granting that group full permissions.

Ownership

Understanding the concept of ownership is crucial to understanding the Microsoft Jet security model. The user who creates an object *owns* that object. This ownership grants that user special privileges for that object; thus, he or she can always assign or revoke permissions for that object. This privilege cannot be revoked by any other user, including members of the Admins group.

Before you establish user-level security, the default Admin user is the owner of the database and all the objects in it. To effectively manage security, you need to change the ownership of the database and all the objects in it. You can do this for all objects except the database itself directly through ADO by using the **SetObjectOwner** method of the **Catalog** object, or in Access on the **Change Owner** tab in the **User And Group Permissions** dialog box (**Tools** menu, **Security** submenu). However, you can't change the owner of a database on the **Change Owner** tab in the same way. When you are using the Access user interface, the only way to transfer the ownership of all the objects and the database itself is to log on as the user that you want to own the database, create a new blank database, and then import all of the objects. However, when you run the User-Level Security Wizard to secure your database, it transfers ownership of the database and all of its objects by using code.

Note These procedures don't change the ownership of queries whose **RunPermissions** property is set to Owner's. You can change ownership of a query only if you own the query, or if its **RunPermissions** property is set to User's. For more information about the **RunPermissions** property, see "Using the Access RunPermissions Property with User-Level Security" later in this chapter.

The owner of the database itself is the user account in use when the database is created. The database owner can always open a database, create new objects in it, and grant or revoke permissions for objects in the database. The database owner can also grant or revoke the permission to open a database. A database owner's permissions for an object can be revoked by using the **User And Group Permissions** dialog box; however, the owner of the database always has the ability to reinstate his or her permissions on that object.

Important If you don't transfer database ownership to a secure user account, any users of Access or Visual Basic can open your database and grant themselves full permissions.

The Workgroup Information File

As mentioned earlier, **User** and **Group** objects and their passwords are not stored in your database. They are stored in a Microsoft Jet database known as the *workgroup information file*, which is also referred to as the *system database* (Figure 18.3). The default name of this database is System.mdw. Although it's structurally no different from the databases you create, it does contain several system tables that the engine uses to store security information. You can't make changes to the contents of those tables by opening a workgroup information file directly; the information stored in them is encrypted and protected. To define user accounts and security groups, you must use the **User** and **Group** objects in ADO code, or use the Access security user interface.

The workgroup information file stores information about each user and group in a workgroup. This information includes which users belong to which groups, encrypted passwords, and the SID for each user and group. When you use Microsoft Jet commands that affect user or group objects or their passwords, the engine reads and writes to the workgroup information file.

Figure 18.3 The Workgroup Information File

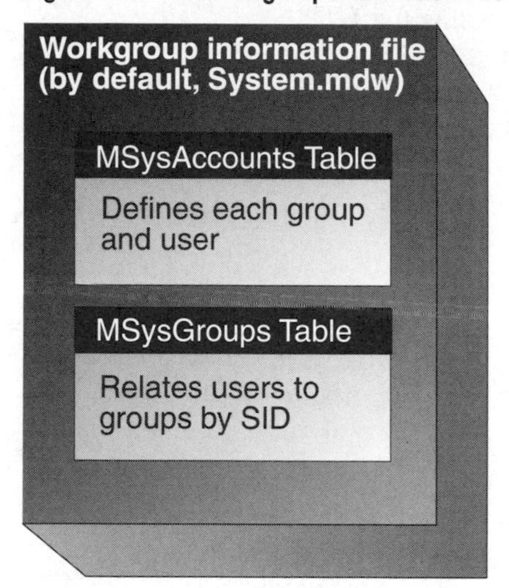

You can use the same workgroup information file for more than one database, in which case the user, group, and password information remains the same across the databases. When a user logs on to Microsoft Jet, the engine looks in the workgroup information file for the user's name and password in order to authenticate the user. From then on, Microsoft Jet uses only the SID that it found for that user.

Keep in mind that when you use the Workgroup Administrator to specify ("join") a workgroup information file, the Workgroup Administrator writes this information to the Windows registry, and that workgroup information file's user and group accounts are used by default until you (or your code) specify another workgroup information file. If you perform operations on other databases while that workgroup information file is current, you may see unexpected results. For this reason, you may want to create a separate workgroup information file for each database that you secure, and then have users open the secured database by using a Windows shortcut that specifies the correct workgroup information file with the Access **/wrkgrp** startup command-line option. For more information about how to do this, see "Access Startup Command-Line Options" later in this chapter. The User-Level Security wizard also provides the option of creating such a shortcut for you.

Note In versions of Microsoft Jet prior to 3.0, the initialization file (usually MSAccess.ini or MSAcc20.ini) is used to store the path and name of the workgroup information file. In Microsoft Jet versions 3.0, 3.5, and 4.0, the path and name of the workgroup information file are stored in the Windows registry. In all versions, the SystemDB registry entry is used to specify the path to the workgroup information file. In Access 2000, the path and name of the default workgroup information file is stored in the \HKEY_LOCAL_MACHINE\SOFTWARE\Microsoft\Office\9.0\Access\Jet\4.0\Engines subkey of the Windows registry.

You can set or return the path for the current location of the workgroup information file when you are opening a database from ADO code by using the **Jet OLEDB:System Database** provider-specific property of the Microsoft OLE DB provider for Jet in the ADO **Properties** collection of the **Connection** object. For example, the following code fragment specifies the path to the workgroup information file to use before opening an Access database in ADO code.

```
Dim cnnOpen As ADODB.Connection

Set cnnOpen = New ADODB.Connection

With cnnOpen
    .Provider = "Microsoft.Jet.OLEDB.4.0"
    .Properties("Jet OLEDB:System Database") = "c:\MyFolder\MySystem.mdw"
    .Open "c:\MyFolder\MyDatabase.mdb", "MyUser", "MyPassword"
End With
```

Opening a database by using the Access user interface automatically establishes an ADO **Connection** object for the current database. Typing the following line of code in the Immediate window in Access and pressing ENTER returns the path to the workgroup information file in use for the current database.

```
? CurrentProject.Connection.Properties("Jet OLEDB:System Database").Value
```

Similarly, the **DBEngine** property of the Access **Application** object will create an instance of DAO even if the DAO type library isn't referenced. This allows you to return the path to the workgroup information file for the current database to the Immediate window in Access by using the DAO **SystemDB** property as shown in the following line of code.

```
? Application.DBEngine.SystemDB
```

Note Once a database is opened, the **Jet OLEDB:System Database** and **SystemDB** properties become read-only. You can't change the path to the workgroup information file for the current database after it is opened.

Access Startup Command-Line Options

You can start Access with the following command-line options, which configure the security environment:

- **/user** *UserName*. Starts Microsoft Jet while using the specified user name.
- **/pwd** *Password*. Starts Microsoft Jet while using the specified password.
- **/profile** *UserProfile*. Starts Microsoft Jet while using the options in the specified Access user profile instead of the standard Windows registry entries that were created when you installed Microsoft Jet. This replaces **/ini**, which is used in previous versions of Microsoft Jet to specify an initialization file.

Access Startup Command-Line Options (*continued*)

- **/wrkgrp** *PathToWorkgroupInformationFile*. Starts Microsoft Jet while using the specified workgroup information file.

Note A user profile that you use to start Access from the command line is not the same thing as a user profile that's defined for logging on to the operating system. An Access user profile applies only to Access, and only when you start Access from the command line. A user profile defined for the operating system applies to every application on the system, and is used to maintain system data for individual users.

These startup command-line options are particularly useful when you are creating a Windows shortcut to open a secured database. For example, instead of using the Workgroup Administrator to specify a workgroup information file before opening a secured database, you can create a shortcut that uses the **/wrkgrp** option to specify the file when the database is opened.

Note that you must include the full path to the Access .exe file, as well as to the database. For example, the following command line starts Access and opens the Northwind sample database by using the MySystem.mdw workgroup information file:

"C:\Program Files\Microsoft Office\Office\MSAccess.exe" "C:\Program Files\Microsoft Office\Office\Samples\Northwind.mdb" /wrkgrp "C:\Windows\System\MySystem.mdw"

The Secured Database

The final element of Microsoft Jet security is your database. This is where the objects that have to be secure are stored. The actual permissions related to specific objects for specific users and groups are stored in system tables in your database. However, the definitions of user or group accounts themselves are not stored here. This information is stored in the workgroup information file.

For example, when a user requests access to an object, Microsoft Jet already has retrieved the SIDs for the user and any groups to which he or she belongs from the workgroup information file when the user logged on. These SIDs are then compared to the SIDs in your database's system tables to verify that the user has sufficient permissions to access the object.

Permissions

Microsoft Jet defines a set of permissions that give you fine control over a user's access to an object. For example, you can allow a user to read an object's contents, but not to change them.

Microsoft Jet supports both *explicit* and *implicit* permissions. Explicit permissions are those you explicitly grant to an individual user. When an explicit permission is granted to a user, no other users are affected. Implicit permissions, on the other hand, are granted to a group. Because a group contains more than one user, all users in a group receive the permissions granted to the group. If a user is added to a group, that user automatically inherits all the implicit permissions of that group. Microsoft Jet uses the least restrictive set of permissions among the permissions granted to a user and all groups to which that user belongs. For example, if a user has explicit read permission for a table but no write permission, and that same user also belongs to a group that has write permission for the table, the user will be able to write to the table because of the higher level of the implicit write permission.

In nearly all cases, the permissions in user-level security will be much easier to manage if you use the following strategy:

1. Revoke all permissions on all objects for the default Users group and remove the default Admin user from the Admins group.
2. Create the appropriate groups for the different levels of access you want to provide to users.
3. Don't assign permissions to individual users; assign permissions only to groups.
4. Assign each user to the appropriate group for the level of access you want the user to have.

You can use the User-Level Security Wizard to perform all of these steps and more for you. For information about how to run the wizard, see "Running the User-Level Security Wizard" later in this chapter.

Microsoft Jet allows you to set permissions on all of the objects in the database except for modules and the links to data access pages. Access provides no form of security for data access page links other than control over who can open a database, but you can password-protect all of the modules stored in a database by locking the VBA project. The Jet database engine also allows you to set permissions for new objects; that is, you can set permissions that will be inherited by any new object of a given type that is created after user-level security is established. You can also set permissions on the database itself to control who can open the database, who can open the database for exclusive access, and who can administer the database. The following table summarizes the permissions you can set as they are identified in the **User and Group Permissions** dialog box.

Permission	Permits a user to	Applies to
Open/Run	Open a database, form, or report, or run a macro	Databases, forms, reports, and macros
Open Exclusive	Open a database with exclusive access	Databases
Read Design	View objects in Design view	Tables, queries, forms, reports, and macros
Modify Design	View and change the design of objects, or delete them	Tables, queries, forms, reports, and macros
Administer	For databases, set database password, replicate a database, and change startup properties For database objects, have full access to objects and data, including ability to assign permissions	Databases, tables, queries, forms, reports, and macros
Read Data	View data	Tables and queries
Update Data	View and modify but not insert or delete data	Tables and queries
Insert Data	View and insert but not modify or delete data	Tables and queries
Delete Data	View and delete but not modify or insert data	Tables and queries

Note Some permissions automatically imply the selection of others, which is reflected when you select a permission in the **User and Group Permissions** dialog box. For example, if you select the Update Data permission for a table, the Read Data and Read Design permissions are automatically selected because you also need these permissions in order to modify the data in a table.

For information about setting permissions by using VBA code, see "Using VBA Code to Work with User-Level Security" later in this chapter.

Securing Your Database with Access

It's important to realize that Microsoft Jet security is always enabled—every time a user performs any action, Microsoft Jet first checks to make sure the user has sufficient permissions to perform that action. However, most Microsoft Jet users never realize that they are logging on and never see a security-related message. How does this happen? This is because the Users group (the default group that contains the default Admin user account) has full permissions for all objects in a database.

This arrangement works well because there are no "back doors" that allow a user to open a Microsoft Jet database without security being in effect. Solutions that don't need the engine's security services still use it, even though it's not apparent.

To establish security successfully, you need to do some advance planning. Make a list of all types of potential users of your solutions, logical groupings of those users, and the operations that each group should be able to perform. Then map this information to the Microsoft Jet security model of users, groups, and object permissions.

Securing your database is a multiple-step process that replaces the default users and groups with your own secure set of users and groups. In Access 2000, the User-Level Security Wizard has been significantly updated to step you through the entire process of securing your Access database. This section outlines each of these steps.

Using Access as a Security Tool

If you're building Microsoft Jet solutions by using a program other than Access (such as Visual Basic or Microsoft Excel), you can secure your solutions by using ADO or DAO. These interfaces give you much of the same functionality that exists in Access. However, to create a secure environment, you must build workgroup information files with the Workgroup Administrator program or the User-Level Security Wizard (**Tools** menu, **Security** submenu, **User-Level Security Wizard** command). These utilities ship only with Access. Because of this, you must use Access to set up the initial elements of a secured system. Although you have full programmatic access to existing security through ADO or DAO, it's often easier to use Access to develop and maintain security in your solution.

Running the User-Level Security Wizard

In previous versions of Access, if you want to fully secure your Access database, you are required to perform a number of steps both before and after running the User-Level Security Wizard. In Access 2000, the new User-Level Security Wizard performs all of these steps for you, and can even be run again on a secured database to modify previous settings. The User-Level Security Wizard performs the following steps to secure your Access database:

1. Creates a new secure workgroup information file by using a secure workgroup ID (WID). You can also choose to use and modify the current workgroup information file created previously by running the User-Level Security Wizard or the Workgroup Administrator. You can choose to make the workgroup information file the default one for the current installation of Access, or the wizard can create a Windows shortcut that uses the **\wrkgrp** startup command-line option to open your secured database by using the workgroup information file.
2. Secures all selected database objects, and sets the permissions that will be assigned to any new objects that users create after running the wizard.
3. Secures the database's VBA project to protect access to all code modules (standalone modules, the modules behind forms and reports, and class modules) by setting a password. If the database's VBA project has been password-protected before running the wizard, you must provide the correct password or the wizard won't be able to secure your code modules.

4. Creates up to seven new predefined group accounts for the following typical user roles: Backup Operators, Full Data Users, Full Permissions, New Data Users, Project Designers, Read-Only Users, and Update Data Users. For more information about the permissions assigned to these predefined groups, see “Assigning Permissions to Users and Groups” later in this chapter.
5. By default, removes permissions on all objects for the default Users group. Optionally, you can grant permissions to the Users group for some objects. This is useful for developers of add-ins and other developers who don’t want to require users to log on to the database and only want to secure certain objects.
6. Creates and adds new user accounts to the workgroup information file, and allows you to assign passwords for each new user. If you choose to create a new workgroup information file by using the first dialog box of the wizard, a new user account is created for you.
7. Assigns users to the default Admins group account, or to the selected predefined group accounts. At least one new user account must be assigned to the Admins group account to serve as the database administrator account, because the wizard will remove the default Admin user from the Admins group to fully secure the database. By default, the new user account created for you in the previous step is assigned to the default Admins group as the new database administrator account.
8. Creates a backup copy of the current database, and secures the current database in place. The objects you selected are secured by revoking all permissions on those objects for the default Users group. Ownership of the database and all objects in it is transferred to the new database administrator account. Finally, the secured database is encrypted. The secured database will have the same name as before, and the backup copy of the database will be named *OriginalDatabaseName*.bak.
9. Formats a report that documents the values used to create the new workgroup information file and user accounts. You should print this report and keep it in a secure location in the event you need to use these values to re-create the workgroup information file if it becomes corrupted. This report also documents which objects have been secured.

▶ To secure your solution with the Access User-Level Security Wizard

1. Open the database you want to secure.
2. On the **Tools** menu, point to **Security**, and then click **User-Level Security Wizard**.
3. Follow the directions in the wizard dialog boxes.

If you log on as a member of the Admins group, you can run the User-Level Security Wizard again on the new, secured database to create new users, modify permissions, and to assign users to groups.

Assigning Permissions to Users and Groups

The User-Level Security Wizard provides the option to create up to seven predefined groups in addition to the default Admins and Users groups. These groups cover many of the typical roles required to manage a secured database. The following table describes each of the groups you can create by using the User-Level Security Wizard and the set of permissions assigned to each group for each object type.

Group name	Description	Database permissions	Table permissions (including new tables)	Query permissions (including new queries)	Form, report, and macro permissions
Full Permissions	Has full permissions on all database objects but cannot assign permissions to other users	Open/Run Open Exclusive	All except Administer	All except Administer	All except Administer
Project Designers	Has full permissions to edit data and all objects, but can't alter the tables or relationships	Open/Run Open Exclusive	Read Design Read Data Update Data Insert Data Delete Data	Read Design Read Data Update Data Insert Data Delete Data Modify Design	Open/Run Read Design Modify Design
Full Data Users	Has full permissions to edit data, but can't alter the design of any database objects	Open/Run Open Exclusive	Read Design Read Data Update Data Insert Data Delete Data	Read Design Read Data Update Data Insert Data Delete Data	Open/Run
Read-Only Users	Can read all data, but can't alter the design of any database objects	Open/Run	Read Design Read Data	Read Design Read Data	Open/Run
Update Data Users	Can read and update data, but can't alter the design of any database objects, or insert or delete data	Open/Run	Read Design Read Data Update Data	Read Design Read Data Update Data	Open/Run

Group name	Description	Database permissions	Table permissions (including new tables)	Query permissions (including new queries)	Form, report, and macro permissions
New Data Users	Can read and insert data, but can't alter the design of any database object, or delete or update data	Open/Run	Read Design Read Data Insert Data	Read Design Read Data Insert Data	Open/Run
Backup Operators	Can open the database exclusively for backup and compacting, but can't see any database objects	Open/Run Open Exclusive	None	None	None

If you want to create additional groups or accounts for new users, you can do so by using the **User And Group Accounts** dialog box, available from the **Security** submenu on the **Tools** menu. If you selected only some of the predefined groups when you originally ran the User-Level Security Wizard, and find that you want to use additional predefined groups, you can run the wizard again to add them. You can also run the wizard again to add new users and to assign them to the appropriate groups. Keep in mind that the user and group accounts created when you run the wizard are stored either in the workgroup information file created by the wizard, or in the file that was being used when you started the wizard (if you chose to modify it). Before running the wizard again or using the **User And Group Accounts** dialog box, be sure to specify the correct workgroup information file when you log on.

As mentioned earlier, it's best to assign permissions to groups rather than to individual users. This way, administering your workgroup becomes simply a matter of assigning users to the appropriate groups. If you use the predefined groups provided by the User-Level Security Wizard, you can assign permissions to any new users by running the wizard again or by using the **User And Group Accounts** dialog box to assign new users to the appropriate groups.

If you find that you need to change the set of permissions for any of the predefined groups, or to assign permissions for any groups you created yourself, use the **User And Group Permissions** dialog box (**Tools** menu, **Security** submenu).

Securing a Front-End/Back-End Solution

There are additional factors to take into account when establishing user-level security for a solution that has been split into a back-end database that contains only tables, and a front-end database that contains the remaining objects plus links to the tables in the back-end database. You may not know the name of the specific network location for the back-end database in advance, or you may want to allow a database administrator to move the back-end database. In either situation, users must be able to relink the tables in the back-end database.

▶ To establish user-level security for a front-end/back-end solution

1. For both databases, follow the procedure described earlier in this section for establishing security with the User-Level Security Wizard.
2. Assign users to the appropriate groups so that they have permissions to read, update, insert, or delete data in tables in the back-end database, or remove all permissions for those tables and create queries in the front-end database that have the **RunPermissions** property set to Owner's, and that use the tables in the back-end database. All users must be assigned to groups that have Open/Run permission for the **Database** object in the back-end database. This is true for all predefined groups created with the User-Level Security Wizard. This is required even if you are using queries with the **RunPermissions** property set to Owner's.

   For more information about the **RunPermissions** property, see "Using the Access RunPermissions Property with User-Level Security" later in this chapter.
3. In the front-end database, grant users Modify Design permission for the table links. (Doing so does *not* grant them the same rights to the tables in the back-end database.)
4. When the users first install your solution, have them run the Linked Table Manager (**Tools** menu, **Add-ins** submenu) from the front-end database to refresh the links to the tables in the back-end database in its new location.

   Tip You can also write code that prompts users during startup to refresh table links. For sample code that refreshes table links, see "Refreshing Links for Linked Tables" in Chapter 14, "Working with the Data Access Components of an Office Solution."

Because users have Modify Design permission for the linked tables in the front-end database, they can reset the links to the back-end tables if the location of the back-end database changes. They can't make any modifications to the design of the actual tables in the back-end database.

Removing Security from a Database

Securing a database is usually a one-way process. However, certain development issues might require you to work with an unsecured copy. You can follow these steps to reverse the process of securing your database.

▶ To remove security from a database

1. Make a backup copy of the database you want to remove security from.
2. Start Access and log on as a member of the Admins group. This can be the administrator account you created when you secured the database, or any member of the Admins group. Be sure you're using your own secure workgroup information file when starting Access.
3. Open the database.
4. On the **Tools** menu, point to **Security**, and then click **User And Group Permissions**.
5. In the **User And Group Permissions** dialog box, assign full permissions to the Users group for the database and all the objects in the database.

   Because all users are automatically part of the Users group in Microsoft Jet, this step has the effect of rendering security "invisible" again.
6. On the **Tools** menu, point to **Security**, and then click **User And Group Accounts**. On the **Users** tab, click **Admin** in the **Name** box, and then click **Clear Password**.

   Clearing the password for the Admin user disables the **Logon** dialog box that displays when you start Access. You and your users will be automatically logged on as the Admin user the next time you or they start Access.

   Important This step disables the **Logon** dialog box for all databases that are using the same workgroup information file.
7. Restart Access.
8. Create a new database and import all objects from the secured database. You can accomplish this easily by using the **Import** command (**File** menu, **Get External Data** submenu).

The new database you created in step 8 is now an unsecured version of the original. As always, Microsoft Jet security is still active, but once again, it's transparent.

Securing Your Database Without Asking Users to Log On

If you want to secure some objects in a database but you don't need to grant various permissions to different groups of users, you might want to consider securing your solution without asking users to log on. You can do this by running the User-Level Security Wizard and granting the permissions you want available for all users to the Users group as described in the following procedure.

▶ To secure your solution without asking users to log on

1. Open the database you want to secure.
2. On the Tools menu, point to Security, and then click User-Level Security Wizard.
3. Follow the directions in the wizard dialog boxes up to the sixth dialog box. In the sixth dialog box, click Yes, I would like to grant some permissions to the Users group. Assign the permissions to the Users group for objects you want to be available to all users. Typical permissions may include Read Data and Update Data permissions for tables and queries, and Open/Run permission for forms and reports. Don't give the Users group the permission to modify the design of tables and queries, or Administer permission for the database.
4. Complete the remaining dialog boxes to secure the database.
5. Distribute the database to users who are using the default workgroup information file that is created when Access is installed, or another file that doesn't have the default Admin user's password set so that the Logon dialog box won't be displayed when users start Access.

Users can now open your database without logging on—that is, they are automatically logged on as the Admin user. They will be able to perform all actions you gave the Users group permission to perform in step 3, but the User-Level Security Wizard will have removed the Admin user from the Admins group, so users won't have any administrative permissions. This works for any workgroup because the Users group is the same in every workgroup information file. Even if a user logs on as a member of the Admins group of some other workgroup information file, that user will be able to perform only actions granted to the Users group, because the SID of the Admins group is unique to each workgroup information file. Only members of the Admins group of the workgroup information file that was in use when you ran the User-Level Security Wizard have full permissions on the objects in your database. To perform administrative functions, you must use the workgroup information file that was in use when you secured the database, and you must log on as one of the members of that file's Admins group.

Important Do not distribute copies of the workgroup information file that was in use when you secured the database in this procedure. If you need to allow a user to administer your database, give a copy of the workgroup information file to that user only.

Using the Access RunPermissions Property with User-Level Security

In order for Access to display a table or query, it needs to read the design of that table or query. For example, it needs to read field names and other field properties, such as the **Format** and **InputMask** properties. As a result, in order for a user to read and display the data in a table or query, that user must also have permission to read the design of the table or query. (This is why selecting the **Read Data** permission check box in the **User And Group Permissions** dialog box automatically selects the **Read Design** check box as well.) If you don't want your users to see the design of your table or query, you can create a query and set its **RunPermissions** property to restrict their access to this information.

The **RunPermissions** property determines whether Access uses the query user's permissions or the query owner's permissions when checking the user-level security permissions for each of the underlying tables in a query. If the **RunPermissions** property is set to User's, the users of a query have only their own permissions to view data in underlying tables. However, if the owner of a query sets the **RunPermissions** property to Owner's, anyone who uses that query will have the same level of permissions to view data in the underlying tables as the query's owner.

By using the **RunPermissions** property, you can create queries to display data to users who don't have permission to access the underlying tables. You can build different views of your data, which will provide record-level and field-level security for a table. For example, suppose you have a secure database with an Employees table and a Salary table. By using the **RunPermissions** property, you can build several views of the two tables: one that allows a user or group to view but not update the Salary field, a second that allows a different user or group to view and update the Salary field, and a third that allows another user or group to view the Salary field only for a certain category of employees.

▶ To prevent users from viewing the design of underlying tables or queries

1. For the users or groups whose access you want to restrict, remove all permissions for the tables or queries whose design you want to secure.
2. Build a new query that includes all the fields you want to include from those tables or queries. You can exclude access to a field by omitting that field. You can also limit access to a certain range of values by defining criteria for your query.
3. In the query's property sheet, set the **RunPermissions** property of the new query to Owner's.

4 Grant appropriate data permissions for the new query to the users and groups that you want to be able to update data, but not to view the design of the underlying table or query. Such permissions typically include Read Design, Read Data, Update Data, Delete Data, and Insert Data.

Tip You can base forms and reports on the new query.

Users can update data in the underlying tables or queries by using the new query or forms based on it. However, they won't be able to view the design of the underlying tables or queries. If they try to view the design of the new query, they receive a message that they don't have permissions to view the source tables or queries.

Important By default, the user who creates a query is its owner, and only the owner of a query can save changes to it if the **RunPermissions** property is set to Owner's. Even members of the Admins group or users with Administer permission are prevented from saving changes to a query created by another user if the **RunPermissions** property is set to Owner's. However, anyone with Modify Design permission for the query can set the **RunPermissions** property to User's and then successfully save changes to the query.

Because the creator of a query owns it by default, having the **RunPermissions** property set to Owner's can create problems if you need to allow more than one user to work with the design of a query. To correct this, ownership of the query can be transferred to a group. To do this, create a group, change the owner of the query to this group on the **Change Owner** tab of the **User And Group Permissions** dialog box, and then add the users who need to modify the query to the new group. Any member of the new group will be able to edit the query and save changes.

Similarly, if a user is otherwise prevented from creating or adding to a table, you can create a make-table or append query and set its **RunPermissions** property to Owner's.

You can also set the **RunPermissions** property for a query in SQL view or in code by using the WITH OWNERACCESS OPTION declaration in an SQL statement. For example, suppose that a user doesn't have permission to view the payroll information in your application. You can create a query like the following example that uses WITH OWNERACCESS OPTION to allow the user to view this information:

```
SELECT LastName, FirstName, Salary
FROM Employees
ORDER BY LastName
WITH OWNERACCESS OPTION;
```

Just as when you use the Access **RunPermissions** property, you can't change the owner of a query created by using the WITH OWNERACCESS OPTION declaration. If you need to do this, you must remove the WITH OWNERACCESS OPTION declaration, change the owner, and then change it back to a query created by using the WITH OWNERACCESS OPTION declaration. Note that only the owner of such a query can save design changes to that query. If you have several developers who need to modify this type of query, assign those developers to a group, and then make the group the owner of the query, by using the steps previously described.

Using VBA Code to Work with User-Level Security

There are three ways to work with user-level security from VBA code in Access databases (.mdb):

- By using the Microsoft ADO Extensions 2.1 for DDL and Security object library
- By using the Microsoft DAO 3.6 object library
- By using Microsoft Jet 4.0 SQL commands, such as CREATE USER, CREATE GROUP, ADD USER, GRANT, and REVOKE

This section provides examples of how to use ADO to work with user-level security. For information about how to use DAO to work with user-level security, search the DAO Reference Help for information about the **Groups** and **Users** collections and the **Permissions** property, or see Chapter 10, "Managing Security" in the *Microsoft Jet Database Engine Programmer's Guide, Second Edition* (Microsoft Press, 1997). You can use the new Microsoft Jet 4.0 SQL commands either from ADO by using the **Execute** method of the **Connection** object, or from DAO by using the **Execute** method of the **Database** object. For information about the Microsoft Jet 4.0 SQL commands and syntax, see the Microsoft Jet SQL Reference Help (C:\Program Files\Microsoft Office\Office\1033\Jetsql40.chm).

Note DAO code that is based on the DAO 3.5 object library will run in Access 2000 if you establish a reference to the new DAO 3.6 object library. For this reason, DAO security code written in previous versions of Access will continue to run correctly after you convert or enable a database to work in Access 2000, and you can write DAO code to work with security in new Access databases after establishing a reference to the DAO 3.6 object library. However, you should be aware that DAO will allow you to get and set permissions on modules in an Access 2000 database. For example, `Set doc = dbs.Containers("Modules") _ .Documents("Module1")` will establish a reference to the Module1 module, and you can get and set permissions on it. But Access 2000 no longer stores modules in the Microsoft Jet Modules **Container** object, and the Jet database engine will ignore any permissions set on modules. To properly secure all modules in an Access 2000 database, you should lock the database's VBA project.

Caution Although the Access user interface may warn you if you are changing security in a way that might lock you out of your database, Microsoft Jet does not. To avoid causing irreparable damage to your database, use caution when making programmatic changes to security. Be especially careful when making changes to permissions for the Admins group or when removing user accounts from the Admins group. Make a backup copy of the database first.

The ADOX Object Model

The ADOX object model extends ADO to include objects for creating, modifying, and deleting database objects such as tables and stored queries. It also includes security objects to maintain users and groups and to grant and revoke permissions on database objects. To use ADOX, you must set a reference to the Microsoft ADO Ext. 2.1 for DDL and Security object library.

To work with security in previous versions of Access, you must use the DAO **Users** and **Groups** collections of the **Workspace** object to create and manage security user accounts, and then use the **Permissions** property of a **Document** object to set a user's or group's permissions on a database object. To use the ADOX object model to work with user-level security, you use the **Users** and **Groups** collections of an open **Catalog** object to create and manage security user accounts, and use the **GetPermissions** and **SetPermissions** methods of the **User** and **Group** objects to set permissions on database objects.

Managing Security Accounts

The **Users** collection of a **Catalog** object contains all users defined for the workgroup information file specified for the **Connection** object that is used to open the **Catalog** object. Similarly, the **Groups** collection contains all groups in that workgroup information file. By manipulating these collections, you define and control the security accounts that Microsoft Jet uses. The **Groups** and **Users** collections are interesting in that they are self-referencing—the **Users** collection contains a **Groups** collection, and the **Groups** collection contains a **Users** collection. By using this structure, you can easily determine which users belong to which groups, and which groups contain which users.

There are a few things to keep in mind when you're working with users and groups:

- To add a new user or group, you first create the user or group by passing a string for the **Name** property for the user or group you want to create to the **Append** method of the **Users** or **Groups** collection. (You can also create a **User** or **Group** object, set its **Name** property, and then pass the object itself to the **Append** method.)

Warning The ADOX **User** and **Group** objects do not use a personal ID (PID) string to create the security ID (SID) for a user or group. This means that there is no way to reliably re-create an identical user or group account if the workgroup information file is deleted or becomes corrupted. To create a user or group account from code by using a PID, you should use the DAO **CreateUser** or **CreateGroup** method instead. For more information about Microsoft Jet SIDs, see "Users and Groups" earlier in this chapter.

After you've created a new **User** object, you must also add the new user to one or more groups. Similarly, after you've created a new **Group** object, you must add users to that group. Because each **User** object has its own **Groups** collection, and each **Group** object has its own **Users** collection, you can work with either collection. You can add a user to a group by appending the user's name to the **Users** collection of that group, or you can "add a group to a user" by appending the name of the group to the **Groups** collection for that user.

- When you use the Access user interface to add a new user, that user is automatically added to the default Users group. However, if you add a user programmatically, you must explicitly add the user to the Users group. That is, you must append the new user's name to the **Users** collection of the default Users group, or append the name of the default Users group ("Users") to the **Groups** collection of the new **User** object.
- If you're using ADOX to manipulate users and groups in an application other than Access, you must set the **Jet OLEDB:System Database** property in the **Properties** collection of the ADO **Connection** object to the path and file name of the workgroup information file you want to work with before opening the database. (Or pass the **Jet OLEDB:System Database** property in the **ConnectionString** property when you use the **Open** method of the **Connection** object.) Otherwise, Microsoft Jet will not know which workgroup information file you want to update. In Access, you can work with the connection to the current database by using the **Connection** property of the **CurrentProject** object. The **Connection** property of the **CurrentProject** object returns the connection string used to open the current database. The string includes the **Jet OLEDB:System Database** property, which is set to the workgroup information file that is active when the database is opened. Just as when you are working with ADO from other Office applications, you can also explicitly open a separate **Connection** to another database and specify the workgroup information file when doing so.

The following examples illustrate how to create and manage user accounts. These examples are available in the modSecurity module in AccessSecurity.mdb in the Samples\CH18 subfolder on the companion CD-ROM.

The following procedure is designed to be used within Access after logging on and opening a database. It creates a new user account, and then appends it to the default Users group in the workgroup information file that is used for the current database.

```
Sub CreateUserInAccess(strUser As String, _
                       Optional strPwd As String)
   Dim catDB As ADOX.Catalog

   Set catDB = New ADOX.Catalog
   With catDB
      ' Open Catalog object by using connection to the current database.
      .ActiveConnection = CurrentProject.Connection
      ' Create new user account.
      .Users.Append strUser, strPwd
```

```
        ' Append new user account to default Users group.
        .Groups("Users").Users.Append strUser
    End With

    ' Close Catalog object.
    Set catDB = Nothing
End Sub
```

The next procedure creates a new user by opening another database while using the specified workgroup information file (system database), and logging in by using the specified user account and password. This procedure can be used from Access or any other Office application that supports VBA.

```
Sub CreateUserInSystemDB(strDB As String, _
                         strSystemDb As String, _
                         strUserID As String, _
                         strUserIDPwd As String, _
                         strNewUser As String, _
                         Optional strNewUserPwd As String)
    Dim catDB As ADOX.Catalog
    Dim cnnDB As ADODB.Connection

    ' Open connection to database by using specified system database, user ID,
    ' and password.
    Set cnnDB = New ADODB.Connection
    With cnnDB
        .Provider = "Microsoft.Jet.OLEDB.4.0"
        .Properties("Jet OLEDB:System Database") = strSystemDb
        .Properties("User ID") = strUserID
        .Properties("Password") = strUserIDPwd
        .Open strDB
    End With

    Set catDB = New ADOX.Catalog
    With catDB
        ' Open Catalog object by using cnnDB.
        .ActiveConnection = cnnDB
        ' Create new user account.
        .Users.Append strNewUser, strNewUserPwd
        ' Append new user account to default Users group.
        .Groups("Users").Users.Append "MyUser"
    End With

    ' Close Catalog object.
    Set catDB = Nothing
    ' Close connection.
    cnnDB.Close
    Set cnnDB = Nothing
End Sub
```

The process of creating a new group is nearly identical to the one used to create a new user. The following procedure creates a new group from within Access after you log on and open a database. To create a new group for a database other than the current database, or from another Office application, open a connection to that database as shown in the previous example and pass this connection to the **ActiveConnection** property of the **Catalog** object.

```
Sub CreateGroupInAccess(strGroup As String)
   Dim catDB As ADOX.Catalog

   Set catDB = New ADOX.Catalog
   With catDB
      ' Open Catalog object by using connection to the current database.
      .ActiveConnection = CurrentProject.Connection
      ' Create new group.
      .Groups.Append strGroup
   End With
   ' Close Catalog object.
   Set catDB = Nothing
End Sub
```

To add a new user account to an existing group, simply append that user's name to the **Users** collection of that group. The following procedure is designed to add a new user account to a group from within the current Access database.

```
Sub AddUserToGroupInAccess(strUser As String, _
                           strGroup As String)
   Dim catDB As ADOX.Catalog

   Set catDB = New ADOX.Catalog
   With catDB
      ' Open Catalog object by using connection to the current database.
      .ActiveConnection = CurrentProject.Connection
      ' Add strUser to strGroup.
      .Groups(strGroup).Users.Append strUser
   End With
   ' Close Catalog object.
   Set catDB = Nothing
End Sub
```

To delete a user or group account, use the **Delete** method of the **Users** or **Groups** collection. The following example deletes a user account from within the current Access database.

```
Sub DeleteUserInAccess(strUser As String)
   Dim catDB As ADOX.Catalog

   Set catDB = New ADOX.Catalog
   With catDB
      ' Open Catalog object by using connection to the current database.
      .ActiveConnection = CurrentProject.Connection
      ' Delete strUser.
      .Users.Delete strUser
   End With
   ' Close Catalog object.
   Set catDB - Nothing
End Sub
```

Keep the following additional points in mind when you are working with **User** and **Group** objects:

- If a user or group account is deleted from the workgroup information file, any object that has specific permissions for that user or group retains those permissions; that is, those permissions are still stored with that object in the database. If that user or group is re-created by using the same user name and PID, those permissions will become active again. For this reason, you should delete a user's or group's permissions before deleting the account.
- Not everyone has permissions to view user and group information. Generally, it's best to be logged on as an administrator account—that is, as a user who is a member of the Admins group—before attempting to retrieve this information. This is also true if you want to modify security settings: You must be logged on as a user with sufficient permissions.

Setting and Reading Permissions

To set and read permissions in Access databases by using ADOX, you use the **SetPermissions** and **GetPermissions** methods. The following sections provide an introduction on how to use these methods.

Setting Permissions

To set permissions on an object by using ADOX, you use the **SetPermissions** method of the group or user you want to grant or revoke permissions for. As mentioned previously, user-level security will be much easier to manage if you set permissions only for groups, and then assign users to the appropriate groups. However, the **SetPermissions** method can be used for users as well as groups.

The syntax for the **SetPermissions** method has the following format:

GroupOrUser.**SetPermissions(***Name***,** *ObjectType***,** *Action***,** *Rights*[**,** *Inherit*][**,** *ObjectTypeID*])

The *Name* argument is a **Variant** value specifying the name of the object to set permissions for. If you want to set permissions for all objects of the specified type, set the *Name* argument to **Null**, and set the optional *Inherit* argument as specified later in this section. If you want to set permissions for the database itself, set the *Name* argument to **Null**, and set the *ObjectType* argument to **adPermObjDatabase**. The *ObjectType* argument is a **Long** value specifying the type of object you are setting permissions for. For Access databases, the *ObjectType* argument can be specified by using the following constants.

Constant	Description
adPermObjProviderSpecific	Object is of a provider-defined type. This constant is required to set permissions for Access forms, reports, and macros. If you use this constant, you must also set the *ObjectTypeID* argument to the appropriate globally unique identifier (GUID), as shown later in this section. An error will occur if the *ObjectType* argument is **adPermObjProviderSpecific** and an *ObjectTypeID* argument value is not supplied.
adPermObjTable	Object is a table.
adPermObjDatabase	Object is a database.
adPermObjView	Object is a query that returns records, such as a select query.
adPermObjProcedure	Object is a query that does not return records, such as an action query.

The *Action* argument is a **Long** value specifying the type of action to perform when setting permissions. For Access databases, the *Action* argument can be specified only when you are using the **adAccessSet** constant. The **adAccessSet** constant specifies that the group or user will have exactly the requested permissions.

The *Rights* argument is a **Long** value containing a bitmask indicating the permissions to set. The *Rights* argument can consist of a single constant or, if you want to set several permissions at once, you can use the **Or** operator to combine the constants for the permissions you want to set. For Access databases, you can specify the *Rights* argument by using the constants in the following table.

Constant	Description
adRightExecute	The group or user has permission to execute the object.
adRightExclusive	The group or user has permission to open the object exclusively.
adRightRead	The group or user has permission to read records.
adRightUpdate	The group or user has permission to update (modify) records.
adRightInsert	The group or user has permission to insert (add) new records.
adRightDelete	The group or user has permission to delete records.
adRightDrop	The group or user has permission to drop (delete) the object.
adRightReference	The group or user has permission to reference the object.
adRightCreate	The group or user has permission to create the object.

Constant	Description
adRightWithGrant	The group or user has permission to grant permissions on the object.
adRightReadDesign	The group or user has permission to read the design of the object.
adRightReadPermissions	The group or user has permission to read permissions on the object.
adRightWriteDesign	The group or user has permission to change the design of the object.
adRightWriteOwner	The group or user has permission to change the owner of the object.
adRightWritePermissions	The group or user has permission to change permissions on the object.
adRightNone	The group or user has no permissions on the object.
adRightMaximumAllowed	The group or user has the maximum allowed permissions on the object. (For Access databases, use the **adRightFull** constant instead.)
adRightFull	The group or user has all permissions on the object.

The *Inherit* argument is an optional **Long** value that is used if you set the *Name* argument to **Null** to determine how permissions will be applied to new objects of the type specified by the *ObjectType* argument. Setting the *Inherit* argument will not affect existing objects of the specified type; only new objects created after setting the *Inherit* argument will be affected. For Access databases (.mdb), you can specify the *Inherit* argument by using the constants in the following table.

Constant	Description
adInheritNone	Permissions will not be inherited by new objects. (Default)
adInheritObjects	Permissions will be inherited by new objects of the type specified in the *ObjectType* argument. Use this setting to set permissions on new objects.
adInheritContainers	This setting doesn't apply to Access databases. However, if you use it, it will have the same effect as using **adInheritObject** because the Microsoft Jet 4.0 OLE DB provider will accept any nonzero value for the *Inherit* argument to apply permissions for new objects.
adInheritBoth	Same as using **adInheritContainers**.
adInheritNoPropagate	Same as using **adInheritContainers**.

For Access databases, to set permissions for forms, reports, and macros you must set the *ObjectType* argument to **adPermObjProviderSpecific** and set the *ObjectTypeID* argument to a **Variant** value that specifies the GUID for the object. The GUIDs to use for Access forms, reports, and macros are listed in the following table.

Object	GUID
Form	{c49c842e-9dcb-11d1-9f0a-00c04fc2c2e0}
Report	{c49c8430-9dcb-11d1-9f0a-00c04fc2c2e0}
Macro	{c49c842f-9dcb-11d1-9f0a-00c04fc2c2e0}

Reading Permissions

To read the permissions of an object by using ADOX, you use the **GetPermissions** method to return a **Long** value that specifies a bitmask for the permissions the group or user has on the object. The syntax for the **GetPermissions** method has the following format:

ReturnValue = *GroupOrUser*.**GetPermissions(***Name*, *ObjectType*[, *ObjectTypeID*])

Just as with the **SetPermissions** method, the *Name* argument is a **Variant** value specifying the name of the object to set permissions for. If you want to read permissions for all new objects of the specified type, set the *Name* argument to **Null**. The *ObjectType* argument is a **Long** value specifying the type of object you are reading permissions for. For forms, reports, or macros, the *ObjectType* argument must be set to **adPermObjProviderSpecific** and the *ObjectTypeID* argument is set to a **Variant** value that specifies the GUID for the corresponding object. If you want to read permissions for the database itself, set the *Name* argument to **Null**, and set the *ObjectType* argument to **adPermObjDatabase**. For *ObjectType* argument constants and form, report, and macro GUIDs for the *ObjectTypeID* argument, see the tables for the **SetPermissions** method in "Setting Permissions" earlier in this chapter.

The **GetPermissions** method is useful for reading permissions to determine what permissions a user or group currently has.

The **GetPermissions** method is also useful when you are adding or removing permissions from an existing set of permissions:

- To add additional permissions to an existing set of permissions, use the **GetPermissions** method to retrieve the bitmask for the current set of permissions and use the **Or** operator with permissions constants to add additional permissions to the bitmask passed to the **SetPermissions** method as the *Rights* argument.
- To remove permissions from the existing set of permissions, use the **GetPermissions** method to retrieve the bitmask for the current set of permissions, and then use the **And Not** operator to remove permissions from the bitmask passed to the **SetPermissions** method. For examples of this technique, see "Permissions Programming Examples" later in this chapter.

An Important Point to Remember

Microsoft Jet user-level security always uses the least restrictive set of permissions among the permissions granted to a user and to all groups to which that user belongs. This can have consequences that you may find confusing when you use the **SetPermissions** and **GetPermissions** methods.

- Using the **SetPermissions** method to revoke permissions for a user account doesn't override permissions granted by any group to which that user belongs.
- Using the **GetPermissions** method to retrieve a user's permissions returns a bitmask that reflects only the permissions granted *explicitly* to that user on that object, not the user's implicit permissions inherited from group membership. If you aren't aware of this, you may be confused by the results returned. For example, suppose you use the **SetPermissions** method on a user with the **adRightNone** constant to remove all permissions for an object. Using **GetPermissions** to check the user's permissions will return **adRightNone**. However, if the user is a member of a group that has permissions on the object, the user will have the permissions he or she inherited from that group.

To avoid these situations, revoke all permissions on all objects for the default Users group (the User-Level Security Wizard will do this for you) and don't assign permissions to individual users; assign permissions only to groups, and then assign users to the appropriate group. If possible, avoid assigning users to more than one group (in addition to the default Users group).

Permissions Programming Examples

The following examples show how to set and read permissions. You can view these examples and additional code samples that work with user and group permissions in the modSecurity module in AccessSecurity.mdb in the Samples\CH18 subfolder on the companion CD-ROM.

The first code fragment shows one method of setting a group's permissions from within the current Access database.

Note This procedure assumes that the value you pass to it as the *lngRights* argument is either a single permissions constant, such as **adRightRead**, or a value created by combining all the constants for the permissions you want to set by using the **Or** operator, such as:

```
adRightRead Or adRightInsert Or adRightUpdate
```

Also, you can use this procedure to set permissions on all new objects of the type specified by the *lngObjectType* argument by passing in **Null** for the *varObjName* argument.

The procedure first revokes all permissions on the specified object, and then grants the specified permissions. This ensures that the group has exactly the permissions specified on the object. The following code fragment is from the SetGroupPermsInAccess procedure, which is available in the modSecurity module in AccessSecurity.mdb in the Samples\CH18 subfolder on the companion CD-ROM.

```
Set catDB = New ADOX.Catalog

With catDB
   ' Open Catalog object by using connection to current database.
   .ActiveConnection = CurrentProject.Connection

   ' Revoke all permissions.
   .Groups(strGroup).SetPermissions varObjName, lngObjectType, adAccessSet, _
      adRightNone, lngInherit, varObjectID

   ' Grant specified permissions.
   .Groups(strGroup).SetPermissions varObjName, lngObjectType, adAccessSet, _
      lngRights, lngInherit, varObjectID

   ' Retrieve current permissions and display them in the Immediate window.
   lngRightsNow = .Groups(strGroup).GetPermissions(varObjName, lngObjectType, _
      varObjectID)
   Debug.Print DecodePerms(lngRightsNow)
End With

Set catDB = Nothing
```

If you only want to add permissions to the existing set, first use the **GetPermissions** method to retrieve the bitmask for the existing permissions, add the new permissions to the bitmask by using the **Or** operator, and then use the new bitmask as the *Rights* argument of the **SetPermissions** method. The following code fragment shows how to do this for the current Access database. The value you pass as the *lngAddRights* argument can be a single permissions constant or several constants combined by using the **Or** operator. Also, you can use this procedure to add permissions for all new objects of the type specified by the *lngObjectType* argument by passing in **Null** for the *varObjName* argument. The following code fragment is from the AddGroupPermsInAccess procedure, which is available in the modSecurity module in AccessSecurity.mdb in the Samples\CH18 subfolder on the companion CD-ROM.

```
Set catDB = New ADOX.Catalog

With catDB
   ' Open Catalog object by using connection to current database.
   .ActiveConnection = CurrentProject.Connection

   ' Retrieve the current set of permissions for the group.
   lngOldRights = .Groups(strGroup).GetPermissions(varObjName, _
      lngObjectType, varObjectID)

   ' Add new permissions to existing permissions bitmask.
   lngNewRights = lngOldRights Or lngAddRights
```

```
    ' Grant specified permissions.
    .Groups(strGroup).SetPermissions varObjName, lngObjectType, adAccessSet, _
       lngNewRights, lngInherit, varObjectID

    ' Retrieve current permissions and display them in the Immediate window.
    lngRightsNow = .Groups(strGroup).GetPermissions(varObjName, lngObjectType)
    Debug.Print DecodePerms(lngRightsNow)
End With

Set catDB = Nothing
```

You can remove rights from the existing set of permissions for a group by changing a single line of code in the previous procedure. Instead of using the **Or** operator to add permissions to the bitmask for the new set of permissions, use the **And Not** operator to remove permissions from the bitmask:

```
' Remove permissions from existing permissions bitmask.
 lngNewRights = lngOldRights And Not lngRemoveRights
```

If a user or group has less than full permissions (**adRightFull**) and more than no permissions (**adRightNone**), you can check to see if a user or group has a specific permission on a object. To do this, perform a bitwise **And** comparison between the value of the permission you want to check and the bitmask value returned by the **GetPermissions** method. If the resulting value is greater than 0, you know that the user or group has the specified permission. The following example shows how to do this for a user account. The value you pass in for the *lngCheckRights* argument can be a single permissions constant, or several constants combined by using the **Or** operator. Also, you can use this procedure to check permissions for all new objects of the type specified by the *lngObjectType* argument by passing in **Null** for the *varObjName* argument. The following code fragment is from the CheckUserPermsInAccess procedure, which is available in the modSecurity module in AccessSecurity.mdb in the Samples\CH18 subfolder on the companion CD-ROM.

```
Set catDB = New ADOX.Catalog

With catDB
    ' Open Catalog object by using connection to current database.
    .ActiveConnection = CurrentProject.Connection

    ' Retrieve the current set of permissions for the group.
    lngCurrentRights = .Users(strUser).GetPermissions(varObjName, _
       lngObjectType, varObjectID)
End With
```

```
' If varObjName is not Null, then caller is checking
' permissions for a specific object.
If Not IsNull(varObjName) Then
   ' Check to see if lngCurrentRights is exactly adRightNone or adRightFull.
   If lngCurrentRights = adRightNone Then
      Debug.Print strUser & " has no permissions for " & varObjName

   ElseIf lngCurrentRights = adRightFull Then
      Debug.Print strUser & " has full permissions for " & varObjName

   ' Otherwise, use the And operator to check if lngCheckRights
   ' is part of the current permissions bitmask.
   ElseIf (lngCurrentRights And lngCheckRights) > 0 Then
      Debug.Print strUser & " has the specified permissions for " & varObjName

   ' User doesn't have the specified permissions.
   Else
      Debug.Print strUser & " doesn't have the specified permissions for " _
         & varObjName
   End If

' Otherwise, the varObjName object variable is Null,
' so the caller is checking permissions for new objects
' of the specified object type (in DAO, a Container object).
Else
   If lngCurrentRights = adRightNone Then
      Debug.Print strUser & " has no permissions for all new objects of " _
         & "the specified type."

   ElseIf lngCurrentRights = adRightFull Then
      Debug.Print strUser & " has full permissions for all new objects of " _
         & "the specified type."
   ElseIf (lngCurrentRights And lngCheckRights) > 0 Then
      Debug.Print strUser & " has the specified permissions for all new " _
            & "objects of the specified type."
   Else
      Debug.Print strUser & " doesn't have the specified permissions for " _
            & " all new objects of the specified type."
   End If
End If

' Display current permissions in the Immediate window.
Debug.Print DecodePerms(lngCurrentRights)

Set catDB = Nothing
```

Setting and Reading Ownership

To set and read ownership in Access databases by using ADOX, you use the **SetObjectOwner** and **GetObjectOwner** methods. The following sections provide an introduction to using these methods.

Setting Ownership

To set the ownership of an object by using ADOX, you use the **SetObjectOwner** method of the **Catalog** object to specify the user or group that owns the object. The syntax for the **SetObjectOwner** method has the following format:

SetObjectOwner(*ObjectName***,** *ObjectType***,** *UserName*[**,** *ObjectTypeID*]**)**

The *ObjectName* argument is a **Variant** value specifying the name of the object to set ownership for, and the *UserName* argument is a **String** value specifying the name of the user or group you want to own the object. The *ObjectType* and *ObjectTypeID* arguments work in the same fashion as those for the **SetPermissions** and **GetPermissions** methods. The *ObjectType* argument is a **Long** value specifying the type of object you are setting ownership for. For forms, reports, or macros, the *ObjectType* argument must be set to **adPermObjProviderSpecific** and the *ObjectTypeID* argument is set to a **Variant** value that specifies the GUID for the corresponding object. If you want to set ownership for the database itself, set the *ObjectName* argument to **Null**, and set the *ObjectType* argument to **adPermObjDatabase**. For *ObjectType* argument constants and form, report, and macro GUIDs for the *ObjectTypeID* argument, see the tables for the **SetPermissions** method in "Setting Permissions" earlier in this chapter.

Reading Ownership

To read the ownership of an object by using ADOX, you use the **GetObjectOwner** method of the **Catalog** object to return a **String** value that specifies the user or group that owns the object. The syntax for the **GetObjectOwner** method has the following format:

ReturnValue **= GetObjectOwner(***ObjectName***,** *ObjectType*[**,** *ObjectTypeID*]**)**

The *ObjectName* argument is a **Variant** value specifying the name of the object to read ownership for. The *ObjectType* and *ObjectTypeID* arguments work in the same fashion as the **SetPermissions** and **GetPermissions** methods. The *ObjectType* argument is a **Long** value specifying the type of object you are reading ownership for. For forms, reports, or macros, the *ObjectType* argument must be set to **adPermObjProviderSpecific** and the *ObjectTypeID* argument must be set to a **Variant** value that specifies the GUID for the corresponding object. If you want to read ownership for the database itself, set the *Name* argument to **Null**, and set the *ObjectType* argument to **adPermObjDatabase**. For *ObjectType* argument constants and form, report, and macro GUIDs for the *ObjectTypeID* argument, see the tables for the **SetPermissions** method in "Setting Permissions" earlier in this chapter.

You can view the SetOwnerInAccess and GetOwnerInAccess procedures, which set and read the ownership of objects, in the AccessSecurity.mdb file in the Samples\CH18 subfolder on the companion CD-ROM.

Security and Database Replication

Database replicas use the same security model as all Microsoft Jet databases: Users' permissions on database objects are determined at the time they start Microsoft Jet and log on. It's up to you, the developer, to make sure the same security information is available at each location where a replica is used.

You can do this by making the identical workgroup information file available to users at each location where a replica is used. Although the workgroup information file cannot be replicated, it can be manually copied to each location.

Alternatively, you can create a new workgroup information file at each location and then re-create the required user and group accounts needed at each location by entering the same user and group names with their associated PIDs.

Note Modifications to permissions are considered design changes and can be made only in the Design Master replica.

Some security permissions control certain aspects of database replication. For example, a user must have Administer permission on the database in order to:

- Convert a database into a replicable database.
- Change the setting of the **ReplicableBool** property, make a local object replicable, or make a replicable object local. Note that these actions can be performed only in the Design Master replica.
- Transfer Design Master status to another replica. This action can be performed in any replica in the set; however, there should never be more than one Design Master replica in a set at a time.

By default, Administer permission is granted to the Users group, the Admins group, and the creator of the database. If security is to be maintained, you must restrict this permission to selected users. For more information about replication, see Chapter 16, "Multiuser Database Applications."

Encrypting a Database

If you want to protect your secured database from unauthorized access by someone who is using a disk editor or other utility program, you can *encrypt* it. Encryption makes a database indecipherable, which protects it from unauthorized viewing or use, particularly during electronic transmission or when it's stored on floppy disk, tape, or compact disc. Encrypting an unsecured database will have no effect because anybody can open the database with Access or VBA and gain full access to all objects in the database.

Important Before you can encrypt or decrypt an Access database, you must be either the owner of the database or, if the database has been secured, a member of the Admins group of the workgroup information file that contains the accounts used to secure the database. You must also be able to open the database in exclusive mode, which, if the database is secured by using user-level security, requires you to have the Open/Run and Open Exclusive permissions.

The User-Level Security Wizard automatically encrypts your database. You can encrypt or decrypt a database by starting Access without opening a database, and then using the **Encrypt/Decrypt Database** command (**Tools** menu, **Security** submenu). When you encrypt a database by using the same file name as that of the original database, Access deletes the original unencrypted file if the encryption process is successful. If an error occurs, Access doesn't delete the original file.

Note Encrypting a database slows its performance by up to 15 percent. Also, an encrypted database cannot be compressed by programs such as DriveSpace or PKZIP. If you try to compress an encrypted database, its size doesn't change.

You can also use the **CompactDatabase** method of the Microsoft Jet and Replication Objects (JRO) 2.1 **JetEngine** object to encrypt or decrypt a database. To use the JRO **JetEngine** object, you must set a reference to the Microsoft Jet and Replication Objects 2.1 object library. When you use the **CompactDatabase** method, you can't save the compacted (and optionally encrypted) database to the same name as the original database. The **CompactDatabase** method takes two arguments to specify the source database and the destination database: *SourceConnection* and *DestConnection.* Both the *SourceConnection* and *DestConnection* arguments take the form of connection strings. Within the connection strings, you specify various connection properties to determine how the source database is opened and how the destination database is compacted. At a minimum, you must use the **Data Source** property in each connection string to specify the path and name of the database. Additionally, to encrypt the database, you must include the **Jet OLEDB:Encrypt Database** property in the connection string for the *DestConnection* argument. The following procedure uses these connection properties to encrypt the database specified by the *strSourceDB* argument to the path and name specified by the *strDestDB* argument:

```
Function EncryptDb(strSourceDB As String, _
                   strDestDB As String) As String
   Dim jetEngine        As JRO.JetEngine
   Dim strSourceConnect As String
   Dim strDestConnect   As String

   ' Build connection strings for SourceConnection and
   ' DestConnection arguments.
   strSourceConnect = "Data Source=" & strSourceDB
   strDestConnect = "Data Source=" & strDestDB & ";" & _
                    "Jet OLEDB:Encrypt Database=True"

   Set jetEngine = New JRO.JetEngine

   ' Compact and encrypt the database specified by strSourceDB
   ' to the name and path specified by strDestDB.
   jetEngine.CompactDatabase strSourceConnect, strDestConnect

   Set jetEngine = Nothing
End Function
```

The EncryptDb procedure is available in the modSecurity module in AccessSecurity.mdb in the Samples\CH18 subfolder on the companion CD-ROM.

If the database you are encrypting or compacting is secured with user-level security or a database password, to open the source database you must specify additional connection properties in the connection string for the *SourceConnection* argument. When specifying additional properties in the connection string, separate each property with a semicolon (;). The following table lists these properties.

Connection property	Description
User ID	The name of the user account used to open the database if the source database is secured with user-level security.
Password	The password for the user account specified by the **User ID** property.
Jet OLEDB:System Database	The path and name of the system database (workgroup information file) that contains the user and group accounts for user-level security.
Jet OLEDB:Database Password	The password required to open the database if the database is password-protected.

The connection string for both the *SourceConnection* and *DestConnection* arguments also accepts the **Provider** property, but the OLE DB provider for Microsoft Jet 4.0 (`Microsoft.Jet.OLEDB.4.0`) is assumed by default, so you don't have to specify it within the string. The connection strings can also include other properties to determine how the database is compacted. For more information about using the JRO **CompactDatabase** method, search Microsoft ADO Help (C:\Program Files\Common Files\System\Ado\Ado210.chm) or the Microsoft Access Visual Basic Reference Help index for "CompactDatabase method."

Data Access Page Security Issues

Data access pages present security concerns in three areas:

- Security for the links to data access pages stored in the **Pages** object list in the Database window in an Access database or Access project
- Security for data access page files themselves
- Controlling access to the database that a data access page is connected to

Security for Data Access Page Links

Access doesn't provide user-level security for the links to data access pages stored in the **Pages** object list in the Database window. When an Access database or Access project is opened with write access to the file, users can add, delete, or rename the links stored in the **Pages** object list in the Database window. For this reason, the only way to prevent users from making changes to data access page links is to make the .mdb or .adp file read-only. You can do this by using file-system access control, such as setting the read-only attribute, or putting the file on a read-only network share.

Security for Data Access Page Files

Data access pages themselves are HTML pages that contain <OBJECT> tag references to the Microsoft Office **Data Source** control and other Microsoft Office Web Components, as well as XML and script. Data access pages aren't actually stored in Access database (.mdb) or Access project (.adp) files; they are stored as .htm files either in the local file system, in a folder on a network share, or on an HTTP server. For this reason, Access has no control over the security of data access page files. To secure a data access page file that is stored on a local or network file system, you must use the file access security available for your operating system. To secure data access page files that are stored on an HTTP server, you must use the security features available on the server itself. For example, if you are using Microsoft Internet Information Server, you can use the Internet Service Manager or FrontPage Server Administrator to control security settings for files stored on the server.

Controlling Database Access from Data Access Pages

There are three primary concerns regarding securing access to a database from a data access page:

- Preventing unauthorized users from opening the database at all
- Controlling the level of access once a database is open
- Preventing malicious scripts from using the user's identity to access other databases

For Access databases, there is the additional concern of controlling access to the database file itself (.mdb) through the file system. All of these issues are addressed in the following sections.

Preventing Unauthorized Access

The method you use to prevent unauthorized access may differ depending on whether you are using an Access database or a SQL Server database as the back end for your data access page. In either case, the back-end database itself must be secured. For an .mdb file, you should secure the database by using user-level security as described earlier in this chapter. For a SQL Server database, you should secure the database by using native SQL Server security accounts or by integrating Windows NT security accounts, which is referred to as *integrated security*. When you are using integrated security, user and group accounts defined for a Windows NT network are used to authenticate users for SQL Server database security. This means that users don't have to log on for security purposes when opening a database; they are identified by the Windows NT user account they used to log on to the network (or by the group account of which that user account is a member). The user or group account's access level still must be defined in the database itself, but you are using the Windows NT user or group accounts instead of using native SQL Server accounts. For more information about how to use security in a SQL Server database, see the documentation provided with SQL Server.

You can also author a data access page against an Access database that is secured with a database password. However, a database password provides control only over who can open the database, and requires that all users know a single password to open the database. If you use database password security to control database access for a data access page, you have two options on how to use it. By default, a database password isn't saved with a data access page, so users are prompted to enter the database password when opening the page. (Similarly, if a database password is set for the database after you author the page, users of your page will be prompted to enter the password before they can use the page.)

If you don't want to prompt users for the database password, you can embed the password in the page; however, when you do so, the password is saved in an unencrypted format in the HTML of the page itself, which makes it fairly easy to discover.

▶ To embed the database password in the page

1 Open the HTML page in Notepad or a text editor.

2 Search for `Jet OLEDB:Database Password=`

3 Delete `""` following the = sign.

4 Type the password following the = sign.

5 Save your changes.

Even though you can edit the value of the **Jet OLEDB:Database Password** property on the **All** tab of the **Data Link Properties** dialog box (which is displayed by right-clicking the database name in the field list and then clicking **Connection**) while authoring a data access page in Access, you aren't allowed to save changes because the database is already in use.

Preventing unauthorized database access from a data access page consists of performing the following steps:

1. Preventing the user ID and password (that you use to access the database while authoring a data access page) from being saved with the page.
2. Determining how users of the page will be authenticated; that is, determining how their logon identities will be entered and validated.
3. Determining how—or if—you can control the level of access for individual users.
4. Preventing unauthorized access from malicious scripts hidden in the page.

Preventing the User ID and Password from Being Saved with the Page

For an Access database back end secured with user-level security, the only way to prevent unauthorized access is to prevent the security account user ID and password from being saved with the information used to connect to the database. This will cause a logon dialog box to be displayed that requires a user to enter a correct logon account name and password before the data access page can connect to the database. This is also appropriate for SQL Server back-end databases regardless of whether you are using native SQL Server security accounts or Windows NT integrated security for authentication. To prevent a logon password from being saved with a data access page's connection information, you must use the **Data Link Properties** dialog box as described in the following procedure.

▶ To prevent the password used to connect to a database from being saved with a data access page

1. Start Access and open the data access page you want to work with in Design view.
2. On the **View** menu, click **Field List**.
3. On the **Database** tab, right-click the database name, and then click **Connection**.
4. Under **Enter information to log on to the server**, make sure the **Allow saving of password** check box is cleared.
5. Click **OK**, and save your changes to the data access page.

Now whenever the data access page is opened, the user must provide the appropriate user name and password to log on to the database, or if you are using integrated security with SQL Server, the user's identity must be passed in from the Windows NT Server network's authentication system.

Determining How Users Are Authenticated

Two major factors determine how users of a data access page will be authenticated to access a secured back-end database:

- How user accounts are defined and authenticated in the back-end database. This differs depending on whether you are using an Access database or a SQL Server database.
- How authentication is configured on the Internet Information Server (IIS) that is used to publish the page.

For Access databases, there is the additional factor of allowing access to the database file itself (.mdb) through the file system. Because the Access database itself is a file, users of a data access page connected to an Access database must have sufficient file-system permissions (defined through the network operating system) to open and possibly write to the database file. These factors must be coordinated in order for authentication to work correctly. The following sections describe the available options for each database type.

Authenticating Users of Data Access Pages Connected to an Access Database Back End

Users of secured Access databases must be authenticated against account information stored in a workgroup information file. For authentication to work correctly for a secured Access database back end, you must also make sure that the connection information for a data access page specifies the correct workgroup information file. To do this, you must also make sure that the workgroup information file is in a location, such as a public network share, that can be accessed by all users who need to open the data access page. The following procedure describes how to specify this information for a data access page.

▶ To specify the workgroup information file to use when opening a data access page that is connected to a secured Access database (.mdb)

1. Start Access and open the data access page you want to work with in Design view.
2. On the **View** menu, click **Field List**.
3. On the **Database** tab, right-click the database name, and then click **Connection**.
4. On the **All** tab, double-click **Jet OLEDB:System database**.
5. Specify the path to the correct workgroup information file in the **Property Value** box. In most cases, this should be a UNC path (*ServerName**ShareName*) to the file on a network share.
6. Click **OK** twice to close the **Data Link Properties** dialog box, and then save your changes to the data access page.

For authentication information to be passed correctly from the IIS server that is used to publish the page to the Jet database engine, you must configure the authentication method used on the IIS server. If you want to use individual user accounts to determine the level of access a user has after opening an Access database through a data access page, you must use IIS Basic Authentication, which prompts the user to enter a user account name and password when opening the page. For information about configuring Basic Authentication, see "Using Basic Authentication" later in this chapter.

If it is acceptable to use a single level of access for all users who open the database through a data access page, you can define an Access user account that matches the name and password of the IIS Anonymous User account and use Anonymous Access authentication on the IIS server. In this case, all users are automatically logged on under the single Anonymous Access user account. For information about configuring Anonymous Access authentication, see "Using Anonymous Access Authentication" later in this chapter.

It is also possible to use Windows NT Challenge/Response authentication, but because the Microsoft Jet database engine can't use Windows NT logon accounts, the database must be secured by granting the desired permissions to the Admin user as described earlier in this chapter in "Securing Your Database Without Asking Users to Log On." For more information about configuring Windows NT Challenge/Response authentication, see "Using Windows NT Challenge/Response Authentication" later in this chapter.

Authenticating Users of Data Access Pages Connected to a SQL Server Back-End Database

How users of secured SQL Server databases are authenticated depends on how security accounts are defined for the back-end database. If you are using native SQL Server security accounts, users are authenticated against information stored on the database server itself. As long as you haven't stored the user ID and password you used while authoring the page, and you are using Basic Authentication on the IIS server, users will be prompted to enter a user ID and password when they open the page, and that logon information will be passed to the server for authentication.

Just as with an Access database, if it's acceptable to specify a single level of access for all users who open the database through a data access page, you can define a native SQL Server user account and password that matches the IIS Anonymous User account and use Anonymous Access authentication on the IIS server. For information about configuring Anonymous Access authentication, see "Using Anonymous Access Authentication" later in this chapter.

If you are using Windows NT integrated security to connect to a SQL Server database from a data access page, only authorized Windows NT accounts will be allowed to open or work with the database—their Windows NT logon identity will be passed to the database. To use Windows NT authentication to connect to a SQL Server database from a data access page, you must use the **Data Link Properties** dialog box as described in the following procedure.

▶ To use Windows NT authentication to connect to a SQL Server database from a data access page

1. Start Access and open the data access page you want to work with in Design view.
2. On the **View** menu, click **Field List**.
3. On the **Database** tab, right-click the database name, and then click **Connection**.
4. Under **Enter information to log on to the server**, click **Use Windows NT Integrated security**.
5. Click **OK**, and save your changes to the data access page.

Whenever the data access page is opened, only Windows NT logon accounts that have been authorized to open and work with the SQL Server database will be allowed to log on to the database. For more information about configuring Windows NT Challenge/Response authentication on the IIS server used to publish the page, see "Using Windows NT Challenge/Response Authentication" later in this chapter.

Important For the highest level of security when you are using an IIS server to share a data access page across a network, your data access page should use three-tier data access against secured Access and SQL Server databases. Using three-tier data access against a secured database requires you to perform additional steps to configure authentication. For information about how to do this, see "Preventing Unauthorized Access from Malicious Scripts" later in this chapter.

Controlling the Level of Access

The strategies for controlling the level of access once a database is opened from a data access page are similar to those used in desktop solutions. For Access databases, you can use either of the following methods after establishing user-level security for the database:

- Define a user account that has the appropriate level of access you want to allow for any user of the data access page. Use the **Data Link Properties** dialog box to save this account name and password in the data access page connection information. This account and password will be used for all users who open the data access page. Also be sure to put the correct workgroup information file in a shared location and specify the path to the file in the **Data Link Properties** dialog box, as described in "Preventing Unauthorized Access" earlier in this chapter.

- Define the appropriate groups and access levels you want to allow for users of the data access page. Create user account names and passwords to distribute to authorized users of the data access page, and assign those users to the appropriate groups. Use the **Data Link Properties** dialog box to prevent the password from being saved in the data access page connection information, as described in "Preventing Unauthorized Access" earlier in this chapter. Be sure to specify the correct workgroup information file in the **Data Link Properties** dialog box. All users of the data access page will be required to enter a valid user name and password before the database can be opened.

For SQL Server databases, the methods you can use are similar to those used with Access databases; in addition, you have the option of using Windows NT authentication:

- Define a native SQL Server user account that has the appropriate level of access you want to allow for any user of the data access page. Use the **Data Link Properties** dialog box to save this account name and password in the data access page's connection information. This account and password will be used for all users who open the data access page. In SQL Server databases that use native security accounts, user and group account information is stored on the server itself, so you don't need to specify a workgroup information file as you do when connecting to a secured Access database.
- Define the appropriate groups and access levels you want to allow for users of the data access page. Either create native SQL Server user account names and passwords to distribute to authorized users of the data access page, or use Windows NT integrated security. Assign users to the appropriate groups. If you use native SQL Server accounts, use the **Data Link Properties** dialog box to prevent the password from being saved in the data access page's connection information so that users of the data access page will be required to enter a valid user name and password before they can open the database. If you use Windows NT integrated security, use the **Data Link Properties** dialog box to specify that the data access page use that method to authenticate users who can open the database the page is connected to.

When you use both Access databases and SQL Server databases with data access pages, if you want to allow users to update information in the database, you must grant the appropriate permissions (such as Update, Insert, and/or Delete permissions) on the tables that contain the data you want to update. Granting permissions on a query (Access) or view (SQL Server) used by the data access page is not sufficient.

Important Depending on the data access method you choose for the data access page, where the database is located on the network relative to the IIS server used to publish the page, and how authentication is defined on the IIS server, you may not be able to control the level of access for individual users. That is, you may only be able to control access based on a single account used for all users who open the page. For more information, see "Configuring Authentication Methods Used on Internet Information Server" later in this chapter.

Preventing Unauthorized Access from Malicious Scripts

A data access page uses the Microsoft Office **Data Source** control (MSODSC) to connect to its data source. When a data access page is open in Internet Explorer or in an HTML-capable mail reader that uses Internet Explorer browsing components, such as Outlook 98 or Outlook 2000, the MSODSC on the page is using the identity of the user to log on to the database. A malicious user could exploit this fact to use script running against the MSODSC to attempt to access databases on servers other than the one the page was downloaded from. Attempts to use the MSODSC to access databases on servers other than the one the page originated from are referred to as *cross-domain data access*.

The mode of data access used by the MSODSC determines whether a data access page is considered inherently safe, or if cross-domain data access is possible from the page. The MSODSC can be configured to use two modes of data access: *two-tier* or *three-tier data access*.

Two-tier data access refers to using a direct connection to a data source in a traditional client/server fashion—the client (first tier) makes a direct connection to the database server (second tier). To perform two-tier data access, the MSODSC makes a direct connection to its data source through an OLE DB provider registered on the user's computer. For an Access database, two-tier data access uses the local computer's Microsoft Jet 4.0 OLE DB provider to connect to an .mdb file located on a network share. For a SQL Server database, two-tier data access uses the local computer's Microsoft OLE DB provider for SQL Server to connect to a database server available on your local network.

Three-tier data access refers to using a third, remote component between the client and database components. Three-tier data access is typically used to access data across the Internet or an intranet. For three-tier data access that uses the MSODSC, this third component is the ADO Remote Data Service (RDS) component running on an Internet Information Server (IIS). To perform three-tier data access, the MSODSC sends a request via HTTP to IIS, and IIS passes the connection information to the RDS component, which then uses an OLE DB provider running on the server computer to connect to the database. Once RDS is connected to the database, it passes the retrieved data back through IIS to the client.

Note If a user opens a data access page that is configured to use three-tier data access through an Internet firewall, that user will be authenticated twice: once as the page is initially opened, and again as the MSODSC binds data to the page. As a result, if the server is configured to use Basic Authentication, the user will have to enter his or her user name and password twice. This occurs because two separate HTTP connections are being made: (1) the connection from Internet Explorer to the Web server to retrieve the page, and (2) the connection from the Microsoft OLE DB Remoting Provider (MSRemote) to the Web server to bind the data.

Any data access page that uses two-tier data access is considered by Internet Explorer to be making a cross-domain access attempt. Depending on the security settings in Internet Explorer, when a user opens a data access page by using two-tier data access, one of three things occurs: the page is automatically disabled, the user is asked whether to allow data access, or the page is automatically enabled.

Internet Explorer security settings also define different security zones. If a page is published from a server in a trusted zone, the cross-domain attempt can be enabled automatically. In a controlled environment, such as a corporate intranet, your data access pages will perform better if you use two-tier data access and make sure that they are published from a server located in a trusted security zone. This is the simplest way to provide security against unauthorized access from malicious scripts. For more information about Internet Explorer data access security settings, see "Configuring Internet Explorer Data Access Security Settings" later in this chapter.

Important If your data access page is connected to multidimensional data through the OLAP Services component of Microsoft SQL Server, you must use two-tier data access because the PivotTable Service, which is the OLE DB for OLAP provider for the OLAP Services component that is used to connect to multidimensional data, doesn't support three-tier data access.

A data access page that uses three-tier data access to connect to a database is considered to be inherently safe regardless of what Internet Explorer security zone it is published from, and will not warn the user about cross-domain access attempts when it is opened if authentication settings have been configured correctly. There are three forms of authentication you can use for HTML pages published with Microsoft Internet Information Server:

- Anonymous Access authentication, which provides an Anonymous User account for all access to the page and its data source
- Windows NT Challenge/Response authentication
- Basic authentication

Each method has certain advantages and disadvantages, and requires additional configuration to work correctly.

Before you can use any of these methods to prevent cross-domain access attempts, you must configure the data access method for the MSODSC on the data access page to use three-tier data access. To configure the data access method used for a data access page, set the **UseRemoteProvider** property of the MSODSC. The default setting is **False**, which configures the MSODSC to use two-tier data access. Using the default two-tier data access method is appropriate while you are developing the data access page (and, in fact, is the only data access method that will work if you are authoring the page using a local HTML file, or against a local copy of a database), but if you want to deploy the page using three-tier data access, you must change a property setting for the MSODSC. By setting the **UseRemoteProvider** property to **True**, you configure the MSODSC to use three-tier data access. The simplest method of configuring the **UseRemoteProvider** property is in the data access page's Design view, as described in the following procedure.

▶ To configure the data access method used for a data access page

1 Start Access and open the data access page you want work with in Design view.

2 Click the title bar of the data access page (to ensure that no other items are selected on the page), and then click **Properties** on the **View** menu.

3 On the **Data** tab, set the **UseRemoteProvider** property to determine how you want to perform data access:

- For two-tier data access, set **UseRemoteProvider** to **False**.
- For three-tier data access, set **UseRemoteProvider** to **True**.

4 Close the property sheet, and save your changes to the data access page.

Configuring Authentication Methods Used on Internet Information Server

After configuring the data access page for three-tier data access, you can determine what form of authentication you want to use with the page. You can configure an authentication method for an individual page or for the entire folder where you are publishing the page on your IIS server. The following procedure describes how to configure an authentication method.

▶ To configure an authentication method used for a data access page

1 On the computer running Internet Information Server, start the Internet Service Manager.

2 Navigate to the Web Site folder where you are publishing your page.

3 Do one of the following:

- To set the authentication method for the entire folder where the page is published, right-click the folder, click **Properties**, click the **Directory Security** tab, and under **Anonymous Access and Authentication Control**, click **Edit**.
- To set the authentication for just the page, navigate to the page, right-click the page, click **Properties**, click the **File Security** tab, and under **Anonymous Access and Authentication Control**, click **Edit**.

4 Select the authentication method(s) you want to use: Anonymous Access, Windows NT Challenge/Response, or Basic. The following sections describe the options available for each method of authentication.

Using Anonymous Access Authentication

If you select **Allow Anonymous Access** for the page or the folder the page is in, IIS will always use the IIS Anonymous Access user account (Internet Guest Account) to access the page's data source. You can work with this account by running the **User Manager** for the IIS server computer's local domain. The account's name will have this format: **IUSR_***ComputerName*. For example, if the name of the computer your IIS server is running on is OurWebServer, the IIS Anonymous Access user account will be named **IUSR_OURWEBSERVER**. If your page is authored against a SQL Server database, this Windows NT user account must be able to make a connection to the SQL Server database and access the data requested by the page. If the SQL Server database is set up to require Windows NT Authentication, the SQL Server administrator must specifically grant database permissions to that user account. If your page is authored against an Access database, the Anonymous User account must be able to access the network share where the database resides. In most cases this will require you to add the Anonymous User account as a domain account so that it will be recognized by both the IIS machine and the database machine, or to define a local account by using the same name and password on both IIS and database machines.

Using Windows NT Challenge/Response Authentication

If you clear the **Allow Anonymous Access** option for the page or the folder the page is in, and select the **Windows NT Challenge/Response Authentication** option, the IIS server will attempt to connect to the database by using the account of the user who opens the page in a browser. An important restriction in Windows NT Server 4.0 is that this connection appears to another computer as a "Null" session attempt with no security context, because a connection's security context can't be delegated to another computer under Windows NT Server 4.0. This means that if the SQL Server or Access database is located on a different computer than the IIS server that was used to publish the page, the connection will usually fail.

The only way to avoid the Windows NT Server restriction is to put the database on the same computer as the one that is running IIS to publish the data access page. For an Access database, the database must reside in a local folder on that computer. Additionally, because an Access database can't recognize Window NT logon accounts, you must secure the database by using the method described in the section "Securing Your Database Without Asking Users to Log On" earlier in this chapter. For a SQL Server database, SQL Server must be installed and running on that computer. Then use a local computer address for the connection's data source. For example, for an Access database, you must set the data source to use a path on the IIS server's local drive, and for a SQL Server database, you need to set the connection's data source to **(local)**.

When you initially author a data access page that uses an Access database as a data source, you may be working against a local copy of the database before you publish it. If this is the case, after you finish authoring the page, create a public share on the computer that is running the copy of IIS that will be used to publish the page, and put a copy of the database in that share. Then reset the page's data source to the path that is local to the computer running IIS (for example, "C:\Databases\MyDatabase.mdb" *not* "\\MyServer\Databases\MyDatabase.mdb"). Similarly, when you initially author a data access page by using a SQL Server database as a data source, the server the database resides on is identified by its network name, such as DATASERVER1. Before you publish the page, you must reset the page's data source to **(local)** so that the MSODSC control treats the database as local to the IIS server computer. The following procedure describes how to do this for both Access and SQL Server data sources.

▶To set a data access page to use the copy of the database that is local to the computer running IIS to publish the page

1. Start Access and open the data access page you want to work with in Design view.
2. On the **View** menu, click **Field List**.
3. On the **Database** tab, right-click the database name, and then click **Connection**.
4. Do one of the following:
   - For an Access database, on the **Connection** tab in the **Data Source** box, change the path to the database to use the drive and path for the copy of the database that is local to the computer running IIS.
   - For a SQL Server database, on the **Connection** tab in the **Select or enter a server name** box, change the server name to **(local)**.
5. Click **OK**, and save your changes to the data access page.

Using Basic Authentication

If you clear the **Allow Anonymous Access** and **Windows NT Challenge/Response Authentication** options for the page or the folder the page is in, and select the **Basic Authentication** option, the IIS server will prompt the user to enter his or her Windows NT user account and password before opening the page. This method of authentication doesn't use delegation and for this reason doesn't have the restrictions described for Windows NT Challenge/Response authentication. However, basic authentication sends user account and password information across the network in an unencrypted format that could be intercepted by a malicious user. If you want to avoid this risk, you can set up your server to publish the data access page by using a Secure Sockets Layer (SSL) encrypted connection. For information about how to enable encryption, see the documentation for Microsoft Internet Information Server.

Strategies for Maintaining Secured Data Access Pages That Use Three-Tier Data Access

There are several ways you can manage how data access pages that use secure three-tier data access are authored and maintained:

- If both the page author's workstation and the IIS server can use the same connection information, the author can view and modify the page in Design view in Access and resave it to the IIS server. One way to satisfy this requirement is to author the page on the IIS machine itself.
- You can author the page with the **UseRemoteProvider** property set to **False**. Then, when you are ready to deploy the page, set the **UseRemoteProvider** property to **True**, change the data source information to **(local)** for a SQL Server database or a local path such as **C:\MyFolder\MyDB.mdb** for an Access database, and then save and copy the page to the IIS server.
- Alternatively, use both a design and production copy of the database. (The design copy resides on the author's workstation, and the production copy resides on the IIS server computer.) If both databases use the same local data source connection information, such as **(local)** for a SQL Server database or **C:\MyFolder\MyDB.mdb** for an Access database, the page will work correctly when it is saved to the IIS server.

Configuring Internet Explorer Data Access Security Settings

To configure the security settings in Internet Explorer, you use the **Security** tab of the **Internet Options** dialog box. In Internet Explorer 5, cross-domain data access is controlled by using the **Access data sources across domains** security setting. To view this setting, click **Internet Options** on the **View** menu, click the **Security** tab, click the zone you want to view settings for, and then click **Customize Settings**. To prevent all attempts to use cross-domain data access, set the **Access data sources across domains** setting to **Disable**. To allow a user who is browsing a data access page to decide whether to allow cross-domain data access, set the **Access data sources across domains** setting to **Prompt**. The default settings for the **Access data sources across domains** setting for each zone in Internet Explorer 5 are shown in the following table.

Zone	Setting
Internet	**Disable**
Local intranet	**Prompt**
Trusted sites	**Enable**
Restricted sites	**Disable**

If you can't or don't want to use three-tier data access with your data access pages, you can publish your pages from a Web site that is located in the **Trusted sites** zone. Using this strategy assumes either that all users who can publish pages to folders on that site are trusted, or that pages are examined and approved by an administrator before they are published on that site.

To control security settings for all users who install and use Internet Explorer 5, a system administrator can use the Internet Explorer Administration Kit (IEAK). For more information about the IEAK, see the Internet Explorer Administration Kit Web site at http://ieak.microsoft.com. For more information about creating and deploying secure data access pages, see the white paper "Creating Secure Data Access Pages" (DAP Security.doc), located in the Appendixes folder on the companion CD-ROM.

Where to Go from Here

For additional information about the subjects discussed in this chapter, see the following sources. If a file name is listed, that file is located in the Appendixes folder on the companion CD-ROM, unless otherwise noted.

General Security Issues

Microsoft Security Advisor Web site
(http://www.microsoft.com/security/)

Administrator Control over Passwords

Microsoft Office 2000 Resource Kit. Redmond, WA: Microsoft Press, 1999.

Microsoft Office 2000 Resource Kit Web site
(http://www.microsoft.com/office/ork/)

Administrator Control over Internet Explorer

Internet Explorer Administration Kit Web site
(http://ieak.microsoft.com/)

Access Virus Information

Access Virus Information Web site
(http://officeupdate.microsoft.com/Articles/antivirus.htm)

Data Access Objects (DAO)

Microsoft Jet Database Engine Programmer's Guide, Second Edition. Redmond, WA: Microsoft Press, 1997

Microsoft Office Developer Web site
(http://www.microsoft.com/officedev/)

ActiveX Data Objects (ADO)

Microsoft Jet Database Engine Programmer's Guide, Third Edition. Redmond, WA: Microsoft Press, 1999.

Microsoft Universal Data Access Web site (http://www.microsoft.com/data/)

Microsoft ActiveX Data Objects Web site (http://www.microsoft.com/data/ado/)

Microsoft Office Developer Web site (http://www.microsoft.com/officedev/)

Internet Information Server Authentication and Encryption Configuration

Microsoft Internet Information Server 4.0 Online documentation (Server Administration\Security\Authentication)

Microsoft Internet Information Server 4.0 Online documentation (Server Administration\Security\Encryption)

Data Access Pages Security

Covington, Clinton. "Creating Secure Data Access Pages." (DAP Security.doc)

Code Samples

The code samples shown in this chapter, along with additional examples demonstrating similar techniques, can be copied from the files in the Samples\CH18 subfolder on the companion CD-ROM.

Appendix

Controls
Members of <globals>
Abs
ActiveDocument
Application
<globals>
AddIn
AddIns
Adjustments
Assistant
<All Libraries>
.On = True
Call Wait(5000)

Object Model Diagrams

This appendix consists of object model diagrams for each Microsoft Office application as well as components available for use within an Office application. The object model diagrams included here show how the objects in an object model fit together.

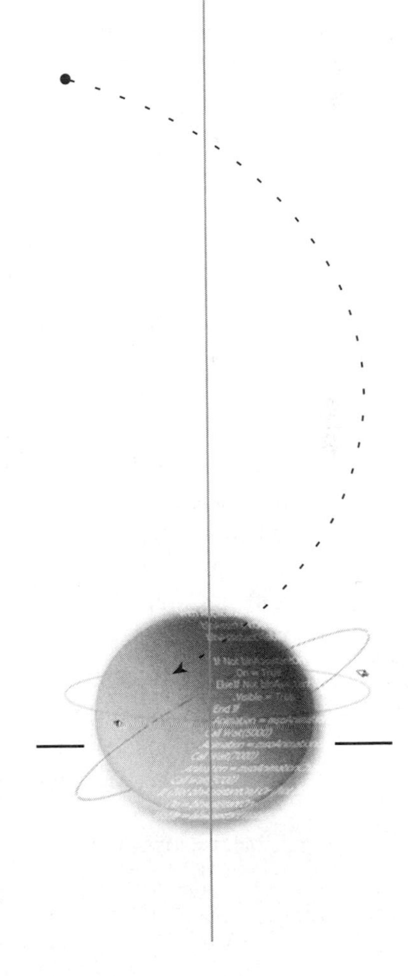

An application or component programmatically exposes its functionality through objects. You work with an object by using its properties and methods. Objects are named according to the portion of an application they represent, and they are ordered in a hierarchy. The topmost tier of each application's object hierarchy is typically occupied by a single object: **Application**. The **Application** object represents the application itself, and all other objects for that application are below the **Application** object. The second tier consists of a high-level categorization of objects. The remaining tiers include a variety of additional objects that are used to access the functionality that the second-tier objects contain.

A group of similar objects can be combined in the hierarchy as a *collection*. You can work with a member of a collection as a single object or as a member of that collection. For example, the Microsoft Excel object model exposes the **Application** object as the top-level object in its object model hierarchy. The **Application** object has a **Workbooks** collection that contains a **Workbook** object for each currently open workbook. Similarly, each **Workbook** object has a **Worksheets** collection that represents the worksheets in a workbook, and so on.

Using These Object Model Diagrams

You can use these diagrams as a handy shortcut to finding the object you want to work with and understanding how that object fits into the overall object model exposed by an application.

The following table shows how objects and collections are represented in the diagrams.

This type of item	Is designated this way
Object	
Collection	

Each diagram contains notes to help you further understand what is depicted. The notes vary from diagram to diagram, but every note includes the name of the type library and its file name, as well as the name of the Help file that contains detailed information about the objects in the object model.

The symbols associated with a diagram indicate special information necessary to help you understand and work with the objects in the specified object model. Some symbols are used globally throughout the appendix; the following table explains what these global symbols mean.

Symbol	Meaning
*	Items marked with this symbol are contained in the Microsoft Office 2000 library, whose objects are shown separately in several object model diagrams in this appendix.
**	Items marked with this symbol are contained in the Microsoft Visual Basic Extensibility 5.3 library, whose object model diagram is shown separately in this appendix.

Where to Find Additional Information

For more information about working with the objects exposed by Microsoft Office applications, see Chapter 4, "Understanding Office Objects and Object Models," and Chapter 6, "Working with Shared Office Components." For information about programming objects in a specific application, see Chapter 5, "Working with Office Applications."

In addition, you'll find detailed reference information about the objects contained in the object models shown here (and their related properties and methods) in the Help topics available for each object model. The easiest way to get help for an object is to select it in the Object Browser and then press F1 to display the related Help topic.

Contents

Microsoft Access 2000

Default location: \Program Files\Microsoft Office\Office

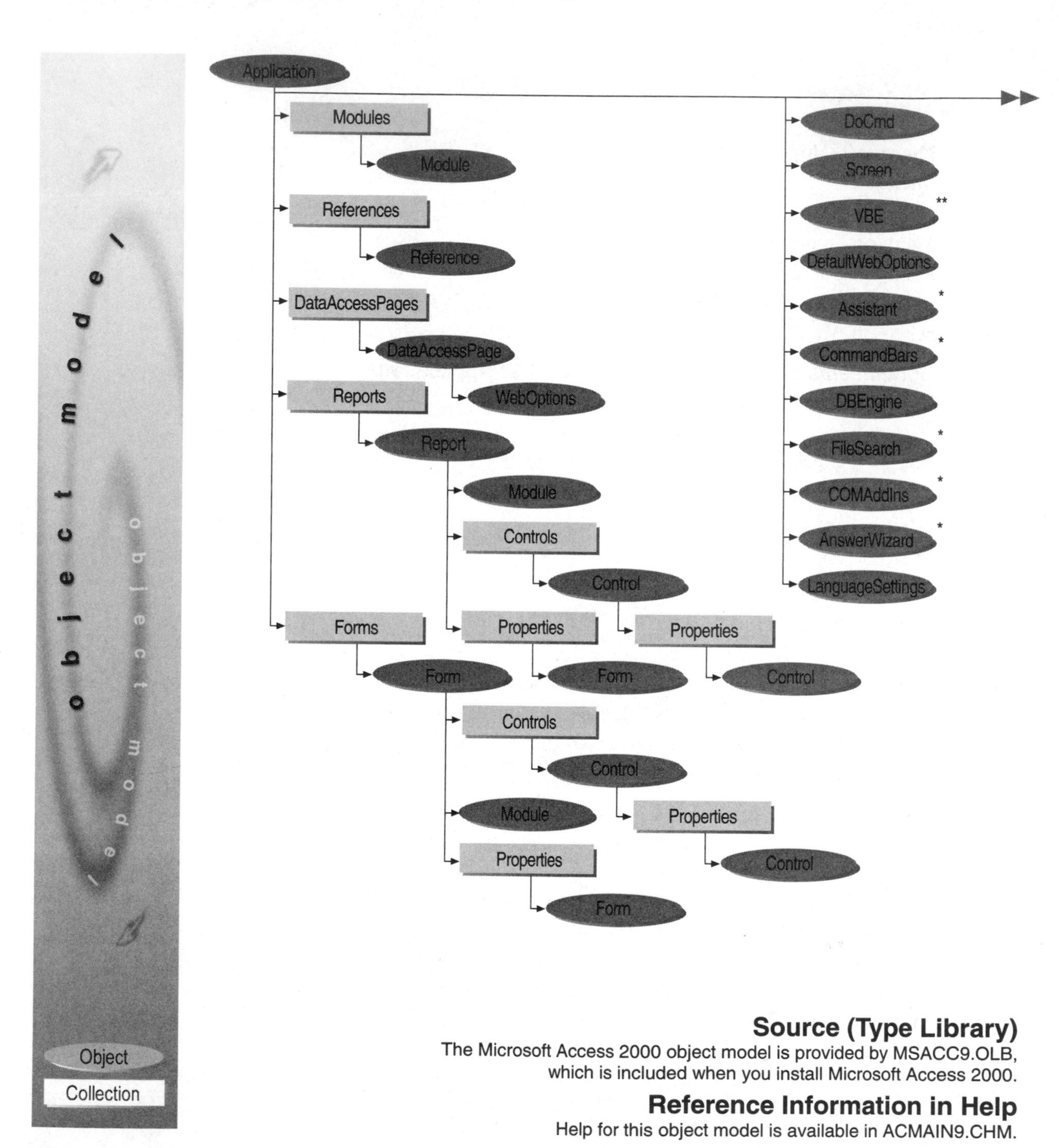

Source (Type Library)

The Microsoft Access 2000 object model is provided by MSACC9.OLB, which is included when you install Microsoft Access 2000.

Reference Information in Help

Help for this object model is available in ACMAIN9.CHM.

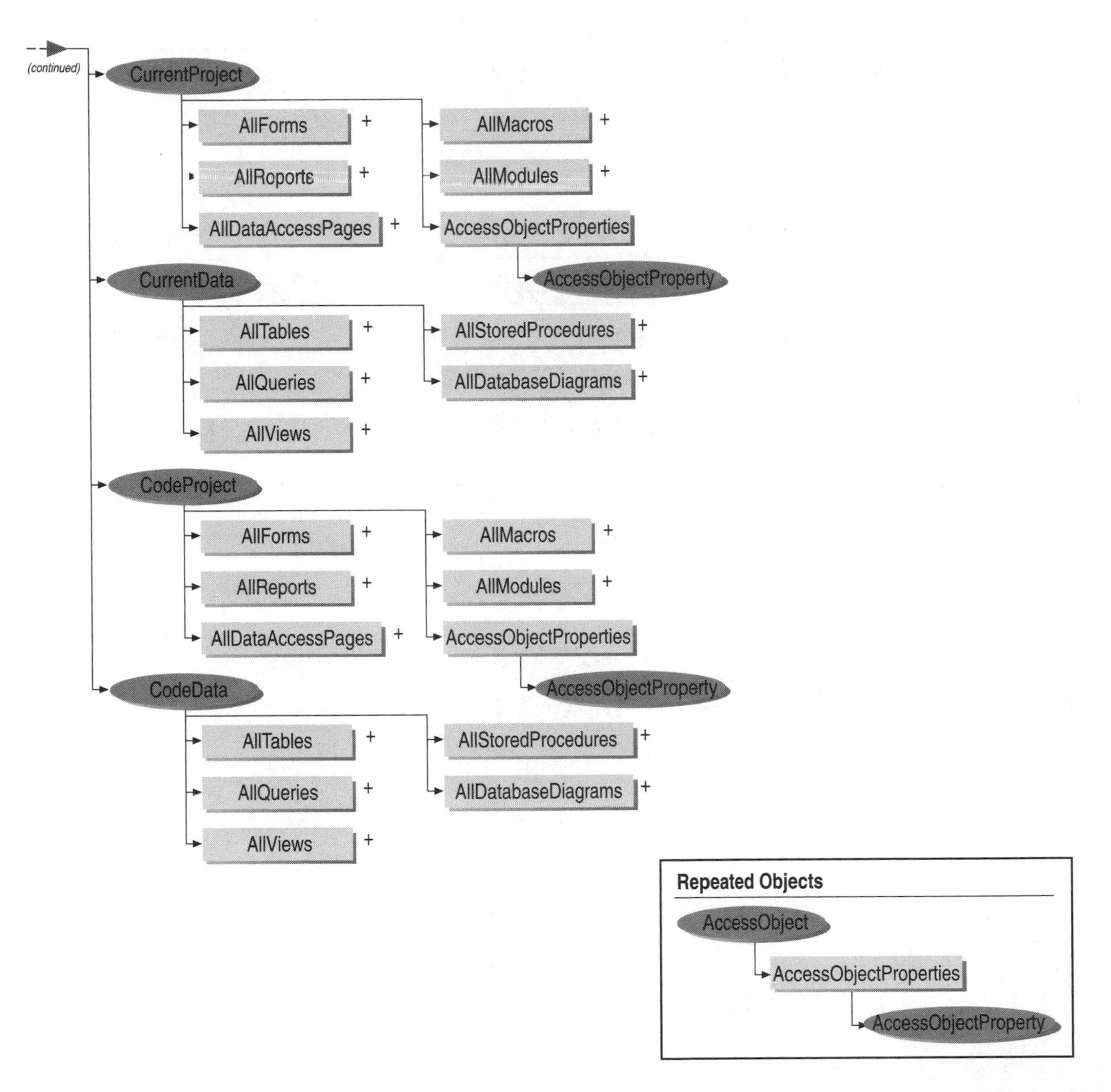

Notes

A plus sign (+) indicates that additional objects or collections are displayed in the "Repeated Objects" portion of this object model diagram.

Microsoft Excel 2000

Default location: \Program Files\Microsoft Office\Office

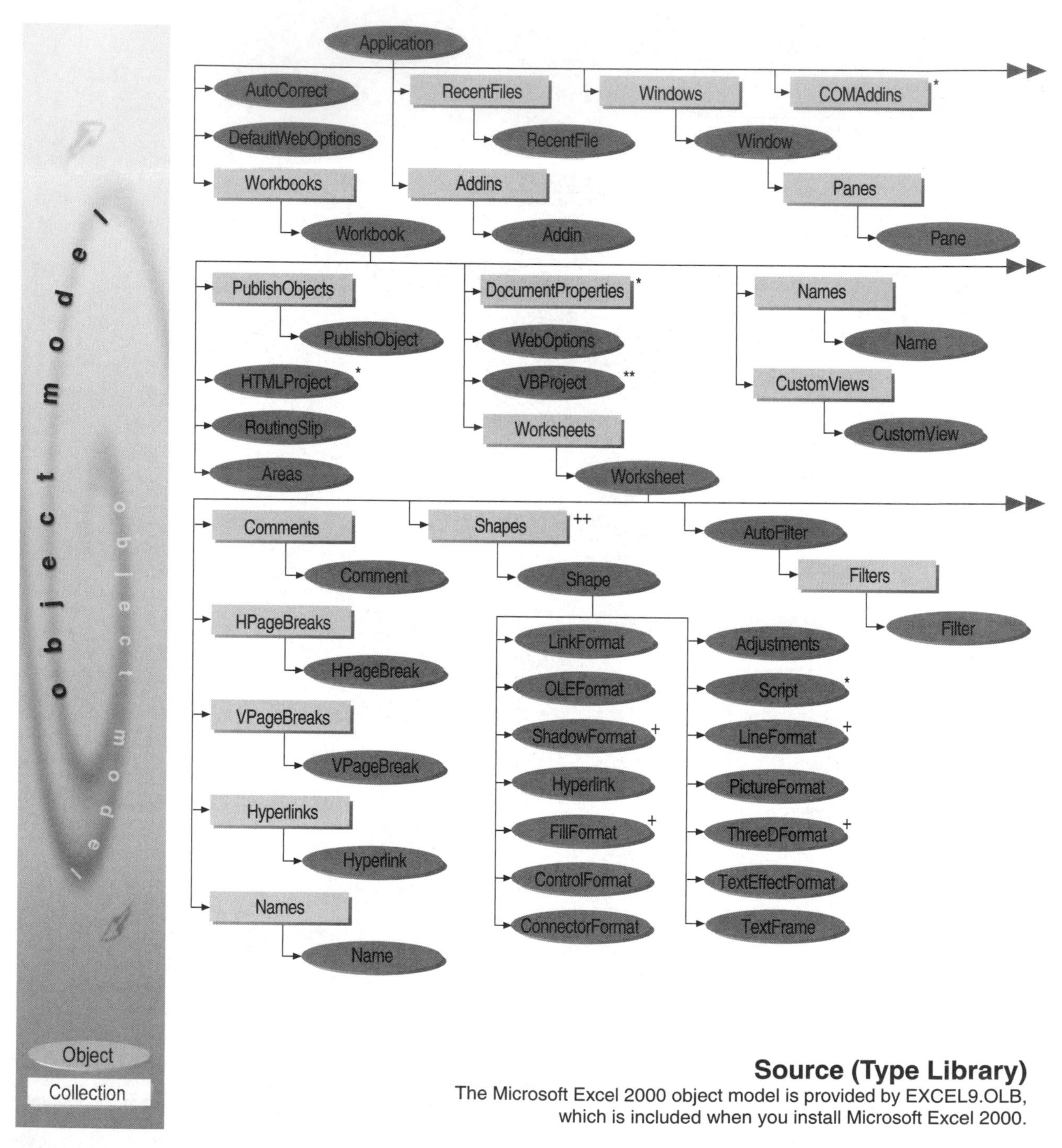

Source (Type Library)

The Microsoft Excel 2000 object model is provided by EXCEL9.OLB, which is included when you install Microsoft Excel 2000.

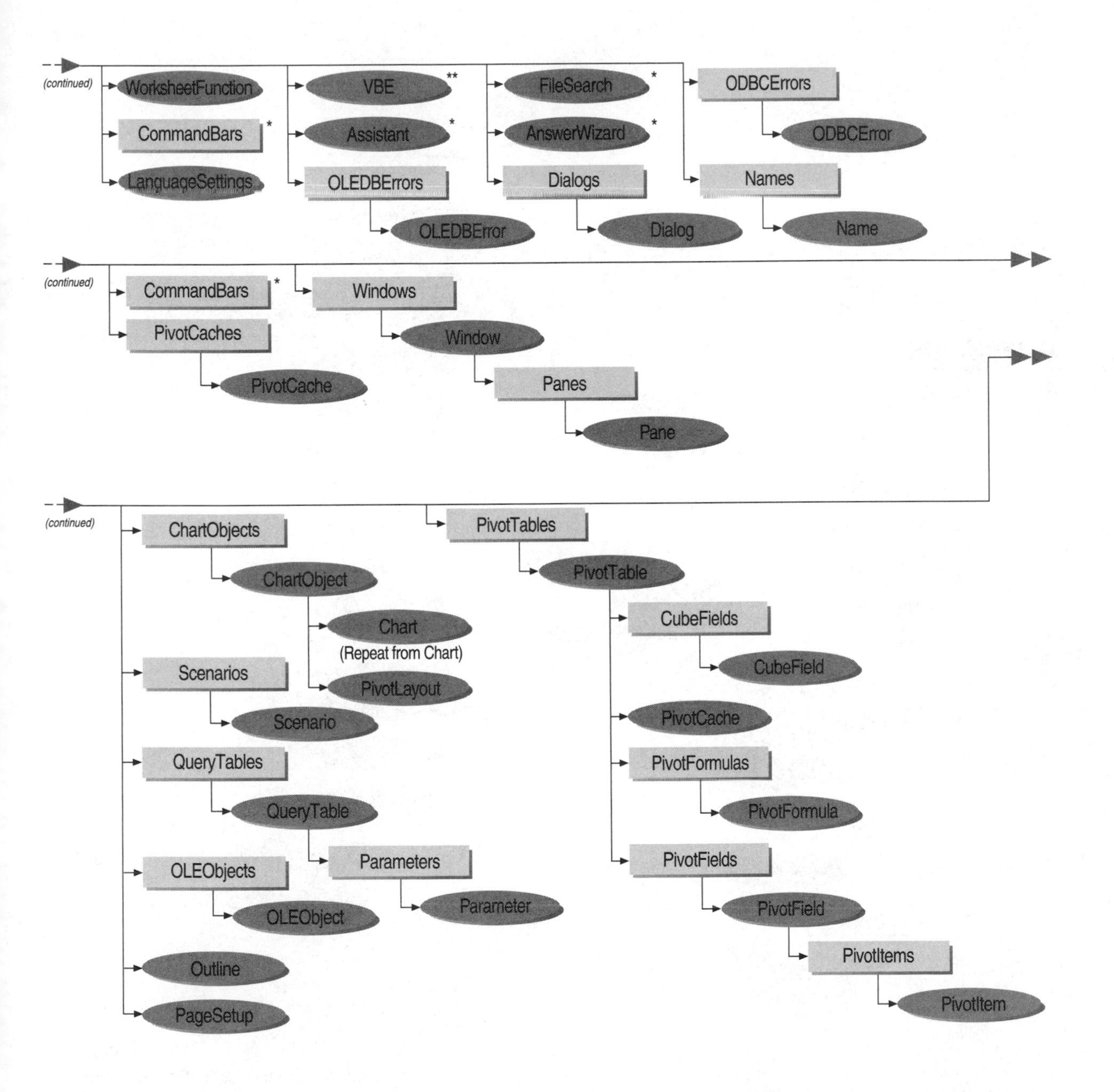

Reference Information in Help

Help for this object model is available in VBAXL9.CHM.

Microsoft Excel 2000 *(continued)*

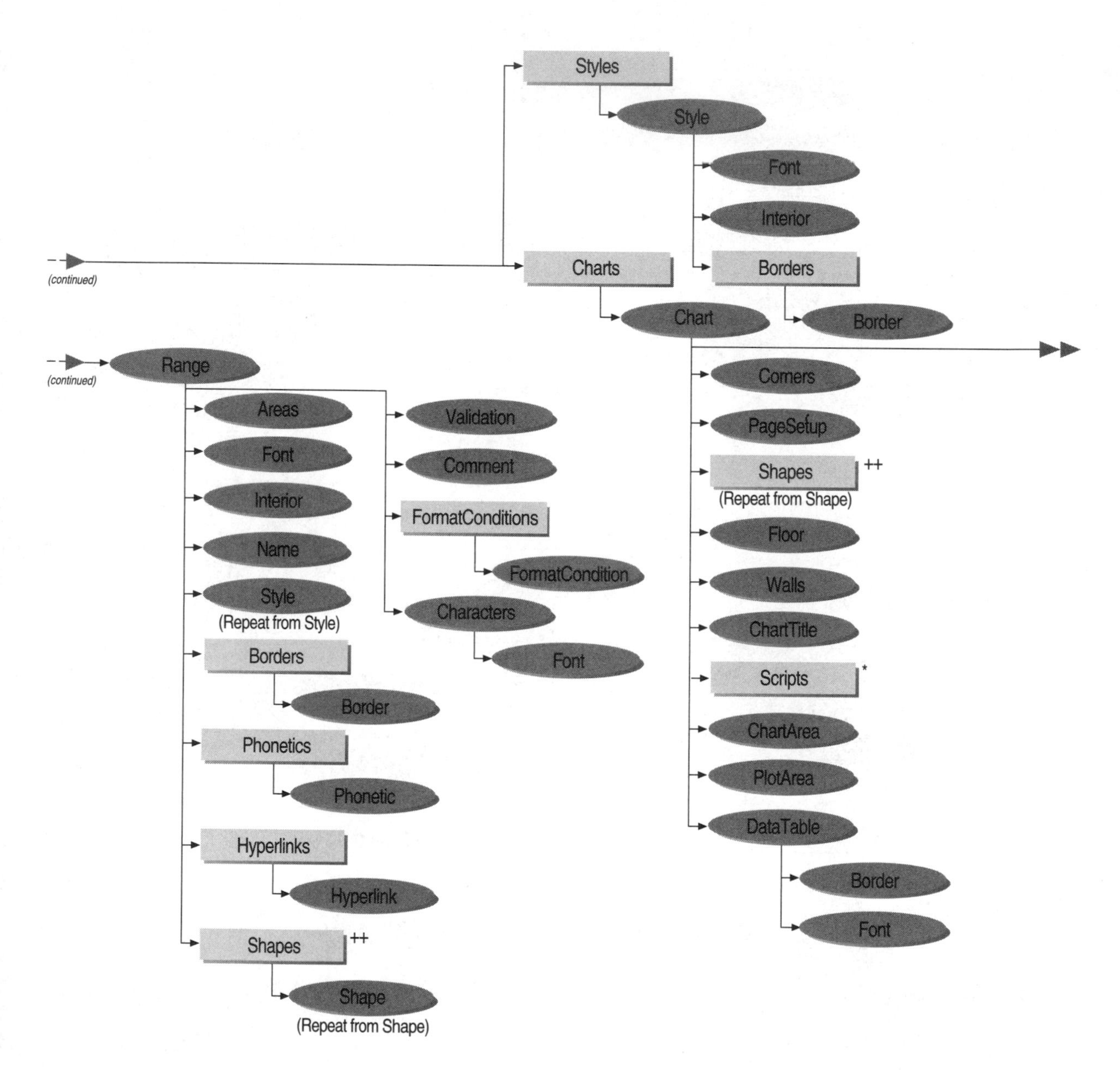

Notes

A single plus sign (+) designates objects with accessors to the **ColorFormat** object.

A double plus sign (++) indicates that the **ShapeRange** objects have been omitted from this diagram. For general purposes, you can think of these objects as occupying the same positions as the **Shape** object.

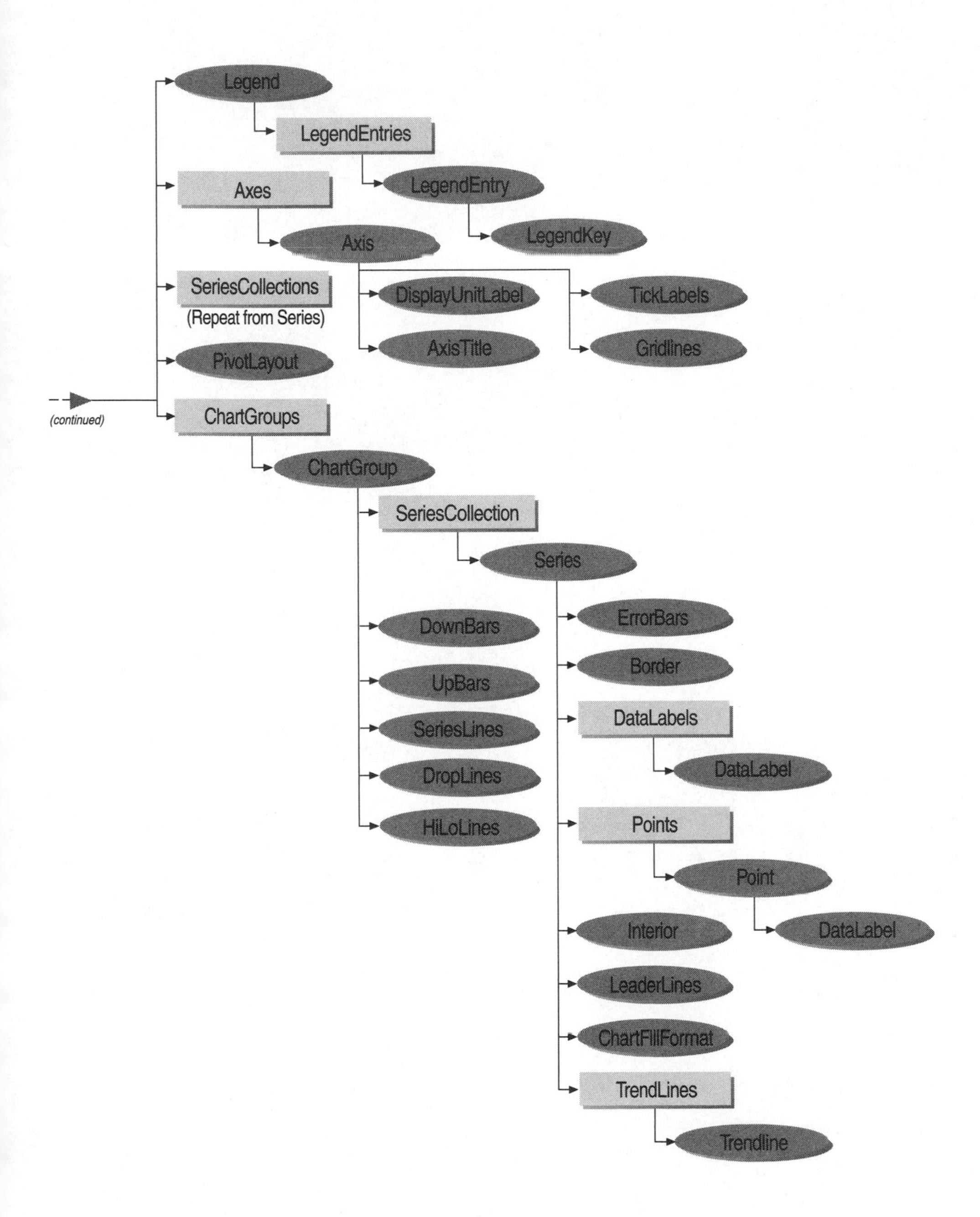

Legend
LegendEntries
Axes
LegendEntry
LegendKey
Axis
SeriesCollections
(Repeat from Series)
DisplayUnitLabel
TickLabels
AxisTitle
Gridlines
PivotLayout
(continued)
ChartGroups
ChartGroup
SeriesCollection
Series
DownBars
ErrorBars
Border
UpBars
SeriesLines
DataLabels
DropLines
DataLabel
HiLoLines
Points
Point
Interior
DataLabel
LeaderLines
ChartFillFormat
TrendLines
Trendline

Microsoft FrontPage 2000

Default location: \Program Files\Microsoft Office\Office

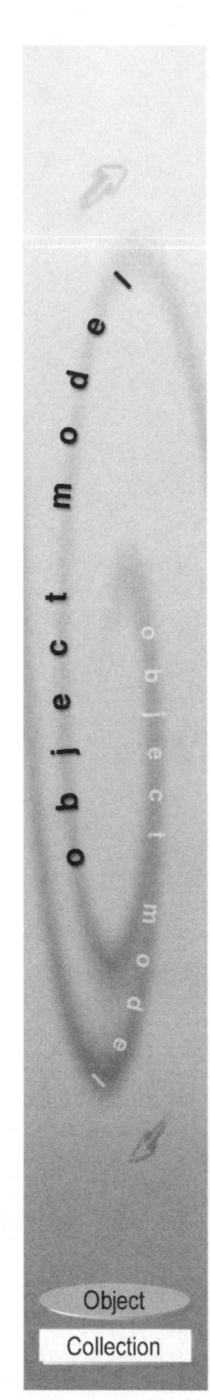

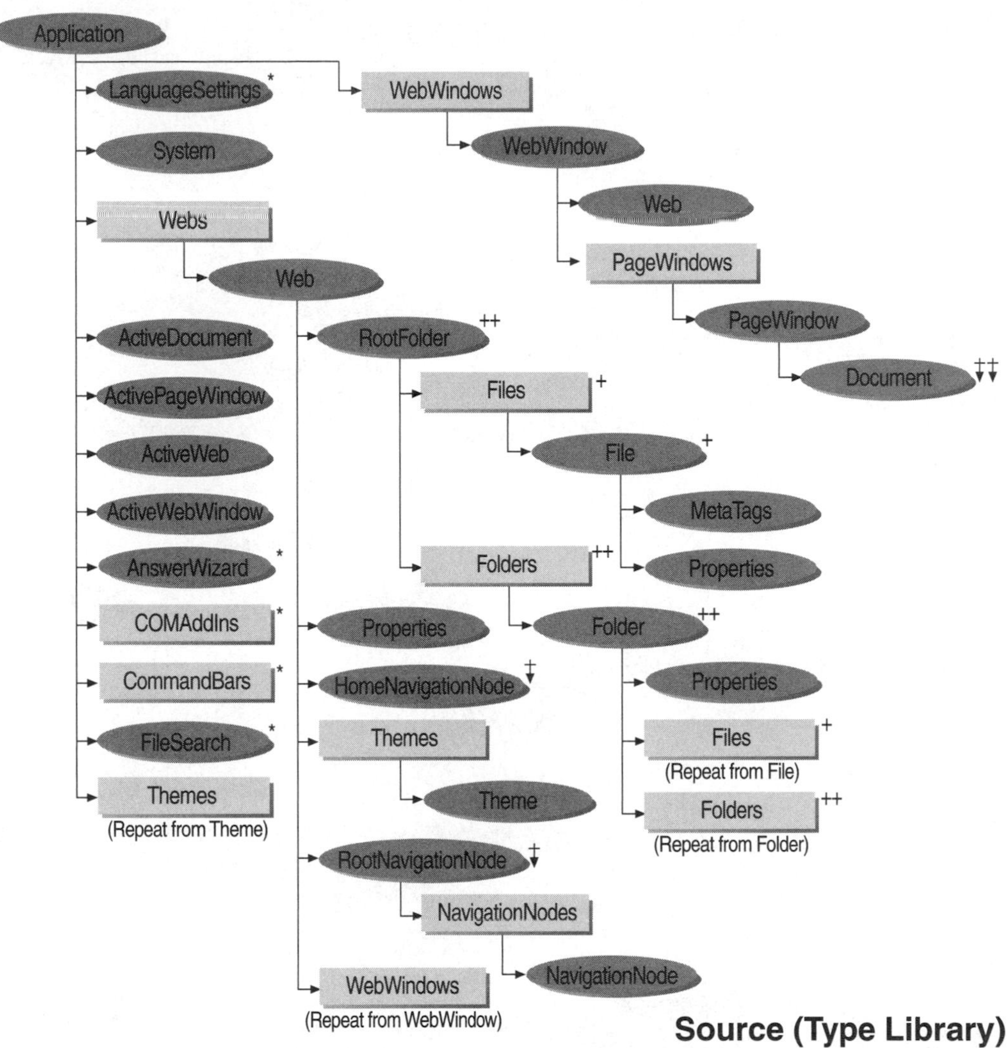

Source (Type Library)

The Microsoft FrontPage object model is provided by FPEDITAX.DLL and FRONTPG.EXE, which are included when you install Microsoft FrontPage 2000.

Reference Information in Help

Help for this object model is available in VBAFP4.CHM.

Notes

Property names are sometimes shown instead of collection and object names. A plus sign (+) indicates that the **Files** and **File** properties return the **WebFiles** collection and the **WebFile** object. A double plus sign (++) indicates that the **Folders** property returns the **WebFolders** collection and that the **RootFolder** and **Folder** properties each return a **WebFolder** object. A ‡ symbol indicates that the **HomeNavigationNode** and **RootNavigationNode** properties return a **NavigationNode** object. A ‡‡ symbol indicates that the **Document** property returns the FrontPage document object model.

Microsoft Outlook 2000

Default location: \Program Files\Microsoft Office\Office

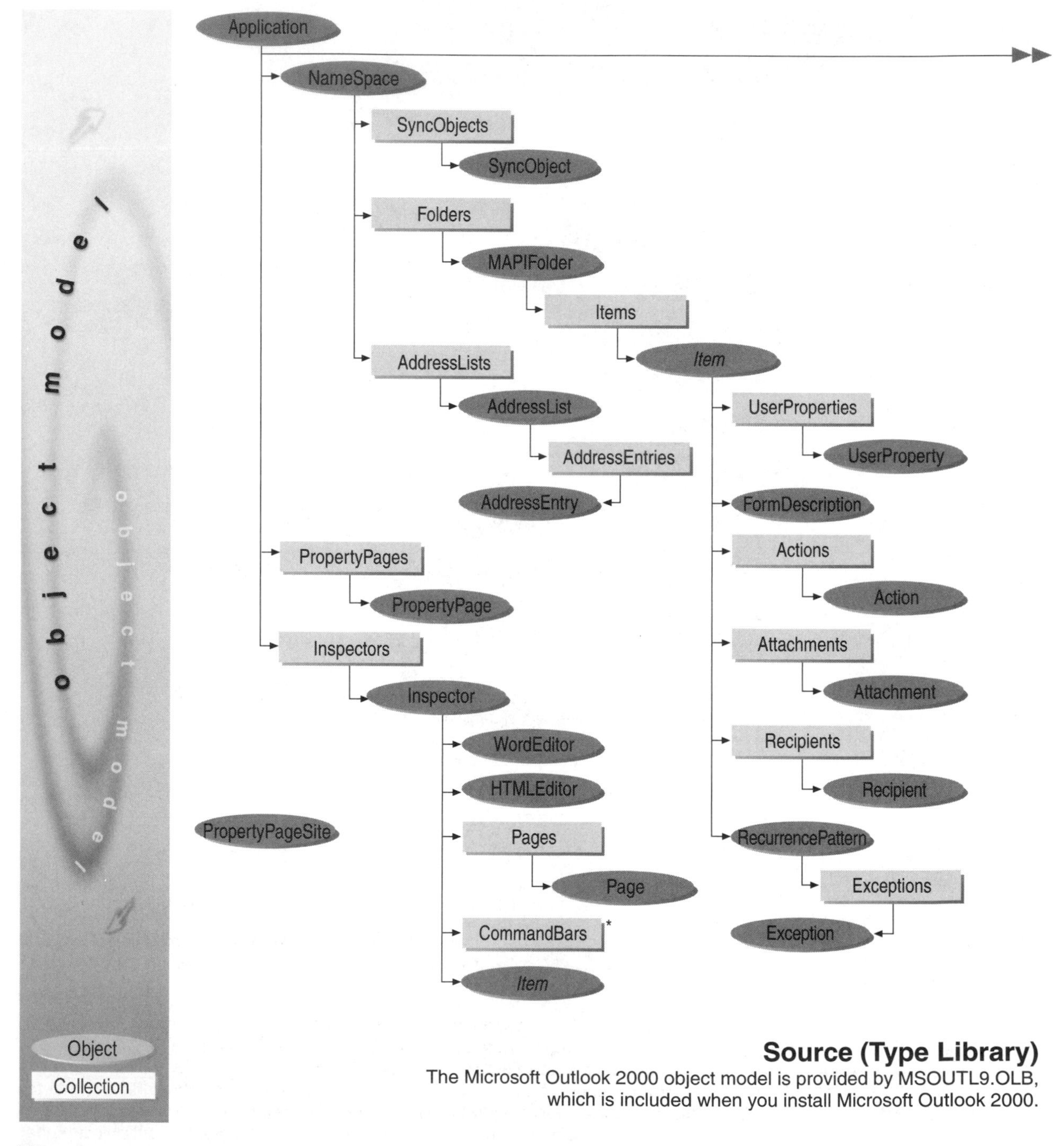

Source (Type Library)

The Microsoft Outlook 2000 object model is provided by MSOUTL9.OLB, which is included when you install Microsoft Outlook 2000.

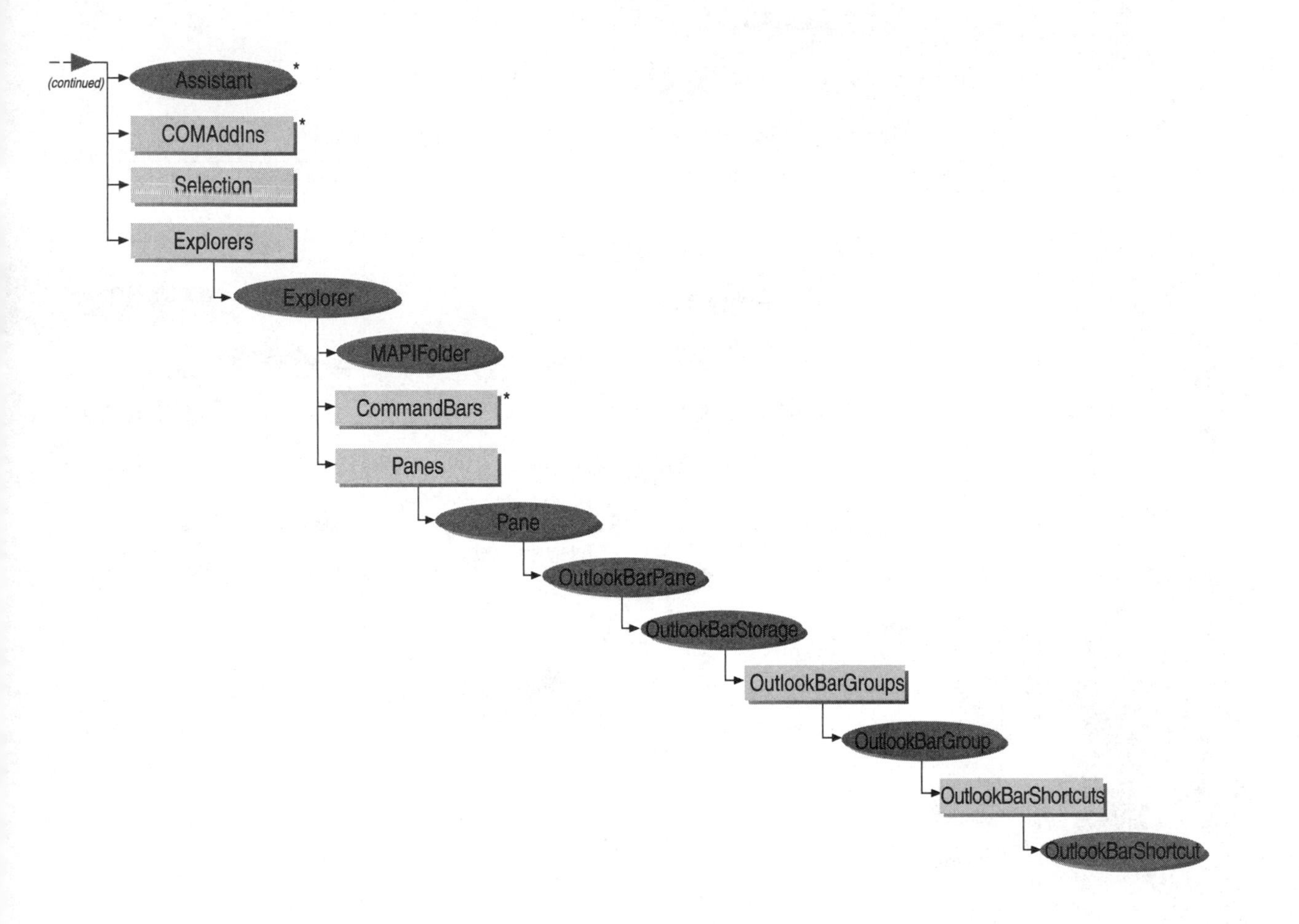

Reference Information in Help

Help for this object model is available in VBAOUTL9.CHM.

Microsoft PowerPoint 2000

Default location: \Program Files\Microsoft Office\Office

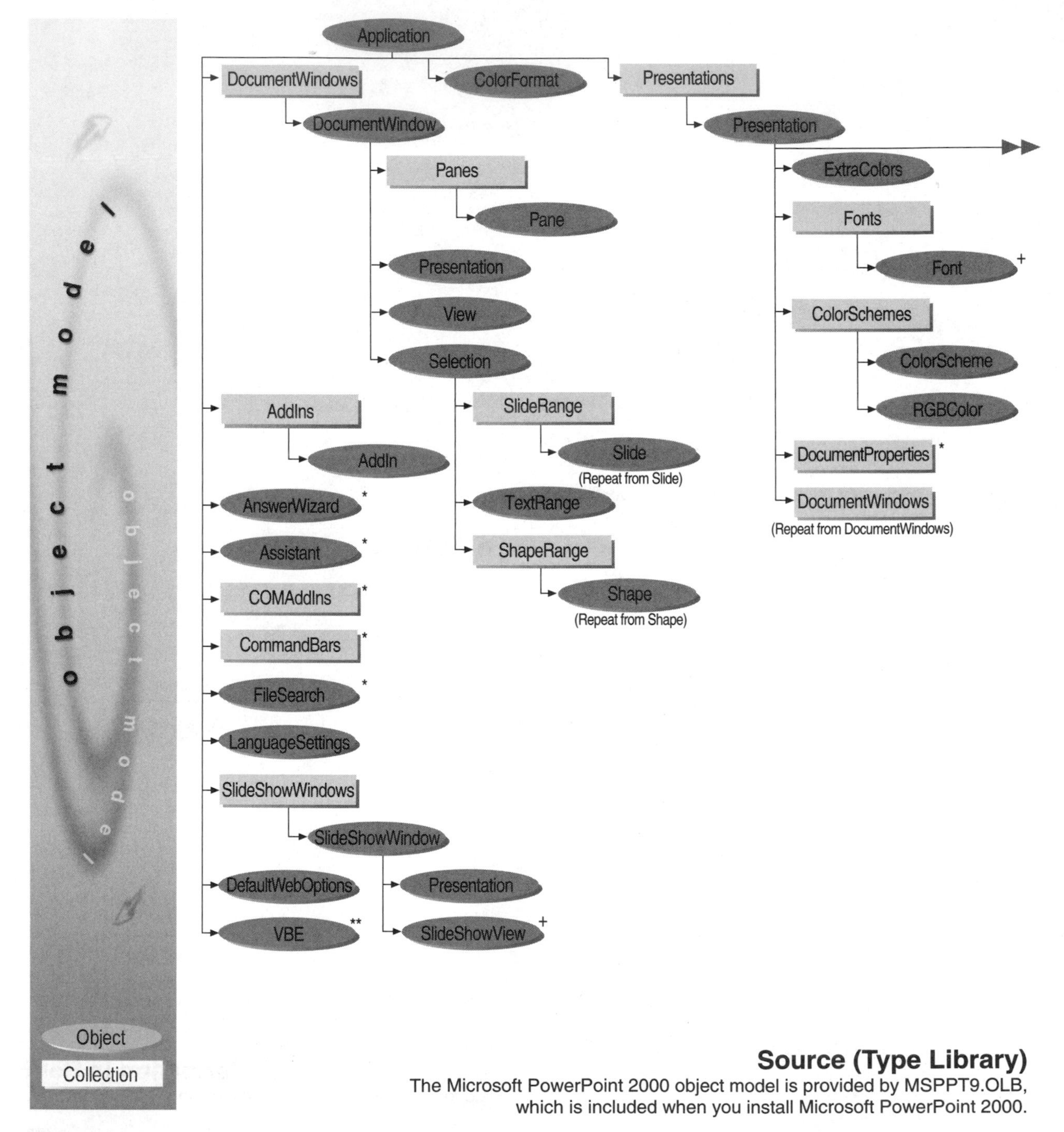

Source (Type Library)

The Microsoft PowerPoint 2000 object model is provided by MSPPT9.OLB, which is included when you install Microsoft PowerPoint 2000.

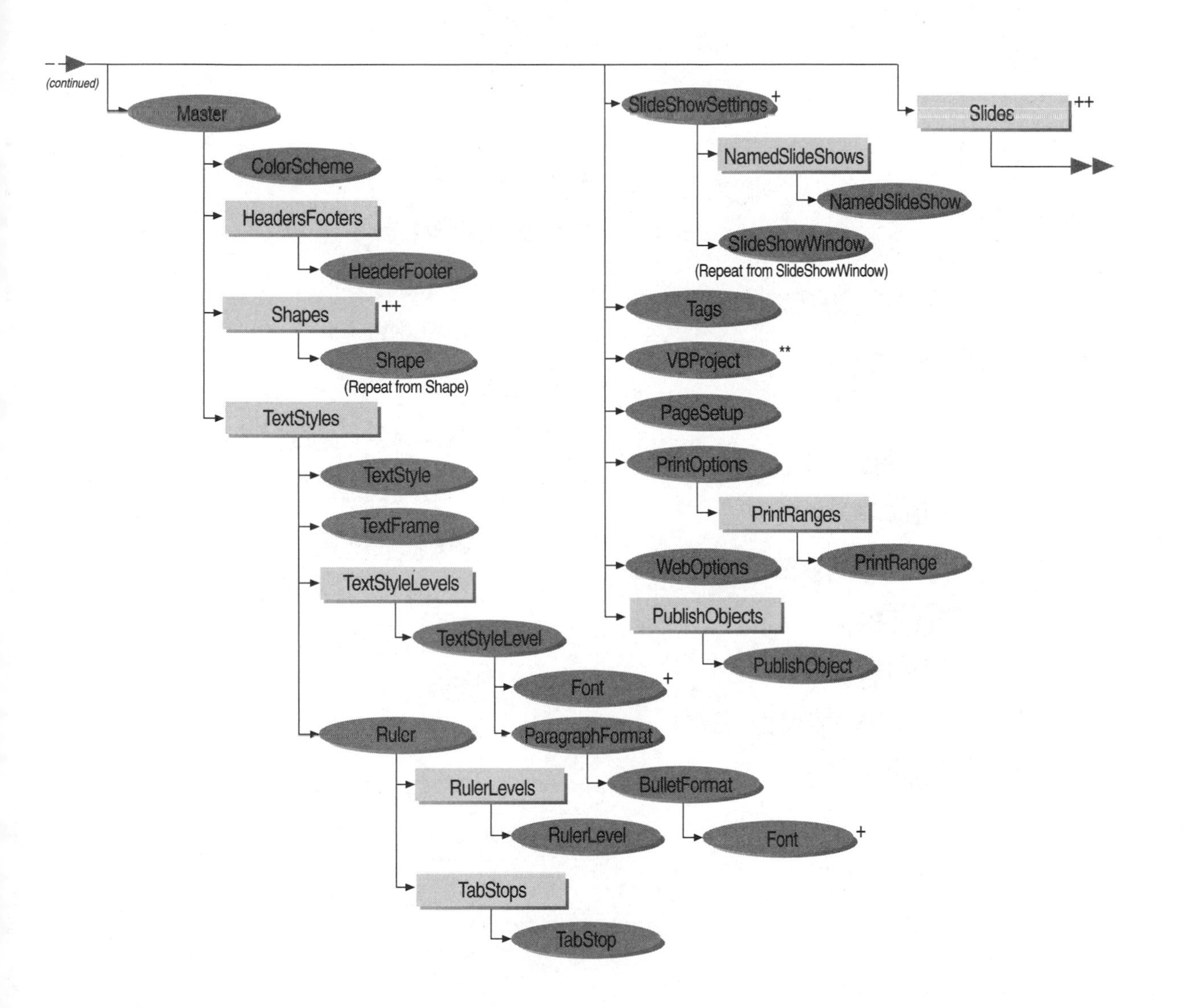

Reference Information in Help

Help for this object model is available in VBAPPT9.CHM.

Microsoft PowerPoint 2000 *(continued)*

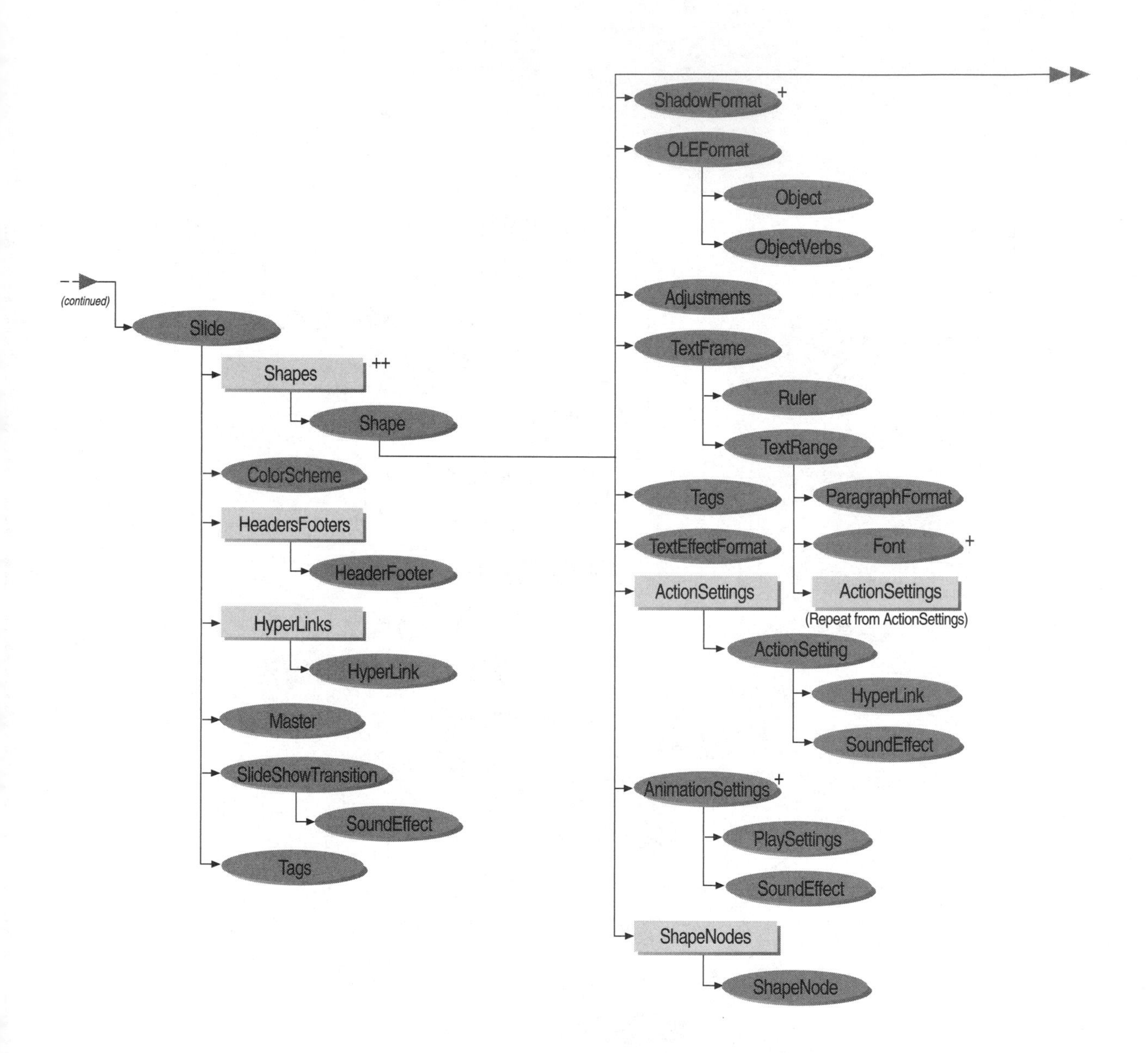

Notes

A single plus sign (+) designates objects with accessors to the **ColorFormat** object. A double plus sign (++) indicates that the **SlideRange** and **ShapeRange** objects have been omitted from this diagram. For general purposes, you can think of these objects as occupying the same positions as the **Slide** and **Shape** objects, respectively.

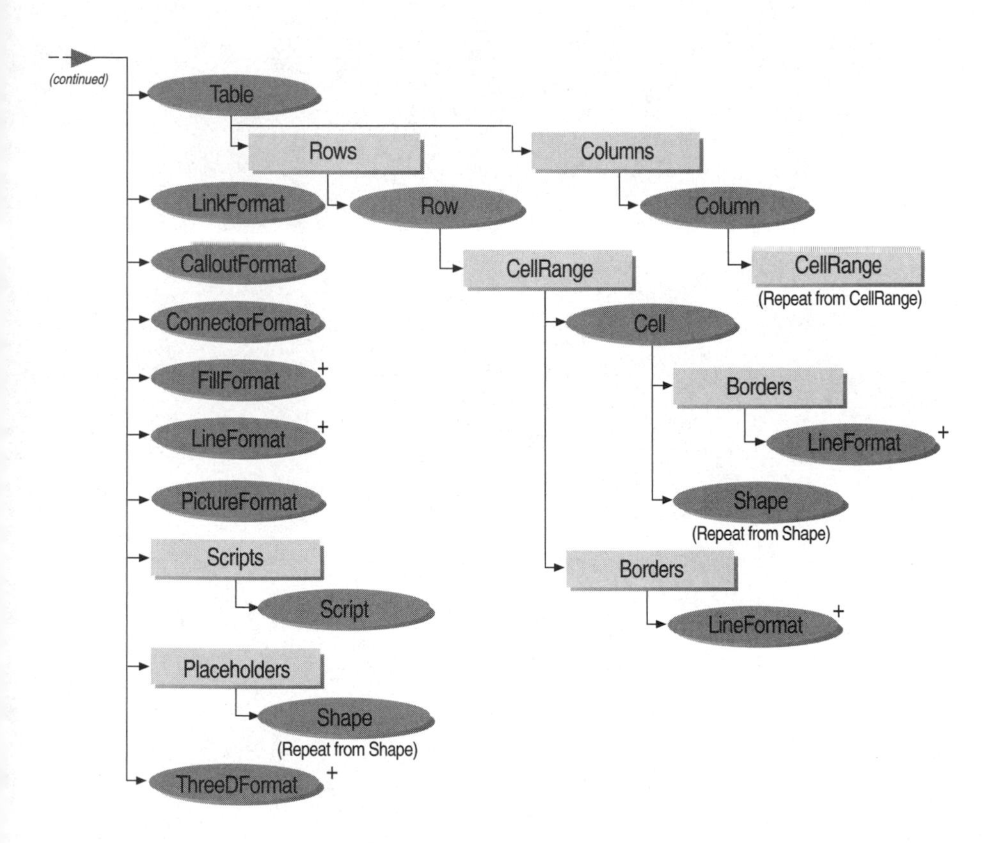
(continued)
Table
Rows
Columns
LinkFormat
Row
Column
CalloutFormat
CellRange
CellRange
(Repeat from CellRange)
ConnectorFormat
Cell
FillFormat
+
Borders
LineFormat
+
LineFormat
+
PictureFormat
Shape
(Repeat from Shape)
Scripts
Borders
Script
LineFormat
+
Placeholders
Shape
(Repeat from Shape)
ThreeDFormat
+

Microsoft Word 2000

Default location: \Program Files\Microsoft Office\Office

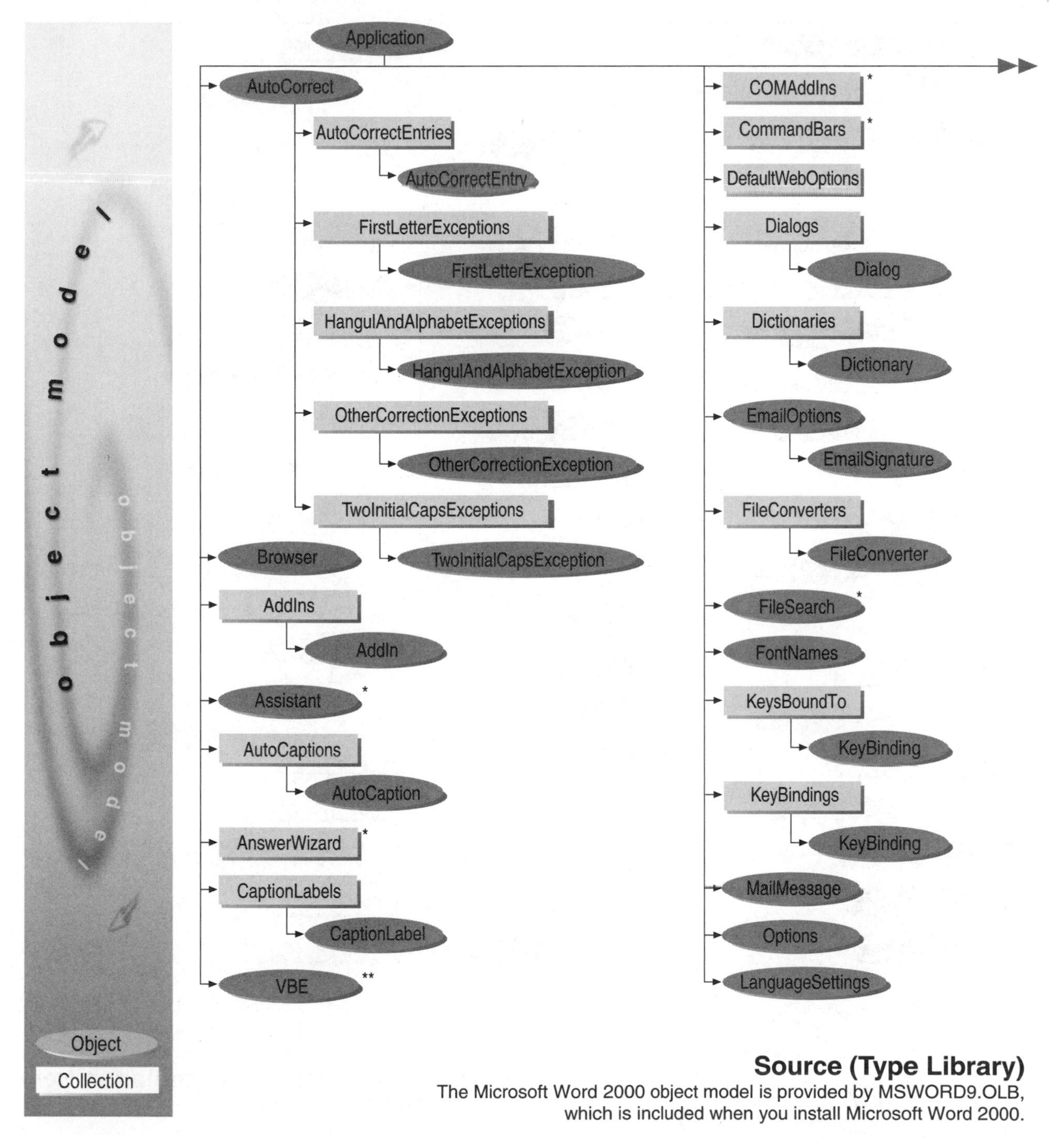

Source (Type Library)

The Microsoft Word 2000 object model is provided by MSWORD9.OLB, which is included when you install Microsoft Word 2000.

Microsoft Word 2000 *(continued)*

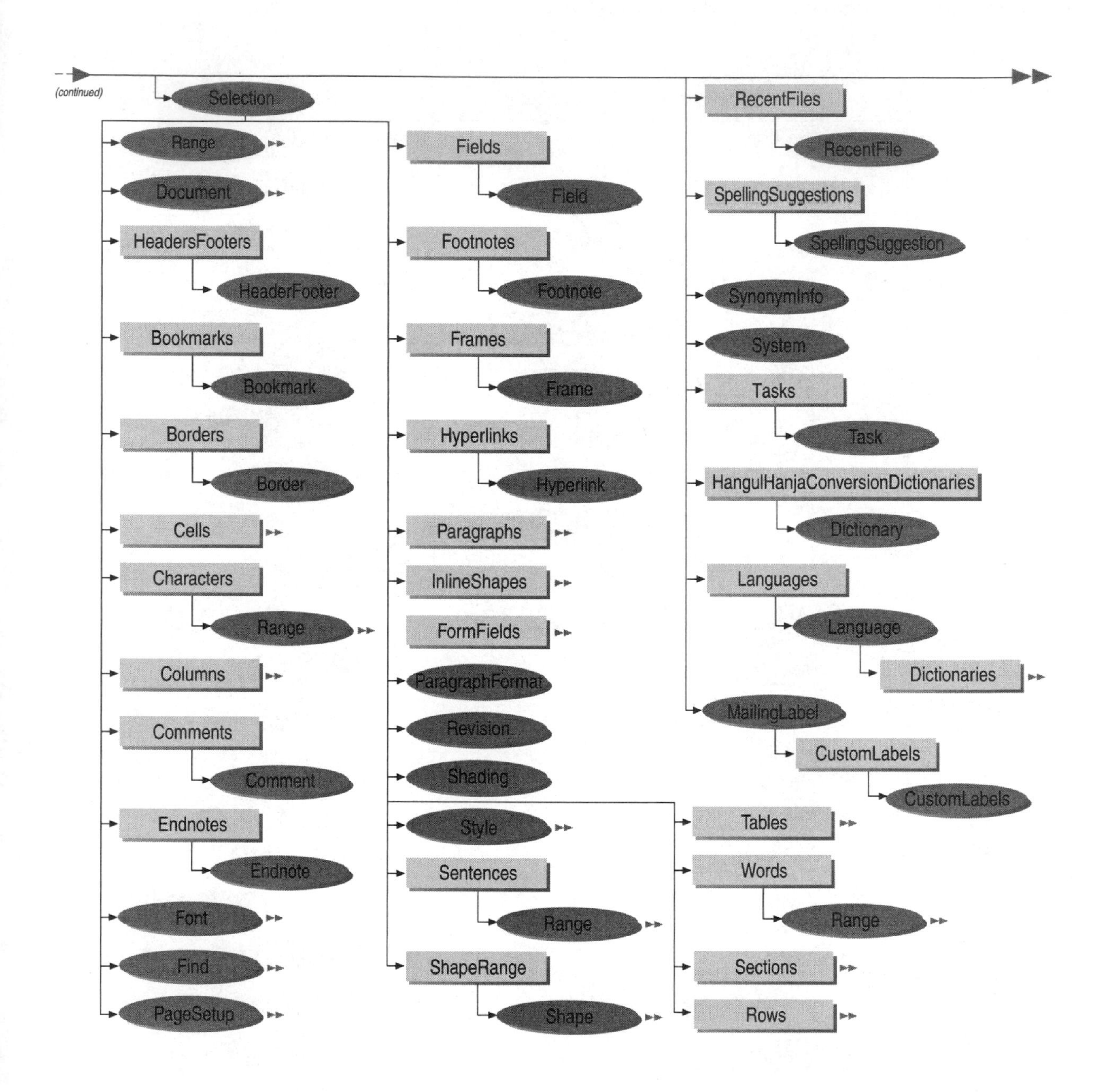

Reference Information in Help

Help for this object model is available in VBAWRD9.CHM.

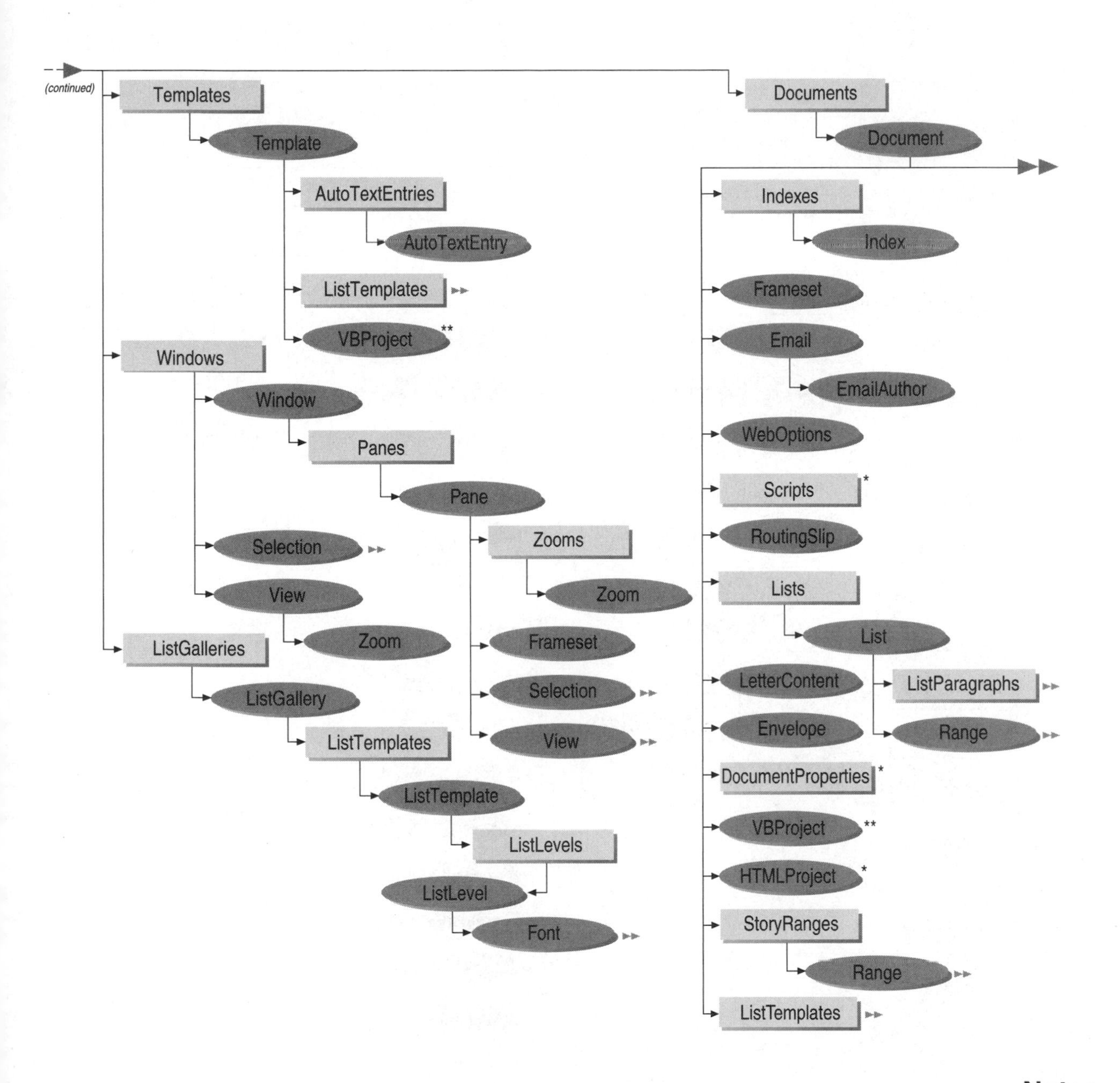

Notes

A single plus sign (+) designates objects with accessors to the **ColorFormat** object.
A double plus sign (++) indicates that the **ShapeRange** objects have been omitted from this diagram.
For general purposes, you can think of these objects as occupying the same positions as the **Shape** object.
A ►► symbol indicates that additional objects are shown elsewhere in this diagram.

Microsoft Word 2000 *(continued)*

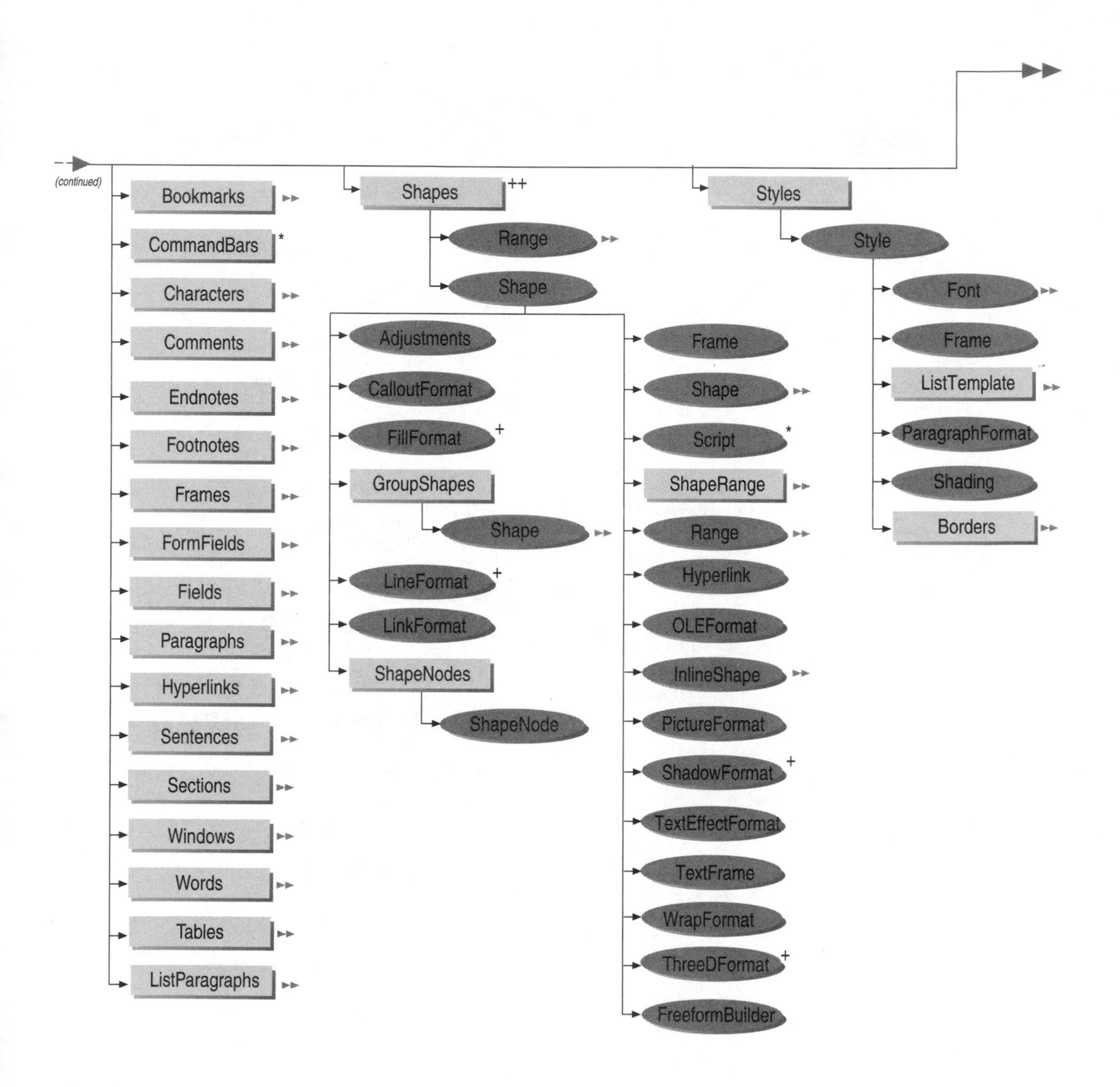

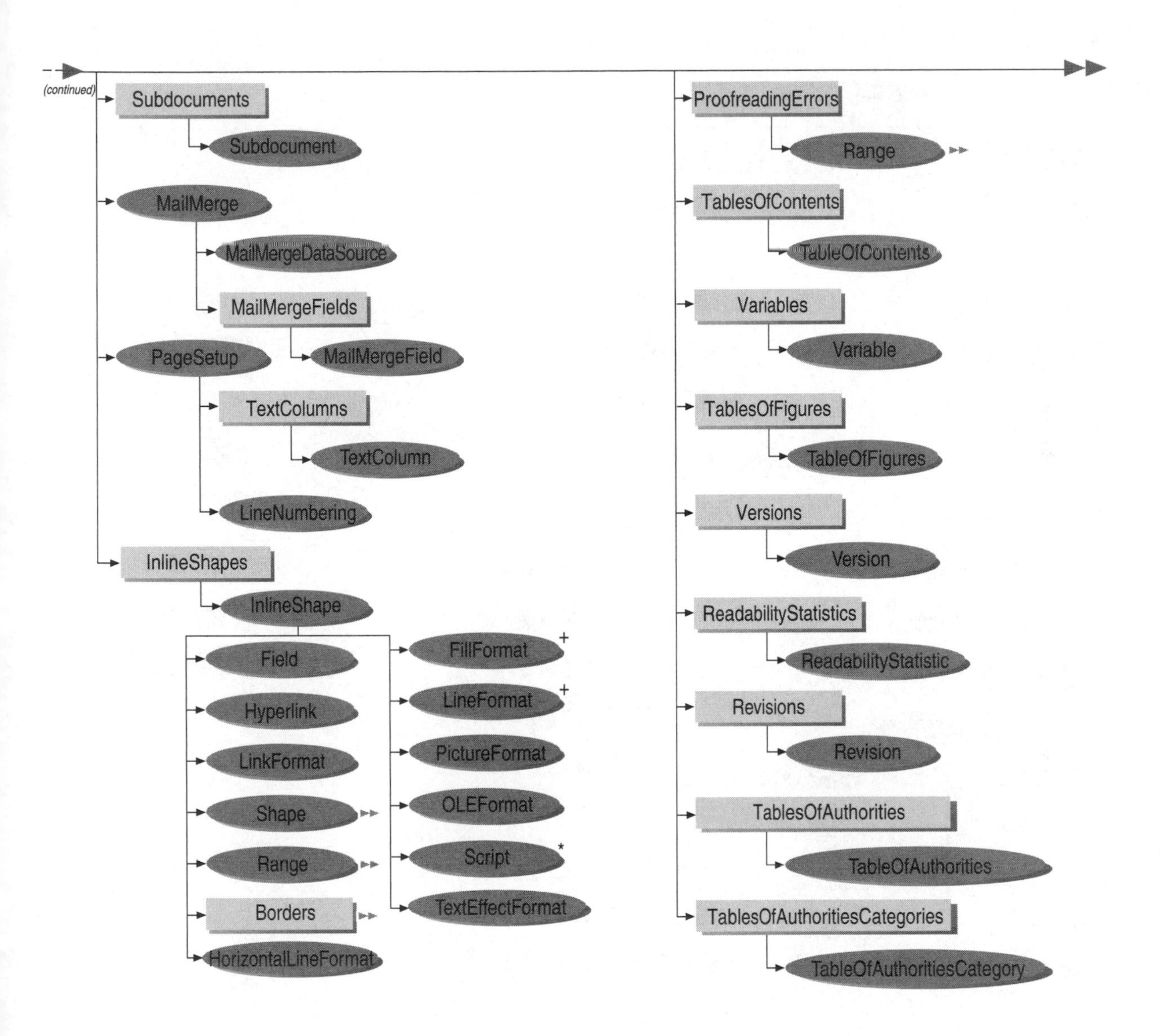

(continued)
Subdocuments
Subdocument
MailMerge
MailMergeDataSource
MailMergeFields
MailMergeField
PageSetup
TextColumns
TextColumn
LineNumbering
InlineShapes
InlineShape
Field
Hyperlink
LinkFormat
Shape
Range
Borders
HorizontalLineFormat
FillFormat
+
LineFormat
+
PictureFormat
OLEFormat
Script
*
TextEffectFormat
ProofreadingErrors
Range
TablesOfContents
TableOfContents
Variables
Variable
TablesOfFigures
TableOfFigures
Versions
Version
ReadabilityStatistics
ReadabilityStatistic
Revisions
Revision
TablesOfAuthorities
TableOfAuthorities
TablesOfAuthoritiesCategories
TableOfAuthoritiesCategory

Microsoft Word 2000 *(continued)*

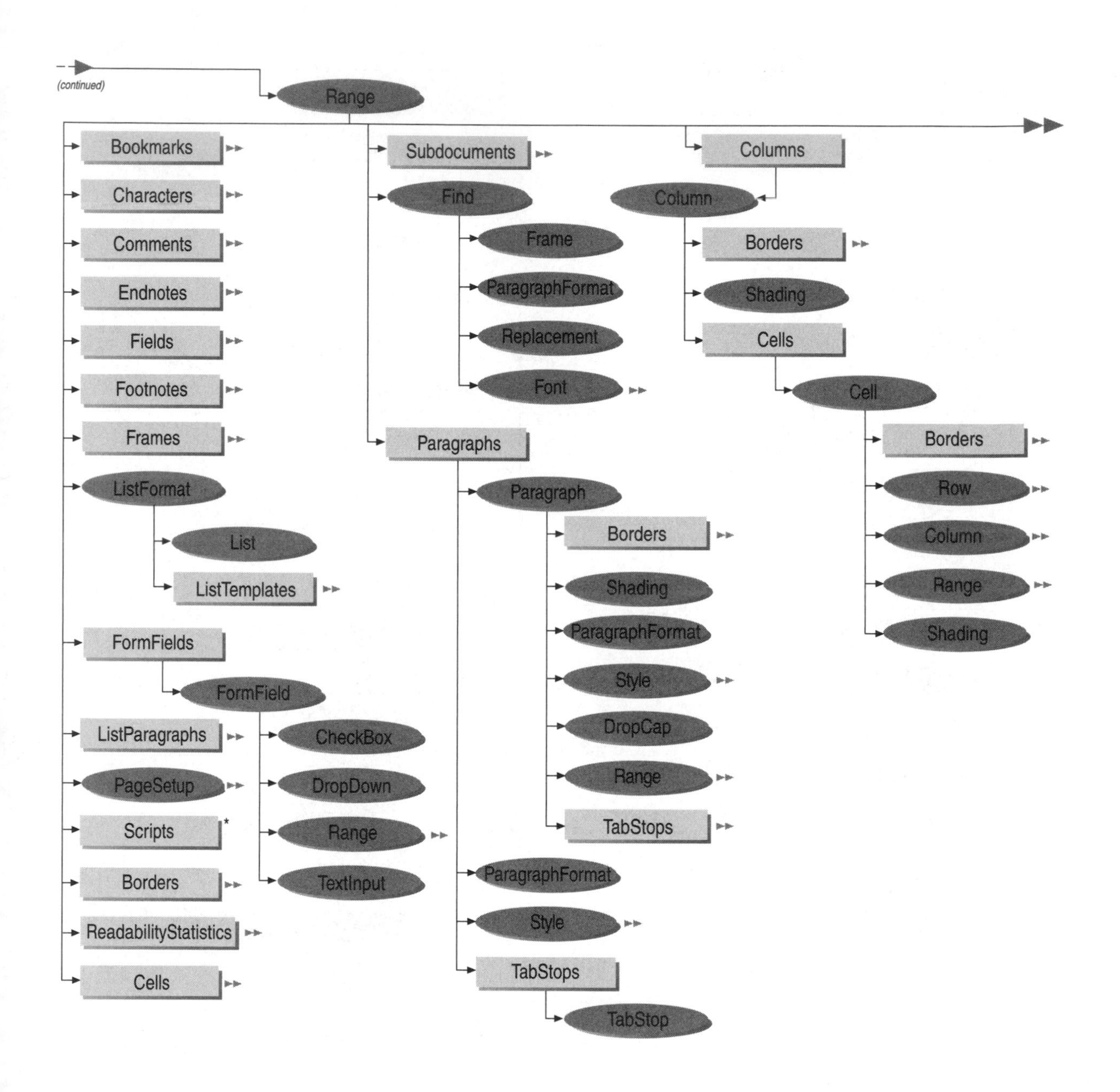

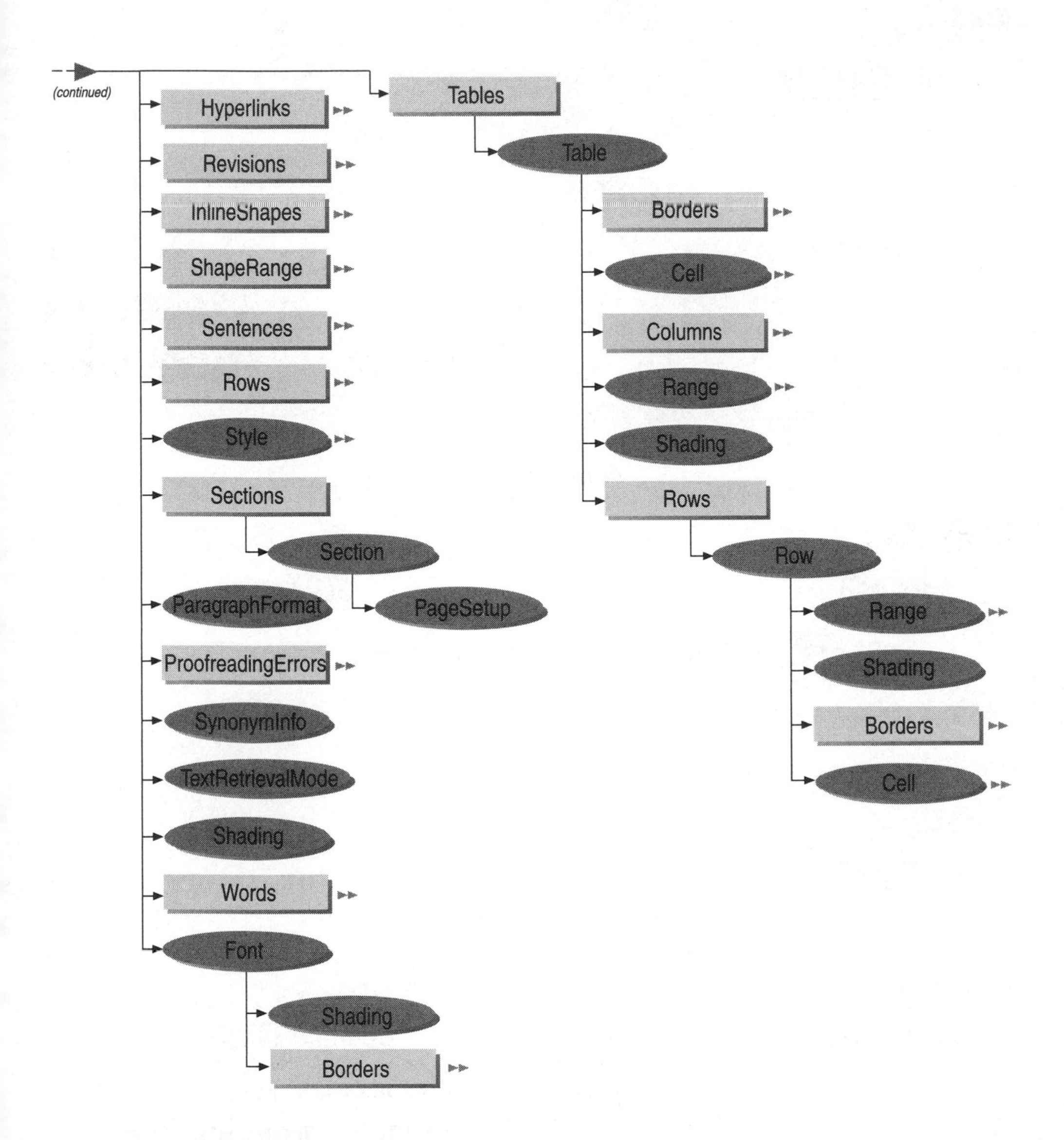
(continued)
Hyperlinks
Revisions
InlineShapes
ShapeRange
Sentences
Rows
Style
Sections
Section
PageSetup
ParagraphFormat
ProofreadingErrors
SynonymInfo
TextRetrievalMode
Shading
Words
Font
Shading
Borders
Tables
Table
Borders
Cell
Columns
Range
Shading
Rows
Row
Range
Shading
Borders
Cell

Microsoft Office Objects

Default location: \Program Files\Microsoft Office\Office

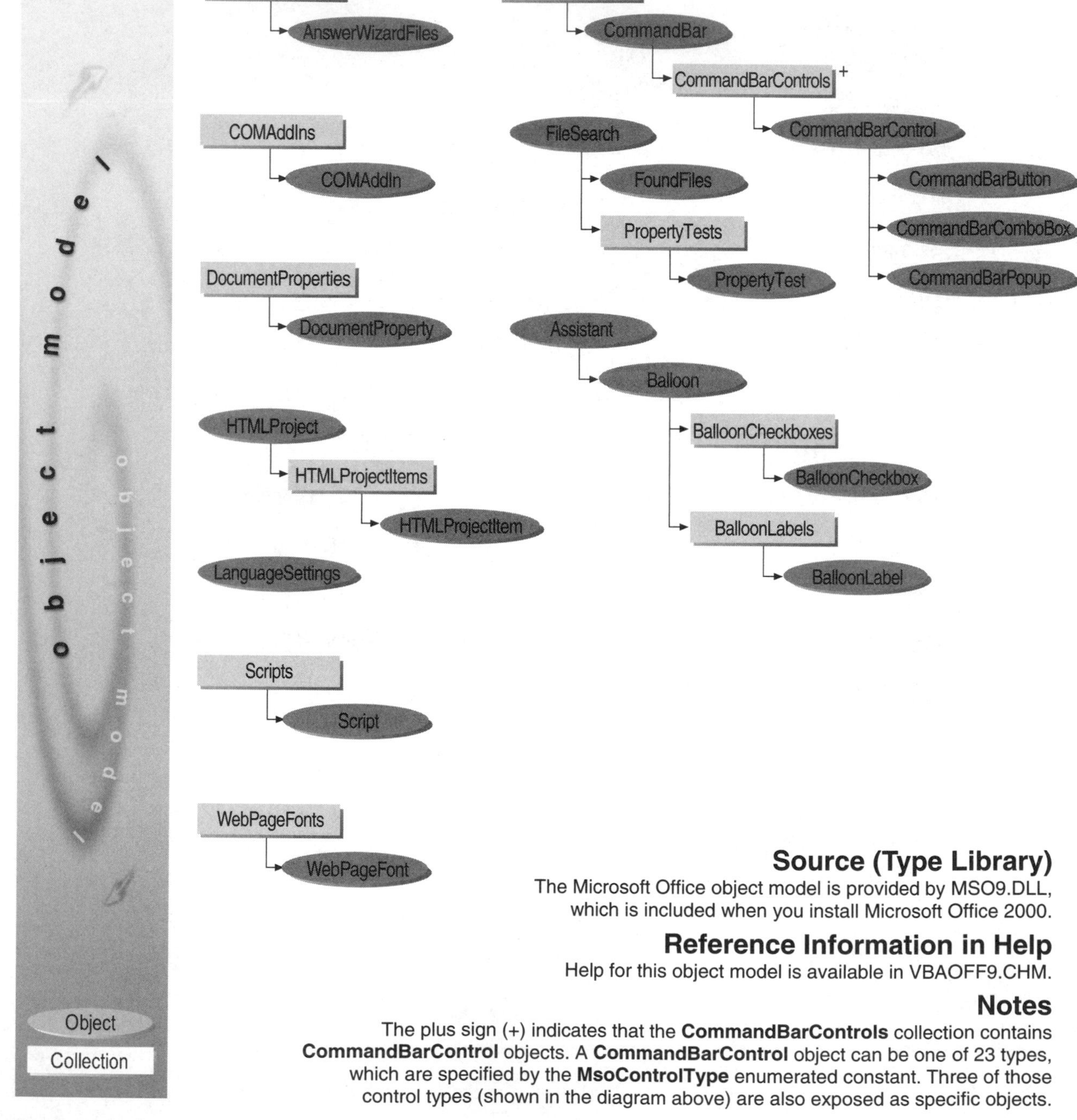

Source (Type Library)

The Microsoft Office object model is provided by MSO9.DLL, which is included when you install Microsoft Office 2000.

Reference Information in Help

Help for this object model is available in VBAOFF9.CHM.

Notes

The plus sign (+) indicates that the **CommandBarControls** collection contains **CommandBarControl** objects. A **CommandBarControl** object can be one of 23 types, which are specified by the **MsoControlType** enumerated constant. Three of those control types (shown in the diagram above) are also exposed as specific objects.

Microsoft Office Binder

Default location: \Program Files\Microsoft Office\Office

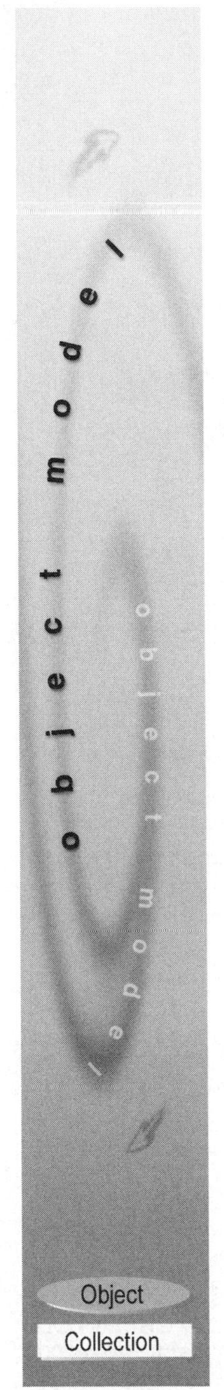

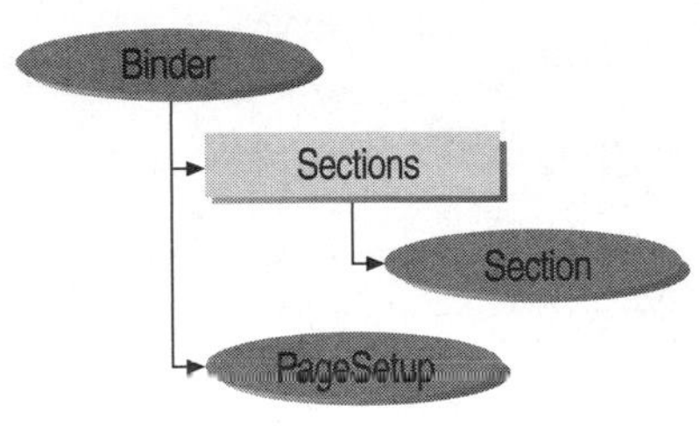

Source (Type Library)

The Microsoft Office Binder object model is provided by MSBDR9.OLB. The Binder type library is installed by selecting Microsoft Binder in the Office Tools category during custom setup.

Reference Information in Help

Help for this object model is available in VBABDR8.HLP.

Microsoft Graph 2000

Default location: \Program Files\Microsoft Office\Office

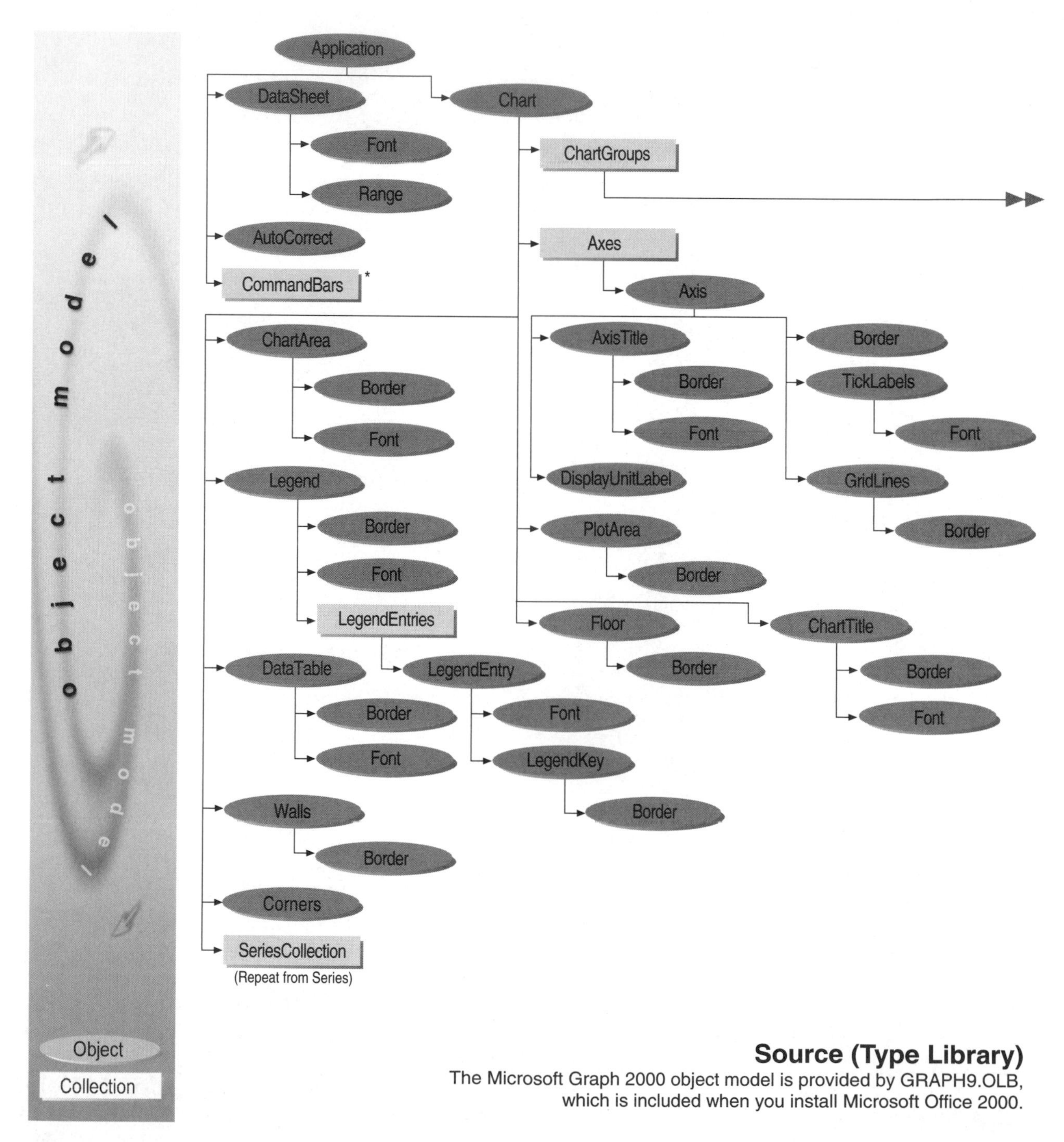

Source (Type Library)

The Microsoft Graph 2000 object model is provided by GRAPH9.OLB, which is included when you install Microsoft Office 2000.

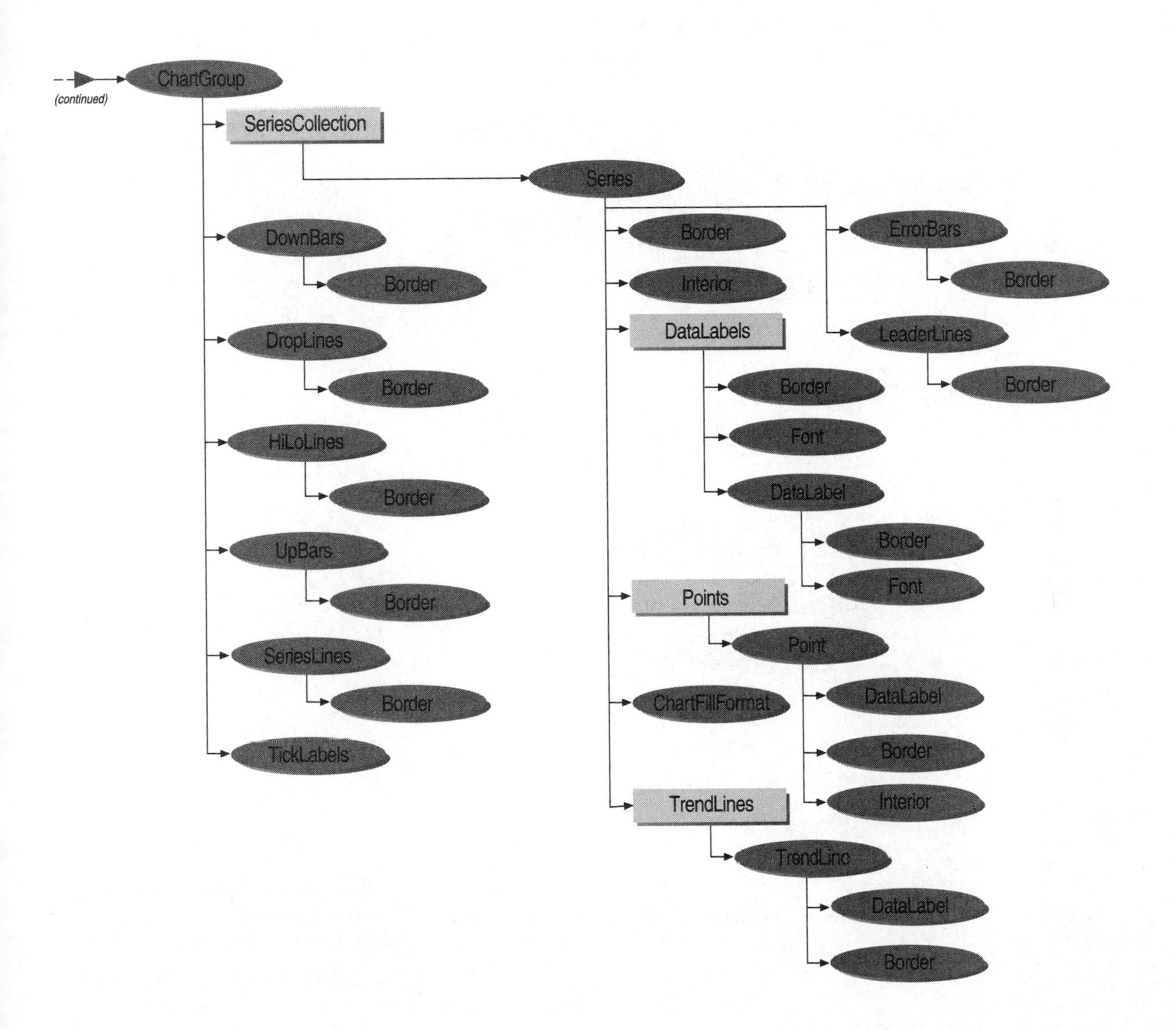

Reference Information in Help

Help for this object model is available in VBAGRP9.CHM.

Microsoft Map

Default location: \Program Files\Common Files\Microsoft Shared\Datamap

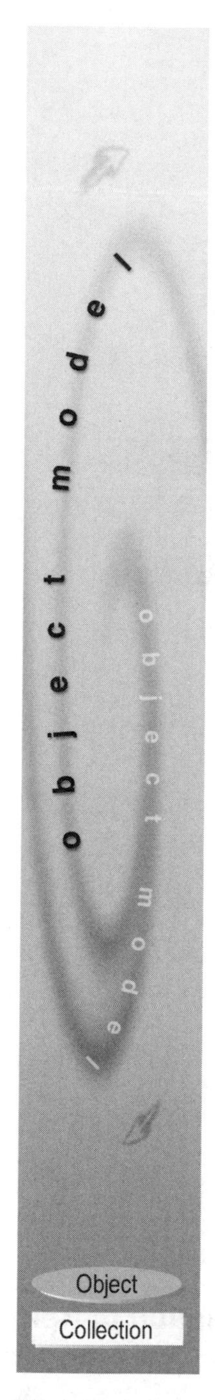

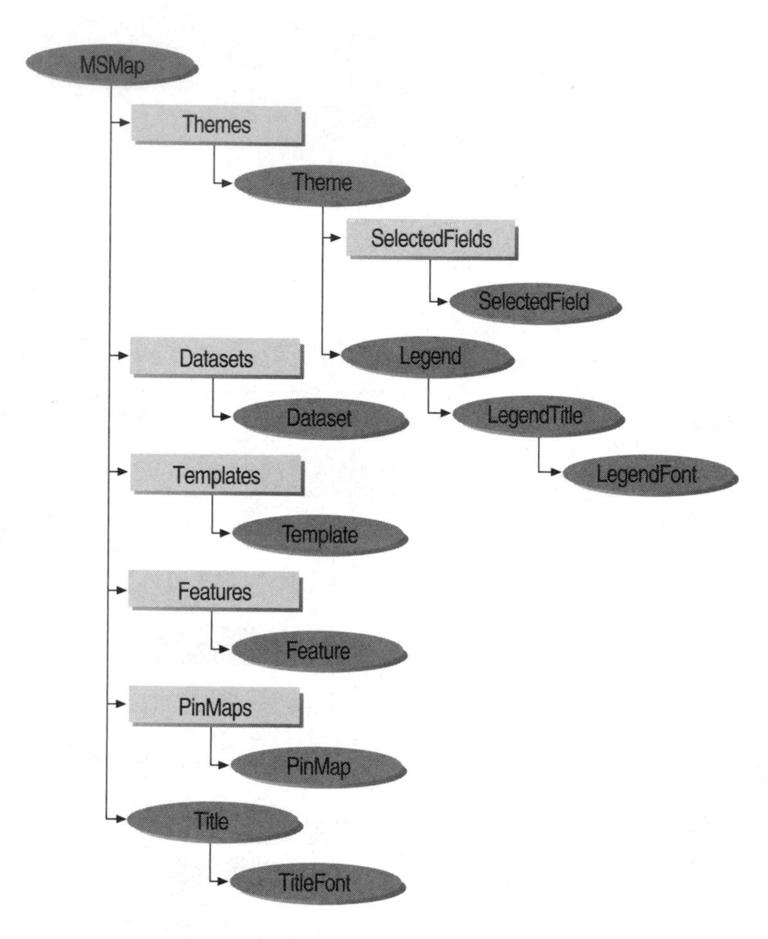

Source (Type Library)

The Microsoft Map object model is provided by MSMAP.TLB, which is included when you install the Microsoft Map feature for Microsoft Excel 2000.

Reference Information in Help

Help for this object model is available in VBAMAP8.HLP.

Notes

Automation for Microsoft Map works only when Microsoft Map is embedded in Microsoft Excel. It will not work when Microsoft Map is embedded in other applications.

Microsoft Forms

Default location: \Windows\System

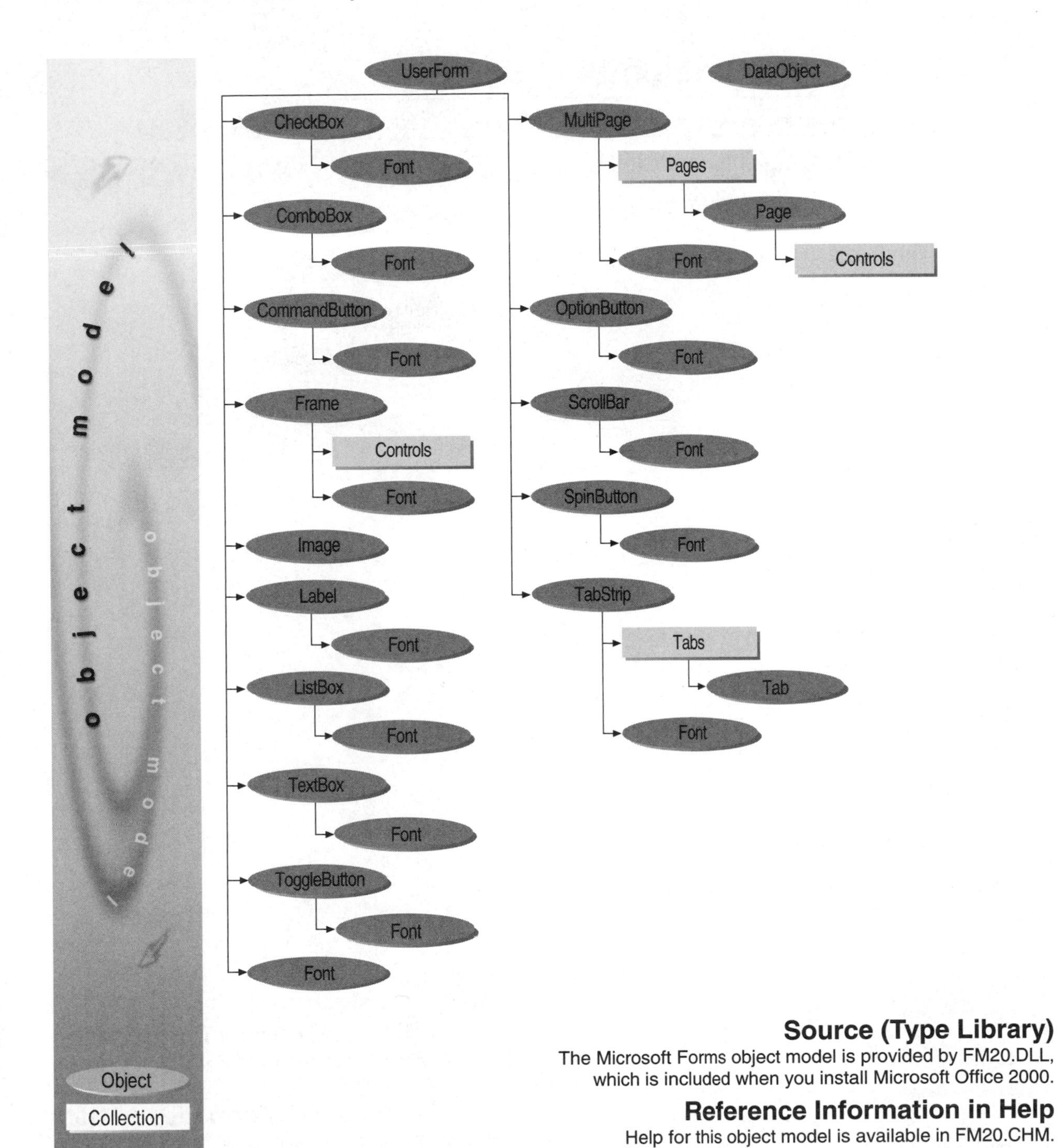

Source (Type Library)

The Microsoft Forms object model is provided by FM20.DLL, which is included when you install Microsoft Office 2000.

Reference Information in Help

Help for this object model is available in FM20.CHM.

Visual Basic Editor

Default location: \Program Files\Common Files\Microsoft Shared\VBA\VBA6

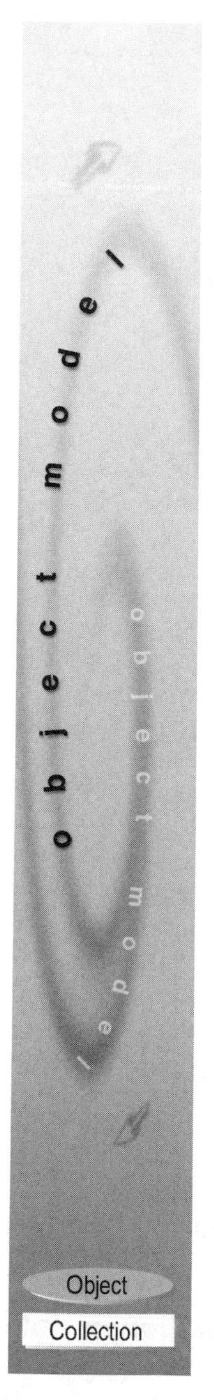

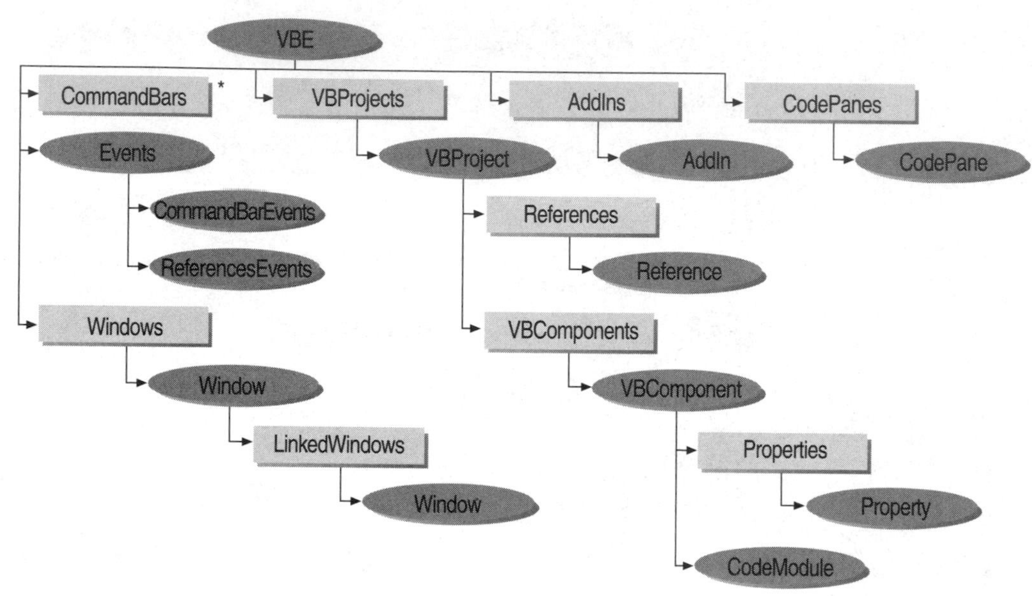

Source (Type Library)

The Visual Basic Editor object model is provided by VBE6EXT.OLB, which is included when you install Microsoft Office 2000.

Reference Information in Help

Help for this object model is available in VBOB6.CHM.

Microsoft ActiveX Data Objects 2.1

Default location: \Program Files\Common Files\System\ADO

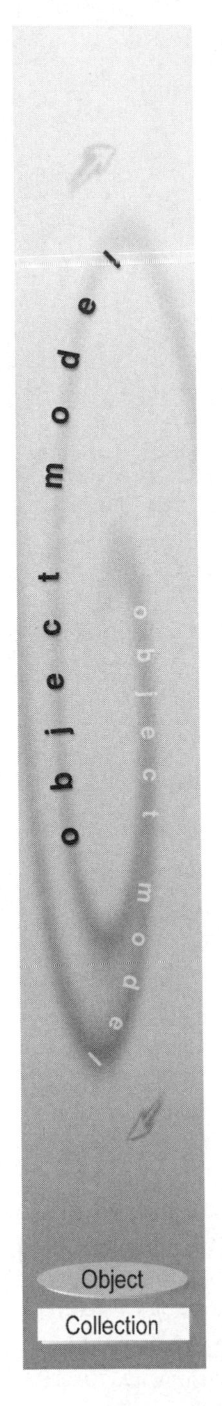

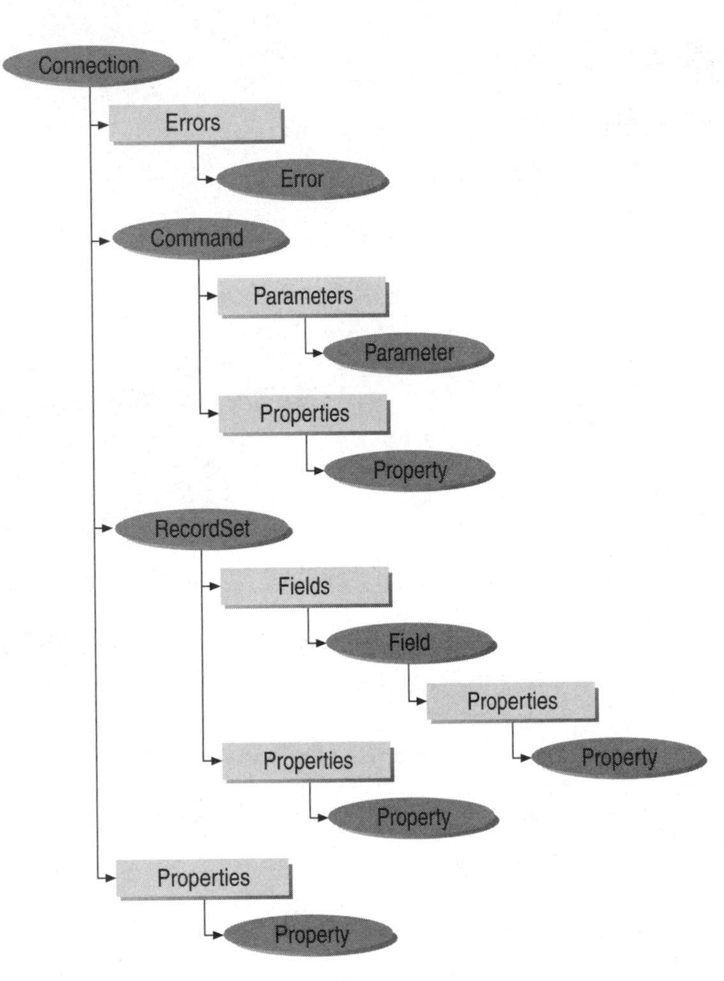

Source (Type Library)

The Microsoft ActiveX Data Objects 2.1 object model is provided by MSADO15.DLL, which is included when you install Microsoft Office 2000.

Reference Information in Help

Help for this object model is available in ADO210.CHM.

Microsoft ADO Extensions 2.1 for DDL and Security

Default location: \Program Files\Common Files\System\ADO

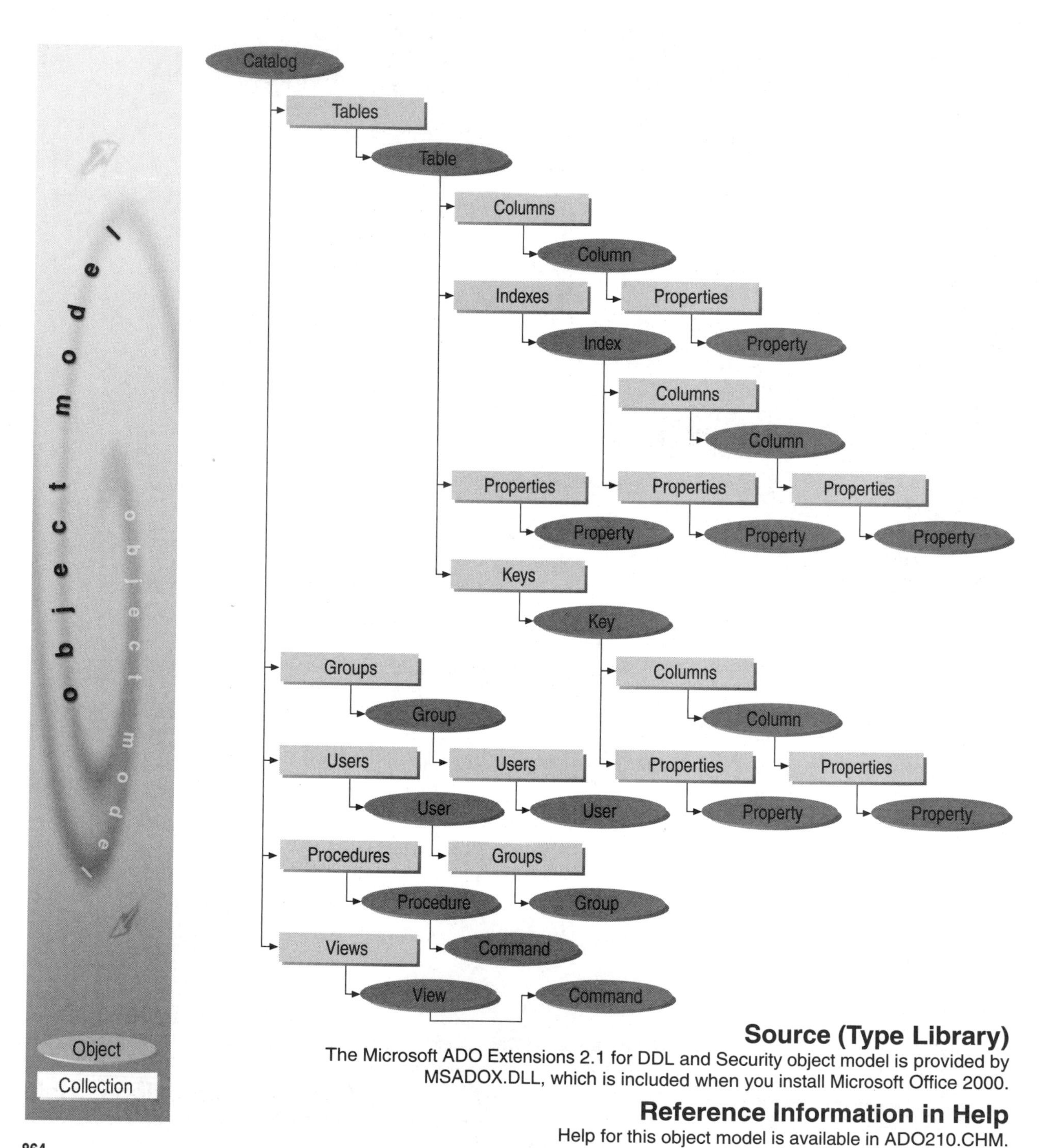

Source (Type Library)

The Microsoft ADO Extensions 2.1 for DDL and Security object model is provided by MSADOX.DLL, which is included when you install Microsoft Office 2000.

Reference Information in Help

Help for this object model is available in ADO210.CHM.

Microsoft ActiveX Data Objects (Multi-Dimensional) 1.0

Default location: \Program Files\Common Files\System\ADO

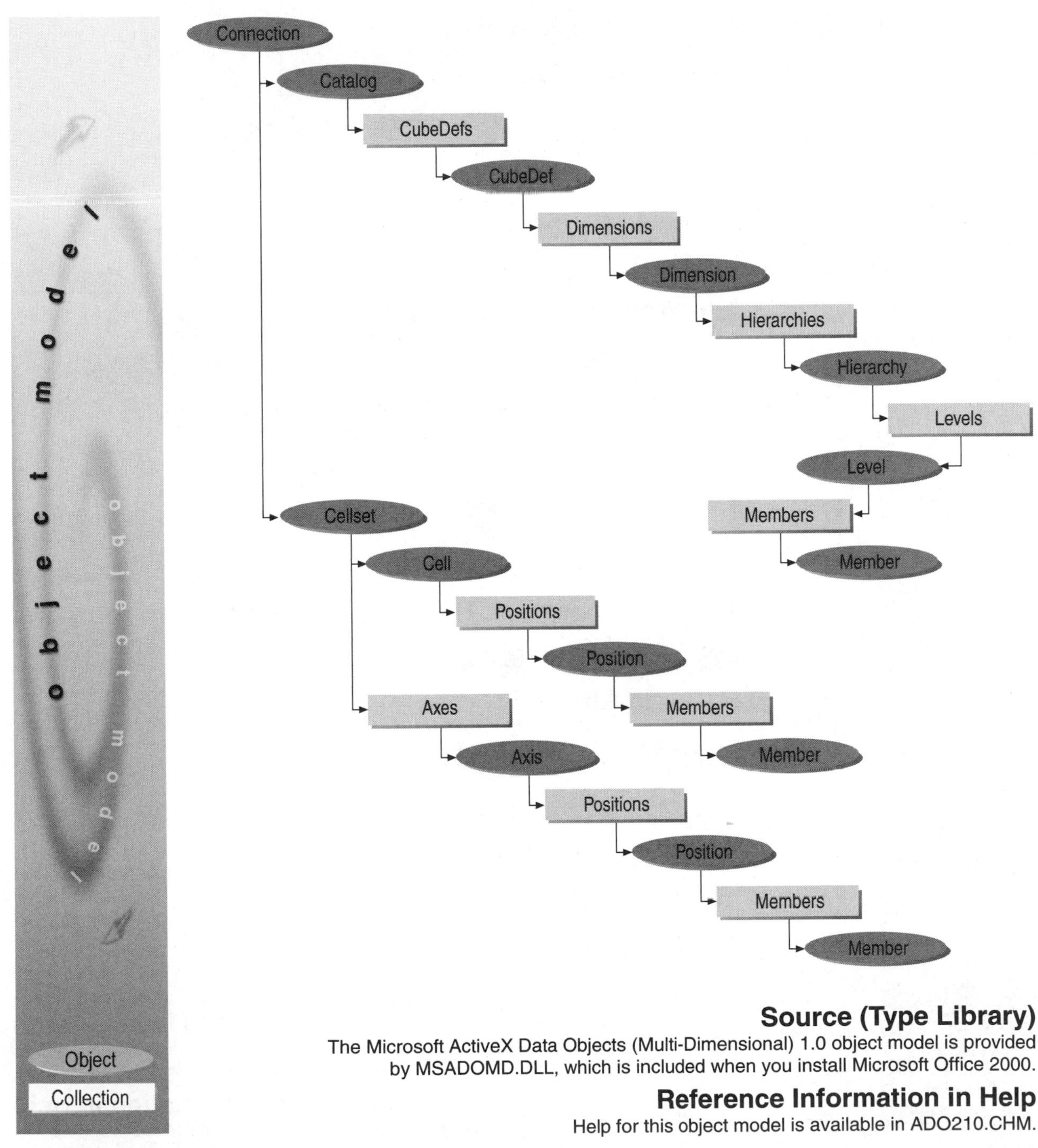

Source (Type Library)

The Microsoft ActiveX Data Objects (Multi-Dimensional) 1.0 object model is provided by MSADOMD.DLL, which is included when you install Microsoft Office 2000.

Reference Information in Help

Help for this object model is available in ADO210.CHM.

Microsoft Data Access Objects (DAO) 3.6 Object Library

Default location: \Program Files\Common Files\Microsoft Shared\DAO

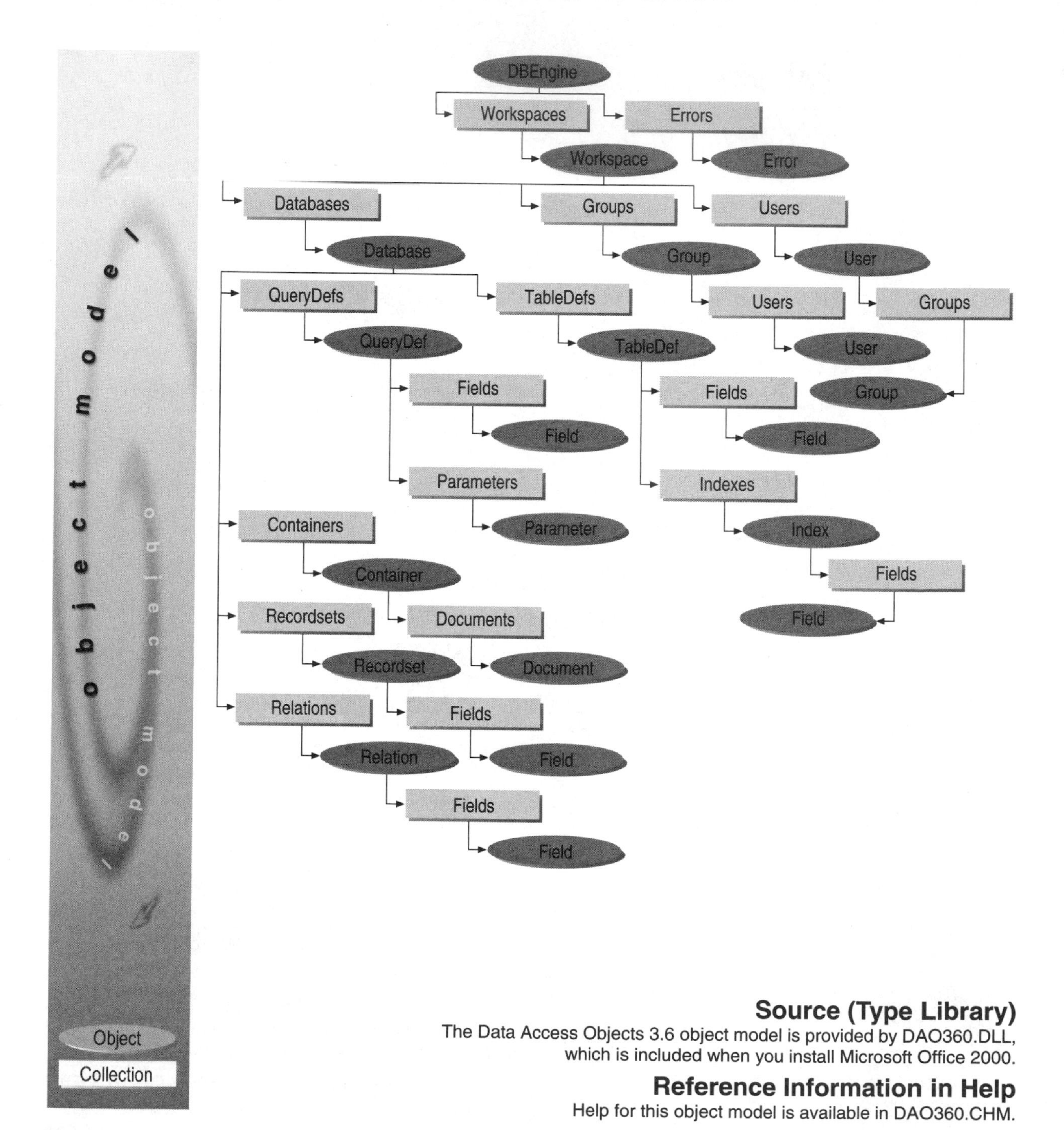

Source (Type Library)

The Data Access Objects 3.6 object model is provided by DAO360.DLL, which is included when you install Microsoft Office 2000.

Reference Information in Help

Help for this object model is available in DAO360.CHM.

Microsoft Jet and Replication Objects 2.1 Library

Default location: \Program Files\Common Files\System\ADO

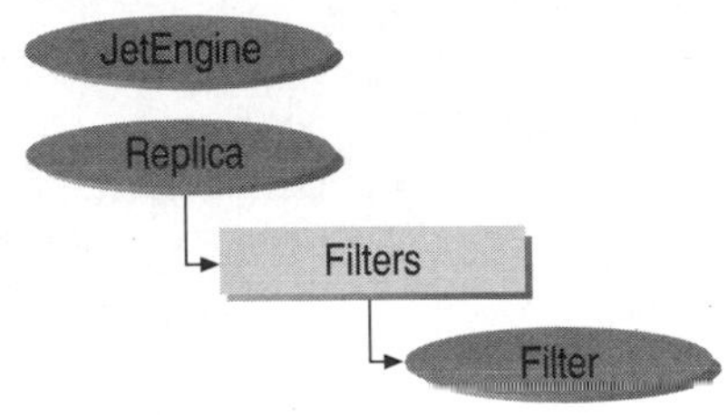

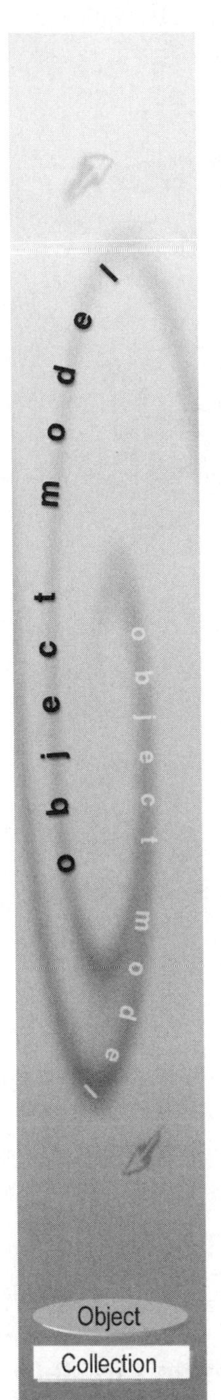

Source (Type Library)

The Microsoft Jet and Replication objects 2.1 object model is provided by MSJRO.DLL, which is included when you install Microsoft Office 2000.

Reference Information in Help

Help for this object model is available in MSJRO.CHM.

Microsoft Internet Explorer 5 and Document Object Model

Default location: \Windows\System

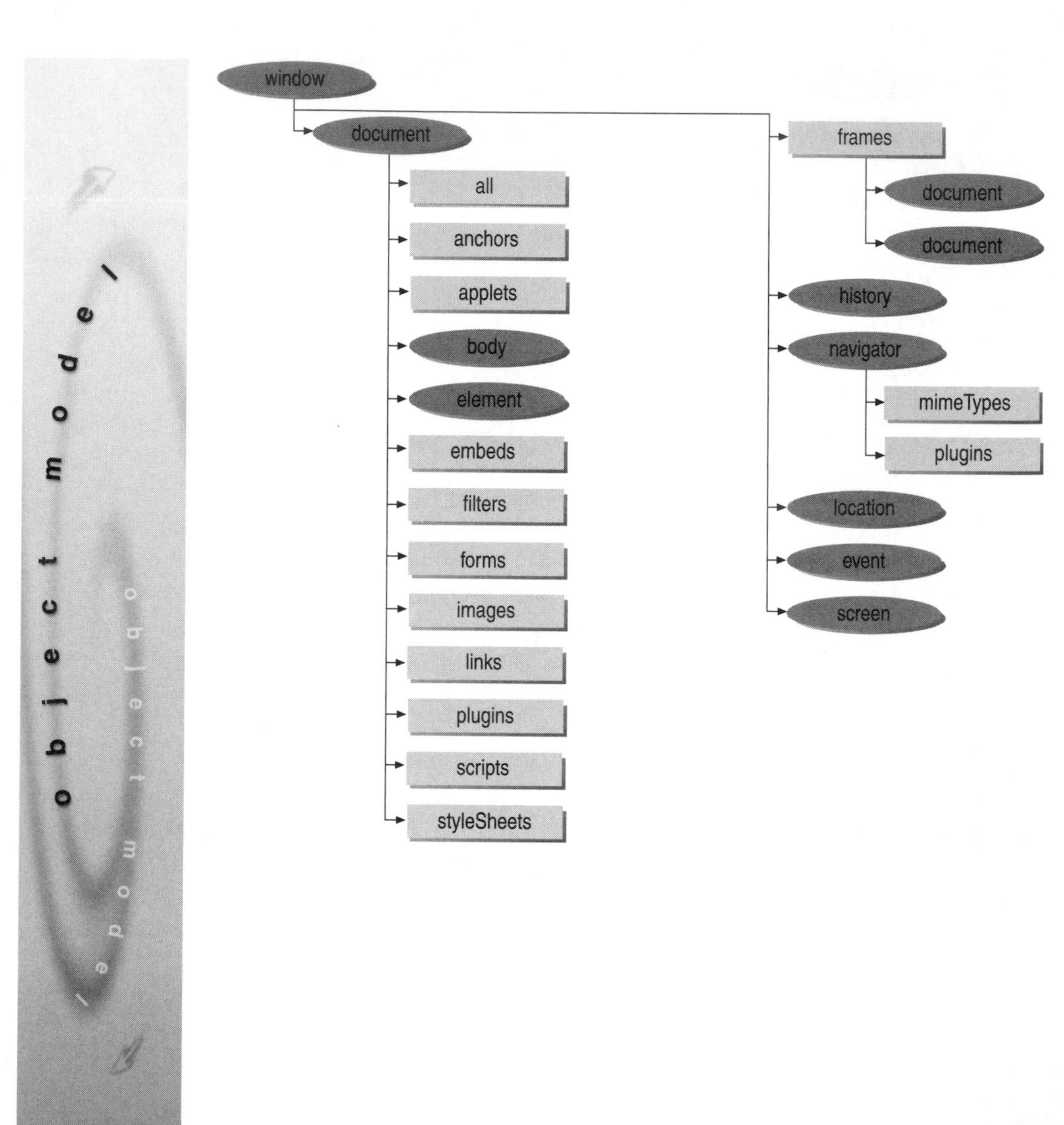

Source (Type Library)

The Microsoft Internet Explorer object model is provided by MSHTML.TLB, which is included when you install Microsoft Office 2000. The objects in this object model are available whenever Internet Explorer is open, so there is no need to refer to a specific type library file.

Reference Information in Help

Help for this object model is available in HTMLREF.CHM.

Microsoft Scripting Runtime

Default location: \Windows\System

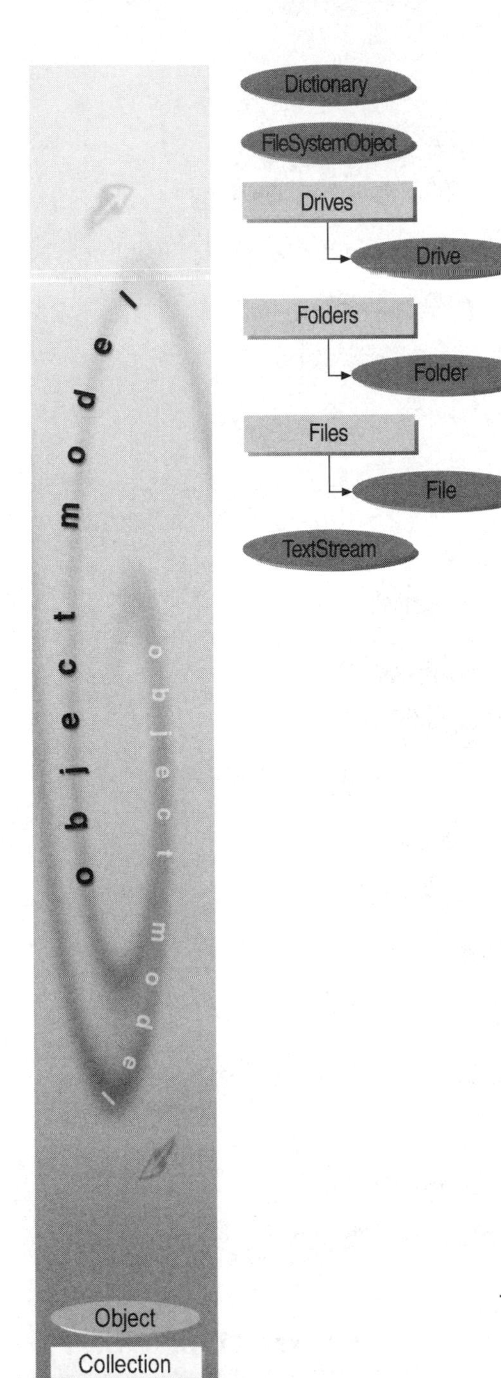

Source (Type Library)

The Microsoft Scripting Runtime object model is provided by SCRRUN.DLL, which is included when you install Microsoft Office 2000.

Reference Information in Help

Help for this object model is available in VBLR6.CHM.

Microsoft Office Chart Component

Default location: \Program Files\Microsoft Office\Office

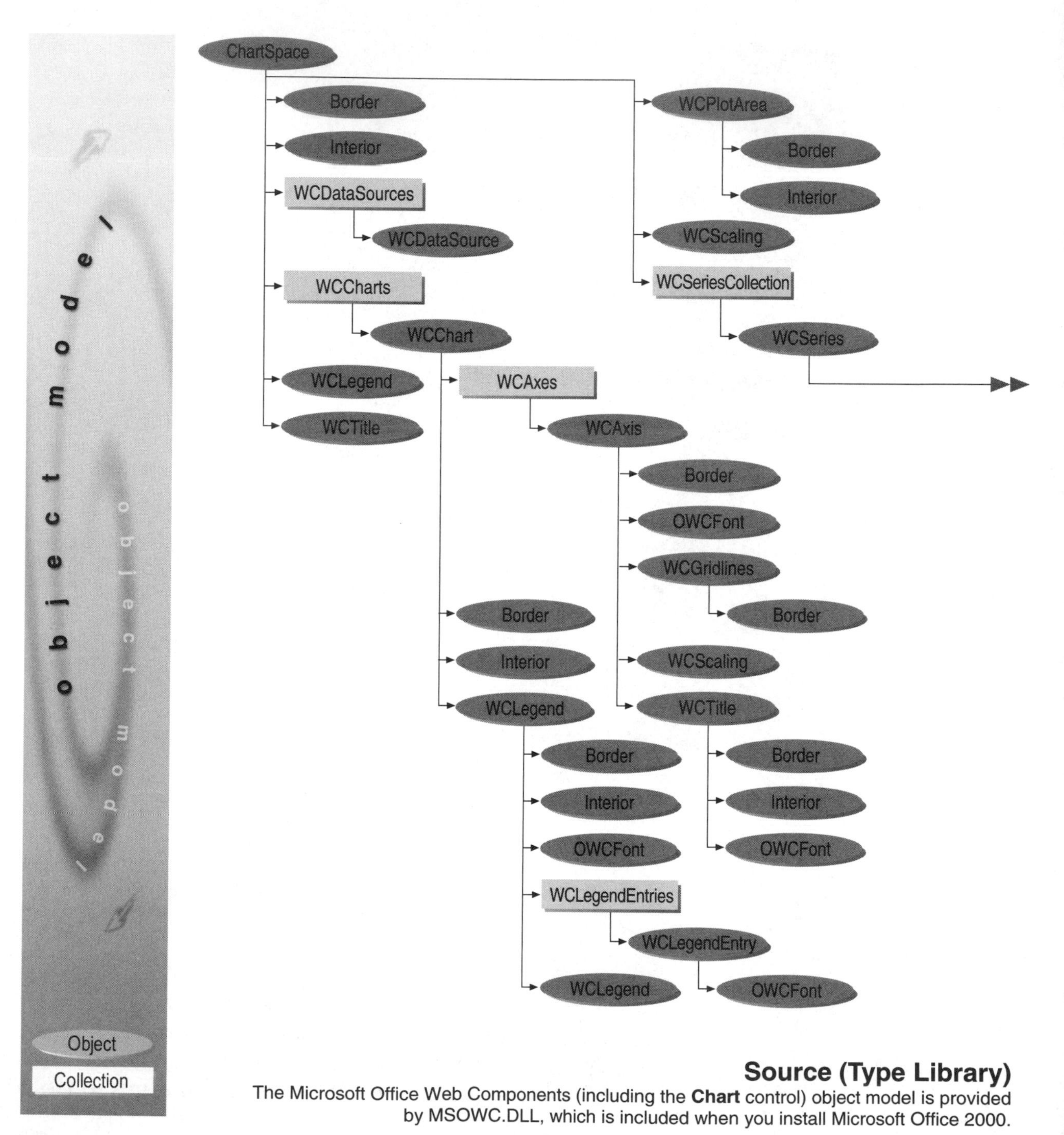

Source (Type Library)

The Microsoft Office Web Components (including the **Chart** control) object model is provided by MSOWC.DLL, which is included when you install Microsoft Office 2000.

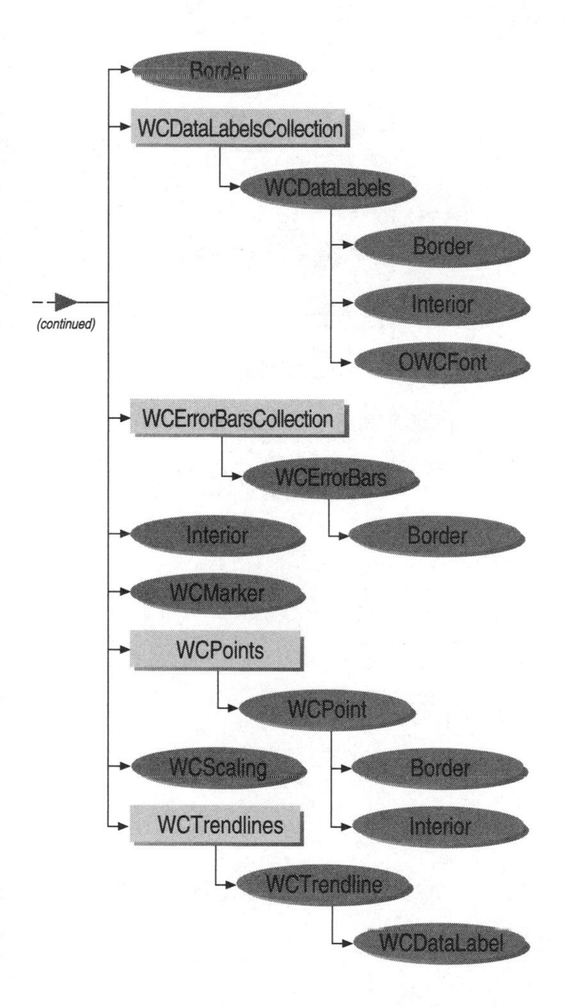

Reference Information in Help

Help for this object model is available in MSOWCVBA.CHM.

Microsoft Office Data Source Control

Default location: \Program Files\Microsoft Office\Office

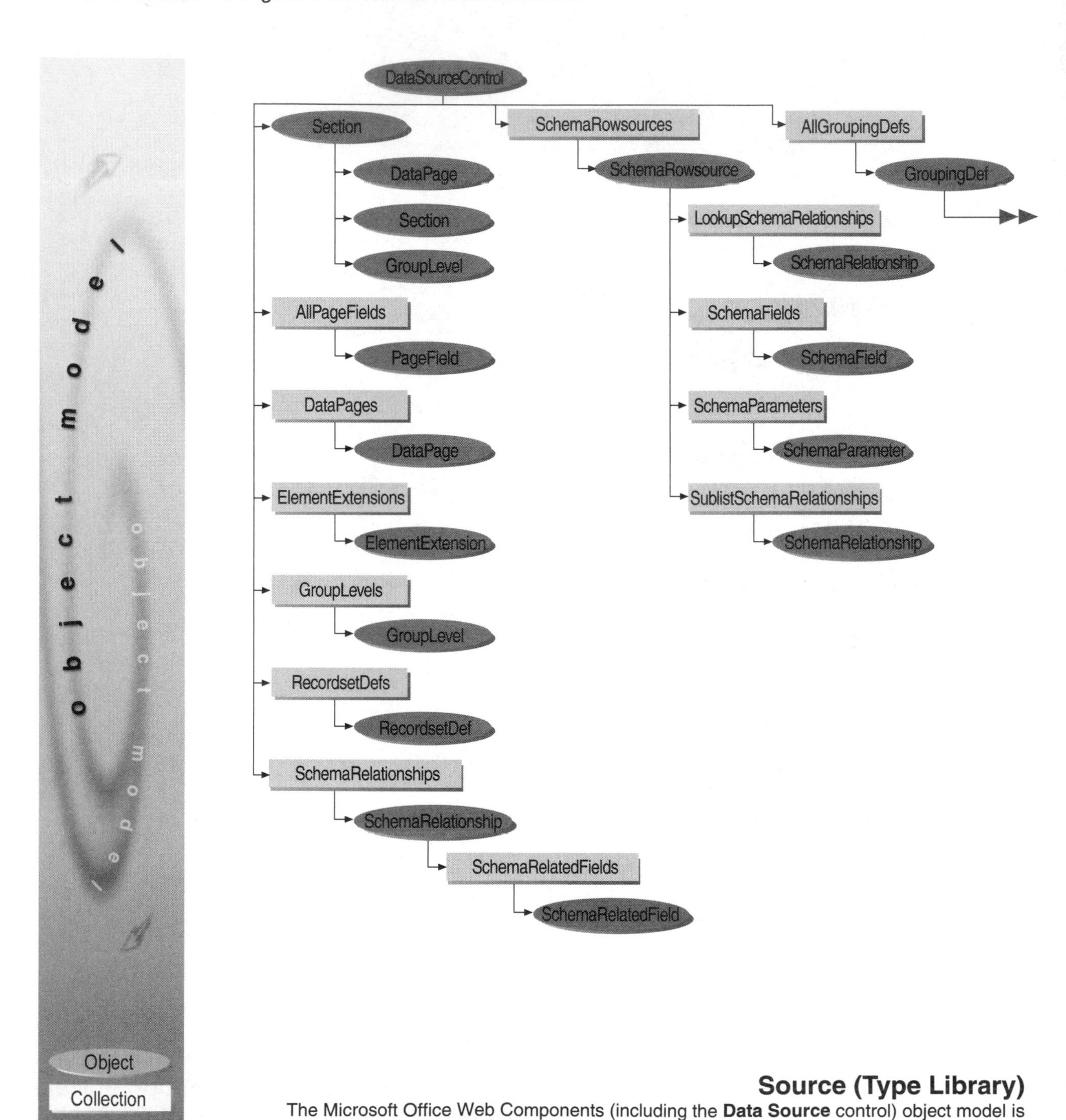

Source (Type Library)

The Microsoft Office Web Components (including the **Data Source** control) object model is provided by MSOWC.DLL, which is included when you install Microsoft Office 2000.

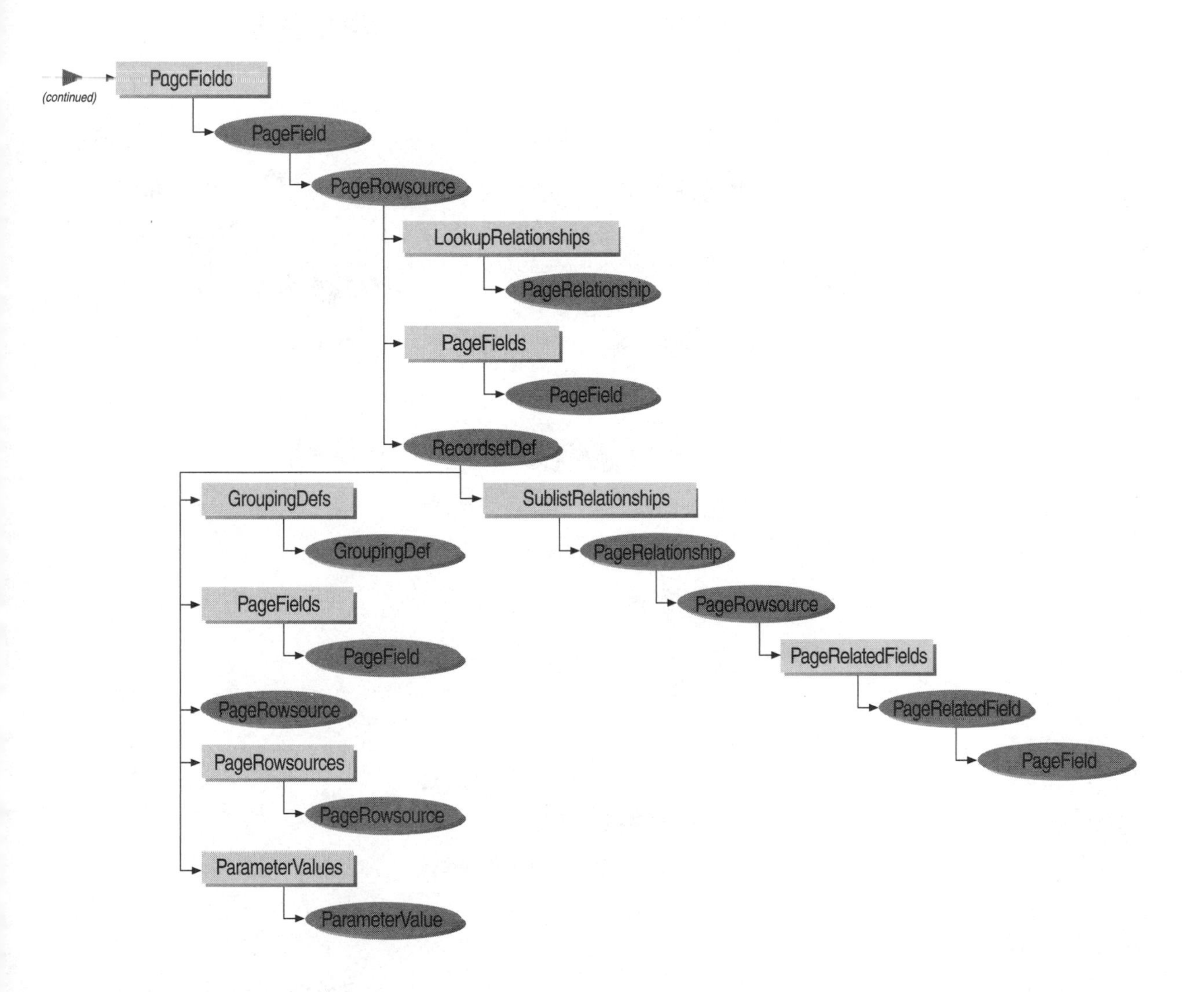

Reference Information in Help

Help for this object model is available in MSOWCVBA.CHM.

Microsoft Office PivotTable Component

Default location: \Program Files\Microsoft Office\Office

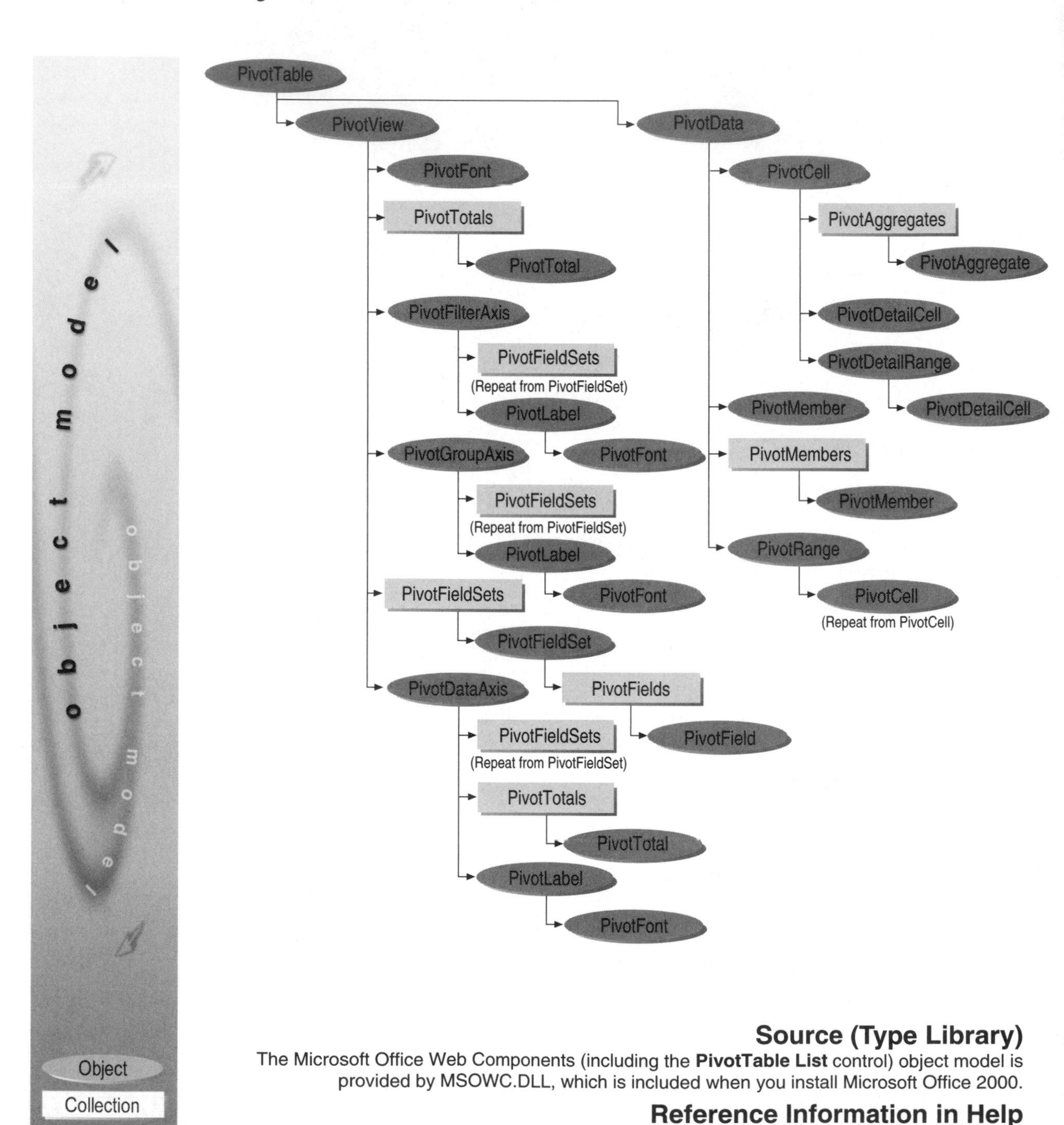

Source (Type Library)

The Microsoft Office Web Components (including the **PivotTable List** control) object model is provided by MSOWC.DLL, which is included when you install Microsoft Office 2000.

Reference Information in Help

Help for this object model is available in MSOWCVBA.CHM.

Microsoft Office Spreadsheet Component

Default location: \Program Files\Microsoft Office\Office

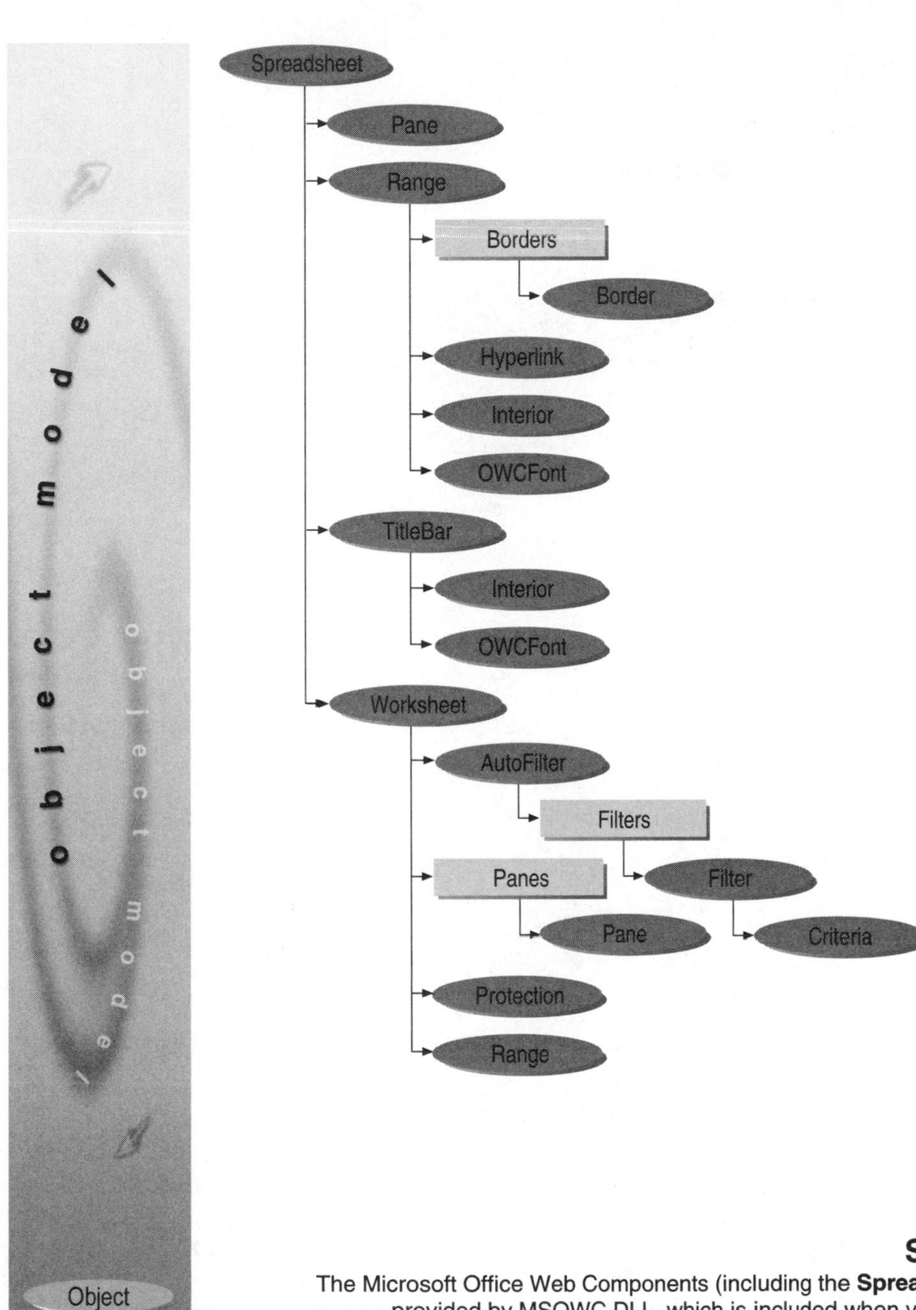

Source (Type Library)

The Microsoft Office Web Components (including the **Spreadsheet** control) object model is provided by MSOWC.DLL, which is included when you install Microsoft Office 2000.

Reference Information in Help

Help for this object model is available in MSOWCVBA.CHM.

Microsoft Office Server Extensions

Default location: \Program Files\Microsoft Office\Office

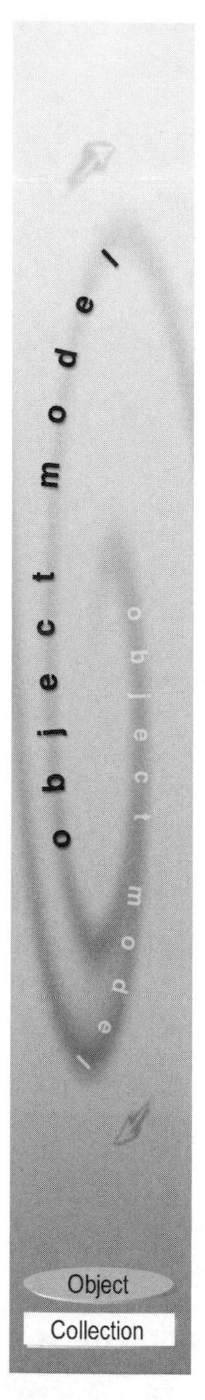

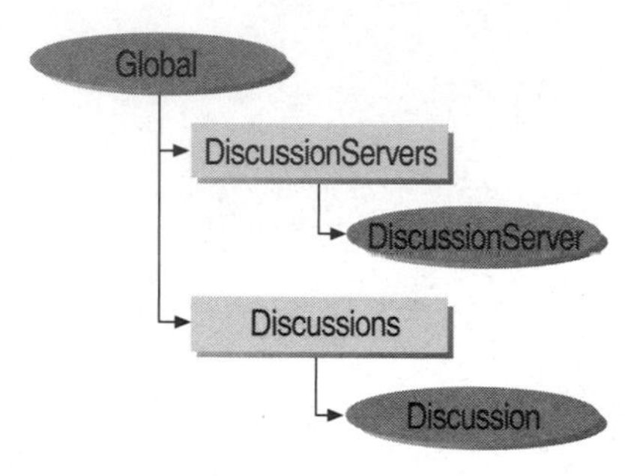

Source (Type Library)

The Microsoft Office Server Extensions object model is provided by OWSDSC.DLL, which is included when you install the Web Discussions feature of Microsoft Office 2000.

Reference Information in Help

Help for this object model is available in OWSVBA.CHM.

Index

Symbols

A

B

C

D

E

F

G

H

K

L

M

N

O

P

Q

R

S

T

W

X

Y

Z

MICROSOFT LICENSE AGREEMENT

Book Companion CD

IMPORTANT—READ CAREFULLY: This Microsoft End-User License Agreement ("EULA") is a legal agreement between you (either an individual or an entity) and Microsoft Corporation for the Microsoft product identified above, which includes computer software and may include associated media, printed materials, and "online" or electronic documentation ("SOFTWARE PRODUCT"). Any component included within the SOFTWARE PRODUCT that is accompanied by a separate End-User License Agreement shall be governed by such agreement and not the terms set forth below. By installing, copying, or otherwise using the SOFTWARE PRODUCT, you agree to be bound by the terms of this EULA. If you do not agree to the terms of this EULA, you are not authorized to install, copy, or otherwise use the SOFTWARE PRODUCT; you may, however, return the SOFTWARE PRODUCT, along with all printed materials and other items that form a part of the Microsoft product that includes the SOFTWARE PRODUCT, to the place you obtained them for a full refund.

SOFTWARE PRODUCT LICENSE

The SOFTWARE PRODUCT is protected by United States copyright laws and international copyright treaties, as well as other intellectual property laws and treaties. The SOFTWARE PRODUCT is licensed, not sold.

1. **GRANT OF LICENSE.** This EULA grants you the following rights:

   a. **Software Product.** You may install and use one copy of the SOFTWARE PRODUCT on a single computer. The primary user of the computer on which the SOFTWARE PRODUCT is installed may make a second copy for his or her exclusive use on a portable computer.

   b. **Storage/Network Use.** You may also store or install a copy of the SOFTWARE PRODUCT on a storage device, such as a network server, used only to install or run the SOFTWARE PRODUCT on your other computers over an internal network; however, you must acquire and dedicate a license for each separate computer on which the SOFTWARE PRODUCT is installed or run from the storage device. A license for the SOFTWARE PRODUCT may not be shared or used concurrently on different computers.

   c. **License Pak.** If you have acquired this EULA in a Microsoft License Pak, you may make the number of additional copies of the computer software portion of the SOFTWARE PRODUCT authorized on the printed copy of this EULA, and you may use each copy in the manner specified above. You are also entitled to make a corresponding number of secondary copies for portable computer use as specified above.

   d. **Sample Code.** Solely with respect to portions, if any, of the SOFTWARE PRODUCT that are identified within the SOFTWARE PRODUCT as sample code (the "SAMPLE CODE"):

      i. **Use and Modification.** Microsoft grants you the right to use and modify the source code version of the SAMPLE CODE, *provided* you comply with subsection (d)(iii) below. You may not distribute the SAMPLE CODE, or any modified version of the SAMPLE CODE, in source code form.

      ii. **Redistributable Files.** Provided you comply with subsection (d)(iii) below, Microsoft grants you a nonexclusive, royalty-free right to reproduce and distribute the object code version of the SAMPLE CODE and of any modified SAMPLE CODE, other than SAMPLE CODE, or any modified version thereof, designated as not redistributable in the Readme file that forms a part of the SOFTWARE PRODUCT (the "Non-Redistributable Sample Code"). All SAMPLE CODE other than the Non-Redistributable Sample Code is collectively referred to as the "REDISTRIBUTABLES."

      iii. **Redistribution Requirements.** If you redistribute the REDISTRIBUTABLES, you agree to: (i) distribute the REDISTRIBUTABLES in object code form only in conjunction with and as a part of your software application product; (ii) not use Microsoft's name, logo, or trademarks to market your software application product; (iii) include a valid copyright notice on your software application product; (iv) indemnify, hold harmless, and defend Microsoft from and against any claims or lawsuits, including attorney's fees, that arise or result from the use or distribution of your software application product; and (v) not permit further distribution of the REDISTRIBUTABLES by your end user. Contact Microsoft for the applicable royalties due and other licensing terms for all other uses and/or distribution of the REDISTRIBUTABLES.

2. **DESCRIPTION OF OTHER RIGHTS AND LIMITATIONS.**

   - **Limitations on Reverse Engineering, Decompilation, and Disassembly.** You may not reverse engineer, decompile, or disassemble the SOFTWARE PRODUCT, except and only to the extent that such activity is expressly permitted by applicable law notwithstanding this limitation.
   - **Separation of Components.** The SOFTWARE PRODUCT is licensed as a single product. Its component parts may not be separated for use on more than one computer.
   - **Rental.** You may not rent, lease, or lend the SOFTWARE PRODUCT.

- **Support Services.** Microsoft may, but is not obligated to, provide you with support services related to the SOFTWARE PRODUCT ("Support Services"). Use of Support Services is governed by the Microsoft policies and programs described in the user manual, in "online" documentation, and/or other Microsoft-provided materials. Any supplemental software code provided to you as part of the Support Services shall be considered part of the SOFTWARE PRODUCT and subject to the terms and conditions of this EULA. With respect to technical information you provide to Microsoft as part of the Support Services, Microsoft may use such information for its business purposes, including for product support and development. Microsoft will not utilize such technical information in a form that personally identifies you.
- **Software Transfer.** You may permanently transfer all of your rights under this EULA, provided you retain no copies, you transfer all of the SOFTWARE PRODUCT (including all component parts, the media and printed materials, any upgrades, this EULA, and, if applicable, the Certificate of Authenticity), **and** the recipient agrees to the terms of this EULA.
- **Termination.** Without prejudice to any other rights, Microsoft may terminate this EULA if you fail to comply with the terms and conditions of this EULA. In such event, you must destroy all copies of the SOFTWARE PRODUCT and all of its component parts.

3. **COPYRIGHT.** All title and copyrights in and to the SOFTWARE PRODUCT (including but not limited to any images, photographs, animations, video, audio, music, text, SAMPLE CODE, REDISTRIBUTABLES, and "applets" incorporated into the SOFTWARE PRODUCT) and any copies of the SOFTWARE PRODUCT are owned by Microsoft or its suppliers. The SOFTWARE PRODUCT is protected by copyright laws and international treaty provisions. Therefore, you must treat the SOFTWARE PRODUCT like any other copyrighted material **except** that you may install the SOFTWARE PRODUCT on a single computer provided you keep the original solely for backup or archival purposes. You may not copy the printed materials accompanying the SOFTWARE PRODUCT.

4. **U.S. GOVERNMENT RESTRICTED RIGHTS.** The SOFTWARE PRODUCT and documentation are provided with RESTRICTED RIGHTS. Use, duplication, or disclosure by the Government is subject to restrictions as set forth in subparagraph (c)(1)(ii) of the Rights in Technical Data and Computer Software clause at DFARS 252.227-7013 or subparagraphs (c)(1) and (2) of the Commercial Computer Software—Restricted Rights at 48 CFR 52.227-19, as applicable. Manufacturer is Microsoft Corporation/One Microsoft Way/Redmond, WA 98052-6399.

5. **EXPORT RESTRICTIONS.** You agree that you will not export or re-export the SOFTWARE PRODUCT, any part thereof, or any process or service that is the direct product of the SOFTWARE PRODUCT (the foregoing collectively referred to as the "Restricted Components"), to any country, person, entity, or end user subject to U.S. export restrictions. You specifically agree not to export or re-export any of the Restricted Components (i) to any country to which the U.S. has embargoed or restricted the export of goods or services, which currently include, but are not necessarily limited to Cuba, Iran, Iraq, Libya, North Korea, Sudan, and Syria, or to any national of any such country, wherever located, who intends to transmit or transport the Restricted Components back to such country; (ii) to any end-user who you know or have reason to know will utilize the Restricted Components in the design, development, or production of nuclear, chemical, or biological weapons; or (iii) to any end-user who has been prohibited from participating in U.S. export transactions by any federal agency of the U.S. government. You warrant and represent that neither the BXA nor any other U.S. federal agency has suspended, revoked, or denied your export privileges.

DISCLAIMER OF WARRANTY

NO WARRANTIES OR CONDITIONS. MICROSOFT EXPRESSLY DISCLAIMS ANY WARRANTY OR CONDITION FOR THE SOFTWARE PRODUCT. THE SOFTWARE PRODUCT AND ANY RELATED DOCUMENTATION IS PROVIDED "AS IS" WITHOUT WARRANTY OR CONDITION OF ANY KIND, EITHER EXPRESS OR IMPLIED, INCLUDING, WITHOUT LIMITATION, THE IMPLIED WARRANTIES OF MERCHANTABILITY, FITNESS FOR A PARTICULAR PURPOSE, OR NONINFRINGEMENT. THE ENTIRE RISK ARISING OUT OF USE OR PERFORMANCE OF THE SOFTWARE PRODUCT REMAINS WITH YOU.

LIMITATION OF LIABILITY. TO THE MAXIMUM EXTENT PERMITTED BY APPLICABLE LAW, IN NO EVENT SHALL MICROSOFT OR ITS SUPPLIERS BE LIABLE FOR ANY SPECIAL, INCIDENTAL, INDIRECT, OR CONSEQUENTIAL DAMAGES WHATSOEVER (INCLUDING, WITHOUT LIMITATION, DAMAGES FOR LOSS OF BUSINESS PROFITS, BUSINESS INTERRUPTION, LOSS OF BUSINESS INFORMATION, OR ANY OTHER PECUNIARY LOSS) ARISING OUT OF THE USE OF OR INABILITY TO USE THE SOFTWARE PRODUCT OR THE PROVISION OF OR FAILURE TO PROVIDE SUPPORT SERVICES, EVEN IF MICROSOFT HAS BEEN ADVISED OF THE POSSIBILITY OF SUCH DAMAGES. IN ANY CASE, MICROSOFT'S ENTIRE LIABILITY UNDER ANY PROVISION OF THIS EULA SHALL BE LIMITED TO THE GREATER OF THE AMOUNT ACTUALLY PAID BY YOU FOR THE SOFTWARE PRODUCT OR US$5.00; PROVIDED HOWEVER, IF YOU HAVE ENTERED INTO A MICROSOFT SUPPORT SERVICES AGREEMENT, MICROSOFT'S ENTIRE LIABILITY REGARDING SUPPORT SERVICES SHALL BE GOVERNED BY THE TERMS OF THAT AGREEMENT. BECAUSE SOME STATES AND JURISDICTIONS DO NOT ALLOW THE EXCLUSION OR LIMITATION OF LIABILITY, THE ABOVE LIMITATION MAY NOT APPLY TO YOU.

MISCELLANEOUS

This EULA is governed by the laws of the State of Washington USA, except and only to the extent that applicable law mandates governing law of a different jurisdiction.

Should you have any questions concerning this EULA, or if you desire to contact Microsoft for any reason, please contact the Microsoft subsidiary serving your country, or write: Microsoft Sales Information Center/One Microsoft Way/Redmond, WA 98052-6399.